28th Edition

P9-CQR-677

Students with Disabilities and Special Education Law

- Compensatory Education

- IEPs

- School Liability

- Private School Tuition

- Stay-Put Placement

- Related Services

- Due Process Hearings

- IDEA

- Mainstreaming

- Student Records and Privacy

Center for
Education & Employment Law

Center for Education & Employment Law
P.O. Box 3008
Malvern, Pennsylvania 19355

First edition 1984
Twenty-eighth edition 2011
Printed in the United States of America

> "This publication is designed to provide accurate and authoritative information
> in regard to the subject matter covered. It is sold with the understanding that the
> publisher is not engaged in rendering legal, accounting or other professional services. If
> legal advice or other expert assistance is required, the services of a competent
> professional person should be sought."—from a Declaration of Principles jointly adopted
> by a Committee of the American Bar Association and a Committee of Publishers and
> Associations.

The Library of Congress has catalogued this book as follows:

Library of Congress Cataloging-in-Publication Data
Students with disabilities and special education. 28th ed.
p. cm.
Includes index.
ISBN 978-1-933043-56-2

Cover design by Katie Reing

1. Special education—Law and legislation—United States. 2. Handicapped children—
    Education—Law and legislation—United States. I. Center for Education & Employment Law
    (Malvern, PA)

LC4031.5875 1999
371.91'0973—dc20

Library of Congress Catalog Card Number: 93-13784

ISBN 978-1-933043-56-2
ISSN 1076-0911

Other Titles Published by Center for Education & Employment Law:

Deskbook Encyclopedia of American School Law
Private School Law in America
Higher Education Law in America
U.S. Supreme Court Education Cases
Deskbook Encyclopedia of Public Employment Law
U.S. Supreme Court Employment Cases
Deskbook Encyclopedia of Employment Law
Statutes, Regulations and Case Law Protecting Individuals with Disabilities
Federal Laws Prohibiting Employment Discrimination

TABLE OF CONTENTS

CHAPTER ONE
The Individuals with Disabilities Education Act

TABLE OF CONTENTS

CHAPTER TWO
Placement

CHAPTER THREE
IDEA Procedural Safeguards

TABLE OF CONTENTS

TABLE OF CONTENTS

CHAPTER EIGHT
School District Operations

CHAPTER NINE
Discrimination

REFERENCE SECTION

INTRODUCTION

Federal law requires that school districts provide each child with a disability a free appropriate education. This volume has been published in response to the need of school administrators and others involved in providing special education services to have a reference available when confronted with any of the multitude of problems in the special education area. The 28th Edition continues to group cases by subject matter and contains the full text of the Individuals with Disabilities Education Act as amended through July, 2005, as well as the full text of the Part 300 federal regulations governing the education of children with disabilities. The full legal citation is given for each reported case, and all cases have been indexed and placed in a Table of Cases following the Table of Contents.

Although the IDEA has undergone several major amendments – from the EHA to the EAHCA to the HCPA and finally to the IDEA – the book generally uses the abbreviation "IDEA" in place of the others for ease of readability and textual flow.

The intent of this volume is to provide professional educators and lawyers with access to important cases, statutory and regulatory law in the field of special education and disabled students' rights.

Steve McEllistrem, Esq.
Senior Legal Editor
Center for Education & Employment Law

ABOUT THE EDITORS

Steve McEllistrem is the senior legal editor at the Center for Education & Employment Law. He is a co-author of *Students with Disabilities and Special Education Law* and *Higher Education Law in America*, and is the former managing editor of the monthly newsletter *Special Education Law Update*. He graduated cum laude from William Mitchell College of Law and received his undergraduate degree from the University of Minnesota. Mr. McEllistrem is admitted to the Minnesota Bar.

James A. Roth is the editor of *Legal Notes for Education* and *Special Education Law Update*. He is a co-editor of *Students with Disabilities and Special Education Law* and an adjunct program assistant professor at St. Mary's University in Minnesota. Mr. Roth is a graduate of the University of Minnesota and William Mitchell College of Law. He is admitted to the Minnesota Bar.

Thomas D'Agostino is a managing editor at the Center for Education & Employment Law and is the editor of *Higher Education Legal Alert*. He is a co-author of *Keeping Your School Safe & Secure: A Practical Guide*. He graduated from the Duquesne University School of Law and received his undergraduate degree from Ramapo College of New Jersey. He is a past member of the American Bar Association's Section of Individual Rights and Responsibilities as well as the Pennsylvania Bar Association's Legal Services to Persons with Disabilities Committee. Mr. D'Agostino is admitted to the Pennsylvania bar.

Curt J. Brown is the Group Publisher of the Center for Education & Employment Law. Prior to assuming his present position, he gained extensive experience in business-to-business publishing, including management of well-known publications such as *What's Working in Human Resources, What's New in Benefits & Compensation, Keep Up to Date with Payroll, Supervisors Legal Update,* and *Facility Manager's Alert*. Mr. Brown graduated from Villanova University School of Law and graduated magna cum laude from Bloomsburg University with a B.S. in Business Administration. He is admitted to the Pennsylvania Bar.

How to Use Your Deskbook

We have designed *Students with Disabilities and Special Education Law* in an accessible format for both attorneys and non-attorneys to use as a research and reference tool toward prevention of legal problems.

Using Your Deskbook to Conduct Research

As a research tool, our deskbook allows you to conduct your research on two different levels – by topics or by cases.

Topic Research

♦ If you have a general interest in a particular **topic** area, our **Table of Contents** provides descriptive section headings with detailed subheadings for each chapter.

    ✓ For your convenience, we also include an individual chapter table of contents at the beginning of each chapter.

Example:

    If you are seeking information on home-schooled students, the Table of Contents indicates that a discussion of that topic takes place in Chapter Five, under "Related Services Under the IDEA," on page 219:

How to Use Your Deskbook

♦ If you have a specific interest in a particular **issue**, our comprehensive **index** collects all of the relevant page references to particular issues.

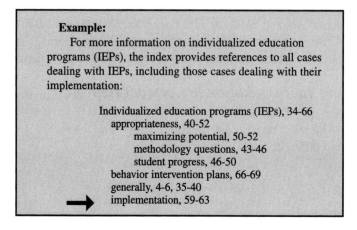

Example:
For more information on individualized education programs (IEPs), the index provides references to all cases dealing with IEPs, including those cases dealing with their implementation:

Individualized education programs (IEPs), 34-66
  appropriateness, 40-52
      maximizing potential, 50-52
      methodology questions, 43-46
      student progress, 46-50
    behavior intervention plans, 66-69
    generally, 4-6, 35-40
➡ implementation, 59-63

Case Research

♦ If you know the **name** of a particular case, our **Table of Cases** will allow you to quickly reference the location of the case.

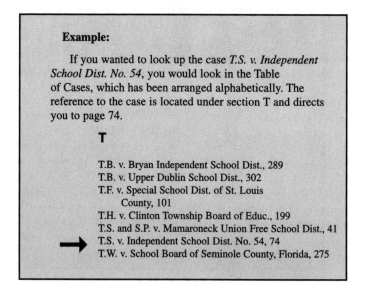

Example:

If you wanted to look up the case *T.S. v. Independent School Dist. No. 54*, you would look in the Table of Cases, which has been arranged alphabetically. The reference to the case is located under section T and directs you to page 74.

T

T.B. v. Bryan Independent School Dist., 289
T.B. v. Upper Dublin School Dist., 302
T.F. v. Special School Dist. of St. Louis
      County, 101
T.H. v. Clinton Township Board of Educ., 199
T.S. and S.P. v. Mamaroneck Union Free School Dist., 41
➡ T.S. v. Independent School Dist. No. 54, 74
T.W. v. School Board of Seminole County, Florida, 275

✓ Each of the cases summarized in the deskbook also contains the case citation that will allow you to access the full text of the case from a law library. See *How to Read a Case Citation*, p. 645.

♦ If your interest lies in cases from a **particular state**, our **Table of Cases by State** will identify the cases from your state and direct you to the page numbers where they are located.

Example:
If cases from Arizona are of interest, the Table of Cases by State, arranged alphabetically, lists all of the Arizona case summaries contained in the deskbook.

ARIZONA

Arizona Dep't of Educ. v. U.S. Dep't of Educ., 372
Arizona State Board for Charter Schools v. U.S. Dep't of Educ., 347
Cain v. Horne, 344, 362
Davis v. Roosevelt Elementary School Dist. No. 66, 155
Hance v. Fountain Hills Unified School Dist., 165

✓ Remember, the judicial system has two court systems – state and federal – which generally function independently of each other. See *The Judicial System*, p. 641. We have included the federal court cases in the table of cases by state according to the state in which the court resides. However, federal court decisions often impact other federal courts within that particular circuit. Therefore, it may be helpful to review cases from all of the states contained in a particular circuit.

Reference Tool

As a reference tool, we have highlighted important resources that provide the framework for many legal issues.

♦ If you would like to see specific wording of the **Individuals with Disabilities Education Act Amendments of 1997**, refer to **Appendix A**.

♦ If you have questions about the **Federal Regulations Implementing the 2006 IDEA Amendments**, we have included the appropriate text in one convenient location, **Appendix B**.

◆ If you would like to review the **Table of Special Education Cases Decided by the U.S. Supreme Court** in a particular subject matter area, our topical list of U.S. Supreme Court case citations located in **Appendix C** will be helpful.

We hope you benefit from the use of *Students with Disabilities and Special Education Law*. If you have any questions about how to use the deskbook, please contact Steve McEllistrem at smcellistrem@pbp.com.

TABLE OF ABBREVIATIONS

The following abbreviations are used in this edition of *Students with Disabilities and Special Education Law*:

ABA – applied behavioral analysis

ADA – Americans with Disabilities Act

ADD – attention deficit disorder

ADHD – attention deficit hyperactivity disorder

ALJ – administrative law judge

ARD – admission, review and dismissal

AVT – auditory-verbal therapy

AYP – adequate yearly progress

CSE – committee on special education

CST – child study team

DTT – discrete trial training

ESY – extended school year

FAPE – free appropriate public education

FERPA – Family Educational Rights and Privacy Act

FMLA – Family and Medical Leave Act

IDEA – Individuals with Disabilities Education Act

IEE – independent educational evaluation

IEP – individualized education program

IFSP – individual family service plan

TABLE OF ABBREVIATIONS

IHO – independent hearing officer

IU – intermediate unit

LEA – local educational agency

LRE – least restrictive environment

MDE – multidisciplinary evaluation

MDT – manifestation determination team

NCLB Act – No Child Left Behind Act

OG – Orton-Gillingham

OT – occupational therapy

PPT – planning and placement team

PT – physical therapy

TA – teaching assistant

TEACCH – Treatment and Education of Autistic and related Communication Handicapped Children

TABLE OF CASES

TABLE OF CASES

TABLE OF CASES

TABLE OF CASES

TABLE OF CASES

TABLE OF CASES

TABLE OF CASES

TABLE OF CASES

TABLE OF CASES

TABLE OF CASES

TABLE OF CASES

TABLE OF CASES

TABLE OF CASES

TABLE OF CASES BY STATE

COLORADO

CONNECTICUT

INDIANA

IOWA

KANSAS

MISSISSIPPI

MISSOURI

MONTANA

NEBRASKA

NEVADA

NORTH CAROLINA

TABLE OF CASES BY STATE

WYOMING

CHAPTER ONE

The Individuals with Disabilities Education Act

I. INDIVIDUALS WITH DISABILITIES EDUCATION ACT

The Individuals with Disabilities Education Act (IDEA), 20 U.S.C. § 1400 et seq., was enacted to ensure that all children with disabilities have available to them a free appropriate public education. The IDEA was reauthorized in 2004 as the Individuals with Disabilities Education Improvement Act.

The new IDEA amendments increase federal funding, adopt terms from the No Child Left Behind Act, and relax some student disciplinary provisions.

Under the new Section 1415(k), for example, schools may "consider any unique circumstances on a case-by-case basis when determining whether to order a change in placement" for a student who violates a code of conduct. A new subsection (G) specifies the special circumstances under which schools may remove a student to an interim alternative educational setting for up to 45 days. For further details on Section 1415(k), see Chapter Two, Section IV.

A. Background

The IDEA was originally passed as the Education of the Handicapped Act of 1970 (EHA). It was intended to assist the states in providing a free appropriate public education to children with disabilities by establishing minimum requirements with which the states had to comply in order to receive federal financial assistance.

Congress amended the EHA in 1975 with the Education for All Handicapped Children Act (EAHCA) (P.L. 94–142), which contains many of the most important legal protections of the legislation now known as the IDEA. The passage of the EAHCA resulted in thousands of administrative challenges and EAHCA lawsuits filed by disabled students and their parents, forcing states, local education agencies, and school districts to bring themselves into compliance with the new federal law.

The Handicapped Children's Protection Act of 1986 (HCPA) (P.L. 99–372), further amended the EHA by specifically authorizing awards of attorneys' fees to the families of students with disabilities who prevailed in EHA lawsuits. The HCPA also expressly allowed disabled students to cumulate their available remedies under Section 504 of the Rehabilitation Act of 1973 (29 U.S.C. § 794) and 42 U.S.C. § 1983. The HCPA is found in the present IDEA at 20 U.S.C. § 1415(i)(3) and Section 1415(*l*).

In 1990, Congress passed the amendment renaming the legislation the Individuals with Disabilities Education Act (IDEA) (P.L. 102–119), and added specific clauses to abrogate sovereign immunity and authorize remedies under both legal and equitable theories (20 U.S.C. § 1403).

In 1994, Congress amended the IDEA as part of the Improving America's Schools Act of 1994, P.L. 103–382, Title III, Amendments to Other Acts, Part A Sections 311–315. The 1994 amendments include language that permits interim placements of up to 45 days for students with disabilities who have brought a weapon to school. The interim placement must be made by the student's individualized education program (IEP) team. If the student's parent requests a due process hearing, the student must remain in the interim placement during the pendency of any IDEA proceeding, unless the parents and local educational agency otherwise agree.

The IDEA requires states and local educational agencies (LEAs) to meet minimum federal special education standards. Although states remain the entities that directly receive IDEA funds, it is the LEAs that must comply with state policies, procedures and programs as specified by 20 U.S.C. § 1413.

Failure to comply with the congressional directives contained in the IDEA may result in a state's retention and use of payments that would otherwise have been available to the LEA. States also bear the risk of losing federal funding eligibility for noncompliance with IDEA requirements, as set forth in 20 U.S.C. §§ 1412 and 1415.

State eligibility requirements under the IDEA appear in 20 U.S.C. § 1412. These include explicit requirements for the provision of a free appropriate education, the state's child find obligation, development of individualized education programs, procedural safeguards, evaluations and student transition from early intervention programs.

The IDEA emphasizes the designing of a free appropriate public education (FAPE) to meet the unique needs of students with disabilities, in order to prepare them for employment and independent living. A multidisciplinary team must consider a number of special factors to the extent applicable to the student.

The focus of the IEP must be on access to general curriculum and the IEP must explain the extent to which a student will not be participating with non-disabled students. An IEP must include a statement of any modifications that are required to enable a student to participate in an assessment.

A student's IEP must establish benchmarks or short-term objectives. 20 U.S.C. § 1414(d).

The IDEA's triennial reevaluation requirement allows evaluation teams to forgo testing where new information is not needed to assist in a placement decision. 20 U.S.C. § 1414(c)(4).

The IDEA requires state and local educational agencies receiving IDEA assistance to offer parents voluntary mediation, with the states being required to establish an informal mediation procedure and to make mediation available whenever a due process hearing is requested.

Some of the most litigated sections of the IDEA concern student discipline and the requirement that a free appropriate public education be made available to all students with disabilities, including those who have been suspended or expelled from school. 20 U.S.C. § 1415(k).

The IDEA specifies that under "special circumstances," students with disabilities can be removed from the classroom and placed in an alternative educational setting for up to 45 days. The special circumstances are: weapons possession; the sale, use or possession of drugs; or infliction of serious bodily injury while at school, on school grounds or at a school event. 20 U.S.C. § 1415(k)(G).

The 1997 IDEA Amendments require an IEP team to review whether the student's inappropriate action was a manifestation of the disability. The student's placement may then be changed, with the consent of the parents, if the behavior is the result of the disability.

The IDEA provides that students with disabilities may be disciplined in the same manner as students without disabilities if the behavior giving rise to the discipline is not a manifestation of the student's disability.

Section 1415(i) allows for a reduction in attorneys' fees awards whenever a court finds that a parent has unreasonably protracted the final resolution of an IDEA dispute, the amount of attorneys' fees is unreasonable or excessive, or the attorney representing a parent has failed to provide the school district with appropriate information. State and local educational agencies may also be penalized for unreasonably protracting the final resolution of an IDEA action.

Under the Early Intervention Program in Part C of the IDEA, each state system must establish procedures to ensure that early intervention services are provided to students in natural environments to the maximum extent appropriate. 20 U.S.C. § 1432(4)(g).

States are required to develop written policies and procedures for submission to the Department of Education as part of each state's funding application. Each individualized family service plan must contain a statement of the natural environments in which services will be provided, and justification for providing services that will not occur in natural environments. 20 U.S.C. § 1436(d)(5).

B. Overview

States and LEAs must have in place a number of statutory policies and procedures in order to ensure the receipt of IDEA funds. State and local agencies are required under 20 U.S.C. § 1414(a) to conduct a full and individual evaluation to determine the educational needs of resident students. If parents refuse to give consent for such evaluations, the agency may pursue available mediation and due process procedures.

As discussed in Section V, below, the IDEA requires educational agencies to provide students with certain procedural protections, the most important of which is the development of an individualized education program (IEP). The IEP constitutes a written statement of each special education student's present level of educational performance, including how the disability affects the student's involvement and progress in the general curriculum, a statement of annual goals including benchmarks or short-term objectives, and a statement of the special education and related services that will be provided to the student.

Special education and related services must be provided so that the student can advance appropriately toward annual goals, be involved and progress in the general curriculum, participate in extracurricular and nonacademic activities, and participate with non-disabled students to the maximum extent appropriate.

IEPs must be reviewed at least annually to evaluate whether the educational agency is providing the student with a free appropriate public education. An important IDEA goal is to integrate students with disabilities into regular classrooms to the extent appropriate for the student and others. An IEP must be in effect for each student with a disability in an educational agency's jurisdiction at the beginning of each school year. 20 U.S.C. § 1414(d)(2)(A).

The IDEA includes sections describing additional requirements for students with disabilities ages three through five, alternative educational placements and requirements for students with disabilities who have been convicted as adults and incarcerated in adult prisons.

Special education means specially designed instruction, at no cost to parents or guardians, to meet the unique needs of a child with a disability, including classroom instruction, home instruction, and instruction in other settings such as hospitals and institutions. 20 U.S.C. § 1401(25).

The IDEA defines a child with a disability at 20 U.S.C. § 1401(3) as a child "(i) with mental retardation, hearing impairments (including deafness), speech or language impairments, visual impairments (including blindness), serious emotional disturbance (... referred to as 'emotional disturbance'), orthopedic impairments, autism, traumatic brain injury, other health impairments, or specific learning disabilities; and (ii) who, by reason thereof, needs special education and related services."

Local educational agencies must provide all children with disabilities with a free appropriate public education, which means "special education and related services that – (A) have been provided at public expense, under public supervision and direction, and without charge; (B) meet the standards of the State educational agency; (C) include an appropriate preschool, elementary, or secondary school education in the State involved; and (D) are provided in conformity with the individualized education program required under section 1414(d)." 20 U.S.C. § 1401(8).

Related services are an important part of an educational agency's obligation to students with disabilities. Such services make access to education possible for students with disabilities.

The IDEA defines related services as "transportation, and such developmental, corrective, and other supportive services (including speech-language pathology and audiology services, psychological services, physical and occupational therapy, recreation, including therapeutic recreation, social work services, counseling services, including rehabilitation counseling, orientation and mobility services, and medical services, except that such medical services shall be for diagnostic and evaluation purposes only) as may be required to assist a child with a disability to benefit from special education, and includes the early identification and assessment of disabling conditions in children." 20 U.S.C. § 1401(22).

Although excluded from the definition of related services, medical services needed by a child for diagnostic and evaluative purposes must be provided free of charge. See *Darlene L. v. Illinois State Board of Educ.*, 568 F.Supp. 1340 (N.D. Ill. 1983). Also, if certain services, like catheterization and tracheostomy suctioning, do not require a physician to perform them, they will not be excluded medical services, and school districts will have to provide them where necessary to enable the student to learn. See *Irving Independent School Dist. v. Tatro* and *Cedar Rapids Community School Dist. v. Garret F.*, Chapter Five, Section III.

The IDEA contains mandatory procedures designed to safeguard the rights of students with disabilities. The general procedural requirements remain in 20 U.S.C. § 1415. State eligibility is described in 20 U.S.C. § 1412, while local eligibility rules appear in 20 U.S.C. § 1413. Procedures for evaluations, eligibility determinations, individualized education programs and placement are located in 20 U.S.C. § 1414.

IDEA safeguards emphasize, among other things, notice to parents and an opportunity for parental participation in the development of a child's special education program. Significantly, 20 U.S.C. § 1415 requires that parents have an opportunity to examine their child's records, and "to participate in meetings with respect to the identification, evaluation, and educational placement of the child, and the provision of a free appropriate public education" to the child.

Parents are entitled to obtain an independent evaluation of their children and to receive prior written notice whenever an educational agency proposes to initiate or change, or refuses to initiate or change, the education of the child, and where the identification, evaluation or placement of the child, or the provision of a FAPE to the child is at issue.

Parents who disagree with an educational agency's proposed IEP or a proposal to change a placement have the right to receive an impartial hearing before a hearing officer who is not an employee of the school district or of the state education department. 20 U.S.C. § 1415(f).

Under 20 U.S.C. § 1415(d), states and LEAs that receive IDEA funds must ensure that a mediation process is available to allow parties to resolve special education disputes. The parents or the school may appeal unfavorable hearing decisions to the state education department after the exhaustion of available administrative procedures. A lawsuit may be commenced by an aggrieved party in either state or federal court after a decision has been reached by the state education agency.

The IDEA stay-put requirement, found at 20 U.S.C. § 1415(j), is a frequently litigated provision requiring the maintenance of a student's current educational placement pending any IDEA proceeding, unless the parties agree otherwise. See Chapter Two, Section III, subsection B for cases interpreting the stay-put requirement.

The Supreme Court has held that the indefinite suspension of a student with a disability violates the stay-put provision. See *Honig v. Doe*, Chapter Two, Section IV.

It's important to remember that the IDEA was enacted to ensure that all children with disabilities, even those with severe disabilities, receive a free appropriate public education (FAPE).

C. Organization of This Book

The subject matter of cases in special education overlaps, perhaps more than in other areas of the law. For example, a case that primarily involves a placement dispute may also contain important information in other subject matter areas such as procedures, private school tuition reimbursement, related services and attorneys' fees.

Many lawsuits filed under the IDEA include causes of action under other federal statutes such as the Americans with Disabilities Act, 42 U.S.C. § 12101 *et seq.*, the Rehabilitation Act of 1973 (29 U.S.C. § 701 *et seq.*) and 42 U.S.C. § 1983. Accordingly, the concerned professional will want to become familiar with all the cases in this volume.

Although some cases appear in more than one chapter of the book because they concern multiple subject matters, the cases have generally been categorized according to the subject matter of the court's most significant holding (in the opinion of the editors).

Unlike the IDEA, which mandates special education standards and procedures, Section 504 of the Rehabilitation Act of 1973 places greater emphasis on employment training and habilitation for individuals with disabilities. It contains an anti-discrimination provision that prohibits entities that receive federal funds from discriminating against individuals with disabilities in their programs or services. 29 U.S.C. § 794.

Since all school districts, states and educational agencies receive federal funds, Section 504 complaints are commonly filed by students seeking educational benefits, by individuals seeking employment or benefits from educational agencies, and by employees claiming disability discrimination. Whereas courts are permitted to award damages under Section 504, claims for monetary damage awards under the IDEA have been dismissed by several courts despite the apparently permissive language of 20 U.S.C. § 1403(b).

For employment discrimination cases under Section 504, see Chapter Seven, Section II, subsection A. For Section 504 cases involving complaints by students for failure to provide them with reasonable accommodations, see Chapter Nine, Section I, subsection A.

The Americans with Disabilities Act of 1990 (ADA) is another important federal statute protecting individuals with disabilities. Although based upon the anti-discrimination principles of Section 504 and its regulations, the ADA's application extends to many public and private entities without restriction to recipients of federal funding. For employment discrimination cases under the ADA, see Chapter Seven, Section II, subsection A. For ADA cases involving complaints by students for failure to provide reasonable accommodation, see Chapter Nine, Section I, subsection B.

II. MINIMUM IDEA STANDARDS UNDER
BOARD OF EDUCATION V. ROWLEY

The IDEA and its regulations focus on procedural requirements and delegate substantive educational issues to the states and their local educational agencies. However, the IDEA has been interpreted by the U.S. Supreme Court as establishing a minimum "floor of educational opportunity" that requires educational agencies to provide educational benefits that are reasonably calculated to enable students with disabilities to receive a free appropriate public education.

States may voluntarily establish their own higher standards as New Jersey, North Carolina, California and Massachusetts have done. According to the U.S. Supreme Court, the IDEA was not enacted to maximize the potential of students with disabilities, but rather to open the door of educational opportunity. The Supreme Court's decision in Board of Education v. Rowley, *458 U.S. 176 (1982), discusses the substantive requirements of the IDEA.*

◆   The parents of an eight-year-old New York student with profound hearing impairments disagreed with their local education board over the student's need for a sign-language interpreter during academic classes. They insisted that the tutoring and hearing aid provided by the school district were insufficient, even though the student performed better than average and advanced educationally. The parents argued that because of the disparity between her achievement and her potential, she was not receiving a FAPE under the IDEA (then known as the EHA). The state commissioner of education affirmed an independent hearing examiner's decision that found the interpreter unnecessary because the student was achieving educationally, academically and socially without this service. A federal court held that because of the disparity between the student's achievement and her potential, she was not receiving a FAPE. The Second Circuit affirmed and the U.S. Supreme Court granted review.

The Court observed that in passing the IDEA, "Congress sought primarily to make public education available to [children with disabilities]. But in seeking to provide such access to public education, Congress did not impose upon the States any greater substantive educational standard than would be necessary to make such access meaningful." According to the Court, the IDEA imposed no requirement on states to provide equal educational opportunities and Congress recognized that educational opportunity differs among students of varying abilities. Because of the "wide spectrum" of abilities, the Court refused to establish a test to determine the adequacy of educational benefits provided by schools under the IDEA. Instead of imposing a general rule, the Court held:

> Insofar as a State is required to provide a handicapped child with a "free appropriate public education," we hold that it satisfies this requirement by providing **personalized instruction with sufficient support services to permit the child to benefit educationally from that instruction**. Such instruction and services must be provided at public expense, must meet the State's educational standards, must approximate the grade levels used in the State's regular education, and must comport with the child's IEP. In addition, the IEP, and therefore the personalized instruction, should be formulated in accordance with the requirements of the Act and, if the child is being educated in the regular classrooms of the public education system, should be **reasonably calculated to enable the child to achieve passing marks and advance from grade to grade**.

The Court ruled that the school board was not required to provide the sign-language interpreter. The IDEA required only the development of an IEP that was reasonably calculated to enable the disabled student to derive some educational benefit. **The IDEA created a minimum floor** for the provision of special education services but did not require states to maximize the potential of each disabled child. In this case, the child was advancing through school easily and was not entitled to an interpreter, despite evidence that this would remedy the disparity between her achievement and her potential. *Board of Educ. v. Rowley*, 458 U.S. 176, 102 S.Ct. 3034, 73 L.Ed.2d 690 (1982).

Board of Education v. Rowley remains a primary source of authority for interpreting the IDEA and is still relied upon by state and federal courts. The following cases concern the standards and policies cited in *Rowley*.

◆   The parents of a Texas student with Williams syndrome sought to have her placed in a Massachusetts residential music academy because research suggested that music could help in her academic development. After they sent her to the music academy, school officials denied their request for tuition reimbursement. They eventually sued, **claiming that the "access with some benefit" standards set by *Board of Educ. v. Rowley* were no longer applicable following the IDEA amendments of 1997 and 2004**. Instead, they claimed, the school district had to maximize the student's potential. A federal court disagreed, noting that the Fifth Circuit (as well as the First Circuit) still relies on *Rowley*. Thus, the district did not have to reimburse the parents for the tuition paid to the music academy. *K.C. ex rel. M.C. v. Mansfield Independent School Dist.*, 618 F.Supp.2d 568 (N.D. Tex. 2009).

♦ A Washington student with learning disabilities attended regular classes and progressed from grade to grade. Her parents became dissatisfied with her education and found an independent evaluator who suggested that no public schools in the state could provide an adequate education. The parents enrolled their daughter in a Massachusetts private school and sought tuition reimbursement. An administrative law judge ruled against them, but a federal court held that the ALJ had improperly used the *Board of Educ. v. Rowley* standard, which had been superseded by amendments to the IDEA. The case reached the Ninth Circuit, which ruled that **the *Rowley* standard was still the appropriate means for determining whether a child received an appropriate education**. Congress never disapproved of the *Rowley* standard in any of the amendments to the IDEA. *J.L. v. Mercer Island School Dist.*, 575 F.3d 1025 (9th Cir. 2009).

♦ The parents of a Connecticut student disagreed with his IEPs for grades five and six. They placed him in a private school with smaller classes, then sought due process, asserting that the board did not fully evaluate him and did not base the IEPs on the recommendations of their experts. The case reached the Second Circuit, which ruled for the board. The IEPs for both grades provided the student with a **basic floor of opportunity** and "prescribed interventions that anticipated the suggestions of the [parents'] experts." *Mr. B. v. East Granby Board of Educ.*, 201 Fed.Appx. 834 (2d Cir. 2006).

♦ In 2002, Missouri amended its special education law to delete the requirement that special education programs maximize the capabilities of students with disabilities. When a disabled student and a public interest law center challenged the amendment as violative of the Missouri Constitution, the case reached the state supreme court. The court held that the amendment did not violate the state constitution. It did not amend the law in a way that changed its original purpose. As a result, **Missouri now uses the federal standard for determining the sufficiency of special education services.** *McEuen v. Missouri State Board of Educ.*, 120 S.W.3d 207 (Mo. 2003).

♦ A California student was on a home/hospital instruction plan during the 1994-95 school year but was not provided with instruction from a teacher with a special education credential until March. For the first three months of the school year, the district provided him with a regular education teacher, and for the next two months, it did not provide any teacher. The next year, the district placed the student in a class for students with serious emotional disturbance, even though he was not seriously emotionally disturbed. A federal court awarded the student compensatory education and his parents reimbursement for various expenses. The Ninth Circuit observed that the student's improper placement in the seriously emotionally disturbed classroom violated the IDEA's least restrictive environment requirement. The district's failure to provide the student any special education services for a significant part of a school year meant that **it did not offer services that were reasonably calculated to provide the student with educational benefits**. The district fell below the minimum "basic floor of opportunity" by failing to provide access to a special education teacher. Parents have an equitable right to reimbursement for the cost of compensatory education when a school district fails to provide a student with a FAPE. Despite the parents' repeated requests for services, the student had not graduated with his class and did not perform at his grade level. Although he had left school, he was entitled to compensatory education. The court affirmed the district court order awarding the parents reimbursement for certain costs and attorneys' fees. *Everett v. Santa Barbara High School Dist.*, 28 Fed.Appx. 683 (9th Cir. 2002) (Unpublished).

♦ A Michigan student was diagnosed as autistic and received services in a trainable mentally impaired classroom operated by an educational services agency. The agency discontinued the program, and the student was placed in a cross-categorical program. The agency special education coordinator notified the parents that the district would offer the student a program equivalent to a favorable program offered at another district. An IEP calling for placement within the district was finalized without the parents' involvement. A hearing officer held that this violated the IDEA. However, a review officer found that the proposed placement provided the student with a FAPE. When the parents sued, the Sixth Circuit observed that even though Michigan special education standards require school boards to maximize the potential of each student with disabilities, the term **"maximum potential" was not well defined in Michigan law and did not necessarily mean the best education possible**. The court required only that the student receive a FAPE that was reasonably calculated to provide educational benefits. The program proposed by the school district met this standard. *Soraruf v. Pinckney Community Schools*, 208 F.3d 215 (6th Cir. 2000).

♦ Although a student struggled in his public school placement, he did not initially qualify for special education services. His parents obtained an independent evaluation, learned that he had dyslexia and attention deficit disorder, and enrolled him in a private school. The student returned to the public school before the end of the year and was eventually referred to an admission, review and dismissal (ARD) committee, which identified reading and language deficiencies. The ARD committee recommended 10 hours per week in a reading and language resource room with weekly speech therapy. The student continued to experience some difficulties in grade four and received extended-year services and compensatory speech therapy. His parents objected to the district's failure to implement certain IEP modifications. A hearing officer found that the district failed to consistently or appropriately implement the student's IEP. For the student's seventh-grade year, the parties failed to agree on an IEP, and the parents placed him in a private setting.

The school district appealed to a federal court, which concluded the student showed improvement and received educational benefit during the disputed time period. The court dismissed the parents' counterclaim for private school compensatory services reimbursement. The parents appealed to the Fifth Circuit, which noted that the test for appropriateness of an IEP includes assessment of whether education is provided in a coordinated and collaborative manner by key stakeholders and asks whether the student is receiving positive academic and nonacademic benefits. Here, the lower court properly determined that any shortcomings in the school district's implementation of the IEP were remedied by the compensatory services it offered. The student received educational benefits. **It was unnecessary for the student to improve in every academic area in order to receive educational benefit from his IEP.** Since he received a FAPE in his public school placement, the claim for private school reimbursement was rejected. *Houston Independent School Dist. v. Bobby R.,* 200 F.3d 341 (5th Cir. 2000).

♦   The parents of a child identified as autistic determined that the child would benefit most from a 40-hour per week, Lovaas-type program of discrete trial training (DTT). Members of the individual family service plan (IFSP) team sought to include other methodologies in the child's program, and the parties began to dispute the frequency and level of services. The county educational service district rejected the parents' request for an extension in services to 40 hours per week of DTT. The parties ultimately agreed on a program of 12.5 hours of weekly early intervention services. The parents voluntarily supplemented this with more intensive home services and private tutoring. They approved the IFSP and did not seek reimbursement for supplemental services. They also approved the county's decision to reduce the weekly services for the child to 7.5 hours during the summer to accommodate vacation schedules. The parents then asserted that the county failed to provide appropriate early intervention services.

The Ninth Circuit observed that **as in the case of K-12 students, infants and toddlers are not entitled to early intervention programs that maximize their potential**. Courts must look to IFSP goals as of the time of implementation, and ask whether the methods were reasonably calculated to confer meaningful educational benefit on the child. Here, the IFSP was sufficient to confer a meaningful benefit. The family was not entitled to reimbursement for the child's school year programming. The reduction in services had erroneously been made in consideration of staff vacation schedules. Although a reduction in hours linked with developmental goals is permissible, this one was not. As a result, the parents were entitled to reimbursement for their expenses in obtaining appropriate services and tutoring during the summer. *Adams v. State of Oregon,* 195 F.3d 1141 (9th Cir. 1999).

III. U.S. SUPREME COURT CASES

The following brief summaries provide an overview of important IDEA cases decided by the U.S. Supreme Court. For the full summary of each case and other cases dealing with issues in the subject matter of the Supreme Court's case, please refer to the chapter and section indicated.

♦   A Maryland student with learning disabilities and a speech impairment attended private schools until the eighth grade, when his parents sought to place him in district schools. The district conducted an evaluation and drafted an IEP that would have placed him in one of two district schools. The parents rejected the offer, seeking a smaller classroom setting with more intensive services. They requested an IDEA due process hearing, where the administrative law judge ruled they had the burden of persuasion and did not meet it. Eventually the case reached the U.S. Supreme Court, which agreed that **parents who challenge IEPs have the burden of proving that the IEPs are not appropriate**. To do otherwise would force courts to assume that every IEP is invalid until the school district demonstrates that it is not. *Schaffer v. Weast*, 546 U.S. 49, 126 S.Ct. 528, 163 L.Ed.2d 387 (2005). See also Chapter Three, Section I.

◆   The U.S. Supreme Court held that a New York statute that created a special school district for a religious community (which had been incorporated as a village) had to be struck down as violative of the Establishment Clause. **The special school district exceeded the bounds of religious neutrality** required by the Constitution. *Board of Educ. of Kiryas Joel Village School Dist. v. Grumet*, 512 U.S. 687, 114 S.Ct. 2481, 129 L.Ed.2d 546 (1994). See also Chapter Eight, Section I.

◆   The parents of a learning disabled Massachusetts student were found by the Court to have violated the IDEA's stay-put provision by unilaterally enrolling him in a private school. Because the proposed IEP had been appropriate, the parents were not entitled to tuition reimbursement and other costs. The Court, however, noted that in some situations parents could be reimbursed even though they unilaterally placed a student in a private school where a court later held that the proposed IEP was educationally inappropriate. **Parents who unilaterally changed their children's placement did so at their own risk**, because if (as in this case) the proposed IEP was appropriate, the parents had to pay the private school costs. *Burlington School Committee v. Dep't of Educ. of Massachusetts*, 471 U.S. 359, 105 S.Ct. 1996, 85 L.Ed.2d 385 (1985). See also Chapter Four, Section I.

◆   The Court held that the failure of a school district to propose an appropriate IEP and placement for a learning disabled student justified an award of private school tuition reimbursement by the district, even though the private school was not approved by the state of South Carolina. This was because the private school placement was appropriate and because South Carolina did not publish a list of approved schools. The IDEA requirement to provide a free appropriate public education did not apply to parental placements. **To recover private school tuition costs, parents must show that the placement proposed by the school district violates the IDEA and that the private school placement is appropriate under the act.** Federal courts have broad discretion in granting relief under the IDEA and may reduce tuition reimbursement awards found to be unreasonably expensive. The Court upheld the lower court decisions in favor of the parents. *Florence County School Dist. Four v. Carter*, 510 U.S. 7, 114 S.Ct. 361, 126 L.Ed.2d 284 (1993). See also Chapter Four, Section I.

◆   The Establishment Clause of the First Amendment did not bar a public school district from **providing a sign-language interpreter to an Arizona student who attended a parochial school**. The provision of the interpreter was a neutral service that provided only an indirect economic benefit to the parochial school. *Zobrest v. Catalina Foothills School Dist.,* 509 U.S. 1, 113 S.Ct. 2462, 125 L.Ed.2d 1 (1993). See also Chapter Four, Section II.

◆ The Court held that Congress did not intend that the IDEA permit monetary damage awards against states in actions brought in federal courts under the doctrine of sovereign immunity. This permitted the Commonwealth of Pennsylvania to avoid liability in an IDEA damage suit brought by a learning disabled student. [In 1990, Congress passed an amendment abrogating sovereign immunity (20 U.S.C. § 1403) in IDEA cases and authorizing both equitable (injunctive and declaratory) and legal (damage award) remedies under the IDEA.] *Dellmuth v. Muth,* 491 U.S. 223, 109 S.Ct. 2397, 105 L.Ed.2d 181 (1989). For a full discussion of sovereign immunity issues, see Chapter Six, Section I.

◆ The suspension or expulsion of a special education student constitutes a change of placement under the IDEA, according to the 1988 decision *Honig v. Doe.* School authorities may not unilaterally exclude a child from classes pending administrative proceedings. However, **the IDEA's stay-put provision (20 U.S.C. § 1415(e)(3), now Section 1415(j)) did not prevent school districts from imposing temporary suspensions of 10 school days or less** upon students who present a threat of harm to other persons. *Honig v. Doe,* 484 U.S. 305, 108 S.Ct. 592, 98 L.Ed.2d 686 (1988). The 1997 Amendments address suspensions for disciplinary reasons in 20 U.S.C. § 1415(k) and allow removal from class for up to 55 days in certain circumstances. See also Chapter Two, Section IV.

◆ A Texas **school district had to provide catheterization services for a disabled student while she attended school because it was a "supportive service" (related service)** under the IDEA, 20 U.S.C. § 1401(22). The Court held that the student's parents were also entitled to receive their attorneys' fees under Section 504 of the Rehabilitation Act. *Irving Independent School Dist. v. Tatro,* 468 U.S. 883, 104 S.Ct. 3371, 82 L.Ed.2d 664 (1984). See also Chapter Five, Section II.

◆ The Supreme Court held that an Iowa school district had to provide a quadriplegic student with a full-time aide to assure his meaningful access to education under the IDEA. **Providing an aide amounted to a necessary related service and not an excluded medical service.** Using a "bright-line" rule, the Court limited medical services to those provided by a physician. *Cedar Rapids Community School Dist. v. Garret F.,* 526 U.S. 66, 119 S.Ct. 992, 143 L.Ed.2d 154 (1999). See also Chapter Five, Section II.

◆ A disabled Rhode Island student was not entitled to recover attorneys' fees despite prevailing in an IDEA lawsuit against his school district in *Smith v. Robinson.* The Court ruled that there was no evidence that the school district had violated any of the student's procedural safeguards under the IDEA. Congress responded to the *Smith* decision by passing the Handicapped

Children's Protection Act of 1986 (P.L. 99–372), which **specifically authorized attorneys' fee awards to students with disabilities who prevailed in IDEA lawsuits**. The same legislation provided that disabled students may cumulate available remedies under Section 504 of the Rehabilitation Act (29 U.S.C. § 794) and 42 U.S.C. § 1983. See 20 U.S.C. § 1415(i)(3) and § 1415(l). *Smith v. Robinson*, 468 U.S. 992, 104 S.Ct. 3457, 82 L.Ed.2d 746 (1984). Because the Handicapped Children's Protection Act of 1986 substantially overruled *Smith v. Robinson*, there is no further summary of the case in this volume.

IV. IDENTIFICATION AND EVALUATION

The IDEA requires each state and LEA to conduct a full and individual evaluation before the initial provision of special education and related services to resident students with disabilities. See 20 U.S.C. § 1414(a)(1)(A). Each state must also demonstrate that each resident student with a disability is identified, located and evaluated under 20 U.S.C. § 1412(a)(3)(c), and is provided with an IEP that meets IDEA requirements described at 20 U.S.C. § 1414(d).

LEAs must comply with the notice and procedural requirements of 20 U.S.C. § 1414(b). The IDEA's triennial reevaluation requirement was modified by the 1997 amendments to allow evaluation teams to forego testing where new information is unnecessary to assist in a placement decision.

Parents who have not allowed an evaluation of their children, or who have refused special education, are barred from later asserting IDEA procedural protections in disciplinary cases.

A. Educational Agency Obligations

1. Child Find

♦   A California student for whom English was a second language was found to be at risk of retention in several early grades. The district found the student's cognitive, perceptual-motor and behavioral function scores to be average, and it denied special education. It offered a Section 504 plan to address his distractibility and homework problems, and he progressed from grade to grade despite his at-risk designation. The parents sued for a violation of the child-find requirement, and a federal court ruled in favor of the district. **Interventions corrected the student's problems, and he was properly denied special education status.** There was no child-find violation. *E.M. v. Pajaro Valley Unified School Dist.*, No. C 06-4694 JF, 2009 WL 2766704 (N.D. Cal. 8/27/09).

♦   An Ohio student diagnosed with ADD, ADHD, oppositional defiance disorder and absence seizures was finally diagnosed with Asperger's syndrome in eighth grade. A dispute arose over the student's IEP, and his parents eventually sued, asserting that the district's failure to diagnose Asperger's syndrome amounted to a violation of the IDEA. A federal court held that **the**

district's failure to correctly label the student's disabilities did not violate the IDEA. The student received special education beginning in his second-grade year. The IDEA does not require schools to place students in specific categories. It only requires that they be given an appropriate education, which the student received. *Pohorecki v. Anthony Wayne Local School Dist.*, 637 F.Supp.2d 547 (N.D. Ohio 2009).

♦ After an evaluation, a Pennsylvania second-grader was thought to have ADHD. However, there was no discrepancy between his ability and his achievement, so he was not placed in special education. By the seventh grade, his performance declined and at the end of the eighth grade he was evaluated again and found to have ADHD. His performance continued to decline over the next two years. He dropped out of school, and his parents sued the district for failing to timely identify him as disabled. A federal court and the Third Circuit ruled against them, finding that **the school district did not rely solely on an ability/achievement analysis in determining that the student didn't need special education at an earlier age**. The district did not violate its child-find duty under the IDEA. *Richard S. v. Wissahickon School Dist.*, 334 Fed.Appx. 508 (3d Cir. 2009).

♦ The mother of Nevada preschool twins with speech and other developmental difficulties took them to a free screening session at a private learning center, which referred them to their school district. The district referred the mother to a "Child Find Day" about six weeks later and did not give her a copy of her IDEA procedural safeguards. The children were not responsive at the Child Find Day, and assessments were scheduled for two months later. Meanwhile, the private center determined that the children had autism. The district eventually agreed with the diagnosis. A hearing officer determined that the district failed to timely evaluate the children, but the Ninth Circuit held that **the delay between when the twins were evaluated and when they began receiving services was reasonable**. The mother was only entitled to be reimbursed for the $1,670 she spent on private evaluations. *JG v. Douglas County School Dist.*, 552 F.3d 786 (9th Cir. 2009).

♦ A Kentucky student was diagnosed with ADHD near the end of his fourth-grade year. His mother claimed the district should have identified him as IDEA-eligible earlier and sought due process. A hearing officer awarded the student 125 hours of compensatory education. A state appeals board affirmed but decided that the student's IEP team should determine how much compensatory education the student should receive. On appeal, the Sixth Circuit held that the IEP team should not have been granted the authority to decide how much compensatory education the student was due. However, **it rejected the mother's claim that the district should have referred the student for special education as early as kindergarten**. Children have different development rates, and referring a child too early can be damaging. The court remanded the case for a re-determination of the compensatory education award. *Board of Educ. of Fayette County, Kentucky v. L.M.*, 478 F.3d 307 (6th Cir. 2007).

♦   When a Pennsylvania student was in first grade, an evaluation by a county intermediate unit (IU) found she had a learning disability. Although the evaluation recommended a public school placement with intensive reading and language therapy services, the parents kept the student in her private school through her sixth-grade year. The district provided the student's private school transportation until she reached grade seven, when she began attending a school outside the district. The parents contested the district's refusal to continue transportation and sought tuition reimbursement for the student's six years in private schools, plus compensatory education for violations of the IDEA's "child-find" duty. A federal court ruled against them. **The district's child-find activities were legally sufficient.** Also, the parents did not give the district an opportunity to provide their daughter a public school education. *Marissa F. v. William Penn School Dist.*, No. Civ.A. 04-286, 2005 WL 2304738 (E.D. Pa. 9/20/05).

♦   The mother of a Pennsylvania private school student told the principal she believed he had a learning disability, but she did not make a written request for his evaluation. Years later, the parents made a written request for an evaluation. The district exceeded the 60-day time limit for completing an evaluation, then crafted an IEP near the end of the school year. The parents approved of the IEP, but requested a due process hearing, alleging that the district violated the IDEA child-find obligation, and claiming tuition reimbursement for the past six years. The hearing officer ruled against them, and a federal court agreed that **the district did not fail in its child-find obligations.** Any delay in completing the evaluation and IEP was harmless because it was highly unlikely the parents would have removed their son from school for the last few weeks of the year. *Alex K. v. Wissahickon School Dist.*, No. Civ.A. 03-854, 2004 WL 286871 (E.D. Pa. 2/12/04).

♦   An Ohio student diagnosed with leukemia at age seven became eligible for special education and related services as "other health impaired" (OHI) under the IDEA. During her eighth-grade year, the district initiated a multi-factored evaluation to determine whether she was still eligible under the OHI designation. It concluded that she was no longer eligible for special education and related services because her academic achievement was commensurate with her general academic ability. Her mother challenged the decision, and a hearing officer ordered the district to continue providing services to the student under her IEP until the district could reevaluate her. He found that the district failed to comply with IDEA procedural safeguards. A state review officer and a federal court agreed with the hearing officer that the student was entitled to continuing services. Here, **the student still had late effects from chemotherapy and radiation** that resulted in cognitive, academic, executive functioning and processing speed deficits, as well as depression, psychomotor retardation and frequent bone fractures. *Elida Local School Dist. Board of Educ. v. Erickson*, 252 F.Supp.2d 476 (N.D. Ohio 2003).

♦   A Tennessee student with learning disabilities and an emotional disturbance never attended public schools. His parents enrolled him in a private Connecticut school for students with learning disabilities. They did not contact the district before making the placement or request an evaluation. When the family requested an evaluation over a year later, the district took more than six months to complete it. The evaluation was hampered by the student's absence from the district and by delays in obtaining information. During a meeting to discuss the student's educational program, his father expressed his intention to keep his son in the Connecticut facility and did not complain about the lengthy evaluation process. The district certified the student for special education and proposed a public school placement. The parents commenced an IDEA action against the district, asserting they were entitled to reimbursement and claiming that the district had an insufficient child find plan.

A federal court found that the district's plan called for the dissemination of information to all area private schools, day care centers, nursery schools, hospitals and other places where medical professionals were likely to encounter children with special education requirements. The district also made local public service announcements and conducted an outreach program. The court found that the school district had made adequate child-find efforts and denied the parents' request for private school tuition reimbursement. The Sixth Circuit affirmed, observing that the parents had never contacted the district about their son's placement before seeking reimbursement. **The district's publicity campaign fulfilled its child-find duties.** The IDEA's child-find obligation does not require districts to pursue the parents of private school students who do not act upon available information. *Doe v. Metropolitan Nashville Public Schools*, 9 Fed.Appx. 453 (6th Cir. 2001).

2. IDEA Eligibility Determinations

◆   The parents of a New York preschool student obtained three evaluations showing that their son had either an autism spectrum disorder, ADHD or serious social issues. They sought special education for him even though his teachers maintained that he made academic progress and his behavior problems were manageable. A due process hearing officer noted that the student's behavior did not adversely impact his education to a degree that indicated a need for special education. A federal court agreed. All the parents could show was that because their son needed frequent redirection, **he was not reaching his full academic potential, which is not the IDEA eligibility standard.** *A.J. v. Board of Educ., East Islip Union Free School Dist.*, 679 F.Supp.2d 299 (E.D.N.Y. 2010).

◆   A Wisconsin student with Ehlers-Danlos Syndrome had chronic pain and fatigue, hypotonic muscles and gastrointestinal problems. Due to modifications and accommodations, he performed in the average range at school and achieved three of his five IEP objectives for adaptive PE. The IEP team then recommended that he no longer be classified as eligible for special education. His parents requested a due process hearing, at which an administrative law judge found him eligible for special education. A federal court agreed that the school improperly found him ineligible, but the Seventh Circuit reversed, finding that the student only received special education for his gym class. And **his doctor evaluated him for a mere 15 minutes before finding that the**

student's pain <u>could</u> affect his educational performance. The court of appeals held that the doctor could not prescribe special education over the judgment of the IEP team. *Marshall Joint School Dist. No. 2 v. C.D.*, 616 F.3d 632 (7th Cir. 2010).

♦ A Hawaii student with ADHD received accommodations and achieved average scores on standardized tests. An eligibility team found the student ineligible for special education. The parents requested an independent education evaluator, who recommended a functional behavioral assessment. The team rejected that recommendation. A hearing officer found that the student's accommodations did not provide him with access to the general education curriculum, and a federal court agreed that the student's ADHD adversely affected his educational performance. He made no progress in science or social studies, and he failed spelling. **The standardized test results did not address the student's ability to perform in a regular classroom setting.** The student was entitled to compensatory education. *State of Hawaii, Dep't of Educ. v. Zachary B.*, No. 08-00499 JMS/LEK, 2009 WL 1585816 (D. Haw. 6/5/09).

♦ A New York student with ADHD and bipolar disorder earned good grades and test scores. Still, her parents placed her in a private school and sought tuition reimbursement. The case reached the Second Circuit, which held that **the student, despite her disabling conditions, was not eligible for special education** and related services under the IDEA. Her academic success made her ineligible. *C.B. v. Dep't of Educ. of City of New York*, 322 Fed.Appx. 20 (2d Cir. 2009).

♦ Before a California student entered grade five his mother asked the district to evaluate him for special education. An IEP assessment team determined that he was not eligible for special education, and the mother challenged that decision. An administrative law judge (ALJ) upheld the denial of services, but a federal court found that the ALJ had not sufficiently explained his decision, apparently **relying on only a single measure** – the Wechsler Intelligence Scale for Children – and disregarding the student's score on the Kaufman Assessment Battery for Children as well as his IQ tests. The court remanded the case for further proceedings. *E.M. v. Pajaro Valley Unified School Dist.*, No. C 06-4694 JF, 2008 WL 4615436 (N.D. Cal. 10/17/08).

♦ A Hawaii third-grader was diagnosed with ADHD, but was found ineligible for special education under the IDEA. The eligibility determination team found no discrepancy between his achievement and ability. Actually, he was achieving at a rate higher than his ability level based on standardized tests. The team also found the student ineligible for services under Section 504. After a hearing officer upheld that decision, a federal court agreed that the student was not entitled to special education or related services under the IDEA or Section 504. The parents failed to show that the student's ADHD more than minimally adversely affected his educational performance. *Ashli C. v. State of Hawaii*, No. 05-00429 HG-KSC, 2007 WL 247761 (D. Haw. 1/23/07).

♦   A California student had difficulty completing tasks, turning her homework in on time, and organizing her belongings. However, she performed at grade level and tested in the fiftieth percentile on the Stanford Achievement Test. She was taking medication for a possible seizure disorder and was placed on a Section 504 accommodation plan. Her parents sought special education for her based on a specific learning disability, claiming that her seizure disorder adversely affected her ability to focus in the classroom. The district found that **she did not qualify for special education and related services because she performed in at least the average range academically**. When the parents placed her in a private school and sought tuition reimbursement, a federal court and the Ninth Circuit ruled for the district. The student did not require special education to meet her needs. *Hood v. Encinitas Union School Dist.*, 486 F.3d 1099 (9th Cir. 2007).

♦   A Maine elementary school student excelled academically, but began having problems with peers and depression. She stayed in public school until sixth grade, when she skipped school, inflicted wounds on herself and had more peer problems. After attempting suicide, she was hospitalized and later diagnosed with Asperger's Syndrome. A school pupil evaluation team identified her as a qualified individual with a disability under Section 504, but determined she was ineligible for special education under the IDEA. She was offered 10 hours of weekly tutoring. Instead, her parents enrolled her in a private school. In the lawsuit that arose over her education, the First Circuit held that **even though the child did not have academic needs, she could still be eligible for special education** under the IDEA. Here, the student's condition adversely affected her educational performance in nonacademic areas. Accordingly, the student was entitled to compensatory education for the period during which she was deemed ineligible. However, she was not entitled to tuition reimbursement for the private school placement. *Mr. I. v. Maine School Administrative Dist. No. 55*, 480 F.3d 1 (1st Cir. 2007).

♦   A Pennsylvania student was diagnosed with ADHD after an independent educational evaluation in 2004. However, the district did not find him eligible for special education. In 2005, his parents placed him in a private school, then sought tuition reimbursement, asserting that the district should have known of his disability as early as 2002. In 2006, the student was identified as having a specific learning disability. In the lawsuit that arose over tuition, a federal court ruled against the parents, noting that **the district had complied with its child-find obligation under the IDEA**. The 2004 evaluation did not automatically signal that the school district believed the student was entitled to special education at that time. The district's IEPs were reasonably calculated to yield meaningful educational progress, and the parents were not entitled to tuition reimbursement. *Daniel S. v. Council Rock School Dist.*, No. 06-3531, 2007 WL 3120014 (E.D. Pa. 10/25/07).

♦   Missouri school district officials sought to evaluate a student whose behavior and academic performance indicated he might have a disability. His parents refused to consent to the evaluation, pulled him from school to educate him at home, obtained a private evaluation and expressly waived IDEA services. When the district continued to pursue an evaluation, the Eighth Circuit held that **the district could not override the parents' wishes and force an evaluation of the student**, who was no longer in district schools. *Fitzgerald v. Camdenton R-III, School Dist.*, 439 F.3d 773 (8th Cir. 2006).

◆   The parent of a student at a District of Columbia public school requested special education evaluations, but the district did not timely complete them. The student transferred to a charter school for the next year and it completed the evaluations. It then filed an IDEA due process hearing request against the district, seeking $1,150 in evaluation costs. The hearing officer held that he did not have jurisdiction, and a federal court agreed that **the charter school could not act on behalf of the parent to recover the evaluation costs**. It had to either follow existing procedures for reimbursement from the district or invoice the parent for its evaluation costs. The parent would then be allowed to initiate a due process request. *IDEA Public Charter School v. District of Columbia*, 374 F.Supp.2d 158 (D.D.C. 2005).

◆   Although she received special education until the fifth grade, a Nebraska student was then deemed ineligible for special education services. When her grades dropped during the seventh grade, her parents questioned the lack of special education. Although they signed a release allowing the school to inspect her medical records, they provided outdated information. Her grades continued to drop and she was placed in a home school program. The parents sued the district and officials under the IDEA, ADA, and Rehabilitation Act Section 504. The court held for the district and officials, and the Eighth Circuit affirmed. Here, the parents did not appropriately respond to the district's requests for current information. **The district performed its obligation to identify and evaluate the student**, and there was no IDEA violation. The ADA and Section 504 claims failed because the student's impairments were only moderately limiting, and she was not disabled under either act. *Costello v. Mitchell Public School Dist. 79*, 266 F.3d 916 (8th Cir. 2001).

3. District Delays and Failures

◆   A Pennsylvania student suffered a severe asthma attack at school. Paramedics arrived within 10 minutes of being called, but the student died three days later at a hospital. When his mother sued the district for violating the child-find requirement of the IDEA, a federal court first ruled that she did not have to exhaust her administrative remedies because she could obtain no relief through the administrative process. However, **the district did not violate the IDEA by failing to identify him as eligible for special education**. He received average grades, was social with other students and had no attendance problems. On the other hand, the mother might be able to attain some relief under Section 504 for failure to reasonably accommodate. A trial was required on that issue. *Taylor v. Altoona Area School Dist.*, 737 F.Supp.2d 474 (W.D. Pa. 2010).

♦   A family moved to Georgia, and their daughter was placed in kindergarten using her former district's test scores. She was evaluated as mildly mentally retarded and was educated that way for 10 years until her parents requested a change in curriculum and brought in an advocate who suggested the student might have autism. A school psychologist concurred with that diagnosis. The parents sought remediation at the Lindamood Bell Center, but the district denied their request. In the lawsuit that followed, a federal court ruled that the district did not violate the IDEA for a 10-year period by placing the student in a mentally disabled program instead of an autism one. However, the two-year statute of limitations did not bar the parents' claim that she was misdiagnosed. Also, **the student should have been provided remedial education once she was diagnosed with autism**. *Gwinnett County School Dist. v. A.A.*, No. 1:09-CV-445-TWT, 2010 WL 2838585 (N.D. Ga. 7/16/10).

♦   The parents of a California student revoked their consent to his IEP and sought to place him in a private school. They claimed that the district denied their son a FAPE by failing to assess him in the area of auditory processing deficits. They asserted that the district failed to conduct a TAPS-3 test in accord with instructions provided by the producer of the test. An administrative law judge and a federal court ruled for the district, noting that **even if the TAPS-3 test was administered incorrectly, many other measures were used to assess the student's eligibility and need for services**. The IDEA did not require an assessment by an audiologist. *M.P. v. Poway Unified School Dist.*, No. 09 CV 1627 JLS (NLS), 2010 WL 2735759 (S.D. Cal. 7/12/10).

♦   Ohio parents sought services for their child based on his suspected autism and language disorder. The district found him ineligible for special education. They obtained private services for him and **two years later presented private speech-language evaluations to support their position**. The district again denied special education, and they placed him in a private school. When they tried to obtain due process, the district's hearing officer held that their complaint did not meet IDEA requirements. Eventually they sued and settled, with state officials agreeing that they were prevailing parties with respect to systemic issues related to sufficiency challenges. A court then awarded them $81,000 in attorneys' fees, and the Sixth Circuit upheld the award. *Keene v. Zelman*, 337 Fed.Appx. 553 (6th Cir. 2009).

♦   A California student with ADHD received As and Bs but began having behavior problems in second grade. He started to freeze when writing unless he knew the exact spelling of a word. The district offered him a Section 504 plan, permitting him to complete 50% of his schoolwork, but he managed to complete only half that. District representatives had him assessed in various areas, but the IEP team found him ineligible for special education and related services. The parents eventually sued, and a federal court held that **the district's failure to assess the student in all areas (including physiological and neurological disorders) violated the IDEA**. The student clearly was impaired in written expression but was never assessed in that area. *W.H. v. Clovis Unified School Dist.*, No. CV F 08-0374 LJO DLB, 2009 WL 1605356 (E.D. Cal. 6/8/09).

◆ A family moved from New York to Delaware. Their daughter had a Section 504 plan from her New York district but did not qualify for special education. The parents sought an occupational therapy evaluation, but they didn't request a special education evaluation. The student began failing her math classes, and in February her mother requested further evaluations. More than 45 school days later, the district evaluated her and found her eligible for special education with a learning disability. It offered an IEP that the parents rejected. Instead, they placed their daughter in a private school and eventually sued for tuition reimbursement. A federal court held that **the delay in the evaluation meant that the district had to pay for a private tutor and Sylvan Learning costs. However, the district did not have to reimburse the parents for the private school tuition** because the parents did not prove that the IEP was inadequate. The Third Circuit affirmed that decision. *Anello v. Indian River School Dist.*, 355 Fed.Appx. 594 (3d Cir. 2009).

◆ The parents of a Connecticut student with a nonverbal learning disability believed their school district should have diagnosed their son as IDEA-eligible for the fourth grade. However, the district did not find him eligible until his sixth-grade year. The parents placed their son in a private school and sued for tuition reimbursement. A federal court ruled against them, noting their failure to prove that district officials "overlooked clear signs of disability." The child-find provision of **the IDEA does not impose liability for every failure to identify a child with a disability**, and nonverbal learning disabilities are difficult to identify. The Second Circuit affirmed, noting that the student's teacher had testified that she thought he was just as capable as other students in her class. The lowest grade he had received before being removed from class was a C+. *A.P. v. Woodstock Board of Educ.*, 370 Fed.Appx. 202 (2d Cir. 2010).

◆ A Pennsylvania student with autism spectrum disorder was diagnosed only as learning disabled when an IEP was developed for her. The IEP called for learning support and "as needed" assistance through a school-based behavioral health program. After kindergarten, the school district eliminated her one-on-one support. Following several assaults on the student, her mother home-schooled her, then filed for due process, claiming the district failed to offer her daughter a FAPE. A federal court held that **the district's failure to diagnose the autism spectrum disorder did not deny the student a FAPE**. The district had properly evaluated the student based on the information available at the time. On further appeal, the Third Circuit affirmed, finding no evidence that a correct diagnosis would have changed the student's placement. *K.R. v. School Dist. of Philadelphia*, 373 Fed.Appx. 204 (3d Cir. 2010).

◆ A Georgia school district **failed to assess a student for special education for four years despite requests from his teachers**. When it finally did evaluate the student, it determined that he had an IQ of 63. It reevaluated the student when he turned 16 and determined that his IQ was 82 – the low end of average. However, the student was still at a third-grade level in reading and math. Eventually, his parents obtained an independent educational evaluation at which he was diagnosed with dyslexia. The parents sought due process, and a hearing officer gave them a choice of additional support at the public school or a private school placement with reimbursement limited to $15,000 a year. The parents chose the private school, and the district appealed. A federal court removed the tuition cap and ordered the district to pay the student's annual tuition of $34,150. On further appeal, the Eleventh Circuit affirmed. Even though the IDEA has a preference for public school placements, a private school placement may be an appropriate compensatory education remedy where the district fails to provide a FAPE. *Draper v. Atlanta Independent School System*, 518 F.3d 1275 (11th Cir. 2008).

◆ A Tennessee student with cerebral palsy, seizures, visual impairments and other disabilities was classified by her district as mentally retarded. Her IEP did not include a behavior modification plan. After several serious behavioral incidents, she was suspended. Her family requested a due process hearing, and an administrative law judge considered the student's prior IEPs in finding that her current IEP resulted in the denial of a free appropriate public education. A federal court supplemented the administrative record with evaluations and ruled that **the student was not receiving FAPE because she had been mistakenly labeled as mentally retarded**. On further appeal, the Sixth Circuit affirmed. The administrative law judge properly considered the student's IEPs from prior years in finding the current IEP inappropriate. And the lower court properly considered the additional evidence. The court of appeals upheld the award of compensatory education to the student. *Metropolitan Board of Public Educ. v. Bellamy*, 116 Fed.Appx. 570 (6th Cir. 2004).

4. Uncooperative Parents

◆ A California student was diagnosed with Pachygyria, a rare disorder associated with seizures, developmental delays and neuropsychiatric dysfunction. **Her parents selected a private school and then sought an evaluation.** School district evaluators, though highly experienced, had never assisted a child with Pachygyria before. They recommended a public school placement and determined that the student's behaviors and anxieties did not disrupt her ability to learn and participate. The parents, however, desiring a private school placement, sought due process and appealed an adverse decision to a federal court. The court ruled that the evaluators' lack of familiarity with Pachygyria did not violate the IDEA and that the district had offered an adequate academic program. *Marcotte v. Palos Verdes Peninsula Unified School Dist.*, No. CV 08-1671 PSG (PLAx), 2009 WL 1873024 (C.D. Cal. 6/29/09).

◆ For seven years, a Hawaii student attended a private special education school at the state's expense. The state then proposed a public middle school placement. The student's father sought to stop the move and alleged a number of IDEA violations. A federal court ruled the state did not violate IDEA evaluation requirements. And **the fact that the father disagreed with the rest of the IEP team did not mean that he was denied full participation** or that the IEP team's determination was incorrect. *Laddie C. v. Dep't of Educ., State of Hawaii*, No. 08-00309 SOM/BMK, 2009 WL 855966 (D. Haw. 3/27/09).

◆ Minnesota parents disagreed over whether their child should be evaluated for special education. **One parent consented and the other did not.** The district asked a court to determine whether it could conduct the evaluation. The court ruled that it could not. Minnesota law imposes a dual consent requirement when more than one parent participates in the decision-making process. *J.H. v. Northfield Public School Dist. No. 659*, No. A08-1213, 2009 WL 1182199 (Minn. Ct. App. 5/5/09).

◆ The parents of a New Hampshire student became concerned that she needed special education, and their school district found she had a learning disability in math. An IEP team suggested a private school placement, to which the parents agreed. The following year, the parents requested due process, claiming the district had denied her a free appropriate public education (FAPE) for the previous five years. They withdrew the student from school and began home-schooling her. The district threatened to file truancy charges against them unless they registered her as a home-schooled student. When the case finally reached a federal court, it held that **the parents acted unreasonably during the IEP process; thus, any delay in developing an IEP did not violate the IDEA**. Also, the truancy threat did not amount to a denial of FAPE. *Kasenia R. v. Brookline School Dist.*, 588 F.Supp.2d 175 (D.N.H. 2008).

◆ The parents of a New York student educated him at home for religious reasons. After the student's grandparent sent a letter to the school district, concerned that the student had a learning disability, the district sought to evaluate the student. The parents refused to allow it, and the district sought due process. A hearing officer denied the parents' motion to dismiss, and they appealed to a federal court. The court noted that the IDEA explicitly recognized parental rights to refuse publicly funded special education services offered by a school district. Here, **since the parents had refused special education services, they could not be compelled to have their son evaluated**. *Durkee v. Livonia Cent. School Dist.*, 487 F.Supp.2d 313 (W.D.N.Y. 2007).

◆ The grandmother (and guardian) of a Texas student with a rare nervous system disorder participated in IEP team meetings and agreed to a mainstream placement. She accompanied the student to class each day the student attended and sat in the back of the classroom, but was disruptive in her care for the student. The teacher barred her from continuing to attend classes, and the student was then pulled from school. When the district later sought a reevaluation of the student, the grandmother refused, claiming it would seriously harm the student. The case reached the Fifth Circuit, which ruled that **the district had to be allowed to evaluate the student to complete the IEP**. The district needed more medical information to provide the special education the grandmother wanted. *Shelby S. v. Conroe Independent School Dist.*, 454 F.3d 450 (5th Cir. 2006).

◆ The parents of a New Jersey student failed to cooperate with their district's request to evaluate their daughter, claiming they did not have to do so because the district forfeited its right to evaluate her by its failure to take note of her underperformance over a period of several years. A lawsuit arose under Section 504 of the Rehabilitation Act, and the district sought pretrial judgment. The court refused to grant it, noting that there were questions of fact over whether the district had failed to take note of the student's underperformance in prior years. However, **the parents would have to make their daughter available for an evaluation in the next 45 days.** *H.G. v. Audubon Board of Educ.*, No. 05-4220 (FLW), 2006 WL 1675072 (D.N.J. 6/15/06).

◆   The parents of a Connecticut child refused to cooperate with their district's attempts to evaluate the child. A due process hearing officer held that the district was entitled to a report of a physician's evaluation with recommendations for accommodations, and a federal court ordered the parents to schedule appointments as soon as possible. The parents refused to comply, asserting that they were denied an opportunity to review and object to a draft order. The court then ordered the parties back to court and held that **the parents had to provide up-to-date evaluations so that the district could determine its IDEA obligations.** The district did not have to exhaust its administrative remedies before reviewing the child's medical records. *Mrs. B. v. Litchfield Board of Educ.*, 321 F.Supp.2d 342 (D. Conn. 2004).

◆   A student enrolled in a public school where he received poor grades and did not interact well with other students. School officials repeatedly asked his mother for permission to evaluate him for special education. She refused, and also refused to provide requested medical records. A neurologist advised school representatives that he had no learning disability. The school implemented a general education intervention plan. The following year, the student played on the basketball team, developed friendships, and made the honor roll. Later, he was cut from the junior varsity basketball team because of tardiness. His mother then asserted that the student had a disability and consented to an evaluation. However, she refused to sign an evaluation consent form and again refused to provide medical records. A hearing officer determined that the school system had not failed to identify the student as eligible for special education. **School officials had made every effort to assist the student and gain parental permission to evaluate him.** The Seventh Circuit agreed that the school system did not fail to identify the student as requiring special education. *P.J. v. Eagle-Union Community School Corp.*, 202 F.3d 274 (7th Cir. 1999).

5. Emotional/Behavioral Issues

◆   A Rhode Island student with oppositional defiant disorder suffered bouts of extreme rage that eventually resulted in her hospitalization for suicidal and homicidal ideation. Her school district determined she was not eligible for special education and did not provide educational services to her during or after her hospitalization. A hearing officer awarded her 21 weeks of compensatory education, and a federal court agreed with that outcome. **The student's problems were so severe that they could not be segregated from the learning process.** *Linda E. v. Bristol Warren Regional School Dist.*, 758 F.Supp.2d 75 (D.R.I. 2010).

◆ A New York student with multiple behavior problems attended a succession of private schools. In grade 11, her parents contacted school officials for an evaluation. However, they went on vacation instead of making their daughter available for the evaluation. They placed her in a private school in Massachusetts, and a few months later they transferred her to another boarding school with a more structured program. The committee on special education found her ineligible under the IDEA, but a federal court found otherwise. **The student had an emotional disturbance that adversely affected her educational performance.** The court awarded tuition reimbursement for the second placement but gave the parents nothing for the first placement or for the district's failure to evaluate the student in a timely fashion. *Eschenasy v. New York City Dep't of Educ.*, 604 F.Supp.2d 639 (S.D.N.Y. 2009).

◆ A New York school district offered an autistic student support from a special education teacher for part of the day and a program assistant for the rest of the day. However, he had behavioral and lack-of-focus problems and his parents placed him in a private school. They sued for tuition reimbursement, alleging that the district violated the IDEA because it failed to offer a functional behavioral assessment (FBA). The Second Circuit ruled that **the district did not have to offer an FBA**. Three key district officials testified that an FBA was not necessary. The IEP adequately addressed the student's behavior, and the parents were not entitled to tuition reimbursement. *A.C. and M.C. v. Board of Educ. of Chappaqua Cent. School Dist.*, 553 F.3d 165 (2d Cir. 2009).

◆ A New York student with ADHD was sexually abused by a cousin and later suspended for fighting and drug possession. His grade point average dropped out of the honor roll range, but he continued to pass his classes. His parents later placed him in a boarding school for troubled students. The committee on special education met and determined that he did not meet the IDEA criteria for a student with severe emotional disturbance. His parents appealed that decision, and the case reached the Second Circuit, which ruled against them. Here, **even if the student exhibited some of the symptomology for an emotional disturbance, his symptoms did not affect his academic performance**. Instead, drug use appeared to be at the root of his school problems. *Mr. and Mrs. N.C. v. Bedford Cent. School Dist.*, 300 Fed.Appx. 11 (2d Cir. 2008).

◆ A California student with a learning disability and a speech/language impairment began to experience anger and frustration, causing negative and truant behavior. A behavior support plan attempted to reduce his disciplinary referrals, but his truancy continued. The IEP team found his behavior support plan no longer appropriate but did not create a functional behavioral assessment. After he got in trouble with the law, a wilderness program placement was offered, but his mother had to fund it. She later sought tuition reimbursement, which the Ninth Circuit denied. Here, **the district did not have to conduct a functional behavioral assessment**, a functional analysis assessment or an environmental assessment because he did not suffer from a serious behavior problem like self-injury or assault on others. The district had created a behavior support plan to address the student's problems and a behavior intervention plan was unnecessary. *Rodriguez v. San Mateo Union High School Dist.*, 357 Fed.Appx. 752 (9th Cir. 2009).

♦   A Texas student with ADHD received special education services until the fourth grade, after which he no longer needed them. He performed well in school but had behavioral problems through the seventh and eighth grades. He nevertheless passed all his classes and met the statewide standards required by the Texas Assessment of Knowledge and Skills. After he robbed a school concession stand, he was placed in an alternative setting. His mother requested a due process hearing, alleging that the district failed to identify him as a student with a disability. The case reached the Fifth Circuit Court of Appeals, which held that even though the student had a qualifying disability (his ADHD), he did not need special education services as a result. **His behavioral problems resulted from non-ADHD occurrences**, such as family problems. *Alvin Independent School Dist. v. Patricia F.*, 503 F.3d 378 (5th Cir. 2007).

♦   A Pennsylvania third-grader with a non-verbal learning disability claimed that she was bullied by her peers and that school officials refused to address the problem. The school collected data and made observations for a functional behavioral assessment. **It found that the student was at fault for some of the conflict.** When the parents requested due process, a hearing officer found for the school. A federal court agreed that the school was not liable under the IDEA or Section 504. The student received a FAPE, and the school did not condone, ignore or approve of inappropriate behavior. It took steps to address the reports of bullying. *Emily Z. v. Mt. Lebanon School Dist.*, No. 06-442, 2007 WL 3174027 (W.D. Pa. 10/29/07).

♦   A Texas student with ADHD received special education until the seventh grade under the other health impaired category. At that time, the school found he was no longer manifesting symptoms and thus no longer required special education or related services. His father agreed to the cessation, but after the student had trouble in seventh grade, the father objected when the school refused to recommend a special education placement for eighth grade. The student had discipline problems and was assigned to an alternative school, where he continued to have disciplinary problems but passed his classes and all parts of the Texas Assessment of Knowledge and Skills except for math. When his parents sought to have him qualified for special education, a federal court ruled against them. **There was no evidence that the student's classroom misbehavior was due to ADHD.** *M.P. v. North East Independent School Dist.*, No. SA-07-CA-004-XR, 2007 WL 4199774 (W.D. Tex. 11/27/07).

♦   A New Jersey student, classified as perceptually impaired, had behavioral problems at home and threatened to kill himself, but his school behavior was less troubled. A school psychologist reevaluated the student at the mother's request and found problems with his family dynamics. At the age of 10, after arguing with his father about a school assignment, the student tried to hang himself at home, sustaining severe and permanent brain damage as a result. The family sued the state, the district and various officials for negligence, and they also filed claims under the IDEA and the ADA. A state court dismissed the claims against the district and its officials. **There was no liability for failing to classify the student as emotionally disturbed**, and the school psychologist had no duty to warn of the student's risk of suicide. *Braski v. State of New Jersey*, 2007 WL 2274886 (N.J. Super. Ct. App. Div. 8/10/07).

♦   The foster parents of an HIV-positive Maryland student told her of her condition just before her fifth-grade year. Her behavior deteriorated sharply over the next two years. She cut herself, heard voices telling her to stab herself, and was hospitalized at five institutions, finally being diagnosed with a psychotic condition. She missed a lot of school, and her academic performance declined during sixth grade. Her mother requested an IEP meeting to determine her eligibility under the IDEA. The IEP team found that although the student engaged in inappropriate behavior or had inappropriate feelings, she did not qualify for special education because her condition caused no adverse educational impact. Eventually the dispute reached the Fourth Circuit, which held that the student was eligible for special education. **Her emotional disturbance affected her educational performance**, despite contrary testimony from school district experts. *Board of Educ. of Montgomery County, Maryland v. S.G.*, 230 Fed.Appx. 330 (4th Cir. 2007).

♦   During an honors student's tenth-grade year, his father contacted school officials, expressing concern about his son's emotional problems and drug use and asking for assistance. The student suffered from ADHD, bipolar disorder, obsessive compulsive disorder and marijuana abuse, but was not deemed eligible for special education. The following year, he became chronically truant. His parents placed him in a Connecticut therapeutic school, where he received treatment for emotional problems. However, he continued to use marijuana and inhalants and was transferred to a residential drug treatment program in Utah. His behavior soon improved and he returned to the Connecticut school, where he completed eleventh grade. He re-enrolled in his public school for grade 12. His parents requested an IDEA due process hearing, arguing that their request for assistance with identification of the student's problems created a duty on the school district to make a special education eligibility determination. They argued that the district's failure to do so denied the student a FAPE. A federal court disagreed. **The student's behavior problems resulted not from an educational disability but from social maladjustment**, as evidenced by his history of drug abuse. The Fourth Circuit affirmed. *Board of Educ. of Frederick County, Maryland v. JD III*, 232 F.3d 886 (4th Cir. 2000).

♦   A New York student, who was classified as speech impaired, received special education through fourth grade. She was placed in a remedial reading program through grade seven, and promoted to ninth grade despite failing multiple subjects in grades seven and eight. She began to experience behavior problems and was hospitalized for depression. Her emotional and behavioral problems resumed after she returned to school and she was again hospitalized. Her family placed her in a residential treatment and educational facility in Connecticut. She was then diagnosed as having conduct disorder, and later, oppositional defiant disorder. Her parents sought payment for the private placement. The district's committee on special education determined that the student was ineligible for special education under the IDEA, but recommended referral for services under Section 504 of the Rehabilitation Act.

A federal court ordered the school committee to reimburse the family for the costs of the private placement. The Second Circuit affirmed. Here, the student had been deprived of appropriate IDEA services due to the school committee's erroneous attempts to classify her. Evidence indicated that the student had demonstrated an inability to learn that could not be explained solely by intellectual, sensory or health factors. Because **the student's academic problems resulted at least in part from her emotional problems**, and most of her medical evaluations indicated symptoms of depression that endured for several years, she was properly deemed eligible for IDEA services due to a serious emotional disturbance. *Muller v. Committee on Special Educ. of East Islip Union Free School Dist.*, 145 F.3d 95 (2d Cir. 1998).

6. Reevaluation

♦ A New Jersey school district evaluated a first-grade student as having a specific learning disability. She received special education through grade four. Near the end of that year, her parents rejected her IEP. Shortly thereafter, the district notified them that **she was no longer eligible for special education because of a reevaluation conducted by a computer program**. An administrative law judge determined that the reevaluation was proper, but a federal court disagreed. It noted that there was still a severe discrepancy between the student's achievement and ability in both reading and math, and the only contrary evidence came from the computer program. She accomplished her work in reading and math only with the help of educational supports. *M.B. and K.H. v. South Orange/Maplewood Board of Educ.*, No. 09-5294 (SRC), 2010 WL 3035494 (D.N.J. 8/3/10).

♦ A Texas student received 60 minutes of weekly speech-language pathology as a related service to address his speech impediment. His district later found that he no longer required such services. However, his mother disagreed and fought to continue them. The district continued to provide them under the stay-put provision, but it sought to reevaluate the student to determine whether he continued to need speech therapy. The mother refused to give her consent for a reevaluation, and a hearing officer ruled that he could not order one. A federal court then held that **the hearing officer could override the lack of parental consent and order a reevaluation**. *M.L. v. El Paso Independent School Dist.*, 610 F.Supp.2d 582 (W.D. Tex. 2009).

♦ A Pennsylvania student with autism spectrum disorder had a behavioral crisis while in a private school funded by the district. A reevaluation led to an evaluation report that used boilerplate language, listing generic goals and principles that might work for any child rather than specifying the student's needs and issues. The IEP also contained much of that boilerplate language. When the parents sought due process, a hearing officer determined that **the IEP**

was inappropriate, but so was the private school placement. The case reached a federal court, which agreed that the IEP was inappropriate and so was the private school. A new IEP would have to be developed. *A.Y. and D.Y. v. Cumberland Valley School Dist.*, 569 F.Supp.2d 496 (M.D. Pa. 2008).

♦   The mother of a New Jersey student sought an independent evaluation for him as well as increased occupational therapy outside of school. After getting an evaluation that supported her desires, she rejected the Child Study Team's (CST's) request for a reevaluation and placed her son in a private school. When she sought reimbursement, the Third Circuit ruled against her. Here, she had obstructed the CST at every turn, and had obtained her evaluation to establish that the school board's services were inadequate, not with the intent of placing her son in public schools. **Her refusal to cooperate in the reevaluation prevented the CST from creating an IEP.** *M.S. and D.S. v. Mullica Township Board of Educ.*, 263 Fed. Appx. 264 (3d Cir. 2008).

♦   A California school district conducted a reevaluation of a special education student who primarily spoke Korean. The mother agreed to have the evaluation conducted in English. However, an audiology assessment could not be conducted because of a buildup of earwax, which the mother failed to have removed. Also, a vision assessment found no hindrance to his education. His parents nonetheless contested the proposed placement and the evaluation. A hearing officer found that the district had conducted appropriate assessments but had denied the student a free appropriate public education for a year and two months. The case reached the Ninth Circuit, which upheld the hearing officer's rulings. **The district did not violate the IDEA in its assessment of the student.** Further, the award of compensatory education – in the form of additional training for the student's teachers – was proper even though it did not directly impact the student. Finally, the lower court had improperly ruled that the student was not a prevailing party. The student obtained enough relief that he was entitled to some attorneys' fees. *Park v. Anaheim Union High School Dist.*, 464 F.3d 1025 (9th Cir. 2006).

♦   The parents of a Michigan student with disabilities asserted that the school district's IEP was inappropriate, denying him a free appropriate public education. They requested a due process hearing, challenging the IEP, then withdrew their son from school and placed him in a private school. The hearing officer dismissed the case upon learning of the unilateral placement. A state-level review officer upheld that decision, as did a federal court. The court noted that the school district **did not violate the IDEA by failing to annually update the student's IEP**. Once an IDEA action has been commenced, the student's most recent IEP continues to operate under the stay-put provision until conclusion of the appeal or litigation. The Sixth Circuit affirmed the ruling in favor of the district. *Kuszewski v. Chippewa Valley School Dist.*, 56 Fed.Appx. 655 (6th Cir. 2003).

B. Independent Evaluations

♦   The father of a Minnesota student complained about the evaluation methods used on his son. He asserted that the district failed to consider a private evaluation he obtained and also failed to use a transitions planning test he preferred to the evaluation model used by the district. In the lawsuit that resulted, the Minnesota Court of Appeals noted that **state regulations required districts to use a variety of evaluation tools and not any single procedure**. The district evaluation was thorough and well-documented, and the father did not have a right to insist on his preferred evaluation methodology. *Heller v. Minnesota Dep't of Educ.*, No. A09-1720, 2010 WL 2035844 (Minn. Ct. App. 5/25/10).

♦   The mother of a New Jersey student with disabilities agreed to an IEP with the district, but she later objected to the IEP and repeated her earlier request for an independent psychological evaluation and a functional behavioral assessment. The district and an administrative law judge denied her request, but a federal court held that she was entitled to the independent evaluation. **She did not need to disagree with the IEP or the eligibility determination to invoke the right to an independent evaluation.** She only needed to disagree with the district's assessment. *K.B. v. Haledon Board of Educ.*, No. 08-4647 (JLL), 2010 WL 2079713 (D.N.J. 5/24/10).

♦   When a North Carolina student's medical condition changed, his parents enrolled him in a private supplemental learning center. They did not request reimbursement for more than a year, at which time they also asked for payment for an independent educational evaluation. They claimed the board didn't respond to their request, so **they paid $3,250 for an evaluation,** only later learning that the board would pay just $800 for an IEE from a list of approved evaluators. A federal court held their claims were largely time-barred by the state's 60-day statute of limitations and that even for those few days when they might be eligible for reimbursement, they could not get it because their son was reading at grade level. *P.L. v. Charlotte-Mecklenburg Board of Educ.*, No. 3:07-CV-170-GCM, 2010 WL 2926129 (W.D.N.C. 7/23/10).

♦   A Pennsylvania student had academic difficulty during her school career. By the fifth grade, she was receiving 45 minutes of daily learning support. In the second half of the year, the district reevaluated her and found her ineligible for special education. **A due process hearing officer ruled that the district violated the IDEA by failing to properly evaluate the student** and ordered compensatory education as well as reimbursement for an independent education evaluation. A review panel largely affirmed that decision. When the district appealed to a federal court, the parents sought money damages for the district's conduct. The court ruled that the IDEA doesn't permit compensatory damages but that they might be available under Section 504. The case would move forward. *Breanne C. v. Southern York County School Dist.*, 665 F.Supp.2d 504 (M.D. Pa. 2009).

♦   A Pennsylvania student with Asperger's syndrome was also designated as a gifted student. A school psychologist later ruled out autism and serious emotional disturbance during an evaluation, concluding that the student's frequent arguments with teachers and his refusal to do school work was willful and not the result of an emotional disturbance. His parents disagreed with the evaluation. They placed him in a private school and obtained an independent educational evaluation, then sought reimbursement. A federal court ruled against them, noting that **the district evaluation was appropriate** and that they were not entitled to a diagnosis with which they agreed. *Jack B. v. Council Rock School Dist.*, No. 06-1968, 2008 WL 4489793 (E.D. Pa. 10/3/08).

♦   A California student spent three years in foster care before reuniting with his mother as a five-year-old, just before beginning kindergarten. He acted out at school and fell out of his chair. He was disciplined by his teacher four times in less than four months at a Los Angeles public school. His mother requested an initial special education assessment, which the district denied because of the student's limited school experience and the lack of general education interventions. The family moved out of the district and the mother requested due process. A hearing officer held that **the district had to pay for an independent educational evaluation**, and a federal court agreed. Although the district did not have to assess the student itself, it had an obligation to fund the independent evaluation. *Los Angeles Unified School Dist. v. D.L.*, 548 F.Supp.2d 815 (C.D. Cal. 2008).

♦   The parents of an Ohio student with ADD and allergies requested due process, seeking an evaluation for him when he was threatened with discipline as a junior in high school. The district found the student ineligible for special education, and the parents then hired a private evaluator to conduct an independent evaluation. They sought reimbursement for the cost of the evaluation. After administrative decisions in favor of the district, a federal court and the Sixth Circuit held that **the parents were not entitled to reimbursement for the independent evaluation**. Here, the parents failed to notify the district in advance of the evaluation. Also, the appropriateness of the district's evaluation had been challenged and confirmed. *P.R. v. Woodmore Local School Dist.*, 256 Fed. Appx. 751 (6th Cir. 2007).

♦   A multiply disabled 11-year-old Massachusetts student had attended a seven-week summer program called "Active Healing" at district expense since her kindergarten year. However, the program was not a state-approved special education program. After a seizure caused the student to regress, her mother sought to have her evaluated during a 12-week extended evaluation at Active Healing. The district refused to pay for the extended evaluation because the program was unapproved, and the mother sought administrative review. A hearing officer ruled that the district had to pay for the evaluation, but a federal court disagreed. Despite the past history of the district funding the summer program, **it could not be ordered to pay for the extended evaluation at an unapproved program**. *Manchester-Essex Regional School Dist. v. Bureau of Special Educ. Appeals*, 490 F.Supp.2d 49 (D. Mass. 2007).

♦   After a Georgia student prevailed in a lawsuit to attain related services, the district sought to reevaluate the student to determine whether he was eligible as "other health impaired." The parents refused to allow the reevaluation, insisting that the district should rely on the independent evaluation they had obtained. They also claimed that the district had retaliated against them after they won the prior lawsuit. The new case reached the Eleventh Circuit, which held that **the parents could not force the district to rely on their independent evaluation**. They had to allow the district to conduct the triennial evaluation. Also, their retaliation claim required them to exhaust their administrative remedies. *M.T.V. v. DeKalb County School Dist.*, 446 F.3d 1153 (11th Cir. 2006).

♦   After a regular education student was suspended, his mother sought to have him evaluated for special education. A district assessment found that the student was not entitled to special education. His mother then sought an independent educational evaluation at district expense. Three weeks later, the district asserted that its assessment had been appropriate. Three months after that, the district filed a due process hearing request. A hearing officer ruled that the district had to pay for an independent evaluation because it failed to show that it conducted its assessment properly. A California federal court agreed. **The delays by the district meant that it waived its right to contest the request for an independent education evaluation.** *Pajaro Valley Unified School Dist. v. J.S.*, No. C 06-0380 PVT, 2006 WL 3734289 (N.D. Cal. 12/15/06).

♦   A Connecticut sophomore with epilepsy was hospitalized after going into a catatonic state. He then began a daytime treatment program and received home tutoring from a school district instructor. The district's planning and placement team obtained the mother's consent for an evaluation but before that happened the mother withdrew her consent. The parents placed their son in a hospital's education program and sought private school tuition reimbursement. The due process hearing officer **agreed with the district that it was entitled to perform a psychological evaluation of the student**. When the parents refused to comply with the order for 20 months, the hearing officer held that they were not entitled to tuition reimbursement. A federal court agreed. The IDEA, at Section 1412(a)(10)(C), allows denial of tuition reimbursement where parents do not make their child available for an evaluation. The Second Circuit affirmed, finding no evidence that an evaluation of the student would be harmful. *P.S. v. Brookfield Board of Educ.*, 186 Fed.Appx. 79 (2d Cir. 2006).

V. INDIVIDUALIZED EDUCATION PROGRAMS

An individualized education program (IEP) is a written statement for each student with a disability that describes the student's present levels of educational performance, progress in the general curriculum, services to be provided, annual goals, and complies with many other statutory requirements. The specific requirements for IEPs are found at 20 U.S.C. § 1414(d). Many of the issues presented in this section of the book are more fully discussed in the closely related area of placement, found in Chapter Two.

A. Generally

Each IEP includes statements of annual goals, including benchmarks or short-term objectives, related to meeting the student's needs that result from the student's disability, to enable involvement and progress in the general curriculum. **IEPs include a statement of the special education and related services to be provided to the student and a statement of the program modifications to be furnished**, which will allow the student to advance appropriately toward attaining the annual goals, and be involved and progress in the general curriculum and participate with other students.

Each IEP must explain the extent to which a student will not participate with non-disabled students in regular classes and a statement of any individual modifications that are needed for the student to participate in state or local student achievement assessments. For students age 14 and over, a statement of the student's necessary transition services under the applicable components of an IEP focusing on courses of study must be included.

For those over 16, a statement of necessary transition services must be included which may describe interagency responsibilities. Beginning at least one year before the student reaches the age of majority under state law, the IEP must include a statement that the student has been advised of IDEA rights that will transfer to the student upon the attainment of the age of majority.

The composition of an IEP team is described at 20 U.S.C. § 1414(d)(1)(B). IEP teams include the student's parents, at least one of the student's regular education teachers, at least one special education teacher of the student, and a local educational agency representative who is qualified to provide or supervise the provision of specially designed instruction to meet the unique needs of the student and who is knowledgeable about the general curriculum and local agency's resources.

♦ The parents of a Missouri student with autism challenged two IEPs used during his fourth- and fifth-grade years after becoming dissatisfied with his progress. They sought a private school placement, which the district rejected. A state hearing panel determined that the IEPs were deficient because they lacked baseline data, but a federal court and the Eighth Circuit ruled that **the IDEA does not explicitly require recitation of baseline data**. It only commands that each IEP include a statement of the "present levels of educational performance," which the IEPs in this case included. Also, the IEPs did not have to include specific behavior goals. It was enough that they described the student's disruptive behaviors and included strategies to address them. *Lathrop R-II School Dist. v. Gray*, 611 F.3d 419 (8th Cir. 2010).

♦ A few months into the 2006-07 school year, a Maryland school board amended a student's IEP to include occupational and physical therapy goals and objectives. The parents objected to both IEPs and placed their child in a private school. An administrative law judge found the first IEP violated IDEA procedural requirements, but that the second IEP provided a FAPE. Tuition reimbursement was denied for the second semester. When the IEP team decided that the school named in the 2006-07 IEPs was no longer appropriate, the parents claimed that was an admission that the second IEP wasn't appropriate after all. A federal court agreed and awarded tuition reimbursement for the second semester, but the Fourth Circuit reversed and remanded the case. A special education supervisor had determined that **the student's needs had changed, so the change in the IEP was not an admission of inappropriateness**. *Lorenzen v. Montgomery County Board of Educ.*, 403 Fed.Appx. 832 (4th Cir. 2010).

♦   The mother of a Hawaii student met with state education department staff but failed to reach an agreement on an IEP. The draft IEP stated that services provided would "include" occupational and speech therapy, but not during an extended school year, and did not specify the particular school that the mother wanted. She rejected the IEP and placed her child in a private school and then contested the IEP. A federal court ruled for the state, finding that **the IEP did not have to specify the school where services would be provided**. Nor did the use of the term "include" denote that the department would not provide real services for the student. *N.S. v. State of Hawaii*, No. 09-00343 SOM/KSC, 2010 WL 2348664 (D. Haw. 6/9/10).

♦   The mother of an autistic student in Kansas grew concerned that her son's IEP was not meeting his needs, particularly in the area of social interaction with his peers. She also found it unacceptable that none of the IEP team members had appropriate training relating to autism. She placed her son in a private school and then sought due process. A hearing officer and a federal court ruled against her. The court noted that **although it would be preferable to have a staff member with extensive experience in a child's particular disability, the IDEA does not require this**. Some IEP team members had relevant autism training, and the school had held two in-service trainings on autism. As a result, the court reached the conclusion that the student received some educational benefit from the district. *Huffman v. North Lyon County School Dist.*, No. 08-2083-KGS, 2009 WL 3185239 (D. Kan. 9/30/09).

♦   A Florida student with multiple disabilities, including ADHD, displayed disruptive behavior. His IEP team considered putting him in a varying exceptionalities program, but his parents sought more time to obtain medical advice before changing his placement. He began taking new medication that resulted in improved behavior, and the IEP team reconsidered his reassignment. His parents ultimately alleged that the district denied him a free appropriate public education because of the delays in developing a final IEP. However, a federal court and the Eleventh Circuit ruled for the district. The IEPs prepared by the district were reasonably calculated to provide a free appropriate public education, and **the sudden success of the new medication made the changes to the draft IEP necessary**. *School Board of Lee County, Florida v. M.M.*, 348 Fed.Appx. 504 (11th Cir. 2009).

◆ An Indiana school district sought to classify a student with delays in expressive language, readiness skills and adaptive skills as a student with autism spectrum disorder. However, his parents wanted him classified as other health impaired. They feared the stigma attached to autism and sought to maintain the communication disorder designation. The case reached a federal court, which noted that the labeling issue was linked to school funding. The district wanted the autism label because that would provide it with more state funding – $2,250 for students with mild and moderate disabilities as opposed to $531 for students with communication disorders. The court held that **the student should be classified as other health impaired rather than autistic** and that his IEP satisfied the IDEA. *B.B. v. Perry Township School Corp.*, No. 1:07-CV-0323-DFH-JMS, 2008 WL 2745094 (S.D. Ind. 7/11/08).

◆ A Pennsylvania school district offered IEPs to a Spanish-speaking student with retardation and epilepsy. The IEPs initially provided for English as a Second Language (ESL), but that element was later removed in favor of 30 minutes of weekly group speech and language therapy. Communications with his father were made in English even though the father did not speak or read English. Eventually, the father sought compensatory education. A federal court held that **the district failed to offer a free appropriate public education once the ESL instruction ended**. Although it set general goals to increase English vocabulary, the district did not have specific goals or measurements and did not reasonably address the student's language needs. *Marple Newtown School Dist. v. Rafael N.*, No. 07-0558, 2007 WL 2458076 (E.D. Pa. 8/23/07).

◆ The school district for a North Carolina student with fragile X syndrome and other disabilities was unable to find an appropriate in-state program for the student and paid for a placement in Maryland. Later, the district found an in-state program that would offer a FAPE and amended the IEP accordingly. The parents challenged the new IEP and lost. However, they delayed sending in the application to the new program and again challenged the district's offer, claiming that the Maryland placement was the student's stay-put placement under the IDEA. A federal court disagreed. **By rejecting the new program, the parents essentially refused to consent to receive special education** and related services. Thus, the district no longer had an obligation to provide their son with a FAPE. *Cone v. Randolph County Schools Board of Educ.*, No. 1:06 CV00579, 2006 WL 3000445 (M.D.N.C. 10/20/06).

◆ An Alaska school district offered an autistic student either a morning or afternoon preschool session for children with disabilities. His parents asked for an all-day ABA therapy program. The district maintained that all-day programming was not appropriate and that its program was similar to the ABA one preferred by the parents, even though it was not labeled "ABA" therapy. The parents withdrew from the IEP process, then sought compensatory education, asserting that the district violated the IDEA. A federal court ruled against the parents, noting that **their withdrawal from the IEP process undercut their argument that the district should have done more**. The district had been open to providing more services if necessary, but the parents' withdrawal had prevented that. *A.M. v. Fairbanks North Star Borough School Dist.*, No. 3:05-cv-179 TMB, 2006 WL 2841054 (D. Alaska 9/29/06).

◆   The Minnesota Department of Education and the state court of appeals found that **a school district violated state law in the treatment of preschool students it had placed at a private early intervention center**. It failed to provide transportation to students it had placed at the center, did not properly implement the IEPs of some students, and did not address the needs of others for extended school year (ESY) services. Further, the district did not properly staff IEP meetings, and was found in violation of certain parent notification requirements. The district was ordered to revise its policies. *Independent School Dist. No. 709 v. Bonney*, 705 N.W.2d 209 (Minn. Ct. App. 2005).

◆   The parents of a New York student with an autistic disorder agreed to his placement, but soon requested an at-home applied behavioral analysis (ABA) program to supplement his school day services. The district denied their request. An independent hearing officer upheld the IEP, as did a state review officer. However, a federal court held that the student was denied a free appropriate public education and awarded him at least 10 hours of at-home ABA therapy. The Second Circuit reversed and remanded the case. It held that **retrospective evidence of a student's progress should not be considered in assessing an IEP**. A school's judgment was not to be judged in hindsight, but rather at the time it is drafted. If it was reasonably calculated to provide an appropriate education, then a lack of progress did not necessarily render the IEP inappropriate. *D.F. v. Ramapo Cent. School Dist.*, 430 F.3d 595 (2d Cir. 2005).

◆   When a New York student was diagnosed with a learning disability, her district's committee on special education found that she could progress in regular education classes with tutoring. After the tenth grade ended, the student's parents requested the eleventh-grade IEP by August 20th. They also asked for student profiles for their daughter's upcoming classes. The district failed to respond by the 20th, and the parents sought a due process hearing. Upon losing there, they appealed. The case reached the Second Circuit, which held that **IEPs do not have to be produced at the time parents demand them**. Also, the district did not have to provide student profiles for classes where enrollment had not yet been finalized. *Cerra v. Pawling Cent. School Dist.*, 427 F.3d 186 (2d Cir. 2005).

◆   When a student with the mental functioning of a 10-month-old was about to enter grade three, her IEP team met to discuss her placement. It later created a draft IEP, which raised concerns for the student's mother. She sought to increase the student's time in regular education classes to 80% of the school day and also objected to the early release of her daughter on Fridays. She claimed that the draft IEP did not represent the product of the IEP team meeting, and requested due process. A hearing officer held for the district, and a Connecticut federal court upheld the hearing officer's findings. **The modifications in the draft IEP did not violate the IDEA.** They reflected the increased information that became available as the school year approached. Further, the district mainstreamed the student to the extent appropriate. *R.L. v. Plainville Board of Educ.*, 363 F.Supp.2d 222 (D. Conn. 2005).

◆ A California student with a language disorder began receiving special education at age three. Her parents and her school district were unable to agree on a placement for kindergarten, with her parents insisting on full inclusion and the district offering a half-day of special education and a half-day of regular kindergarten. Due process proceedings were not completed until near the end of the following school year. In the lawsuit that arose, a federal court found that for the year prior to kindergarten, the district failed to offer a free appropriate public education because it did not provide for any mainstreaming. However, for the student's kindergarten year, the proposed IEP complied with the IDEA. The student would not receive an educational benefit from a full inclusion placement. Also, **the district had no obligation under the IDEA to "adequately discuss mainstreaming" with the parents** at IEP team meetings. The Ninth Circuit affirmed. The kindergarten placement offered by the district provided the student with educational opportunity. As for the preschool placement, the district failed to show that the student could not have developed social skills in a mainstream setting. *Katherine G. v. Kentfield School Dist.*, 112 Fed.Appx. 586 (9th Cir. 2004).

◆ A Virginia student with autism received extended school year (ESY) services prior to his kindergarten year. In kindergarten, he progressed in all but two of the 27 goals stated in his IEP. His parents sought to continue the one-on-one services he received during the summer but were unable to agree with the district on an IEP. A hearing officer and a federal court ruled that the purpose of ESY services was to make reasonable progress on unmet goals. The court found that the district's IEP was adequate. The Fourth Circuit Court of Appeals then noted that ESY services are necessary only when the regular school year **benefits to a student will be significantly jeopardized in the absence of summer programming**. The court remanded the case to the hearing officer for a redetermination of the appropriateness of ESY services using the correct standard. *JH ex rel. JD v. Henrico County School Board*, 326 F.3d 560 (4th Cir. 2003).

◆ A Louisiana student with cerebral palsy, bladder incontinence and developmental delays used a wheelchair. When he was 18, his mother requested a due process hearing, asserting that the district had denied him a free appropriate public education. She alleged deficiencies in his IEPs and that his high school lacked accessible facilities. An administrative hearing officer and a state-level review panel ruled against her, and she later sued the school board under the IDEA, the ADA, and the Rehabilitation Act. She also sued the state, state board of education and department of education. A federal court ruled against her, and the Fifth Circuit affirmed. Although the defendants were not entitled to Eleventh Amendment immunity, they did not violate the IDEA, ADA or Section 504. The student's IEP had been reasonably calculated to provide him with a FAPE. **He raised his grade point average in several areas**, though he did not improve in every area. Nevertheless, he received an educational benefit under his IEP. Further, the board had provided him with aides to assist him in getting around the school and using the lavatory. Thus, it had provided him with reasonable accommodations under the ADA and the Rehabilitation Act. *Pace v. Bogalusa City School Board*, 403 F.3d 272 (5th Cir. 2005).

♦   When a preschool student was three years old, his parents started a home-based discrete trial training (DTT) program and notified the district that he had autism. A psychologist selected by the parents submitted a written proposal for a DTT program including staff training at a tape-recorded IEP conference. The district's director of special education drafted a new proposal calling for placement in a mainstream kindergarten class, without DTT. The parents objected. A due process hearing officer ruled that the taped proposal was an IEP that should have been implemented and that the parents were entitled to reimbursement. A Michigan hearing review officer reversed. A federal court concluded the district had conducted a proper evaluation of the student and proposed an IEP designed to address his needs. The parents appealed to the Sixth Circuit, which disagreed that the taped IEP proceeding was a final IEP. It noted that **the IEP prepared by the district took into account the unique needs of the student, set out his goals and included detailed daily schedules addressing each goal**. His program included group instruction and one-to-one therapy. The IEP complied with the IDEA. *Burilovich v. Board of Educ. of Lincoln Consolidated Schools*, 208 F.3d 560 (6th Cir. 2000).

B. Predetermined Placement

♦   A nonprofit operating a New York school for disabled children and a group of parents sued the state education department after the department changed its policy and ordered the school to stop placing students in 12:2:2 classes, instead requiring 6:1:1 classes. The department sought to have the case dismissed, but a federal court refused to do so. The IEPs called for 12:2:2 class sizes, and the parents maintained that the larger classes were necessary to allow the students to obtain meaningful educational opportunities. **If the department in fact predetermined class sizes under the new policy, that would violate the IDEA** and Section 504. The case was allowed to proceed. *Kalliope R. v. New York State Dep't of Educ.*, No. 09-CV-1718 (JFB) (WDW), 2010 WL 2243278 (E.D.N.Y. 6/10/10).

♦   For three years, the parents of an autistic student objected to the full-time autistic program placement the district wanted. The district refused to consider a placement with typically developing peers on the grounds that it had already been determined not to be an appropriate program. It also allegedly ignored the mother's questions. When the parents sued, claiming the district had predetermined their son's placement, **the district asserted that the mere presence of the parents at IEP meetings was sufficient to avoid a ruling of predetermination**. However, a federal court disagreed. It ordered the district to create a new IEP with the parents' input, it but refused to award monetary damages. *D.B. and L.B. v. Gloucester Township School Dist.*, 751 F.Supp.2d 764 (D.N.J. 2010).

♦ The mother of a California student rejected an initial IEP that would have placed her daughter in a district school. The parties agreed on a private preschool. Negotiations over an IEP for the next year broke down, and an administrative law judge determined that the district did not predetermine a placement for the student. However, the IEP improperly called for moving the student from special day classes to general education classes in a manner that created too many transitions. The judge awarded $6,100 for the cost of the private preschool. A federal court upheld the award as well as the finding that **the district did not predetermine the child's placement**. It also ruled that the mother was not entitled to be paid for personally providing supplemental ABA therapy services to her daughter at home. *K.A.D. v. Solana Beach School Dist.*, No. 08-CV-622 W(WVG), 2010 WL 2925569 (S.D. Cal. 7/23/10).

♦ Before an autistic New York student reached kindergarten age, his school district provided him with 30-35 hours per week of home-based Applied Behavioral Analysis (ABA) therapy as well as speech and occupational therapy. The committee on special education (CSE) recommended a special education placement but without the intensive ABA home therapy sessions. His parents rejected the IEP and sought due process. A hearing officer ruled for the district, and the Second Circuit ultimately agreed that the district did not have to provide the home-based ABA therapy. Appropriate supports and services were included in the IEP to ease the student's transition to school. And **the parents failed to show that the CSE had predetermined a kindergarten placement**. *T.S. and S.P. v. Mamaroneck Union Free School Dist.*, 554 F.3d 247 (2d Cir. 2009).

♦ An Illinois student with Rett Syndrome engaged in self-injurious behavior and sometimes struck others. In her first year of high school, she head-butted two staff members, breaking their noses. The district sought a special education setting, but the parents objected, instead settling for keeping the student at home. Eventually she was returned to her neighborhood school, where she made limited academic progress. When the district again tried to place the student in a special education setting, the parents requested due process, asserting that the IEP meeting was a sham to mask a "predetermined placement." A hearing officer, a federal court and the Seventh Circuit ruled for the district, noting that **the parents received a meaningful opportunity to participate in the development and review of their daughter's IEP**. Also, even though the district did not include a transition plan in the IEP, the student was unable to benefit from one at that time, so the lack of a transition plan did not violate the IDEA. *Board of Educ. of Township High School Dist. No. 211 v. Ross*, 486 F.3d 267 (7th Cir. 2007).

♦ The parents of a West Virginia student with autism began a home-based program of discrete trial training, ABA and Lovaas. They sought an IEP meeting to discuss incorporating the home program into a school setting with a LEAP program. The final IEP took many of the parents' suggestions into account, but it did not include a 1:1 aide or the ABA therapy they wanted. They requested a due process hearing, **asserting that the district had**

predetermined their son's placement and that they were not allowed to meaningfully participate in the IEP process. The Fourth Circuit affirmed the ruling that the district had considered information from the parents at IEP meetings and that the parents had derailed the IEP process by preventing thorough discussions. The use of a draft IEP did not show predetermination. *J.D. v. Kanawha County Board of Educ.*, 357 Fed.Appx. 515 (4th Cir. 2009).

♦ Prior to an IEP meeting, a California school district decided to move a private school student with autism to a public school placement with other autistic children. The parents attended the IEP meeting but offered no alternative placements for the student. Later, they requested due process and eventually sued, claiming the district had predetermined their son's placement. After a federal court held that the district violated the IDEA by predetermining the student's placement, the Ninth Circuit reversed. It found that more facts were needed to ascertain **whether the district predetermined the child's placement.** Because the parents had not offered an alternative to the district's proposal, it was difficult to discern the district's intent and whether the district would have considered an alternative placement had one been offered. A new hearing was required. *H.B. v. Las Virgenes Unified School Dist.*, 239 Fed.Appx. 342 (9th Cir. 2007).

♦ A Connecticut student with serious emotional disturbance had increasing behavioral problems as he entered middle school. He was transferred to a state-approved special education day school, where he achieved good grades. However, his parents sought a private school placement, fearing he was not being sufficiently challenged. After an evaluation, the school board adopted several of the parents' suggested changes to the IEP and offered to place the student in a regional school for students with emotional and behavioral difficulties. The parents rejected the IEP and sought due process. A hearing officer, a federal court and the U.S. Court of Appeals, Second Circuit, decided the issue in favor of the school board. School boards comply with the IDEA when parents have adequate opportunities to participate in the development of the IEP. **Nothing in the IDEA required that parents consent to an IEP.** Because the initial and revised IEPs were sufficient, the school board offered an appropriate education. *A.E. v. Westport Board of Educ.*, 251 Fed. Appx. 685 (2d Cir. 2007).

♦ An Ohio student began experiencing disciplinary problems in sixth grade and his IEP was changed twice. His mother rejected his seventh-grade IEP on the grounds that it had been predetermined. She eventually sued, and the case reached the Sixth Circuit. The court of appeals held that predetermination is not the same as preparation and that **the IEP team members could prepare reports and come to meetings with pre-formed opinions** about the best course of action for a student. That kind of work did not amount to predetermination. Here, the parties had met 16 times over a two-year period and had daily communications about homework. The school district's preparation work prior to the IEP meeting did not violate the IDEA. *Nack v. Orange City School Dist.*, 454 F.3d 604 (6th Cir. 2006).

C. Appropriateness of IEP

1. Methodology Questions

♦ A New Jersey preschool student with autism resisted one-on-one ABA therapy but made significant progress when a developmental individual relationship (DIR)-based Floortime methodology was used. When she aged out of early intervention services, the district offered a placement that used only ABA therapy. The parents refused to sign the IEP and placed her in a private school that offered the DIR-Floortime methodology. They sued for tuition reimbursement, which a federal court granted. **The district refused to even consider the DIR-Floortime methodology** even though one of the school board's own witnesses knew of the student's progress with that programming and believed its use should continue. Also, the IEP included no behavior modification plan and did not address the student's need for sensory education. *Dumont Board of Educ. v. J.T.*, No. 09-5048 (JLL) 2010 WL 1875584 (D.N.J. 5/10/10).

♦ The parents of a California student with autism claimed their school district had not offered an appropriate IEP because the district had not properly obtained an IQ score for her. They believed that she needed 30 hours of weekly ABA therapy to adequately progress under her IEPs. When they sued, a federal court ruled against them, noting that although the child's progress was slow, it was adequate under the IDEA. Further, the parents could not dictate the methodology used to educate their daughter. And **one expert had noted that up to 50% of autistic children do not benefit from ABA therapy**. Each of the student's IEPs built on earlier IEPs and the foundational skills the student acquired under them. *K.S. v. Fremont Unified School Dist.*, 679 F.Supp.2d 1046 (N.D. Cal. 2009).

♦ A Virginia student with autism and a significant communication disorder made little progress in the public school system, mastering only one IEP objective in six years. His parents requested a due process hearing, suggesting a one-on-one Lindamood-Bell Center placement. After the hearing, **the school system acknowledged that the student should be classified as having multiple disabilities but refused to provide one-on-one instruction**. The parents placed their son in the Lindamood-Bell program for four years and then sought tuition reimbursement. A hearing officer found three of the IEPs invalid but also found the center to be an inappropriate placement. A federal court agreed, but the Fourth Circuit vacated and remanded the case for a year-by-year IEP analysis. If the parents could show that the center placement was appropriate, they might be entitled to tuition reimbursement. *M.S. v. Fairfax County School Board*, 553 F.3d 315 (4th Cir. 2009).

♦ The parents of an Arizona child with autism signed off on his IEPs, and the district employed multiple instructional and behavioral methods and strategies, including the TEACCH method. It also paid for a summer program using the ABA method. The child made slow but observable progress, leading his parents to seek additional tutoring. **The district complied with their request for two** autism specialists to train paraprofessionals in ABA methodology. When the parents sued anyway, a federal court not only ruled against them but also awarded attorneys' fees and costs to the district as the prevailing party – more than $140,000. *Parenteau v. Prescott Unified School Dist.*, No. CV 07-8072-PCT-NVW, 2009 WL 2169154 (D. Ariz. 7/17/09).

♦ The mother of a Washington student with autism **believed that the in-home ABA therapists provided by her district were not properly trained**. She began taking him to a private therapist. The school district then began offering ABA therapy and discontinued paying for the private therapist. The mother refused to let her son attend an ESY program because she believed the staff was improperly trained. She rejected another IEP offer. The case reached the Washington Court of Appeals, which noted that the IEP offered a FAPE even though the IEP team ultimately rejected the mother's position. She had attended IEP meetings with an advocate and an autism consultant. *Hensley v. Colville School Dist.*, 148 Wash.App.1032 (Wash. Ct. App. 2009).

♦ The IEP team for a Tennessee student with autism rejected several parental proposals for ABA Lovaas programming. His parents placed him in a private school and requested a due process hearing, at which it was determined that the school district violated IDEA procedural requirements by predetermining the student's placement under an unofficial policy of refusing to consider "Lovaas style ABA." It also violated the IDEA by failing to ensure that regular education teachers attended IEP team meetings. The case reached the Sixth Circuit, which noted that **differences in outcomes between two methodologies can sometimes be so great that the provision of a lesser program amounts to a denial of FAPE.** Here, the question of whether the district had provided the student with a meaningful educational benefit had to be gauged in relation to the child's potential. On remand, the court held that the school district's proposals were substantively appropriate for the student. It denied the parents full reimbursement for ABA services, but awarded them half their costs of such services. The parents appealed and the Sixth Circuit affirmed. Since the district's IEPs were reasonably calculated to offer the student a meaningful educational benefit, the reduction in the amount of reimbursement was reasonable. *Deal v. Hamilton County Dep't of Educ.*, 258 Fed. Appx. 863 (6th Cir. 2008).

♦ The parents of a Virginia student with dyslexia and other disabilities removed her from her public school in favor of a Lindamood-Bell program, then placed her in a private school. They rejected an IEP for her eighth-grade year because it placed her back at the public school, and they placed her in the Kildonan School for ninth grade. They also rejected an IEP for tenth grade. A hearing officer eventually found that the board had offered the student a FAPE, and a federal court upheld that determination. The Fourth Circuit affirmed, finding that the parents failed to meet their burden of showing that the hearing officer's findings were erroneous. **The student was not entitled to a Lindamood-Bell program.** *Fairfax County School Board v. Knight*, 261 Fed. Appx. 606 (4th Cir. 2008).

♦ A New Hampshire school district prepared an IEP for an 18-year-old student, whose parents' relationship with the district had deteriorated. The IEP was nearly 60 pages long and contained nine pages of transition services. The parents rejected the IEP but refused to make any modifications to the plan or even to specify which parts of the IEP were objectionable other than to say they disagreed with the behavior aspects of the IEP. The district unsuccessfully tried to put the rest of the IEP into effect, then sought due process. A hearing officer ruled in its favor, and a federal court affirmed. **The district did not have to comply with the parents' unspecified vision of the perfect IEP.** Here, the district offered a detailed and comprehensive IEP that more than adequately addressed the student's needs. *Lessard v. Wilton-Lyndeborough Cooperative School Dist.*, No. 05-CV-192-SM, 2007 WL 1221103 (D.N.H. 4/23/07).

♦ A Florida student with profound bilateral sensorial hearing loss began auditory-verbal therapy (AVT) at the age of nine months. After she received a cochlear implant, a surgeon stated that AVT was the best therapy for her. When she turned three, the district found her eligible for special education but rejected the parents' request to continue the AVT program and instead offered the verbotonal approach to develop her oral communication skills. After a hearing in favor of the district, the parents sued. A federal court and the Eleventh Circuit ruled for the district, noting that **the verbotonal approach was an accepted, proven therapeutic methodology** and that the district did not have to provide the best program possible under the IDEA. *M.M. v. School Board of Miami-Dade County*, 437 F.3d 1085 (11th Cir. 2006).

♦ An Indiana student with autism received one-on-one ABA therapy in his home prior to entering kindergarten. When he was to start kindergarten, the district proposed placing him in a small group with individual instruction in the mornings and regular kindergarten classes in the afternoon. His parents objected, seeking continued ABA therapy and a full-time ABA-trained therapist for his kindergarten classes. A hearing officer ruled that the district was offering a free appropriate public education, and a federal court agreed. **The district's flexible and varied approach was properly individualized for the student and its methodology was not improper.** *Z.F. v. South Harrison Community School Corp.*, No. 404CV0073DFHWGH, 2005 WL 2373729 (S.D. Ind. 9/1/05).

♦ When a student with autism moved to Rhode Island, his new school district assembled an IEP team and proposed an interim IEP within two weeks. The district wanted to place the student in a newly established self-contained classroom that used a modified version of the TEACCH method. **The parents asserted that only the DTT methodology was appropriate.** They rejected the IEP and notified the district that they would be placing their son in a private school. They then rejected a second IEP developed by the district. A due process hearing officer ruled for the parents, but a federal court and the First Circuit Court of Appeals ruled for the district, noting that the IDEA did not require the best possible education for students with disabilities. Here, the IEP was reasonably calculated to provide the student with an appropriate education. The classroom was half the size of his previous placement, and the teachers had extensive experience and training with autistic children. Further, many of the elements of DTT would be available through the use of the TEACCH methodology, including considerable one-on-one instruction. *L.T. on Behalf of N.B. v. Warwick School Committee*, 361 F.3d 80 (1st Cir. 2004).

2. Student Progress

♦   A Pennsylvania school district cut the learning support offered to a student with a specific learning disability in reading and written expression. The following year, the district reevaluated the student and, **despite a report of numerous areas of decline, put her on a "monitoring IEP," under which she received no direct special education**. Her parents obtained private tutoring for her and pursued legal action. A hearing officer and a federal court ruled that the district violated the student's IDEA rights by putting her on the "monitoring IEP." She was entitled to compensatory education of an hour per day for three years. *Breanne C. v. Southern York County School Dist.*, 732 F.Supp.2d 474 (M.D. Pa. 2010).

♦   A New York school psychologist **found a student would benefit from larger classrooms** and recommended a change from self-contained classes to consultant teacher services for his grade-seven IEP. The school's committee on special education took the evaluation into account and drafted an IEP that did not specify "building supports," which were regular education services. Instead, the IEP called for an integrated daily consultant teacher program in English and social studies. The student's mother challenged the IEP, but a federal court ruled against her. The district used the evaluation results in determining the IEP, and it did not have to include the regular education services in the IEP it drafted. *M.F. v. Irvington Union Free School Dist.*, 719 F.Supp.2d 302 (S.D.N.Y. 2010).

♦   A New Jersey high school student designated as "other health impaired" received special education and did well in his programs but tested poorly in standardized tests. His parents became concerned with his education and requested due process, where they noted that his reading skills were at a third-grade level. His teachers and other school employees testified that standardized test scores were unreliable and that academic progress was a better indicator of success, but an administrative law judge disagreed and ruled for the parents. A federal court reversed that decision, but the Third Circuit reversed the lower court, holding that **the student's good grades did not indicate that he was making educational progress**. The district failed to incorporate necessary recommendations made by the parents' experts and by the student's teachers and evaluators. *D.S. v. Bayonne Board of Educ.*, 602 F.3d 553 (3d Cir. 2010).

♦   A Pennsylvania student with dyslexia and learning disabilities attended a private high school for two years. A district reevaluation recommended that she attend district schools for her junior and senior years. She began her junior year reading at a fourth-grade level but raised it to a sixth-grade level during the year. Her parents nonetheless challenged the IEP, citing the six-grade gap between her reading level and that of her peers. A hearing officer and a federal court ruled for the school district, noting the two-year increase in reading level accomplished in a single year, and noting also that **the student had made meaningful progress in math and especially writing**, where she was nearly at a collegiate level. *High v. Exeter Township School Dist.*, No. 09-2202, 2010 WL 363832 (E.D. Pa. 2/1/10).

◆ A dyslexic New York student with a learning disability had an IEP that called for weekly reading and writing intervention periods as well as daily multi-sensory reading periods in a resource room. However, the district did not provide the daily resource room component, instead offering inclusion programming with support, and providing multi-sensory reading on alternate days. The student's reading skills regressed, and **he showed satisfactory progress in only two of 29 short-term IEP goals, but the district didn't change his IEP**. His parents placed him in a private school and sought tuition reimbursement. A federal court awarded them tuition because of the district's failure to modify the IEP. *Bougades v. Pine Plains Cent. School Dist.*, No. 05 Civ. 02861 (PGG), 2009 WL 2603110 (S.D.N.Y. 8/25/09).

◆ A New Jersey student who suffered from epileptic seizures was classified as "other health impaired." After surgeries, his seizures stopped and his IQ increased to the low average range. During his eighth-grade year, a neuropsychologist evaluated him in class and found he had trouble keeping pace with his peers. She felt his current IEP did not address his needs adequately and recommended a quiet environment. The parents sought an out-of-district placement, which the district denied. A due process hearing officer relied on two standardized tests (in which the student went from a higher score to a lower one over a one-year period) and ordered the out-of-district placement. However, a federal court reversed, noting that **the hearing officer should also have considered the student's high grades in assessing his progress**. *D.S. v. Bayonne Board of Educ.*, No. 2:08-CV-01726 (WJM) (MF), 2008 WL 4960055 (D.N.J. 11/19/08).

◆ A student with ADHD attended a Massachusetts charter school that emphasized performing arts in the context of a demanding but ungraded academic curriculum. The school had a competency-based educational philosophy, requiring its students to achieve the equivalent of at least a B in courses to reach the "competency" level. For his ninth-grade year, his parents rejected his IEP, seeking measurable goals. The case eventually reached a federal court, which held that the parents failed to show a violation of the IDEA. The school had graduation standards that far exceeded Massachusetts state standards, and **the competency-based system satisfied legal requirements**. *Claudia C-B v. Board of Trustees of Pioneer Valley Performing Arts Charter School*, 539 F.Supp.2d 474 (D. Mass. 2008).

◆ The parents of an Arkansas student with Asperger's Syndrome became dissatisfied with his IEP and challenged it unsuccessfully. They later convinced the district to make some big changes to the IEP, requiring the student to be graded on all work and not just what he chose to complete. He then began failing some classes and his father became upset. He expressed hostility toward the superintendent and was arrested. After a restraining order was issued against the father, he arranged for homebound instruction and was then charged with truancy. Eventually, the district agreed to the offsite education and hired the person recommended by the father. After the student graduated at his parents' request, the parents sued the district for IDEA and Section 504 violations. A federal court and the Eighth Circuit credited the district's expert, who testified that the student had made educational progress. **The district tried to give the student the best education it could.** *Bradley v. Arkansas Dep't of Educ.*, 443 F.3d 965 (8th Cir. 2005).

♦   A Pennsylvania student contracted a chronic illness that left him unable to attend school. After a three-month delay, the district provided him weekly home instruction. He completed grade seven with straight As and academic honors. He remained unable to attend school in eighth grade, and the district resumed homebound instruction. A district tutor resigned and some were rejected by the parents. The parents also refused to accommodate district tutors at times when private tutors were scheduled to teach their son. The student received straight As for grade eight, won the school geography bee and qualified for the Junior National Honor Society. **His test scores in standardized national tests increased over prior school years.** The parents rejected an offer by the district to make up 55 hours of missed instruction during the summer after the student's eighth-grade year. They sought reimbursement for their privately hired tutors and for his high school tuition. The U.S. Court of Appeals, Third Circuit, ruled that the district provided the student with meaningful educational benefits, despite some failures. Reimbursement was denied. *Falzett v. Pocono Mountain School Dist.*, 152 Fed.Appx. 117 (3d Cir. 2005).

♦   A Connecticut student performed inconsistently in school. A comprehensive evaluation determined that she was functioning within the average range. However, her math skills were significantly below her intellectual potential and her anxiety was clinically significant. After an IEP called for regular classes, with three hours of weekly special education, her parents placed her in a private school, then sought tuition reimbursement. A hearing officer found that the board's IEP proposal was reasonably calculated to confer educational benefits on the student, and denied tuition reimbursement. A federal court found sufficient objective evidence in this case that **the student had progressed under prior IEPs**, and that the IEP proposed for her fifth-grade year would have provided her with a free appropriate education. *B.L. v. New Britain Board of Educ.*, 394 F.Supp.2d 522 (D. Conn. 2005).

♦   A Maryland student with a specific learning disability and ADHD was placed in a private school at district expense for three years. **The district then proposed a public school placement based on his progress at the private school.** His parents objected and kept him at the private school for the following year. When they sought tuition reimbursement, an administrative law judge ruled against them. A federal court affirmed, noting that the proposed IEP would have provided the student at least 20 hours a week of special education in his weaker subjects. Also, the failure to have a general education teacher at his IEP meeting, although a procedural violation of the IDEA, did not materially violate the act. *Lundvall v. Board of Educ. of Anne Arundel County*, No. Civ. JFM-05-646, 2005 WL 2123724 (D. Md. 8/31/05).

♦ A learning disabled student with a major depressive disorder attended school under inclusive IEPs. In grade five, testing indicated significant regression in word decoding, and his parents refused to sign the next IEP. They requested an independent evaluation, which revealed even greater regression than was first believed. A special education hearing panel conducted a hearing and determined that the student was entitled to two years of compensatory education. A trial court reversed, but the Supreme Court of Delaware reversed the trial court. Here, **the student's IEPs from grade three through six contained the same objectives despite his regression** or "plateaus." This was a denial of FAPE. *Fisher v. Board of Educ. of Christina School Dist.*, 856 A.2d 552 (Del. 2004).

♦ The parents of a sixth-grade student with dyslexia requested a due process hearing because of dissatisfaction with the IEP developed for the following year. They then unilaterally placed the student in a summer program at a residential school. The hearing officer determined that the IEP was inappropriate and ordered the school district to convene an IEP meeting within 15 days. She also held that a residential placement was not justified and that the parents were not entitled to compensatory education. A West Virginia federal court agreed, and so did the Fourth Circuit Court of Appeals. **The parents had not shown that a residential placement was appropriate or that the student needed extended year programming.** They had to participate in the IEP process. *Morgan v. Greenbrier County Board of Educ.*, 83 Fed.Appx. 566 (4th Cir. 2003).

♦ A learning disabled student had an IQ in the 140 range. In ninth grade, he took a higher number of courses than recommended, including two honors classes. He received all Bs except for his honors classes. His father filed a due process challenge to the IEP. A hearing officer upheld the IEP, and a federal court agreed with that decision. Here, the student's progress was hampered by his participation on the school ski team, which caused him to miss six days of class over a six-week period. Also, his father forbade the district from reducing his ski team participation and refused to take an active role in monitoring his son's homework. **The student's failure to progress at the rate expected by his parents was not evidence that he failed to make educational progress.** Despite the father's adversarial posture, the district properly implemented the student's IEP. *Michael D.M. v. Pemi-Baker Regional School Dist.*, No. Civ. 02-541-SM, 2004 WL 1932813 (D.N.H. 8/31/04).

♦ A Minnesota student with brain lesions and a long history of psychiatric illness had many disciplinary incidents in his public school setting, including the use of physical restraints. However, he showed academic progress there. His mother eventually agreed to a home instruction plan, but then placed him in a private school, where he continued to experience behavioral difficulties. She requested a due process hearing, seeking tuition reimbursement and alleging that the school district's lack of positive behavioral interventions, as well as the high number of physical restraints, prevented the student from receiving a free appropriate public education. The hearing officer ruled in favor of the student, but the state level review officer reversed. A federal court and the Eighth Circuit Court of Appeals affirmed. Here, contrary to the mother's assertions, the student's **academic progress was not irrelevant to the question of the adequacy of his IEP.** Also, the fact that more behavioral interventions could have been made did not mean the school district had not acted in good faith in assisting the student with his educational goals. Tuition reimbursement was disallowed. *CJN v. Minneapolis Public Schools, Special School Dist. No. 1*, 323 F.3d 630 (8th Cir. 2003).

3. Maximizing Potential

♦   The parents of a New Jersey preschool student with autism rejected the IEP offered by their district. The IEP called for a public school ABA program four and a-half days a week as well as speech therapy, and staff and parent training sessions. The IEP could be further molded to fit the student's specific needs upon his enrollment. But the parents placed their son in a private school and sought tuition reimbursement. A federal court ruled against them. The IDEA does not require a school district to maximize a student's potential or provide the best education possible, and **the district properly considered the student's potential and educational needs.** The district's program was extremely flexible in adapting programs for preschool students who were receiving their first educational services. *G.B. v. Bridgewater-Raritan Regional Board of Educ.*, No. 07-4300 (JJH), 2009 WL 512122 (D.N.J. 2/27/09).

♦   After a Pennsylvania student's fourth-grade year, his parents rejected an IEP proposed by the district. They requested a due process hearing, but settled the case, with the district agreeing to fund a private school placement for the fifth grade. At the end of the fifth grade, the parents again rejected the IEP because the district did not consider continuing the private school placement. They challenged the IEP and lost. A hearing officer and a federal court noted that **an IEP does not need to provide the best possible education.** Here, the IEP offered a highly structured program with ample time to address the student's needs in small group settings. *J.G. and L.G. v. Abington School Dist.*, No. 08-CV-00734, 2008 WL 4633380 (E.D. Pa. 10/15/08).

♦   The parents of a severely dyslexic Rhode Island student who received extended school year and extended school day services rejected his IEP for seventh grade and placed him in an uncertified private school for students with learning disabilities. When they sought tuition reimbursement, a hearing officer denied their request. A federal court noted that the student had made gains in reading despite his dyslexia. And the district had modified his seventh-grade IEP, increasing the level of proposed services for middle school. Since **the IDEA did not require the optimization of services**, the district's IEP offered the student a free appropriate public education. *Slater v. Exeter-West Greenwich Regional School Dist.*, No. CA 06-527 ML, 2007 WL 2067719 (D.R.I. 7/16/07).

♦   A Hawaii student with Asperger's syndrome became anxious and overwhelmed at changes in his routine and environment. When his paraprofessional skills trainer left during his eighth-grade year, a replacement came and went, followed by another replacement, neither of whom had experience teaching students with autism. At an emergency IEP meeting held at the mother's request, the school refused to hire a skills trainer the mother desired. She enrolled her son in a private school and sought tuition reimbursement. A hearing officer and a federal court ruled against her. **The student was not entitled to the best skills trainer available**, and his special education teacher was outstanding. *B.V. v. Dep't of Educ., State of Hawaii*, 451 F.Supp.2d 1113 (D. Haw. 2005).

♦   A child with a high-functioning form of autism was classified as eligible for special education two years before kindergarten. In the summer before kindergarten, he received extended school year (ESY) special education services. His IEP for kindergarten called for six hours of one-on-one therapy and two hours of speech/language services each day, plus two hours of occupational therapy each week. When the parties put together an extended school year IEP for the summer after kindergarten, his therapists proposed a peer modeling approach. However, his parents preferred one-on-one services. The ESY IEP provided for 151 hours of services, including eight hours of direct speech and occupational therapy. A due process hearing officer concluded that the school board should have provided the level of services requested by the parents. However, he refused to order reimbursement. The parents sued, seeking reimbursement and a goal of "mastery" of the various skills listed in the IEP. A federal court ruled in favor of the district, finding the hearing officer had too heavily relied on the testimony of various expert witnesses over the testimony of the student's therapists when he concluded that the IEP should have provided the level of services requested by the parents. On appeal, the Fourth Circuit noted that **extended school year services were only necessary where the benefits a student gains during the school year will be significantly jeopardized if he receives no education during the summer**. The court remanded the case for a determination of ESY eligibility. *JH ex rel. JD v. Henrico County School Board*, 326 F.3d 560 (4th Cir. 2003).

♦   An Indiana school district approved a full-time public school program for a student with autism and determined that he was eligible for eight hours of speech therapy to avoid regression in his communication skills during the summer. Before the school year, the parents agreed to an IEP that called for the student's placement in a district program employing an eclectic approach that included the picture exchange communication system, one-on-one instruction and some of the "applied behavior analysis" (ABA) and "discrete trial training" (DTT) techniques. The parents also decided to provide the student with a home ABA/DTT program administered by a private provider. For the next year, the parents sought district funding of a program of at least 40 hours per week of combined home and school training under the provider's supervision. The district proposed an IEP calling for 20 hours of weekly programming. A due process hearing officer upheld the district's IEPs as appropriate.

A federal court stated that the parents' criticisms of the IEP were based on their belief that "nothing short of total commitment" to the ABA/DTT approach was appropriate. However, **the district was not legally obligated to provide the student with the best education possible.** The district provided the student a FAPE and its IEPs were reasonably calculated to continue providing him with educational benefits. Further, while the law forbids a district from using cost as a reason for denying a FAPE or when implementing an IEP that has already been formulated, schools may consider cost when formulating an IEP. The hearing officer's decision was affirmed. *J.P. v. West Clark Community Schools*, 230 F.Supp.2d 910 (S.D. Ind. 2002).

♦ A North Carolina seventh-grader's grades dropped sharply and he often failed to complete assignments. After being identified as academically gifted, he was diagnosed with a learning disability that primarily affected his writing skills. The district agreed to certain accommodations, but an IEP was never completed due to disagreements. The student's mother filed a complaint with the state department of public instruction and office for civil rights, asserting that the system failed to identify her son as having a disability and mishandled the IEP process. A state investigation indicated no failure by the school system. The student's performance deteriorated in grade eight, which resulted in further modifications to his draft IEP, but he managed to pass the eighth grade. A due process hearing officer ruled that the school failed to provide a FAPE and did not consistently implement the student's IEPs.

The case reached the Fourth Circuit, which held that the student had been evaluated by seven different evaluators and four of them recommended the minimization of writing. The school system followed these recommendations by providing for reduced handwriting through the use of computers and tape recorders. The student's IEPs contained specific goals and a means to assess his performance. **Any deficiency in the IEPs did not deny the student a FAPE or diminish his opportunity to achieve his full potential as required by North Carolina law.** The court ruled in favor of the school system. *D.B. v. Craven County Board of Educ.*, 210 F.3d 360 (4th Cir. 2000).

D. Procedural Violations

♦ The parents of a Vermont student with a disability asserted that their school district violated the IDEA because the student's applied media instructor (regular education teacher) missed some IEP meetings. They claimed his increased presence might have led to a different placement. When they initiated due process proceedings, the case eventually reached the Second Circuit, which ruled against them. The court of appeals noted that **the mere absence of a regular educator at any given IEP meeting was not necessarily a procedural violation** of the IDEA. Here, the instructor's participation was appropriate under the circumstances. He attended some meetings, and the parents decided to enroll their child in a particular applied media course without regard to the instructor's opinion. Thus, they suffered no harm. *K.L.A. v. Windham Southeast Supervisory Union*, 371 Fed.Appx. 151 (2d Cir. 2010).

♦ The parents of a New York student who had problems in large group settings attended committee on special education (CSE) meetings at which the student's IEP was changed from a classroom of 24 students to a 12:1:1 setting. The parents rejected the proposed IEP and placed the student in a private school, then sought tuition reimbursement. A federal court found the IEP procedurally deficient because the student's special education teacher did not attend the CSE meetings. However, the Second Circuit reversed, noting that **the IEP coordinator at the student's school had attended the CSE meetings along with the student's general education teacher**, and that the IEP was reasonably calculated to provide educational benefits. No tuition was awarded. *A.H. v. Dep't of Educ. of City of New York*, 394 Fed.Appx. 718 (2d Cir. 2010).

♦ A California school district scheduled an IEP meeting without first checking the parents' availability. The parents had a history of not attending such meetings, and they did not return a signed copy of this IEP meeting notice. The mother asked the district to reschedule the meeting, but the district held the meeting in their absence. The parents later filed an administrative action against the district. Eventually the case reached the Ninth Circuit, which ruled that **regardless of the parents' history of non-attendance and the reason for their unavailability on the date in question, the district had an affirmative duty to comply with the IDEA**. *Drobnicki v. Poway Unified School Dist.*, 358 Fed.Appx. 788 (9th Cir. 2009).

♦ A New York committee on special education convened to discuss a student's IEP for grade five. **No additional parent member of the team was available to attend the meeting, so the student's parents agreed to proceed with their private psychologist in attendance.** They rejected the IEP, asserting that it placed their daughter in a male-dominated classroom and that at times she would be the only female student in class. Instead they placed her in a private school and sought tuition reimbursement. A federal court found no procedural violation justifying tuition reimbursement. The student had been offered a FAPE, and her IEP was not predetermined. *R.R. and D.R. v. Scarsdale Union Free School Dist.*, 615 F.Supp.2d 283 (S.D.N.Y. 2009).

♦ The parents of a Colorado three-year-old with autism rejected the draft IEP offered by their school district, which would have placed their son in an integrated setting, and kept their son at home, continuing the one-on-one therapy program he had been receiving. The district failed to finalize the IEP for that year. The next year, the parents again rejected the district's IEP calling for an integrated placement with five hours of discrete trial training a week. The district finalized that IEP, but the parents selected a private school, then sought tuition reimbursement. A hearing officer ruled for the district, but a federal court found the parents were entitled to tuition for the first year because the district failed to finalize the IEP. The Tenth Circuit reversed, noting that **procedural violations of the IDEA are not sufficient to prove an IDEA violation; there**

must also be a substantive violation that results in lost educational opportunity. On remand, the district court held that the unfinished IEP failed to offer the student needed one-on-one services. As a result, the parents were entitled to their tuition costs. *Sytsema v. Academy School Dist. No. 20*, No. 03-CV-2582-RPM, 2009 WL 3682221 (D. Colo. 10/30/09).

♦   A California school district convened an IEP team meeting that included a student's adaptive physical education (PE) teacher from three years earlier. Given the student's disabilities, adaptive PE was one of his most significant IEP components. The PE teacher had recently visited his school to evaluate his education needs and was familiar with his current situation. His parents claimed an IDEA violation because his most current special education providers did not attend the meeting. However, the Ninth Circuit ruled against them, noting that **the IDEA does not require the most current teacher to attend**. Rather, it requires a special education teacher or provider who has actually taught the student. Not all a student's special education teachers need to attend the IEP meeting. *A.G. v. Placentia-Yorba Linda Unified School Dist.*, 320 Fed.Appx. 519 (9th Cir. 2009).

♦   The parents of an autistic student in California claimed that their district violated the IDEA when it put together an IEP. No teacher from the student's private school attended IEP team meetings. The case reached the Ninth Circuit, which ruled that the district provided a valid IEP effectively tailored to his needs and reasonably calculated to provide meaningful educational benefit. **The exclusion of a private school teacher from IEP team meetings did not result in lost educational opportunities.** However, the district did have to continue to co-fund an in-home intervention program while the appeals process occurred. The stay-put provision required the district to maintain the student's current educational placement during the appeals process even though the IDEA did not specifically require it. *Joshua A. v. Rocklin Unified School Dist.*, 559 F.3d 1036 (9th Cir. 2009).

♦   After a Pennsylvania student with disabilities turned 16, his new IEP left sections of his mandatory transition plan largely blank, instead noting that he would meet with a school counselor to discuss his prerequisites for college and other issues. At the next IEP team meeting, the district offered the student an alternative special education day placement at an in-state private school. His parents instead opted for a residential school in New York. When they sought tuition reimbursement, the district failed to submit the due process request for more than three months. However, a hearing officer still ruled in favor of the district, finding the proposed placement appropriate. A federal court and the Third Circuit affirmed. Here, **the dispute over the transition plan and the delay in submitting the due process request did not add up to an IDEA violation** where the proposed IEP was appropriate. *Sinan v. School Dist. of Philadelphia*, 293 Fed.Appx. 912 (3d Cir. 2008).

♦   A California student with ADHD and reactive detachment disorder, who had also been abused, was expelled from three preschool programs for classroom misconduct. In first grade, the district declared her ineligible for special education under the IDEA, but eligible for an accommodation under Section 504. She continued to have behavior problems in elementary school. Her mother placed her in a private residential facility in Montana, then sought tuition reimbursement. The district convened an IEP team meeting, but no representative from the Montana school attended. When the team again found the student ineligible for special education, a hearing officer held that the improperly formed IEP team meeting did not result in any lost opportunity for the student and thus did not justify tuition reimbursement. A federal court and the Ninth Circuit upheld that ruling. **Any procedural error by the district in failing to properly staff the IEP team meeting was harmless** because the student failed to show that she had a qualifying disability under the IDEA. Her emotional problems did not affect her ability to build and maintain relationships with teachers and peers. And her achievement scores were at or above grade level. *R.B. v. Napa Valley Unified School Dist.*, 496 F.3d 932 (9th Cir. 2007).

♦ A New Jersey student with ADHD, developmental writing disorder and dyslexia was classified under the category of specific learning disability. Her parents sought changes to her sixth-grade IEP, but rejected the offer made by the district because it would remove her from some mainstream classes. They challenged the IEP, **asserting the IEP did not have adequate goals and objectives**. A federal court held that even though the district committed a procedural violation of the IDEA because the IEP was missing goals and objectives, the parents failed to prove that this resulted in the denial of a free appropriate public education. The student received educational benefits, moving from grade to grade and attaining at least average test scores, and her parents participated in the IEP process. *G.N. v. Board of Educ. of Township of Livingston*, No. 05-3325 (JAG), 2007 WL 2265035 (D.N.J. 8/6/07).

♦ The parents of a student with an IQ of 140 and a neuropsychiatric disability enrolled him in a private school and then attended an IEP meeting where only one specific goal was agreed upon. The district later offered the student an IEP with four goals, largely based on a previous IEP. The parents then sought reimbursement, claiming that the failure to complete the IEP at the meeting denied their son a free appropriate public education. A Wisconsin federal court disagreed. Although a procedural violation of the IDEA can be so severe as to cause a loss of educational opportunity, that was not the case here. The district had determined that the student could remain in its schools and offered to meet with the parents to discuss any changes they believed were appropriate. The parents appealed to the Seventh Circuit, which **rejected their claim that the district violated the IDEA by not having a representative from the private school at the IEP meeting**. That was only required if the district made a private school placement. The court also held that the district did not predetermine the student's IEP. Finally, the parents were only interested in discussing the private school placement they had made. Their intransigence did not result in a procedural violation by the district. *Hjortness v. Neenah Joint School Dist.*, 507 F.3d 1060 (7th Cir. 2007).

♦   A Virginia student with Asperger's syndrome and a nonverbal learning disability was subjected to teasing and assaults by other students. At the IEP meeting for his ninth-grade year, the discussion focused on levels of performance and goals and objectives. The team decided the student would be placed at an unspecified private day school even though the student's mother believed neither of two suggested schools was appropriate. The district applied at five schools on the student's behalf; two schools invited him and his parents to visit. After the visits, the parents found both schools inappropriate because of concerns about continued teasing and bullying. They sought placement in a residential school, and the Fourth Circuit ultimately agreed with that decision. Here, **the district's failure to identify a particular school in the IEP amounted to an IDEA violation.** The IEP team comments about certain private schools did not equate to a written IEP offer. *A.K. v. Alexandria City School Board*, 484 F.3d 672 (4th Cir. 2007).

On remand, the federal court held that the district had to pay the parents over $135,000 in tuition and transportation costs. *A.K. v. Alexandria City School Board*, 544 F.Supp.2d 487 (E.D. Va. 2008).

♦   A District of Columbia charter school student with disabilities was reclassified from "specific learning disability" to "multiple disabilities." The school decided he required a full-time special education program, which it could not provide. It convened a Multi-Disciplinary Team meeting to determine a new placement and offered a public school placement in the fifth grade. The student's mother objected to the offer, seeking a private school placement. A hearing officer ruled for the district, and a federal court affirmed. **Even though the district did not have a classroom for the student's grade level at the school selected, he would be in classes with age-appropriate peers who functioned at his comparable academic ability.** So even if the district committed a procedural violation of the IDEA, it did not violate his substantive due process rights. *Holdzclaw v. District of Columbia*, 524 F.Supp.2d 43 (D.D.C. 2007).

♦   The mother of a Hawaii student claimed she did not receive a copy of her son's IEP until near the end of the school year, at which time she learned that his special education services had been reduced from 1,440 minutes to 600 per week. A hearing officer found that she was unable to meaningfully participate in three IEP meetings and that her son had been denied a free appropriate public education. A federal court agreed. **The procedural violation resulted in a loss of opportunity to participate in the IEP process and a denial of FAPE.** *Hawaii Dep't of Educ. v. D.K.*, No. 05-00560 ACK/LEK, 2006 WL 1646093 (D. Haw. 6/6/06).

♦   A Washington student with autism and other cognitive and behavioral disabilities was placed in a self-contained program for non-disabled students with behavior problems. The IEP team recommended that the student not return to the program for the following year out of safety concerns, but the district then decided to place the student there despite failing to hold an IEP team meeting before the school year began. The student's grandparents (guardians) placed him in a private school and requested a due process hearing. An administrative law judge determined that the district violated the IDEA and found the private school placement appropriate. The Washington Court of Appeals upheld that decision. **The failure to create a timely IEP justified the private school placement.** *North Kitsap School Dist. v. K.W.*, 123 P.3d 469 (Wash. Ct. App. 2005).

♦ Eleven days after an autistic Indiana student's third birthday, his school district completed his IEP, basing it on a communication disorder. His parents asked for reclassification and a home-based program of applied behavioral analysis (ABA) therapy as well as occupational therapy. The district reevaluated the student, reclassified him as developmentally delayed and placed him in a home program. His parents asked for more services, requesting that they be provided evenings, weekends and holidays. The district refused. When it sought to transition the student to an in-school program, the parents objected. A due process hearing officer found that the district violated state rules by not developing an IEP by the student's third birthday. A federal court found **the 11-day delay in beginning services to the student was minimal.** Also, the student's IEP was adequate. There were technical IDEA procedural violations, but no harm resulted. *J.K. v. Metropolitan School Dist. of Southwest Allen County*, No. 1:04-CV-293-TS, 2005 WL 2406046 (N.D. Ind. 9/27/05).

♦ The parents of a 10-year-old student with autism placed him in a private school at their own expense, pending a special education evaluation by their school district. After conducting an assessment, the district declared the student eligible for special education. The parents rejected the district's proposal for a public school special day program, asked for an administrative hearing and sought to have their expert observe the special day program. The district refused to let the expert observe the program. When the parents sued, the California Court of Appeal ruled that **their expert should have been allowed to observe the public school special day program.** *Benjamin G. v. Special Educ. Hearing Office*, 131 Cal.App.4th 875, 32 Cal.Rptr.3d 366 (Cal. Ct. App. 2005).

♦ A Texas student with Asperger's syndrome, ADHD and oppositional defiant disorder attended a public school in a highly structured behavior modification classroom. After experiencing severe behavior problems at home, his parents placed him in a private residential treatment facility. The following year, the school district removed his "emotional disturbance" eligibility, but he remained IDEA-eligible as a student with autism. Although the student's behavior improved with the assistance of a personal aide, the district's proposed IEP did not call for a full-time aide. The parents rejected the IEP, and a hearing officer ruled in favor of the district. The case reached the Fifth Circuit Court of Appeals, which upheld the ruling against the parents. It noted that **any procedural defects in the development of the IEP did not deprive the student of educational opportunity.** The parents actively participated in the IEP process, and the IEP was appropriately individualized for the student. *Adam J. on behalf of Robert J. v. Keller Independent School Dist.*, 328 F.3d 804 (5th Cir. 2003).

♦ A Tennessee student with ADHD also had serious behavior problems and received special education under an IEP for a number of years. However, the school's team of evaluators eventually concluded that her behavioral problems were volitional and not the result of her disability. At the subsequent IEP team meeting, the IEP team considered the evaluation team's report and determined that the student was ineligible for services under the IDEA and Section 504 of the Rehabilitation Act. At the due process hearing, the student's mother complained that some of the IEP team members had met prior to the IEP team meeting and decided to find the student ineligible for services. The administrative law judge ruled against the mother, but a federal court ruled that the team denied the mother her right to participate in the initial determination of eligibility. The Sixth Circuit reversed, noting that **experts and IEP team members can confer prior to an IEP team meeting**. There is no substantive harm caused by pre-meeting discussions where a parent fully participates in IEP team meetings. *N.L. v. Knox County Schools*, 315 F.3d 688 (6th Cir. 2003).

♦ An Ohio student with obsessive compulsive disorder, Tourette syndrome and Asperger's syndrome passed all his seventh- and eighth-grade classes and made progress in his socialization skills, but his mother told school officials that other students victimized him and that his behavior at home made her life "a living hell." The school district proposed an IEP for the student's freshman year that had similar goals to the IEP of the previous year. The parents attended two meetings held to address their son's proposed IEP, at which a consultant's report was discussed, but they were not allowed to attend a third "staff meeting." They challenged their exclusion. The Sixth Circuit held that the school district offered their son an appropriate IEP. The district had revised the student's IEP after reviewing the consultant's report and in view of the student's deteriorating behavior. **The parents were properly excluded from the third meeting**, which was an "in-service" to train teachers in accordance with the consultant's report and was not conducted to revise the student's IEP. *Kings Local School Dist. v. Zelazny*, 325 F.3d 724 (6th Cir. 2003).

♦ A New York second-grader's school district developed an IEP for her and began providing special education services during the last month of the school year. During the summer, her parents unilaterally placed her in a private school that used the Orton-Gillingham methodology. For the next three years, the student remained at the private school. Her parents challenged the district's IEPs but lost at the administrative level. A federal court then held that the district failed to comply with IDEA procedures on all three challenged IEPs because of extensive delays in developing and reviewing the IEPs. The court also held that the district's "formulaic articulation of goals and strategies" evaluating the student's progress violated the IDEA as generic rather than individualized IEPs. The Second Circuit reversed, finding that **the delays did not affect the student's education** because the parents did not show that they would have changed her placement had there been more timely decisions on her IEPs. The parents were not entitled to tuition reimbursement. *Grim v. Rhinebeck Cent. School Dist.*, 346 F.3d 377 (2d Cir. 2003).

◆ The IEP of a third-grade student with Down syndrome called for 30 minutes weekly of direct occupational therapy (OT). The therapist who provided OT services to the student received her master's degree before the start of the school year but did not obtain her license until near the end of the year. Using the results of the student's triennial evaluation, the district proposed an IEP for the student's fourth-grade year that called for 30 minutes of monthly OT consultation and less physical therapy than the parents desired. They rejected the IEP. A due process hearing officer rejected the parents' claims of IEP deficiencies for nine of the 11 areas they identified. However, she held that the district should provide 60 minutes weekly of direct OT services as compensatory services during the fourth grade because the occupational therapist was unlicensed and improperly supervised during the third grade. An Illinois federal court ordered the district to provide the OT services the hearing officer required. The Seventh Circuit agreed that **the 60 minutes of direct OT services each week was appropriate** given the failure of the district in the third-grade year to properly supervise the unlicensed occupational therapist. *Evanston Community Consolidated School Dist. No. 65 v. Michael M.*, 356 F.3d 798 (7th Cir. 2004).

◆ A Nevada student was placed in her school district's early childhood program before her third birthday after a psychologist determined that she had moderately low communication and daily living skills. The next year, two school psychologists evaluated the student, reaching mixed conclusions. One determined that she was "severely autistic," but this was not communicated to the parents. A district eligibility team found the student eligible for special education. The district denied the mother's request for copies of her daughter's assessment reports, instead sending her a two-page summary. After the family moved to California, the student was diagnosed as autistic and began an in-home intervention program using discrete trial training. The parents then learned of the earlier evaluation indicating severe autism, which had not been included in the summary.

Eventually the Ninth Circuit noted that **the right to examine all records relating to a child and to participate in meetings to identify, evaluate and place a child is guaranteed to parents by the IDEA**. Districts are specifically required to give parents a copy of their procedural safeguards as well as a copy of the evaluation report and documentation regarding the determination of eligibility. The district here did not provide the parents with copies of reports indicating the possibility of autism or the need for further evaluation, resulting in a blatant violation of the IDEA. By failing to disclose the student's full records upon request, the district denied a FAPE to the student. *Amanda J. v. Clark County School Dist.*, 267 F.3d 877 (9th Cir. 2001).

E. Implementation of IEPs

◆ A student with multiple disabilities was home-educated through the California Virtual Academy under an IEP that the parents agreed to for one year. However, they rejected the IEP for the following year and eventually agreed to an IEP that would place the student in a third-grade classroom with appropriate supports. Since the academy had no general education classrooms, the student was enrolled in a district school, but the district failed to implement the IEP within 30 days because of insufficient time to evaluate the student. IEP meetings were then scheduled and rescheduled, and the parents sued the district. Their son died during the case, but the Ninth Circuit held **the IDEA does not require a district to implement a transfer student's IEP within 30 days** if the IEP was never implemented by the sending district. *A.M. v. Monrovia Unified School Dist.*, 627 F.3d 773 (9th Cir. 2010).

♦ After a due process hearing, an IEP was created for an Illinois student authorizing a summer program and therapeutic day school placement as well as compensatory education services. Within two weeks, the parents filed a new due process request, asserting that the district had failed to implement the IEP within 10 days as specified by Illinois regulations. A hearing officer ruled for the parents, and a federal court affirmed. Here, there was no distinction between compensatory services and other services under the IDEA, and **the law required implementing an IEP within 10 days of notice**. *Board of Educ. of City of Chicago v. Illinois State Board of Educ.*, 741 F.Supp.2d 920 (N.D. Ill. 2010).

♦ The parents of a Massachusetts student missed five IEP meetings scheduled by the district. They instead sought to hold two "emergency" IEP meetings, which the district refused to agree to. After placing their son in a private school, the parents requested due process, asserting that the district had failed to have an IEP in place at the start of the school year. A hearing officer and a federal court noted that **the delay was due primarily to the parents' failure to attend scheduled IEP meetings**. Further, while there were some recordkeeping lapses by the district, the student had continued to receive an adequate IEP while in district schools. The court refused to award tuition reimbursement to the parents. *Doe v. Hampden-Wilbraham Regional School Dist.*, 715 F.Supp.2d 185 (D. Mass. 2010).

♦ The mother of a Maine student challenged her daughter's 2007-08 placement decision after previously filing a complaint about the 2006-07 school year. A hearing officer ruled that the 2007-08 placement was appropriate even though the district did not have an IEP in place at the start of the year. The hearing officer then ruled that the 2006-07 placement denied the student a free appropriate public education. On appeal, a federal court held that the 2007-08 placement violated the IDEA because **the district failed to have an IEP in place at the start of the year**. The court also stated that the hearing officer had the power to expand the hearing to include the 2006-07 school year. However, the hearing officer had improperly held that the 2006-07 placement violated the IDEA. *Millay v. Surry School Dep't*, 707 F.Supp.2d 56 (D. Me. 2010).

♦ A New York school department's committee on special education developed an IEP for a student with autism. The IEP stated that the student would attend school in District 75 (a group of schools for students with disabilities) but did not specify which school he would attend. Instead, a citywide placement officer would make that determination. The student's parents objected to the school that was eventually proposed, but rather than visit a second school, they enrolled their son in a private school. When they sought tuition reimbursement, a federal court and the Second Circuit ruled against them. **The IDEA does not require a school district to name the particular location for receiving special education services.** *T.Y. v. New York City Dep't of Educ.*, 584 F.3d 412 (2d Cir. 2009).

♦   The parents of a New Jersey student with autism claimed that their son's IEP did not address his educational needs. A hearing officer ordered the district to provide the student with a positive behavioral plan and 15 hours of weekly ABA services. The district was also ordered to revise the student's IEP goals. The parents then filed an action in federal court, claiming the district was not properly implementing the hearing officer's order. The court ruled that **the district was largely in compliance with the order** and could not be held in contempt. The district had revised the IEP and was logging daily minutes of individualized instruction, small group instruction, behavioral programming and consultation. *L.J. v. Audubon Board of Educ.*, No. 06-5350 (JBS), 2007 WL 3252240 (D.N.J. 11/5/07).

♦   A severely autistic Oregon student transitioned from elementary to middle school, where his father claimed the district failed to implement key parts of his IEP. He requested a due process hearing, and the administrative law judge found that the district was adequately implementing the student's IEP, except for math instruction. She ordered the district to remedy that aspect of the IEP, and a federal court affirmed her ruling. The U.S. Court of Appeals for the Ninth Circuit then largely upheld the decision in favor of the district. It noted that **minor failures in implementing an IEP are not automatic violations of the IDEA.** Only a material failure to implement an IEP violates the IDEA. "A material failure occurs when the services a school provides to a disabled child fall significantly short of the services required by the child's IEP." Because the district had remedied the math instruction deficiency, there were no substantive IDEA violations. *Van Duyn v. Baker School Dist. 5J*, 481 F.3d 770 (9th Cir. 2007).

♦   The parents of a California student with deafness and autism grew dissatisfied with her education at the California School for the Deaf. The school proposed transferring the student to a special day class at an elementary school but the parents rejected that offer, believing it to be inappropriate. Ultimately they sued for discrimination as well as IDEA violations, and the district sought pretrial judgment. A federal court found issues of fact requiring a trial. Here, the parents alleged that the school did not properly implement their daughter's IEP because it disallowed her participation in certain activities and **failed to educate her in her primary language (American Sign Language).** *J.C. v. California School for Deaf*, No. C 06-02337 JSW, 2006 WL 2850376 (N.D. Cal. 10/5/06).

◆   A New York student was placed in a private school for seventh grade after her parents became dissatisfied with her educational progress. The grade-eight IEP called for non-integrated classes in four subjects. However, when the parents inspected a self-contained science classroom after the IEP meeting, they determined that it was not non-integrated and again enrolled their daughter in a private school. When they sued for tuition reimbursement, they lost. A federal court ruled that **the district did not have to have the accommodations it was planning to offer the student in place prior to the student's attendance**. *Schied v. Board of Educ. of Penfield Cent. School Dist.*, No. 05-CV-6255CJS (P), 2006 WL 2927875 (W.D.N.Y. 10/12/06).

◆   The parents of three preschool children with disabilities brought a class action suit against the New York City Board of Education, requesting immediate implementation of all services required in their IEPs. The students had received IEPs but, because educational services could not immediately be found for all required services, they were forced to wait for certain services. The case reached the Second Circuit Court of Appeals, which held that **IEPs must be implemented as soon as possible after being developed. The IDEA does not require immediate implementation.** The regulations merely specify that there can be no undue delay. *D.D. v. New York City Board of Educ.*, 465 F.3d 503 (2d Cir. 2006).

◆   A Minnesota school district convened an IEP team meeting for a sixth-grade student with a specific learning disability. The student's case manager brought a draft IEP to the meeting, which the student's mother rejected. She described it as a "proposed IEP." When the team met again, the mother insisted that her son receive one-to-one instruction. The district refused, and a lawsuit resulted. A federal court held that the district did not have to defend bringing a draft IEP to the team meeting. **A draft IEP was not a predetermination of IEP in violation of the IDEA**, and the IEP team had discussed a range of reading services for the student. *Grant v. Independent School Dist. No. 11*, No. Civ. 02-795 ADM/AJB, 2005 WL 1539805 (D. Minn. 6/30/05).

◆   A California school district provided a qualified speech/language therapist to a student. Her parents initiated a due process hearing, asserting that the district had to provide therapy through a private provider due to **frequent staff turnover**. The hearing officer disagreed. So did the Ninth Circuit. Although staff turnover interrupted the continuity of therapy services on occasion, the district offered the student a free appropriate public education, and it did not intentionally discriminate against the student by its actions. There was no IDEA or Section 504 violation. *Zasslow v. Menlo Park City School Dist.*, 60 Fed.Appx. 27 (9th Cir. 2003).

◆   The IEP for a seven-year-old kindergarten student with cerebral palsy, hydrocephalus and a seizure disorder called for a full-time aide. At the end of the school year, the district transferred him to another school and contracted with a health-services employer for aides. These employees frequently arrived late, left early or did not show up at all. The school sometimes assigned first-grade students to accompany the student to his locker. On one such occasion, the student was knocked down by other students, resulting in his hospitalization for three weeks. The state education department conducted an investigation but was unable to determine whether the district had complied with the IEP. The family requested a due process hearing, which resulted in a decision that the district did not deprive the student of a FAPE.

The student then sued the district and state education department in a federal court, which noted that his IEP called for a program aide to assist him each day he attended school. The IEP also included the goal of safe independent mobility in the school environment. The court refused to dismiss the education department from the case, holding that it had failed to fulfill its obligations under the IDEA. It should have continued its investigation until it found enough information to make a determination one way or the other. Inclusion of an aide was a significant element of the IEP and made it possible for the student to be in a general education setting. The district was bound to provide the services actually listed in the IEP. **Even though there was evidence the student was progressing educationally, this could not be used to insulate the district from adequately implementing his IEP.** The school had no discretion to unilaterally decide that a listed service not be provided. The court ordered the district to re-enroll the student in his former school with appropriate implementation of his IEP. *Manalansan v. Board of Educ. of Baltimore City*, No. Civ. A.MD 01-312, 2001 WL 939699 (D. Md. 8/14/01).

F. Transfer Students

♦ A family moved to Montana from New Jersey after a doctor determined that the son's performance had an autistic component, and after an IEP was crafted providing the student with speech/language therapy. **The IEP team at his new school refused to consider the New Jersey doctor's evaluation** and reduced the student's speech/language therapy. After two months, the IEP team referred the student to a child development center for free autism testing. Five months later, a report came back confirming that his behavior was consistent with autism spectrum disorder. By that time the school year was almost over. The IEP team met to develop an IEP for the next year and determined that the student did not need extended school year services. The parents brought a challenge that reached the Ninth Circuit. The court of appeals held that the referral of the student to the child development center did not comply with the IDEA. The district failed to meet its obligation to evaluate the student. *N.B. and C.B. v. Hellgate Elementary School Dist.*, 541 F.3d 1202 (9th Cir. 2008).

♦ An Alabama student with diabetes and ADHD had an unacceptable attendance level at school. He sought to transfer to another school, but his request was denied. His parents then sued under the ADA and Section 504, seeking a preliminary order that would permit him to transfer to the new school. A federal court refused to grant the order and the Eleventh Circuit Court of Appeals affirmed. Here, **the student failed to show that he would be irreparably harmed by not being allowed to immediately transfer to the new school**. He would continue to receive educational services at his neighborhood school while the case was pending. *C.B. v. Board of School Commissioners of Mobile County, Alabama*, 261 Fed.Appx. 192 (11th Cir. 2008).

◆   The mother of a Michigan special education student sought to enroll him in a neighboring school district, which had accepted 67 applications from nonresidents under the state's school choice law. However, because the process was less streamlined for special education students due to the higher costs, the two districts were unable to reach an agreement and the neighboring district rejected the student's application. His mother sued for discrimination and the case reached the Sixth Circuit. The court of appeals held that the school choice law did not violate equal protection. **There was a rational reason for the stricter transfer requirements for special education students.** *Clark v. Banks*, 193 Fed.Appx. 510 (6th Cir. 2006).

◆   A student attended a private school under an IEP drafted by the Glendale School District. The family moved into the Hart School District, which conducted a meeting without the parents, asserting its right to provide a 30-day "interim placement" for the student under California Education Code § 56325(a). When the school district requested another IEP team meeting, the parents commenced due process proceedings, seeking an order preserving the student's private school placement under the stay-put provision. A hearing officer denied the parents' request for a stay-put order, and a federal court affirmed. After the school year, the hearing officer found that the Hart School District failed to provide the student a FAPE during the first half of the 30-day interim period. The parents were entitled to reimbursement for private school tuition for those days. The hearing officer reduced the award based on the "unreasonable, dilatory actions" of the parents' attorney and ordered the parties to meet to consider a placement for the next school year.

The district then asserted that the parents had been intentionally deceptive when changing school districts, but the court rejected its argument that equitable principles should be considered when determining the appropriate stay-put placement. California Education Code § 56325(a) allowed the school district to determine an appropriate interim placement. The Ninth Circuit has recognized that school districts need not, and probably cannot, provide the exact program as that created by another district when a student transfers. Thus, the interim placement created by Section 56325 was the student's stay-put placement. In order to account for the reality of a shift in responsible educational agencies, the decision creating an interim placement rested with the new educational agency. **The interim placement designed by the Hart School District was the student's stay-put placement and it did not have to be identical to the IEP drafted by Glendale.** *Termine ex rel. Termine v. William S. Hart Union High School Dist.*, 219 F.Supp.2d 1049 (C.D. Cal. 2002), *aff'd*, 354 F.3d 1004 (9th Cir. 2004), *see also* 90 Fed.Appx. 200 (9th Cir. 2004).

◆   A student attended a private special education school under an IEP formulated by the District of Columbia Public Schools. When the student's family moved to Pennsylvania, his new school district proposed placing him in a learning support or combined learning/emotional support program. The family rejected these proposals and unilaterally enrolled the student in a private school. His student's parents sought tuition reimbursement. A hearing officer held that because state standards differ, the adoption of an IEP from another state would require the receiving state to approve of standards that would not necessarily be applicable under the receiving state's standards. A federal court held that a receiving school district is not required to accept an IEP drafted by a district in another state pending an appeal involving an intrastate transfer.

The family appealed to the Third Circuit, which observed that the stay-put provision does not specifically address student transfers between states. Where a parent unilaterally removes a student from a placement determined under state procedures, the stay-put provision is inoperative until the parties reach a new agreement. Because the student was without a "then current educational placement" in Pennsylvania, he was not entitled to stay-put protection. Moreover, **whenever a student moves into a new state, the receiving state is not obligated to automatically effectuate a prior IEP from another state**, and parents maintain the risk of unilateral private school placements. The school district did not have to preserve a private school placement on the basis of the IEP prepared in Washington, D.C. *Michael C. v. Radnor Township School Dist.*, 202 F.3d 642 (3d Cir. 2000).

♦ A profoundly deaf student with a cochlear implant attended a private school in Missouri that practiced oral education, pursuant to an IEP. His school district completed another IEP for the student shortly before he and his family moved to Minnesota. Minnesota school officials proposed placing him in an "Early Childhood Special Education" (ECSE) classroom. The parents instead informed the district that they intended to enroll their son in a private school. A private assessment recommended placing the student in a cued speech program, which was not offered by the private school. The district developed an IEP calling for the student's placement in a district classroom with six or seven other students. The parents rejected the proposal. A hearing officer concluded that the district IEP offered the student a FAPE. A federal court held that **the district was under no obligation to automatically adopt an IEP from another state**, as Congress left the primary responsibility for providing a free appropriate public education under the IDEA to the states themselves. The district's willingness to make the necessary modifications to allow the student to hear in the ECSE classroom indicated that he could receive educational benefits there. The court reinstated the IHO's decision. *Grafe v. Independent School Dist. No. 834*, No. CIV.00-1690 (MJD/JGL), 2001 WL 1631455 (D. Minn. 7/17/01).

♦ A student with autism moved from Georgia to Florida. Instead of implementing the Georgia IEP, as the parents wished, the Florida school board advised the family that additional evaluations were required before a permanent IEP could be adopted. It placed the student under an interim IEP. The board conducted several evaluations to create a permanent IEP, but the parents objected and requested an independent evaluation. The board determined that the student met the criteria for its program for students with autism and should receive speech and occupational therapy. However, the parents refused to consent to the IEP until the completion of the independent evaluation. They removed the student from the district and challenged the use of the interim IEP. The hearing officer held that the IEP was appropriate, that the district had performed adequate evaluations for developing a permanent IEP, that the student had received a free appropriate public education, and that the family had suffered no harm due to any defective notices by the board.

A federal court affirmed the hearing officer's decision. It rejected the parent's equal protection argument that **the administrative code's allowance of up to six months for school districts to formulate a permanent IEP for students moving to Florida from other states** treated such students less favorably than disabled students transferring between in-state schools. In those cases, districts are required to formulate a new IEP within 30 days. Because the IDEA requires only the provision of an education meeting the standards of the state educational agency, the administrative code did not violate federal law. The six-month time frame for students moving from out of state allowed school districts the necessary time to gather evaluation information and determine a student's eligibility for Florida programs. On further appeal, the Eleventh Circuit Court of Appeals affirmed. *Weiss v. School Board of Hillsborough County*, 141 F.3d 990 (11th Cir. 1998).

G. Behavior Intervention Plans

◆ The mother of a Hawaii student with behavioral problems unilaterally placed him in a private school because she thought the public school wasn't adequately addressing his behavior problems. When she sought approval for the private placement, the Hawaii Court of Appeals ruled against her, noting that her son was receiving an educational benefit in school, earning passing grades and advancing from grade to grade. It seemed that **his behavioral problems largely occurred at home**. His IEP addressed his emotional and self-esteem and confidence issues. And even if the private school improved his behavior, the state did not have an obligation to maximize the student's potential. *State of Hawaii Dep't of Educ. v. M.S. and J.S.*, 243 P.3d 1054 (Haw. Ct. App. 2010).

◆ A Connecticut student with Down syndrome had serious behavioral issues. Her parents were critical of the proposed behavior intervention plan and asked the district to hire a behavior specialist. After the district adopted an IEP that incorporated the specialist's plan (which avoided aversive, negative or punishing interventions), the student shoved and punched her tutor and then threatened to poke a teacher in the eye with a hanger. The district suspended the student for 10 days and placed her in an interim homebound program, assuming her behavior was a manifestation of her disability. The district then sought an out-of-district placement and the parents sued, alleging that the behavior plan the district had implemented was a failure. A federal court found that the district had offered the student an appropriate behavior plan. Indeed, it was the parents' plan. **The fact that the student could not be educated in district schools did not mean that the district had violated the IDEA.** *L. v. North Haven Board of Educ.*, 624 F.Supp.2d 163 (D. Conn. 2009).

◆   The mother of a New York student with Asperger's disorder signed him up for a private school before the school district prepared an IEP for the upcoming year. The IEP, when completed, maintained his "other health impaired" classification but placed him in a more restrictive special education class. The mother sought tuition reimbursement, and a hearing officer found that the district's failure to obtain a **functional behavior analysis (FBA)** entitled the mother to tuition reimbursement. A review officer reversed, and a federal court agreed that **the lack of an FBA was not fatal to the IEP**. School districts must consider using positive behavioral interventions and supports as well as other strategies to address behavior, so the mere failure to conduct an FBA would not violate the IDEA. *Connor v. New York City Dep't of Educ.*, No. 08 Civ. 7710 (LBS), 2009 WL 3335760 (S.D.N.Y. 10/13/09).

◆   A Nevada school district proposed removing an autistic student from a general math class to a resource room. His parents sought due process, alleging the student should have a behavior intervention plan in his IEP. A hearing officer found the lack of a behavior intervention plan did not deny him a FAPE. However, a review officer disagreed, and a federal court agreed with the review officer that **the student needed a behavior intervention plan** in his IEP. Further, there was no point in keeping him in general math classes because he was making no progress there. *Yates v. Washoe County School Dist.*, No. 03-07-CV-00200-LRH-RJJ, 2008 WL 4106816 (D. Nev. 8/28/08).

◆   The parents of a New York student with autism had a number of concerns about their school district's IEPs and began to home-school their son. For the student's third-grade year, the IEP team specified a 12:1:2 placement, a behavior intervention plan and a transition plan for bringing the child back to school. Before that transition occurred, the parents became upset at the quality of home instruction their son was receiving and challenged the IEPs for the previous few years. The case reached a federal court, which held that the lack of a behavior intervention plan in earlier IEPs was not an IDEA violation. The court also upheld the IEP with respect to the transition plan and the other challenged elements. The Second Circuit affirmed the ruling for the district, finding that **the absence of a behavior intervention plan did not violate the IDEA because his IEPs addressed his needs**. *E.H. and K.H. v. Board of Educ. of Shenendehowa Cent. School Dist.*, 361 Fed.Appx 156 (2d Cir. 2009).

◆   An emotionally and behaviorally disabled Minnesota student verbally and physically abused teachers and classmates, made sexual comments and left his classroom to wander around the school. He was placed in a setting for students with serious emotional and behavioral needs. His tenth-grade IEP included a behavior intervention plan, and for the first half of the year he performed well. However, his behavior later deteriorated and he clashed with the police liaison officer on numerous occasions, seeking her out to provoke her and engage her in a power struggle. His behavior incidents increased from 91 in the first semester to 304 in the second. His mother sought due process over the implementation of his IEP, and eventually the question of compensatory education reached a federal court. The court found no IDEA violation. *P.K.W.G. v. Independent School Dist. No. 11, Anoka-Hennepin School Dist.*, No. 07-4023 ADM/AJB, 2008 WL 2405818 (D. Minn. 6/11/08).

♦   A New Hampshire student with multiple disabilities attended a day school program for special needs students. When she reached age 18, her mother met with the school IEP team on at least four occasions to discuss her IEP, but no agreement was reached. She refused to sign the district's proposed IEP – which contained a transition plan but no behavior plan – but she did not communicate any specific objections to it. Several months later, the district presented her with a new IEP, which contained a behavior plan and a full-blown transition plan. The mother again refused to sign it, so the district filed a due process hearing request. A hearing officer upheld the IEP plan, and the mother appealed. A federal court and the First Circuit agreed that the IEP should be put into effect. The court of appeals noted that the IDEA does not require transition plans to be articulated as a separate component of an IEP. Nor were behavior plans necessary unless certain disciplinary actions had been taken. Thus, **the first proposed IEP, which discussed a behavior plan without specifically including it, did not violate the IDEA**. And the lateness of the second IEP was caused by the mother's conduct. *Lessard v. Wilton-Lyndeborough Coop School Dist.*, 518 F.3d 18 (1st Cir. 2008).

♦   A Minnesota student with a behavior disorder and other disabilities received special education and related services under the IDEA. When behavioral incidents occurred at school, paraprofessionals assigned to him escorted him to a separate room so he would have a place to calm down. His family contested his education and the parties agreed to develop an IEP that would address his needs as he transitioned to high school. The IEP called for a written behavior intervention plan (BIP), but none was created by the deadline. The family sued, and the case reached the Eighth Circuit. The court of appeals held that **nothing in state or federal law required a written BIP in a student's IEP**. The school had responded to the student's behavioral incidents using set procedures, and there was no substantive or procedural violation of the IDEA. *School Board of Independent School Dist. No. 11 v. Renollett*, 440 F.3d 1007 (8th Cir. 2006).

♦   An Alabama school district created IEPs for an autistic student, but failed to include behavior intervention plans and also did not identify measurable goals. For example, it referred to an 80% accuracy objective without specifying what that accuracy applied to. The student's mother requested a due process hearing on both those flaws and a hearing officer agreed that the IEPs were deficient. On appeal by the district, a federal court upheld the hearing officer's decision. **The ambiguous goals of the IEPs and their failure to address his behavior problems made them improper under the IDEA** because they could not confer an educational benefit. *Escambia County Board of Educ. v. Benton*, 406 F.Supp.2d 1248 (S.D. Ala. 2005).

♦   A Pennsylvania student with Down syndrome and severe behavioral problems had outbursts that included kicking, screaming, hitting and spitting.

Her school hired a specialist to help determine the causes of her misconduct. The specialist recommended incorporating a behavior support plan into her IEP. However, while the behavioral assessment was ongoing, the student's mother removed her from school. She claimed the school violated the IDEA by improperly using physical restraints and isolation to avoid developing a behavioral plan. The case reached the Third Circuit, which ruled for the school, noting that **it had properly handled the student's frequent behavior outbursts**. Security guards would remove her from class and take her to a time-out area in an unused office, where an aide would give her work to do and encourage her to return to class. The school did not fail to implement the student's IEP. *Melissa S. v. School Dist. of Pittsburgh*, 183 Fed.Appx. 184 (3d Cir. 2006).

◆ A student with a neurological disorder began exhibiting behavioral problems during grade two. A school psychologist conducted a functional behavioral assessment and prepared a functional behavioral analysis for him. Before a behavior intervention plan could be implemented, the student became increasingly violent, injuring teachers and fellow students in several attacks that resulted in suspensions. His IEP had to be revised several times. His mother then requested a due process hearing, and the hearing officer held that the district did not create an IEP that was reasonably calculated to provide the student with educational benefits. An Illinois federal court and the Seventh Circuit disagreed. Since **the IDEA does not create specific substantive requirements for behavior intervention plans**, the district's plan did not violate the IDEA. Also, the district appropriately considered the student's disruptive impact on other students as a relevant consideration in determining the adequacy of his program. *Alex R. v. Forrestville Community Unit School Dist. #221*, 375 F.3d 603 (7th Cir. 2004).

◆ An autistic student with a learning disability was prone to inappropriate behavior that prevented him from interacting with peers when unmanaged. His Missouri school district drafted an IEP that called for placement in a self-contained classroom and the use of a paraprofessional, but it did not include a behavior management plan. The student's behavior problems increased dramatically, but the school did not formulate a behavior management plan until near the end of the school year. At a due process hearing, the parents brought in an autism expert who testified that the student required a formal behavior management plan. A state administrative panel ordered the district to craft an appropriate behavior management plan. A federal court upheld the panel's decision, and the Eighth Circuit affirmed. The district's **failure to create a cohesive behavior management plan prevented the student from achieving a meaningful educational benefit**. The minimal academic and social progress gained by the student were offset by the behavior problems not addressed by the IEP. Also, the parents were prevailing parties entitled to attorneys' fees, but they were not entitled to expert witness fees under the IDEA. *Neosho R-V School Dist. v. Clark*, 315 F.3d 1022 (8th Cir. 2003).

VI. GRADUATION

◆   A Massachusetts student with disabilities made progress toward all his IEP goals in grade 11. His mother agreed to his grade-12 IEP, which stated that he was working toward graduation. As graduation neared, however, his mother asserted that he needed to attend a residential program. She placed him there after graduation and claimed the proctor had changed her son's answers on the standardized test. A hearing officer found the student had unmet deficits in emotional control and navigating social situations, among other things. The case reached a federal court, which ruled that no private tuition was required. **The student had been properly graduated despite failing to meet two IEP goals.** The student's emotional and social deficits would follow him all his life and could not be eliminated with additional services from the district. *Doe v. Marlborough Public Schools*, No. 09-11118-WGY, 2010 WL 2682433 (D. Mass. 6/30/10).

◆   An Indiana school district offered special education to a learning disabled student until his parents decided to home-school him. Later, they sought to reintegrate him into public schools and obtained private evaluations showing he had autism. The district did not identify an autism spectrum disorder until he was 17. When he was 19, the district awarded him a diploma. His parents challenged the graduation, asserting that the student should continue to receive special education. Using the stay-put provisions of the IDEA, federal court ordered the district to continue educating the student in a college preparatory program. **The parents' challenge to the validity and good faith of the decision to graduate their son warranted a stay-put placement.** *Tindell v. Evansville-Vanderburgh School Corp.*, No. 309-CV-00159-SEB-WGH, 2010 WL 557058 (S.D. Ind. 2/10/10).

◆   A New York student with ADHD and bipolar disorder was suspended numerous times for cutting classes and insubordinate behavior, including cursing at staff. **After he graduated, he sought his transcript. He claimed that it wrongly lowered his grades.** However, the school district asserted that it properly lowered the grades due to the suspensions caused by his behavior problems. He then claimed that the district interfered with his second SAT exam because he was not given accommodations for that test. When he sued, he lost. A federal court noted that the grades were accurately recorded. He did not receive accommodations for his second SAT because he did not take the test at the scheduled time, and the approved accommodations expired by the time he took the test. *Rafano v. Patchogue-Medford School Dist.*, No. 06-CV-5367 (JFB) (ARL), 2009 WL 789440 (E.D.N.Y. 3/20/09).

◆   A 19-year-old special education student in Florida became incarcerated. He completed the math part of his studies while in prison and obtained his general equivalency diploma (GED). He then claimed that the state Department of Corrections and the Department of Education violated the IDEA by granting him his GED. A federal court held that the adult educational program at the correctional facility was not contrary to the state's FAPE obligation under the

IDEA. **By acquiring his GED, the student essentially graduated**, completing his secondary education. He was no longer entitled to special education services. *MP v. Florida Dep't of Corrections*, No. 4:06CV52-SPM/WCS, 2008 WL 4525134 (N.D. Fla. 9/30/08).

◆ The parents of a Florida student with Asperger's syndrome disagreed with their school's decision to graduate him and asked for an IEP meeting after the district sent them a notice informing them that it expected he would meet his graduation requirements by May 13, 2004. The notice stated that the IEP meeting would be held on May 21. The student graduated on May 20, and his parents then asserted that the school improperly graduated him. A federal court agreed, but the Eleventh Circuit reversed. **It found no evidence that the school district intended to avoid holding the IEP meeting if the student failed to graduate on time.** The case returned to the federal court, which held that the student, now 22, was not entitled to stay-put protection or compensatory education. *Sammons v. Polk County School Board*, No. 8:04-CV-2657-T-24 EAJ, 2007 WL 4358266 (M.D. Fla. 12/10/07).

◆ A Florida high school notified the parents of a nonverbal student with autism that the student would graduate at the end of the year if he received all of his academic credits. The parents requested a new IEP meeting or mediation and new evaluations. Less than two weeks before graduation, the board advised the parents it would hold an IEP meeting to discuss a diploma and review the IEP the day after the graduation ceremony. Although the student graduated with a 3.09 grade average and passed the Florida Comprehensive Assessment Test, the parents asked for an emergency order to preserve his placement. The Eleventh Circuit held that **his placement could not be preserved under the IDEA's stay-put provision since the parents did not request a due process hearing until after he graduated**. However, it remanded the case with instructions to decide if a preliminary order should be issued allowing the student to stay in school. *Sammons v. Polk County School Board*, 165 Fed.Appx. 750 (11th Cir. 2006).

◆ A Louisiana student with spondylolisthesis **missed a mandatory practice session for commencement exercises because she slept through her alarm after taking a painkiller.** She was barred from the graduation ceremony as a result, though she did receive her diploma. When she sued for discrimination under Section 504 and the ADA, a federal court ruled against her. It noted that her back condition did not substantially limit her ability to perform major life activities. Thus, she was not protected by either statute. *Soirez v. Vermilion Parish School Board*, No. 6:04 CV 00959, 2005 WL 2286951 (W.D. La. 9/16/05).

◆ A high school senior in Washington became pregnant and failed a quiz near the end of the year. Hours before the graduation ceremony, she and her mother were told that her grade could not be raised under the class grading policy. As a result, she could not participate in the ceremony. Later, the district superintendent met with the family and suggested that a Section 504 plan could be used to increase the student's point total for the failed course. This resulted in an increase in points earned, allowing the student to graduate. She then sued the district for refusing to allow her to participate in the graduation ceremony. A jury awarded her damages, but the Washington Court of Appeals reversed. **She had no constitutional right to attend her graduation ceremony** and no state law granted her that right either. *Nieshe v. Concrete School Dist.*, 128 Wash.App. 1029 (Wash. Ct. App. 2005).

♦   A Minnesota student with chronic fatigue syndrome missed a large number of classes because of his condition and was no longer on track to graduate with his peers. A hearing officer found the student eligible for special education despite the district's doubts about the validity of his condition, and ordered the district to "consider how [the student] may participate in the graduation ceremony with his class." The IEP team rejected the student's request to participate in commencement exercises, and the student sued for an injunction. A federal court ordered the district to allow the student to participate. *Olson v. Robbinsdale Area School Dist.*, No. Civ. 04-2707 RHK/AJB, 2004 WL 1212081 (D. Minn. 5/28/04).

♦   A student was born with cerebral palsy, no hands and only one foot and was diagnosed with learning disabilities and a low IQ. He attended a public school under an IEP and eventually received a special education diploma. His parents placed him in a state-run vocational program, and he improved his reading ability to the eighth-grade level. His parents commenced an IDEA administrative proceeding against the district, asserting that the student was entitled to further educational services. An administrative law judge denied their claim, and a federal court held that the case was moot in view of the student's receipt of a special education diploma.

The parents appealed to the Sixth Circuit, where they argued that despite the student's learning disabilities, he had greater ability than the district acknowledged in his IEPs. The court noted that one of the student's former teachers had testified that he was capable of making progress beyond what was specified in his IEPs. There was also evidence that when the student failed to make progress in any given year, the district did not recommend any changes to the instructional methods being used, even though those methods had failed. **Despite having received a special education diploma, the student had potential claims against the district**; therefore, the case was not moot. The court vacated the judgment and remanded the case with instructions to consider further evidence on whether the removal of the student from district school mooted the case and whether he was capable of progressing in his education beyond what was stated in his individualized education program. *Barnett v. Memphis City Schools*, 50 Fed.Appx. 219 (6th Cir. 2002).

♦   A group of Indiana students with disabilities asserted that the state violated student due process rights by imposing a graduation qualification examination (GQE) as a condition of high school graduation beginning in the 1999-2000 school year. Students with disabilities were previously exempt from the exam and they claimed they received no instruction in the material being tested. A second subclass of students claimed that they were denied testing accommodations and adaptations in violation of the IDEA. They alleged the state denied them permission to use many of the accommodations specified in their IEPs.

The case reached the Indiana Court of Appeals, which observed that the GQE is part of the Statewide Testing for Educational Progress program applicable to all students. The court agreed with the students that they had property interests in diplomas if they met graduation requirements. This interest was protected by the right to due process, including adequate notice of the examination and exposure to the material being tested. The state had provided school districts with at least five years' notice about the GQE and the students learned of it at least three years in advance. This notice was adequate, in view of the multiple, free opportunities the students received for remediation and retaking the GQE, if necessary. Also, the students were exposed to the curriculum tested on the GQE. School systems were required to align their curriculum with state standards as of 1996. The court noted that the proper remedy for failing to teach students the subjects tested on the GQE was remediation, not the award of diplomas. It stated that **the IDEA does not require specific results such as the award of a diploma, but instead mandates that students with disabilities receive access to specialized and individualized educational services.** Denying diplomas to these students did not violate the IDEA's FAPE requirement. The state only prohibited accommodations such as reading aloud questions that were designed to measure reading comprehension or allowing students unlimited testing time. The state was not required to provide the accommodations specified in student IEPs during the GQE. *Rene v. Reed*, 751 N.E.2d 736 (Ind. Ct. App. 2001).

◆   At the beginning of his senior year, a student requested a due process hearing, claiming that his school district denied him a FAPE by devising an IEP for him that did not identify his weakness in typing and did not provide modifications for two classes. A hearing officer held that the IEP was appropriate, and that decision was affirmed on appeal. The student did not appeal, but just before his last day of school, he requested another due process hearing. The district determined that he graduated before the second request for due process was received and was not entitled to any relief under the IDEA. A hearing officer held that he lacked jurisdiction to hold another hearing and an appeals officer affirmed. This time, the student appealed to a federal court, which held that the administrative decisions were correct.

The Tenth Circuit held that if a student graduates from high school and does not contest the validity of the graduation, the case is moot. This rule does not apply to cases in which graduated former students seek compensatory relief. Here, the student claimed that the district should have provided him with formal notification of his impending graduation and an "exit IEP meeting." He asserted that the district was required to evaluate him prior to any determination that he was no longer eligible for special education. While IDEA regulations provide that graduation with a regular diploma is a change of placement requiring prior notice, the student did not claim that the lack of notice rendered his graduation invalid. By failing to directly challenge the validity of his graduation, the student conceded that he suffered no harm. At best, the failure to provide a formal written notice of graduation was a harmless technical procedural defect. The IDEA does not specify an "exit IEP meeting," and IDEA regulations at 34 C.F.R. § 300.534 provide that an evaluation is not required before the termination of educational benefits due to graduation with a regular diploma. The district's obligation to the student ceased upon his graduation with a regular diploma. **At the time he submitted his request for a second hearing, he had completed his graduation requirements and was no longer entitled to IDEA protections and benefits, including a hearing.** The court upheld the administrative decisions. *T.S. v. Independent School Dist. No. 54*, 265 F.3d 1090 (10th Cir. 2001).

♦ An 18-year-old with cerebral palsy reported to school officials that her mother was abusing her. She was then placed in protective custody pending a court determination of her competency. The school scheduled an IEP meeting to consider the student's placement for the following school year, without providing notice to the mother. School officials determined that it was in the student's best interest to graduate early. She agreed. The district never notified the mother of the graduation decision. The student later agreed to return to her mother, and then filed a complaint against the district with the state department of education, alleging her graduation was rushed. The complaint was rejected. The mother sued the school district, school officials, the state Department of Human Services and several of its employees, asserting that she had been deprived of adequate notice of the graduation decision in violation of the IDEA, Section 504 and the ADA. The court dismissed the IDEA claim.

The mother appealed to the Eighth Circuit, which noted that state and federal law required the education of students with disabilities until the age of 21 or the completion of a secondary education program. **The district's failure to provide the mother with written notice of the graduation decision violated the IDEA**, as the student was under 21 years old and had not completed the state's secondary education program at the time the graduation decision was made. The Eighth Circuit reversed that part of the judgment, and remanded the case to determine the nature and extent of a compensatory education award. *Birmingham v. Omaha School Dist.*, 220 F.3d 850 (8th Cir. 2000).

CHAPTER TWO

Placement

I. PLACEMENT IN SPECIAL EDUCATION PROGRAMS

The IDEA requires local education agencies to provide students with disabilities in the jurisdiction with an appropriate program of special education and related services that is individualized and reasonably calculated to confer educational benefits.

The placement must also take into consideration the least restrictive appropriate environment to maximize the student's contact with regular education students – also known as mainstreaming. The placement must comply with state educational standards, which in some cases exceed the IDEA minimum standard, and the agency may be required to locate and pay for a private school placement if it is necessary for the student to realize educational benefits.

A. Educational Benefit Generally

◆   The parents of a New Jersey student objected to the IEP proposed by their school district because it largely duplicated his third-grade program. Under the IEP, the student was graded on effort rather than achievement. He also suffered from depression and suicidal tendencies, and he endured harassment and physical abuse at the hands of his classmates. The Third Circuit held that the parents had properly placed the student in a private school. They were entitled to tuition reimbursement. **The district's proposed IEP provided only superficial attention to the student's significant difficulties** and failed to offer educational benefit. *Montgomery Township Board of Educ. v. S.C.*, 135 Fed.Appx. 534 (3d Cir. 2005).

◆   A Pennsylvania student with learning disabilities in math, reading and written language attended a private school at the district's expense for three years until the district determined that he should attend a public school. His parents objected to the new IEP offered by the district, but a hearing officer found that the IEP was reasonably calculated to provide the student with meaningful educational benefits. A federal court upheld that decision. **The district did not have to perform the full scope of testing required for an initial evaluation when it reevaluated the student for the transfer to public school.** Nor did it have to create a separate behavior intervention plan or a transition plan. The IEP properly addressed the student's skills and needs, and it did not violate the IDEA. *Robert B. v. West Chester Area School Dist.*, No. Civ. A. 04-CV-2069, 2005 WL 2396968 (E.D. Pa. 9/27/05).

◆   A New Jersey school district proposed placing a disabled student in a resource room for social studies rather than a regular classroom, even though he had earned a B the prior year. His parents objected. They also claimed the district violated the IDEA by changing the student's grading to pass-fail in science without notifying them, because his IEP called for letter grades. An administrative law judge ruled for the district, but a federal court reversed. **The ALJ did not take into account the least restrictive environment when finding the resource room placement acceptable.** Also, the district failed to show that the pass-fail change was necessary, and it should have provided notice before attempting to change the IEP. *D.E.R. v. Board of Educ. of Borough of Ramsey*, No. Civ. 04-2274 (DRD), 2005 WL 1177944 (D.N.J. 5/18/05).

◆   A Minnesota student with multiple disabilities attended an elementary school under an IEP integrating her with non-disabled peers for over 70% of the school day. When she entered middle school, her parents proposed full integration while the district proposed a segregated, center-based program for special education students that focused on structured teaching strategies for 30% of the day. A hearing officer and a federal court determined that the district's proposed placement was appropriate. Because the student was still not reading, **a mix of programs would provide her with the structured environment she needed while also allowing social interaction** in her mainstream classes. The district did not violate the IDEA by failing to classify the student as deaf/hard of hearing because the parents could not show that she lost any educational benefits as a result. Further, the district did not have to provide extended school year (ESY) services in the interim IEP because when it expired, the ESY services in the earlier IEP would become effective unless a new agreement was reached. The parents appealed to the Eighth Circuit Court of Appeals, which affirmed the decision in favor of the district. The least restrictive environment requirement of the IDEA does not apply where the student cannot achieve educational progress in a mainstream environment. *Pachl v. Seagren*, 453 F.3d 1064 (8th Cir. 2006).

♦   Two students with multiple disabilities attended a private center for special learning for four years. They transferred to public schools in their district, and their parents provided the district with their IEPs, evaluations and test results. The district obtained the parents' consent to perform its own evaluations. After reevaluating the students, the district proposed a life skills program in a neighboring district. The parents objected to the proposal and requested a due process hearing, seeking compensatory education. They asserted that the district should have implemented the private school IEPs. The hearing officer disagreed, as did the Commonwealth Court of Pennsylvania. **Nothing in the state's special education regulations required a district to follow an IEP from a private school.** The students were not entitled to compensatory education. *Schuylkill Haven Area School Dist. v. Rhett P.*, 857 A.2d 226 (Pa. Commw. Ct. 2004).

♦   A Maryland student had difficulty in the use of phonic and structural analysis to decode words. His IEP team altered his fourth-grade IEP, and his parents approved it. Prior to his fifth-grade year, his parents had him tested by a speech/language pathologist, who recommended regular speech/language therapy sessions. The district accepted the test results and created new goals and objectives for the student. However, his parents placed him in a private school unilaterally. At due process, they claimed that the district failed to provide a free appropriate public education (FAPE). An administrative law judge ruled for the district, and a federal court upheld that ruling. Here, the parents were never denied the chance to participate as IEP team members, and the district did not violate the student's IDEA procedural rights. As for his substantive rights, the court also found no IDEA violation. His **failure to progress in the single area of phonics and structural analysis to decode words** was insufficient to show he was deprived of a FAPE, especially considering his IEP's overall success and his significant progress in other areas. *Alexis v. Board of Educ., Baltimore Public Schools*, 286 F.Supp.2d 551 (D. Md. 2003).

◆ A student with ADD attended a resource program and received social work services but failed most of his classes, was truant and refused to cooperate with his teachers. Eventually the district recommended he attend a public alternative high school. His mother rejected the proposed placement, preferring additional accommodations in the student's regular education classes. He was suspended for possession of alcohol and marijuana on one occasion. When his parents requested a due process hearing, seeking a private school placement, the student was a fifth-year senior with only two years of high school credit. A hearing officer upheld the district's primary disability classification and its placement recommendation, and ordered the district to devise a new IEP, provide compensatory education and reimburse the parents for the cost of an independent evaluation.

A federal court noted that **state and federal law do not require districts to guarantee students will remain in school long enough to receive a diploma**. While the district had failed to prepare a behavior intervention plan for the student, there was also evidence that it was aware of his behavioral difficulties and was actively implementing accommodations to address his problems. The lack of a behavior intervention plan and other procedural flaws did not deny the student a FAPE. The alternative school was appropriate, and the court upheld the district's IEP proposal. The court also expanded the award of compensatory education to include one semester of summer school and eight months of compensatory social work services. *Edwin K. v. Jackson*, No. 01 C 7115, 2002 WL 1433722 (N.D. Ill. 7/2/02).

◆ The kindergarten IEP for a student with autism called for her to spend 20% of her day in regular education. While her instruction included numerous methods of teaching, it relied most heavily on the TEACCH method. The student continued to attend a mix of regular and special education classes in subsequent years, with instruction in a curriculum that was primarily based on TEACCH. During her second-grade year, her parents requested district funding for a 40-hour-per-week home Lovaas program. The district denied this request. The student's third-grade program called for 25.5 hours of weekly applied behavioral analysis, including 12.5 hours of discrete trial training. Although the student made considerable progress that year, the parents sought a 40-hour program of weekly, year-round individual direct instruction.

A federal court found that while Lovaas programming benefits some students, its general applicability to all students with autism remains unclear. The district had included methods of direct teaching in the student's program and her teacher regularly used drills during the school day. The district's TEACCH-based methodology was reasonably calculated to provide the student with some educational benefit. **Since the school had provided the student with access to specialized instruction and related services that were individually designed to provide her with educational benefits, the district did not deny her a FAPE.** However, the failure to include a knowledgeable district representative as part of the student's second-grade IEP team was a procedural violation that denied the parents an opportunity to meaningfully participate in the IEP process. *Pitchford v. Salem-Keizer School Dist. No. 24J*, 155 F.Supp.2d 1213 (D. Or. 2001).

♦ A Tennessee school system proposed a placement calling for six hours of daily instruction three times a week in a special education classroom, including auditory training and speech/language therapy, for a student with a hearing impairment and dyspraxia. The parents objected to the proposed special education classroom on the grounds that it was not suitable for a student with hearing impairments and that the teacher had little experience. They sought reimbursement for the costs of a private program they enrolled the student in. The case reached the Tennessee Court of Appeals, which ruled that the IEP proposed by the school system was inappropriate and that the private hearing and speech facility was an appropriate placement. **School witnesses admitted the failure of the school system to modify the proposed classroom.** The classroom had a comprehensive development curriculum designed for special education students, and did not emphasize speech and language for students with hearing impairments or dyspraxia. Also, the special education classroom teacher had no formal training or certification in deaf education or speech/language pathology. The student required an acoustically treated classroom with minimal visual distraction and a curriculum that consistently emphasized and reinforced speech and language development. Tuition reimbursement and attorneys' fees were awarded. *Wilson County School System v. Clifton*, 41 S.W.3d 645 (Tenn. Ct. App. 2000).

1. Segregated Placement

♦ An Illinois school district funded a private day school placement for twin girls who were severely disabled by Rett syndrome. When the girls' parents sought to have the children educated in a regular education setting in a public school, the district refused. A hearing officer found that the district provided a free appropriate public education for the three years in question, and a federal court upheld that decision. **A mainstream setting would not be the appropriate forum** for the twins' education because their needs for therapy and medical care were excessive. The segregated placement was the least restrictive environment. *Kerry M. v. Manhattan School Dist. #114*, No. 03 C 9349, 2006 WL 2862118 (N.D. Ill. 9/29/06).

♦ A learning disabled student attended a private school, where he had behavior issues. When the school did not invite him back for the following year, the district's IEP team recommended a special day program at the student's neighborhood school. However, the student's parents paid tuition at another private school without notifying the district, then challenged the IEP, claiming it did not offer the least restrictive environment. A California federal court ruled for the district, noting that the mainstreaming requirement of the IDEA was not absolute. Instead, students were to be mainstreamed to the maximum extent appropriate. Here, **the student's behavior issues would be better addressed in the special day program**. *L.S. v. Newark Unified School Dist.*, No. C 05-03241 JSW, 2006 WL 1390661 (N.D. Cal. 5/22/06).

♦ A Michigan student with an IQ of 36 attended regular classes with his peers, but worked with an aide on materials completely different than his classmates. When he approached middle school, the district recommended a segregated categorical placement, which his mother rejected. She rejected three other IEPs calling for varying amounts of segregated time, insisting on full inclusion. Eventually, she placed her son in a private religious school and sought tuition reimbursement. A federal court ruled against her, noting that the least restrictive environment requirement of the IDEA does not necessarily entitle a student to full inclusion. Here, **the student would not benefit from regular instruction.** *Dick-Friedman v. Board of Educ. of West Bloomfield Public Schools,* 427 F.Supp.2d 768 (E.D. Mich. 2006).

◆   A Kansas student with Down syndrome scored in the 0.1 percentile on the knowledge and skills portion of the Woodcock-Johnson achievement test. His district proposed placing him in a self-contained classroom. His parents objected, and a trial placement was made in a regular classroom. However, the student could not keep up with his classmates and became frustrated. He engaged in disruptive behavior. A hearing officer determined that **a self-contained classroom was the least restrictive environment.** A federal court and the Tenth Circuit agreed. The student would continue to have interaction with regular education students in nonacademic classes. *T.W. v. Unified School Dist. No. 259, Wichita, Kansas,* 136 Fed.Appx. 122 (10th Cir. 2005).

◆   An Illinois second-grader with a speech/language disorder was frequently distracted, went off-task, refused to do school work and became angry when he didn't get his way. His behavior worsened in third grade. He destroyed property, assaulted fellow students and staff, and left the school building. He was found in muddy water in a cornfield after a search of several hours. The district then placed him in a self-contained program for behavior disordered students. His mother initiated due process, and a hearing officer agreed with her that the district failed to provide her son with a free appropriate public education. A federal court then ruled in favor of the school district, finding that the hearing officer had substituted her judgment for that of school administrators. Here, the district continually updated and evaluated the student's IEP. It met frequently to address a rapidly deteriorating situation, and it was responsive to the mother's request to undertake a formal behavior implementation plan. **The district could take the student's disruptive behavior into account in its placement decision.** *Forrestville Board of Educ. v. Illinois State Board of Educ.,* No. 02 C 50373, 2003 WL 22287388 (N.D. Ill. 9/30/03).

◆   Before her hospitalization for attempting suicide, a high school student with emotional problems achieved good grades in regular education classes with limited special education services. Her transition back to school was difficult, she failed to take advantage of extra help offered to her, and she began to miss classes. In response, her IEP team suggested she participate in the school's intensive alternative program for students with serious emotional problems. The student's IEP called for her to remain in her general education setting, with access to the alternative program when needed. The placement proved unsuccessful. When the student's problems worsened, her parents requested placement in a private therapeutic program. The district instead offered to increase her participation in the school's intensive alternative program, known as Interlude. The parents challenged that proposal, and a hearing officer agreed that the Interlude placement was inappropriate. He based his decision partially on the student's strong objection. The hearing officer concluded the proper placement was a private therapeutic day school.

A federal court then concluded that the hearing officer had failed to defer to the judgment of educational experts, who had "uniformly and consistently testified" that the student would benefit from the Interlude program. There was evidence that the program's small class sizes and structure would allow her to make educational progress. The hearing officer's decision allowed the student to dictate her placement, which was not appropriate. The hearing officer overlooked the program's many benefits, and the evidence indicated that **the IEP calling for the student's placement in the Interlude program was reasonably calculated to enable the student to receive educational benefit.** *Arlington County School Board v. Smith*, 230 F.Supp.2d 704 (E.D. Va. 2002).

♦ When a student with significant learning disabilities was in the eighth grade, her parents and local school system met to develop her IEP for the ninth grade and to determine an appropriate placement. For the first eight years of school, the student was enrolled in a private school, and the parents wanted her placed in an out-of-state residential school. The district recommended the student be placed in a nonresidential public school in a fundamental life skills program. The parents rejected the placement offer and enrolled their daughter in the residential school. A due process hearing officer upheld the proposed placement. The district's placement proposal afforded the student the opportunity to receive a FAPE. The parents then sued the school district for IDEA violations, adding claims under Section 504 of the Rehabilitation Act and seeking an award of money damages under 42 U.S.C. § 1983. A federal magistrate judge observed that **the district's placement recommendation for the student's first year in high school would provide her with a FAPE.** She needed fundamental skills instruction to prepare her for everyday life, and it would be difficult for her to attend a diploma-track program. *Steinberg v. Weast*, 132 F.Supp.2d 343 (D. Md. 2001).

2. Home-Bound Instruction

♦ A New Hampshire student with mental retardation, orthopedic impairment and other disabilities attended a rehabilitation day center for four years under an IEP. However, when she was 19 and the IEP team recommended a continued placement there, her parents refused to consent to the IEP and withdrew her from school. They sought a home- and community-based program to help her with basic life skills and community interaction. The case reached the First Circuit, which ruled for the school district. The student's behavior appeared to be improving, and **the day center was a less restrictive placement than the home service setting the parents wanted.** Further, the IEP called for a significant increase in services in the area of pre-vocational skills. *Lessard v. Lyndeborough Cooperative School Dist.*, 592 F.3d 267 (1st Cir. 2010).

♦   A California student diagnosed with autism received early intervention services through a one-to-one, in-home behavioral program. When he reached age three and his transition to school was discussed, his parents refused the district's offer of an elementary school placement. They kept the student at home but visited the school proposed in the IEP. However, their psychologist was limited to 20 minutes of classroom observation time. They sought payment for the private services and claimed that the 20-minute limitation violated the IDEA. The case reached the Ninth Circuit, which held that **even though the district's 20-minute observation policy violated California education law, it did not undermine the law's purpose.** The parents were still able to participate in the due process hearing, and their psychologist was still able to give them advice. The district did not have to pay for the private services. *L.M. v. Capistrano Unified School Dist.*, 538 F.3d 1261 (9th Cir. 2008).

♦   The parents of a California student with autism **sought to continue the home-based program of applied behavior analysis (ABA)** when the district proposed an IEP calling for placement in a special day class with 18.75 hours a week of special education. The district also sought to assess the student for his needs but the parents believed the assessment done earlier by a private institute was sufficient. After several hearings, a federal court determined that the district had offered an appropriate IEP and that the district's proposed evaluation was indeed necessary. The parents had meaningfully participated in the IEP team meetings, and the IEP team had considered multiple programs, including the student's home ABA program. *L.M. v. Capistrano Unified School Dist*, No. 2:05-CV-0194-MCE-DAD, 2006 WL 2830172 (E.D. Cal. 9/29/06).

♦   A student with autism was characterized as unable to function in social settings that were not highly structured. After his unmanageable behavior continued through various placements, the district assigned him to home instruction pending determination of an appropriate placement. At a due process hearing, an administrative law judge (ALJ) held that the district denied the student a FAPE and failed to diagnose him as autistic. He determined that the district should not have placed the student in a restrictive home setting without services for a full month while it determined an appropriate placement. Also, it should have given more consideration to a regular school placement with a full-time aide. A federal court reversed, and the student's guardian appealed to the Seventh Circuit, which noted that not even a full-time aide could "restrain this wild child when he started kicking and biting people, tearing his clothes, breaking furniture, and otherwise acting out as he had been doing for years, with no sign of improvement." **District administrators did not unreasonably assign the student to a temporary homebound placement. He had a "disastrous history" in regular school** and did not function well in any setting except a residential facility. The ALJ had improperly focused on the district's failure to categorize the student as autistic. Labels were irrelevant in this case, as there was no evidence that a formal diagnosis of autism would show it was unreasonable to keep the student out of school. *School Dist. of Wisconsin Dells v. Z.S.*, 295 F.3d 671 (7th Cir. 2002).

♦ When a student with hypotonic and autistic behaviors and a developmental disability was 15 months old, her parents enrolled her in First Steps, a program operated by the Missouri Department of Mental Health. They became dissatisfied with her progress and enrolled her in an intensive, home-based program of individualized therapy for 12 hours a day. They requested district funding for the program when the student turned three. The district prepared a proposed IEP calling for instruction in a classroom with developmentally disabled students, as well as some non-disabled students, supplemented by individualized speech, occupational and physical therapy. The parents' proposal for in-home individualized training was discussed at an IEP meeting, but was ultimately rejected because of the lack of interaction with other students. The parents left the meeting before it ended. They challenged the proposed IEP at due process and lost. A federal court reversed the hearing panel's decision, but the Eighth Circuit reversed again, holding that the parents had received a meaningful opportunity to participate in the development of the IEP. By abruptly leaving the meeting, they had truncated their own procedural rights to participate in the IEP development process. **The district proposal significantly expanded the time the student would spend in therapy.** *Blackmon v. Springfield R-XII School Dist.*, 198 F.3d 648 (8th Cir. 1999).

♦ A New York preschool student was identified with autistic symptoms, and his parents enrolled him in a home-based program in which he received 40 hours per week of one-on-one instruction using the Applied Behavioral Analysis method. Following an evaluation and assessment by a multi-disciplinary team, the district recommended placement in a private nursery school for autistic children, and called for 25 hours of ABA instruction. The student's father requested a due process hearing, at which the hearing officer upheld the proposed IEP. A state review officer affirmed, but a New York federal court reversed. It found substantial evidence that the 40-hour intensive one-on-one ABA program was appropriate since it was supported by a psychological and behavioral evaluation and a neuropsychological evaluation of the student. There was also evidence that the 25 hours of instruction proposed by the district would not be intensive and would therefore be inappropriate. **The court rejected the district's assertion that the home-based placement violated the IDEA.** Some students with disabilities must be educated in segregated facilities because of their disruptive behavior or because the gains from inclusive instruction may be marginal. *Mr. X v. New York State Educ. Dep't*, 975 F.Supp. 546 (S.D.N.Y. 1997).

B. Neighborhood Placement

♦ A Kentucky school board declined to place a diabetic student in his neighborhood school because there was no full-time nurse there and he needed daily insulin injections. It offered a placement at a school with a nurse, as well as transportation. The parents argued that other staff members ought to be able to give the injections at the neighborhood school, but the district used state law to assert that it couldn't do so. In the lawsuit that resulted, a federal court held that **the district did not have to place the student at the neighborhood**

school. The placement offered by the district did not deny the student any educational rights or benefits. *R.K. v. Board of Educ of Scott County*, 755 F.Supp.2d 800 (E.D. Ky. 2010).

♦ An Illinois school district placed a student with severe developmental dyslexia and a learning disorder in a neighborhood school, offering her special education services for about half of her school day. Her parents declined extended school year services. They became frustrated by her lack of progress and placed her in a private school, then requested due process. A hearing officer and a federal court ruled that the student was properly placed in the neighborhood school and that the parents were not entitled to tuition reimbursement. The IEPs created by the district stated broad annual goals and listed short-term objectives that showed the district had offered an appropriate education. And **the student made some academic progress at the neighborhood school**. *James D. v. Board of Educ. of Aptakisic-Tripp Community Consolidated School Dist. No. 102*, 642 F.Supp.2d 804 (N.D. Ill. 2009).

♦ The mother of a Kansas student with Down syndrome challenged the IEP proposed for his entry into high school, as it would require a long bus ride to a high school in another town. She sought to place him in the high school in their town. An educational cooperative serving eight school districts ran a "level program" (also known as a cluster system) that used a functional educational approach. A hearing officer and a federal court found that **the Level IV program at the distant high school was the least restrictive placement** and that the neighborhood school had no teachers qualified to teach the student. The student's inability to focus in regular classrooms was documented, and the Level IV program provided a continuum of placements and support services. Although neighborhood placements are preferred under the IDEA, they are not an enforceable right. *M.M. v. Unified School Dist. No. 368*, No. 07-2291-JTM, 2008 WL 4950987 (D. Kan. 11/18/08).

♦ A nine-year-old Mississippi student functioned at a four-month cognitive level and a nine-month linguistic level. Her school district proposed a placement in a program offered by another district under an inter-agency agreement. Her parents objected, asserting that this wasn't the least restrictive environment, and that the district had come up with this option after the IEP meeting ended. A federal court disagreed. The parents produced no evidence that the IEP was cobbled together after they left the meeting. Also, **the student could obtain more sophisticated resources at the program in the other district**. And the district had the discretion to determine the geographic location of the educational placement. *Russell v. Water Valley School Dist.*, No. 3:06-CV-101-SAA, 2008 WL 723842 (N.D. Miss. 3/17/08).

♦ A student with Rett Syndrome and apraxia had disruptive vocalizations that often lasted more than a minute. She also engaged in self-injurious behavior and sometimes struck others. After a triennial evaluation, her school district sought to remove her from her neighborhood school and place her in a special education setting. Her parents objected. A lengthy administrative process ensued. Sometimes the student did not attend school. Other times she had to be removed because of her vocalizations and behavior. She attended only five full school days in the first two months of the year. When the case reached an Illinois federal court, it ruled in favor of the district, finding that it had made good faith efforts to carry out the IEP. **Its decision to remove the student from her neighborhood placement did not violate the IDEA.** *Board of Educ. of Township High School Dist. No. 211 v. Michael R.*, No. 02 C 6098, 2005 WL 2008919 (N.D. Ill. 8/15/05).

◆   A Louisiana school district transferred a student with deafness from his neighborhood school to a cluster school about four miles farther away from his home. His parents claimed that the transfer was a change in placement under the IDEA that required the district to give them prior written notice. They requested a due process hearing. After a question about bias by a review officer was resolved, a federal court upheld the district's decision to transfer the student. The parents appealed to the Fifth Circuit Court of Appeals, which ruled that **the few changes the student experienced as a result of the transfer to the new school did not amount to a change in placement** under the IDEA. Riding a special bus for disabled students instead of a regular school bus and sharing a transliterator with another student instead of having his own were not fundamental changes to his IEP. *Veazey v. Ascension Parish School Board*, 121 Fed.Appx. 552 (5th Cir. 2005).

◆   The mother of a private school student met with the special education coordinator at the local high school. She claimed she provided evaluations, prior IEPs and progress reports, and notified the school that **she did not want her son's placement changed until there was a determination that the neighborhood school was appropriate**. She claimed that the school did not contact her again. She requested due process, seeking tuition reimbursement. A hearing officer found that she was not interested in any placement the district had to offer and failed to give the district written permission for an evaluation. Thus, she was not entitled to reimbursement. A federal court reversed, noting that the hearing officer should have made findings on whether the district violated the IDEA before skipping ahead to the question of reimbursement. *Goldstrom v. District of Columbia*, 319 F.Supp.2d 5 (D.D.C. 2004).

◆   A New Jersey school district placed a student with profound sensorineural hearing loss in a public school for deaf children outside the district. The next year, it proposed placing the student in a self-contained school for the deaf located in the neighborhood school the student would have attended if not for her special needs. It did not explain why it failed to propose that placement previously, or what had changed to make the new placement appropriate. The student's family challenged the placement, and an administrative law judge (ALJ) ruled in their favor. A federal court held that the ALJ "got it wrong" without explaining why the decision was incorrect. The Third Circuit Court of Appeals reversed, finding the district's emphasis on least restrictive environment to be misplaced. **The district had not shown that the new**

placement would provide meaningful educational benefit. Here, the neighborhood school offered the student minimal mainstreaming opportunities. The district was not allowed to change the student's placement. *S.H. v. State-Operated School Dist. of City of Newark*, 336 F.3d 260 (3d Cir. 2003).

♦   The IEP team for a Michigan student with Down syndrome felt that she needed a categorical classroom placement to meet her IEP goals. The only categorical classroom placement in the district was at a school 7.3 miles from her home. Her parents rejected that proposal and asked for a resource room placement. A due process hearing officer upheld the IEP team's proposal, focusing on the appropriateness of the classroom placement, and a state level review officer agreed with that decision. However, a federal court ruled that the least restrictive environment requirement of the IDEA mandated that the student be educated at her neighborhood school. The Sixth Circuit Court of Appeals reversed, noting that the IDEA regulation requiring placement "as close as possible to the child's home" did not apply if a necessary program was unavailable at a neighborhood school. Since **the categorical classroom placement was appropriate, and unavailable at the neighborhood school**, the proposed IEP complied with the IDEA. *McLaughlin v. Holt Public Schools Board of Educ.*, 320 F.3d 663 (6th Cir. 2003).

♦   A hearing-impaired Louisiana student attended a public school with the assistance of a cued speech transliterator, who supplemented spoken information in his classes. Although hearing-impaired students who used American Sign Language attended neighborhood schools, the cued speech transliterator served only at a centralized location. The student achieved academic benefits and success at the centralized school. However, his parents decided he should attend his neighborhood school for social reasons. The district denied their transfer request. A hearing officer agreed with the district, but a federal court ruled that the student was entitled to attend his neighborhood school with the transliterator. The Fifth Circuit reversed. Here, the student's IEP satisfied the IDEA, and **his parents were seeking the neighborhood placement for primarily social reasons**. They did not have veto power over the district's decision to provide the transliterator only at the central location. *White v. Ascension Parish School Board*, 343 F.3d 373 (5th Cir. 2003).

♦   An 11-year-old Rhode Island student had a respiratory condition that required a tracheal tube for breathing and a full-time nurse. His parents objected to the implementation of his IEP at the location designated by the school district, which was three miles away. They argued that the district should reassign its only full-time nurse from that school to the student's neighborhood school. A federal court rejected the parents' claim that the nurse should be transferred to the neighborhood school. **The need to respond to a possible medical emergency overcame the IDEA's presumption in favor of a neighborhood school placement.** The First Circuit affirmed, noting that the site selected by the school district was only three miles from the student's home and was readily accessible to the student. *Kevin G. by Robert G. v. Cranston School Committee*, 130 F.3d 481 (1st Cir. 1997).

C. Mainstreaming

1. Appropriateness

♦   An 18-year-old Pennsylvania student with multiple disabilities was non-verbal and not toilet trained. Her district proposed placing her in a full-time life skills support class and mainstreaming her in school assemblies, lunch, homeroom and recess. Her parents filed a due process hearing request, asserting that the placement would deny her a FAPE because it was too restrictive. A hearing officer agreed with them and ordered compensatory education, but an appeals panel held that the student required mainstreaming only for lunch, recess, physical education, homeroom, music, art and a single academic class. The award of compensatory education was reversed. A federal court and the Third Circuit upheld that decision, noting that **the student was making progress in her life skills class and her frequent loud vocalizations had a negative effect on other students**. *A.G. v. Wissahickon School Dist.*, 374 Fed.Appx. 330 (3d Cir. 2010).

♦   The parents of a California autistic student challenged his IEP for two school years, claiming that he should have been kept in a regular language arts program instead of a blended language arts program. They sought tuition reimbursement for a private placement. A federal court and the Ninth Circuit ruled against them, noting that the benefits of a mainstream placement were minimal in comparison with the blended program. The IEP was suited to the student's unique abilities, and **there was a sufficient basis to overcome the preference for mainstreaming**. *B.S. v. Yorba-Linda Unified School Dist.*, 306 Fed.Appx. 397 (9th Cir. 2009).

♦   A student with ADHD struggled socially and academically, and engaged in numerous disruptive behaviors until he was assigned a 1:1 behavior paraprofessional, at which time his behavior improved markedly. The school district then placed him in a 12:1:1 classroom in a specialized school serving only disabled students, and discontinued his 1:1 behavior paraprofessional. The student sought to attend a private school program offering a 15:1 setting for college-bound disabled students with minor emotional issues. Students in the program attended homeroom, gym and lunch with non-disabled students. The district rejected that option. The parents challenged that decision and placed him in the private school. A New York federal court eventually agreed with the parents that the district's IEP was inappropriate because it did not place the student in the least restrictive environment. **The student's improved behavior justified the more inclusive setting,** and the district had to reimburse the parents for the private school tuition. *Jennifer D. v. New York City Dep't of Educ.*, 550 F.Supp.2d 420 (S.D.N.Y. 2008).

♦   An Illinois student with multiple disabilities had severe behavioral and academic problems in his public elementary school, where he attended a self-contained special education classroom. He had lunch and physical education with non-disabled peers, but he exhibited immature and inappropriate behavior around them. An IEP team determined that he should be placed in a Christian special education school, and he made significant educational gains there. When he reached high school, the district sought to return him to public school, proposing a plan similar to what it had offered while he was in elementary school. His mother challenged the IEP, and a federal court eventually agreed with the hearing officer that the Christian school was the appropriate placement. Here, the district was proposing to repeat an unsuccessful program from his elementary school days. **Mainstreaming was part of the student's problem.** He needed a small educational setting, noise avoidance, a very structured classroom, repetition of routines and the elimination of distractions. *Board of Educ. of Homewood Flossmoor Community High School Dist. No. 233 v. Illinois State Board of Educ.*, No. 06 C 0676, 2008 WL 1968790 (N.D. Ill. 5/1/08).

♦   A Connecticut school district behavioral consultant notified the parents of a student with Down syndrome and other impairments that because of his behavior problems it was becoming more difficult to keep the student in a regular classroom. A performance and planning team drafted an IEP that called for only 60% regular classroom placement instead of the 80% urged by the parents. The district hired a consultant who recommended gradually increasing the student's time in regular classrooms to 80%, and the district agreed to increase the time to 74%. However, the parents were determined to achieve 80% time in regular classrooms. A federal court and the Second Circuit eventually upheld the IEP, noting that while mainstreaming is an important objective, it has to be weighed against the need for appropriate education. **Mandating a percentage of time in regular classes would be inconsistent with the individualized approach of the IDEA.** *P. v. Newington Board of Educ.*, 546 F.3d 111 (2d Cir. 2008).

♦   A New York student with autism-spectrum disorders began to withdraw from reality. Her mother removed her from the private day school placement specified by her IEP and placed her in an unapproved private school in Connecticut. The district reimbursed her for the amount of tuition that would have been charged by the New York private school. The following year, the district recommended a public school placement. The mother rejected the IEP and sought tuition reimbursement. A federal court overturned the hearing officer and review officer, and held that the IEP was inadequate. However, the Second Circuit reversed, finding considerable evidence to support the administrative decisions in favor of the district. The student's recent social progress indicated **she could make educational progress in an environment consistent with the IDEA's preference for mainstreaming.** *Cabouli v. Chappaqua Cent. School Dist.*, 202 Fed.Appx. 519 (2d Cir. 2006).

♦   A Texas school district and the parents of a student with Down syndrome, mental retardation and speech impairments disagreed over his placement. The district maintained that he needed to be educated in a resource room for math and language arts, while the parents believed he should be educated in a regular classroom with increased use of aides. An independent hearing officer determined that the student should be educated in a resource room for math and language arts. A federal court agreed. **Full inclusion is not appropriate where a regular classroom cannot meet a disabled child's needs.** The student needed special instruction in math and language arts, and he would have ample time for socialization in other classes. *Cody H. v. Bryan Independent School Dist.*, No. Civ.A. H-03-5598, 2005 WL 1515389 (S.D. Tex. 6/24/05).

◆ A school district recommended placing an autistic student in a 1:6+1 special education program (one teacher, six students, plus a special education aide) outside the mainstream setting. His parents objected, and a due process hearing officer ruled for the parents. A state review officer held that the student should remain in the special education placement pending appeals. Eventually, the case reached a federal court, which ruled that **the school district did not violate the IDEA by failing to place the student in an integrated classroom.** Later hearing officers had agreed that the district's methodology was the appropriate means of educating the student. *J.K. v. Springville-Griffith Institute Cent. School Dist. Board of Educ.*, No. 02-CV-765S, 2005 WL 711886 (W.D.N.Y. 3/28/05).

◆ A Texas first-grader had trouble with science and social studies under his IEP, which called for regular classroom placements in those subjects. The IEP for the second grade called for placement in a special education setting for science and social studies, with regular education placement for all nonacademic instruction. His parents challenged the IEP, and a due process hearing officer ruled for the district, noting that the student was not progressing in a general education setting. A federal court reversed, but the Fifth Circuit reversed. The IDEA does not require regular education teachers to devote most of their time to one student or to modify the regular education program beyond recognition. **Mainstreaming here would require unduly burdensome modifications to the regular education curriculum** so that the student would not have to learn any of the skills normally taught. *Brillon v. Klein Independent School Dist.*, 100 Fed.Appx. 309 (5th Cir. 2004).

◆ The parents of a Utah preschooler with autism met with school officials to discuss their daughter's IEP. The district declined to place her in a mainstream private preschool and instead offered to place her in a preschool class consisting mostly of disabled students. It also offered to increase the number of typically developing students in the classroom and to provide speech therapy, occupational therapy and 8-15 hours of applied behavioral analysis (ABA) therapy per week. The parents declined the district's offer and kept the student in a mainstream private preschool, where she progressed with the help of a supplementary aide and 35-40 hours of weekly ABA therapy. A hearing officer and a federal court ruled for the district, finding the parents' placement the most restrictive, but the Tenth Circuit Court of Appeals reversed. Here, **the student could be educated in a regular classroom.** She was not disruptive in a mainstream setting. And her primary need was to improve her social skills – best achieved in a mainstream classroom. *L.B. v. Nebo School Dist.*, 379 F.3d 966 (10th Cir. 2004).

♦ A Maryland student attended a private Christian school from kindergarten through grade three, at which time the school proposed that he repeat the third grade because of his difficulties in reading, language and spelling. The student's mother removed him from the school, obtained an evaluation that showed the student was in the high average range in verbal and full scale IQ, and placed him in a public school for fourth grade. An IEP team initially determined he did not have a learning disability, but after several disputes with the mother, during which she obtained another evaluation, it recommended 31.25 hours of weekly general education with nine hours of special education a week. The mother rejected the offer and placed the student in a private school. A due process hearing officer ruled that the district's evaluation process, though lengthy, had been appropriate. The hearing officer found that the student did not need all-day special education and that **the IEP proposal placed him in the least restrictive setting**. A federal court reversed the hearing officer's decision, but the Fourth Circuit reversed the district court. Here, the lower court had improperly substituted its own views for those of the school district, which did not have to rely on the mother's two private evaluations or maximize the student's educational potential. Because the student received an educational benefit from the district, the the public school placement in the proposed IEP was best. *A.B. v. Board of Educ. of Anne Arundel County*, 354 F.3d 315 (4th Cir. 2004).

♦ A Texas student with a high-functioning form of autism attended advanced placement classes as well as regular classes, received instruction in a special communication class and had a behavioral intervention plan in place for the seventh grade. Although his grades were fine, his parents felt his behavior had regressed. They placed him in a preparatory school for disabled students. A hearing officer ordered the district to reimburse the parents for the costs of the private school, but a federal court reversed. The Fifth Circuit then held that the student's IEP was sufficiently individualized and that he was appropriately mainstreamed. Also, the IEP was developed in a coordinated and collaborative manner between "key stakeholders." And he received positive academic and nonacademic benefits from his IEP. Even though his behavior incidents had increased during grade seven, that was related to the new system adopted for notification about his offenses. The court affirmed the ruling for the district, **finding the mainstream placement appropriate**. *Lewisville Independent School Dist. v. Charles W.*, 81 Fed.Appx. 843 (5th Cir. 2003).

♦ An Illinois student with Rett Syndrome, which is characterized as a form of autism, was placed in a regular kindergarten class at the insistence of her parents. By second grade, her IEP team recommended placing her in an Educational Life Skills (ELS) program, where she would spend most school days in a segregated classroom. Her parents rejected this offer. A due process hearing officer held the district's proposal appropriate, and a federal court agreed. There was evidence that the student would gain nothing from attending regular classes. On further appeal, the Seventh Circuit noted that although the student had been in regular classrooms for seven years, she was unable to fully participate in the curriculum and received very little benefit from those placements. The ELS setting recommended by the district offered many opportunities for mainstreaming during nonacademic classes, certain social studies and science classes, and for lunch, recess, assemblies and field trips. The district also used reverse mainstreaming, in which non-disabled peers came into the ELS classroom for interaction. The court upheld the placement proposed by the district as appropriate. **Although the IDEA contains a strong preference for mainstreaming or LRE, it does not suggest doing so when a regular classroom setting provides an unsatisfactory education.** The ELS setting satisfied both the FAPE and LRE requirements of the IDEA. *Beth B. v. Van Clay*, 282 F.3d 493 (7th Cir. 2002).

◆ A Connecticut planning and placement team decided to transition a residential school student to a public high school based on progress he made in maintaining appropriate behavior. His father disagreed, urging that the student be placed at a private, non-special education, all-male, college preparatory boarding school. The school board rejected the father's request to pay for a summer program at the boarding school, and he unilaterally placed the student there for the next academic year. A due process hearing officer held that the student did not require a residential placement or a therapeutic day program in order to obtain educational benefits. He found that the public school transition plan would have provided the student with a FAPE and that the district did not commit any procedural violations of the IDEA. A federal court and the Second Circuit agreed. The board's recommended placement was reasonably calculated to enable the student to receive educational benefits. Also, **it was consistent with the IDEA's requirement that students with disabilities receive education in the least restrictive environment.** *A.S. by P.B.S. v. Board of Educ. of the Town of West Hartford*, 47 Fed. Appx. 615 (2d Cir. 2002).

2. Services and Aids

◆ A New Jersey student with reading and writing disorders received pull-out resource room instruction until sixth grade, when her parents became concerned about low self-esteem and sought to have her mainstreamed full time, with homework accommodations and supplemental multi-sensory reading instruction. School team members prepared two draft IEPs, one calling for continued pull-out instruction and the other calling for mainstream instruction but without the homework accommodations and reading supplements that the parents wanted. The parents rejected the IEPs and placed the student in a private school. When they sued for tuition reimbursement, they lost. The Third Circuit held that **the final, mainstream IEP offered the student a free appropriate public education in the least restrictive environment.** The lack of the homework accommodations and reading supplements did not render the IEP ineffective. *G.N. and S.N. v. Board of Educ. of Township of Livingston*, 309 Fed.Appx. 542 (3d Cir. 2009).

◆ An autistic student in New York attended general education classes in eighth grade for all classes except English. The district prepared an IEP for ninth grade that would remove him from the general education history class as well, but his parents rejected the IEP and sought due process. Evidence at the hearing indicated that the student had trouble with language-based subjects like history and English. A hearing officer upheld the IEP, and a federal court agreed that **removing the student from history class did not violate the IDEA**. Even though the student had passed his general education history class after the hearing officer issued his opinion, he had done so with many services and accommodations, and he gained greater benefits from his self-contained special education classes. *J.S. v. North Colonie Cent. School Dist.*, 586 F.Supp.2d 74 (N.D.N.Y. 2008).

♦   A Pennsylvania county intermediate unit (IU) prepared an IEP for a four-year-old with Down syndrome that called for a full-time specialized classroom. The student's parents rejected the placement and requested a due process hearing, seeking a regular classroom placement with supplemental aids and services at a private community preschool near their home. A hearing officer held that the student had to be educated in a full-time segregated classroom, and the parents appealed. A federal court held that the hearing officer had failed to place the burden of proof on the IU to justify its IEP. This was required under *Oberti v. Board of Educ.*, 995 F.2d 1204 (3d Cir. 1993). Since the IU had failed to show that it attempted to mainstream the student to the extent possible, and since there was evidence that the student had attended a Sunday school classroom with non-disabled peers without creating disruption, it seemed likely that the student could be mainstreamed. The court remanded the case to the hearing officer, and **ordered that the student be initially mainstreamed with supplemental aids and services**. *Blount v. Lancaster-Lebanon Intermediate Unit*, No. Civ.A. 03-579, 2003 WL 22988892 (E.D. Pa. 11/25/03).

♦   Through the third grade, a student with neurological and visual impairments was placed in her school district's developmental handicapped (DH) program. The district mainstreamed her in fourth grade with the assistance of an aide and an independent consultant. The student remained in regular education settings through grade seven. For her first year of high school, the district proposed a DH program that emphasized vocational and life skills training, with mainstreaming for selected nonacademic classes. The student's parents objected, and the district provided her with supportive services and modifications to her regular education curriculum. A due process hearing officer determined that both the regular education program and the proposed DH placement were inappropriate. He ordered the development of a new IEP. A federal court then agreed that the student's IEP goals were inappropriate. **The district did not make reasonable efforts to accommodate the student in regular classes** because it did not consider a broad spectrum of appropriate supplemental services. There was evidence that the student could progress toward her IEP goals in a regular education environment with appropriate supplemental aids and services. *A.S. ex rel. S. v. Norwalk Board of Educ.*, 183 F.Supp.2d 534 (D. Conn. 2002).

♦   A student with neurological impairments, hyperactivity, perseverative behaviors, speech and language delays and impaired comprehension was about to enter the fifth grade. For that year, his planning and placement team (PPT) prepared an IEP calling for regular education in math, homeroom, art and music; with the rest of his academic subjects in a self-contained special education classroom. The IEP specified that the student would receive extended time, study material modification and a paraprofessional. He received good grades but met only 16 of his 49 IEP goals during fifth grade. The PPT then proposed changing his placement to a life skills program for the sixth grade. His parents rejected this placement, preferring mainstreaming. When the parties could not reach agreement, a due process hearing officer ordered placement in a self-contained special education room or multi-categorical program for most academic subjects. The district then proposed an IEP calling for 18.75 hours of weekly special education, with 7.5 hours of weekly mainstream instruction with related services. The parents sued.

A federal court held that the PPT did not make reasonable efforts to accommodate the student in his regular education classes, and failed to propose appropriate modifications or accommodations. The district also failed to provide the student with a paraprofessional, despite including this service in an IEP. **The student's past inability to progress in the mainstream did not indicate that he could not succeed with appropriate supports.** The school board violated the IDEA by failing to consider what aids and services would enable him to succeed in regular classrooms. There was no evidence of any negative impact on other students in his classes. Thus, a self-contained placement violated the IDEA's mainstreaming requirement. *Warton v. New Fairfield Board of Educ.*, 217 F.Supp.2d 261 (D. Conn. 2002).

◆ For the sixth grade, a Pennsylvania school district proposed placing a student with an IQ of 36 in a part-time life-skills support placement for academic subjects and a school in another district for nonacademic subjects. Before this time, the student was placed in a regular education classroom while receiving special education instruction from an aide. His parents objected to the recommendation. The case reached a federal court, which found that the school district was required to make reasonable efforts to accommodate the student in a regular education setting. It was **required to consider a range of supplemental aids and services and to make efforts to modify the regular education program to accommodate his needs**. The district had failed to give the requisite consideration to the student in this case. It had assigned all responsibility for the student's education to his aide, rather than his teachers. While the student was placed in regular classes, the school did not meaningfully attempt to instruct him as inclusively as required by the IDEA. The district also failed to provide supplementary aids and services to the student. The district had to develop an IEP considering all available supplementary aides and services. *Girty v. School Dist. of Valley Grove*, 163 F.Supp.2d 527 (W.D. Pa. 2001).

D. Private School Placement

◆ The mother of a Texas student with ADHD, bipolar disorder, and oppositional defiant disorder complained to the district about her child's home behavior and educational problems but got no response. She placed the student in an out-of-district private school but did not file a due process complaint until the following school year. The case came before a hearing officer more than a year after the placement, so the hearing officer found most of her claims were time-barred, including her claim that the district failed to hold an annual IEP meeting for the student. A federal court upheld that determination, noting that **the placement of the student in the out-of-district private school ended the district's duty to conduct the IEP meeting.** *D.C. v. Klein Independent School Dist.*, 711 F.Supp.2d 739 (S.D. Tex. 2010).

♦   A District of Columbia high school student received mostly failing grades. An evaluator diagnosed him with a learning disorder, and the district's multidisciplinary team agreed to fund a private school placement in a highly structured, supervised classroom with a low student-staff ratio. At the private school, the student earned much better grades. When the student sought compensatory education, a hearing officer ruled that **the district had remedied the prior denial of a FAPE by making the private school placement** and that no additional services were needed to "undo damage caused by prior violations." Thus, he was not entitled to compensatory education. A federal court and the D.C. Circuit Court of Appeals upheld that determination. *Wheaton v. District of Columbia*, No. 10-7105, 2010 WL 5372181 (D.C. Cir. 12/28/10).

♦   A Texas school district determined that a child with autism should receive weekly speech therapy and attend an early childhood public school classroom with both special education students and typically developing students. His parents agreed to the placement, but when his behavior regressed, they asked for a summer school placement. When the district didn't respond, they placed him in his old private school and sought tuition reimbursement. A hearing officer, a federal court and the Fifth Circuit all ruled for the school district, holding that the child had been placed in the least restrictive environment and that **he made enough progress in the public school setting to demonstrate that his IEP was providing him a FAPE.** *R.H. v. Plano Independent School Dist.*, 607 F.3d 1003 (5th Cir. 2010).

♦   A Minnesota student made little progress in public schools, slipping behind his peers each year and never progressing beyond a first-grade reading level. After fourth grade, the district offered a placement in a Coordinated Learning for Academic and Social Success (CLASS) program, but the parents rejected it and instead placed him in a private school for students with IEPs and other learning or attention issues. When they sought tuition reimbursement, a hearing officer ruled in their favor. However, a federal court reversed, noting that **the private school offered similar services to the CLASS program but in a more segregated placement.** Therefore, the private school was not the appropriate placement and no tuition reimbursement was allowed. *C.B. v. Special School Dist. No. 1*, 641 F.Supp.2d 850 (D. Minn. 2009).

♦   A 14-year-old Arizona student suffered traumatic brain injury that confined him to a wheelchair and made him dependent on caregivers for daily activities. He was considered the most severely disabled student in his school district. His IEP team determined that he had a better chance of achieving his IEP goals if he were placed at a particular private day school 35 miles away. His parents objected, seeking instead to keep him in his neighborhood school with his non-disabled peers. A hearing officer found that the student failed to respond despite the district's best efforts and that the private day placement was best. The Arizona Court of Appeals agreed. **The student's severe disability made continued mainstreaming inappropriate.** *Stallings v. Gilbert Unified School Dist. No. 41,* No. 1 CA-CV 08-0625, 2009 WL 3165452 (Ariz. Ct. App. 10/1/09).

♦ A New York student unilaterally placed in an unapproved private school made progress the first year, then regressed the second. He had shown progressive improvement while in public schools. Nevertheless, the parents rejected the district's IEP for eighth grade that included ESY services, an inclusive setting and special instruction in English, math, science, social studies and reading. They sought tuition reimbursement for the private school. A hearing officer determined that the district failed to prove it had offered an adequate IEP, and found the private school placement appropriate even though the student received no speech and language therapy and was provided no behavior intervention plan. The state review officer reversed, and a federal court upheld the review officer's decision. The Second Circuit affirmed, noting that **the student's regression at the private school demonstrated that the private school placement was not appropriate** and prevented the parents from recovering tuition reimbursement. *Matrejek v. Brewster Cent. School Dist.,* 293 Fed.Appx. 20 (2d Cir. 2008).

♦ The parents of an Ohio student disagreed with the district's placement of their autistic son and placed him in a private school. They initiated due process, and a local independent hearing officer found the IEP inappropriate, ordering the district to fund the private school placement. However, the parents then assumed that the local hearing officer's decision amounted to an agreement between them and the state to change their son's placement. The state disagreed and a federal court ruled for the state. Only a state-level hearing officer could bind the state to an agreement, not a local hearing officer. *Winkelman v. Ohio Dep't of Educ.,* 616 F.Supp. 2d 714 (N.D. Ohio 2008).

♦ Massachusetts school district representatives met with the mother of a student with specific learning disabilities to discuss the student's IEP. School members of the IEP team eventually concluded that he no longer met the criteria for special education eligibility. The student was reevaluated, and the district eventually issued a finding of no eligibility. A due process hearing was postponed on two occasions so that the district could consider the mother's expert's report. After another IEP team meeting, the team found the student eligible for special education. The district offered compensatory education, but the mother sought due process. **A hearing officer ordered 78 compensatory education sessions but refused to order a private school placement** as the mother wished. A federal court agreed with the hearing officer that the school district could provide a free appropriate public education. Also, the district had provided valid reasons for the hearing date postponements. *Wanham v. Everett Public Schools,* 550 F.Supp.2d 152 (D. Mass. 2008).

♦ The parents of a disabled New Hampshire student home-schooled her during parts of her fourth-, fifth- and sixth-grade years. They then agreed to a public school placement on a diagnostic IEP. However, after a year they became dissatisfied with her education, insisting that the district had failed to properly implement the IEP. They requested several due process hearings, at which **the mother commented on her daughter's unhappiness and made sweeping declarations about the necessity of an out-of-district placement**. The hearing officers and a federal court ruled for the district, finding the testimony of district witnesses more credible. Thus, the parents were not entitled to prospective payment for tuition in a private school. *Mr. G. and Ms. K. v. Timberlane Regional School Dist.*, No. 1 CA-CV 08-625, 2007 WL 54819 (D.N.H. 1/4/07).

♦ A New Jersey student with an IQ of 135 had several learning disabilities and lagged behind her classmates in elementary school. When she reached sixth grade, her parents became frustrated at her lack of progress and opted to follow the advice of their psychologist, placing the student in a private school with similarly performing students. The parents then sought tuition reimbursement from the district. An administrative law judge denied the request, but a federal court ordered reimbursement. Here, **the district failed to modify its IEPs despite six years without progress**, and the student's performance at the private school increased dramatically. *F.D. & S.D. v. Holland Township Board of Educ.*, No. 05-5237(AET), 2007 WL 2021782 (D.N.J. 7/9/07).

♦ A New York student with gastrointestinal problems due to anxiety about school performance was referred for special education evaluations in grades six and eight. He was ruled ineligible. During ninth grade, the committee on special education (CSE) offered to refer the student for a Section 504 accommodation plan. His parents instead placed him in a private school that was "essentially ungraded." Later, the CSE classified the student as emotionally disturbed. When the parents sought tuition reimbursement, a federal court denied their claim. It held that **the private school was not the least restrictive environment**. In addition to the no-grades policy, only four to seven students attended the school while the student was there. *Pinn v. Harrison Cent. School Dist.*, 473 F.Supp.2d 477 (S.D.N.Y. 2007).

♦ A learning-disabled student in New Jersey with an IQ of 94 attended a public school under an IEP. His mother became concerned about his lack of academic progress in reading and writing, and she sought an out-of-district placement specializing in language-based learning disabilities. The district noted that the student's IQ had increased to 114 and found his current placement appropriate. However, a hearing officer disagreed, noting that the student remained two years behind his peers in reading and writing. Deciding that the student required intensive teaching in multisensory techniques, **the hearing officer ordered the district to pay for a private school placement that utilized the Orton-Gillingham approach**. A federal court reversed, but the Third Circuit reversed the federal court. Here, the lower court failed to give proper weight to the hearing officer's decision. *Ringwood Board of Educ. v. K.H.J.*, 258 Fed.Appx. 399 (3d Cir. 2007).

♦   After a student enrolled in a California school district, her mother claimed that the district failed to properly implement the IEP (by keeping her daughter out of general education classes) and that her daughter should have been placed in a particular private school with which it already had contracts. She placed her daughter in the private school. **A hearing officer agreed that the district materially failed to implement the IEP.** The case reached the Ninth Circuit, which held that the district failed to make a timely interim placement of the student, and when it finally made a placement, the placement was not in conformity with the IEP. However, the district only had to reimburse the mother for half of the private school tuition because the mother had contributed to delays in assessment and other proceedings. *Termine v. William S. Hart Union High School Dist.*, 249 Fed.Appx. 583 (9th Cir. 2007).

♦   The parents of a private school student sought greater special education for him but wanted to keep him in his private school. The district offered a public school placement that would give him psychological counseling he was not receiving at the private school. The parents, after due process hearings, took the case to the U.S. Court of Appeals, D.C. Circuit, which noted that **the student's placement could not be based on the mere preference of his parents that he stay in the private school.** The public school placement would comply with the IDEA requirement to offer the student some educational benefits. *Paolella v. District of Columbia*, 210 Fed.Appx. 1 (D.C. Cir. 2006).

♦   A sixth-grader's academic performance deteriorated and his parents requested a special education evaluation. His school district conducted two evaluations and found him ineligible for special education. His parents then notified the district they were removing him from public schools and seeking tuition reimbursement. They placed the student in a private school with small classes, where he showed significant improvement. Eventually, the district agreed that the student was IDEA-eligible, but it refused to accommodate him with small classes. A lawsuit resulted and a federal court ruled that the parents were entitled to tuition reimbursement. **The district failed to show that it could provide the student with a free appropriate public education.** *Gellert v. District of Columbia Public Schools*, 435 F.Supp.2d 18 (D.D.C. 2006).

♦   The parents of a 15-year-old Massachusetts student with language and auditory disabilities objected to a series of IEPs proposed by the school committee, but they continued to accept the services proposed for her in the IEPs. They sought a private school placement 60 miles away even though the student did not want to attend that school. **The hearing officer took into account the student's desire to stay at the public school** and determined that the student's IEP could be modified with a series of services to meet her needs. The parents appealed. A federal court ruled that the school's modified IEP provided a free appropriate public education and was the least restrictive environment for the student. The IEP did not have to be ideal but only appropriate. *Parents of Danielle v. Massachusetts Dep't of Educ.*, 430 F.Supp.2d 3 (D. Mass. 2006).

♦   The parents of a learning disabled student rejected his IEP for the 1999-2000 school year and enrolled him in a private school. They sought tuition reimbursement and a hearing officer held that the district's IEP provided FAPE. A state review officer reversed, a federal court affirmed, and the district reimbursed the parents. For the 2000-2001 school year, the parents again rejected the district's IEP and re-enrolled the student in the private school. This time the state review officer agreed with the hearing officer that the district's IEP provided FAPE, but the decision was not made until five months after the school year ended. A New York federal court held that the parents were not entitled to any tuition reimbursement for that year, but the Second Circuit reversed. Here, **the review officer's initial decision was an agreement to change the student's placement to the private school.** Thus, the district had to pay part of the student's tuition because of the late decision. *Mackey v. Board of Educ. for Arlington Cent. School Dist.*, 386 F.3d 158 (2d Cir. 2004).

♦   Vermont law permits school districts that do not maintain a public high school to pay tuition on behalf of resident students at approved public or independent high schools. The majority of high school students residing in the St. Johnsbury School District attend St. Johnsbury Academy. The academy maintains programs for students with disabilities, including a resource room and an individualized services program (ISP). In order to attend the resource room program and regular academic classes, the school requires students to perform at least at a fifth-grade level. A St. Johnsbury student with disabilities was admitted to the academy, but was denied permission to attend mainstream academic classes because he did not read at a fifth-grade level. His parent refused to send him to the academy as an ISP student, since his IEP for grade nine called for regular education placement in English and social studies. The district offered an alternative placement, which the parent rejected. In the lawsuit that followed, a federal court ordered the academy to admit the student into the specified mainstream academic classes.

The Second Circuit noted that the academy, as a private school, was not directly subject to IDEA standards. **The IDEA applies only to state and local agencies, and expressly contemplates that federal IEP and LRE requirements will be enforced by a public agency when it places a student in a private school.** Even when a private school conducts and revises IEPs, the public agency remains responsible for IDEA compliance. The student had no IDEA cause of action against the academy, which was not a local education agency under the IDEA. *St. Johnsbury Academy v. D.H.*, 240 F.3d 163 (2d Cir. 2001).

E. Residential School Placement

1. Appropriateness

♦   An Oregon student with ADHD and depression made progress in school but engaged in defiant and risky behavior at home. Her parents sought a more restrictive placement for her, but the school district ruled it out because she was earning good grades when she did her work. Her parents unilaterally placed her in a residential facility, but she was expelled for having sex with another student. Her parents then placed her in an out-of-state facility and sought tuition reimbursement, which the Ninth Circuit denied. **The student did not require residential placement for any educational reason.** She was not disruptive in class and was well regarded by teachers. *Ashland School Dist. v. Parents of Student R.J.*, 588 F.3d 1004 (9th Cir. 2009).

♦   A New York mother claimed that her son was improperly restrained at the Massachusetts school she had agreed to send him to. She sued in both states. A New York appellate court held that she could not sue her school district because she had consented to the Massachusetts placement, and the Massachusetts court had found the use of the restraints reasonable. Further, the district had contracted out the duty to supervise the use of restraints to the Massachusetts school with her consent. *Nicholson v. Freeport Union Free School Dist.*, 74 A.D.3d 926, 902 N.Y.S.2d 192 (N.Y. App. Div. 2010).

♦   A Texas student with autism and other disorders regressed significantly in the summer before her ninth-grade year. Her IEP was revised, but her behavior and academic problems increased. She ran away from school and had sexual contact with fellow students in a lavatory. Her parents sought to place her at a residential school, and a hearing officer agreed with that decision. A federal court affirmed, awarding over $110,000 plus $36,000 in attorneys' fees. However, the Fifth Circuit reversed, noting that although the district had failed to offer a free appropriate public education, **the parents had not yet shown that the residential placement was necessary for educational (rather than medical or behavioral) reasons.** The court remanded the case for further proceedings. *Richardson Independent School Dist. v. Michael Z.*, 580 F.3d 286 (5th Cir. 2009).

♦   An Oregon student began having emotional problems in school, but performed well academically. He was later hospitalized for migraines and attempted suicide. His doctors recommended a residential placement. His parents sought his placement in an alternative school, but the district refused because it couldn't monitor him properly there. The parents then placed him in a residential school without giving proper notice to the district. When they sued for tuition reimbursement, a federal court and the Ninth Circuit ruled against them. **Ample evidence indicated that the placement was made for medical reasons** and that the parents did not provide proper notice. *Ashland School Dist. v. Parents of Student E.H.*, 587 F.3d 1175 (9th Cir. 2009).

♦   The parents of a New York student with disabilities sought to place her in a private treatment facility. The school district declined, asserting that the private therapeutic high school day placement in which she was enrolled satisfied the IDEA. The parents placed her in the residential facility and sought tuition reimbursement, but a due process hearing officer ruled for the district. A court reversed, finding the day program inadequate, but the Second Circuit reversed the lower court, noting that schools are not required to maximize student potential. **Generally, students must be regressing in day placements to be**

eligible for residential placement. Here, the student was progressing in her day placement. *M.H. v. Monroe-Woodbury Cent. School Dist.*, 296 Fed.Appx. 126 (2d Cir. 2008).

♦ A Colorado student with autism and mental retardation had numerous behavioral problems (including crying, screaming, tantrums and other resistance) at school. He was even worse at home. His school behavior incidents lasted up to 40 minutes a day. His parents sought a residential placement and requested tuition reimbursement. A federal court held they were entitled to it. Here, even though the hearing officer had improperly used a "self-sufficiency" standard, the district failed to offer an appropriate placement option, and the student was not receiving educational benefit from his IEP because of his behavior problems. However, the Tenth Circuit held that the parents were not entitled to tuition reimbursement. Here, **every evaluation of the student while he was in public schools determined that he was making some progress.** It was only away from school that his behavior was "unmanageable." And even though generalization of learned skills to home and other locations was critical for self-sufficiency and independence, the school district was not required to assure this goal. *Thompson R2-J School Dist. v. Luke P.*, 540 F.3d 1143 (10th Cir. 2008).

♦ After a family moved from New York to Florida, the Florida school district considered the New York draft IEP recommending a residential placement for the parents' son, who had serious emotional, behavioral and social problems. Ultimately, the district decided on a therapeutic day school placement. After a violent episode at home over the summer, the parents unilaterally placed the student at a residential health care facility, then hospitalized him. Later, they put him in a residential school. After an administrative law judge denied them tuition reimbursement, a federal court and the Eleventh Circuit agreed with that decision. Here, **the residential placement was not the least restrictive environment. Nor did the parents show that it was educationally necessary,** let alone appropriate. The student had not been hospitalized to address educational concerns. *L.G. v. School Board of Palm Beach County, Florida*, 255 Fed.Appx. 360 (11th Cir. 2007).

♦ The parents of a Maine student placed her in a private residential facility before the district could evaluate her. They then demanded a due process hearing and met with the district to consider her eligibility for IDEA services. The hearing was delayed while an independent evaluation was conducted. At an IEP meeting, the parents insisted on a therapeutic residential placement while the district asserted that a non-residential public school setting would be appropriate. The parents challenged the district's placement, claiming it failed to offer a finalized IEP. A federal court and the First Circuit ruled for the district, noting that **the IEP was never finalized because the parents disrupted the IEP process. Their fixation on a residential placement at district expense caused the breakdown of the IEP process.** *C.G. and B.S. v. Five Town Community School Dist.*, 513 F.3d 279 (1st Cir. 2008).

♦   A Washington student of average intelligence had severe learning disabilities affecting her ability to read and write. She failed to meet IEP objectives in writing and met only three of seven goals in reading during eighth and ninth grades. A neuropsychologist recommended placement in a residential facility, but the district determined she did not need it. After the parents unilaterally placed her in the residential school, they sought reimbursement. An administrative law judge ruled for the district, and the parents appealed. A federal court held that the IDEA Amendments of 1997 changed the purpose of the act from providing access to education (under *Rowley*), to addressing low expectations and working toward preparing students for self-sufficiency. The district's IEPs failed in that regard. Later, the court held **the district would have to pay for the student's twelfth-grade placement at the residential school as compensatory education**. *J.L. v. Mercer Island School Dist.*, No. C06-494MJP, 2007 WL 2253304 (W.D. Wash. 8/2/07).

♦   A Maryland student's psychologist believed the only acceptable placement for his emotional and educational needs was a therapeutic residential school. The parents argued for that at the IEP meeting, and the IEP team offered the name of a residential program available to some students, indicating that it would be up to the facility to determine if the student was eligible. At the end of the IEP meeting, the team offered a written IEP that recommended a private day school. The parents signed the IEP without objection. **The residential school later accepted their son, and they claimed the district had to pay for it.** The Fourth Circuit disagreed. Here, a school official who was present at the IEP meeting testified that the student did not need a residential placement for educational reasons, and that the parents did not object to the IEP calling for a day school placement. *Avjian v. Weast*, 242 Fed.Appx. 77 (4th Cir. 2007).

♦   Missouri parents rejected their son's fifth-grade IEP and placed him in a private school. He attended private schools until eighth grade, when he was expelled for bad behavior. They then sought services from the school district, which reevaluated him and proposed a program that would divide his time between a special high school program and a private facility, with counseling and therapy as well. The parents **insisted that only a residential placement was appropriate** and sent him to such a school. When they sued for tuition reimbursement, a federal court and the Eighth Circuit ruled against them. Here, the district's proposed program offered the student a unique combination of services he had not previously experienced that satisfied the IDEA. *T.F. v. Special School Dist. of St. Louis County*, 449 F.3d 816 (8th Cir. 2006).

♦   A North Carolina student with Fragile X syndrome spent two years in a Maryland facility for students with developmental disabilities. When state mental health officials identified an in-state residential program known as Partners in Autism Treatment and Habilitation (PATH) that they believed was appropriate for him, they notified school district staff and encouraged them to investigate the program. Two staff members toured PATH facilities and, at an IEP meeting, the PATH placement was adopted by the IEP team over the parents' objections. After a due process hearing, the case reached a federal court, which found that the student's IEP could be successfully implemented in the PATH program. The parents were not denied adequate participation in the IEP process, and **state officials did not unilaterally impose the PATH placement on the IEP team**. *Cone v. Randolph County Schools*, 302 F.Supp.2d 500 (M.D.N.C. 2004).

◆ An autistic student was placed by his Florida school district in a day program for exceptional children. For three years, he attended an autism program with family counseling and in-home behavioral counseling under IEPs. His parents then insisted that he attend a particular residential school, while school representatives argued that residential placement was unnecessary. A due process hearing officer found the IEP for that year inappropriate because it failed to provide the student a FAPE. However, the officer disagreed with the parents' assertion that a residential placement was necessary. A federal court held the IEP appropriate. A residential placement was not required. The parents appealed to the Eleventh Circuit, which affirmed. **When the student arrived at the school, he was largely uncontrollable and unable to establish relationships. Under his current IEP, he progressed** in 26 out of 27 areas and learned skills that could be displayed across settings. Since the student benefited from his district placement, the residential placement sought by the parents was not warranted. *Devine v. Indian River County School Board*, 249 F.3d 1289 (11th Cir. 2001).

◆ A Connecticut student had serious social and emotional problems, including hyperactivity, inability to interact with others and lack of self-confidence. Although she was in the average intelligence range, she failed to progress academically and met only four of 32 objectives stated in her IEP. A public school evaluator recommended placement in a residential facility, but the board refused the recommendation. However, the placement was arranged through the state Department of Child and Youth Services. The student attended the residential facility, where her academic and social skills improved. The school board maintained that the placement was nonacademic and was made necessary by the student's mother's manipulative behavior. The mother sought complete funding for the placement, and the Second Circuit observed that, **notwithstanding the nonacademic reasons for the residential placement, the student had failed to progress in her public school placement** and the school board had failed to take action to remedy her serious academic regression. The residential placement was necessary to enable the student to obtain academic benefits, and it was appropriate for the board to fund the noneducational portion of the residential placement despite the other factors that were present in the decision to place her there. *Mrs. B. v. Milford Board of Educ.*, 103 F.3d 1114 (2d Cir. 1997).

2. Behavioral/Emotional Problems

◆ An adopted student in Maryland with learning disabilities and emotional disturbance exhibited suicidal tendencies and clinical depression. Her IEP team placed her in a private special education day school. She later self-mutilated and attempted suicide. Her parents placed her in a residential school even though a school psychologist found that she should be placed in a therapeutic school for students with serious emotional issues. When the parents sought reimbursement, a federal court and the Fourth Circuit ruled against them, noting that **the placement was based on the parents' desire to ensure that she did not harm herself.** It was not made for educational reasons and was not the least restrictive environment. She made progress in the day school when her mental health issues stabilized. *Shaw v. Weast*, 364 Fed.Appx. 47 (4th Cir. 2010).

◆   A Pennsylvania student with worsening psychological problems attended private schools at the district's expense. After she was kicked out of a residential school in New Mexico, her parents placed her in a psychiatric residential treatment center that provided no educational services. Her parents sought reimbursement for the costs. The case reached the Third Circuit, which held that **the district did not have to pay for the treatment center placement because her admission there was necessitated by her acute medical condition.** And her medical and educational needs could be separated. Further, once the student's condition stabilized, the district began providing services again. *Mary v. School Dist. of Philadelphia*, 575 F.3d 235 (3d Cir. 2009).

◆   New York school districts sent hundreds of students to a Massachusetts private residential facility that used aversive interventions (skin shocks, restraints and contingent food programs) for behavior modification. In 2006, the New York State Department of Education issued an emergency regulation generally banning the use of aversive interventions. **A group of parents then sued to continue the use of aversive interventions.** They claimed that the regulation violated federal law. A New York federal court issued a preliminary injunction, but the Second Circuit reversed, noting that the lower court should have first determined whether irreparable harm would occur to the parents if the injunction was not issued. The lower court would also have to determine the likelihood of either party prevailing on the merits. *Alleyne v. New York State Educ. Dep't*, 516 F.3d 96 (2d Cir. 2008).

◆   The mother of a Minnesota student with emotional behavioral disorders sought a residential placement for her son. A hearing officer found the student's behavioral issues were separate and distinct from his educational needs, making a residential placement not warranted. She then **claimed that school and county officials conspired to deprive her son of a residential placement** by repeatedly causing him to be arrested, detained and charged in juvenile court. A federal court ruled in favor of the district. Here, the student had made progress towards his IEP goals while he was in school, and school officials did not refer him to the juvenile court system in order to keep him from receiving a residential placement. *J.E.B. v. Independent School Dist. No. 720*, No. 06-3017 (JRT/FLN), 2007 WL 1544611 (D. Minn. 5/24/07).

◆   A New York principal initiated a "person in need of supervision" (PINS) proceeding for a student with disabilities who had excessive absenteeism and who had admitted to using marijuana at school. The principal did not seek a change in the student's educational placement. The family court granted the petition for a PINS placement outside the home, and the Supreme Court, Appellate Division, affirmed that decision. The IDEA did not deprive the family court of jurisdiction, and **the student's proper placement was outside the home due to his two suicide attempts while in his mother's care.** *In re Charles U.*, 837 N.Y.S.2d 356 (N.Y. App. Div. 2007).

♦   A Texas student with disabilities and behavioral disorders passed his tenth-grade mainstream program and the first grading period of eleventh grade despite skipping classes and using profanity. His behavior problems at home were even worse. After the school's admission, review and dismissal committee proposed changes to his IEP, including to his behavior intervention plan, his parents rejected the changes and placed him in a residential placement. A hearing officer found that to be appropriate, but a Texas federal court disagreed. **The hearing officer had changed the student's placement from mainstream to residential without considering the spectrum of options between the two opposites.** This violated the continuum of services requirement of the IDEA. The district's intermediate proposals were the least restrictive option. *Corpus Christi Independent School Dist. v. Christopher N.*, No. C.A. C-04-318, 2006 WL 870739 (S.D. Tex. 3/31/06).

♦   A student had behavioral problems at home and also missed 12 school days. However, she completed the ninth grade with a 3.68 average. The next year her parents enrolled her in a private school. She continued to "go into rages" against her parents and missed 20 days of school, but completed the tenth grade with a B average. After she was arrested for hitting her father, her parents sought a residential placement. The district recommended a day placement, which the parents rejected. When they sought tuition reimbursement for a residential placement, an administrative law judge ruled in their favor, but a federal court reversed. **The district did not have to fund a residential placement for medical, social or emotional problems that could be segregated from the learning process.** *West-Windsor Plainsboro Regional School Dist. Board of Educ. v. J.S.*, No. CIV 04-3459 (SRC), 2005 WL 2897494 (D.N.J. 10/31/05).

♦   A Wisconsin student had emotional and behavioral crises at home and school. After he attempted suicide, his parents sought to place him in a residential school in Illinois that specialized in adolescents with emotional and behavioral issues. The IEP team determined that a residential placement was not necessary. The district agreed to fund the educational component of the placement at the Illinois school ($23,000 annually) but not the residential and therapeutic components ($70,000 annually). A federal court agreed with the administrative ruling that **the district did not have to fund the residential placement.** The parents' desire for the residential setting was motivated by the student's inability to control himself, not educational necessity. *Doe v. Shorewood School Dist.*, No. 03 C 743, 2005 WL 2387717 (E.D. Wis. 9/28/05).

♦   A Missouri student with multiple disabilities was a "severely handicapped child" under state law. She attended local public schools until her behavior deteriorated significantly, at which time her parents placed her in a Massachusetts residential facility. The district agreed that a residential placement was necessary. It referred her to the Missouri School for the Blind (MSB), which claimed to have no appropriate program for her. State education department officials pushed for the student's placement at the MSB, but a due process hearing panel held that the MSB could not provide a free appropriate public education (FAPE). The case reached the Eighth Circuit Court of Appeals, which ruled that **the state had to fund the placement at the Massachusetts facility because the district had notified the state that it could not adequately educate the student.** The burden was on the state to provide FAPE. The state had to pay the residential school's tuition, less the district's local tax effort. *Missouri Dep't of Elementary and Secondary Educ. v. Springfield R-12 School Dist.*, 358 F.3d 992 (8th Cir. 2004).

♦   A New Jersey student with autism had increasing behavior problems during his time in a day program for students with special needs. His parents sought to place him in a residential placement to control his behavior problems and reverse his academic regression. After the district denied the request, a due process hearing officer heard testimony from a witness with expertise in the education of students with autism. The expert stated that **the student required a 24-hour behavior modification program** or else he would regress. The hearing officer then ordered the district to place the student in a residential facility, and a federal court upheld that decision. The school district was unable to counter the evidence in favor of a residential placement. *S.C. v. Deptford Township Board of Educ.*, 248 F.Supp.2d 368 (D.N.J. 2003).

♦   By the fifth grade, a child with superior intellectual ability and ADHD was placed in a special education program for emotionally disturbed children and was hospitalized twice because of concerns about him harming himself or others. He was diagnosed with schizo-affective, oppositional defiant and personality disorders, and he eventually became uncontrollable at home. A Wisconsin court adjudicated him a child in need of protection and placed him in a residential treatment facility. The court ordered his father to contribute to his support under a state law. The school district in which the residential facility was located convened an IEP meeting and recommended implementation at the facility. The father asked for relief from the child-support order, arguing that he was exempt from the cost of the placement under the IDEA. The court disagreed, ruling that the child had been placed at the residential facility for mental health reasons rather than educational reasons.

The Wisconsin Supreme Court held that the case could be resolved by determining whether the residential placement was for educational purposes under the IDEA. A residential placement that is required as "a necessary predicate for learning" is covered by the IDEA. By contrast, a placement that is in response to medical, social or emotional problems is not considered an educational placement under the IDEA. The child was placed in the residential facility under a child-protection order that was initiated by the father and based on the child's mental illness. The placement came in response to his psychiatric and emotional problems and was separate from his special education needs. The child had been hospitalized for months prior to the initiation of the child-protection proceeding and he was recommended for a residential placement by hospital staff. **The IEP prepared after his placement in the residential facility did not demonstrate that a residential placement was necessary to meet his educational needs.** The court affirmed the order requiring continuation of the child-support obligation. *State of Wisconsin v. Randall H.*, 257 Wis.2d 57, 653 N.W.2d 503 (Wis. 2002).

♦   A Minnesota student with emotional and behavioral disorders repeatedly exhibited inappropriate behavior and engaged in truancy. In non-school settings she used alcohol and illegal drugs, was promiscuous, ran away, and was hospitalized three times. Her mother sought a residential placement, even locating an Idaho facility, but the district only offered to pay the educational portion of the placement. An independent evaluator diagnosed the student with a conduct disorder and strongly recommended placement in a secure facility. The case reached the Eighth Circuit Court of Appeals, which stated that if a student cannot reasonably be expected to benefit from instruction in a less restrictive setting, residential placement is educationally necessary, and the state must then pay for it. Here, the court found that the student was entitled to a residential placement based on evidence that her behavior and attendance problems were a result of her emotional disturbance. **Because the evidence did not indicate that the student's behavior problems could be separated from the learning process, she would not receive educational benefit until her behavior was addressed.** *Independent School Dist. No. 284 v. A.C.*, 258 F.3d 769 (8th Cir. 2001).

♦   A 17-year-old student with autism had a history of temper tantrums at home. He attended a residential school in Boston for nine years, demonstrating some progress. His parents sought approval for the Boston placement, or placement in a comparable residential facility, from the Puerto Rico Department of Education. They asserted that the department was required to pay for a residential placement as part of its obligation to provide the student with a FAPE. The department proposed an IEP that did not call for a residential placement. An administrative hearing officer held that the proposed IEP was sufficient under the IDEA, but ordered the department to include additional services. A federal court affirmed the IEP but ordered the inclusion of some services intended to facilitate his transition into Puerto Rico schools.

The parents appealed to the First Circuit, arguing that the district court did not take into account the student's past behavioral difficulties at home by allowing a nonresidential placement. The court observed that there are no clear lines between a student's educational needs and social problems at home. **The IDEA does not require a residential program to remedy a poor home setting.** Contrary to the parents' argument, the district court had given due consideration to the student's problems at home and ordered the department to change his IEP to address them. There was support for the district court's finding that the student's home behavior could be effectively managed through the amended IEP. The court affirmed the judgment for the department. *Gonzalez v. Puerto Rico Dep't of Educ.*, 254 F.3d 350 (1st Cir. 2001).

II. CONTAGIOUS DISEASES AND PLACEMENT

Courts have held that students with hepatitis, HIV and AIDS may have disabilities as defined by law and can be admitted to public school programs if their enrollment is not a health threat to the school community. This result follows from the case of School Board of Nassau County v. Arline, *480 U.S. 273, 107 S.Ct. 1123, 94 L.Ed.2d 307 (1987), see Chapter Seven, Section II. In that case, the U.S. Supreme Court ruled that persons with contagious diseases such as tuberculosis may be considered disabled under Section 504 of the Rehabilitation Act if they are otherwise qualified to participate in a program and able to perform essential job duties. For more Rehabilitation Act cases, see Chapter Nine.*

♦   A federal court held that **three brothers who were hemophiliacs and who had tested positive for HIV could not be excluded from public school classes**. The school district contended that although no actual physical harm had been done to their classmates or teachers due to the brothers' class attendance, there was the possibility of future harm. This future harm allegedly included transmission of the HIV virus in the classroom setting and liability of the school district for allowing the brothers to attend classes. The court also cited the Supreme Court's decision in *School Board of Nassau County v. Arline*, where the Supreme Court held that a person with tuberculosis could be considered an individual with a disability under Section 504 of the Rehabilitation Act. Because Section 504 prohibits recipients of federal funds from discriminating against the disabled solely because of their disability, the school district could not exclude the brothers from class. *Ray v. School Dist. of Desoto County*, 666 F.Supp. 1524 (N.D. Fla. 1987).

♦   A girl born with respiratory distress received 39 blood transfusions during the first four months of her life and was diagnosed with AIDS at the age of three. She was classified as trainable mentally handicapped (TMH). By age six she had a mental age of between one-and-a-half years in expressive language and three-and-a-half years in perceptual motor skills. She was incontinent and was observed by doctors to drool and suck her thumb continually. In the past, she had developed skin lesions. When these occurred, her mother kept her home. When the girl approached school age her mother attempted to enroll her in a Florida public school. The school district operated two schools which each maintained classes for TMH children. However, the school district excluded her from public schools based upon her incontinence. It recommended that she be educated in its homebound program. The girl appealed to the Florida State Division of Administrative Hearings. The school district prevailed after an evidentiary hearing. The administrative decision was appealed to a federal court, which held in favor of the school district. *Martinez v. School Board of Hillsborough County, Florida*, 675 F.Supp. 1574 (M.D. Fla. 1987).

In 1988, the U.S. District Court for the Middle District of Florida held a full trial on the matter of placing the student. The court allowed the student to join the school's TMH classroom with heavy restrictions. It noted that the student was still incontinent and sucked her thumb and fingers continuously. Because there was a remote theoretical possibility of transmitting AIDS through bodily secretions, the court again ruled that the student could not be mainstreamed. It ordered the school district to construct a separate room within the TMH classroom. The school board was also required to provide a full-time aide to remain with the student in her room at all times. Other children in the TMH class who had written parental waivers could be allowed into the separate room during class time. *Martinez v. School Board of Hillsborough County, Florida,* 692 F.Supp. 1293 (M.D. Fla. 1988).

The U.S. Court of Appeals, Eleventh Circuit, first determined that the student was entitled to a free appropriate education under the IDEA. She suffered from two disabilities under Section 504 as she was both mentally retarded and had AIDS. **The appropriate educational placement was the regular TMH classroom.** The district court's finding of a "remote theoretical possibility" of transmission of AIDS was insufficient to exclude her from the TMH classroom. Because the district court had failed to make findings concerning the overall risk of transmitting AIDS through bodily secretions, it had failed to determine whether the student was "otherwise qualified" to attend the TMH classroom. If the court found on remand that the student was not "otherwise qualified" to attend the TMH classroom, it was bound to consider whether reasonable accommodations would qualify her. The lower court would also be required to hear evidence concerning the stigmatizing effect of segregating the student in a separate room. The appeals court vacated the district court's decision and remanded the case.

On remand, the court noted that the American Academy of Pediatrics had eliminated its recommendation that students who could not control their bodily secretions be placed in more restrictive environments. It also noted that the Centers for Disease Control had stated that the risk of transmission of HIV and HBV from feces, nasal secretion, saliva, sweat, tears, urine and vomit was extremely low or nonexistent unless visible blood was actually present. The student's behavior had changed since the initial consideration of the case. She sucked her fingers less often and was becoming toilet trained. The court ruled that she could join the TMH classroom. It also required the school board to provide an educational program for parents whose children would be in the classroom. *Martinez v. School Board of Hillsborough County, Florida,* 711 F.Supp. 1066 (M.D. Fla. 1989). In 1989, Eliana Martinez died at the age of six from complications attributable to AIDS.

◆ A 12-year-old student contracted the AIDS virus through blood transfusions when he underwent open-heart surgery as a child. When the board of education of an Illinois school district learned that he had the AIDS virus, it excluded him from attending the school's regular education classes and extracurricular activities. The student sued in federal court, seeking an order to allow him to return to his regular classes as a full-time student. In order to prevail under Section 504 of the Rehabilitation Act, he had to be an individual with a disability and "otherwise qualified" to attend school.

The court found that the student would likely be considered an individual with a disability. As an AIDS victim, he was regarded as being impaired and this impairment substantially limited one or more of the student's major life activities. The court also deemed the student "otherwise qualified" to attend school. Medical authorities found no significant risk of transmission of AIDS in the classroom. The student had been harmed by loss of self-esteem, which could be partially alleviated by returning him to the classroom. Any injury that might occur by issuing the order was insufficient to outweigh the harm to the student. In addition, it would not be a disservice to the public interest to allow the student to return to school, since the threat of the student transmitting the AIDS virus to others was minimal. **The court required carefully drawn procedures to ensure that any potential risk of harm to the student's classmates and teachers was eliminated.** *Doe v. Dolton Elementary School Dist. No. 148*, 694 F.Supp. 440 (N.D. Ill. 1988).

◆   A California school district learned that an 11-year-old hemophilic student had been exposed to the AIDS virus. The district instructed the student not to enroll in school and required him to study at home until it formulated an AIDS policy. The student's guardian was unhappy with the home tutor program and repeatedly requested to have the student returned to regular classes. On each occasion the district told her that the student could not attend school until an AIDS policy had been formulated. The guardian filed a complaint in a California trial court, seeking both a preliminary and a permanent order allowing the student to return to school. The guardian also sought attorneys' fees. The court issued an injunction ordering the school district to allow the student to attend a regular school within its district, subject to its evaluation of his medical condition every six months. Shortly after the court's order, the district's policy on AIDS and infectious diseases became effective. The matter then proceeded to trial, where the court found for the guardian. An order was granted, which required the school district to allow the student to attend a regular school, subject to periodic medical examinations. The guardian was also awarded attorneys' fees. The school district appealed to the California Court of Appeal, Fourth District. On appeal, the school district argued that the trial court abused its discretion in issuing a permanent order. It insisted that a permanent order was not necessary because the student had been attending school. Alternatively, it contended that even if the order was proper, attorneys' fees were not warranted. The court ruled that **the district had unreasonably delayed the formulation of its AIDS policy for more than five months.** The permanent order was proper even though the school district had decided to allow the student to attend class. The record suggested that the student was allowed to attend solely because it was mandated by the court order. Also, attorneys' fees were appropriately awarded, as the lawsuit was instrumental in motivating the school district to address the issue of AIDS and to effectuate an appropriate policy without impairing the rights of students. *Phipps v. Saddleback Valley Unified School Dist.*, 251 Cal.Rptr. 720 (Cal. Ct. App. 1988).

◆   The Appellate Court of Illinois considered the appropriate educational placement of a trainable mentally disabled child with Down syndrome who was also a carrier of Hepatitis B. Local school officials contended that because of the risk of the child transmitting the disease to other children, the appropriate placement for her was in a "homebound" setting. The child maintained that the risk of transmission of the disease was remote and therefore not a sufficient reason to exclude her from classroom participation. The Appellate Court of Illinois noted **a major goal of the educational process is the socialization process that takes place in the regular classroom, with the resulting capacity to interact in a social way with one's peers**. The superintendent of education recognized this and determined that the risk of transmission of the disease did not outweigh the injury to the child if she remained isolated from her peers. The court concluded that the child could be integrated into the classroom if appropriate sanitary procedures were followed. *Community High School Dist. 155 v. Denz*, 463 N.E.2d 998 (Ill. App. Ct. 1984).

III. CHANGES IN PLACEMENT

The IDEA requires school districts to provide parents with prior written notice of any proposed change in the educational placement of a child with a disability. See 20 U.S.C. § 1415(b)(1)(C). This notice requirement also applies when an LEA proposes graduating a student with a disability and awarding the student a regular education diploma. See 34 C.F.R. § 300.122(a)(3)(iii). A hearing must be granted to parents wishing to contest a change in placement. Under the IDEA "stay-put" provision, school officials are prevented from removing a child from a current placement over the parents' objection pending completion of review proceedings.

◆   The Texas Education Agency conducted a hearing to discuss suspending school operations at a charter school that served special education students. After the agency voted to suspend school operations, notices were sent to parents advising them of the closure and providing lists of other schools. The parents of 14 students sued the agency, alleging a violation of the IDEA because closing the school amounted to a change in placement. The agency countered that **any transfer of students was only a change in location**, and a federal court agreed that closing the charter school was not grounds for a temporary order preventing it. The parents didn't identify any specific elements that would be modified or eliminated from their children's IEPs as a result of the school's closure. *Comb v. Benji's Special Educ. Academy*, 745 F.Supp.2d 755 (S.D. Tex. 2010).

◆   A Hawaii student with mental retardation and a heart condition reported feeling unsafe while at his home school. The state Department of Education (DOE) held an IEP meeting to discuss a placement for the 2004-05 school year at a location where the student would feel safe. The DOE offered to place him at a large public school building, but the parents rejected the placement as being intimidating to the student. They placed the student in a home program and a private academy, then sought reimbursement. A hearing officer ruled against them, but a federal court reversed. **Although a change in schools is not necessarily a change in placement, it was a change in placement here.** Placing him in the larger school could be emotionally, educationally and psychologically detrimental. No one at the IEP meeting, apart from the parents, had information about the student. It was apparent that the DOE had pre-determined the physical location of the student's placement and thus violated the IDEA. The parents were entitled to reimbursement. *Melodee H. v. Dep't of Educ., State of Hawaii*, 2008 WL 2051757 (D. Haw. 5/13/08).

A. Notice and Hearing

♦   The parents of a 20-year-old student with Down syndrome sought to have him participate in the Virginia Alternate Assessment Program (VAAP) (used to assess students who have traditionally been exempt from other tests). They also requested sign-language services, but the IEP team was unable to agree on an IEP for the school year. At a due process hearing, the parents learned that their son had been promoted to grade 12, making him ineligible for the VAAP. The hearing officer held that the promotion violated the IDEA, and the Fourth Circuit ultimately agreed. **Promoting the student without notifying his parents was just an attempt to avoid placing him in the VAAP.** *County School Board of York County v. A.L.*, 194 Fed.Appx. 173 (4th Cir. 2006).

♦   An Ohio school district made addendums to a student's IEP in three consecutive months during his sixth-grade year. The third addendum sought to phase out a point reward system used to reinforce his behavior. The addendum also stated if the target behavior was not maintained, the original IEP would be reinstated. The parents did not agree to the third addendum at an IEP meeting. They did not learn that the addendum was being implemented until the district sent them a certified letter several days after the meeting. The parents challenged the addendum to the IEP, asserting that it fundamentally changed their child's placement. The case reached the Ohio Court of Appeals, which noted that the addendum was neither a fundamental change in nor an elimination of a basic element of the IEP. The original IEP called for a behavior plan that would eventually thin the reinforcers. **Not every change to an IEP constitutes a change in placement.** *Stancourt v. Worthington City School Dist.*, No. 07AP-835, 2008 WL 4151623 (Ohio Ct. App. 9/9/08).

♦   A Georgia student attended regular education classes through the sixth grade. He then attended a private school, and a psychologist diagnosed him with a nonverbal learning disability. Weeks before the end of his eighth-grade year, his mother informed the district that she wanted to enroll him in public school. The district formulated an interim IEP for the ninth grade, and the student began attending the public school. However, he remained there for only five days. His mother then sent a letter rejecting the IEP and stating that she intended to enroll her son in the private school. When the parents sought tuition reimbursement, an administrative law judge held for the school district, finding the parents did not provide sufficient notice to the district, and that they deprived it of a reasonable chance to accommodate the student by yanking him out of school after only five days. A federal court granted summary judgment to the district, finding the parents' conduct unreasonable as a matter of law. However, the Eleventh Circuit vacated and remanded the case. It noted that the lower court should have considered whether the district complied with IDEA procedures and provided a FAPE in addition to examining the parents' actions. Even though **the parents' failure to provide the requisite 10-day rejection notice might allow the denial of their reimbursement claim**, a trial was required. *Loren F. v. Atlanta Independent School System*, 349 F.3d 1309 (11th Cir. 2003).

♦ After an Illinois school district completed an IEP for a student with Down syndrome, the parents elected to place their son in a parochial school. Before the next school year, the district again proposed a public school placement. The parents objected, again placing the student in the parochial school. The due process hearing officer ruled that the public school placement was appropriate under the IDEA. However, when the student was supposed to start at the public school, there was a miscommunication, and the district failed to arrange for bus transportation on the first day of school. It also failed to register him in the public school and failed to notify a teacher that the student would be starting at the public school that day. In the lawsuit that followed, a federal court ruled that **the confusion surrounding the student's first day at the public school did not violate the IDEA**. *Peter G. v. Chicago Public School Dist. No. 299 Board of Educ.*, No. 02 C 0687, 2003 WL 121932 (N.D. Ill. 1/13/03).

♦ A New Jersey school district placed a student at a private school under an IEP. The private school contractually agreed to comply with the IDEA as well as state special education law. Under the contract for educational services, the school or district could terminate the arrangement upon 15 days' written notice. When the student did not get along with a new teacher, a school executive terminated his placement two days after giving oral notice. After the student missed 17 days of instruction, the district found him a new private school placement. His parents requested a due process hearing. The hearing officer held that the private school did not provide the requisite 15-day notice, but she also held that she had no jurisdiction over the private school. She further held that the student was not entitled to compensatory education because he found a new placement after just 17 days. A federal court found that the hearing officer erred in letting the private school off the hook. It had agreed to be bound by the IDEA and state special education law, and it failed to provide the requisite notice when terminating the student's placement. The district was also liable for compensatory education because it failed to convene an IEP meeting without delay when it learned of the placement termination. Plus, the district's obligations under the IDEA were not delegable. **The district and private school had to share liability for the improper termination of the student's placement.** *P.N. and G.N. v. Greco*, 282 F.Supp.2d 221 (D.N.J. 2003).

♦ After a student with an emotional disturbance was tardy 20 times during one year and was disruptive in class, a truancy petition was filed. The family court denied a motion by the student's guardian to dismiss the petition on the grounds that it called for a change in placement in violation of the stay-put provision. The court placed the student under county supervision. The New York Supreme Court, Appellate Division, agreed that the filing of the truancy petition triggered the stay-put provision and that the county failed to exhaust required IDEA and state administrative remedies prior to filing the petition.

School officials appealed to the New York Court of Appeals, which observed that the stay-put provision requires that parents or guardians of students with disabilities receive prior written notice whenever an education agency proposes to initiate or change the identification, evaluation or educational placement of a student. The key phrase was "change in educational placement," which is not defined in the IDEA. **The determination of whether a change in placement has occurred must be made on a case-by-case basis under which a number of factors are considered:** whether the student's IEP has been revised, whether the student will be educated with non-disabled students to the same extent as before, whether the student will have the same participation opportunities in nonacademic and extracurricular programs, and whether the new placement option is the same option on the continuum of alternative placements. Here, school officials were not seeking a change of placement by filing the petition. To the contrary, they sought to enforce his program through probation. Under probation, the student attended the same school, same classes and received the same type and level of services. *In re Beau II,* 715 N.Y.S.2d 686 (N.Y. 2000).

♦ A Maine student with a learning disability received special education from his local public school. In third grade, his parents requested his removal from the school based on their perception that the school administration, teachers, students, and a bus driver were harassing him. The school agreed to provide tutoring in the superintendent's office for the rest of the school year, but the IEP developed for grade four called for continuing placement at the school. The parents instead decided to provide a home-school curriculum and then sought placement in a neighboring school system 30 miles away. The district prepared a new IEP calling for special education and mainstreaming at the local school, but a due process hearing officer determined that hostility between the family and school staff prevented a successful education program at the student's former school. He ordered the implementation of the student's IEP at a different school. A federal court held that the IDEA allowed consideration of parental objections to a proposed IEP. The hearing officer had properly focused on the student's inability to gain educational benefits from his placement and recognized that **his anxiety prevented a successful placement at his former school**. The court affirmed the hearing officer's decision. *Greenbush School Committee v. Mr. and Mrs. K.,* 949 F.Supp. 934 (D. Me. 1996).

B. Stay-Put Provision

1. Settlements and Administrative Rulings

♦ A New Jersey student with autism endured bullying and ridicule until a new IEP allowed his placement in an accredited K-12 Christian School. However, after he entered high school, a state official notified the district and his parents that his placement violated the state's Naples Act because they did not get approval from the state education department and the school was not nonsectarian. The district later proposed a public school placement. The parents appealed, seeking to keep their son at the Christian school under the stay-put placement. A federal court allowed the student to stay at the school during the litigation. **Even though the placement had been mistakenly made, it was the student's stay-put placement under the IDEA.** *R.S. v. Somerville Board of Educ.*, No. 10-4215 (MLC), 2011 WL 32521 (D.N.J. 1/5/11).

♦ After a Minnesota student spent time in juvenile and adult detention facilities, his mother claimed IDEA violations and requested a due process hearing. She reached a settlement with the school district, agreeing on a level of services that did not continue the provisions of his stay-put IEP and releasing any claims arising out of his education at the time of the agreement. Before being transferred to a state prison, the student complained that his district failed to provide a FAPE during his incarceration. A federal court eventually held that **the settlement agreement superseded the stay-put IEP** and that the student's mother's waiver was valid under the IDEA. *D.B.A. v. Special School Dist. No. 1, Minneapolis, Minnesota*, No. 10-1045 (PAM/FLN), 2010 WL 5300946 (D. Minn. 12/20/10).

♦ An 18-year-old Georgia student requested a due process hearing, alleging that he had been misdiagnosed as mentally retarded (rather than dyslexic) since the third grade. An administrative law judge (ALJ) found that the district had misdiagnosed the student and made no effort to reevaluate him for five years. The ALJ offered the student two options for continuing his education at the district's expense. An appeal was taken to a federal court, with the district seeking to prevent enforcement of the ALJ's order. The court noted that the ALJ's decision changed the student's placement. **The option the student selected became his new stay-put placement. It did not matter that he did not request that option prior to the due process hearing.** The ALJ's order would be enforced. *Draper v. Atlanta Independent School System*, No. Civ.A. 1:06 CV487-MHS, 2006 WL 1734257 (N.D. Ga. 6/20/06).

♦ The parents of an autistic or developmentally delayed North Carolina student challenged their district's IEP, which did not contain an offer of ABA therapy. They contested two consecutive IEPs and sought funding for the cost of home-based programming. A hearing officer found the earlier IEP violated the IDEA, but a state review officer reversed, finding both IEPs valid. When the parents claimed that they were entitled to the cost of the home-based programming under the IDEA's stay-put provision, a federal court disagreed. It noted that under North Carolina's two-tiered system (hearing officer, then review officer), **a hearing officer's decision did not amount to an agreement by the parties as to the child's stay-put placement**. It was the review officer's decision that mattered. *Wittenburg v. Winston-Salem/Forsyth County Board of Educ.*, 2006 WL 1932672, 2006 WL 2568937 (M.D.N.C. 7/11/06, 9/1/06).

♦ A due process hearing officer ruled that an Alabama school board violated an autistic student's right to a free appropriate public education by offering him an improper IEP for two years. It also failed to conduct a functional behavior assessment and an appropriate behavior intervention plan. The school board appealed, then sought to invoke the stay-put provision to block the hearing officer's order to develop a behavior modification plan within 30 days. An

Alabama federal court held that **the school board could not use the stay-put provision to appeal a ruling favorable to a student**. Hearing officer decisions are deemed to be an agreement between the parties as to the student's placement. *Escambia County Board of Educ. v. Benton,* 358 F.Supp.2d 1112 (S.D. Ala. 2005).

♦   A student with a learning disability attended public schools in New York for two years until his parents became dissatisfied with his progress. They placed him in a private, unapproved school and commenced due process proceedings against the district, seeking tuition reimbursement. The district conceded it failed to appropriately place the student, and the hearing officer ordered the district to reimburse the parents for two years at the private school. A state review officer upheld that determination. When the district recommended returning the student to public school, the parents objected, claiming that **the private school was the student's current placement under the stay-put provision**. A federal court and the Second Circuit agreed, holding that the district had to pay the private school tuition until the parties reached a new placement agreement. The administrative decision constituted an agreement between the parties to maintain the student's private school placement for purposes of the stay-put provision. The district then brought an action in state court, seeking reimbursement from the state education department because of the year its review officer took to decide the case. The New York Supreme Court, Appellate Division, ruled against the district. It was not entitled to reimbursement from the state. *Pawling Cent. School Dist. v. New York State Educ. Dep't,* 771 N.Y.S.2d 572 (N.Y. App. Div. 2004).

♦   A Connecticut school district classified a student as developmentally delayed and placed him in an integrated public preschool program. His parents obtained an independent evaluation diagnosing the student with an autistic spectrum disorder. They initiated due process proceedings, and a hearing officer required the district to: 1) change the student's classification from other health impaired to autism, and 2) reimburse the parents for in-home therapy while continuing to provide or fund additional ongoing therapy at school. The school board sued to reverse the order and the parents sued to enforce it. A federal court ruled that the hearing officer's decision had to be treated as an agreement between the district and the parents under the stay-put provision. Thus, **the hearing officer's order represented the child's current educational placement**, and the district had to comply with the order until a trial or other court order. *Greenwich Board of Educ. v. Torok,* No. Civ. A. 3:03-CV1407JCH, 2003 WL 22429016 (D. Conn. 10/22/03).

♦   An educational consultant reviewed a New York student's IEP and helped his parents prepare for meetings of his committee on special education. She eventually recommended that the student be placed in a private school in Connecticut. The parents unilaterally made the placement and then initiated due process proceedings. An independent hearing officer ruled that the district denied the student a free appropriate public education and upheld the private school placement. A state review officer largely upheld that decision but reversed the award of speech therapy costs. The district then prepared an IEP for the following year, which the parents rejected. They re-enrolled the student in the private school, and the district appealed. A federal court held that **the private school was the student's current educational placement**, and the Second Circuit affirmed. It noted that an administrative order based on a finding of inadequacy of an IEP is a "change in the child's current educational placement," justifying an order requiring the district to pay the private school tuition. The district had to reimburse the parents until there was a change in the student's placement pursuant to the IDEA. *Murphy v. Arlington Cent. School Dist. Board of Educ.*, 297 F.3d 195 (2d Cir. 2002).

2. Transfers and Grade Changes

◆ An Illinois student with Down syndrome received co-teaching services in middle school, but his high school district asserted that it could not provide such services. It instead offered to increase the observation time for the student's special education teacher during his general education classes. The parents rejected the IEP and sought due process, where the hearing officer upheld the district's IEP and ruled that the IEP satisfied the IDEA's stay-put requirement. A federal court revised the student's IEP, but the Seventh Circuit ruled that it had improperly done so. The district had not been informed that the court planned to address the correctness of the IEP. Also, the stay-put issue was complicated by the student's transition to high school, so the court had to consider that there might not be a status quo. **The district had to provide services that approximated the student's old IEP as closely as possible.** And the old IEP did not specify co-teaching. The case returned to the district court, which noted that the parties had continued to work together and that the student was in his last semester of school before graduating. As a result, the parents could no longer use the stay-put provision to compel an academic approach. Transition services still needed to be provided, and compensatory education might be available. *John M. v. Board of Educ. of Evanston Township High School Dist. 202*, No. 05 C 6720, 2009 WL 691276 (N.D. Ill. 3/16/09).

◆ The parents of an Illinois eighth-grader placed him in a private school and sought funding from their school district, claiming that the district could not provide services to address the student's severe dyslexia. The district agreed to fund the placement for nine weeks until the student turned 15 and became the high school district's responsibility. However, when the student turned 15, the high school district did not authorize the private school placement. The parents invoked the stay-put provision to keep the student at the private school and the Seventh Circuit Court of Appeals upheld that temporary placement. **The shift to the high school district did not affect the stay-put provision.** *Casey K. v. St. Anne Community High School Dist. No. 302*, 400 F.3d 508 (7th Cir. 2005).

◆ A California student attending a regular education program in kindergarten received 120 minutes of daily service with a behavioral health specialist (BHS) outside his classroom. Near the end of the school year, his parents disputed his educational program. Before the case reached a due process hearing officer, the student advanced to first grade. A district employee wrote a letter to the parents proposing the elimination of daily BHS services now that the school day was full time instead of half time. The parents objected, and the case reached a federal court. The court held that the parents never agreed to a change in the student's placement. Under the stay-put provision, **the placement upon a change in grade should replicate, as closely as possible, the placement that existed at the time the dispute arose**, taking into account the changed circumstances. Here, eliminating the BHS services would constitute a change in placement. *Van Scoy v. San Luis Coastal Unified School Dist.*, 353 F.Supp.2d 1083 (C.D. Cal. 2005).

♦ A Virginia special education student with an emotional disability attended a gifted and talented program in an elementary school. He persuaded a classmate to place a threatening note in another student's computer file stating: "death awaits you." The district assembled a manifestation determination review committee, which found no relationship between the student's disabilities and the threatening note. It recommended expelling the student, but the district instead transferred him to a gifted and talented program at a nearby school for the remainder of the year. His parents objected to the transfer decision and requested a due process hearing. The hearing officer ruled against the parents, and the Fourth Circuit affirmed, noting that **the student's transfer to a nearly identical program at a nearby school did not implicate the IDEA's stay-put provision**. Also, his IEP was appropriate. *A.W. v. Fairfax County School Board*, 372 F.3d 674 (4th Cir. 2004).

♦ When a student with a learning disability reached the seventh grade, his parents removed him from his public school, claiming that the school failed to protect him from daily harassment and bullying. They requested a due process hearing, but attended an IEP meeting at which the district declined to change the student's IEP. A hearing panel ruled in favor of the school district, and the parents appealed to a federal court. The parties held an IEP meeting just before the student was to begin eighth grade, and the district agreed to provide homebound services. The parents refused to sign an IEP offered for the student's transition to high school for ninth grade, asserting that he was entitled to remain in his homebound placement.

The district discontinued homebound services, and the student did not attend school as ninth grade began. His parents sought an order requiring the district to provide homebound services under the stay-put provision. The court observed that the Third Circuit has ruled that a student's "last functioning IEP" determines the student's "then-current placement" under the stay-put provision. **The last IEP to which the parties had agreed was the homebound placement for grade eight.** The court rejected the district's assertion that the eighth-grade IEP was limited in duration to that school year. While other courts have ruled that review of an IEP is limited to the terms of the document itself, the IEP in this case was silent as to duration. Because the eighth-grade IEP was the "last functioning IEP" that was agreed upon and signed by the parties, it was the student's stay-put placement. *W.E.B. v. Appoquinimink School Dist.*, No. Civ. A. 01-499-SLR, 2002 WL 31641642 (D. Del. 11/21/02).

♦ A sixth-grade student with cerebral palsy underwent surgery to implant a pump in his abdomen. He received home instruction through grade seven due to complications. Meanwhile, the relationship between his parents and school officials deteriorated. The district determined that his home was no longer an appropriate learning environment and notified the parents that it would provide him the same services at school. The parents refused to bring him to school and he received no services until a federal court issued a preliminary order 10 months later. A due process hearing panel held that the district provided the student with a FAPE and did not violate the stay-put provision with its unilateral action. However, the panel ordered the district to provide the student with ESY services and other relief while phasing out his home schooling. A federal court then held that the decision to change the location of the student's program from home to school violated the stay-put provision.

The Eighth Circuit Court of Appeals affirmed, holding that **the stay-put provision is to be literally and rigorously enforced in order to strip schools of the unilateral authority they formerly employed to exclude students with disabilities from school.** The district argued that its action did not change the student's placement since it called for the provision of identical services at a different location. The lower court had employed a "fact intensive" approach and then made findings on the impact of the change in setting to the student's education. There was no error in this analysis, and the findings were not clearly erroneous. The remedy ordered by the lower court – to provide the student with ESY services – was also well within its discretion. *Hale v. Poplar Bluff R-I School Dist.*, 280 F.3d 831 (8th Cir. 2002).

3. Individual Family Service Plans

♦ A New Jersey student diagnosed with autism at the age of two attended a special nursery school and received applied behavioral analysis (ABA) services under an individualized family service plan. The school district proposed an IEP for preschool that included ABA services different than what the student had previously received. His parents challenged the IEP, and a federal court held that **they did not have to place their son in the class before challenging the IEP.** They could seek reimbursement for private services despite language in the IDEA stating that reimbursement was available only where a student has been denied FAPE and "previously received special education and related services from a public agency." *D.L. and K.L. v. Springfield Board of Educ.*, 536 F.Supp.2d 534 (D.N.J. 2008).

♦ Florida triplets with autism aged out of Part C eligibility under the IDEA when they reached three years old. They then became eligible for services under IDEA Part B. However, their parents rejected the temporary IEPs offered by their school district and sought to continue the individualized family service plans (IFSPs) the triplets had received until they aged out of Part C. The parents claimed that the IFSPs were the triplets' stay-put placement under the IDEA. The school district disagreed, and the Eleventh Circuit sided with the school district. **IFSPs don't necessarily focus on educational needs as IEPs do.** Therefore, the IFSPs were not the triplets' stay-put placement. The stay-put placement does not apply to an initial public school application. *D.P. v. School Board of Broward County*, 483 F.3d 725 (11th Cir. 2007).

♦ When a Pennsylvania preschooler with cerebral palsy approached age three, the intermediate unit responsible for her education conducted a reevaluation so as to transition her from the individual family service plan (IFSP) to an IDEA Part B individualized education program (IEP). Her parents rejected the IEP because it did not include conductive education, which she had been receiving. Prior to a due process hearing, her parents sued to require the continuation of conductive education through the stay-put provision. The court ruled that the stay-put provision did not apply to an IFSP because **the IFSP was not a "current educational placement"** under Section 1415(j). Even though the intermediate unit was offering them the IEP on a "take it or leave it" basis, it did not have to replicate the IFSP services the child received. Under 34 C.F.R. § 300.514, if a dispute arises about a child's initial placement in public schools, the IDEA stay-put placement is the public school IEP. On appeal, the Third Circuit reversed, holding that **Congress did not intend to use a prospective IEP as a student's stay-put placement**. The "then current educational placement" referred to by the IDEA connotes the operative placement actually functioning at the time the dispute arises. The school district had to continue providing conductive education to the student until the question of whether it should be in her IEP was resolved. *Pardini v. Allegheny Intermediate Unit*, 420 F.3d 181 (3d Cir. 2005).

♦ Before he turned three, a California student received services from a regional center under an individualized family service plan (IFSP) calling for 35 hours of weekly individualized therapy with 10 hours of weekly supervision. When he turned three, responsibility for his education shifted to his local school district. After his parents refused to consent to the district's IEP, the district proposed an interim placement with the same goals and objectives as the IFSP, calling for 35 hours of weekly discrete trial training in a home setting. The parents sought to preserve the status quo and made a separate request for a stay-put order. A hearing officer ordered the district to maintain the student's educational placement and the services as described in the IFSP, but noted that it did not have to use the same vendors. The parents appealed to a federal court, which denied their request for preliminary relief.

On appeal, the Ninth Circuit stated that while the IFSP constituted the student's current educational placement for stay-put purposes, the district argued persuasively that it could provide a comparable placement. The hearing officer and district court had properly analogized the case to that of an incoming transfer student. When a student transfers from one public agency to another, the receiving agency is required only to provide a program that conforms with the last agreed-upon placement, not to provide the exact same program. **The change in responsibility for the student's education necessarily changed the status quo, and the hearing officer properly found that the district needed to provide an interim placement that conformed to the IFSP.** The modification of educational vendors in this case involved only changes to plan supervisors. Since district personnel were highly qualified to supervise the student's program, the stay-put order correctly determined the student's current educational placement and he suffered no irreparable harm. *Johnson v. Special Educ. Hearing Office*, 287 F.3d 1176 (9th Cir. 2002).

4. IEP Determines Stay-Put Placement

♦   An emotionally handicapped Florida student struggled academically. His frequent behavior problems led to juvenile offenses. He was placed in a wilderness institute for non-violent juvenile offenders, but his behavior worsened. After he was incarcerated in a juvenile facility, his IEP team proposed placing him back in his day treatment program upon his release. His parents objected and insisted on a stay-put placement. They were unable to agree with the school board on a new IEP, then sought due process and eventually sued the school board for refusing to revise his IEP. The Eleventh Circuit held that **the school board did not have to revise the IEP while due process proceedings were pending**. Because the parents invoked the IDEA's stay-put provision, the school board could not revise the IEP without their consent. *CP v. Leon County School Board*, 483 F.3d 1151 (11th Cir. 2007).

♦   The parents of a Michigan student with disabilities objected to the placement described in his IEP and unilaterally placed him in a private school. Their first attempt to recover tuition reimbursement was rejected by a federal court due to their failure to exhaust administrative remedies. They then commenced an administrative proceeding. A local hearing officer heard six days of testimony, then terminated the proceeding as moot when the parents announced that they intended to place the student in a private school. A state review officer affirmed, and the parents appealed to federal court.

The court agreed that the local hearing officer had erroneously failed to consider whether the student had received a FAPE. However, the error was corrected when the state review officer fully reviewed the IEP. The court rejected the parents' argument that the student was entitled to have his IEPs updated during the pendency of the case, which was now in its fifth year of litigation. **The district had prepared a new IEP in 1998 pursuant to the court's order, and the IDEA's stay-put provision required the district to maintain that IEP as the student's current educational placement pending the outcome of the proceedings.** In examining the district's proposed IEP, the court agreed with the review officer's conclusion that it was reasonably calculated to enable the student to receive educational benefits under the IDEA. It also satisfied Michigan's higher standard of "maximum potential," which does not require the best education possible. Accordingly, the court denied the parents' request for private educational expenses and attorneys' fees. *Kuszewski v. Chippewa Valley School Dist.*, 131 F.Supp.2d 926 (E.D. Mich. 2001).

♦   A Minnesota school district and the parents of a student with autism debated an appropriate placement. The district contended an in-school placement could adequately serve the student's needs, while the parents sought an in-home applied behavioral analysis program. At due process, a level-one hearing officer agreed with the school district's IEP. A level-two hearing officer modified the district's IEP. A court affirmed, but during the appeal, the district sought to implement the administrative decision. It rejected the parents' requests to pay for the 30 hours of home-based services specified in the student's IEP. After the parties failed to agree on a new IEP, the district threatened to file a truancy report against the student. The parents applied to home-school the student and filed a complaint against the district with the state commissioner of the Department of Children, Families and Learning. The commissioner found the district in violation of the IDEA and ordered it to reimburse the parents for their home-based educational expenses pending appeal. The Minnesota Court of Appeals found that the IDEA required the district to provide services in conformity with the applicable IEP pending appeal. Further, **the commissioner had the authority to order the district to reimburse the parents for the costs of the home-based program pending appeal** because the commissioner had the power to determine whether the district violated the stay-put provision. The district's obligation to fund the home-based program did not cease once the parents elected to home-school their son. *Special School Dist. No. 1 v. E.N.*, 620 N.W.2d 65 (Minn. Ct. App. 2000).

♦   A student with bipolar disorder and learning disabilities received two hours of occupational therapy weekly. One hour was devoted to hippotherapy, a therapy involving horses. At an IEP meeting, the school district proposed reducing the number of occupational therapy hours per week to one and eliminating hippotherapy. The student's mother agreed to the reduction, but objected to the elimination of hippotherapy. A due process hearing officer held that the school district violated the IDEA's stay-put provision by discontinuing hippotherapy during the administrative proceedings and that it violated the IDEA by determining prior to the IEP meeting that occupational therapy would be provided at school and not at an outside facility. He also awarded the student one semester of hippotherapy as compensatory education. An appeal officer held that the district was entitled to change the location of services. The district did not violate the stay-put provision, and because the proposed IEP offered the student a FAPE, he was not entitled to compensatory education. The family appealed to a federal court, which upheld the appeal officer's decision. The elimination of hippotherapy was a change in methodology, not a change in educational placement that triggered the stay-put provision.

On appeal, the Tenth Circuit disagreed with the mother's assertion that the district had to continue providing two hours of weekly occupational therapy including the hour of hippotherapy until resolution of her appeal. Here, the mother had agreed to the reduction in services. **The stay-put provision is inapplicable when a parent and school district agree to change the level of services in an educational program.** The district court had properly found that hippotherapy is a treatment modality, and not an educational placement. The student's IEP did not specify service providers or modalities and the elimination of hippotherapy was permissible because the district continued to provide occupational therapy addressing the same issues and did not fundamentally change a basic element of the student's program. The proposed IEP was appropriate and the claim for compensatory education was dismissed. *Erickson v. Albuquerque Public Schools*, 199 F.3d 1116 (10th Cir. 1999).

5. Other Stay-Put Issues

♦ A disabled New Jersey student attended a charter school. Near the end of a school year, his parents and the charter school agreed on an IEP that called for an out-of-district private school placement for the next year. The district challenged the IEP, and the parents asserted that the private school should be his stay-put placement. A hearing officer denied the request, and a federal court held that the charter school should be his stay-put placement. The case reached the Third Circuit, which noted that **the private school could not be his stay-put placement because he had not yet received any services under the new IEP.** Further, the district had the right to object to the placement. It continued to maintain that it could provide a FAPE in the least restrictive environment. *L.Y. v. Bayonne Board of Educ.*, 384 Fed.Appx. 58 (3d Cir. 2010).

♦ Hawaii and its state teachers union agreed to school shutdowns on 17 Fridays during a school year because of a fiscal crisis. A student with disabilities challenged the shutdowns, asserting that they amounted to a change in his placement. Other disabled students joined the lawsuit. The case reached the Ninth Circuit Court of Appeals, which ruled that the shutdowns did not amount to a change in placement because they did not constitute moving the students from one type of program to another. Congress did not intend the IDEA to apply to system-wide administrative decisions, and **the across-the-board reduction in school days did not single out disabled students.** The court refused to issue a stay-put order to keep the schools open. *N.G. v. Hawaii Dep't of Educ.*, 600 F.3d 1104 (9th Cir. 2010).

♦ A Pennsylvania student became involved in two fights during his junior year. His IEP team conducted a functional behavioral assessment and modified his IEP. He was suspended, and a manifestation determination hearing found that his fighting was unrelated to his hearing disability. The district sought to place him in an alternative school, but his mother requested a due process hearing, seeking to place him at his old high school where he would have the supports he needed. A federal court ruled that **the stay-put provision of the IDEA required the student to be placed at his old high school during due process proceedings.** *George A. v. Wallingford Swarthmore School Dist.*, 655 F.Supp.2d 546 (E.D. Pa. 2009).

♦ The parents of a Texas student with disabilities disagreed with the district's proposed IEP for grade two and placed her in a private school. They sought due process and obtained a ruling from the hearing officer that the district did not make an appropriate placement. Thus, the parents were entitled to tuition reimbursement. By the time the administrative ruling was issued, the school year was nearly over. When the district appealed to a federal court, the parents did not ask for tuition reimbursement for another school year. As a result, when the court ruled on the case over a year later, it held that they were not entitled to tuition reimbursement. However, the Fifth Circuit reversed, finding that **another year of tuition was due under the stay-put provision.** *Houston Independent School Dist. v. V.P.*, 582 F.3d 576 (5th Cir. 2009).

♦   A Pennsylvania student had a specific learning disability. His parents and the school district disagreed on a placement after his third-grade year. Over the next two years, his third-grade IEP became his stay-put placement under the IDEA. The district proposed providing itinerant learning support primarily in a regular classroom, instead of the daily hour of resource room support specified in the third-grade IEP. The parents rejected that proposal, arguing that it amounted to a change in placement. In the lawsuit that followed, the Third Circuit held that the district provided the same services to the student in the inclusive setting, on a daily basis and with the same special education teacher. Thus, **providing the itinerant learning support was not a change in placement so as to violate the IDEA's stay-put provision.** *In re Educ. Assignment of Joseph R.*, 318 Fed.Appx. 113 (3d Cir. 2009).

♦   The parents of a Florida student with autism sought a residential placement to address his maladaptive behaviors. A federal court agreed, and the student attended a residential program in Kansas for one year. For the following year, the school district proposed a non-residential placement in a Florida school. The parents objected and invoked the stay-put placement provision. An administrative law judge ruled for the parents, **finding the proposed IEP inadequate, partly because it contained no behavior intervention plan.** No changed circumstances warranted terminating the residential placement. A federal court then agreed that a residential placement was appropriate. However, the Kansas facility might not be necessary if the school district could find another appropriate facility in Florida. *School Board of Lee County, Florida v. E.S.*, 561 F.Supp.2d 1282 (M.D. Fla. 2008).

♦   The mother of a severely disabled, autistic child placed him in a Kansas residential facility, which the Hawaii Department of Education funded. However, the department notified the mother that it would stop funding the placement when the student turned 20 over the summer. It asserted that state rules required a student to be under age 20 on the first day of school to be eligible. The mother disagreed and asked a federal court to intervene under the IDEA's stay-put provision. **The court noted inconsistencies in state law, making it unclear that age 20 had to be reached prior to the first day of school.** It ordered the department to continue paying the student's tuition until the action was completed or the student turned 21. *B.T. v. Dep't of Educ., State of Hawaii*, No. 08-00356 DAE-BMK, 2008 WL 3891867 (D. Haw. 8/21/08).

♦   An Oregon student challenged his IEP, and a hearing officer agreed that the district failed to provide him with a free appropriate public education. Thus, the parents were justified in removing him from district schools, and the district was ordered to pay for his private school tuition. The district offered a new IEP and appealed to a federal court, **asserting that it should not have to pay tuition as part of the stay-put placement because it had offered a new IEP.** The court disagreed, citing the district's appeal as evidence that proceedings were continuing. The district had to pay the tuition until the proceedings ended. *Ashland School Dist. v. V.M.*, 494 F.Supp.2d 1180 (D. Or. 2007).

♦   The parents of a Connecticut student unilaterally placed him in a residential school. The school board later agreed to the placement through yearly agreements that bound both parties to work toward transitioning the student to the public school for the following year. The agreements also stated that the parents waived their right to an interim private placement under the stay-put provision in the event of due process. After three years, the parents challenged the school board's IEP (calling for a public school placement), and a hearing officer ruled for the school board. When the parents sought to invoke the stay-put provision of the IDEA, a federal court refused to let them. Here, **in exchange for tuition reimbursement, they had waived their right to invoke the stay-put provision**. Further, none of the agreements designated the residential school as the student's stay-put placement. *K.G. v. Plainville Board of Educ.*, No. 3:06 CV 1907 (CFD), 2007 WL 80671 (D. Conn. 1/9/07).

♦   The parents of a Virginia student with disabilities rejected their school district's IEP and placed him in a private program. A hearing officer found that the school's IEP did not provide sufficient one-on-one instruction, but nevertheless denied reimbursement because the private program was not reasonably calculated to confer educational benefits on the student. Multiple claims arose from the dispute, including one related to the failure of the district to provide sufficient one-on-one instruction. However, **the parents could not seek to enforce a stay-put order through 42 U.S.C. § 1983 because it was not a final order and they had other options under the IDEA**. *M.S. v. Fairfax County School Board*, No. 1:05CV1476 (JCC), 2006 WL 721372 (E.D. Va. 3/20/06).

♦   A Florida high school student with emotional and behavioral problems was frequently tardy, slept in class and was failing three classes. His attendance and behavior worsened until he was arrested and sent to juvenile detention. His parents initiated a due process hearing request against their school board. They invoked the stay-put provision of the IDEA. A hearing officer ruled that the IEP satisfied the IDEA, and the parents appealed. The board notified the parents that because they had invoked the stay-put provision, no new IEP would be developed for the next year. The parents then asserted that the board should have revised their son's IEP despite the stay-put provision. The Eleventh Circuit held that **the stay-put provision does not require annual updating of an IEP**. *CP v. Leon County School Board*, 466 F.3d 1318 (11th Cir. 2006).

♦   A Maine student with Down syndrome had behavioral difficulties. He received some IEP services in a work opportunities program off campus. His IEP team proposed a new IEP for 2000-2001 that placed him at the off-campus training program for the entire school day. His parents objected to the IEP and obtained a stay-put order requiring the student to remain in his 1999-2000 educational placement pending the resolution of the dispute. During the course of legal proceedings, the student "aged out" of IDEA eligibility. A federal court then held that the district could be responsible for providing compensatory education for the 2000-2001 school year, during which the 1999-2000 IEP was in place. The stay-put order did not absolve the district from the compensatory education claim. Because the district held 10 meetings with the parents during that year to discuss the IEP, and because it devised a substantially different IEP during the year, it should have known that **it failed to provide a free appropriate public education even as it complied with the stay-put order**. The court remanded the case to the hearing officer for a determination as to how much compensatory education the student should receive. *Mr. and Mrs. R. v. Maine School Administrative Dist. No. 35*, 295 F.Supp.2d 113 (D. Me. 2003).

♦   A New York principal initiated a family court proceeding to determine if a student was in need of supervision based on 16 unexcused absences from school during a two-month period. The family court ordered the school's committee on special education to conduct an evaluation, which found that the student was emotionally disturbed and had a disability. After the court placed the student on probation for a year, he appealed. The New York Supreme Court, Appellate Division, ruled that the adjudication of the student as a child in need of supervision did not constitute a change in placement under the IDEA. Here, **the student's placement was not changed** by the court's ruling. He was simply ordered to attend school and participate in his IEP. *Erich D. v. New Milford Board of Educ.*, 767 N.Y.S.2d 488 (N.Y. App. Div. 2003).

♦   A Maryland student with autism received a home Lovaas therapy program under an IEP, which specified that the therapy would be given by a community services provider that was the only state-approved provider of Lovaas therapy in Maryland. When the relationship between the student's parents and the provider's employees deteriorated, the provider discontinued services. The school board then proposed a public school placement. The parents sought a due process hearing, asserting that the school board had a duty under the stay-put provision to seek out a comparable placement for the student. The case reached the Fourth Circuit, which noted that **the stay-put provision did not impose any affirmative duty on local education agencies**. Here, through no fault of the district, the placement became unavailable. Ordering the district to create a new placement amounted to using the stay-put provision to implement change. On remand, the court held that the administrative law judge had correctly applied the two-step analysis of *Board of Educ. v. Rowley*, 458 U.S. 176 (1982). Although the district did not fully comply with IDEA requirements, the violations did not result in the loss of any educational opportunities. Also, "the IDEA does not demand that any particular set or level of services be maintained for a student merely because they were previously provided to that student." **The lack of services was due to the unavailability of a proper stay-put placement.** *Wagner v. Board of Educ. of Montgomery County*, 340 F.Supp.2d 603 (D. Md. 2004).

IV. SUSPENSION AND EXPULSION

The suspension or expulsion of students with disabilities from school may be a change in placement for purposes of the IDEA under the U.S. Supreme Court's decision in Honig v. Doe, *484 U.S. 305, 108 S.Ct. 592, 98 L.Ed.2d 686*

(1988). Indefinite suspensions violate the IDEA's stay-put provision found at 20 U.S.C. § 1415(e)(3); however, suspensions for up to 10 days do not constitute a change in placement.

In recent years, courts have considered cases filed by regular education students who claim to have disabilities and seek the protection of the stay-put provision to avoid a pending suspension or expulsion. The issue has been addressed in recent IDEA Amendments, which provide that where a school district does not have knowledge that a child is a child with a disability, the child may be subjected to the same disciplinary measures as those applied to non-disabled children.

The IDEA also provides that a student may be removed from the classroom for up to 55 days if he or she is placed in an appropriate interim alternative educational setting. See 20 U.S.C. § 1415(k). This section is applicable to students who possess weapons at school or school functions, who possess, sell or use drugs at school or a school function, or who inflict or are substantially likely to inflict serious bodily to the self or others.

♦ *Honig v. Doe* involved two emotionally disturbed children in California who were given five-day suspensions from school for misbehavior that included destroying school property and assaulting other students. Pursuant to state law, the suspensions were continued indefinitely during the pendency of expulsion proceedings. The students sued the school district in federal court contesting the extended suspensions on the ground that they violated the stay-put provision, which provides that a student must be kept in his or her "then current" educational placement during the pendency of proceedings that contemplate a change in placement. The court issued an injunction preventing the expulsion of any disabled student for misbehavior resulting from the student's disability, and the school district appealed. The Ninth Circuit determined that the indefinite suspensions constituted a prohibited change in placement under the IDEA and that no dangerousness exception existed in the stay-put provision. It ruled that indefinite suspensions or expulsions of disabled children for misconduct arising out of their disabilities violate the IDEA. It also ruled, however, that fixed suspensions of up to 30 school days did not constitute a change in placement. It determined that a state must provide services directly to a disabled child when a local school district fails to do so.

The U.S. Supreme Court declared that the purpose of the stay-put provision was to prevent schools from changing a child's educational placement over his or her parents' objection until all review proceedings were completed. While the IDEA provided for interim placements where parents and school officials were able to agree on one, no emergency exception for dangerous students was included. However, **where a disabled student poses an immediate threat to the safety of others, school officials may temporarily suspend him or her for up to 10 school days**. This authority ensured that school officials can: 1) protect the safety of others by removing dangerous students, 2) seek a review of the student's placement and try to persuade the student's parents to agree to an interim placement, and 3) seek court rulings to exclude students whose parents adamantly refuse to permit any change in placement. School officials could seek such a court order without exhausting IDEA administrative remedies "only by showing that maintaining the child in his or her current placement is substantially likely to result in injury either to himself or herself, or to others." Indefinite suspensions violate the IDEA's stay-put provision. Suspensions up to 10 days do not constitute a change in placement. The Court also upheld the court of appeals' decision that states could be required to provide services directly to disabled students where a local school district fails to do so. *Honig v. Doe*, 484 U.S. 305, 108 S.Ct. 592, 98 L.Ed.2d 686 (1988).

A. Generally

♦ The parents of a New Jersey student made vague claims that their son had been improperly suspended for 10 days near the end of a school year when he had already been suspended nine different times earlier in the year for a total of 19 days. **They requested due process but never provided details about why their son was suspended.** As a result, the hearing officer, a federal court and the Third Circuit dismissed their case. Without proper notice, there was no way for the district to defend itself. *M.S.-G. v. Lenape Regional High School Dist. Board of Educ.*, 306 Fed.Appx. 772 (3d Cir. 2009).

♦ Four Michigan teachers and their union brought a lawsuit against their school board, **asserting that it improperly failed to expel students who had assaulted them.** They maintained that state law required the expulsion of students who assaulted others, and argued that school administrators who failed to follow the law should have their contracts cancelled. The Court of Appeals of Michigan ruled against them, holding that they did not have standing to pursue the case. On further appeal, the Michigan Supreme Court held that the teachers had standing to pursue their action. They were likely to suffer an injury that other members of the public wouldn't face. Thus, they had a substantial and distinct interest in enforcing the law that a student be expelled for assaulting a teacher. *Lansing Schools Educ. Ass'n MEA/NEA v. Lansing Board of Educ.*, 792 N.W.2d 686 (Mich. 2010).

♦ The divorced, noncustodial mother of a New Hampshire student with a disability sought to be notified whenever he was suspended for fighting or dismissed for illness. However, a federal court ruled that **she had received due process in the custody proceedings and was not now entitled to notice before her son was released to his father**. *Vendouri v. Gaylord*, No. 10-CV-277-SM, 2010 WL 4236856 (D.N.H. 2010).

♦ A Michigan student with Tourette's Disorder and related disabilities received special education services and had a behavioral plan. After his school district suspended him for 10 days in successive years, it petitioned a state court to find him guilty of school incorrigibility because of his repeated rules violations. The court found the student guilty, and the Michigan Court of Appeals affirmed that decision. The filing of a juvenile petition was not a change in placement under the IDEA. And **since the student was never**

suspended for more than 10 days, he was not entitled to a manifestation determination hearing. *In re Nicholas Papadelis*, No. 291536, 2010 WL 3447892 (Mich. Ct. App. 9/2/10).

◆ A South Dakota learning disabled student got into a fight after bringing a knife to school. The assistant principal suspended him and, at a manifestation determination meeting, school officials determined that his misconduct was not a manifestation of his disability. After missing four days of school, he was placed in an alternative educational setting. His grandmother asked for a school board hearing but was informed that was not possible because the student was no longer suspended. In his alternative placement, the student received two hours of instruction four days a week instead of his usual 30 hours per week – a 73% reduction. When a lawsuit arose over the district's actions, a federal court found that the alternative placement amounted to a long-term suspension that exceeded 10 days. However, the Eighth Circuit reversed, noting that **the student had only been suspended for four days**, and that the student's grandmother had agreed to the alternative placement. *Doe v. Todd County School Dist.*, 625 F.3d 459 (8th Cir. 2010).

◆ A Washington student threatened his older sisters at home with scissors and a knife. The girls barricaded themselves in their room and called their father, who called 911. Police took the student into custody and notified school officials, who expelled the student on an emergency basis. After a therapist found he was not a risk to himself or others, he was allowed to return to school. He then sued the school district for violating his due process rights, arguing that he should have been given notice and some kind of hearing before his expulsion. A federal court and the Ninth Circuit disagreed. The court of appeals noted that the student and his mother met with a district official, who gave them oral notice of the exclusion pending a meeting with the superintendent. Also, the superintendent later met with the student and his mother for several hours to discuss the incident. Thus, **the student received adequate notice and a hearing under** *Goss v. Lopez*, 419 U.S. 565 (1975). *Doe v. Mercer Island School Dist. No. 400*, 288 Fed.Appx. 426 (9th Cir. 2008).

◆ A Minnesota student with emotional and behavioral disabilities was suspended several times for fighting with other girls. Her suspensions added up to more than 10 days out of class. The district offered home-schooling services, but the student's mother rejected the offer. After conducting a functional behavioral assessment, the district offered to place the student in an emotional behavioral disability setting that included boys, but the mother rejected this placement as well, preferring an all-girl setting. An administrative law judge held that the district denied the student a FAPE because of the suspensions and the district's failure to modify the student's IEP. However, the Eighth Circuit Court of Appeals reversed, finding that the district did not violate the IDEA. Here, the mother rejected the district's offer of home schooling, and **the mixed-gender setting was appropriate given that all the student's serious behavior problems involved altercations with other girls.** *M.M. v. Special School Dist. No. 1*, 512 F.3d 455 (8th Cir. 2008).

◆ A Minnesota first-grader was involved in over 50 behavioral incidents and was disciplined many times. His placement was changed from a Level I setting to a Level III setting, so he would be in an emotional behavioral disorder classroom for the entire day. Later, the student received a suspension after he threatened to kill a classmate. His father then filed a complaint against the district, using the state department of education process. The department investigated, found numerous violations and imposed corrective action. The school district appealed, and the Minnesota Court of Appeals reversed. Here, **the truncated investigation of the complaint was not properly carried out in compliance with federal regulations**. The investigator conducted numerous interviews with the father, but never contacted school staff and made no on-site investigation. *Independent School Dist. No. 192 (Farmington) v. Minnesota Dep't of Educ.*, 742 N.W.2d 713 (Minn. Ct. App. 2007).

◆ An Oregon student with ADHD and ongoing disciplinary issues, together with the school's quarterback, created counterfeit money. Both students were caught passing the fake bills at school. The ADHD student received a harsher suspension than the quarterback. He transferred to another school, then sued for equal protection violations, claiming he was treated more harshly because of behavior issues arising from his learning disabilities. A federal court rejected his claims. **The difference between the two students' disciplinary histories allowed for the greater punishment.** This did not violate equal protection. *Schneider v. Corvallis School Dist.*, No. CIV 05-6375 TC, 2006 WL 3827457 (D. Or. 12/27/06).

◆ An Ohio student with Asperger's syndrome asked for a break as allowed by his IEP, but then became very agitated and head-butted an intervention specialist. He was sent home with his mother. The principal called the mother to suspend the student. A month later, before a hearing had taken place on the mother's appeal of the first suspension, the student was suspended again for failing to leave an icy area of the playground as instructed and for grabbing an office worker by the blouse. A due process hearing was finally conducted three months later, and the hearing officer upheld the first suspension, reducing the second suspension by half. A trial court upheld the suspensions, but the Court of Appeals of Ohio reversed. Here, **the principal violated state law and district regulations by failing to provide written notice before the first suspension.** As for the second suspension, it constituted a change in placement because the student had been removed from school for more than 10 days. And the district failed to conduct a manifestation determination. The court reversed the first suspension and ordered the student's records expunged. *Grine v. Sylvania Schools Board of Educ.*, No. L-04-1137, 2004 WL 2924335 (Ohio Ct. App. 12/17/04).

◆ A fourth-grade special education student in Minnesota received 25 disciplinary write-ups for harassment and inappropriate comments on his school bus, including lewd statements to girls. When his class was given the opportunity to visit the Minnesota Vikings training camp, he was excluded for his bus misconduct. He maintained that the real reason was because he was a

Green Bay Packers fan and pointed to two previous incidents: he drew a picture of a Packer instead of a Viking for a class display, and his picture was left out; and he was excluded from participating in a holiday parade when he did not dress in Vikings colors. When he sued, a federal court ruled against him, and the Eighth Circuit affirmed. Elementary school students do not have a constitutional right to wear a Green Bay Packers jersey to school, and school officials could require him to follow directions on a school project (drawing a Vikings player). Also, there was no showing that he was excluded from the field trip because of his ADHD. Rather, **the discipline was based on his documented misconduct.** *Sonkowsky v. Board of Educ. for Independent School Dist. No. 721*, 327 F.3d 675 (8th Cir. 2003).

B. Manifestation Determination

◆   An Ohio student with ADD received interventions in grades one and two but was determined not to need an IEP. In third grade, she became physically aggressive and was referred to a mental health agency. Later, she was suspended for threatening behavior. Her mother requested a manifestation determination review (MDR) and an evaluation, which found her eligible for special education. Her mother then sought due process for various IDEA violations, and a hearing officer awarded compensatory education for the delay in identifying the student as IDEA-eligible. A federal court agreed that **the district should have conducted an MDR before suspending the student**. It also ordered the discipline wiped from her record. *Jackson v. Northwest Local School Dist.*, No. 1-09-CV-300, 2010 WL 3452333 (S.D. Ohio 8/3/10).

◆   Florida brothers with ADHD as well as cognitive and academic deficits attended school under IEPs. The younger brother attacked another student and was suspended for 10 days. A few weeks later, the older brother threatened to shoot and kill classmates and was also suspended for 10 days. Both brothers received manifestation hearings, which determined that their misconduct did not relate to their disabilities. After the older brother was expelled, the mother challenged the decision. An administrative ruling favored the school district, and a federal court affirmed that decision. **The students' misconduct was not a manifestation of their disabilities,** and the mother failed to show there was any discrimination or violation of the IDEA. *Lewellyn v. Sarasota County School Board*, No. 8:07-CV-1712-T-33TGW, 2009 WL 5214983 (M.D. Fla. 12/29/09).

◆   A Pennsylvania student who caused a bomb scare at his school had previously been ruled eligible for a Section 504 plan but ineligible for special education under the IDEA. The district refused his parents' request for a manifestation determination hearing and ultimately expelled the student. His parents sued, but a federal court held that **a manifestation determination is required only under the IDEA, not Section 504**. As a result, the student had not been denied due process by the failure to conduct a manifestation determination. *Centennial School Dist. v. Phil L.*, 559 F.Supp.2d 634 (E.D. Pa. 2008).

◆ A student from New Jersey moved to North Carolina to live with his aunt. While there, he was suspended for bringing a razor to school, among other reasons. An IEP team determined that his conduct was a manifestation of his disabilities, but it upheld a recommendation to suspend him. An administrative law judge reversed the suspension, but a review officer reinstated it. The student moved back to New Jersey, then sued the North Carolina school district for violating the IDEA. The district sought to have the case dismissed, but a federal court refused to do so. **The student could seek to have references to his suspension purged from his disciplinary records**, which might be considered by other schools. *L.K. v. North Carolina State Board of Educ.*, No. 5:08-CV-85-BR, 2008 WL 2397696 (E.D.N.C. 6/9/08).

◆ An emotionally disabled Virginia student, along with several friends, vandalized his school by shooting the building and some school buses with paintball guns. The principal recommended that he be expelled, which triggered an IDEA manifestation determination review. The review committee found that the student's behavior was not a manifestation of his disability, and a hearing officer recommended suspending the student for the rest of the year. His parents objected and sought due process. The hearing officer found no IDEA violation, and a federal court upheld that determination. There was no IDEA requirement that the review committee members know the student personally, as the parents had argued. **And the student was not drawn into the vandalism by his friends. Rather, he had been an instigator.** *Fitzgerald v. Fairfax County School Board*, 556 F.Supp.2d 543 (E.D. Va. 2008).

◆ A Tennessee student with ADHD received accommodations under a Section 504 plan, but was ruled ineligible for special education under the IDEA. After he got into a fight with a classmate, he became subject to discipline. The manifestation determination hearing found his behavior was not a manifestation of his disability. His parents requested due process, at which a hearing officer ruled that **the student should have received special education under the IDEA because his Section 504 plan was not meeting his needs**. The district appealed, arguing that it should not have to comply with the hearing officer's order and that the order should not be considered the student's stay-put placement because the student had not been identified as needing special education under the IDEA. The court ruled for the parents, finding the stay-put placement applied to the student because the district had denied the student a free appropriate public education by failing to develop an IEP for him. *Williamson County Board of Educ. v. C.K.*, No. 3:07-0826, 2007 WL 3023616 (M.D. Tenn. 10/11/07).

◆ A Pennsylvania student began having behavioral problems in elementary school and was diagnosed with ADHD and oppositional defiant disorder. He took medication that helped him in class, and he performed at grade level in reading, writing, math, science and social studies. In grade seven, the district found him eligible for a Section 504 accommodation plan. The student's behavior deteriorated; he threatened to shoot a teacher and burn down the school, and was suspended. His parents asserted that the district had failed him under both the IDEA and Section 504. After a hearing officer found the district had adequately addressed the student's attention and organization problems, the parents sued. A federal court held that **the student did not have a serious emotional disturbance so as to be entitled to IDEA disciplinary protections like a manifestation determination**. He understood the consequences of his behavior, and the district accommodated his needs. *Brendan K. v. Easton Area School Dist.*, No. 05-4179, 2007 WL 1160377 (E.D. Pa. 4/16/07).

◆ A learning disabled student who was also an accomplished track athlete was called a "faggot" and "PLC," which stood for "prescriptive learning class." A fight broke out and the student was suspended for five days, with notice of a hearing. The superintendent accepted the hearing officer's recommendation for another five-day suspension pending a manifestation hearing. **The school's committee on special education found that the student's behavior was not a manifestation of his disability**, and the superintendent then planned to suspend the student for the rest of the year. The student sued, and a New York federal court held that the student was entitled to a preliminary injunction, ordering the student's reinstatement from his suspension during his administrative appeal so that he would be able to participate in track and graduate with his classmates. After the student graduated, he sued for his attorneys' fees. The Second Circuit held that he should have exhausted his administrative remedies before suing. Thus, he was not entitled to fees. Further, he had no right to graduate at a particular time from a particular school, and the fact that he was a superior athlete on the verge of graduation did not create an emergency. *Coleman v. Newburgh Enlarged City School Dist.*, 503 F.3d 198 (2d Cir. 2007).

◆ A New Jersey student with attention deficit disorder – based on test scores, achievement levels, evaluations and medical diagnoses – was found to be ineligible for special education. He was later determined to be using marijuana and was suspended. He then tested positive for marijuana again, and **a manifestation hearing determined that the drug use was not a manifestation of his disability**. After the board voted to expel the student on his sixteenth birthday, he appealed. The case reached a federal court, which ruled that his Fourth Amendment and due process rights were not violated. However, he could pursue his IDEA and Section 504 claims because he was entitled to a free appropriate public education until age 18. *Gutin v. Washington Township Board of Educ.*, 467 F.Supp.2d 414 (D.N.J. 2006).

◆ The principal of a Texas school questioned a student about a fire in a lavatory. The student confessed to setting the fire, and the principal called the police, who arrested him. The student's parents were not contacted until later. They rejected a Section 504 hearing offered by the district, insisting that their son was entitled to a manifestation hearing under the IDEA. After the student was expelled, they sued the district for violating Section 504. A magistrate judge recommended pretrial judgment for the district, finding no evidence of a Section 504 violation. **By insisting on an IDEA hearing, the parents waived their rights to a Section 504 hearing.** *Ron J. v. McKinney Independent School Dist.*, No. 4:05 CV257, 2006 WL 2927446 (E.D. Tex. 10/11/06).

♦   A disabled New Jersey student was caught smoking marijuana after she had previously been suspended for refusing a drug test. She again refused to take a drug test and was suspended for 20 days. She requested an expedited due process hearing, which was adjourned because her mother refused to participate. An administrative law judge then ordered the student returned to class because the school had improperly suspended the student for more than 10 days without a manifestation hearing. A federal court reversed that ruling. Under the IDEA, **a student can be suspended for up to 45 days, without a manifestation determination, for drug or weapon possession**. *A.P. v. Pemberton Township Board of Educ.*, No. 05-3780 (RBK), 2006 WL 1344788 (D.N.J. 5/15/06).

♦   An Illinois student with emotional disabilities brought a letter opener to school and threatened two classmates with it. The school suspended him for three days and referred him for a safety evaluation. **The IEP team determined that the incident was a manifestation of the student's disability and that his placement should be changed** to an alternative day school. The student's parents sued and lost because they failed to exhaust their administrative remedies. Also, although the IDEA limits a school's ability to unilaterally change a student's placement, a school can change a placement for up to 45 days if a student brings a weapon to school. However, this exception does not apply if a school proposes permanently changing a student's placement, as the school did here. If the parents requested a due process hearing, the stay-put provision would be triggered and the student would have to be returned to his then-current placement. *Kaczmarski v. Wheaton Community Unit School Dist. #200*, No. 04-2976, 2004 WL 1093348 (N.D. Ill. 5/4/04).

♦   An eighth-grade student with a learning disability brought marijuana to school and sold it. After a 10-day suspension, the school board expelled him for the rest of the year at a disciplinary hearing. The next day, the district special education director attempted to schedule a manifestation review meeting. The district's attempts to schedule the meeting within the 10 days were unsuccessful, and the hearing was held 12 days after the expulsion decision. At the meeting, it was determined that the student's misconduct was not a manifestation of his disability. An IEP for the remainder of the student's expulsion called for two hours of in-home, one-to-one instruction in core subjects and two hours of weekly specialized reading instruction.

A federal court noted that although Section 1415(k)(4)(A) requires a manifestation determination within 10 days of a change in placement, the two-day delay that occurred in this case did not result in any harm. The delay had no effect on the parties' participation in the meeting, the meeting's result, or the student's educational program. Also, the IEP developed at the manifestation review meeting did not deny the student a FAPE. It **allowed him to participate in and progress in the general curriculum during his expulsion**, as required by 20 U.S.C. § 1415(k)(3)(B). The court ordered the district and the parents to arrange for a functional behavioral assessment. *Farrin v. Maine School Administrative Dist. No. 59*, 165 F.Supp.2d 37 (D. Me. 2001).

C. Interim Placement

♦   A District of Columbia student eligible for special education taunted a substitute teacher and refused to follow several instructions. Because he had two prior infractions in the same school year, he was suspended for 54 days and placed in an alternative educational setting as a result of this Level II infraction. A manifestation determination review found his behavior was not a manifestation of his disability. After a hearing officer reduced the suspension to 10 days, an assistant district superintendent raised it to 45 days. **Another hearing officer found that the alternative placement was not appropriate under the IDEA and reduced the suspension to 11 days.** When the district challenged that decision, the D.C. Circuit upheld it because the alternative placement denied the student a FAPE. The hearing officer did not exceed his authority in modifying the suspension. *District of Columbia v. Doe*, 611 F.3d 888 (D.C. Cir. 2010).

♦   A middle school student ran out of classrooms and his school building without permission. This was a particular danger because the school was located near a major highway. The student also chased other students in his classroom, hit teachers and students with a folder or crumpled paper, and chewed on sharp objects while leaning back in his chair. The school sought to suspend the student by placing him on homebound instruction pending a psychiatric evaluation and review by the district's committee on special education. A state trial court extended the suspension from school and placement of the student on homebound instruction. The New York Supreme Court, Appellate Division, noted that under 20 U.S.C. § 1415(k)(2)(A), school districts are authorized to extend a student's suspension upon showing that maintaining a current placement is substantially likely to result in injury to the student or others. The district's evidence clearly demonstrated that **allowing the student to return to the regular classroom was substantially likely to result in injury to himself or others.** The trial court properly extended the suspension. *Roslyn Union Free School Dist. v. Geoffrey W.*, 740 N.Y.S.2d 451 (N.Y. App. Div. 2002).

♦   During the seventh grade, a student with ADHD, pervasive development disorder and a history of aggression and violent outbursts wrote a story for a class about a student who gets revenge on his school, designed a computer game called "101 Ways to Destroy the School," and asked a classmate about obtaining guns. The student was suspended pending a manifestation determination. The district concluded that he should not return to school because of his propensity for violence and the danger he presented to others. Since no alternative sites were available, the mother suggested an "interim homebound placement." The school district agreed and promised weekly tutoring and social work therapy while searching for an alternative setting for grade eight. The team concluded that the student's conduct was related to his disability, but did not change the student's IEP, related services or behavior plan.

A federal court later held that the district's numerous procedural errors resulted in the denial of a FAPE. The district had to address the student's behavior after determining that his conduct was related to his disability. Such a finding requires an IEP team to change the IEP, discuss ways to address behavioral problems, or consider what in-school remedies or services could address the behavior. The district instead removed the student from school without considering realistic alternatives. **It violated the IDEA by offering an interim homebound setting without first seeking the expedited due process hearing procedure under 20 U.S.C. § 1415(k) for students posing a threat.** *Community Consolidated School Dist. No. 93 v. John F.*, No. 00 CV 1347 (N.D. Ill. 2000).

♦ A student with emotional and learning disabilities was disciplined numerous times for fighting, disobedience, profanity and other misconduct. He slashed another student in the face with a box cutter, and was placed in juvenile detention and suspended. A manifestation hearing determined that the incident was not a manifestation of his disability. The principal recommended expulsion for the rest of the school year and the following year. However, the committee instead placed the student in a temporary homebound program. At a second meeting, the committee released the student from the homebound program and placed him in an alternative school. During the summer, the school committee again met and decided to resume the alternative school placement. The student was not allowed to return to the high school so that he could play football. An administrative law judge held that the alternative school placement provided the student with FAPE and was his stay-put placement.

On appeal, a federal court found that the district had provided the student with FAPE. **The alternative school furnished a basic floor of opportunity and was the least restrictive environment in view of his history of aggressive behavior and violence.** While the student's behavior had improved at the alternative school and there was evidence that it had improved further under his juvenile justice program, there was evidence that he would still present a danger to himself or others in a regular school setting. *Parent v. Osceola County School Board*, 59 F.Supp.2d 1243 (M.D. Fla. 1999).

♦ An Illinois high school freshman with a learning disability was accused of marijuana possession at a school dance. The school board suspended him for 10 days, held a multidisciplinary conference, and then determined that his misconduct was unrelated to his disability. It voted to expel the student for the rest of the semester, a decision that was affirmed by a federal court. The Seventh Circuit held that the pre-1997 IDEA did not require the provision of educational services to a student expelled for misconduct unrelated to a disability. The IDEA stay-put provision was inapplicable since the school board had determined that the student's disabilities had nothing to do with his marijuana possession. The court affirmed the judgment for the board, acknowledging that **the IDEA Amendments of 1997 mandate that a FAPE be made available to all students with disabilities, including those who have been suspended or expelled.** Since the misconduct had occurred prior to the effective date of the amendments, the court held them inapplicable. *Doe v. Board of Educ. of Oak Park and River Forest High School Dist. 200*, 115 F.3d 1273 (7th Cir. 1997).

♦ A 15-year-old Arizona student with emotionally disabling conditions brought a knife to school. His immediate short-term suspension was extended to a 175-day expulsion following a meeting of school officials, who determined that his misconduct was unrelated to his disabling condition. The district maintained a written policy that educational services for students with disabilities could be discontinued entirely during a long-term suspension or expulsion for conduct unrelated to the disability. The student claimed that the district violated the IDEA when it failed to consider providing him with alternative educational services. The student's father requested an IEP meeting, which was held, but resulted in no alternative educational placement. The student was placed in the juvenile court system with no educational services after his conviction on state weapons charges. The student and his father sued the school district, seeking a declaration that the long-term suspension and expulsion order violated the IDEA.

The court rejected the district's assertion that it need not provide IDEA procedural protections or educational services for a student with a disability expelled for misconduct unrelated to his disabling condition. **Since the expulsion of a student with disabilities constitutes a change in placement for IDEA purposes, the district had violated the IDEA stay-put provision and was presently violating the IDEA by refusing to provide educational services.** Because the district continued to violate the IDEA, the court left open the possibility of an award of compensatory services and ordered the school to ensure that the student received appropriate services within 10 days. It ordered the district to refrain from discontinuing educational services for students with disabilities during long-term suspensions or expulsions and granted the student's summary judgment motion. *Magyar v. Tucson Unified School Dist.*, 958 F.Supp. 1423 (D. Ariz. 1997).

♦ A Missouri student with multiple mental disabilities exhibited aggressive behavior toward students and teachers. She was placed in a public school's self-contained classroom for students with mental disabilities and provided with two-on-one staffing at all times. She was also enrolled in several regular classes. Despite this placement, her aggressive behavior continued to the point that daily lesson plans were not completed and the parents of other students complained of the negative effect on their children. Her IEP team reevaluated the placement. Shortly thereafter, the student hit another student on the head three times during art class. The school imposed a 10-day suspension, and the parents filed a lawsuit seeking to set it aside. The school district sought to remove the student from school during the revision of the IEP, based on her aggressive behavior and the substantial risk of injury she presented to herself and others. The court granted the district's motion for an order allowing it to remove the student from school. The parents appealed to the Eighth Circuit, which found **substantial evidence in the record of a likelihood of injury based on almost daily episodes of aggressive behavior by the student.** Accordingly, removal of the student had been proper and temporary placement at a segregated facility for students with disabilities was appropriate. The interim placement proposed by the school district was appropriate during the administrative review process. *Light v. Parkway C-2 School Dist.*, 41 F.3d 1223 (8th Cir. 1994).

D. Regular Education Students

Section 1415(k)(8) of the IDEA addresses the issue of regular education students seeking IDEA protections in disciplinary cases. A student who has not been determined to be eligible for special education and related services under the IDEA may assert the act's procedural protections if the LEA has knowledge that the student was a child with a disability prior to the misconduct giving rise to discipline.

In order to impute such knowledge to an LEA, the parents must have expressed written concerns of the student's special education needs or a teacher must have expressed "specific concerns about a pattern of behavior demonstrated by the child" to the special education director or supervisory personnel.

◆   The parents of a Connecticut student whose IEP goals had been met agreed to have him dismissed from his special education program in high school. When he was a senior, he was involved in two fights and left racist voice mails with a classmate. The school informed the parents that it intended to expel the student for the voice mails. They filed a due process hearing request, which resulted in a favorable ruling for the school district. After the student was expelled, he sued for IDEA violations, claiming he should have been granted "stay-put" protections. A federal court disagreed. **He was not entitled to stay-put protections because he had been out of special education for two years** and the district was not on notice that he was disabled. *E.K. v. Stamford Board of Educ.*, No. 3:07CV800, 2007 WL 1746201 (D. Conn. 6/15/07).

◆   After a student transferred schools, her new school noticed that she took medication at home for ADD. Despite the fact that she failed all of her ninth-grade classes, she was not referred for a special needs evaluation. The following year, she was suspended for giving or selling drugs to at least one classmate. She denied providing drugs to others, but the school expelled her after an expulsion hearing. The expulsion notice stated that the student could return to school at the start of the following school year, conditioned on her completion of a drug program and passing a drug test. The student appealed, arguing that the school had knowledge of a qualifying disability when it expelled her, and that it violated the IDEA by failing to provide her with IDEA disciplinary procedures. A hearing officer ordered the school district to evaluate the student. A manifestation determination hearing found that she did not have a disability under the IDEA. The school then sought dismissal of the administrative proceedings, but the student argued that she was entitled to remain in school under the stay-put provision. The hearing officer held for the school. The student commenced a second IDEA proceeding appealing her expulsion. At the start of the next school year, the school readmitted the student.

The family then sued the school district, asserting claims under the IDEA, Section 504 of the Rehabilitation Act and the Due Process Clauses of the Massachusetts and federal Constitutions. The court ruled in favor of the school district on the Section 504 and due process claims. With respect to the IDEA claims, the court held that **students who have not yet been formally identified as disabled within the meaning of the IDEA are entitled to assert IDEA protections if the school is "deemed to have knowledge" of a disability**. This can occur when "the behavior or performance of the child" demonstrates the need for special education and related services. Here, the student stated the minimal factual basis for an IDEA claim by asserting that the school had knowledge of a disability at the time it initiated expulsion proceedings. The court rejected the school's argument that it could rely on the outcome of the manifestation determination hearing for determining that she was not disabled. The student should have been kept in school under the stay-put provision. *S.W. v. Holbrook Public Schools*, 221 F.Supp.2d 222 (D. Mass. 2002).

◆ An Alabama student of normal intelligence experienced academic and behavioral difficulties. His foster parent initially resisted any attempt to place him in special education classes. School administrators recommended a voluntary behavior management plan. After a number of disciplinary referrals, the school district transferred him to an alternative school for 45 days as an interim measure to avoid expulsion. The foster parent then asked the district to evaluate the student for special education. Five teachers and the parent completed surveys designed to identify an emotional disturbance. The surveys of the parent and two of the teachers yielded clinically significant results, but those of the other teachers suggested no disturbance. A hearing officer found the data supplied by the parent incredible, based on bias and possible lack of sincerity, and held that the student did not qualify for special education as emotionally disturbed.

The student appealed to a federal court, where he argued that the survey results should have automatically entitled him to special education. The court stated that the hearing officer had properly discounted the value of the surveys rating the student's emotional disturbance as clinically significant. Only two of the five teacher surveys indicated emotional disturbance, and the parent's survey was clouded by bias. **The parent had changed his position on special education once it was clear that his son could avoid severe discipline by obtaining classification under a special education category.** Multiple experienced educators testified that the student often acted appropriately. The evidence indicated that the student was not emotionally disturbed under state and federal law, and the parent could not force the school district to provide the accommodations requested. *Maricus W. v. Lanett City Board of Educ.*, 142 F.Supp.2d 1327 (M.D. Ala. 2001).

◆ Although a student struggled academically and had repeated fourth grade, he was not identified as a student with disabilities. His parents believed that he had an attention deficit disorder. During his sixth-grade year, he brought a miniature Swiss army knife to school. He also admitted to possessing a home-made knife. The school held a disciplinary hearing that resulted in a recommendation of expulsion for one year, but suspended most of the punishment. The school board overruled the recommendation and approved the student's suspension for a full calendar year under its zero-tolerance policy.

The student appealed to a federal court, claiming that the district should have identified him as having disabilities, and that it violated his procedural rights under the IDEA. He sought preliminary relief from the court preventing the expulsion, asserting that the use of the zero-tolerance policy violated his constitutional rights to due process. The court noted that **the student failed to show that he was a child with a disability as defined by the IDEA.** He presented only lay witnesses, who could not prove that he had ADD. However, the school board did violate his due process rights by deferring to the blanket expulsion policy rather than engaging in an independent consideration of the relevant facts and circumstances of the student's case. Because the board here had "blindly meted out the student's punishment," the court remanded the case to the board for reconsideration. If the board reinstated the student to school, it would have to formally test the student to determine whether he had a learning disability. *Colvin v. Lowndes County School Dist.*, 114 F.Supp.2d 504 (N.D. Miss. 2000).

♦   Maryland school officials questioned a high school student enrolled in a regular education course of study about her possible possession of controlled substances. After signing a written admission that she had brought LSD onto school grounds, she was expelled. The student appealed to the state board of education, which affirmed the local board's decision, and the student appealed to a Maryland circuit court, arguing that the admission had been coerced and that the school district had failed to first assess her special education needs before taking disciplinary action. The court affirmed the expulsion order, and the student appealed. The Court of Special Appeals of Maryland rejected the student's assertion that the district was required to perform a special education evaluation prior to taking disciplinary action against her because it possessed evidence that she had attention deficit hyperactivity disorder. **The procedural safeguards of state special education law applied only to students who were unable to achieve their educational potential in general education programs.** A parental request for a special education evaluation did not bring regular disciplinary proceedings to a halt. The court also rejected the student's claim that her oral admission had been coerced. She had ratified the admission in writing and again at her hearing where she was represented by an attorney. The court affirmed the expulsion order. *Miller v. Board of Educ. of Caroline County*, 114 Md. App. 462, 690 A.2d 557 (Md. Ct. Spec. App. 1997).

♦   An Indiana fourth-grader with diabetes attended a public school as a regular education student. Her blood sugar tested at a low level on a morning that she went on a class field trip. Her teacher suggested that she eat some fruit, and after doing so her blood sugar rose to a level identified by her doctor as unlikely to cause unusual behavior. However, on the return trip to school, she used a nail file instrument containing a small knife blade to threaten two students who had been harassing her. The school's principal suspended her for five days. A hearing officer recommended a six-week expulsion, but was not notified of the student's diabetic condition. The student's parents appealed to the school board, and presented evidence that her actions had been caused by her diabetes. The board upheld the expulsion and found that the evidence did not support the argument that the student's behavior was affected by low blood sugar levels. The parents sued. The court held that **the board had not acted arbitrarily or capriciously by expelling the student without finding that her behavior was causally related to her disability**. The district was not obligated to make this finding, since she had not been identified as disabled. The expulsion decision had not been based solely upon the student's aggressive behavior; it was also based on a violation of the state code prohibiting possession of a knife at a school activity. *Brown v. Metropolitan School Dist. of Lawrence Township*, 945 F.Supp. 1202 (S.D. Ind. 1996).

V. EXTENDED SCHOOL YEAR

Extended school year (ESY) services must be provided where necessary to provide students with a free appropriate public education. ESY services were designed to assist students with disabilities who experience significant regression of critical life skills because of an interruption in the instructional program.

♦ A student who received ESY services when he lived in California did not receive them after he and his family moved to Washington. His new district, after a disciplinary incident, agreed to place him in a private school, but justified the refusal to offer ESY services on the lack of data needed from the private school. The case reached the Court of Appeals of Washington, which noted that **the district could not shift the duty for collecting student data to the private school**. It should have conducted tests, evaluations or assessments on its own rather than wait for the information to be provided by the private school. The district had to provide the student with the number of hours of counseling or instruction he would have received had he attended an ESY program. *A.D. v. Sumner School Dist.*, 166 P.3d 837 (Wash. Ct. App. 2007).

♦ A Colorado school district found an autistic student eligible for ESY services, which would help him maintain learned skills over the summer. **His parents instead wanted the district to focus on developing skills identified in his IEPs for the prior and upcoming years.** They obtained private ESY services and requested due process. A hearing officer first found that the state ESY guidelines did not violate the IDEA. However, before the hearing officer ruled on whether the district denied the student a FAPE, the parents appealed to a federal court. The case reached the Tenth Circuit, which held that the parents should have exhausted their administrative remedies before suing. The case was dismissed. *McQueen v. Colorado Springs School Dist. No. 11*, 488 F.3d 868 (10th Cir. 2007).

♦ A Hawaii student with specific learning disabilities was unilaterally placed in a private school, then sent to an Illinois residential school. Her parents sought to return her to a Hawaii school, but rejected the IEP placing her in a public school. They believed she needed extended school year services and that the district/state predetermined her public school placement. A hearing officer rejected their claims and a federal court agreed. **The lack of ESY services did**

not amount to a denial of a free appropriate public education. Also, the lack of a specific transition plan did not mean that the district/state had predetermined where the student should attend school. Since she was only a sophomore, the transition plan did not yet need to be specific. However, there was a question as to whether the district/state had conducted IEP meetings or evaluations while the student was in the private schools. And the parents might be entitled to some tuition reimbursement. The case was remanded to the hearing officer for further action. *Virginia S. v. Dep't of Educ., State of Hawaii*, No. 06-00128 JMS/LEK, 2007 WL 80814 (D. Haw. 1/8/07).

◆   A student who received extended school year services turned 21 on August 21, 2006 and his ESY services ended. He claimed he was entitled to receive funding for his residential placement through the end of the 2006-07 school year. The district disagreed and a lawsuit resulted. A New Jersey federal court held that the student was entitled to educational benefits through the end of the 2006-07 school year (the school year during which he turned 21). **The date the ESY program ended was not the time frame to be used for determining the student's school-year eligibility.** ESY programs are not actually extensions of school years, but rather "additional special education services outside the normal [educational] program." *C.T. v. Verona Board of Educ.*, 464 F.Supp.2d 383 (D.N.J. 2006).

◆   The parent of a disabled Minnesota student rejected the district's IEP, and a due process hearing was conducted on, among other issues, whether the district had failed to develop a timely extended school year (ESY) program. The hearing officer held that the district had always intended to offer ESY services and that the parent had not cooperated in discussing ESY issues. The Eighth Circuit ultimately affirmed that decision, ruling that the student was not entitled to compensatory education for the delay, and that **IDEA regulations do not prescribe the time in which an ESY proposal must be made.** *Reinholdson v. School Board of Independent School Dist. No. 11*, 187 Fed.Appx. 672 (8th Cir. 2006).

◆   The mother of a Minnesota student with multiple disabilities sought one-to-one paraprofessional support services for her son when he moved from elementary school to middle school. The district determined that one-to-one support was not needed and waited until late in the year to create an extended school year (ESY) program. When the mother eventually sued under the IDEA, a federal court ruled for the district, noting that the student actually did better with less paraprofessional assistance by seeking cues from his environment and peers. Also, **nothing in the IDEA or state law required an IEP team to determine ESY services by a specific date.** *Reinholdson v. School Board of Independent School Dist. No. 11*, No. Civ. 02-4225 ADM/AJB, 2005 WL 1819976 (D. Minn. 8/2/05).

◆   The IEP team for a Minnesota student with epilepsy and other disabilities agreed that she needed extended school year (ESY) services but did not specify the services, location, goal or objectives. The student's father proposed a residential program in South Dakota and eventually placed her there. He then requested a due process hearing, claiming the district's proposed ESY program was deficient. The hearing officer ruled for the district and a federal court agreed. Here, **the IEP team did not have to draft an ESY program at the same time it drafted the rest of the student's IEP**. The team was allowed to wait until spring to determine what ESY services would be provided. Also, since ESY services are designed to prevent regression and not advance IEP goals, ESY services could differ from school year IEPs. *Pachl v. School Board of Independent School Dist. No. 11*, No. Civ. 02-4065 ADM/AJB, 2005 WL 428587 (D. Minn. 2/23/05).

◆ The mother of a student with a mild, high-functioning pervasive developmental disorder made a number of complaints about her son's education. She objected to a particular consultant, complained that the district's extended school year (ESY) offer did not specify the length of the school day, and asserted that the district kept poor track of data that would allow her to monitor her son's progress. When she withdrew her son from school and sued, a California federal court ruled against her. The IDEA does not specify how a student's progress is to be monitored, and the ESY offer complied with the IDEA. **The ESY did not have to detail exact class times and teacher names.** *Jack P. v. Auburn Union Elementary School Dist.*, No. 5-04-896 LKK/PAN, 2005 WL 2042269 (E.D. Cal. 8/23/05).

◆ The parents of an Ohio student with disabilities entered into two settlement agreements with their school district after disputes over extended school year services, behavioral reinforcements and the provision of tutoring services. After the first agreement, the tutor became ill and the superintendent offered to provide another tutor for the student, but only two sessions were provided because of a conflict between student and tutor. After the second agreement, limited tutoring was provided because the parents refused to transport the student to the tutor. The parents sued the district for breach of contract, but a federal court ruled against them. **The district had lived up to its obligations under the agreements.** If the parents were dissatisfied with its actions, they should have requested due process. *Popson v. Danbury Local School Dist.*, No. 304CV7056, 2005 WL 1126732 (N.D. Ohio 4/28/05).

CHAPTER THREE

IDEA Procedural Safeguards

I. DUE PROCESS HEARINGS

The procedural safeguards of the IDEA provide the means for students with disabilities and their parents to enforce their rights under the act. The safeguards include the right to an "impartial due process hearing" under 20 U.S.C. § 1415(f) when parents or guardians are dissatisfied with any matter relating to the identification, evaluation, or educational placement of the child, or the provision of a free appropriate public education to the child.

The state or local educational agency responsible for providing services conducts the hearing with the assistance of an impartial hearing officer. The initial due process hearing may be provided at the state or local educational agency level. If held at the local level, either party may appeal to the state educational agency, which shall conduct an impartial review of such hearing. See 20 U.S.C. § 1415(g). Unless appealed, the initial hearing officer's decision becomes final. Likewise, the state officer's decision becomes final unless a party brings a challenge in state or federal court. See 20 U.S.C. § 1415(i)(2).

A. Generally

♦ A Pennsylvania student with ADHD took medication for his condition. His district found him ineligible for special education under both the IDEA and Section 504. After he scrawled a bomb threat on a school lavatory wall, his parents sought a manifestation determination, which request was denied. A hearing officer found him eligible under Section 504 but also found no due process violation. The case reached a federal court, which stated that **Section 504 students do not have the same protections as IDEA students**. The student was not denied due process. However, the hearing officer should have considered the effect of the medication on the student's condition before determining that he was eligible under Section 504. *Centennial School Dist. v. Phil L.*, No. 08-982, 2010 WL 1174206 (E.D. Pa. 3/26/10).

♦ A Minnesota student's parents filed a due process hearing request. Both the parents and the school district sought delays, and the hearing officer then asked for an extension of the 45-day time limit for due process hearing decisions. When the parents complained to the state department of education, an investigation determined that **the delay was caused by requests from both parties**. Eventually, the hearing officer approved the student's IEP and behavior intervention plan. The student sued the state for failing to ensure compliance with the 45-day deadline, but the federal court dismissed the state from the lawsuit. The state was not responsible for any delay. *Renollett v. State of Minnesota*, No. Civ. 03-6452 ADM/AJB, 2004 WL 1576716 (D. Minn. 7/13/04).

♦ The parents of a student with sensitivities to many chemicals (including pesticides) rejected a Section 504 plan for their daughter – not wanting to use the local hospital in case of emergency, not wanting to label her "disabled," and rejecting provisions for adaptive physical education. **The school district requested a due process hearing**, and a special education hearing officer found the Section 504 plan appropriate, allowing the student to attend a school not surrounded by fields and farms. The parents withdrew their daughter from school and sued the district for abusing its power. A Pennsylvania federal court ruled for the district, finding no abuse of power in requesting a due process hearing or in any of the Section 504 procedures it used. *Sutton v. West Chester Area School Dist.*, No. Civ.A. 03-3061, 2004 WL 999144 (E.D. Pa. 5/5/04).

♦ New Jersey students with disabilities left their public school to enroll in charter schools, which then transferred them to private schools. The charter schools sought tuition reimbursement from the school district under the IDEA provision of the Charter School Act. The district paid the tuition, even though it was not consulted about the placements, but objected to the transfers and complained to the state department of education. It requested that school districts have input into private school placements by charter schools. When the department did not provide relief, the district sued the charter schools and the department in a federal court, arguing that the department's application of the Charter School Act conflicted with and was preempted by the IDEA mainstreaming requirement. The court ruled against the district, finding that it had **no private right of action to dispute the placement of students by charter schools** without first requesting a due process hearing. This, it failed to do. *Asbury Park Board of Educ. v. Hope Academy Charter School*, 278 F.Supp.2d 417 (D.N.J. 2003).

◆   A hearing-impaired student and his family moved from Michigan to Indiana. His parents sought compensatory education from their old school district, asserting that the district failed to provide their son with a properly endorsed teacher, necessary speech/language services and an interpreter. The state education department determined that the student was entitled to compensatory speech/language services, but otherwise exonerated the district. The parents requested due process, but a hearing officer dismissed the case because the student had moved from the district. A state review officer reversed. A Michigan federal court then held that the district had properly asserted that it had no obligation to provide services to a student residing outside its boundaries. However, **the district could not deny the student a hearing just because the due process request came after he moved out of the district**. It would be able to provide him with compensatory services by contracting with an out-of-state entity to fulfill its obligations. The student was entitled to a due process hearing. *Lewis Cass Intermediate School Dist. v. M.K.*, 290 F.Supp.2d 832 (W.D. Mich. 2003).

◆   A student with disabilities attended a Catholic elementary school in New Hampshire but received special education services from a public school district. He was transported to a speech/language program at a public school for one hour a week, then returned to the private school. His parents sought compensatory education from the district after it failed to provide him with services for parts of two school years and caused him to miss speech/language sessions because of unreliable transportation. They requested a due process hearing, which was refused because of their voluntary placement of their son in a private school. A federal court agreed that they were not entitled to a due process hearing. Laws that set conditions on the ability to receive government benefits are not invalid. And **private school students do not have individually enforceable rights under the IDEA**. *Andrew S. v. Manchester School Dist.*, 241 F.Supp.2d 111 (D.N.H. 2003).

◆   A Virginia student with autistic spectrum disorder attended public schools in a class-based, noncategorical program. His father sought intensive one-to-one Applied Behavioral Analysis training, which the school district refused to provide. The father rejected the proposed IEP, and the district responded with an explanation of its reasoning. It also notified him of his right to a due process hearing or administrative review. The father enrolled his son in a private school and, more than 29 months later, filed a due process hearing request. A hearing officer held that he had waited too long, but a federal court ruled that the district should have given him notice of Virginia's two-year statute of limitations. The Fourth Circuit reversed, noting that **nothing in the IDEA requires school districts to provide parents with notice of appropriate limitations periods**. *R.R. v. Fairfax County School Board*, 338 F.3d 325 (4th Cir. 2003).

◆   A school district agreed to place a student with autism in a private school for six months. Near the end of this period, the parties met at an IEP meeting, where the district proposed changing his placement to a public school. The parents instead requested a placement at a different private school and notified the district of their intention to enroll the student there. When the parties could not agree on an IEP, the district requested a due process hearing to determine the student's placement. The parents moved to dismiss the action as "premature" because they had not yet filed any claim for tuition or transportation reimbursement. An administrative law judge held that there was "no case or controversy" for him to decide and that the district lacked standing to file a due process request. A federal court then held that **under Maryland special education regulations, the district had standing to resolve the placement dispute, whether initiated by the parents or a school district**. If the parents' argument were accepted, a district would be unable to provide the education it deemed appropriate, and teachers would be unable to devise an IEP based on personal knowledge of the student. This would improperly transfer decision-making authority from the school board to the parents. *Yates v. Charles County Board of Educ.*, 212 F.Supp.2d 470 (D. Md. 2002).

◆   A student with a learning disability and communication disorder was removed from school when his parents felt his local school district was unwilling to provide him with an appropriate IEP. The parents placed him in a private school and commenced due process proceedings. The parties initially agreed upon a hearing officer, but the district withdrew its consent and the selected officer recused himself. A state special education compliance officer appointed a replacement. At the hearing, the compliance officer appeared as an expert witness on behalf of the school district. The hearing officer then denied relief to the parents. They sought review by a state special education appeals panel, but the parties were unable to agree on the composition of the panel. The state superintendent of public instruction appointed a three-member panel, which affirmed the hearing officer's decision. The parents then sued state and local education officials and entities, asserting that the hearing process violated the IDEA.

The court held that **under the IDEA, procedural due process is afforded where a party has legal representation and the opportunity to cross-examine witnesses. The parents received these rights**, and the officials and agencies were entitled to pretrial judgment. Also, state officials had not acted improperly and with bias for the district, since the parents did not allege specific factual determinations demonstrating bias. *L.C. v. Utah State Board of Educ.*, 188 F.Supp.2d 1330 (D. Utah 2002).

◆   The mother of a Florida student claimed that the district failed to provide an appropriate IEP for her child, who had mental and physical disabilities. She commenced an administrative action against the school board that was resolved through a settlement agreement prior to a final hearing. The board agreed to place the student in a particular school and provide her with transportation for a four-month period in 1999. It also agreed to pay the family up to $17,000 for attorneys' fees in return for their waiver of any further claims in a formal administrative proceeding. During the four-month period, the student's mother claimed that the board breached the agreement by failing to provide the student with agreed-upon services. She commenced a new due process action against the board, which was dismissed in view of the settlement agreement. The Florida Second District Court of Appeal affirmed the decision, and the mother filed a new administrative action against the board, seeking rescission of the settlement agreement and damages for breaching it.

The hearing officer held that he was without jurisdiction to consider the case, which sought only to enforce, interpret or rescind the prior settlement agreement and did not relate to the student's present educational placement. The board appealed to the district court of appeal, seeking to dismiss the action. The court held that the hearing officer had correctly found himself without jurisdiction to consider the case. The agreement pertained to a specific time period for which services had allegedly been withheld from the student. It was not the typical special education dispute in which a family sought to ensure an appropriate placement. **There was no current claim that the student's IEP was improper or needed to be changed.** Issues such as breach of contract, rescission and attorneys' fees were properly before a state circuit court, and the court affirmed the administrative order. *School Board of Lee County v. M.C.*, 796 So.2d 581 (Fla. Dist. Ct. App. 2001).

♦ The parents of a student with disabilities filed a due process complaint against their school district to determine whether it would continue providing him with reading and comprehension tutoring services. The parties reached a settlement agreement during the administrative proceedings. The following year, the parents initiated a due process proceeding with the California Special Education Hearing Office (SEHO), primarily asserting that the district failed to comply with the parties' settlement agreement from the prior administrative action. The hearing officer held that he lacked jurisdiction to hear any issue related to the previous hearing order, since due process orders are considered final under the state education code. Compliance with SEHO orders was an issue for the state education department's compliance office, and the hearing officer dismissed the case. The parents then filed a federal court action against the school district, arguing that the SEHO had jurisdiction to hear compliance issues related to previous due process proceedings.

The court affirmed the hearing officer's order, and the parents appealed to the Ninth Circuit. On appeal, they asserted that the SEHO had jurisdiction over several of their claims because they related to the settlement agreement. The circuit court disagreed, holding that the SEHO hearing officer lacked jurisdiction to hear issues arising from a final hearing order. The California Education Code states that a special education due process hearing is the final determination in a special education dispute and is binding on all parties. Once a decision is rendered by the SEHO, it becomes final and is not subject to further review on the same issue. Here, the hearing officer had properly found that the prior order dismissing the case was final. **The appropriate recourse for the parents to address alleged noncompliance by the school district was an action before the state education department's compliance office.** *Wyner v. Manhattan Beach Unified School Dist.*, 223 F.3d 1026 (9th Cir. 2000).

♦   The Delaware Office of Disciplinary Counsel (ODC) petitioned the state board on the Unauthorized Practice of Law for a ruling that a New Jersey non-profit advocacy center was engaging in the unauthorized practice of law by attempting to represent students during Delaware special education due process proceedings. The board agreed with the ODC, and the center appealed to the state supreme court, asserting that the IDEA authorized it to argue on behalf of students with disabilities in state due process hearings, and that Delaware was the only state that did not permit lay advocates to do so. Its petition was supported by the U.S. Department of Justice.

The court observed that hearings were conducted by three-person panels that included a lay person with a demonstrated interest in the education of students with disabilities, a certified educator or post-secondary educator of students with disabilities, and an attorney licensed to practice law in Delaware. Hearings were relatively informal, but parties presented evidence through witnesses and cross-examined adverse witnesses. Parties also made closing statements and were sometimes asked to file written submissions. The court found that **the IDEA was ambiguous, apparently conferring joint authority upon attorneys and non-lawyers to accompany and advise parents at IDEA due process hearings**. The court concluded that Delaware had the authority to exclude non-attorneys from adversarial hearings such as state due process hearings. *In the Matter of Arons*, 756 A.2d 867 (Del. 2000).

B. Evidence

♦   When a Maryland private school student with learning, language and other health impairments did not succeed despite the school's small size, significant accommodations and his receipt of additional services, his parents contacted a school district and sought special education. The district found the student eligible and proposed a draft IEP calling for the student's placement in a public middle school. The parents requested a due process hearing and enrolled the student in a different private school. The administrative law judge (ALJ) assigned the burden of proof to the parents. Since they could not meet this burden, the district prevailed. On appeal, a federal court held that the hearing officer had erroneously allocated the burden of proof to the parents. The Fourth Circuit vacated and remanded the case, and the ALJ held for the parents, finding that the IEP offered by the district was inadequate.

A federal court agreed with the ALJ's conclusion that the district did not provide the student with a FAPE during the year it first proposed an IEP. It awarded the parents full reimbursement for the costs of private school during the first year. Because the parents did not exhaust their administrative remedies concerning the two subsequent years of private school tuition, the court denied those claims. The Fourth Circuit reversed the district court, and the case reached the U.S. Supreme Court, which agreed with the court of appeals that **parents who challenge IEPs have the burden of proving that the IEPs are not appropriate**. To do otherwise would force courts to assume that every IEP is invalid until the school district demonstrates that it is not. *Schaffer v. Weast*, 546 U.S. 49, 126 S.Ct. 528, 163 L.Ed.2d 387 (2005).

On remand, the parents challenged the student's eighth-grade IEP by presenting evidence of the changes made to his 10th-grade IEP. The school district countered with evidence that the student had graduated with a 3.4 grade point average. A Maryland federal court ruled for the district and the Fourth Circuit affirmed. Using the 10th-grade IEP to challenge the eighth-grade IEP would promote a hindsight-based review that conflicted with the IDEA's structure and purpose. *Schaffer v. Weast*, 554 F.3d 470 (4th Cir. 2009).

♦   The parents of a Virginia student with autism became dissatisfied with his public school education and requested due process. The hearing officer determined that he could not resolve the case on the basis of the credibility of the witnesses because they were all credible. Nevertheless, he ruled for the school district, finding that it offered the student a FAPE by providing a self-contained special education classroom, a full-time instructional aide and opportunities for ABA. A federal court reversed the hearing officer's award, making its own findings of fact and determining that the private school placement sought by the parents was appropriate. The Fourth Circuit then vacated the lower court's ruling, noting that **the district court should not have questioned the hearing officer's findings**. The IDEA did not require the hearing officer to offer a more detailed explanation of credibility assessments. *Peterson v. County School Board of Hanover County, Virginia*, 516 F.3d 254 (4th Cir. 2008).

♦   When the parents of a learning-disabled Missouri student challenged his IEP, a special education panel found that the district denied the student a free appropriate public education (FAPE) after putting the burden of proving compliance with the IDEA on the district. A federal court largely upheld that decision. The Eighth Circuit reversed, noting that **the burden of proof was on the parents**, as the parties challenging the IEP, to show noncompliance with the IDEA. Since this was a close case, putting the burden on the parents might result in a decision for the district. *West Platte R-II School Dist. v. Wilson*, 439 F.3d 782 (8th Cir. 2006).

♦   By the ninth grade, a student with emotional disturbance and learning disabilities had extreme anxiety about school and refused to attend. His parents placed him in a private school and gave district officials an individualized program prepared by the private school. When the district prepared an IEP that specified a public school placement with speech/language therapy and 21 hours of weekly special education, the parents requested a due process hearing. The district's only witness was a special education coordinator who had never met the student or reviewed his evaluations. The hearing officer ruled that the IEP was appropriate, but a District of Columbia federal court reversed. It noted that **the district failed to present any competent evidence that the proposed placement was appropriate**. The parents had presented five witnesses in support of their claims. They were entitled to tuition reimbursement for the prior year. *Scorah v. District of Columbia*, 322 F.Supp.2d 12 (D.D.C. 2004).

♦   A Virginia preschool student with autism was enrolled in a private center, where the school board conducted evaluations concerning his performance level. When the board proposed placing him in a public elementary school that employed the TEACCH methodology, instead of the ABA methodology employed by the center, the parents rejected the IEP. At an administrative hearing, the board provided three expert witnesses, who testified that the TEACCH program offered the student a free appropriate public education and that other students with similar abilities were succeeding in the program. The hearing officer instead credited the testimony of the parents' witnesses in finding that the board did not offer the student a free appropriate public education. A federal court then ruled that **the school board was deprived of the opportunity to show it offered a free appropriate public education**. The hearing officer had placed too much reliance on the parents' witnesses, who had no knowledge of the TEACCH program and the educational benefits it offered. The court held in favor of the school board. The parents appealed to the Fourth Circuit, which noted that the hearing officer's findings of fact were presumptively correct and that the lower court did not explain what was wrong with them. The court remanded the case for reconsideration of the IEP, giving deference to the hearing officer's decision. *County School Board of Henrico County, Virginia v. Z.P.*, 399 F.3d 298 (4th Cir. 2005).

♦ A 21-year-old student had cerebral palsy, mental retardation, a degree of cortical blindness and the expressive language level of a two-year-old. Her parents expressed dissatisfaction with her IEPs by filing complaints against their school district with the U.S. Department of Education's Office for Civil Rights (OCR) and the Florida Education Department, which ordered the district to provide the student with transition planning. The parties settled the OCR complaint through an agreement to transfer the student to a high school for which the parents expressed a placement preference. After the student was transferred, the parents filed a due process complaint against the school district. An administrative law judge (ALJ) ordered the district to provide the student with a qualified speech and language pathologist or therapist. He found that the school's speech and language teacher was unqualified, since she was teaching outside the areas for which she was certified and had received only six hours of field course work in speech pathology. The order noted three deficiencies in the student's IEP, but otherwise held for the school board.

The Florida Court of Appeal found that the ALJ had applied proper IDEA legal standards when considering the IEP. However, he exceeded his authority by ordering the district to attempt to ensure the attendance of an outside agency at future transition service meetings. **The ALJ also abused his discretion by determining that the student's speech therapist was not qualified simply because she was teaching outside her field of certification.** There was no evidence to support this finding. There was evidence indicating that the student had significantly improved her communication skills through augmentative communication and that she had increased her verbal skills. The court reversed the decision in part. *School Board of Lee County v. S.W.*, 789 So.2d 1162 (Fla. Dist. Ct. App. 2001).

♦ The parents of an eight-year-old student with autism rejected a proposed IEP and unilaterally enrolled her in a private school. They requested tuition reimbursement and sought a due process hearing. An administrative law judge held that the IEP prepared by the school district did not comply with the IDEA and awarded the parents reimbursement. The school district appealed to a Georgia federal court, seeking to present additional evidence. The court required a proffer of evidence by the district and it responded with a list of 19 witnesses and three categories of documentary evidence. The court excluded most of the evidence offered by the school district, finding it was cumulative and/or irrelevant, and affirmed the decision for the parents. The school district appealed to the Eleventh Circuit, which observed that the determination of what additional evidence should be allowed was within the discretion of the trial court. In *Town of Burlington v. Dep't of Educ.*, 471 U.S. 359 (1985), the U.S. Supreme Court affirmed a decision construing the IDEA's "additional evidence" clause as not authorizing trial witnesses to repeat or embellish their administrative testimony. The lower court decision was affirmed. *Walker County School Dist. v. Bennett*, 203 F.3d 1293 (11th Cir. 2000).

♦ A nine-year-old Pennsylvania student was identified as having attention deficit disorder with hyperactivity (ADHD). Her school district conducted a multidisciplinary evaluation and determined that she was not entitled to special education. The multidisciplinary team found that although she exhibited ADHD symptoms, she had strong verbal skills, achievement levels and abilities that were at or above average, and that she could be educated in regular classrooms. A school IEP team agreed. The student's parents requested a hearing, which resulted in reversal of the proposed placement decision. A state appeals panel reversed, and a federal court affirmed. In doing so, the court disallowed the family's attempt to supplement the record and held that it was confined to a review of the administrative record. It also held that the IDEA preempted other claims by the student, including those filed under Section 504 of the Rehabilitation Act, the Americans with Disabilities Act and Pennsylvania law. The family appealed. The Third Circuit Court of Appeals noted that **language in the IDEA required a district court to hear additional evidence at the request of a party**. Although a district court should exclude cumulative evidence and testimony offered only to bolster the record, it must consider evidence acquired after the administrative hearing that pertains to the reasonableness of a school district's initial placement decision or denial of special education services. The district court erroneously held that the IDEA preempted other state and federal claims. The IDEA expressly allowed students to advance multiple claims under state and federal law after exhausting their administrative remedies. The court vacated and remanded the district court's decision. *Susan N. v. Wilson School Dist.*, 70 F.3d 751 (3d Cir. 1995).

C. Hearing Officer Bias and Authority

♦ The parents of a Maine student requested a due process hearing, seeking tuition reimbursement. After the hearing officer ruled against them, they challenged her decision on the grounds that she was **not an impartial hearing officer because she had also served as a complaint investigator** for the state. A federal court disagreed with them. Hearing officers enjoy a presumption of honesty and integrity. Further, the parents did not timely object to the hearing officer or exhaust their administrative remedies. *Mr. and Mrs. V. v. York School Dist.*, 434 F.Supp.2d 5 (D. Me. 2006).

♦   The parents of a 12-year-old gifted high school student with Asperger's syndrome and significant difficulties in writing and interpersonal skills filed a complaint with the Maine education department. A complaint investigator concluded that the district had failed to implement some of the student's IEP goals, objectives and modifications, failed to provide the parents with certain notices, and did not address the extent to which the student would participate with non-disabled students. At a pre-hearing due process conference, the hearing officer commented that the investigator's findings were not binding on him. After he issued a ruling for the school district, the parents appealed.

A magistrate judge found nothing improper in the conduct of the hearing by the hearing officer. Other than the issue of the appropriateness of the IEP and the existence of a behavior plan, he had confined the issues to those identified in the pre-conference hearing. The parents themselves had acquiesced to the addition of the "IEP/modification or implementation" issue. They had brought up the issue of the lack of behavior intervention plan in the first place, and could not now argue that the issue was improperly before the hearing officer. **The hearing officer had the power and responsibility to make independent determinations of law and was not bound by the factual findings of the complaint investigator.** *Donlan v. Wells Ogunquit Community School Dist.*, 226 F.Supp.2d 261 (D. Me. 2002).

♦   When a school district and the parents of a gifted student were unable to agree on his IEP for the 2000-2001 school year, a hearing officer ordered the parties to develop a new IEP and required the district to give the student certain credits toward graduation. At the resulting IEP meeting, the district proposed an IEP calling for the student's graduation in 2002, with an agreement that if he completed the 28.5 credits he needed for graduation, he would graduate a semester early. The parents challenged the 2002 graduation decision. A hearing officer upheld the district's IEP and the 2002 graduation date. A due process appeals panel reversed, finding that the IEP contained both substantive and procedural errors. The panel ordered the student classified as a member of the 2000-2001 class, provided he completed the required number of credits. The school district was ordered to provide certain personnel involved in the student's education with 10 hours of special education in-service education, and to hire an outside expert to help develop an appropriate IEP.

The Pennsylvania Commonwealth Court noted that **although appeals panels have the authority to order remedies such as compensatory education, the appeals panel was not authorized under Pennsylvania law to order the special education in-service it ordered in this case.** Since the panel lacked the authority to order district personnel to participate in an in-service session, this part of the panel's decision was reversed. Under Pennsylvania special education regulations, the composition of the IEP team is the school district's responsibility. Because the inclusion of an outside expert was not a statutory requirement for the composition of an IEP team, the panel lacked the authority to order the inclusion of an outside expert on the student's IEP team. Also, the district could not be forced to graduate the student before he earned the statutorily established minimum number of credits toward graduation. The student had to earn 28.5 credits, since this was the graduation requirement when he started high school. The court reversed the appeals panel's order. *Saucon Valley School Dist. v. Robert O.*, 785 A.2d 1069 (Pa. Commw. Ct. 2001).

◆ A Maine school committee and the parents of a student with disabilities went to due process over the parents' decision to unilaterally place the student in a private school. The hearing officer ordered the school committee to reimburse the parents for their tuition. Shortly after the hearing concluded, the committee learned the hearing officer had a disabled student who attended private school. When the committee requested a new hearing to consider the family's failure to cooperate with requested evaluations of the student, the same hearing officer was appointed. The committee requested she recuse herself. She declined to do so, and the school committee appealed her original decision on the grounds that she had a disqualifying personal interest and was biased. The court observed that Maine special education regulations permit the challenge of a hearing officer only on the grounds of conflict of interest or bias. The appearance of impartiality alone was insufficient to disqualify a hearing officer. **The fact that the hearing officer had a child with moderate hearing loss in private schools did not indicate any conflict of interest, bias, hostility or prejudgment** against the school committee. The alleged conversations with the parents had been about the hearing officer's son, not the student whose case was being considered. The court disallowed the committee's request for further fact finding. *Falmouth School Committee v. B.*, 106 F.Supp.2d 69 (D. Me. 2000).

◆ A hearing officer made the list of independent hearing officers available to preside over special education hearings in Indiana. Because state and federal law require that hearing officers be independent from public education agencies, he was not a state employee and was not compensated unless he was actually selected to hear a case. After serving in this capacity for several years, the hearing officer decided a case in favor of a student that resulted in an order requiring the state to reimburse the parents for over $121,000. The decision was reversed by the state board of special education appeals, which expressed concern over the hearing officer's handling of the case. The board's attorney found that the officer had made several inaccurate factual findings and argumentative conclusions of law. The state superintendent of public instruction informed the hearing officer that he would be removed from the list of available hearing officers. The hearing officer sued the superintendent for constitutional rights violations, asserting the right to a hearing prior to the termination action. The Indiana Court of Appeals noted that the hearing officer was not a state employee who was entitled to the same constitutional due process protections that government officials enjoy. The placement of his name on a list of hearing officer candidates did not create a contract and did not guarantee that he would actually be assigned to hear any cases. **Since he had no constitutionally protectable property interest, he was not entitled to due process protections.** *Reed v. Schultz*, 715 N.E.2d 896 (Ind. Ct. App. 1999).

II.   EXHAUSTION OF ADMINISTRATIVE REMEDIES

The exhaustion of remedies doctrine, as articulated by the U.S. Supreme Court in Myers v. Bethlehem Shipbuilding Corp.*, 303 U.S. 41, 58 S.Ct. 459, 82 L.Ed. 638 (1938), provides that "no one is entitled to judicial relief for a supposed or threatened injury until the prescribed administrative remedy has been exhausted." The U.S. Supreme Court, in* McKart v. U.S.*, 395 U.S. 185, 89 S.Ct. 1657, 23 L.Ed.2d 194 (1968), explained that the doctrine allows for the development of an accurate factual record, thereby allowing more informed judicial review, encouraging "expeditious decision making," and taking advantage of agency expertise.*

Exhaustion is usually required when either IDEA violations or related claims are involved. Courts have reached varying conclusions with respect to whether exhaustion is required when a claim is brought seeking money damages in the context of a special education dispute. In those circuits that allow claims for money damages to be brought under the IDEA, courts have reached varying conclusions as to whether exhaustion of administrative remedies is required or excused. As a result, whether exhaustion is required in these cases depends on what state or circuit the claim arises in. For more information about claims for money damages, see Chapter Six, Section IV, C.

A.   Operation of the Exhaustion Doctrine

Parents or guardians of a child with a disability generally have the duty to exhaust all administrative channels before resorting to a state or federal court. Where a student adds other claims to an IDEA lawsuit, the exhaustion requirement remains in effect and subjects all claims to dismissal upon failure to exhaust agency remedies.

♦   The guardian of a California student with mental health problems entered into a settlement whereby the student was placed in a Colorado residential treatment facility. After she turned 18, she sued state officials, challenging California's failure to make in-state residential services available to emotionally disturbed students over age 18 who had not graduated and would not do so by age 19. A federal court ruled that she had to exhaust her administrative remedies first. **The settlement agreement did not satisfy the exhaustion requirement.** *Washington v. California Dep't of Educ.*, No. 2:10-CV-0186 FCD KJM, 2010 WL 4157139 (E.D. Cal. 10/19/10).

♦   The father of two disabled New Hampshire students claimed that his daughter was sexually abused by another disabled student and that his son was left without adult supervision. He sued the district for discrimination. A federal court dismissed the action on the grounds that he failed to exhaust his administrative remedies under the IDEA. **He should have filed a due process request because his discrimination claim was based on an IDEA violation.** *Hatch v. Milford School Dist.*, No. 10-CV-263-JD, 2010 WL 3489037 (D.N.H. 9/2/10).

♦ A California student with severe autism was placed in a different school than the one his siblings attended, which prompted a due process complaint from his family. After the case was settled, the family brought another complaint alleging that the district had violated the settlement agreement. A hearing officer ruled for the district, and the family then sued, adding other claims against the district. However, a federal court held that **the family failed to exhaust its administrative remedies** on those other claims. They should have gone before the hearing officer. *Andrew W. v. Menlo Park City School Dist.*, No. C-10-0292 MMC, 2010 WL 3001216 (N.D. Cal. 7/29/10).

♦ Parents of an Illinois child with autism objected to a change in her placement and requested due process. They later sought to amend their complaint and their attorney withdrew from the case, so they then asked for an extension and a continuance. The hearing officer rejected their request. They found another attorney but were still denied continuances. As a result, they sued the district, claiming that exhaustion of administrative remedies would be futile. A federal court ruled against them. Despite the procedural hurdles, they still had to exhaust their administrative remedies. *C.S. v. Oak Lawn-Hometown School Dist. 123*, No. 09 C 2246, 2009 WL 3444776 (N.D. Ill. 10/22/09).

♦ A New York parent sued a school district for money damages, claiming that the district committed multiple offenses against his son. He included a claim under the IDEA because his son was not only limited-English proficient but also had significant language impairments. A federal court dismissed the lawsuit for failure to exhaust administrative remedies. **Even though race was the reason claimed for much of the mistreatment, the parent still had to exhaust administrative remedies.** *Dallas v. Roosevelt Union Free School Dist.*, 644 F.Supp.2d 287 (E.D.N.Y. 2009).

♦ The Ninth Circuit held that a California student's non-IDEA claims had to be addressed by a hearing officer before a lawsuit could be filed. **Exhaustion was required even though the district had found the student ineligible for special education.** The student was pursuing identification, evaluation and placement claims, as well as a Section 504 claim. *Huson v. Simi Valley Unified School Dist.*, 346 Fed.Appx. 150 (9th Cir. 2009).

♦ An Arizona parent believed her daughter had a learning disability and transferred her to another district. She then initiated due process against the old district and obtained some relief, with the old district remedying certain aspects of its IDEA procedures. The parent then filed another administrative complaint, seeking a new hearing. A hearing officer dismissed the case and she sued. However, the Arizona Court of Appeals upheld the dismissal of the lawsuit because she did not exhaust her administrative remedies. *Davis v. Roosevelt Elementary School Dist. No. 66*, No. 1 CA-CV 08-0628, 2009 WL 2032029 (Ariz. Ct. App. 7/14/09).

♦ A Connecticut parent of two biracial children claimed that the school district improperly denied special education services to one of them and provided insufficient special education to the other. She also alleged that her children were bullied and physically harmed by other students. She sued for race discrimination and equal protection violations, and she brought a bullying claim under state law. A federal court dismissed her lawsuit for failure to exhaust her administrative remedies. **She was alleging denial of special educational services and it didn't matter that the asserted reason was race discrimination.** Also, the bullying statute provided no private right to sue. *Karlen v. Westport Board of Educ.*, 638 F.Supp.2d 293 (D. Conn. 2009).

◆   A New York student who attended both district schools and a Bridges Program for students at risk of leaving school brought a lawsuit against the school district and various officials, claiming violations of the IDEA, Section 504 and the Constitution. A federal court held that he was required to exhaust his administrative remedies even though the district and the Board of Cooperative Educational Services had a long history of failing him. The Second Circuit U.S. Court of Appeals affirmed that decision. **The student was not claiming systemic failures so as to justify an exception to the exhaustion requirement.** *Levine v. Greece Cent. School Dist.*, No. 09-0910-CV, 2009 WL 3765813 (2d Cir. 11/12/09).

◆   Parents of two autistic students in Arizona claimed that their school district had no autism program and no qualified teachers. They sued the district, but a federal court and the Ninth Circuit ruled that they had failed to exhaust their administrative remedies. They failed to show that the district had admitted it could not serve their children and that any administrative due process hearing would be futile. *Wiatt v. Prescott Unified School Dist.*, 357 Fed.Appx. 28 (9th Cir. 2009).

◆   A West Virginia student with ADHD, a depressive disorder and a low-average IQ graduated from high school and then had trouble finding a job. The Social Security Administration found him functionally illiterate, unable to perform activities within a schedule, and unable to maintain regular attendance. He was declared eligible for Social Security Income benefits. When he later sued the school district for providing a defective education, the Supreme Court of Appeals of West Virginia upheld lower court decisions to dismiss the lawsuit. He had failed to exhaust his administrative remedies under the IDEA during his schooling. *Sturm v. Board of Educ. of Kanawha County*, 672 S.E.2d 606 (W. Va. 2008).

◆   The parents of a California student waited until after he graduated to challenge his education, bringing a Section 504 claim against the school district. A federal court dismissed the case, and the U.S. Court of Appeals for the Ninth Circuit affirmed that decision. Although Section 504 imposes slightly different obligations on school districts than those set by the IDEA, **parties seeking Section 504 relief that is also available under the IDEA must exhaust their administrative remedies** to the same extent as they would for IDEA claims. *Fraser v. Tamalpais Union High School Dist.*, 281 Fed.Appx. 746 (9th Cir. 2008).

♦   A Louisiana school board decided to consolidate two high schools that served at least 27 students with disabilities. Some of the parents sued in federal court to prevent the closing of the one school, asserting that their children would be forced to endure excessively long and dangerous bus rides and attend unsafe schools that were labeled as "in decline." They also asserted that their children would not receive all the services specified in their IEPs. The court ruled that they should have exhausted their administrative remedies first. Here, even though due process could not address their concerns over the school closing, **due process could address the issues of long bus rides, insufficient services and the inability to participate in extracurricular activities.** *J.I. and N.I. v. Beauregard Parish School Board*, No. 2:08 CV 535, 2008 WL 2340214 (W.D. La. 6/6/08).

♦   An Alaska student's family complained to the state department of education and early development that their district failed to provide the student with periodic speech, language, and occupational and physical therapy sessions. When the department found no violations of law, the family failed to file a due process action, instead suing the department under the IDEA. A federal court and the Ninth Circuit ruled against them, noting that **they were required to exhaust their administrative remedies even though they were claiming a systemic challenge.** They failed to show that the state had an unlawful policy of refusing to enforce district compliance with state educational requirements. *Brooke M. v. State of Alaska, Dep't of Educ. and Early Development*, 293 Fed.Appx. 452 (9th Cir. 2008).

♦   A Virginia student with Asperger's syndrome used his cell phone to take multiple pictures up a female classmate's skirt without her knowledge. The school suspended the student for 10 days and recommended expelling him. The IEP team determined that his misconduct was not a manifestation of his disability. A hearing officer ruled that he should be suspended for 18 days and then reassigned to another school. The school board agreed and offered interim services, but the parents instead appealed to a federal court, seeking money damages. The court dismissed their lawsuit, noting that they failed to exhaust their administrative remedies. *A.W. v. Fairfax County School Board*, 548 F.Supp.2d 219 (E.D. Va. 2008).

♦   The mother of a Florida autistic student pursued at least six due process complaints against the school district, appealing to a federal court after a hearing officer ruled in favor of the district. The court first noted that the mother failed to exhaust her administrative remedies with respect to her claim that the district retaliated against her for vigorous advocacy of her son's rights. Next, the court stated that although the Supreme Court had recognized parental rights under the IDEA, the mother could not pursue her discrimination claims without the assistance of legal counsel. *N.N.J. v. Broward County School Board*, No. 06-61282-CIV, 2007 WL 3120299 (S.D. Fla. 10/23/07).

♦   A disabled Georgia student sustained injuries while attending an after-school program. His parents reached a settlement with the district, but claimed that the school later retaliated against them at IEP meetings, sending them intimidating letters and needlessly testing their son. When the parents sued under the IDEA, a federal court held that they failed to exhaust their administrative remedies. All their claims related to their son's education within the meaning of the IDEA. Accordingly, they should have exhausted administrative remedies before suing. *J.P. v. Cherokee County Board of Educ.*, 218 Fed.Appx. 911 (11th Cir. 2007).

◆   A Pennsylvania fourth-grader with a visual motor disability, fine motor disability and handwriting needs received occupational therapy and classroom accommodations under a Section 504 service plan. After a third-grade teacher allegedly bullied him – staring at him, making fun of his handwriting, brushing against him and stepping on his finger, among other things – the student's parents sued the district under the IDEA, Section 504 and the Constitution. A federal court held that the parents were required to exhaust their administrative remedies before bringing their lawsuit because **most of their claims stemmed from the student's right to a free appropriate public education under the IDEA**. *M.M. v. Tredyffrin/Easttown School Dist.*, No. 06-1966, 2006 WL 2561242 (E.D. Pa. 9/1/06).

◆   The parents of a Kentucky student became dissatisfied with her progress and filed a due process action that was dismissed. They placed her in a private school through grade 12, then filed a complaint against the district using state complaint resolution procedures. The state education department found that the student was entitled to compensatory education for approximately three years. The district agreed to provide computer training for 104 weeks, and the state concluded that it had complied with its obligations. The parents then sued for further relief, but the Sixth Circuit ruled against them because they failed to exhaust their administrative remedies. *Long v. Dawson Springs Independent School Dist.*, 197 Fed.Appx. 427 (6th Cir. 2006).

◆   A Wisconsin student received four to six hours of therapy per week until his district discontinued the therapist's services. His parents then sued the district for a preliminary order preventing that action. A federal court dismissed the parents' lawsuit, finding that they failed to exhaust their administrative remedies. **They could not avoid requesting a due process hearing by adding a Section 1983 claim to the IDEA action.** *Greaves v. Stoughton Area School Dist.*, No. 05-C-0102-C, 2005 WL 567817 (W.D. Wis. 2/25/05).

◆   A special education student in the eighth grade who was a ward of the state earned enough credits to advance to ninth grade. However, the state department of health, a social worker, a teacher and his guardian ad litem advocated for his return to the eighth grade. The student's surrogate parent, foster parents and school personnel favored placement in the ninth grade. The guardian ad litem filed a motion in family court to have the student retained in eighth grade, and the court granted the order. The Supreme Court of Hawaii reversed. It found that the family court did not have the power to exercise jurisdiction here. **The guardian ad litem failed to exhaust IDEA administrative remedies.** *In the Interest of Doe Children*, 93 P.3d 1145 (Haw. 2004).

♦ A New York committee on special education (CSE) reclassified a student as non-handicapped and recommended no further special education or related services. The student's mother obtained an independent evaluation and private tutoring services, then requested a due process hearing. The parties reached a settlement in which the school board agreed to pay for the independent evaluation and the tutoring services. The hearing officer then sent the case back to the CSE, which again found the student was not disabled. The mother sued and a federal court ruled that she failed to exhaust her administrative remedies. **If the mother was displeased with the second determination to declassify the student, she had to once again seek a due process hearing.** *Combier v. Biegelson*, No. 03 CV 10304 (GBD), 2005 WL 477628 (S.D.N.Y. 2/28/05).

♦ The parents of a Connecticut student with disabilities agreed to a new IEP, but later alleged that the district did not adequately staff and implement it. A due process hearing officer issued an interim order requiring the district to immediately implement the IEP. When the parents felt it was still not being implemented properly, they complained to the state education department, which concluded that it lacked the authority to implement an interim order. The parents sued the state and the district. A federal court held that the parents failed to exhaust their administrative remedies with respect to the state. **Even though the IDEA requires the state to step in and provide the student with a free appropriate public education upon the local board's failure, this did not excuse the exhaustion requirement.** The parents could, however, seek compensatory education against the district. *B.H. v. Southington Board of Educ.*, 273 F.Supp.2d 194 (D. Conn. 2003).

♦ A Nevada student with severe emotional and behavioral problems alleged that school district and police officers twice violated the discipline provisions of his IEP – once by handcuffing him and putting him in the back of a squad car, and the other time by trying to get him to sign a citation without notifying his guardian. He claimed both incidents caused him emotional distress, and he sued the school district and the police under the IDEA. A federal court dismissed his claims for failure to exhaust his administrative remedies, and the Ninth Circuit affirmed. **A hearing officer had the power to award psychological counseling** as a related service. Thus, the student could not show that pursuing administrative remedies would be futile. *Fliess v. Washoe County School Dist.*, 90 Fed.Appx. 240 (9th Cir. 2004).

♦ A Rhode Island student with neurological deficits was reclassified from IDEA-eligible to Section 504-eligible at her mother's request. Subsequently, her mother contested the accommodation plan, challenging parts she claimed did not work. She later requested a Section 504 due process hearing. When the district superintendent appointed a school administrator to serve as the impartial hearing officer, she objected and later removed the student from district schools. After the student graduated, the mother filed a complaint with the state education department, seeking four years of compensatory education. A hearing officer held that the district had violated Section 504 procedural safeguards, but that the violations did not deprive the student of a free appropriate public education. No compensatory education was ordered. The mother, instead of appealing to the state board of regents, filed a lawsuit, which a federal court dismissed. It ruled that **Section 504 required her to exhaust her administrative remedies because she was alleging the denial of FAPE**. *Weber v. Cranston Public School Committee*, 245 F.Supp.2d 401 (D.R.I. 2003).

♦   Although a Massachusetts student with ADHD received a high school diploma, her family sued the school committee and several of its employees for monetary damages under 42 U.S.C. § 1983 based on alleged violations of her right to receive a FAPE under the IDEA. The student also included claims for damages resulting from violations of other federal laws. The court observed that students with disabilities may seek relief under other laws in an IDEA action or in a case seeking relief that is available under the IDEA, but the IDEA requires exhaustion of administrative procedures "to the same extent as would be required had the action been brought under" the IDEA. **Administrative exhaustion was required even where a party was seeking relief under Section 1983**, since the underlying basis for the claim was rooted in alleged IDEA violations. On appeal, the First Circuit affirmed the dismissal of the case. *Frazier v. Fairhaven School Committee*, 276 F.3d 52 (1st Cir. 2002).

B. Exceptions to the Exhaustion Doctrine

There are several instances where the exhaustion doctrine will not apply or exhaustion will be excused. The exhaustion doctrine does not apply when it would be futile or cause irreparable harm. Delay by an agency in making a decision, or the fact that the agency may not be empowered to grant relief, may excuse the exhaustion requirement. The unavailability of a state or local remedy or a predetermined result by an agency may also excuse the requirement.

♦   The parents of an autistic Missouri student sued their school district after the district dismissed their daughter from school two hours early every day for two years. The Department of Education's Office for Civil Rights had found that the student was denied the same educational opportunities as her non-disabled peers, in violation of the ADA and Section 504 of the Rehabilitation Act. The district sought to dismiss the claims for failure to exhaust administrative remedies, but the court refused to do so. **There was no exhaustion requirement where the parents were challenging a blanket, system-wide violation of law.** Plus, under the Supreme Court's ruling in *Winkelman*, the parents had independent and enforceable rights under the IDEA. The lawsuit could continue. *K.F. v. Francis Howell R-III School Dist.*, No. 4:07CV01691 ERW, 2008 WL 723751 (E.D. Mo. 3/17/08).

♦   An autistic Florida student sued his school board under 42 U.S.C. § 1983, claiming that it violated his civil rights by retaining a teacher who used corporal punishment and abused many students over a period of years before she was finally arrested. The school board sought to have the case dismissed. A federal court held that he could proceed with the lawsuit. **He did not have to request a due process hearing before suing because he was seeking relief that was**

not available under the IDEA. The exhaustion requirement was excused. *J.V. v. Seminole County School Board*, No. 604CV1889ORL28JGG, 2005 WL 1243756 (M.D. Fla. 5/25/05).

◆   The non-custodial divorced father of a student with disabilities who attended a private school wrote to the school district complaining about the private school, requesting reevaluation and a mainstream placement. The district rejected both requests. He wrote the district again, requesting a reevaluation and transfer of the student to a mainstream setting for math and language arts. He also sought to join the student's IEP team. The district responded that the father had no say in the student's classification and placement because he was a non-custodial parent. District staff advised the father to contact a lawyer but failed to inform him about state due process hearing procedures. Subsequently, the father attempted to inspect his son's educational records. The district denied the request. He asked a family court for an order that would require the district to reevaluate the student and place him in a regular education setting. The family court denied his requests because he was not the custodial parent.

The father then sued the district, which moved to dismiss the case for failure to exhaust administrative remedies. The court stated that New York special education regulations require districts to inform parents of their state law procedural rights and safeguards. The district here had violated the law by failing to give the father notice of his IDEA due process hearing rights. **Instead of referring the father to the administrative process, the district referred him to a private attorney and his ex-wife.** Thus, the father could not be penalized for not exhausting his administrative remedies. The court allowed the father, who was acting as his own attorney, to hire an attorney in order to pursue further action. However, the father instead appealed to the Second Circuit, which held that his claims had been properly dismissed. As a non-attorney parent, he had to be represented by counsel when suing on behalf of his child. *Fauconier v. Committee on Special Educ., Dist. 3, New York City Board of Educ.*, 112 Fed.Appx. 85 (2d Cir. 2004).

◆   Students with disabilities who attended different schools in a New York district brought a lawsuit under the IDEA, Section 504 and other laws, claiming they were denied a free appropriate public education. The district sought to dismiss the lawsuit for failure to exhaust administrative remedies, but the federal court refused to do so. The Second Circuit Court of Appeals affirmed. Where due process hearings would be futile, students do not have to exhaust their administrative remedies. Here, **the students were alleging systemic violations of federal law that could not be remedied by administrative hearings.** Since it was the framework and procedures for assessing and placing students that were being challenged, the students could proceed with their lawsuit. *J.S. v. Attica Cent. Schools*, 386 F.3d 107 (2d Cir. 2004).

◆   The parents of a New York student rejected a proposed IEP, believing that the student needed more home-based services. A hearing officer ordered the district to place the student in a day program with significant home-based services. After the district failed to provide a substantial part of the services ordered, the parents filed another due process request, and the hearing officer ordered the district to increase the level of home-based services and search for a center-based program. Claiming the district still failed to provide ordered services, the parents sued. A New York federal court held that the parents did not have to file another due process request before bringing suit. **Another due process request would be futile in this case.** *SJB v. New York City Dep't of Educ.*, No. 03 Civ. 6653 (NRB), 2004 WL 1586500 (S.D.N.Y. 7/14/04).

◆   When a student with autism was 12 years old, his parents filed a due process complaint with the state special education hearing office (SEHO), alleging the district failed to provide the student with a FAPE. The SEHO agreed and ordered the district to provide compensatory education. However, the district did not implement a full compensatory education program. The parents hired a tutor, then sued the district in a federal court to enforce the SEHO order and seeking an award of monetary damages. The court dismissed the case, agreeing with the district that since California had established a complaint resolution procedure (CRP) that vested the state education department with the power to enforce SEHO decisions, the family had to file a CRP against the district to enforce the compensatory education award.

The parents appealed to the Ninth Circuit, which noted that IDEA regulations permit the filing of a complaint under either the CRP or the due process hearing procedure. Although the regulations permitted parents to file a CRP and a due process hearing request, they did not state that a parent had to exhaust a CRP to enforce a due process decision in a court proceeding. Also, California regulations did not specify that parents exhaust the CRP before filing a lawsuit under the IDEA. The parents here had exhausted the due process hearing procedure and received an SEHO order in their favor. Neither party had appealed the order, making it final and binding under the IDEA and California law. The Ninth Circuit had held in a 2000 case that the SEHO lacked jurisdiction to enforce its own orders, so the parents were correct in asserting that further administrative review was futile. **Neither the courts nor the U.S. Education Department had ever interpreted CRP regulations as requiring a CRP filing to exhaust administrative remedies.** As only the due process hearing procedure had to be exhausted, the court reversed the lower court's decision. *Porter v. Board of Trustees of Manhattan Beach Unified School Dist.*, 307 F.3d 1064 (9th Cir. 2002).

◆   A Kansas student suffered from several disabling conditions including Asperger's syndrome, a high-functioning form of autism. Her parents claimed that her school district failed to provide her with a FAPE and sued the district and officials in a federal court. The district and officials moved to dismiss the case for failure to exhaust administrative remedies. The parents admitted that they had not availed themselves of Kansas' state administrative review process, but claimed that they were excused from the requirement because the state's administrative process was "not adequate." The court observed that the Tenth Circuit has held that **administrative remedies may be found inadequate or futile where a complaining party alleges "structural" or "systematic"**

failures requiring system-wide reforms. The parents here alleged only that the student's IEP was improperly formulated and implemented. This did not call into question the structural or due process concerns of the state and therefore did not excuse the exhaustion requirement. The family's allegations had to do with the student's educational program and were squarely within the scope of the IDEA. The court found no reason to excuse the administrative exhaustion requirement and dismissed the case. *Marlana G. v. Unified School Dist. No. 497, Douglas County, Kansas,* 167 F.Supp.2d 1303 (D. Kan. 2001).

◆   A Tennessee student attended a public special education program at the Knoxville Adaptive Education Center until graduating with a special education diploma. His mother alleged that the school system and its employees locked him in a time-out enclosure on various occasions during a four-year period. She asserted that the system used the enclosure for disciplinary reasons, and that it was a dark, vault-like box about four feet by six, with a concrete floor and no heat, furniture or ventilation. She claimed that the student was repeatedly locked in the enclosure and was often left there unsupervised. She filed a complaint against the school system and officials with the Tennessee Department of Education. The system denied the allegations and she requested an IDEA due process hearing, asserting that her son had been improperly disciplined. The hearing was repeatedly delayed over the next three years.

Before a hearing was ever held, the parent sued the system and its officials in federal court for civil rights violations under 42 U.S.C. § 1983, adding state law claims for intentional infliction of emotional distress and false imprisonment. The complaint asserted no IDEA violations, but the system moved to dismiss on grounds of failure to exhaust administrative remedies. The school system argued that the claims involved IDEA subject matter, since they revolved around allegations of improper disciplinary measures under the student's IEP. The court agreed with the school system, but the U.S. Court of Appeals, Sixth Circuit, reversed and remanded. Without determining whether the parent's claim arose under the IDEA, the court held that it would be futile for her to seek administrative relief in this case. The student had graduated, and non-monetary relief could not redress his claimed injuries. **Under the unique circumstances of this case, proceeding through the state's administrative process would be futile.** *Covington v. Knox County School System,* 205 F.3d 912 (6th Cir. 2000).

C. Regular Education Students

◆   An Oregon student with ADHD had a Section 504 plan. He got suspended for accessing a school database to change his grades. A hearing was conducted to consider expulsion, but the student's father claimed he received improper notice and thought the meeting was just for fact-finding. The district agreed to further investigate, and the family filed a Section 504 complaint, challenging the suspension and seeking restoration of class credit. A hearing officer ordered the school district to give the student the opportunity to recover lost credits. The student graduated with a regular diploma but sued the district under Section 504 and the IDEA, seeking to modify his final grades and also asking for money damages. A federal court dismissed the case, holding that **even though he had graduated, he should still have pursued administrative remedies** before suing. *Ruecker v. Sommer*, 567 F.Supp.2d 1276 (D. Or. 2008).

♦   A Massachusetts student with Crohn's disease and depression attended the Boston Latin School, a competitive public school that relies on an entrance test and grade point average for admission. He was unable to complete his studies for ninth grade, and he applied for a third year in grade nine. The school denied him admission until it was ordered to admit him by a special education hearing officer, who found a Section 504 violation. The city appealed the finding of a Section 504 violation, and the parents counterclaimed for money damages. The city's claims were dismissed after the student was unable to complete grade nine for a third time and re-enrolled for the fourth time, and the court held that the parents' claims were barred by their failure to exhaust their administrative remedies. **Even though their son had been given a general education placement, he met the definition of a "child with a disability" under the IDEA. Thus, administrative exhaustion was required.** *City of Boston v. Bureau of Special Educ. Appeals*, No. 06-11703-RWZ, 2008 WL 2066989 (D. Mass. 4/30/08).

♦   A regular education student failed one high school math course, and on seven occasions failed the math portion of the Texas Assessment of Academic Skills (TAAS). After modifications, she was able to pass the TAAS and graduate. She then sued the district for failing to refer her for special education. A federal court held that **she was required to exhaust her administrative remedies even though she had graduated**. The student's mother (a special education teacher) never made a written request for school assistance, so the IDEA's child-find duty was never triggered. And since compensatory education could be awarded after graduation, pursuing administrative remedies would not be futile. *Oliver v. Dallas Independent School Dist.*, No. Civ.A. 3:01-CV-2627, 2004 WL 1800878 (N.D. Tex. 8/11/04).

♦   The Tenth Circuit Court of Appeals upheld pretrial judgment against an Oklahoma student who alleged race and disability discrimination by his school district and unlawful disclosure of private information by a former teacher. There was no evidence of discriminatory intent, and **even though the student was never identified as a student with disabilities, he had to exhaust available administrative procedures under the IDEA prior to filing a lawsuit**. Applying a recent U.S. Supreme Court decision, the court also found that his privacy claim failed. The dispute between the parents and the district arose partially from the parents' refusal to approve the homebound teacher the district assigned. As a result, the student did not have a teacher for a year. The family's Section 504 claims had to be dismissed because of the family's failure to follow procedures under the IDEA. Even though the student had never been identified as a student with disabilities under the IDEA, a student with a disability who brings a claim alleging educational deficiencies must exhaust IDEA administrative remedies before filing suit. The student's condition would have qualified him as eligible for services under the IDEA. *Cudjoe v. Independent School Dist. No. 12*, 297 F.3d 1058 (10th Cir. 2002).

♦   A Pennsylvania student was enrolled in public school regular education classes for two years. His father met with a school principal to discuss enrolling the student in a special education program to address an attention deficit disorder. The father alleged that the principal and other administrators refused to respond to his requests for special education services and told him that the student "could not learn, and that it was a waste of time for him to be in school." According to the father, school officials at one point called the police with a false report that the student possessed a gun. The student withdrew from school, after which his father sued the district and administrators, seeking monetary damages for violations of the IDEA, Title IX of the Education Amendments of 1972 and the U.S. and Pennsylvania Constitutions.

The court rejected the father's argument that administrative exhaustion was futile here. There were factual issues that could be resolved in an administrative proceeding. Exhaustion of IDEA procedures was important, since **the parties disputed whether the student should be classified as disabled, and he had yet to be evaluated or placed in a special education program**. The court disagreed with the father's assertion that since the family sought only monetary damages, an administrative proceeding was unnecessary. The primary dispute in this case was one of appropriate classification, and an administrative proceeding was essential to resolve this question. The claims under the constitutions and Title IX were also dismissed. *Blanck v. Exeter School Dist.*, No. Civ. 01-1402, 2002 WL 31247983 (E.D. Pa. 10/2/02).

D. Claims for Money Damages

♦   The parents of an Arizona student with autism became frustrated with her school situation and moved out of the district. They claimed that the district failed to implement an IEP and used a makeshift system of security guards and student aides to guide their daughter between classes rather than facilitated socialization and mobility navigation assistance. Seeking only money damages, they sued the district. However, a federal court held that they were still required to exhaust their administrative remedies despite moving out of the district and asking only for money damages. The case later reached the Court of Appeals of Arizona, which agreed that **the parents had to exhaust their administrative remedies despite their assertion that their claims arose under tort (personal injury) law**. Regardless of the language in their lawsuit, the parents were alleging a breach of duties that arose under the IEP. *Hance v. Fountain Hills Unified School Dist.*, No. 1 CA-CV 09-0281, 2010 WL 2773545 (Ariz. Ct. App. 7/13/10).

♦   The mother of Pennsylvania students with disabilities alleged that their school district retaliated against her for contesting her children's IEP and writing an article about the school board for the local newspaper. She and her husband sued the district in a federal court, but the court held that they should have pursued a due process action first. **They were not seeking purely money damages but also declaratory relief, and they made no persuasive argument for not filing a due process request.** *Hesling v. Avon Grove School Dist.*, No. 02-8565, 2010 WL 2649909 (E.D. Pa. 6/30/10).

♦   The family of a California student with disabilities had a history of disagreeing with their school district. After the district proposed a placement in a class with disabled students regardless of age, grade or specific disability, the family rejected the placement, removed the student from school and sued for discrimination, seeking money damages. A federal court and the Ninth Circuit dismissed the lawsuit because the family should have requested a due process hearing first. **The issues raised by the lawsuit were educational in nature** and should have been considered by a due process hearing officer. *Kutasi v. Las Virgenes Unified School Dist.*, 494 F.3d 1162 (9th Cir. 2007).

♦   A Washington teacher allegedly locked a seven-year-old disabled student in a "safe room" as a form of classroom discipline. The student then became fearful and routinely urinated and defecated on himself. His parents sued the school district, asserting that they did not have to exhaust their administrative remedies because they were seeking monetary damages unavailable under the IDEA. A federal court ruled that they should have requested due process because **a claim based on emotional distress, humiliation, embarrassment and psychological injury might be remedied by the provision of related services** under the IDEA, such as psychological counseling. They were not excused from the requirement to exhaust administrative remedies. *Payne v. Peninsula School Dist.*, No. C05-5780 RBL, 2007 WL 128884 (W.D. Wash. 1/12/07).

♦   The mother of a Washington student represented her son at a due process hearing, where it was determined that the district did not properly implement his IEP. Compensatory education was ordered. Over the next two years, the mother filed four additional due process hearing requests, seeking to implement and modify the IEP. She then sued the district for money damages, claiming she lost income and suffered emotional distress during the IDEA challenge. After the Ninth Circuit held that she did not have to exhaust her administrative remedies before suing, the case reached the Ninth Circuit again. This time, it held that **she could not recover lost wages or pain and suffering under the IDEA on her own behalf**. Nor could she sue under 42 U.S.C. § 1983. *Blanchard v. Morton School Dist.*, 504 F.3d 771 (9th Cir. 2007).

♦   The parents of a Rhode Island student filed a due process hearing request, but the hearing was postponed and rescheduled several times. The parents agreed to the first delay; the others resulted from problems within the school district. **The parents then refused to participate any further and sued the district for money damages** under 42 U.S.C. § 1983. The case reached the Supreme Court of Rhode Island, which held that they should have exhausted their administrative remedies. The 45-day period for resolving complaints was not nearly as strict as the parents had argued and could be extended by continuances and postponements. They failed to show that exhausting their administrative remedies would be futile. *Doe v. East Greenwich School Dep't*, 899 A.2d 1258 (R.I. 2006).

♦   The parents of a Tennessee student with Down syndrome requested a due process hearing, **asserting that the student's classmates had physically and**

verbally abused him, and that the school's staff did nothing to prevent it. Before a ruling was issued, the parents sued the district and a classmate's parent. A federal court held that they were required, as part of the exhaustion of administrative remedies, to wait for the hearing officer's ruling before they could sue. Since they failed to do so, their lawsuit was dismissed. *R.R. v. Board of Educ., Kingsport City Schools*, No. 2:05-CV-50, 2006 WL 1211163 (E.D. Tenn. 4/28/06).

◆ The parents of a disabled student expressed their dissatisfaction with the district's proposed IEP because it did not address crisis episodes relating to the student's acute adrenal insufficiency. Such crisis episodes were life threatening. The state education department found the district was not complying with its IDEA duties and obligations, and the district then allegedly retaliated against the student by forbidding all teachers and district personnel from administering an emergency adrenal injection. The parties agreed to resolve the due process proceeding through mediation, and the U.S. Department of Education closed an investigation of discrimination because the parties were cooperating to resolve their dispute. No due process hearing was ever held. When the parents later sued for money damages, a California federal court ruled that their **failure to exhaust their administrative remedies** barred their claims under the IDEA. Here, they were seeking money damages for the deprivation of educational services that could be remedied under the IDEA. *Tyler B. and Brandy B. v. San Antonio School Dist.*, 253 F.Supp.2d 1111 (N.D. Cal. 2003).

◆ A student with behavioral and social problems attended public schools in the same district from kindergarten until age 13 under an IEP. His parents unilaterally removed him from school after stating that the district deprived him of educational opportunities and caused him emotional injury. They requested a due process hearing under the IDEA but then removed the student from school and abandoned the proceeding. No hearing was ever held, but the parents sued the district, school officials and an agency under contract with the district to provide special education services. The court dismissed based on failure to exhaust IDEA administrative remedies, and the parents appealed to the Seventh Circuit. There, they asserted that exhaustion should be excused because the filing of any administrative proceeding would have been futile.

The appeals court held that parties cannot avoid administrative exhaustion merely by seeking monetary damages. IDEA procedures cover any matter with respect to the identification, evaluation and placement of student with disabilities. **The parents were not permitted to bypass IDEA administrative processes by seeking money damages.** Because administrative relief was available in this case, the district court had properly found that the parents failed to exhaust their administrative remedies. *C.T. v. Necedah Area School Dist.*, 39 Fed.Appx. 420 (7th Cir. 2002).

◆ The Ninth Circuit joined the majority of circuit courts that have held a party seeking relief under the IDEA cannot avoid the statute's administrative exhaustion requirement by limiting the requested relief to monetary damages. The case arose from a dispute over the peer tutoring provided to a student with cerebral palsy. Her parents sued the district and school officials for violations of the IDEA, seeking monetary damages under 42 U.S.C. § 1983. The complaint sought to compensate the family for lost educational opportunities, emotional distress, humiliation, embarrassment and psychological injury. The court dismissed the case for lack of jurisdiction, ruling that the family had to exhaust administrative remedies under the IDEA. On appeal, the Ninth Circuit joined the First, Sixth, Seventh, Tenth and Eleventh Circuits in ruling that parents cannot avoid the IDEA's administrative exhaustion requirement by limiting their requested relief to monetary awards. *Robb v. Bethel School Dist. No. 403,* 308 F.3d 1047 (9th Cir. 2002).

III.   LIMITATION OF ACTIONS

The IDEA does not specify a time limitation in which parties may bring suit in state or federal court after exhausting administrative remedies or in which they may appeal adverse administrative decisions. Federal courts are required to apply the most analogous state statute of limitations from the district in which they are located, consistent with underlying IDEA policies. State laws govern administrative procedures and often specify a relatively brief limitation on appeals. Parties also often make claims for attorneys' fees, requiring courts to determine if the claim constitutes an independent claim or a claim subject to the limitations period.

♦   In a case from Pennsylvania, the Third Circuit held that a 2004 IDEA amendment limiting the time to appeal compensatory education claims applied retroactively. The amendment included a seven-month grace period for parents to file claims that had already accrued. Thus, the amendment barred claims going back more than two years. *Steven I. v. Cent. Bucks School Dist.,* 618 F.3d 411 (3d Cir. 2010).

A. Administrative Appeals

♦   Parents of a Pennsylvania student with a learning disability appealed a mixed administrative ruling to a federal court on the 90th day after the ruling – the last day allowed by the IDEA. The school district filed a counterclaim 70 days later, and the parents claimed it was untimely. They asserted that the district should have filed the counterclaim on the same day they filed their appeal. The Third Circuit ruled for the district, noting that **since the counterclaim was "reactive" rather than the bringing of an action, the district was not bound by the 90-day limit**. *Jonathan H. v. Souderton Area School Dist.,* 562 F.3d 527 (3d Cir. 2009).

♦   A multiply disabled New York student who graduated from high school in 2003 was placed in an occupational training center. Although her entitlement to a free appropriate public education had expired, the department of education agreed to fund the placement in exchange for the mother's promise to release it from any liability for claims that the student did not receive a FAPE. In 2006, the student's mother sued under the IDEA, seeking continued funding. The

Second Circuit dismissed her lawsuit, noting that it was barred by the IDEA's two-year statute of limitations. *Somoza v. New York City Dep't of Educ.*, 538 F.3d 106 (2d Cir. 2008).

♦ A Georgia student with autism and a language disorder was found eligible for IDEA Part C services at age one. His parents placed him in a private school. At age three, the Department of Education and the local school district prepared for his transition to Part B services. The parents disagreed with the proposed IEP and sought to keep their son in the private school. At the due process hearing, the administrative law judge found that the department was responsible for the student's placement at the private school under the IDEA's stay-put provision and ordered it to reimburse the parents for their tuition as well as for speech and language services. The department appealed to a federal court nearly six months later, but the court then dismissed the appeal as untimely. The Eleventh Circuit Court of Appeals affirmed the dismissal. Here, the department failed to comply with the Georgia Administrative Procedure Act's **30-day statute of limitations**. *Georgia State Dep't of Educ. v. Derrick C.*, 314 F.3d 545 (11th Cir. 2002).

♦ A gifted student was eligible for special education and related services under the IDEA. When he disagreed with the recommended assignment for his senior year, he requested a due process hearing, at which he challenged his IEPs for the past six years. The hearing officer held that the statute of limitations had passed on the IEPs from seventh to tenth grade, and that his IEPs for eleventh and twelfth grade were adequate. A review panel awarded the student compensatory education on the grounds that his IEPs did not include programming for his individual needs and were not reasonably calculated to enable meaningful educational progress. The Pennsylvania Commonwealth Court ruled that **the student could only challenge an IEP from the one-year period prior to the due process hearing**. Also, if the student was entitled to compensatory education, he would be limited to the education available within the school's curriculum. The court remanded the case. *Carlynton School Dist. v. D.S.*, 815 A.2d 666 (Pa. Commw. Ct. 2003).

♦ A Connecticut family believed their daughter was improperly denied special education services. They unilaterally removed her from district schools and placed her in another district, where they had to pay tuition. Later, they moved out of the district. Four years after changing their daughter's placement, the parents filed a due process request against the district for tuition reimbursement. A federal court dismissed the action, and the Second Circuit affirmed. The parents had **waited too long to bring their action** against the district, and they were not entitled to reimbursement. The two-year limitation period on challenges to educational placements had long passed. *M.D., Mr. and Mrs. D. v. Southington Board of Educ.*, 334 F.3d 217 (2d Cir. 2003).

♦ A 17-year-old special education student with mild mental retardation, attention deficit/hyperactivity disorder, seizures and chronic depression pushed a teacher, wandered the halls and disrupted classes on December 2, 1999. A manifestation determination team (MDT) determined the student's behavior was unrelated to his disability, and the district's disciplinary tribunal expelled him. Several days later, the student's mother requested a due process hearing, challenging the MDT procedures and findings. On January 20, 2000, an administrative law judge upheld all the procedures and findings of the MDT. On February 8 the student's mother sued the school district. However, she voluntarily dismissed the action three months later. On August 4 the student's mother sued the school district again in federal court, challenging the final administrative determination of the MDT. The court found the 30-day statute of limitations from the Georgia Administrative Procedure Act (APA) applicable and concluded that the lawsuit had not been timely filed.

The mother appealed to the Eleventh Circuit, asserting that the proper limitations period to be applied was the state's two-year statute of limitations for personal injury actions. **The appeals court stated that the 30-day limitations period from the Georgia APA was the appropriate statute of limitations for review of an administrative decision.** A personal injury action is an independent claim that does not involve review of agency decisions. The Georgia APA was the most appropriate state statute to use for determining the limitations period. Further, since the goal of the IDEA is to empower disabled children to reach their fullest potential by providing a FAPE tailored to their individual needs, the most effective way to ensure that empowerment is to provide prompt resolution of disputes over students' IEPs. The Eleventh Circuit affirmed the ruling in favor of the school district. *Cory D. ex rel. Diane D. v. Burke County School Dist.*, 285 F.3d 1294 (11th Cir. 2002).

◆ The parents of an Oregon student with disabilities sought tuition reimbursement from their school district, claiming that it denied him a FAPE. The district asserted that the parents' administrative claim was barred by a two-year limitations period. A hearing officer ruled that a state law allowing two years for personal injury claims against a government entity was the proper limitations period, and that this period applied to the initiation of the parents' request for a due process hearing. A federal court reversed, and the parents appealed to the Ninth Circuit.

The circuit court employed the same analysis for determining the correct limitations period for commencing an administrative hearing as used by courts to determine when to limit civil actions under the IDEA. The parents' claim could reasonably be characterized as one arising from liability created by a statute, as the district court had done. However, the school district was a "public body" as defined by the Oregon Tort Claims Act. The IDEA was the source of the district's alleged duty, and the student's claim was within the statutory definition of "tort." Because the two-year limitation period employed by the hearing officer applied specifically to breaches of duty by public bodies, and a two-year limitations period was consistent with underlying IDEA policies, the court reversed the district court's judgment and reinstated the hearing officer's decision. **The two-year statute of limitations best served IDEA policies because it was short enough to allow expeditious claims resolution, but long enough for parents to protect their children's rights.** *S.V. v. Sherwood School Dist.*, 254 F.3d 877 (9th Cir. 2001).

♦   The families of two students with autism moved to North Carolina and brought separate actions against their school districts after their requests for funding of Lovaas programs were denied. In the first case, the family filed a due process petition, which an administrative law judge rejected as untimely filed under the state's 60-day limitation law. In the second case, a school district proposed a full-day TEACCH program for successive school years. The district did not explain that it was making a final decision or refer to the 60-day state law limitations period in its interactions with the parents.

The Fourth Circuit consolidated the cases. It found the North Carolina statute unique in that it specifically referred to special education cases. For this reason, the court did not have to determine the most appropriate local limitations period in the jurisdiction. It noted that **while local limitations periods are most frequently raised as a defense to a late-filed court action, the same policy concerns applied to the commencement of an administrative appeal**. While the court had previously held that a very short limitations period, such as 30 days, was disfavored under the IDEA, the North Carolina limitations period was entitled to special deference. The 60-day period was twice as long as the one previously held insufficient and took account of all relevant federal policies under the IDEA. The state statute required school authorities to clearly and fully notify parents in writing of the 60-day limitations period. In both cases, the school districts failed to provide the notice required. As a result, the limitations periods could not be applied. *CM v. Board of Educ. of Henderson County*, 241 F.3d 374 (4th Cir. 2001).

On remand, the district court noted that even after the parents asked for contribution toward Lovaas therapy, they still raised no complaint or objection to the IEP. As a result, the due process notice requirement of state law had never been triggered. **In the absence of a complaint by the parents, the county could not be faulted for failing to provide a due process notice.** The parents were not entitled to reimbursement for the 1993-1996 years, since there was no showing that the IEPs proposed for those years was inadequate. *CM v. Board of Public Educ. of Henderson County*, 184 F.Supp.2d 466 (W.D.N.C. 2002).

♦   An Ohio student with a severe form of dyslexia attended public schools through the start of his fourth-grade year. His parents grew dissatisfied with his lack of progress. When the district refused to modify his existing IEP, the parents unilaterally placed him in a private special education school where he experienced success for three years. He later attended two other special education schools. More than six years after withdrawing the student, and after having spent over $150,000 on private schools, the parents requested a due process hearing to obtain tuition reimbursement. A hearing officer determined that the parents had failed to timely initiate due process procedures and dismissed the action. A federal court upheld that decision.

The parents appealed to the Sixth Circuit. While the parents did not request a due process hearing for almost seven years after the start of the present dispute, they had maintained interaction with the district at various times through the years. They had attempted to negotiate the return of their son to public school two years before their formal hearing request, but had been rebuffed by school officials. The special education director had incorrectly advised them that the student had to be re-enrolled before the district had any obligation to prepare him a new IEP. The district was excused from taking no action for the first five years in which the student attended private schools, as there was evidence that the parents knew of their due process rights but sat on them during that time period. However, **it was not excused from claims arising during the next two years, since there was evidence the district had refused to prepare a pre-enrollment IEP.** This violated the IDEA. The parents' request for a due process hearing preserved this claim, and it was not barred under either the two- or four-year statutory limitation periods of Ohio law. *James v. Upper Arlington City School Dist.*, 228 F.3d 764 (6th Cir. 2000).

♦   A Rhode Island student with mental disabilities was entitled to receive 230 days of special education services under state special education regulations. However, the state school department failed to provide her with 50 days of summer educational services in three consecutive years, and the department admitted that she was entitled to a total of 150 additional days of special education. The department refused to provide services when it learned that the student had moved to Pennsylvania. A review officer held that the student was entitled to compensatory education services even though she now lived in Pennsylvania. The school department didn't receive that decision until almost two weeks later. It appealed to a federal court within 30 days of its receipt of the decision, but 41 days after the issuance of the decision. The First Circuit held that the state Administrative Procedure Act was most analogous to the IDEA and **because its 30-day time limit did not begin to run until the receipt of an administrative decision, the appeal had been timely.** *Providence School Dep't v. Ana C.*, 108 F.3d 1 (1st Cir. 1997).

B. Attorneys' Fees

♦   Parents contended that their school district unilaterally changed the placement of their three children without prior notice or consultation. A due process hearing officer ultimately agreed with them and held that the district violated the IDEA. A state appeals board affirmed the decision, and the district did not appeal further. More than nine months later, the parents filed separate suits in a federal court seeking attorneys' fees. The court consolidated the cases and held that the parents were prevailing parties in an IDEA action and thus entitled to an award of fees. It also adopted their argument that Kentucky's five-year limitation on actions for liability created by a statute should apply to their claim, and it awarded them over $37,000. The district appealed to the Sixth Circuit, asserting that the state's 30-day limitation on appeals from administrative proceedings barred the claims.

The Sixth Circuit noted that U.S. circuit courts have been divided on the issue, with some accepting the notion that a claim for fees was a separate action from IDEA due process procedures. The Eleventh Circuit has accepted this view. The Seventh Circuit has found that claims for attorneys' fees are a part of the due process procedure. The court agreed with this view, finding that **claims for attorneys' fees were another phase of the administrative proceeding**. Because the claims were not independent of the administrative action, the 30-

day limitation period applied. The case was reversed and remanded for further proceedings. *King v. Floyd County Board of Educ.*, 228 F.3d 622 (6th Cir. 2000).

♦   A parent challenged the educational program provided for her son at an administrative hearing. The hearing officer determined that the school board failed to provide the student with a FAPE under the IDEA. Forty days later, the parent filed a federal court action for recovery of her legal fees. The board moved for summary judgment, asserting that an Alabama law requiring appeal from an administrative hearing within 30 days was the most analogous state limitation period for IDEA actions. The parent asserted that a two-year limitations period on actions for injury to the person or rights of another was more appropriate. The court stated that the IDEA does not contain a limitations period for attorneys' fees actions, and courts must look to the local limitations statute most analogous to the case that is consistent with federal policies. An award of attorneys' fees is not analogous to an administrative appeal. Instead, actions for attorneys' fees are founded on statutory liability. **Alabama had no limitations period governing actions founded on statutory liability, and its two-year limit on actions arising from injury to the person or rights of another, was most analogous to the claim for attorneys' fees.** Because the action for attorneys' fees was filed within two years, it was not time barred, and the court denied the board's motion for summary judgment. *Dickerson ex rel. Ingram v. Brodgen*, 80 F.Supp.2d 1319 (S.D. Ala. 1999).

♦   A New Jersey student needed care for his basic needs due to cerebral palsy. His school district classified him as multiply disabled and placed him in a regional day school clinic where he had occupational, physical and speech therapy and a full-time aide. His mother demanded full inclusion in his neighborhood school, which the district rejected. The parties reached a settlement at which the district agreed to the neighborhood placement and agreed to conduct another IEP conference. However, the mother later rejected the neighborhood school placement since it was in a self-contained classroom with no mainstreaming opportunities. She filed a petition for emergency relief to enforce the mediation agreement and allow the student to attend a resource room, pending placement in a more inclusive setting. The parties reached a partial agreement, but the school was unable to fully accommodate the student's personal needs. The mother came to school to care for him in the absence of a full-time aide. She later commenced a due process hearing that resulted in another settlement by which the district modified the IEP and placed the student in four regular classes at the neighborhood school.

Two years later, the parent sought her attorneys' fees from the mediation and administrative proceedings. She also sought reimbursement for her own services at the school and for interest accrued on her credit cards to pay dispute-related expenses. The court stated that claims for attorneys' fees must be brought within a reasonable time. **Because the mother here had changed attorneys during the dispute, the two-year delay was not unreasonable** and the action was not barred. However, there were factual disputes concerning whether the school district had changed the IEP as a result of the threatened due process hearing. The court also denied the parent's claim for her personal care of the student at school and her credit card interest. It ordered a hearing to resolve the remaining factual disputes. *B.K. v. Toms River Board of Educ.*, 998 F.Supp. 462 (D.N.J. 1998).

♦   Seven students with disabilities and their families prevailed in separate administrative proceedings brought under the IDEA against an Iowa school district. They individually sought reimbursement for their attorneys' fees for successfully prosecuting their cases at the administrative level. When the district failed to pay any of the attorneys' fees claims, the families filed lawsuits. The U.S. District Court for the Northern District of Iowa considered the district's motion for summary judgment on the basis of the passage of a 30-day limitation period taken from Iowa administrative law. The court found that this time restriction was far too short to allow for effective settlement negotiations. Instead, **the court agreed with the students and parents that either a two- or five-year statute of limitations from Iowa personal injury law was the most analogous to the IDEA.** Under either statute, the claims for attorneys' fees were not barred. *Curtis K. by Delores K. v. Sioux City Community School Dist.*, 895 F.Supp. 1197 (N.D. Iowa 1995).

IV. OTHER IDEA PROCEEDINGS

A. Class Actions

♦   After a lawsuit by students with disabilities, the Chicago Public Schools and the Illinois State Board of Education entered into a consent decree over the segregative placement of disabled students. A court-appointed monitor set 20% as the target for the highest acceptable percentage of students with disabilities in any school. For five years, the Chicago Public Schools failed to seek a single waiver to the 20% cap. Then just before the deadline, it sought waivers for 96 schools without providing adequate information to support the requests. It claimed it either had to violate the consent decree or transfer students in violation of the IDEA. The Seventh Circuit dismissed the lawsuit, holding that it was not yet ripe for action as no concrete action had yet been taken against the Chicago Public Schools. *Corey H. v. Board of Educ. of City of Chicago*, 534 F.3d 683 (7th Cir. 2008).

♦   New York parents and students brought a class action lawsuit against state and local education officials, claiming that they failed to comply with certain provisions of the No Child Left Behind (NCLB) Act. They asserted that the officials did not meet parental notification requirements and provisions allowing the transfer of students to better schools. The officials asked for dismissal of the case, and a federal court granted their request. It held that **the NCLB Act did not create any individual entitlement**, and that it could not be enforced through a private action. *Ass'n of Community Organizations for Reform Now v. New York City Dep't of Educ.*, 269 F.Supp.2d 338 (S.D.N.Y. 2003).

♦ Nine special education students and their families pursued administrative due process actions against a Minnesota school district and its officials, utilizing the two-step procedure specified by state special education law. The students all obtained decisions that were unfavorable at least in part. Instead of appealing individually in separate actions, the families pursued a federal class action suit in which they included state education officials as defendants. The state and local officials moved for dismissal. The court stated that all the claims by the would-be class members were subject to dismissal, as the issues they raised required a detailed, case-by-case analysis of educational program eligibility and availability that could not be addressed in a class action. While a state agency can be named as a defendant in an IDEA action if the action involves claims of "systemic violations," the families in this case had only voiced dissatisfaction with the outcome of their administrative proceedings. A claim is not systemic if it involves only substantive issues, which the administrative process is capable of correcting. **The court denied the students' motion for class certification.** Each student had to refile a separate action naming only the district as a defendant. *Reinholdson v. State of Minnesota*, No. CIV. 02-795 ADM/AJB, 2002 WL 31026580 (D. Minn. 9/9/02).

♦ A California elementary school district with a long history of non-compliance with the IDEA was the subject of an extensive corrective action plan. The plan was adopted as the result of a class action lawsuit brought on behalf of students who attended or would attend district schools. Under the plan, the district was to come into compliance with the IDEA, and the plan included specific actions for the district to take, described the expected results, contained a timeline for completing the goals, identified the responsible individual for each objective and established measures for determining compliance. A federal court approved the plan in January 2000, and a court-appointed monitor began overseeing the district. The plaintiff class requested that the court sanction the district, arguing that it was not complying with the plan or attempting to follow it. At a hearing in April 2001, the court gave the district three additional months to show its commitment to complying with the plan and ordered the California Department of Education to furnish additional assistance to the district. After the district's IDEA compliance did not improve dramatically within the three-month period, the court noted that there was no dispute over the district's failure to comply with its order. **There was little evidence that district personnel were committed to implementing the plan, and there appeared to be an entrenched resistance to the plan among district employees, including the superintendent.** Although the court held the district in contempt, it gave the district seven months to demonstrate its commitment to compliance with the plan. *Emma C. v. Eastin*, No. C96-4179 T E H (N.D. Cal. 2001).

♦ A New York City student with a learning disability in reading received resource room instruction from grades five through seven. When he was 15 years old, his mother filed an administrative action against the board of education, challenging the lack of individual instruction. A hearing officer ordered the city to provide him with instruction in a more restrictive modified instruction services class setting with a student-teacher ratio of 3-to-1. A 12-year-old New York City student with a learning disability also received resource room instruction for years in groups of about eight students without any individual assistance. The students later sued the city school board, seeking to represent a class of New York students with learning disabilities who were denied necessary individual instruction because of placement in resource rooms with inappropriately high student-teacher ratios.

The court found that **neither student could adequately represent the class because they had obtained relief addressing their educational needs that separated their interests from other students in the proposed class.** The 12-year-old student no longer attended resource rooms, and thus could not fairly or effectively represent a class seeking relief from deficient instruction in resource rooms. The 15-year-old student admitted that the hearing officer's order modifying his IEP fully addressed his educational needs. The court held that because the intervening decisions by the administrative officers had substantially altered the status of the case, the action should be dismissed without prejudice to allow the amendment of the complaint to reflect these changed circumstances. *Adrian R. v. New York City Board of Educ.*, No. 99CIV9064(WK), 2001 WL 77066 (S.D.N.Y. 1/30/01).

◆   Despite a history of deficient performance by a District of Columbia institution for detained and committed students, the appointment of a receiver by a trial court was inappropriate in view of the creation by Congress of a new District financial authority and the appointment of a new superintendent. **The District of Columbia Court of Appeals held that the appointment of a receiver was a drastic remedy that should be employed only as a last resort.** The dispute arose from a class action brought against the District, which alleged the defendants failed to provide students confined to juvenile facilities with appropriate care, rehabilitation and treatment. A consent decree was entered into by the parties, and a special master was eventually appointed to help the defendants comply with the consent decree and related orders. The students later requested the appointment of a receiver to oversee the institution's education system. *District of Columbia v. Jerry M.*, 738 A.2d 1206 (D.C. 1999).

B. Expert Witness Fees

◆   After the parents of a special education student obtained reimbursement for tuition at a private school, they sought reimbursement for the cost of an educational consultant they used during the course of litigation. A New York federal court awarded them $8,650 of the $29,350 in fees they claimed, reducing the award because the consultant did not keep contemporaneous time records. The Second Circuit upheld the award, noting that the IDEA permits the recovery of fees and costs for individuals with "special knowledge." The consultant qualified as an expert entitled to those fees. On further appeal, the U.S. Supreme Court reversed, holding that **the IDEA does not authorize prevailing parents to recover expert fees.** The Court noted that the IDEA was enacted under the Spending Clause, and that it does not even hint that the acceptance of IDEA funds makes a state responsible for reimbursing prevailing parents for the services of experts. The statute simply adds reasonable attorneys' fees to the list of recoverable costs. Further, the expert witness fees could not be deemed costs so as to be reimbursable. *Arlington Cent. School Dist. Board of Educ. v. Murphy*, 548 U.S. 291, 126 S.Ct. 2455, 165 L.Ed.2d 526 (2006).

♦   The District of Columbia had a policy authorizing the payment of expert witness fees in due process hearings. However, in 2006, the U.S. Supreme Court held that expert fees could not be recovered by prevailing parties in IDEA cases. When the parents of a disabled student sought to recover their expert fees as prevailing parties, the U.S. Court of Appeals, D.C. Circuit, held that they could not do so. **Even though they had sought their expert fees prior to the Supreme Court's decision, that ruling took precedence.** *Fisher v. District of Columbia*, 517 F.3d 570 (D.C. Cir. 2008).

♦   After prevailing in IDEA due process hearings, the families of five students with disabilities sought to recover their expert witness fees. A federal court denied the fees, and the U.S. Court of Appeals, D.C. Circuit, affirmed. **There is no language in the IDEA allowing expert witness fees to prevailing parties.** Only "reasonable attorneys' fees" are provided for by Section 1415. *Goldring v. District of Columbia*, 416 F.3d 70 (D.C. Cir. 2005).

♦   The parents of a disabled New York student prevailed in an IDEA hearing, then filed an action seeking $84,000 in attorneys' fees and $5,375 for an independent evaluator. The court reduced their attorneys' fees to $52,500 and denied the evaluator's fee, stating that the IDEA provides no explicit authorization for the reimbursement of an expert witness. The Supreme Court, Appellate Division, noted that **the parents' claim failed to explain the evaluator's role or significance.** Nor did they explain why an evaluation at public expense would have been insufficient. The court affirmed the denial of the evaluator's fee. *Pawling Cent. School Dist. v. Munoz*, 788 N.Y.S.2d 267 (N.Y. App. Div. 2005).

♦   A North Carolina student with ADHD obtained an administrative order holding that his school board's IEP was inappropriate and that his parents' decision to place him in a Wisconsin public school (where he lived with his grandparents) was appropriate. A state review officer affirmed the administrative order for the reimbursement of certain costs associated with evaluations, private tutoring, travel and related expenses. However, she reversed the part of the order allowing the parents to recover claims for lost wages and other incidental expenses and for two independent evaluations. The review officer also found that the IEP devised for the student for a subsequent school year was appropriate, and she denied recovery for any expenses during that year. The parents filed a federal court action seeking attorneys' fees and expert witness fees. The court noted that **the IDEA makes no provision for expert witness fees. The parents were thus entitled only to the $40 fee allowed under federal law.** Also, 42 U.S.C. § 1988, a federal civil rights statute, did not provide an alternative means of recovering expert witness fees. *Eirschele by Eirschele v. Craven County Board of Educ.*, 7 F.Supp.2d 655 (E.D.N.C. 1998).

C. Parent Actions and Representation

◆ Ohio parents disagreed with the IEP prepared for their autistic son and placed him in a private school. They filed a due process hearing request, but lost at two administrative levels. Without the assistance of an attorney, the parents appealed to a federal court. The court held for the school district, and the U.S. Court of Appeals, Sixth Circuit, then held that they could not pursue the case unless they hired an attorney. The U.S. Supreme Court agreed to review the parents' appeal and held that **the IDEA accorded the parents independent enforceable rights**. It would be inconsistent with the statutory scheme to bar the parents from continuing to assert these rights in federal court. Because the IDEA did not differentiate between the rights of disabled children and their parents, the Court reversed the judgment, permitting the parents to pursue their case. *Winkelman v. Parma City School Dist.*, 550 U.S. 516, 127 S.Ct. 1994, 167 L.Ed.2d 904 (2007).

◆ The mother of a North Carolina student reached a settlement with the school district over her son's special education. However, a state department of public instruction investigation revealed that the district was not in compliance with the agreement. She sued the district on her son's behalf, alleging constitutional violations, but a federal court ruled against her. Also, **as a non-attorney, she could not pursue an action on her son's behalf**. *R.W. v. Wake County Public Schools*, No. 5:07-CV-136-F3, 2010 WL 3452376 (E.D.N.C. 9/1/10).

◆ An Oklahoma parent sued school officials on his child's behalf, asserting that the school used physical force to restrain the student in violation of the IEP. However, the court dismissed his lawsuit, noting that **non-attorney parents can't represent their children in court**. And the parent failed to exhaust his administrative remedies for any violation on his own behalf. As a result, the child would have to pursue any claims regarding the improper restraints via due process. *M.D.F. v. Independent School Dist. No. 50 of Osage County*, No. 09-CV-548-GKF-PJC, 2010 WL 2326260 (N.D. Okla. 6/3/10).

◆ The parents of a disabled New York child divorced, with the mother taking custody of the child. The father later challenged the special education services the student was receiving, and the question of a non-custodial parent's rights to direct the child's education came before the state's highest court. The New York Court of Appeals held that **although a non-custodial parent has the right to participate in a child's education, that parent does not have the right to "control educational decisions"** absent an express provision in the custody agreement. Thus, the father could not challenge the student's educational services. *Fuentes v. Board of Educ. of City of New York*, 907 N.E.2d 696 (N.Y. 2009).

◆ The parents of an Ohio special education student had a contentious relationship with their school district, filing numerous administrative complaints. They sought to tape IEP meetings without prior consent and objected to the presence of the school district's attorney at the meetings. As a result of the disputes, the parties were unable to negotiate an IEP. The district filed a due process request and the case reached a federal court, which held that the district's attorney could be present at the IEP meetings. Further, **canceling IEP meetings because of the conditions the parents imposed did not deprive them of any due process rights.** *Horen v. Board of Educ. of Toledo City School Dist.*, 594 F.Supp.2d 833 (N.D. Ohio 2009).

♦   The mother of an Indiana student with a disability complained that a teacher harassed her daughter and allowed other students to do the same. However, when she sued the school district without an attorney, a federal court dismissed the lawsuit, noting that **non-lawyer parents cannot represent their children in federal court.** Further, the mother failed to exhaust her administrative due process remedies. *Lenker v. Gray*, No. 2:07-CV-274-PRC, 2008 WL 4613534 (N.D. Ind. 10/10/08).

♦   The parents of an Illinois student with disabilities claimed that their district denied their son a free appropriate public education under the IDEA by ignoring or flouting many provisions of his IEP. During administrative proceedings, the student died and a hearing officer dismissed the case. The parents continued the action in a federal court, which also dismissed the case. Without an attorney, the parents appealed to the Seventh Circuit Court of Appeals, which ruled **that they could not represent their son's estate without a lawyer.** They were given 60 days to find an attorney. *Malone v. Nielson*, 474 F.3d 934 (7th Cir. 2007).

♦   In an effort to obtain private school tuition reimbursement, the mother of a Connecticut student sued the school board without the assistance of an attorney. A federal court ruled that she could not represent her son in an IDEA action. Eight days before the student turned 18, his mother sought to include him as a party. The court refused to let her. However, the Second Circuit held that the son should have been allowed to join the lawsuit. **Once he became 18, he could represent himself without a lawyer.** *Cortese v. New Fairfield Board of Educ.*, 210 Fed.Appx. 83 (2d Cir. 2006).

♦   Under a settlement agreement, a New Jersey parent agreed to apply to a private day school for her son if the district would provide a number of independent evaluations. She balked at sending her son to the private school until the evaluations were completed, and the district sued to enforce the settlement agreement by requiring the parent to send her son to the school. She did not hire a lawyer to represent her son. A federal court issued a preliminary order requiring the parent to send her son to the private school, and she appealed. The Third Circuit held that **she was entitled to a rehearing because she should not have been allowed to represent her son.** The case was returned to the lower court. *Montclair Board of Educ. v. M.W.D.*, 182 Fed.Appx. 136 (3d Cir. 2006).

♦   The attorney-father of a New York student with health and learning impairments challenged a change to the student's IEP and represented her at the due process hearing. He later sued to recover his attorneys' fees and the case reached the Second Circuit. The court of appeals agreed with the Third and Fourth Circuits that **parent attorneys cannot recover fees in IDEA cases in which they represent their own children.** *S.N. v. Pittsford Cent. School Dist.*, 448 F.3d 601 (2d Cir. 2006).

♦   The parents of a California student with autism sought reimbursement from their school district for educational services they paid for during a school year and an extended school year. They requested a due process hearing that resulted in a decision for the district. They appealed to a federal court without an attorney. The district claimed they could not represent their child without an attorney, but the court ruled that **they had substantive rights of their own that were enforceable** even though they were not the intended recipients of the education. The court refused to dismiss the case. *D.K. v. Huntington Beach Union High School Dist.*, 482 F.Supp.2d 1088 (C.D. Cal. 2006).

♦   The father of a disabled New Hampshire student filed due process proceedings against two school districts, challenging his son's IEPs. Both hearings went against him, and he sought judicial review. The question then arose as to **whether the father – a non-attorney – could represent his son in court.** The First Circuit Court of Appeals held that he could. It stated that since parents could request due process hearings, they were parties to the hearings and were logically "parties aggrieved" when hearing officers ruled in favor of school districts. And since they were "parties aggrieved" under the IDEA, they could proceed on behalf of their children regardless of whether they were alleging procedural or substantive violations of the IDEA. *Maroni v. Pemi-Baker Regional School Dist.*, 346 F.3d 247 (1st Cir. 2003).

♦   The U.S. Court of Appeals, Second Circuit, held that **a Vermont parent who was not an attorney could not bring an appeal in federal court on behalf of her son** after an adverse due process decision under the IDEA unless she obtained the assistance of counsel. *Tindall v. Poultney High School Dist.*, 414 F.3d 281 (2d Cir. 2005).

♦   A non-custodial Texas father disagreed with a school district's decision to retain his daughter in the fifth grade for another year. However, he did not challenge the IEP or its goals, the services his daughter received, her evaluations or any other criteria related to her educational placement. A hearing officer dismissed the father's complaint, finding it was unrelated to the student's educational placement under the IDEA. A federal court upheld the hearing officer's decision. Here, **the divorce decree gave the student's mother exclusive rights to make educational decisions** after consultation with the father. Also, the father had no standing to bring an action under the IDEA. *Schares v. Katy Independent School Dist.*, 252 F.Supp.2d 364 (S.D. Tex. 2003).

♦   The parent of a student with disabilities brought a due process hearing against her son's school district and won. She then alleged that the district refused to implement the decision and sued it in a Delaware federal court. She did not hire an attorney, and she was not an attorney herself. The court dismissed her action because, while the IDEA allows lay parents to represent their children in administrative proceedings, **it does not permit lay parents to represent their children in federal court proceedings**. *Hayes v. Board of Educ. for Cape Henlopen School Dist.*, No. Civ.A. 02-55-SLR, 2003 WL 105482 (D. Del. 1/3/03).

♦   The divorce decree of the parents of a student with dyslexia awarded the mother custody and vested her with authority to make decisions about his education. The decree allowed the father to inspect school records and communicate with school personnel about the student's progress. The father disagreed with the district's IEP proposal and requested a due process hearing. An administrative hearing officer dismissed the father's hearing request on grounds that he was not the custodial parent and had no decision-making authority to request a due process hearing. A federal court agreed that a non-custodial parent could not bring an IDEA suit challenging a child's educational plan. The Seventh Circuit reversed in part, finding that the father could not bring a claim on behalf of the student without hiring a lawyer. The appeals court found that the divorce decree did not eliminate all of the father's rights. Since the father was challenging the student's educational plan, and the divorce decree did not appear to bar this type of challenge, the lower court had erroneously dismissed the father's claim without examining the decree.

On remand, the district court observed that the mother was content with the student's IEP. The IDEA did not override the state's allocation of authority to the mother to determine her son's education. **While the father retained certain rights under the divorce decree, his interests were relevant only if they were compatible with the mother's parental rights.** He could not challenge the mother's decision to adopt the IEP proposed by the school district, and the district was entitled to summary judgment on the IEP dispute. The case was remanded to a hearing officer for consideration of whether the district had provided him with sufficient notice of an IEP meeting and access to the student's records. When the father appealed, the Seventh Circuit held that the father's only potential IDEA claim was a procedural one that had been sent back to a state tribunal and was not properly before the court. *Navin v. Park Ridge School Dist. 64,* 49 Fed.Appx. 69 (7th Cir. 2002).

♦   The parents of an autistic Florida student disagreed with the IEP proposed by their school district. They urged the school board to place the student in a private Massachusetts facility. When the school board denied the requested placement, the parents requested a due process hearing. The hearing officer agreed that the IEP was insufficient but denied the request for a residential placement. The parents appealed to a federal court on several grounds, including claims that the student was entitled to an order for extended eligibility, an award of monetary damages and the residential placement. The family contracted with an attorney, who represented them through the first day of trial, but then discharged him. The student's father asked the court to allow the attorney's withdrawal and to grant permission to proceed on behalf of his son. The court refused, and the father appealed to the Eleventh Circuit. The court found that **while the IDEA allows parents to bring lawsuits on behalf**

of their children, it does not authorize them to act as their children's counsel. This is true even though parents have a right to represent their children in due process hearings. There was no authority in the federal rules of civil procedure or other federal law allowing parties to be represented by non-attorney parents. The court affirmed the order denying the father's motion. *Devine v. Indian River County School Board*, 121 F.3d 576 (11th Cir. 1997).

D. Settlement

◆ The parents of a disabled student believed their district was denying their son special education. They requested an IDEA due process hearing. Before the hearing, the district allegedly agreed to a settlement with the parents. It sought to have the settlement enforced, but a hearing panel ruled that it did not have the authority to do so. The district appealed to the Missouri Court of Appeals, which ruled that **the hearing panel in fact had the authority to determine the settlement's enforceability**. Disputes over settlements relate to the provision of FAPE. *State of Missouri v. Missouri Dep't of Elementary and Secondary Educ.*, 307 S.W.3d 209 (Mo. Ct. App. 2010).

◆ The mother of a Pennsylvania student with autism challenged his educational program and eventually entered into a settlement agreement with the district, returning her son to his neighborhood school. However, she and the district deadlocked on one issue and she then sought to withdraw her consent from the entire settlement agreement. A federal court and the Third Circuit ruled that **she could not withdraw her consent just because she had later found it inadequate**. There was no change in circumstances that would make enforcement of the agreement improper. *Muse B. v. Upper Darby School Dist.*, 282 Fed.Appx. 986 (3d Cir. 2008).

◆ A private school contracted with a Virginia school district to provide educational services for an autistic student. The contract allowed either party to terminate the agreement upon 30 days' notice. The school could also terminate the contract if the student committed a serious incident. When the school sought to discharge the student over safety concerns, his parents objected and requested due process. A hearing officer ordered the school to comply with the stay-put provision, finding that its contract with the district required it to comply with the IDEA. The school sued to challenge the order, then reached a settlement with the district releasing it from the contract. The federal court then refused to intervene in the dispute, leaving the due process hearing (over the decision to expel the student) to the hearing officer. *Virginia Institute of Autism v. Virginia Dep't of Educ.*, 537 F.Supp.2d 817 (E.D. Va. 2008).

◆ The mother of a Pennsylvania student with Down syndrome rejected an IEP offer to place her daughter in a life skills support class for most of each school day. She believed a largely mainstream setting was appropriate and requested a due process hearing. A hearing officer ruled in her favor, but an appeals panel reversed that decision. She appealed to a federal court but settled on the morning of the trial. However, she then changed her mind and sought to revoke the settlement, claiming duress and lack of effective counsel. The court rejected her request, and the Third Circuit affirmed. Here, **any pressure of time constraints did not amount to duress** that would justify revoking the settlement. *Ballard v. Philadelphia School Dist.*, 273 Fed.Appx. 184 (3d Cir. 2008).

◆ The parents of an Illinois student sued their school district over her education, then reached a settlement agreement and signed a release of all claims against the district. Later, the student reached the age of majority and sued the district on her own for discriminating against her. The Seventh Circuit dismissed her claims, noting that even though she was asserting different legal theories, **her claims were based on the same set of events as had defined the earlier settlement**. It did not matter that her parents had brought the earlier lawsuit. The parties were still the same. *Ross v. Board of Educ. of Township High School Dist. No. 211*, 486 F.3d 279 (7th Cir. 2007).

◆ New Jersey parents entered into a settlement agreement with their school district arising from a due process action brought on behalf of their autistic son. The administrative law judge instructed both parties to write to the state director of special education programs if they thought the terms of the settlement were not being properly implemented. Subsequently, the parents sued to enforce the settlement, and the district sought to have the case dismissed. The court held that **despite the order to write to the director of special education, the parents could sue to enforce the settlement**. They were permitted but not required to write to the director as an alternative to a lawsuit. *W.K. v. Sea Isle City Board of Educ.*, No. 06-1815 (JEI), 2007 WL 433323 (D.N.J. 2/5/07).

◆ A class representing juvenile inmates in South Dakota sued under the IDEA and the Prison Litigation Reform Act over such issues as restraints, discipline, length of confinement, lack of mental health services and inadequate staff training. Eventually, the parties settled the case, and a federal court approved the settlement. It also awarded attorneys' fees to the class because of the settlement's positive impact on conditions at the correctional facility school. However, the Eighth Circuit reversed the award, noting that attorneys' fees are available only where there is an enforceable judgment or a consent decree. Here, **the approval of the settlement agreement did not create a consent decree**. *Christina A. v. Bloomberg*, 315 F.3d 990 (8th Cir. 2003).

◆ The parent of a New York student with disabilities sued his school district, alleging violations of the IDEA and 42 U.S.C. § 1983. The parent's attorney informed the court during the course of a hearing that the parties had reached a tentative settlement pending approval. The judge agreed to discontinue the action so that the school district could obtain the necessary approval, and stated that the parties were entitled to reopen the matter if the settlement fell through within 45 days. He also said that the case could be reopened by means of a letter to the court rather than a formal motion. Within three weeks of the hearing, the parent wrote the court a letter stating that she was firing her attorney and wished to reopen the matter. However, the court held that the district had ratified the settlement and that the case was closed. Eleven months later, the parent appealed to the Second Circuit, which noted that the 45-day period specified by the court applied to both parties and that the court had indicated that the parties could reopen the case if the settlement fell through. **Since the mother had followed the court's suggested procedure for abandoning the settlement by mailing a letter to the court within 45 days, it should have granted her motion to reopen the case.** The 11-month delay in bringing an appeal was not grounds for barring the challenge since there was no evidence of undue delay or prejudice to the school district. The court reversed and remanded the case. *Cappillino v. Hyde Park Cent. School Dist.*, 135 F.3d 264 (2d Cir. 1998).

E. Other Proceedings

♦   Michigan school districts attempted to pursue an IDEA action against the state department of education, asserting that it had unlawfully exercised its power over an administrative appeal involving a student with autism. However, since the student had settled with the districts, the Sixth Circuit held that the districts could no longer sue the state. **School districts are not "aggrieved parties" under the IDEA**, and the statute does not give districts the right to sue state agencies. *Traverse Bay Area Intermediate School Dist. v. Michigan Dep't of Educ.*, 615 F.3d 622 (6th Cir. 2010).

♦   The mother of a Pennsylvania student with disabilities sought a Mandarin Chinese translation of the transcript from due process proceedings. When the school district refused to provide such a transcript, she sued. The Pennsylvania Commonwealth Court held that she was not entitled to a translated transcript. **Although due process may require a translator during administrative proceedings, that right does not extend to the provision of a transcript in any language.** *Bethlehem Area School Dist. v. Zhou*, 976 A.2d 1284 (Pa. Commw. Ct. 2009).

♦   Florida parents of two students with disabilities claimed the students were improperly sent to a new school, where they were bullied and subjected to unfair punishment by teachers. They requested private school placements, which were denied. When they sought due process, a hearing officer dismissed their cases as moot because the school year had ended. They appealed to a federal court, which held that **their lawsuit could proceed even though the hearing officer had failed to compile an administrative record on their IDEA claims**. *Lewellyn v. Sarasota County School Board*, No. 8:07-CV-1712-T-33TGW, 2009 WL 1515737 (M.D. Fla. 6/1/09).

♦   The mother of a New Jersey special education student sent him to live with his aunt in another district, which approved the student's attendance as a resident. Later the mother again took custody of the student, claiming that she now lived in the district and producing a lease agreement, a copy of her driver's license and a sworn statement of residency. The school district nevertheless rejected her claim of residency. It asserted that the lease agreement was fraudulent and relied on investigative evidence showing the student and parent leaving from a non-district residence four days in a row. Before an administrative law judge, the mother again produced her documentation, while the district's attorney argued that the documentation was worthless. The ALJ ruled for the district, but a New Jersey appellate court ruled that a new hearing was required. **The district could not simply rely on its attorney's arguments to prove nonresidency.** *Y.E. ex rel. E.E. v. State-Operated School Dist. of City of Newark*, 2008 WL 2492258 (N.J. Super. Ct. App. Div. 6/24/08).

♦ The parents of two disabled New Jersey students filed an administrative complaint against their school board rather than seek due process. They alleged violations of the IDEA, and they brought the complaint under the dispute resolution procedure described in federal regulations at 34 C.F.R. Part 300.661. The state education department's Office of Special Education Programs resolved the complaint in their favor, and the school board sought review. The Superior Court of New Jersey, Appellate Division, ruled that OSEP's final decision was not reviewable in the courts. **The complaint resolution procedure described in the regulations was designed to be a low-cost alternative to due process actions.** *Board of Educ. of Lenape Regional HS Dist. v. New Jersey State DOE, OSEP*, 945 A.2d 125 (N.J. Super. Ct. App. Div. 2008).   •

♦ Two Minnesota students who were brothers claimed that fellow students harassed and discriminated against them. One student was disabled and the other was perceived to be a homosexual. They eventually sued the district in a federal court and reached a waiver and release of the disabled student's claims under the IDEA. The court ruled for the district on the other claims. Rather than appeal, the students filed another lawsuit in state court. The Minnesota Court of Appeals held that **the claims were essentially the same as the ones disposed of in the earlier lawsuit.** Thus, the case had to be dismissed. *S.A.S. v. Hibbing Public Schools*, No. A06-688, 2007 WL 1322337 (Minn. Ct. App. 5/8/07).

♦ A California school district drew up an IEP for an autistic student. The IEP contained a behavior intervention plan allowing staff to physically restrain the student to address his violent outbursts. The parents later withdrew their consent for any physical restraint. They requested a due process hearing, claiming that staff members were still restraining the student. After a settlement and claims by the parents that the student's teacher was not abiding by the settlement's terms, the district got a temporary restraining order barring the student from school. The parents sued under 42 U.S.C. § 1983, and a federal court ruled against them. **The IDEA was their sole remedy for IDEA violations.** They could not use Section 1983 to enforce the student's rights under the IDEA. *Alex G. v. Board of Trustees of Davis Joint Unified School Dist.*, 332 F.Supp.2d 1315 (E.D. Cal. 2004).

♦ Two Kansas students with disabilities received special education services from a school district. When the district learned that their mother and her boyfriend might be living outside the district's boundaries, an investigator confirmed that suspicion. The district sued the mother and boyfriend in a state court seeking nonresident tuition and an order prohibiting the children from attending district schools. The mother, boyfriend and children then brought a lawsuit against the district in federal court. The court ruled against them, and the Tenth Circuit affirmed. **The federal court could not grant any relief against the district without first determining whether the children were entitled to be educated in the district** – which was the very subject of the state court lawsuit. Also, the boyfriend had no standing to sue. *D.L. v. Unified School Dist. No. 497*, 392 F.3d 1223 (10th Cir. 2004).

♦ After a due process hearing concerning an autistic student's IEP, the student appealed to a federal court. During the pretrial discovery process, the school district sought to protect certain documentation as irrelevant or duplicative. This included e-mail and other written communications about the student's lawsuit as well as all program and behavior data collected on the student over a two-year period. The court ruled that the documents were potentially admissible as "additional evidence" under the IDEA. The potential harm to the district in producing them was outweighed by their relevance. **The district had to produce the requested documents**, except for certain documents dated before the conclusion of the due process hearing, which were not necessary to supplement the record. *Johnson v. Olathe Dist. Schools*, 212 F.R.D. 582 (D. Kan. 2003).

CHAPTER FOUR

Private School Tuition

I. TUITION REIMBURSEMENT

In Burlington School Committee v. Dep't of Educ. of Massachusetts, *below, the U.S. Supreme Court ruled that parents who unilaterally place children in private schools may nevertheless receive tuition reimbursement from the school district if the IEP proposed by the school is later found to be inappropriate. If the proposed IEP is found to be appropriate, however, the parents will not be entitled to reimbursement for the tuition and related expenses incurred in unilaterally changing their child's placement.*

♦ In the *Burlington* case, the father of a learning disabled third-grader became dissatisfied with his son's lack of progress in the public school system. A new IEP called for placement in a different public school. The father, however, unilaterally withdrew his son from school, placing him instead at a state-approved private facility. He then sought reimbursement for tuition and transportation expenses, contending that the proposed IEP was educationally inappropriate. The state Board of Special Education Appeals ruled that the proposed IEP was inappropriate and that the father was entitled to reimbursement. The school committee appealed. A Massachusetts federal court held that the parents had violated the IDEA by enrolling their child in the private school without the agreement of public school officials. Thus, they were not entitled to reimbursement. The First Circuit reversed, and the school committee appealed to the U.S. Supreme Court.

In upholding the court of appeals, the Supreme Court ruled that parents who place a disabled child in a private educational facility are entitled to reimbursement for the child's tuition and living expenses if a court

187

later determines that the school district proposed an inappropriate IEP. Conversely, reimbursement could not be ordered if the school district's proposed IEP was appropriate. The Court observed that to bar reimbursement claims under all circumstances would violate the IDEA, which requires appropriate interim placement for children with disabilities. In addition, under the school committee's reading of the IDEA's stay-put provision, parents would be forced to leave children in what might later be determined to be an inappropriate educational placement, or would obtain the appropriate placement only by sacrificing any claim for reimbursement. This result was not intended by Congress. However, **parents who unilaterally change the placement of a child during the pendency of IDEA proceedings do so at their own financial risk**. If the courts ultimately determine that a proposed IEP is appropriate, the parents are barred from obtaining reimbursement for an unauthorized private school placement. *Burlington School Committee v. Dep't of Educ. of Massachusetts*, 471 U.S. 359, 105 S.Ct. 1996, 85 L.Ed.2d 385 (1985).

A. Unilateral Placement by Parents

1. Behavioral Challenges

◆   The parents of a Pennsylvania student with ADHD removed her from public school and placed her in a Friends school. They later sought tuition reimbursement, claiming that her IEPs for grades 9 through 11 were inappropriate. The case reached the Third Circuit, which noted that the student's distractability was part of her disability and that the district had notice that her IEP wasn't working. However, **the Friends school was not an appropriate placement because it did not address the student's most critical behavior problems**. Accordingly, tuition reimbursement was denied. *Lauren P. v. Wissahickon School Dist.*, 310 Fed.Appx. 552 (3d Cir. 2009).

◆   A Maine student with behavioral problems and severe depression had difficulty attending school and obtained an IEP allowing for in-home tutoring for eighth grade. For grade nine, however, the pupil evaluation team (PET) placed him in public school but increased his tutorial time. He quit attending classes halfway through the year. The PET recommended hospitalization or residential placement, but the student did not qualify for either program identified because he was not violent or suicidal. His mother then placed him in a wilderness program and, after he completed that, a boarding school. The PET refused to approve either placement, instead arguing for an in-state day program that was not yet operational. When the mother sought over $80,000 at a due process hearing, the hearing officer ruled in her favor. A federal court agreed that **the district had failed to address the student's emotional and behavioral problems as well as his attendance problems**. It failed to provide a FAPE and thus was liable for tuition reimbursement. *Lamoine School Committee v. Mrs. Z.*, 353 F.Supp.2d 18 (D. Me. 2005).

◆   A New York student with a genetic disorder that caused multiple disabilities had increasing academic and social problems in the sixth grade. Although she had behavior problems at home, she managed to stay on the honor roll and make social progress in the classroom. After the committee on special education denied the parents' request to place her in a self-contained classroom, instead modifying her IEP, her parents notified the school they intended to place her in a private school for seventh grade and requested a due process hearing, seeking tuition reimbursement. Following administrative rulings in favor of the district, a federal court affirmed. The student was benefiting socially from an inclusive IEP, she was on the honor roll, and **she generally behaved appropriately in school. Tuition reimbursement was denied.** *J.R. v. Board of Educ., City of Rye School Dist.*, 345 F.Supp.2d 386 (S.D.N.Y. 2004).

◆   From kindergarten through eighth grade, a New Jersey student endured harassment and bullying. He made repeated complaints to school administrators, but they were unable to resolve the situation. He became depressed, his grades suffered and he was declared eligible for special education. After he attempted suicide, his parents sought to place him in a neighboring district for high school. The child study team rejected the placement. His parents placed him there anyway and requested a due process hearing. The hearing officer ordered the district to reimburse the parents for their out-of-district tuition and costs. The Third Circuit Court of Appeals upheld that decision. **The district failed to show that it could remedy a situation it had failed to remedy since kindergarten.** *Shore Regional High School Board of Educ. v. P.S.*, 381 F.3d 194 (3d Cir. 2004).

◆   An elementary school student was hospitalized several times for a serious emotional and mental illness. After the third hospitalization, his parents admitted him to a private mental health facility. Once he was discharged, the district developed an IEP calling for homebound services. He experienced more behavior problems, and his parents eventually placed him in a day treatment program at the mental health facility. A hearing panel denied the parents' requests for tuition and other costs. The parents appealed. A federal court noted that the IDEA authorizes placement in private facilities at public expense only when the nature and severity of a disability makes placement in regular classes with supplemental services unsatisfactory. Here, **the private facility was overly restrictive.** The student had no peer role models at the school and rarely engaged in interactive play with classmates. The lack of any inclusive component in the placement made it inappropriate. The district proposed that he receive instruction in a self-contained classroom and be included in activities with non-disabled peers. The facility's focus was on behavior, not education. The parents were not entitled to tuition reimbursement and related costs, but the student should receive compensatory education. *Reese v. Board of Educ. of Bismarck R-V School Dist.*, 225 F.Supp.2d 1149 (E.D. Mo. 2002).

◆   A high school student earned high grades despite her emotional disabilities, which included obsessive-compulsive disorder, bipolar disorder and severe ADHD. During tenth grade, she was declared eligible for special education and her parents admitted her to a psychiatric hospital. The district agreed to pay for the educational component of the placement. After the student's release, her parents enrolled her in a private boarding school in Maine that lacked a special education program. Several months later, they sought tuition reimbursement. The district prepared an IEP that proposed placing the student in a local private day school. The parents rejected the IEP and kept the student in the Maine school. A due process hearing officer found that the IEP proposed by the district met IDEA requirements, but ordered the district to reimburse the parents for the cost of a "suitable local private day program." A Virginia federal court found that the district's IEP offer was proper in view of the student's hospitalization and did not prevent the parents from participating in the IEP process. Its proposed IEP was designed to meet the student's unique needs. **The parents were entitled to reimbursement only for the cost of the educational services provided at the psychiatric hospital.** The Fourth Circuit agreed. *Jennings v. Fairfax County School Board*, 39 Fed.Appx. 921 (4th Cir. 2002).

2.   Preferred Placement or Methodology

♦   A Pennsylvania student attended private schools through grade nine, when she withdrew due to problems with ADHD. She switched to a public school and, after an evaluation, the district issued an IEP that proposed a public school placement. Her parents rejected the IEP and placed her in a different private school. They requested due process, but the district did not process the request for more than a year. A hearing officer eventually found that the IEP would have provided the student with a free appropriate public education. The parents appealed, arguing that the delay required awarding them tuition reimbursement, but the Third Circuit disagreed. **The IEP offered an appropriate education, and the parents didn't dispute that.** *C.W. v. The Rose Tree Media School Dist.*, 395 Fed.Appx. 824 (3d Cir. 2010).

♦   The parents of a New York student with dyslexia lost faith in their district's ability to teach him and placed him in a private residential school. They later sought tuition reimbursement, but a federal court denied it. The court stated that the district provided adequate IEPs and that it used multisensory instruction, even though it didn't provide the Orton-Gillingham multisensory methodology preferred by the parents. Further, the self-contained program in the private school was too restrictive. The parents were not entitled to tuition reimbursement just because **the education they sought was perhaps superior to the appropriate education available** in the district. *D.G. v. Cooperstown Cent. School Dist.*,746 F.Supp.2d 435 (N.D.N.Y. 2010).

♦   An Illinois student with Type 1 diabetes and a social anxiety disorder began missing classes and instead enrolled at a community college. She sought reimbursement for her tuition there, but a federal court and the Seventh Circuit ruled against her. She had a Section 504 plan in place for her diabetes and was not IDEA eligible. Also, **there was no medical evidence that she stopped attending high school because her anxiety had worsened**. There was no medical basis for her better attendance and performance at the community college. *Loch v. Edwardsville School Dist. No. 7*, 327 Fed.Appx. 647 (7th Cir. 2009).

♦   A county special services agency recommended a private school placement for a New Jersey boy. The school district corresponded with the parents, sending them a draft IEP and expressing a desire to meet with them. Instead, the parents placed their son in an unapproved private school. When they requested due process, an administrative law judge found that **their agreement with the private school meant that they had failed to meaningfully engage in the IEP process**. The ALJ also found that the district had offered a free appropriate public education. A federal court agreed. Here, the parents, by registering their son in the private school, did not negotiate with the school district in good faith. Further the district's draft IEP was thorough and comprehensive. The parents were not entitled to tuition reimbursement. *S.G. v. Lakeland Regional High School Board of Educ.*, No. 05-3607 (GEB), 2007 WL 174172 (D.N.J. 1/22/07).

♦   After a federal court awarded tuition reimbursement to Massachusetts parents, their school district developed a substantially improved IEP. The parents rejected it, even though it utilized three teachers who had been at the private school and were familiar with their daughter. A new due process hearing resulted in a decision for the district, and the parents appealed. This time, **the federal court denied reimbursement, noting that the new IEP was substantially different than the previous one**. It had significant remedial instruction and was individualized to the student. *David T. v. City of Chicopee*, 431 F.Supp.2d 180 (D. Mass. 2006).

♦   A 17-year-old with a learning disability and emotional disturbance attended a public school under an IEP that gave him 11.5 hours of specialized instruction weekly. The district placement specialist recommended a neighborhood school placement that offered a part-time special education program. The parents insisted on 30 hours of specialized instruction each week, which the district agreed to. They later enrolled their son in a private school. A hearing officer and a District of Columbia federal court held that **there was no justification for the increase in specialized instruction except as a transparent attempt to circumvent the IDEA** and obtain a private school placement. No new information about the student was presented at the March meeting to justify the change. The parents were simply trying to "game the system to obtain a private placement." *R.D. v. District of Columbia*, 374 F.Supp.2d 84 (D.D.C. 2005).

♦   The parents of a New Hampshire student with speech/language difficulties abandoned IEP discussions with the district and placed her in a private school. The district provided occupational and speech/language therapies at the private school. The student returned to public school for grade four and progressed in almost all areas, so her fifth-grade IEP was substantially similar. However, her progress was not as good that year, and her parents pushed for a private school placement. They unilaterally enrolled her in the private school, refused to sign IEP documents and cancelled an IEP meeting. They sought tuition reimbursement for the private school, but a federal court ruled against them. Here, the hearing officer had properly found that the IEP complied with IDEA procedures, was sufficient to meet the student's needs and could be implemented by the school district. **It did not matter if the private school**

placement was better because the IEP was reasonably calculated to provide the student with educational benefits. *Galina C. v. Shaker Regional School Dist.*, No. Civ. 03-34-B, 2004 WL 626833 (D.N.H. 3/30/04).

♦   A New York school district offered a learning-disabled student IEPs calling for resource room placement and speech/language therapy. It incorporated a resource room teacher with training in Orton-Gillingham (OG), a methodology often used with students with dyslexia and other learning disabilities. The student continued to experience difficulties, and the school recommended increasing his resource room time and adding a self-contained reading class to his IEP, while his parents sought more instruction under the OG method. When the IEP proposal for the following school year was substantially unchanged, the parents unilaterally placed the student in a private school and sought tuition reimbursement. Before a federal court, they argued that the student's disability required instruction by a teacher fully trained in the OG method. However, their expert witness admitted that **the district couldn't fully provide the OG methodology because students received instruction from different teachers for each subject.** The court ruled for for the district, finding that the appropriateness of the placement should not be determined by comparison with a private placement preferred by parents. *M.B. v. Arlington Cent. School Dist.*, No. 99 CIV. 9973(SAS), 2002 WL 389151 (S.D.N.Y. 3/12/02).

♦   By the fifth grade, a student with a learning disability read at a grade 1.7 level. His parents agreed to a proposed IEP for the sixth grade, but within a month requested private school tuition reimbursement. After the parents placed the student in a private school, the district requested a due process hearing. A hearing officer concluded the district IEP was not appropriate and ordered the district to reimburse the parents. A state appeals panel affirmed, but the Pennsylvania Commonwealth Court reversed. **The fact that the student achieved greater success in the private school reading program than he did in his public school placement did not establish that the district's program was inappropriate.** The proposed IEP would confer a meaningful educational benefit. *Daniel G. by Robert G. v. Delaware Valley School Dist.*, 813 A.2d 36 (Pa. Commw. Ct. 2002).

3.   Regular Education Students

♦   A student attended Oregon public schools through grade 11. He had problems paying attention and finishing work, but he was able to pass his classes with help from family members at home. The district evaluated him but found him ineligible for special education and related services. After he exhibited multiple behavioral problems, a psychologist determined that he had ADHD, depression and other issues. His parents enrolled him in a three-week wilderness program, then a private residential school. They then sought due process. A hearing officer found the student disabled and eligible for IDEA services, but held that the district only had to pay for the residential placement, not the wilderness program or the evaluation. The district appealed, and the Ninth Circuit held that **the fact that the student had never received special**

education from the district was not a categorical bar to reimbursement. On further appeal, the U.S. Supreme Court noted that the district's failure to provide an IEP was at least as serious a violation of its responsibilities under the IDEA as a failure to provide an adequate IEP. It rejected the district's argument that the student first had to receive special education and related services from the district to advance any claim for tuition reimbursement. The 1997 Amendments did not mandate a different result from *Burlington* (pp.187-188). *Forest Grove School Dist. v. T.A.*, 129 S.Ct. 2484, 174 L.Ed.2d 168 (U.S. 2009).

On remand, a federal court held that the district did not have to pay the student's tuition because the parents failed to notify the district of their private school selection until well after making it, and because **the district had found that the student did not need special education or even a Section 504 plan**. Here, the parents seemingly chose the private school because of the student's drug use and behavioral problems. *Forest Grove School Dist. v. T.A.*, 675 F.Supp.2d 1063 (D. Or. 2009).

◆   A New York sixth-grader received Bs and Cs in regular education classes with support. His parents nevertheless enrolled him in an unapproved private residential school, insisting that his IEP had been predetermined and that there should have been a behavioral intervention plan. When they sued for tuition, a federal court ruled against them, noting that the student had never been sent to the principal for discipline, had worked cooperatively in groups and was making progress in his regular placement. Thus, no tuition reimbursement was granted. *Z.D. v. Niskayuna Cent. School Dist.*, No. 1:06-CV-1190 (FJS/DRH), 2009 WL 1748794 (N.D.N.Y. 6/19/09).

◆   When the Hawaii Department of Education rescinded a dyslexic student's special education eligibility, his parents enrolled him in a private school. After the student's support team found him ineligible for Section 504 services, the parents sought tuition reimbursement under Section 504, citing to an IDEA regulation (34 C.F.R. Part 300.403(c)). A federal court rejected their argument that an IDEA regulation applied to a Section 504 claim. Further, **the parents failed to show that their son was entitled to Section 504 services**. *Janet G. v. Hawaii Dep't of Educ.*, 410 F.Supp.2d 958 (D. Haw. 2005).

◆   A Missouri student who had attended his neighborhood elementary school began middle school. He came home after the first day with a stomachache, vomiting, crying and other physical symptoms that he continued to experience throughout the school year. A psychiatrist determined that he had general and separation anxiety but had no impediment to attending school. The student completed seventh grade, receiving mostly As and Bs and showing marked improvement in managing his anxiety. However, he began to cry when he returned home from his first day in eighth grade, and his parents unilaterally enrolled him in a private school. They later sued for reimbursement, and a court ruled for the district, finding that the student was not disabled under the IDEA because his anxiety did not cause his academic performance to fall below his age level. The Eighth Circuit affirmed. **Here, the district had received no**

opportunity to provide an appropriate public education through possible accommodations. Because the district had been excluded from the parents' decision-making process, reimbursement was inappropriate. *Schoenfeld v. Parkway School Dist.*, 138 F.3d 379 (8th Cir. 1998).

4. Failure to Cooperate

◆   The mother of a Delaware student with disabilities placed him in a private school after a dispute about his IEP. The district agreed to fund the placement for one year and began the formal IEP process for the next year. However, the mother failed to return the form requesting permission to evaluate her son until midway through the summer. She also claimed she could not attend an IEP meeting because of scheduling conflicts. She then returned her son to the private school and refused to participate in the IEP process any more, asserting that FAPE was denied because the IEP was not in place at the start of the school year. A federal court ultimately ruled against her when she sued for tuition reimbursement, noting that **the delays were at least partly her fault and did not deny her son FAPE.** On further appeal, the Third Circuit affirmed, noting that not all procedural violations of the IDEA result in a denial of FAPE. Here, the parents' non-cooperation caused the delay. *C.H. v. Cape Henlopen School Dist.*, 606 F.3d 59 (3d Cir. 2010).

◆   The parents of an Indiana student with a traumatic brain injury sought placement for him in a full-day kindergarten program. The district did not offer such a program, so attending both sessions would be duplicative and would not constitute special education. They eventually stopped communicating with the district and enrolled their son in a private Lindamood Bell program. When they sought reimbursement for their costs, they lost. A federal district court noted that **they had stopped participating in conferences** and that the student had been progressing in his placement. Thus, they were not entitled to reimbursement. *M.B. v. Hamilton Southeastern Schools*, No. 1:09-CV-0304-TWP-TAB, 2010 WL 3168666 (S.D. Ind. 8/10/10).

◆   The mother of a student with a learning disability rejected the sixth-grade IEP offered by the New York City Department of Education (DOE) and placed him in an unapproved private school. She kept him there for four years, always rejecting the IEPs proposed by the DOE. The DOE eventually agreed to pay for the placement but refused to pay tuition after four years. Instead it offered another public school placement. The mother re-enrolled her son in the private school without informing the DOE that she was rejecting the IEP. The contract relieved her of any responsibility to pay tuition, with the school assuming the risk that it might not be paid. In January, she filed a due process request, only then notifying the DOE that she was rejecting the IEP. The case reached a federal court, which ruled against her. **Her lack of good faith, combined with the private school contract relieving her of liability for tuition, meant that she was not entitled to tuition reimbursement.** *S.W. v. New York City Dep't of Educ.*, 646 F.Supp.2d 346 (S.D.N.Y. 2009).

◆   A New York five-year-old with an emotional disturbance faced expulsion from his preschool for misbehavior. His parents submitted an application to a private school for both its summer program and the following year. They paid a nonrefundable deposit, then asked the school district's committee on special education to develop an IEP. The CSE recommended a private school, but the parents refused to visit, claiming this would traumatize their son. When they sought tuition reimbursement for the placement they had already made, a federal court ruled against them. **Their failure to cooperate with the CSE made the denial of reimbursement appropriate.** *Bettinger v. New York City Board of Educ.*, No. 06 CV 6889 (PAC), 2007 WL 4208560 (S.D.N.Y. 11/20/07).

◆   A California school district evaluated a low-performing second-grade student and determined he did not have a disability and was therefore not eligible for special education under the IDEA. His parents then placed him in a private school and got a private evaluation that indicated the student was dyslexic and had ADD. They did not notify the district of the assessment until the end of the seventh-grade year. An IEP team met early in the student's eighth-grade year. The parents rejected a public school placement and then sought tuition reimbursement for grades two through eight. A hearing officer found the district violated the IDEA child find obligation for the years leading up to the IEP team meeting, but that **the parents suffered no compensable loss because they had no intention of placing their son in public school.** A federal court agreed with that ruling. No tuition reimbursement was available through the date of the IEP team meeting. *Miller ex rel. Miller v. San Mateo-Foster City Unified School Dist.*, 318 F.Supp.2d 851 (N.D. Cal. 2004).

◆   A New Jersey school district proposed placing a student with disabilities (including Asperger's syndrome) in a co-ed classroom of eight students, instructed by a teacher familiar with Asperger's syndrome and assisted by at least two paraprofessionals. The student would also receive one-to-one instruction in certain subjects, related services and a behavior modification plan. Her parents rejected the placement and placed her in a private school. They then requested a due process hearing, seeking three years of tuition. An administrative law judge determined that the parents did not give the district an opportunity to provide the student with FAPE. A federal court reversed, but the Third Circuit reversed the lower court. By preemptively placing the student in the private school, **the parents denied the district an opportunity to provide FAPE.** Their concern about possible regression at the public school and their desire to compare the private and public schools were irrelevant to the question of whether the district's proposed placement was appropriate. *H.W. ex rel. A.W. v. Highland Park Board of Educ.*, 108 Fed.Appx. 731 (3d Cir. 2004).

◆   The parents of a Maryland student with multiple disabilities agreed to an IEP and then began the application process for putting her in a private school. They signed a contract with the private school for the following year and made a nonrefundable deposit. During the summer, an independent speech and language assessment was made. When the school district discussed objectives and goals for the following year at the IEP meeting, they did not object, instead asking to discuss the proposed IEP with their expert. Later, they rejected the proposed IEP and enrolled their daughter in the private school. At that point, they finally disclosed the results of the summer assessment. When they sought tuition reimbursement, an administrative law judge denied it on the grounds that they had acted in bad faith, never intending to accept a public school placement. A federal court agreed. **Where parents fail to cooperate in the development of an IEP, they can be denied tuition reimbursement.** *S.M. v. Weast*, 240 F.Supp.2d 426 (D. Md. 2003).

◆   The mother of an Illinois student with a history of emotional and behavioral problems placed him in a private residential school in Maine without consulting with the district and without allowing him to be evaluated. She sought tuition reimbursement. A federal court denied the claim, and the Seventh Circuit Court of Appeals affirmed. **Parents who fail to cooperate with a school district's attempts to evaluate children with disabilities, and make unilateral private placements, forfeit their claims for tuition reimbursement.** Courts will look harshly upon any party's failure to reasonably cooperate under the IDEA. Here, the mother did not cooperate with school officials by placing the student in an out-of-state residential school and declining to allow district officials to evaluate him in the state of Illinois. *Patricia P. v. Board of Educ. of Oak Park*, 203 F.3d 462 (7th Cir. 2000).

◆   A Kentucky student with Pervasive Development Disorder attended a preschool program in the county school system. His parents obtained an evaluation from a Boston private school and later sought to place him there. They asked school officials to delay formulation of the student's IEP because he had been accepted for a summer program at the Boston school and they wished to incorporate his expected progress there into the IEP. Before the IEP was developed, the parents placed the student at the Boston school for the regular school year. The school district offered placement in a general ungraded primary school. A hearing officer held that the school district did not offer an appropriate placement, but a state appeal board reversed. The parents appealed, seeking an order that the student should remain in the Boston school as well as tuition reimbursement for two years. A federal court stated that **the parents had failed to give the district an opportunity to develop an appropriate IEP for the first school year and were not entitled to any expenses for either year.** The U.S. Court of Appeals, Sixth Circuit, affirmed. The district had proposed an appropriate, comprehensive IEP. *Tucker by Tucker v. Calloway County Board of Educ.*, 136 F.3d 495 (6th Cir. 1998).

5. Least Restrictive Environment

◆   A Pennsylvania student with a specific learning disability needed social modeling and did not meaningfully interact with his peers. His parents placed him in a private school and rejected the district's IEP proposal, claiming that it did not meet their child's need for intensive and rigorous instruction. They sought tuition reimbursement, which a hearing officer and a federal court denied. Here, the IEP would offer the student a meaningful educational benefit.

The district's teachers were well trained in the Orton-Gillingham method, and **the public school setting was the least restrictive environment**. As the private school was not an appropriate setting, the parents were not entitled to tuition reimbursement. On appeal, the Third Circuit affirmed, noting that the IEP called for social interaction with non-disabled peers and that it was reasonably calculated to provide meaningful educational benefits. *N.M. v. School Dist. of Philadelphia*, 394 Fed.Appx. 920 (3d Cir. 2010).

♦   A Virginia student with mental retardation and a significant communication disorder was diagnosed with autism. However, his IEP did not identify him as having autism until the parents presented evidence of the diagnosis. They sought to place their son in a Lindamood-Bell program. The district offered to place him there for up to 12 weeks, provided he then return to district schools. The district's IEP offered the student 23.5 hours of weekly special education in small groups but no one-on-one instruction. The parents unilaterally placed their son in a private Lindamood-Bell center. Two years later, they sought tuition reimbursement. A federal court held that they were not entitled to it because **even though the district failed to provide appropriate IEPs for the three years in question (by failing to provide one-on-one instruction), the private placement was also inappropriate (overly restrictive)** and focused almost exclusively on communication skills. *M.S. v. Fairfax County School Board*, No. 1:05CV1476 (JCC), 2007 WL 1378545 (E.D. Va. 5/8/07).

♦   A New York school district proposed placing a female student with a severe communication speech disorder in a 12:1:1 self-contained classroom with boys who had behavior problems. Her parents rejected the IEP and placed her in a private school. Under a settlement, the district agreed to pay $8,750 for tuition, damages and attorneys' fees. Shortly before the next school year was to begin, **the district proposed an even more restrictive 8:1:1 placement, then admitted it did not have an appropriate placement** for the student. In the lawsuit that followed, a federal court held that the parents were entitled to tuition reimbursement. Also, the parents could pursue a claim for damages under Section 504 because the district's delays and placement suggestions could be construed as gross negligence or reckless indifference. *Gabel v. Board of Educ. of Hyde Park Cent. School Dist.*, 368 F.Supp.2d 313 (S.D.N.Y. 2005).

♦   An Illinois student exhibited behavior problems by second grade but was not identified as disabled or eligible for special education until the end of her eighth-grade year. Her elementary school district offered two summer placement options and a primarily mainstream placement for grade nine. Although the student failed several eighth-grade classes, she was "placed" in ninth grade. Two weeks prior to the next IEP team meeting, the student's mother enrolled her in a residential facility in Maine that utilized controversial methods. The IEP team then proposed placement in a self-contained program with some regular education, counseling and community-based services. The student's mother did not attend the meeting, instead seeking reimbursement.

A federal court stated that the high school district appropriately intervened by helping develop the IEP and placing the student in an adequate program in a highly structured environment. The student's mother had signed the IEP, and it was in accord with the recommendations of the student's therapist and psychologist. Although an administrator's inappropriate comments about residential placement prompted the student's mother to seek a private placement, she should have waited for the scheduled meeting before making her decision, since she knew the IEP team would be discussing the case. Moreover, **the private school was inappropriate, as it employed a controversial method contrary to the recommendations of the student's own experts.** The placement segregated the student with disabled students, in violation of the IDEA's least restrictive environment requirement. While the elementary district had not acted with urgency to evaluate the student despite her deteriorating performance, the IEP was approved within IDEA deadlines. Because the districts had offered her an appropriate placement, and the placement selected by her mother was inappropriate, the court denied tuition reimbursement. *Board of Educ. of Arlington Heights School Dist. No. 25 v. Illinois State Board of Educ.*, No. 98 C 5370, 2001 WL 585149 (N.D. Ill. 3/19/01).

◆ The parents of an Indiana student with dyslexia objected to the school district's proposed IEP near the end of his seventh-grade year. During the summer, they placed the student in a private school. A hearing officer held that the district was required to provide the student with weekly sessions for remedial reading and accommodation strategies and provide compensatory education during the next two summers to make up for failing to provide this assistance prior to the hearing. However, the decision rejected further summer education and affirmed the proposed placement in a mainstream public school setting. The parents placed the student full time at the private school. A federal court and the Seventh Circuit held that **private school tuition reimbursement was inappropriate because the extra summer sessions and the continuation of the mainstream public school program would be preferable to the segregated placement.** Even though the public school had fallen behind in providing extra services to the student, this did not require a private school placement. *Linda W. v. Indiana Dep't of Educ.*, 200 F.3d 504 (7th Cir. 1999).

6. Students Never Enrolled in Public Schools

◆ The parents of a California student with autism placed their child in a private Lovaas program after obtaining an independent educational evaluation. **They never gave the district an opportunity to make a formal placement offer.** When they sought tuition reimbursement, a federal court and the Ninth Circuit ruled against them. The courts noted that the student had never received special education and related services from a public agency. Therefore, reimbursement was unauthorized by IDEA Section 1412(a)(10)(C). *C.S. v. Governing Board of Riverside Unified School Dist.*, 321 Fed.Appx. 630 (9th Cir. 2009).

◆ The mother of a disabled student alleged that the Hawaii Department of Education (DOE) violated the IDEA by failing to offer her son an IEP for three consecutive years. An impartial hearing officer agreed, noting that the DOE's proposal to place the student in fully self-contained classes for an unspecified period while an IEP was developed did not meet the requirements of the IDEA. The hearing officer granted tuition reimbursement and a federal court upheld that decision. **Even though the student had never been enrolled in public schools, his mother had repeatedly tried to enroll him, only placing him in the private school when no IEP was timely offered.** *Dep't of Educ., State of Hawaii v. E.B.*, 2006 WL 1343681 (D. Haw. 5/15/06).

◆   A New Jersey school district provided a student with supportive services but did not classify her as disabled. Her parents then moved to their summer home in another district and got her classified as eligible for special education. They moved back to their old district and placed her in a private school, then sought tuition reimbursement. The old district evaluated the student and found her eligible for special education but proposed an IEP specifying in-class support. A hearing officer and a federal court **denied the parents' request for tuition reimbursement because the student had never received special education services from the district** – a prerequisite for tuition reimbursement under state law and the IDEA. *T.H. v. Clinton Township Board of Educ.*, No. Civ. 05-3709 SRC, 2006 WL 1128713 (D.N.J. 4/25/06).

◆   The adoptive parents of a New York ADHD student kept him in private schools through the fourth grade. They then contacted their school board and the student was identified as learning disabled. However, the committee on special education rejected the recommendations of an independent evaluation (small classes with an aide) and suggested a regular education placement with related services. The parents rejected the offer and sought a due process hearing, at which the district conceded its IEP was inappropriate. Eventually, the case reached the Second Circuit, which ruled that **the parents were entitled to tuition reimbursement even though their child had never received special education from a public agency.** The IDEA allows courts to award tuition where appropriate. *Frank G. v. Board of Educ. of Hyde Park*, 459 F.3d 356 (2d Cir. 2006).

◆   A New York kindergartner with learning disabilities attended a private school. His parents asked for an evaluation to determine an appropriate placement for the next year, and the district recommended a public school placement. The parents instead kept the student in the private school. When they sought tuition reimbursement, a federal court ruled against them. **The IDEA does not allow for tuition reimbursement where private school students have not previously received special education from a public agency.** *Board of Educ. of City of New York v. Tom F.*, No. 04-CV-6596L, 2005 WL 17838 (W.D.N.Y. 1/4/05).

◆   The parents of a Maryland student with multiple disabilities placed her in private schools for kindergarten and first grade. Soon after making the first-grade placement, they contacted the principal at a public elementary school about enrollment procedures. The elementary school staff lost a certified letter from the parents containing required information for enrollment and three evaluations of their daughter. As a result, the staff took no further action to develop an IEP. The parents requested a due process hearing more than six months later. The school finally found the missing letter. An administrative law judge awarded tuition reimbursement for most of the student's first-grade year. However, a federal court reversed. **Even though the failure to develop an IEP denied the student a free appropriate public education, the parents were not eligible for tuition reimbursement.** The IDEA allows reimbursement only where the disabled student was at one time receiving "special education and related services from a public agency." *Baltimore City Board of School Commissioners v. Taylorch*, 395 F.Supp.2d 246 (D. Md. 2005).

7. Other Issues

◆   The mother of a severely disabled, autistic child placed him in a Kansas residential facility, which the Hawaii Department of Education funded. However, the department notified the mother it would stop funding the placement when the student turned 20 over the summer. It asserted that state rules required a student to be under age 20 on the first day of school to be eligible. The mother sued, seeking tuition reimbursement and arguing that the automatic bar for special education students at age 20 was improper because there was no such bar for general education students at age 20. A federal court agreed, noting that the state admitted 100% of over-age general education students who sought enrollment. Thus, the state department of education **could not deny special education services based solely on the attainment of age 20**. The state had to provide special education services through age 21. *B.T. v. Dep't of Educ., State of Hawaii*, No. 08-00356 DAE-BMK, 2009 WL 4884447 (D. Haw. 12/17/09).

◆   The parents of a Maine student sought tuition reimbursement from a school district, which sought coverage under an educator's liability policy. The insurer denied coverage on the grounds that "reimbursement" was not covered by the policy. When the district sued the insurer, the case reached the First Circuit, which held that **the underlying claim for reimbursement under the IDEA was covered by the policy because it was a claim for "money damages,"** which included equitable monetary relief under Maine law. *School Union No. 37 v. United National Ins. Co.*, 617 F.3d 554 (1st Cir. 2010).

◆   A New York fifth-grader's IEP stated that his homework assignments would be broken down into manageable parts. However, in sixth grade, his parents requested that that accommodation be discontinued. He struggled in grade six, and his parents sought tuition reimbursement for a private school placement. A hearing officer found that the discontinuation of the homework modifications played a part in the student's lack of progress in sixth grade, along with a lack of daily multi-sensory reading classes. The parties agreed that the student needed daily reading instruction, and the hearing officer ruled that no tuition reimbursement was necessary. A federal court reversed, but the Second Circuit reversed the lower court, finding **the hearing officer's refusal to grant reimbursement supported by the evidence**. *Bougades v. Pine Plains Cent. School Dist.*, 376 Fed.Appx. 95 (2d Cir. 2010).

♦ A Pennsylvania student with learning disabilities received special education in reading, math and writing. In the sixth grade, his parents placed him in a private school and sought tuition reimbursement as well as compensatory education for the prior two years. After **a federal court upheld the student's-sixth grade IEP**, the Third Circuit agreed that it addressed his deficiencies. And the lack of occupational therapy in the student's seventh-grade IEP was attributable to the delay by the parents in providing an OT evaluation. Once they did so, a revised IEP provided for reevaluation for potential OT needs within 30 days of his return to a district school. *Souderton Area School Dist. v. J.H.*, 351 Fed.Appx. 755 (3d Cir. 2009).

♦ The parents of a Connecticut student with autism placed him in a private school after failing to reach an agreement with the public school about his IEP. The district denied their request for tuition reimbursement, but a hearing officer found that **the district's IEPs for two years lacked adequate transition plans, training, assistive technology, follow-up meetings and transportation**. As a result, the parents were entitled to tuition reimbursement for those two years. A federal court agreed. *Regional School Dist. No. 9 Board of Educ. v. Mr. & Mrs. P.*, No. 3:06 CV 01278 (CFD), 2009 WL 103376 (D. Conn. 1/12/09).

♦ The parents of an autistic student met with their school district to discuss an IEP for their son's kindergarten year. The IEP called for a 6:1:1 placement in a specialized school, but it did not identify the specific school the student would attend. The parents made a nonrefundable deposit to a private school, then rejected the district's placement offer just before the start of the school year and sought tuition reimbursement for the private school. A federal court refused their request for tuition, noting that **the delay in identifying a particular school did not violate the IDEA**. *Tarlowe v. New York City Board of Educ.*, No. 07 Civ. 7936 (GEL), 2008 WL 2736027 (S.D.N.Y. 7/3/08).

♦ The mother of a New Hampshire wheelchair-bound student claimed that the district failed to follow his IEP and erroneously decertified him from eligibility for special education. She filed a complaint with the state department of education. After an administrative ruling against her, she placed her son in a private school outside the district. When she sued under the IDEA and Section 504, a federal court held that **most of her claims failed because the private school was outside the district and she did not intend to return her son to district schools**. The court then determined that tuition reimbursement was not in order because the student's classroom performance demonstrated that he was no longer qualified as a child with a disability under the IDEA. *J.P.E.H. v. Hooksett School Dist.*, No. 07-CV-276-SM, 2009 WL 1883885 (D.N.H. 6/30/09).

♦ The parents of a disabled Pennsylvania student placed her in a private school for grade eight and reached an agreement with the district for funding, waiving any remaining claims against the district. For grades nine and ten, the board approved private school tuition, but no final agreement was reached because the parents refused to waive their claims against the district. For grade eleven, the district proposed an IEP that would move the student back to the public school. The parents fought it and kept their daughter in private school through grade twelve. When they sought tuition reimbursement, a hearing officer, a federal court and the Third Circuit all agreed that the claims for grade eight and earlier were barred by the settlement agreement. Also, the district was liable for tuition for grades nine and ten. Finally, **the district was not entitled to recover the tuition it paid for grades eleven and twelve even though it offered an appropriate IEP** for grade eleven because of another agreement it made with the parents. *Lauren W. ex rel. Jean W. v. Deflaminis*, 480 F.3d 259 (3d Cir. 2007).

♦   The parents of a student with disabilities enrolled him in a private school and sought tuition reimbursement. A hearing officer ruled that the parents had failed to notify the district at least 10 days in advance, so they were not eligible for reimbursement for the first year of the private school placement. However, the hearing officer determined that the district had failed to provide a free appropriate public education, thus making the district liable for tuition in the following year. The Indiana Board of Special Education Appeals reversed, and the district then asserted that it did not have to pay the student's tuition for the second year at the private school. A federal court disagreed. Here, **the placement ordered by the hearing officer was treated as "agreed upon" by the parties even though it was later reversed.** *L.B. v. Greater Clark County Schools*, 458 F.Supp.2d 845 (S.D. Ind. 2006).

♦   The parents of a Massachusetts student with disabilities agreed to his seventh-grade IEP, but they did not formally accept or reject another one until he was in the eleventh grade and an IEP for the twelfth grade had been proposed. They filed a due process hearing request. The student graduated from the vo-tech high school where they had placed him and enrolled in college. His parents sought tuition reimbursement for a year of college. The hearing officer awarded a half-year of tuition, but a federal court found that no tuition reimbursement was required. **Because the parents never formally rejected the student's IEPs for the years in question, they were deemed to have accepted them under the IDEA's stay-put provision.** *Shawsheen Valley Regional Vocational Technical School Dist. Committee v. Massachusetts Bureau of Special Educ. Appeals*, 367 F.Supp.2d 44 (D. Mass. 2005).

♦   The parents of a New York student decided to place her in a private school for grade four after disagreeing with the program proposed by the district. The district deactivated the student's file for grade five and did not develop an IEP. The parents kept her in the private school and also requested tuition reimbursement for that year. Finally the parents rejected the district's proposed IEP for grade six and again requested tuition reimbursement. A hearing officer awarded tuition reimbursement for grades four and five, but a state review officer (SRO) found that the private school was the appropriate placement only for grade five. The SRO issued that decision over a year late. When the question of tuition reimbursement for grade six came before a federal court, the court ruled that because of the SRO's decision, the private school was the stay-put placement for grade six, which meant that **the student was entitled to tuition**

reimbursement for that grade despite the lateness of the SRO's decision. *Board of Educ. of Poughkeepsie City School Dist. v. O'Shea*, 353 F.Supp.2d 449 (S.D.N.Y. 2005).

♦ Parents of a Michigan student unilaterally placed him in a private residential school based on a doctor's recommendation. They then sought tuition reimbursement from their school district. A due process hearing officer ruled for the parents, a state review officer reversed, and a federal court held that the school district committed procedural and substantive violations of the IDEA by failing to timely advise the parents of their rights. The district also failed in its child-find obligations, such that an IEP was not created for the student until seven months after he was placed in the residential facility. The court ordered reimbursement, but limited it to the seven months prior to the development of the IEP. The Sixth Circuit affirmed. **The IEP that was eventually developed was adequate** to provide the student with a free appropriate public education. Further, the district's failure to include the student's doctor on the IEP team did not violate the IDEA because the district considered all relevant educational and medical information. *Lakin v. Birmingham Public Schools*, 70 Fed.Appx. 295 (6th Cir. 2003).

B. Placement in Unapproved Schools

The U.S. Supreme Court's decision in *Florence County School Dist. Four v. Carter*, below, held that parents who placed their child in an unapproved private facility were entitled to tuition reimbursement despite the lack of state approval of the facility.

The Court's analysis focused on the appropriateness of the placement selected by the parents and the inability of the local school district to provide an appropriate alternative.

While state approval remains a factor in selecting an appropriate placement, the lack of state approval by itself no longer determines the appropriateness of the placement.

♦ The parents of a South Carolina ninth-grader with a learning disability disagreed with the IEP proposed by their school district. The IEP called for mainstreaming in most subjects, with individual instruction three periods a week, and specific goals of increasing the student's reading and mathematics levels by four months for the entire school year. The parents requested due process and unilaterally placed their daughter in a private school that specialized in teaching students with disabilities. A hearing officer held that the IEP was adequate. After the student raised her reading comprehension three full grades in one year at the private school, the parents sued the school district for tuition reimbursement. A federal court found that the educational program and achievement goals of the proposed IEP were "wholly inadequate" under the IDEA. Even though the private school did not comply with all IDEA procedures – by employing noncertified staff members, for example – it provided the student with an excellent education that complied with IDEA substantive requirements. The court awarded tuition reimbursement, a result upheld by the Fourth Circuit. The school district appealed to the U.S. Supreme Court.

The Court expanded upon its decision in *Burlington School Committee v. Dep't of Educ. of Massachusetts*, subsection A, above, where it held that parents had the right to unilaterally change their children's placement at their own financial risk. To recover private school tuition costs, parents must show that the placement proposed by the school district violates the IDEA and that the private school placement is appropriate under the act. Here, **the failure by the school district to provide an appropriate placement entitled the parents to an award of tuition reimbursement, even though the private school was not approved by the state**, because the education provided at the private school had been determined by the district court to be appropriate. The decisions in favor of the parents were upheld. *Florence County School Dist. Four v. Carter*, 510 U.S. 7, 114 S.Ct. 361, 126 L.Ed.2d 284 (1993).

♦   After being bullied, a New York student began to experience anxiety about school. He was diagnosed with severe anxiety and depression, and the committee on special education found him eligible under the IDEA with emotional disturbance. The district developed an IEP specifying individualized counseling, resource room services and test modifications. The parents later withdrew their consent for the IEP and sought home tutoring. The district then recommended several alternative high school placements. **The parents unilaterally placed their son in an unapproved private school without informing the district, then rejected the district's recommendations.** When they sought tuition reimbursement, the Second Circuit ruled against them. The private school lacked a therapeutic setting, and was inappropriate. *Gagliardo v. Arlington Cent. School Dist.*, 489 F.3d 105 (2d Cir. 2007).

♦   A New York school district offered to provide a student with 27.5 hours of special education per week, as well as ABA therapy. However, the parents requested a higher level of services. The committee on special education authorized a private school placement but neither the parents nor the district were able to locate an approved placement. The parents unilaterally placed the student in a private pre-school program and arranged for in-home ABA therapy. When they sought to recover their costs and tuition, a hearing officer ruled that the parents' placement, although better than the district's, was not appropriate because the student received only nine hours of ABA therapy a week under it. A review officer affirmed, but a federal court reversed. **The hearing and review officers had improperly held the parents to a higher standard than the one to which school districts are held.** *C.B. v. New York City Dep't of Educ.*, No. 02 CV 4620 (CLP), 2005 WL 1388964 (E.D.N.Y. 6/10/05).

♦   A New York school district and the parents of a student with emotional and psychological problems agreed on a residential placement but did not agree on a school. The district's committee on special education recommended a therapeutic placement but no representative of the recommended facility attended the meeting to propose that placement. The parents then unilaterally placed their son in a private school and sought tuition reimbursement. A federal court denied reimbursement because **even though the district had violated the IDEA by failing to have a representative at the meeting, the parents could not show that the placement they made was appropriate**. The private school did not prepare written behavior plans for students with behavioral difficulties and did not provide counseling services as part of the normal program. *Werner v. Clarkstown Cent. School Dist.*, 363 F.Supp.2d 656 (S.D.N.Y. 2005).

◆   A two-year-old with developmental delay and autism was eligible for early intervention services. The New York City Early Intervention Program devised an individualized family service plan for him that included treatment at a development center, social work and speech therapy. The parents requested the inclusion of applied behavioral analysis (ABA) therapy, but the city did not provide it for students under three. The parents arranged for in-home ABA therapy and withdrew the student from the city program. Their social worker trained the parents and six college students to provide ABA therapy. The parents then requested a hearing to obtain reimbursement for the in-home therapy. An administrative law judge agreed that the city program was inappropriate and ordered the city to reimburse the parents for in-house therapy. The city and state department of developmental health appealed.

A federal court dismissed the case, and the Second Circuit affirmed. The right of parents to unilaterally withdraw a student from a state-approved program must be preserved where the local education agency's program is inappropriate. In this case, **the city's placement decision was inappropriate**, there was a demonstrated lack of ABA therapists in the area, and evidence indicated that the students were qualified to provide the services. *Still v. DeBuono*, 101 F.3d 888 (2d Cir. 1996).

◆   The parents of an emotionally disturbed student requested their school district evaluate the student for special education. They placed the student at a private school that offered small classes and employed unlicensed professionals. The district convened an IEP meeting; however, it excluded the parents from the development of the IEP in violation of IDEA § 1415(b). The placement team's confidential report was not signed by all multidisciplinary team members and was not created with the input of the student's current teachers, which also violated the IDEA. A due process hearing officer ruled that the placement outlined in the IEP was deficient. The district proposed another placement without developing a new IEP. A second due process hearing found that **the district had not made an appropriate placement because of the lack of parental participation in the IEP, but the private school placement was inappropriate**. A District of Columbia federal court agreed that there could be no tuition reimbursement. This would be contrary to the IDEA's requirement for an appropriate education, defined in 20 U.S.C. § 1401(a)(18) as "special education and related services that ... meet the standards of the State Educational Agency." Even though the school district had repeatedly failed to include the parents in the IEP process, they were not entitled to tuition reimbursement. *Fagan v. District of Columbia*, 817 F.Supp. 161 (D.D.C. 1993).

◆   A 20-year-old New Jersey student was entitled to special education services under the IDEA because of autism and severe behavioral problems. The state Division of Developmental Disabilities (DDD) placed her in a Delaware school that was not an approved special education facility. Her mother sought a transfer to a residential facility located in the family's home town. When the DDD refused to transfer the student, an administrative law judge ordered it to place the student at the residential facility in the family's home town. The DDD failed to transfer the student, and the case then reached a New Jersey federal court. Before the district court, the DDD changed its position, arguing that the Delaware school retained a "conditional approval" for special education. The student's mother argued that the programs were comparable and that the IDEA's requirement of placement in the least restrictive environment included placing the student as close as possible to the family's home. The district court agreed, citing 34 C.F.R. § 300.552(a)(3), a regulation which requires school districts to take into account the location of the placement, "particularly in a residential program." **Because the educational program available to the student in her hometown was comparable to the Delaware placement, it was the appropriate placement.** The court affirmed the decision for the student and awarded attorneys' fees and costs. *Remis v. New Jersey Dep't of Human Services,* 815 F.Supp. 141 (D.N.J. 1993).

C. Notice

The IDEA contains provisions requiring notice when parents decide to unilaterally enroll their child in a private school. These provisions are listed at 20 U.S.C. § 1412(a)(10)(C)(iii), which states when reimbursement for the costs of a unilateral private school placement can be limited, and 20 U.S.C. § 1415.

Before reimbursement can be limited under 20 U.S.C. § 1412(a)(10)(C)(iii), the school district must have previously provided the parents with all applicable IDEA notices and in most cases, the parents are required to notify the district, in writing, of their objections to the district's program and their intent to enroll the child in a private program before actually doing so. Some states have comparable statutory provisions.

◆   A New Jersey student with a specific learning disability made tremendous progress in a mainstream setting with resource support. The following year, his child-study team ruled him ineligible for special education. Several years later, he was suspended after a positive marijuana test. His parents placed him in an outback treatment center in Utah without notifying the district and then placed him in an adolescent treatment center, where he earned his diploma. Two years later, they filed a due process action against the school district seeking tuition reimbursement. A hearing officer and a New Jersey federal district court ruled against them, noting that **they had waited too long to challenge the declassification and had failed to give timely notice of their private placement.** *Mittman v. Livingston Township Board of Educ.,* No. 09-4754 (DRD), 2010 WL 3947548 (D.N.J. 10/7/10).

♦   After an Illinois student was hospitalized, her parents placed her in a private residential facility. Three days later, they notified the district of their intent to seek their costs. The district agreed to pay the educational and therapeutic costs but not the residential costs. At due process, a hearing officer found that the parents did not provide prior written notice and so were not entitled to reimbursement for the eight months prior to obtaining state approval for the placement. However, a federal court held relief still could be awarded under the IDEA. **Under 20 U.S.C. § 1412(a)(1)(C)(ii), private school reimbursement "may" be reduced or denied if parents fail to provide at least 10 days written notice. However, the statute does not say reimbursement "shall" be denied.** Thus, reimbursement might still be appropriate. A hearing officer would have to decide the matter. *Erin K. v. Naperville School Dist. No. 203*, No. 08 C 6997, 2009 WL 3271954 (N.D. Ill. 10/6/09).

♦   The mother of a Maine student with disabilities placed the student in public schools for five years, then home-schooled him for a while before placing him in a series of out-of-state private schools. She never objected to the IEPs prepared for him while he was in public schools. And she received tuition for the placements, supplemented by an amount for special education services, under the state's "local choice" option. After the student reached age 19, his mother sought reimbursement for room, board, transportation and related expenses. A hearing officer awarded her $52,000, but a federal court held that she waited too long to seek reimbursement. The First Circuit agreed with the lower court that **her delay in seeking reimbursement prejudiced the school district's ability to defend the IEPs it had offered.** *School Union No. 37 v. Ms. C.*, 518 F.3d 31 (1st Cir. 2008).

♦   The parents of a Maryland student with ADHD placed him in a private school after he began suffering academic and emotional problems. Their district agreed to fund the placement through 2001-02. When they sought to continue the placement through 2002-03, the district notified them that the school had not yet been approved as a fundable special education school for that year. The district recommended another private school, but the parents kept their son where he was. The school was approved as a fundable special education school for the 2003-04 year, and the parents then sought tuition reimbursement for the 2002-03 year. The case reached the Fourth Circuit, which denied reimbursement because **the district had offered a free appropriate public education at the other private school, and the parents did not properly notify the district of their intent to reject the IEP.** *Z.W. v. Smith*, 210 Fed.Appx. 282 (4th Cir. 2006).

♦   The parents of a New Jersey student with disabilities rejected their school board's proposed IEP advancing their son to first grade. They placed him in a private school, then wrote a series of letters to school officials, informing them that the student would be placed in the private school the next year and asking what services the board might provide. The board did not hold a child study team meeting or prepare an IEP for the next year. When the parents sought tuition reimbursement for the two years, a hearing officer and a federal court determined that they were entitled to reimbursement for the second year because **they had given proper notice and the board had failed to have an IEP ready at the start of the year**. However, they were not entitled to reimbursement for the first year because they did not properly notify the board of their intent with respect to that year. *A.Z. v. Mahwah Township Board of Educ.*, No. Civ. A. 04-4003(KSH), 2006 WL 827791 (D.N.J. 3/30/06).

◆ The mother of a New Jersey student with ADHD placed him in a residential school during the summer after he stole her car and led police on a high speed chase. Although she had signed the student's IEP for the following year, she kept him in the residential school and notified the district her son would not be attending a district school that year. Halfway through the year, she sought tuition reimbursement. A federal court refused to dismiss her claim because even though she did not provide proper notice to the district of her intent to seek reimbursement, **there was a question about whether providing notice before the placement would have harmed the student**. *J.M. v. Kingsway Regional School Dist.*, No. Civ. 04-4046(RBK), 2005 WL 2000179 (D.N.J. 8/18/05).

◆ The parents of a learning disabled child home-schooled her until she was 14. They did not provide their school district with their daughter's educational records for much of the time she was home-schooled, nor did they express any concerns that she had a learning disability. They subsequently placed her in a private school and moved to a new district. Less than a month before a new school year, they notified the new district of her learning disability and sought special education services. Because of the lack of time, the student was placed again at the private school. When the parents sought tuition reimbursement, a federal court ruled against them, overruling the hearing officer's decision. Here, **the parents did not notify the district of their daughter's needs until after making a unilateral placement**. They clearly did not intend to cooperate and, in fact, actively concealed what they knew about their daughter's needs in order to recover tuition reimbursement for the private school placement they desired. *Carmel Cent. School Dist. v. V.P.*, 373 F.Supp.2d 402 (S.D.N.Y. 2005).

◆ The parents of a learning disabled student recently diagnosed with Asperger's syndrome attended an IEP team meeting near the end of the school year. The team proposed an IEP for general education with one hour of specialized instruction and 30 minutes of counseling per week as well as a full-time aide. The parents did not object. They signed the IEP but later sent a letter announcing their intent to place the student in a private school for the following year. When they sought tuition reimbursement for that year, a due process hearing officer ruled in favor of the school, and a federal court affirmed. Although later evidence showed that the private school was in fact the appropriate placement, **the parents acted unreasonably by failing to formally object to the IEP and did not provide adequate notice to the school**. *Schoenback v. District of Columbia*, 309 F.Supp.2d 71 (D.D.C. 2004).

◆ An Ohio student with profound hearing loss received speech and language therapy and pre-tutoring of new vocabulary and concepts from a school district through grade four. His school performance dropped during that year, when he earned Ds and Fs in math. His IEP team recommended promoting him to grade five with resource room placement for part of the day. His parents agreed to the placement. However, two months later, they notified the district of their intent to place the student in a private school that did not offer special education. They then sought tuition reimbursement. A hearing officer denied reimbursement because the parents **failed to properly notify the district of their placement decision**. The Sixth Circuit agreed that the parents had failed to inform the district of their objections to the IEP prior to removing the student from school. Also, the private school placement was not appropriate because it did not provide the student with any of the special education services he required, including the pre-tutoring services the parents had insisted upon from the district. *Berger v. Medina City School Dist.*, 348 F.3d 513 (6th Cir. 2003).

◆ The pupil evaluation team (PET) for a Maine student with disabilities declared him eligible for special education and, over the next three years, increased his services. When the student reached fifth grade, his mother, who also had a learning disability, presented the PET with a statement of her concerns about his lack of progress. She unilaterally placed him in a private school for grade six, then sought tuition reimbursement, **claiming that she did not have to comply with the notice requirements of the IDEA because she was illiterate**. A hearing officer found that, as a high school graduate, she was literate within the meaning of the IDEA. She also admitted receiving notices from the district regarding her procedural obligations. A federal court and the First Circuit Court of Appeals agreed with the hearing officer that the mother was not entitled to tuition reimbursement. *Ms. M., ex rel. K.M. v. Portland School Committee*, 360 F.3d 267 (1st Cir. 2004).

◆ The parents of a Maryland student with disabilities agreed to an IEP proposed during March of one school year, without mentioning that they had submitted an application to a private school. After the student was accepted in June, the family's attorney sent a letter to the public school principal, stating that the parents intended to place their son at the private school. He enclosed new assessments and requested that the school system consider the private school as the student's appropriate placement. The system recommended placement in a public school. The student attended the private school for the remainder of the year, and the parents sought tuition reimbursement. The district argued that the IDEA required the parents to provide prior notice of the rejection of an IEP as a prerequisite to reimbursement. An administrative law judge (ALJ) denied reimbursement.

The parents sued the school system and officials in a federal court, which awarded pretrial judgment to the district and officials. On appeal to the Fourth Circuit, the court noted that although the parents now asserted they had expressed reservations about signing the IEP, they did not inform school officials they were rejecting it. **The letter from the parents' attorney did not serve as a proper rejection, as it did not explain that they no longer considered the IEP legally adequate.** The parents thus waived the issue of whether they failed to provide timely notice of their son's enrollment in the private school. The claim for tuition reimbursement was properly denied. *Pollowitz v. Weast*, 90 Fed.Appx. 438 (4th Cir. 2001).

♦   Because a student with disabilities did not perform well in a district middle school, his parents transferred him to a private residential school in Connecticut. They requested reimbursement and a reevaluation. Before an IEP was approved, they requested a hearing on their tuition reimbursement claim on grounds that the district failed to provide a residential placement for the student. The district later approved an IEP calling for a 45-day diagnostic placement, but the plan was not approved until after the hearing date. The board moved to dismiss the administrative proceeding on grounds that the family failed to provide it with a notice required by Maryland law. An administrative law judge granted the board's motion and the parents appealed to a federal court. The court granted pretrial judgment to the board.

On appeal, the parents argued that the state law did not apply in their case, because the board had not proposed an IEP at the time they enrolled the student in the residential school. The court of appeals agreed with the parents, noting that **because there was no IEP for them to reject, the notice contemplated by the state law was impossible.** The law applied only when an IEP has actually been proposed by a school district prior to the time a student is enrolled in a nonpublic school. The Fourth Circuit reversed and remanded the case. *Sandler v. Hickey*, 5 Fed. Appx. 233 (4th Cir. 2001).

II. RELIGIOUS SCHOOLS

Public aid to students who attend private religious schools implicates the Establishment Clause of the First Amendment. Public school funding for students with disabilities for private religious school education and related services has been held constitutionally permissible, as the benefit to the private school is only attenuated. In contrast, a direct payment of government funds to a private religious school would violate the U.S. Constitution.

♦   An Arizona student attended a school for the deaf from grades one through five and then transferred to a public school for grades six through eight. During his public school attendance, the school district furnished him with a sign-language interpreter. His parents enrolled him in a parochial high school for ninth grade and asked the district to continue providing a sign-language interpreter. The district refused, and the student's parents sued. The court ruled for the school district. The Ninth Circuit affirmed, determining that the furnishing of a sign-language interpreter to a parochial school student had the primary effect of advancing religion in violation of the Establishment Clause of the U.S. Constitution. The placement of a public school employee in a parochial school would create the appearance that the government was a joint sponsor of the private school's activities. The U.S. Supreme Court granted the parents' petition for review. On appeal, the school district cited 34 C.F.R. § 76.532(a)(1), an IDEA regulation, as authority for the prohibition against using federal funds for private school sign-language interpreters.

The Court stated that the Establishment Clause did not completely prohibit religious institutions from participating in publicly sponsored benefits. If this were the case, religious groups would not even enjoy police and fire protection or have use of public roads and sidewalks. Government programs that neutrally provide benefits to broad classes of citizens are not subject to Establishment Clause prohibition simply because some religiously affiliated institutions receive "an attenuated financial benefit." Providing a sign-language interpreter under the IDEA was part of a general program for distribution of benefits in a neutral manner to qualified students. **The provision of the interpreter provided only an indirect economic benefit to the parochial school and was a neutral service** that was part of a general program not "skewed" toward religion. A sign-language interpreter, unlike an instructor or counselor, was ethically bound to transmit everything said in exactly the same way as it was intended. Because the Establishment Clause did not prevent the district from providing the student with a sign-language interpreter under the IDEA, the Court reversed the court of appeals' decision. *Zobrest v. Catalina Foothills School Dist.*, 509 U.S. 1, 113 S.Ct. 2462, 125 L.Ed.2d 1 (1993).

◆ The New York City Board of Education attempted to implement Title I programs at parochial schools by allowing public employees to instruct students on private school grounds during school hours. In 1985, the U.S. Supreme Court agreed with a group of taxpayers that this violated the Establishment Clause in *Aguilar v. Felton,* 473 U.S. 402, 105 S.Ct. 3232, 87 L.Ed.2d 290 (1985). On remand, a federal court ordered the city board to refrain from using Title I funds for any plan or program under which public school teachers and counselors furnished services on sectarian school grounds. In response to *Aguilar,* local education boards modified Title I programs by moving classes to remote sites, including mobile instructional units parked near sectarian schools. A new group of parents and parochial school students filed motions seeking relief from the permanent order.

The court denied the motions, and the Second Circuit affirmed. On further appeal, the U.S. Supreme Court agreed with the city board and students that recent Supreme Court decisions required a new ruling on the question of government aid to religious schools. For example, the provision of a sign-language interpreter by a school district at a private school was upheld in *Zobrest v. Catalina Foothills School Dist.,* 509 U.S. 1 (1993), above. The Court held that it would no longer presume that the presence of a public school teacher on parochial school grounds creates a symbolic union between church and state. The provision of Title I services at parochial schools resembled the provision of a sign-language interpreter under the IDEA. **New York City's Title I program was constitutionally permissible because it did not result in government indoctrination, define funding recipients by reference to religion or create excessive entanglement between education officials and religious schools.** The Court reversed the lower court judgments. In the process, the Court substantially overruled *Aguilar* and its companion case, *School Dist. of Grand Rapids v. Ball,* 473 U.S. 373, 105 S.Ct. 3216, 87 L.Ed.2d 267 (1985). *Agostini v. Felton,* 521 U.S. 203, 117 S.Ct. 1997, 138 L.Ed.2d 391 (1997).

♦   When the parents of a multiply disabled student rejected a school district's IEP, they placed their son in a Quaker school and requested a due process hearing seeking tuition reimbursement. The hearing officer dismissed the action, holding that Pennsylvania law prohibited tuition reimbursement for unilateral sectarian school placements. A federal court overturned that decision. It noted that 34 C.F.R. § 403(c) specifies that unilateral placements need not meet state standards; the placement must simply be appropriate, and the district must have denied a free appropriate public education to the student. Also, **paying religious school tuition did not violate the Establishment Clause** because it was the parents who decided where the money was going, not the government. The court remanded the case for a determination of whether the district had provided FAPE to the student. If not, the hearing officer would have to determine whether the Quaker school placement was appropriate. *L.M. v. Evesham Township Board of Educ.*, 256 F.Supp.2d 290 (D.N.J. 2003).

♦   A Pennsylvania school district developed an IEP for a student's sixth-grade year including mainstream classes with learning disabled resource room support. Her academic performance declined through the seventh grade and she was diagnosed with ADHD in eighth grade. That year, her academic and behavior problems became severe. Her mother placed the student in a private Quaker school that was not state approved. Although the student excelled at the private school, the district's proposed IEP for the following year called for a different placement. The student's mother rejected the IEP. A due process hearing officer determined that because the placement selected by the mother was for a private, sectarian institution, the state could not be compelled to fund it. She also ordered the district to provide an appropriate IEP for tenth grade, but the district failed to do so until April of the student's tenth-grade year.

A federal court affirmed the denial of tuition for the ninth grade. There was evidence that the district IEP had been reasonably calculated to enable the student to receive educational benefits. However, the district had failed to act on the administrative orders to devise an appropriate placement for the tenth grade. The student was therefore entitled to private school tuition reimbursement for tenth grade. **There was no merit to the school district's argument that payment of private school tuition to a sectarian school violated the Establishment Clause.** *Christen G. v. Lower Merion School Dist.*, 919 F.Supp. 793 (E.D. Pa. 1996).

♦   A blind person sought vocational rehabilitative services from the state of Washington's Commission for the Blind pursuant to a state law, which provided that visually disabled persons were eligible for educational assistance to enable them to "overcome vocational handicaps and to obtain the maximum degree of self-support and self-care." However, because the plaintiff was a private school student intending to pursue a career of service in the church, the Commission for the Blind denied his request for assistance. The Washington Supreme Court upheld this decision on the ground that the First Amendment prohibited state funding of a student's education at a religious college. The U.S. Supreme Court reversed, finding that Washington's program was such that the commission paid money directly to the student, who would then attend the school of his or her choice. **The fact that the student in this case chose to attend a religious college did not constitute state support of religion** because the individual, not the state, made the decision to support religious education. The First Amendment was therefore not offended. The case was remanded to the Washington Supreme Court. *Witters v. Washington Dep't of Services for the Blind*, 474 U.S. 481, 106 S.Ct. 748, 88 L.Ed.2d 846 (1986).

On remand, the Washington Supreme Court reconsidered the matter under the Washington Constitution, which provides a more strict prohibition on the expenditure of public funds for religious instruction than the U.S. Constitution. **The disbursement of vocational assistance funds for the student's religious education violated the state constitution** because it would result in the expenditure of public money for religious instruction. The court rejected the student's argument that the restriction on public expenditures would violate his right to free exercise of religion. Also, denial of funds to the student did not violate the Fourteenth Amendment's Equal Protection Clause because the commission had a policy of denying any student's religious vocational funding. The classification was directly related to the state's interest in ensuring the separation between church and state. The court reaffirmed its previous order disallowing financial assistance. *Witters v. State Comm'n for the Blind*, 771 P.2d 1119 (Wash. 1989).

CHAPTER FIVE

Related Services

I. RELATED SERVICES UNDER THE IDEA

The IDEA requires states to provide a free appropriate education to each child with a disability. Related services are part of the state's obligation to provide that free appropriate education.

Related services are defined by the IDEA, at 20 U.S.C. § 1401(22), to include transportation, speech pathology, psychological services, physical and occupational therapy, recreation and medical services that are necessary for the student to receive an educational benefit. Other services, such as sign-language interpreters, rehabilitation services, family counseling, transition services and extracurricular activities may also be required for children with disabilities.

A. Voluntarily Enrolled Private School Students

♦ A New York first-grader with ADHD sought a 1:1 aide at his private school, and administrative rulings agreed that the aide would be sent to the private school. The district then sought a court ruling that the aide should be provided only at the public school. The Supreme Court, Appellate Division, held that state law permitted a school district to provide services at a private school. It ruled that the decision must be made on a case-by-case basis, with the student's needs in the least restrictive environment serving as a guide. The New York Court of Appeals affirmed, noting that **the state's dual enrollment statute was intended to offer private school students with disabilities "equal access** to the full array of specialized public school programs." *Board of Educ. of Bay Shore Union Free School Dist. v. Thomas K.*, 14 N.Y.3d 289 (N.Y. 2010).

♦   The parents of a New Hampshire student with disabilities placed him in a Catholic school and then met with a school district team to develop an IEP. The IEP called for transportation to and from a public school speech/language program for one hour per week. Later, the parents challenged the IEP, asserting that some services were not provided and that the district had furnished unreliable transportation. A hearing officer held that they were not entitled to a due process hearing because they had voluntarily placed their son at the religious school. The First Circuit Court of Appeals agreed. By placing their son in the private school, the parents had to accept the disadvantages as well as the benefits. And **Congress had chosen not to provide the same benefits to private school students** as it did to public school students. *Gary S. v. Manchester School Dist.*, 374 F.3d 15 (1st Cir. 2004).

♦   A disabled student attending a parochial school in Rhode Island received resource services at her school because it was within "walking distance" of a public school. When she began attending a religious school in another town, the school committee stopped providing services on site. Although she initially received such services at a public school, her parents later sought to have the services provided at the private school. They claimed that the unwritten "walking distance" rule was unfair to their daughter. A due process hearing officer agreed with the parents, stating that because the school committee provided resource services to other parochial school students in the district (who were within walking distance of a public school), it had to provide them to the student here. A federal court overturned the hearing officer's decision. **The IDEA regulation that permits on-site services could not be used to require on-site services.** The hearing officer's decision resulted from her "sense of arm-chair equity" and was improper. *Bristol Warren Regional School Committee v. Rhode Island Dep't of Educ.*, 253 F.Supp.2d 236 (D.R.I. 2003).

♦   A county intermediate unit provided speech and language services to a parochial school student during his kindergarten year. It then notified the family that it intended to discontinue services to Diocesan schools. A multidisciplinary team devised an IEP calling for biweekly speech/language therapy sessions, on the condition that the student be exclusively enrolled in district schools. The parents rejected the IEP. A hearing officer held that the district did not have to provide the student with services while he was enrolled in a private school. A state appeals panel affirmed.

The parents appealed to the Pennsylvania Commonwealth Court, which agreed with the parents that a state law, 24 Pa. Stat. § 5-502, prevented the district from denying their child services by reason of his attendance at a parochial school. The IDEA did not relieve school districts of their obligation to provide services to private school students with disabilities; it only freed them from having to provide services at nonpublic schools. **State and federal special education law did not permit school districts to dictate the conditions imposed on private school students in order to receive services.** The district did not assert that it had no room for the student or that his attendance in district programs would cause significant expenditures. It also failed to assert that it expended a proportionate share of federal funds in other ways that benefited private school students. State law did not prevent dual enrollment, and state guidelines recommended dual enrollment as a "genuine opportunity for equitable participation." Services offered to private school students had to reflect a genuine opportunity to participate in programs. *Veschi v. Northwestern Lehigh School Dist.*, 772 A.2d 469 (Pa. Commw. Ct. 2001).

♦ A student with spinal meningitis required constant medical care and supervision. He lived with his parents and received special educational services at home from the school district. His parents placed him in a licensed nursing facility within the school district for noneducational reasons. The district discontinued his educational services, and his parents objected. A hearing officer held that the parents were not entitled to relief because they had unilaterally placed the student at the nursing facility. On appeal, a federal court held that state law and the IDEA required the school district to provide the student with services at the nursing facility.

The district appealed to the Eighth Circuit, which noted that the district remained willing to provide the student with a FAPE at school facilities or at his home. The parents had chosen the nursing facility for noneducational reasons and had acted without the consent or approval of the student's IEP team. **Local education agencies are not required to pay the cost of a private school education if they have offered a FAPE to the student and the parents nonetheless make a voluntary private school placement.** Under the Nebraska Special Education Act, on-site teaching services were listed as just one of the authorized methods by which a school district may provide a FAPE. School districts were not required to pay for the costs of educating a student with a disability at a nonpublic school or facility if the school district made a FAPE available. Since the district offered the student a FAPE, the district complied with both the IDEA and Nebraska special education law. *Jasa v. Millard Public School Dist. No. 17*, 206 F.3d 813 (8th Cir. 2000).

♦ An Oregon student with blindness and cerebral palsy initially attended public schools. He received physical therapy and services from a vision specialist, along with special equipment. After his parents transferred him to a sectarian school, the district continued to provide him with braillers, computers, and other special equipment, but declined to provide a vision specialist. Instead, it provided the service at a nearby fire hall, with transportation. The family sued the school district and state superintendent of public instruction, seeking an order requiring the district to furnish the services at the sectarian school. A court determined that the IDEA did not require the district to provide the services at the sectarian school. However, a state regulation requiring the provision of services for private school students in religiously neutral settings violated the Free Exercise, Establishment, and Equal Protection Clauses of the U.S. Constitution. The district and superintendent appealed.

The Ninth Circuit held that the 1997 IDEA amendments do not require the provision of services on site at a private school and affirmed that part of the judgment. It rejected the family's assertion that the state regulation violated the Free Exercise Clause. **The regulation did not force the family to choose between enrolling the student in a sectarian school and forgoing services,**

and it did not burden their free exercise of religion. Moreover, the regulation did not discriminate against religious school students or suppress religion or religious conduct. Further, the regulation did not violate the Establishment Clause or the Equal Protection Clause. The regulation did not violate the family's constitutional rights, and the lower court judgment was reversed. *KDM v. Reedsport School Dist.*, 196 F.3d 1046 (9th Cir. 1999).

◆   When the parents of a New York student with mental retardation requested that the student receive special education services at a parochial school, the district refused, stating that complying with the parents' request would violate the Establishment Clause. The case reached the U.S. Court of Appeals, Second Circuit, which held that individualized special education services must be made available to private school students on the same basis as public school students. However, the U.S. Supreme Court vacated and remanded the case in view of the 1997 Amendments to the IDEA. On remand, the Second Circuit held that the IDEA amendments do not require that on-site special education services be provided to voluntarily placed private school students. A school district need only allocate a proportionate share of IDEA funds to such students. **While the district had the discretion to provide such services on-site at private schools, it was not bound to do so by the IDEA.** The case was sent back to the district court for further analysis. *Russman v. Board of Educ. of the Enlarged City School Dist. of Watervliet,* 150 F.3d 219 (2d Cir. 1998).

◆   A Louisiana student with hearing impairments attended a public school under an IEP that included sign-language interpretation services. His parents then enrolled him at a parochial school and requested on-site sign-language interpretation services. The school board refused. A hearing officer upheld the board's decision and the parents appealed to a federal court, claiming IDEA violations. The court granted summary judgment to the parents and ordered the board to provide a sign-language interpreter at the parochial school, even though the parties had previously agreed that the student's public school IEP was appropriate. The U.S. Court of Appeals for the Fifth Circuit issued a decision that was favorable to the student in some respects, but it remanded the case for further consideration. It then solicited an opinion from the U.S. Department of Education, which stated that the IDEA does not require school districts to expend non-IDEA funds for students voluntarily enrolled in private schools. **A local education agency's obligation is to make a FAPE available to all disabled students and provide a proportionate share of IDEA funds to students enrolled in private schools.** The court accepted this opinion, and added that the IDEA Amendments of 1997 specify that an education agency need only provide students enrolled in private schools with a proportionate share of IDEA funds. Because the district had offered the student an appropriate public school IEP, it was not required to provide him with an on-site interpreter. *Cefalu v. East Baton Rouge Parish School Board,* 117 F.3d 231 (5th Cir. 1997).

◆   A multiply disabled Indiana student attended public school with assistance for positioning, self-help skills, motor movements, mobility and expression. Her parents chose to enroll her in a private school and requested the assistance of an on-site instructional assistant. When the school district denied the request, a hearing officer held that the school district was not obligated to provide the student with an instructional assistant at the private school. The parents appealed to a federal court, asserting IDEA violations. The court held that IDEA regulations required the district to provide related services to private school students that were comparable to those received by public school students. The district appealed to the Seventh Circuit.

The court of appeals held that public schools need not provide voluntarily placed private school students with related services that are comparable to those received by public school students. School districts maintain the discretion to decide what benefits will be provided to private school students and need only provide voluntarily placed private school students with a genuine opportunity for equitable participation. **The 1997 amendments relieve a local education agency from the obligation to pay for a private school student's special education and related services if the agency has made a FAPE available and the parents voluntarily place the child in the private school.** Because the school district had afforded the student a genuine opportunity to receive a FAPE, the court reversed the district court judgment. *K.R. by M.R. v. Anderson Community School Corp.*, 125 F.3d 1017 (7th Cir. 1997).

♦ Two Minnesota students with disabilities attended private religious schools. Their school districts denied requests to furnish on-site paraprofessional services. The families then became financially unable to continue paying tuition. A group representing parents of Minnesota students with disabilities joined the two families in suing the two school districts, the state education commissioner and other education officials, claiming state regulations and policies implementing the IDEA were unconstitutional and that state and local officials had violated the IDEA by denying their requests. The case reached the Eighth Circuit, which noted that the district's policy of denying on-site special education services to students with disabilities who attended sectarian schools while providing services to students who were home-schooled or attended non-sectarian schools appeared to be unconstitutional. The evidence suggested impermissible religious discrimination by the district. Turning to the IDEA claims, the court stated that under IDEA 1997, the student was not entitled to on-site services at a sectarian school. However, **the denial of on-site services before the effective date of IDEA 1997 was improper.** Under the old version of the IDEA, the student was entitled to special education services that were "comparable in quality, scope, and opportunity for participation" to the services furnished to public school students. *Peter v. Wedl*, 155 F.3d 992 (8th Cir. 1998).

B. Home-Schooled Students

♦ The parents of a home-schooled student who needed speech therapy requested the service from their school district and indicated their willingness to bring the student to a public school for therapy. The district rejected the request. The state department of education denied mediation and due process hearing requests by the parents, and they sued. A trial court found that the student was entitled to a pro rata allocation of federal funds available for New Jersey nonpublic school students. It also held that the department had improperly engaged in rulemaking, in violation of the state administrative procedure act, when it created its regulatory definition of "nonpublic school." Moreover, the department and district violated the student's state equal protection right to receive special education. The court ordered the department and district to reimburse the family for the student's weekly speech therapy sessions.

On appeal, the New Jersey Superior Court, Appellate Division, noted that the IDEA allows school districts to treat nonpublic-school students and home-schooled students differently. IDEA regulations state that local districts must provide services to students in "private schools" under a funding formula that compares the number of private school students with the total number of students with disabilities in the district. Because the student in this case was not attending a "nonpublic school," he was not included in this calculation. Although New Jersey school districts could differentiate between nonpublic-school students and those who received home education, the district in this case violated the student's equal protection rights by refusing entirely to provide him with services, even after his parents agreed to follow a recommended treatment plan that was to take place at a public school in the district. **Because the district did not provide the student with services it provided other students (at the same cost to the district), the district violated the student's equal protection rights.** *Forstrom v. Byrne*, 775 A.2d 65 (N.J. Super. Ct. App. Div. 2001).

♦   A special education student's parents received an exemption from the state's compulsory attendance law by providing him with home education services. Their school district denied their request for speech therapy services under a policy stating that home-schooled students "do not have access to instruction and/or ancillary services with the public schools." The administration explained that the policy complied with Nevada law and suggested that the parents either seek an exception or enroll the student in the district. The parents instead filed a complaint with the state department of education, which was denied on the basis of a 1992 Office of Special Education Programs policy letter declaring that states have discretion to determine whether or not home education qualifies as a private school or facility that implicates IDEA coverage. The parents then sued the school district, alleging that its policy violated the IDEA and the Equal Protection Clause of the Fourteenth Amendment. They sought speech therapy services and an award of attorneys' fees.

A federal court ruled for the school district, and the Ninth Circuit affirmed. Although the district now had to provide speech therapy to the student due to a change in Nevada law, that did not solve the question of reimbursement for speech therapy costs and attorneys' fees. The court noted that nothing in the IDEA requires the provision of services to children who are not enrolled in a school. States were permitted to determine whether home education should be considered an IDEA-qualifying "private school or facility." Moreover, **the district had offered the student a free appropriate education and nothing in the IDEA required it to provide services to children whose parents reject an offer of education** but fail to enroll them in any "school." The parents were not entitled to reimbursement or attorneys' fees. *Hooks v. Clark County School Dist.*, 228 F.3d 1036 (9th Cir. 2000).

C. Sign-Language Interpreters and Hearing Services

♦   An Arizona school district furnished a sign-language interpreter to a student with hearing impairments who attended public schools. When the student's parents enrolled him in a parochial school, they requested that the school district continue providing the sign-language interpreter. The district refused to provide this service on Establishment Clause grounds, and the parents sued. Appeal reached the U.S. Supreme Court, which held that **the provision of a sign-language interpreter is a religiously neutral distribution of IDEA benefits that provides only an indirect financial benefit to a parochial school**. The Court held that the Establishment Clause did not prohibit the school district from sending the sign-language interpreter to the parochial school for the student's benefit. *Zobrest v. Catalina Foothills School Dist.*, 509 U.S. 1, 113 S.Ct. 2462, 125 L.Ed.2d 1 (1993). For a full summary of this case, see Chapter Four, Section II.

♦   Parents of students with cochlear implants sued the Department of Education in a District of Columbia federal court, seeking a declaration that cochlear implant mapping should be a related service under the IDEA. The department had issued **a regulation excluding cochlear implant mapping as a related service** because cochlear implants are surgical implants. The department's interpretation of the law was entitled to deference, and the regulation was upheld. *Petit v. U.S. Dep't of Educ.*, 756 F.Supp.2d 11 (D.D.C. 2010).

♦   A Connecticut student with deafness and a specific language learning disability was not fluent in sign language. As a result, his IEP called for captioning to be provided for all classes, group meetings and assemblies. However, the planning and placement team "tabled" the discussion of how to accommodate him with respect to the daily morning news broadcasts. After three years of no action on the issue, he sued the state and the district to force the district to caption the broadcasts. A federal court held that the state could not be sued. It also ruled that **the news broadcasts were not a limited public forum but rather a closed forum, justifying the district's decision not to caption them**. *Quatroche v. East Lyme Board of Educ.*, 604 F.Supp.2d 403 (D. Conn. 2009).

♦   The parents of a student at the Delaware School for the Deaf became concerned when he began performing below grade level. They requested a general education placement with a full-time American Sign-Language interpreter, and they also sought a private school placement with a small class size. The district responded that **a sign-language interpreter would be provided only if the student attended district schools**. After the parents placed their son in a private school, a hearing officer held that the district should have provided a sign-language interpreter. A federal court reversed. Nothing in the IDEA or its regulations conferred upon parentally placed private school students an individual right to receive special education and related services that they would receive in public schools. The IDEA only required districts to allocate a proportional share of IDEA funds to private schools, which the district had done here. *Board of Educ. of Appoquinimink School Dist. v. Johnson*, 543 F.Supp.2d 351 (D. Del. 2008).

♦ A California student with a cochlear implant received one-on-one deaf and hard of hearing services in his family's home. However, when his family moved to Nevada, the school district there offered the services in his neighborhood school under an interim IEP. His parents objected, asserting that the school location violated the IEP in place in California. They hired a private provider and sought reimbursement. A hearing officer and a federal court held that the district had offered comparable services to the transfer student. **The IDEA did not require the Nevada district to adopt the California IEP in its exact form.** *Sterling A. v. Washoe County School Dist.*, No. 3:07-CV-00245-LRH-RJJ, 2008 WL 4865570 (D. Nev. 11/10/08).

♦ The parents of a second-grade student asked that he be provided a sign-language interpreter, but the Puerto Rico Department of Education denied their request. An administrative law judge ordered the school to provide an interpreter, but none was provided. By the third grade, when the student still did not have an interpreter, the parents sued under the IDEA, the ADA and Section 504. The First Circuit Court of Appeals held that the parents should be deemed "aggrieved parties" even though they prevailed at the administrative level. They could sue for a violation of the stay-put provision as well as the free appropriate public education guarantee. The student was entitled to an order for injunctive relief, and possibly money damages under the ADA and Section 504 if it could be shown that Puerto Rico intentionally discriminated against him. *Nieves-Marquez v. Comwlth. of Puerto Rico*, 353 F.3d 108 (1st Cir. 2003).

♦ Three Nebraska students with hearing impairments required the use of sign-language interpreters in their classrooms. Their school district provided a modified SEE-II system. However, the students used strict SEE-II signing systems at home, and their parents made numerous requests to use strict SEE-II systems at school. After the district refused to do so, the parents filed a complaint, alleging that the modified signing system did not provide their children with an adequate individualized special education program. The hearing officer held for the school district but imposed on it the requirement to develop IEPs for each student that called for interpreters during both academic and nonacademic activities. A federal court affirmed, and the Eighth Circuit also affirmed. The IDEA does not require a school to maximize the educational potential of each student. **Parents and students could not compel a school district to provide a specific signing system of choice as a related service.** Although ADA regulations required a public entity to provide an auxiliary aid or service of choice to an individual with disabilities, the public entity was allowed to demonstrate that another effective means of communication existed. The school district had complied with the ADA by providing the modified SEE-II system as an effective means of communication. The lower court decision was affirmed. *Petersen v. Hastings Public Schools*, 31 F.3d 705 (8th Cir. 1994).

D. Transition Services

Transition services must be included in each IEP as a part of the duty to provide a FAPE. Under IDEA 1997 and the corresponding regulations, transition services must be considered by the IEP team starting at age 14, or earlier if deemed appropriate by the student's IEP team.

Transition services help students prepare for post-school life by teaching them employment and independent living skills, or by teaching them how to deal with an advance to another type of school (e.g., from an IFSP to an IEP). Further, transition services can be a related service if required to assist a student with a disability in benefiting from special education.

◆   A Hawaii student who received Part C services through an Individualized Family Support Plan was supposed to receive Part B services under an IEP, but because of a dispute over which school he would be attending, the department of education offered him no services for about a month. A lawsuit erupted and a federal court held that **the failure of the department to transition the student to an IEP violated the IDEA.** This failure resulted in lost educational opportunities that required a hearing officer to consider an appropriate placement and compensatory education. *Shaun M. v. Hamamoto*, No. 09-00075 DAE/BMK, 2009 WL 3415308 (D. Haw. 10/22/09).

◆   The parents of a Pennsylvania student with dyslexia, memory disorder and ADHD agreed on a twelfth-grade IEP that called for transition services in a college prep program in Maryland. The district did not provide the transition services, but at the end of the year, it recommended that the student be graduated. The parents objected, and the IEP team met without the parents to finalize an IEP for a thirteenth year of services that also did not include transition services. A due process hearing officer found that the student had received a free appropriate public education, but a state review panel reversed. The Commonwealth Court of Pennsylvania upheld the review panel's decision. Here, the district had **failed to provide agreed-upon transition services**, then scheduled the student's graduation. The district had to provide a year of compensatory education in the college preparatory program. *Susquehanna Township School Dist. v. Frances J.*, 823 A.2d 249 (Pa. Commw. Ct. 2003).

◆   The parents of a 20-year-old student requested a due process hearing over their school district's diagnosis of the student. An administrative order required the district to conduct an evaluation and devise a new IEP. The parents disputed the resulting IEP and arranged for independent evaluations. They did not participate in further IEP and multidisciplinary team meetings and requested a second hearing. A hearing officer held for the school district, and a state appeals panel affirmed. The panel denied the parents' request for reimbursement of the costs of the independent evaluations. It held that the IEPs for the student's three most recent school years were inadequate in the areas of transition planning and assistive technology. As relief, the student was awarded more than 600 hours of compensatory education. A federal court examined the transition services issue and noted that the IDEA requires a statement of transition services for students no later than age 16. In this case, **the transitional evaluation prepared by the school multidisciplinary team was inadequate because the team did not include personnel who had evaluated the student's transition needs.** The district also failed to include aspects of transition planning in the student's IEP. The court adopted the panel's decision, finding that the IEP was not sufficiently tailored to meet the student's needs. Accordingly, compensatory education was appropriate, though the amount was slightly decreased. *East Penn School Dist. v. Scott B.*, No. Civ. A. 97-1989, 1999 WL 178363 (E.D. Pa. 2/23/99).

♦ A 17-year-old South Dakota student with cerebral palsy was classified as orthopedically impaired. Her special education program provided adaptive physical education, physical therapy and transportation. After she completed her physical education requirements in ninth grade, the district advised her parents that she was no longer eligible for special education. Her parents requested a due process hearing, claiming that the district had failed to provide transition services. A hearing officer determined that even if the student was not eligible for special education, the need for transition services alone justified providing them. The district had to provide training in independent living skills and self-advocacy as necessary transition services and develop a transition plan in coordination with other agencies. A federal court agreed.

The school district appealed to the Eighth Circuit, which affirmed. If not for the specialized accommodations, instruction and services provided, the student's grades would be adversely affected. The district had failed to incorporate the services it was providing the student into her written IEP and her need for the services had not ended. **The student was entitled to receive transition services from the district until age 21 or her graduation date.** *Yankton School Dist. v. Schramm*, 93 F.3d 1369 (8th Cir. 1996).

E. Occupational Therapy and Rehabilitation Services

♦ A New Jersey student with developmental delays due to complications from his premature birth received occupational therapy (OT) as part of his pre-school IEP. The IEP specified that he receive 30 minutes of OT per week. His mother sought an independent evaluation, which recommended 60 minutes of OT per week. She asked the school district for more OT and requested that it pay for the increased OT she was providing. **The child study team sought to conduct a reevaluation of the child**, but his mother removed him from school and placed him in a private school, where he received OT six times a week. She then sought tuition reimbursement, which a federal court denied. Not only did she fail to cooperate with the school district, but the district also provided a free appropriate public education for her son. *M.S. and D.S. v. Mullica Township Board of Educ.*, 485 F.Supp.2d 555 (D.N.J. 2007).

♦ A Hawaii student with multiple disabilities received one hour a week of occupational therapy (OT) and one hour a week of speech/language therapy. Her 2004-05 IEP stated that extended school year (ESY) services were appropriate for the summer of 2005, but it did not specify how much therapy the student should receive during the summer. She nevertheless received one hour per week of OT and speech/language therapy. The following year, settlement of an earlier dispute raised the student's OT and speech/language therapy levels to two hours per week of each. However, the IEP team decided to reduce to 90 minutes per week the OT and speech/language therapy the student would receive during the 2006 ESY. The parents challenged that decision and a federal court ruled in their favor. **By challenging the ESY IEP, the parents effectively invoked the stay-put provision, requiring the school to provide two hours a week of both OT and speech/language therapy.** *Dep't of Educ., State of Hawaii v. A.F.*, No. 06-00488 SOM/BMK, 2007 WL 1080085 (D. Haw. 4/9/07).

◆   A Pennsylvania school district determined that a student was not IDEA-eligible, but that he was eligible for occupational therapy under Section 504. The student's parents enrolled him in a private school, but also dually enrolled him in public schools so that he would be able to get occupational therapy at a public school. The district refused to provide the services, but a court ordered it to do so. Here, the student was not seeking tuition reimbursement or even related services at a private school. He was merely seeking Section 504 services at a public facility. And he was "enrolled" in the district. He did not have to actually attend classes to be eligible for occupational therapy. The Supreme Court of Pennsylvania then ruled that the student was entitled to Section 504 services. **Federal regulations didn't require the student to attend classes in the district to qualify for Section 504 services.** Further, Section 504 required schools to seek out eligible beneficiaries based on residency, not school attendance. *Lower Merion School Dist. v. Doe*, 931 A.2d 640 (Pa. 2007).

◆   An Illinois student with Down syndrome was entitled to occupational therapy under his IEP. His district provided the therapy, but its **occupational therapist was unlicensed** and could only work in the district with more supervision than she actually received. After his parents rejected his IEP, a hearing officer found that the hiring of the therapist was a violation of the IDEA. She awarded the student 60 minutes of weekly direct occupational therapy services. A federal court then ruled that the student was entitled to a year of compensatory education, reimbursement for the independent evaluation and attorneys' fees. On appeal, the Seventh Circuit reversed the order to reimburse for the independent evaluation, but otherwise affirmed. Noncompliance with the state licensure requirements was not a minor procedural violation of the IDEA. *Evanston Community Consolidated School Dist. No. 65 v. Michael M.*, 356 F.3d 798 (7th Cir. 2004).

◆   A preschooler with ataxic cerebral palsy received occupational, physical and speech therapy services from a Texas school district's early childhood program. The district prepared an IEP for the student calling for 30 minutes of occupational therapy per week. The family moved to Mississippi and their new school district adopted the Texas district's IEP, providing him with occupational and physical therapy for the rest of the school year and summer. As the district prepared a revised IEP for the upcoming school year, the parents decided to enroll the student in a private religious school. The district discontinued occupational therapy and quit developing an IEP. The parents requested a due process hearing, seeking continuation of related services. A hearing officer ordered the district to provide occupational therapy, and the district appealed to a federal court. The court found that there was no merit to the district's argument that it had satisfied IDEA obligations by simply offering related services to the student should the family decide to return him to public schools. **The district had to make meaningful efforts to provide educational benefits to the student and could not condition the provision of services on whether the family decided to enroll the student in public schools.** The court affirmed this aspect of the hearing officer's decision but held that he should not have ordered the district to provide the student with an occupational therapist. Because the IEP prepared by the Texas school district was still in place, the student was entitled to receive the 30 minutes of occupational therapy it specified. *Natchez-Adams School Dist. v. Searing*, 918 F.Supp. 1028 (S.D. Miss. 1996).

F. Other Services

Any service that might be required in order for a student to benefit from special education will generally be deemed a related service that the school district will have to provide.

♦ An Illinois autistic student had daily tantrums, an eating disorder and episodes of running on impulse. A doctor prescribed a service dog, which the family obtained two years later. This calmed the student greatly. However, at a preschool IEP meeting, district officials told the mother the service dog could not accompany him to school because even though the dog was hypoallergenic, another student was highly allergic to dogs. The family then sought an order defining the dog as a "service animal" that would allow it to accompany the student to school. The Appellate Court of Illinois found that **the dog met the state's definition of a "service animal"** even though the commands to assist the student came from staff members and not the student himself. The student could bring the dog to school. *K.D. v. Villa Grove Community Unit School Dist. No. 302*, 936 N.E.2d 690 (Ill. App. Ct. 2010).

♦ A New York student with autism received related services in addition to what he received in a special education classroom. He later won a lottery to attend an autism charter school, which used an ABA model and lowered his student-teacher-aide ratio from 8:1:2 to 4:1:3. His parents nevertheless asserted that he should continue to receive related services even though they were embedded within the charter school's curriculum. A due process hearing officer disagreed with them, and a federal court affirmed that decision. The student's IEP addressed his individual needs, and **he was making educational progress with the embedded related services in the school' curriculum.** *M.N. v. New York City Dep't of Educ.*, 700 F.Supp.2d 356 (S.D.N.Y. 2010).

♦ A Missouri student with multiple disabilities attended a state school for severely disabled persons for 12 years. His parent challenged his educational program, alleging that staff failed to engage him in stretching exercises and that as a result his body began to conform to his wheelchair shape and his motor skills regressed. The parent sought audiovisual surveillance as part of the relief, and a federal court ruled that **audiovisual surveillance could be a related service under the IDEA**. It therefore denied the motion to dismiss that part of the lawsuit. The court also allowed the claim for compensatory education to proceed. *J.T. v. Missouri State Board of Educ.*, No. 4:08CV1431RWS, 2009 WL 262094 (E.D. Mo. 2/4/09).

◆   The parents of a Minnesota child sought to have accommodations provided for extracurricular activities in which she might wish to engage. However, they didn't identify any specific activity at that time. The student later identified volleyball and after-school clubs as activities she was interested in. Her parents also sought accommodations so that she could attend an off-campus fifth-grade graduation party. The district refused to provide accommodations to the party because it was a private event sponsored by the parent-teacher organization. In the lawsuit that followed, the Minnesota Court of Appeals held that **the district did not have to accommodate the child's attendance at the PTA-sponsored, fifth-grade graduation party**. However, it did have to provide accommodations for volleyball and after-school clubs, the specific activities she had identified. The Minnesota Supreme Court affirmed in part. The student didn't have to prove that she would receive educational benefits from extracurricular and nonacademic activities in order to qualify for supplemental aides and services. But the IEP team had to consider whether the extracurricular and nonacademic activities were appropriate. *Independent School Dist. No. 12, Centennial v. Minnesota Dep't of Educ.*, 788 N.W.2d 907 (Minn. 2010).

◆   A New Jersey student's IEP called for a personal aide for the full school day as well as 10 hours of at-home tutoring a week at district expense. Aides were to be Lovaas trained. **When the district could not find a Lovaas-trained aide, the student's mother did so and the district hired him.** The aide later resigned. It took the district a while to replace him, during which time the mother kept her son at home and hired another Lovaas-trained aide, whom the district also hired. She made extra payments to the aides the district provided, then sought reimbursement for those payments, but a federal court and the Third Circuit ruled against her. Here, the school board had no idea she was making the payments. Further, the delay in finding a replacement aide did not amount to a denial of a free appropriate public education. *Fisher v. Stafford Township Board of Educ.*, 289 Fed.Appx. 520 (3d Cir. 2008).

◆   A California student with multiple disabilities could not swallow food. Instead, he received nutrition through a surgical opening into his stomach called a gastrostomy tube or "G-tube." His mother claimed he developed a severe reflux disorder from liquids, necessitating that he be fed only pureed foods. She used a syringe plunger even though standard medical practice called for using a gravity methodology. A dispute arose over the method of feeding her son, and she kept him at home for a while and then sought compensatory education. A federal court ultimately ruled that **the mother could not dictate the method to be used to feed her son**. The doctor's prescription did not specify the plunge method, and the mother never provided the IEP team with evidence that the gravity method would not work. No compensatory education was due. *C.N. v. Los Angeles Unified School Dist.*, No. CV 07-03642 MMM (SSx), 2008 WL 4552951 (C.D. Cal. 10/9/08).

♦   A Pennsylvania school district offered an incoming kindergartner with autism an IEP that included ABA therapy and verbal behavior (VB) services in an autistic support class, but reduced the student's ABA therapy from his early intervention IEP, and also reduced his occupational therapy. His parents challenged the IEP and reached a settlement in which the student was to receive two hours of ABA and VB therapy a day. The district then provided three hours a day, exceeding the interim IEP requirements. Later, the district proposed reducing the ABA/VB therapy for the rest of the school year and for the ESY program in the summer. Again the parents objected. The case reached a federal court, which ruled for the district. **The district could provide less than three hours of ABA therapy a day**, and it did not have to provide more than 1.5 hours a day during the summer. It had already provided more ABA therapy than the interim IEP required. *Travis G. v. New Hope-Solebury School Dist.*, 544 F.Supp.2d 435 (E.D. Pa. 2008).

♦   A Minnesota school district provided developmental adapted physical education (DAPE) swimming to special education students. It later conducted a study that resulted in a recommendation to discontinue the program. The district's board informed parents that the DAPE program was under review, but it did not notify parents when it finally canceled the program. Instead, parents were notified during IEP meetings. After a parent complained, the state education department found that **the district violated the IDEA by canceling the DAPE program without proper notice** to the parents. It ordered the district to restore DAPE swimming services at the beginning of the next school year and to provide a year of compensatory DAPE swimming for the year in which such services ended. The Minnesota Court of Appeals affirmed that decision. *Independent School Dist. No. 281 v. Minnesota Dep't of Educ.*, No. A06-1617, 2007 WL 2774337 (Minn. Ct. App. 9/25/07).

♦   A Tennessee student with profound bilateral hearing loss received a cochlear implant at the age of 14 months. Her school district later developed an IEP for her, offering to place her in a new collaborative program that was being developed with Head Start, and which served low-income students, many of whom did not have disabilities. The district also proposed to discontinue the mapping service (optimization of the implant) it had been providing for the student. When the parents objected, a hearing officer held that the district's placement met IDEA requirements, but that it had to continue the mapping services. A federal court then held that **the 2004 IDEA Amendments excluded the mapping of a cochlear implant as a related service** under the IDEA. *A.U. v. Roane County Board of Educ.*, 501 F.Supp.2d 1134 (E.D. Tenn. 2007).

♦   A California student's IEP did not include extended school year (ESY) services. Her parents unilaterally placed her in "Camp Kodiak," then sought placement in a Utah residential treatment facility called the "Alpine Academy."

They asserted that the district had failed to provide counseling sessions required by the IEP. A hearing officer agreed that the parents should be compensated for the counseling sessions, but held that the ESY services and the residential placement were not necessary. A federal court upheld that determination. Although **the failure to provide all the counseling sessions specified in the IEP was a denial of a free appropriate public education**, it did not justify the residential placement or ESY services. *Roxanne J. v. Nevada County Human Services Agency*, No. Cir. 5-05-2602 KJM, 2006 WL 3437494 (E.D. Cal. 11/28/06).

♦   After a dispute with their district over placement, the parents of a Pennsylvania student with deaf-blindness finally agreed on an IEP. However, they then withdrew their son from school and sued the district, alleging that it failed to comply with the requirements of the IEP. A federal court held that the district had largely complied. It had assigned its Supervisor of Hearing and Vision Support Programs to serve as the student's deaf-blind coordinator. However, the district had not properly given the certified "intervener" one-on-one training. **The district had to provide further training to the intervener**, but it did not have to replace her based on the parents' preferences. *Derrick F. v. Red Lion Area School Dist.*, Civil No. 1:06-CV-1463, 2006 WL 2547050 (M.D. Pa. 9/1/06).

♦   A Georgia student with a disability complained that words became fuzzy or three dimensional when he tried to read. A behavioral optometrist diagnosed accommodative and convergence disorder, and recommended visual therapy to reduce vision loss. The district refused to pay for such therapy on the grounds that the student was receiving a free appropriate public education. The parents paid for the therapy, then sought due process. An administrative hearing officer and a federal court found that the parents were entitled to reimbursement for the therapy as a related service. The Eleventh Circuit agreed. **Although the student's condition had not yet caused poor academic performance, it did prevent him from receiving a FAPE.** *DeKalb County School Dist. v. M.T.V.*, 164 Fed.Appx. 900 (11th Cir. 2006).

♦   An Illinois student with autism was placed in a Boston school under an IEP that sought to control his behavior and teach his parents skills and strategies that would allow him to return home. Although the first IEP included reimbursement for the parents for up to 12 trips to Boston per year, either for training or to drop off or pick up their son, the next year's IEP called for only six trips. The parents objected to the modification, and a lawsuit resulted. An Illinois federal court ruled that **travel for parental training can be a related service** under the IDEA, but that six trips per year were sufficient to meet the statute's requirements. *Aaron M. v. Yomtoob*, No. 00 C 7732, 2003 WL 223469 (N.D. Ill. 2/3/03).

♦   The IEPs for a Kentucky student with cerebral palsy and delayed cognitive development addressed his ongoing behavior issues. His parents believed he was regressing and sought direct occupational therapy for him as well as a summer placement. Ultimately, the district rejected extended school year (ESY) programming for the student's next school year. The parents unilaterally placed the student in a residential facility that offered summer programs and requested a due process hearing. A hearing officer ruled for the district, but an appeals board and a federal court reversed. On further appeal, the Sixth Circuit reversed the lower court. **ESY programming was the exception, not the rule.** And the parents would have to show that ESY was necessary to avoid something more than "adequately recoupable regression." *Kenton County School Dist. v. Hunt*, 384 F.3d 269 (6th Cir. 2004).

♦   The parents of a disabled Minnesota student hired a personal care attendant to assist their daughter in school. The IEP team agreed to incorporate the attendant's services into the student's IEP. Subsequently, the district sought to replace the attendant with a district employee. The parents objected and removed their daughter from school. They initiated a due process hearing, asserting that the IEP required them to appoint their daughter's attendant. The hearing officer and a review officer disagreed, as did a federal magistrate judge. Under the IDEA, **districts have the sole discretion to assign staff.** Therefore, the district's decision to replace the attendant with a district employee did not violate the IDEA. *Slama v. Independent School Dist. No. 2580*, 259 F.Supp.2d 880 (D. Minn. 2003).

♦   A New Hampshire student with hearing impairments underwent surgery for a cochlear implant and later had 19 separate appointments with audiologists for the mapping of his speech processor. His parents sought reimbursement from the school district for their mileage to the appointments as well as reimbursement for the $10 office co-pays for each mapping appointment. The district refused to reimburse them and a hearing officer determined that the mapping services were necessary related services under the IDEA. A federal court agreed. His IEP included the cochlear implant as his method of communication and confirmed that the educational methodology selected for him was a necessary part of a free appropriate public education. **The cochlear implant mapping was a related service** under the IDEA. *Stratham School Dist. v. Beth P.*, No. Civ. 02-135-JD, 2003 WL 260728 (D.N.H. 2/5/03).

♦   The parents of a student with autism commenced due process proceedings, seeking an order requiring their school district to assign the student an aide who had previously worked in his home program. The hearing officer agreed. The school district appealed to a federal court, which concluded the district had provided the student with a FAPE, despite deciding to assign him an aide without experience in his home program. The Ninth Circuit Court of Appeals held that neither the IDEA nor the student's IEP required the district to employ a classroom aide with previous work experience in the student's home program. A behavioral consultant had suggested that **an aide without any knowledge of the student could help his classroom teacher implement his behavior plan and enable the student to receive educational benefits.** And the school's proposed classroom aide had the necessary qualifications to serve as the student's aide. She had completed college course work in education and psychology, and she had 13 years of experience, including experience with a high-functioning autistic student. The court of appeals affirmed the decision in favor of the school district. *Gellerman v. Calaveras Uniform School Dist.*, 43 Fed.Appx. 28 (9th Cir. 2002).

♦ A Connecticut hearing officer denied a student's parents' request for reimbursement of the cost of psychological services because the student's IEP for grade seven called only for school counseling. The parents appealed to a federal court, which held that they were entitled to reimbursement for the costs of the psychological counseling services. On appeal, the Second Circuit reversed. Under the IDEA, no-cost psychological counseling is required only if the services are required to assist the student to benefit from special education. **Psychological counseling reimbursement is barred where parents arrange for the services without first notifying their school boards of dissatisfaction** with an IEP. The parents brought the issue to the district's attention about eight months after the services were obtained, making it impossible for the district to determine whether the expenditures were necessary. *M.C. v. Voluntown Board of Educ.*, 226 F.3d 60 (2d Cir. 2000).

II. MEDICAL SERVICES

The IDEA specifically excludes medical services from its definition of related services, unless provided for diagnostic or evaluative purposes. In determining whether a service is an excluded medical service, courts tend to focus on who has to provide the service and the nature of the service being provided to determine whether it is part of the school district's obligation under the IDEA.

♦ In 1984, the U.S. Supreme Court ruled that clean intermittent catheterization (CIC) is a related service not subject to the "medical service" exclusion of the IDEA. The parents of an eight-year-old girl born with spina bifida brought suit against a local Texas school district after the district refused to provide catheterization for the child while she attended school. The parents pursued administrative and judicial avenues to force the district to train staff to perform the simple procedure. After a federal court held against the parents, they appealed to the U.S. Court of Appeals, Fifth Circuit, which reversed. The school district then appealed to the U.S. Supreme Court. The Supreme Court affirmed that portion of the court of appeals decision that held CIC is a "supportive service," not a "medical service," within the meaning of the IDEA. The Court was not persuaded by the school district's argument that catheterization is a medical service because it is provided in accordance with a physician's prescription and under a physician's supervision, even though it may be administered by a nurse or trained layperson. The Court listed four criteria to determine a school's obligation to provide services that relate to both the health and education of a child. First, to be entitled to related services, a child must be disabled so as to require special education. Second, **only those services necessary to aid a child with disabilities to benefit from special education must be provided**, regardless of how easily a school nurse or layperson could furnish them. Third, IDEA regulations state that school nursing services must be performed by a nurse or other qualified person, not by a physician. Fourth, the child's parents in this case were seeking only the services of a qualified person at the school; they were not asking the school to provide equipment. The Court reversed those portions of the court of appeals ruling which held the school district liable under the Rehabilitation Act and which held that the parents were entitled to attorneys' fees. *Irving Independent School Dist. v. Tatro*, 468 U.S. 883, 104 S.Ct. 3371, 82 L.Ed.2d 664 (1984).

♦ In 1999, the Supreme Court decided another case involving the extent of a school district's obligation to provide medical services, adopting a bright-line, physician/non-physician test to determine whether a requested service is a related service or a medical service. An Iowa student suffered a spinal cord injury that left him quadriplegic and ventilator dependent. For several years, his family provided him with personal attendant services at school. When the student entered grade five, his mother asserted that the district should provide him with continuous one-on-one nursing services. The district refused. A due process hearing officer determined that the school district had to reimburse the family for nursing costs in the current school year and provide the services in the future. A federal court ruled for the family, and the U.S. Court of Appeals, Eighth Circuit, found that the services provided for the student were related services as defined by the IDEA that were necessary to enable him to benefit from special education. The court rejected the school district's argument that the services were medical services excluded under the IDEA and state law. Because the district's nurse could provide the required services, they were not excluded from IDEA coverage as medical services.

On appeal, the U.S. Supreme Court affirmed the Eight Circuit's opinion, agreeing that the requested services were not medical services. The Court based its decision on the IDEA definition of related services, the *Tatro* decision, and the purpose of the IDEA to make special education available to all disabled students. **Adopting a bright-line, physician/non-physician standard, the court held that since the disputed services could be performed by someone other than a physician, the district had to provide them.** The district's assertion that a multi-factor standard that includes cost as a consideration was appropriate was rejected. *Cedar Rapids Community School Dist. v. Garret F.*, 526 U.S. 66, 119 S.Ct. 992, 143 L.Ed.2d 154 (1999).

♦ A Michigan school district's insurer sued the district to enforce its rights under state law with respect to the provision of nursing services to a student. It sought reimbursement for services it believed the district was providing and it was paying for. However, when the case reached the court of appeals, it noted that the student's IEPs did not specify the services in dispute and that **the services being provided by the district were not being paid for by the insurer**. Further, the insurer had no right to try to determine, through a lawsuit, whether the district should be providing nursing services to the student. *Progressive Michigan Insurance Co. v. Calhoun Intermediate School Dist.*, No. 290564, 2010 WL 2680112 (Mich. Ct. App. 7/6/10).

♦   A West Virginia student with medical problems suffered abuse and neglect at the hands of his parents. He was placed in foster care. Thirteen years later, a state court conducted a review of his pending abuse and neglect petition and **ordered the school board to provide and pay for a full-time nurse even though the board received no notice or opportunity to appear at the review hearing**. The Supreme Court of Appeal of West Virginia then issued an order in favor of the board, finding that it should have been given notice and an opportunity to be heard so that it could have helped shed light on the best interests of the student. For example, its records showed that the student hadn't suffered a seizure in two years and that he hadn't had a full-time nurse assigned to him for four of his 11 years in the school system. *State of West Virginia v. Beane*, 680 S.E.2d 46 (W. Va. 2009).

♦   A Maryland student with disabilities received two types of medication from the school nurse under an agreement signed by her treating/prescribing psychiatrist. When teachers and other staff members observed that the student was lethargic and drowsy, the psychiatrist prescribed another medication. However, the student's fatigue continued. The nurse sought clarification from the doctor on giving the student medication when symptoms contraindicated further drug administration. The parents told the doctor not to provide further information to the nurse or other district employees regarding the student's medical condition and treatment. The district then refused to continue medicating the student. When the parents challenged that decision, they lost. The Court of Appeals of Maryland held that the dispute was about medical treatment and not special education. **The nurse could not be forced to medicate the student without free communication with the doctor.** *John A. v. Board of Educ. for Howard County*, 929 A.2d 136 (Md. 2007).

♦   **A Virginia school board did not have to reimburse a disabled student for hospitalization costs** that were paid years earlier by his father's group health insurance, even though the payments counted against the lifetime medical benefits limit of the policy. The father made several requests to recover the $200,000 cost of the hospitalization from the board, but did not request a due process hearing for almost 10 years. The hearing officer held the action was barred by a one-year Virginia statute of limitations. A federal district court affirmed. The Fourth Circuit agreed that the action was untimely. Also, the student was now an adult and was no longer covered by his father's insurance policy. He had his own Medicaid coverage, and this insurance was not affected by the decrease in lifetime medical benefits to his father's plan. *Emery v. Roanoke City School Board*, 432 F.3d 294 (4th Cir. 2005).

♦   A student had over 150 absences and numerous behavioral referrals during her sophomore year of high school. She also exhibited signs of drug use. A school support team began an initial evaluation for special education, and a social worker urged her parents to have her tested for drug use late in her junior year. Two days later, the mother confronted the student about drug use and the student threatened to kill her mother. The student was hospitalized and tested positive for marijuana. She underwent a special education evaluation that resulted in her classification as emotionally impaired. She spent time in a juvenile detention center but eventually completed a residential program at another hospital during the summer. She received tutoring and graduated the following spring. Her parents filed an administrative action against state education officials seeking reimbursement for the hospitalization costs, characterizing them as IDEA-related services. A hearing officer concluded that the costs were reimbursable and awarded the parents $7,713.

The Hawaii education department appealed to a federal court, which noted that a state or local education agency is deemed to have knowledge that a child has a disability if behavior or performance demonstrates the need for special education and related services. The hearing officer had found reason to suspect that the student was disabled and that she might need special education services to address her emotional impairment as early as the beginning of her junior year. She was absent from school 79 times and had many behavior referrals the previous year. The court rejected the state's argument that the student's graduation under the IEP it eventually developed satisfied its obligation to provide a FAPE. The student's receipt of some educational benefit was not determinative, because instruction was not provided under an appropriate IEP, despite numerous warning signs, before the end of her junior year. The state violated the IDEA's child-find provisions by failing to evaluate her earlier. **The services provided at the hospital were diagnostic and for evaluation.** While they had been precipitated by a crisis, the student's disability might never have been addressed and she might not have ever received IDEA services if not for her hospitalization. The parents were entitled to reimbursement for the hospitalization costs. *Dep't of Educ., State of Hawaii v. Cari Rae S.*, 158 F.Supp.2d 1190 (D. Haw. 2001).

◆   After an Indiana student was released from a medical center, her parents contacted local school officials, seeking a residential placement. The parties met at an IEP conference and agreed on the need for a residential placement. While the student awaited the outcome of the administrative process, she was placed in a psychiatric hospital for over sixth months, incurring significant costs for psychiatric counseling, medication and therapy. Her parents then sought to have her involuntarily committed. The court found that the student was mentally ill and required long-term education in a residential placement. She remained in the hospital for an additional five months, since the least restrictive appropriate facility had no available space. The hospital notified the court that she was no longer a threat to herself or others and recommended termination of her civil commitment. In a separate action, a class of Indiana students with disabilities and their parents sued the Indiana Department of Education, alleging that the department's long delays in residential placement matters violated the IDEA. That lawsuit settled under an order that provided for recovery of certain educational and related services costs from the state where there was a delay between the date of the IEP and the date of placement. The state agreed to place eligible students in residential facilities within 30 days of the development of their IEPs, "except where special circumstances require otherwise." The student and her parents joined the action and sought reimbursement for the services she received while hospitalized.

The case reached the Seventh Circuit, which held that the hospitalization charges incurred by the student resulted from "special circumstances" as described in the settlement order; therefore, the delay in placing her in a residential facility, as called for in her IEP, did not violate the terms of the settlement agreement. Her IEP was designed for homebound services and contemplated a residential placement for her educational needs, not a placement based on medical treatment. The student's unstable condition made hospitalization necessary and resulted in her inability to be placed at a residential facility. **The hospital placement was for medical reasons related to the student's psychiatric crisis; therefore, reimbursement was not warranted.** The student's IEP team had unanimously concluded that she did not require hospitalization, and her parents had failed to challenge the adequacy of the IEP. The hospital was not equipped to serve as an educational provider. *Butler v. Evans*, 225 F.3d 887 (7th Cir. 2000).

♦   The mother of a Rhode Island student who was profoundly retarded, paraplegic and required a ventilator challenged the student's IEP. The city school department prevailed in administrative proceedings, and the mother appealed. However, she voluntarily dismissed the action. At that time, an IEP team meeting was already one month overdue under state law. A state education department compliance officer requested an IEP review meeting. Although a meeting was held, it was not attended by any representative from the city school department. The state education department then initiated compliance proceedings against the city school department for failure to conduct an annual IEP review.

Following a hearing, the education department authorized the compliance officer to take necessary action to develop a revised IEP. At a final hearing in the compliance action, the officer testified that nursing services were appropriate in order to provide the student with a safe environment in which to receive a FAPE. The city later refused to pay for a full-time nurse to assist the student, and the commissioner deducted almost $55,000 from the city's operation aid to pay for nursing services rendered. The case then came before the Rhode Island Superior Court, which found that the state's general laws authorized the commissioner to deduct funds from a city's operation aid for a violation or neglect of law, or for a municipality's violation or neglect of rules and regulations. Here, the city had violated state special education law by failing to timely arrange for an IEP meeting. Withholding of funds had therefore been appropriate. Also, **full-time nursing services were necessary for the student to maintain her health and safety while she received education**. She was technology-dependent, in need of respiratory suctioning, special feeding, catheterization and a ventilator. The disputed services could be provided by a nurse and were thus not subject to the IDEA's medical services exclusion. *City of Warwick v. Rhode Island Dep't of Educ.*, No. PC 98-3189, 2000 WL 1879897 (R.I. Super. 12/5/00).

♦   An eight-year-old Ohio student with spina bifida required regular suctioning of her tracheostomy tube. Despite her impairment, she was bright and highly motivated. The special education services provided by her school district were limited to one hour of home instruction per day. She received no physical or speech therapy. Her mother requested additional home instruction or an in-school placement. The school board denied an in-school placement, stating that the student's disability required the services of a full-time licensed practical nurse and that this would be an excluded medical service. A hearing officer determined that the student's IEP should be modified to include placement at a school for disabled students with the services of an attendant at regular intervals. A state level review officer reversed, finding that the student was receiving a free appropriate public education under her present IEP. A court then held that the district's failure to place the student in a school with necessary related services violated the IDEA and the Rehabilitation Act. The Court of Appeals of Ohio affirmed. **The evidence here overwhelmingly demonstrated that the single hour of home instruction provided by the district each day was inadequate for the student to receive educational benefits.** *Tanya v. Cincinnati Board of Educ.*, 651 N.E.2d 1373 (Ohio Ct. App. 1995).

III. TRANSPORTATION

The IDEA expressly requires school districts to furnish students with disabilities necessary transportation as a related service. School districts must also furnish transportation to disabled students attending private schools if necessary for the student to receive a FAPE. Transportation includes travel to and from school and between schools, as well as travel in and around school buildings. It also includes any specialized equipment that might be needed.

◆   The parents of a disabled child in Hawaii sued after the state failed to reimburse them for **mileage incurred in transporting the child to school**. The case reached the Ninth Circuit, which held that the state rightly withheld reimbursement. The parents failed to provide proof of insurance and did not submit reimbursement forms as required. *Russell v. Dep't of Educ.*, 377 Fed.Appx. 595 (9th Cir. 2010).

◆   A California parent **sought a temporary order for transportation costs for her son's attendance at a charter school that was outside their district** of residence. She claimed that district officials retaliated against her for her efforts to provide a FAPE for her son and that the state department of education failed to ensure that the district would comply with its obligations under the IDEA. A federal court refused to grant the temporary relief, holding that she was not alleging irreparable harm. If she prevailed in later proceedings, she could be reimbursed for her transportation costs. *Stassart v. Lakeside School Dist.*, No. C 09-1131 JF (HRL), 2009 WL 2566717 (N.D. Cal. 8/18/09).

◆   The grandparents of an Ohio student with Asperger's Syndrome requested two due process hearings over two school years – once to deal with extended school year issues, and once to resolve issues relating to her return to school after worsening behavior kept her at home. Both times the grandparents reached mediated settlement agreements stating that all educational issues in dispute were resolved. However, after the tutor provided for by the second agreement had to stop transporting the student because he lacked the proper certification, the grandparents sued. A federal court and the Sixth Circuit ruled against them. The mediated agreements prevented court review, and **the tutor remained available except for his inability to transport the student**, so there was no breach of contract by the district. *Amy S. v. Danbury Local School Dist.*, 174 Fed.Appx. 896 (6th Cir. 2006).

♦   A Maine student with cerebral palsy, visual impairments, a seizure disorder and mental retardation received in-home services after school from a developmental disabilities provider. However, the provider could not always be at the bus stop when the student was dropped off. Nor could his mother. His IEP described an informal protocol that applied when no adult was there to meet him at the bus stop. The bus driver violated the protocol on two occasions by dropping him off when no adult was there to meet him. The district offered to let him ride a special education bus, but his mother rejected that offer because it would result in increased time on the bus. A hearing officer found that the school district did not violate the IDEA, and a federal court agreed. **The student's mother here was seeking assistance related to child care**, not special education. The district had mainstreamed the student to the maximum extent appropriate under the IDEA. *Ms. S. v. Scarborough School Committee*, 366 F.Supp.2d 98 (D. Me. 2005).

♦   Two autistic students in New Jersey resided in a group home and were transported to special education programs located in other districts. The students' parents resided in districts other than the one where the group home was located. The parents' districts asked the state education commissioner for an order requiring the group home district to pay for the transportation costs. The case reached the Superior Court of New Jersey, Appellate Division, which ruled that **the parents' districts had to fund the transportation**. Under state law, the students were deemed to be residents of their parents' homes, making those districts liable for transportation costs. *Board of Educ. of West Windsor-Plainsboro Regional School Dist. v. Board of Educ. of Township of Delran*, 825 A.2d 1215 (N.J. Super. Ct. App. Div. 2003).

♦   A South Dakota student who suffered epileptic seizures was provided transportation both to and from school by her district as a related service under the IDEA. She was accompanied by a nurse during the ride. Although parents could designate different pick-up and drop-off sites within a specific boundary, students were not transported outside the boundary unless it was necessary to obtain an educational benefit under an IEP. When the student's mother asked the district to drop off her daughter at a daycare center outside the boundary, it refused to do so. The state Office of Special Education ordered the district to pay for transportation to the day care center, but a hearing examiner ruled that was not necessary. A federal court and the Eighth Circuit agreed that **the district did not have to provide transportation to the daycare center**. Here, the request was for the mother's own convenience and was not necessary to provide the student with educational benefit. *Fick v. Sioux Falls School Dist. 49-5*, 337 F.3d 968 (8th Cir. 2003).

♦   An Illinois student with autism attended a private Boston school under an IEP that called for the school district to pay for 12 round trips a year for the parents. Four years later, the district reduced the number of paid annual visits from 12 to six. The parents requested a due process hearing, at which the hearing officer noted that the parents had never made more than six trips a year and determined that six trips a year were appropriate. The parents appealed, and a federal court ruled for the district. During the 38-month period from the time of the due process hearing request to the court's decision, the parents took 12 trips to Boston in addition to the six specified in the IEP. When the district sought to be reimbursed for the extra 12 trips the parents had taken, the court refused to force the parents to repay the district (over $13,000). **Even though the parents seemingly took advantage of the stay-put provision by increasing their visits during litigation**, IDEA policies justified allowing them to keep the money. *Aaron M. v. Yomtoob*, No. 00 C 7732, 2003 WL 22836308 (N.D. Ill. 11/25/03).

♦   A school district placed a student with autistic-like behaviors in a private school for students and provided him with transportation from the private school to his home each day. His parents petitioned the school district's committee for special education to add a private after-school program to the student's IEP, pay for the after-school program, and provide transportation to and from the program twice a week. The district declined the request. A due process hearing officer upheld the decision not to add the program to the student's IEP and the refusal to provide transportation. A state review officer annulled the portion of the hearing officer's decision denying transportation, but affirmed the decision that the program need not be added to the student's IEP. On appeal to the New York Supreme Court, Appellate Division, the court observed that the review officer had correctly held that the district was not required to fund the after-school program in order to provide the student a FAPE, since his private school placement met his educational needs. Since the student's IEP was appropriate, the district was not required to modify it by adding the after-school program. **The obligation to provide equal opportunities for students to participate in nonacademic and extracurricular activities did not extend to the provision of equivalent or alternative transportation** simply because a district's after-school program was unsuitable for students with disabilities. There was no evidence that the district had excluded the student from its existing extracurricular programs. To the contrary, it had offered to modify its existing program to accommodate him. The district did not deprive the student of any opportunities that he would have received had he attended a district school. Access to the after-school program was not required by the IDEA or state law, and the district did not have to pay for transportation home from the alternate after-school program chosen by the parents. *Roslyn Union Free School Dist. v. Univ. of State of New York, State Educ. Dep't*, 711 N.Y.S.2d 582 (N.Y. App. Div. 2000).

♦   An Iowa student with severe disabilities, including cerebral palsy and spastic quadriplegia, participated in the special education program of her regularly assigned, neighborhood school. She was transported there with a lift bus that traveled a special route for her. Her parents sought to transfer her to a different school under the intra-district transfer program and asked for special transportation despite the program requirement that they furnish their own transportation. The district approved the transfer but denied the transportation request. An administrative law judge held that the parents had established no need for special transportation beyond parental preference for placement at a specific school. A federal court reversed the administrative decision, ruling that the district had impermissibly limited the student's opportunity to participate in the transfer program.

The district appealed to the Eighth Circuit, which found that the student was not denied the benefit of participating in the intra-district transfer program, since she was allowed to participate in it on the same terms as other applicants. There was no evidence of discrimination in the administration of the transfer program, and the student was not denied access to it on the basis of her disability. Instead, her parents did not wish to comply with "the main condition of the program applicable to all students who wish[ed] to participate - parental transportation." **Requiring the district to spend additional funds on transportation to the transfer program would fundamentally alter this requirement, creating an undue burden on the school district.** The court reversed and remanded the district court decision. *Timothy H. v. Cedar Rapids Community School Dist.*, 178 F.3d 968 (8th Cir. 1999).

♦   A parochial academy attended by a student with speech impairments was located three blocks from a public school that offered a speech therapy program. The school board agreed to provide the student with speech therapy at the public school under an IEP but declined to furnish transportation or to send a speech therapist to the private school. The student's mother filed an administrative appeal, and a hearing officer upheld the board's decision. The mother appealed to the U.S. District Court for the Southern District of Alabama, which found that the student was not entitled to receive transportation or speech therapy services at the parochial school. The mother appealed to the U.S. Court of Appeals, Eleventh Circuit.

The court stated that public schools need to provide only those services that are necessary to help a student with disabilities benefit from special education. In determining whether a student with disabilities needs transportation as a related service, the court must **consider the student's age, the distance the student must travel, the nature of the area over which the student must travel, the availability of private assistance, and the availability of public transit and crossing guards**. Here, the student was only six years old but was only required to travel a short distance. His mother failed to show that she was unavailable to provide private transportation, and there was no evidence that the school was in a high crime or high traffic area. Because the student was unable to establish that he could not reach the public school without the board's assistance, the board did not need to provide transportation. There was no evidence that the offering of a speech therapy class at the public school denied the student access to a free appropriate public education. The court affirmed the judgment for the school board. *Donald B. by Christine B. v. Board of School Commissioners of Mobile County, Alabama*, 117 F.3d 1371 (11th Cir. 1997).

♦   A Pennsylvania student with disabilities attended a public school where he
was enrolled in a hearing-impaired support resource room program. His parents
were divorced and had a joint physical custody arrangement by which his
residence alternated between parents each week. The mother resided within the
school district, but the father lived outside the district, and school officials
refused to provide transportation to and from his residence. The
Commonwealth Court of Pennsylvania observed that transportation is a related
service under the IDEA that must be provided where it is an integral part of the
student's IEP and is required to assist the student in benefiting from a special
education program. Although the Fifth Circuit has approved of supplemental
transportation outside a school district where required to prevent significant
regression of a student's educational progress, **the requested transportation
here did not address the student's special education needs**. Transportation to
the father's residence served only to accommodate the custody arrangement of
the parents. It did not have to be provided. *North Allegheny School Dist. v.
Gregory P.*, 687 A.2d 37 (Pa. Commw. Ct. 1996).

CHAPTER SIX

School Liability

I. GOVERNMENTAL IMMUNITY

The doctrine of governmental immunity, based on the Eleventh Amendment to the U.S. Constitution, prohibits lawsuits against the government and its officials. However, the doctrine has been limited in several aspects by legislative action or judicial decisions.

Eleventh Amendment immunity protects against lawsuits brought by individuals in federal court for money damages, not lawsuits seeking prospective relief, like injunctions.

A. Federal Suits

Generally, the Eleventh Amendment protects states or state officials in their official capacities from (a) federal court lawsuits (b) brought by individuals (c) seeking money damages. However, local political subdivisions do not constitute "states" and they are thus subject to suit.

Additionally, the Eleventh Amendment does not attach to suits brought by the federal government against a state, or lawsuits brought in state court. Nor does it protect against lawsuits that seek only injunctive relief, like court orders preventing continued harassment or discrimination.

◆ In 1974, a Pennsylvania state school and hospital resident brought a class action suit against the school and its officials as well as various state and local mental health administrators. The resident claimed that conditions at the institution violated Section 504 of the Rehabilitation Act, the Developmentally Disabled Assistance and Bill of Rights Act, 42 U.S.C. §§ 6001-6081 (DDABRA), Pennsylvania mental health legislation, and the Eighth and Fourteenth Amendments to the U.S. Constitution. A federal court held that the state legislation provided a right to adequate habilitation, but did not determine whether the student and class had habilitation rights in the least restrictive environment. On appeal, the U.S. Court of Appeals, Third Circuit, affirmed, ruling that the class had habilitation rights in the least restrictive environment based on its interpretation of the DDABRA. The U.S. Supreme Court reversed, holding that the DDABRA created no substantive rights. It remanded the case to the court of appeals. *Pennhurst State School and Hospital v. Halderman*, 451 U.S. 1, 101 S.Ct. 1531, 67 L.Ed.2d 694 (1981).

On remand, the court of appeals affirmed its previous decision. The U.S. Supreme Court again reversed and remanded the case. **It held that the Eleventh Amendment prohibited federal courts from ordering state officials to conform their conduct to their own state laws.** On remand, the court of appeals would be permitted to consider a judgment based on the federal legislation. *Pennhurst State School and Hospital v. Halderman*, 465 U.S. 89, 104 S.Ct. 900, 79 L.Ed.2d 67 (1984).

◆ A Georgia teacher often engaged in horseplay with a disabled student. One day, the teacher shoved the student's head into a trash can and then pulled him out by his legs. The student and his family sued, asserting violations of the student's constitutional rights. A federal court and the Eleventh Circuit ruled against them, noting that there was no evidence of any injury suffered by the student. Further, **the teacher did not act with malice or intent to injure**. Because there was no constitutional violation, the defendants were entitled to immunity. *Mahone v. Ben Hill County School System*, 377 Fed.Appx. 913 (11th Cir. 2010).

◆ The mother of a Virginia child with cerebral palsy and a seizure disorder became concerned that the student's teacher was improperly confining her to a wheelchair for most of the day. She hid recording equipment in the child's wheelchair, got information that corroborated her concerns, and then sued the teacher, the school board and the superintendent for violating her child's right to bodily integrity under the Due Process Clause. The defendants sought immunity, but the Fourth Circuit held that they were not entitled to it. The student had a clearly established right to be free from bodily restraint, and the mother alleged that the confinement was intentional and excessive. **If staff members indeed restrained the child for hours at a time as alleged, they would have violated clearly established law.** The court remanded the case for further proceedings. *H.H. v. Moffett*, 335 Fed.Appx. 306 (4th Cir. 2009).

♦ A mother and daughter sued their Pennsylvania school district, claiming it did not take action to stop harassment by a special education student against the daughter, and that it retaliated against the mother for complaining about school safety and harassment issues. The mother worked as a vision specialist for an agency that served the district and was transferred after complaining about the fact that her daughter was harassed by the disabled student for over four years. The school district talked to the disabled student, but he continued to harass the daughter. It also removed his behavior plan. At one point, he found the daughter alone in a school weight room and prevented her from leaving for half an hour. Another time he tried to get into her car on a school parking lot. Eventually, the district reinstated a behavior plan and assigned aides to monitor him in school. **A federal court refused to dismiss the Title IX and free speech claims** by the daughter and mother, finding evidence that the district's response was unreasonable. A trial was required. *Jones v. Indiana Area School Dist.*, 397 F.Supp.2d 628 (W.D. Pa. 2005).

♦ A Virginia student with ADHD brought a pellet gun to school. District officials sought to expel him, and a manifestation committee determined that his behavior was unrelated to his disability, such that expulsion was proper. An impartial hearing officer reversed the finding of the manifestation committee but ruled that it did not commit procedural violations. Before a review officer could consider the case, the parents sued under Section 504, alleging that the board's policies and procedures were inadequate. They did not allege disability discrimination. A federal court dismissed the lawsuit, noting that although Section 504 confers a private right of action to enforce discrimination claims, **it does not provide a private right of action to assert procedural violations.** The case was remanded to the review officer. *Power v. School Board of City of Virginia Beach*, 276 F.Supp.2d 515 (E.D. Va. 2003).

♦ A 13-year-old student with Tourette's syndrome, asthma, ADHD and emotional problems alleged that staff at his school repeatedly abused him during a three-year period. He asserted that district personnel strangled him and subjected him to a "take down procedure" in which he was pinned to the ground with his arms and legs forcibly crossed behind him while a teacher applied pressure. A 12-year-old student with autism, cognitive impairment and ADHD who attended the same school also asserted that the school's staff severely abused him by subjecting him to the "take down procedure," spraying him in the face with cold water and forcing him to run on a treadmill with ankle weights, among other things. The students' families sued the district and school officials in a federal court, which awarded summary judgment to the district and school officials on the basis of Eleventh Amendment immunity. The Ninth Circuit reversed the grant of immunity to the district. Nevada did not treat public schools as a statewide or central government function, and each school district had the power to sue and be sued. Although Nevada districts were not autonomous government corporations, each district board was a corporation. **The factors for determining whether to apply the Eleventh Amendment weighed against the district's arguments for immunity.** The students' claims against the school officials in their individual and official capacities survived dismissal. *Eason v. Clark County School Dist.*, 303 F.3d 1137 (9th Cir. 2002).

◆   Two Arkansas families filed a lawsuit alleging that the state education department violated the IDEA, Section 504 and other state and federal laws. A federal court refused to dismiss one family's IDEA claims against the department and an education department employee. The court also denied dismissal of the Section 504 claim against the department in the second family's case, which named various other defendants. The second family asserted that their child, a student with autism, should have been provided with Lovaas programming. The court refused to dismiss the IDEA claims, finding the defendant state officials were not entitled to immunity, but they were entitled to immunity on the Section 504 claim. The Eighth Circuit affirmed the determination that Section 504 was a valid exercise of Congressional spending power and that Arkansas had waived its immunity under Section 504 by accepting federal funds.

Later, the case returned to the Eighth Circuit, which explained that qualified immunity is more than a defense to liability. It prevents any action against a person or agency from going to a trial. **The officials here were entitled to qualified immunity because the parents were unable to demonstrate any violation of their clearly established rights.** The parents failed to show specific facts that amounted to gross misjudgment or bad faith, which must be shown to proceed in a Section 504 action. The parents also could not proceed with an action for damages under the IDEA or Section 1983, since the IDEA does not allow compensatory or punitive damages. *Bradley v. Arkansas Dep't of Educ.*, 301 F.3d 952 (8th Cir. 2002).

◆   A student with disabilities had a history of severe behavior problems. When she returned to school after being hospitalized, her behavior problems escalated, to the point that she spat at a counselor and head-butted him. School staff members began to wrap her in a sheet or blanket to ensure her safety, and when she escaped the wrap, they began to secure it with safety pins or duct tape. On one occasion, they wrapped her in a blanket and secured it to a cot with tape. The student's mother removed her from school for about three months because of this treatment but later returned her. Even though the school discontinued the practice of wrapping or taping the student, the mother sued.

The mother asserted that the school's restraint methods violated the student's constitutional rights, the Texas Education Code and other state laws. School personnel testified that the wrapping incidents were not designed to punish the student but were intended to protect her and those around her. The court held that the school officials were entitled to qualified immunity. **There was no legal authority for the mother's claim that her daughter had a constitutional right to be free from restraint.** The asserted right to bodily integrity was not sufficiently well established to create liability. An emotionally disturbed student does not have a due process right to be free from restraints to control outbursts that prevent harm to herself or others. School officials relied on the professional judgment of a therapist who testified that the wrapping technique was preferable to allowing the student to injure herself. *Doe v. S & S Consolidated Independent School Dist.*, 149 F.Supp.2d 274 (E.D. Tex. 2001).

♦ A 16-year-old New Mexico special education student had psychological and emotional problems. He twice mentioned suicide to a school aide. The principal reprimanded and suspended the student for threatening physical harm to a teacher. She then instructed the teacher to drive the student home, without first contacting the parents. She did, however, call the police with instructions to detain the student if he returned to school. The school's disciplinary policy called for the temporary suspension of a special education student on the same basis as regular students, but provided that students should remain at school if their parents were not home. The teacher also failed to contact the parents and dropped the student off at home, where he committed suicide.

His parents sued the district, its board and certain employees in a federal court under 42 U.S.C. § 1983, alleging constitutional and IDEA violations. The court found that the reasonableness of taking a potentially suicidal student home without notifying his parents was a question that should be considered by a jury. The Tenth Circuit agreed. There can be liability under Section 1983 only where government officials violate clearly established rights of which a reasonable person would know. Here, **it was possible that by suspending the student and taking him home without notice to his parents, the actions of the principal and teacher placed him in danger or increased the risk of harm.** There was evidence that the principal and teacher had knowledge of the student's suicidal threats and knew that he had access to firearms. *Armijo v. Wagon Mound Public Schools*, 159 F.3d 1253 (10th Cir. 1998).

B. IDEA

Congress may remove a state's Eleventh Amendment protection by specifically abrogating it for particular and specified purposes. In the 1990 amendments to the IDEA, Congress authorized lawsuits against the states for violations of the IDEA.

♦ In 1989, the U.S. Supreme Court, in *Dellmuth v. Muth*, 491 U.S. 223, 109 S.Ct. 2397, 105 L.Ed.2d 181 (1989), ruled that while local school districts could be sued under the IDEA, states were immune from IDEA liability under the Eleventh Amendment. In response, Congress passed the Education of the Handicapped Act Amendments of 1990 – known as the Individuals with Disabilities Education Act (IDEA), and included a new section, 20 U.S.C. § 1403, which specifically abrogates a state's Eleventh Amendment immunity to suit in federal court for violations of the IDEA. This section allows suits against a state for both legal and equitable remedies in federal court.

♦ A Nevada student with tuberous sclerosis (a neurological disease that causes tumors) also suffered from autism and was non-verbal. An IDEA lawsuit was brought on his behalf against his school district and teacher. In it, he alleged that his teacher slapped him repeatedly and body-slammed him into a chair. He also claimed that school officials knew about his teacher's violent conduct but did nothing to prevent it. The teacher and the school district asked for qualified immunity, but a federal court and the Ninth Circuit refused to grant it. The court of appeals noted that **no reasonable special education teacher would believe it was lawful to seriously beat a disabled four-year-old**. The case was allowed to proceed. *Preschooler II v. Clark County School Board of Trustees*, 479 F.3d 1175 (9th Cir. 2007).

♦ A Georgia student with a tracheotomy tube entered an early childhood center under an IEP. On his second day there, he collapsed while on the playground. His teacher and a paraprofessional attempted to resuscitate him and noticed that his tracheotomy tube was dislodged. Paramedics took him to the emergency room, where he died from asphyxiation. His mother sued the school district in federal court for wrongful death and IDEA violations. The district sought to have the lawsuit dismissed, and the Eleventh Circuit agreed. It held that **personal injury claims for tort-type damages are not available under the IDEA**. *Ortega v. Bibb County School Dist.*, 397 F.3d 1231 (11th Cir. 2005).

♦ A New Jersey student made only minimal progress in reading, writing and spelling over his 12 years in public schools. When he turned 19, he sued state and local officials and agencies for failing to diagnose his dyslexia such that he was denied a free appropriate public education under the IDEA. He also claimed violations of Section 504 and 42 U.S.C. § 1983. The state officials sought to have the case dismissed on grounds of immunity, but the Third Circuit Court of Appeals ruled against them. Congress clearly expressed an intent to **condition the receipt of funds under Section 504 and the IDEA on the relinquishment of immunity** by the states. The lawsuit could proceed. *A.W. v. Jersey City Public Schools*, 341 F.3d 234 (3d Cir. 2003).

♦ After a student was suspended without a due process hearing, he sued his school district and a district administrator for violations of the IDEA and the Due Process Clause. The district and administrator moved for summary judgment, but the court denied it to the district on the due process claims. The district argued that the administrator was entitled to qualified immunity from suit for the IDEA claims against him in his individual capacity. Public officials who perform "discretionary functions" generally have qualified immunity from civil damage claims unless they violate clearly established federal rights of which a reasonable person would have known. A court must consider whether the official could have believed that his or her acts were lawful in view of clearly established law and the information the official possessed at the time of the action. Here, the student alleged that the administrator violated his right to a FAPE by suspending him without providing a due process hearing. The court found no decision by the Tenth Circuit or the U.S. Supreme Court involving facts like those alleged by the student in this case. **Because the administrator was not on notice of such clearly established law, he was entitled to summary judgment on the IDEA claims brought against him in his individual capacity.** The student's case could proceed on the remaining issues, including the IDEA and due process claims against the district and the administrator in his official capacity. *D.L. v. Unified School Dist. No. 497*, Civ. No. 00-2439-CM, 2002 WL 31296445 (D. Kan. 10/1/02).

C. State Statutory Immunity

Congress enacted the Federal Tort Claims Act to allow individuals to sue the federal government in limited circumstances. Many states have enacted similar legislation wherein they effectively consent to be sued in certain instances. The following cases address immunity for tort claims – which are claims for civil wrongs other than breach of contract.

♦ An Oklahoma student with disabilities **claimed that a teacher, an aide and a principal punished him by confining and restraining him in a dark room.** He also claimed that he was slapped and held down for long periods of time. When he sued for negligent supervision, assault, battery, false imprisonment and due process violations, the school officials sought to have the case dismissed. A federal court dismissed the state law claims because of the Oklahoma Governmental Tort Claims Act. However, it refused to dismiss claims for intentional infliction of emotional distress and constitutional claims against the teacher and two others. It also allowed claims against the school system for battery, assault, false imprisonment, negligent supervision and negligent hiring to proceed. *Muskrat v. Deer Creek Public Schools*, No. CIV-08-1103-L, 2010 WL 356659 (W.D. Okla. 1/27/10).

♦ Ohio parents grew frustrated with their school district, which had implemented a policy of not allowing students to be dropped off before 8:45 a.m. and requiring them to be picked up by 3:30 p.m. The parents became confrontational and had a number of run-ins with school staff. The police were called, and the mother was charged with criminal trespass. Various court actions followed, and the parents then sued the district for multiple violations of law. The case reached the Ohio Court of Appeals, which held that the district was entitled to governmental immunity on all the parents' claims. **School employees were engaged in governmental functions when they denied the parents early access to the school.** *Horen v. Board of Educ. of City of Toledo Public Schools*, No. L-09-1143, 2010 WL 3064394 (Ohio Ct. App. 8/6/10).

♦ A Michigan school system operated a school for 18- to 26-year-old students with physical and cognitive disabilities from throughout the county. A student with cognitive impairments and a seizure disorder was practicing for a Special Olympics event in a system pool, with a lifeguard and a paraprofessional. When they turned away for a minute, he somehow drowned despite the almost-immediate administration of CPR. His estate sued the school system and staff members for gross negligence. The Court of Appeals of Michigan ruled that **the school system was entitled to immunity for hosting the Special Olympics event**. However, the court refused to grant the staff members immunity without further findings regarding whether they were being paid by the Special Olympics or the government. *Ryan v. Lamphere Public School System*, No. 286741, 2010 WL 934243 (Mich. Ct. App. 3/16/10).

◆ The family of an Ohio student with Down syndrome sued their district and several employees, alleging that a substitute teacher did not monitor their child's classroom on many occasions and that the student was assaulted by a known abuser as a result. The Court of Appeals of Ohio granted the district immunity because **the failure to monitor was within the scope of the employees' official job duties**. However, the individual employees might be liable for their "recklessness." The court remanded the case for a trial on that issue. *E.F. v. Oberlin City School Dist.*, No. 09CA009640, 2010 WL 1227703 (Ohio Ct. App. 3/31/10).

◆ According to a Michigan student with cerebral palsy and partial paralysis, a teacher's aide pushed him to a concrete floor and pushed him again when he tried to stand up. The aide later pled guilty to assault in an unrelated criminal case. When the student sued the district to recover for his injuries, the district claimed immunity and the Michigan Court of Appeals granted it. **The aide was not acting within the course and scope of his employment when he allegedly pushed the student to the floor.** Therefore, the district was entitled to immunity for his actions unless it committed gross negligence, which was not the case here. *Booker v. Detroit Public Schools*, No. 290071, 2010 WL 1052275 (Mich. Ct. App. 3/23/10).

◆ Police questioned a learning-disabled Massachusetts student after a classmate accused him of grabbing and squeezing her breasts. A school rule required administrators to make an effort to protect students' rights in police interrogations, but **the assistant principal left before the police interrogation was over**. The student admitted to grabbing the girl. He was suspended and convicted of indecent assault and battery. He then sued the district and the assistant principal for negligence and infliction of emotional distress because of the assistant principal's failure to diminish the consequences of the police interview, but the Court of Appeals of Massachusetts ruled that the defendants were entitled to immunity. *Jones v. Maloney*, 910 N.E.2d 412 (Mass. App. Ct. 2009).

◆ An assistant principal in North Carolina called a disabled student's mother to report some sexual experimentation between the student and another boy. The mother believed the contact was not consensual. She sued the school board for negligence, also asserting state constitutional claims. The school board sought immunity, but the North Carolina Supreme Court ruled that the lawsuit could proceed. Sovereign immunity was created by the courts, but constitutional rights trumped. And **granting immunity to the board would**

leave the student and his mother without an adequate state remedy. The court made clear that this did not mean the student and his mother should win. It meant only that they have the possibility of gaining relief. *Craig v. New Hanover County Board of Educ.*, 678 S.E.2d 351 (N.C. 2009).

◆ A disabled female student in Ohio rode the bus home every afternoon with three disabled male students. No bus aide accompanied them because none was required by any of the students' IEPs. The student was abused by a male student during the rides home. A bus aide present on the morning drive eventually discovered the abuse, and the parents sued the district for her injuries. They claimed that the motor vehicle exception to immunity allowed them to sue, while the district asserted that the exception applied only to the action of driving the bus. The case reached the Ohio Supreme Court, which ruled in favor of the district. **Immunity protected the district because the motor vehicle exception applied only to the driving of the bus** and not the supervision of students by the driver. *Doe v. Marlington Local School Dist. Board of Educ.*, 907 N.E.2d 706 (Ohio 2009).

◆ A Texas student sustained injuries when her wheelchair fell from a school bus loading ramp. Her guardian sued the school district for negligence, and it sought immunity under the state's tort claims act. The district claimed the bus was parked at the time of the accident and was not being "used or operated" within the meaning of the statute. However, a state court and the Texas Court of Appeals ruled against the district. **The mechanical lift and the ramp were being used at the time of the accident, so the district was not entitled to immunity.** *El Paso Independent School Dist. v. Apodaca*, No. 08-07-00163-CV, 2009 WL 383758 (Tex. Ct. App. 2/12/09).

◆ A North Carolina teacher's aide allegedly force-fed a student to the point of choking on several occasions. The aide also allegedly used abusive language and pulled his hair. The student stopped eating and had to be hospitalized. His parents sued the aide, the school board, administrators and a teacher for claims including infliction of emotional distress. The teacher sought immunity, but a trial court and the court of appeals rejected her claim. Here, **the teacher was not a public official exercising discretion but rather a public employee**. There was evidence that she refused to act in the face of widespread abuse by the aide, and the claims involved clearly established constitutional rights of which she would have known. *Farrell v. Transylvania County Board of Educ.*, 682 S.E.2d 224 (N.C. Ct. App. 2009).

◆ During a field trip to an Ohio recreation center, a Kentucky special education student with profound mental disabilities fell while on a pair of roller skates. His teacher arrived after he fell. She looked at his ankle after he indicated that it hurt, but **she saw no obvious injuries. Later, the student's doctor discovered the broken ankle.** The parents then sued the school board and the teacher to recover for his injuries. A trial court held that the board and the teacher were entitled to immunity. The Court of Appeals of Kentucky agreed. Public employees have qualified immunity where they perform acts involving the exercise of discretion and judgment, if those acts are taken in good faith and within the scope of employment authority. Here, the teacher had to exercise discretion and her personal judgment a number of times during the day, including on how to implement the student's IEP and how to supervise him. She also acted in good faith and within the course and scope of her employment. *Pennington v. Greenup County Board of Educ.*, No. 2006-CA-001942-MR, 2008 WL 1757209 (Ky. Ct. App. 4/18/08).

♦ A disabled student asked to change his work schedule at the student store so he could join his friends for lunch. When his request was denied, he became upset and went to a school parking lot to calm down. His IEP permitted "cool down" time when he was angry or upset. However, the principal told the campus police officer to go after the student because he had bipolar disorder, epilepsy and a history of getting on buses without permission. The latter claim was untrue. The student was taken for a psych evaluation, but was not detained. He then sued the principal and the district, who sought immunity. The California Court of Appeal **refused to grant immunity to the principal or the district on the false claims with respect to getting on buses**, which led to his psych evaluation. *Orterry v. Mt. Diablo Unified School Dist.*, No. A117392, 2008 WL 948363 (Cal. Ct. App. 4/9/08).

♦ A Georgia father claimed that school officials denied him access to records, report cards and progress reports regarding his disabled daughter. He sued, seeking $12 million in general damages and $2 million in punitive damages. His lawsuit was dismissed on immunity grounds, and the Georgia Court of Appeals upheld that ruling. **The actions in this case were purely discretionary**, involving the evaluation, placement or delivery of educational services, and the father presented no evidence of malice or reckless disregard for his or his daughter's rights. *Chisolm v. Tippens*, 658 S.E.2d 147 (Ga. Ct. App. 2008).

♦ A 14-year-old Texas student who was sent to the assistant principal's office was suspended for truancy and insubordination. When the assistant principal could not find her name in the school's electronic database, he allowed her to call her "uncle." She left with him without checking in with the assistant principal, then was sexually abused. She sued the district and the assistant principal, but lost. **The assistant principal was entitled to immunity because he did not have a duty to protect her from third-party violence.** There was no special relationship between the student and school giving rise to an increased duty, nor did the assistant principal demonstrate deliberate indifference to her well-being. *Doe v. San Antonio Independent School Dist.*, 197 Fed.Appx. 296 (5th Cir. 2006).

♦ The parents of a special-needs student sued a special education aide for negligence, **alleging she dropped the student and fell on him while attempting to transfer him from a wheelchair to a changing table.** She sought to dismiss the case, asserting immunity, but the Court of Civil Appeals of Alabama held that there was a fact issue as to whether she was exercising judgment so as to be entitled to immunity. All she offered to support her position was her sworn statement that she was exercising discretion. A trial was required. *Wilson v. Colbert County Board of Educ.*, 952 So.2d 1122 (Ala. Civ. App. 2006).

♦   After a disabled North Carolina student was allegedly abused by a teacher's aide, who allegedly force-fed him to the point of choking, the student and his parents sued the school board and various officials for negligence. The question of immunity for the director of federal programs reached the North Carolina Court of Appeals, which ruled that the director was entitled to official immunity. **She performed discretionary acts**, including ensuring that students were treated in compliance with state law, and supervising all special education teachers and aides for the county. *Farrell v. Transylvania County Board of Educ.*, 625 S.E.2d 128 (N.C. Ct. App. 2006).

♦   A Tennessee student with a history of aggressive behavior was evaluated for a disability. His evaluation results were inconsistent, and the IEP team found him ineligible for special education. However, it indicated that further evaluation was warranted. Less than a month later, the student struck his teacher in the face, and the principal suspended him for 10 days. Afterward, the principal decided to return the student to the classroom with a teacher's aide assigned to him. On the first day back, he assaulted the teacher and the aide. The teacher sued the school board for negligence. The Tennessee Court of Appeals held that **the school board was entitled to immunity for the principal's discretionary decision**. Here, she balanced the zero-tolerance policy against the IDEA's stay-put provision in deciding to allow the student to return to class. *Babb v. Hamilton County Board of Educ.*, No. E2004-00782-COA-R3-CV, 2004 WL 2094538 (Tenn. Ct. App. 9/21/04).

II. LIABILITY FOR NEGLIGENCE

In the absence of immunity, courts have held schools and their agents liable for personal injuries that resulted from the negligent failure to provide a reasonably safe environment, failure to warn of known hazards or to remove known dangers where possible, failure to properly instruct participants in an activity, or failure to provide adequate supervision.

♦   The teacher of a learning disabled New Hampshire student heard him say he wanted to "blow his brains out." The teacher notified the guidance counselor, who called the student's mother and told her he was doing better and had returned to class. The counselor had the student sign a contract for safety. Several weeks later the student was suspended for poor behavior. His mother took him home, where he hanged himself. His mother then sued the counselor and the school administrative unit for negligence and infliction of emotional distress. The Supreme Court of New Hampshire ruled that **the counselor had no duty to prevent the student's suicide at home**. *Mikell v. School Administrative Unit #33*, 972 A.2d 1050 (N.H. 2009).

♦   The parents of a Florida student eligible for special education were allegedly told by a school district that a particular school in the district provided students with a "best practices" curriculum. After moving into the district and placing their son at the school, the parents became disenchanted. They placed the student in a private school and then **sued the school board for fraudulent inducement and negligent misrepresentation**. The court determined that the claims were essentially re-packaged educational malpractice claims and dismissed them, but the Court of Appeal reversed. The parents' claims were not for educational malpractice, and they had to be allowed to amend their complaint to try to prove their claims. *Simon v. Celebration Co.*, 883 So.2d 826 (Fla. Dist. Ct. App. 2004).

A. Negligent Supervision

1. Student Injuries

♦   An autistic Pennsylvania student stood up and screamed obscenities at other students. His aide placed her hand over his mouth, allegedly after filling it with hand sanitizer. She admitted that she used hand sanitizer but claimed she didn't do what he alleged. His parents took him to a doctor even though he didn't complain of any injuries or exhibit any symptoms of poisoning. When the family sued, a Pennsylvania federal district court ruled against them, noting that **the aide had a pedagogical objective for using force** to prevent him from spewing obscenities, and that he suffered no apparent physical injuries. *JGS v. Titusville Area School Dist.*, 737 F.Supp.2d 449 (W.D. Pa. 2010).

♦   A Kentucky student with autism, who was largely nonverbal, wandered out of a class. The teacher's aide assigned to watch him noticed his absence and notified school officials, who began searching the adjoining neighborhood. With the help of police, he was found several hours later a number of blocks from the school, naked and covered in mud. His parents sued the district for violating his substantive due process rights to be secure at school, but a federal court and the Sixth Circuit ruled against them. **The student apparently suffered no physical or psychological harm** while away from school. *Parker v. Fayette County Public Schools*, 332 Fed.Appx. 229 (6th Cir. 2009).

♦   A Florida school bus driver activated her flashing lights so a deaf child could cross the street and board the bus. The driver heard a pickup speeding down the street and **tried to signal the child not to cross, but the child crossed anyway**. She was struck and injured by the pickup. The pickup's driver was sentenced to five years for reckless driving, and the family sued the school board for negligence. A jury found the board 20% at fault, the student 10% at fault and the pickup driver 70% at fault. The family then sought to hold the board liable for a greater percentage, but the Florida District Court of Appeal refused to do so. *Petit-Dos v. School Board of Boward County*, 2 So.3d 1022 (Fla. Dist. Ct. App. 2009).

♦   A Kansas bus driver inadvertently left a four-year-old special education student on the bus, and the student woke up after school started. He began to walk to his mother's workplace and was spotted by a relative, who brought him to his mother. He became traumatized by the incident and was diagnosed with post-traumatic stress disorder. When he sued the special educational cooperative for negligent infliction of emotional distress, the Court of Appeals of Kansas held that **he could not recover without establishing that he suffered some sort of physical injury** as well as the emotional injury he claimed. This he failed to do. *Ware v. ANW Special Educ. Cooperative No. 603*, 180 P.3d 610 (Kan. Ct. App. 2008).

♦   A Down syndrome student in Illinois had a tendency to eat his food too quickly, risking choking himself as a result. School employees, aware of his condition, cut up his food into small pieces, feeding him gradually. On a classmate's birthday, the student received a cupcake, which he ate under a paraprofessional's observation. As the meal ended, the paraprofessional got up to clean the area but kept an eye on the student. He ran around the table and grabbed another cupcake, which he stuffed into his mouth. He began to choke. The paraprofessional and the student's teacher tried to remove the food from his mouth without success. School nurses also were unable to help. An ambulance took the student to a hospital, where he remained in an induced coma for some time, suffering injuries as a result. When his mother sued the district for negligence, she lost. The Appellate Court of Illinois found **no evidence of indifference to or conscious disregard for the student's safety**. *Mitchell v. Special Educ. Joint Agreement School Dist. No. 208*, 897 N.E.2d 352 (Ill. App. Ct. 2008).

♦   A North Carolina student with hydrocephalus and a shunt in his brain used a walker and was accompanied to the lavatory by a staff member. Although he had used the lavatory successfully more than 1,450 times in the past three years, **on this occasion he slipped on some urine and fell**, hitting his head on the toilet seat and causing the shunt in his brain to malfunction. He sued the school district for negligence but lost because he was unable to prove that the district had breached its duty of care to him. *Foster v. Nash-Rocky Mount County Board of Educ.*, 665 S.E.2d 745 (N.C. Ct. App. 2008).

♦   A Tennessee student with asthma and mental retardation had trouble breathing during and after a physical education class. The PE coach was unaware of his medical conditions and made him continue running even after he grabbed his chest and stopped. The student, after being hospitalized for six months, sued the district for negligence. A jury awarded him $3 million, which the court reduced to $130,000 – the limit under the state's Governmental Tort Liability Act. The state court of appeals upheld the award. Here, **the district did not follow its own policy when it failed to provide the student's medical information to the coach**. This was an "operational act" for which the district had no immunity. *Small v. Shelby County Schools*, No. W2007-00045-COA-R3-CV, 2008 WL 360925 (Tenn. Ct. App. 2/12/08).

♦   The mother of an asthmatic New York kindergartner gave the school nurse his asthma medication, an inhaler, and an authorization and directive from his pediatrician. One day, the student's teacher and aide noticed he was coughing and took him to the nurse's office, where the nurse administered medication. He was reported as "breathing, alert and in no distress," so he was returned to class and his mother was called. She picked him up an hour later. He became ill in the car and later died at home. When she sued the school district, her lawsuit was dismissed. **The boy had been removed from school premises to the custody of his mother.** *Williams v. Hempstead School Dist.*, 46 A.D.3d 550 (N.Y. App. Div. 2007).

♦   An 11-year-old Nevada student with a severe learning disability pestered his teacher to cut his hair. She told him he needed permission from his mother. The student then told her that his mother had given her consent but that he'd left the permission slip at home. **After the teacher cut his hair in front of the class, he claimed that she did a bad job and that his classmates teased him.** His mother complained to the school, and an admonishment letter was placed in the teacher's file. When the student and his mother sued the school for constitutional rights violations and negligence, a federal court largely dismissed the action, finding no constitutional rights violations, but allowing a single claim for negligent training to proceed. *Cox v. Clark County School Dist.*, No. 2:05-CV-0928-RLH-PAL, 2007 WL 316300 (D. Nev. 1/31/07).

♦   The teacher of an Indiana student (who was non-verbal and had seizure disorder, hyptonia and cerebral ataxia) allegedly placed the student in a harness and put him in a lavatory stall for several hours. His parents sued the teacher and the school district for bias as well as for violating the student's constitutional rights. A federal court ruled for the district, noting that **the teacher's negligence was not intentional bias under the ADA.** Nor did the district have a policy of depriving students of their constitutional rights. The teacher's negligence was not sufficient to create constitutional liability. *A.D. v. Nelson*, No. 2:07-CV-116-PRC, 2007 WL 2446729 (N.D. Ind. 8/20/07).

♦   A mentally disabled eight-year-old with a history of aggressive behavior was secured to his seat on the bus by a child-proof restraining harness. However, he freed himself from the harness on two consecutive days. On the second day, he opened the emergency exit and fell from the bus, sustaining injuries. His family sued the district for negligence. The Court of Appeals of Texas explained that the district was entitled to immunity because **the student's injuries did not arise out of the negligent operation of the bus, but rather the student's own affirmative act of jumping from it.** *Montoya v. Houston Independent School Dist.*, 177 S.W.3d 332 (Tex. Ct. App. 2006).

♦   A 14-year-old Ohio student with mild asthma had trouble breathing during gym class and asked to go to his locker to retrieve his inhaler. His teacher allowed him to do so. A few minutes later, another teacher found the student on the locker room floor, unconscious and not breathing. He died, and his family sued the school board for negligence. A jury held for the school board, and the

Court of Appeals of Ohio upheld that determination. A doctor had testified that **the student's death was a "one in a million" chance that doctors could have foreseen.** *Spencer v. Lakeview School Dist.*, No. 2005-T-0083, 2006 WL 1816452 (Ohio Ct. App. 6/30/06).

♦   A California third-grader began experiencing emotional problems when his mother and stepfather divorced. He was hospitalized for a week and raped by a 14-year-old boy. He was then found eligible for special education and was placed at a private school under an IEP. Several years later, after exhibiting self-destructive behavior and attempting suicide on more than one occasion, he left the school without permission after telling staff he had not taken his medication that day. The school notified his mother eight minutes later that he had left campus. He was found three days later, after being sexually assaulted by an adult. Three months after that, he committed suicide. His mother sued the school for negligence and emotional distress. The California Court of Appeal reversed a jury verdict in her favor of $3.6 million. **Neither the suicide nor the sexual assault while the student was AWOL were foreseeable.** *Allison C. v. Advanced Educ. Services*, 28 Cal.Rptr.3d 605 (Cal. Ct. App. 2005).

♦   A bus driver picked up a student with disabilities on the first day of school and then got lost. He drove around for four hours until he found the school. The student, meanwhile, had urinated on himself and appeared to be dehydrated. The child began having nightmares and wetting the bed. His parents sued the school system for negligence and false imprisonment. A jury awarded emotional distress damages to the son despite the lack of a physical injury, but the Florida District Court of Appeal reversed. Emotional harm must flow from the physical injuries suffered from an impact. Here, the lack of a physical injury precluded a recovery for emotional distress. Further, **there was no intent to confine the student: the driver simply got lost.** *Florida v. Trujillo*, 906 So.2d 1109 (Fla. Dist. Ct. App. 2005).

♦   When an Idaho student with Asperger's syndrome was verbally aggressive toward his teachers, they called a police officer who had been able to calm him in past episodes. She took the student to the floor, handcuffed him and hobbled his legs. The student later sued the district and the officer, claiming the district was negligent and the officer used excessive force. A federal court and the Ninth Circuit ruled against him. **The district was not negligent because it could not have foreseen that the officer would harm the student.** Also, the officer was entitled to qualified immunity because there was no clearly established right to be free of the kind of force used in this case. *Hayenga v. Nampa School Dist. No. 131*, 123 Fed.Appx. 783 (9th Cir. 2005).

♦   The parents of an Illinois student with a rare form of muscular dystrophy sent his school a letter from his doctor detailing the student's muscle wasting. It clearly stated that **vigorous exercise was to be avoided** due to the risk of permanent muscle and kidney damage. The student's IEP called for adaptive physical education with limited exertion. However, a few days before the end of the semester, his physical education teacher ordered him to run laps and do push-ups if he did not want to get an F. After complying with the teacher's commands, the student had to go to the emergency room, where he was diagnosed with permanent kidney damage. He sued the district, but a federal court dismissed for failure to exhaust administrative remedies. The Seventh Circuit reversed, noting that the claims were not educational and could not be remedied by changing the student's IEP. The lawsuit could proceed. *McCormick v. Waukegan School Dist. #60*, 374 F.3d 564 (7th Cir. 2004).

2. Student-on-Student Injuries

Where a student injures another student, schools can be liable if the injury was foreseeable and if they failed to take reasonable steps to prevent it.

◆   A Massachusetts kindergartner told her parents that a third-grader on her school bus bullied her into lifting her skirt whenever she wore one. The parents complained to the principal, who investigated but could not corroborate the student's story. Later, the student told her parents that the boy made her pull down her underpants and spread her legs. Police became involved but could not find sufficient evidence to bring criminal charges against the third-grade boy. The principal did not discipline the third-grader, instead offering to transfer the kindergartner to a different bus. The family sued the school district under Title IX and 42 U.S.C. § 1983. A federal court and the First Circuit found no Title IX violation and also held that the family could not sue under Section 1983. The U.S. Supreme Court reversed, holding that the family could pursue a Section 1983 claim. **Title IX was not the exclusive mechanism for addressing gender discrimination.** *Fitzgerald v. Barnstable School Committee*, 555 U.S. 246, 129 S.Ct. 788, 172 L.Ed.2d 582 (2009).

◆   A Georgia student complained to her teacher of sexual harassment by a male student. The teacher did not immediately notify the principal. Although the harassing student was eventually charged with sexual battery, school officials took no action against him. The student sued the school board in a federal court under Title IX of the Education Amendments of 1972, which prohibits sex discrimination by education programs receiving federal assistance. The court dismissed the case. The U.S. Court of Appeals, Eleventh Circuit, affirmed. However, the U.S. Supreme Court reversed, holding that **school districts may be liable for deliberate indifference to known acts of peer sexual harassment under Title IX** in cases where the response of school administrators is clearly unreasonable under the circumstances. A recipient of federal funds may be liable for student-on-student sexual harassment where it is deliberately indifferent to known student sexual harassment and the harasser is under the recipient's disciplinary authority. In order to create Title IX liability, the harassment must be so severe, pervasive and objectively offensive that it deprives the victim of access to the funding recipient's educational opportunities or benefits. The Supreme Court stated that the harassment alleged by the student in this case was sufficiently severe to avoid pretrial dismissal. *Davis v. Monroe County Board of Educ.*, 526 U.S. 629, 119 S.Ct. 1661, 143 L.Ed.2d 839 (1999).

♦   A New York student with a history of behavior problems that included aggression at home, setting fires, stealing and threatening others attended school under an IEP. He made better social progress after being placed in a community residence and displayed no aggressive behaviors for two years. When he was 11 years old, he called a kindergartner his girlfriend while on a school bus. Her mother asked that they be separated. Later, he exposed himself to the kindergartner and forced her to touch him. Her mother sued the district for negligence. The Court of Appeals of New York ruled that she could not recover for her daughter's injuries because **the molestation by the 11-year-old was not foreseeable**. His past conduct did not indicate any sexually aggressive behavior. *Brandy B. v. Eden Cent. School Dist.*, 934 N.E.2d 304 (N.Y. 2010).

♦   After a California minor student was raped by a knife-wielding disabled student, she sued the district for negligence, **asserting that the teacher and principal knew the disabled student often brought a folding utility knife to school**, which he wore outside his pants and in plain view. The district claimed it had no inkling the disabled student might attempt sexual misconduct, while the principal and teacher claimed they had no knowledge that the disabled student carried a knife. Although the minor student sought the disabled student's juvenile records, asserting they contained a statement by the principal indicating an awareness that the disabled student carried a knife, a court accepted the district's version of the facts. The state court of appeal reversed, finding issues of fact. *Sheaffer v. Scott Valley Union High School Dist.*, No. C059862, 2010 WL 109724 (Cal. Ct. App. 1/13/10).

♦   An Arizona special education student was assaulted by other students after he was left unattended. His parents sued the district for negligence, **asserting that the school failed to constantly supervise the students involved in the assault** in violation of an internal policy, and that this violated the student's due process rights. A federal court and the Ninth Circuit ruled against them. They failed to show that the district had a policy or custom of deliberate indifference to student due process rights. *Ramirez v. Glendale Union High School Dist. No. 205*, 319 Fed.Appx. 683 (9th Cir. 2009).

♦   A disabled California student had an IEP that called for full-time adult supervision. She had held hands with a male student on more than one occasion and later went with him unsupervised to a greenhouse on campus, where he made sexual advances toward her. Her family sued the district for negligence and lost. **The student's IEP did not require the district to supervise her every minute** she was on campus. Further, the hand-holding did not make it foreseeable that the male student would make sexual advances toward her during one brief, unsupervised period. *M.P. v. Chico Unified School Dist.*, No. C057770, 2009 WL 226005 (Cal. Ct. App. 2/2/09).

♦   A male special needs student approached a multiply handicapped female student in the cafeteria and led her to a hidden alcove under a stairway, where he sexually assaulted her. Her representatives sued the Los Angeles school district for negligence, asserting that it had a special relationship with the disabled student and that it breached its affirmative duty of care to her. A state court granted pretrial judgment to the school district, but the court of appeal reversed, noting that **the harm in this case was foreseeable**. The yellow chain across the alcove designating it as off limits would not keep out a child who could not appreciate danger. *Jennifer C. v. Los Angeles Unified School Dist.*, 168 Cal.App.4th 1320, 86 Cal.Rptr.3d 274 (Cal. Ct. App. 2008).

♦   A disabled New York student was injured when a classmate picked him up and dropped him on the lavatory floor. His parents sued the school district, claiming it should have known not to let the students use the lavatory together. They alleged that the other student had picked up their son during class and spun him around with the knowledge of school staff. The Supreme Court, Appellate Division, refused to grant pretrial judgment to the district. It found that **the district had some notice of the classmate's dangerous behavior**. And the district had not shown that its lack of supervision was not a cause of the injury. *Johnson v. Ken-Ton Union Free School Dist.*, 850 N.Y.S.2d 813 (N.Y. App. Div. 2008).

♦   A disabled Kentucky student claimed she was sexually assaulted by a male student while the class was watching a movie and the teacher was playing a computer game. The student sued the school board under Title IX and the Kentucky Civil Rights Act, and a federal court found no federal violations. A state court then ruled for the school board on the Kentucky Civil Rights Act claims, and it refused to let her add a claim against the teacher and associate principal for **negligent supervision**. The Kentucky Court of Appeals held she should have been allowed to add those claims. They addressed different issues than those considered by the federal court. *A.R. v. Fayette County Board of Educ.*, No. 2004-CA-002377-ME, 2007 WL 127775 (Ky. Ct. App. 1/19/07).

♦   A Michigan student with disabilities was repeatedly threatened by another disabled student. His mother complained to the principal and a teacher, both of whom assured her that her son would be protected. The classmate was suspended for a week, but then returned to the student's classroom. After class one day, the classmate assaulted the student, pushing him into a locker. The mother removed the student from school and they moved to North Carolina. When she sued the school board, a federal court held that she did not have to exhaust her administrative remedies. However, the school board was not liable for her son's injuries because **it did not increase the risk of harm to the student by allowing the classmate to return to the classroom. The assault took place in the hallway.** *Molina v. Board of Educ. of School Dist. for the City of Detroit*, No. 07-10948, 2007 WL 4454928 (E.D. Mich. 12/14/07).

♦   A Connecticut high school freshman with ADHD stood four feet seven inches tall and weighed 75 pounds. While attending a public school under an IEP, he was subjected to harassment and bullying by fellow students, including being stuffed into a backpack and being treated like a baby. After his parents removed him from the school, they sued the school board and officials under 42 U.S.C. § 1983. A federal court ruled against them, noting that **the student had**

been discriminated against and bullied because of his size, not his disability. Although the treatment by his fellow students was repugnant, it did not amount to a constitutional violation. *Smith v. Guilford Board of Educ.*, No. Civ.A. 303 CV 1829 (WWE), 2005 WL 3211449 (D. Conn. 11/30/05).

♦   An 18-year-old Texas student with Down syndrome was passing between classes when a male student grabbed her, pulled her into a boys' lavatory and sexually assaulted her. The student's stepmother sued the district for constitutional rights violations, claiming it failed to supervise and properly train the staff, leading to the assault. A federal court ruled against her, noting that **the district did not have a special relationship with the student** that required providing increased protection. *Teague v. Texas City Independent School Dist.*, 386 F.Supp.2d 893 (S.D. Tex. 2005).

♦   After a classmate teased and then hit a disabled student in the eye, the student's mother sued the school board under 42 U.S.C. § 1983, alleging constitutional violations. An Alabama federal court ruled against the mother, finding no due process violation based on **the school's alleged deliberate indifference** to a risk of harm by a third party. Even if the school was deliberately indifferent to the student's rights, that was not enough for liability under Section 1983. *Walton v. Montgomery County Board of Educ.*, 371 F.Supp.2d 1318 (M.D. Ala. 2005).

♦   A Florida student with known developmental problems and sexually aggressive behavior sexually assaulted a kindergartner in the lavatory. The assault occurred when the regular teacher was absent and a substitute did not abide by the school's lavatory pass procedure. The kindergartner sued the school board for **negligence in failing to inform the substitute about the sexually aggressive student** and the lavatory pass procedure. A jury awarded the kindergartner money damages, and the Florida District Court of Appeal upheld the award. *Miami-Dade County School Board v. A.N.*, 905 So.2d 203 (Fla. Dist. Ct. App. 2005).

♦   A mentally retarded eighth-grade student who functioned at the third-grade level was dropped off by his mother about 7:15 each day. The school provided specific supervisory duties for teachers at 7:45, but before that time had only a general supervision policy. The student was subjected to teasing and ridicule on a daily basis. After a disabled classmate with a history of defiance and aggressive behavior sexually assaulted the student on two separate occasions, the student told his mother about the attacks. The classmate was then arrested and expelled. Two years later, the student attempted suicide after classmates locked him in a portable toilet. He sued the school district for negligence, and a jury awarded him almost $2.4 million in damages. The California Court of Appeal affirmed the award, noting that **schools have a special relationship with students that imposes a duty to protect**. Further, the state constitution mandated that students have the right to safe, secure and peaceful campuses. The court found that the assault was reasonably foreseeable given the classmate's many grave acts of defiance and violent behavior. Also, the school district was not entitled to immunity because the principal had no discretion with respect to protecting students. *M.W. v. Panama Buena Union School Dist.*, 1 Cal.Rptr.3d 673 (Cal. Ct. App. 2003).

♦   A disabled New York student with a medical port attended a special education class for students with behavioral problems. While being supervised by a teacher and a teaching assistant, he told a male classmate to stop bothering a female classmate. In response, the male classmate kicked him in the chest, breaking his medi-port and causing him injury. His family sued the school district and lost. The Appellate Division affirmed. Here, **the incident occurred without warning, and it could not have been prevented by any level of supervision**. Since the district provided a level of supervision at least as high as what a prudent parent would have provided, no liability attached. *Cranston v. Nyack Public Schools*, 756 N.Y.S.2d 610 (N.Y. App. Div. 2003).

♦   During the seventh grade, a student with epilepsy became the subject of taunting and teasing. She and her mother complained to the school on many occasions that other students called her "ugly dog," "seizure girl" and "lesby." Various school officials met with some of the boys accused of teasing the student and explained that their behavior was unacceptable. The vice principal informed teachers that they should send students to his office immediately if anyone said any harassing things to the student. Despite these measures, the student's parents removed her from school. When they sued, they lost because there was no evidence that the board was deliberately indifferent to the student. **The school responded each and every time the student or her mother complained.** The court dismissed the case. *Biggs v. Board of Educ. of Cecil County, Maryland*, 229 F.Supp.2d 437 (D. Md. 2002).

3. Injuries to Others

♦   A New York child with severe autism hit and kicked an occupational therapist, who then sued the child's parents and the district for negligence. An appellate division court upheld the ruling against the therapist because the parents had no ability to control their child in school and they had **no duty to warn the therapist because the therapist knew of the student's condition** and it could also be readily observed. *Johnson v. Cantie*, 905 N.Y.S.2d 384 (N.Y. App. Div. 2010).

♦   A New York City special education teacher initiated a Type Three referral to remove an aggressive student from her class, and contemplated quitting because of his behavior. Her supervisors told her to "hang in there" because a Type Three referral could take up to 60 days. Forty-one days after the referral was initiated, the student attacked another child and the teacher intervened. She sustained injuries while attempting to protect the other child from the aggressor. She then sued the city for negligence, alleging that a "special relationship" supported her claim. A jury awarded her more than $512,000, but the New York Court of Appeals struck down the award of damages. It noted that **the teacher had no rational basis for relying on the assurances of the board of**

education. Thus, she was not lulled into a false sense of security that justified a finding of liability against the board. *DiNardo v. City of New York*, 921 N.E. 2d 585 (N.Y. 2009).

♦ An Ohio school aide supervised an autistic student who had previously injured fellow students on the bus. The aide rode with the student on the bus, and was hit and bitten by the student on one occasion. Later, the aide accompanied the student on a field trip to a bowling alley, where the aide intervened to protect another student from the autistic student's attack. The aide sustained injuries and sued the school board for negligence and civil rights violations, asserting a "state-created danger" theory. A federal court and the Sixth Circuit ruled in favor of the school board, noting that **the state did not create the danger or increase the risk to the aide**. The board was attempting to discharge its duties under the IDEA at the time of the injury. *Hunt v. Sycamore Community School Dist. Board of Educ.*, 542 F.3d 529 (6th Cir. 2008).

♦ An Illinois teacher sued a student's mother after the student attacked her in class, charging her with a scissors and screaming obscenities. She managed to disarm the student but sustained emotional injuries. A federal court held that the mother could not be liable for the teacher's injuries unless she knew of specific prior conduct by the student putting her on notice that the assault was likely to occur. Because the student's mother was not at the school and was thus not in a position to exercise immediate control over her son, and because **there was no proof that the mother should have known her son was likely to attack the teacher**, the lawsuit was dismissed. *Bland v. Candioto*, No. 04 C 8361, 2006 WL 2735501 (N.D. Ill. 9/21/06).

♦ After a school nurse in Pennsylvania was attacked by a special education student, she sued the district under 42 U.S.C. § 1983, alleging a "state-created danger." The judge applied a two-year statute of limitations on her claim and a jury found that none of the conduct alleged by the nurse occurred within that two-year period. She appealed, **asserting that she should be able to use the continuing violation doctrine to recover damages from the district**. The Third Circuit rejected her argument, finding no school actions in the past two years that were sufficient to extend the limitations period. *Buchholz v. Midwestern Intermediate Unit IV*, 128 Fed.Appx. 890 (3d Cir. 2005).

♦ On a school bus, two emotionally disabled teenagers in North Carolina discussed committing robbery and murder with a gun that one student had access to. A bus attendant overheard the conversation and told the bus driver, but neither reported it to the school board, the police department or the mental health authority that ran the school they attended. A week later at 8:15 p.m., and not on school property, one of the students shot a person, severely injuring her. She sued the school board for negligence. The case reached the Supreme Court of North Carolina, which noted that the school board could not be held liable for the actions of third parties, such as the students, unless it had some "special relationship" with the students. As **no special relationship created a duty of**

supervision for the board at the time and place of the shooting, the board was not liable for negligence. *Stein v. Asheville City Board of Educ.*, 626 S.E.3d 263 (N.C. 2006).

♦   When the Indianapolis Public Schools (IPS) accidentally delivered a disabled three-year-old to the wrong house, the student's mother became frantic while waiting for the bus. She contacted the police department, and the student was finally returned to his home about three hours later. His mother sued the IPS for negligent infliction of emotional distress. The case reached the Court of Appeals of Indiana, which ruled for the IPS. Even though the mother did not have to prove she had suffered an actual physical impact to recover, **the delivery of her son to the wrong house did not create the grounds for a claim of negligent infliction of emotional distress.** *Ritchhart v. Indianapolis Public Schools*, 812 N.E.2d 189 (Ind. Ct. App. 2004).

♦   An Idaho physical therapist incurred injuries while helping a wheelchair-bound student off a bus. The reason she tried to help the student was because the aide provided by the school for assisting the student had a bad back. She sued the district for negligence, asserting that she was not limited to workers' compensation remedies because she was an independent contractor and not an employee of the school district. The case reached the Supreme Court of Idaho, which agreed with the lower court that **the district did not owe the therapist a legal duty.** Without a legal duty, there can be no breach of duty – an essential element of a negligence case. The school could not have foreseen that she would try to maneuver the student's wheelchair off the bus. Thus, even though she was an independent contractor, she could not sue the district for negligence. *Daleiden v. Jefferson County Joint School Dist.*, 80 P.3d 1067 (Idaho 2003).

♦   A special education teacher was assigned to a public school for students with severe behavioral problems, emotional disturbance and learning disabilities. The teacher agreed to drive a bus for special education students and began to document frequent and serious behavioral incidents on bus routes. His repeated requests for a monitor to supervise students during bus trips were denied. A student sprayed the teacher with a fire extinguisher while he was driving the bus. Although he was able to bring the bus to a safe stop, he suffered permanent injuries that rendered him unable to drive a bus or teach. He sued the school district in federal court, asserting due process violations for knowingly creating a dangerous environment on the bus and acting with deliberate indifference to his safety. He sought monetary damages under 42 U.S.C. § 1983 based on a "state-created danger theory," state law negligence and the Texas Tort Claims Act.

When the court ruled for the district, the teacher appealed to the Fifth Circuit, which affirmed. The Due Process Clause of the Fourteenth Amendment does not generally require the government to protect citizens from private parties. Even if there was a viable claim under this theory, the teacher failed to show that the district's conduct increased any danger he faced. **The students created any dangers present on the bus, and the fire extinguisher attack might have occurred regardless of whether a bus monitor was in place.** The district was not liable because it did not create or increase the danger to the teacher, and district officials were not deliberately indifferent to known dangers. *McKinney v. Irving Independent School Dist.*, 309 F.3d 308 (5th Cir. 2002).

♦   A psychologist diagnosed a Wisconsin grade school student as having ADHD. After the student repeatedly kicked, bit, spit, and yelled at other students and teachers, his psychologist prescribed Dexedrine, a medicine designed to reduce impulsive and aggressive behavior. The parents kept him on the medication for one term but then discontinued it without consulting the psychologist, teachers, or any member of the special education staff. The student again became disruptive. On one occasion, he pulled a teacher's hair, causing her to fall down a flight of stairs and suffer a herniated disc. The teacher sued the parents and their homeowner's insurer, alleging that the parents were negligent in failing to inform anyone at the school that they had stopped the student's medication. A state trial court held for the teacher, but an appeals court reversed. The teacher appealed.

The Supreme Court of Wisconsin held that **the parents' negligent conduct was a substantial cause of the teacher's injury.** They had inadequately researched both the consequences of discontinuing Dexedrine and alternative forms of treatment. They had also neglected to inform the school that the medication had been discontinued, precluding development of a plan to manage the student's behavior. The parents were negligent in failing to control the student, and their negligence was a substantial factor in causing the teacher's injuries. No public policy considerations precluded a finding of liability, and the supreme court reinstated the trial court's decision. *Nieuwendorp v. American Family Insurance Co.*, 529 N.W.2d 594 (Wis. 1995).

♦   The mother of a Florida student was severely injured when she was struck in the mouth by a 16-year-old junior high school student as she walked down a school corridor. The student had a long history of disciplinary problems. The injured parent sued the school board, claiming that it had breached a duty to protect her from a known or foreseeable threat of violence. A trial court granted the board summary judgment, stating that there was no evidence of prior violence by the student toward non-students and non-teachers that would place the school board on actual notice of an attack. The court of appeal noted that **the school board owed visitors a duty to keep reasonably safe conditions,** including a duty to protect parents and other visitors from reasonably foreseeable student attacks. Evidence indicated that the student was "extremely volatile and was becoming more difficult, unruly, and violent as time went on." The court reversed and remanded the case for a trial. *Garufi v. School Board of Hillsborough County*, 613 So.2d 1341 (Fla. Dist. Ct. App. 1993).

B. Negligent Placement

♦   A Massachusetts student who attended a middle school program for students with special needs was brutally beaten by a classmate. The classmate had recently transferred from another school, where he had allegedly threatened another student with a weapon. When the classmate arrived at the school, he was placed in a restrictive program for students with serious behavioral disorders. The program did not expressly apply to after-school activities. On the day of the beating, the classmate beat the student instead of boarding a school bus. The student suffered a permanent closed-head injury. Although the classmate was found delinquent in the state juvenile justice system, he returned to the school and was never disciplined. The student's parents sued the school committee, special education director, school psychologist and principal. The school defendants sought summary judgment on the parents' claims.

The court observed that school officials have no general constitutional duty to protect students from harmful conduct by classmates. Compulsory school attendance laws did not create a "special relationship" between the officials and the student that entitled him to heightened protection. At most, the officials demonstrated poor judgment by accepting the classmate into the restrictive program and failing to supervise him after school. This conduct did not rise to the level of a constitutional rights violation. The Massachusetts Torts Claims Act provided immunity for claims based on the exercise of discretion. **The placement of the student in a program involved a high degree of discretion and judgment by a special education team.** Also, the state tort claims act could not be used to hold public schools liable for the release of students after the regular school day. The officials were entitled to summary judgment. *Willhauck v. Town of Mansfield*, 164 F.Supp.2d 127 (D. Mass. 2001).

♦   A Virginia high school student was identified as having a learning disability when he was 18 years old. His parents claimed that the school district's failure to identify his disability while he was in the fourth grade violated a number of his rights. An administrative hearing officer denied their request for compensatory and punitive damages. They appealed to a federal court, seeking damages under the IDEA, Section 504, Virginia law and the U.S. Constitution for failing to identify the student's disability. The court dismissed the lawsuit, observing that the IDEA does not create a private cause of action for educational malpractice. Also, the Section 504 claim failed to state a valid cause of action because any damage recovery under Section 504 required a showing of intentional discrimination or bad faith, which the student had failed to allege. The parents appealed to the Fourth Circuit, which agreed with the district court that **the IDEA claim was indistinguishable from one for educational malpractice, which Virginia does not recognize**. Also, compensatory or punitive damages in an IDEA case were inconsistent with the IDEA's statutory scheme, and would transform the IDEA into a personal injury statute. Although other courts have allowed monetary damage awards on claims filed under Section 504, such claims require proof of bad faith or gross misjudgment, which had not been alleged here. The district court had properly dismissed the Rehabilitation Act and 42 U.S.C. § 1983 claims, and the court affirmed the judgment. *Sellers v. School Board of City of Manassas, Virginia*, 141 F.3d 524 (4th Cir. 1998).

♦   A New York student encountered great difficulty in his classes but consistently scored well on standardized citywide tests. The tests indicated that he was an above-average student, which resulted in his being placed in regular classes. He did not receive any special education services. The student finally received a learning disabled classification when he entered high school, and he was then placed in appropriate classes. He claimed that the school district's earlier failure to evaluate and properly place him constituted educational malpractice. He also claimed that his elementary school principal had altered his citywide test answer sheets, which had the effect of denying him access to special education programs and services. He sued for educational malpractice. The court refused to dismiss the lawsuit at the pretrial stage. The New York Supreme Court, Appellate Division, stated that New York did not recognize a legal cause of action for educational malpractice. Those portions of the complaint were dismissed. However, **the student's allegations of fraud and other intentional wrongdoing could be viable if properly pleaded and proven at trial**. The court allowed him an opportunity to refile claims for fraud and intentional tort. It would also be possible for the student to raise the question of the city board of education's knowledge of the principal's alleged wrongdoing based on the dramatic improvement in the ranking of his school as the result of city-wide test results. *Helbig v. City of New York*, 622 N.Y.S.2d 316 (N.Y. App. Div. 1995).

III. LIABILITY FOR INTENTIONAL CONDUCT

Parties injured as the result of intentional conduct by school employees or third parties, including students, have sought to hold school districts and their officials liable for constitutional rights violations. Courts have rejected claims for school district liability based on intentional conduct except where a special relationship exists between the victim and district and where proof of an official policy of deliberate indifference to the victim's clearly established constitutional rights exists. State compulsory attendance laws have been held not to create the required special relationship; instead, the victim must be completely dependent upon and in the custody of the agency for liability to attach, such as in cases of involuntary commitment or incarceration.

A. School Employees

♦ The parents of a Georgia student with autism suspected wrongdoing by his teacher because he came home with unexplained injuries. **They sewed a recording device into his shirt** and obtained audio of the teacher allegedly beating him and letting him eat garbage. She also allegedly taunted and ridiculed him. When they sued her for due process violations and emotional distress, she asked that the case be dismissed, but a federal court allowed the lawsuit to proceed. *Atlanta Independent School System v. S.F.*, 740 F.Supp.2d 1335 (N.D. Ga. 2010).

♦ A Florida teacher tried to break up a fight between two disabled students instead of calling the trained first responders she was supposed to call and simply using verbal commands to try to stop the fighting. She fell on her knee during the action and sustained injuries. Later, she sued the school board, asserting intentional conduct that qualified for an exception to the exclusivity of workers' compensation. However, the court of appeal ruled against her, noting that she was only entitled to collect workers' compensation for her injuries. She **failed to follow the school policy** requiring her to give only verbal instructions to the fighters until trained staff could arrive. *Patrick v. Palm Beach County School Board*, 50 So.3d 1161 (Fla. Dist. Ct. App. 2010).

◆   The parents of a mentally disabled Arizona student claimed her school bus aide allowed the driver to grab the child by the ankles and choke her for about two minutes. They also asserted the aide lifted their daughter by the wrist and failed to report the driver's misconduct. When they sued the district and the aide under Section 1983 for a violation of their daughter's constitutional rights, the aide sought to be dismissed from the case, but a federal court refused to do so. Since the parents **alleged that the aide participated in the misconduct** by grabbing their daughter's wrist and lifting her, the lawsuit could continue. *Rodriguez v. Case Grande Elementary School Dist. #4*, No. CV10-1904-PHX-DGC, 2010 WL 4629914 (D. Ariz. 11/8/10).

◆   A South Carolina special education teacher formed a close bond with a student and let him use her car, unaware that he did not have a license. She also gave him school computer passwords and wrote him excuses from his classes. The principal, after learning of her activity, fired her. She was also arrested and charged with contributing to the delinquency of a minor, but the charges were dropped. Later, the principal told a staff member that she had "cleaned [them] out," referring to the fact that when she left, she took a great deal of equipment that she had purchased. She sued the principal for defamation, among other claims, and the state court of appeals held that **she could pursue the defamation claim against the principal** because she was accused of a crime involving moral turpitude. *McBride v. School Dist. of Greenville County*, 698 S.E.2d 845 (S.C. Ct. App. 2010).

◆   The teacher of a Minnesota student took her to her resource room as a result of a behavior incident, as specified in her IEP, which also included a behavior intervention plan. On the way, she denied the student lavatory use, causing the student to have an accident. An investigation found that **the denial of lavatory use was merely a lapse in judgment**, so the teacher was not disciplined. The student's mother sued the district, but a federal court and the Eighth Circuit ruled against her, noting that the mother failed to allege anything that was "shocking to the contemporary conscience," and that there had been no due process or Fourth Amendment violation. *C.N. v. Willmar Public Schools, ISD No. 347*, 591 F.3d 624 (8th Cir. 2010).

◆   A Georgia student with emotional and behavioral issues as well as ADHD **made suicidal comments to staff members but told a school psychologist he had been kidding** about them. He was hospitalized for two weeks and then released. The school placed him in its time-out room for most of two days due to disruptive behavior. He made suicidal threats again. Several days later, after picking a fight with another student, he was sent to the time-out room again, where he hanged himself. His parents sued the school system and the state department of education. The Georgia Court of Appeals ruled against them, noting that the defendants did not disregard the student's rights in a manner that could be deemed deliberately indifferent. Apparently, the time-out monitors had not been made aware of the student's prior suicidal threats. *King v. Pioneer Regional Educ. Service Agency*, 688 S.E.2d 7 (Ga. Ct. App. 2009).

◆ After a Florida special education teacher was found guilty of a single count of aggravated child abuse, an autistic student sued the school board, asserting that the teacher had improperly restrained him, cursed him and hit him on the knees. He claimed she also abused other students, which caused him psychological harm. A federal court ruled against the student, noting that **the restraints had been to prevent the student from running away** and that he had never sought any treatment for his knee injuries. Also, the student had previously stated that the teacher was a good teacher and that she was nice. This helped defeat his claims. *G.C. v. School Board of Seminole County, Florida*, 639 F.Supp.2d 1295 (M.D. Fla. 2009).

◆ A Minnesota special education cooperative conducted daily searches of disabled students at segregated facilities. Many of the students attending the program had serious behavior problems, and a primary disability for several of them was emotional/behavior disorder. Five students sued the co-op, asserting that the searches violated their Fourth Amendment rights. A federal court agreed with the students that the searches violated the Fourth Amendment. The programs were educational in nature and not punitive, thereby granting the students greater privacy rights. **Daily, suspicionless searches were unreasonable and unconstitutional.** *Hough v. Shakopee Public Schools*, 608 F.Supp.2d 1087 (D. Minn. 2009).

◆ A New Mexico student with severe emotional and mental health problems had an IEP with a behavior intervention plan designed to teach him to control his dangerous outbursts. The IEP authorized placement in supervised timeouts when his behavior was disruptive. To be released from the timeout room, he had to remain calm and silent for five minutes, and he was sometimes carried into the timeout room. His mother eventually challenged the use of the timeout room, claiming it violated the IDEA and the Fourth Amendment as an unlawful seizure. The case reached the Tenth Circuit, which ruled that the IEP and the use of the timeout room did not violate the student's rights. *Couture v. Board of Educ. of Albuquerque Public Schools*, 535 F.3d 1243 (10th Cir. 2008).

◆ An Ohio student's mother had a deteriorating relationship with their school district, partly over a dispute relating to the administration of insulin shots to the student during the school day. She refused to tell the school nurse what her daughter ate at home, considering that an invasion of privacy. She wrote a letter to a paper expressing her concerns about the way her child was being treated at school. An anonymous tip to family services resulted in a complaint against the mother that was later dismissed. She then sued the school board for retaliating against her. A federal court dismissed the lawsuit, finding no protected First

Amendment right in the mother's letter to the newspaper because her comments addressed only her daughter's treatment and not a matter of public concern. There was also no invasion of privacy by the nurse who sought dietary information. On appeal, the Sixth Circuit reversed. **All the mother's comments were protected under the First Amendment.** And a jury could conclude that the superintendent's actions were retaliatory. However, the school board could not be held liable as it had no policy or custom of depriving parents of their civil rights. *Jenkins v. Rock Hill School Dist.*, 513 F.3d 580 (6th Cir. 2008).

◆   The parents of a Missouri student with autism sued their school district, claiming that the principal stalked and harassed their son. However, the Eighth Circuit Court of Appeals noted that they stated only conclusions rather than specific facts. Further, **they did not suggest that their son was deprived of access to educational benefits as a result of the alleged harassment,** nor did they assert that he did not receive the services mandated by his IEP. *Stringer v. St. James R-I School Dist.*, 446 F.3d 799 (8th Cir. 2006).

◆   A Florida child with multiple personality disorder had a history of violence, including threats against his teachers. The district **placed him in a new school without informing his teachers of his propensity for violence.** After he attacked and injured a teacher, she sued the district under the intentional tort exception to workers' compensation immunity. Before trial, the court held that workers' compensation was her exclusive remedy. The District Court of Appeal reversed, finding a trial was necessary. If the district "should have known" that its conduct was substantially certain to result in injury, it would not be entitled to immunity. *Patrick v. Palm Beach County School Board*, 927 So.2d 973 (Fla. Dist. Ct. App. 2006).

◆   An 11-year-old disabled student pointed a toy gun at a teaching assistant and yelled, "Bang!" The teaching assistant claimed she suffered mental and emotional trauma, and she collected workers' compensation benefits from the school board. The school board then sought to recover its costs from the student's mother, but the Court of Appeal of Louisiana ruled against it. Even though parents are liable for damages caused by their children that create an unreasonable risk of injury to others, **the board failed to show that an 11-year-old disabled child should have reasonably foreseen psychological injury** to the teaching assistant. The school board could not recover its costs. *Lafayette Parish School Board v. Cormier*, 901 So.2d 1197 (La. Ct. App. 2005).

◆   A Washington student with autism inflicted frequent injuries on students and staff. After a change in his medication, his behavior worsened, and he injured students or teachers more than once a week. He pushed one teacher who tried to intervene during one of his attacks, and she fell to the floor, where she was knocked unconscious. The next day, he bit another teacher on the breast as she tried to distract him from other students. Both teachers received workers' compensation benefits and then sued the school district for additional damages, **asserting that it deliberately intended their injuries.** A court ruled for the district, and the Supreme Court of Washington affirmed. An employer's failure to observe safety laws and procedures does not constitute specific intent to injure. Here, the district had attempted a series of increasingly restrictive strategies for bringing the student's behavior under control. The employees did not show that the district could have been certain they would fail. *Vallandigham v. Clover Park School Dist. No. 400*, 109 P.3d 805 (Wash. 2005).

♦ A Kansas paraprofessional began working with a 12-year-old student who had behavior problems and had threatened suicide. The principal later became concerned about the paraprofessional's numerous requests to see the student but did not suspect any inappropriate behavior by the paraprofessional. As time went by, the student became friends with the paraprofessional's son and occasionally slept over at the paraprofessional's house. At one point, after the student made an inappropriate comment during a sleepover, the paraprofessional reported it and was told not to have further contact with the student. Nevertheless, she continued to see the student. Subsequently, she admitted to having sexual contact with the student. The student sued the school district for negligence, but a federal court and the Tenth Circuit U.S. Court of Appeals ruled against him. Here, **the paraprofessional's molestation was not foreseeable**, so the district could not be liable for negligent hiring and retention. *Kurtz v. Unified School Dist. No. 308*, 65 Fed.Appx. 257 (10th Cir. 2003).

B. Sexual Abuse Reporting

♦ A teacher's aide observed irritation and swelling when changing the diaper of a severely disabled nine-year-old student and contacted the principal, who contacted the police. A state trooper and a social worker became involved and, after two later occurrences where it looked like the student had been sexually abused, the principal, trooper and social worker took the student to a doctor for an examination. The doctor found no evidence of sexual abuse. When the student's parents sued the teacher's aide, principal, trooper and social worker, a court ruled for the defendants. The Michigan Court of Appeals agreed that the teacher's aide and principal were immune. It also found the trooper and social worker could not be held liable for their warrantless search of the student's person because of probable cause and exigent circumstances. *Britton v. Beauchaine*, No. 244640, 2003 WL 22462122 (Mich. Ct. App. 10/30/03).

♦ A teacher's aide noticed abnormalities in the genital area of a nine-year-old student with severe disabilities and alerted the teacher, who notified the principal, who contacted a state trooper. Although the trooper suspected child abuse, she could not verify her suspicions and asked school employees to inform her immediately if they discovered further symptoms. Several weeks later, the principal reported additional symptoms. The trooper instructed the principal to take the student to a doctor's office immediately. However, the trooper did not obtain a court order allowing an examination. A child protection worker signed a consent form purporting to authorize the exam. The laboratory results did not indicate sexual abuse. The trooper then met with the student's parents and accused the father of molesting his daughter. No evidence of abuse was discovered, and no charges were ever filed.

The student's conservator sued the aide, principal, trooper and child protection worker, alleging false imprisonment, battery and constitutional rights violations. The court ruled for the government employees, finding they were entitled to immunity under the state Child Protection Law since they were engaged in a good-faith investigation of child abuse. The Michigan Court of Appeals agreed that there could be no personal monetary liability by government employees for constitutional rights violations arising from an unlawful search and seizure. **The trial court had properly dismissed the remaining claims against the aide and principal under the Child Protection Law, which immunizes persons who act in good faith in reporting abuse, or otherwise cooperating or assisting in an investigation.** The aide's observations created reasonable cause to believe that the student was a victim of child abuse. Even though no charges were ever filed against the parents, the principal acted in good faith when she took the student to the doctor's office. However, the trooper and child protection worker were not entitled to immunity under the Child Protection Law because they made no effort to obtain a court order prior to the exam. *Lavey v. Mills*, 639 N.W.2d 261 (Mich. Ct. App. 2001).

◆   Three special education students were sexually abused by a teacher. Allegedly, they informed their homeroom teacher about the abuse, but she did not report it for several weeks. According to the students, the teacher's abuse did not stop until a doctor reported it to the Massachusetts Department of Social Services (DSS). The DSS took immediate action after receiving the report. The homeroom teacher eventually reported the allegations to a city civil rights officer. She asserted that she was unaware that state law and Boston Public Schools policy required immediate reporting of such incidents to the DSS. The civil rights officer also failed to contact DSS, as did a school special education supervisor and school principal who learned of the suspected abuse. The students sued the city and a number of school employees in a federal court under Title IX, 42 U.S.C. § 1983 and state law.

The city had a written policy requiring teachers to immediately report sexual abuse charges to the DSS. However, **there was evidence to support a finding that the city failed to train employees under this policy or to ensure employees were aware of their reporting requirements**. The court denied the city's motion for dismissal on the Section 1983 and Title IX claims. It rejected the city's argument that it was not on "actual notice" of the abuse. There was evidence the school principal had knowledge of the allegations before the doctor made his report. Also, all four school employees who were notified of the teacher's abuse had the power to stop it. The Title IX and Section 1983 claims against the city would proceed to trial. *Booker v. City of Boston*, No. CIV.A.97-CV-12534MEL, 2000 WL 1868180 (D. Mass. 12/12/00).

◆   A Texas family enrolled their four-year-old child in a school for speech therapy. Although a teacher had received only one training session in the use of facilitated communication (FC), she decided to use FC with the student without the parents' consent. Despite the student's inability to read or write, she produced messages indicating her father had sexually abused her. A state agency then initiated parental rights termination proceedings. The father was denied contact with the student for three years, and the mother was allowed only supervised visits, even though there was no medical evidence of abuse. The state dismissed the parental termination action, but the parents asserted that the charges destroyed their marriage, cost the father his job and deprived them of three years of contact with their child. They sued the teacher, school district and others. When the court denied the teacher's motion for summary judgment, she appealed to the Fifth Circuit.

The court stated that the right to family integrity was clearly protected by the Constitution, and the district court had correctly determined that a teacher's fabrication of sexual abuse by a parent was shocking to the conscience. The use of a highly controversial FC device with a four-year-old who could not read or write was a clear abuse of governmental power. **The teacher was deemed to know that she could not manufacture false evidence of sexual abuse.** Accordingly, she was not entitled to immunity. *Morris v. Dearborne*, 181 F.3d 657 (5th Cir. 1999).

The district court then considered the motion for summary judgment filed by the Texas Department of Protective and Regulatory Services and the employees named in the suit. It held that the county employees were not entitled to immunity. They depended on unreliable information and omitted pertinent information in official reports. No sensible person would defend the belief that holding an illiterate child's wrists would make her capable of generating the disputed reports, and the county employees' actions shocked the conscience. The employees conducted a sham investigation, withheld evidence, violated state law and agency policies and procedures, and misrepresented facts to a court. *Morris v. Dearborne*, 69 F.Supp.2d 868 (E.D. Tex. 1999).

C. Third Parties

◆ A Minnesota teacher was threatened by a parent who demanded speech therapy for her son. The teacher obtained a state court harassment restraining order against the parent. The order did not prevent the parent from coming to school, but it did prevent her from coming near the teacher's second-floor classroom. On two later occasions, the teacher saw the parent at school. The first time, she called 911 and left early. The second time, she told the principal to take her students to the bus and also left early. After the school admonished her, she sued it for negligence. The Minnesota Court of Appeals agreed with the school that it was entitled to immunity. **The district's anti-harassment policy did not apply to parents**, and school officials did not commit any willful or malicious wrong. *Ellison-Harpole v. Special School Dist. No. 1*, No. A07-1070, 2008 WL 933537 (Minn. Ct. App. 4/8/08).

◆ A disabled Wisconsin student with physical deformities endured verbal attacks and mockery by other students. Two boys in shop class also threw pieces of wood at him. He sustained injuries; they were suspended. He was allowed to leave classes early so he could avoid others in the hallway. A third shop student then threw safety glasses at him, causing a concussion and cracked teeth. That student was also suspended. When the disabled student sued the school board and the shop teacher for violating his equal protection and due process rights by failing to protect him from his fellow students, a Wisconsin federal court noted that **he could not prove intentional discrimination**. The shop teacher did not treat him differently than non-disabled students, and the attacks came from different students. There was also no ADA or Rehabilitation Act violation. *Werth v. Board of Directors of the Public Schools of City of Milwaukee*, 472 F.Supp.2d 1113 (E.D. Wis. 2007).

♦   A California school district suspended and counseled a defiant and violent student after various troubling incidents. The student was classified as having an emotional disturbance. His parents insisted he remain in a regular classroom. One day the student knocked down a classmate, and his teacher accompanied him to the bus to ensure he sat right behind the driver. However, the student charged the teacher, knocking her down and injuring her. She obtained workers' compensation benefits and sought an additional award on the grounds that the district had engaged in serious and willful misconduct by failing to remove the student from class. After an administrative ruling in her favor, the California Court of Appeal reversed, holding that **the district did not deliberately or consciously fail to take action for the teacher's safety**. *Elk Grove Unified School Dist. v. Workers' Compensation Appeals Board*, No. C052945, 2007 WL 1169336 (Cal. Ct. App. 4/20/07).

♦   A 13-year-old African-American student with autism transitioned to junior high school and became aggressive in response to some teasing and new classroom experiences. She was led to the school office, where a police officer was stationed, and grew more aggressive when he confronted her. According to the parents, the officer "panicked and pepper-sprayed" their daughter in the face, then handcuffed her, which aggravated the situation. The parents sued the district and municipal police department in a California federal court for civil rights violations and discrimination relating to the handcuffing and later exclusion of the student from the district. The court dismissed the federal claims against the district as barred by the Eleventh Amendment. However, the pepper-spraying and handcuffing of a 13-year-old mentally disabled child was shocking. **The district had a duty to protect the student from the use of excessive force by the police**, based on a special relationship. The due process claim required a trial. *Banks v. Modesto City School Dist.*, No. CVF046284RECSMS, 2005 WL 2233213 (E.D. Cal. 9/9/05).

♦   A New York high school student with learning disabilities had behavior problems and was transferred to a learning center operated by a board of cooperative services. However, he continued to hang around the school. While in the school hallway, he punched another student in the mouth. The injured student's family sued the school district for negligence, but the Supreme Court, Appellate Division, ruled that the school district should have had the case dismissed. Here, **the incident was unforeseeable**, sudden, unprovoked and of extremely short duration. The student would have been injured by the punch regardless of the level of supervision. *Nocilla v. Middle Country Cent. School Dist.*, 757 N.Y.S.2d 300 (N.Y. App. Div. 2003).

◆ The parents of a student with a visual impairment sued their school district, alleging the district committed civil rights violations when it placed the student in a fourth-grade class with another student who had tormented and abused her the previous school year. The district was allegedly aware of the abuse. A New York federal court ruled in favor of the district, and the Second Circuit affirmed. Although **Section 1983 claims are not barred if state officials in some way assist in creating a danger or increasing the risk of harm** to the complaining party, the student's parents failed to allege that the school district was warned of the classmate's alleged abusive conduct during grade three. The mother's sworn statement indicated only that she had requested that the students be separated and that the request had been refused. This was insufficient for a reasonable jury to conclude that the classmate had abused the student. *Robertson v. Arlington Cent. School Dist.*, 229 F.3d 1136 (2d Cir. 2000).

D. Sexual Assault

◆ A 16-year-old Philadelphia student with mild mental retardation and a language disorder was led by a male student to an auditorium balcony normally closed to students. Five male students managed to gain entry to the area and sexually assaulted her there. Her family sued the district and various school officials for constitutional violations as well as for negligence. However, a federal court ruled for the defendants, noting that no action by the district or its officials caused the injury to the student. And **the male students had no prior record of sexual assault** to put the officials on notice that they might attack the girl. *Brown v. School Dist. of Philadelphia*, No. 08-2787, 2010 WL 2991741 (E.D. Pa. 7/28/10).

◆ A California student with an IQ of 55 often flirted with a male friend on the bus. One day, she reported that he kissed her buttocks and breast over her clothing after she said, "Kiss my ass." Police were called, but the driver had seen nothing and the officers believed the incident was merely teenage flirting that had gotten out of hand. The student's mother filled out a citizen's arrest form and insisted on the friend's removal from school. Later, she sued the district for negligence. A jury ruled for the district, and the court of appeal affirmed. **The student failed to prove that she was sexually assaulted by her long-time friend**, and the trial court properly admitted evidence of the student's own sexual conduct, which went to the issue of the student's emotional distress. *Brittany P. v. Sweetwater Union High School Dist.*, No. D053932, 2009 WL 4817839 (Cal. Ct. App. 12/15/09).

◆ A Minnesota student with an emotional-behavioral disorder and a history of sexually inappropriate behavior was supposed to sit alone behind the bus driver, and his transportation form included that directive. However, the form did not detail his past history. He was allowed to move back in the bus at some point, and he sexually assaulted another student. When the other student sued the district, the Minnesota Court of Appeals held that **the district had immunity with respect to its decision to withhold the student's prior history of sexual misbehavior**. However, with respect to the failure to follow directions and keep the student in the seat behind the driver, the bus service had no immunity. *J.W. v. 287 Intermediate Dist.*, 761 N.W.2d 896 (Minn. Ct. App. 2009).

♦   A Michigan middle school student endured harassment and taunting by his peers and became withdrawn. The school talked to individual students who then stopped harassing him, but overall the harassment continued. After being identified as emotionally impaired and eligible for special education, he was allowed to use a resource room, whose teacher helped him cope with the harassment. When he moved on to ninth grade, he was not allowed to use the resource room anymore even though it adjoined the high school building. The harassment continued and he was then sexually assaulted. His family sued the district for violating Title IX, but a federal court granted pretrial judgment to the district. The Sixth Circuit reversed, finding issues of fact that required a trial. **The refusal to let the student use the resource room might be deliberate indifference** if the school knew its efforts to halt the harassment weren't working. *Patterson v. Hudson Area Schools*, 551 F.3d 438 (6th Cir. 2008).

♦   **Over a 16-year period, an Alabama physical education teacher was accused of five incidents of inappropriate touching and comments.** The district's personnel director investigated three of the incidents, which occurred at the high school. The teacher denied misconduct on each occasion and, after the investigations, written reports were placed in his personnel file. After the third incident, the teacher was transferred to an elementary school. The other two incidents did not involve physical contact but rather inappropriate comments. An 11-year-old fifth-grader with speech and learning disabilities was then allegedly raped by the teacher, though she did not report it until after she transferred out of his class and to another school. When she finally told a school counselor, the personnel director placed the teacher on administrative leave and began investigating. The teacher retired before the board made any final employment decision. Eventually the student sued the board and the personnel director for civil rights violations. The Supreme Court of Alabama ruled that the board was not entitled to immunity. However, the director was. *Madison County Board of Educ. v. Reaves*, 1 So.3d 980 (Ala. 2008).

♦   A seven-year-old Alabama student attended an intensive therapeutic placement center, which was described as an "alternative school for students with behavioral and emotional problems." Each day, the student rode a special education bus about 30 miles to the center. According to the student, a classmate sexually assaulted him on a day when a substitute driver drove the bus. The classmate denied the molestation, stating the two boys had only exposed themselves to each other. The student's parents sued the board and school officials in a federal court for negligence and civil rights violations. The case reached the Eleventh Circuit, which held that the Due Process clause does not require a state entity to protect citizens from private misconduct. **The student's special education status did not form a "special relationship"** creating a duty by the board to protect him from the classmate. *Worthington v. Elmore County Board of Educ.*, 160 Fed.Appx. 877 (11th Cir. 2005).

♦ An Illinois student attended a school for maladjusted boys. He rode a school bus with a disabled student who had been declared a sexually aggressive child and youth ward (SACY) and who had been placed under a protective plan requiring that he never be left with other children unsupervised. When the attendant who normally supervised students on the bus called in sick one day, the SACY assaulted the student. He and his family sued the Chicago School Board for negligence, alleging that the board knew or should have known that supervision was required on the bus at all times. The question of immunity reached the Supreme Court of Illinois, which ruled that the board was not entitled to it. Here, **the student had alleged "willful and wanton conduct" in the failure to supervise a dangerous student.** *Doe v. Chicago Board of Educ.*, 820 N.E.2d 418 (Ill. 2004).

♦ A resident advisor at a Delaware public school for the hearing impaired was also a recent graduate of the school. He had been the senior class president and a good student, with no indications that he might harbor sexually inappropriate thoughts. After graduating, he took the resident advisor position and then sexually abused a student every evening for three months until he was caught and arrested. The victimized student subsequently sued the school, and a state court found that the school was not liable. Here, it did not know, nor did it have reason to believe, that the resident advisor posed any danger to children at the school. Further, there could be no vicarious liability because **the abuse could not be deemed to have occurred within the scope of the resident advisor's employment at the school.** *Simms v. Christina School Dist.*, No. C.A. 02C-07-043 JTV, 2004 WL 344015 (Del. Super. Ct. 1/30/04).

E. Corporal Punishment

♦ A Florida student with autism sued his former teacher and school board based on five incidents of corporal punishment. He claimed that she violated his due process rights and also violated the Rehabilitation Act by abusing him in class, and pointed to her suspension and later conviction on one count of child abuse. However, he lost because four of the incidents he cited were related to his refusal to go to the cool-down room or his calling the teacher names or threatening her. The fifth incident involved her tripping him, which was not corporal punishment. And **in each case of corporal punishment, the teacher used restraint on the student only until he calmed down** or agreed to comply with her instructions. *T.W. v. School Board of Seminole County, Florida*, 610 F.3d 588 (11th Cir. 2010).

♦ An Alabama teacher administered corporal punishment to a student who had been held behind in school. She claimed that she struck him once, but he asserted that she repeatedly struck him, injuring his legs and one of his arms. He enrolled in another school and sued her and the school board for negligence. The teacher argued that she should be entitled to immunity without a trial, but the Supreme Court of Alabama ruled against her. **She violated the education board's own policy, which required her to have a witness present whenever corporal punishment was being administered.** Despite her and her supervisors' assertion that she couldn't leave the other students alone to go find a witness, a further inquiry into the matter was necessary. *Ex Parte Monroe County Board of Educ.*, No. 1090387, 2010 WL 1946266 (5/14/10).

♦ An Alabama student with disabilities, including autism, ADHD and impulse control disorder, was very disruptive one day, kicking his teacher in the shins. She attempted to calm him by placing him in a Rifton chair in the hallway for the approximately 10 minutes left until his mother was scheduled to pick him up. His mother found him alone and crying in the chair. When she sued the district for due process violations, a federal court ruled against her, noting that there was no claim of excessive force, the student was left alone for only 10 minutes, and **the teacher was trying to calm him by putting him in the Rifton chair**. *D.D. v. Chilton County Board of Educ.*, 701 F.Supp.2d 1236 (M.D. Ala. 2010).

♦ An autistic student claimed that **his special education teacher placed him in belts or straps in another student's wheelchair** and locked him in a darkened lavatory for up to 10 minutes on at least four occasions to punish him for off-task behavior. He sued the school board, alleging that the corporal punishment violated his Fourteenth Amendment due process rights, and the school board sought to dismiss the case. A federal court refused to do so, finding issues of fact that needed to be pursued. Here, the student's injuries appeared to be largely psychological, but he could not effectively communicate the extent of his injuries. *O.H. v. Volusia County School Board*, No. 6:07-CV-1545-Orl-22DAB, 2008 WL 2901044 (M.D. Fla. 7/23/08).

♦ Severely autistic twins in California attended an education center where "deep pressure" and other touching techniques were used. After staff members accused the twins' special education teacher of improper conduct, the principal investigated and made some suggestions. She also observed him in the classroom. Later, the twins' parents sued the school district for negligence, asserting that the teacher had committed a battery against them, pinching the girl and using too much pressure on the boy. A jury ruled for the district, finding no battery, and the California Court of Appeal affirmed. Here, the teacher did not intend to harm or offend the twins. **He used deep pressure on the boy to calm him, and pinched the girl to teach her not to pinch others.** State law contained a privilege for teachers to use the same degree of physical control over students that a parent could exercise. *Austin B. v. Escondido Union School Dist.*, 149 Cal.App.4th 860, 57 Cal.Rptr.3d 454 (Cal. Ct. App. 2007).

♦ The parents of an autistic Nevada student claimed that his teacher and teacher's aide assaulted, grabbed and threw him. They sued state and local officials. A federal court dismissed most of their claims, noting that there was no evidence the officials acted with deliberate indifference to the student's federally protected rights. However, there was **a possibility the parents could prove that the teacher and aide acted with malice while using corporal punishment on their son.** This due process claim required a trial. *Doe v. State of Nevada*, No. 02:03CV01500LRHRJJ, 2006 WL 2583746 (D. Nev. 9/7/06).

♦ A Kansas special education student with a history of behavioral issues, including hitting teachers, was issued a demerit by her teacher. She cursed and argued, so the teacher asked the student proctor to escort the student from the room. When the student continued to yell, the teacher slapped her face, leaving red marks. The student required no medical treatment and the teacher was reprimanded, although the extent of the discipline was not made known to the student. She later sued the district for violating her due process rights. A federal court ruled that **the single slap did not amount to a due process violation.** Further, the student had no property interest in knowing what discipline was taken against the teacher. *Holloman v. Unified School Dist. 259*, No. 05-1180-JTM, 2006 WL 1675932 (D. Kan. 6/15/06).

♦ An autistic student, while having what appeared to be a seizure, was placed on his stomach by school staff, with his shoulders and legs held down and his hands behind his back. After the student became non-responsive (about 45 minutes later), he was transported to a hospital, where he died of prolonged physical restraint. The Autism Society of Michigan then sued the school board for constitutional rights violations arising out of its restraint policies. A federal court held that **the autism society had no standing to sue** and dismissed the case. *Autism Society of Michigan v. Fuller*, No. 05:05-CV-73, 2006 WL 1519966 (W.D. Mich. 5/26/06).

♦ After a Tennessee student with autism refused to turn off a computer and kicked his aide, **the aide kicked the student and threw him to the floor.** The student was not seriously injured, but his parents sued the aide and the district for violating the student's Fourteenth Amendment right to be free from bodily injury. A federal court held that the aide's conduct did not "shock the conscience." The aide simply used excessive force to restrain or discipline the student. Also, the parents were not entitled to an award for negligent failure to train or supervise the aide. *Fessler v. Giles County Board of Educ.*, No. 1-00-0120, 2005 WL 1868793 (M.D. Tenn. 7/27/05).

♦ A teacher's aide in Mississippi, while escorting an autistic student in a hallway, **had to grab the student and hold his arms to prevent him from hurting himself** after the student had an outburst caused by a ringing bell and a rush of students. When the student's father discovered bruises, he sued the district, teacher and aide for negligence and for using excessive force. The case reached the Court of Appeals of Mississippi, which ruled for the defendants. State law allows corporal punishment that is reasonably administered. Here, the aide's restraint of the student was intended to control and discipline him, and was not done with wanton or willful disregard of his rights or safety. *Pigford v. Jackson Public School Dist.*, 910 So.2d 575 (Miss. Ct. App. 2005).

♦ A student with ADHD had a history of misconduct, including violence against others. His parents agreed to a behavior management plan but rejected corporal punishment as an option. After the student bit a classmate during recess, the assistant principal administered three strokes to the student's buttocks with a regulation wooden paddle. The parents sued the school board for negligence and obtained an award of $45,000. The Louisiana Court of Appeal reversed, finding that the board's duty to provide a safe, disciplined school environment exceeded any private duty that might have resulted from the parents' request to refrain from paddling their child. Here, the student had a longstanding pattern of continual misbehavior, and **the paddling was administered only after other methods of punishment had failed.** *Setliff v. Rapides Parish School Board*, 888 So.2d 1156 (La. Ct. App. 2004).

◆   A Wisconsin student with mild autism had an IEP that instructed his teachers to take him to a particular room when he became anxious and frustrated. During an English class, the student began to cry when a disagreement arose among students in his group. He refused to comply with the teacher's instruction to report to the room specified in his IEP. The teacher pushed the student to the wall to get him to stop struggling, then physically removed him from the classroom. He sued the district and some employees for battery and negligence, but the Wisconsin Court of Appeals ruled against him. The teacher lacked the intent to hurt the student. Further, **removing the student from class in accordance with his IEP was not corporal punishment.** *Loy v. Dodgeville School Dist.*, 688 N.W.2d 783 (Wis. Ct. App. 2004).

IV. AWARDS AND DAMAGES

A. Attorneys' Fees

In *Smith v. Robinson*, 468 U.S. 992, 104 S.Ct. 3457, 82 L.Ed.2d 746 (1984), the U.S. Supreme Court held that attorneys' fees were not recoverable for special education claims made under the IDEA. Congress responded by enacting the Handicapped Children's Protection Act (HCPA) (20 U.S.C. § 1415(i)(3)), a 1986 amendment to the IDEA, which allows recovery of attorneys' fees where a student or guardian prevails in "any action or proceeding." The HCPA overruled *Smith*.

1. Administrative Proceedings

◆   The parents of a California student repeatedly challenged their son's classification, believing he had autism. District evaluations indicated that the student had mental retardation. The parents hired the student's grandmother as their attorney, and an administrative law judge determined that the student should have been classified under both categories, but that he was not denied a FAPE because he received special education services. When the parents sought their attorneys' fees, the Ninth Circuit ruled that they were entitled to them. The grandmother was not barred from receiving attorneys' fees, and the parents were prevailing parties in the administrative proceedings **because the correct classification made the student eligible for teachers with relevant qualifications.** *Weissburg v. Lancaster School Dist.*, 591 F.3d 1255 (9th Cir. 2009).

♦ West Virginia parents entered into mediation with their school board over the education of their autistic son. Eventually they rejected the board's settlement offer. A hearing officer then ruled for the parents on four of five issues but found that the board had offered an appropriate IEP. The parents appealed the IEP issue and sought attorneys' fees of $112,292. A federal court upheld the IEP decision and ruled that the board could not assert that its settlement offer was better than what the parents received from the hearing officer because mediation discussions are confidential and the parties had signed an agreement prohibiting releasing that information to anyone, including a judge. **The court reduced the attorneys' fee award to $34,072 to reflect the failure to prevail on the IEP issue.** *J.D. v. Kanawha County Board of Educ.*, 571 F.3d 381 (4th Cir. 2009).

♦ New York parents reached a favorable agreement with a school district over eligibility for one student and evaluation and additional services for another student receiving special education. However, the district refused to pay their attorneys' fees. The parents requested due process and, just before the hearing, agreed to a consent decree that included a provision for attorneys' fees. The hearing officer signed the consent decrees, and the parents then sought to be paid attorneys' fees. The case reached the Second Circuit, which held that **they became prevailing parties when the hearing officer signed the consent decrees.** *V.G. v. Auburn Enlarged Cent. School Dist.*, 349 Fed.Appx. 582 (2d Cir. 2009).

♦ A Hawaii student with a major depressive disorder (and a history of difficulty with transitions) transitioned from elementary school to intermediate school. However, the Hawaii Department of Education (DOE) did not increase the hours of mental health services she received to help with the transition despite her therapist's recommendations. She had a "meltdown" on the second day. Her mother challenged the DOE's refusal to increase mental health services, and a hearing officer ruled in her favor. **The DOE later offered an IEP with appropriate mental health services.** When the mother sought attorneys' fees, a federal court held that she was entitled to prevailing party status, and thus her fees. *Dep't of Educ., State of Hawaii v. Leialoha J.*, Civ. No. 08-00077 ACK-BMK, 2008 WL 4761793 (D. Haw. 10/29/08).

♦ The mother of a California student filed a due process request against the school district for failing to conduct a timely eligibility assessment and inappropriately finding the student ineligible for special education. The school then began an assessment of the student. After a hearing officer ruled that the district had denied the student a free appropriate public education, the mother sought attorneys' fees. The Ninth Circuit U.S. Court of Appeals held that attorneys' fees were indicated in this case because without the hearing officer's decision that the student had a qualifying disability under the IDEA, the school would not have had to conduct the assessment of the student. This made the mother the prevailing party. *V.S. v. Los Gatos-Saratoga Joint Union High School Dist.*, 484 F.3d 1230 (9th Cir. 2007).

♦   The mother of a California student challenged the implementation of his IEP, raising 27 issues. **A hearing officer ruled in her favor on four of the 27 issues.** She then petitioned for her attorneys' fees as a prevailing party. A federal court awarded her about half of the $42,000 she sought, noting that she had prevailed on a significant issue in litigation. The Ninth Circuit, however, vacated the judgment and ordered the lower court to consider the mother's degree of success when awarding the fees, keeping in mind that she prevailed on only four issues. *Aguirre v. Los Angeles Unified School Dist.*, 461 F.3d 1114 (9th Cir. 2006).

♦   The parents of an autistic New Jersey student challenged the amount of at-home ABA therapy he was to receive per week. They also challenged the methodology used by the district in educating him while he was in school. They reached a written agreement on one of the issues in dispute. A hearing officer then denied the district's request to reduce ABA therapy to six hours a week, but also refused to increase it to 21 hours a week as the parents wished. When the parents sued for their attorneys' fees as prevailing parties, a federal appeals court ruled that **they could recover only 20% of their attorneys' fees because they did not prevail on the issue of methodology** of instruction, which was one of the most significant issues in dispute. *A.S. v. Colts Neck Board of Educ.*, 190 Fed.Appx. 140 (3d Cir. 2006).

♦   The parents of a New Jersey student filed a due process request, challenging their district's classification, assessment and methodology. They wanted to place their son in a private school; the district sought to place the student in a particular alternative middle school. An administrative law judge found that neither side had proposed an appropriate placement for the student. When the parents then sued for their attorneys' fees, a federal court ruled against them. **Since neither side had received the relief it sought, the parents were not prevailing parties** entitled to their attorneys' fees. *R.G. v. Union Township Board of Educ.*, Civil No. 05-2302 (GEB), 2006 WL 2668202 (D.N.J. 9/11/06).

♦   The parents of a Wisconsin student with disabilities rejected a district proposal to place their son in a regular classroom for half a day and asked for a due process hearing. The administrative law judge ruled that the student would not receive a satisfactory education in a regular classroom and ordered the IEP team to reconvene to revise the IEP and include appropriate mainstreaming opportunities. The parents then sought to recover their attorneys' fees. A federal court and the Seventh Circuit ruled against them. **The parents' success in getting the order for the IEP team to meet was minimal.** *Linda T. v. Rice Lake Area School Dist.*, 417 F.3d 704 (7th Cir. 2005).

♦   In separate administrative proceedings, four sets of parents obtained favorable settlement agreements with the New York City Education Department. They then sought to recover their attorneys' fees. The case reached the Second Circuit Court of Appeals, which held that they were entitled to "prevailing party" status because a federal court had issued orders implementing the points of agreement between the parties. Thus, **the** administrative orders were "administrative consent decrees." *A.R. v. New York City Dep't of Educ.*, 407 F.3d 65 (2d Cir. 2005).

♦ A Connecticut student with autism was placed in a neighboring district until that district decided to stop accepting non-resident, tuition-paying students. The student's residence district offered to place him in one of its schools, but the parents declined and obtained a stay-put order to allow him to stay in the neighboring school. A hearing officer then ruled that the neighboring district did not have to keep the student in the program it was terminating, and that the residence district offered a FAPE. The parents asked for their attorney fees and lost. **The stay-put victory did not change the legal relationship of the parties so as to make the parents prevailing parties** under the IDEA. *Mr. and Mrs. G. v. Trumbull, Connecticut Board of Educ.*, No. 3:04CV1653MRK, 2005 WL 544711 (D. Conn. 2/24/05).

♦ New York parents objected to their son's IEP because it called for a segregated placement in a special education classroom. A due process hearing officer found that the IEP was invalid because it lacked required information and procedural safeguards. The hearing officer also rejected the placement proposed by the parents, instead ordering the district to reevaluate the student and make a new placement recommendation. The parties later agreed to a mainstream placement. When the parents sued for their attorneys' fees, a federal court awarded them. Here, **the parents had obtained the necessary level of success to be deemed prevailing parties** even though they did not get the exact placement they wanted. *D.M. v. Board of Educ. Center, Moriches Union Free School Dist.*, 296 F.Supp.2d 400 (E.D.N.Y. 2003).

♦ Parents of a student who attended a full-time, center-based program sought additional educational services, which the school board denied. At a due process hearing, they prevailed. When they requested attorneys' fees of $44,000, the board asserted their **attorney's hourly rate of up to $375 per hour** was unreasonable. A New York federal court disagreed. An hourly rate of $125 to $200 was reasonable for negotiated cases, but here the hearing took place over five dates and the subject matter was complex. After a downward adjustment, the court awarded over $30,000. *Z.E. v. New York City Board of Educ.*, No. 02 Civ. 1067(DC), 2003 WL 42017 (S.D.N.Y. 1/6/03).

♦ The father and attorney-mother of a Georgia student disputed the result of an assistive technology evaluation of their son and requested an independent evaluation. When the district did not agree, they requested a due process hearing and paid for an independent evaluation. They submitted a bill to the district for $491, which the district paid just prior to a hearing, at which the mother represented the student. The hearing officer held the district should have either requested a due process hearing or provided an evaluation at public expense. When the mother sought attorneys' fees, a federal court held that she was not entitled to them. Although a parent-attorney can be eligible for attorneys' fees under the IDEA, **the student was not a prevailing party here where the district made a voluntary payment before the hearing started**, and there was no judicial approval or formal agreement of the settlement. *Matthew V. v. DeKalb County School System*, 244 F.Supp.2d 1331 (N.D. Ga. 2003).

♦   The parents of an Illinois student with disabilities challenged their son's placement, among other issues. Although the hearing officer refused to find that the school district denied the student a free appropriate public education, the parents received partial relief on four of the eight issues they raised, including reimbursement for half the cost of a neuropsychologist at an IEP meeting, and reimbursement for a home-based tutor. The value of the services covered in the award was approximately $3,000. When the parents sought attorneys' fees of over $102,000, a federal court granted them only $18,000. Although they were **not entitled to a full recovery of attorneys' fees**, they prevailed on some of the issues and thus qualified for a partial recovery. *Koswenda v. Flossmoor School Dist. No. 161*, 227 F.Supp.2d 979 (N.D. Ill. 2002).

♦   A Pennsylvania student with mental retardation and Down syndrome attended a private school. His parents requested that certain programs and services be offered on site at the private school, but the school district refused, instead offering the services at the public school. When the parents sued for reimbursement, a federal court issued a preliminary order requiring the district to provide the student with speech and occupational therapy, a teacher's aide and an itinerant teacher for his secular subjects. The district appealed and refused to provide the relief ordered. Eventually, the parties settled, the parents agreed to an IEP, and the student began attending public school. When his parents sought to recover their attorneys' fees, a federal court denied their request. The Third Circuit affirmed. The parents were not entitled to fees under the "catalyst" theory and **they were not prevailing parties despite the preliminary order in their favor**. Because the preliminary order did not concern the merits of the student's claims, it was an insufficient basis for an award of attorneys' fees. *John T. by Paul T. and Joan T. v. Delaware County Intermediate Unit*, 318 F.3d 545 (3d Cir. 2003).

♦   After a student with behavioral problems was suspended three times during the 1999-2000 school year, he received limited home instruction. While on suspension, his school sought an order from the New Jersey special education agency that would affirm his placement in a program of home instruction until an appropriate placement could be located. The mother sought an order requiring the student to be reinstated to his high school, a behavioral specialist to perform a functional behavioral assessment, a behavior intervention plan and further assessments. She also sought instruction to compensate the student for the time he was at home and an order preventing the board from suspending him again without complying with the IDEA. An administrative law judge ordered the board to reinstate the student and hire a behavioral specialist to perform assessments and establish a behavior plan. The family moved out of the school district, and the mother petitioned a federal court for an award of attorneys' fees and costs. The court denied the request, ruling that the administrative order was not a permanent resolution of the merits of the family's claims.

The Third Circuit affirmed, rejecting the mother's argument that she obtained the primary goal of the lawsuit. The order reinstating the student provided only interim relief. The temporary order did not concern his permanent educational placement. And the administrative order was not based on the merits of the case. **The family was not entitled to prevailing party status based on an interim order**, and attorneys' fees were unavailable. *J.O. ex rel. C.O. v. Orange Township Board of Educ.*, 287 F.3d 267 (3d Cir. 2002).

♦ After an evaluation, a school planning and placement team (PPT) found inconsistencies in a regular education student's grades and signs that he had ADHD, but did not find him in need of special education. The next year, the student allegedly vandalized a bus. His parents contested his expulsion and sought an independent evaluation. The PPT determined that the student had a disability and that his actions on the school bus manifested his disability. The PPT drafted an IEP that provided all the relief the parents sought. A hearing officer declined to adopt the PPT decision as an official order but allowed it to be read into the hearing record. The hearing officer then issued a final decision dismissing the hearing as moot. The parents sought attorneys' fees from the board, asserting that they were prevailing parties. A Connecticut federal court awarded them $14,140 in attorneys' fees and costs. The school board appealed to the Second Circuit, which noted that **PPT meetings are mechanisms for compromise and cooperation, not adversarial confrontation**. The parents were not entitled to an award of fees under the IDEA or Section 504. *J.C. v. Regional School Dist. 10, Board of Educ.*, 278 F.3d 119 (2d Cir. 2002).

2. Court Proceedings

♦ The mother of a Pennsylvania student sued to challenge an adverse administrative decision and a court agreed that **the student's IEP had not been properly implemented for part of the year**. When she then sought attorneys' fees, the Third Circuit ruled that she was entitled to more than $104,000. *Damian J. v. School Dist. of Philadelphia*, 358 Fed.Appx. 333 (3d Cir. 2009).

♦ An attorney in New Jersey represented a student with autism, winning a new IEP for the student. When he sought attorneys' fees of $400 per hour, he submitted statements by an environmental law attorney who charged $575 an hour and a veteran Philadelphia special education attorney who charged $375 an hour. The court awarded him only $250 per hour and reduced the hours chargeable from 236 to 177. He appealed, but the Third Circuit ruled against him. It noted his **"unprofessional and contentious" performance in the litigation**, and also found that lawyers in his community with similar experience were paid much less than he claimed. *L.J. v. Audubon Board of Educ.*, 373 Fed.Appx. 294 (3d Cir. 2010).

♦ A three-year-old Hawaii student was denied special education for a 26-day period during the transition from IDEA Part C to Part B. The delay was largely due to a dispute between the parents and educator over the school he would attend. After a court ruled that the failure to implement the IEP was material and significant, the parents sought their attorneys' fees. **The court awarded the**

parents over $48,000 even though school officials were still appealing the earlier ruling. *Shaun M. v. Hamamoto*, No. 09-00075 DAE, 2010 WL 346451 (D. Haw. 1/27/10).

♦   A dispute arose between a New Jersey school district and the parents of a student over extended school year (ESY) services and transportation. A federal court ruled for the district on the ESY and transportation claims but awarded 17 days of compensatory education due to the district's failure to serve the student for the same number of days at the start of his fifth-grade year. The family then sought costs and attorneys' fees of $118,787. The court modified the award but still granted them all their costs and $71,850 in attorneys' fees because **even though they were successful on only one claim, their claims were all related.** *L.T. v. Mansfield Township School Dist.*, No. 04-1381 (NLH), 2009 WL 1971329 (D.N.J. 7/1/09).

♦   A number of families in the District of Columbia sued to recover attorneys' fees for administrative or court actions under the IDEA. They sought more than the $4,000 per action authorized by the District of Columbia Appropriations Act of 2005, claiming that the lawsuits to obtain payment should not be considered part of the same action as the underlying action to obtain relief under the IDEA. The U.S. Court of Appeals, D.C. Circuit, ruled that the requests for attorneys' fees should be considered part of the same action as the underlying IDEA disputes, thus **limiting the amounts payable to $4,000 per action.** *Kaseman v. District of Columbia*, 444 F.3d 637 (D.C. Cir. 2006).

♦   The parents of an Arizona student enrolled her in a Missouri school for students with hearing impairments. Arizona then created a program for hearing-impaired students, but the parents again sent their daughter to the Missouri school. They obtained an attorney not licensed to practice in Arizona who got permission from a state court to represent the family. An administrative law judge then held that the parents were entitled to a year of tuition. When they sought attorneys' fees, the Ninth Circuit held that **they were prevailing parties entitled to fees from the time the attorney was properly licensed by the state.** *Shapiro v. Paradise Valley Unified School Dist. No. 69*, 374 F.3d 857 (9th Cir. 2004).

♦   After a hearing officer ruled that a Pennsylvania school district denied a student a free appropriate public education for the first three days of a school year, three days of compensatory education were ordered. On appeal, a review panel and a federal court upheld that determination. The court also awarded the student's attorney over $20,000 in fees. The student then moved from the district, which appealed to the Third Circuit, asserting that the case had become moot. The court of appeals refused to issue a ruling eliminating the attorneys' fees but noted that **the district would be entitled to victory if the student was no longer interested in pursuing the action.** The court remanded the case. *Cent. Dauphin School Dist. v. Rashawn S.*, 65 Fed.Appx. 394 (3d Cir. 2003).

♦   **An attorney had no right to retain $50,000 in fees awarded by a federal court in an action under the IDEA after the court's judgment was reversed.**

The Seventh Circuit held that courts have inherent powers to order the repayment of such fees and to regulate the conduct of attorneys practicing before them. The fees were awarded after a federal court upheld a state hearing officer's decision requiring a school district to fund the residential placement of a disruptive and frequently truant student. The district paid the fees but appealed to the Seventh Circuit, which held that the residential placement chosen by the student's mother was "a jail substitute" that did not provide the student psychological services or treat his depression and conduct disorder. After the U.S. Supreme Court refused to review the case, the federal court ordered the family's attorney to return the award of fees to the school district. When the attorney refused, the district appealed to the Seventh Circuit, which rejected the attorney's argument that the federal court lacked the power to order her to return the funds. Courts have inherent power to regulate the conduct of attorneys who practice before them. *Dale M. v. Board of Educ. of Bradley Bourbonnais High School Dist. No. 307*, 282 F.3d 984 (7th Cir. 2002).

♦ Following IDEA proceedings, a federal court ordered an Arkansas school district to provide a special education student with compensatory education. The court affirmed an IEP for the student, which was accepted through her attorney. However, the parties disputed how the IEP would be carried out, with the mother insisting that the district provide a private teacher to the family at their home. The court eventually ruled that the district was not required to pay for a private instructor because it provided the student with a qualified teacher. The student moved for reconsideration of the order, arguing that the parties had never reached agreement on the IEP and that it was insufficient. The court denied the motion as untimely but awarded attorneys' fees to the family.

While the student's appeal was pending, she declined the compensatory education services specified in the IEP. The Eighth Circuit found no error with respect to the lower court's decision about the student's IEP. The only dispute was over whether the IEP would be implemented by a district teacher or a private instructor. There was no evidence that the district's special education teacher was unqualified, and school districts are not required to pay for private placements if they can provide the same services. **The court rejected the district's argument that the family was no longer entitled to "prevailing party" status because the student declined the relief authorized** by the court when she rejected the proposed compensatory education services. The district violated the IDEA, and the court's previous order altered the legal relationship of the parties by granting the student a legal right that had previously been denied. The fact that the family refused to allow compensatory education did not change its prevailing party status. The court affirmed the award and the compensatory education plan approved by the lower court. *Birmingham v. Omaha School Dist.*, 298 F.3d 731 (8th Cir. 2002).

♦ The parents of a student with cerebral palsy unilaterally enrolled him in a private religious school and asked their school district to provide an on-site assistant. The district refused. The parents initiated a state administrative proceeding, which resulted in a decision for the district. The parents then sued the district and state education department. The court held that the denial of services violated Iowa special education law and awarded attorneys' fees to the parents as prevailing parties. It awarded fees against the department for its advocacy in support of the administrative decision. The district and department appealed to the Eighth Circuit, which explained that the lower court had correctly found that the parents prevailed. The IDEA places primary responsibility on state education agencies to ensure local compliance with the act. However, the lower court should not have imposed liability against the department for the parents' attorneys' fees incurred during the administrative proceedings, because the department did not participate in those proceedings. **The department was liable for a portion of the fees for its opposition to the federal court decision in the parents' favor.** *John T. ex rel. Robert T. v. Iowa Dep't of Educ.*, 258 F.3d 860 (8th Cir. 2001).

3. Settlement

♦ New York parents rejected a 12:1:1 IEP placement for their autistic son and placed him in a private therapeutic setting. A hearing officer found the IEP inadequate, and a new IEP called for a 6:1:1 placement with a behavior intervention plan. The parents rejected that IEP too. Later, the school department agreed to pay for private services. The parents nevertheless sued, but a federal court ruled against them, noting that **the lawsuit appeared to be nothing more than an attempt to recover attorneys' fees**. Since the parents had already received full compensation for their private expenditures, they were not entitled to relief. *M.S. v. New York City Dep't of Educ.*, 734 F.Supp.2d 271 (E.D.N.Y. 2010).

♦ After a Texas student failed the state's standardized test three years in a row, his father requested a special education evaluation. The district instead set up a committee to evaluate the student's placement and found it appropriate. The student failed the test again, and his father requested due process. At a pre-hearing resolution meeting, the district offered the father all the relief he sought, including $3,000 in reasonable attorneys' fees. He rejected the offer and sued, obtaining the same relief as well as $45,000 in attorneys' fees. However, the Fifth Circuit reversed the award of attorneys' fees, noting that **rejecting the settlement offer protracted the proceedings**. He got no greater relief after the settlement offer. *El Paso Independent School Dist. v. Richard R.*, 591 F.3d 417 (5th Cir. 2009).

♦ Wisconsin parents became upset when their school district didn't evaluate their son for special education. They removed him from district schools and placed him in a private school, from which he graduated. They then requested due process and sought tuition reimbursement of $15,638. **The district voluntarily paid the amount sought**, but the parents continued with their due process hearing, seeking attorneys' fees. The case reached the Seventh Circuit Court of Appeals, which held that they were not entitled to them because of the district's voluntary payment. However, the district might be entitled to attorneys' fees for defending the action. *Bingham v. New Berlin School Dist.*, 550 F.3d 601 (7th Cir. 2008).

♦   After a California parent refused to agree to an IEP for her child, the school district filed for due process. The parties then reached an agreement, and the district's complaint was dismissed. Subsequently, the parent filed a lawsuit, claiming the hearing officer should not have dismissed the case, and seeking to recover attorneys' fees. A federal court and the Ninth Circuit ruled for the district, noting that the parent did not suffer any injury by the dismissal of the district's complaint, and that the sole reason for filing the lawsuit seemed to be to obtain attorneys' fees. *Levina v. San Luis Coastal Unified School Dist.*, 514 F.3d 866 (9th Cir. 2007).

♦   The father of an emotionally disturbed Connecticut student filed a due process hearing request to challenge his son's placement. Following a series of hearings, he and the district notified the hearing officer that they were discussing a settlement. The hearing officer set two deadlines for the settlement to be reached, but both passed, so the case was dismissed. A settlement was later reached and the father then sued for his attorneys' fees as a prevailing party. The Second Circuit Court of Appeals refused to award them because **the private settlement was not judicially or administratively sanctioned**. Thus, he was not a prevailing party under the IDEA. *Mr. L. v. Sloan*, 449 F.3d 405 (2d Cir. 2006).

♦   The parents of a New Jersey student, who was expelled one year and suspended the next, filed for due process to get the student returned to school, as well as reimbursement for psychological services, a Section 504 plan and an independent evaluation. They settled the dispute before a due process hearing was held, and the student returned to school with accommodations and an evaluation, while the parents were reimbursed for the psychological services. When they sued to recover their attorneys' fees, a federal court ruled against them, but the Third Circuit reversed. **Even though the administrative law judge lacked the jurisdiction to enforce the terms of the settlement agreement, judicial enforcement was available** and the parents received all they sought. *P.N. by M.W. v. Clementon Board of Educ.*, 442 F.3d 848 (3d Cir. 2006).

♦   The parents of a Michigan student filed a due process action against their district after a four-year dispute. The district proposed a settlement that provided substantially enhanced services, but also explicitly stated that the parents would not be reimbursed for their legal fees. They signed the settlement agreement but rejected the legal fees part of it and eventually sued for their attorneys' fees. The case reached the Sixth Circuit, which noted that **they could not accept part of the settlement while rejecting the legal fees provision**. The parents had waived their right to attorneys' fees. *Tompkins v. Troy School Dist.*, 199 Fed.Appx. 463 (6th Cir. 2006).

♦   The parents of a Pennsylvania child brought an administrative action under the IDEA to compel their child's dual enrollment in a public and private school. They entered into a settlement agreement with the school district. The agreement contained a clause providing that the settlement would "have the effect of a judicial consent decree." When they later sued for their attorneys' fees as prevailing parties under the IDEA, the Third Circuit U.S. Court of Appeals ruled against them. **They could not create judicial approval by stipulation.** *Nathan F. v. Parkland School Dist.*, 136 Fed.Appx. 511 (3d Cir. 2005).

◆   The mother of a Pennsylvania student filed numerous due process hearing requests against her school district, seeking to enforce her daughter's IEP. The parties finally reached a voluntary agreement on the student's IEP, deeming it a "consent decree" even though the hearing officer did not retain jurisdiction over the case. When the mother sought to recover her attorneys' fees, the Third Circuit ruled against her. **Attorneys' fees are not available for actions voluntarily settled and not accompanied by any order.** *Maria C. v. School Dist. of Philadelphia*, 142 Fed.Appx. 78 (3d Cir. 2005).

◆   The parents of a Massachusetts student with severe mental disabilities sought a placement for their daughter in a private day school. However, the IEP team rejected that request in favor of a public school placement. The parents asked for a due process hearing, and they reached a settlement just before the hearing that allowed the student to attend the private school for the current year. The hearing officer dismissed the IDEA claims. When the parents sued for their attorneys' fees, the First Circuit ruled against them. It held that they were not "prevailing parties" under the IDEA because **they did not reach a judicially sanctioned settlement with the district.** *Doe v. Boston Public Schools*, 358 F.3d 20 (1st Cir. 2004).

4. Other Proceedings and Issues

◆   A Texas student entitled to speech therapy missed some sessions because of a shortage of qualified therapists. The school offered a settlement of one hour of compensatory services for each hour missed by the student, plus attorneys' fees. The parent rejected the offer and eventually sued. A court found that **the parent's attorney "stonewalled" attempts to resolve disputes with the district**, including refusing to allow a reevaluation and not participating in the review committee process. It ordered the parent's attorney to pay $10,000 in attorneys' fees to the school district, and the Fifth Circuit affirmed that decision. *El Paso Independent School Dist. v. Berry*, 400 Fed.Appx. 947 (5th Cir. 2010).

◆   A private school in Ohio provided special education services to a student but later expelled him over a dispute concerning the IEP. His parents sued the private school and the school district. After the private school was dismissed from the case, it sought its attorneys' fees from the parents, but the Sixth Circuit ruled that it was not entitled to them. The IDEA only allows for attorneys' fees to be paid to prevailing parents or to state and local educational agencies. The private school was neither. *Children's Center for Developmental Enrichment v. Machle*, 612 F.3d 518 (6th Cir. 2010).

◆   A Texas third-grader with ADHD was found ineligible for special education, but was provided accommodations under Section 504. In sixth grade, he was progressively disciplined for misconduct and was reassigned to a special school. His parents challenged the reassignment, claiming that he should have been declared eligible for special education. A hearing officer ordered the district to reconsider his eligibility. A federal court then awarded partial attorneys' fees to the student, but the Fifth Circuit reversed, noting that **a student who is not deemed a "child with a disability" under the IDEA cannot obtain attorneys' fees**. If he was later ruled IDEA eligible, he could seek attorneys' fees at that time. *T.B. v. Bryan Independent School Dist.*, 628 F.3d 240 (5th Cir. 2010).

◆   The mother of a D.C. student with disabilities filed a due process complaint against a charter school, asserting various IEP failures. However, when school officials met with her during a resolution meeting, she refused to cooperate, claiming that only a "full time out of district placement" would do, and that the school she'd selected was appropriate. A hearing officer later determined that her claims were frivolous because the IEPs were developed with the mother's full participation. The school then sought its attorneys' fees as a prevailing party, and a federal court held that it could sue to recover the fees. **The mother's lawsuit lacked any factual or legal basis**, and the school she had selected did not even offer the kind of placement she insisted was necessary. *Bridges Public Charter School v. Barrie*, 709 F.Supp.2d 94 (D.D.C. 2010).

◆   The parents of a Georgia student with autism settled their dispute with the school district. The district agreed to provide a functional behavior analysis at a clinic. Six months later, the district determined that the student should return to his local high school placement. The parents disagreed and requested due process, seeking to keep the student in his stay-put placement. An administrative law judge agreed with them, and they then pursued a claim for attorneys' fees. However, the Eleventh Circuit ruled against them, noting that **a stay-put placement victory is not the same thing as prevailing on the merits**. *Robert K. v. Cobb County School Dist.*, 279 Fed.Appx. 798 (11th Cir. 2008).

◆   A New Jersey student who molested two younger siblings was placed in a public high school and underwent several independent evaluations. After the district's child study team met several times and determined that the student was not eligible for special education and related services, his parents sought due process. A state administrative law judge denied the parents' request for relief. They appealed to a state court, which ordered the student placed in a treatment facility, with the school district paying for the educational component. The district again found the student ineligible for special education. When the parents then sued for attorneys' fees, a federal court and the Third Circuit ruled against them. **Because the student was never identified as a student in need of special education, attorneys' fees were unavailable.** It did not matter that the parents obtained some relief in getting their child committed. *D.S. v. Neptune Township Board of Educ.*, 264 Fed.Appx. 186 (3d Cir. 2008).

♦   The mother of a multiply disabled Ohio student sought door-to-door transportation for him. After she and the district agreed to delay the due process hearing, the district offered to reimburse her for the $368 she had spent on transportation to that point, as well as $1,000 for her attorneys' fees. It also offered to have an aide escort her son from her apartment to the bus stop. She rejected the offer and sued the district, receiving essentially the same relief the district had offered, as well as $57,000 in attorneys' fees. The Ohio Court of Appeals reversed the award of attorneys' fees, finding that she failed to exhaust her administrative remedies prior to suing the district, and that **she received substantially what the district had offered**. *Olivas v. Cincinnati Public Schools*, 872 N.E.2d 962 (Ohio Ct. App. 2007).

♦   The parents of a Hawaii student who became overwhelmingly afraid of school decided to educate him at home with tutoring and a private math class. The state brought an educational neglect (truancy) petition against the parents in family court and lost because the department of education did not address the student's psychological needs with an offer of mental health services. When the parents sought their attorneys' fees as prevailing parties, a federal court ruled against them, noting that **the family court action was not an IDEA action**. *Melodee H. v. Dep't of Educ., State of Hawaii*, 374 F.Supp.2d 886 (D. Haw. 2005).

♦   Parents of a Massachusetts student rejected his proposed IEP, placed him in a private school and requested a due process hearing. A hearing officer awarded tuition reimbursement and the district did not appeal that decision. More than 30 days later, the parents sued to recover their attorneys' fees. The district moved for dismissal on the grounds that the statute of limitations had passed and that no attorneys' fees could be awarded for an administrative action. When the parents did not respond, the court granted the motion. The First Circuit Court of Appeals affirmed. *Pomerleau v. West Springfield Public Schools*, 362 F.3d 143 (1st Cir. 2004).

♦   A New Jersey school district refused to evaluate a child until he could be observed in a preschool setting. His parents requested a due process hearing, and an administrative law judge (ALJ) ordered the district to classify the child as eligible for special education. The ALJ also ordered the parents to let the district conduct a speech/language evaluation. The parents and their attorney walked out of an IEP meeting ordered by the ALJ. At another due process hearing, the ALJ ruled that the IEP was invalid. When the parents sought their attorneys' fees, a federal court and the Third Circuit denied them. **The parents and their attorney had needlessly delayed the resolution of the dispute.** *J.T. v. Medford Board of Educ.*, 118 Fed.Appx. 605 (3d Cir. 2004).

♦   A Michigan court denied a request for attorneys' fees by the parents of students with disabilities who settled a special education dispute under the Michigan Mandatory Special Education Act (MMSEA). **The court found no basis for awarding fees under the act, stating that the Michigan legislature could have explicitly authorized fees** but did not do so. A school district disputed its obligation to provide services to certain students, claiming that they were not residents of the district. The parents commenced a lawsuit alleging MMSEA violations. The parties resolved their dispute and a state trial court entered a consent judgment incorporating the settlement terms. The parents then sought attorneys' fees, asserting that since the IDEA authorizes attorneys' fee awards to prevailing parties, the MMSEA did so by implication. The Michigan Court of Appeals disagreed. *Schill v. Washtenaw Intermediate School Dist.*, No. 230356, 2002 WL 31188429 (Mich. Ct. App. 10/1/02).

◆   A mediation agreement between an Illinois family and a school district did not confer prevailing party status on the family under the IDEA. The hearing officer made no findings or rulings, so the mediation agreement was a private settlement, not an enforceable consent decree. The agreement was read into the record before a hearing officer, who did not make any findings of fact or deliver a ruling. The mother sued the district, seeking attorneys' fees and costs. The court found that a consent decree is a contract between parties that is entered into the record with the court's approval and sanction. The hearing officer had not approved or sanctioned the agreement in this case. **The settlement agreement resembled a private settlement, not a consent decree, and did not confer prevailing party status on the mother.** The court awarded summary judgment to the school district. *Luis R. v. Joliet Township High School Dist.*, No. 01 C 4798, 2002 WL 54544 (N.D. Ill 1/1/5/02).

◆   Prior to a student's junior year in high school, his parents and school district unsuccessfully sought to create an IEP for him. The student had been diagnosed with attention deficit disorder and had a history of not attending classes. His parents requested a due process hearing, believing the student should receive an independent educational evaluation (IEE), a transition planning consultant, and modification of his IEP to build on his strengths and provide more positive behavioral reinforcement. The district agreed to mediate the dispute and to pay for a second IEE and the transition consultant. The parties reached a settlement agreement incorporating the suggestions from the IEE into the student's IEP. The district reduced the number of credits he needed to graduate and provided a detailed list of classroom modifications, including a short school day and off-site tutoring. The plan proved to be ineffective, as the student continued cutting classes and did not graduate.

His parents sued the district to recover their legal fees associated with the mediation proceedings. A Wisconsin federal court ruled against them, and they appealed to the Seventh Circuit. The court of appeals observed that the parents were not entitled to a second IEE under the IDEA because they did not significantly disagree with the first one. They also failed to identify any areas of disagreement with the school district's diagnosis or methodology. **Their claim to attorneys' fees could not rest only on the district's agreement to pay for a second evaluation.** The granting of interim relief such as ordering the second IEE did not make the parents prevailing parties. The court affirmed the judgment for the school district. *Edie F. v. River Falls School Dist.*, 243 F.3d 329 (7th Cir. 2001).

♦   The parents of a student with autism made informal complaints to the Oregon education department about their son's education program, then filed a formal complaint under the state complaint resolution procedure (CRP), alleging IDEA violations. The department conducted an investigation of the school district, identified IDEA violations and ordered the district to hold an IEP meeting. The parties agreed on a revised IEP for the student, and the parents sued the district for reimbursement of attorneys' fees incurred for their attorney's attendance at the department-ordered IEP meetings. The court granted the request, and the Ninth Circuit affirmed. Here, the IEP-team meeting had arisen from an order pursuant to the CRP. The parents were prevailing parties who **could recover attorneys' fees for their lawyer's attendance at the department-ordered IEP meetings.** *Lucht v. Molalla River School Dist.*, 225 F.3d 1023 (9th Cir. 2000).

B. Compensatory Education

Compensatory education involves the belated provision of necessary educational services by a school district to a student with a disability. Courts may award compensatory education to students with disabilities who have been deprived of their right to a free appropriate public education pursuant to 20 U.S.C. § 1415(i)(2)(B)(iii), which recognizes the power of a court to grant such relief as it deems appropriate in IDEA cases. In recent years, courts have shown an increased willingness to award compensatory education beyond the age of 21.

1. Generally

♦   A New York school district was found to have violated a student's rights under the IDEA. The case reached the Second Circuit, which ruled that the student still had two years of eligibility for compensatory education and that **his parents should be paid for five of the nine classes he attended at college.** It also found the reimbursement award should be reduced by the amount of financial aid and scholarships the student received. The parents were entitled to reimbursement for a laptop and reading software as well as the cost of an independent neuropsychological evaluation. *Streck v. Board of Educ. of East Greenbush Cent. School Dist.*, 408 Fed.Appx. 411 (2d Cir. 2010).

♦   A deaf/hard of hearing student in California had IEPs until she entered a media arts middle school, which exited her from special education eligibility. A stay-put order kept her placement intact until she entered a media arts high school. She withdrew from school but requested another due process hearing, seeking compensatory education. The district claimed that her case became moot when she withdrew from school, but a federal court held that **compensatory education could be a remedy for failure to provide FAPE.** The court allowed her lawsuit to proceed. *Alexis R. v. High Tech Middle Media Arts School*, No. 07CV830 BTM (WMC), 2009 WL 2382429 (S.D. Cal. 8/3/09).

♦   A New Jersey student with multiple disabilities attended a private school at the district's expense. When he sought to attend a public school for the fourth grade, the principal allegedly refused to meet with his parents and declined to take their calls. No IEP was in place for the first 17 days of the school year, so the student received a limited amount of homebound instruction during that time. His parents asserted violations of the IDEA and Section 504, and a federal court agreed that **the district "recklessly disregarded" the student's educational needs at the start of the year**. Accordingly, he was entitled to compensatory education for the lost time. *L.T. v. Mansfield Township School Dist.*, No. 04-1381 (NLH), 2009 WL 737108 (D.N.J. 3/17/09).

♦ A student was diagnosed with pervasive developmental disorder and was offered an IEP with 10 hours of 1:1 behavior and speech therapy. Near the end of the school year, it was determined that he needed more intense therapy and that he had autism. The parents sought compensatory education to make up for the less intense therapy the student had received during the school year. The case reached a New York federal court, which noted that **compensatory education ought to be available only for a gross violation of the IDEA**, resulting in a near total denial of educational services to an individual who is no longer eligible for public education due to age. Here, the student was five years old and had not been substantially excluded from school. Also, the district had provided positive behavioral interventions and supports. *J.A. and E.A. v. East Ramapo Cent. School Dist.*, 603 F.Supp.2d 684 (S.D.N.Y. 2009).

♦ The parents of an 11-year-old Pennsylvania student who had never attended public schools requested an evaluation for special education after obtaining a private evaluation. They did not sign the consent forms for a public evaluation, instead enrolling the student in a private school recommended by their evaluator. Eventually the district was able to conduct an evaluation and prepare an IEP, which the parents rejected. When they sought compensatory education for the delay, claiming that they'd asked for an evaluation during the student's kindergarten year, the Third Circuit ruled against them. It noted that **they were not entitled to compensatory education because they had no intention of placing their son in public school** and that there was no evidence they'd asked for an evaluation during kindergarten. *P.P. v. West Chester Area School Dist.*, 585 F.3d 727 (3d Cir. 2009).

♦ The parents of a Pennsylvania student with autism removed her from school and challenged her IEPs for a five-year period, seeking compensatory education for each year. A hearing officer found that her IEPs lacked present levels of educational performance, measurable annual goals and progress monitoring. As a result, she was entitled to 450 days of compensatory education. However, she was not entitled to compensatory education for the current year because her parents had unilaterally removed her from school while administrative decisions were pending. A federal court largely agreed, noting that the IEPs failed to address the student's lack of progress and did not suggest changes in instruction. **The IEPs remained nearly identical from year to year.** On the other hand, her current IEP was carefully prepared and had a comprehensive report of her progress and abilities. *Laura P. v. Haverford School Dist.*, No. 07-5395, 2008 WL 5000461 (E.D. Pa. 11/21/08).

♦   A New Mexico student with a specific learning disability began having academic performance and significant disciplinary problems. She skipped school 136 times during the fall semester, and she began using drugs and alcohol. After she was arrested for attacking her mother and brother, she was sent to a juvenile detention center, where a one-page form served as her interim IEP. It stated merely that her reading was good and that she needed help in math. The following year, she returned to school and a new IEP was then developed for her. But she continued to skip classes. Eventually, she sought compensatory education. The case reached the Tenth Circuit, which noted that she was seeking the very services she would have received if only she had attended classes. Even though the school district violated the IDEA by using the poor interim IEP and by not having an IEP ready for her upon her return to school, **the district's failure was immaterial because of the student's truancy and behavior problems**. *Garcia v. Board of Educ. of Albuquerque Public Schools*, 520 F.3d 1116 (10th Cir. 2008).

♦   After the District of Columbia offered a disabled student limited special education, without a behavioral intervention plan or extended school year services, and after the D.C. public schools dropped the student's speech/language impairment classification and failed to provide some of the services specified in his IEPs, his mother requested due process. A hearing officer granted her compensatory education, but applied the two-year statute of limitations from the 2004 IDEA Improvement Act. On appeal, a federal court held that the hearing officer should not have applied the two-year statute of limitations to claims arising before 2004. Prior to that, a three-year limitations period was applied by courts. The court remanded the case to the hearing officer to reformulate an appropriate compensatory education award, and to consider that **there might be a continuing violation of the IDEA that justified going back further**. *Anthony v. District of Columbia*, 463 F.Supp.2d 37 (D.D.C. 2006).

♦   The mother of a District of Columbia second-grader met with his teacher and principal to discuss his behavior, academic and attention problems. After the school district promoted him to third grade, the student attended school in California the following year but returned for grade four. At the end of that year, the student was identified with ADHD and a learning disability, and an IEP was developed. By the end of the next school year, the district again sought to hold him back, and his mother filed a due process hearing request. A hearing officer ruled that the district failed to identify the student as in need of special education for three years in violation of the child-find obligation and awarded one hour of compensatory education for each day he was denied FAPE. The mother appealed, and a federal court upheld the hearing officer's decision. On further appeal, the U.S. Court of Appeals, DC Circuit, reversed, finding that the one-hour-for-one-day award granted by the hearing officer was not properly supported by reasoning or factual findings. It also rejected the mother's argument that compensatory education should be one-day-for-one-day. On remand, **the court would have to design a proper remedy of compensatory education**. *Reid v. District of Columbia*, 401 F.3d 516 (D.C. Cir. 2005).

♦ A Texas student with multiple disabilities had an IEP that included a goal for the student to initiate communications about his need to go to the bathroom. The district used a voice-output device for him to communicate this need and gave a device to his parents for home use, explaining its proper use with his mother. The student regressed in his ability to use the device at home and in his extended school year program, and he wet the bed every morning. His parents challenged the IEP's schedule of in-home and parent training. A hearing officer noted that the district provided only four of ten scheduled training sessions, and ordered 150 minutes of compensatory training. However, a federal court ruled that **the student's regression in this area was not a failure to implement a significant portion of the IEP**. The award of compensatory training was reversed. *Clear Creek Independent School Dist. v. J.K.*, 400 F.Supp.2d 991 (S.D. Tex. 2005).

♦ Although a three-year-old had been diagnosed with autism, his public school classified him as speech-language impaired. For the next three years, he was placed in a school with no autism program under an IEP with no management plan. When his mother challenged the IEP, the hearing officer agreed that the school district did not comply with the IDEA. However, the hearing officer denied the mother's request for three years of applied behavior analysis (ABA) as compensatory education and reassigned the student to the same school. On appeal, a District of Columbia federal court overturned the hearing officer's decision and awarded four years of ABA therapy as compensatory education. **The school district repeatedly misdiagnosed and mishandled the student's program** and presented no evidence to support its IEPs. *Diatta v. District of Columbia*, 319 F.Supp.2d 57 (D.D.C. 2004).

♦ When a Maine student with Down syndrome was 19, his school district prepared an IEP that called for mornings to be spent in high school, with afternoons at a work-site training program. Because of behavior problems, his parents requested a modification of the IEP. The district proposed an IEP for the following year that would have placed the student at the work-site program all day, with various related services. The parents rejected the IEP. The district then sought a court order preventing the student from returning to school because he posed a threat to himself or others. The court denied the order, keeping the student in school. The parents then asked for attorneys' fees and sought compensatory education on the ground that the work-site placement was inadequate. When the student turned 20 and graduated, the district asked to have the case dismissed as moot. The First Circuit ruled that **a claim for compensatory education could survive a student's graduation if it was timely filed**, as it was here. Next, the parents were entitled to attorneys' fees because of their success in the "stay-put" action. *Maine School Administrative Dist. No. 35 v. Mr. and Mrs. R.*, 321 F.3d 9 (1st Cir. 2003).

2. Beyond Age 21

♦ The parents of a 21-year-old Pennsylvania student with autism asserted that she was deprived of a FAPE while in district schools. Their district set up a trust fund to pay for future educational costs for three years of compensatory education. However, the district sought to cease creating IEPs and no longer wished to serve as her local educational agency. The problem was that the private school the student attended required all students to have IEPs and required a district to serve as an LEA. The case reached the Third Circuit, which held that the student was eligible for relief despite the fact that she was now 24 years old. **The compensatory education was for the denial of FAPE while she was still IDEA-eligible**, and the trust fund by itself was not a sufficient remedy because the private school required an IEP and a district to serve as her LEA. *Ferren C. v. School Dist. of Philadelphia*, 612 F.3d 712 (3d Cir. 2010).

♦ A District of Columbia charter school entered into three settlement agreements concerning remedial education for a student with disabilities. However, his mother contended that the district failed to provide the required services. She sought compensatory education for him and was awarded more than 3,000 hours. But the D.C. Public Schools appealed and sought a stay of the award. A magistrate judge ruled against the school system, noting that the student was 25 years old and **the school system was attempting to avoid paying for its failures from more than seven years prior**. *Friendship Edison Public Charter School Collegiate Campus v. Nesbitt*, 704 F.Supp.2d 50 (D.D.C. 2010).

♦ A 19-year-old Tennessee student with no hands, one foot and cerebral palsy was dropped while school district attendants were attempting to move him from his wheelchair. His parents sued for his injuries and received his complete academic record for the first time. They believed his IEPs had been inappropriate and requested a due process hearing. A hearing officer ruled for the school system, but a federal court held that the system violated the IDEA by failing to relay information from the student's previous assessments. The court also held, however, that the student received a FAPE, and it denied his request for compensatory education. After the student received a special education diploma, the Sixth Circuit reversed, ordering the district court to determine whether the case was moot in view of the issuance of a diploma. The district court then held that the student's compensatory education claim was based on his assertion that the school system had denied him a FAPE at a time when he remained eligible for services. Even though he was now 24 and had a special education diploma, **his compensatory education request involved past violations and not future ones**. The case was not moot.

The case returned to the Sixth Circuit, which affirmed the ruling for the student. The case was not moot despite the special education diploma, and the failure to share evaluations with the parents was a procedural violation of the IDEA. Further, even after the student failed to reach his IEP goals, the district did not recommend any different instructional approaches for him. *Barnett v. Memphis City Schools*, 113 Fed.Appx. 124 (6th Cir. 2004).

♦ The mother of a student with disabilities petitioned the West Virginia Supreme Court of Appeals for an order compelling the school district to provide her child with certain special education services she claimed he was entitled to but had not received. After numerous court proceedings, a special master issued a report in favor of the mother, finding that the district did not perform its obligations from 1993 to 1995. Moreover, the district's performance of make-up services did not compensate the student for depriving him of them at the time they were actually required, justifying compensatory education. The district challenged the action in a federal court, which dismissed the action because the district failed to exhaust administrative remedies. When mediation attempts failed, the mother requested relief based on allegations of "a 14-year history of inadequate, bad-faith malfeasance" by the district. She sought a private placement as well as a court-appointed monitor and reimbursement for the costs of all the services she had previously arranged for the student. The court held that the record supported the special master's finding that the district did not comply with its legal duty to provide the student with special education from 1993 to 1995, and that the corrective measures it took did not fully address the lack of services during this period. The record also supported her finding that a new IEP and medical evaluation were necessary. The court granted the mother's request for relief, ordering the parties to create a new IEP. The mother was ordered to permit a full physical and psychological examination of her son. **The district was responsible for providing special education services for two additional years beyond the student's statutory entitlement to compensate him for past service deficiencies.** *State of West Virginia ex rel. Justice v. Board of Educ. of County of Monongalia*, 539 S.E.2d 777 (W.Va. 2000).

♦ A 15-year-old New York student suffered severe brain injuries in an automobile accident. After he was transferred to a rehabilitation facility in Pennsylvania, his district's committee on special education recommended a daily special services program that it attempted to implement by contract with a Pennsylvania school district. The student returned to a hospital in New York where only part of the IEP was implemented, with some services withheld. The parents requested a due process hearing to address the failure to provide services, which the district had discontinued on the basis of the lack of medical information. The hearing officer ordered the school committee to prepare a new IEP for the upcoming school year but did not address the lack of services for the current school year. A state-level review officer held that the school district had failed to provide the services described in the IEP, but denied the parents' request for compensatory special education and related services.

A New York federal court found the IEP appropriate and affirmed the administrative decisions. Later, the court found that **compensatory education is a permissible form of relief for a student over 21 years of age where there has been a gross violation of the IDEA.** However, the parents had failed to show that the student's condition regressed because of the failure to provide a free appropriate education. The court agreed with the administrative decisions that compensatory education and related services would not be appropriate to remedy the lack of services during the year after the injury. On appeal, the Second Circuit affirmed, noting that an award of compensatory special education and related services beyond a student's 21st birthday was inappropriate, and that the IDEA does not provide for monetary damage awards. *Wenger v. Canastota Cent. School Dist.*, 208 F.3d 204 (2d Cir. 2000).

C. Monetary Damages

Courts seem unable to agree on whether money damages are available under the IDEA. Although the IDEA allows courts to award any appropriate relief, some courts have taken the position that the only form of money damages available is for reimbursement of the costs incurred in providing a necessary placement or services.

Other courts have stated that compensatory monetary damages may be available under the IDEA.

Given the lack of decisions awarding money damages for IDEA violations, it remains to be seen which view will prevail. For more cases addressing monetary damages and whether plaintiffs seeking monetary damages under the IDEA must exhaust administrative remedies before filing a lawsuit, see Chapter Three, Section II.

♦   The parents of a Pennsylvania student with mental retardation brought numerous due process hearing requests over her school career. By the time she reached age 18, a hearing officer determined that her school district owed her 3,180 hours of compensatory education arising from four different school years. He required over $200,000 to be placed into a trust for her benefit. The parents then sued for compensatory damages, but a federal court and the Third Circuit ruled against them. Although the IDEA permits parents to advance claims on their own behalf, **the parents here sought only money damages, to which they were not entitled.** *Chambers v. School Dist. of Philadelphia Board of Educ.*, 587 F.3d 176 (3d Cir. 2009).

♦   Two Hawaii sisters with autism spectrum disorders were misclassified by the Hawaii Department of Education for several years. Eventually the students were classified as having autism. Their parents brought an administrative challenge, and a hearing officer found that the department had failed to provide autism services to the girls for about four years. Later, the parents sued for money damages under Section 504 and the IDEA. A federal court granted pretrial judgment to the department, but the Ninth Circuit reversed and remanded the case. It held that the department would be liable under Section 504 if it denied the students reasonable accommodations by failing to provide access to the benefits of public education despite knowing the services were necessary and available. Issues of fact required a trial. *Mark H. v. Hamamoto*, 620 F.3d 1090 (9th Cir. 2010).

♦   The parents of a Hawaii student with autism brought a series of administrative complaints against the state department of education for IDEA violations. The case eventually reached a federal court, which held that the student was entitled to tuition reimbursement for a defective IEP in 2005-06. **It awarded the student nearly $63,000 as compensation.** *Blake C. v. Dep't of Educ., State of Hawaii*, 593 F.Supp.2d 1199 (D. Haw. 2009).

♦ The parents of an Ohio student expressed concerns about his reading ability to his kindergarten teacher, but the district's evaluation found the student ineligible for special education. The parents obtained a private evaluation that diagnosed their son with a language-based learning disability. Eventually, the district acknowledged his eligibility for special education. The student continued to fall behind in grades three and four. When the parents ultimately sued the district and various officials, seeking emotional distress damages for the officials' intentional failure to deny their child a FAPE, a federal court ruled that the officials could not be sued. **The IDEA permits no monetary claims against individuals.** Any wrongdoing the parents might be able to show in further proceedings would be attributed to the district alone. *Doe v. Westerville City School Dist.*, No. 2:07-CV-00683, 2008 WL 2323526 (S.D. Ohio 6/2/08).

♦ The parents of a severely autistic Pennsylvania student had numerous run-ins with their school district, requesting multiple due process hearings over the student's educational career. A hearing officer eventually agreed that the district had denied the student an appropriate education for the previous three years. She ordered the district to provide 3,180 hours of compensatory education at a cost of $209,000. The parents then sued the district for $8 million for life care, pain, suffering, financial losses and compensation for loss of companionship. They claimed the student would never fully develop her communication skills. However, a federal court ruled that they could not pursue a claim against the district in their own right. **The IDEA does not confer substantive rights on the parents of disabled students.** *Ronald E. v. School Dist. of Philadelphia Board of Educ.*, No. 05-2535, 2007 WL 4225584 (E.D. Pa. 11/29/07).

♦ A New Jersey student with palsy affecting his hands and arms excelled academically, but alleged that he was not given the accommodations required under his Section 504 plan. He sued the board of education, two teachers and the principal for discrimination under various laws. After the jury was instructed that the school board was responsible for all damages, it awarded the student $500,000 against the board, $150,000 against the principal, $75,000 against his French teacher and $25,000 against his math teacher. The Appellate Division court ruled that a new trial on the issue of damages was required. **The jury should not be told that the school board would be responsible for the damage awards**, as that could result in a completely arbitrary allocation of damages. *Grinbaum v. Township of Livingston Board of Educ.*, No. L-4153-01, 2007 WL 1362716 (N.J. Super. Ct. App. Div. 5/10/07).

♦ The parents of three adopted disabled girls filed a lawsuit against their New Hampshire school district under the IDEA, ADA, Section 1983 and FERPA, seeking $250,000 in damages, claiming that the district had failed to properly investigate their complaints about how the district was addressing their daughters' needs. A federal court held that the IDEA and FERPA claims had to be dismissed because those statutes did not allow for money damages. Also, **the ADA and Section 1983 claims were dismissed because they were closely related to the identification, evaluation and placement of their daughters under the IDEA.** *Burke v. Brookline School Dist.*, No. 06-CV-317-JD, 2007 WL 268947 (D.N.H. 1/29/07).

♦ The parents of an Illinois student sued their district's former special education director under 42 U.S.C. § 1983, alleging that she was reckless in developing a defective IEP for their son. They sought money damages from her, **claiming that she committed the same violations in a previous case and thus knew her actions violated the IDEA**. The director asked to have the lawsuit dismissed, but the court refused to do so. If she acted with recklessness or callous indifference to the student's IDEA rights, she could be liable for money damages. The court allowed the lawsuit to proceed. *Board of Educ. of Elmhurst Community Unit School Dist. 205 v. Daniel M.*, No. CIVA 06 C 2218, 2006 WL 2579679 (N.D. Ill. 9/5/06).

♦ The parents of a disabled Puerto Rico student maintained that swimming was the only sport their daughter could participate in safely. However, public schools lacked swimming pools and school officials refused to pay for private swim lessons. The parents enrolled their daughter in a private school and sought tuition reimbursement as well as money damages, which a jury awarded. The First Circuit reversed in part, noting that **personal injury damages are not available under the IDEA**. The only monetary relief available is for educational and transportation costs paid on a student's behalf. *Diaz-Fonseca v. Comwlth. of Puerto Rico*, 451 F.3d 13 (1st Cir. 2006).

♦ The mother of a Nevada student with autism took her son to a childhood autism program ordered by a hearing officer as compensatory education. The district was required to pay "all out-of-pocket expenses" – nearly $65,000. When the mother sought an additional $26,515 to fully compensate her for lost wages and benefits while transporting her son to the program, the Supreme Court of Nevada held that she was not entitled to them. **The out-of-pocket expenses the district had to pay did not include lost income.** *Gumm v. Nevada Dep't of Educ.*, 113 P.3d 853 (Nev. 2005).

♦ A Virginia student received special education until he moved to a new district, which denied his mother's request for an evaluation. Two years later, the district finally conceded that he was eligible for special education. The mother then sued the district for violations of the IDEA and Section 504. She also sought money damages under 42 U.S.C. § 1983. The IDEA claim settled, and the other two claims reached the Fourth Circuit. The court of appeals held that **she was not entitled to money damages under Section 1983**. The IDEA established a comprehensive remedial scheme, and the student obtained all the relief he was due under that statute. However, the Section 504 claim could proceed. *Duck v. Isle of Wight County School Board*, 402 F.3d 468 (4th Cir. 2005).

♦ A Florida student who had problems with grades and behavior in school was found to be ineligible for special education under the IDEA despite his mother's assertions that he had ADD. After the student was suspended for threatening to kill a teacher who gave him poor grades, his parents requested an IDEA due process hearing and copies of his grades and discipline records. The district denied the due process request and failed to provide the records within 30 days, as required by state rule. The parents then sued for money damages under Section 1983, which a jury awarded. The Eleventh Circuit reversed, noting that **there was no policy or custom of denying students access to due process or records that would justify such an award**. No other student had been denied a due process hearing, and the records delay was caused by the winter holiday. *K.M. v. School Board of Lee County, Florida*, 150 Fed.Appx. 953 (11th Cir. 2005).

♦   The parents of a New Jersey student with autism disagreed with their school district over how to educate the student. An administrative law judge ordered the district to provide a full-day regular education program incorporating discrete trial therapy, compensatory education, occupational therapy and the cost of independent evaluations. The district appealed and the parents moved away shortly thereafter. When they sued the district under the IDEA for money damages, asserting that it had forced them to move because of a policy of refusing to comply with administrative orders, a federal court ruled against them. It found **no evidence that the parents were forced to move to obtain necessary services**. *Deptford Township School Dist. v. H.B.*, Civil No. 01-0784 (JBS), 2005 WL 1400752 (D.N.J. 6/15/05).

♦   The mother of a Philadelphia seventh-grade student made several verbal and written requests for an evaluation. After the eighth grade, the district complied. It completed an IEP that the mother did not agree with, and the parties reached a settlement on the day of the due process hearing. The district agreed to review the student's IEP by a certain date and provide tutoring for the next two years. It also agreed to provide 200 hours of compensatory education and a computer. The district failed to live up to its obligations, and a second agreement was reached regarding those delays. After the district again failed to abide by the agreement, the mother sued. A federal court ordered the district to pay the student $10,000 for an "educational advocate" who would help the family make the most of the compensatory education and other services the district had to provide. **Money damages were appropriate where the compensatory education remedy was not sufficient**. *Reid v. School Dist. of Philadelphia*, No. Civ. A. 03-1742, 2004 WL 1926324 (E.D. Pa. 8/27/04).

♦   A New York student with autism and a history of aggressive behavior punched the principal and struck a teacher in the face several times. He was suspended, and the district requested an expedited hearing to determine an interim alternative education setting (IAES) for him. His parents objected to the proposed IAES, and a hearing officer found the two hours of daily instruction specified in the IAES insufficient. A lawsuit followed, and a New York federal court held that the student's family could proceed with its claim for money damages under 42 U.S.C. § 1983. **The student was entitled to some amount of damages for the school board's failure to provide FAPE for the three months after his suspension**. *Zahran v. Board of Educ. of Niskayuna Cent. School Dist.*, 306 F.Supp.2d 204 (N.D.N.Y. 2004).

♦   Parents of a student with disabilities removed him from school and placed him in a home-based program because of alleged inadequacies in the district's IEP. They then sued the district for punitive damages, among other things. A

Pennsylvania federal court pointed to *Barnes v. Gorman*, 536 U.S. 181 (2002), wherein the Supreme Court held that punitive damages were not available in an action under Title VI because Congress placed contract-like conditions on the grant of Title VI funds. Since punitive damages are not available in breach of contract cases, they were not available in Title VI cases. Here, the court noted that the IDEA had similar funding conditions to Title VI. As a result, **punitive damages were not available under the IDEA**. *T.B. v. Upper Dublin School Dist.*, No. Civ.A. 03-2120, 2003 WL 22717391 (E.D. Pa. 11/17/03).

♦   A New York student with visual impairments graduated in 1997. During her senior year, she sued her school district in a federal court, asserting that she was denied academic honors, study materials, tutoring and a FAPE. She included claims under the Americans with Disabilities Act (ADA), Section 504 of the Rehabilitation Act, 42 U.S.C. § 1983, and the state and federal constitutions. She sought a declaration that her rights had been violated, plus reinstatement of academic honors, reimbursement for educational expenses, her attorneys' fees, and compensatory and punitive damages. After a trial, the court found that the board intentionally discriminated against the student in violation of the ADA and Section 504 and it awarded her $30,000 in compensatory damages.

The board appealed to the Second Circuit, which noted that monetary damages are available for IDEA violations through Section 1983. Since there was no remaining Section 1983 claim in this case, the issue was whether monetary damages were available directly under the IDEA. **The Second Circuit found that at least five other federal appeals courts have found monetary damages unavailable under the IDEA and agreed with them that damages should remain unavailable**, as the purpose of the IDEA is to provide educational services, not compensate for personal injury. The other relief sought by the student, including an order bestowing her with academic honors and reimbursement, was available under the IDEA. A full remedy was available to the student under the IDEA, and she was not excused from IDEA procedures based on the argument that doing so was futile. The administrative process could have provided her with appropriate and expeditious relief, and she should have filed a due process request instead of pursuing the case in court. The district court judgment was vacated, and the case was remanded for dismissal. *Polera v. Board of Educ. of Newburgh Enlarged City School Dist.*, 288 F.3d 478 (2d Cir. 2002).

♦   A Missouri student with behavior problems sued his school district after a security guard sprayed him with mace for behavior that could have been attributed to his mental illness. He alleged that the action caused an unlawful change in placement in violation of the IDEA's stay-put provision, and that it violated his right to procedural due process. The student also sought monetary damages under 42 U.S.C. § 1983 for pain and emotional distress against the guard, the school district and its insurer. The court dismissed the claims, and the student appealed. The U.S. Court of Appeals, Eighth Circuit, agreed with the school district that the student failed to allege that he had undergone any change of placement in violation of the IDEA stay-put provision. It also held that **the IDEA does not allow the recovery of monetary damages in an action under**

42 U.S.C. § 1983. The student's procedural due process claim failed because he did not allege that the school district maintained a policy or custom of requiring the use of mace to discipline students, or that any school official made an executive decision to have him maced. The court affirmed the district court judgment for the district. *Wolverton v. Doniphan R-1 School Dist.*, 16 Fed.Appx. 523 (8th Cir. 2001).

♦ After an incident in which the teacher of a nonverbal student with Down syndrome allegedly spat water in the student's face, his parents learned that she had restrained the student by strapping him to a chair without their consent. The new teacher assigned to the student after this incident physically restrained him at least once. Shortly thereafter, the parents rejected a proposed behavior management plan that allowed physical restraint. They challenged both the district's provision of a FAPE and its proposed summer program. After resolution of the administrative proceedings, the parents sued for attorneys' fees. The district agreed to pay $15,500 in settlement of both actions. The parents then sued the school board and school officials for federal civil rights violations and the special education teachers for assault and intentional infliction of emotional distress. The parents included a claim for monetary damages under 42 U.S.C. § 1983.

The court held that **the school board, as a municipal entity, could not be held liable for any Section 1983 violations**, since the harm suffered by the student was not the result of an official board policy or custom of physically restraining disabled students. There was insufficient evidence to create supervisory liability for the Section 1983 claims against the superintendent and the director of pupil services. However, the district supervisor of special education might be liable. She was apparently familiar with the student's IEP and behavioral management plan. She was in a position to know that the methods used by the teachers were not included in the student's IEPs and were not agreed to by the parents. The teachers were entitled to immunity concerning the claims for assault and intentional infliction of emotional distress, as they acted pursuant to the delegated state responsibility. A trial was required. *M.H. v. Bristol Board of Educ.*, 169 F.Supp.2d 21 (D. Conn. 2001).

♦ The mother of a student with medical and developmental disabilities and a history of behavior problems brought a stroller to school for transporting the student from class to the resource room. However, the district allegedly used the stroller for physically restraining the student during time-outs. On one such occasion, the student fell out of the stroller and fractured her skull. The parents sued the district and five employees for compensatory damages under the IDEA through 42 U.S.C. § 1983. The case reached the Tenth Circuit Court of Appeals, which held that **the IDEA provided a comprehensive remedial framework that foreclosed Section 1983 as a remedy**. *Padilla v. School Dist. No. 1, City and County of Denver, Colorado*, 233 F.3d 1268 (10th Cir. 2000).

♦ The parents of a student with autism claimed that school employees had frequently strapped the student to a chair with a vest-like device, resulting in bruises and psychological trauma. They asserted that on one occasion he became hysterical and passed out when resisting the restraint. The family filed an administrative action against the school board, asserting that it had violated the IDEA by failing to provide the student with a free appropriate public education. The parties reached a settlement concerning the implementation of goals and objectives for his program, the location of his placement, and his classification. The proceeding was dismissed pursuant to the settlement, and the parents sued the board for monetary damages and injunctive relief arising from use of the restraining device.

The court granted summary judgment to the school board, ruling that the settlement agreement and the IDEA precluded the action, and that the parents had failed to exhaust administrative remedies prior to filing suit. They appealed to the Supreme Court of Appeals of West Virginia, which found that **the settlement agreement did not mention the use of the restraint, was limited to IDEA issues and did not bar the action for damages**. The family had already exhausted all available IDEA remedies by pursuing the action before the state board. Further administrative consideration would have been futile in view of the fact that the settlement and the damage claim neither referred to nor related to the IDEA claim. The court reversed and remanded the case to the circuit court. At trial in 1999, a jury awarded the parents $339,000 in damages. *Ronnie Lee S. v. Mingo County Board of Educ.*, 500 S.E.2d 292 (W. Va. 1997).

CHAPTER SEVEN

Employment

I. DISCIPLINE AND DISCHARGE

Each state establishes permissible grounds for disciplinary action against a teacher, typically reserving discretion to the school district for necessary action. Two of the most frequently stated grounds for employee discipline are misconduct and incompetence. Courts that review employee suspension and discharge actions must analyze each case under applicable state laws, collective bargaining agreements and school board policies and procedures. Constitutional issues arise when a school board is charged with violating fundamental employee rights such as free speech.

A. Misconduct

♦ While a school nurse in Florida was tube-feeding a seizure-prone quadriplegic, he was called by a teacher to assess another student who might be having a seizure. He clamped the feeding tube and left the student to conduct a brief assessment of the other pupil, and the school board then tried to fire him for not following procedures. **An administrative law judge recommended a written reprimand, but the school board instead fired him.** However, the District Court of Appeal ruled that the school board acted improperly. *Resnick v. Flagler County School Board*, 46 So.3d 1110 (Fla. Dist. Ct. App. 2010).

♦ A Delaware school board charged a special education teacher with four incidents of misconduct and/or immorality, including **"selling" higher grades to students for cash**, sleeping during the school day and swearing at a high school football game. A hearing officer recommended discharge, and the board fired the teacher. He appealed to the Supreme Court of Delaware, which upheld the termination. His claims of due process violations and insufficient evidence for the termination did not hold up. The board properly heard all evidence that could conceivably shed light on the controversy before making its decision, and substantial evidence justified the firing. *Bethel v. Board of Educ. of Capital School Dist.*, 985 A.2d 389 (Del. 2009).

♦ After being injured on two occasions by developmentally disabled students, an employee of an Illinois school went to work in the kitchen, where students were not allowed. When a student later came into the kitchen, she complained to the HR department about the unsafe environment. She asked for an FMLA certification form and went to a doctor, who filled out the form and certified her condition as severe recurrent headaches and pain in her upper body from the student attacks. The employee added the words "plus previous depression" to the form and turned it in late. The school denied her FMLA request and fired her for excessive absenteeism. When she sued, she lost. The Seventh Circuit held that **she was not entitled to FMLA leave after altering the certification form**, even though she would have qualified for such leave had she not done so. *Smith v. Hope School*, 560 F.3d 694 (7th Cir. 2009).

♦ A distinguished California special education teacher withheld food from several aggressive students for behavior reinforcement. An aide reported the teacher and an investigation was conducted. The teacher admitted to the infraction and no parents filed a complaint. The district nevertheless sought to fire the teacher. When the teacher appealed, the state commission on professional competence found no cause for dismissal. The California Court of Appeal agreed. **The teacher had shown remorse for his misconduct and cooperated in the investigation.** He accepted full responsibility, and the misconduct was unlikely to recur. *Grossmont Union High School Dist. v. Comm'n on Professional Competence*, No. D052932, 2009 WL 777639 (Cal. Ct. App. 3/25/09).

♦ A New Jersey school board member whose son received special education from the district sought extended at-home day services and also requested payment to his spouse for services rendered to their son. The school board tried to have the board member removed for creating a conflict of interest, and the board member fought that action. The case reached the New Jersey Supreme Court, which noted that not all special education disagreements result in a conflict of interest. Here, however, **the demand for monetary relief for the**

board member's spouse crossed the line into a substantial conflict. The board member could be removed from his position. *Board of Educ. of City of Sea Isle City v. Kennedy*, 951 A.2d 987 (N.J. 2008).

♦ An elementary school teacher in Delaware taught art for eight years before becoming involved with a former student who was then 17. Their relationship evolved into a sexual one, and the former student told a friend about it. Police arrested the teacher and charged him with fourth-degree sexual rape. After the charge was dropped, the school board notified the teacher that it intended to fire him based on immorality and/or misconduct. He was fired, then sued, claiming his positive evaluations proved that he could still teach. He also asserted that he had not engaged in criminal activity, and that his former student did not attend district schools. The case reached the Supreme Court of Delaware, which upheld his termination. Here, the teacher compromised his position of trust and his status as a role model. And **his sexual relationship with his former student impacted his ability to teach**. *Lehto v. Board of Educ. of Caesar Rodney School Dist.*, 962 A.2d 222 (Del. 2008).

♦ A school district maintenance supervisor in Utah operated his own electrical contracting business at the same time. After other district employees reported that he was performing personal work on district time, local police conducted an investigation and confirmed that he left work early on most days. He also used his district vehicle to visit non-district work sites on district time. The district suspended him, and he then pled guilty to misdemeanor charges of communications fraud. The district then fired him and he sued for breach of contract, among other claims. The case reached the Supreme Court of Utah, which upheld his termination. **It disregarded his argument that as long as he had his cell phone with him, he was still working for the district.** The district properly followed its procedures for a termination "for cause." *Oman v. Davis School Dist.*, 194 P.3d 956 (Utah 2008).

♦ An Oklahoma special education teacher went to look for a student who had left class, fearing the student might leave school grounds. He found the student in the office and slapped him twice on the face, but not very hard, according to a secretary. The teacher then went to the student's home to apologize. He was fired under the state Teacher Due Process Act for physical or mental abuse of a child. He then filed for reinstatement with full pay and expungement of his personnel file. A court ordered his reinstatement, and the district appealed to the Oklahoma Supreme Court, which affirmed the ruling. Here, the student was on medication; he had left school grounds in the past; he had been slapped by his grandmother "to stop him from throwing fits"; the teacher's slaps had not been hard; and the parents had said they would not oppose the teacher's return to classroom instruction. The lower court had properly determined that **the teacher did not physically or mentally abuse the student**. *Hagen v. Independent School Dist. No. I-004*, 157 P.3d 738 (Okla. 2007).

♦ A certified special education teacher who had 12 years of experience was **fired after he provided students with answers for state-mandated testing**

and failed to keep current IEPs for some students. He challenged his dismissal unsuccessfully and then applied for the vacancy his termination created. The school board instead hired a teacher with an emergency certificate in special education. He sued the board, claiming it had to hire a certificated teacher such as himself over one with an emergency credential. The Kentucky Court of Appeals disagreed. He was unsuitable for appointment under state law, permitting the board to hire the emergency-credentialed teacher. *Hicks v. Floyd County Board of Educ.*, No. 2006-CA-000499-MR, 2007 WL 3226983 (Ky. Ct. App. 11/2/07).

◆ A Pennsylvania special education teacher got a note from a student expressing suicidal thoughts. She took the note to the principal, then got verbal permission from the student's parent to take the student to an outside psychologist. After her conduct was questioned, she was disciplined for going outside the scope of her duties. The student's IEP did not call for psychological services and she should have obtained the parent's written permission before arranging for psychological therapy. When she sued, claiming equal protection violations and constructive discharge, a federal court ruled against her. She appealed to the Third Circuit, which considered her claim to First Amendment protection and her claim of retaliation under Section 504. First, the court held that **her conduct in transporting the student to therapy (and attending the sessions) did not amount to protected free speech**. Next, the court held that she was not entitled to protection under Section 504 because she was simply providing assistance to a disabled person; she was not advocating on the student's behalf. The lower court decision was affirmed. *Montanye v. Wissahickon School Dist.*, 218 Fed.Appx. 126 (3d Cir. 2007).

◆ A physical education instructor at the Georgia School for the Deaf was **involved in two incidents of corporal punishment on the same day**, having to physically restrain two students. One involved a student who repeatedly hit a classmate on the head with a dodgeball; the other involved a student who violently kicked an aide. The state education department conducted a hearing, then issued a notice of dismissal against the teacher for violating the code of ethics standards governing the abuse of students and professional conduct. An administrative law judge upheld the firing, but the state personnel board reversed. The Georgia Court of Appeals ruled that the personnel board had the authority to reverse the termination. *Georgia Dep't of Educ. v. Niemeier*, 616 S.E.2d 861 (Ga. Ct. App. 2005).

◆ A special education assistant in an Oregon school received favorable employment evaluations for six years. She was then arrested for shoplifting $300 in merchandise from a department store, but wasn't prosecuted. The school district fired her because she was no longer an effective role model and could not be relied on to exercise good judgment. Her union filed a grievance on her behalf, and an arbitrator ordered the district to reinstate her. The Oregon Court of Appeals upheld the arbitrator's decision, noting that **the arbitrator's reinstatement ruling did not violate public policy**. Also, the employee had been arrested for what would have been a second-degree theft, had she been charged. This was not within the class of felony crimes that prevented employment by Oregon school districts. *Salem-Keizer Ass'n of Classified Employees v. Salem-Keizer School Dist. 24J*, 61 P.3d 970 (Or. Ct. App. 2003).

◆ A teacher employed by the Kansas State School for the Deaf (KSSD) asked an assistant football coach to recruit players to help him improve property he owned. Part of the improvement project involved moving discarded railroad ties that weighed 150 pounds. The school's head teacher turned down a written request for a field trip to the property, but later signed the request form. Two students and the assistant football coach went with the teacher to the property. When the teacher left to prepare lunch, one of the students was struck and killed by a train. The KSSD board performed an investigation and adopted a motion terminating the teacher's employment. The teacher appealed to a hearing committee, which held for the teacher, finding that the board did not show by substantial evidence that the teacher displayed a lack of professional judgment. The case reached the Kansas Supreme Court, which agreed that **no school policy or student safety regulations applied to the case.** While the teacher did not inform parents about the nature of the field trip, this was the head teacher's duty. There was evidence that the practice of taking railroad ties from railroad property was common and not inappropriate. The court upheld the committee's ruling for the teacher. *Kansas State Board of Educ. v. Marsh*, 50 P.3d 9 (Kan. 2002).

◆ Three teacher aides were noncertified, untenured employees who worked under annual contracts. They refused to attend a required training session on clean intermittent urinary catheterization. After attending individual conferences to discuss their refusal to attend the training session, a new session was arranged. They were advised that failure to attend the rescheduled training session would be considered insubordination, for which they could be discharged. The aides again refused to attend, and were fired. A court held that the board had arbitrarily terminated their contracts, and it awarded them pay and benefits for the remainder of their contract terms. An appeals court awarded them damages even beyond their contracts, but the Tennessee Supreme Court held that **awarding damages for a period beyond the term stated in the contracts would put the aides in a better position than they would have enjoyed if they had fully performed their contracts.** They had no reasonable expectation of continued employment beyond their contract terms and were ineligible for protection under the state Teacher Tenure Act. The aides were entitled only to payment for the remainder of their contract terms. *Cantrell v. Knox County Board of Educ.*, 53 S.W.3d 659 (Tenn. 2001).

B. Incompetence

◆ Los Angeles school officials observed a veteran special education teacher on four occasions and issued below-standard evaluations and a notice that cause existed for termination. The teacher requested a hearing before the Commission on Professional Competence (CPC), which found that 1) **the administrators had no training or expertise in special education and** 2) **they simply disagreed with the teacher's skills or style.** Further, the students were simply difficult to teach and manage, and their behaviors were characteristic of special education students. The CPC rejected the attempt to fire the teacher, and the California Court of Appeal affirmed. The court also ruled that the teacher was entitled to $180,000 in attorneys' fees. *Los Angeles Unified School Dist. v. Comm'n on Professional Competence*, No. B204963, 2009 WL 596766 (Cal. Ct. App. 3/10/09).

♦ A probationary special education teacher in Louisiana received numerous complaints about her performance at a school for the visually impaired. She was offered counseling on at least four occasions, without success. The school superintendent placed her on exigent leave with pay, pending her discharge at the end of the school year. She sued the state board of elementary and secondary education (BESE) for reinstatement and back pay, claiming that school officials ignored provisions of the BESE manual, which governs the employment terms of personnel working in the state's special schools. The Louisiana Court of Appeal upheld her termination, noting that as a probationary employee, she could be discharged upon the written recommendation of the superintendent, so long as valid reasons accompanied that recommendation. Here, **the teacher had failed to implement instruction for multiply handicapped students and had lost her composure,** yelling at students and parents. *Muse v. Louisiana State Board of Elementary and Secondary Educ.*, No. 2007 CA 1146, 2008 WL 426483 (La. Ct. App. 2/8/08).

♦ A Missouri **special education teacher failed to properly complete the paperwork for her IEPs** during two years. She met with the special education director four times in one month to discuss incomplete IEPs and review Missouri special education standards. After two extensions, she managed to complete the necessary paperwork. The following year, she was again late with her paperwork, and the material she submitted contained errors. She was fired for incompetence, inefficiency and insubordination. The Missouri Court of Appeals upheld her discharge over her complaint that special education paperwork requirements were unduly burdensome. The timely completion of paperwork was inextricable from teaching duties and could result in the denial of an appropriate education. *Hellmann v. Union R-XI School Dist.*, 170 S.W.3d 52 (Mo. Ct. App. 2005).

♦ A Texas school district employed a special education teacher for several years under a continuing contract until notifying her of its intention to terminate the contract based on myriad deficiencies, including: failure to fulfill her duties and responsibilities; incompetency and insufficiency in performing classroom duties; inability to maintain classroom discipline; failure to comply with reasonable district requirements for professional improvement and growth; and failure to attain stated goals in consecutive school years. Following a hearing, the district accepted the hearing examiner's findings of good cause to terminate the teacher's contract. The state commissioner of education adopted the findings. The Texas Court of Appeals held that **the evidence supported the hearing examiner's finding that the teacher had failed to fulfill her job duties and responsibilities,** particularly with regard to adequate classroom management and discipline. It agreed that the teacher's performance was so deficient that the district was not required to offer her the opportunity for remediation. The teacher also failed to teach in accordance with student IEPs, which violated the IDEA. *Ramirez v. Edgewood Independent School Dist.*, No. 04-00-00137-CV, 2001 WL 22043 (Tex. Ct. App. 2001).

♦   A South Dakota school district contracted for 15 years with a community health nurse to provide sex education for elementary students. However, the school board never pre-screened the program. After a video presentation by the nurse, a teacher with 29 years of experience in the district solicited questions from a group of boys, as had been the practice for 15 years. The teacher responded to a question about homosexual practices in explicit language, prompting complaints from parents. At the hearing to consider the teacher's discharge, only two parents testified that they were bothered by his statements, and the principal testified that there was no evidence that students had been harmed or that there had been an increase in discipline problems. However, the school board voted to discharge him.

A trial court upheld the discharge, but the Supreme Court of South Dakota reversed. Although a single incident may be sufficient to support a finding of incompetency, the teacher's conduct here did not rise to that level since **there was no showing that his teaching ability had been impaired or that students were detrimentally affected.** The school administration had abdicated its control over the sex education program, and no school officials ever took steps to place limits upon it. The teacher had participated in the questioning for the past 15 years without incident. Accordingly, the one ill-advised answer did not support the finding of incompetence. The court remanded the case for reinstatement of the teacher. *Collins v. Faith School Dist. No. 46-2*, 574 N.W.2d 889 (S.D. 1998).

C. Speech Rights and Retaliation

1. Speech Rights

♦   A Michigan special education teacher' probationary contract was not renewed. The district told her that she failed to timely and appropriately complete required Medicaid and IEP reports, that she improperly delegated responsibilities to teaching assistants, and that she failed to provide students their required instructional time. She asserted that the real reason was that she complained her class size was larger than the law allowed. When she sued under the First Amendment, she lost. A federal court and the Sixth Circuit noted that her complaint only went to her supervisor, and it was part of her job duties to address her caseload. Thus, **her statement was not protected under the First Amendment.** *Fox v. Traverse City Area Public Schools Board of Educ.*, 605 F.3d 345 (6th Cir. 2010).

♦   The New York City Board of Education required employees to maintain a posture of complete neutrality regarding political candidates while on duty or in contact with students. This meant that teachers were prohibited from wearing political buttons in school buildings. The board also prohibited the distribution of political material in staff mailboxes or on union bulletin boards. Several teachers and the president of a union sued, claiming that the board's regulations violated the First Amendment. **A federal court upheld the ban on political buttons**, noting that the board had legitimate pedagogical reasons for maintaining neutrality on controversial issues. However, the board could not prohibit the distribution of political material in staff mailboxes and on union bulletin boards where students were unlikely to encounter it. *Weingarten v. Board of Educ. of City of New York*, 591 F.Supp.2d 511 (S.D.N.Y. 2008).

◆ Idaho amended its Right to Work Act to permit all state and political subdivision employees to continue authorizing payroll deductions for general union dues, but not for political activities. A state and local education association challenged the amendment as violating the First and Fourteenth Amendments. The case reached the U.S. Supreme Court, which upheld the prohibition on payroll deductions for political causes. Here, **the state was not abridging the employees' speech rights. It was merely refusing to provide payroll deductions for political speech.** *Ysursa v. Pocatello Educ. Ass'n*, 555 U.S. 353, 129 S.Ct. 1093, 172 L.Ed.2d 770 (2009).

◆ A New York contractor who provided special education services sued education officials claiming that her contract was terminated because of a letter she wrote. A federal court held that **the letter addressed internal administrative matters and did not address a matter of public concern** so as to allow for First Amendment protections. The Second Circuit Court of Appeals agreed. However, it noted that the contractor might be able to amend her complaint to allege that she was speaking as a citizen engaged in public speech when she made statements about the provision of services to special needs children as a group. Thus, if she properly amended her complaint within 45 days, her lawsuit would be allowed to continue. *McGuire v. Warren*, 207 Fed.Appx. 34 (2d Cir. 2006).

◆ A Delaware school psychologist began reporting incidents of non-compliance with the IDEA as soon as she started her job. After her contract was not renewed, she sued, claiming that she was not rehired because of her efforts to bring the school district into compliance with the IDEA. A federal court held that she was not speaking as a citizen on a matter of public concern when she reported alleged IDEA violations. This was because **one of her job duties was to report on non-compliance**. Since her speech was not protected by the First Amendment, her lawsuit failed. *Houlihan v. Sussex Technical School Dist.*, 461 F.Supp.2d 252 (D. Del. 2006).

◆ A district assistant superintendent for curriculum and program accountability was reassigned to an administrative assistant position. She asserted that she was improperly reassigned for reporting misconduct by district employees associated with the Texas Assessment of Academic Skills (TAAS). She claimed that teachers "paced" students on the untimed TAAS and that the district exempted a disproportionate number of recent immigrants and special education students from taking the test. She sued the district, board and superintendent, asserting federal civil rights violations and a claim against the district under the Texas Whistleblower Act. The court found **no evidence of deliberate indifference to her constitutional rights by the district in her reassignment**. The superintendent was entitled to qualified immunity because the administrator's allegations of testing improprieties were not protected forms of speech, since they did not involve a public interest or a public controversy. It was not clear that the practice of pacing, by itself, violated Texas law. She had no firsthand knowledge that pacing actually took place, and her report was therefore not in good faith. The superintendent reassigned her for failing to follow orders. *Rodriguez v. Board of Trustees of Laredo Independent School Dist.*, 143 F.Supp.2d 727 (S.D. Tex. 2001).

♦ A group of Arkansas special education teachers worked at a middle school that was the site of increasing tension over the needs of special education students. The principal allegedly instructed teachers not to discuss incidents involving special education students. However, one teacher was quoted in a local newspaper, and another teacher then told her she should leave the school. The staff became deeply divided. In a lawsuit, a group of teachers claimed that the principal lowered their performance evaluations, stifled their personal speech rights and violated their right to equal protection. A federal court denied the principal's motion for immunity, but the Eighth Circuit reversed.

The court of appeals held that the teachers offered no evidence that they were treated differently than other teachers. Also, although the teachers' speech about special education students involved a matter of public concern, there was undisputed evidence that it resulted in disharmony and created factions that negatively affected the efficient administration of the school. **Where a teacher's speech causes upheaval, it does not outweigh the interest of efficient school administration even if it touches on a matter of public concern.** Under these circumstances, the principal should have been granted qualified immunity. *Fales v. Garst*, 235 F.3d 1122 (8th Cir. 2000).

♦ A teacher with more than 12 years of experience teaching socially and emotionally disturbed high school students underwent "a dramatic conversion to Christianity." After being admonished against discussing religious topics in his classes, he did not abide by a cease and desist memo. The special education director suspended him indefinitely for violating the directive, which was later adjusted to a six-month suspension. The teacher then signed an affirmation indicating that he would adhere to the directive, but wrote a letter to the director requesting clarification. The director reassigned the teacher to a comprehensive development skills class attended by students with autism and other disabilities. After a student's parent sent a tape of religious songs to calm his son at school, the teacher sent him a thank you note containing religious references. The teacher's supervisor advised him that the letter violated the directive but took no disciplinary action. The teacher responded by suing the board for violating his speech rights, and claimed that the directive was unconstitutionally vague.

The case reached the Second Circuit, which found that schools have the ability to restrain teacher speech rights in view of legitimate government interests, such as avoiding litigation over possible Establishment Clause violations. In this case, the teacher's letter introduced religious content into a curricular matter. The directive did not infringe on the teacher's speech rights, and **there was no merit to the teacher's claim that the directive was unconstitutionally vague, since its basic meaning gave him fair notice of what he was not supposed to do**. *Marchi v. Board of Cooperative Educ. Services of Albany*, 173 F.3d 469 (2d Cir. 1999).

◆   A Massachusetts special needs teacher supervised a small therapy session attended by seventh-grade male students. During a discussion of words with multiple meanings, one student interrupted the discussion with an obscenity. The teacher allowed the discussion to continue, as the word had multiple meanings. The last 10 minutes of the class were devoted to a discussion of similar words and their literal definitions. At the end of class, the teacher admonished students not to use these words and to consult an adult or dictionary if they had further questions. When a parent complained, the superintendent suspended the teacher for two days and refused to recommend her for reappointment. The teacher did not gain tenure. She sued the school committee. The case reached the Supreme Judicial Court of Massachusetts, which stated that the teacher had demonstrated that she was not rehired because of the discussion. **The district's resource room discipline guidelines required her to respond to difficult situations in creative ways** without sending students to the principal's office for discipline. The teacher had responded to the situation appropriately. Accordingly, she was entitled to be reinstated for one year of untenured service as well as economic damages. *Hosford v. School Committee of Sandwich*, 421 Mass. 708, 659 N.E.2d 1178 (Mass. 1996).

2. Retaliation

◆   A probationary teacher in California complained about a student in her class who had severe behavior issues. Another student's parent threatened a lawsuit against her because the student was not receiving special education. The teacher had a poor relationship with her director of special education, partly due to the placement of her own child. After her contract was not renewed, she sued, asserting that she had engaged in whistleblowing activity by complaining about the education plans of students in her class. However, the state court of appeal ruled against her, noting that **her complaints about unruly students were made in the context of internal personnel or administrative matters**. *Conn v. Western Placer Unified School Dist.*, 186 Cal.App.4th 1163 (Cal. Ct. App. 2010).

◆   A New York special education teacher received poor job evaluations. He claimed they were in retaliation for advocating on behalf of students, but the Second Circuit ruled against him. It cited evidence that **he was unable to teach to the level of his special needs students, even before he began to make complaints** about school policies. The negative evaluations were not causally related to his allegedly protected activity. *Valtchev v. City of New York*, 400 Fed.Appx. 586 (2d Cir. 2010).

◆   A recently hired Mississippi special education teacher berated a colleague (in front of the colleague's students) for using corporal punishment on an autistic boy. A few months later, the teacher learned that her contract would not be renewed. She sued, claiming age discrimination and that the non-renewal was in retaliation for protected speech. A federal court disagreed. It found that age was not a factor because the teacher had been hired shortly before the incident, and **the speech was not protected because it was made pursuant to her official duties**. *Lamb v. Booneville School Dist.*, No. 1:08CV254-SA-JAD, 2010 WL 457576 (N.D. Miss. 2/3/10).

◆   A California special education teacher filed a complaint with the U.S. Department of Education's Office for Civil Rights (OCR), alleging that her county education office denied students appropriate services. Allegedly, she was then subjected to intimidation, exclusion from important meetings, changed work assignments and a reduced workload despite the increase in the number of disabled students in the district. She filed an OCR complaint that resulted in a finding of retaliation. When she sued, a federal court found that she couldn't pursue legal action because she wasn't disabled. However, the Ninth Circuit ruled that she could continue her lawsuit. **Section 504 and the ADA protect against retaliation for advocating on behalf of the disabled.** *Barker v. Riverside County Office of Educ.*, 584 F.3d 821 (9th Cir. 2009).

◆   A part-time special education teacher in New York made allegations of discrimination on a Friday. On the following Tuesday, she was informed that her position would probably be eliminated because of a projected decrease in enrollment. The district terminated her only to realize that enrollment would not decrease and that it needed a full-time teacher. It did not offer her the job. When she sued for retaliation, a federal court granted pretrial judgment to the district. The Second Circuit, however, found issues of fact that required a trial. Here, **the timing was such that an inference of retaliation was possible**. Also, the refusal to rehire her hinted at a retaliatory motive. A jury would have to decide the matter. *Wood v. Pittsford Cent. School Dist.*, No. 07-0892, 2008 WL 5120494 (2d Cir. 12/8/08).

◆   An Idaho school employee assisted with school security, preventing crime, and supervising the parking lot, grounds and hallways. Although the principal told him to update the school emergency plan, his policy-making responsibilities were unclear. He composed a letter to various school officials complaining about the principal's handling of some of his reports. At the end of that school year, his position was eliminated. He sued under the First Amendment. A federal court granted pretrial judgment to the school district, but the Ninth Circuit reversed, finding issues of fact that required a trial. Here, the employee's speech was on a matter of public concern. However, under the Supreme Court's ruling in *Garcetti* [547 U.S. 410 (2006)], **if he was speaking pursuant to his official duties, then his speech was not protected**. On remand, this issue would have to be addressed. *Posey v. Lake Pond Oreille School Dist.*, 546 F.3d 1121 (9th Cir. 2008).

◆   An Illinois special education teacher dealt with students who frequently misbehaved. She claimed that the principal and vice principal placed a disruptive student in her classroom and failed to discipline him. They also harassed students and ran a private business during school hours, which hindered their ability to properly run the school. **She was forced to file a grievance to obtain "assault leave" after a confrontation with a student.** She also notified authorities about the private business the administrators were running. They fired her after the school year, and she sued for retaliation under several laws. The board of education sought to dismiss the case, but a federal court allowed the teacher to proceed on a number of fronts, including her claim under the Rehabilitation Act and her claim under the federal Whistleblowers Protection Act. The case would have to proceed to trial. *Blazquez v. Board of Educ. of City of Chicago*, No. 05-CV-4389, 2006 WL 3320538 (N.D. Ill. 11/14/06).

◆   A Pennsylvania school nurse enjoyed outstanding employment ratings for five years. She then began advocating for two disabled students, complaining that the district kept two sets of records on the children and that the principal was gathering information to remove the students from their homes. She also filed two complaints with the state office for civil rights. Her employment ratings fell. She claimed she was then targeted for harassment that forced her to resign. She sued the district for retaliation under the First Amendment. A federal court ruled for the district, but the Third Circuit reversed. Here, **the nurse's speech addressed a matter of public concern** and did not disrupt school operations. *McGreevy v. Stroup*, 413 F.3d 359 (3d Cir. 2005).

◆   After a probationary special education teacher wrote letters to district officials criticizing its special education programs and policies, the district did not renew her contract. It cited her low performance evaluations (including her deficiency in writing IEPs) which were made after she wrote the letters. She sued the district in an Oregon federal court, and a jury awarded her over $900,000 in compensatory damages and $50,000 in punitive damages. The case reached the Ninth Circuit Court of Appeals, which upheld the award. It found little evidence that her input into the drafting of IEPs was deficient. Also, **her speech was on a matter of public concern and outweighed any disruptive effect it had on the district**. Her letters went through proper channels and may have actually had a harmonizing effect rather than a disruptive one. *Settlegoode v. Portland Public Schools*, 371 F.3d 503 (9th Cir. 2004).

◆   A special education administrator for a Connecticut regional service center claimed that her supervisor yelled at her for failing to inform the center that she had cancer. Also, she refused to give a negative performance evaluation to an African-American co-worker despite orders to do so because she believed a negative performance evaluation was not deserved. After the school year, the administrator was transferred to a new position. She sued the center, asserting retaliation. A federal court found that the the administrator **failed to show that the allegedly retaliatory action of transferring her to another job constituted an adverse employment action**, because she could not show that her changed work environment was "unreasonably inferior." *St. Ledger v. Area Cooperative Educ. Services*, 228 F.Supp.2d 66 (D. Conn. 2002).

♦   During her fourth year of employment by a New York school district, a teacher was called to testify before an impartial hearing officer in IDEA proceedings. Her testimony supported the position advocated by a student's parent, who prevailed in the IDEA proceeding. Almost five years later, the district superintendent of instruction notified the teacher by letter that she would be terminated. The letter stated that the teacher had refused to turn in a grade for a student, failed to respond to repeated requests for work samples by the same student, failed to schedule an appointment with the superintendent, and cited her "record of instruction." The school district fired her. When she sued, a federal court and the Second Circuit ruled against her. **She failed to make out a claim for retaliation under the First Amendment or demonstrate that the district deprived her of any due process rights** under the Fourteenth Amendment. *Reynolds v. Board of Educ. of Wappingers Cent. School Dist.*, 208 F.3d 203 (2d Cir. 2000).

♦   An Oklahoma school administrator was suspended and reprimanded for insubordination and not getting along with a co-worker during his service as an elementary school principal. He filed an Equal Employment Opportunity Commission (EEOC) claim, which he later voluntarily withdrew. He became active in unionizing district administrative employees and was eventually reassigned to serve as an assistant high school principal. He filed a second EEOC claim, which he also lost, alleging that the reassignment was discriminatory and that a reprimand issued to him was retaliatory. He continued having difficulties and received poor performance evaluations. The principal's refusal to change an evaluation led to a third EEOC claim. The board then voted to discharge him. He sued, alleging his termination was retaliatory. The Tenth Circuit Court of Appeals rejected his arguments that he had been discharged for his union activities and EEOC complaints, finding no evidence that the decision to fire him was based on his union activities or previous EEOC charges. Further, **there was no evidence that the legitimate, nondiscriminatory reasons offered by the board for the discharge were a pretext for retaliation.** The administrator had a history of not getting along with co-workers, and the individual who recommended his termination was also a union official. *Grady v. Shawnee Public School Dist. I-93,* 166 F.3d 347 (10th Cir. 1998).

♦   A Dallas high school math teacher alleged that his principal told him to give a student-athlete a passing grade even though the student was failing. After the teacher refused to change the grade, the principal allowed the student to transfer to another class. The Texas Education Agency (TEA) investigated the school and disqualified it from the state football playoffs. The school district then transferred the teacher to a middle school, placed him on probation, froze his salary and gave him an unsatisfactory performance rating. An administrative panel upheld the school board's decision, but the TEA reversed it. Although he prevailed in the TEA action, the teacher resigned and sued the district and certain officials. The Court of Appeals of Texas held that **the teacher had no**

constitutional right to refuse to assign a grade to a student. This was not an example of academic freedom protected by the First Amendment. *Bates v. Dallas Independent School Dist.*, 952 S.W.2d 543 (Tex. Ct. App. 1997).

II. EMPLOYMENT DISCRIMINATION

State and federal anti-discrimination laws prohibit specific forms of employment discrimination. Title VII of the Civil Rights Act of 1964 is the primary federal law prohibiting discrimination on grounds including race, sex, national origin and religion. State civil rights acts are based upon Title VII, often directly incorporating its language and standards.

Discrimination on the basis of disability may violate Section 504 of the Rehabilitation Act, the Americans with Disabilities Act (ADA) and/or analogous state laws. Many other state and federal acts prohibit employment discrimination on the basis of other grounds, such as age.

A. Disability

The following employment discrimination cases arise under Section 504, the ADA and related state laws. For Section 504 and ADA cases involving students, please see Chapter Nine.

◆   The Supreme Court held that Congress did not show a history and pattern of irrational employment discrimination by the states against individuals with disabilities when it enacted the ADA. In determining whether two Alabama state employees were subjected to disability discrimination, the Supreme Court noted that **although Congress had identified negative attitudes and biases against individuals with disabilities as reasons for enacting the ADA, it did not identify a pattern of irrational discrimination by the states against them**. Since there was no pattern of unconstitutional behavior by the states, the employees could not sue the state for money damages. The Eleventh Amendment barred any such claims. Congress did not validly abrogate states' immunity. *Board of Trustees of Univ. of Alabama v. Garrett*, 531 U.S. 356, 121 S.Ct. 955, 148 L.Ed.2d 866 (2001).

◆   In a 2002 case, the U.S. Supreme Court restricted the number of individuals covered by the ADA, finding **the statute applies only to persons with impairments that prevent or severely restrict them from activities that are of central importance to daily life**. The plaintiff in the case was restricted from performing certain aspects of her manufacturing position due to carpal tunnel syndrome. When the employer allegedly refused to accommodate the employee, she sued under the ADA. The Supreme Court agreed to review the case to consider the proper standard for determining when an ADA claimant is substantially limited in the major life activity of performing manual tasks. The court held that this standard is met only where a person has "an impairment that prevents or severely restricts [her] from doing activities that are of central importance to most people's daily lives. *Toyota Motor Manufacturing, Kentucky, Inc. v. Williams*, 534 U.S. 184, 122 S.Ct. 681, 151 L.Ed.2d 615 (2002).

♦ Twin sisters with uncorrected vision of 20/200 or worse but corrected vision of 20/20 or better were denied jobs as global airline pilots with an airline because their uncorrected vision did not meet the airline's minimum uncorrected vision standard. The Supreme Court found that the sisters had not demonstrated they were disabled as defined by the ADA. The Court concluded that **mitigating measures** had to be taken into account when evaluating whether an individual was disabled, and that, because glasses or contacts corrected the sisters' vision to 20/20 or better, they were not substantially limited in a major life activity. The sisters were also not regarded as having a disability because the airline did not perceive them to be substantially limited in a major life activity. *Sutton v. United Air Lines, Inc.*, 527 U.S. 471, 119 S.Ct. 2139, 144 L.Ed.2d 450 (1999).

The Supreme Court also held that a mechanic with high blood pressure who was fired from his job was not disabled under the ADA. Because **the mechanic was able to control his high blood pressure with medication**, he was not substantially limited in a major life activity. He was also not regarded as disabled. At most, the employer regarded the mechanic as being unable to perform the single, particular job of mechanic because it believed his high blood pressure exceeded the U.S. Department of Transportation's requirements for drivers of commercial motor vehicles. *Murphy v. United Parcel Service, Inc.*, 527 U.S. 516, 119 S.Ct. 2133, 144 L.Ed.2d 484 (1999).

However, the ADA was amended in 2008 to provide that mitigating measures, such as medications, not be considered when determining whether someone is substantially limited in a major life activity.

The ADA Amendments Act of 2008 also expands the definition of "major life activity" to include a non-exhaustive list of physical activities. And it clarifies that an episodic impairment or one in remission is a disability if it substantially limits a major life activity when active.

♦ The U.S. Supreme Court ruled that an individual with tuberculosis may be considered an individual with a disability under Section 504 of the Rehabilitation Act. Federal regulations published under Section 504 define an individual with a disability as "any person who (i) has a physical or mental impairment which substantially limits one or more of such person's major life activities, (ii) has a record of such impairment or (iii) is regarded as having such an impairment." It defines "physical impairment" as a disorder affecting, among other things, the respiratory system and defines "major life activities" as "functions such as caring for one's self … and working."

The case involved a Florida elementary school teacher who was discharged because of the continued recurrence of tuberculosis. The teacher sued the school board under Section 504 but a federal court dismissed her claims. However, the U.S. Court of Appeals, Eleventh Circuit, reversed the district court's decision and held that persons with contagious diseases fall within Section 504's coverage. The school board appealed to the U.S. Supreme Court.

The Supreme Court ruled that **the teacher was a person with a disability under Section 504 because her tuberculosis affected her respiratory system and her ability to work**. The school board contended that in defining an individual with a disability under Section 504, the contagious effects of a disease can be distinguished from the disease's physical effects. However, the Court reasoned that the teacher's contagion and her physical impairment both resulted from tuberculosis. It would be unfair to allow an employer to distinguish between a disease's potential effect on others and its effect on the afflicted employee in order to justify discriminatory treatment. Allowing discrimination based on the contagious effects of a physical impairment would be inconsistent with the underlying purpose of Section 504. Contagion cannot remove a person from Section 504 coverage. The Supreme Court remanded the case to the district court to determine whether the teacher was "otherwise qualified" for her job and whether the school board could reasonably accommodate her as an employee. *School Board of Nassau County v. Arline*, 480 U.S. 273, 107 S.Ct. 1123, 94 L.Ed.2d 307 (1987).

On remand, the district court held that the teacher was "otherwise qualified" to teach. The teacher posed no threat of spreading tuberculosis to her students. When she was on medication, medical tests indicated a limited number of negative cultures. Her family members tested negative and she had limited contact with students. The court ordered reinstatement or front pay in the amount of $768,724 for earnings until retirement. *Arline v. School Board of Nassau County*, 692 F.Supp. 1286 (M.D. Fla. 1988).

◆   A Michigan school district transferred a long-time special education teacher on two occasions because of increasing budget deficits. The teacher claimed the transfers forced her retirement and asserted they were in retaliation for her opposition to discriminatory policies. However, the state court of appeals ruled against her, noting that **her earlier objection to the transfers never referenced discrimination laws**. *Rott v. Madison Dist. Public Schools*, No. 294291, 2010 WL 5175457 (Mich. Ct. App. 12/21/10).

◆   A New York teacher with dyslexia sought accommodations when she was required to take the liberal arts and sciences part of the teacher certification test. She wanted a dictionary, extra time, frequent breaks and an oral examination. However, since the test partly measured proper sentence structure, grammar and punctuation, the National Evaluation Systems (NES) denied her request. Eventually the NES agreed to some accommodations, but she had already lost her teaching position and therefore sued under the ADA and the Rehabilitation Act. A federal court ruled against her, noting that **all the accommodations she sought would have given her an advantage over non-disabled persons**, which neither act required. *Falchenberg v. New York State Dep't of Educ.*, 567 F.Supp.2d 513 (S.D.N.Y. 2008).

◆   A Washington school district assistant cook wore hearing aids for her clinical deafness. She had problems with a supervisor and transferred several times. After she disregarded a supervisor's order to use sick time to have a hearing aid repaired (for safety reasons), the food services director escorted her out of the kitchen. She quit and sued for disability discrimination, constructive discharge and retaliation. The Court of Appeals of Washington ruled in favor of the school district. Here, even though she qualified as disabled under state law, **she failed to show that the district refused to accommodate her**. Her transfer requests had all been granted, and her problems getting along with her supervisor did not support a claim for constructive discharge. Nor did the safety-based order to repair her hearing aid. *Townsend v. Walla Walla School Dist.*, 196 P.3d 748 (Wash. Ct. App. 2008).

♦ For 17 years, an Ohio special education teacher received disability retirement benefits due to an inner eyelid infection that caused a film over his eyes. The medical review board of the teachers' retirement system then asked an ophthalmologist to review the teacher's condition. The ophthalmologist found the teacher incapable of resuming his teaching duties due to the 17-year absence. However, **the ophthalmologist did not find a physiological condition that rendered the teacher totally and permanently disabled**. The board then terminated the teacher's benefits. He appealed, and the Supreme Court of Ohio upheld the decision. The board had exclusive authority to determine his eligibility for benefits and could terminate them where the medical findings did not support the continuation of benefits. *Ackerman v. State Teachers Retirement Board*, 883 N.E.2d 445 (Ohio 2008).

♦ Parents and teachers accused an Illinois principal of mishandling disciplinary issues and being unavailable. Before the school board could implement a performance improvement plan for him, he took a medical leave for stress and depression. He sought a shortened work day and other accommodations, which were denied. He then returned to work, where he was reassigned as a teacher for budgetary reasons. When he sued for disability discrimination, he lost. The Seventh Circuit held that **his short-term depression did not qualify as a disability** under the ADA. *Cassimy v. Board of Educ. of Rockford Public Schools*, 461 F.3d 932 (7th Cir. 2006).

♦ A wheelchair-bound teacher asserted that her employing district and superintendent made inadequate accommodations, and that the offered accommodations caused her physical injuries and emotional distress. She further alleged that the superintendent had made derogatory comments about her disability. She requested compensatory and punitive damages. The district and superintendent moved to dismiss the action, asserting immunity under Article 5, Section 20 of the Arkansas Constitution. The court denied the motion, ruling that school districts are not entitled to immunity under that provision of the state constitution. The district and superintendent appealed to the Arkansas Supreme Court, which affirmed. School districts, which were considered political subdivisions, **were creatures of the state that could not avail themselves of constitutional immunity safeguards**. State law granted immunity to political subdivisions that was not as comprehensive as that provided to state agencies under the Arkansas Constitution. This protection limited immunity to the extent political subdivisions were covered by liability insurance, prohibiting recovery for any excess over that amount. *Dermott Special School Dist. v. Johnson*, 32 S.W.3d 477 (Ark. 2000).

♦ A school bus driver was employed by an Ohio school district for seven years, and then transferred to a custodial position. After he was observed drinking beer at an elementary school, the school board recommended discharging him. The employee was allowed to keep his job after signing a last chance agreement. The school district later rejected the employee for a part-time bus driver/garage worker position, even though he was the most senior applicant. He filed a grievance and won the position after arbitration and a lawsuit. However, he received no back pay or other benefits. He sued the board, asserting violations of federal and state disability discrimination laws. A federal court held for the board because it found that the employee had no disability, perceived or real. On appeal, the Sixth Circuit affirmed. **An employer may hold an alcoholic employee to the same performance and behavior standards to which it holds other employees.** The ADA did not require the district to put a person guilty of drinking on the job in a bus driver position. There was a serious risk that the employee might drink on the job, run the risk of an accident, and potentially subject the district to liability. *Martin v. Barnesville Exempted Village School Dist. Board of Educ.*, 209 F.3d 931 (6th Cir. 2000).

♦ A visually impaired Illinois social worker applied at an alternative high school for students with behavior disorders. The school served students described as the toughest two percent of the student population, including those with conduct and emotional disorders who sometimes required physical restraint. School officials determined that the applicant should have a two-day trial observation period. When evaluators noticed that she failed to detect cues from students that indicated the possibility of imminent violent behavior, the school decided not to hire her. She filed a complaint with the state human rights commission, asserting discrimination on the basis of her visual disabilities. The commission found that her visual impairment interfered with her ability to recognize impending aggressive situations, and that the employment decision was unrelated to her disability. The applicant appealed to the Appellate Court of Illinois, which found that she was inexperienced with the behavior-disordered population and that **her application had been denied on the basis of legitimate safety concerns.** She failed to show that she could perform the job. Also, an employer's duty to provide reasonable accommodations does not attach until an employee asserts the ability to perform essential job functions if afforded a reasonable accommodation. Since the applicant had presented no evidence that she had even asked for a reasonable accommodation, the court affirmed the commission's decision dismissing the complaint. *Truger v. Dep't of Human Rights*, 688 N.E.2d 1209 (Ill. App. Ct. 1997).

♦ An Illinois elementary school custodian complained that certain staff members were trying to get rid of him. He exhibited behavior that caused the school's principal to fear for her personal safety. After a meeting, the district placed the custodian on a paid leave of absence pending a psychiatric examination. A psychiatrist diagnosed the custodian with paranoid psychotic symptoms that could predispose an individual to violent behavior. The district later allowed the custodian to return to work but issued a disciplinary letter warning him that insubordination, baseless accusations and threats would not be tolerated. The custodian filed a grievance to protest the psychiatric examination and disciplinary letter. An arbitrator held that the examination was appropriate but that the letter was improper. The school district removed the letter from the custodian's file, but he sued the district, asserting ADA and Title VII claims. The court rejected his argument that the psychiatric examination requirement violated the ADA. **The district had shown that the examination was job-related and consistent with business necessity since there was concern for the safety of others.** *Miller v. Champaign Community Unit School Dist. No. 4,* 983 F.Supp. 1201 (C.D. Ill. 1997).

♦ A New York school librarian sustained serious neurological injuries in an automobile accident. She was unable to completely recover, but obtained a job several years later as a library teacher at two elementary schools. As her probationary employment term reached a conclusion, two evaluators determined that she had difficulty controlling her library skills class and that she had improperly remained seated during class. When she was denied tenure, she sued the school district in a federal court, claiming that the district had violated Section 504 of the Rehabilitation Act. The court granted pretrial judgment to the school district, and the librarian appealed to the Second Circuit.

The court noted that if an employer is aware of the disability, it has an affirmative obligation to make reasonable accommodations available unless they present an undue hardship, such as an excessively burdensome cost. The complaining party must demonstrate that a reasonable accommodation exists that makes employment feasible. Here, **the librarian had presented evidence that an aide could help her control unruly students.** Rehabilitation Act regulations specifically mention that aides may be used as reasonable accommodations for employees with disabilities. The school district had failed to present any evidence concerning its budget, the cost of providing an aide or any other relevant factors indicating whether the proposed accommodation presented an undue hardship. So the court of appeals vacated and remanded the case. *Borkowski v. Valley Cent. School Dist.,* 63 F.3d 131 (2d Cir. 1995).

B. Title VII and Related State Laws

1. Sex Discrimination

♦ A school district employee met with two male co-workers to review psychological evaluation reports from job applicants. She alleged that during one meeting, her supervisor read from a report that one applicant had commented to a co-worker, "I hear making love to you is like making love to the Grand Canyon," and that the supervisor then said, "I don't know what that means." According to the complaining employee, the other employee responded, "Well, I'll tell you later," and then both male employees chuckled. She asserted that when she complained that this constituted sexual harassment, she was transferred to another position in retaliation. The transfer took place 20 months after the alleged harassment. The employee filed a federal court action against the school district. The court awarded summary judgment to the district. The Ninth Circuit reversed, observing that the employee had a reasonable belief that the harassing incident violated Title VII.

The U.S. Supreme Court held that no reasonable person could have believed that the single incident leading to the lawsuit violated Title VII. Sexual harassment is actionable only if it is so severe or pervasive as to alter the conditions of the victim's employment and create an abusive working environment. **Simple teasing, offhand comments and isolated incidents that are not extremely serious will not amount to discriminatory changes in the terms and conditions of employment.** Here, the employee conceded that it did not upset her to read the written remark in the applicant's file. The supervisor's comment and the male employee's response was at worst "an isolated incident" that could not remotely be considered serious. The Court found "no causality at all" between the job transfer proposed by the school district and the employee's complaint. It noted that there must be a very close proximity in time between an employer's knowledge of an employee's protected conduct and an adverse employment action if this is the employee's only evidence of retaliation. The Court reversed the Ninth Circuit's judgment, in effect reinstating the district court's summary judgment order for the school district. *Clark County School Dist. v. Breeden*, 532 U.S. 268, 121 S.Ct. 1508, 149 L.Ed.2d 509 (2001).

◆   A 63-year-old special education director in Louisiana claimed that she was demoted because of her age, race and gender, and that she was replaced by a younger man of a different race. However, the Fifth Circuit held that **the school board properly replaced her after she mishandled the reporting of her school system's special education to state authorities.** And a comment about projecting an image of youth and vitality did not amount to age bias. *Crary v. East Baton Rouge Parish School Board*, 340 Fed.Appx. 239 (5th Cir. 2009).

◆   A Mississippi school district employee of African-American descent served as a secretary to various administrators. She alleged that when a district superintendent resigned and the district decided not to replace him immediately for budgetary reasons, she took on many of his duties. A district administrator later challenged that assertion, stating that the superintendent's duties were spread out to a number of employees. When a white male was hired at a higher salary to become the central office administrative coordinator, she quit and sued under Title VII and the Equal Pay Act, claiming race and sex discrimination. A federal court and the Fifth Circuit ruled against her, noting that **the white male's duties and responsibilities were different than hers, justifying his higher salary.** *Stover v. Hattiesburg Public School Dist.*, 549 F.3d 985 (5th Cir. 2008).

◆   A Delaware teacher with an emergency certification for special education was repeatedly harassed by a 14-year-old disabled student, who made sexual comments and propositions, and caused other disruptions. She told the principal about the incidents. The student was suspended. When he returned, he grabbed the teacher and pretended to have sex with her, then continued making sexual comments for 11 days. He was removed from her classroom, and his misconduct was determined to be a manifestation of his disability. The teacher's contract for the next year was not renewed based on her lack of certification. She sued, claiming discrimination and retaliation. A federal court ruled for the district. **Although the teacher could sue the district for harassment by the student, the harassment was not severe enough** to create liability for the district. *Mongelli v. Red Clay Consolidated School Dist.*, 491 F.Supp.2d 467 (D. Del. 2007).

◆   A 55-year-old New York state special education school employee claimed that her supervisor made sexual remarks and derogatory comments about her age. After she was fired, she sued the supervisor and school in a federal court, claiming violations of Title VII of the Civil Rights Act of 1964 and the Age Discrimination in Employment Act (ADEA). She also alleged violations of New York law, asserting that her supervisor had sexually harassed her and discriminated against her. The court considered the supervisor's dismissal motions. It observed that the statutory language of Title VII and the ADEA provided that a supervisor could not be sued in an individual capacity under those federal acts. Only entities with 15 or more employees are subject to Title VII and ADEA liability. However, New York's highest court has determined that a supervisor discriminating on the basis of age or sex may be held subject to liability under the state Human Rights Law. This depends upon the supervisor's ownership interest in the employing entity or the ability to hire or fire the complaining party. **Because the employee alleged that the supervisor had participated in the creation of a hostile work environment by his remarks, the state human rights claims could not be dismissed prior to a trial.** *Storr v. Anderson School*, 919 F.Supp. 144 (S.D.N.Y. 1996).

2.   Race Discrimination and Affirmative Action

◆   An African-American special education teacher in Virginia was suspended for five days after she called a referee "the n-word" at a school basketball game. **She claimed that the use of the n-word between African-Americans was culturally acceptable,** and she sued for discrimination. The Fourth Circuit ruled against her, finding no due process violations or discriminatory action. *Parker v. Albemarle County Public Schools*, 332 Fed.Appx. 111 (4th Cir. 2009).

◆   State law prohibited the California Commission for Teacher Preparation and Licensing (CTPL) from issuing credentials, permits or certificates to applicants who were unable to demonstrate reading, writing and mathematics skills in English. CTPL used a basic skills proficiency test to make this assessment. Groups representing minority educators asserted that they historically failed the test at a higher rate than Caucasians, and that the test had a disproportionately adverse impact on minorities that violated Title VII. A federal court awarded summary judgment to the state.

The Ninth Circuit noted that discriminatory employment tests are unlawful unless they are proven to be predictive or significantly correlated with important elements of work behavior that are relevant to the job. Here, the complaining parties successfully showed that the test requirement had a disparate impact upon minority applicants. However, **the test was properly validated in that it had a manifest relationship to school employment.** It adequately identified specific job duties to which the test could be correlated, and it established a minimum level of competence in three areas of basic education skills. Validation studies adequately considered the specific positions for which the test was required, and the skills measured by it were important elements of work behavior for employment in public schools. The state did not set passing scores at an impermissible level. For these reasons, the test requirement did not violate Title VII. *Ass'n of Mexican-American Educators v. State of California*, 231 F.3d 572 (9th Cir. 2000).

◆   The University of Nevada used an unwritten affirmative action policy to achieve balance in the faculty's racial composition. A white female instructor was hired at a substantially lower wage than that paid to an African-American male hired for a similar job. She sued the state university system for violation of the Equal Pay Act and Title VII. A jury awarded her $40,000. The university system appealed to the Supreme Court of Nevada, which observed the tension between affirmative action goals and Title VII's prohibition on employment discrimination. **The affirmative action plan did not violate Title VII because it included nonracial criteria** such as educational background, publishing history, and work experience. The plan did not violate the Equal Pay Act because there was a legitimate business reason for the wage disparity between the two employees. The court reversed the case. *Univ. and Community College System of Nevada v. Farmer*, 930 P.2d 730 (Nev. 1997).

III. LABOR RELATIONS

Collective bargaining agreements between local education agencies and their employees are contracts that are subject to interpretation under a state education code as well as a state labor code. Since collective bargaining agreements typically refer employment disputes to an arbitrator, the jurisdiction of the courts to consider disputes arising under collective bargaining agreements is usually limited to the consideration of major issues, most frequently those arising under the category of unfair labor practices.

A. State Law Conflicts

◆   Ohio public university regents can set standards for faculty instructional workloads in order to emphasize undergraduate instruction, according to the U.S. Supreme Court. A state law required public universities to adopt faculty workload policies and made them an inappropriate subject for collective bargaining. Any university policy prevailed over the contrary provisions of collective bargaining agreements. One university adopted a workload policy pursuant to the law and notified its professors' collective bargaining agent that it would not bargain over the policy. The professors' union filed a state court action, seeking an order that the law violated public employee equal protection rights. The Supreme Court of Ohio struck down the law. The U.S. Supreme Court then held that the Ohio state legislature could properly conclude that **collective bargaining would interfere with the legitimate goal of achieving uniformity in faculty workloads.** The Court reversed and remanded the case. *Cent. State Univ. v. American Ass'n of Univ. Professors, Cent. State Univ. Chapter*, 526 U.S. 124, 143 L.Ed.2d 227, 119 S.Ct. 1162 (1999).

On remand, the Supreme Court of Ohio concluded that the statute did not violate either the state equal protection clause or the provision of the state constitution authorizing the legislature to pass laws regarding certain employment matters. *American Ass'n of Univ. Professors, Cent. State Univ. Chapter v. Cent. State Univ.*, 87 Ohio St. 3d 55, 717 N.E.2d 286 (Ohio 1999).

◆ The California Department of Education issued a legal advisory stating that trained but unlicensed employees could administer insulin to students at school if a Section 504 plan or IEP required it and no licensed person was available. A nurses union sued, challenging the advisory as inconsistent with the state Nursing Practices Act. A court held that the advisory was invalid, and the California Court of Appeal affirmed. The courts rejected the department's assertion that invalidating the advisory would make it impossible for many students to receive required insulin injections. Despite a general shortage of nurses in the state, **school districts could locate and contract for licensed nursing services.** *American Nurses Ass'n v. O'Connell*, 185 Cal.App.4th 393 (Cal. Ct. App. 2010), *review granted* 116 Cal.Rptr.3d 194 (2010).

◆ A Connecticut board of education filed a lawsuit seeking a declaration that class size limits for special education classes contained in the teachers' collective bargaining agreement were illegal and unenforceable under the IDEA. A federal court disagreed with the board, finding that the board could comply with the class size limitations by creating additional sections for students in inclusion classes or hiring more teachers. Further, **no evidence existed that any student was ever denied services required by an IEP as a result of the class size limitations.** *New Britain Board of Educ. v. New Britain Federation of Teachers, Local 871*, 754 F.Supp.2d 407 (D. Conn. 2010).

◆ Teachers unions in West Virginia brought a lawsuit challenging **a random, suspicionless drug testing policy for employees in "safety sensitive" positions, which included teachers**, coaches, plumbers, handymen, cabinetmakers and superintendents. A federal court struck down the policy because there was no evidence of an underlying problem with employee drug abuse. Here, there was not a sufficient safety reason for the policy. The risk of harm from impaired school employees did not approach that of an impaired worker on a train, in a customs office or at a nuclear reactor. Further, teachers and other school employees did not have a reduced expectation of privacy that would justify random, suspicionless testing. *American Federation of Teachers-West Virginia, AFL-CIO v. Kanawha County Board of Educ.*, 592 F.Supp.2d 883 (S.D. W. Va. 2009).

♦ A school nurse filed a grievance against the school committee after a principal ordered her to administer medication to a special education student. Her union argued that any increase in her workload was not covered by the collective bargaining agreement (CBA) and that the non-emergency medication of special education students attending the collaborative program at the school was not permitted. According to the union, the matter had to be negotiated by the parties and the collaborative program was not a party to the agreement. An arbitrator held that a school administrator could not order the nurse to dispense medication to a student who was not a member of the regular student body. A state court upheld the arbitrator's decision, and the school committee appealed.

The Rhode Island Supreme Court observed that the school district had a non-delegable managerial duty to provide health services to students attending the collaborative education program. The district had to operate a school health program and provide special education programs. These duties were non-delegable and could not be bargained away in a CBA. State law and regulations provided that special education students in the collaborative program were within the public school system and entitled to receive health services. There was no collective bargaining provision limiting the provision of services to students within the exclusive control of the school district. **The principal acted according to law when he ordered the nurse to provide medication to the student.** *Woonsocket Teachers' Guild, Local 951, AFT v. Woonsocket School Committee*, 770 A.2d 834 (R.I. 2001).

♦ A school district subcontracted its printing services to a Board of Cooperative Education Services (BOCES) district with the consent of its only printing employee, who continued performing his duties in the same shop. The employee association filed an improper practice charge with the state Public Employment Relations Board (PERB), claiming the printing services could not be subcontracted out without first submitting the matter to collective bargaining. An administrative law judge held that the district's actions constituted an improper practice. The case reached the New York Court of Appeals, which held that **the school district's decision to subcontract its printing services to the BOCES district was not subject to mandatory collective bargaining**. *Vestal Employees Ass'n, NEA/NY v. Public Employment Relations Board of State of New York*, 94 N.Y.2d 409 (N.Y. 2000).

♦ A Pennsylvania school district and the education association representing its teachers were unable to reach a new agreement upon the expiration of their collective bargaining agreement. After six months, the association called a two-day strike that ended with an agreement to extend the terms of the expired agreement. As the school year reached its end, the association called a second strike because of continuing unsuccessful negotiations. The strike jeopardized the district's ability to provide 180 days of instruction per year as required by state law. The state secretary of education sued the association for a preliminary order to compel a return to work because the district had provided only 163 days of instruction for the year. The court granted the request and ordered the association and school board to engage in court-monitored bargaining. The case reached the Supreme Court of Pennsylvania, where the board and district argued that the state Public Employee Relations Act did not grant state courts the authority to order negotiations between parties to collective bargaining agreements. The court ruled that the Public Employee Relations Act must be read in conjunction with **the state public school code, which empowers the secretary of education to compel a return to work in order to provide at least 180 days of instruction annually**. Because the trial court had correctly construed the statutes together in ordering the parties to resume bargaining, its order was affirmed. *Carroll v. Ringgold Educ. Ass'n*, 680 A.2d 1137 (Pa. 1996).

B. Unfair Labor Practices

◆   A Connecticut special ed teacher quit early in a school year, causing the special education director to reassign his caseload. The four remaining special ed teachers had to work between 10 and 14 more hours per week. When they complained to the director, she advised them not to pursue a complaint through the union and suggested that they lie about the union's actions on their behalf. In the lawsuit that followed, the Supreme Court of Connecticut held that their work level was not substantially greater than it had been in past years, so they failed to show a unilateral change in a condition of employment. However, **the director's actions amounted to unlawful direct dealing with the teachers** to erode the union's status as their collective bargaining representative. *Board of Educ. of Region 16 v. State Board of Labor Relations*, 299 Conn. 63 (Conn. 2010).

◆   A New Jersey physical education teacher of students with disabilities also served as a union representative, speaking out about student violence, drug use, smoking and inadequate discipline at school. Near the end of his career, he was accused of kicking a student – an allegation that proved to be unfounded. He later sued for retaliation, claiming he was put in danger by behavior-disordered students who weren't properly disciplined. His lawsuit failed because he could not show any retaliatory acts by school officials. **School officials were allowed to increase his class sizes under the bargaining agreement**, and the school's mission was primarily to serve emotionally disturbed children. Any injuries he suffered were caused by his students, not school officials. *Nead v. Union County Educ. Services Comm'n*, 378 Fed.Appx. 175 (3d Cir. 2010).

◆   The New York City Board of Education created collaborative team teaching classrooms and staffed each one with a regular education and a special education teacher, who worked together, incorporating a range of modalities. However, the board did not assign two teachers to those classrooms during times when one of the regularly assigned teachers had a preparation period. The teachers association filed several grievances, claiming the board's action violated the collective bargaining agreement. An arbitrator agreed, and a state court upheld the arbitrator's decision. The arbitration award did not interfere with the board's obligation to provide educational programs and services to students with disabilities. *Board of Educ. of City of New York v. United Federation of Teachers, Local 2, American Federation of Teachers, AFL-CIO*, 800 N.Y.S.2d 342 (N.Y. Sup. Ct. 2005).

♦ When a school committee's director of special education sought to transfer a teacher to a special needs class with older and more severely disabled students, inferior resources and different working hours, the teacher rejected the transfer. She also noted that accepting it would mean a loss of a $2,500 annual stipend for being her school's technology integrator. The director decided to go through with the transfer anyway, and the teacher filed a grievance. The arbitrator ruled that the matter was subject to grievance procedures, and that the committee **violated the collective bargaining agreement by transferring the teacher to a position that was not comparable**. The Massachusetts Supreme Judicial Court upheld the arbitrator's decision. The Education Reform Act did not allow the committee to involuntarily transfer the teacher. *School Committee of Pittsfield v. United Educators of Pittsfield*, 784 N.E.2d 11 (Mass. 2003).

♦ A school district declared an impasse after bargaining with an education association. Pursuant to the rules of impasse, the district implemented its "last best offer," which called for replacing the reduction in force and recall policy from the previously negotiated agreement in favor of a non-negotiated board policy. The education association filed an unfair labor practices complaint against the district with the South Dakota Department of Labor, which held that the unilateral modification of the policy was an unfair labor practice. A state court affirmed the decision, and the district appealed.

The South Dakota Supreme Court explained that for public employees, a negotiable item is one that relates to rates of pay, wages, hours of employment and other conditions of employment. A subject is negotiable only if it "intimately and directly affects the work and welfare of public employees" and is a matter on which negotiated agreement would not significantly interfere with the employer's inherent management prerogatives. An item is not negotiable if it has been preempted by a statute or regulation. In this case, the reduction in force and recall policy intimately and directly affected the work and welfare of teachers working under the collective bargaining agreement. There was no state law or regulation preempting the policy, and there was no statutory basis for preempting the policy from negotiation. Finally, **negotiation of the policy did not significantly interfere with the exercise of the district's inherent management prerogatives**. The court distinguished between a public employer's substantive decision to transfer or assign employees, which came within the employer's managerial discretion, and procedural processes to be followed after making a decision, which were mandatory subjects of negotiation. Because the policy in this case involved only procedures, the court affirmed the judgment in favor of the association. *Webster Educ. Ass'n v. Webster School Dist.*, 631 N.W.2d 202 (S.D. 2001).

♦ The University of Alaska adopted a non-smoking policy applicable to all university facilities and motor vehicles. Prior to the adoption of the policy, a union representing certain university employees requested bargaining. One union member continued to smoke in a vehicle assigned to him and was censured. He circulated a petition asking the union to negotiate the policy. The university refused to bargain, but the parties reached a collective bargaining agreement without any reference to the non-smoking policy. The union filed an unfair labor practice complaint against the university, asserting that the policy was a mandatory subject of bargaining. The Supreme Court of Alaska observed that because the collective bargaining agreement contained no reference to the non-smoking policy, **the union had contractually waived its right to bargain the issue by agreeing to the contract**. The union could also be deemed to have waived its right to bargain under the management rights section of the agreement. *Univ. of Alaska v. Univ. of Alaska Classified Employees Ass'n*, 952 P.2d 1182 (Alaska 1998).

♦   A Wisconsin school district established a pilot program to increase the promotion rate among ninth-graders in its schools. Each teacher in the program was directed to call the parents of participating students. However, the teachers' association advised the school that the calling would create a burden upon teachers that could not be unilaterally imposed. It filed a prohibited practice complaint with the state employment relations commission, asserting that the district had a duty to bargain over the subject. The commission dismissed the complaint, finding that the calling had no impact on teacher wages, hours or employment conditions. A trial court affirmed the decision, and the teachers' association appealed. The Court of Appeals of Wisconsin agreed with the commission that **telephoning parents is fairly within the scope of a teacher's regular job duties**. It required only five to six hours during the first two weeks of school and did not adversely affect teacher wages, hours or working conditions. The telephone contact was expected of teachers and did not represent a new duty for them. The court affirmed the judgment in favor of the school district. *Madison Teachers, Inc. v. Wisconsin Employment Relations Comm'n*, 580 N.W.2d 375 (Wis. Ct. App. 1998).

♦   A New Jersey school board adopted a 186-day school calendar providing for three additional makeup days for school closings due to weather emergencies. Because of severe weather, schools in the district were closed for 12 days during the school year and the school superintendent proposed eliminating several school holidays including the spring break, with additional makeup days to be added to the end of the school year. Although he notified parents and employees of the proposed changes, he presented the changes to the school board without consulting the employees' labor organization. After the board unilaterally adopted a revised calendar, the employees' association filed an unfair labor practices complaint, alleging that the changes affected terms and conditions of employment that could not be unilaterally changed by the board.

   The Superior Court of New Jersey, Appellate Division, noted that the establishment of a school calendar is a traditional management decision that is not a term or condition of employment. However, even non-negotiable management decisions may have an effect on terms and conditions of employment that are negotiable. **A case-by-case analysis must be applied to non-negotiable management decisions to determine whether negotiating their impact upon employees would significantly encroach upon a management prerogative.** The court remanded the case. *Piscataway Township Educ. Ass'n v. Piscataway Township Board of Educ.*, 307 N.J. Super. 263, 704 A.2d 981 (N.J. Super. Ct. App. Div. 1998).

♦ The collective bargaining agreement between a New Hampshire education board and the union representing its custodians expired. The agreement generally provided for full-time employment for represented employees at a stated wage. During negotiations for a new contract, the board announced a reorganization under which full-time custodians would be laid off and replaced by part-time employees working for $2 per hour less with no benefits. The union filed an unfair labor practice charge against the board, asserting that the layoff and hiring of part-time employees was a unilateral change in the conditions of employment in violation of the collective bargaining agreement. The state Public Employee Labor Relations Board (PELRB) ordered the board to pay part-time custodians at the contractual hourly rate with prorated benefits. The board appealed to the Supreme Court of New Hampshire, which found that **the reorganization was a mandatory subject of collective bargaining**. The reorganization was not reserved to the board's exclusive managerial authority; it affected terms and conditions of employment; and it did not involve governmental functions. The court affirmed the PELRB's order. *Appeal of City of Nashua Board of Educ.*, 695 A.2d 647 (N.H. 1997).

IV. TENURE, DUE PROCESS AND OTHER RIGHTS

State tenure laws protect qualified school employees by establishing minimum procedural protections for adverse employment actions proposed by an education agency. These protections, in conjunction with existing contract rights and constitutional rights to notice and an opportunity to be heard, are referred to as due process rights.

A. Tenure and Due Process Rights

♦ A Pennsylvania state university police officer was charged with felony counts related to marijuana possession. State police notified the university about the charges, and the university immediately suspended the officer without pay pursuant to a state executive order requiring such action where a state employee is formally charged with a felony. University officials demoted the officer but did not inform him that they had obtained his confession from police records. He sued university officials contesting his suspension without pay. The court granted summary judgment to the officials, but the U.S. Court of Appeals, Third Circuit, reversed and remanded the case. The U.S. Supreme Court agreed to hear the case, and **held that the university did not have to suspend the officer with pay pending a hearing**. The criminal complaint established an independent basis for believing that he had committed a felony, and the suspension did not violate his due process rights. The Court reversed and remanded the case. *Gilbert v. Homar*, 520 U.S. 924, 117 S.Ct. 1807, 138 L.Ed.2d 120 (1997).

♦ A Connecticut teacher began posting profiles on MySpace to communicate with students. A guidance counselor learned of the profile and found pictures of naked men there, as well as "inappropriate comments" posted near student pictures. Conversations posted on the page were very peer-to-peer oriented, with students telling the teacher about their social activities and problems. After the counselor complained to the teacher, he took down the profile and created a new one that was very similar. When a number of students complained about the MySpace profile, school officials informed the teacher that his contract would not be renewed for the following year. He sought a formal hearing, at which the non-renewal decision was upheld. He then sued, claiming violations of his First and Fourteenth Amendment rights. A federal court held that **he had no due process right to continued employment because he was not tenured**. Further, school officials complied with the collective bargaining agreement by providing timely written notice of the non-renewal. Finally, there was no First Amendment violation because even though he had posted an anti-war poem, most of his MySpace postings were not of public concern, and he could not prove that the non-renewal was because of the single poem. *Spanierman v. Hughes*, 576 F.Supp.2d 292 (D. Conn. 2008).

♦   A Louisiana teacher with 18 years of experience took a job as a probationary special education teacher at a correctional center for youth. She signed two consecutive annual teaching contracts. After her second year, her contract was not renewed, but no reason was given for the action. She sued the board of education, alleging that it attempted to circumvent state law by disguising her firing as a non-renewal. The case reached the Supreme Court of Louisiana, which agreed with the teacher that **the board had to state the valid reasons for a recommendation of discharge at any time during the probationary period**, even the conclusion of a school year. A decision not to renew a contract was the same as a discharge. Since regular education teachers were entitled to the reasons for a discharge, special education teachers were entitled to the same protections. *Palmer v. Louisiana State Board of Elementary and Secondary Educ.*, 842 So.2d 363 (La. 2003).

♦   A principal's first-year evaluation expressed concerns, and she received a preliminary notice of contract non-renewal the next year. After a hearing, the board renewed her contract. At the start of the principal's third year, a district administrator developed a formal assistance plan for her. During the same school year, a group of students violently and aggressively assaulted a student. When the principal called law enforcement and suspended the students, their parents began to actively denounce her. The district administrator initially voiced support for the principal, and he recommended renewal of her contract. When a complaining parent reported that the closed board vote renewing the principal's contract violated the state open meetings law, the board rescinded its action and held a second meeting. By the time the board met again, it was bound by state law to renew the contract. However, all district employees were notified that the board had revised the principal's title and job description. Subsequently, the principal resigned, stating that the removal of her main job duties amounted to constructive discharge.

She sued the school district, school board, and district administrator in federal court, asserting violation of an asserted constitutional property right in continued employment duties, constructive discharge, and violation of her liberty interest in her reputation. The court ruled for the board and administrator, and the Seventh Circuit affirmed. Wisconsin law and the principal's contract did not encompass any right to perform particular job duties. The district did not transfer the principal, and she retained her title and salary. **Her expectation of retaining certain job duties did not create a protectable property interest.** Accordingly, she had no constitutionally protected claims against the board, district or administrator. Her constructive discharge claim failed because she had abruptly resigned and had declined the opportunity to participate in the creation of her new job duties. There was no violation of her liberty interest in reputation because a charge of mismanagement or incompetence does not rise to a constitutionally protected level. *Ulichny v. Merton Community School Dist.*, 249 F.3d 686 (7th Cir. 2001).

◆ Two Kentucky special education teachers were assigned to a school that had some of the lowest scores in the state on student tests, tense relations among faculty and the administration, and significant problems with student discipline. Six staff members, including the special education teachers, who had opposed a recommended school improvement plan, received notices on the last day of school that they would be transferred for "good cause and extenuating circumstances" pursuant to the collective bargaining agreement. Neither teacher received an opportunity for a hearing. They sued the superintendent in a federal court, asserting that they had been transferred based on the exercise of their speech rights. Days before school resumed, the court held that the superintendent had not violated the First Amendment rights of the teachers when deciding to transfer them, but had deprived them of their due process rights. The morning before school resumed, the superintendent provided the teachers with written notices of the transfers, listing the reasons for them, and scheduling hearings for a few hours later that same day. The transfers were upheld, and the teachers appealed.

The Sixth Circuit observed that the teachers had clearly spoken on matters of public concern. The essential requirements of due process are notice and an opportunity to respond. The district court had correctly ruled that **the teachers received all the process they were due**. Although they received little time to prepare for their hearings, their attorneys had advised the court that they were prepared to be heard. There was an urgency for immediate hearings, since school was to start the following day, and the teachers could still file grievances against the board under the collective bargaining agreement. The court affirmed the judgment. *Leary v. Daeschner*, 228 F.3d 729 (6th Cir. 2000).

◆ A New York special education teacher was assigned to teach, for one year, a regular education class in which six learning disabled students were mainstreamed. The following year, the same class was assigned to a regular education teacher who had a probationary appointment. Two years later, the school district abolished four positions and determined that the special education teacher had more seniority in the elementary tenure area than did the regular education teacher. It did not renew the regular education teacher's position, and she sued. The court held that the special education teacher had more seniority in the elementary tenure area than the regular education teacher.

She was thus entitled to seniority credit for the year she had served as a regular education teacher, even though the district had not expressly notified her that this assignment was outside her initial special education tenure area appointment as required by New York education regulations.

The case reached the Court of Appeals of New York, which stated that **the regulation protected teacher tenure and should not be applied to prevent the special education teacher from receiving seniority credit** to which she was entitled. Although the regular education teacher's argument was technically correct, a teacher assigned out of a tenure area could waive entitlement to the statutory notice and consent if enforcement of these requirements would work to the teacher's detriment. The special education teacher was entitled to receive her elementary tenure area credit even though some of her students had learning disabilities. *Kaufman v. Fallsburg Cent. School Dist. Board of Educ.*, 91 N.Y.2d 57, 666 N.Y.S.2d 1000, 689 N.E.2d 894 (N.Y. 1997).

♦ New York Education Law requires teachers to serve a three-year probationary period to obtain tenure. The law allows regular substitutes to earn credit toward tenure but does not define "regular substitute." A teacher served as a substitute for two terms. Although she later received a probationary special education teaching position, her employer decided not to renew her position just prior to the expiration of the three-year probationary term. The substitute sued. The Court of Appeals of New York held that **a substitute teacher is entitled to earn credit for continuously performing the duties of a regular substitute for at least one term.** This is without regard to whether the employer designates the substitute as a regular or per diem substitute. *Speichler v. Board of Cooperative Educ. Services*, 90 N.Y.2d 110, 659 N.Y.S.2d 199, 681 N.E.2d 366 (N.Y. 1997).

B. Seniority and Reductions in Force

♦ A California school district reduced or discontinued five positions, including a full-time equivalent psychologist position. Rather than rehire two part-time psychologists for the new full-time job, the district hired a less-senior full-time psychologist. The part-time employees challenged that decision and the case reached the California Court of Appeal, which ruled in favor of the district. School districts have broad discretion to define jobs and establish requirements, and **the district was within its rights when defining the position as full time.** *Hildebrandt v. St. Helena Unified School Dist.*, 172 Cal.App.4th 334 (Cal. Ct. App. 2009).

♦ A New York board of cooperative educational services laid off nine teaching assistants (TAs) due to declining student enrollment, but did not make the layoffs according to seniority. Five of the laid-off TAs sued, claiming that they could only be laid off according to seniority under Section 3013(2) of the New York Education Law. The case reached the New York Court of Appeals, which **held that TAs are "teachers" covered by Section 3013(2) and that they should be laid off according to seniority.** The law was intended to protect the tenure and due process rights of professional educators, not just teachers, and the TAs qualified for protection as such. *Madison-Oneida Board of Cooperative Educ. Services v. Mills*, 4 N.Y.3d 51 (N.Y. 2005).

♦ A South Dakota school district and its teachers association negotiated a collective bargaining agreement that set out mandatory procedures for reductions in force. If normal attrition did not succeed in reducing the work force, teachers with less than full certification would be released first, followed by those without continuing contract status, then those with continuing contract status, according to "length of service." The board voted for a work force reduction and notified a teacher and a teacher/coach that they were subject to release. The teacher/coach had three years of continuous service to the district, but the other teacher had more than five years of overall service. She had worked as a substitute, taught summer school and worked as a full-time contract teacher. The board determined that because the teacher/coach would reach continuing contract status first, he had seniority. However, the state labor department held that the reduction-in-force policy measured seniority by "length of service," not "continuous service." Because the teacher's overall service was greater, the board should have retained her.

The South Dakota Supreme Court agreed. The teacher's case was governed by the collective bargaining agreement, not the contract renewal statute. By acting under the agreement, the district had to abide by its terms and could not add words that the parties left out of it. **The agreement enumerated the specific protocol for implementing a reduction in force**, using a principle of seniority measured by length of service within the school system. The board was not permitted to insert or delete contract language to make it mean more than its plain words. The contract included no language such as "continuous" or "uninterrupted" to define length of service, and the teacher should have been retained. *Gettysburg School Dist. 53-1 v. Larson*, 631 N.W.2d 196 (S.D. 2001).

♦ In order to fund an alternative learning center, a Kentucky school board reduced extended employment days for 46 of its 600 certified employees based on a "budget allocation." Several of the teachers sued the school board for violations of state law. The court held that the reduction in extended employment days had been accomplished according to a uniform plan in compliance with state law, and that there had been no violation of the state open meetings law. The court of appeals stated that Ky. Rev. Stat. § 161.760 provided that teacher salaries shall not be lowered unless the reduction is part of a uniform plan affecting all teachers in the entire district and there is a reduction in responsibilities. The reduction in extended employment days was a reduction of responsibilities under the law. The board's records indicated that the plan included only 46 of 600 certified employees and that specific teachers were targeted for reductions. **While a school board could adjust its budget to meet district needs, there had to be uniformity when making such adjustments so that no teacher or class of teachers was "sacrificed."** All teachers were to be encompassed in such a plan, even though not all were affected by the implementation of the plan, to prevent arbitrary salary reductions of a targeted class. The court remanded the case for further proceedings. *Pigue v. Christian County Board of Educ.*, 65 S.W.3d 540 (Ky. Ct. App. 2001).

♦   An Oklahoma school superintendent advised his school board that the district should eliminate four teaching positions in order to reduce the annual budget. The board eliminated a driver education position occupied by a tenured teacher with 19 years of experience. The district retained some non-tenured, probationary teachers who instructed classes in academic areas in which the tenured teacher was also certified to teach. He sued the district, claiming breach of employment contract. The court granted summary judgment to the school district, and the court of appeals affirmed.

The Supreme Court of Oklahoma stated that school boards were allowed to exercise discretion when making necessary reductions in force but were required to conform their actions to the state tenure act. Although boards were allowed to make necessary economic adjustments, they were **required to retain tenured teachers before rehiring non-tenured or probationary teachers pursuant to any reduction in force**. Because the tenured teacher presented evidence that he was certified to teach in other areas and also showed that the school district could have accommodated him through minimal efforts, the summary judgment order had been improper. The case was reversed and remanded. *Barton v. Independent School Dist. No. I-99, Custer County*, 914 P.2d 1041 (Okla. 1996).

♦   A West Virginia special education school devoted itself primarily to mentally retarded students. Federal law required the school district that operated the school to provide certain seriously disabled students with education and related services beyond the normal 180-day school year to prevent educational regressions during summer vacation. The school could not charge tuition or fees for this summer session. The school's principal posted the job vacancies for the special education summer program and then conducted interviews with the applicants. The principal's decision on whom to hire focused on the applicants' relationship with the students, giving preference to those who had existing relationships with the students. An applicant who was not hired brought a grievance, claiming that his seniority required the principal to hire him. A hearing examiner ordered the board of education to pay the teacher back wages and benefits. A West Virginia trial court reversed, holding the examiner's decision to be contrary to the law. The teacher appealed to the Supreme Court of Appeals of West Virginia.

On appeal, the teacher argued that West Virginia law on summer schools mandated that the more experienced teacher be hired. The supreme court disagreed. The court stated that **the special education summer session was not a traditional summer school and was not governed by the normal hiring mandates** of West Virginia law. IDEA hiring requirements for special education summer programs are governed by West Virginia law. Under that law, vacant teaching positions are filled according to the applicants' qualifications. Seniority is only considered for otherwise equal applicants. The principal had made a diligent, professional, and reasonable attempt to hire the best-qualified teachers. Therefore, there was no basis for an award of back pay or benefits. *Board of Educ. v. Enoch*, 414 S.E.2d 630 (W. Va. 1992).

C. Certification Issues

♦ A Kentucky special education teacher applied for a special education teacher/director position, but **the school board instead hired a non-certified but otherwise qualified applicant who held an emergency certification**. The teacher sued, but the Kentucky Court of Appeals ruled that there was sufficient evidence that the teacher was not qualified for the job. A former employer "absolutely did not recommend him for employment," and the Education Professional Standards Board was apparently reviewing him at the time of his application. *Hicks v. Magoffin County Board of Educ.*, 292 S.W.3d 335 (Ky. Ct. App. 2009).

♦ Based on exigent circumstances, an Ohio school board hired a teacher for a multi-disabled/intervention (MD) class even though she did not hold the required licensure. In addition, she had allowed all her certificates to lapse. She received a substitute license that allowed her to teach for a year while working toward full credentials as an MD teacher. When she failed to complete the required work to obtain her MD licensure, the school board terminated her contract. She sued, claiming that she was replaced by an unqualified teacher at a substantial savings. The Ohio Court of Appeals ruled against her, holding that **the superintendent had the discretion not to rehire her after she failed to obtain the proper licensure** and showed no progress toward completing her course work. *Hamilton v. Governing Board of Madison-Champaign Educ. Service*, No. 08-CA-22, 2009 WL 1002982 (Ohio Ct. App. 4/10/09).

♦ An Ohio teacher reviewed the math portion of the Ohio Achievement Test (OAT) and changed the directions on a practice worksheet. She distributed copies to other teachers and told them not to let the students take the copies home. She also asked them to destroy the copies when they were done. When similarities were noticed between the worksheet and actual test problems, the Ohio State Board of Education notified the teacher of its intent to suspend her teaching certificates for violating test security. A state hearing officer recommended suspending her teaching certificates for one year, and the Court of Appeals of Ohio upheld that recommendation. Here, the teacher created questions that were similar or identical to questions on the current OAT. **This amounted to cheating in violation of state law and justified the suspension of her teaching certificates.** *Luscre-Miles v. Dep't of Educ.*, No. 2008P-0048, 2008 WL 5330522 (Ohio Ct. App. 12/19/08).

♦ In a related case, shortly before the district court ordered the ISBE to implement the transitional rules governing the new teacher certification standards, a group of downstate Illinois students and special education teachers sought to join the action, asserting that the ISBE violated the IDEA and the Constitution. The court denied a motion by the would-be intervenors, and they filed a separate action seeking declaratory and injunctive relief based on the same claims they raised in their motion to intervene. The court denied the request for relief by the downstate teachers and students, and they appealed. The Seventh Circuit held that the students' claim was entirely speculative. **There was no reason to believe either the new or transition rules would**

result in the assignment of teachers outside their certification areas so as to deny the students appropriate educational services. Also, the teachers lacked standing to join the lawsuit because they could not show any injury traceable to the ISBE. The students and special education teachers could not intervene in the lawsuit. *Reid L. v. Illinois State Board of Educ.*, 358 F.3d 511 (7th Cir. 2003).

D. Other Rights

◆ Parents of severely disabled Illinois students claimed that a special education teacher and aide screamed at, degraded, force-fed, pushed, slapped and abandoned students in a time-out room or lavatory. An investigation forced the resignations of the teacher and aide. The parents raised new concerns, and the school board proposed installing security cameras with both audio and video in open locations of classrooms. A group of special education teachers sued, claiming a violation of the Fourth Amendment and the Illinois Eavesdropping Act. A state court found no Fourth Amendment violation because **the teachers had no reasonable expectation of privacy in a classroom.** The Appellate Court of Illinois then held that the surveillance would violate the Eavesdropping Act because the act defined "conversation" to include oral communications, which was what the teachers were engaged in while teaching. *Plock v. Board of Educ. of Freeport School Dist. No. 145*, 920 N.E.2d 1087 (Ill. App. Ct. 2009).

CHAPTER EIGHT

School District Operations

I.   BUDGET AND FINANCE

Local educational agencies that receive federal funding are required to comply with federal law requirements. The oversight role of the federal government often includes the threat of withholding funds for local noncompliance with federal requirements. Since local educational agencies depend upon a combination of state, federal and local tax revenues, reviewing courts have been presented with challenges involving funding at all levels of government.

A. State and Local Educational Funding

♦   The Ohio General Assembly adopted the Ohio Pilot Scholarship Program in 1995. The voucher program applied only to the Cleveland school system and allowed public financing of up to $2,500 in scholarships for students to attend public or private schools, including religiously affiliated schools or public schools in adjacent districts. The Supreme Court of Ohio struck down the program on state constitutional grounds in 1999. The general assembly reauthorized the program in time for the 1999-2000 school year, and a new lawsuit challenging the program was commenced in federal court. The court permanently enjoined the state from administering the program under *Committee for Public Educ. and Religious Liberty v. Nyquist*, 413 U.S. 756

(1973), which concluded that direct aid from states to sectarian schools "in whatever form is invalid." State officials appealed to the Sixth Circuit, which found that there was no evidence the use of vouchers was a neutral form of state assistance. According to the circuit court, the program had the primary effect of advancing religion, endorsed religion and provided a direct monetary subsidy to religious institutions that was prohibited by the Establishment Clause. The Supreme Court agreed to review the case.

The program offered two basic kinds of assistance to parents, including tuition aid and tutorial aid for students who chose to remain enrolled in public schools. Any private school could participate so long as it was within the district's boundaries and met statewide standards. Adjacent public schools were eligible to receive an extra grant for accepting program students. The Court cited three decisions that won the case for Ohio officials and voucher advocates: *Mueller v. Allen*, 463 U.S. 388 (1983), *Witters v. Washington Dep't of Services for the Blind*, 474 U.S. 481 (1986) and *Zobrest v. Catalina Foothills School Dist.*, 509 U.S. 1 (1993). Under these cases, where government aid is religiously neutral and provides direct assistance to a broad class of citizens who, in turn, direct that aid to religious schools wholly as a result of independent choice, the aid will survive an Establishment Clause challenge. The Court found that **the Cleveland program allowed government aid to reach religious institutions only because of the deliberate choices of the individual recipients**. Any incidental advancement of religion, or perceived endorsement of a religious message, was reasonably attributable to individual recipients, not to the government, thus avoiding an Establishment Clause violation. The Sixth Circuit decision was reversed. *Zelman v. Simmons-Harris*, 536 U.S. 639, 122 S.Ct. 2460, 153 L.Ed.2d 604 (2002).

♦   After the New York Court of Appeals held that school districts had to make special education services available to all students residing within district boundaries even if they were attending private schools, the New York legislature enacted a statute that created a new school district whose boundaries were coterminous with a Hasidic community (whose residents demanded education of their children in accordance with their tradition of segregating the sexes in school). Taxpayers and an association representing New York school districts sued for a declaration that the statute was unconstitutional. A trial court held that the statute violated the state and federal constitutions, and the Supreme Court, Appellate Division, affirmed. The Court of Appeals of New York held that the statute had the primary effect of establishing a symbolic union of church and state that could be perceived as an endorsement of religion. Because the legislation conveyed a message of governmental endorsement of religion, it violated the Establishment Clause of the U.S. Constitution.

The U.S. Supreme Court agreed to review the matter and held that a state may not delegate authority to a group chosen by religion. Although the statute did not expressly identify the Hasidic community as a recipient of governmental authority, it had clearly been passed to benefit them. The result was a purposeful and forbidden fusion of governmental and religious functions. **The creation of a school district for the religious community violated the Establishment Clause.** The legislation extended a special franchise to the Hasidic community that violated the constitutional requirement of religious neutrality by the government. The statute crossed "the line from permissible accommodation to impermissible establishment," and the Supreme Court affirmed the judgment of the court of appeals. *Board of Educ. of Kiryas Joel Village School Dist. v. Grumet*, 512 U.S. 687, 114 S.Ct. 2481, 129 L.Ed.2d 546 (1994).

♦ The New York legislature promptly repealed the statute and abolished the Kiryas Joel Village School District, passing two statutes that provided a mechanism for the organization of new school districts. They authorized school districts consisting of the entire territory of a municipality coterminous with preexisting school districts when the educational interests of the community required such action, and where certain student enrollment and property tax requirements were satisfied. The taxpayers sought a declaration that the new statutes were unconstitutional. The New York Supreme Court, Appellate Division, held that the new legislative criteria for authorizing school districts created the same result as under the prior unconstitutional law. One of the criteria was apparently meaningless and had been included only to limit the applicability of the statute and afford special treatment to village residents. **The legislation had no educational purpose, was not generally applicable and had been enacted as a subterfuge to avoid the prior U.S. Supreme Court decision.** The Court of Appeals of New York agreed to review the case and found that despite the apparently neutral criteria in the amendments, the Hasidic village was the only municipality that could ever avail itself of the statutory mechanism, and the legislation impermissibly favored that group. The court affirmed the judgment for the taxpayers. *Grumet v. Cuomo*, 90 N.Y.2d 57, 659 N.Y.S.2d 173, 681 N.E.2d 340 (N.Y. 1997).

In 1997, the legislature passed yet another law, but broadened its applicability to municipalities that were as yet unformed. A school district for Kiryas Joel was reconstituted under the new act, and a new challenge was mounted. The court of appeals held that while the 1997 law was facially neutral with respect to religion, its actual effect benefited only the Kiryas Joel district, and its potential benefit extended to only one other district in the state. Since other religious groups would be unable to benefit from the law in the manner enjoyed by the Satmar sect in Kiryas Joel, the law was not neutral in effect. The law violated the Establishment Clause by preferring one religion to others. *Grumet v. Pataki*, 93 N.Y.2d 677, 720 N.E.2d 66 (N.Y. 1999).

♦ An alliance of school districts in Washington sued the state, asserting that it was not fully funding special education. The state provided a basic allotment as well as excess funding at 0.939 times the basic allotment and a safety net for districts that showed they needed more than the basic allotment and excess funding. The court of appeals found that the alliance failed to show the funding violated the state's constitution, and the Supreme Court of Washington affirmed. Any perceived special education deficit disappeared when the basic allotment was included in the calculations for how special education was funded. **Special education funding was in addition to the basic allotment and not in place of it.** *School Districts' Alliance for Adequate Funding of Special Educ. v. State of Washington*, 244 P.3d 1 (Wash. 2010).

♦   A New Mexico sixth-grader with autism would not go to school. His district refused to help the parents bring him to school, but it sent homework to the parents for a few weeks before dropping the student from its attendance rolls. The parents sent an informal complaint to the state department of education and spoke with a liaison officer. They filed a due process request against the district and the state. A hearing officer found that the district had denied the student a FAPE. After the district reached a settlement with the parents, the Tenth Circuit held that **the state education department did not have to provide direct services to the student while he was pursuing his due process action against the district.** However, it could be financially liable for the district's failure to provide a FAPE. *Chavez v. New Mexico Public Educ. Dep't*, 621 F.3d 1275 (10th Cir. 2010).

♦   After the California Legislature slashed statewide funding of mental health services for special education students to $1,000, San Diego County obtained a court ruling that this was an unfunded state mandate, such that it did not have to provide the services. **The California Department of Education then required local school districts to absorb the costs of mental health services for special education students.** One school district later sued for an order that it did not have to pay the costs. However, the Court of Appeal ruled that the district should have first exhausted its administrative remedies before the Commission on State Mandates. *Grossmont Union High School Dist. v. California Dep't of Educ.*, 86 Cal.Rptr.3d 890 (Cal. Ct. App. 2008).

♦   Arizona legislators enacted a voucher program that allowed public school students with disabilities to attend a private school or a public school outside their own districts. They also enacted a program that permitted children in foster care to attend private schools. Opponents of the programs sued, claiming violations of the state constitution. The case reached the state supreme court, which agreed that **the programs violated the Arizona Constitution's "Aid Clause," which prohibited the payment of any public funds to a private school.** *Cain v. Horne*, 202 P.3d 1178 (Ariz. 2009).

♦   A Wisconsin county brought a child protection action against a disabled student, which led to a residential placement. The county funded the educational component of the student's placement until he turned 18, at which time the residential placement ended. The student was transferred to a community-based residential facility, and the county sought to have the school district of residence pay for the educational component of the new placement. The Wisconsin Court of Appeals agreed that **the school district had to pay for the student's education** because the student had not moved to the district to obtain education. He was there for other reasons. *Oconomowoc Area School Dist. v. Burmaster*, 747 N.W.2d 528 (Wis. Ct. App. 2008).

♦   After 56 of Richmond's 60 public schools were found to be out of compliance with the ADA and state law (because they lacked wheelchair ramps, elevators and accessible lavatories), a lawsuit resulted. The school board approved a three-year remediation plan, but a settlement made the board's obligations "contingent on the School Board receiving funding from the city of Richmond." The families who had sued the city and school board appealed to the Fourth Circuit Court of Appeals, which held that the city could not be required to fund the retrofitting of Richmond's public schools. **The agreement that bound the school board was not binding on the city**, which played no part in depriving the families of their rights under the law. The city did not have to fund the settlement. *Bacon v. City of Richmond, Virginia*, 475 F.3d 633 (4th Cir. 2007).

♦ An Illinois student who lived in the Proviso school district was placed in a drug and alcohol treatment facility in the Antioch school district by the Cook County Juvenile Probation Department. The Antioch district sought tuition reimbursement for the educational part of the placement from the Proviso district where the student lived. The Appellate Court of Illinois ruled that **the Proviso district would have had to reimburse the Antioch district only if the placement was made for an educational purpose**. However, since it was made under the juvenile court act, Antioch was not entitled to reimbursement from Proviso. *Antioch Community High School Dist. 17 v. Board of Educ., Proviso Township High School Dist. 209*, 868 N.E.2d 1068 (Ill. App. Ct. 2007).

♦ An administrative law judge (ALJ) ordered a residential placement for a student with autism. As part of its appeal of the ALJ's decision, the district filed a third-party complaint against the New Jersey Department of Education and Department of Human Services, Division of Developmental Disabilities (DDD), asserting that these agencies were obligated under the IDEA to pay for the residential portion of the placement. On appeal, the Third Circuit Court of Appeals held that **the school district could not file a lawsuit under the IDEA to recover the annual placement costs from the state** and the DDD. *Lawrence Township Board of Educ. v. State of New Jersey*, 417 F.3d 368 (3d Cir. 2005).

♦ A group of school districts sued the state of Michigan, alleging that it created an unfunded mandate that violated the state constitution by requiring them to maintain and report data they would not otherwise collect. The case reached the court of appeals, which held that the districts had failed to prove that the data was only for the state's purposes and that they would have no use for it. Evidence supported the state's argument that **the recordkeeping mandate was more efficient, secure and user-friendly than prior reporting methods**. The Supreme Court of Michigan vacated and remanded the case for a reevaluation of the claims, noting that the court of appeals applied the wrong standard. If the state forced the districts to maintain data that the state required for its own purposes (without providing the necessary funds), then an actionable claim existed. *Adair v. State of Michigan*, 712 N.W.2d 702 (Mich. 2006).

♦ An Illinois student who received special education and related services was charged with lighting fireworks and throwing them at others. A juvenile court adjudicated him delinquent and placed him on probation. When he violated probation, his probation officer recommended a residential placement. His mother moved to a new school district, which was notified that it should appear in juvenile court regarding its potential liability for funding the student's placement. The juvenile court agreed with the probation officer that the student should be residentially placed, and it ordered the district to fund the placement. The district challenged that decision and won. The Illinois Supreme Court held that **the student's placement was not made under the School Code, but under the Juvenile Court Act**. It was made to remedy a probation violation, not the student's educational needs. Also, the district was not given the opportunity to show that it could educate the student. The state had to fund the placement. *In re D.D.*, 819 N.E.2d 300 (Ill. 2004).

B. Federal Funding Issues

♦   The Federal Impact Aid Program provides financial assistance to local school districts whose ability to finance public school education is adversely affected by a federal presence – e.g., where a significant amount of federal land is exempt from local property taxes. The statute prohibits a state from offsetting this federal aid by reducing state aid to a local district. To avoid unreasonably interfering with a state program that seeks to equalize per-pupil expenditures, the statute contains an exception permitting a state to reduce its own local funding on account of the federal aid where the Secretary of Education finds that the state program "equalizes expenditures" among local school districts. Two New Mexico school districts disputed certain calculations under the act and the case reached the U.S. Supreme Court, which held that the Secretary of Education could identify the school districts that should be "disregarded" by looking to the number of a district's pupils as well as to the size of the district's expenditures per pupil. Thus, **the state could factor in the receipt of federal Impact Aid funds when making its own distributions of educational aid to its school districts**. *Zuni Public School Dist. No. 89 v. Dep't of Educ.*, 127 S.Ct. 1534, 167 L.Ed.2d 449 (U.S. 2007).

♦   A group of Louisiana citizens sued the Jefferson Parish School Board in 1985 for violating the First Amendment, alleging that the board improperly provided Chapter Two funds to parochial schools for the purpose of acquiring library materials and media equipment. The group asserted that expenditures for books, computers, software and other audiovisual equipment violated the Establishment Clause, since 41 of 46 participating private schools were religiously affiliated. A federal court agreed that the funding failed the religious advancement test from *Lemon v. Kurtzman*, 403 U.S. 602 (1971). It also found that the loan of materials to sectarian schools constituted impermissible direct government aid to the schools. Two years later, the court reversed itself in post-judgment activity, citing an intervening U.S. Supreme Court decision in which the Court held that a state could provide a sign-language interpreter on site at a parochial school. The citizens appealed to the U.S. Court of Appeals, Fifth Circuit, which held that the Chapter Two grants were unconstitutional.
    The U.S. Supreme Court found that the use of the funds by private schools did not result in government indoctrination of religion, because eligibility was determined on a neutral basis and through private choices made by parents. Chapter Two had no impermissible content and did not define its recipients by

reference to religion. Chapter Two funding in the school district did not create an improper incentive for parents to select religious schools. A broad array of schools was eligible for assistance without regard to religious affiliation. **The program was neutral with regard to religion, and private decision-making controlled the allocation of funds to private schools.** Students who attended schools receiving Chapter Two funds were the ultimate beneficiaries of the assistance, even though the schools used them to purchase computers, software, books and other equipment. The Court upheld the board's use of Chapter Two funding. The parish did not need to exclude religious schools from the program. *Mitchell v. Helms*, 530 U.S. 793, 120 S.Ct. 2530, 147 L.Ed.2d 660 (2000).

◆ Title I of the Elementary and Secondary Education Act of 1965 provides federal funding through states to local educational agencies to provide remedial education, guidance and job counseling to at-risk students and students residing in low-income areas. Title I requires that funding be made available for all eligible students, including those attending private schools. Local agencies retain control over Title I funds and materials. The New York City Board of Education attempted to implement Title I programs at parochial schools by allowing public employees to instruct students on private school grounds during school hours. The U.S. Supreme Court agreed with a group of taxpayers that this violated the Establishment Clause in *Aguilar v. Felton*, 473 U.S. 402 (1985). In response to *Aguilar*, local education boards modified Title I programs by moving classes to remote sites including mobile instructional units parked near sectarian schools. However, a new group of parents and parochial school students filed motions seeking relief.

The district court denied the motions, and the U.S. Court of Appeals, Second Circuit, affirmed. On further appeal, the U.S. Supreme Court agreed with the city board and students that recent Supreme Court decisions required a new ruling on the question of government aid to religious schools. For example, the provision of a sign-language interpreter by a school district at a private school was upheld in *Zobrest v. Catalina Foothills School Dist.*, 509 U.S. 1 (1993). The Court held that **it would no longer presume that the presence of a public school teacher on parochial school grounds creates a symbolic union between church and state.** The provision of Title I services at parochial schools resembled the provision of a sign-language interpreter under the IDEA. New York City's Title I program was constitutionally permissible because it did not result in government indoctrination, define funding recipients by reference to religion or create excessive entanglement between education officials and religious schools. The Court reversed the lower court judgments. *Agostini v. Felton*, 521 U.S. 203, 138 L.Ed.2d 391, 117 S.Ct. 1997 (1997).

◆ After a U.S. Department of Education audit concluded that the Arizona Department of Education had improperly awarded IDEA and Elementary and Secondary Education Act (ESEA) funds to for-profit entities that operated charter schools in the state, a lawsuit resulted. The case reached the Ninth Circuit, which held that **for-profit entities cannot receive federal funds under the IDEA** and ESEA. *Arizona State Board for Charter Schools v. U.S. Dep't of Educ.*, 464 F.3d 1003 (9th Cir. 2006).

C. Residency Disputes

♦   A New Jersey student with multiple disabilities was placed in a residential program. Her parents paid $14,500 annually toward the cost of the placement, and their school district paid the remainder. Three years later, the program dismissed the student. Her father then placed her in a children's hospital in Virginia, with his insurer picking up the tab for a while. When that funding ended, the father sought reimbursement from the district. However, the parents were divorced by now (with joint legal and physical custody) and the student's mother had moved into another district. A federal court and the Third Circuit ruled that **because the student did not have a clear domicile, both districts should share the educational costs** of the placement. *Cumberland Regional HSD Board of Educ. v. Freehold Regional HSD Board of Educ.*, 293 Fed.Appx. 900 (3d Cir. 2008).

♦   The grandparents of a Nebraska student with developmental disabilities and behavioral problems were his legal guardians. They became unable to care for him and he was eventually declared a ward of the state. He was placed in a group home in another county and, after he turned 19, his grandparents' county asserted that the county where he now lived should be responsible for the cost of educating him. The Supreme Court of Nebraska disagreed. It held that **the grandparents' county was responsible for the cost of educating the student because he had resided there until becoming a ward of the state**. *Board of Educ. of Jefferson County School Dist. No. 8 v. Board of Educ. of York County School Dist. No. 12*, 703 N.W.2d 257 (Neb. 2005).

♦   The parents of a Massachusetts child with a disability divorced, sharing joint legal custody. Later, they placed the child with the department of social services (DSS), which then placed the child in a private residential school. Because the parents lived in separate cities, **the DSS apportioned the cost of educating the student between the two districts the parents lived in**. The mother's district appealed, but the Supreme Judicial Court of Massachusetts upheld the DSS determination. Apportioning the costs between the two districts would prevent one district from incurring unfair costs. *City of Salem v. Bureau of Special Educ. Appeals of Dep't of Educ.*, 829 N.E.2d 641 (Mass. 2005).

♦   A student in the Manchester, New Hampshire, school district was left blind and severely developmentally delayed after an accident when she was three months old. Her parents placed her in a children's home in Pittsfield, New Hampshire, with the assistance of the state Division of Children and Youth Services. The parents moved and had little or no contact with the student. When they divorced, the father retained legal custody. After three years, a service provider affiliated with a state agency sought a determination of responsibility for payment of the student's educational expenses. The state department of education held that Manchester remained responsible for these costs under Section 193:29 of the state code, which assigns liability for the educational costs of a student placed in a children's home to the district in which the student has most recently resided prior to placement. When the student's father moved to Ohio, an unsuccessful attempt was made to place the student in a residential school there. Seven years later, the student's surrogate parent became her legal guardian and Manchester renewed its efforts to avoid liability for her educational costs. A hearing officer ruled against Manchester, and a federal court upheld that decision. Manchester appealed to the First Circuit.

The court of appeals disagreed with Manchester's assertion that the IDEA, not state law, resolved the liability dispute. The IDEA contains no language determining which particular state agency or school district must assume financial liability for a student's education. **The state law definition of "sending district" remained the district in which the child most recently resided prior to the placement, regardless of legal residency.** Manchester remained liable for the student's educational costs. *Manchester School Dist. v. Crisman*, 306 F.3d 1 (1st Cir. 2002).

◆ During the seventh grade, the attendance of a Rhode Island student with disabilities worsened due to family disruption and her mother's cancer diagnosis. A dispute arose between the mother and the school district over the student's IEPs, and the mother enrolled the student in a Kentucky reading center at the start of her eighth-grade year. The mother requested a due process hearing, asserting IDEA procedural violations by the school committee, which initiated a residency hearing against the family. During the residency hearing proceedings, the mother admitted that she lived in Massachusetts while recuperating from brain cancer, but asserted that her residency remained in Rhode Island. The state education department commissioner stayed any ruling on the residency proceeding until the IDEA due process hearing concluded. The hearing officer held that the student's 1998 and 1999 IEPs were inadequate and inappropriate but deemed the Kentucky placement inappropriate.

The mother appealed to the First Circuit, which upheld the denial of tuition reimbursement, as the student did not study any subject in the Kentucky facility other than reading. Also, in order to preserve a claim for private school tuition reimbursement under the IDEA, parents must provide a school district with at least 10 days' prior written notice that a proposed IEP is being rejected and explain that they are removing their child from public school. Although the mother asserted that her illness prevented her from complying with this requirement, the evidence indicated that she was able to complete application materials for the Kentucky facility during the same time period. Further, the committee did not convene the residency hearing in retaliation for the mother's request for a due process hearing. **There were obvious, non-retaliatory reasons for initiating the hearing, as several facts indicated that the mother and student did not reside in the state.** The court affirmed the judgment for the school committee. *Rafferty v. Cranston Public School Committee*, 315 F.3d 21 (1st Cir. 2002).

◆ A New Jersey student was classified as neurologically impaired by the Somerville school system, where her parents lived before they divorced. The divorce decree provided for joint legal and shared physical custody. The mother moved into the Manville school district, while the father continued to reside in Somerville. The IEP prepared by the Somerville district placed the student in a third district, and the Somerville and Manville school boards orally agreed to split the cost. Manville then determined that it should not continue paying tuition. Somerville sued for a declaration that the student was jointly domiciled in both districts and that the agreement to share tuition expenses remained enforceable. Manville sought the amount it had already contributed. The court held that the student was domiciled in Somerville, which should bear the costs of educating her in the future. Manville was liable only for the balance of the student's current tuition. The New Jersey Superior Court, Appellate Division, reversed, finding that a child may be domiciled in both parental households if the evidence indicates actual residence with both parents. Fairness dictated that Manville and Somerville equally share the costs.

The Manville school district appealed to the New Jersey Supreme Court, which noted that **the parties had voluntarily agreed to share the costs of educating the student and had agreed to share state and federal categorical aid on an alternating annual basis**. The district paying tuition for a given year would count the student for the purposes of receiving state and federal assistance. The parties had also agreed to share the responsibility of providing transportation. The court affirmed the appellate court's decision. *Somerville Board of Educ. v. Manville Board of Educ.*, 768 A.2d 779 (N.J. 2001).

♦   The parents of a Kansas student divorced when he was two. The student lived with his mother until age 10, then with his father, and eventually moved in with an adult sister. He attended a number of schools, some with IDEA financing and some financed by his mother. The mother moved from the Wichita school district to the Andover school district in March 1995. Eight months later, the student pled guilty to criminal charges. The court ordered him to serve 24 months of probation and complete a program at a private residential facility. The mother sought public financing from the Wichita school district. She placed him in the private facility before an IEP was prepared. Wichita refused to fund the placement. A due process hearing officer found that the student was not a resident of the Wichita district as of the time of his conviction, and therefore Wichita did not have to fund the placement. A review officer and a federal court affirmed. The student's mother appealed to the Tenth Circuit.

The court of appeals noted that the student had lived within the Wichita school district boundaries all his life. The mother's residency was not relevant, as the student did not live with her and his residency controlled the case. However, **Wichita was not liable for any residential placement costs. Neither parent resided in Wichita** and the student's adult sister was not a "person acting as a parent" within the meaning of state law. The mother's unilateral placement of her son in the residential facility was "manipulative, was not undertaken for education purposes, and essentially obstructed the IDEA process." The court affirmed the judgment for the school districts and officials. *Joshua W. v. Unified School Dist. 259 Board of Educ., Wichita Public Schools*, 211 F.3d 1278 (10th Cir. 2000) (Unpublished).

♦   A special education student, his mother and his brother lived in a rented townhouse located in the Cumberland Valley School District during the week and spent some weekends and holidays with the father, who lived in a different school district. After the student was hospitalized twice, a private placement was recommended. Cumberland Valley school officials refused to fund a private placement, stating that the family had never established residency in the district. The parents unilaterally enrolled the student in a private school for students with learning disabilities. An administrative board determined the townhouse was a temporary residence and concluded that the family resided in the district within which their home was located. A Pennsylvania court concluded that the student's residence was the place of his physical presence. Accordingly, Cumberland Valley had to provide the student with a FAPE and was obligated to pay the costs of the private school.

Cumberland Valley officials appealed the residency issue to the Pennsylvania Supreme Court, which concluded that under the state public school code, a student is a resident of the district in which his parent or guardian resides. The board had erroneously interpreted "resides" to refer to the custodial parent's primary residence and domicile. Under the board's interpretation, primary residence and domicile were largely equivalent, which would result in children being able to claim residency in the district of their choice, regardless of where the parents paid property taxes. **The court agreed with the lower courts that a person resides in the place where he is physically present.** This definition of resides was appropriate for use when interpreting the school code. As a general rule, the court noted that a minor has the same residence as the parent with whom he lives. The court affirmed the judgment in favor of the family. *In re Residence Hearing Before the Board of School Directors, Cumberland Valley School Dist.*, 744 A.2d 1272 (Pa. 2000).

♦   The parents of a New York student with Down syndrome placed him in a group residence home. When they moved to Massachusetts, their old school district discontinued funding the student's educational program. The commissioner of education interpreted state law as creating a presumption that children reside with their parents, even where they are not physically present in the parents' home. The parents sued the education commissioner in a federal court, arguing that this interpretation violated the Constitution and IDEA. The court held that the commissioner's interpretation did not violate the Equal Protection Clause because it furthered the legitimate educational interest of preserving special education services for legitimate state residents and reserving local control over education. However, the law as applied in this case violated the Due Process Clause. The commissioner appealed to the Second Circuit, which ruled for him on both constitutional issues.

The parents then sought an order that the school district could not seek tuition reimbursement from them for the student's residence home costs. They claimed that the state of Massachusetts was now liable for the student's tuition. However, **the Massachusetts school district had never been afforded the opportunity to evaluate or place the student.** Consequently, the old district could seek reimbursement from the parents without suing Massachusetts first. *Catlin v. Sobol*, 988 F.Supp. 85 (N.D.N.Y. 1997).

♦   The parents of an Illinois student with disabilities voluntarily transferred custody of their son to licensed foster parents. The parents retained legal guardianship of their son while the foster parents became his primary care givers. Three years later, the foster parents moved to a different county and enrolled the student in special education classes in the county school district. When the school district in which the foster parents lived learned that they were not the student's legal guardians, it sought reimbursement for special education costs from the natural parents and their district of residence. The request was denied, and the foster parents' residence district sued the parents' residence district for reimbursement. The Appellate Court of Illinois held that **Illinois law defines the school district of residence as the district in which the parent or guardian of a student resides when the parent has legal guardianship and resides in the state**. The foster parents' district was entitled to reimbursement. *Board of Educ. of Community Unit School Dist. No. 428 v. Board of Educ. of High School Dist. No. 214*, 680 N.E.2d 450 (Ill. App. Ct. 1997).

◆   A 16-year-old Florida student with special needs lived with his mother until she became unable to care for him. The student then went to live with his grandmother in North Carolina and applied to the local school board for enrollment as a student with special needs. School administrators denied the application, stating that he was neither a resident nor a domiciliary of the district. The student appealed to the state office of administrative hearings, which found that he was a resident of the county and that his grandmother acted as his guardian. The student was entitled to a free appropriate education. This decision was affirmed by a state court as well as the Court of Appeals of North Carolina. It noted that the statute pertaining to students with special needs specifies that each local education agency provide free appropriate special education services to all students with special needs residing in the district. The specific requirements of state special education law imposed **an obligation on the district to provide a free appropriate education for each student with disabilities residing in the district**. *Craven County Board of Educ. v. Willoughby*, 466 S.E.2d 334 (N.C. Ct. App. 1996).

II.   STUDENT RECORDS AND PRIVACY

The federal Family Educational Rights and Privacy Act (FERPA) prohibits the unauthorized release by an educational agency of personally identifiable student information without prior parental consent. State laws also impose obligations upon local educational agencies to protect student privacy. These laws occasionally come into conflict with public information disclosure acts.

◆   A student who claimed that a university violated FERPA could not sue under 42 U.S.C. § 1983 to enforce his "rights" under the act. The student attended a private university in Washington, intending to teach in the state's public school system after his graduation. At the time, the state required new teachers to obtain an affidavit of good moral character from the dean of their college or university. When the university's teacher certification specialist overheard a conversation implicating the student in sexual misconduct with a classmate, she commenced an investigation of the student and reported the allegations against him to the state teacher certification agency. She later informed the student that the university would not provide him with the affidavit of good moral character required for certification as a Washington teacher. The student sued the university and the specialist under state law and under 42 U.S.C. § 1983, alleging a violation of FERPA. A jury awarded him over $1 million in damages. The case reached the U.S. Supreme Court, which ruled that **FERPA creates no personal rights that can be enforced under Section 1983**. Congress enacted FERPA to force schools to respect students' privacy with respect to educational records. It did not confer upon students enforceable rights. As a result, the Court reversed and remanded the case for further proceedings. *Gonzaga Univ. v. Doe*, 536 U.S. 273, 122 S.Ct. 2268, 153 L.Ed.2d 309 (2002).

◆ An Oklahoma mother asserted that her school district's allowance of peer grading was embarrassing to her children, one of whom received special education. Peer grading policies allow students to grade each other's assignments and call out the results in class. She sued the school district and school administrators for violations of FERPA, the IDEA and the Constitution (through 42 U.S.C. § 1983). A court held that the policy did not violate any constitutional privacy rights and did not involve "education records" under FERPA. She appealed to the Tenth Circuit, which rejected her constitutional claim, ruling that school work did not rise to the level of constitutionally protected information. It further held that neither FERPA nor the IDEA created constitutional privacy rights. However, FERPA could establish the basis for a suit for damages under 42 U.S.C. § 1983. FERPA was intended to protect student and parent privacy rights and creates a binding obligation on schools not to disclose personally identifying student information without permission. The district court decision was reversed on the FERPA claim.

The U.S. Supreme Court agreed to review whether the peer grading policy violated FERPA. It observed that FERPA defines an education record as one that is "maintained by an educational agency or institution," or by a person acting for an agency or institution. Student papers are not maintained under FERPA when students correct them or call out grades in class. The word "maintain" suggested that FERPA records were kept in files or cabinets in a "records room at the school or on a permanent secure database." The momentary handling of assignments by students did not conform to this definition. FERPA's language implies that education records are "institutional records…, not individual assignments handled by many student graders in their separate classrooms." The court of appeals committed error by deciding that a student acted for an educational institution under FERPA when assisting with grading. **The Court noted the educational benefits of peer grading, such as teaching the same material a different way, demonstrating how to assist and respect classmates and reinforcement of concepts, and held that FERPA should not be construed to prohibit these techniques.** Because Congress did not intend to intervene in drastic fashion with traditional state functions by exercising minute control over specific teaching methods, the Court reversed and remanded the case. *Owasso Independent School Dist. No. I-011 v. Falvo*, 534 U.S. 426, 122 S.Ct. 934, 151 L.Ed.2d 896 (2002).

♦   The parents of a California student with autism made a written request to the county education office for copies of all electronic mail sent or received by the agency that concerned or personally identified the student. The agency sent the parents hard copies of e-mails that had been printed and placed in the student's permanent file, but it refused to provide electronically formatted e-mails. The parents then filed a complaint with the California Department of Education, which found that the e-mails were not education records under FERPA and that the agency did not have to release them. When the parents sued, a federal court held that the agency's interpretation of the law was correct. **Only those e-mails "maintained" by the county that personally identified the student were education records.** E-mails on a central mail server or in individual e-mail inboxes were not "maintained" by the county. *S.A. v. Tulare County Office of Educ.*, No. CV F 08-1215 LJO GSA, 2009 WL 3126322 (E.D. Cal. 9/24/09).

♦   A special education student in New Jersey was suspended after crossing out pictures of other students in his yearbook and stating that they were now mere memories. He also said he hoped they experienced the "pain and agony" he had. His parents placed him in a private school and sued the district under the IDEA and the Family Educational Rights and Privacy Act (FERPA). The case reached the Third Circuit, which noted that the parents had failed to exhaust their administrative remedies and that **they could not bring a private claim to enforce FERPA.** *Woodruff v. Hamilton Township Public Schools*, 305 Fed.Appx. 833 (3d Cir. 2009).

♦   Alaska's Disability Law Center sought to investigate abuse and neglect allegations involving developmentally disabled students in the Anchorage school district. The district refused to provide contact information for student guardians or legal representatives on grounds of privacy rights under FERPA. The case reached the Ninth Circuit, which held that FERPA did not bar the release of the requested information. **The center would be duty-bound to maintain the confidentiality of any student records it received, so there was little risk of public disclosure of private student information.** And it didn't matter that the suspected aide and teacher no longer worked at the school. *Disability Law Center of Alaska v. Anchorage School Dist.*, 581 F.3d 936 (9th Cir. 2009).

♦   A Wisconsin teacher was involved in a disciplinary grievance proceeding where she was represented by a union-appointed attorney. She provided the attorney with a copy of a student's IEP. The district reprimanded her in writing for releasing a student record to an unauthorized third party without written consent. The reprimand matter was submitted to an arbitrator, who found that the teacher could provide the IEP to her attorney. On appeal, the Wisconsin Court of Appeals noted that the disclosure violated two school board policies intended to comply with FERPA. However, an arbitration award can be overturned only if it is a "perverse misconstruction" or "manifest disregard of the law," or if it is illegal or violates public policy. Here, none of those conditions were met, and FERPA probably did not apply to individual teachers. **The teacher, therefore, could not be reprimanded for disclosing the**

student's IEP to her attorney. *Madison Metropolitan School Dist. v. Madison Teachers*, 746 N.W.2d 605 (Wis. Ct. App. 2008).

◆   A California student with a speech-language impairment received three hours of weekly behavioral support services and 30 minutes of monthly speech therapy, provided on a consulting basis. When the school district changed providers, there was a two-week gap in services. However, the new provider averaged four hours per week even though the IEP called for only three. The district withheld the student's report card for the second and third trimesters of her eighth-grade year because she lost or defaced textbooks and her mother refused to pay for them. After a dispute between the district and the student's mother, a federal court held that **the district did not violate the IDEA by withholding the report cards** because it sent IEP progress reports to the mother via e-mail. Also, the absence of the speech therapist from the IEP meeting was a harmless error because the student's resource teacher was the appropriate person to help her meet her IEP goals. *Sarah Z. v. Menlo Park City School Dist.*, No. C 06-4098 PJH, 2007 WL 1574569 (N.D. Cal. 5/30/07).

◆   A lawsuit arose under the Health Insurance Portability and Accountability Act (HIPAA) over whether the Wyoming Protection and Advocacy (P&A) System could access records without the authorization of the individuals to investigate abuse and neglect allegations. A federal court held that the HIPAA privacy rule did not bar the state hospital and state training school from disclosing protected health information without the authorization of the individual so long as the disclosure was mandated by another federal law. It stated that the purpose of all the laws could be met by **allowing the P&A system to access incident reports with names withheld** to make probable cause determinations of abuse or neglect. If probable cause was found, the P&A system could then seek more information. *Protection and Advocacy System v. Freudenthal*, 412 F.Supp.2d 1211 (D. Wyo. 2006).

◆   A New York school district created a policy wherein a staff member who learned of a student's pregnancy "should" immediately report it to a school social worker, who would "encourage" the student to tell her parents. If she refused, the social worker, after consultation with the principal and superintendent, "should" inform the parents. When a teachers' association sued the school board over the policy, a federal court ruled it lacked standing to bring the lawsuit because it had suffered no injury. **The policy was not mandatory and staff members faced no repercussions if they violated it.** Finally, FERPA might even require disclosure of the pregnancy to the parents. *Port Washington Teachers' Ass'n v. Board of Educ. of Port Washington Union Free School Dist.*, No. 04-CV1357TCPWDW, 2006 WL 47447 (E.D.N.Y. 1/4/06).

◆   The father of a disabled Illinois student became dissatisfied with her progress and requested a copy of her early childhood program records. When he received no response, he filed a due process hearing request. He later **sued the district for improperly denying him access to his daughter's educational records** and for improperly releasing the records to the district's attorneys. The case reached the Appellate Court of Illinois, which ruled that the district did not violate the law by releasing the student's records to its attorneys so they could represent it in proceedings concerning the student's placement. *Ibata v. Board of Educ. of Edwardsville Community Unit School Dist. No. 7*, 851 N.E.2d 658 (Ill. App. Ct. 2006).

♦   A learning disabled and speech-impaired Georgia student progressed to the fifth grade, his basic skills scores rising at least one grade level every year. His parents brought an attorney to an IEP meeting to discuss his sixth-grade IEP. The district agreed to provide extended school year services and a private psychological evaluation. The parents then claimed their son made no measurable progress in district schools. At a due process hearing, the hearing officer ruled against the parents. They appealed to a federal court, asserting that the district denied them access to 700 pages of their son's educational records. The court disagreed. **Writing samples, daily work and teacher private notes did not constitute educational records** under FERPA or the IDEA. *K.C. v. Fulton County School Dist.*, No. 1:03-CV-3501-TWT, 2006 WL 1868348 (N.D. Ga. 6/30/06).

♦   Connecticut's Office of Protection and Advocacy for Persons with Disabilities sought access to student records and asked to observe and interview students at an academy for students with serious emotional disturbance. The request came after parents complained of improper restraints and seclusion. The district that ran the academy cited the IDEA and FERPA in denying the request. However, the Second Circuit held that **the district had to provide access to the students as well as disclose names and contact information**. Three federal laws – the Protection and Advocacy for Individuals with Mental Illness Act, the Developmental Disabilities Assistance and Bill of Rights Act, and the Protection and Advocacy of Individual Rights Act – required the disclosure of the information to protect the students. *State of Connecticut Office of Protection and Advocacy for Persons with Disabilities v. Hartford Board of Educ.*, 464 F.3d 229 (2d Cir. 2006).

♦   A student told his mother two other students were flashing around papers with information on him and calling him "stupid" and "retarded." After learning that the other students had found copies of the student's assessment summary report in a parking lot near the trash dumpster, the mother sued the district for violating the Minnesota Government Data Practices Act. A jury awarded $140,000 in damages plus $47,000 in attorneys' fees. The state court of appeals upheld the award, noting that the act protects individuals against the inadvertent disclosure of student records and that **the district did not have in place a policy for destroying documents**. However, the attorneys' fee award had to be reconsidered. *Scott v. Minneapolis Public Schools, Special Dist. No. 1*, No. A05-649, 2006 WL 997721 (Minn. Ct. App. 4/18/06).

♦   The father of a California student with special needs **requested copies of his son's test protocols prior to a scheduled IEP team meeting**. The district refused to provide a copy of the copyrighted protocols for an achievement test because doing so would violate federal copyright law. A lawsuit resulted, and a federal court held that the district had to provide the test protocols in accordance with state education law. Here, the father would only receive the part of the test identifiable with his son. This was a "fair use" under copyright law. *Newport-Mesa Unified School Dist. v. State of California Dep't of Educ.*, 371 F.Supp.2d 1170 (C.D. Cal. 2005).

◆ The Connecticut Office of Protection and Advocacy for Persons with Disabilities (OPA) received complaints that a school for seriously emotionally disturbed students had injured some students by using inappropriate restraints and seclusion. It began an investigation, but the Hartford Board of Education refused the OPA's request for access to students and records. A federal court then **ordered the board to provide physical access and contact information for the students' parents** and guardians so that the investigation could proceed. Since the OPA was required to maintain confidentiality of student records, it would follow the privacy dictates of the Family Educational Rights and Privacy Act. *State of Connecticut OPA v. Hartford Board of Educ.*, 355 F.Supp.2d 649 (D. Conn. 2005).

◆ After students complained that a special education teacher mistreated them, the school installed cameras in her classroom to monitor her performance. She later made a request under the state Open Records Act to view the videotapes. The principal denied her request, finding the tapes to be "educational records" under the Family Educational Rights and Privacy Act as well as state law. The question of whether the teacher could view the tapes reached the Kentucky Court of Appeals, which held that **the district would have to prove that the teacher lacked any legitimate educational interest in the classroom videotapes in order to deny access to them**. There was no confidentiality issue because the teacher obviously had knowledge of her own students. *Medley v. Board of Educ. of Shelby County*, 168 S.W.3d 398 (Ky. Ct. App. 2004).

◆ A Florida superintendent's investigation report addressed a school principal's misconduct, but also referenced other faculty members and included confidential student information. When the superintendent offered copies of the report to the principal and faculty members if they signed confidentiality agreements or agreed to have student identifying information redacted (blacked out), the faculty members refused the offer and sued, asking that the report be released with no restrictions on data. A court held that state law only protected the privacy rights of exceptional students. Therefore, information relating to regular education students should not be redacted. The District Court of Appeal of Florida reversed. Under state law, all personally identifiable student records and reports are confidential and exempt from disclosure. **The law did not differentiate between students with disabilities and students who were not disabled.** The teachers had no access rights to confidential student information. *Johnson v. Deluz*, 875 So.2d 1 (Fla. Dist. Ct. App. 2004).

◆ A divorce decree awarded a father custody and the right to make educational decisions. The mother got the right to reasonable information regarding their child's progress in school and her health and safety. The summer before the child was to begin fifth grade, an IEP team determined that she had an emotional-behavioral disability. The mother was initially excluded from the IEP team, but later joined. When her request for an independent educational evaluation was denied, she sought due process. A hearing officer found that the custody order deprived her of standing to request a hearing. She challenged the accuracy of the child's educational files and unsuccessfully sought to change aspects of her records. She commenced an IDEA and FERPA action.

The Second Circuit held that because the Vermont family court had vested the father with the right to make the child's educational decisions, the mother could not demand a due process hearing to determine the appropriateness of an IEP. She also couldn't pursue her records access claim under FERPA, which is enforced by education agencies, not by private lawsuits under 42 U.S.C. § 1983. **The mother's claimed right to amend the child's records was properly dismissed, as the father was given all legal rights over the child's education** in the divorce decree. However, the district court should not have dismissed the IDEA action based on access to records, as the information the mother sought might be considered "reasonable information" she was entitled to receive. *Taylor v. Vermont Dep't of Educ.*, 313 F.3d 768 (2d Cir. 2002).

♦ A school district acted reasonably by submitting a student's schoolwork to local law enforcement officers for comparison to racist graffiti found on school grounds. The Massachusetts Supreme Judicial Court held that the use of student papers as handwriting samples did not violate state regulations or student privacy expectations. A school vice principal provided the police with written samples of the student's schoolwork to help determine whether it matched racist and obscene writing found at the school and in the student's classroom. A handwriting expert determined that the student had likely written the graffiti. The commonwealth of Massachusetts commenced proceedings against the student for malicious destruction of property and violation of civil rights. A trial court held that the handwriting samples had been obtained in violation of a state law requiring student or parental consent prior to the release of a "student record." On appeal, the Supreme Judicial Court rejected the student's argument that his handwriting samples were protected "student records" within the meaning of state law. **The handwriting samples provided to the police were not student records and were not protected by state confidentiality requirements.** *Comwlth. of Massachusetts v. Buccella*, 434 Mass. 473, 751 N.E.2d 373 (Mass. 2001).

III. GIFTED STUDENT PROGRAMS

The IDEA does not create rights or entitlements for gifted and exceptional students. State laws may establish gifted student programs and requirements, but they do not confer a property interest in gifted student program participation.

♦ Chicago students in a gifted education program designed a class T-shirt depicting a boy with an enormous head, misshapen teeth, a dilated pupil and a missing hand. The word "Gifties" was on the back. When the "Gifties" shirt lost in the school election, some of the gifted students protested what they thought was a rigged election and wore the shirts to school in defiance of the principal's orders. They were confined to their homerooms for a time, then allowed to wear the shirts. When they sued under the First Amendment, a federal court and the Seventh Circuit ruled against them. **The shirts did not contain a statement or symbolic message protected by the First Amendment.** *Brandt v. Board of Educ. of City of Chicago*, 480 F.3d 460 (7th Cir. 2007).

♦   A Pennsylvania five-year-old with an IQ at or under 130 entered first grade a year ahead of schedule. His parents wanted him identified as gifted – IQ of 130 or higher plus multiple criteria indicating gifted ability – but the district believed that being in the first grade was enough of an enrichment given his anxiety and the way he interacted with his peers. The Pennsylvania Commonwealth Court ruled that **the district had appropriately kept the student in first grade, rather than accelerate his education further.** Although he displayed some characteristics of giftedness, the district properly considered his personality and interpersonal style. *E.N. v. M. School Dist.*, 928 A.2d 453 (Pa. Commw. Ct. 2007).

♦   After a gifted student began attending UCLA at 13, his mother sued state education officials, seeking the cost of a college education. The California Court of Appeal noted that the state's free school guarantee did not mandate a K-12 education individually tailored to each student's particular needs. Also, **the gifted student was not a child with exceptional needs** so as to be eligible for a free appropriate public education under the IDEA. That statute is limited to preschool, elementary and secondary education; it does not include college education. *Levi v. O'Connell*, 144 Cal.App.4th, 50 Cal.Rptr.3d 691 (Cal. Ct. App. 2006).

♦   The Commonwealth Court of Pennsylvania held that **a gifted student was entitled to one hour of compensatory education for each school day he was denied appropriate educational services.** The gifted IEP for one school year failed to sufficiently describe the student's present abilities or needs, lacked necessary test scores and descriptive goals, and failed to provide individualized instruction. Nevertheless, the student was not entitled to day-for-day compensatory education. *B.C. v. Penn Manor School Dist.*, 906 A.2d 642 (Pa. Commw. Ct. 2006).

♦   A gifted Pennsylvania student attended some fourth-grade classes midway through her third-grade year and excelled at them. The IEP for the following year called for her to skip fourth grade and enter fifth grade, but the school district unilaterally removed the grade-skipping provision. After due process hearings, the Commonwealth Court of Pennsylvania held that **the district should not have unilaterally removed the grade-skipping provision from the student's IEP.** The grade-skipping provision was reinstated, and the student would receive 60 minutes of compensatory education per day. *York Suburban School Dist. v. S.P.*, 872 A.2d 1285 (Pa. Commw. Ct. 2005).

♦   A gifted student with an IQ in the 140-range also had ADHD and a learning disability. His parents rejected special education services for three years, instead opting for a Section 504 plan. After he was accepted into a private preparatory high school, the parents sought to have his placement changed. A hearing officer ruled that **the school district had offered the student FAPE**, and a New Hampshire federal court upheld that decision. The student had made academic progress and advanced from grade to grade. Also, the district was not required to seek a due process hearing when the parents rejected special education, so it did not violate the IDEA. The district did not have to maximize the student's potential. *Michael M. v. Plymouth School Dist.*, No. Civ. 01-469-M, 2004 WL 768896 (D.N.H. 4/12/04).

♦   Before a gifted Vermont student with emotional and behavior problems entered grade 10, his parents expressed concerns about his program. Their psychologist recommended that the district classify the student as having an emotional and behavioral disability, provide him with counseling and place him in an academically challenging program with his intellectual peers. A school evaluation and planning team determined that the student had an emotional-behavioral disability, but concluded that his disability did not "adversely affect" his educational performance. A Section 504 team determined that the student was eligible for accommodations and offered him a support program. The parents unilaterally enrolled the student in an out-of-state higher education boarding school for academically gifted students and requested funding from the district. The Section 504 team rejected the placement selected by the parents. A hearing officer held that the student was ineligible for special education under the IDEA, and that the district did not have to place the student among his intellectual peers.

The case reached the Second Circuit, which noted that **the student consistently performed above the mean in basic skills**. Accordingly, his educational performance was not adversely affected by his disability and he was ineligible for special education under the IDEA. The court also rejected the Section 504 claim, since the IEP proposal was a reasonable accommodation. The school had offered him individual counseling, and the refusal to fund his college-level program did not amount to discrimination. The student was essentially claiming that the proposed accommodation was not an optimal placement, and Section 504 did not require "potential-maximizing education." *J.D. v. Pawlet School Dist.*, 224 F.3d 60 (2d Cir. 2000).

♦   A Connecticut special education statute defined "gifted children" as being "exceptional children" who did not progress effectively without special education. Although this definition coincided with the state law definition of children with disabilities, the statute did not mandate special education for gifted students, as it did for students with disabilities. The parents of a Connecticut student identified as gifted demanded that his school board provide him with special education individually designed to meet his needs. The board refused to provide an IEP for the student, and the parents sued for a declaration that he was entitled to special education. The court granted summary judgment motions by the state and local education boards and the state commissioner of education, finding that gifted children did not have a right to special education under the state statute or constitution.

The Supreme Court of Connecticut observed that although the legislature had categorized gifted children within the definition of exceptional children, **the statute did not create a right to special education for gifted children.** Special education was mandatory only for students with disabilities. Because students with disabilities had different needs than gifted children, there was a rational basis for the legislature to treat the two groups differently, and there was no violation of the state constitution on equal protection grounds. The board did not have to provide individualized education for the gifted student. The lower court holding was affirmed. *Broadley v. Board of Educ. of the City of Meriden*, 229 Conn. 1, 639 A.2d 502 (Conn. 1994).

IV. STATE REGULATORY AUTHORITY

Cases in this section involve state law conflicts arising from the exercise of state or school district authority and the operation of state compulsory attendance and delinquency laws. Because school districts are government entities that have only the powers granted to them by state law, a reviewing court may set aside a local decision as an abuse of authority. Courts have approved innovative educational approaches including charter schools and community service obligations when challenged on constitutional grounds.

A. State and School District Authority

◆   The mother of an Alabama student became dissatisfied with her child's education and sued the school board, the state department of education and several officials. A federal court dismissed the department and the officials from the lawsuit, noting that the IDEA does not provide for individual liability and that **the mother failed to show any widespread systemic breakdown by the department in carrying out its mandate under the IDEA.** *B.I. v. Montgomery County Board of Educ.*, 750 F.Supp.2d 1280 (M.D. Ala. 2010).

◆   The mother of a Washington student with ADHD stopped taking care of him because of substance abuse. She completed a treatment program and stayed sober for more than a year, but the state nevertheless sought to terminate her parental rights and provided foster parent training to someone else. In the lawsuit that resulted, the Supreme Court of Washington held the state had overstepped its bounds. **The state could not terminate the mother's parental rights without at least offering to provide the same training to her that it provided to the foster parent.** *In re Welfare of C.S.*, 225 P.3d 953 (Wash. 2010).

◆   With the consent of parents, a residential school in Massachusetts used shock therapy on students when other positive and non-intrusive behavioral procedures were ineffective. The school sought to be certified by the California Department of Education as a nonpublic, nonsectarian school authorized to serve students with IEPs. The department refused to grant the certification, and the California Court of Appeal upheld that determination. **The school's written policy authorized corporal punishment, in violation of the California Education Code**, and it was not entitled to a waiver of that prohibition. *Judge Rotenberg Educ. Center v. Office of Administrative Hearings*, No. C056194, 2009 WL 162066 (Cal. Ct. App. 1/26/09).

♦   Arizona lawmakers enacted a law that would give students with disabilities who attended public schools up to $5,000 for tuition and fees at private schools. The program included both sectarian and nonsectarian private schools in its scope. Objectors to the program sued state officials asserting constitutional violations. The case reached the Arizona Court of Appeals, which held that **although the program did not violate the Religion Clause of the state constitution, it did violate the Aid Clause**, which prohibits the appropriation of public money made in aid of private or sectarian schools. Even though the payments would be made to the students, who would then give the money to the schools, the program would still transfer state funds to private schools. *Cain v. Horne*, 183 P.3d 1269 (Ariz. Ct. App. 2008).

♦   An Illinois school district received allegations of abuse and decided to install audio/visual recording equipment in plain view in the classrooms. Special education teachers sought a court order that would prohibit the operation of the audio recording equipment. They asserted that the audio recording violated the Fourth Amendment as well as the Illinois Eavesdropping Act. A federal court examined the Fourth Amendment claim and held that **the teachers did not have a reasonable expectation of privacy in their classrooms**, which were not the private property of any teacher. The court remanded the case to state court for a decision on the other claim. *Plock v. Board of Educ. of Freeport School Dist. No. 145*, 545 F.Supp.2d 755 (N.D. Ill. 2007).

♦   The parents of a disabled Minnesota student who attended a private school asked their local school district about his eligibility for ESY services. The district told them it provided no summer services for non-public school students with disabilities. The parents complained to the state Department of Education, and the district began voluntarily providing 60 minutes of math instruction per week for four weeks. **The Department of Education then found that the district's policy of denying ESY services to non-public school students violated state law.** It ordered the district to take corrective action. The district appealed. The Minnesota Court of Appeals held that the Department of Education had the authority to investigate the legality of district policies and, when necessary, to order corrective action. *Independent School Dist. No. 281 (Robbinsdale) v. Minnesota Dep't of Educ.*, 743 N.W.2d 315 (Minn. Ct. App. 2008).

♦   A New York private school authorized to serve students with language and communications disorders through third grade sued the state when its application to serve students in higher grades was denied. A federal court upheld the denial of the application. The state's education policies capping reimbursement for certain special education placements did not violate the school's rights. The policies were intended to encourage placements in the least restrictive environments and ensure compliance with the IDEA. **The school was unable to prove that the caps on enrollment resulted in the denial of FAPE** to students. Finally, the caps were flexible, and they were allowed to expand upon a showing of regional need. *School for Language and Communication Development v. New York State Dep't of Educ.*, No. 02-CV-0269(JS)(JO), 2006 WL 2792754 (E.D.N.Y. 9/26/06).

◆ After a charter school in the District of Columbia elected to be its own LEA under the IDEA, it challenged a hearing officer's decision in an IDEA action and sought to include the district in the lawsuit. A federal court ruled against it, noting that **its election to serve as its own LEA made it individually responsible for providing a FAPE** under the IDEA. The district was dismissed from the case. *Hyde Leadership Public Charter School v. Lewis*, No. Civ. 05-0487 RJL, 2006 WL 2639514 (D.D.C. 9/11/06).

◆ A Minnesota school district removed two disabled siblings from school because it believed their mother no longer resided in the district. When she proved she was still a resident six days later, the students were readmitted. The mother filed a complaint with the state education department, which found that the students did not suffer educational harm. However it **ordered the district to provide due process before seeking removal of any disabled student (for nonresidency) in the future**. The district claimed the department had overstepped its authority, but the Minnesota Court of Appeals upheld the action as consistent with the IDEA. *Independent School Dist. No. 623 Roseville Area Schools v. Minnesota Dep't of Educ.*, No. A05-361, 2005 WL 3111963 (Minn. Ct. App. 11/22/05).

◆ After certain private schools in California had their certification for teaching special education suspended or revoked, a lawsuit resulted. The association representing them argued that the state could not revoke or suspend certifications without first providing an administrative hearing. The California Court of Appeal disagreed. **Neither state law nor education regulations required hearings prior to the suspension or revocation of certification.** Hearings after the fact were sufficient. *California Ass'n of Private Special Education Schools v. California Dep't of Educ.*, 45 Cal.Rptr.3d 888 (Cal. Ct. App. 2006).

◆ An Indiana school board entered into an agreement with a nonpublic high school to operate an alternate education program. The board agreed to pay the high school $2,334 per semester for each student enrolled in the program, based upon a statutory formula that included state and local funds. A group of taxpayers, some of whom had children attending public schools in the district, sued the state department of education, state board of education, local educational agency and the high school, challenging the agreement. The taxpayers sought recovery of the monies paid under the agreement, asserting that the Indiana Constitution and state law prohibited the arrangement. The case and reached the Court of Appeals of Indiana, which held that in order to attain standing to bring a lawsuit, a party must demonstrate a personal stake in the outcome of the case and show immediate danger of suffering a direct injury as a result of the conduct at issue. The parents claimed that they would suffer direct injury due to the agreement, since public money used to fund the high school would result in less money for other programs attended by their children. The court disagreed, finding no threat of a direct injury to them as a result of the school board's action. Taxpayers typically have only a general interest in the spending of public funds that is common to all members of the public, and **the taxpayers here had no personal stake in the expenditure of funds**. Since the taxpayers had no standing, the case was dismissed. *Fort Wayne Educ. Ass'n v. Indiana Dep't of Educ.*, 692 N.E.2d 902 (Ind. Ct. App. 1998).

♦   A North Carolina school board adopted a student accountability policy to provide that **students in grades three through eight who failed a state-developed standardized test would be retained in their grade** instead of promoted. The policy contained a waiver for students who achieved passing grades during the school year and received teacher and principal approval. A group of North Carolina public school students and their parents sued school officials, challenging the constitutionality of the policy. The court held that the students failed to present the court with a valid constitutional claim, since a student who was not promoted would be given a remedial year to catch up on skills in which future performance could be enhanced. Public policy discourages a federal court from substituting its judgment for that of publicly elected school board members. The policy employed rational means to further a legitimate academic purpose. The court denied the motion for a preliminary order. *Erik V. by Catherine V. v. Causby*, 977 F.Supp. 384 (E.D.N.C. 1997).

B. Compulsory Attendance and Delinquency

State compulsory attendance and delinquency laws impose obligations on students that conflict when a juvenile court order requires incarceration of the student. Many states have acted to create alternative placements for students who would otherwise be suspended or expelled for violation of state laws. For a full discussion on the rights of students with disabilities in suspension and expulsion cases, please see Chapter Two, Section IV.

♦   An Alabama school handbook provided for referral to an "early warning program" conducted by the county juvenile court system where a student had three unexcused absences in a semester. After a student accumulated a tenth tardy in a single semester (for a total of 40 minutes), her principal reported her to the school truant officer. The principal did not refer her to the early warning program or contact her parents, as specified in the handbook. A court adjudicated the student a child in need of supervision and placed her on probation for the rest of the school year. She appealed to the Alabama Court of

Civil Appeals, admitting to being tardy on 10 occasions, but asserting that a medical condition had made it difficult for her to be on time for school. And after receiving prescription medication, she was not late for school again. The court upheld the lower court's ruling, noting that **nothing in state law required the principal to investigate the causes of the student's tardiness**. Also, the principal did not violate the student's due process rights by failing to follow the handbook's progressive discipline procedures. The handbook placed a duty on the student to provide a timely excuse for her absences. *S.H. v. State of Alabama*, 868 So.2d 1110 (Ala. Civ. App. 2003).

◆   A Massachusetts student with a long record of disruptive behavior was not identified as a student with a disability under the IDEA but was the subject of numerous school disciplinary actions. A school administrator referred him for a psycho-educational evaluation, which did not indicate the student needed special education. Three years later, a teacher observed the student participate in what appeared to be a drug transaction. The principal called the police and questioned the student in the presence of an officer. When the student emptied his pockets, he produced two homemade pipes and a wallet that contained two small packages of marijuana and cash. The student was adjudicated delinquent and sentenced to one year of probation, with the condition that he continue his education or maintain employment.

The student appealed to the Massachusetts Appeals Court, where he argued that the juvenile court proceeding constituted a change of placement that violated the IDEA's stay-put provision. He claimed that the school violated the IDEA by failing to immediately provide the police with his school records. The court noted that even if the student had a disability, he was not entitled to the relief he sought. The police, not the school, had initiated the delinquency proceeding. **The IDEA does not prevent state law enforcement and judicial authorities from exercising their responsibilities when students with disabilities commit crimes.** School officials did not violate the IDEA by failing to immediately deliver his records to the police. While the IDEA requires an agency reporting a crime by a disabled student to transmit the student's educational and disciplinary records to law enforcement authorities, it does not specify when this must occur. The juvenile court was provided with the student's psycho-educational evaluation results and notices of his school disciplinary incidents. The court affirmed the finding of delinquency. *Comwlth. of Massachusetts v. Nathaniel N.*, 764 N.E.2d 883 (Mass. App. Ct. 2002).

◆   An Illinois student was identified as behavior-disordered and declared eligible for special education services in sixth grade. He demonstrated repeated truancy, poor impulse control, lack of cooperation with school staff, low self-confidence and failing grades. Despite his academic failure, the IEP designed for seventh grade reflected no change, and he repeated the eighth grade. The IEP team determined that the student should be enrolled in a therapeutic day program, where he successfully completed eighth grade. Meanwhile, the state filed a petition to declare the student a ward of the state, and a juvenile court judge adjudicated him a delinquent minor. His attendance at the therapeutic day program deteriorated and the program discharged him. The juvenile court judge then ordered him placed in a Utah facility for troubled minors. When the student's mother moved into the Oak Park River Forest High School District, the district received notice from the juvenile court of its potential obligation to fund the educational component of the student's Utah placement.

The juvenile court judge ordered the district to pay the educational cost of the Utah placement, and the district appealed. The Appellate Court of Illinois found that under the School Code, where a district could not meet the needs of a student in the district, it had to pay for placements that could be public or private, inside or outside the state of Illinois. The Juvenile Code, on the other hand, provided for making a minor a ward of the state when it was in the minor's best interest. The court rejected the district's assertion that it could not be held liable for the Utah placement because it had not been made a party to the juvenile court proceeding. However, state law typically made the parents or guardians of a delinquent minor responsible for paying for the minor's needs. The juvenile court had violated statutory provisions for the needs of a delinquent minor by ordering the district to fund the cost of the educational component of the Utah placement. **Illinois law did not grant juvenile courts the power to require districts to pay for the educational component of a delinquent minor's residential placement.** The court reversed the juvenile court order. *In re D.D.*, 788 N.E.2d 10 (Ill. App. Ct. 2002).

◆ The Pennsylvania Department of Public Welfare contracted with a private children and youth agency to operate a day treatment program located within the Bethlehem Area School District. The program served students attending school in the Bethlehem district and nonresident students who had been ordered into treatment by the county juvenile court. The facility had an educational component for which the agency sought reimbursement from Bethlehem. When Bethlehem refused, the agency sought a court order requiring Bethlehem to either pay for the educational services provided by the facility to nonresident students or provide the services to students regardless of their residency. The court granted the requested order. Bethlehem appealed to the Commonwealth Court of Pennsylvania, arguing that state law imposed no duty upon it to pay for the education of nonresident students, but created an option to provide or purchase services for its own students while the home districts of nonresident students were required to pay for the education of those students. The court disagreed, finding that Bethlehem **had an obligation to provide for the educational component of all students attending the day treatment program**. It had to either provide the services or pay another district to provide them. Providing an education to all students assigned to a day treatment program is the responsibility of the school district in which the program is located. The court affirmed the judgment. *Community Service Foundation, Inc. v. Bethlehem Area School Dist.*, 706 A.2d 882 (Pa. Commw. Ct. 1998).

V. INCARCERATED STUDENTS

Section 1412(a)(1)(B)(ii) of the IDEA provides that a FAPE need not be provided to children with disabilities "aged 18 through 21 to the extent that

State law does not require that special education and related services under this part be provided to children with disabilities who, in the educational placement prior to their incarceration in an adult correctional facility" were not identified as a child with a disability or did not have an IEP.

Section 1412(a)(11)(C) allows states discretion as to whether they will provide services to students with disabilities who are convicted as adults under state law and subsequently incarcerated in adult prisons. As a result of these provisions, cases have arisen over exactly what obligations states have to incarcerated students with disabilities, primarily under state law.

♦ A Tennessee school district, in conjunction with the sheriff's department, conducted a random canine drug sweep in the parking lot of a high school. One of the dogs alerted to the presence of drugs in a learning disabled student's car. The officers present handcuffed him and searched his vehicle, finding 10 bottles of beer. The student spent a month at an alternative school, then sued under the Fourth Amendment. A federal court held that he did not have a reasonable expectation of privacy in a parking lot accessible to the public. Further, **the dog sniff was not a "search," although it did give the officers probable cause to search his vehicle.** And the handcuffing was a reasonable seizure designed to prevent him from fleeing and to minimize risk to the officers. *Hill v. Scharber,* 544 F.Supp.2d 670 (M.D. Tenn. 2008).

♦ A 17-year-old special education student in the District of Columbia was incarcerated in Maryland and sought an order requiring the district to provide him with private special education services while he was in prison. The district agreed to provide services, but Maryland officials refused to let the private provider into the prison for security reasons. Instead, Maryland developed an IEP for him and provided him with services under that. Two years later, the student sued the district for failing to provide him with services. He sought compensatory education. The U.S. Court of Appeals, D.C. Circuit, ruled against him. Here, the district was unable to perform its contractual obligations because of an event not contemplated by the contract. Therefore, its duty was discharged. *Hester v. District of Columbia,* 505 F.3d 1283 (D.C. Cir. 2007).

♦ A 21-year-old Connecticut student had an IQ of 61 and was classified as educable mentally retarded. He attended a self-contained special education program at a public high school until being arrested and hospitalized. The Connecticut Office of Protection and Advocacy for Persons with Disabilities assisted him in obtaining services from the state department of children and families, and a child-student team at the hospital implemented his IEP. However, the hospital released the student and returned him to the custody of the correctional center, where he was admitted to the mental health unit. An evaluation determined that he was mentally retarded and needed a supervised, but not institutional, setting. A consultant informed the center that the student was a special education student with an IEP. The center began providing services to the student in a segregated housing unit and an IEP team meeting was convened. The student then inflicted wounds on himself and was placed in a restrictive housing unit due to chronic disciplinary problems.

After a stalemate concerning the student's transition plan, the office of protection and advocacy requested a due process hearing. A hearing officer awarded one year of compensatory education, and a Connecticut trial court affirmed. The special school district appealed. The court of appeals stated that the district knew the student was entitled to special education services when the center received a call from the consultant. It was the district's responsibility to comply with the IDEA, not the student's. Any delay could not be attributed to the office of protection and advocacy for educational entitlements. **The district was charged with the responsibility of identifying students with special educational needs. It was required to follow IDEA procedural requirements** and was charged with the knowledge that he had an IEP from the time of the consultant's call. The district had no IEP for the student and was required to implement a program for him. Because the district failed to provide him with a free appropriate public education, he was entitled to compensatory education, even though he was over 21. *Unified School Dist. No. 1 v. Connecticut Dep't of Educ.*, 780 A.2d 154 (Conn. App. Ct. 2001).

◆ Pennsylvania law provided that persons under age 21 who are confined to adult county correctional facilities and otherwise eligible for educational services are entitled to services to the extent expelled students are. The law differentiated between juveniles convicted as adults based on their place of incarceration, since those placed in state facilities received full education programs. Generally, juveniles sentenced to two years or less were confined in county facilities, while those sentenced to terms of five years or more were confined in state facilities. Sentences of between two and five years could be served at either type of facility. Students over age 17 in county facilities received no educational services at all, since state law did not provide for any services to expelled students. A group representing juveniles incarcerated in adult county facilities sued, asserting violation of their constitutional right to equal protection. The Third Circuit held that **the state was required only to show that the disproportionate allocation of state educational resources had some rational relationship to a legitimate end. The state had met this showing** by providing four justifications for the distinction between county and state adult corrections facilities. County correctional institutions, unlike state facilities, had space limitations. State facilities also had higher youth populations, reducing the cost of providing education there. *Brian B. v. Comwlth. of Pennsylvania Dep't of Educ.*, 230 F.3d 582 (3d Cir. 2000).

◆ The Washington legislature enacted a law in 1998 providing for the education of juveniles incarcerated in adult prisons. After two school districts began providing services at correctional facilities under the new law, a group of inmates brought a class-action lawsuit against the state, the school districts, and a number of state officials, alleging that the various entities failed to provide special education services in violation of state and federal law. They also asserted violations of the U.S. and Washington Constitutions. The court granted summary judgment to the inmates on their state law claims and invalidated the 1998 legislation as unconstitutional because it failed to provide special educational opportunities. The court dismissed all the federal claims, and the parties appealed.

The Washington Supreme Court observed that the legislature had specifically acted to exempt incarcerated juveniles from the state compulsory school attendance law. State special education law did not specifically address the education of juveniles incarcerated in adult facilities. Inmates were outside the state's school system and were exempt from the state special education act. The court rejected the inmates' argument that the state constitution required basic and special education for all inmates in adult prisons up to age 22. The provision of education to inmates up to age 18 satisfied the U.S. Constitution. The 1998 legislation did not violate the Washington Constitution, since the state had no obligation to provide an identical education to all children, regardless of circumstances. The court rejected the inmates' assertion that the state had a duty under the IDEA to provide special education to students with disabilities under age 22. **IDEA language specifically exempts the states from their duty to provide special education services "where its application would be inconsistent with state law or practice" for students age 18 through 21.** It also exempted those students who were not identified as disabled or did not have IEPs prior to incarceration. The state did not have to provide special education to students over age 18 if it did not also provide education services to students without disabilities in this age group. Since inmates were only entitled to education until age 18, the inmates' IDEA and Section 504 claims were properly dismissed. *Tunstall v. Bergeson*, 5 P.3d 691 (Wash. 2000).

♦ The Maryland Court of Special Appeals held that **a juvenile court judge could not order a county education board to provide educational services to a delinquent student who was ordered to attend a children's institute**. The board was not a party to the delinquency proceeding, and the court lacked the power to order it to provide the student with services. The student was adjudicated delinquent at age 13. A judge placed him in a regional institute for children and adolescents. As part of the order, the judge required the student's school board to provide him with educational services at the institute. The board appealed to the state court of special appeals, where it argued that the juvenile court had no authority to enter the order and that the order violated the constitutional separation of powers. The court of special appeals noted that the Juvenile Causes Act's relevant provisions did not authorize a juvenile court to order a school system to provide educational services to juveniles. The separation of powers doctrine prohibited the judge's order in this case. *In re Nicholas B.*, 768 A.2d 735 (Md. Ct. Spec. App. 2001).

♦ A 1985 amendment to a New Hampshire statute required school districts to perform evaluations, develop individualized education plans and hold staffings for incarcerated special education students between the ages of 18 and 21 in their jurisdictions. It also made school districts that sent students to residential schools in other districts liable for all special education costs associated with these placements. Prior to the amendment, liability for the cost of a court-ordered juvenile placement in a residential school was placed on the town in which the student lived. A New Hampshire school district sued the state, claiming that the amendment created an unfunded mandate in violation of the state constitution. The district argued that the amendment unfairly required school districts to provide services for incarcerated special education students between the ages of 18 and 21. The court upheld the amendment, and the district appealed to the Supreme Court of New Hampshire.

The court held that the 1985 amendment did not create an unconstitutional unfunded mandate because it represented no new, expanded, or modified program for school districts that might require additional local expenditures. Although recognizing the burden of the responsibility for districts to enter state prisons to perform evaluations, conduct IEPs and hold annual staffings, school districts bore the responsibility for the education of each child residing in their jurisdiction. **The school district was responsible for developing plans for each of its resident incarcerated students between the ages of 18 and 21**, and the court affirmed the judgment for the state. *Nashua School Dist. v. State of New Hampshire*, 667 A.2d 1036 (N.H. 1995).

VI. NO CHILD LEFT BEHIND

The No Child Left Behind Act (NCLB) is actually a reauthorization of the 1965 Elementary and Secondary Education Act (ESEA). Some of its controversial reporting and testing provisions give teeth to requirements that were already in place in previous incarnations of the ESEA. It differs from previous reauthorizations by its emphasis on accountability.

Under NCLB, schools must maintain adequate yearly progress (AYP) toward achieving state academic standards. If schools fail to make adequate yearly progress, districts must implement certain corrective actions, such as replacing staff, implementing new curricula and providing supplemental educational services.

Every state is required to: 1) set standards for grade-level achievement, and 2) develop a system to measure the progress of all students and subgroups of students in meeting those state-determined grade-level standards.

Although NCLB mandates annual testing for all states, it does not provide federal standards for testing practices. Individual states create their own approaches for testing students through either norm-referenced or criterion-referenced tests. Norm-referenced tests measure progress against a comparison group, while criterion-referenced tests measure progress against pre-established standards of academic performance.

Under NCLB, students who attend Title I schools that do not make adequate yearly progress, as defined by states, for two consecutive years have the option of transferring to a higher-performing public school or a charter school within their district.

Students with disabilities must be included in state and district-wide assessment programs. These assessments measure how well students with disabilities have learned required material in reading and mathematics. Students with the most significant cognitive disabilities can have results from specially designed alternate assessments used in accountability decisions instead. States may include proficient scores from such assessments in making AYP decisions. Those scores are capped at 1% of the total tested population.

NCLB requires all teachers to be highly qualified by the end of the 2005-2006 school year. It requires highly qualified teachers to: 1) have a bachelor's degree, 2) have full state certification or licensure, and 3) prove that they know each subject they teach.

State Requirements: NCLB requires states to: 1) measure the extent to which all students have highly qualified teachers, particularly minority and disadvantaged students, 2) adopt goals and plans to ensure all teachers are highly qualified and, 3) publicly report plans and progress in meeting teacher quality goals.

Demonstration of Competency: Teachers (in middle and high school) must prove that they know the subject they teach with: 1) a major in the subject they teach, 2) credits equivalent to a major in the subject, 3) passage of a state-developed test, 4) HOUSSE (for current teachers only, see below), 5) an advanced certification from the state, or 6) a graduate degree.

High, Objective, Uniform State Standard of Evaluation (HOUSSE): NCLB allows states to develop an additional way for current teachers to demonstrate subject-matter competency and meet highly qualified teacher requirements. Proof may consist of a combination of teaching experience, professional development, and knowledge in the subject garnered over time in the profession.

NCLB offers some flexibility for teachers to demonstrate that they are highly qualified.

Rural: Teachers in eligible rural districts who are highly qualified in at least one subject will have three years to become highly qualified in the additional subjects they teach.

Science: States may allow science teachers to demonstrate that they are highly qualified either in "broad field" science or individual fields of science (such as physics, biology or chemistry).

Multi-subject: States may streamline the evaluation process for the highly qualified requirement by developing a method for current multi-subject teachers to demonstrate through one process that they are highly qualified in each of their subjects and maintain the same high standards in subject-matter mastery.

Special Education: The highly qualified teacher requirements apply only to teachers providing direct instruction in core academic subjects. Special educators who do not directly instruct students in core academic subjects or who provide only consultation to highly qualified teachers in adapting curricula, using behavioral supports and interventions or selecting appropriate accommodations, do not need to demonstrate subject-matter competency in those subjects.

♦ Connecticut officials asked for a waiver from certain testing provisions of the NCLB. The U.S. Secretary of Education denied the waiver and sought more information while stating that a policy change for special education students was forthcoming. However, **the new policy did not permit testing of special education students at their instructional level**, even if consistent with the students' IEPs. The state then sued over the unfunded mandates provision of the act, but a federal court and the Second Circuit held that the challenges to the unfunded mandates provision could not be litigated because Connecticut was in compliance with the NCLB and continued to receive federal funds under the law. *Connecticut v. Duncan*, 612 F.3d 107 (2d Cir. 2010).

♦ A group of Newark parents brought a class action lawsuit under NCLB against the public school system, claiming they were denied adequate notice of their right to obtain transfers for their children to better-performing schools, to receive supplemental educational services and to learn about the qualifications of teachers. A federal court dismissed the case, and the Third Circuit upheld that decision. NCLB focuses on aggregate level compliance and **does not create individual rights** to enforce it. *Newark Parents Ass'n v. Newark Public Schools*, 547 F.3d 199 (3d Cir. 2008).

♦ The Arizona Department of Education entered into an agreement with the U.S. Department of Education that would allow it the discretion to exclude the test scores of certain limited English proficiency students in adequate yearly progress calculations under NCLB. The agreement also allowed the state to grant appeals under 20 U.S.C. § 6316(b)(2)(B) to schools that did not achieve adequate yearly progress. After **the U.S. Department of Education issued a report finding that Arizona's practice of granting appeals and excluding limited-English proficiency students violated NCLB**, Arizona's Department of Education sued. However, a federal court held that the lawsuit was actually a "pre-enforcement" challenge to the Secretary of Education's interpretation of Section 6316(b)(2)(B) and was thus not within the court's jurisdiction. Arizona would have to wait until after the Secretary commenced an enforcement action to challenge the U.S. Department of Education's action. *Arizona Dep't of Educ. v. U.S. Dep't of Educ.*, No. CV-06-1719-PHX-DGC, 2007 WL 433581 (D. Ariz. 2/6/07).

♦ A supplemental educational services company approved by the state of Michigan to provide tutoring services for underachieving students enrolled about 1,000 Detroit students during the 2005-06 school year. The Detroit school district terminated the contract during the year for failure to provide services and failure to pay its employees. It also refused to recognize the company as an approved provider for the following year. The company sued the district in federal court, claiming relief under NCLB. The court ruled for the district, finding **no private right of action under NCLB**. Further, any breach of contract claim would have to be brought in state court. *Alliance For Children, Inc. v. City of Detroit Public Schools*, 475 F.Supp.2d 655 (E.D. Mich. 2007).

◆   Two Illinois school districts, along with the families of four disabled students, sued the U.S. Department of Education (DOE) alleging that by complying with NCLB, they had to violate provisions of the IEPs of some students. The lawsuit **claimed that NCLB ignored the unique needs of students with disabilities** by imposing the requirement that they meet state standards based on all students. And the only feasible corrective action was to change the curriculum of disabled students, which meant changing their IEPs without accounting for their individual needs. A federal court ruled for the DOE, holding that the districts did not have standing to sue. The districts and parents appealed to the Seventh Circuit, which agreed that the case should be dismissed. The court noted that if there truly were a conflict between the two laws, the more recently enacted 2004 IDEA amendments would prevail over the 2001 NCLB. *Board of Educ. of Ottawa Township High School Dist. 140 v. Spellings*, 517 F.3d 922 (7th Cir. 2008).

◆   School districts from Michigan, Texas and other states joined the National Education Association and several state affiliates in a challenge to the Secretary of Education's enforcement of NCLB. They argued that states need not comply with the NCLB's requirements where federal funds did not cover the increased costs of compliance with the act. They also sought an injunction against the withholding of federal funds for noncompliance with NCLB. A federal court dismissed the case, holding that the states had to comply with NCLB regardless of any federal funding shortfall. The full Sixth Circuit upheld the district court decision, with eight judges voting to reverse and eight judges voting to affirm. *School Dist. of City of Pontiac v. Secretary of U.S. Dep't of Educ.*, 584 F.3d 253 (6th Cir. 2009).

◆   Pennsylvania's education secretary identified 13 schools in a district as failing to achieve adequate yearly progress under the No Child Left Behind Act. Seven schools were placed on a warning list and the others (Title I schools) were placed in school improvement. The district appealed, asserting that the Pennsylvania System of State Assessment was discriminatory because it did not provide for native language testing. It also claimed it was entitled to greater levels of state assistance. The Pennsylvania Commonwealth Court agreed with the secretary that **it would not be practicable to provide native language testing at present**. Further, the state had provided appropriate technical assistance and was planning to offer more technical assistance in the future. The court upheld the secretary's designation of the schools as failing. *Reading School Dist. v. Dep't of Educ.*, 855 A.2d 166 (Pa. Commw. Ct. 2004).

The district then submitted its plans to bring the six schools into compliance, estimating the cost at $26 million for the following school year. Since the district would only receive $8 million in federal funding, it asked the state to make up the difference. The state did not respond to the request for funds, but found that the six schools and the district failed to achieve adequate yearly progress (AYP). The district appealed, asserting that the state education department had created an unfunded mandate prohibited by NCLB. The state's education secretary dismissed the appeal because it violated the department's new appeal policy. However, a Pennsylvania court held that the new appeal policy violated the district's due process rights. *Reading School Dist. v. Dep't of Educ.*, 875 A.2d 1218 (Pa. Commw. Ct. 2005).

♦   An Ohio provider of "supplemental educational services" (SES) as defined under the NCLB sued a school board, claiming that the board had misappropriated NCLB funds by hiring other SES providers while excluding it from the bidding process. A federal court noted that NCLB requires districts that do not make adequate yearly progress for a specified time period to arrange for SES. However, NCLB does not provide a procedure for individual entities to enforce its provisions. The only penalties available are the withholding of funds from the states. Since **there was no private right of action to enforce the NCLB**, the court dismissed the case. *Fresh Start Academy v. Toledo Board of Educ.*, 363 F.Supp.2d 910 (N.D. Ohio 2005).

CHAPTER NINE

Discrimination

I. FEDERAL ANTI-DISCRIMINATION LAWS

The Rehabilitation Act of 1973 and the Americans with Disabilities Act of 1990 (ADA) prohibit discrimination against individuals with disabilities. They state that no individual with a disability is to be excluded from employment, programs, or services if the individual is otherwise qualified to participate in the program or to receive benefits to which he or she is entitled.

Under the statutes, it is discriminatory for a school or educational facility to impose eligibility criteria that screen out disabled individuals. It is also discriminatory for the facilities to fail to reasonably accommodate disabled individuals. This chapter deals primarily with disabled students. However, there is a substantial body of disability employment cases in Chapter Seven, Section II, subsection A. For cases involving the placement of students with disabilities, see Chapter Two.

A. Generally

♦ The U.S. Supreme Court concluded that **no private cause of action exists to enforce federal regulations published under Title VI of the Civil Rights Act** of 1964. It dismissed a class action suit advanced by non-English speakers who claimed that Alabama's exclusive reliance on English for state driver's license examinations had a discriminatory effect based on national origin. Title VI is one of the principal federal laws preventing discrimination on the basis of race, color, or national origin. It prohibits federal funding recipients, including educational institutions, from discriminating in any covered program or activity and is commonly cited in education cases alleging discrimination. The Supreme Court noted that Title VI prohibits only intentional discrimination and cannot be used to enforce a disparate impact action. Thus, there could be no private right of action to enforce Title VI disparate impact regulations. *Alexander v. Sandoval,* 532 U.S. 275, 121 S.Ct. 1511, 149 L.Ed.2d 517 (2001).

♦ The mother of a Maine student with emotional and mental disorders claimed that their school district's IEP discriminated against her son. She sued under § 504. However, a federal court dismissed the action, noting that § 504 is broader in scope than the IDEA, which limits a person's ability to pursue damage awards under other federal laws, including § 504. Here, **the mother's claim turned entirely on rights created by the IDEA, so she had no alternative but to pursue relief under that statute.** *Doe v. Wells-Ogunquit Community School Dist.*, 698 F.Supp.2d 219 (D. Me. 2010).

♦ When she was in the fifth grade, an Indiana student learned that she had been born with HIV. She discussed her condition on social media sites in sixth grade and was harassed by two students as a result. A counselor warned the harassers and met with their parent. In seventh grade, another student warned a fellow pupil not to kiss her because he could get AIDS. Again, the counselor intervened and met with the parent. In eighth grade, her soccer coach asked if she had AIDS. The principal met with the coach afterwards. When the student then dropped out of school and sued for harassment, she lost. A federal court held that **the school acted immediately upon learning of the harassing incidents** and was thus not deliberately indifferent to them so as to be liable under the ADA and Section 504. *P.R. v. Metropolitan School Dist. of Washington Township*, No. 1:08-CV-1562-WTC-DML, 2010 WL 4457417 (S.D. Ind. 11/1/10).

♦ A Houston student had trouble finishing his work and following directions. His mother sought to have him tested to see if he needed special education services, but the district failed to do so. During the winter holiday of his first-grade year, his mother enrolled him in another district, where he was immediately referred for special education testing. She later sued the Houston district for discrimination under the ADA and Section 504, but a federal court and the Fifth Circuit ruled against her. **The untimely diagnosis was at most negligence.** *D.A. v. Houston Independent School Dist.*, 629 F.3d 450 (5th Cir. 2010).

♦ A Georgia school district assigned a one-on-one assistant to an aggressive autistic student for an after-school daycare program and also devised a behavior intervention plan. A custodian with a special needs son received training and served as the assistant but often had to be away to attend to his own child. On a day when the custodian was absent, the student became agitated and left the building. Eventually, several staff members placed him in his time-out room, where he hit the window and kicked the walls. A police officer handcuffed him until his father could come and pick him up. The father later sued for disability discrimination under Section 504 and the ADA, but **a federal court found no evidence of intentional discrimination against the student. At most, staff members acted negligently.** *J.D.P. v. Cherokee County, Georgia School Dist.*, 735 F.Supp.2d 1348 (N.D. Ga. 2010).

♦ A hearing-impaired California student challenged his special educational services under the IDEA and lost, except for a ruling that extended school year services should have been provided for one summer. He then brought claims against the district under Section 504, seeking money damages. However, a federal court held that **he failed to present any evidence that the district had treated him less well than non-disabled students**. The Ninth Circuit affirmed, finding that the district's offer to mainstream him was reasonably calculated to provide him with educational benefits. *J.W. v. Fresno Unified School Dist.*, 626 F.3d 431 (9th Cir. 2010).

♦ A disabled Texas student with an alleged history of violence and displaying pornography was left alone with a female student for 15 to 20 minutes. He exposed himself to her, grabbed her, kissed her and lifted her dress. He was separated from her after she reported the incident and was later transferred to another school. Her family sued the district for sexual harassment under Title IX. A federal court and the Fifth Circuit ruled against them. **The single incident of misconduct was not so severe, pervasive and objectively unreasonable as to deprive the female student of an education.** Further, the district responded promptly to her report of the incident. *Watkins v. La Marque Independent School Dist.*, 308 Fed.Appx. 781 (5th Cir. 2009).

♦ A student with oppositional defiance disorder had an IEP. She sought admission to the New Mexico Military Institute, a college preparatory school. Her application was denied based on several factors, including behavior problems and past drug use. She sued for violations of the IDEA, Section 504 and the ADA. A federal court and the Tenth Circuit ruled against her. The institute complied with the IDEA and she also failed to exhaust her administrative remedies under that statute. Further, even though she was IDEA-eligible, she failed to show that she was "disabled" under Section 504 and the ADA. She could not demonstrate that she was "substantially limited in the major life activity of learning." **A person can be IDEA-eligible and not disabled under Section 504 or the ADA.** *Ellenberg v. New Mexico Military Institute*, 572 F.3d 815 (10th Cir. 2009).

♦ Two male students chased a female special education student around a classroom, grabbing her breasts and privates. The teacher apparently failed to intervene even though the student screamed for help. A friend of the student reported the incident, and the two male students were suspended for 87 days. After they returned to school, the student suffered panic attacks upon seeing them. She sued the district for violating Title IX. A federal court refused to dismiss the case. **There was a question as to whether the teacher knew an assault was taking place and failed to intervene.** If so, that might lead to liability under Title IX. *T.Z. v. City of New York*, 634 F.Supp.2d 263 (E.D.N.Y. 2009).

♦ The parents of two disabled students in California sued the county office of education. They said a teacher and an aide had abused their children, tying one to his wheelchair and making him sit in his own feces and forcing the other to stand on a chair for prolonged periods, resulting in her falling at least once. The county sought to have the lawsuit dismissed, but a federal court refused to do so. **The parents had asserted legitimate claims under Section 504 and the**

ADA – alleging that their children were treated differently than non-disabled children, and that county officials knew about the abuse and failed to take corrective action. Their state law claims could also proceed. *D.K. v. Solano County Office of Educ.*, 667 F.Supp. 2d 1184 (E.D. Cal. 2009).

◆ An Indiana high school student with epilepsy suffered a seizure and injured a teacher who was trying to help him. The school created a protocol for how to handle future seizures, including calling his parents and an ambulance, but not calling the police. However, the superintendent, without notifying the parents, decided that the police should be called. The student missed 10 days. After he returned, he suffered another seizure and police were called. One of them injured the student, who later sued the school for discrimination under Section 504. A federal court ruled that **the missed school and the calling of the police did not amount to a violation of Section 504** despite the fact that the school failed to follow the Section 504 plan. *Sandlin v. Switzerland County School Corp.*, No. 4:08-CV-0047-DFH-WGH, 2009 WL 2563470 (S.D. Ind. 8/17/09).

◆ A New Jersey vice principal suspended an African-American preschool student on two occasions after the student assaulted teachers and fellow students. The district determined that the misbehavior was a manifestation of the student's disability and placed him out of district. The student's parents sued for race discrimination, asserting that the vice principal had made a racial comment about their son. A federal court dismissed the claims against the district, finding no official policy or custom (and no district-wide pattern or practice) of race discrimination. However, **the parents were entitled to a trial against the vice principal on their claims of discrimination**. *Clark v. Board of Educ. of Franklin Township Public Schools*, No. 06-2736 (FLW), 2009 WL 1586940 (D.N.J. 6/4/09).

◆ A District of Columbia student with multiple disabilities attended a private school paid for by the D.C. Public Schools (DCPS). However, as his graduation approached, the DCPS failed to identify him as a student who might be eligible for benefits from the D.C. Rehabilitation Service Agency (RSA). As a result, **he did not learn about the tuition assistance the RSA provided until after he had incurred the obligation to pay the first semester's tuition** at a Florida college. When he applied for benefits, the RSA granted them going forward, but not for the first semester. He appealed, but the D.C. Court of Appeals ruled against him. According to the Rehabilitation Act, the RSA was not responsible for identifying him as a qualifying student and it did not have to pay for an obligation he had already incurred. *Takahashi v. District of Columbia Dep't of Human Services*, 952 A.2d 869 (D.C. 2008).

◆ The mother of an African-American student in Philadelphia claimed that the district failed to meet its child-find obligations under the IDEA for five years, refusing to evaluate her son and instead suspending him for behavior problems as well as referring him for truancy. Eventually she reached a settlement with the district, but was only able to get a year of compensatory education because of the IDEA's two-year limitations period. She then sued for race and disability discrimination. The district sought to have the case dismissed, but a federal court refused to do so. She produced sufficient evidence to warrant further consideration of those claims. *James S. v. School Dist. of Philadelphia*, 559 F.Supp.2d 600 (E.D. Pa. 2008).

◆   A 14-year-old African-American junior high school student with ADHD brought a .45 caliber pistol to school and gave it to another student. His Section 504 committee found that his ADHD did not impair his ability to understand the impact and consequences of his behavior, and he was expelled for the rest of the year. **His parents sued for discrimination, arguing that a white nine-year-old with ADHD was not expelled** by the district for bringing a toy gun to his intermediate school. His Section 504 committee found a relationship between his disability and his behavior. An Arkansas federal court held that the circumstances were different enough that the two cases could not be compared for the purpose of divining a discrimination claim. *Griffin v. Crossett School Dist.*, No. 07-CV-1015, 2008 WL 2669115 (W.D. Ark. 7/1/08).

◆   The parents of a New Jersey student with Down syndrome objected to her placement in a segregated institution where she was taught life skills rather than academics. A due process hearing officer upheld the district's decision and the parents appealed to a federal court. They also added claims on their own behalf for discrimination under the ADA and Section 504. The court ruled against them, noting that **they could not pursue discrimination claims under the ADA and Section 504** even though the Supreme Court had allowed parents to pursue claims on their own behalf under the IDEA. *D.A. v. Pleasantville School Dist.*, No. 07-4341 (RBK), 2008 WL 2684239 (D.N.J. 6/30/08).

◆   A Connecticut high school student enrolled in special education was frequently asked by a male student to have sex. Her teacher advised the assistant principal of the situation, and the male student was then educated at home. However, before he was officially withdrawn from school, he was able to penetrate the female student sexually. Her parents sued the school board for violating Title IX, and the school board sought to have the case dismissed. A federal court refused to dismiss the lawsuit, finding **some evidence that the board made the student more vulnerable to harassment** after the teacher informed the assistant principal but before the male student was educated at home. *M. v. Stamford Board of Educ.*, 2008 WL 2704704, 2008 WL 4197047 (D. Conn. 7/7/08).

◆   A Minnesota student's IEP team determined that she was not eligible for extended school year (ESY) services, but provided curb-to-curb transportation, as well as an aide, for one summer. The next summer it required the student to use general education transportation without an aide. After a driver sexually abused her, the district fired the driver, and the parents sued the district for violating Section 504. A federal court and the Eighth Circuit ruled for the district, noting that **the discontinuation of the aide and the abuse by the driver did not amount to discrimination** because the district did not act with bad faith or gross misjudgment. It followed the IEP, which stated that she was ineligible for ESY and related services such as transportation. *M.Y. v. Special School Dist. No. 1*, 544 F.3d 885 (8th Cir. 2008).

♦ On two occasions, a severely disabled Oklahoma student rolled or fell off the changing table at school while a special education teacher changed his diaper. The table had no straps or other securing devices, and the student was prone to uncontrolled spastic movements. His guardians sued the school district for negligence and discrimination under Section 504. The district sought pretrial judgment on the discrimination claims, which a federal court denied. Here, **there was evidence that the district was deliberately indifferent to the student's well-being.** Despite knowledge of his spastic movements, the district did not obtain a changing table with security restraints. A trial was required. *Miles v. Cushing Public Schools*, No. CIV-06-1431-D, 2008 WL 4619857 (W.D. Okla. 10/16/08).

♦ The parents of an Arkansas student with mental retardation and serious heart disease sued their school district for discrimination under the Rehabilitation Act and ADA. They alleged that a group of non-disabled students pretended to befriend their son, then confined him in a dog cage and forced him to eat dog feces. They also stole from him, sexually abused him and exposed his body to non-disabled peers. The parents claimed they discussed the bullying with school officials repeatedly, but that the district did nothing to stop the abuse. The district sought to have the claims dismissed for failure to exhaust administrative remedies, but a federal court refused to do so. Here, **there was some evidence that the district acted with bad faith or gross misjudgment.** The case was allowed to proceed. *R.P. v. Springdale School Dist.*, No. 06-5014, 2007 WL 552117 (W.D. Ark. 2/21/07).

♦ An Arkansas student with ADHD was provided with a written Section 504 accommodation plan in her final year of middle school. In high school, the student had multiple disciplinary referrals. However, she was selected for the cheerleading squad as a ninth-grader. When she wasn't selected for the squad as a tenth-grader, she sued for discrimination under the IDEA and Section 504. A federal court held that her IDEA claims failed because she did not exhaust her administrative remedies. And **her Section 504 claims failed because she failed to show that she was treated any differently than any of the other competitors for the cheerleading position.** *Doe v. Rousseau*, No. 4:06CV0911 JMM, 2007 WL 2445305 (E.D. Ark. 8/23/07).

♦ A Louisiana student sued school officials under the ADA and Rehabilitation Act, alleging that he was denied access to the auditorium stage and that he had to take alternate routes to his classrooms because of a lack of wheelchair accessibility. The case reached the Fifth Circuit, which ruled against him. Here, **although the stage was not wheelchair accessible while he was in the drama club, he never auditioned for any plays and did not need to be on stage** while in the club. The school also had the option of moving plays to the gymnasium, which it had done in the past for wheelchair accessibility reasons. Finally, the school completed a ramp after the student quit drama club. *Logwood v. Louisiana Dep't of Educ.*, 197 Fed.Appx. 302 (5th Cir. 2006).

♦ After a Georgia student with a tracheotomy tube collapsed on the playground and died, his mother sued the school district for discrimination under the ADA and the Rehabilitation Act, alleging a failure to provide qualified personnel and necessary medical services. A federal court ruled that the mother could seek compensatory damages, but that she had to prove her son's death resulted from intentional discrimination to succeed in her lawsuit. A jury held for the school board and the mother asked the court to set aside the verdict. The court refused to do so. **There was no merit to the mother's claim that the mere failure to accommodate the student's disability could amount to intentional discrimination.** *Ortega v. Bibb County School Dist.*, No. 5:00-CV-366-2(HL), 2006 WL 3534685 (M.D. Ga. 12/7/06).

♦ The parents of a Puerto Rico student with autism had substantial disagreements with their son's teacher over his education. The teacher believed the parents were neglecting their son, noticing bruises on his arms and being unable to reach the parents when he had seizures at school. The teacher and principal **reported the parents to the local child protection agency, after which the parents sued for retaliation**. The First Circuit held that the parents failed to prove retaliation under the Rehabilitation Act. School providers are obligated by law to report situations of abuse and neglect of a minor and they reasonably believed the parents' intransigence was negligence in this case. *Vives v. Fajardo*, 472 F.3d 19 (1st Cir. 2007).

♦ A New York student with pervasive development disorder and dyslexia claimed that he was harassed and bullied on numerous occasions over two years, alleging that he was body-slammed and beaten and had his books thrown in the trash at least five times. His mother also complained to school officials. Eventually, he was admitted to a hospital psychiatric emergency room. He was then sent to another school at the district's expense. His mother nevertheless sued the district and superintendent under the Rehabilitation Act and the ADA. The court refused to dismiss the case, finding **issues over the credibility of school employees who professed ignorance to the harassment and bullying despite numerous incident reports**. A trial was required. *K.M. v. Hyde Park Cent. School Dist.*, 381 F.Supp.2d 343 (S.D.N.Y. 2005).

♦ Due to budget constraints, a California school district informed parents of autistic students that the autism class would end at noon every Tuesday. A parent filed a complaint resolution procedure request with the state department of education, and the district then extended the school day on Tuesdays by 30 minutes. It included lunch and recess as instructional time and asserted that it was in compliance with state regulations that require the school day to be the same length for special education students as it is for regular education students. The department of education took no further action, and the students sued for discrimination. A federal court dismissed the case for failure to exhaust administrative remedies, but the Ninth Circuit Court of Appeals reversed the lower court decision. **There was little reason to require a due process hearing when assessing the validity of a district-wide policy.** Further, lunch and recess did not qualify as instructional time unless specified in individual IEPs, which was not the case here. *Christopher S. v. Stanislaus County Office of Educ.*, 384 F.3d 1205 (9th Cir. 2004).

♦   A Colorado student with hearing and visual impairments received special education and related services from a school district. In her second-grade year, her parents moved out of the district, but she continued to attend the school. The district also allowed her to attend the same school in her third- and fourth-grade years, but it denied admission for her fifth-grade year because the special education program now exceeded the district's capacity. The parents then moved back into the district, re-enrolled their daughter, and sued the district under the state's school choice law, the IDEA, Section 504 and the ADA. A court ruled for the district, and the Colorado Court of Appeals affirmed. Student re-enrollment rights were limited to students who became nonresidents between school years, and the right did not extend beyond the following school year. Although the school choice law allowed the student to enroll for subsequent years, the district could rely on the statute to deny her attempt to enroll for the fifth grade. A district regulation specified that a program would be closed to nonresidents if enrollment caused the program to exceed the district's staffing standard. The court also held that **the limitation on the number of nonresident students was not an illegal quota**. *Bradshaw v. Cherry Creek School Dist. No. 5*, 98 P.3d 886 (Colo. Ct. App. 2003).

♦   A Wyoming student with cerebral palsy attended school in a district that initially did not have accessible buildings. The district hired a full-time aide to assist her during the school day. During her entire school career, the student continued to have accessibility issues, like the inability to use accessible seating in the gym and being locked out of school because the accessible door was not working. Also, during her senior year, her aide frequently missed school due to a personal situation. When the student sued the district under Section 504 and the ADA, the district sought to have the case dismissed. The court refused to do so, noting that **the mere hiring of the full-time aide did not mean that the district had not intentionally discriminated against the student**. Not only was the aide absent at times during the school day, but she was also not present for extracurricular activities and events. A trial would have to be held. *Swenson v. Lincoln County School Dist.*, 260 F.Supp.2d 1136 (D. Wyo. 2003).

♦   A New Jersey student with disabilities had substantial fatigue that made her unable to attend school for a full day. Under her IEP, she attended morning classes and received home instruction from school staff during the afternoon. Despite her disability, she earned a weighted GPA of 4.6894 and scored 1570 out of 1600 possible points on the SAT. Although she was the highest-ranked student in her class, the district superintendent changed district policy to allow for multiple valedictorians. The student sued under Section 504 and the ADA, asserting that the district's action discriminated against her on the basis of her disability. A federal court agreed. Here, her home placement actually put her at a disadvantage because she was unable to take some Advanced Placement courses that could have lifted her GPA even higher. Her IEP did not give her an advantage; it merely leveled the playing field. **The district could not retroactively change its policy to allow for multiple valedictorians.** *Hornstine v. Township of Moorestown*, 263 F.Supp.2d 887 (D.N.J. 2003).

♦ A student with a history of chronic illness missed extensive amounts of school during the seventh grade. Although her mother furnished a pediatrician's note excusing her from school, school officials insisted she attend. After the student was diagnosed with chronic fatigue syndrome, her mother decided to home-school her. The parties were unable to agree on the appropriate placement once the student returned to school. The student and her mother sued the school district, board and numerous education officials, asserting disability discrimination and retaliation under Section 504, the ADA, the IDEA, and other state and federal laws. The court concluded that because the student did not have a learning disability, she was unprotected by federal anti-discrimination laws. The Second Circuit noted that **the district court had erroneously dismissed the Section 504 and ADA claims based on its finding that the student was not learning-disabled and therefore was not substantially limited in the major life activity of learning**. The student was "disabled" under both acts. She was substantially impaired in major life activities such as walking, exerting herself and attending school. The district failed to reasonably accommodate the student by denying her any meaningful education for much of her seventh-grade year. Also, the student's retaliation claim should not have been dismissed. The complaint contained many examples of threats to initiate child welfare investigations against the mother, along with the refusal to evaluate the student and appropriately place her. *Weixel v. Board of Educ. of City of New York*, 287 F.3d 138 (2d Cir. 2002).

♦ A Kentucky ninth-grader with hemophilia and hepatitis B joined the junior varsity basketball team. Upon learning of the student's medical condition, the high school's principal instructed the coach to put the student on "hold" pending further investigation into whether it was medically appropriate for him to play. After obtaining information from his physician, the principal directed the coach to allow the student to play. Before this decision was communicated to the family, the student decided that he no longer wanted to play. The family sued the school board, asserting violations of Section 504 and the ADA. The court ruled for the school district and officials, and the family appealed.

The Sixth Circuit noted that under either Section 504 or the ADA, a person with disabilities may be excluded from a program if their participation presents a direct threat to the health and safety of others. In this case, the student was placed on hold while **the school district was legitimately attempting to determine whether his participation on the junior varsity basketball team presented a serious health risk to others**. School officials never actually removed the student from the team and reasonably placed him on hold status while awaiting medical advice. The school district had not violated the student's rights, and the circuit court affirmed the judgment in its favor. *Doe v. Woodford County Board of Educ.*, 213 F.3d 921 (6th Cir. 2000).

B. Reasonable Accommodation

Under the ADA and the Rehabilitation Act, educational facilities, as well as many other entities, are required to make reasonable accommodations for disabled individuals.

For places of public accommodation, such as schools, this entails the reasonable modification of policies, practices or procedures when such modifications are necessary for disabled individuals to participate in the schools' programs or to benefit from their services.

However, modifications that would fundamentally alter the schools' programs or services, or that would result in an undue burden or hardship, are not required.

♦ A wheelchair-bound student in Arkansas sued the district superintendent under the ADA, seeking a preliminary injunction that would require the district to modify its facilities to help him and others gain full access. He claimed that he was exposed to rain on an uncovered walkway and that only two lavatories were wheelchair accessible. He also made several other assertions of noncompliance with the ADA. A federal court rejected his request for an injunction. Here, **the district's program as a whole was accessible, so even if individual elements were not in compliance, the district itself was.** For example, on rainy days, an aide carried a large umbrella and walked beside him on the uncovered walkway. And he did not show that the two wheelchair-accessible lavatories were insufficient to meet his needs. *Littlefield v. Kirspel*, No. 4:08-CV-00201-WRW, 2008 WL 4015743 (E.D. Ark. 8/25/08).

♦ A Kentucky student with diabetes attended her neighborhood school, which did not have a nurse working there. Because she required insulin shots, her mother arranged to have someone give them to her. However, the mother then sought to have the district hire a nurse for the school. The district instead offered to transfer the student to a nearby school where a nurse worked. The mother rejected this option because of the extra transportation time it would involve. She later sued the district under the Rehabilitation Act and the ADA. A federal court ruled against her, noting that **the district had offered a reasonable accommodation, which the mother had refused.** *B.M. v. Board of Educ. of Scott County, Kentucky*, No. 5:07-153-JMH, 2008 WL 4073855 (E.D. Ky. 8/29/08).

♦ A Massachusetts student with Asperger's syndrome applied for admission to an agricultural high school, seeking entry into its landscaping program. He scored only 32 of 55 possible points under the school's admissions policy and was placed on the waiting list. The school admitted 16 other students with IEPs, and at least 25 other students with IEPs ranked ahead of him on the waiting list. Eventually, his parents sued, claiming the school discriminated against him on the basis of his disability. A federal court found no discrimination under the ADA or Section 504. **The school's admissions policy was neutral, and other disabled students had been selected under its criteria.** The school did not have to modify its admissions requirements because that would constitute a fundamental change in its program. *Cordeiro v. Driscoll*, No. 06-10854-DPW, 2007 WL 763907 (D. Mass. 3/8/07).

♦   A diabetic student with emotional disabilities attended high school under a Section 504 plan but was not eligible for special education under the IDEA. During her sophomore year, she left school and began attending a community college, then sued her district for failing to accommodate her diabetes. One of her allegations was that **a teacher, unaware of her condition, refused to let her leave class so she could test her blood sugar level.** An Illinois federal court refused to dismiss her lawsuit. Her allegations, if true, would evidence a violation of both the IDEA and Section 504. *Loch v. Board of Educ. of Edwardsville Community School Dist. No. 7*, No. 3:06-CV-17-MJR, 2007 WL 1468675 (S.D. Ill. 5/18/07).

♦   A hearing-impaired student in New York was provided with a sign-language interpreter, a teacher for the hearing impaired, a note-taker, a microphone system, a closed-caption device and preferential classroom seating. His parents asked high school officials if he could bring a **service dog** to school each day. They claimed it was necessary to alert him to alarms, people calling his name and traffic noises. The school denied the request, and the parents sued for discrimination. The Second Circuit held that the parents should have exhausted their administrative remedies before suing. Rejecting the parents' claim that exhaustion wasn't required, the court noted that the decision to deny access to the service dog was made by the school's committee on special education, and that it implicated the student's IEP. *Cave v. East Meadow Union Free School Dist.*, 514 F.3d 240 (2d Cir. 2008).

♦   A learning disabled student attended a Quaker school in Pennsylvania and was allowed certain accommodations, like extra time for tests. However, **when the school refused other accommodation requests, the student sued** under the ADA. A federal court noted that although private schools are places of public accommodation under Title III of the ADA, religious schools are not places of public accommodation and are exempt from the requirements of Title III. On appeal, the Third Circuit held that the student had to be allowed to conduct discovery to determine whether the school had strayed so far from its religious foundation so as to be no longer eligible for the religious exemption under the ADA. The court vacated and remanded the case. *Doe v. Abington Friends School*, 480 F.3d 252 (3d Cir. 2007).

♦   A student with a learning disability, but no IEP or Section 504 plan, was dropped from the football team when he failed to maintain a 2.0 GPA. His parents sued the district under Section 504 and 42 U.S.C. § 1983, claiming the district denied their son a reasonable accommodation for his learning disability. A California federal court held that the parents should have exhausted their administrative remedies first. Even though their son did not have an IEP, **all the alleged injuries arose from the educational program provided to the student,** and should have been addressed by a due process hearing. The court dismissed the case. *Fraser v. Tamalpais Union High School Dist.*, No. C-06-1255 MMC, 2006 WL 1348427 (N.D. Cal. 5/17/06).

♦ A Michigan student's reading and writing skills were well below average, and tests administered during eighth and ninth grade revealed deficits in his literacy aptitude. His psychologist diagnosed him with developmental dyslexia, and the school district declared him eligible for Section 504 accommodations. It assigned him to its standard remedial program for students with literacy impairments. Although the psychologist identified the program as similar in approach and effectiveness to Orton-Gillingham instruction, the parents rejected the program and enrolled the student in a private program. They then sought tuition reimbursement, **asserting that the district's program was not a reasonable accommodation under Section 504.** A hearing officer, a federal court and the Sixth Circuit all ruled in favor of the school district. Here, the parents could not show that their son had been deliberately excluded from a federally funded program because of his disability. They could not show that the district failed to reasonably accommodate their son. *Campbell v. Board of Educ. of Centerline School Dist.*, 58 Fed. Appx. 162 (6th Cir. 2003).

♦ A 12-year-old student with AIDS sought admission to group karate classes at a private school, and his parents signed an application for admission asserting that he was in good health and suffered from no illness or condition that would pose a threat to other students. Students learned techniques that involved substantial body contact, and often received minor but bloody injuries from sparring. After the student's first class, the owner was informed that the student had AIDS. The owner banned the student from further group classes based on the belief that the student posed a direct threat to the health and safety of other class members. Instead, the owner offered to give the student private lessons. This offer was rejected and the family sued the school under Title III of the ADA. A court held that the student's condition threatened the health of others and refused to order the school to admit him. The Fourth Circuit agreed that the school did not violate Title III of the ADA. **The offer of private lessons was a reasonable accommodation, and placement in the group classes posed too great a risk to the safety of other students.** Also, the school was not required to fundamentally alter the nature of its karate program. *Montalvo v. Radcliffe*, 167 F.3d 873 (4th Cir. 1999).

♦ A Nevada elementary school music instructor volunteered as a helping dog trainer, which required her to have the dog lie down or sleep next to her for extended time periods. The instructor asked to bring a golden retriever she was training to class each day to lie down or sleep under her desk. The school district denied the request, fearing a distraction and that students might be afraid of or allergic to the dog. The teacher sued under a Nevada law making it an unlawful practice for a place of public accommodation to refuse admittance to a person with a helping dog or service animal. The court granted her request for a temporary order allowing her to bring the dog to class pending further consideration, subject to any serious difficulties or dangers created by the presence of the dog at school. The district appealed. The Supreme Court of

Nevada observed that **the district had refused to negotiate a reasonable compromise, despite the mandatory language of the statute requiring a place of public accommodation to allow a training dog**. The trial court had correctly granted the instructor's request for an injunction, as there was a high probability that she would succeed on the merits of her claim. If a legitimate health concern could be proven, the employer could place reasonable restrictions on the right to train the helping dog as necessary to prevent health problems. The court affirmed the trial court order. *Clark County School Dist. v. Buchanan*, 924 P.2d 716 (Nev. 1996).

II. STUDENTS WITH DISABILITIES IN SCHOOL ATHLETICS

Students with disabilities may not be excluded from any athletic activity conducted by a school receiving federal financial assistance as long as the student is "otherwise qualified" to participate in spite of his or her disability. However, problems can occur where students with disabilities have been held back one or more years. In such cases, students are sometimes prohibited from participating in interscholastic athletics.

♦ A New York student with cerebral palsy served as the football team manager. Because of minor architectural barriers, he had to take a detour to and from the school's athletic fields, costing him 20 minutes, which reduced his participation as team manager and nearly halved his time in a typical PE class. When he sued under Section 504 and the ADA, a jury ruled in his favor, and the Second Circuit largely affirmed. The jury had sufficient evidence that **the district denied him "meaningful access" to the school's athletic fields**, and the student offered plausible, simple remedies that the district could have implemented. *Celeste v. East Meadow Union Free School Dist.*, 373 Fed.Appx. 85 (2d Cir. 2010).

♦ An African-American student, who had an IEP, became involved in a fight with other African-American students in the cafeteria. He was charged with disorderly conduct and was suspended from school. He was also removed from the high school football team, and he finished his high school studies at home and acquired a diploma. He then sued the state department of education for race and disability discrimination, but a Hawaii federal court ruled against him. **He failed to show that he was treated differently than other students because of race or disability**. *Scott v. State of Hawaii Dep't of Educ.*, No. 07-00575 SOM/BMK, 2009 WL 564709 (D. Haw. 3/5/09).

♦ A visually impaired student in New York sought to participate in school swim activities as well as track and field. The school denied her requests, and her grades fell significantly. She had a history of safe and successful participation in swimming, using a kickboard at the end of the swimming lane to prevent collisions and allow her to reverse directions. However, she had no history of safe participation in running. A court ruled that **she had to be allowed to participate in swimming because it was in her best interests**. But she was not entitled to an order requiring her participation in track and field. *Baker v. Farmingdale Union Free School Dist.*, 887 N.Y.S. 2d 766 (N.Y. Sup. Ct. 2009).

◆ When a Tennessee sixth-grader with asthma did not bring his gym clothes to class, his teacher told him to do jumping jacks and sit-ups and to walk for the rest of the class, as required by school policy. This caused an asthma attack that required him to see a doctor. He sued the school board and officials for constitutional and ADA violations, and the defendants sought to have the case dismissed. A federal court dismissed only in part. **The school board knew about his asthma and should have modified its standard punishment** to accommodate his condition. Also, he could pursue his Fourteenth Amendment due process claim (asserting a right to be free from bodily harm). *Moss v. Shelby County*, 401 F.Supp.2d 850 (W.D. Tenn. 2005).

◆ A Mississippi 19-year-old senior with learning disabilities transferred to another school and sought a temporary restraining order that would allow him to play basketball. He sued under the ADA, IDEA and the Constitution. A federal court refused to grant the relief requested, finding no justification for disrupting the status quo. The state high school athletic association had found that **the transfer was made for athletic reasons**, and he failed to show a substantial likelihood of success on the merits. Nor could he show irreparable injury. His lawsuit essentially argued that if he was not allowed to play, he would be less likely to get a professional NBA contract. This could be remedied by a claim for money damages. *Newsome v. Mississippi High School Activities Ass'n, Inc.*, No. 1:07CV293-D-D, 2007 WL 4268771 (N.D. Miss. 11/30/07).

◆ A Colorado student with ADD stopped taking medication for the condition in eighth grade. When he entered high school, he was given extra time to take tests and complete homework assignments. His parents divorced and he contracted a sinus infection, missing weeks of school and causing him to repeat ninth grade. However, he then progressed to grade twelve, where he sought a waiver of the state's "eight-semester rule" so he could play football. The Colorado Court of Appeals denied him an extra year of sports eligibility. He could not claim the protection of anti-discrimination laws because **his ADD did not substantially limit him in a major life activity**. *Tesmer v. Colorado High School Activities Ass'n*, 140 P.3d 249 (Colo. Ct. App. 2006).

◆ An Ohio high school student with specific learning disabilities received instruction under IEPs. He failed his English final during his junior year because he did not receive the testing accommodations specified in his IEP. His English teacher misunderstood the school's and her own responsibilities under the IEP. He was allowed to make up the work so that he became eligible to play football. However, an Ohio High School Athletic Association (OHSAA) bylaw prohibited makeup work from satisfying academic standards for the final grading period of a year. As a result, the student was told he could not play football in the fall of his senior year. After a hearing officer ruled that the school did not properly implement the student's IEP, a federal court held that the

OHSAA unreasonably interpreted its bylaw to prevent the student from playing football. **The bylaw should not have excluded from eligibility a disabled student whose school failed to properly implement his IEP.** The student was eligible to play for the remaining three games of the season. *Ingram v. Toledo City School Dist. Board of Educ.*, 339 F.Supp.2d 998 (N.D. Ohio 2004).

♦ The IEP for a student with learning disabilities, who was classified as educable mentally retarded, called for his participation in extracurricular activities as part of his need for socialization and education. The student turned 19 prior to the start of his fourth year of high school, 28 days before the date when a Pennsylvania Interscholastic Athletic Association (PIAA) bylaw operated to exclude him from further interscholastic sports eligibility. The PIAA rejected his request for a waiver, and he sued it under the ADA, Section 504 and the IDEA. The court denied his motion for a temporary order that would have allowed him to compete in football, wrestling and track. He had administrative remedies under the IDEA, and the PIAA was not a recipient of federal funding, as required to create Section 504 liability. As for the ADA claim, the court found that **the student's participation in football and track would not fundamentally alter the nature of interscholastic competition, as he lacked a competitive advantage.** He was entitled to an order prohibiting the PIAA from enforcing its age bylaw unless it did so under a waiver rule. The court's order did not extend to the student's request to participate on the wrestling team, as there was evidence he excelled in wrestling and might have a competitive advantage if allowed to participate. *Cruz v. Pennsylvania Interscholastic Athletic Ass'n*, 157 F.Supp.2d 485 (E.D. Pa. 2001).

III. CIVIL RIGHTS REMEDIES

A 1986 amendment to the IDEA, known as the Handicapped Children's Protection Act, expressly allows disabled students to cumulate all available remedies under federal law. One of the most commonly used federal civil rights statutes is 42 U.S.C. § 1983, a post-Civil War statute that protects individuals from violations of their constitutional rights by state actors.

♦ A Georgia student spent most of his early years in a special education classroom for students with mild intellectual disabilities. However, he was not diagnosed with dyslexia until his tenth-grade year. An administrative law judge awarded him compensatory education services, including money for private school tuition. He then sued under the Rehabilitation Act, but the Eleventh Circuit held that he could not do so because of his earlier IDEA action involving the same facts. *Draper v. Atlanta Independent School System*, 377 Fed.Appx. 937 (11th Cir. 2010).

♦ A Connecticut student with a learning disability, an IQ of 57 and obesity had to withdraw from school due to severe harassment by peers. He was home-schooled for a while, but his parents later sought to return him to school. That didn't happen. His parents ultimately sued their district for negligence, also **asserting civil rights claims based on the repeated harassment**. The

Connecticut Superior Court ruled against them, noting that the district had immunity with respect to many of the claims. It could only be liable for harassment that occurred on school buses, and those claims also failed because the parents couldn't provide sufficient evidence that harassment had occurred on buses. *Silano v. Board of Educ. of City of Bridgeport*, No. CV990367741, 2010 WL 1795094 (Conn. Super. Ct. 4/7/10).

♦ A Minnesota school district created an alternative school for immigrant students with limited English skills and little or no formal education. Students from Ethiopia and Somalia refugee camps attended the school. A lawsuit later resulted from several school policies, including one in which students were not tested for special education eligibility until they had at least three years of English Language Learner instruction. The lawsuit alleged discrimination under Title VI. A federal court ruled for the school, noting that the students failed to prove the school intended to discriminate against them. Further, the school stopped its policy of delaying special education testing after being notified by the state of its invalidity. The Eighth Circuit affirmed, noting that **a policy treating ELL students differently than others is not discrimination on the basis of national origin**. *Mumid v. Abraham Lincoln High School*, 618 F.3d 789 (8th Cir. 2010).

♦ A Minnesota student wrote an essay detailing a fantasy murder-suicide inspired by the school shooting that took place at Columbine High School. The essay included many threats against his teacher. He placed the essay in his folder, but his teacher did not read it for several weeks. After the teacher reported the essay's disturbing and graphic content, a child protection worker obtained a court order placing the student in protective custody. He was released after 72 hours, when an evaluation determined that he was not a threat to himself or others. He sued the district and various officials for violating his First and Fourth Amendment rights. A federal court and the Eighth Circuit ruled against him. **The First Amendment does not protect true threats**, and the seizure of his person was reasonable. It did not matter that the essay sat in his file for weeks because school shootings can require extensive planning. *Riehm v. Engelking*, 538 F.3d 952 (8th Cir. 2008).

♦ A 15-year-old student with depression, ADHD, bipolar disorder and schizophrenia **jumped off a moving school bus after the driver refused to allow him to get off at a location that was not designated as a bus stop**. The student died from the fall and his mother sued school officials, claiming disability discrimination and civil rights violations. A Tennessee federal court and the Sixth Circuit ruled against her, noting that the school board had no policy or custom of deliberate indifference to student rights, and its conduct was not the moving force or cause of his death. *Hill v. Bradley County Board of Educ.*, 29J Fed.Appx. 740 (6th Cir. 2008).

♦ A Wisconsin student with fragile bones was allowed to join other students outside at recess on a day in which there was freezing rain and snow. Although the custodian had put down about 600 pounds of salt, the student slipped and fell while walking to the basketball court to watch her friends play. She broke a leg and a wrist. Her parents sued the school district under the ADA and also asserted constitutional due process claims. A federal court ruled for the school district, noting that the district had no obligation under the ADA to provide accommodations for temporary conditions like snowfall. Also, **the district had no constitutional duty to protect her from dangerous conditions like freezing rain**. *Edwards v. School Dist. of Baraboo*, 570 F.Supp.2d 1077 (W.D. Wis. 2008).

◆ A Washington student with a genitor-urinary defect and self-esteem issues, eligible for a Section 504 plan, moved to a new school district, which **failed to follow the Section 504 plan because the family did not disclose the nature of the student's condition**. The student began failing classes, and his family finally disclosed the nature of his disability. He was promoted to grade nine but was not allowed to walk in graduation ceremonies with his class. His parents sued for discrimination because of the district's failure to follow the Section 504 plan, but a federal court ruled against them. They had not informed the district of their son's condition in a timely manner. *S.L.-M. v. Dieringer School Dist. No. 343*, 614 F.Supp.2d 1152 (W.D. Wash. 2008).

◆ A Kentucky student with ADHD and bipolar disorder took medication at school for her condition. On the last day of the school year, the nurse returned the bottle of medicine to her with four pills in it. She gave a pill to a fellow student who pestered her for it. On the first day of the next year, the assistant principal had her write out a statement regarding the incident. He suspended both students for a day, and referred them to the juvenile justice system. The student opted for a diversion agreement, then sued the school board under the Fourth and Fifth Amendments. A federal court and the Sixth Circuit ruled that **there was no Fourth or Fifth Amendment violation**. The assistant principal acted reasonably based on the violation of school rules and did not have to read the student her *Miranda* rights. Further, her Section 504 claim failed because she did not exhaust her administrative remedies. *S.E. v. Grant County Board of Educ.*, 544 F.3d 633 (6th Cir. 2008).

◆ A high-functioning autistic student claimed his teacher used improper restraints and aversive techniques against him. He sued under 42 U.S.C. § 1983, alleging constitutional violations as well as abuse claims under the IDEA. A federal court allowed the constitutional claims to proceed, but held that the IDEA claims had to be addressed by the IDEA's comprehensive remedial scheme. Those claims were dismissed. *Kimberly F. v. Northeastern Educ. Intermediate Unit 19*, No. 3:06-CV-01901, 2007 WL 2844934 (M.D. Pa. 9/26/07).

◆ A Massachusetts student with fetal alcohol syndrome and developmental delays had a number of sexual contacts with another boy in his special education class. His foster mother reported several incidents, including oral sex on the school bus, and the district then placed the boys on separate buses. Teachers and aides were instructed to monitor the boys, and no substantial contact was reported between them for 18 months. Later, they were found together in a bathroom stall and admitted they'd been touching each other for some time. The mother then sued the town for sexual harassment under Title IX. After a jury awarded the family $250,000 in damages, the First Circuit reversed. It found **no evidence of deliberate indifference by the town**, or that the town knew the other boy was harassing the student. *Porto v. Town of Tewksbury*, 488 F.3d 67 (1st Cir. 2007).

◆ A learning-disabled Colorado high school student told her mother she did not want to attend school anymore because boys teased her. The mother told the principal that certain boys were "bothering" her daughter. Later, the student told a school counselor that one boy had repeatedly called her to ask for oral sex and that two boys had coerced her into sexual conduct. The school resource officer then investigated, but the mother refused to cooperate on "advice of counsel." The district attorney declined to prosecute the case because of the difficulty of proving the activity was not consensual and because of the trauma to which the student would be subjected. When the student had a psychotic episode that required hospitalization, the family moved away, and then sued the school district under Title IX. A federal court and the Tenth Circuit ruled for the district, finding that **the district did not have actual knowledge of the sexual harassment until the student told the counselor about it**. Nor did the district have a policy of allowing student-on-student sexual harassment. Finally, the district was not required to discipline the boys for sexual harassment. *Rost v. Steamboat Springs RE-2 School Dist.*, 511 F.3d 1114 (10th Cir. 2008).

◆ A ninth-grade Connecticut student with ADHD was under five feet tall and weighed 75 pounds. He endured harassment and bullying by his classmates, which he claimed school officials knew about and did nothing to stop. After withdrawing from school, he and his family sued the school board for violating his civil rights and the IDEA. The Second Circuit held that the school did not violate the student's due process or equal protection rights. However, there was a question as to whether they denied him a free appropriate public education so as to entitle him to money damages. *Smith v. Guilford Board of Educ.*, 226 Fed.Appx. 58 (2d Cir. 2007).

◆ A Pennsylvania student with autism sued his teacher, intermediate unit and supervisory employees under 42 U.S.C. § 1983, claiming that the teacher had used improper restraints and aversive techniques such as a Rifton chair. The teacher also allegedly squeezed his ears, stepped on his insteps, grabbed him violently, forced him to the floor, forced him to undress, refused him a snack and verbally abused him. A federal court refused to dismiss the claims. Here, **if the teacher had committed the acts alleged, the student's due process and equal protection rights would have been violated**. *Kimberly F. v. Northeastern Educ. Intermediate Unit*, No. 3:06-CV-01901, 2007 WL 1450364 (M.D. Pa. 5/15/07).

◆ A New Jersey student sued his school district under 42 U.S.C. Section 1983, asserting that school district officials deprived him of his right to a free appropriate public education by failing to identify his dyslexia. The district officials sought qualified immunity, challenging the student's use of Section 1983 as a remedy for an IDEA violation. A federal court refused to grant them immunity, relying on *W.B. v. Matula*, but **the Third Circuit reconsidered the Matula case and decided that the student could not enforce his IDEA or Section 504 rights under 42 U.S.C. § 1983**. The IDEA has an enforcement scheme that precludes Section 1983 remedies. *A.W. v. Jersey City Public Schools*, 486 F.3d 791 (3d Cir. 2007).

♦ An 18-year-old Texas student with Down syndrome told a school official that another student forced her into a lavatory and sexually assaulted her. She claimed that she was then escorted to a security office where she was forced to disrobe. Her family sued the school district for civil rights violations under 42 U.S.C. § 1983. The school district sought pretrial judgment on the grounds that no "special relationship" existed between it and the student, even though she was in special education in a segregated classroom. The court agreed. **Because the student was 18 and not subject to compulsory attendance laws, she was not in a special relationship with the district** such that it had to protect her from third-party harm. Also, even if she was forced to disrobe in front of a teacher, there was no official policy or custom causing that injury, so the district was not liable for that either. *Teague v. Texas City Independent School Dist.*, 386 F.Supp.2d 893 (S.D. Tex. 2005).

♦ A Michigan parent sought to place her disabled son in a kindergarten where she worked rather than in her residential school district. However, under the state's "school of choice law," districts had to have a written agreement regarding the costs of special education prior to permitting a student to attend a public school of his or her choice. Because there was no written agreement, the student could not attend kindergarten in the mother's work district. She sued, alleging that the law violated equal protection and disability rights but a federal court ruled against her. It found the distinction between special and general education students to be rationally based. *B.C. v. Banks*, No. 5:04-CV-155, 2005 WL 2001159 (W.D. Mich. 8/17/05).

♦ A disabled Kentucky student missed 7.5 days of school for various reasons. His mother sought to send him to a one-week camp as part of his IEP, but did not get a determination of whether his absences from school would be considered "excused." The son accumulated unexcused absences while at the camp, putting him at 16 absences and making him habitually truant. After the mother was found not guilty of truancy, she sued the school board for discrimination and civil rights violations. A federal court ruled against her. The board had not been motivated by anything other than its statutory duty to enforce state compulsory attendance laws. *Sudekamp v. Fayette County Board of Educ.*, No. Civ. A. 04-467-JBC, 2005 WL 2137739 (E.D. Ky. 9/1/05).

♦ A school district expelled three students for marijuana possession. Two were regular education students, and the third was a special education student. He continued to receive the educational services described in his IEP, but the two regular education students did not receive alternative education. They were adjudicated delinquent, and the juvenile court held that they were entitled to a free appropriate education during their expulsion period. The Supreme Court of Wyoming disagreed. Although education is a fundamental right under the state constitution, the district could temporarily deny the students educational services if their conduct threatened the safety and welfare of others and interfered with the district's obligation to provide equal opportunities to all its students. **The government had a compelling interest in treating disabled students differently than non-disabled students**, and the district did not violate the non-disabled students' equal protection rights by refusing to provide them with an alternative education. *In re R.M.*, 102 P.3d 868 (Wyo. 2004).

♦ A group of current and former special education students in a New York school district, identified as "high need" due to its low wealth, sued the district and the state, asserting that the defendants violated the IDEA and Section 504. They alleged that the district failed to timely refer cases to a committee on special education, properly evaluate students with disabilities, include necessary information in IEPs, retain certified teachers, follow due process hearing procedures, properly group students, and provide guidance programs for students in grades K-6. The district agreed to pay the students $735,000 in damages and to submit to monitoring. The action against the state then went to trial, with the students claiming that state officials should have withheld IDEA funds from the district for being out of compliance for eight years. A federal court ruled that withholding IDEA funds would have harmed students. **Cutting off federal funds would not have had a positive impact on the quality of special education** the district provided. There was no evidence that such action would somehow have forced the district into compliance with the IDEA. The state education department's flexible oversight approach did not violate the IDEA. *A.A. v. Board of Educ., Cent. Islip Union Free School Dist.*, 255 F.Supp.2d 119 (E.D.N.Y. 2003).

On appeal, the Second Circuit held that nothing in the IDEA required the state to cut off federal funds or use those funds to directly provide special education services to students based on local noncompliance. The state also did not have a duty to conduct monitoring visits on any particular schedule. Further, nothing in the IDEA gave the state specific guidance on how to ensure local compliance. *A.A. v. Philips*, 386 F.3d 455 (2d Cir. 2004).

♦ In March 1992, a New Jersey student with severe behavior problems was classified as emotionally disturbed and his school district agreed to a residential placement. Only the school preferred by the district agreed to admit the student. The day after the student entered the school, he got into a fight with other residents. A staff worker intervened, and he suffered fatal injuries. His parents sued the state and others for damages under the IDEA, Section 504 and 42 U.S.C. § 1983. A federal court dismissed most of the claims. It characterized the defendants' violations of the IDEA as merely technical and, consequently, not the proximate cause of the student's death. On appeal, the Third Circuit affirmed. By agreeing to the student's temporary placement at the school, the parents could not argue that his placement there without an IEP violated the IDEA. **The parents could not establish an IDEA violation because they**

were unable to show that the school did not provide an education that would confer a "meaningful benefit" on the student. Moreover, the parents were unable to demonstrate that either the curriculum or the nature of the residents at the school led to the student's death. There was no evidence of an IDEA violation that was the proximate cause of the student's death. *Tallman v. Barnegat Board of Educ.*, 43 Fed.Appx. 490 (3d Cir. 2002).

♦ After a middle school student with mental retardation, ADHD and Cohen syndrome was told she and other special education students "did not belong" at a school dance, the assistant principal telephoned the student's mother and told her she did not belong at the dance because she was a sixth-grader. The mother explained that the student was in fact a seventh-grader, but the assistant principal stated that she could not remain at the dance. The parents sued the school district and officials, including the assistant principal, in a federal court, which referred the matter to a magistrate for a recommendation. The complaint alleged violations of Section 504 and the ADA, among other claims. A magistrate judge recommended dismissal of the Section 504 and ADA claims against the officials in their individual capacities. They were also entitled to dismissal of the claims based on the Maine Human Rights Act. **Because Section 504 and the ADA contain their own comprehensive remedial schemes, the student was not entitled to advance a claim for damages under 42 U.S.C. § 1983 based on alleged Section 504 and ADA violations.** The officials were entitled to dismissal of the Section 1983 claim based on IDEA violations. If the magistrate's recommendations were adopted, the federal claims would have to be resolved. *Smith v. Maine School Administrative Dist. No. 6*, No. 00-284-P-C, 2001 WL 68305 (D. Me. 1/29/01).

♦ A student with Asperger's syndrome attended a public school during the first grade. Two different IEPs for that year had a goal of improving his classroom behavior and authorized physical restraint when necessary for safety reasons. The student told his mother that his teacher and an aide used a restraint hold that suffocated him or caused a choking sensation on many occasions. He stated that school employees held his wrists, crossed his arms in front of his body and pushed his head into his chest so he could not breathe. The parents did not take the student to a doctor to determine if he had suffered any physical injury, but took him to a psychotherapist almost two years later for emotional problems. The psychotherapist diagnosed the student as having post-traumatic stress disorder. The family sued school officials and employees, including the teacher and aide, in a federal court for civil rights violations, including claims arising under 42 U.S.C. § 1983.

A leading case concerning Section 1983 claims arising from excessive corporal punishment is *Hall v. Tawney*, 621 F.2d 607 (4th Cir. 1980), which established a test for official liability in such cases that considers whether force applied by a school employee caused severe injury, was disproportionate to the need presented, and was so inspired by malice or sadism or an unwise excess of zeal as to be a brutal and inhumane abuse of official power that literally shocks the conscience. Here, the student failed to meet this high standard for liability. Applying the *Hall* factors, the court granted the teachers summary judgment, finding that **no reasonable jury could find that the student's injuries were severe or that the alleged abuse rose to the level of a constitutional rights violation**. The method of restraint was not disproportionate to the student's behavior and was not shocking to the conscience. The teacher and aide both testified that they only restrained the student when necessary because he was a danger to himself or others, and they did not act with malice when restraining him. *Brown v. Ramsey*, 121 F.Supp.2d 911 (E.D.Va. 2000).

◆ When a student with congenital hydrocephalus was nine years old, a substitute school nurse gave her an overdose of her medication. A month later, the student's parents contended that the district performed an unauthorized medical inspection. The next school year, the student was transferred to another classroom. She then refused to stand and recite the Pledge of Allegiance or participate in other aspects of her class's morning routine. Her teacher scolded her in front of other students, took her to the principal's office as punishment, and allegedly imposed other disciplinary sanctions. The family sued the school district, teacher, principal and other school officials in a federal court for civil rights violations arising under 42 U.S.C. § 1983.

The court ruled that **there could be no liability for the overdose or unauthorized medical examination**. There was no evidence that the district had a policy or custom of over-medicating students or subjecting them to unauthorized examinations. However, the court refused to dismiss the student's First Amendment claims based on the allegation that she was forced to stand and say the Pledge of Allegiance. It is well-established that **a school may not require students to stand and recite the Pledge of Allegiance** or punish any student for not doing so. Because there was evidence that the student's teacher compelled her to stand and recite the Pledge of Allegiance against her will, the First Amendment claims required a trial. Also, the principal's behavior and acquiescence to the special education teacher's conduct was attributable to the district. *Rabideau v. Beekmantown Cent. School Dist.*, 89 F.Supp.2d 263 (N.D.N.Y. 2000).

APPENDIX A

The statutory text of the Individuals with Disabilities Education Act, as amended through July, 2005, is reproduced below in its entirety. It includes the most recent amendments to the statute.

An Act

To reauthorize the Individuals with Disabilities Education Act, and for other purposes.

Be it enacted by the Senate and House of Representatives of the United States of America in Congress assembled,

SEC. 1. SHORT TITLE.

This Act may be cited as the 'Individuals with Disabilities Education Improvement Act of 2004'.

SEC. 2. ORGANIZATION OF THE ACT.

This Act is organized into the following titles:
Title I—Amendments to the Individuals With Disabilities Education Act.
Title II—National Center for Special Education Research.
Title III—Miscellaneous Provisions.

TITLE I—AMENDMENTS TO THE INDIVIDUALS WITH DISABILITIES EDUCATION ACT

SEC. 101. AMENDMENTS TO THE INDIVIDUALS WITH DISABILITIES EDUCATION ACT.

Parts A through D of the Individuals with Disabilities Education Act (20 U.S.C. 1400 et seq.) are amended to read as follows:

PART A—GENERAL PROVISIONS

SEC. 601. SHORT TITLE; TABLE OF CONTENTS; FINDINGS; PURPOSES.

(a) SHORT TITLE – This title may be cited as the 'Individuals with Disabilities Education Act'.

(b) TABLE OF CONTENTS – The table of contents for this title is as follows:

SUBPART 3—SUPPORTS TO IMPROVE RESULTS FOR CHILDREN WITH DISABILITIES

SUBPART 4—GENERAL PROVISIONS

(c) FINDINGS- Congress finds the following:

(1) Disability is a natural part of the human experience and in no way diminishes the right of individuals to participate in or contribute to society. Improving educational results for children with disabilities is an essential element of our national policy of ensuring equality of opportunity, full participation, independent living, and economic self-sufficiency for individuals with disabilities.

(2) Before the date of enactment of the Education for All Handicapped Children Act of 1975 (Public Law 94-142), the educational needs of millions of children with disabilities were not being fully met because—

(A) the children did not receive appropriate educational services;

(B) the children were excluded entirely from the public school system and from being educated with their peers;

(C) undiagnosed disabilities prevented the children from having a successful educational experience; or

(D) a lack of adequate resources within the public school system forced families to find services outside the public school system.

(3) Since the enactment and implementation of the Education for All Handicapped Children Act of 1975, this title has been successful in ensuring children with disabilities and the families of such children access to a free appropriate public education and in improving educational results for children with disabilities.

(4) However, the implementation of this title has been impeded by low expectations, and an insufficient focus on applying replicable research on proven methods of teaching and learning for children with disabilities.

(5) Almost 30 years of research and experience has demonstrated that the education of children with disabilities can be made more effective by—

(A) having high expectations for such children and ensuring their access to the general education curriculum in the regular classroom, to the maximum extent possible, in order to—

(i) meet developmental goals and, to the maximum extent possible, the challenging expectations that have been established for all children; and

(ii) be prepared to lead productive and independent adult lives, to the maximum extent possible;

(B) strengthening the role and responsibility of parents and ensuring that families of such children have meaningful opportunities to participate in the education of their children at school and at home;

(C) coordinating this title with other local, educational service agency, State, and Federal school improvement efforts, including improvement efforts under the Elementary and Secondary Education Act of 1965, in order to ensure that such children benefit from such efforts and that special education can become a service for such children rather than a place where such children are sent;

(D) providing appropriate special education and related services, and aids and supports in the regular classroom, to such children, whenever appropriate;

(E) supporting high-quality, intensive preservice preparation and professional development for all personnel who work with children with disabilities in order to ensure that such personnel have the skills and knowledge necessary to improve the academic achievement and functional performance of children with disabilities, including the use of scientifically based instructional practices, to the maximum extent possible;

(F) providing incentives for whole-school approaches, scientifically based early reading programs, positive behavioral interventions and supports, and early intervening services to reduce the need to label children as disabled in order to address the learning and behavioral needs of such children;

(G) focusing resources on teaching and learning while reducing paperwork and requirements that do not assist in improving educational results; and

(H) supporting the development and use of technology, including assistive technology devices and assistive technology services, to maximize accessibility for children with disabilities.

(6) While States, local educational agencies, and educational service agencies are primarily responsible for providing an education for all children with disabilities, it is in the national interest that the Federal Government have a supporting role in assisting State and local efforts to educate children with disabilities in order to improve results for such children and to ensure equal protection of the law.

(7) A more equitable allocation of resources is essential for the Federal Government to meet its responsibility to provide an equal educational opportunity for all individuals.

(8) Parents and schools should be given expanded opportunities to resolve their disagreements in positive and constructive ways.

(9) Teachers, schools, local educational agencies, and States should be relieved of irrelevant and unnecessary paperwork burdens that do not lead to improved educational outcomes.

(10)(A) The Federal Government must be responsive to the growing needs of an increasingly diverse society.

(B) America's ethnic profile is rapidly changing. In 2000, 1 of every 3 persons in the United States was a member of a minority group or was limited English proficient.

(C) Minority children comprise an increasing percentage of public school students.

(D) With such changing demographics, recruitment efforts for special education personnel should focus on increasing the participation of minorities in the teaching profession in order to provide appropriate role models with sufficient knowledge to address the special education needs of these students.

(11)(A) The limited English proficient population is the fastest growing in our Nation, and the growth is occurring in many parts of our Nation.

(B) Studies have documented apparent discrepancies in the levels of referral and placement of limited English proficient children in special education.

(C) Such discrepancies pose a special challenge for special education in the referral of, assessment of, and provision of services for, our Nation's students from non-English language backgrounds.

(12)(A) Greater efforts are needed to prevent the intensification of problems connected with mislabeling and high dropout rates among minority children with disabilities.

(B) More minority children continue to be served in special education than would be expected from the percentage of minority students in the general school population.

(C) African-American children are identified as having mental retardation and emotional disturbance at rates greater than their White counterparts.

(D) In the 1998-1999 school year, African-American children represented just 14.8 percent of the population aged 6 through 21, but comprised 20.2 percent of all children with disabilities.

(E) Studies have found that schools with predominately White students and teachers have placed disproportionately high numbers of their minority students into special education.

(13)(A) As the number of minority students in special education increases, the number of minority teachers and related services personnel produced in colleges and universities continues to decrease.

(B) The opportunity for full participation by minority individuals, minority organizations, and Historically Black Colleges and Universities in awards for grants and contracts, boards of organizations receiving assistance under this title, peer review panels, and training of professionals in the area of special education is essential to obtain greater success in the education of minority children with disabilities.

(14) As the graduation rates for children with disabilities continue to climb, providing effective transition services to promote successful post-school employment or education is an important measure of accountability for children with disabilities.

(d) PURPOSES- The purposes of this title are—

(1)(A) to ensure that all children with disabilities have available to them a free appropriate public education that emphasizes special education and related services designed to meet their unique needs and prepare them for further education, employment, and independent living;

(B) to ensure that the rights of children with disabilities and parents of such children are protected; and

(C) to assist States, localities, educational service agencies, and Federal agencies to provide for the education of all children with disabilities;

(2) to assist States in the implementation of a statewide, comprehensive, coordinated, multidisciplinary, interagency system of early intervention services for infants and toddlers with disabilities and their families;

(3) to ensure that educators and parents have the necessary tools to improve educational results for children with disabilities by supporting system improvement activities; coordinated research and personnel preparation; coordinated technical assistance, dissemination, and support; and technology development and media services; and

(4) to assess, and ensure the effectiveness of, efforts to educate children with disabilities.

SEC. 602. DEFINITIONS.

Except as otherwise provided, in this title:

(1) ASSISTIVE TECHNOLOGY DEVICE-

(A) IN GENERAL- The term 'assistive technology device' means any item, piece of equipment, or product system, whether acquired commercially off the shelf, modified, or customized, that is used to increase, maintain, or improve functional capabilities of a child with a disability.

(B) EXCEPTION- The term does not include a medical device that is surgically implanted, or the replacement of such device.

(2) ASSISTIVE TECHNOLOGY SERVICE- The term 'assistive technology service' means any service that directly assists a child with a disability in the selection, acquisition, or use of an assistive technology device. Such term includes—

(A) the evaluation of the needs of such child, including a functional evaluation of the child in the child's customary environment;

(B) purchasing, leasing, or otherwise providing for the acquisition of assistive technology devices by such child;

(C) selecting, designing, fitting, customizing, adapting, applying, maintaining, repairing, or replacing assistive technology devices;

(D) coordinating and using other therapies, interventions, or services with assistive technology devices, such as those associated with existing education and rehabilitation plans and programs;

(E) training or technical assistance for such child, or, where appropriate, the family of such child; and

(F) training or technical assistance for professionals (including individuals providing education and rehabilitation services), employers, or other individuals who provide services to, employ, or are otherwise substantially involved in the major life functions of such child.

(3) CHILD WITH A DISABILITY-

(A) IN GENERAL- The term 'child with a disability' means a child—

(i) with mental retardation, hearing impairments (including deafness), speech or language impairments, visual impairments (including blindness), serious emotional disturbance (referred to in this title as 'emotional disturbance'), orthopedic impairments, autism, traumatic brain injury, other health impairments, or specific learning disabilities; and

(ii) who, by reason thereof, needs special education and related services.

(B) CHILD AGED 3 THROUGH 9- The term 'child with a disability' for a child aged 3 through 9 (or any subset of that age range, including ages 3 through 5), may, at the discretion of the State and the local educational agency, include a child—

(i) experiencing developmental delays, as defined by the State and as measured by appropriate diagnostic instruments and procedures, in 1 or more of the following areas: physical development; cognitive development; communication development; social or emotional development; or adaptive development; and

(ii) who, by reason thereof, needs special education and related services.

(4) CORE ACADEMIC SUBJECTS- The term 'core academic subjects' has the meaning given the term in section 9101 of the Elementary and Secondary Education Act of 1965.

(5) EDUCATIONAL SERVICE AGENCY- The term 'educational service agency'—

(A) means a regional public multiservice agency—

(i) authorized by State law to develop, manage, and provide services or programs to local educational agencies; and

(ii) recognized as an administrative agency for purposes of the provision of special education and related services provided within public elementary schools and secondary schools of the State; and

(B) includes any other public institution or agency having administrative control and direction over a public elementary school or secondary school.

(6) ELEMENTARY SCHOOL- The term 'elementary school' means a nonprofit institutional day or residential school, including a public elementary charter school, that provides elementary education, as

determined under State law.

(7) EQUIPMENT- The term 'equipment' includes—

(A) machinery, utilities, and built-in equipment, and any necessary enclosures or structures to house such machinery, utilities, or equipment; and

(B) all other items necessary for the functioning of a particular facility as a facility for the provision of educational services, including items such as instructional equipment and necessary furniture; printed, published, and audio-visual instructional materials; telecommunications, sensory, and other technological aids and devices; and books, periodicals, documents, and other related materials.

(8) EXCESS COSTS- The term 'excess costs' means those costs that are in excess of the average annual per-student expenditure in a local educational agency during the preceding school year for an elementary school or secondary school student, as may be appropriate, and which shall be computed after deducting—

(A) amounts received—

(i) under part B;

(ii) under part A of title I of the Elementary and Secondary Education Act of 1965; and

(iii) under parts A and B of title III of that Act; and

(B) any State or local funds expended for programs that would qualify for assistance under any of those parts.

(9) FREE APPROPRIATE PUBLIC EDUCATION- The term 'free appropriate public education' means special education and related services that—

(A) have been provided at public expense, under public supervision and direction, and without charge;

(B) meet the standards of the State educational agency;

(C) include an appropriate preschool, elementary school, or secondary school education in the State involved; and

(D) are provided in conformity with the individualized education program required under section 614(d).

(10) HIGHLY QUALIFIED-

(A) IN GENERAL- For any special education teacher, the term 'highly qualified' has the meaning given the term in section 9101 of the Elementary and Secondary Education Act of 1965, except that such term also—

(i) includes the requirements described in subparagraph (B); and

(ii) includes the option for teachers to meet the requirements of section 9101 of such Act by

meeting the requirements of subparagraph (C) or (D).

(B) REQUIREMENTS FOR SPECIAL EDUCATION TEACHERS- When used with respect to any public elementary school or secondary school special education teacher teaching in a State, such term means that—

(i) the teacher has obtained full State certification as a special education teacher (including certification obtained through alternative routes to certification), or passed the State special education teacher licensing examination, and holds a license to teach in the State as a special education teacher, except that when used with respect to any teacher teaching in a public charter school, the term means that the teacher meets the requirements set forth in the State's public charter school law;

(ii) the teacher has not had special education certification or licensure requirements waived on an emergency, temporary, or provisional basis; and

(iii) the teacher holds at least a bachelor's degree.

(C) SPECIAL EDUCATION TEACHERS TEACHING TO ALTERNATE ACHIEVEMENT STANDARDS- When used with respect to a special education teacher who teaches core academic subjects exclusively to children who are assessed against alternate achievement standards established under the regulations promulgated under section 1111(b)(1) of the Elementary and Secondary Education Act of 1965, such term means the teacher, whether new or not new to the profession, may either—

(i) meet the applicable requirements of section 9101 of such Act for any elementary, middle, or secondary school teacher who is new or not new to the profession; or

(ii) meet the requirements of subparagraph (B) or (C) of section 9101(23) of such Act as applied to an elementary school teacher, or, in the case of instruction above the elementary level, has subject matter knowledge appropriate to the level of instruction being provided, as determined by the State, needed to effectively teach to those standards.

(D) SPECIAL EDUCATION TEACHERS TEACHING MULTIPLE SUBJECTS- When used with respect to a special education teacher who teaches 2 or more core academic subjects exclusively to children with disabilities, such term means that the teacher may either—

(i) meet the applicable requirements of section 9101 of the Elementary and Secondary Education Act of 1965 for any elementary, middle, or secondary school teacher who is new or not new to the profession;

(ii) in the case of a teacher who is not new to the profession, demonstrate competence in all the core academic subjects in which the teacher teaches in the same manner as is required for an elementary, middle, or secondary school teacher who is not new to the profession under section 9101(23)(C)(ii) of such Act, which may include a single, high objective uniform State standard of evaluation covering multiple subjects; or

(iii) in the case of a new special education teacher who teaches multiple subjects and who is highly qualified in mathematics, language arts, or science, demonstrate competence in the other core academic subjects in which the teacher teaches in the same manner as is required for an elementary, middle, or secondary school teacher under section 9101(23)(C)(ii) of such Act, which may include a single, high objective uniform State standard of evaluation covering multiple subjects, not later than 2 years after the date of employment.

(E) RULE OF CONSTRUCTION- Notwithstanding any other individual right of action that a parent or student may maintain under this part, nothing in this section or part shall be construed to create a right of action on behalf of an individual student or class of students for the failure of a particular State educational agency or local educational agency employee to be highly qualified.

(F) DEFINITION FOR PURPOSES OF THE ESEA- A teacher who is highly qualified under this paragraph shall be considered highly qualified for purposes of the Elementary and Secondary Education Act of 1965.

(11) HOMELESS CHILDREN- The term 'homeless children' has the meaning given the term 'homeless children and youths' in section 725 of the McKinney-Vento Homeless Assistance Act (42 U.S.C. 11434a).

(12) INDIAN- The term 'Indian' means an individual who is a member of an Indian tribe.

(13) INDIAN TRIBE- The term 'Indian tribe' means any Federal or State Indian tribe, band, rancheria, pueblo, colony, or community, including any Alaska Native village or regional village corporation (as defined in or established under the Alaska Native Claims Settlement Act (43 U.S.C. 1601 et seq.)).

(14) INDIVIDUALIZED EDUCATION PROGRAM; IEP- The term 'individualized education program' or 'IEP' means a written statement for each child with a disability that is developed, reviewed, and revised in accordance with section 614(d).

(15) INDIVIDUALIZED FAMILY SERVICE PLAN- The term 'individualized family service plan' has the meaning given the term in section 636.

(16) INFANT OR TODDLER WITH A DISABILITY- The term 'infant or toddler with a disability' has the meaning given the term in section 632.

(17) INSTITUTION OF HIGHER EDUCATION- The term 'institution of higher education'—

(A) has the meaning given the term in section 101 of the Higher Education Act of 1965; and

(B) also includes any community college receiving funding from the Secretary of the Interior under the Tribally Controlled College or University Assistance Act of 1978.

(18) LIMITED ENGLISH PROFICIENT- The term 'limited English proficient' has the meaning given the term in section 9101 of the Elementary and Secondary Education Act of 1965.

(19) LOCAL EDUCATIONAL AGENCY-

(A) IN GENERAL- The term 'local educational agency' means a public board of education or other public authority legally constituted within a State for either administrative control or direction of, or to perform a service function for, public elementary schools or secondary schools in a city, county, township, school district, or other political subdivision of a State, or for such combination of school districts or counties as are recognized in a State as an administrative agency for its public elementary schools or secondary schools.

(B) EDUCATIONAL SERVICE AGENCIES AND OTHER PUBLIC INSTITUTIONS OR AGENCIES- The term includes—

(i) an educational service agency; and

(ii) any other public institution or agency having administrative control and direction of a public elementary school or secondary school.

(C) BIA FUNDED SCHOOLS- The term includes an elementary school or secondary school funded by the Bureau of Indian Affairs, but only to the extent that such inclusion makes the school eligible for programs for which specific eligibility is not provided to the school in another provision of law and the school does not have a student population that is smaller than the student population of the local educational agency receiving assistance under this title with the smallest student population, except that the school shall not be subject to the jurisdiction of any State educational agency other than the Bureau of Indian Affairs.

(20) NATIVE LANGUAGE- The term 'native language', when used with respect to an

individual who is limited English proficient, means the language normally used by the individual or, in the case of a child, the language normally used by the parents of the child.

(21) NONPROFIT- The term 'nonprofit', as applied to a school, agency, organization, or institution, means a school, agency, organization, or institution owned and operated by 1 or more nonprofit corporations or associations no part of the net earnings of which inures, or may lawfully inure, to the benefit of any private shareholder or individual.

(22) OUTLYING AREA- The term 'outlying area' means the United States Virgin Islands, Guam, American Samoa, and the Commonwealth of the Northern Mariana Islands.

(23) PARENT- The term 'parent' means—

(A) a natural, adoptive, or foster parent of a child (unless a foster parent is prohibited by State law from serving as a parent);

(B) a guardian (but not the State if the child is a ward of the State);

(C) an individual acting in the place of a natural or adoptive parent (including a grandparent, stepparent, or other relative) with whom the child lives, or an individual who is legally responsible for the child's welfare; or

(D) except as used in sections 615(b)(2) and 639(a)(5), an individual assigned under either of those sections to be a surrogate parent.

(24) PARENT ORGANIZATION- The term 'parent organization' has the meaning given the term in section 671(g).

(25) PARENT TRAINING AND INFORMATION CENTER- The term 'parent training and information center' means a center assisted under section 671 or 672.

(26) RELATED SERVICES-

(A) IN GENERAL- The term 'related services' means transportation, and such developmental, corrective, and other supportive services (including speech-language pathology and audiology services, interpreting services, psychological services, physical and occupational therapy, recreation, including therapeutic recreation, social work services, school nurse services designed to enable a child with a disability to receive a free appropriate public education as described in the individualized education program of the child, counseling services, including rehabilitation counseling, orientation and mobility services, and medical services, except that such medical services shall be for diagnostic and evaluation purposes only) as may be required to assist a child with a disability to benefit from special education, and includes the early identification and assessment of disabling conditions in children.

(B) EXCEPTION- The term does not include a medical device that is surgically implanted, or the replacement of such device.

(27) SECONDARY SCHOOL- The term 'secondary school' means a nonprofit institutional day or residential school, including a public secondary charter school, that provides secondary education, as determined under State law, except that it does not include any education beyond grade 12.

(28) SECRETARY- The term 'Secretary' means the Secretary of Education.

(29) SPECIAL EDUCATION- The term 'special education' means specially designed instruction, at no cost to parents, to meet the unique needs of a child with a disability, including—

(A) instruction conducted in the classroom, in the home, in hospitals and institutions, and in other settings; and

(B) instruction in physical education.

(30) SPECIFIC LEARNING DISABILITY-

(A) IN GENERAL- The term 'specific learning disability' means a disorder in 1 or more of the basic psychological processes involved in understanding or in using language, spoken or written, which disorder may manifest itself in the imperfect ability to listen, think, speak, read, write, spell, or do mathematical calculations.

(B) DISORDERS INCLUDED- Such term includes such conditions as perceptual disabilities, brain injury, minimal brain dysfunction, dyslexia, and developmental aphasia.

(C) DISORDERS NOT INCLUDED- Such term does not include a learning problem that is primarily the result of visual, hearing, or motor disabilities, of mental retardation, of emotional disturbance, or of environmental, cultural, or economic disadvantage.

(31) STATE- The term 'State' means each of the 50 States, the District of Columbia, the Commonwealth of Puerto Rico, and each of the outlying areas.

(32) STATE EDUCATIONAL AGENCY- The term 'State educational agency' means the State board of education or other agency or officer primarily responsible for the State supervision of public elementary schools and secondary schools, or, if there is no such officer or agency, an officer or agency designated by the Governor or by State law.

(33) SUPPLEMENTARY AIDS AND SERVICES- The term 'supplementary aids and

services' means aids, services, and other supports that are provided in regular education classes or other education-related settings to enable children with disabilities to be educated with nondisabled children to the maximum extent appropriate in accordance with section 612(a)(5).

(34) TRANSITION SERVICES- The term 'transition services' means a coordinated set of activities for a child with a disability that—

(A) is designed to be within a results-oriented process, that is focused on improving the academic and functional achievement of the child with a disability to facilitate the child's movement from school to post-school activities, including post-secondary education, vocational education, integrated employment (including supported employment), continuing and adult education, adult services, independent living, or community participation;

(B) is based on the individual child's needs, taking into account the child's strengths, preferences, and interests; and

(C) includes instruction, related services, community experiences, the development of employment and other post-school adult living objectives, and, when appropriate, acquisition of daily living skills and functional vocational evaluation.

(35) UNIVERSAL DESIGN- The term 'universal design' has the meaning given the term in section 3 of the Assistive Technology Act of 1998 (29 U.S.C. 3002).

(36) WARD OF THE STATE-

(A) IN GENERAL- The term 'ward of the State' means a child who, as determined by the State where the child resides, is a foster child, is a ward of the State, or is in the custody of a public child welfare agency.

(B) EXCEPTION- The term does not include a foster child who has a foster parent who meets the definition of a parent in paragraph (23).

SEC. 603. OFFICE OF SPECIAL EDUCATION PROGRAMS.

(a) ESTABLISHMENT- There shall be, within the Office of Special Education and Rehabilitative Services in the Department of Education, an Office of Special Education Programs, which shall be the principal agency in the Department for administering and carrying out this title and other programs and activities concerning the education of children with disabilities.

(b) DIRECTOR- The Office established under subsection (a) shall be headed by a Director who shall be selected by the Secretary and shall report directly to the Assistant Secretary for Special Education and Rehabilitative Services.

(c) VOLUNTARY AND UNCOMPENSATED SERVICES- Notwithstanding section 1342 of title 31, United States Code, the Secretary is authorized to accept voluntary and uncompensated services in furtherance of the purposes of this title.

SEC. 604. ABROGATION OF STATE SOVEREIGN IMMUNITY.

(a) IN GENERAL- A State shall not be immune under the 11th amendment to the Constitution of the United States from suit in Federal court for a violation of this title.

(b) REMEDIES- In a suit against a State for a violation of this title, remedies (including remedies both at law and in equity) are available for such a violation to the same extent as those remedies are available for such a violation in the suit against any public entity other than a State.

(c) EFFECTIVE DATE- Subsections (a) and (b) apply with respect to violations that occur in whole or part after the date of enactment of the Education of the Handicapped Act Amendments of 1990.

SEC. 605. ACQUISITION OF EQUIPMENT; CONSTRUCTION OR ALTERATION OF FACILITIES.

(a) IN GENERAL- If the Secretary determines that a program authorized under this title will be improved by permitting program funds to be used to acquire appropriate equipment, or to construct new facilities or alter existing facilities, the Secretary is authorized to allow the use of those funds for those purposes.

(b) COMPLIANCE WITH CERTAIN REGULATIONS- Any construction of new facilities or alteration of existing facilities under subsection (a) shall comply with the requirements of—

(1) appendix A of part 36 of title 28, Code of Federal Regulations (commonly known as the 'Americans with Disabilities Accessibility Guidelines for Buildings and Facilities'); or

(2) appendix A of subpart 101-19.6 of title 41, Code of Federal Regulations (commonly known as the 'Uniform Federal Accessibility Standards').

SEC. 606. EMPLOYMENT OF INDIVIDUALS WITH DISABILITIES.

The Secretary shall ensure that each recipient of assistance under this title makes positive efforts to employ and advance in employment qualified individuals with disabilities in programs assisted under this title.

SEC. 607. REQUIREMENTS FOR PRESCRIBING REGULATIONS.

(a) IN GENERAL- In carrying out the provisions of this title, the Secretary shall issue regulations under this title only to the extent that such regulations are necessary to ensure that there is compliance with the specific requirements of this title.

(b) PROTECTIONS PROVIDED TO CHILDREN- The Secretary may not implement, or publish in final form, any regulation prescribed pursuant to this title that—

(1) violates or contradicts any provision of this title; or

(2) procedurally or substantively lessens the protections provided to children with disabilities under this title, as embodied in regulations in effect on July 20, 1983 (particularly as such protections related to parental consent to initial evaluation or initial placement in special education, least restrictive environment, related services, timelines, attendance of evaluation personnel at individualized education program meetings, or qualifications of personnel), except to the extent that such regulation reflects the clear and unequivocal intent of Congress in legislation.

(c) PUBLIC COMMENT PERIOD- The Secretary shall provide a public comment period of not less than 75 days on any regulation proposed under part B or part C on which an opportunity for public comment is otherwise required by law.

(d) POLICY LETTERS AND STATEMENTS- The Secretary may not issue policy letters or other statements (including letters or statements regarding issues of national significance) that—

(1) violate or contradict any provision of this title; or

(2) establish a rule that is required for compliance with, and eligibility under, this title without following the requirements of section 553 of title 5, United States Code.

(e) EXPLANATION AND ASSURANCES- Any written response by the Secretary under subsection (d) regarding a policy, question, or interpretation under part B shall include an explanation in the written response that—

(1) such response is provided as informal guidance and is not legally binding;

(2) when required, such response is issued in compliance with the requirements of section 553 of title 5, United States Code; and

(3) such response represents the interpretation by the Department of Education of the applicable statutory or regulatory requirements in the context of the specific facts presented.

(f) CORRESPONDENCE FROM DEPARTMENT OF EDUCATION DESCRIBING INTERPRETATIONS OF THIS TITLE-

(1) IN GENERAL- The Secretary shall, on a quarterly basis, publish in the Federal Register, and widely disseminate to interested entities through various additional forms of communication, a list of correspondence from the Department of Education received by individuals during the previous quarter that describes the interpretations of the Department of Education of this title or the regulations implemented pursuant to this title.

(2) ADDITIONAL INFORMATION- For each item of correspondence published in a list under paragraph (1), the Secretary shall—

(A) identify the topic addressed by the correspondence and shall include such other summary information as the Secretary determines to be appropriate; and

(B) ensure that all such correspondence is issued, where applicable, in compliance with the requirements of section 553 of title 5, United States Code.

SEC. 608. STATE ADMINISTRATION.

(a) RULEMAKING- Each State that receives funds under this title shall—

(1) ensure that any State rules, regulations, and policies relating to this title conform to the purposes of this title;

(2) identify in writing to local educational agencies located in the State and the Secretary any such rule, regulation, or policy as a State-imposed requirement that is not required by this title and Federal regulations; and

(3) minimize the number of rules, regulations, and policies to which the local educational agencies and schools located in the State are subject under this title.

(b) SUPPORT AND FACILITATION- State rules, regulations, and policies under this title shall support and facilitate local educational agency and school-level system improvement designed to enable children with disabilities to meet the challenging State student academic achievement standards.

SEC. 609. PAPERWORK REDUCTION.

(a) PILOT PROGRAM-

(1) PURPOSE- The purpose of this section is to provide an opportunity for States to identify ways to reduce paperwork burdens and other administrative duties that are directly associated with the requirements of this title, in order to increase the time and resources available for instruction and other activities aimed at improving educational and functional results for children with disabilities.

(2) AUTHORIZATION-

(A) IN GENERAL- In order to carry out the purpose of this section, the Secretary is authorized to grant waivers of statutory requirements of, or regulatory requirements relating to, part B for a period of time not to exceed 4 years with respect to not more than 15 States based on proposals submitted by States to reduce excessive paperwork and noninstructional time burdens that do not assist in improving educational and functional results for children with disabilities.

(B) EXCEPTION- The Secretary shall not waive under this section any statutory requirements of, or regulatory requirements relating to, applicable civil rights requirements.

(C) RULE OF CONSTRUCTION- Nothing in this section shall be construed to—

(i) affect the right of a child with a disability to receive a free appropriate public education under part B; and

(ii) permit a State or local educational agency to waive procedural safeguards under section 615.

(3) PROPOSAL-

(A) IN GENERAL- A State desiring to participate in the program under this section shall submit a proposal to the Secretary at such time and in such manner as the Secretary may reasonably require.

(B) CONTENT- The proposal shall include—

(i) a list of any statutory requirements of, or regulatory requirements relating to, part B that the State desires the Secretary to waive, in whole or in part; and

(ii) a list of any State requirements that the State proposes to waive or change, in whole or in part, to carry out a waiver granted to the State by the Secretary.

(4) TERMINATION OF WAIVER- The Secretary shall terminate a State's waiver under this section if the Secretary determines that the State—

(A) needs assistance under section 616(d)(2)(A)(ii) and that the waiver has contributed to or caused such need for assistance;

(B) needs intervention under section 616(d)(2)(A)(iii) or needs substantial intervention under section 616(d)(2)(A)(iv); or

(C) failed to appropriately implement its waiver.

(b) REPORT- Beginning 2 years after the date of enactment of the Individuals with Disabilities Education Improvement Act of 2004, the Secretary shall include in the annual report to Congress submitted pursuant to section 426 of the Department of Education Organization Act information related to the effectiveness of waivers granted under subsection (a), including any specific recommendations for broader implementation of such waivers, in—

(1) reducing—

(A) the paperwork burden on teachers, principals, administrators, and related service providers; and

(B) noninstructional time spent by teachers in complying with part B;

(2) enhancing longer-term educational planning;

(3) improving positive outcomes for children with disabilities;

(4) promoting collaboration between IEP Team members; and

(5) ensuring satisfaction of family members.

SEC. 610. FREELY ASSOCIATED STATES.

The Republic of the Marshall Islands, the Federated States of Micronesia, and the Republic of Palau shall continue to be eligible for competitive grants administered by the Secretary under this title to the extent that such grants continue to be available to States and local educational agencies under this title.

PART B—ASSISTANCE FOR EDUCATION OF ALL CHILDREN WITH DISABILITIES

SEC. 611. AUTHORIZATION; ALLOTMENT; USE OF FUNDS; AUTHORIZATION OF APPROPRIATIONS.

(a) GRANTS TO STATES-

(1) PURPOSE OF GRANTS- The Secretary shall make grants to States, outlying areas, and freely associated States, and provide funds to the Secretary of the Interior, to assist them to provide special education and related services to children with disabilities in accordance with this part.

(2) MAXIMUM AMOUNT- The maximum amount of the grant a State may receive under this section—

(A) for fiscal years 2005 and 2006 is—

(i) the number of children with disabilities in the State who are receiving special education and related services—

(I) aged 3 through 5 if the State is eligible for a grant under section 619; and

(II) aged 6 through 21; multiplied by

(ii) 40 percent of the average per-pupil expenditure in public elementary schools and secondary schools in the United States; and

(B) for fiscal year 2007 and subsequent fiscal years is—

(i) the number of children with disabilities in the 2004-2005 school year in the State who received special education and related services—

(I) aged 3 through 5 if the State is eligible for a grant under section 619; and

(II) aged 6 through 21; multiplied by

(ii) 40 percent of the average per-pupil expenditure in public elementary schools and secondary schools in the United States; adjusted by

(iii) the rate of annual change in the sum of—

(I) 85 percent of such State's population described in subsection (d)(3)(A)(i)(II); and

(II) 15 percent of such State's population described in subsection (d)(3)(A)(i)(III).

(b) OUTLYING AREAS AND FREELY ASSOCIATED STATES; SECRETARY OF THE INTERIOR-

(1) OUTLYING AREAS AND FREELY ASSOCIATED STATES-

(A) FUNDS RESERVED- From the amount appropriated for any fiscal year under subsection (i), the Secretary shall reserve not more than 1 percent, which shall be used—

(i) to provide assistance to the outlying areas in accordance with their respective populations of individuals aged 3 through 21; and

(ii) to provide each freely associated State a grant in the amount that such freely associated State received for fiscal year 2003 under this part, but only if the freely associated State meets the applicable requirements of this part, as well as the requirements of section 611(b)(2)(C) as such section was in effect on the day before the date of enactment of the Individuals with Disabilities Education Improvement Act of 2004.

(B) SPECIAL RULE- The provisions of Public Law 95-134, permitting the consolidation of grants by the outlying areas, shall not apply to funds provided to the outlying areas or the freely associated States under this section.

(C) DEFINITION- In this paragraph, the term 'freely associated States' means the Republic of the Marshall Islands, the Federated States of Micronesia, and the Republic of Palau.

(2) SECRETARY OF THE INTERIOR- From the amount appropriated for any fiscal year under subsection (i), the Secretary shall reserve 1.226 percent to provide assistance to the Secretary of the Interior in accordance with subsection (h).

(c) TECHNICAL ASSISTANCE-

(1) IN GENERAL- The Secretary may reserve not more than 1/2 of 1 percent of the amounts appropriated under this part for each fiscal year to provide technical assistance activities authorized under section 616(i).

(2) MAXIMUM AMOUNT- The maximum amount the Secretary may reserve under paragraph (1) for any fiscal year is $25,000,000, cumulatively adjusted by the rate of inflation as measured by the percentage increase, if any, from the preceding fiscal year in the Consumer Price Index For All Urban Consumers, published by the Bureau of Labor Statistics of the Department of Labor.

(d) ALLOCATIONS TO STATES-

(1) IN GENERAL- After reserving funds for technical assistance, and for payments to the outlying areas, the freely associated States, and the Secretary of the Interior under subsections (b) and (c) for a fiscal year, the Secretary shall allocate the remaining amount among the States in accordance with this subsection.

(2) SPECIAL RULE FOR USE OF FISCAL YEAR 1999 AMOUNT- If a State

received any funds under this section for fiscal year 1999 on the basis of children aged 3 through 5, but does not make a free appropriate public education available to all children with disabilities aged 3 through 5 in the State in any subsequent fiscal year, the Secretary shall compute the State's amount for fiscal year 1999, solely for the purpose of calculating the State's allocation in that subsequent year under paragraph (3) or (4), by subtracting the amount allocated to the State for fiscal year 1999 on the basis of those children.

(3) INCREASE IN FUNDS- If the amount available for allocations to States under paragraph (1) for a fiscal year is equal to or greater than the amount allocated to the States under this paragraph for the preceding fiscal year, those allocations shall be calculated as follows:

(A) ALLOCATION OF INCREASE-

(i) IN GENERAL- Except as provided in subparagraph (B), the Secretary shall allocate for the fiscal year—

(I) to each State the amount the State received under this section for fiscal year 1999;

(II) 85 percent of any remaining funds to States on the basis of the States' relative populations of children aged 3 through 21 who are of the same age as children with disabilities for whom the State ensures the availability of a free appropriate public education under this part; and

(III) 15 percent of those remaining funds to States on the basis of the States' relative populations of children described in subclause (II) who are living in poverty.

(ii) DATA- For the purpose of making grants under this paragraph, the Secretary shall use the most recent population data, including data on children living in poverty, that are available and satisfactory to the Secretary.

(B) LIMITATIONS- Notwithstanding subparagraph (A), allocations under this paragraph shall be subject to the following:

(i) PRECEDING YEAR ALLOCATION- No State's allocation shall be less than its allocation under this section for the preceding fiscal year.

(ii) MINIMUM- No State's allocation shall be less than the greatest of—

(I) the sum of—

(aa) the amount the State received under this section for fiscal year 1999; and

(bb) 1/3 of 1 percent of the amount by which the amount appropriated under subsection (i) for the fiscal year exceeds the amount appropriated for this section for fiscal year 1999;

(II) the sum of—

(aa) the amount the State received under this section for the preceding fiscal year; and

(bb) that amount multiplied by the percentage by which the increase in the funds appropriated for this section from the preceding fiscal year exceeds 1.5 percent; or

(III) the sum of—

(aa) the amount the State received under this section for the preceding fiscal year; and

(bb) that amount multiplied by 90 percent of the percentage increase in the amount appropriated for this section from the preceding fiscal year.

(iii) MAXIMUM- Notwithstanding clause (ii), no State's allocation under this paragraph shall exceed the sum of—

(I) the amount the State received under this section for the preceding fiscal year; and

(II) that amount multiplied by the sum of 1.5 percent and the percentage increase in the amount appropriated under this section from the preceding fiscal year.

(C) RATABLE REDUCTION- If the amount available for allocations under this paragraph is insufficient to pay those allocations in full, those allocations shall be ratably reduced, subject to subparagraph (B)(i).

(4) DECREASE IN FUNDS- If the amount available for allocations to States under paragraph (1) for a fiscal year is less than the amount allocated to the States under this section for the preceding fiscal year, those allocations shall be calculated as follows:

(A) AMOUNTS GREATER THAN FISCAL YEAR 1999 ALLOCATIONS- If the amount available for allocations is greater than the amount allocated to the States for fiscal year 1999, each State shall be allocated the sum of—

(i) the amount the State received under this section for fiscal year 1999; and

(ii) an amount that bears the same relation to any remaining funds as the increase the State received under this section for the preceding fiscal year over fiscal year 1999 bears to the total of all such increases for all States.

(B) AMOUNTS EQUAL TO OR LESS THAN FISCAL YEAR 1999 ALLOCATIONS-

(i) IN GENERAL- If the amount available for allocations under this paragraph is equal to or less than the amount allocated to the States for fiscal year 1999, each State shall be allocated the amount the State received for fiscal year 1999.

(ii) RATABLE REDUCTION- If the amount available for allocations under this paragraph is insufficient to make the allocations described in clause (i), those allocations shall be ratably reduced.

(e) STATE-LEVEL ACTIVITIES-

(1) STATE ADMINISTRATION-

(A) IN GENERAL- For the purpose of administering this part, including paragraph (3), section 619, and the coordination of activities under this part with, and providing technical assistance to, other programs that provide services to children with disabilities—

(i) each State may reserve for each fiscal year not more than the maximum amount the State was eligible to reserve for State administration under this section for fiscal year 2004 or $800,000 (adjusted in accordance with subparagraph (B)), whichever is greater; and

(ii) each outlying area may reserve for each fiscal year not more than 5 percent of the amount the outlying area receives under subsection (b)(1) for the fiscal year or $35,000, whichever is greater.

(B) CUMULATIVE ANNUAL ADJUSTMENTS- For each fiscal year beginning with fiscal year 2005, the Secretary shall cumulatively adjust—

(i) the maximum amount the State was eligible to reserve for State administration under this part for fiscal year 2004; and

(ii) $800,000, by the rate of inflation as measured by the percentage increase, if any, from the preceding fiscal year in the Consumer Price Index For All Urban Consumers, published by the Bureau of Labor Statistics of the Department of Labor.

(C) CERTIFICATION- Prior to expenditure of funds under this paragraph, the State shall certify to the Secretary that the arrangements to establish responsibility for services pursuant to section 612(a)(12)(A) are current.

(D) PART C- Funds reserved under subparagraph (A) may be used for the administration of part C, if the State educational agency is the lead agency for the State under such part.

(2) OTHER STATE-LEVEL ACTIVITIES-

(A) STATE-LEVEL ACTIVITIES-

(i) IN GENERAL- Except as provided in clause (iii), for the purpose of carrying out State-level activities, each State may reserve for each of the fiscal years 2005 and 2006 not more than 10 percent from the amount of the State's allocation under subsection (d) for each of the fiscal years 2005 and 2006, respectively. For fiscal year 2007 and each subsequent fiscal year, the State may reserve the maximum amount the State was eligible to reserve under the preceding sentence for fiscal year 2006 (cumulatively adjusted by the rate of inflation as measured by the percentage increase, if any, from the preceding fiscal year in the Consumer Price Index For All Urban Consumers,

published by the Bureau of Labor Statistics of the Department of Labor).

(ii) SMALL STATE ADJUSTMENT- Notwithstanding clause (i) and except as provided in clause (iii), in the case of a State for which the maximum amount reserved for State administration is not greater than $850,000, the State may reserve for the purpose of carrying out State-level activities for each of the fiscal years 2005 and 2006, not more than 10.5 percent from the amount of the State's allocation under subsection (d) for each of the fiscal years 2005 and 2006, respectively. For fiscal year 2007 and each subsequent fiscal year, such State may reserve the maximum amount the State was eligible to reserve under the preceding sentence for fiscal year 2006 (cumulatively adjusted by the rate of inflation as measured by the percentage increase, if any, from the preceding fiscal year in the Consumer Price Index For All Urban Consumers, published by the Bureau of Labor Statistics of the Department of Labor).

(iii) EXCEPTION- If a State does not reserve funds under paragraph (3) for a fiscal year, then—

(I) in the case of a State that is not described in clause (ii), for fiscal year 2005 or 2006, clause (i) shall be applied by substituting 9.0 percent for 10 percent; and

(II) in the case of a State that is described in clause (ii), for fiscal year 2005 or 2006, clause (ii) shall be applied by substituting 9.5 percent for 10.5 percent.

(B) REQUIRED ACTIVITIES- Funds reserved under subparagraph (A) shall be used to carry out the following activities:

(i) For monitoring, enforcement, and complaint investigation.

(ii) To establish and implement the mediation process required by section 615(e), including providing for the cost of mediators and support personnel.

(C) AUTHORIZED ACTIVITIES- Funds reserved under subparagraph (A) may be used to carry out the following activities:

(i) For support and direct services, including technical assistance, personnel preparation, and professional development and training.

(ii) To support paperwork reduction activities, including expanding the use of technology in the IEP process.

(iii) To assist local educational agencies in providing positive behavioral interventions and supports and appropriate mental health services for children with disabilities.

(iv) To improve the use of technology in the classroom by children with disabilities to enhance learning.

(v) To support the use of technology, including technology with universal design principles and assistive technology devices, to maximize accessibility to the general education curriculum for children with disabilities.

(vi) Development and implementation of transition programs, including coordination of services with agencies involved in supporting the transition of children with disabilities to postsecondary activities.

(vii) To assist local educational agencies in meeting personnel shortages.

(viii) To support capacity building activities and improve the delivery of services by local educational agencies to improve results for children with disabilities.

(ix) Alternative programming for children with disabilities who have been expelled from school, and services for children with disabilities in correctional facilities, children enrolled in State-operated or State-supported schools, and children with disabilities in charter schools.

(x) To support the development and provision of appropriate accommodations for children with disabilities, or the development and provision of alternate assessments that are valid and reliable for assessing the performance of children with disabilities, in accordance with sections 1111(b) and 6111 of the Elementary and Secondary Education Act of 1965.

(xi) To provide technical assistance to schools and local educational agencies, and direct services, including supplemental educational services as defined in 1116(e) of the Elementary and Secondary Education Act of 1965 to children with disabilities, in schools or local educational agencies identified for improvement under section 1116 of the Elementary and Secondary Education Act of 1965 on the sole basis of the assessment results of the disaggregated subgroup of children with disabilities, including providing professional development to special and regular education teachers, who teach children with disabilities, based on scientifically based research to improve educational instruction, in order to improve academic achievement to meet or exceed the objectives established by the State under section 1111(b)(2)(G) the Elementary and Secondary Education Act of 1965.

(3) LOCAL EDUCATIONAL AGENCY RISK POOL-

(A) IN GENERAL-

(i) RESERVATION OF FUNDS- For the purpose of assisting local educational agencies (including a charter school that is a local educational agency or a consortium of local educational agencies) in addressing the needs of high need children with disabilities, each State shall have the option to reserve for each fiscal year 10 percent of the amount of funds the State reserves for State-level activities under paragraph (2)(A)—

(I) to establish and make disbursements from the high cost fund to local educational agencies in accordance with this paragraph during the first and succeeding fiscal years of the high cost fund; and

(II) to support innovative and effective ways of cost sharing by the State, by a local educational agency, or among a consortium of local educational agencies, as determined by the State in coordination with representatives from local educational agencies, subject to subparagraph (B)(ii).

(ii) DEFINITION OF LOCAL EDUCATIONAL AGENCY- In this paragraph the term 'local educational agency' includes a charter school that is a local educational agency, or a consortium of local educational agencies.

(B) LIMITATION ON USES OF FUNDS-

(i) ESTABLISHMENT OF HIGH COST FUND- A State shall not use any of the funds the State reserves pursuant to subparagraph (A)(i), but may use the funds the State reserves under paragraph (1), to establish and support the high cost fund.

(ii) INNOVATIVE AND EFFECTIVE COST SHARING- A State shall not use more than 5 percent of the funds the State reserves pursuant to subparagraph (A)(i) for each fiscal year to support innovative and effective ways of cost sharing among consortia of local educational agencies.

(C) STATE PLAN FOR HIGH COST FUND-

(i) DEFINITION- The State educational agency shall establish the State's definition of a high need child with a disability, which definition shall be developed in consultation with local educational agencies.

(ii) STATE PLAN- The State educational agency shall develop, not later than 90 days after the State reserves funds under this paragraph, annually review, and amend as necessary, a State plan for the high cost fund. Such State plan shall—

(I) establish, in coordination with representatives from local educational agencies, a definition of a high need child with a disability that, at a minimum—

(aa) addresses the financial impact a high need child with a disability has on the budget of the child's local educational agency; and

(bb) ensures that the cost of the high need

child with a disability is greater than 3 times the average per pupil expenditure (as defined in section 9101 of the Elementary and Secondary Education Act of 1965) in that State;

(II) establish eligibility criteria for the participation of a local educational agency that, at a minimum, takes into account the number and percentage of high need children with disabilities served by a local educational agency;

(III) develop a funding mechanism that provides distributions each fiscal year to local educational agencies that meet the criteria developed by the State under subclause (II); and

(IV) establish an annual schedule by which the State educational agency shall make its distributions from the high cost fund each fiscal year.

(iii) PUBLIC AVAILABILITY- The State shall make its final State plan publicly available not less than 30 days before the beginning of the school year, including dissemination of such information on the State website.

(D) DISBURSEMENTS FROM THE HIGH COST FUND-

(i) IN GENERAL- Each State educational agency shall make all annual disbursements from the high cost fund established under subparagraph (A)(i) in accordance with the State plan published pursuant to subparagraph (C).

(ii) USE OF DISBURSEMENTS- Each State educational agency shall make annual disbursements to eligible local educational agencies in accordance with its State plan under subparagraph (C)(ii).

(iii) APPROPRIATE COSTS- The costs associated with educating a high need child with a disability under subparagraph (C)(i) are only those costs associated with providing direct special education and related services to such child that are identified in such child's IEP.

(E) LEGAL FEES- The disbursements under subparagraph (D) shall not support legal fees, court costs, or other costs associated with a cause of action brought on behalf of a child with a disability to ensure a free appropriate public education for such child.

(F) ASSURANCE OF A FREE APPROPRIATE PUBLIC EDUCATION- Nothing in this paragraph shall be construed—

(i) to limit or condition the right of a child with a disability who is assisted under this part to receive a free appropriate public education pursuant to section 612(a)(1) in the least restrictive environment pursuant to section 612(a)(5); or

(ii) to authorize a State educational agency or local educational agency to establish a limit on what may be spent on the education of a child with a disability.

(G) SPECIAL RULE FOR RISK POOL AND HIGH NEED ASSISTANCE PROGRAMS IN EFFECT AS OF JANUARY 1, 2004- Notwithstanding the provisions of subparagraphs (A) through (F), a State may use funds reserved pursuant to this paragraph for implementing a placement neutral cost sharing and reimbursement program of high need, low incidence, catastrophic, or extraordinary aid to local educational agencies that provides services to high need students based on eligibility criteria for such programs that were created not later than January 1, 2004, and are currently in operation, if such program serves children that meet the requirement of the definition of a high need child with a disability as described in subparagraph (C)(ii)(I).

(H) MEDICAID SERVICES NOT AFFECTED- Disbursements provided under this paragraph shall not be used to pay costs that otherwise would be reimbursed as medical assistance for a child with a disability under the State medicaid program under title XIX of the Social Security Act.

(I) REMAINING FUNDS- Funds reserved under subparagraph (A) in any fiscal year but not expended in that fiscal year pursuant to subparagraph (D) shall be allocated to local educational agencies for the succeeding fiscal year in the same manner as funds are allocated to local educational agencies under subsection (f) for the succeeding fiscal year.

(4) INAPPLICABILITY OF CERTAIN PROHIBITIONS- A State may use funds the State reserves under paragraphs (1) and (2) without regard to—

(A) the prohibition on commingling of funds in section 612(a)(17)(B); and

(B) the prohibition on supplanting other funds in section 612(a)(17)(C).

(5) REPORT ON USE OF FUNDS- As part of the information required to be submitted to the Secretary under section 612, each State shall annually describe how amounts under this section—

(A) will be used to meet the requirements of this title; and

(B) will be allocated among the activities described in this section to meet State priorities based on input from local educational agencies.

(6) SPECIAL RULE FOR INCREASED FUNDS- A State may use funds the State reserves under paragraph (1)(A) as a result of

inflationary increases under paragraph (1)(B) to carry out activities authorized under clause (i), (iii), (vii), or (viii) of paragraph (2)(C).

(7) FLEXIBILITY IN USING FUNDS FOR PART C- Any State eligible to receive a grant under section 619 may use funds made available under paragraph (1)(A), subsection (f)(3), or section 619(f)(5) to develop and implement a State policy jointly with the lead agency under part C and the State educational agency to provide early intervention services (which shall include an educational component that promotes school readiness and incorporates preliteracy, language, and numeracy skills) in accordance with part C to children with disabilities who are eligible for services under section 619 and who previously received services under part C until such children enter, or are eligible under State law to enter, kindergarten, or elementary school as appropriate.

(f) SUBGRANTS TO LOCAL EDUCATIONAL AGENCIES-

(1) SUBGRANTS REQUIRED- Each State that receives a grant under this section for any fiscal year shall distribute any funds the State does not reserve under subsection (e) to local educational agencies (including public charter schools that operate as local educational agencies) in the State that have established their eligibility under section 613 for use in accordance with this part.

(2) PROCEDURE FOR ALLOCATIONS TO LOCAL EDUCATIONAL AGENCIES- For each fiscal year for which funds are allocated to States under subsection (d), each State shall allocate funds under paragraph (1) as follows:

(A) BASE PAYMENTS- The State shall first award each local educational agency described in paragraph (1) the amount the local educational agency would have received under this section for fiscal year 1999, if the State had distributed 75 percent of its grant for that year under section 611(d) as section 611(d) was then in effect.

(B) ALLOCATION OF REMAINING FUNDS- After making allocations under subparagraph (A), the State shall—

(i) allocate 85 percent of any remaining funds to those local educational agencies on the basis of the relative numbers of children enrolled in public and private elementary schools and secondary schools within the local educational agency's jurisdiction; and

(ii) allocate 15 percent of those remaining funds to those local educational agencies in accordance with their relative numbers of children living in poverty, as determined by the State educational agency.

(3) REALLOCATION OF FUNDS- If a State educational agency determines that a local educational agency is adequately providing a free appropriate public education to all children with disabilities residing in the area served by that local educational agency with State and local funds, the State educational agency may reallocate any portion of the funds under this part that are not needed by that local educational agency to provide a free appropriate public education to other local educational agencies in the State that are not adequately providing special education and related services to all children with disabilities residing in the areas served by those other local educational agencies.

(g) DEFINITIONS- In this section:

(1) AVERAGE PER-PUPIL EXPENDITURE IN PUBLIC ELEMENTARY SCHOOLS AND SECONDARY SCHOOLS IN THE UNITED STATES- The term 'average per-pupil expenditure in public elementary schools and secondary schools in the United States' means—

(A) without regard to the source of funds—

(i) the aggregate current expenditures, during the second fiscal year preceding the fiscal year for which the determination is made (or, if satisfactory data for that year are not available, during the most recent preceding fiscal year for which satisfactory data are available) of all local educational agencies in the 50 States and the District of Columbia; plus

(ii) any direct expenditures by the State for the operation of those agencies; divided by

(B) the aggregate number of children in average daily attendance to whom those agencies provided free public education during that preceding year.

(2) STATE- The term 'State' means each of the 50 States, the District of Columbia, and the Commonwealth of Puerto Rico.

(h) USE OF AMOUNTS BY SECRETARY OF THE INTERIOR-

(1) PROVISION OF AMOUNTS FOR ASSISTANCE-

(A) IN GENERAL- The Secretary of Education shall provide amounts to the Secretary of the Interior to meet the need for assistance for the education of children with disabilities on reservations aged 5 to 21, inclusive, enrolled in elementary schools and secondary schools for Indian children operated or funded by the Secretary of the Interior. The amount of such payment for any fiscal year shall be equal to 80 percent of the amount allotted under subsection (b)(2) for that fiscal year. Of the amount described in the preceding sentence—

(i) 80 percent shall be allocated to such schools by July 1 of that fiscal year; and

(ii) 20 percent shall be allocated to such schools by September 30 of that fiscal year.

(B) CALCULATION OF NUMBER OF CHILDREN- In the case of Indian students aged 3 to 5, inclusive, who are enrolled in programs affiliated with the Bureau of Indian Affairs (referred to in this subsection as the 'BIA') schools and that are required by the States in which such schools are located to attain or maintain State accreditation, and which schools have such accreditation prior to the date of enactment of the Individuals with Disabilities Education Act Amendments of 1991, the school shall be allowed to count those children for the purpose of distribution of the funds provided under this paragraph to the Secretary of the Interior. The Secretary of the Interior shall be responsible for meeting all of the requirements of this part for those children, in accordance with paragraph (2).

(C) ADDITIONAL REQUIREMENT- With respect to all other children aged 3 to 21, inclusive, on reservations, the State educational agency shall be responsible for ensuring that all of the requirements of this part are implemented.

(2) SUBMISSION OF INFORMATION- The Secretary of Education may provide the Secretary of the Interior amounts under paragraph (1) for a fiscal year only if the Secretary of the Interior submits to the Secretary of Education information that—

(A) demonstrates that the Department of the Interior meets the appropriate requirements, as determined by the Secretary of Education, of sections 612 (including monitoring and evaluation activities) and 613;

(B) includes a description of how the Secretary of the Interior will coordinate the provision of services under this part with local educational agencies, tribes and tribal organizations, and other private and Federal service providers;

(C) includes an assurance that there are public hearings, adequate notice of such hearings, and an opportunity for comment afforded to members of tribes, tribal governing bodies, and affected local school boards before the adoption of the policies, programs, and procedures related to the requirements described in subparagraph (A);

(D) includes an assurance that the Secretary of the Interior will provide such information as the Secretary of Education may require to comply with section 618;

(E) includes an assurance that the Secretary of the Interior and the Secretary of Health and Human Services have entered into a memorandum of agreement, to be provided to the Secretary of Education, for the coordination of services, resources, and personnel between their respective Federal, State, and local offices and with State and local educational agencies and other entities to facilitate the provision of services to Indian children with disabilities residing on or near reservations (such agreement shall provide for the apportionment of responsibilities and costs, including child find, evaluation, diagnosis, remediation or therapeutic measures, and (where appropriate) equipment and medical or personal supplies as needed for a child to remain in school or a program); and

(F) includes an assurance that the Department of the Interior will cooperate with the Department of Education in its exercise of monitoring and oversight of this application, and any agreements entered into between the Secretary of the Interior and other entities under this part, and will fulfill its duties under this part.

(3) APPLICABILITY- The Secretary shall withhold payments under this subsection with respect to the information described in paragraph (2) in the same manner as the Secretary withholds payments under section 616(e)(6).

(4) PAYMENTS FOR EDUCATION AND SERVICES FOR INDIAN CHILDREN WITH DISABILITIES AGED 3 THROUGH 5-

(A) IN GENERAL- With funds appropriated under subsection (i), the Secretary of Education shall make payments to the Secretary of the Interior to be distributed to tribes or tribal organizations (as defined under section 4 of the Indian Self-Determination and Education Assistance Act) or consortia of tribes or tribal organizations to provide for the coordination of assistance for special education and related services for children with disabilities aged 3 through 5 on reservations served by elementary schools and secondary schools for Indian children operated or funded by the Department of the Interior. The amount of such payments under subparagraph (B) for any fiscal year shall be equal to 20 percent of the amount allotted under subsection (b)(2).

(B) DISTRIBUTION OF FUNDS- The Secretary of the Interior shall distribute the total amount of the payment under subparagraph (A) by allocating to each tribe, tribal organization, or consortium an amount based on the number of children with disabilities aged 3 through 5 residing on reservations as reported annually, divided by the total of those children served by all tribes or tribal organizations.

(C) SUBMISSION OF INFORMATION- To receive a payment under this paragraph, the tribe or tribal organization shall submit such figures to the Secretary of the Interior as required to determine the amounts to be allocated under subparagraph (B). This information shall be compiled and submitted to the Secretary of Education.

(D) USE OF FUNDS- The funds received by a tribe or tribal organization shall be used to assist in child find, screening, and other procedures for the early identification of children aged 3 through 5, parent training, and the provision of direct services. These activities may be carried out directly or through contracts or cooperative agreements with the BIA, local educational agencies, and other public or private nonprofit organizations. The tribe or tribal organization is encouraged to involve Indian parents in the development and implementation of these activities. The tribe or tribal organization shall, as appropriate, make referrals to local, State, or Federal entities for the provision of services or further diagnosis.

(E) BIENNIAL REPORT- To be eligible to receive a grant pursuant to subparagraph (A), the tribe or tribal organization shall provide to the Secretary of the Interior a biennial report of activities undertaken under this paragraph, including the number of contracts and cooperative agreements entered into, the number of children contacted and receiving services for each year, and the estimated number of children needing services during the 2 years following the year in which the report is made. The Secretary of the Interior shall include a summary of this information on a biennial basis in the report to the Secretary of Education required under this subsection. The Secretary of Education may require any additional information from the Secretary of the Interior.

(F) PROHIBITIONS- None of the funds allocated under this paragraph may be used by the Secretary of the Interior for administrative purposes, including child count and the provision of technical assistance.

(5) PLAN FOR COORDINATION OF SERVICES- The Secretary of the Interior shall develop and implement a plan for the coordination of services for all Indian children with disabilities residing on reservations covered under this title. Such plan shall provide for the coordination of services benefiting

those children from whatever source, including tribes, the Indian Health Service, other BIA divisions, and other Federal agencies. In developing the plan, the Secretary of the Interior shall consult with all interested and involved parties. The plan shall be based on the needs of the children and the system best suited for meeting those needs, and may involve the establishment of cooperative agreements between the BIA, other Federal agencies, and other entities. The plan shall also be distributed upon request to States, State educational agencies and local educational agencies, and other agencies providing services to infants, toddlers, and children with disabilities, to tribes, and to other interested parties.

(6) ESTABLISHMENT OF ADVISORY BOARD- To meet the requirements of section 612(a)(21), the Secretary of the Interior shall establish, under the BIA, an advisory board composed of individuals involved in or concerned with the education and provision of services to Indian infants, toddlers, children, and youth with disabilities, including Indians with disabilities, Indian parents or guardians of such children, teachers, service providers, State and local educational officials, representatives of tribes or tribal organizations, representatives from State Interagency Coordinating Councils under section 641 in States having reservations, and other members representing the various divisions and entities of the BIA. The chairperson shall be selected by the Secretary of the Interior. The advisory board shall—

(A) assist in the coordination of services within the BIA and with other local, State, and Federal agencies in the provision of education for infants, toddlers, and children with disabilities;

(B) advise and assist the Secretary of the Interior in the performance of the Secretary of the Interior's responsibilities described in this subsection;

(C) develop and recommend policies concerning effective inter- and intra-agency collaboration, including modifications to regulations, and the elimination of barriers to inter- and intra-agency programs and activities;

(D) provide assistance and disseminate information on best practices, effective program coordination strategies, and recommendations for improved early intervention services or educational programming for Indian infants, toddlers, and children with disabilities; and

(E) provide assistance in the preparation of information required under paragraph (2)(D).

(7) ANNUAL REPORTS-

(A) IN GENERAL- The advisory board established under paragraph (6) shall prepare and submit to the Secretary of the Interior and to Congress an annual report containing a description of the activities of the advisory board for the preceding year.

(B) AVAILABILITY- The Secretary of the Interior shall make available to the Secretary of Education the report described in subparagraph (A).

(i) AUTHORIZATION OF APPROPRIATIONS- For the purpose of carrying out this part, other than section 619, there are authorized to be appropriated—

(1) $12,358,376,571 for fiscal year 2005;

(2) $14,648,647,143 for fiscal year 2006;

(3) $16,938,917,714 for fiscal year 2007;

(4) $19,229,188,286 for fiscal year 2008;

(5) $21,519,458,857 for fiscal year 2009;

(6) $23,809,729,429 for fiscal year 2010;

(7) $26,100,000,000 for fiscal year 2011; and

(8) such sums as may be necessary for fiscal year 2012 and each succeeding fiscal year.

SEC. 612. STATE ELIGIBILITY.

(a) IN GENERAL- A State is eligible for assistance under this part for a fiscal year if the State submits a plan that provides assurances to the Secretary that the State has in effect policies and procedures to ensure that the State meets each of the following conditions:

(1) FREE APPROPRIATE PUBLIC EDUCATION-

(A) IN GENERAL- A free appropriate public education is available to all children with disabilities residing in the State between the ages of 3 and 21, inclusive, including children with disabilities who have been suspended or expelled from school.

(B) LIMITATION- The obligation to make a free appropriate public education available to all children with disabilities does not apply with respect to children—

(i) aged 3 through 5 and 18 through 21 in a State to the extent that its application to those children would be inconsistent with State law or practice, or the order of any court, respecting the provision of public education to children in those age ranges; and

(ii) aged 18 through 21 to the extent that State law does not require that special education and related services under this part be provided to children with disabilities who, in the educational placement prior to their incarceration in an adult correctional facility—

(I) were not actually identified as being a child with a disability under section 602; or

(II) did not have an individualized education program under this part.

(C) STATE FLEXIBILITY- A State that provides early intervention services in accordance with part C to a child who is eligible for services under section 619, is not required to provide such child with a free appropriate public education.

(2) FULL EDUCATIONAL OPPORTUNITY GOAL- The State has established a goal of providing full educational opportunity to all children with disabilities and a detailed timetable for accomplishing that goal.

(3) CHILD FIND-

(A) IN GENERAL- All children with disabilities residing in the State, including children with disabilities who are homeless children or are wards of the State and children with disabilities attending private schools, regardless of the severity of their disabilities, and who are in need of special education and related services, are identified, located, and evaluated and a practical method is developed and implemented to determine which children with disabilities are currently receiving needed special education and related services.

(B) CONSTRUCTION- Nothing in this title requires that children be classified by their disability so long as each child who has a disability listed in section 602 and who, by reason of that disability, needs special education and related services is regarded as a child with a disability under this part.

(4) INDIVIDUALIZED EDUCATION PROGRAM- An individualized education program, or an individualized family service plan that meets the requirements of section 636(d), is developed, reviewed, and revised for each child with a disability in accordance with section 614(d).

(5) LEAST RESTRICTIVE ENVIRONMENT-

(A) IN GENERAL- To the maximum extent appropriate, children with disabilities, including children in public or private institutions or other care facilities, are educated with children who are not disabled, and special classes, separate schooling, or other removal of children with disabilities from the regular educational environment occurs only when the nature or severity of the disability of a child is such that education in regular classes with the use of supplementary aids and services cannot be achieved satisfactorily.

(B) ADDITIONAL REQUIREMENT-

(i) IN GENERAL- A State funding mechanism shall not result in placements that violate the requirements of subparagraph (A), and a State shall not use a funding mechanism by which the State distributes funds on the basis of the type of setting in which a child is served that will result in the failure to provide a child with a disability a free appropriate public education according to the unique needs of the child as described in the child's IEP.

(ii) ASSURANCE- If the State does not have policies and procedures to ensure compliance with clause (i), the State shall provide the Secretary an assurance that the State will revise the funding mechanism as soon as feasible to ensure that such mechanism does not result in such placements.

(6) PROCEDURAL SAFEGUARDS-

(A) IN GENERAL- Children with disabilities and their parents are afforded the procedural safeguards required by section 615.

(B) ADDITIONAL PROCEDURAL SAFEGUARDS- Procedures to ensure that testing and evaluation materials and procedures utilized for the purposes of evaluation and placement of children with disabilities for services under this title will be selected and administered so as not to be racially or culturally discriminatory. Such materials or procedures shall be provided and administered in the child's native language or mode of communication, unless it clearly is not feasible to do so, and no single procedure shall be the sole criterion for determining an appropriate educational program for a child.

(7) EVALUATION- Children with disabilities are evaluated in accordance with subsections (a) through (c) of section 614.

(8) CONFIDENTIALITY- Agencies in the State comply with section 617(c) (relating to the confidentiality of records and information).

(9) TRANSITION FROM PART C TO PRESCHOOL PROGRAMS- Children participating in early intervention programs assisted under part C, and who will participate in preschool programs assisted under this part, experience a smooth and effective transition to those preschool programs in a manner consistent with section 637(a)(9). By the third birthday of such a child, an individualized education program or, if consistent with sections 614(d)(2)(B) and 636(d), an individualized family service plan, has been developed and is being implemented for the child. The local educational agency will participate in transition planning conferences arranged by the designated lead agency under section 635(a)(10).

(10) CHILDREN IN PRIVATE SCHOOLS-

(A) CHILDREN ENROLLED IN PRIVATE SCHOOLS BY THEIR PARENTS-

(i) IN GENERAL- To the extent consistent with the number and location of children with disabilities in the State who are enrolled by their parents in private elementary schools and secondary schools in the school district served by a local educational agency, provision is made for the participation of those children in the program assisted or carried out under this part by providing for such children special education and related services in accordance with the following requirements, unless the Secretary has arranged for services to those children under subsection (f):

(I) Amounts to be expended for the provision of those services (including direct services to parentally placed private school children) by the local educational agency shall be equal to a proportionate amount of Federal funds made available under this part.

(II) In calculating the proportionate amount of Federal funds, the local educational agency, after timely and meaningful consultation with representatives of private schools as described in clause (iii), shall conduct a thorough and complete child find process to determine the number of parentally placed children with disabilities attending private schools located in the local educational agency.

(III) Such services to parentally placed private school children with disabilities may be provided to the children on the premises of private, including religious, schools, to the extent consistent with law.

(IV) State and local funds may supplement and in no case shall supplant the proportionate amount of Federal funds required to be expended under this subparagraph.

(V) Each local educational agency shall maintain in its records and provide to the State educational agency the number of children evaluated under this subparagraph, the number of children determined to be children with disabilities under this paragraph, and the number of children served under this paragraph.

(ii) CHILD FIND REQUIREMENT-

(I) IN GENERAL- The requirements of paragraph (3) (relating to child find) shall apply with respect to children with disabilities in the State who are enrolled in private, including religious, elementary schools and secondary schools.

(II) EQUITABLE PARTICIPATION- The child find process shall be designed to ensure the equitable participation of parentally placed private school children with disabilities and an accurate count of such children.

(III) ACTIVITIES- In carrying out this

clause, the local educational agency, or where applicable, the State educational agency, shall undertake activities similar to those activities undertaken for the agency's public school children.

(IV) COST- The cost of carrying out this clause, including individual evaluations, may not be considered in determining whether a local educational agency has met its obligations under clause (i).

(V) COMPLETION PERIOD- Such child find process shall be completed in a time period comparable to that for other students attending public schools in the local educational agency.

(iii) CONSULTATION- To ensure timely and meaningful consultation, a local educational agency, or where appropriate, a State educational agency, shall consult with private school representatives and representatives of parents of parentally placed private school children with disabilities during the design and development of special education and related services for the children, including regarding—

(I) the child find process and how parentally placed private school children suspected of having a disability can participate equitably, including how parents, teachers, and private school officials will be informed of the process;

(II) the determination of the proportionate amount of Federal funds available to serve parentally placed private school children with disabilities under this subparagraph, including the determination of how the amount was calculated;

(III) the consultation process among the local educational agency, private school officials, and representatives of parents of parentally placed private school children with disabilities, including how such process will operate throughout the school year to ensure that parentally placed private school children with disabilities identified through the child find process can meaningfully participate in special education and related services;

(IV) how, where, and by whom special education and related services will be provided for parentally placed private school children with disabilities, including a discussion of types of services, including direct services and alternate service delivery mechanisms, how such services will be apportioned if funds are insufficient to serve all children, and how and when these decisions will be made; and

(V) how, if the local educational agency disagrees with the views of the private school officials on the provision of services or the types of services, whether provided directly or through a contract, the local educational

agency shall provide to the private school officials a written explanation of the reasons why the local educational agency chose not to provide services directly or through a contract.

(iv) WRITTEN AFFIRMATION- When timely and meaningful consultation as required by clause (iii) has occurred, the local educational agency shall obtain a written affirmation signed by the representatives of participating private schools, and if such representatives do not provide such affirmation within a reasonable period of time, the local educational agency shall forward the documentation of the consultation process to the State educational agency.

(v) COMPLIANCE-

(I) IN GENERAL- A private school official shall have the right to submit a complaint to the State educational agency that the local educational agency did not engage in consultation that was meaningful and timely, or did not give due consideration to the views of the private school official.

(II) PROCEDURE- If the private school official wishes to submit a complaint, the official shall provide the basis of the noncompliance with this subparagraph by the local educational agency to the State educational agency, and the local educational agency shall forward the appropriate documentation to the State educational agency. If the private school official is dissatisfied with the decision of the State educational agency, such official may submit a complaint to the Secretary by providing the basis of the noncompliance with this subparagraph by the local educational agency to the Secretary, and the State educational agency shall forward the appropriate documentation to the Secretary.

(vi) PROVISION OF EQUITABLE SERVICES-

(I) DIRECTLY OR THROUGH CONTRACTS- The provision of services pursuant to this subparagraph shall be provided—

(aa) by employees of a public agency; or

(bb) through contract by the public agency with an individual, association, agency, organization, or other entity.

(II) SECULAR, NEUTRAL, NONIDEOLOGICAL- Special education and related services provided to parentally placed private school children with disabilities, including materials and equipment, shall be secular, neutral, and nonideological.

(vii) PUBLIC CONTROL OF FUNDS- The control of funds used to provide special education and related services under this subparagraph, and title to materials, equipment, and property purchased with those funds, shall be in a public agency for the uses and purposes provided in this title, and a public agency shall administer the funds and property.

(B) CHILDREN PLACED IN, OR REFERRED TO, PRIVATE SCHOOLS BY PUBLIC AGENCIES-

(i) IN GENERAL- Children with disabilities in private schools and facilities are provided special education and related services, in accordance with an individualized education program, at no cost to their parents, if such children are placed in, or referred to, such schools or facilities by the State or appropriate local educational agency as the means of carrying out the requirements of this part or any other applicable law requiring the provision of special education and related services to all children with disabilities within such State.

(ii) STANDARDS- In all cases described in clause (i), the State educational agency shall determine whether such schools and facilities meet standards that apply to State educational agencies and local educational agencies and that children so served have all the rights the children would have if served by such agencies.

(C) PAYMENT FOR EDUCATION OF CHILDREN ENROLLED IN PRIVATE SCHOOLS WITHOUT CONSENT OF OR REFERRAL BY THE PUBLIC AGENCY-

(i) IN GENERAL- Subject to subparagraph (A), this part does not require a local educational agency to pay for the cost of education, including special education and related services, of a child with a disability at a private school or facility if that agency made a free appropriate public education available to the child and the parents elected to place the child in such private school or facility.

(ii) REIMBURSEMENT FOR PRIVATE SCHOOL PLACEMENT- If the parents of a child with a disability, who previously received special education and related services under the authority of a public agency, enroll the child in a private elementary school or secondary school without the consent of or referral by the public agency, a court or a hearing officer may require the agency to reimburse the parents for the cost of that enrollment if the court or hearing officer finds that the agency had not made a free appropriate public education available to the child in a timely manner prior to that enrollment.

(iii) LIMITATION ON REIMBURSEMENT- The cost of reimbursement described in clause (ii) may be reduced or denied—

(I) if—

(aa) at the most recent IEP meeting that the parents attended prior to removal of the child from the public school, the parents did not inform the IEP Team that they were rejecting the placement proposed by the public agency to provide a free appropriate public education to their child, including stating their concerns and their intent to enroll their child in a private school at public expense; or

(bb) 10 business days (including any holidays that occur on a business day) prior to the removal of the child from the public school, the parents did not give written notice to the public agency of the information described in item (aa);

(II) if, prior to the parents' removal of the child from the public school, the public agency informed the parents, through the notice requirements described in section 615(b)(3), of its intent to evaluate the child (including a statement of the purpose of the evaluation that was appropriate and reasonable), but the parents did not make the child available for such evaluation; or

(III) upon a judicial finding of unreasonableness with respect to actions taken by the parents.

(iv) EXCEPTION- Notwithstanding the notice requirement in clause (iii)(I), the cost of reimbursement—

(I) shall not be reduced or denied for failure to provide such notice if—

(aa) the school prevented the parent from providing such notice;

(bb) the parents had not received notice, pursuant to section 615, of the notice requirement in clause (iii)(I); or

(cc) compliance with clause (iii)(I) would likely result in physical harm to the child; and

(II) may, in the discretion of a court or a hearing officer, not be reduced or denied for failure to provide such notice if—

(aa) the parent is illiterate or cannot write in English; or

(bb) compliance with clause (iii)(I) would likely result in serious emotional harm to the child.

(11) STATE EDUCATIONAL AGENCY RESPONSIBLE FOR GENERAL SUPERVISION-

(A) IN GENERAL- The State educational agency is responsible for ensuring that—

(i) the requirements of this part are met;

(ii) all educational programs for children with disabilities in the State, including all such programs administered by any other State agency or local agency—

(I) are under the general supervision of individuals in the State who are responsible for educational programs for children with disabilities; and

(II) meet the educational standards of the State educational agency; and

(iii) in carrying out this part with respect to homeless children, the requirements of subtitle B of title VII of the McKinney-Vento Homeless Assistance Act (42 U.S.C. 11431 et seq.) are met.

(B) LIMITATION- Subparagraph (A) shall not limit the responsibility of agencies in the State other than the State educational agency to provide, or pay for some or all of the costs of, a free appropriate public education for any child with a disability in the State.

(C) EXCEPTION- Notwithstanding subparagraphs (A) and (B), the Governor (or another individual pursuant to State law), consistent with State law, may assign to any public agency in the State the responsibility of ensuring that the requirements of this part are met with respect to children with disabilities who are convicted as adults under State law and incarcerated in adult prisons.

(12) OBLIGATIONS RELATED TO AND METHODS OF ENSURING SERVICES-

(A) ESTABLISHING RESPONSIBILITY FOR SERVICES- The Chief Executive Officer of a State or designee of the officer shall ensure that an interagency agreement or other mechanism for interagency coordination is in effect between each public agency described in subparagraph (B) and the State educational agency, in order to ensure that all services described in subparagraph (B)(i) that are needed to ensure a free appropriate public education are provided, including the provision of such services during the pendency of any dispute under clause (iii). Such agreement or mechanism shall include the following:

(i) AGENCY FINANCIAL RESPONSIBILITY- An identification of, or a method for defining, the financial responsibility of each agency for providing services described in subparagraph (B)(i) to ensure a free appropriate public education to children with disabilities, provided that the financial responsibility of each public agency described in subparagraph (B), including the State medicaid agency and other public insurers of children with disabilities, shall precede the financial responsibility of the local educational agency (or the State agency responsible for developing the child's IEP).

(ii) CONDITIONS AND TERMS OF REIMBURSEMENT- The conditions, terms, and procedures under which a local educational agency shall be reimbursed by other agencies.

(iii) INTERAGENCY DISPUTES- Procedures for resolving interagency disputes (including procedures under which local educational agencies may initiate proceedings) under the agreement or other mechanism to secure reimbursement from other agencies or otherwise implement the provisions of the agreement or mechanism.

(iv) COORDINATION OF SERVICES PROCEDURES- Policies and procedures for agencies to determine and identify the interagency coordination responsibilities of each agency to promote the coordination and timely and appropriate delivery of services described in subparagraph (B)(i).

(B) OBLIGATION OF PUBLIC AGENCY-

(i) IN GENERAL- If any public agency other than an educational agency is otherwise obligated under Federal or State law, or assigned responsibility under State policy pursuant to subparagraph (A), to provide or pay for any services that are also considered special education or related services (such as, but not limited to, services described in section 602(1) relating to assistive technology devices, 602(2) relating to assistive technology services, 602(26) relating to related services, 602(33) relating to supplementary aids and services, and 602(34) relating to transition services) that are necessary for ensuring a free appropriate public education to children with disabilities within the State, such public agency shall fulfill that obligation or responsibility, either directly or through contract or other arrangement pursuant to subparagraph (A) or an agreement pursuant to subparagraph (C).

(ii) REIMBURSEMENT FOR SERVICES BY PUBLIC AGENCY- If a public agency other than an educational agency fails to provide or pay for the special education and related services described in clause (i), the local educational agency (or State agency responsible for developing the child's IEP) shall provide or pay for such services to the child. Such local educational agency or State agency is authorized to claim reimbursement for the services from the public agency that failed to provide or pay for such services and such public agency shall reimburse the local educational agency or State agency pursuant to the terms of the interagency agreement or other mechanism described in subparagraph (A)(i) according to the procedures established in such agreement pursuant to subparagraph (A)(ii).

(C) SPECIAL RULE- The requirements of subparagraph (A) may be met through—

(i) State statute or regulation;

(ii) signed agreements between respective

agency officials that clearly identify the responsibilities of each agency relating to the provision of services; or

(iii) other appropriate written methods as determined by the Chief Executive Officer of the State or designee of the officer and approved by the Secretary.

(13) PROCEDURAL REQUIREMENTS RELATING TO LOCAL EDUCATIONAL AGENCY ELIGIBILITY- The State educational agency will not make a final determination that a local educational agency is not eligible for assistance under this part without first affording that agency reasonable notice and an opportunity for a hearing.

(14) PERSONNEL QUALIFICATIONS-

(A) IN GENERAL- The State educational agency has established and maintains qualifications to ensure that personnel necessary to carry out this part are appropriately and adequately prepared and trained, including that those personnel have the content knowledge and skills to serve children with disabilities.

(B) RELATED SERVICES PERSONNEL AND PARAPROFESSIONALS- The qualifications under subparagraph (A) include qualifications for related services personnel and paraprofessionals that—

(i) are consistent with any State-approved or State-recognized certification, licensing, registration, or other comparable requirements that apply to the professional discipline in which those personnel are providing special education or related services;

(ii) ensure that related services personnel who deliver services in their discipline or profession meet the requirements of clause (i) and have not had certification or licensure requirements waived on an emergency, temporary, or provisional basis; and

(iii) allow paraprofessionals and assistants who are appropriately trained and supervised, in accordance with State law, regulation, or written policy, in meeting the requirements of this part to be used to assist in the provision of special education and related services under this part to children with disabilities.

(C) QUALIFICATIONS FOR SPECIAL EDUCATION TEACHERS- The qualifications described in subparagraph (A) shall ensure that each person employed as a special education teacher in the State who teaches elementary school, middle school, or secondary school is highly qualified by the deadline established in section 1119(a)(2) of the Elementary and Secondary Education Act of 1965.

(D) POLICY- In implementing this section,

a State shall adopt a policy that includes a requirement that local educational agencies in the State take measurable steps to recruit, hire, train, and retain highly qualified personnel to provide special education and related services under this part to children with disabilities.

(E) RULE OF CONSTRUCTION- Notwithstanding any other individual right of action that a parent or student may maintain under this part, nothing in this paragraph shall be construed to create a right of action on behalf of an individual student for the failure of a particular State educational agency or local educational agency staff person to be highly qualified, or to prevent a parent from filing a complaint about staff qualifications with the State educational agency as provided for under this part.

(15) PERFORMANCE GOALS AND INDICATORS- The State—

(A) has established goals for the performance of children with disabilities in the State that—

(i) promote the purposes of this title, as stated in section 601(d);

(ii) are the same as the State's definition of adequate yearly progress, including the State's objectives for progress by children with disabilities, under section 1111(b)(2)(C) of the Elementary and Secondary Education Act of 1965;

(iii) address graduation rates and dropout rates, as well as such other factors as the State may determine; and

(iv) are consistent, to the extent appropriate, with any other goals and standards for children established by the State;

(B) has established performance indicators the State will use to assess progress toward achieving the goals described in subparagraph (A), including measurable annual objectives for progress by children with disabilities under section 1111(b)(2)(C)(v)(II)(cc) of the Elementary and Secondary Education Act of 1965; and

(C) will annually report to the Secretary and the public on the progress of the State, and of children with disabilities in the State, toward meeting the goals established under subparagraph (A), which may include elements of the reports required under section 1111(h) of the Elementary and Secondary Education Act of 1965.

(16) PARTICIPATION IN ASSESSMENTS-

(A) IN GENERAL- All children with disabilities are included in all general State and districtwide assessment programs, including assessments described under section 1111 of the Elementary and Secondary Education Act of 1965, with appropriate accommodations and alternate assessments where necessary and as indicated in their respective individualized education programs.

(B) ACCOMMODATION GUIDELINES- The State (or, in the case of a districtwide assessment, the local educational agency) has developed guidelines for the provision of appropriate accommodations.

(C) ALTERNATE ASSESSMENTS-

(i) IN GENERAL- The State (or, in the case of a districtwide assessment, the local educational agency) has developed and implemented guidelines for the participation of children with disabilities in alternate assessments for those children who cannot participate in regular assessments under subparagraph (A) with accommodations as indicated in their respective individualized education programs.

(ii) REQUIREMENTS FOR ALTERNATE ASSESSMENTS- The guidelines under clause (i) shall provide for alternate assessments that—

(I) are aligned with the State's challenging academic content standards and challenging student academic achievement standards; and

(II) if the State has adopted alternate academic achievement standards permitted under the regulations promulgated to carry out section 1111(b)(1) of the Elementary and Secondary Education Act of 1965, measure the achievement of children with disabilities against those standards.

(iii) CONDUCT OF ALTERNATE ASSESSMENTS- The State conducts the alternate assessments described in this subparagraph.

(D) REPORTS- The State educational agency (or, in the case of a districtwide assessment, the local educational agency) makes available to the public, and reports to the public with the same frequency and in the same detail as it reports on the assessment of nondisabled children, the following:

(i) The number of children with disabilities participating in regular assessments, and the number of those children who were provided accommodations in order to participate in those assessments.

(ii) The number of children with disabilities participating in alternate assessments described in subparagraph (C)(ii)(I).

(iii) The number of children with disabilities participating in alternate assessments described in subparagraph (C)(ii)(II).

(iv) The performance of children with disabilities on regular assessments and on alternate assessments (if the number of children with disabilities participating in those assessments is sufficient to yield statistically reliable information and reporting that information will not reveal personally identifiable information about an individual student), compared with the achievement of all children, including children with disabilities, on those assessments.

(E) UNIVERSAL DESIGN- The State educational agency (or, in the case of a districtwide assessment, the local educational agency) shall, to the extent feasible, use universal design principles in developing and administering any assessments under this paragraph.

(17) SUPPLEMENTATION OF STATE, LOCAL, AND OTHER FEDERAL FUNDS-

(A) EXPENDITURES- Funds paid to a State under this part will be expended in accordance with all the provisions of this part.

(B) PROHIBITION AGAINST COMMINGLING- Funds paid to a State under this part will not be commingled with State funds.

(C) PROHIBITION AGAINST SUPPLANTATION AND CONDITIONS FOR WAIVER BY SECRETARY- Except as provided in section 613, funds paid to a State under this part will be used to supplement the level of Federal, State, and local funds (including funds that are not under the direct control of State or local educational agencies) expended for special education and related services provided to children with disabilities under this part and in no case to supplant such Federal, State, and local funds, except that, where the State provides clear and convincing evidence that all children with disabilities have available to them a free appropriate public education, the Secretary may waive, in whole or in part, the requirements of this subparagraph if the Secretary concurs with the evidence provided by the State.

(18) MAINTENANCE OF STATE FINANCIAL SUPPORT-

(A) IN GENERAL- The State does not reduce the amount of State financial support for special education and related services for children with disabilities, or otherwise made available because of the excess costs of educating those children, below the amount of that support for the preceding fiscal year.

(B) REDUCTION OF FUNDS FOR FAILURE TO MAINTAIN SUPPORT- The Secretary shall reduce the allocation of funds under section 611 for any fiscal year following the fiscal year in which the State fails to comply with the requirement of subparagraph (A) by the same amount by which the State fails to meet the requirement.

(C) WAIVERS FOR EXCEPTIONAL OR UNCONTROLLABLE CIRCUMSTANCES- The Secretary may waive the requirement of subparagraph (A) for a State, for 1 fiscal year at a time, if the Secretary determines that—

(i) granting a waiver would be equitable due to exceptional or uncontrollable circumstances such as a natural disaster or a precipitous and unforeseen decline in the financial resources of the State; or

(ii) the State meets the standard in paragraph (17)(C) for a waiver of the requirement to supplement, and not to supplant, funds received under this part.

(D) SUBSEQUENT YEARS- If, for any year, a State fails to meet the requirement of subparagraph (A), including any year for which the State is granted a waiver under subparagraph (C), the financial support required of the State in future years under subparagraph (A) shall be the amount that would have been required in the absence of that failure and not the reduced level of the State's support.

(19) PUBLIC PARTICIPATION- Prior to the adoption of any policies and procedures needed to comply with this section (including any amendments to such policies and procedures), the State ensures that there are public hearings, adequate notice of the hearings, and an opportunity for comment available to the general public, including individuals with disabilities and parents of children with disabilities.

(20) RULE OF CONSTRUCTION- In complying with paragraphs (17) and (18), a State may not use funds paid to it under this part to satisfy State-law mandated funding obligations to local educational agencies, including funding based on student attendance or enrollment, or inflation.

(21) STATE ADVISORY PANEL-

(A) IN GENERAL- The State has established and maintains an advisory panel for the purpose of providing policy guidance with respect to special education and related services for children with disabilities in the State.

(B) MEMBERSHIP- Such advisory panel shall consist of members appointed by the Governor, or any other official authorized under State law to make such appointments, be representative of the State population, and be composed of individuals involved in, or concerned with, the education of children with disabilities, including—

(i) parents of children with disabilities (ages birth through 26);

(ii) individuals with disabilities;

(iii) teachers;

(iv) representatives of institutions of higher education that prepare special education and related services personnel;

(v) State and local education officials, including officials who carry out activities under subtitle B of title VII of the McKinney-Vento Homeless Assistance Act (42 U.S.C. 11431 et seq.);

(vi) administrators of programs for children with disabilities;

(vii) representatives of other State agencies involved in the financing or delivery of related services to children with disabilities;

(viii) representatives of private schools and public charter schools;

(ix) not less than 1 representative of a vocational, community, or business organization concerned with the provision of transition services to children with disabilities;

(x) a representative from the State child welfare agency responsible for foster care; and

(xi) representatives from the State juvenile and adult corrections agencies.

(C) SPECIAL RULE- A majority of the members of the panel shall be individuals with disabilities or parents of children with disabilities (ages birth through 26).

(D) DUTIES- The advisory panel shall—

(i) advise the State educational agency of unmet needs within the State in the education of children with disabilities;

(ii) comment publicly on any rules or regulations proposed by the State regarding the education of children with disabilities;

(iii) advise the State educational agency in developing evaluations and reporting on data to the Secretary under section 618;

(iv) advise the State educational agency in developing corrective action plans to address findings identified in Federal monitoring reports under this part; and

(v) advise the State educational agency in developing and implementing policies relating to the coordination of services for children with disabilities.

(22) SUSPENSION AND EXPULSION RATES-

(A) IN GENERAL- The State educational agency examines data, including data disaggregated by race and ethnicity, to determine if significant discrepancies are occurring in the rate of long-term suspensions and expulsions of children with disabilities—

(i) among local educational agencies in the

State; or

(ii) compared to such rates for nondisabled children within such agencies.

(B) REVIEW AND REVISION OF POLICIES- If such discrepancies are occurring, the State educational agency reviews and, if appropriate, revises (or requires the affected State or local educational agency to revise) its policies, procedures, and practices relating to the development and implementation of IEPs, the use of positive behavioral interventions and supports, and procedural safeguards, to ensure that such policies, procedures, and practices comply with this title.

(23) ACCESS TO INSTRUCTIONAL MATERIALS-

(A) IN GENERAL- The State adopts the National Instructional Materials Accessibility Standard for the purposes of providing instructional materials to blind persons or other persons with print disabilities, in a timely manner after the publication of the National Instructional Materials Accessibility Standard in the Federal Register.

(B) RIGHTS OF STATE EDUCATIONAL AGENCY- Nothing in this paragraph shall be construed to require any State educational agency to coordinate with the National Instructional Materials Access Center. If a State educational agency chooses not to coordinate with the National Instructional Materials Access Center, such agency shall provide an assurance to the Secretary that the agency will provide instructional materials to blind persons or other persons with print disabilities in a timely manner.

(C) PREPARATION AND DELIVERY OF FILES- If a State educational agency chooses to coordinate with the National Instructional Materials Access Center, not later than 2 years after the date of enactment of the Individuals with Disabilities Education Improvement Act of 2004, the agency, as part of any print instructional materials adoption process, procurement contract, or other practice or instrument used for purchase of print instructional materials, shall enter into a written contract with the publisher of the print instructional materials to—

(i) require the publisher to prepare and, on or before delivery of the print instructional materials, provide to the National Instructional Materials Access Center electronic files containing the contents of the print instructional materials using the National Instructional Materials Accessibility Standard; or

(ii) purchase instructional materials from the publisher that are produced in, or may be rendered in, specialized formats.

(D) ASSISTIVE TECHNOLOGY- In carrying out this paragraph, the State educational agency, to the maximum extent possible, shall work collaboratively with the State agency responsible for assistive technology programs.

(E) DEFINITIONS- In this paragraph:

(i) NATIONAL INSTRUCTIONAL MATERIALS ACCESS CENTER- The term 'National Instructional Materials Access Center' means the center established pursuant to section 674(e).

(ii) NATIONAL INSTRUCTIONAL MATERIALS ACCESSIBILITY STANDARD- The term National Instructional Materials Accessibility Standard' has the meaning given the term in section 674(e)(3)(A).

(iii) SPECIALIZED FORMATS- The term 'specialized formats' has the meaning given the term in section 674(e)(3)(D).

(24) OVERIDENTIFICATION AND DISPROPORTIONALITY- The State has in effect, consistent with the purposes of this title and with section 618(d), policies and procedures designed to prevent the inappropriate overidentification or disproportionate representation by race and ethnicity of children as children with disabilities, including children with disabilities with a particular impairment described in section 602.

(25) PROHIBITION ON MANDATORY MEDICATION-

(A) IN GENERAL- The State educational agency shall prohibit State and local educational agency personnel from requiring a child to obtain a prescription for a substance covered by the Controlled Substances Act (21 U.S.C. 801 et seq.) as a condition of attending school, receiving an evaluation under subsection (a) or (c) of section 614, or receiving services under this title.

(B) RULE OF CONSTRUCTION- Nothing in subparagraph (A) shall be construed to create a Federal prohibition against teachers and other school personnel consulting or sharing classroom-based observations with parents or guardians regarding a student's academic and functional performance, or behavior in the classroom or school, or regarding the need for evaluation for special education or related services under paragraph (3).

(b) STATE EDUCATIONAL AGENCY AS

PROVIDER OF FREE APPROPRIATE PUBLIC EDUCATION OR DIRECT SERVICES- If the State educational agency provides free appropriate public education to children with disabilities, or provides direct services to such children, such agency—

(1) shall comply with any additional requirements of section 613(a), as if such agency were a local educational agency; and

(2) may use amounts that are otherwise available to such agency under this part to serve those children without regard to section 613(a)(2)(A)(i) (relating to excess costs).

(c) EXCEPTION FOR PRIOR STATE PLANS-

(1) IN GENERAL- If a State has on file with the Secretary policies and procedures that demonstrate that such State meets any requirement of subsection (a), including any policies and procedures filed under this part as in effect before the effective date of the Individuals with Disabilities Education Improvement Act of 2004, the Secretary shall consider such State to have met such requirement for purposes of receiving a grant under this part.

(2) MODIFICATIONS MADE BY STATE- Subject to paragraph (3), an application submitted by a State in accordance with this section shall remain in effect until the State submits to the Secretary such modifications as the State determines necessary. This section shall apply to a modification to an application to the same extent and in the same manner as this section applies to the original plan.

(3) MODIFICATIONS REQUIRED BY THE SECRETARY- If, after the effective date of the Individuals with Disabilities Education Improvement Act of 2004, the provisions of this title are amended (or the regulations developed to carry out this title are amended), there is a new interpretation of this title by a Federal court or a State's highest court, or there is an official finding of noncompliance with Federal law or regulations, then the Secretary may require a State to modify its application only to the extent necessary to ensure the State's compliance with this part.

(d) APPROVAL BY THE SECRETARY-

(1) IN GENERAL- If the Secretary determines that a State is eligible to receive a grant under this part, the Secretary shall notify the State of that determination.

(2) NOTICE AND HEARING- The Secretary shall not make a final determination that a State is not eligible to receive a grant under this part until after providing the State—

(A) with reasonable notice; and

(B) with an opportunity for a hearing.

(e) ASSISTANCE UNDER OTHER FEDERAL PROGRAMS- Nothing in this title permits a State to reduce medical and other assistance available, or to alter eligibility, under titles V and XIX of the Social Security Act with respect to the provision of a free appropriate public education for children with disabilities in the State.

(f) BY-PASS FOR CHILDREN IN PRIVATE SCHOOLS-(1) IN GENERAL- If, on the date of enactment of the Education of the Handicapped Act Amendments of 1983, a State educational agency was prohibited by law from providing for the equitable participation in special programs of children with disabilities enrolled in private elementary schools and secondary schools as required by subsection (a)(10)(A), or if the Secretary determines that a State educational agency, local educational agency, or other entity has substantially failed or is unwilling to provide for such equitable participation, then the Secretary shall, notwithstanding such provision of law, arrange for the provision of services to such children through arrangements that shall be subject to the requirements of such subsection.

(2) PAYMENTS-

(A) DETERMINATION OF AMOUNTS- If the Secretary arranges for services pursuant to this subsection, the Secretary, after consultation with the appropriate public and private school officials, shall pay to the provider of such services for a fiscal year an amount per child that does not exceed the amount determined by dividing—

(i) the total amount received by the State under this part for such fiscal year; by

(ii) the number of children with disabilities served in the prior year, as reported to the Secretary by the State under section 618.

(B) WITHHOLDING OF CERTAIN AMOUNTS- Pending final resolution of any investigation or complaint that may result in a determination under this subsection, the Secretary may withhold from the allocation of the affected State educational agency the amount the Secretary estimates will be necessary to pay the cost of services described in subparagraph (A).

(C) PERIOD OF PAYMENTS- The period under which payments are made under subparagraph (A) shall continue until the Secretary determines that there will no longer be any failure or inability on the part of the State educational agency to meet the requirements of subsection (a)(10)(A).

(3) NOTICE AND HEARING-

(A) IN GENERAL- The Secretary shall not take any final action under this subsection until the State educational agency affected by such action has had an opportunity, for not less than 45 days after receiving written notice thereof, to submit written objections and to appear before the Secretary or the Secretary's designee to show cause why such action should not be taken.

(B) REVIEW OF ACTION- If a State educational agency is dissatisfied with the Secretary's final action after a proceeding under subparagraph (A), such agency may, not later than 60 days after notice of such action, file with the United States court of appeals for the circuit in which such State is located a petition for review of that action. A copy of the petition shall be forthwith transmitted by the clerk of the court to the Secretary. The Secretary thereupon shall file in the court the record of the proceedings on which the Secretary based the Secretary's action, as provided in section 2112 of title 28, United States Code.

(C) REVIEW OF FINDINGS OF FACT- The findings of fact by the Secretary, if supported by substantial evidence, shall be conclusive, but the court, for good cause shown, may remand the case to the Secretary to take further evidence, and the Secretary may thereupon make new or modified findings of fact and may modify the Secretary's previous action, and shall file in the court the record of the further proceedings. Such new or modified findings of fact shall likewise be conclusive if supported by substantial evidence.

(D) JURISDICTION OF COURT OF APPEALS; REVIEW BY UNITED STATES SUPREME COURT- Upon the filing of a petition under subparagraph (B), the United States court of appeals shall have jurisdiction to affirm the action of the Secretary or to set it aside, in whole or in part. The judgment of the court shall be subject to review by the Supreme Court of the United States upon certiorari or certification as provided in section 1254 of title 28, United States Code.

SEC. 613. LOCAL EDUCATIONAL AGENCY ELIGIBILITY.

(a) IN GENERAL- A local educational agency is eligible for assistance under this part for a fiscal year if such agency submits a plan that provides assurances to the State educational agency that the local educational agency meets each of the following conditions:

(1) CONSISTENCY WITH STATE POLICIES- The local educational agency, in providing for the education of children with disabilities within its jurisdiction, has in effect policies, procedures, and programs that are consistent with the State policies and procedures established under section 612.

(2) USE OF AMOUNTS-

(A) IN GENERAL- Amounts provided to the local educational agency under this part shall be expended in accordance with the applicable provisions of this part and—

(i) shall be used only to pay the excess costs of providing special education and related services to children with disabilities;

(ii) shall be used to supplement State, local, and other Federal funds and not to supplant such funds; and

(iii) shall not be used, except as provided in subparagraphs (B) and (C), to reduce the level of expenditures for the education of children with disabilities made by the local educational agency from local funds below the level of those expenditures for the preceding fiscal year.

(B) EXCEPTION- Notwithstanding the restriction in subparagraph (A)(iii), a local educational agency may reduce the level of expenditures where such reduction is attributable to—

(i) the voluntary departure, by retirement or otherwise, or departure for just cause, of special education personnel;

(ii) a decrease in the enrollment of children with disabilities;

(iii) the termination of the obligation of the agency, consistent with this part, to provide a program of special education to a particular child with a disability that is an exceptionally costly program, as determined by the State educational agency, because the child—

(I) has left the jurisdiction of the agency;

(II) has reached the age at which the obligation of the agency to provide a free appropriate public education to the child has terminated; or

(III) no longer needs such program of special education; or

(iv) the termination of costly expenditures for long-term purchases, such as the acquisition of equipment or the construction of school facilities.

(C) ADJUSTMENT TO LOCAL FISCAL EFFORT IN CERTAIN FISCAL YEARS-

(i) AMOUNTS IN EXCESS- Notwithstanding clauses (ii) and (iii) of subparagraph (A), for any fiscal year for which the allocation received by a local educational agency under section 611(f) exceeds the amount the local educational agency received for the previous fiscal year, the local educational agency may reduce the level of expenditures otherwise required by subparagraph (A)(iii) by not more than 50 percent of the amount of such excess.

(ii) USE OF AMOUNTS TO CARRY OUT ACTIVITIES UNDER ESEA- If a local educational agency exercises the authority under clause (i), the agency shall use an amount of local funds equal to the reduction in expenditures under clause (i) to carry out activities authorized under the Elementary and Secondary Education Act of 1965.

(iii) STATE PROHIBITION- Notwithstanding clause (i), if a State educational agency determines that a local educational agency is unable to establish and maintain programs of free appropriate public education that meet the requirements of subsection (a) or the State educational agency has taken action against the local educational agency under section 616, the State educational agency shall prohibit the local educational agency from reducing the level of expenditures under clause (i) for that fiscal year.

(iv) SPECIAL RULE- The amount of funds expended by a local educational agency under subsection (f) shall count toward the maximum amount of expenditures such local educational agency may reduce under clause (i).

(D) SCHOOLWIDE PROGRAMS UNDER TITLE I OF THE ESEA- Notwithstanding subparagraph (A) or any other provision of this part, a local educational agency may use funds received under this part for any fiscal year to carry out a schoolwide program under section 1114 of the Elementary and Secondary Education Act of 1965, except that the amount so used in any such program shall not exceed—

(i) the number of children with disabilities participating in the schoolwide program; multiplied by

(ii)(I) the amount received by the local educational agency under this part for that fiscal year; divided by

(II) the number of children with disabilities in the jurisdiction of that agency.

(3) PERSONNEL DEVELOPMENT- The local educational agency shall ensure that all personnel necessary to carry out this part are appropriately and adequately prepared, subject to the requirements of section 612(a)(14) and section 2122 of the Elementary and Secondary Education Act of 1965.

(4) PERMISSIVE USE OF FUNDS-

(A) USES- Notwithstanding paragraph (2)(A) or section 612(a)(17)(B) (relating to commingled funds), funds provided to the local educational agency under this part may be used for the following activities:

(i) SERVICES AND AIDS THAT ALSO BENEFIT NONDISABLED CHILDREN- For the costs of special education and related services, and supplementary aids and services, provided in a regular class or other education-related setting to a child with a disability in accordance with the individualized education program of the child, even if 1 or more nondisabled children benefit from such services.

(ii) EARLY INTERVENING SERVICES- To develop and implement coordinated, early intervening educational services in accordance with subsection (f).

(iii) HIGH COST EDUCATION AND RELATED SERVICES- To establish and implement cost or risk sharing funds, consortia, or cooperatives for the local educational agency itself, or for local educational agencies working in a consortium of which the local educational agency is a part, to pay for high cost special education and related services.

(B) ADMINISTRATIVE CASE MANAGEMENT- A local educational agency may use funds received under this part to purchase appropriate technology for recordkeeping, data collection, and related case management activities of teachers and related services personnel providing services described in the individualized education program of children with disabilities, that is needed for the implementation of such case management activities.

(5) TREATMENT OF CHARTER SCHOOLS AND THEIR STUDENTS- In carrying out this part with respect to charter schools that are public schools of the local educational agency, the local educational agency—

(A) serves children with disabilities attending those charter schools in the same manner as the local educational agency serves children with disabilities in its other schools, including providing supplementary and related services on site at the charter school to the same extent to which the local educational agency has a policy or practice of providing such services on the site to its other public schools; and

(B) provides funds under this part to those charter schools—

(i) on the same basis as the local educational agency provides funds to the local educational agency's other public schools, including proportional distribution based on relative enrollment of children with disabilities; and

(ii) at the same time as the agency

distributes other Federal funds to the agency's other public schools, consistent with the State's charter school law.

(6) PURCHASE OF INSTRUCTIONAL MATERIALS-

(A) IN GENERAL- Not later than 2 years after the date of enactment of the Individuals with Disabilities Education Improvement Act of 2004, a local educational agency that chooses to coordinate with the National Instructional Materials Access Center, when purchasing print instructional materials, shall acquire the print instructional materials in the same manner and subject to the same conditions as a State educational agency acquires print instructional materials under section 612(a)(23).

(B) RIGHTS OF LOCAL EDUCATIONAL AGENCY- Nothing in this paragraph shall be construed to require a local educational agency to coordinate with the National Instructional Materials Access Center. If a local educational agency chooses not to coordinate with the National Instructional Materials Access Center, the local educational agency shall provide an assurance to the State educational agency that the local educational agency will provide instructional materials to blind persons or other persons with print disabilities in a timely manner.

(7) INFORMATION FOR STATE EDUCATIONAL AGENCY- The local educational agency shall provide the State educational agency with information necessary to enable the State educational agency to carry out its duties under this part, including, with respect to paragraphs (15) and (16) of section 612(a), information relating to the performance of children with disabilities participating in programs carried out under this part.

(8) PUBLIC INFORMATION- The local educational agency shall make available to parents of children with disabilities and to the general public all documents relating to the eligibility of such agency under this part.

(9) RECORDS REGARDING MIGRATORY CHILDREN WITH DISABILITIES- The local educational agency shall cooperate in the Secretary's efforts under section 1308 of the Elementary and Secondary Education Act of 1965 to ensure the linkage of records pertaining to migratory children with a disability for the purpose of electronically exchanging, among the States, health and educational information regarding such children.

(b) EXCEPTION FOR PRIOR LOCAL PLANS-

(1) IN GENERAL- If a local educational agency or State agency has on file with the State educational agency policies and procedures that demonstrate that such local educational agency, or such State agency, as the case may be, meets any requirement of subsection (a), including any policies and procedures filed under this part as in effect before the effective date of the Individuals with Disabilities Education Improvement Act of 2004, the State educational agency shall consider such local educational agency or State agency, as the case may be, to have met such requirement for purposes of receiving assistance under this part.

(2) MODIFICATION MADE BY LOCAL EDUCATIONAL AGENCY- Subject to paragraph (3), an application submitted by a local educational agency in accordance with this section shall remain in effect until the local educational agency submits to the State educational agency such modifications as the local educational agency determines necessary.

(3) MODIFICATIONS REQUIRED BY STATE EDUCATIONAL AGENCY- If, after the effective date of the Individuals with Disabilities Education Improvement Act of 2004, the provisions of this title are amended (or the regulations developed to carry out this title are amended), there is a new interpretation of this title by Federal or State courts, or there is an official finding of noncompliance with Federal or State law or regulations, then the State educational agency may require a local educational agency to modify its application only to the extent necessary to ensure the local educational agency's compliance with this part or State law.

(c) NOTIFICATION OF LOCAL EDUCATIONAL AGENCY OR STATE AGENCY IN CASE OF INELIGIBILITY- If the State educational agency determines that a local educational agency or State agency is not eligible under this section, then the State educational agency shall notify the local educational agency or State agency, as the case may be, of that determination and shall provide such local educational agency or State agency with reasonable notice and an opportunity for a hearing.

(d) LOCAL EDUCATIONAL AGENCY COMPLIANCE-

(1) IN GENERAL- If the State educational agency, after reasonable notice and an opportunity for a hearing, finds that a local educational agency or State agency that has been determined to be eligible under this section is failing to comply with any

requirement described in subsection (a), the State educational agency shall reduce or shall not provide any further payments to the local educational agency or State agency until the State educational agency is satisfied that the local educational agency or State agency, as the case may be, is complying with that requirement.

(2) ADDITIONAL REQUIREMENT- Any State agency or local educational agency in receipt of a notice described in paragraph (1) shall, by means of public notice, take such measures as may be necessary to bring the pendency of an action pursuant to this subsection to the attention of the public within the jurisdiction of such agency.

(3) CONSIDERATION- In carrying out its responsibilities under paragraph (1), the State educational agency shall consider any decision made in a hearing held under section 615 that is adverse to the local educational agency or State agency involved in that decision.

(e) JOINT ESTABLISHMENT OF ELIGIBILITY-

(1) JOINT ESTABLISHMENT-

(A) IN GENERAL- A State educational agency may require a local educational agency to establish its eligibility jointly with another local educational agency if the State educational agency determines that the local educational agency will be ineligible under this section because the local educational agency will not be able to establish and maintain programs of sufficient size and scope to effectively meet the needs of children with disabilities.

(B) CHARTER SCHOOL EXCEPTION- A State educational agency may not require a charter school that is a local educational agency to jointly establish its eligibility under subparagraph (A) unless the charter school is explicitly permitted to do so under the State's charter school law.

(2) AMOUNT OF PAYMENTS- If a State educational agency requires the joint establishment of eligibility under paragraph (1), the total amount of funds made available to the affected local educational agencies shall be equal to the sum of the payments that each such local educational agency would have received under section 611(f) if such agencies were eligible for such payments.

(3) REQUIREMENTS- Local educational agencies that establish joint eligibility under this subsection shall—

(A) adopt policies and procedures that are consistent with the State's policies and procedures under section 612(a); and

(B) be jointly responsible for implementing programs that receive assistance under this part.

(4) REQUIREMENTS FOR EDUCATIONAL SERVICE AGENCIES-

(A) IN GENERAL- If an educational service agency is required by State law to carry out programs under this part, the joint responsibilities given to local educational agencies under this subsection shall—

(i) not apply to the administration and disbursement of any payments received by that educational service agency; and

(ii) be carried out only by that educational service agency.

(B) ADDITIONAL REQUIREMENT- Notwithstanding any other provision of this subsection, an educational service agency shall provide for the education of children with disabilities in the least restrictive environment, as required by section 612(a)(5).

(f) EARLY INTERVENING SERVICES-

(1) IN GENERAL- A local educational agency may not use more than 15 percent of the amount such agency receives under this part for any fiscal year, less any amount reduced by the agency pursuant to subsection (a)(2)(C), if any, in combination with other amounts (which may include amounts other than education funds), to develop and implement coordinated, early intervening services, which may include interagency financing structures, for students in kindergarten through grade 12 (with a particular emphasis on students in kindergarten through grade 3) who have not been identified as needing special education or related services but who need additional academic and behavioral support to succeed in a general education environment.

(2) ACTIVITIES- In implementing coordinated, early intervening services under this subsection, a local educational agency may carry out activities that include—

(A) professional development (which may be provided by entities other than local educational agencies) for teachers and other school staff to enable such personnel to deliver scientifically based academic instruction and behavioral interventions, including scientifically based literacy instruction, and, where appropriate, instruction on the use of adaptive and instructional software; and

(B) providing educational and behavioral evaluations, services, and supports, including scientifically based literacy instruction.

(3) CONSTRUCTION- Nothing in this subsection shall be construed to limit or create a right to a free appropriate public education

under this part.

(4) REPORTING- Each local educational agency that develops and maintains coordinated, early intervening services under this subsection shall annually report to the State educational agency on—

(A) the number of students served under this subsection; and

(B) the number of students served under this subsection who subsequently receive special education and related services under this title during the preceding 2-year period.

(5) COORDINATION WITH ELEMENTARY AND SECONDARY EDUCATION ACT OF 1965- Funds made available to carry out this subsection may be used to carry out coordinated, early intervening services aligned with activities funded by, and carried out under, the Elementary and Secondary Education Act of 1965 if such funds are used to supplement, and not supplant, funds made available under the Elementary and Secondary Education Act of 1965 for the activities and services assisted under this subsection.

(g) DIRECT SERVICES BY THE STATE EDUCATIONAL AGENCY-

(1) IN GENERAL- A State educational agency shall use the payments that would otherwise have been available to a local educational agency or to a State agency to provide special education and related services directly to children with disabilities residing in the area served by that local educational agency, or for whom that State agency is responsible, if the State educational agency determines that the local educational agency or State agency, as the case may be—

(A) has not provided the information needed to establish the eligibility of such local educational agency or State agency under this section;

(B) is unable to establish and maintain programs of free appropriate public education that meet the requirements of subsection (a);

(C) is unable or unwilling to be consolidated with 1 or more local educational agencies in order to establish and maintain such programs; or

(D) has 1 or more children with disabilities who can best be served by a regional or State program or service delivery system designed to meet the needs of such children.

(2) MANNER AND LOCATION OF EDUCATION AND SERVICES- The State educational agency may provide special education and related services under paragraph (1) in such manner and at such locations (including regional or State centers) as the State educational agency considers appropriate. Such education and services shall be provided in accordance with this part.

(h) STATE AGENCY ELIGIBILITY- Any State agency that desires to receive a subgrant for any fiscal year under section 611(f) shall demonstrate to the satisfaction of the State educational agency that—

(1) all children with disabilities who are participating in programs and projects funded under this part receive a free appropriate public education, and that those children and their parents are provided all the rights and procedural safeguards described in this part; and

(2) the agency meets such other conditions of this section as the Secretary determines to be appropriate.

(i) DISCIPLINARY INFORMATION- The State may require that a local educational agency include in the records of a child with a disability a statement of any current or previous disciplinary action that has been taken against the child and transmit such statement to the same extent that such disciplinary information is included in, and transmitted with, the student records of nondisabled children. The statement may include a description of any behavior engaged in by the child that required disciplinary action, a description of the disciplinary action taken, and any other information that is relevant to the safety of the child and other individuals involved with the child. If the State adopts such a policy, and the child transfers from 1 school to another, the transmission of any of the child's records shall include both the child's current individualized education program and any such statement of current or previous disciplinary action that has been taken against the child.

(j) STATE AGENCY FLEXIBILITY-

(1) ADJUSTMENT TO STATE FISCAL EFFORT IN CERTAIN FISCAL YEARS- For any fiscal year for which the allotment received by a State under section 611 exceeds the amount the State received for the previous fiscal year and if the State in school year 2003-2004 or any subsequent school year pays or reimburses all local educational agencies within the State from State revenue 100 percent of the non-Federal share of the costs of special education and related services, the State educational agency, notwithstanding paragraphs (17) and (18) of section 612(a) and section 612(b), may reduce the level of expenditures from State sources for the education of children with disabilities by not

more than 50 percent of the amount of such excess.

(2) PROHIBITION- Notwithstanding paragraph (1), if the Secretary determines that a State educational agency is unable to establish, maintain, or oversee programs of free appropriate public education that meet the requirements of this part, or that the State needs assistance, intervention, or substantial intervention under section 616(d)(2)(A), the Secretary shall prohibit the State educational agency from exercising the authority in paragraph (1).

(3) EDUCATION ACTIVITIES- If a State educational agency exercises the authority under paragraph (1), the agency shall use funds from State sources, in an amount equal to the amount of the reduction under paragraph (1), to support activities authorized under the Elementary and Secondary Education Act of 1965 or to support need based student or teacher higher education programs.

(4) REPORT- For each fiscal year for which a State educational agency exercises the authority under paragraph (1), the State educational agency shall report to the Secretary the amount of expenditures reduced pursuant to such paragraph and the activities that were funded pursuant to paragraph (3).

(5) LIMITATION- Notwithstanding paragraph (1), a State educational agency may not reduce the level of expenditures described in paragraph (1) if any local educational agency in the State would, as a result of such reduction, receive less than 100 percent of the amount necessary to ensure that all children with disabilities served by the local educational agency receive a free appropriate public education from the combination of Federal funds received under this title and State funds received from the State educational agency.

SEC. 614. EVALUATIONS, ELIGIBILITY DETERMINATIONS, INDIVIDUALIZED EDUCATION PROGRAMS, AND EDUCATIONAL PLACEMENTS.

(a) EVALUATIONS, PARENTAL CONSENT, AND REEVALUATIONS-

(1) INITIAL EVALUATIONS-

(A) IN GENERAL- A State educational agency, other State agency, or local educational agency shall conduct a full and individual initial evaluation in accordance with this paragraph and subsection (b), before the initial provision of special education and related services to a child with a disability under this part.

(B) REQUEST FOR INITIAL EVALUATION- Consistent with subparagraph (D), either a parent of a child, or a State educational agency, other State agency, or local educational agency may initiate a request for an initial evaluation to determine if the child is a child with a disability.

(C) PROCEDURES-

(i) IN GENERAL- Such initial evaluation shall consist of procedures—

(I) to determine whether a child is a child with a disability (as defined in section 602) within 60 days of receiving parental consent for the evaluation, or, if the State establishes a timeframe within which the evaluation must be conducted, within such timeframe; and

(II) to determine the educational needs of such child.

(ii) EXCEPTION- The relevant timeframe in clause (i)(I) shall not apply to a local educational agency if—

(I) a child enrolls in a school served by the local educational agency after the relevant timeframe in clause (i)(I) has begun and prior to a determination by the child's previous local educational agency as to whether the child is a child with a disability (as defined in section 602), but only if the subsequent local educational agency is making sufficient progress to ensure a prompt completion of the evaluation, and the parent and subsequent local educational agency agree to a specific time when the evaluation will be completed; or

(II) the parent of a child repeatedly fails or refuses to produce the child for the evaluation.

(D) PARENTAL CONSENT-

(i) IN GENERAL-

(I) CONSENT FOR INITIAL EVALUATION- The agency proposing to conduct an initial evaluation to determine if the child qualifies as a child with a disability as defined in section 602 shall obtain informed consent from the parent of such child before conducting the evaluation. Parental consent for evaluation shall not be construed as consent for placement for receipt of special education and related services.

(II) CONSENT FOR SERVICES- An agency that is responsible for making a free appropriate public education available to a child with a disability under this part shall seek to obtain informed consent from the parent of such child before providing special education and related services to the child.

(ii) ABSENCE OF CONSENT-

(I) FOR INITIAL EVALUATION- If the parent of such child does not provide consent for an initial evaluation under clause (i)(I), or the parent fails to respond to a request to provide the consent, the local educational agency may pursue the initial evaluation of the child by utilizing the procedures described in section 615, except to the extent inconsistent with State law relating to such parental consent.

(II) FOR SERVICES- If the parent of such child refuses to consent to services under clause (i)(II), the local educational agency shall not provide special education and related services to the child by utilizing the procedures described in section 615.

(III) EFFECT ON AGENCY OBLIGATIONS- If the parent of such child refuses to consent to the receipt of special education and related services, or the parent fails to respond to a request to provide such consent—

(aa) the local educational agency shall not be considered to be in violation of the requirement to make available a free appropriate public education to the child for the failure to provide such child with the special education and related services for which the local educational agency requests such consent; and

(bb) the local educational agency shall not be required to convene an IEP meeting or develop an IEP under this section for the child for the special education and related services for which the local educational agency requests such consent.

(iii) CONSENT FOR WARDS OF THE STATE-

(I) IN GENERAL- If the child is a ward of the State and is not residing with the child's parent, the agency shall make reasonable efforts to obtain the informed consent from the parent (as defined in section 602) of the child for an initial evaluation to determine whether the child is a child with a disability.

(II) EXCEPTION- The agency shall not be required to obtain informed consent from the parent of a child for an initial evaluation to determine whether the child is a child with a disability if—

(aa) despite reasonable efforts to do so, the agency cannot discover the whereabouts of the parent of the child;

(bb) the rights of the parents of the child have been terminated in accordance with State law; or

(cc) the rights of the parent to make educational decisions have been subrogated by a judge in accordance with State law and consent for an initial evaluation has been given by an individual appointed by the judge to represent the child.

(E) RULE OF CONSTRUCTION- The screening of a student by a teacher or specialist to determine appropriate instructional strategies for curriculum implementation shall not be considered to be an evaluation for eligibility for special education and related services.

(2) REEVALUATIONS-

(A) IN GENERAL- A local educational agency shall ensure that a reevaluation of each child with a disability is conducted in accordance with subsections (b) and (c)—

(i) if the local educational agency determines that the educational or related services needs, including improved academic achievement and functional performance, of the child warrant a reevaluation; or

(ii) if the child's parents or teacher requests a reevaluation.

(B) LIMITATION- A reevaluation conducted under subparagraph (A) shall occur—

(i) not more frequently than once a year, unless the parent and the local educational agency agree otherwise; and

(ii) at least once every 3 years, unless the parent and the local educational agency agree that a reevaluation is unnecessary.

(b) EVALUATION PROCEDURES-

(1) NOTICE- The local educational agency shall provide notice to the parents of a child with a disability, in accordance with subsections (b)(3), (b)(4), and (c) of section 615, that describes any evaluation procedures such agency proposes to conduct.

(2) CONDUCT OF EVALUATION- In conducting the evaluation, the local educational agency shall—

(A) use a variety of assessment tools and strategies to gather relevant functional, developmental, and academic information, including information provided by the parent, that may assist in determining—

(i) whether the child is a child with a disability; and

(ii) the content of the child's individualized education program, including information related to enabling the child to be involved in and progress in the general education curriculum, or, for preschool children, to participate in appropriate activities;

(B) not use any single measure or assessment as the sole criterion for determining whether a child is a child with a disability or determining an appropriate educational program for the child; and

(C) use technically sound instruments that may assess the relative contribution of cognitive and behavioral factors, in addition to physical or developmental factors.

(3) ADDITIONAL REQUIREMENTS- Each local educational agency shall ensure that—

(A) assessments and other evaluation materials used to assess a child under this section—

(i) are selected and administered so as not to be discriminatory on a racial or cultural basis;

(ii) are provided and administered in the language and form most likely to yield accurate information on what the child knows and can do academically, developmentally, and functionally, unless it is not feasible to so provide or administer;

(iii) are used for purposes for which the assessments or measures are valid and reliable;

(iv) are administered by trained and knowledgeable personnel; and

(v) are administered in accordance with any instructions provided by the producer of such assessments;

(B) the child is assessed in all areas of suspected disability;

(C) assessment tools and strategies that provide relevant information that directly assists persons in determining the educational needs of the child are provided; and

(D) assessments of children with disabilities who transfer from 1 school district to another school district in the same academic year are coordinated with such children's prior and subsequent schools, as necessary and as expeditiously as possible, to ensure prompt completion of full evaluations.

(4) DETERMINATION OF ELIGIBILITY AND EDUCATIONAL NEED- Upon completion of the administration of assessments and other evaluation measures—

(A) the determination of whether the child is a child with a disability as defined in section 602(3) and the educational needs of the child shall be made by a team of qualified professionals and the parent of the child in accordance with paragraph (5); and

(B) a copy of the evaluation report and the documentation of determination of eligibility shall be given to the parent.

(5) SPECIAL RULE FOR ELIGIBILITY DETERMINATION- In making a determination of eligibility under paragraph (4)(A), a child shall not be determined to be a child with a disability if the determinant factor for such determination is—

(A) lack of appropriate instruction in reading, including in the essential components of reading instruction (as defined in section 1208(3) of the Elementary and Secondary Education Act of 1965);

(B) lack of instruction in math; or

(C) limited English proficiency.

(6) SPECIFIC LEARNING DISABILITIES-

(A) IN GENERAL- Notwithstanding section 607(b), when determining whether a child has a specific learning disability as defined in section 602, a local educational agency shall not be required to take into consideration whether a child has a severe discrepancy between achievement and intellectual ability in oral expression, listening comprehension, written expression, basic reading skill, reading comprehension, mathematical calculation, or mathematical reasoning.

(B) ADDITIONAL AUTHORITY- In determining whether a child has a specific learning disability, a local educational agency may use a process that determines if the child responds to scientific, research-based intervention as a part of the evaluation procedures described in paragraphs (2) and (3).

(c) ADDITIONAL REQUIREMENTS FOR EVALUATION AND REEVALUATIONS-

(1) REVIEW OF EXISTING EVALUATION DATA- As part of an initial evaluation (if appropriate) and as part of any reevaluation under this section, the IEP Team and other qualified professionals, as appropriate, shall—

(A) review existing evaluation data on the child, including—

(i) evaluations and information provided by the parents of the child;

(ii) current classroom-based, local, or State assessments, and classroom-based observations; and

(iii) observations by teachers and related services providers; and

(B) on the basis of that review, and input from the child's parents, identify what additional data, if any, are needed to determine—

(i) whether the child is a child with a disability as defined in section 602(3), and the educational needs of the child, or, in case of a reevaluation of a child, whether the child continues to have such a disability and such educational needs;

(ii) the present levels of academic achievement and related developmental needs of the child;

(iii) whether the child needs special education and related services, or in the case of a reevaluation of a child, whether the child continues to need special education and related services; and

(iv) whether any additions or modifications to the special education and related services are needed to enable the child to meet the measurable annual goals set out in the individualized education program of the child and to participate, as appropriate, in the general education curriculum.

(2) SOURCE OF DATA- The local educational agency shall administer such assessments and other evaluation measures as may be needed to produce the data identified by the IEP Team under paragraph (1)(B).

(3) PARENTAL CONSENT- Each local educational agency shall obtain informed parental consent, in accordance with subsection (a)(1)(D), prior to conducting any reevaluation of a child with a disability, except that such informed parental consent need not be obtained if the local educational agency can demonstrate that it had taken reasonable measures to obtain such consent and the child's parent has failed to respond.

(4) REQUIREMENTS IF ADDITIONAL DATA ARE NOT NEEDED- If the IEP Team and other qualified professionals, as appropriate, determine that no additional data are needed to determine whether the child continues to be a child with a disability and to determine the child's educational needs, the local educational agency—

(A) shall notify the child's parents of—

(i) that determination and the reasons for the determination; and

(ii) the right of such parents to request an assessment to determine whether the child continues to be a child with a disability and to determine the child's educational needs; and

(B) shall not be required to conduct such an assessment unless requested to by the child's parents.

(5) EVALUATIONS BEFORE CHANGE IN ELIGIBILITY-

(A) IN GENERAL- Except as provided in subparagraph (B), a local educational agency shall evaluate a child with a disability in accordance with this section before determining that the child is no longer a child with a disability.

(B) EXCEPTION-

(i) IN GENERAL- The evaluation described in subparagraph (A) shall not be required before the termination of a child's eligibility under this part due to graduation from secondary school with a regular diploma, or due to exceeding the age eligibility for a free appropriate public education under State law.

(ii) SUMMARY OF PERFORMANCE-

For a child whose eligibility under this part terminates under circumstances described in clause (i), a local educational agency shall provide the child with a summary of the child's academic achievement and functional performance, which shall include recommendations on how to assist the child in meeting the child's postsecondary goals.

(d) INDIVIDUALIZED EDUCATION PROGRAMS-

(1) DEFINITIONS- In this title:

(A) INDIVIDUALIZED EDUCATION PROGRAM-

(i) IN GENERAL- The term 'individualized education program' or 'IEP' means a written statement for each child with a disability that is developed, reviewed, and revised in accordance with this section and that includes—

(I) a statement of the child's present levels of academic achievement and functional performance, including—

(aa) how the child's disability affects the child's involvement and progress in the general education curriculum;

(bb) for preschool children, as appropriate, how the disability affects the child's participation in appropriate activities; and

(cc) for children with disabilities who take alternate assessments aligned to alternate achievement standards, a description of benchmarks or short-term objectives;

(II) a statement of measurable annual goals, including academic and functional goals, designed to—

(aa) meet the child's needs that result from the child's disability to enable the child to be involved in and make progress in the general education curriculum; and

(bb) meet each of the child's other educational needs that result from the child's disability;

(III) a description of how the child's progress toward meeting the annual goals described in subclause (II) will be measured and when periodic reports on the progress the child is making toward meeting the annual goals (such as through the use of quarterly or other periodic reports, concurrent with the issuance of report cards) will be provided;

(IV) a statement of the special education and related services and supplementary aids and services, based on peer-reviewed research to the extent practicable, to be provided to the child, or on behalf of the child, and a statement of the program modifications or supports for school personnel that will be provided for the child—

(aa) to advance appropriately toward attaining the annual goals;

(bb) to be involved in and make progress in the general education curriculum in accordance with subclause (I) and to participate in extracurricular and other nonacademic activities; and

(cc) to be educated and participate with other children with disabilities and nondisabled children in the activities described in this subparagraph;

(V) an explanation of the extent, if any, to which the child will not participate with nondisabled children in the regular class and in the activities described in subclause (IV)(cc);

(VI)(aa) a statement of any individual appropriate accommodations that are necessary to measure the academic achievement and functional performance of the child on State and districtwide assessments consistent with section 612(a)(16)(A); and

(bb) if the IEP Team determines that the child shall take an alternate assessment on a particular State or districtwide assessment of student achievement, a statement of why—

(AA) the child cannot participate in the regular assessment; and

(BB) the particular alternate assessment selected is appropriate for the child;

(VII) the projected date for the beginning of the services and modifications described in subclause (IV), and the anticipated frequency, location, and duration of those services and modifications; and

(VIII) beginning not later than the first IEP to be in effect when the child is 16, and updated annually thereafter—

(aa) appropriate measurable postsecondary goals based upon age appropriate transition assessments related to training, education, employment, and, where appropriate, independent living skills;

(bb) the transition services (including courses of study) needed to assist the child in reaching those goals; and

(cc) beginning not later than 1 year before the child reaches the age of majority under State law, a statement that the child has been informed of the child's rights under this title, if any, that will transfer to the child on reaching the age of majority under section 615(m).

(ii) RULE OF CONSTRUCTION- Nothing in this section shall be construed to require—

(I) that additional information be included in a child's IEP beyond what is explicitly required in this section; and

(II) the IEP Team to include information under 1 component of a child's IEP that is already contained under another component of such IEP.

(B) INDIVIDUALIZED EDUCATION PROGRAM TEAM- The term 'individualized education program team' or 'IEP Team' means a group of individuals composed of—

(i) the parents of a child with a disability;

(ii) not less than 1 regular education teacher of such child (if the child is, or may be, participating in the regular education environment);

(iii) not less than 1 special education teacher, or where appropriate, not less than 1 special education provider of such child;

(iv) a representative of the local educational agency who—

(I) is qualified to provide, or supervise the provision of, specially designed instruction to meet the unique needs of children with disabilities;

(II) is knowledgeable about the general education curriculum; and

(III) is knowledgeable about the availability of resources of the local educational agency;

(v) an individual who can interpret the instructional implications of evaluation results, who may be a member of the team described in clauses (ii) through (vi);

(vi) at the discretion of the parent or the agency, other individuals who have knowledge or special expertise regarding the child, including related services personnel as appropriate; and

(vii) whenever appropriate, the child with a disability.

(C) IEP TEAM ATTENDANCE-

(i) ATTENDANCE NOT NECESSARY- A member of the IEP Team shall not be required to attend an IEP meeting, in whole or in part, if the parent of a child with a disability and the local educational agency agree that the attendance of such member is not necessary because the member's area of the curriculum or related services is not being modified or discussed in the meeting.

(ii) EXCUSAL- A member of the IEP Team may be excused from attending an IEP meeting, in whole or in part, when the meeting involves a modification to or discussion of the member's area of the curriculum or related services, if—

(I) the parent and the local educational agency consent to the excusal; and

(II) the member submits, in writing to the parent and the IEP Team, input into the development of the IEP prior to the meeting.

(iii) WRITTEN AGREEMENT AND CONSENT REQUIRED- A parent's agreement under clause (i) and consent under clause (ii) shall be in writing.

(D) IEP TEAM TRANSITION- In the case of a child who was previously served under part C, an invitation to the initial IEP meeting shall, at the request of the parent, be sent to the part C service coordinator or other representatives of the part C system to assist with the smooth transition of services.

(2) REQUIREMENT THAT PROGRAM BE IN EFFECT-

(A) IN GENERAL- At the beginning of each school year, each local educational agency, State educational agency, or other State agency, as the case may be, shall have in effect, for each child with a disability in the agency's jurisdiction, an individualized education program, as defined in paragraph (1)(A).

(B) PROGRAM FOR CHILD AGED 3 THROUGH 5- In the case of a child with a disability aged 3 through 5 (or, at the discretion of the State educational agency, a 2-year-old child with a disability who will turn age 3 during the school year), the IEP Team shall consider the individualized family service plan that contains the material described in section 636, and that is developed in accordance with this section, and the individualized family service plan may serve as the IEP of the child if using that plan as the IEP is—

(i) consistent with State policy; and

(ii) agreed to by the agency and the child's parents.

(C) PROGRAM FOR CHILDREN WHO TRANSFER SCHOOL DISTRICTS-

(i) IN GENERAL-

(I) TRANSFER WITHIN THE SAME STATE- In the case of a child with a disability who transfers school districts within the same academic year, who enrolls in a new school, and who had an IEP that was in effect in the same State, the local educational agency shall provide such child with a free appropriate public education, including services comparable to those described in the previously held IEP, in consultation with the parents until such time as the local educational agency adopts the previously held IEP or develops, adopts, and implements a new IEP that is consistent with Federal and State law.

(II) TRANSFER OUTSIDE STATE- In the case of a child with a disability who transfers school districts within the same academic year, who enrolls in a new school, and who had an IEP that was in effect in another State, the local educational agency shall provide such child with a free appropriate public education, including services comparable to those described in the previously held IEP, in consultation with the parents until such time as

the local educational agency conducts an evaluation pursuant to subsection (a)(1), if determined to be necessary by such agency, and develops a new IEP, if appropriate, that is consistent with Federal and State law.

(ii) TRANSMITTAL OF RECORDS- To facilitate the transition for a child described in clause (i)—

(I) the new school in which the child enrolls shall take reasonable steps to promptly obtain the child's records, including the IEP and supporting documents and any other records relating to the provision of special education or related services to the child, from the previous school in which the child was enrolled, pursuant to section 99.31(a)(2) of title 34, Code of Federal Regulations; and

(II) the previous school in which the child was enrolled shall take reasonable steps to promptly respond to such request from the new school.

(3) DEVELOPMENT OF IEP-

(A) IN GENERAL- In developing each child's IEP, the IEP Team, subject to subparagraph (C), shall consider—

(i) the strengths of the child;

(ii) the concerns of the parents for enhancing the education of their child;

(iii) the results of the initial evaluation or most recent evaluation of the child; and

(iv) the academic, developmental, and functional needs of the child.

(B) CONSIDERATION OF SPECIAL FACTORS- The IEP Team shall—

(i) in the case of a child whose behavior impedes the child's learning or that of others, consider the use of positive behavioral interventions and supports, and other strategies, to address that behavior;

(ii) in the case of a child with limited English proficiency, consider the language needs of the child as such needs relate to the child's IEP;

(iii) in the case of a child who is blind or visually impaired, provide for instruction in Braille and the use of Braille unless the IEP Team determines, after an evaluation of the child's reading and writing skills, needs, and appropriate reading and writing media (including an evaluation of the child's future needs for instruction in Braille or the use of Braille), that instruction in Braille or the use of Braille is not appropriate for the child;

(iv) consider the communication needs of the child, and in the case of a child who is deaf or hard of hearing, consider the child's language and communication needs, opportunities for direct communications with peers and professional personnel in the child's language and communication mode, academic level, and full range of needs, including opportunities for direct instruction in the child's language and communication mode; and

(v) consider whether the child needs assistive technology devices and services.

(C) REQUIREMENT WITH RESPECT TO REGULAR EDUCATION TEACHER- A regular education teacher of the child, as a member of the IEP Team, shall, to the extent appropriate, participate in the development of the IEP of the child, including the determination of appropriate positive behavioral interventions and supports, and other strategies, and the determination of supplementary aids and services, program modifications, and support for school personnel consistent with paragraph (1)(A)(i)(IV).

(D) AGREEMENT- In making changes to a child's IEP after the annual IEP meeting for a school year, the parent of a child with a disability and the local educational agency may agree not to convene an IEP meeting for the purposes of making such changes, and instead may develop a written document to amend or modify the child's current IEP.

(E) CONSOLIDATION OF IEP TEAM MEETINGS- To the extent possible, the local educational agency shall encourage the consolidation of reevaluation meetings for the child and other IEP Team meetings for the child.

(F) AMENDMENTS- Changes to the IEP may be made either by the entire IEP Team or, as provided in subparagraph (D), by amending the IEP rather than by redrafting the entire IEP. Upon request, a parent shall be provided with a revised copy of the IEP with the amendments incorporated.

(4) REVIEW AND REVISION OF IEP-

(A) IN GENERAL- The local educational agency shall ensure that, subject to subparagraph (B), the IEP Team—

(i) reviews the child's IEP periodically, but not less frequently than annually, to determine whether the annual goals for the child are being achieved; and

(ii) revises the IEP as appropriate to address—

(I) any lack of expected progress toward the annual goals and in the general education curriculum, where appropriate;

(II) the results of any reevaluation conducted under this section;

(III) information about the child provided

to, or by, the parents, as described in subsection (c)(1)(B);

(IV) the child's anticipated needs; or

(V) other matters.

(B) REQUIREMENT WITH RESPECT TO REGULAR EDUCATION TEACHER- A regular education teacher of the child, as a member of the IEP Team, shall, consistent with paragraph (1)(C), participate in the review and revision of the IEP of the child.

(5) MULTI-YEAR IEP DEMONSTRATION-

(A) PILOT PROGRAM-

(i) PURPOSE- The purpose of this paragraph is to provide an opportunity for States to allow parents and local educational agencies the opportunity for long-term planning by offering the option of developing a comprehensive multi-year IEP, not to exceed 3 years, that is designed to coincide with the natural transition points for the child.

(ii) AUTHORIZATION- In order to carry out the purpose of this paragraph, the Secretary is authorized to approve not more than 15 proposals from States to carry out the activity described in clause (i).

(iii) PROPOSAL-

(I) IN GENERAL- A State desiring to participate in the program under this paragraph shall submit a proposal to the Secretary at such time and in such manner as the Secretary may reasonably require.

(II) CONTENT- The proposal shall include—

(aa) assurances that the development of a multi-year IEP under this paragraph is optional for parents;

(bb) assurances that the parent is required to provide informed consent before a comprehensive multi-year IEP is developed;

(cc) a list of required elements for each multi-year IEP, including—

(AA) measurable goals pursuant to paragraph (1)(A)(i)(II), coinciding with natural transition points for the child, that will enable the child to be involved in and make progress in the general education curriculum and that will meet the child's other needs that result from the child's disability; and

(BB) measurable annual goals for determining progress toward meeting the goals described in subitem (AA); and

(dd) a description of the process for the review and revision of each multi-year IEP, including—

(AA) a review by the IEP Team of the child's multi-year IEP at each of the child's natural transition points;

(BB) in years other than a child's natural

transition points, an annual review of the child's IEP to determine the child's current levels of progress and whether the annual goals for the child are being achieved, and a requirement to amend the IEP, as appropriate, to enable the child to continue to meet the measurable goals set out in the IEP;

(CC) if the IEP Team determines on the basis of a review that the child is not making sufficient progress toward the goals described in the multi-year IEP, a requirement that the local educational agency shall ensure that the IEP Team carries out a more thorough review of the IEP in accordance with paragraph (4) within 30 calendar days; and

(DD) at the request of the parent, a requirement that the IEP Team shall conduct a review of the child's multi-year IEP rather than or subsequent to an annual review.

(B) REPORT- Beginning 2 years after the date of enactment of the Individuals with Disabilities Education Improvement Act of 2004, the Secretary shall submit an annual report to the Committee on Education and the Workforce of the House of Representatives and the Committee on Health, Education, Labor, and Pensions of the Senate regarding the effectiveness of the program under this paragraph and any specific recommendations for broader implementation of such program, including—

(i) reducing—

(I) the paperwork burden on teachers, principals, administrators, and related service providers; and

(II) noninstructional time spent by teachers in complying with this part;

(ii) enhancing longer-term educational planning;

(iii) improving positive outcomes for children with disabilities;

(iv) promoting collaboration between IEP Team members; and

(v) ensuring satisfaction of family members.

(C) DEFINITION- In this paragraph, the term 'natural transition points' means those periods that are close in time to the transition of a child with a disability from preschool to elementary grades, from elementary grades to middle or junior high school grades, from middle or junior high school grades to secondary school grades, and from secondary school grades to post-secondary activities, but in no case a period longer than 3 years.

(6) FAILURE TO MEET TRANSITION OBJECTIVES- If a participating agency, other than the local educational agency, fails to provide the transition services described in the IEP in accordance with paragraph (1)(A)(i)(VIII), the local educational agency shall reconvene the IEP Team to identify alternative strategies to meet the transition objectives for the child set out in the IEP.

(7) CHILDREN WITH DISABILITIES IN ADULT PRISONS-

(A) IN GENERAL- The following requirements shall not apply to children with disabilities who are convicted as adults under State law and incarcerated in adult prisons:

(i) The requirements contained in section 612(a)(16) and paragraph (1)(A)(i)(VI) (relating to participation of children with disabilities in general assessments).

(ii) The requirements of items (aa) and (bb) of paragraph (1)(A)(i)(VIII) (relating to transition planning and transition services), do not apply with respect to such children whose eligibility under this part will end, because of such children's age, before such children will be released from prison.

(B) ADDITIONAL REQUIREMENT- If a child with a disability is convicted as an adult under State law and incarcerated in an adult prison, the child's IEP Team may modify the child's IEP or placement notwithstanding the requirements of sections 612(a)(5)(A) and paragraph (1)(A) if the State has demonstrated a bona fide security or compelling penological interest that cannot otherwise be accommodated.

(e) EDUCATIONAL PLACEMENTS- Each local educational agency or State educational agency shall ensure that the parents of each child with a disability are members of any group that makes decisions on the educational placement of their child.

(f) ALTERNATIVE MEANS OF MEETING PARTICIPATION- When conducting IEP team meetings and placement meetings pursuant to this section, section 615(e), and section 615(f)(1)(B), and carrying out administrative matters under section 615 (such as scheduling, exchange of witness lists, and status conferences), the parent of a child with a disability and a local educational agency may agree to use alternative means of meeting participation, such as video conferences and conference calls.

SEC. 615. PROCEDURAL SAFEGUARDS.

(a) ESTABLISHMENT OF PROCEDURES- Any State educational agency, State agency, or local educational agency that receives assistance under this part shall establish and maintain procedures in accordance with this section to ensure that children with disabilities and their parents are guaranteed procedural safeguards with respect to the provision of a free appropriate public education by such agencies.

(b) TYPES OF PROCEDURES- The procedures required by this section shall include the following:

(1) An opportunity for the parents of a child with a disability to examine all records relating to such child and to participate in meetings with respect to the identification, evaluation, and educational placement of the child, and the provision of a free appropriate public education to such child, and to obtain an independent educational evaluation of the child.

(2)(A) Procedures to protect the rights of the child whenever the parents of the child are not known, the agency cannot, after reasonable efforts, locate the parents, or the child is a ward of the State, including the assignment of an individual to act as a surrogate for the parents, which surrogate shall not be an employee of the State educational agency, the local educational agency, or any other agency that is involved in the education or care of the child. In the case of—

(i) a child who is a ward of the State, such surrogate may alternatively be appointed by the judge overseeing the child's care provided that the surrogate meets the requirements of this paragraph; and

(ii) an unaccompanied homeless youth as defined in section 725(6) of the McKinney-Vento Homeless Assistance Act (42 U.S.C. 11434a(6)), the local educational agency shall appoint a surrogate in accordance with this paragraph.

(B) The State shall make reasonable efforts to ensure the assignment of a surrogate not more than 30 days after there is a determination by the agency that the child needs a surrogate.

(3) Written prior notice to the parents of the child, in accordance with subsection (c)(1), whenever the local educational agency—

(A) proposes to initiate or change; or

(B) refuses to initiate or change,the identification, evaluation, or educational placement of the child, or the provision of a free appropriate public education to the child.

(4) Procedures designed to ensure that the notice required by paragraph (3) is in the native language of the parents, unless it clearly is not feasible to do so.

(5) An opportunity for mediation, in accordance with subsection (e).

(6) An opportunity for any party to present a complaint—

(A) with respect to any matter relating to the identification, evaluation, or educational placement of the child, or the provision of a free appropriate public education to such child; and

(B) which sets forth an alleged violation that occurred not more than 2 years before the date the parent or public agency knew or should have known about the alleged action that forms the basis of the complaint, or, if the State has an explicit time limitation for presenting such a complaint under this part, in such time as the State law allows, except that the exceptions to the timeline described in subsection (f)(3)(D) shall apply to the timeline described in this subparagraph.

(7)(A) Procedures that require either party, or the attorney representing a party, to provide due process complaint notice in accordance with subsection (c)(2) (which shall remain confidential)—

(i) to the other party, in the complaint filed under paragraph (6), and forward a copy of such notice to the State educational agency; and

(ii) that shall include—

(I) the name of the child, the address of the residence of the child (or available contact information in the case of a homeless child), and the name of the school the child is attending;

(II) in the case of a homeless child or youth (within the meaning of section 725(2) of the McKinney-Vento Homeless Assistance Act (42 U.S.C. 11434a(2)), available contact information for the child and the name of the school the child is attending;

(III) a description of the nature of the problem of the child relating to such proposed initiation or change, including facts relating to such problem; and

(IV) a proposed resolution of the problem to the extent known and available to the party at the time.

(B) A requirement that a party may not have a due process hearing until the party, or the attorney representing the party, files a notice that meets the requirements of subparagraph (A)(ii).

(8) Procedures that require the State educational agency to develop a model form to assist parents in filing a complaint and due process complaint notice in accordance with paragraphs (6) and (7), respectively.

(c) NOTIFICATION REQUIREMENTS-

(1) CONTENT OF PRIOR WRITTEN NOTICE- The notice required by subsection

(b)(3) shall include—

(A) a description of the action proposed or refused by the agency;

(B) an explanation of why the agency proposes or refuses to take the action and a description of each evaluation procedure, assessment, record, or report the agency used as a basis for the proposed or refused action;

(C) a statement that the parents of a child with a disability have protection under the procedural safeguards of this part and, if this notice is not an initial referral for evaluation, the means by which a copy of a description of the procedural safeguards can be obtained;

(D) sources for parents to contact to obtain assistance in understanding the provisions of this part;

(E) a description of other options considered by the IEP Team and the reason why those options were rejected; and

(F) a description of the factors that are relevant to the agency's proposal or refusal.

(2) DUE PROCESS COMPLAINT NOTICE-

(A) COMPLAINT- The due process complaint notice required under subsection (b)(7)(A) shall be deemed to be sufficient unless the party receiving the notice notifies the hearing officer and the other party in writing that the receiving party believes the notice has not met the requirements of subsection (b)(7)(A).

(B) RESPONSE TO COMPLAINT-

(i) LOCAL EDUCATIONAL AGENCY RESPONSE-

(I) IN GENERAL- If the local educational agency has not sent a prior written notice to the parent regarding the subject matter contained in the parent's due process complaint notice, such local educational agency shall, within 10 days of receiving the complaint, send to the parent a response that shall include—

(aa) an explanation of why the agency proposed or refused to take the action raised in the complaint;

(bb) a description of other options that the IEP Team considered and the reasons why those options were rejected;

(cc) a description of each evaluation procedure, assessment, record, or report the agency used as the basis for the proposed or refused action; and

(dd) a description of the factors that are relevant to the agency's proposal or refusal.

(II) SUFFICIENCY- A response filed by a local educational agency pursuant to subclause (I) shall not be construed to preclude such local educational agency from asserting that the parent's due process complaint notice was insufficient where appropriate.

(ii) OTHER PARTY RESPONSE- Except as provided in clause (i), the non-complaining party shall, within 10 days of receiving the complaint, send to the complaint a response that specifically addresses the issues raised in the complaint.

(C) TIMING- The party providing a hearing officer notification under subparagraph (A) shall provide the notification within 15 days of receiving the complaint.

(D) DETERMINATION- Within 5 days of receipt of the notification provided under subparagraph (C), the hearing officer shall make a determination on the face of the notice of whether the notification meets the requirements of subsection (b)(7)(A), and shall immediately notify the parties in writing of such determination.

(E) AMENDED COMPLAINT NOTICE-

(i) IN GENERAL- A party may amend its due process complaint notice only if—

(I) the other party consents in writing to such amendment and is given the opportunity to resolve the complaint through a meeting held pursuant to subsection (f)(1)(B); or

(II) the hearing officer grants permission, except that the hearing officer may only grant such permission at any time not later than 5 days before a due process hearing occurs.

(ii) APPLICABLE TIMELINE- The applicable timeline for a due process hearing under this part shall recommence at the time the party files an amended notice, including the timeline under subsection (f)(1)(B).

(d) PROCEDURAL SAFEGUARDS NOTICE-

(1) IN GENERAL-

(A) COPY TO PARENTS- A copy of the procedural safeguards available to the parents of a child with a disability shall be given to the parents only 1 time a year, except that a copy also shall be given to the parents—

(i) upon initial referral or parental request for evaluation;

(ii) upon the first occurrence of the filing of a complaint under subsection (b)(6); and

(iii) upon request by a parent.

(B) INTERNET WEBSITE- A local educational agency may place a current copy of the procedural safeguards notice on its Internet website if such website exists.

(2) CONTENTS- The procedural safeguards notice shall include a full explanation of the procedural safeguards, written in the native language of the parents (unless it clearly is not feasible to do so) and

written in an easily understandable manner, available under this section and under regulations promulgated by the Secretary relating to—

(A) independent educational evaluation;

(B) prior written notice;

(C) parental consent;

(D) access to educational records;

(E) the opportunity to present and resolve complaints, including—

(i) the time period in which to make a complaint;

(ii) the opportunity for the agency to resolve the complaint; and

(iii) the availability of mediation;

(F) the child's placement during pendency of due process proceedings;

(G) procedures for students who are subject to placement in an interim alternative educational setting;

(H) requirements for unilateral placement by parents of children in private schools at public expense;

(I) due process hearings, including requirements for disclosure of evaluation results and recommendations;

(J) State-level appeals (if applicable in that State);

(K) civil actions, including the time period in which to file such actions; and

(L) attorneys' fees.

(e) MEDIATION-

(1) IN GENERAL- Any State educational agency or local educational agency that receives assistance under this part shall ensure that procedures are established and implemented to allow parties to disputes involving any matter, including matters arising prior to the filing of a complaint pursuant to subsection (b)(6), to resolve such disputes through a mediation process.

(2) REQUIREMENTS- Such procedures shall meet the following requirements:

(A) The procedures shall ensure that the mediation process—

(i) is voluntary on the part of the parties;

(ii) is not used to deny or delay a parent's right to a due process hearing under subsection (f), or to deny any other rights afforded under this part; and

(iii) is conducted by a qualified and impartial mediator who is trained in effective mediation techniques.

(B) OPPORTUNITY TO MEET WITH A DISINTERESTED PARTY- A local educational agency or a State agency may establish procedures to offer to parents and schools that choose not to use the mediation process, an opportunity to meet, at a time and location convenient to the parents, with a disinterested party who is under contract with—

(i) a parent training and information center or community parent resource center in the State established under section 671 or 672; or

(ii) an appropriate alternative dispute resolution entity, to encourage the use, and explain the benefits, of the mediation process to the parents.

(C) LIST OF QUALIFIED MEDIATORS- The State shall maintain a list of individuals who are qualified mediators and knowledgeable in laws and regulations relating to the provision of special education and related services.

(D) COSTS- The State shall bear the cost of the mediation process, including the costs of meetings described in subparagraph (B).

(E) SCHEDULING AND LOCATION- Each session in the mediation process shall be scheduled in a timely manner and shall be held in a location that is convenient to the parties to the dispute.

(F) WRITTEN AGREEMENT- In the case that a resolution is reached to resolve the complaint through the mediation process, the parties shall execute a legally binding agreement that sets forth such resolution and that—

(i) states that all discussions that occurred during the mediation process shall be confidential and may not be used as evidence in any subsequent due process hearing or civil proceeding;

(ii) is signed by both the parent and a representative of the agency who has the authority to bind such agency; and

(iii) is enforceable in any State court of competent jurisdiction or in a district court of the United States.

(G) MEDIATION DISCUSSIONS- Discussions that occur during the mediation process shall be confidential and may not be used as evidence in any subsequent due process hearing or civil proceeding.

(f) IMPARTIAL DUE PROCESS HEARING-

(1) IN GENERAL-

(A) HEARING- Whenever a complaint has been received under subsection (b)(6) or (k), the parents or the local educational agency involved in such complaint shall have an opportunity for an impartial due process hearing, which shall be conducted by the State educational agency or by the local educational agency, as determined by State law or by the

State educational agency.

(B) RESOLUTION SESSION-

(i) PRELIMINARY MEETING- Prior to the opportunity for an impartial due process hearing under subparagraph (A), the local educational agency shall convene a meeting with the parents and the relevant member or members of the IEP Team who have specific knowledge of the facts identified in the complaint—

(I) within 15 days of receiving notice of the parents' complaint;

(II) which shall include a representative of the agency who has decisionmaking authority on behalf of such agency;

(III) which may not include an attorney of the local educational agency unless the parent is accompanied by an attorney; and

(IV) where the parents of the child discuss their complaint, and the facts that form the basis of the complaint, and the local educational agency is provided the opportunity to resolve the complaint, unless the parents and the local educational agency agree in writing to waive such meeting, or agree to use the mediation process described in subsection (e).

(ii) HEARING- If the local educational agency has not resolved the complaint to the satisfaction of the parents within 30 days of the receipt of the complaint, the due process hearing may occur, and all of the applicable timelines for a due process hearing under this part shall commence.

(iii) WRITTEN SETTLEMENT AGREEMENT- In the case that a resolution is reached to resolve the complaint at a meeting described in clause (i), the parties shall execute a legally binding agreement that is—

(I) signed by both the parent and a representative of the agency who has the authority to bind such agency; and

(II) enforceable in any State court of competent jurisdiction or in a district court of the United States.

(iv) REVIEW PERIOD- If the parties execute an agreement pursuant to clause (iii), a party may void such agreement within 3 business days of the agreement's execution.

(2) DISCLOSURE OF EVALUATIONS AND RECOMMENDATIONS-

(A) IN GENERAL- Not less than 5 business days prior to a hearing conducted pursuant to paragraph (1), each party shall disclose to all other parties all evaluations completed by that date, and recommendations based on the offering party's evaluations, that the party intends to use at the hearing.

(B) FAILURE TO DISCLOSE- A hearing officer may bar any party that fails to comply with subparagraph (A) from introducing the relevant evaluation or recommendation at the hearing without the consent of the other party.

(3) LIMITATIONS ON HEARING-

(A) PERSON CONDUCTING HEARING- A hearing officer conducting a hearing pursuant to paragraph (1)(A) shall, at a minimum—

(i) not be—

(I) an employee of the State educational agency or the local educational agency involved in the education or care of the child; or

(II) a person having a personal or professional interest that conflicts with the person's objectivity in the hearing;

(ii) possess knowledge of, and the ability to understand, the provisions of this title, Federal and State regulations pertaining to this title, and legal interpretations of this title by Federal and State courts;

(iii) possess the knowledge and ability to conduct hearings in accordance with appropriate, standard legal practice; and

(iv) possess the knowledge and ability to render and write decisions in accordance with appropriate, standard legal practice.

(B) SUBJECT MATTER OF HEARING- The party requesting the due process hearing shall not be allowed to raise issues at the due process hearing that were not raised in the notice filed under subsection (b)(7), unless the other party agrees otherwise.

(C) TIMELINE FOR REQUESTING HEARING- A parent or agency shall request an impartial due process hearing within 2 years of the date the parent or agency knew or should have known about the alleged action that forms the basis of the complaint, or, if the State has an explicit time limitation for requesting such a hearing under this part, in such time as the State law allows.

(D) EXCEPTIONS TO THE TIMELINE- The timeline described in subparagraph (C) shall not apply to a parent if the parent was prevented from requesting the hearing due to—

(i) specific misrepresentations by the local educational agency that it had resolved the problem forming the basis of the complaint; or

(ii) the local educational agency's withholding of information from the parent that was required under this part to be provided to the parent.

(E) DECISION OF HEARING OFFICER-

(i) IN GENERAL- Subject to clause (ii), a decision made by a hearing officer shall be made on substantive grounds based on a determination of whether the child received a free appropriate public education.

(ii) PROCEDURAL ISSUES- In matters alleging a procedural violation, a hearing officer may find that a child did not receive a free appropriate public education only if the procedural inadequacies—

(I) impeded the child's right to a free appropriate public education;

(II) significantly impeded the parents' opportunity to participate in the decisionmaking process regarding the provision of a free appropriate public education to the parents' child; or

(III) caused a deprivation of educational benefits.

(iii) RULE OF CONSTRUCTION- Nothing in this subparagraph shall be construed to preclude a hearing officer from ordering a local educational agency to comply with procedural requirements under this section.

(F) RULE OF CONSTRUCTION- Nothing in this paragraph shall be construed to affect the right of a parent to file a complaint with the State educational agency.

(g) APPEAL-

(1) IN GENERAL- If the hearing required by subsection (f) is conducted by a local educational agency, any party aggrieved by the findings and decision rendered in such a hearing may appeal such findings and decision to the State educational agency.

(2) IMPARTIAL REVIEW AND INDEPENDENT DECISION- The State educational agency shall conduct an impartial review of the findings and decision appealed under paragraph (1). The officer conducting such review shall make an independent decision upon completion of such review.

(h) SAFEGUARDS- Any party to a hearing conducted pursuant to subsection (f) or (k), or an appeal conducted pursuant to subsection (g), shall be accorded—

(1) the right to be accompanied and advised by counsel and by individuals with special knowledge or training with respect to the problems of children with disabilities;

(2) the right to present evidence and confront, cross-examine, and compel the attendance of witnesses;

(3) the right to a written, or, at the option of the parents, electronic verbatim record of such hearing; and

(4) the right to written, or, at the option of the parents, electronic findings of fact and decisions, which findings and decisions—

(A) shall be made available to the public consistent with the requirements of section 617(b) (relating to the confidentiality of data, information, and records); and

(B) shall be transmitted to the advisory panel established pursuant to section 612(a)(21).

(i) ADMINISTRATIVE PROCEDURES-

(1) IN GENERAL-

(A) DECISION MADE IN HEARING- A decision made in a hearing conducted pursuant to subsection (f) or (k) shall be final, except that any party involved in such hearing may appeal such decision under the provisions of subsection (g) and paragraph (2).

(B) DECISION MADE AT APPEAL- A decision made under subsection (g) shall be final, except that any party may bring an action under paragraph (2).

(2) RIGHT TO BRING CIVIL ACTION-

(A) IN GENERAL- Any party aggrieved by the findings and decision made under subsection (f) or (k) who does not have the right to an appeal under subsection (g), and any party aggrieved by the findings and decision made under this subsection, shall have the right to bring a civil action with respect to the complaint presented pursuant to this section, which action may be brought in any State court of competent jurisdiction or in a district court of the United States, without regard to the amount in controversy.

(B) LIMITATION- The party bringing the action shall have 90 days from the date of the decision of the hearing officer to bring such an action, or, if the State has an explicit time limitation for bringing such action under this part, in such time as the State law allows.

(C) ADDITIONAL REQUIREMENTS- In any action brought under this paragraph, the court—

(i) shall receive the records of the administrative proceedings;

(ii) shall hear additional evidence at the request of a party; and

(iii) basing its decision on the preponderance of the evidence, shall grant such relief as the court determines is appropriate.

(3) JURISDICTION OF DISTRICT COURTS; ATTORNEYS' FEES-

(A) IN GENERAL- The district courts of the United States shall have jurisdiction of actions brought under this section without regard to the amount in controversy.

(B) AWARD OF ATTORNEYS' FEES-

(i) IN GENERAL- In any action or proceeding brought under this section, the court, in its discretion, may award reasonable attorneys' fees as part of the costs—

(I) to a prevailing party who is the parent of a child with a disability;

(II) to a prevailing party who is a State educational agency or local educational agency against the attorney of a parent who files a complaint or subsequent cause of action that is frivolous, unreasonable, or without foundation, or against the attorney of a parent who continued to litigate after the litigation clearly became frivolous, unreasonable, or without foundation; or

(III) to a prevailing State educational agency or local educational agency against the attorney of a parent, or against the parent, if the parent's complaint or subsequent cause of action was presented for any improper purpose, such as to harass, to cause unnecessary delay, or to needlessly increase the cost of litigation.

(ii) RULE OF CONSTRUCTION- Nothing in this subparagraph shall be construed to affect section 327 of the District of Columbia Appropriations Act, 2005.

(C) DETERMINATION OF AMOUNT OF ATTORNEYS' FEES- Fees awarded under this paragraph shall be based on rates prevailing in the community in which the action or proceeding arose for the kind and quality of services furnished. No bonus or multiplier may be used in calculating the fees awarded under this subsection.

(D) PROHIBITION OF ATTORNEYS' FEES AND RELATED COSTS FOR CERTAIN SERVICES-

(i) IN GENERAL- Attorneys' fees may not be awarded and related costs may not be reimbursed in any action or proceeding under this section for services performed subsequent to the time of a written offer of settlement to a parent if—

(I) the offer is made within the time prescribed by Rule 68 of the Federal Rules of Civil Procedure or, in the case of an administrative proceeding, at any time more than 10 days before the proceeding begins;

(II) the offer is not accepted within 10 days; and

(III) the court or administrative hearing officer finds that the relief finally obtained by the parents is not more favorable to the parents than the offer of settlement.

(ii) IEP TEAM MEETINGS- Attorneys' fees may not be awarded relating to any meeting of the IEP Team unless such meeting is convened as a result of an administrative proceeding or judicial action, or, at the discretion of the State, for a mediation described in subsection (e).

(iii) OPPORTUNITY TO RESOLVE COMPLAINTS- A meeting conducted pursuant to subsection (f)(1)(B)(i) shall not be considered—

(I) a meeting convened as a result of an administrative hearing or judicial action; or

(II) an administrative hearing or judicial

action for purposes of this paragraph.

(E) EXCEPTION TO PROHIBITION ON ATTORNEYS' FEES AND RELATED COSTS- Notwithstanding subparagraph (D), an award of attorneys' fees and related costs may be made to a parent who is the prevailing party and who was substantially justified in rejecting the settlement offer.

(F) REDUCTION IN AMOUNT OF ATTORNEYS' FEES- Except as provided in subparagraph (G), whenever the court finds that—

(i) the parent, or the parent's attorney, during the course of the action or proceeding, unreasonably protracted the final resolution of the controversy;

(ii) the amount of the attorneys' fees otherwise authorized to be awarded unreasonably exceeds the hourly rate prevailing in the community for similar services by attorneys of reasonably comparable skill, reputation, and experience;

(iii) the time spent and legal services furnished were excessive considering the nature of the action or proceeding; or

(iv) the attorney representing the parent did not provide to the local educational agency the appropriate information in the notice of the complaint described in subsection (b)(7)(A), the court shall reduce, accordingly, the amount of the attorneys' fees awarded under this section.

(G) EXCEPTION TO REDUCTION IN AMOUNT OF ATTORNEYS' FEES- The provisions of subparagraph (F) shall not apply in any action or proceeding if the court finds that the State or local educational agency unreasonably protracted the final resolution of the action or proceeding or there was a violation of this section.

(j) MAINTENANCE OF CURRENT EDUCATIONAL PLACEMENT- Except as provided in subsection (k)(4), during the pendency of any proceedings conducted pursuant to this section, unless the State or local educational agency and the parents otherwise agree, the child shall remain in the then-current educational placement of the child, or, if applying for initial admission to a public school, shall, with the consent of the parents, be placed in the public school program until all such proceedings have been completed.

(k) PLACEMENT IN ALTERNATIVE EDUCATIONAL SETTING-

(1) AUTHORITY OF SCHOOL PERSONNEL-

(A) CASE-BY-CASE DETERMINATION- School personnel may consider any unique circumstances on a case-by-case basis when determining whether to order a change in placement for a child with a disability who violates a code of student conduct.

(B) AUTHORITY- School personnel under this subsection may remove a child with a disability who violates a code of student conduct from their current placement to an appropriate interim alternative educational setting, another setting, or suspension, for not more than 10 school days (to the extent such alternatives are applied to children without disabilities).

(C) ADDITIONAL AUTHORITY- If school personnel seek to order a change in placement that would exceed 10 school days and the behavior that gave rise to the violation of the school code is determined not to be a manifestation of the child's disability pursuant to subparagraph (E), the relevant disciplinary procedures applicable to children without disabilities may be applied to the child in the same manner and for the same duration in which the procedures would be applied to children without disabilities, except as provided in section 612(a)(1) although it may be provided in an interim alternative educational setting.

(D) SERVICES- A child with a disability who is removed from the child's current placement under subparagraph (G) (irrespective of whether the behavior is determined to be a manifestation of the child's disability) or subparagraph (C) shall—

(i) continue to receive educational services, as provided in section 612(a)(1), so as to enable the child to continue to participate in the general education curriculum, although in another setting, and to progress toward meeting the goals set out in the child's IEP; and

(ii) receive, as appropriate, a functional behavioral assessment, behavioral intervention services and modifications, that are designed to address the behavior violation so that it does not recur.

(E) MANIFESTATION DETERMINATION-

(i) IN GENERAL- Except as provided in subparagraph (B), within 10 school days of any decision to change the placement of a child with a disability because of a violation of a code of student conduct, the local educational agency, the parent, and relevant members of the IEP Team (as determined by the parent and the local educational agency) shall review all relevant information in the student's file, including the child's IEP, any teacher observations, and any relevant information provided by the parents to determine—

(I) if the conduct in question was caused by, or had a direct and substantial relationship to, the child's disability; or

(II) if the conduct in question was the direct result of the local educational agency's failure to implement the IEP.

(ii) MANIFESTATION- If the local educational agency, the parent, and relevant members of the IEP Team determine that either subclause (I) or (II) of clause (i) is applicable for the child, the conduct shall be determined to be a manifestation of the child's disability.

(F) DETERMINATION THAT BEHAVIOR WAS A MANIFESTATION- If the local educational agency, the parent, and relevant members of the IEP Team make the determination that the conduct was a manifestation of the child's disability, the IEP Team shall—

(i) conduct a functional behavioral assessment, and implement a behavioral intervention plan for such child, provided that the local educational agency had not conducted such assessment prior to such determination before the behavior that resulted in a change in placement described in subparagraph (C) or (G);

(ii) in the situation where a behavioral intervention plan has been developed, review the behavioral intervention plan if the child already has such a behavioral intervention plan, and modify it, as necessary, to address the behavior; and

(iii) except as provided in subparagraph (G), return the child to the placement from which the child was removed, unless the parent and the local educational agency agree to a change of placement as part of the modification of the behavioral intervention plan.

(G) SPECIAL CIRCUMSTANCES- School personnel may remove a student to an interim alternative educational setting for not more than 45 school days without regard to whether the behavior is determined to be a manifestation of the child's disability, in cases where a child—

(i) carries or possesses a weapon to or at school, on school premises, or to or at a school function under the jurisdiction of a State or local educational agency;

(ii) knowingly possesses or uses illegal drugs, or sells or solicits the sale of a controlled substance, while at school, on school premises, or at a school function under the jurisdiction of a State or local educational agency; or

(iii) has inflicted serious bodily injury upon another person while at school, on school premises, or at a school function under the jurisdiction of a State or local educational agency.

(H) NOTIFICATION- Not later than the date on which the decision to take disciplinary action is made, the local educational agency shall notify the parents of that decision, and of all procedural safeguards accorded under this section.

(2) DETERMINATION OF SETTING- The interim alternative educational setting in subparagraphs (C) and (G) of paragraph (1) shall be determined by the IEP Team.

(3) APPEAL-

(A) IN GENERAL- The parent of a child with a disability who disagrees with any decision regarding placement, or the manifestation determination under this subsection, or a local educational agency that believes that maintaining the current placement of the child is substantially likely to result in injury to the child or to others, may request a hearing.

(B) AUTHORITY OF HEARING OFFICER-

(i) IN GENERAL- A hearing officer shall hear, and make a determination regarding, an appeal requested under subparagraph (A).

(ii) CHANGE OF PLACEMENT ORDER- In making the determination under clause (i), the hearing officer may order a change in placement of a child with a disability. In such situations, the hearing officer may—

(I) return a child with a disability to the placement from which the child was removed; or

(II) order a change in placement of a child with a disability to an appropriate interim alternative educational setting for not more than 45 school days if the hearing officer determines that maintaining the current placement of such child is substantially likely to result in injury to the child or to others.

(4) PLACEMENT DURING APPEALS- When an appeal under paragraph (3) has been requested by either the parent or the local educational agency—

(A) the child shall remain in the interim alternative educational setting pending the decision of the hearing officer or until the expiration of the time period provided for in paragraph (1)(C), whichever occurs first, unless the parent and the State or local educational agency agree otherwise; and

(B) the State or local educational agency shall arrange for an expedited hearing, which shall occur within 20 school days of the date the hearing is requested and shall result in a determination within 10 school days after the hearing.

(5) PROTECTIONS FOR CHILDREN NOT YET ELIGIBLE FOR SPECIAL EDUCATION AND RELATED SERVICES-

(A) IN GENERAL- A child who has not been determined to be eligible for special education and related services under this part and who has engaged in behavior that violates a code of student conduct, may assert any of the protections provided for in this part if the local educational agency had knowledge (as determined in accordance with this paragraph) that the child was a child with a disability before the behavior that precipitated the disciplinary action occurred.

(B) BASIS OF KNOWLEDGE- A local educational agency shall be deemed to have knowledge that a child is a child with a disability if, before the behavior that precipitated the disciplinary action occurred—

(i) the parent of the child has expressed concern in writing to supervisory or administrative personnel of the appropriate educational agency, or a teacher of the child, that the child is in need of special education and related services;

(ii) the parent of the child has requested an evaluation of the child pursuant to section 614(a)(1)(B); or

(iii) the teacher of the child, or other personnel of the local educational agency, has expressed specific concerns about a pattern of behavior demonstrated by the child, directly to the director of special education of such agency or to other supervisory personnel of the agency.

(C) EXCEPTION- A local educational agency shall not be deemed to have knowledge that the child is a child with a disability if the parent of the child has not allowed an evaluation of the child pursuant to section 614 or has refused services under this part or the child has been evaluated and it was determined that the child was not a child with a disability under this part.

(D) CONDITIONS THAT APPLY IF NO BASIS OF KNOWLEDGE-

(i) IN GENERAL- If a local educational agency does not have knowledge that a child is a child with a disability (in accordance with subparagraph (B) or (C)) prior to taking disciplinary measures against the child, the child may be subjected to disciplinary measures applied to children without disabilities who engaged in comparable behaviors consistent with clause (ii).

(ii) LIMITATIONS- If a request is made for an evaluation of a child during the time period in which the child is subjected to disciplinary measures under this subsection, the evaluation shall be conducted in an expedited manner. If the child is determined to be a child with a disability, taking into consideration information from the evaluation conducted by the agency and information provided by the parents, the agency shall provide special education and related services in accordance with this part, except that, pending the results of the evaluation, the child shall remain in the educational placement determined by school authorities.

(6) REFERRAL TO AND ACTION BY LAW ENFORCEMENT AND JUDICIAL AUTHORITIES-

(A) RULE OF CONSTRUCTION- Nothing in this part shall be construed to prohibit an agency from reporting a crime committed by a child with a disability to appropriate authorities or to prevent State law enforcement and judicial authorities from exercising their responsibilities with regard to the application of Federal and State law to crimes committed by a child with a disability.

(B) TRANSMITTAL OF RECORDS- An agency reporting a crime committed by a child with a disability shall ensure that copies of the special education and disciplinary records of the child are transmitted for consideration by the appropriate authorities to whom the agency reports the crime.

(7) DEFINITIONS- In this subsection:

(A) CONTROLLED SUBSTANCE- The term 'controlled substance' means a drug or other substance identified under schedule I, II, III, IV, or V in section 202(c) of the Controlled Substances Act (21 U.S.C. 812(c)).

(B) ILLEGAL DRUG- The term 'illegal drug' means a controlled substance but does not include a controlled substance that is legally possessed or used under the supervision of a licensed health-care professional or that is legally possessed or used under any other authority under that Act or under any other provision of Federal law.

(C) WEAPON- The term 'weapon' has the meaning given the term 'dangerous weapon' under section 930(g)(2) of title 18, United States Code.

(D) SERIOUS BODILY INJURY- The term 'serious bodily injury' has the meaning given the term 'serious bodily injury' under paragraph (3) of subsection (h) of section 1365 of title 18, United States Code.

(l) RULE OF CONSTRUCTION- Nothing in this title shall be construed to restrict or limit the rights, procedures, and remedies available under the Constitution, the Americans with Disabilities Act of 1990, title V of the Rehabilitation Act of 1973, or other Federal laws protecting the rights of children with disabilities, except that before the filing of a civil action under such laws seeking relief that is also available under this part, the procedures under subsections (f) and (g) shall be exhausted to the same extent as would be required had the action been brought under this part.

(m) TRANSFER OF PARENTAL RIGHTS AT AGE OF MAJORITY-

(1) IN GENERAL- A State that receives amounts from a grant under this part may provide that, when a child with a disability reaches the age of majority under State law (except for a child with a disability who has been determined to be incompetent under State law)—

(A) the agency shall provide any notice required by this section to both the individual and the parents;

(B) all other rights accorded to parents under this part transfer to the child;

(C) the agency shall notify the individual and the parents of the transfer of rights; and

(D) all rights accorded to parents under this part transfer to children who are incarcerated in an adult or juvenile Federal, State, or local correctional institution.

(2) SPECIAL RULE- If, under State law, a child with a disability who has reached the age of majority under State law, who has not been determined to be incompetent, but who is determined not to have the ability to provide informed consent with respect to the educational program of the child, the State shall establish procedures for appointing the parent of the child, or if the parent is not available, another appropriate individual, to represent the educational interests of the child throughout the period of eligibility of the child under this part.

(n) ELECTRONIC MAIL- A parent of a child with a disability may elect to receive notices required under this section by an electronic mail (e-mail) communication, if the agency makes such option available.

(o) SEPARATE COMPLAINT- Nothing in this section shall be construed to preclude a parent from filing a separate due process complaint on an issue separate from a due process complaint already filed.

SEC. 616. MONITORING, TECHNICAL ASSISTANCE, AND ENFORCEMENT.

(a) FEDERAL AND STATE MONITORING-

(1) IN GENERAL- The Secretary shall—

(A) monitor implementation of this part through—

(i) oversight of the exercise of general supervision by the States, as required in section 612(a)(11); and

(ii) the State performance plans, described in subsection (b);

(B) enforce this part in accordance with subsection (e); and

(C) require States to—

(i) monitor implementation of this part by local educational agencies; and

(ii) enforce this part in accordance with paragraph (3) and subsection (e).

(2) FOCUSED MONITORING- The primary focus of Federal and State monitoring activities described in paragraph (1) shall be on—

(A) improving educational results and functional outcomes for all children with disabilities; and

(B) ensuring that States meet the program requirements under this part, with a particular emphasis on those requirements that are most closely related to improving educational results for children with disabilities.

(3) MONITORING PRIORITIES- The Secretary shall monitor the States, and shall require each State to monitor the local educational agencies located in the State (except the State exercise of general supervisory responsibility), using quantifiable indicators in each of the following priority areas, and using such qualitative indicators as are needed to adequately measure performance in the following priority areas:

(A) Provision of a free appropriate public education in the least restrictive environment.

(B) State exercise of general supervisory authority, including child find, effective monitoring, the use of resolution sessions, mediation, voluntary binding arbitration, and a system of transition services as defined in sections 602(34) and 637(a)(9).

(C) Disproportionate representation of racial and ethnic groups in special education and related services, to the extent the representation is the result of inappropriate identification.

(4) PERMISSIVE AREAS OF REVIEW- The Secretary shall consider other relevant information and data, including data provided by States under section 618.

(b) STATE PERFORMANCE PLANS-

(1) PLAN-

(A) IN GENERAL- Not later than 1 year after the date of enactment of the Individuals with Disabilities Education Improvement Act of 2004, each State shall have in place a performance plan that evaluates that State's efforts to implement the requirements and purposes of this part and describes how the State will improve such implementation.

(B) SUBMISSION FOR APPROVAL- Each State shall submit the State's performance plan to the Secretary for approval in accordance with the approval process described in subsection (c).

(C) REVIEW- Each State shall review its State performance plan at least once every 6 years and submit any amendments to the Secretary.

(2) TARGETS-

(A) IN GENERAL- As a part of the State performance plan described under paragraph (1), each State shall establish measurable and rigorous targets for the indicators established under the priority areas described in subsection (a)(3).

(B) DATA COLLECTION-

(i) IN GENERAL- Each State shall collect valid and reliable information as needed to report annually to the Secretary on the priority areas described in subsection (a)(3).

(ii) RULE OF CONSTRUCTION- Nothing in this title shall be construed to authorize the development of a nationwide database of personally identifiable information on individuals involved in studies or other collections of data under this part.

(C) PUBLIC REPORTING AND PRIVACY-

(i) IN GENERAL- The State shall use the targets established in the plan and priority areas described in subsection (a)(3) to analyze the performance of each local educational agency in the State in implementing this part.

(ii) REPORT-

(I) PUBLIC REPORT- The State shall report annually to the public on the performance of each local educational agency located in the State on the targets in the State's performance plan. The State shall make the State's performance plan available through public means, including by posting on the website of the State educational agency, distribution to the media, and distribution through public agencies.

(II) STATE PERFORMANCE REPORT- The State shall report annually to the Secretary on the performance of the State under the State's performance plan.

(iii) PRIVACY- The State shall not report to the public or the Secretary any information on performance that would result in the disclosure of personally identifiable information about individual children or where the available data is insufficient to yield statistically reliable information.

(c) APPROVAL PROCESS-

(1) DEEMED APPROVAL- The Secretary shall review (including the specific provisions described in subsection (b)) each performance plan submitted by a State pursuant to subsection (b)(1)(B) and the plan shall be deemed to be approved by the Secretary unless the Secretary makes a written determination, prior to the expiration of the 120-day period beginning on the date on which the Secretary received the plan, that the plan does not meet the requirements of this section, including the specific provisions described in subsection (b).

(2) DISAPPROVAL- The Secretary shall not finally disapprove a performance plan, except after giving the State notice and an opportunity for a hearing.

(3) NOTIFICATION- If the Secretary finds that the plan does not meet the requirements, in whole or in part, of this section, the Secretary shall—

(A) give the State notice and an opportunity for a hearing; and

(B) notify the State of the finding, and in such notification shall—

(i) cite the specific provisions in the plan that do not meet the requirements; and

(ii) request additional information, only as to the provisions not meeting the requirements, needed for the plan to meet the requirements of this section.

(4) RESPONSE- If the State responds to the Secretary's notification described in paragraph (3)(B) during the 30-day period beginning on the date on which the State received the notification, and resubmits the plan with the requested information described in paragraph (3)(B)(ii), the Secretary shall approve or disapprove such plan prior to the later of—

(A) the expiration of the 30-day period beginning on the date on which the plan is resubmitted; or

(B) the expiration of the 120-day period described in paragraph (1).

(5) FAILURE TO RESPOND- If the State does not respond to the Secretary's notification described in paragraph (3)(B) during the 30-day period beginning on the date on which the State received the notification, such plan shall be deemed to be disapproved.

(d) SECRETARY'S REVIEW AND DETERMINATION-

(1) REVIEW- The Secretary shall annually review the State performance report submitted pursuant to subsection (b)(2)(C)(ii)(II) in accordance with this section.

(2) DETERMINATION-

(A) IN GENERAL- Based on the information provided by the State in the State performance report, information obtained through monitoring visits, and any other public information made available, the Secretary shall determine if the State—

(i) meets the requirements and purposes of this part;

(ii) needs assistance in implementing the requirements of this part;

(iii) needs intervention in implementing the requirements of this part; or

(iv) needs substantial intervention in implementing the requirements of this part.

(B) NOTICE AND OPPORTUNITY FOR A HEARING- For determinations made under clause (iii) or (iv) of subparagraph (A), the Secretary shall provide reasonable notice and an opportunity for a hearing on such determination.

(e) ENFORCEMENT-

(1) NEEDS ASSISTANCE- If the Secretary determines, for 2 consecutive years, that a State needs assistance under subsection (d)(2)(A)(ii) in implementing the requirements of this part, the Secretary shall take 1 or more of the following actions:

(A) Advise the State of available sources of technical assistance that may help the State address the areas in which the State needs assistance, which may include assistance from the Office of Special Education Programs, other offices of the Department of Education, other Federal agencies, technical assistance providers approved by the Secretary, and other federally funded nonprofit agencies, and require the State to work with appropriate entities. Such technical assistance may include—

(i) the provision of advice by experts to address the areas in which the State needs assistance, including explicit plans for addressing the area for concern within a specified period of time;

(ii) assistance in identifying and implementing professional development, instructional strategies, and methods of instruction that are based on scientifically based research;

(iii) designating and using distinguished superintendents, principals, special education administrators, special education teachers, and other teachers to provide advice, technical assistance, and support; and

(iv) devising additional approaches to providing technical assistance, such as collaborating with institutions of higher education, educational service agencies, national centers of technical assistance supported under part D, and private providers of scientifically based technical assistance.

(B) Direct the use of State-level funds under section 611(e) on the area or areas in which the State needs assistance.

(C) Identify the State as a high-risk grantee and impose special conditions on the State's grant under this part.

(2) NEEDS INTERVENTION- If the Secretary determines, for 3 or more consecutive years, that a State needs intervention under subsection (d)(2)(A)(iii) in implementing the requirements of this part, the following shall apply:

(A) The Secretary may take any of the actions described in paragraph (1).

(B) The Secretary shall take 1 or more of the following actions:

(i) Require the State to prepare a corrective action plan or improvement plan if the Secretary determines that the State should be able to correct the problem within 1 year.

(ii) Require the State to enter into a compliance agreement under section 457 of the General Education Provisions Act, if the Secretary has reason to believe that the State cannot correct the problem within 1 year.

(iii) For each year of the determination, withhold not less than 20 percent and not more than 50 percent of the State's funds under section 611(e), until the Secretary determines the State has sufficiently addressed the areas in which the State needs intervention.

(iv) Seek to recover funds under section 452 of the General Education Provisions Act.

(v) Withhold, in whole or in part, any further payments to the State under this part pursuant to paragraph (5).

(vi) Refer the matter for appropriate enforcement action, which may include referral to the Department of Justice.

(3) NEEDS SUBSTANTIAL INTERVENTION- Notwithstanding paragraph (1) or (2), at any time that the Secretary determines that a State needs substantial intervention in implementing the requirements of this part or that there is a substantial failure to comply with any condition of a State educational agency's or local educational agency's eligibility under this part, the Secretary shall take 1 or more of the following actions:

(A) Recover funds under section 452 of the General Education Provisions Act.

(B) Withhold, in whole or in part, any further payments to the State under this part.

(C) Refer the case to the Office of the Inspector General at the Department of Education.

(D) Refer the matter for appropriate enforcement action, which may include referral to the Department of Justice.

(4) OPPORTUNITY FOR HEARING-

(A) WITHHOLDING FUNDS- Prior to withholding any funds under this section, the Secretary shall provide reasonable notice and an opportunity for a hearing to the State educational agency involved.

(B) SUSPENSION- Pending the outcome of any hearing to withhold payments under subsection (b), the Secretary may suspend payments to a recipient, suspend the authority of the recipient to obligate funds under this part, or both, after such recipient has been given reasonable notice and an opportunity to show cause why future payments or authority to obligate funds under this part should not be suspended.

(5) REPORT TO CONGRESS- The Secretary shall report to the Committee on Education and the Workforce of the House of Representatives and the Committee on Health, Education, Labor, and Pensions of the Senate within 30 days of taking enforcement action pursuant to paragraph (1), (2), or (3), on the specific action taken and the reasons why enforcement action was taken.

(6) NATURE OF WITHHOLDING-

(A) LIMITATION- If the Secretary withholds further payments pursuant to paragraph (2) or (3), the Secretary may determine—

(i) that such withholding will be limited to programs or projects, or portions of programs or projects, that affected the Secretary's determination under subsection (d)(2); or

(ii) that the State educational agency shall not make further payments under this part to specified State agencies or local educational agencies that caused or were involved in the Secretary's determination under subsection (d)(2).

(B) WITHHOLDING UNTIL RECTIFIED- Until the Secretary is satisfied that the condition that caused the initial withholding has been substantially rectified—

(i) payments to the State under this part shall be withheld in whole or in part; and

(ii) payments by the State educational agency under this part shall be limited to State agencies and local educational agencies whose actions did not cause or were not involved in the Secretary's determination under subsection (d)(2), as the case may be.

(7) PUBLIC ATTENTION- Any State that has received notice under subsection (d)(2) shall, by means of a public notice, take such

measures as may be necessary to bring the pendency of an action pursuant to this subsection to the attention of the public within the State.

(8) JUDICIAL REVIEW-

(A) IN GENERAL- If any State is dissatisfied with the Secretary's action with respect to the eligibility of the State under section 612, such State may, not later than 60 days after notice of such action, file with the United States court of appeals for the circuit in which such State is located a petition for review of that action. A copy of the petition shall be transmitted by the clerk of the court to the Secretary. The Secretary thereupon shall file in the court the record of the proceedings upon which the Secretary's action was based, as provided in section 2112 of title 28, United States Code.

(B) JURISDICTION; REVIEW BY UNITED STATES SUPREME COURT- Upon the filing of such petition, the court shall have jurisdiction to affirm the action of the Secretary or to set it aside, in whole or in part. The judgment of the court shall be subject to review by the Supreme Court of the United States upon certiorari or certification as provided in section 1254 of title 28, United States Code.

(C) STANDARD OF REVIEW- The findings of fact by the Secretary, if supported by substantial evidence, shall be conclusive, but the court, for good cause shown, may remand the case to the Secretary to take further evidence, and the Secretary may thereupon make new or modified findings of fact and may modify the Secretary's previous action, and shall file in the court the record of the further proceedings. Such new or modified findings of fact shall be conclusive if supported by substantial evidence.

(f) STATE ENFORCEMENT- If a State educational agency determines that a local educational agency is not meeting the requirements of this part, including the targets in the State's performance plan, the State educational agency shall prohibit the local educational agency from reducing the local educational agency's maintenance of effort under section 613(a)(2)(C) for any fiscal year.

(g) RULE OF CONSTRUCTION- Nothing in this section shall be construed to restrict the Secretary from utilizing any authority under the General Education Provisions Act to monitor and enforce the requirements of this title.

(h) DIVIDED STATE AGENCY RESPONSIBILITY- For purposes of this section, where responsibility for ensuring that the requirements of this part are met with respect to children with disabilities who are convicted as adults under State law and incarcerated in adult prisons is assigned to a public agency other than the State educational agency pursuant to section 612(a)(11)(C), the Secretary, in instances where the Secretary finds that the failure to comply substantially with the provisions of this part are related to a failure by the public agency, shall take appropriate corrective action to ensure compliance with this part, except that—

(1) any reduction or withholding of payments to the State shall be proportionate to the total funds allotted under section 611 to the State as the number of eligible children with disabilities in adult prisons under the supervision of the other public agency is proportionate to the number of eligible individuals with disabilities in the State under the supervision of the State educational agency; and

(2) any withholding of funds under paragraph (1) shall be limited to the specific agency responsible for the failure to comply with this part.

(i) DATA CAPACITY AND TECHNICAL ASSISTANCE REVIEW- The Secretary shall—

(1) review the data collection and analysis capacity of States to ensure that data and information determined necessary for implementation of this section is collected, analyzed, and accurately reported to the Secretary; and

(2) provide technical assistance (from funds reserved under section 611(c)), where needed, to improve the capacity of States to meet the data collection requirements.

SEC. 617. ADMINISTRATION.

(a) RESPONSIBILITIES OF SECRETARY- The Secretary shall—

(1) cooperate with, and (directly or by grant or contract) furnish technical assistance necessary to, a State in matters relating to—

(A) the education of children with disabilities; and

(B) carrying out this part; and

(2) provide short-term training programs and institutes.

(b) PROHIBITION AGAINST FEDERAL MANDATES, DIRECTION, OR CONTROL- Nothing in this title shall be construed to authorize an officer or employee of the Federal Government to mandate, direct, or control a State, local educational agency, or school's specific instructional content, academic achievement standards and assessments, curriculum, or program of instruction.

(c) CONFIDENTIALITY- The Secretary shall take appropriate action, in accordance with section 444 of the General Education Provisions Act, to ensure the protection of the confidentiality of any personally identifiable data, information, and records collected or maintained by the Secretary and by State educational agencies and local educational agencies pursuant to this part.

(d) PERSONNEL- The Secretary is authorized to hire qualified personnel necessary to carry out the Secretary's duties under subsection (a), under section 618, and under subpart 4 of part D, without regard to the provisions of title 5, United States Code, relating to appointments in the competitive service and without regard to chapter 51 and subchapter III of chapter 53 of such title relating to classification and general schedule pay rates, except that no more than 20 such personnel shall be employed at any time.

(e) MODEL FORMS- Not later than the date that the Secretary publishes final regulations under this title, to implement amendments made by the Individuals with Disabilities Education Improvement Act of 2004, the Secretary shall publish and disseminate widely to States, local educational agencies, and parent and community training and information centers—

(1) a model IEP form;

(2) a model individualized family service plan (IFSP) form;

(3) a model form of the notice of procedural safeguards described in section 615(d); and

(4) a model form of the prior written notice described in subsections (b)(3) and (c)(1) of section 615 that is consistent with the requirements of this part and is sufficient to meet such requirements.

SEC. 618. PROGRAM INFORMATION.

(a) IN GENERAL- Each State that receives assistance under this part, and the Secretary of the Interior, shall provide data each year to the Secretary of Education and the public on the following:

(1)(A) The number and percentage of children with disabilities, by race, ethnicity, limited English proficiency status, gender, and disability category, who are in each of the following separate categories:

(i) Receiving a free appropriate public education.

(ii) Participating in regular education.

(iii) In separate classes, separate schools or facilities, or public or private residential facilities.

(iv) For each year of age from age 14 through 21, stopped receiving special education and related services because of program completion (including graduation with a regular secondary school diploma), or other reasons, and the reasons why those children stopped receiving special education and related services.

(v)(I) Removed to an interim alternative educational setting under section 615(k)(1).

(II) The acts or items precipitating those removals.

(III) The number of children with disabilities who are subject to long-term suspensions or expulsions.

(B) The number and percentage of children with disabilities, by race, gender, and ethnicity, who are receiving early intervention services.

(C) The number and percentage of children with disabilities, by race, gender, and ethnicity, who, from birth through age 2, stopped receiving early intervention services because of program completion or for other reasons.

(D) The incidence and duration of disciplinary actions by race, ethnicity, limited English proficiency status, gender, and disability category, of children with disabilities, including suspensions of 1 day or more.

(E) The number and percentage of children with disabilities who are removed to alternative educational settings or expelled as compared to children without disabilities who are removed to alternative educational settings or expelled.

(F) The number of due process complaints filed under section 615 and the number of hearings conducted.

(G) The number of hearings requested under section 615(k) and the number of changes in placements ordered as a result of those hearings.

(H) The number of mediations held and the number of settlement agreements reached through such mediations.

(2) The number and percentage of infants and toddlers, by race, and ethnicity, who are at risk of having substantial developmental delays (as defined in section 632), and who are receiving early intervention services under part C.

(3) Any other information that may be required by the Secretary.

(b) DATA REPORTING-

(1) PROTECTION OF IDENTIFIABLE DATA- The data described in subsection (a) shall be publicly reported by each State in a manner that does not result in the disclosure of

data identifiable to individual children.

(2) SAMPLING- The Secretary may permit States and the Secretary of the Interior to obtain the data described in subsection (a) through sampling.

(c) TECHNICAL ASSISTANCE- The Secretary may provide technical assistance to States to ensure compliance with the data collection and reporting requirements under this title.

(d) DISPROPORTIONALITY-

(1) IN GENERAL- Each State that receives assistance under this part, and the Secretary of the Interior, shall provide for the collection and examination of data to determine if significant disproportionality based on race and ethnicity is occurring in the State and the local educational agencies of the State with respect to—

(A) the identification of children as children with disabilities, including the identification of children as children with disabilities in accordance with a particular impairment described in section 602(3);

(B) the placement in particular educational settings of such children; and

(C) the incidence, duration, and type of disciplinary actions, including suspensions and expulsions.

(2) REVIEW AND REVISION OF POLICIES, PRACTICES, AND PROCEDURES- In the case of a determination of significant disproportionality with respect to the identification of children as children with disabilities, or the placement in particular educational settings of such children, in accordance with paragraph (1), the State or the Secretary of the Interior, as the case may be, shall—

(A) provide for the review and, if appropriate, revision of the policies, procedures, and practices used in such identification or placement to ensure that such policies, procedures, and practices comply with the requirements of this title;

(B) require any local educational agency identified under paragraph (1) to reserve the maximum amount of funds under section 613(f) to provide comprehensive coordinated early intervening services to serve children in the local educational agency, particularly children in those groups that were significantly overidentified under paragraph (1); and

(C) require the local educational agency to publicly report on the revision of policies, practices, and procedures described under subparagraph (A).

SEC. 619. PRESCHOOL GRANTS.

(a) IN GENERAL- The Secretary shall provide grants under this section to assist States to provide special education and related services, in accordance with this part—

(1) to children with disabilities aged 3 through 5, inclusive; and

(2) at the State's discretion, to 2-year-old children with disabilities who will turn 3 during the school year.

(b) ELIGIBILITY- A State shall be eligible for a grant under this section if such State—

(1) is eligible under section 612 to receive a grant under this part; and

(2) makes a free appropriate public education available to all children with disabilities, aged 3 through 5, residing in the State.

(c) ALLOCATIONS TO STATES-

(1) IN GENERAL- The Secretary shall allocate the amount made available to carry out this section for a fiscal year among the States in accordance with paragraph (2) or (3), as the case may be.

(2) INCREASE IN FUNDS- If the amount available for allocations to States under paragraph (1) for a fiscal year is equal to or greater than the amount allocated to the States under this section for the preceding fiscal year, those allocations shall be calculated as follows:

(A) ALLOCATION-

(i) IN GENERAL- Except as provided in subparagraph (B), the Secretary shall—

(I) allocate to each State the amount the State received under this section for fiscal year 1997;

(II) allocate 85 percent of any remaining funds to States on the basis of the States' relative populations of children aged 3 through 5; and

(III) allocate 15 percent of those remaining funds to States on the basis of the States' relative populations of all children aged 3 through 5 who are living in poverty.

(ii) DATA- For the purpose of making grants under this paragraph, the Secretary shall use the most recent population data, including data on children living in poverty, that are available and satisfactory to the Secretary.

(B) LIMITATIONS- Notwithstanding subparagraph (A), allocations under this paragraph shall be subject to the following:

(i) PRECEDING YEARS- No State's allocation shall be less than its allocation under this section for the preceding fiscal year.

(ii) MINIMUM- No State's allocation shall be less than the greatest of—

(I) the sum of—

(aa) the amount the State received under this section for fiscal year 1997; and

(bb) 1/3 of 1 percent of the amount by which the amount appropriated under subsection (j) for the fiscal year exceeds the amount appropriated for this section for fiscal year 1997;

(II) the sum of—

(aa) the amount the State received under this section for the preceding fiscal year; and

(bb) that amount multiplied by the percentage by which the increase in the funds appropriated under this section from the preceding fiscal year exceeds 1.5 percent; or

(III) the sum of—

(aa) the amount the State received under this section for the preceding fiscal year; and

(bb) that amount multiplied by 90 percent of the percentage increase in the amount appropriated under this section from the preceding fiscal year.

(iii) MAXIMUM- Notwithstanding clause (ii), no State's allocation under this paragraph shall exceed the sum of—

(I) the amount the State received under this section for the preceding fiscal year; and

(II) that amount multiplied by the sum of 1.5 percent and the percentage increase in the amount appropriated under this section from the preceding fiscal year.

(C) RATABLE REDUCTIONS- If the amount available for allocations under this paragraph is insufficient to pay those allocations in full, those allocations shall be ratably reduced, subject to subparagraph (B)(i).

(3) DECREASE IN FUNDS- If the amount available for allocations to States under paragraph (1) for a fiscal year is less than the amount allocated to the States under this section for the preceding fiscal year, those allocations shall be calculated as follows:

(A) ALLOCATIONS- If the amount available for allocations is greater than the amount allocated to the States for fiscal year 1997, each State shall be allocated the sum of—

(i) the amount the State received under this section for fiscal year 1997; and

(ii) an amount that bears the same relation to any remaining funds as the increase the State received under this section for the preceding fiscal year over fiscal year 1997 bears to the total of all such increases for all States.

(B) RATABLE REDUCTIONS- If the amount available for allocations is equal to or less than the amount allocated to the States for fiscal year 1997, each State shall be allocated

the amount the State received for fiscal year 1997, ratably reduced, if necessary.

(d) RESERVATION FOR STATE ACTIVITIES-

(1) IN GENERAL- Each State may reserve not more than the amount described in paragraph (2) for administration and other State-level activities in accordance with subsections (e) and (f).

(2) AMOUNT DESCRIBED- For each fiscal year, the Secretary shall determine and report to the State educational agency an amount that is 25 percent of the amount the State received under this section for fiscal year 1997, cumulatively adjusted by the Secretary for each succeeding fiscal year by the lesser of—

(A) the percentage increase, if any, from the preceding fiscal year in the State's allocation under this section; or

(B) the percentage increase, if any, from the preceding fiscal year in the Consumer Price Index For All Urban Consumers published by the Bureau of Labor Statistics of the Department of Labor.

(e) STATE ADMINISTRATION-

(1) IN GENERAL- For the purpose of administering this section (including the coordination of activities under this part with, and providing technical assistance to, other programs that provide services to children with disabilities) a State may use not more than 20 percent of the maximum amount the State may reserve under subsection (d) for any fiscal year.

(2) ADMINISTRATION OF PART C- Funds described in paragraph (1) may also be used for the administration of part C.

(f) OTHER STATE-LEVEL ACTIVITIES- Each State shall use any funds the State reserves under subsection (d) and does not use for administration under subsection (e)—

(1) for support services (including establishing and implementing the mediation process required by section 615(e)), which may benefit children with disabilities younger than 3 or older than 5 as long as those services also benefit children with disabilities aged 3 through 5;

(2) for direct services for children eligible for services under this section;

(3) for activities at the State and local levels to meet the performance goals established by the State under section 612(a)(15);

(4) to supplement other funds used to develop and implement a statewide coordinated services system designed to improve results for children and families, including children with disabilities and their families, but not more than

1 percent of the amount received by the State under this section for a fiscal year;

(5) to provide early intervention services (which shall include an educational component that promotes school readiness and incorporates preliteracy, language, and numeracy skills) in accordance with part C to children with disabilities who are eligible for services under this section and who previously received services under part C until such children enter, or are eligible under State law to enter, kindergarten; or

(6) at the State's discretion, to continue service coordination or case management for families who receive services under part C.

(g) SUBGRANTS TO LOCAL EDUCATIONAL AGENCIES-

(1) SUBGRANTS REQUIRED- Each State that receives a grant under this section for any fiscal year shall distribute all of the grant funds that the State does not reserve under subsection (d) to local educational agencies in the State that have established their eligibility under section 613, as follows:

(A) BASE PAYMENTS- The State shall first award each local educational agency described in paragraph (1) the amount that agency would have received under this section for fiscal year 1997 if the State had distributed 75 percent of its grant for that year under section 619(c)(3), as such section was then in effect.

(B) ALLOCATION OF REMAINING FUNDS- After making allocations under subparagraph (A), the State shall—

(i) allocate 85 percent of any remaining funds to those local educational agencies on the basis of the relative numbers of children enrolled in public and private elementary schools and secondary schools within the local educational agency's jurisdiction; and

(ii) allocate 15 percent of those remaining funds to those local educational agencies in accordance with their relative numbers of children living in poverty, as determined by the State educational agency.

(2) REALLOCATION OF FUNDS- If a State educational agency determines that a local educational agency is adequately providing a free appropriate public education to all children with disabilities aged 3 through 5 residing in the area served by the local educational agency with State and local funds, the State educational agency may reallocate any portion of the funds under this section that are not needed by that local educational agency to provide a free appropriate public education to other local educational agencies in the State

that are not adequately providing special education and related services to all children with disabilities aged 3 through 5 residing in the areas the other local educational agencies serve.

(h) PART C INAPPLICABLE- Part C does not apply to any child with a disability receiving a free appropriate public education, in accordance with this part, with funds received under this section.

(i) STATE DEFINED- In this section, the term 'State' means each of the 50 States, the District of Columbia, and the Commonwealth of Puerto Rico.

(j) AUTHORIZATION OF APPROPRIATIONS- There are authorized to be appropriated to carry out this section such sums as may be necessary.

PART C—INFANTS AND TODDLERS WITH DISABILITIES

SEC. 631. FINDINGS AND POLICY.

(a) FINDINGS- Congress finds that there is an urgent and substantial need—

(1) to enhance the development of infants and toddlers with disabilities, to minimize their potential for developmental delay, and to recognize the significant brain development that occurs during a child's first 3 years of life;

(2) to reduce the educational costs to our society, including our Nation's schools, by minimizing the need for special education and related services after infants and toddlers with disabilities reach school age;

(3) to maximize the potential for individuals with disabilities to live independently in society;

(4) to enhance the capacity of families to meet the special needs of their infants and toddlers with disabilities; and

(5) to enhance the capacity of State and local agencies and service providers to identify, evaluate, and meet the needs of all children, particularly minority, low-income, inner city, and rural children, and infants and toddlers in foster care.

(b) POLICY- It is the policy of the United States to provide financial assistance to States—

(1) to develop and implement a statewide, comprehensive, coordinated, multidisciplinary, interagency system that provides early intervention services for infants and toddlers with disabilities and their families;

(2) to facilitate the coordination of payment for early intervention services from Federal, State, local, and private sources (including public and private insurance coverage);

(3) to enhance State capacity to provide quality early intervention services and expand and improve existing early intervention services being provided to infants and toddlers with disabilities and their families; and

(4) to encourage States to expand opportunities for children under 3 years of age who would be at risk of having substantial developmental delay if they did not receive early intervention services.

SEC. 632. DEFINITIONS.

In this part:

(1) AT-RISK INFANT OR TODDLER- The term 'at-risk infant or toddler' means an individual under 3 years of age who would be at risk of experiencing a substantial developmental delay if early intervention services were not provided to the individual.

(2) COUNCIL- The term 'council' means a State interagency coordinating council established under section 641.

(3) DEVELOPMENTAL DELAY- The term 'developmental delay', when used with respect to an individual residing in a State, has the meaning given such term by the State under section 635(a)(1).

(4) EARLY INTERVENTION SERVICES- The term 'early intervention services' means developmental services that—

(A) are provided under public supervision;

(B) are provided at no cost except where Federal or State law provides for a system of payments by families, including a schedule of sliding fees;

(C) are designed to meet the developmental needs of an infant or toddler with a disability, as identified by the individualized family service plan team, in any 1 or more of the following areas:

(i) physical development;

(ii) cognitive development;

(iii) communication development;

(iv) social or emotional development; or

(v) adaptive development;

(D) meet the standards of the State in which the services are provided, including the requirements of this part;

(E) include—

(i) family training, counseling, and home visits;

(ii) special instruction;

(iii) speech-language pathology and audiology services, and sign language and cued language services;

(iv) occupational therapy;

(v) physical therapy;

(vi) psychological services;

(vii) service coordination services;

(viii) medical services only for diagnostic or evaluation purposes;

(ix) early identification, screening, and assessment services;

(x) health services necessary to enable the infant or toddler to benefit from the other early intervention services;

(xi) social work services;

(xii) vision services;

(xiii) assistive technology devices and assistive technology services; and

(xiv) transportation and related costs that are necessary to enable an infant or toddler and the infant's or toddler's family to receive another service described in this paragraph;

(F) are provided by qualified personnel, including—

(i) special educators;

(ii) speech-language pathologists and audiologists;

(iii) occupational therapists;

(iv) physical therapists;

(v) psychologists;

(vi) social workers;

(vii) nurses;

(viii) registered dietitians;

(ix) family therapists;

(x) vision specialists, including ophthalmologists and optometrists;

(xi) orientation and mobility specialists; and

(xii) pediatricians and other physicians;

(G) to the maximum extent appropriate, are provided in natural environments, including the home, and community settings in which children without disabilities participate; and

(H) are provided in conformity with an individualized family service plan adopted in accordance with section 636.

(5) INFANT OR TODDLER WITH A DISABILITY- The term 'infant or toddler with a disability'—

(A) means an individual under 3 years of age who needs early intervention services because the individual—

(i) is experiencing developmental delays, as measured by appropriate diagnostic instruments and procedures in 1 or more of the areas of cognitive development, physical development, communication development, social or emotional development, and adaptive development; or

(ii) has a diagnosed physical or mental

condition that has a high probability of resulting in developmental delay; and

(B) may also include, at a State's discretion—

(i) at-risk infants and toddlers; and

(ii) children with disabilities who are eligible for services under section 619 and who previously received services under this part until such children enter, or are eligible under State law to enter, kindergarten or elementary school, as appropriate, provided that any programs under this part serving such children shall include—

(I) an educational component that promotes school readiness and incorporates pre-literacy, language, and numeracy skills; and

(II) a written notification to parents of their rights and responsibilities in determining whether their child will continue to receive services under this part or participate in preschool programs under section 619.

SEC. 633. GENERAL AUTHORITY.

The Secretary shall, in accordance with this part, make grants to States (from their allotments under section 643) to assist each State to maintain and implement a statewide, comprehensive, coordinated, multidisciplinary, interagency system to provide early intervention services for infants and toddlers with disabilities and their families.

SEC. 634. ELIGIBILITY.

In order to be eligible for a grant under section 633, a State shall provide assurances to the Secretary that the State—

(1) has adopted a policy that appropriate early intervention services are available to all infants and toddlers with disabilities in the State and their families, including Indian infants and toddlers with disabilities and their families residing on a reservation geographically located in the State, infants and toddlers with disabilities who are homeless children and their families, and infants and toddlers with disabilities who are wards of the State; and

(2) has in effect a statewide system that meets the requirements of section 635.

SEC. 635. REQUIREMENTS FOR STATEWIDE SYSTEM.

(a) IN GENERAL- A statewide system described in section 633 shall include, at a minimum, the following components:

(1) A rigorous definition of the term 'developmental delay' that will be used by the State in carrying out programs under this part in order to appropriately identify infants and toddlers with disabilities that are in need of services under this part.

(2) A State policy that is in effect and that ensures that appropriate early intervention services based on scientifically based research, to the extent practicable, are available to all infants and toddlers with disabilities and their families, including Indian infants and toddlers with disabilities and their families residing on a reservation geographically located in the State and infants and toddlers with disabilities who are homeless children and their families.

(3) A timely, comprehensive, multidisciplinary evaluation of the functioning of each infant or toddler with a disability in the State, and a family-directed identification of the needs of each family of such an infant or toddler, to assist appropriately in the development of the infant or toddler.

(4) For each infant or toddler with a disability in the State, an individualized family service plan in accordance with section 636, including service coordination services in accordance with such service plan.

(5) A comprehensive child find system, consistent with part B, including a system for making referrals to service providers that includes timelines and provides for participation by primary referral sources and that ensures rigorous standards for appropriately identifying infants and toddlers with disabilities for services under this part that will reduce the need for future services.

(6) A public awareness program focusing on early identification of infants and toddlers with disabilities, including the preparation and dissemination by the lead agency designated or established under paragraph (10) to all primary referral sources, especially hospitals and physicians, of information to be given to parents, especially to inform parents with premature infants, or infants with other physical risk factors associated with learning or developmental complications, on the availability of early intervention services under this part and of services under section 619, and procedures for assisting such sources in disseminating such information to parents of infants and toddlers with disabilities.

(7) A central directory that includes information on early intervention services, resources, and experts available in the State and research and demonstration projects being

conducted in the State.

(8) A comprehensive system of personnel development, including the training of paraprofessionals and the training of primary referral sources with respect to the basic components of early intervention services available in the State that—

(A) shall include—

(i) implementing innovative strategies and activities for the recruitment and retention of early education service providers;

(ii) promoting the preparation of early intervention providers who are fully and appropriately qualified to provide early intervention services under this part; and

(iii) training personnel to coordinate transition services for infants and toddlers served under this part from a program providing early intervention services under this part and under part B (other than section 619), to a preschool program receiving funds under section 619, or another appropriate program; and

(B) may include—

(i) training personnel to work in rural and inner-city areas; and

(ii) training personnel in the emotional and social development of young children.

(9) Policies and procedures relating to the establishment and maintenance of qualifications to ensure that personnel necessary to carry out this part are appropriately and adequately prepared and trained, including the establishment and maintenance of qualifications that are consistent with any State-approved or recognized certification, licensing, registration, or other comparable requirements that apply to the area in which such personnel are providing early intervention services, except that nothing in this part (including this paragraph) shall be construed to prohibit the use of paraprofessionals and assistants who are appropriately trained and supervised in accordance with State law, regulation, or written policy, to assist in the provision of early intervention services under this part to infants and toddlers with disabilities.

(10) A single line of responsibility in a lead agency designated or established by the Governor for carrying out—

(A) the general administration and supervision of programs and activities receiving assistance under section 633, and the monitoring of programs and activities used by the State to carry out this part, whether or not such programs or activities are receiving assistance made available under section 633, to ensure that the State complies with this part;

(B) the identification and coordination of all available resources within the State from Federal, State, local, and private sources;

(C) the assignment of financial responsibility in accordance with section 637(a)(2) to the appropriate agencies;

(D) the development of procedures to ensure that services are provided to infants and toddlers with disabilities and their families under this part in a timely manner pending the resolution of any disputes among public agencies or service providers;

(E) the resolution of intra- and interagency disputes; and

(F) the entry into formal interagency agreements that define the financial responsibility of each agency for paying for early intervention services (consistent with State law) and procedures for resolving disputes and that include all additional components necessary to ensure meaningful cooperation and coordination.

(11) A policy pertaining to the contracting or making of other arrangements with service providers to provide early intervention services in the State, consistent with the provisions of this part, including the contents of the application used and the conditions of the contract or other arrangements.

(12) A procedure for securing timely reimbursements of funds used under this part in accordance with section 640(a).

(13) Procedural safeguards with respect to programs under this part, as required by section 639.

(14) A system for compiling data requested by the Secretary under section 618 that relates to this part.

(15) A State interagency coordinating council that meets the requirements of section 641.

(16) Policies and procedures to ensure that, consistent with section 636(d)(5)—

(A) to the maximum extent appropriate, early intervention services are provided in natural environments; and

(B) the provision of early intervention services for any infant or toddler with a disability occurs in a setting other than a natural environment that is most appropriate, as determined by the parent and the individualized family service plan team, only when early intervention cannot be achieved satisfactorily for the infant or toddler in a natural environment.

(b) POLICY- In implementing subsection (a)(9), a State may adopt a policy that includes making ongoing good-faith efforts to recruit and hire appropriately and adequately trained personnel to provide early intervention services to infants and toddlers with disabilities, including, in a geographic area of the State where there is a shortage of such personnel, the most qualified individuals available who are making satisfactory progress toward completing applicable course work necessary to meet the standards described in subsection (a)(9).

(c) Flexibility To Serve Children 3 Years of Age Until Entrance Into Elementary School-

(1) IN GENERAL- A statewide system described in section 633 may include a State policy, developed and implemented jointly by the lead agency and the State educational agency, under which parents of children with disabilities who are eligible for services under section 619 and previously received services under this part, may choose the continuation of early intervention services (which shall include an educational component that promotes school readiness and incorporates preliteracy, language, and numeracy skills) for such children under this part until such children enter, or are eligible under State law to enter, kindergarten.

(2) REQUIREMENTS- If a statewide system includes a State policy described in paragraph (1), the statewide system shall ensure that—

(A) parents of children with disabilities served pursuant to this subsection are provided annual notice that contains—

(i) a description of the rights of such parents to elect to receive services pursuant to this subsection or under part B; and

(ii) an explanation of the differences between services provided pursuant to this subsection and services provided under part B, including—

(I) types of services and the locations at which the services are provided;

(II) applicable procedural safeguards; and

(III) possible costs (including any fees to be charged to families as described in section 632(4)(B)), if any, to parents of infants or toddlers with disabilities;

(B) services provided pursuant to this subsection include an educational component that promotes school readiness and incorporates preliteracy, language, and numeracy skills;

(C) the State policy will not affect the right of any child served pursuant to this subsection to instead receive a free appropriate public education under part B;

(D) all early intervention services outlined in the child's individualized family service plan

under section 636 are continued while any eligibility determination is being made for services under this subsection;

(E) the parents of infants or toddlers with disabilities (as defined in section 632(5)(A)) provide informed written consent to the State, before such infants or toddlers reach 3 years of age, as to whether such parents intend to choose the continuation of early intervention services pursuant to this subsection for such infants or toddlers;

(F) the requirements under section 637(a)(9) shall not apply with respect to a child who is receiving services in accordance with this subsection until not less than 90 days (and at the discretion of the parties to the conference, not more than 9 months) before the time the child will no longer receive those services; and

(G) there will be a referral for evaluation for early intervention services of a child who experiences a substantiated case of trauma due to exposure to family violence (as defined in section 320 of the Family Violence Prevention and Services Act).

(3) REPORTING REQUIREMENT- If a statewide system includes a State policy described in paragraph (1), the State shall submit to the Secretary, in the State's report under section 637(b)(4)(A), a report on the number and percentage of children with disabilities who are eligible for services under section 619 but whose parents choose for such children to continue to receive early intervention services under this part.

(4) AVAILABLE FUNDS- If a statewide system includes a State policy described in paragraph (1), the policy shall describe the funds (including an identification as Federal, State, or local funds) that will be used to ensure that the option described in paragraph (1) is available to eligible children and families who provide the consent described in paragraph (2)(E), including fees (if any) to be charged to families as described in section 632(4)(B).

(5) RULES OF CONSTRUCTION-

(A) SERVICES UNDER PART B- If a statewide system includes a State policy described in paragraph (1), a State that provides services in accordance with this subsection to a child with a disability who is eligible for services under section 619 shall not be required to provide the child with a free appropriate public education under part B for the period of time in which the child is receiving services under this part.

(B) SERVICES UNDER THIS PART- Nothing in this subsection shall be construed to require a provider of services under this part to provide a child served under this part with a free appropriate public education.

SEC. 636. INDIVIDUALIZED FAMILY SERVICE PLAN.

(a) ASSESSMENT AND PROGRAM DEVELOPMENT- A statewide system described in section 633 shall provide, at a minimum, for each infant or toddler with a disability, and the infant's or toddler's family, to receive—

(1) a multidisciplinary assessment of the unique strengths and needs of the infant or toddler and the identification of services appropriate to meet such needs;

(2) a family-directed assessment of the resources, priorities, and concerns of the family and the identification of the supports and services necessary to enhance the family's capacity to meet the developmental needs of the infant or toddler; and

(3) a written individualized family service plan developed by a multidisciplinary team, including the parents, as required by subsection (e), including a description of the appropriate transition services for the infant or toddler.

(b) PERIODIC REVIEW- The individualized family service plan shall be evaluated once a year and the family shall be provided a review of the plan at 6-month intervals (or more often where appropriate based on infant or toddler and family needs).

(c) PROMPTNESS AFTER ASSESSMENT- The individualized family service plan shall be developed within a reasonable time after the assessment required by subsection (a)(1) is completed. With the parents' consent, early intervention services may commence prior to the completion of the assessment.

(d) CONTENT OF PLAN- The individualized family service plan shall be in writing and contain—

(1) a statement of the infant's or toddler's present levels of physical development, cognitive development, communication development, social or emotional development, and adaptive development, based on objective criteria;

(2) a statement of the family's resources, priorities, and concerns relating to enhancing the development of the family's infant or toddler with a disability;

(3) a statement of the measurable results or outcomes expected to be achieved for the infant or toddler and the family, including pre-literacy and language skills, as developmentally appropriate for the child, and the criteria, procedures, and timelines used to determine the degree to which progress toward achieving the results or outcomes is being made and whether modifications or revisions of the results or outcomes or services are necessary;

(4) a statement of specific early intervention services based on peer-reviewed research, to the extent practicable, necessary to meet the unique needs of the infant or toddler and the family, including the frequency, intensity, and method of delivering services;

(5) a statement of the natural environments in which early intervention services will appropriately be provided, including a justification of the extent, if any, to which the services will not be provided in a natural environment;

(6) the projected dates for initiation of services and the anticipated length, duration, and frequency of the services;

(7) the identification of the service coordinator from the profession most immediately relevant to the infant's or toddler's or family's needs (or who is otherwise qualified to carry out all applicable responsibilities under this part) who will be responsible for the implementation of the plan and coordination with other agencies and persons, including transition services; and

(8) the steps to be taken to support the transition of the toddler with a disability to preschool or other appropriate services.

(e) PARENTAL CONSENT- The contents of the individualized family service plan shall be fully explained to the parents and informed written consent from the parents shall be obtained prior to the provision of early intervention services described in such plan. If the parents do not provide consent with respect to a particular early intervention service, then only the early intervention services to which consent is obtained shall be provided.

SEC. 637. STATE APPLICATION AND ASSURANCES.

(a) APPLICATION- A State desiring to receive a grant under section 633 shall submit an application to the Secretary at such time and in such manner as the Secretary may reasonably require. The application shall contain—

(1) a designation of the lead agency in the State that will be responsible for the administration of funds provided under section 633;

(2) a certification to the Secretary that the arrangements to establish financial responsibility for services provided under this part pursuant to section 640(b) are current as of the date of submission of the certification;

(3) information demonstrating eligibility of the State under section 634, including—

(A) information demonstrating to the Secretary's satisfaction that the State has in effect the statewide system required by section 633; and

(B) a description of services to be provided to infants and toddlers with disabilities and their families through the system;

(4) if the State provides services to at-risk infants and toddlers through the statewide system, a description of such services;

(5) a description of the uses for which funds will be expended in accordance with this part;

(6) a description of the State policies and procedures that require the referral for early intervention services under this part of a child under the age of 3 who—

(A) is involved in a substantiated case of child abuse or neglect; or

(B) is identified as affected by illegal substance abuse, or withdrawal symptoms resulting from prenatal drug exposure;

(7) a description of the procedure used to ensure that resources are made available under this part for all geographic areas within the State;

(8) a description of State policies and procedures that ensure that, prior to the adoption by the State of any other policy or procedure necessary to meet the requirements of this part, there are public hearings, adequate notice of the hearings, and an opportunity for comment available to the general public, including individuals with disabilities and parents of infants and toddlers with disabilities;

(9) a description of the policies and procedures to be used—

(A) to ensure a smooth transition for toddlers receiving early intervention services under this part (and children receiving those services under section 635(c)) to preschool, school, other appropriate services, or exiting the program, including a description of how—

(i) the families of such toddlers and children will be included in the transition plans required by subparagraph (C); and

(ii) the lead agency designated or established under section 635(a)(10) will—

(I) notify the local educational agency for the area in which such a child resides that the child will shortly reach the age of eligibility for preschool services under part B, as determined in accordance with State law;

(II) in the case of a child who may be eligible for such preschool services, with the approval of the family of the child, convene a conference among the lead agency, the family, and the local educational agency not less than 90 days (and at the discretion of all such parties, not more than 9 months) before the child is eligible for the preschool services, to discuss any such services that the child may receive; and

(III) in the case of a child who may not be eligible for such preschool services, with the approval of the family, make reasonable efforts to convene a conference among the lead agency, the family, and providers of other appropriate services for children who are not eligible for preschool services under part B, to discuss the appropriate services that the child may receive;

(B) to review the child's program options for the period from the child's third birthday through the remainder of the school year; and

(C) to establish a transition plan, including, as appropriate, steps to exit from the program;

(10) a description of State efforts to promote collaboration among Early Head Start programs under section 645A of the Head Start Act, early education and child care programs, and services under part C; and

(11) such other information and assurances as the Secretary may reasonably require.

(b) ASSURANCES- The application described in subsection (a)—

(1) shall provide satisfactory assurance that Federal funds made available under section 643 to the State will be expended in accordance with this part;

(2) shall contain an assurance that the State will comply with the requirements of section 640;

(3) shall provide satisfactory assurance that the control of funds provided under section 643, and title to property derived from those funds, will be in a public agency for the uses and purposes provided in this part and that a public agency will administer such funds and property;

(4) shall provide for—

(A) making such reports in such form and containing such information as the Secretary may require to carry out the Secretary's functions under this part; and

(B) keeping such reports and affording such access to the reports as the Secretary may find necessary to ensure the correctness and verification of those reports and proper disbursement of Federal funds under this part;

(5) provide satisfactory assurance that Federal funds made available under section 643

to the State—

(A) will not be commingled with State funds; and

(B) will be used so as to supplement the level of State and local funds expended for infants and toddlers with disabilities and their families and in no case to supplant those State and local funds;

(6) shall provide satisfactory assurance that such fiscal control and fund accounting procedures will be adopted as may be necessary to ensure proper disbursement of, and accounting for, Federal funds paid under section 643 to the State;

(7) shall provide satisfactory assurance that policies and procedures have been adopted to ensure meaningful involvement of underserved groups, including minority, low-income, homeless, and rural families and children with disabilities who are wards of the State, in the planning and implementation of all the requirements of this part; and

(8) shall contain such other information and assurances as the Secretary may reasonably require by regulation.

(c) STANDARD FOR DISAPPROVAL OF APPLICATION- The Secretary may not disapprove such an application unless the Secretary determines, after notice and opportunity for a hearing, that the application fails to comply with the requirements of this section.

(d) SUBSEQUENT STATE APPLICATION- If a State has on file with the Secretary a policy, procedure, or assurance that demonstrates that the State meets a requirement of this section, including any policy or procedure filed under this part (as in effect before the date of enactment of the Individuals with Disabilities Education Improvement Act of 2004), the Secretary shall consider the State to have met the requirement for purposes of receiving a grant under this part.

(e) MODIFICATION OF APPLICATION- An application submitted by a State in accordance with this section shall remain in effect until the State submits to the Secretary such modifications as the State determines necessary. This section shall apply to a modification of an application to the same extent and in the same manner as this section applies to the original application.

(f) MODIFICATIONS REQUIRED BY THE SECRETARY- The Secretary may require a State to modify its application under this section, but only to the extent necessary to ensure the State's compliance with this part, if—

(1) an amendment is made to this title, or a Federal regulation issued under this title;

(2) a new interpretation of this title is made by a Federal court or the State's highest court; or

(3) an official finding of noncompliance with Federal law or regulations is made with respect to the State.

SEC. 638. USES OF FUNDS.

In addition to using funds provided under section 633 to maintain and implement the statewide system required by such section, a State may use such funds—

(1) for direct early intervention services for infants and toddlers with disabilities, and their families, under this part that are not otherwise funded through other public or private sources;

(2) to expand and improve on services for infants and toddlers and their families under this part that are otherwise available;

(3) to provide a free appropriate public education, in accordance with part B, to children with disabilities from their third birthday to the beginning of the following school year;

(4) with the written consent of the parents, to continue to provide early intervention services under this part to children with disabilities from their 3rd birthday until such children enter, or are eligible under State law to enter, kindergarten, in lieu of a free appropriate public education provided in accordance with part B; and

(5) in any State that does not provide services for at-risk infants and toddlers under section 637(a)(4), to strengthen the statewide system by initiating, expanding, or improving collaborative efforts related to at-risk infants and toddlers, including establishing linkages with appropriate public or private community-based organizations, services, and personnel for the purposes of—

(A) identifying and evaluating at-risk infants and toddlers;

(B) making referrals of the infants and toddlers identified and evaluated under subparagraph (A); and

(C) conducting periodic follow-up on each such referral to determine if the status of the infant or toddler involved has changed with respect to the eligibility of the infant or toddler for services under this part.

SEC. 639. PROCEDURAL SAFEGUARDS.

(a) MINIMUM PROCEDURES- The procedural safeguards required to be included in a statewide system under section 635(a)(13) shall provide, at a minimum, the following:

(1) The timely administrative resolution of complaints by parents. Any party aggrieved by the findings and decision regarding an administrative complaint shall have the right to bring a civil action with respect to the complaint in any State court of competent jurisdiction or in a district court of the United States without regard to the amount in controversy. In any action brought under this paragraph, the court shall receive the records of the administrative proceedings, shall hear additional evidence at the request of a party, and, basing its decision on the preponderance of the evidence, shall grant such relief as the court determines is appropriate.

(2) The right to confidentiality of personally identifiable information, including the right of parents to written notice of and written consent to the exchange of such information among agencies consistent with Federal and State law.

(3) The right of the parents to determine whether they, their infant or toddler, or other family members will accept or decline any early intervention service under this part in accordance with State law without jeopardizing other early intervention services under this part.

(4) The opportunity for parents to examine records relating to assessment, screening, eligibility determinations, and the development and implementation of the individualized family service plan.

(5) Procedures to protect the rights of the infant or toddler whenever the parents of the infant or toddler are not known or cannot be found or the infant or toddler is a ward of the State, including the assignment of an individual (who shall not be an employee of the State lead agency, or other State agency, and who shall not be any person, or any employee of a person, providing early intervention services to the infant or toddler or any family member of the infant or toddler) to act as a surrogate for the parents.

(6) Written prior notice to the parents of the infant or toddler with a disability whenever the State agency or service provider proposes to initiate or change, or refuses to initiate or change, the identification, evaluation, or placement of the infant or toddler with a disability, or the provision of appropriate early intervention services to the infant or toddler.

(7) Procedures designed to ensure that the notice required by paragraph (6) fully informs the parents, in the parents' native language, unless it clearly is not feasible to do so, of all procedures available pursuant to this section.

(8) The right of parents to use mediation in accordance with section 615, except that—

(A) any reference in the section to a State educational agency shall be considered to be a reference to a State's lead agency established or designated under section 635(a)(10);

(B) any reference in the section to a local educational agency shall be considered to be a reference to a local service provider or the State's lead agency under this part, as the case may be; and

(C) any reference in the section to the provision of a free appropriate public education to children with disabilities shall be considered to be a reference to the provision of appropriate early intervention services to infants and toddlers with disabilities.

(b) SERVICES DURING PENDENCY OF PROCEEDINGS- During the pendency of any proceeding or action involving a complaint by the parents of an infant or toddler with a disability, unless the State agency and the parents otherwise agree, the infant or toddler shall continue to receive the appropriate early intervention services currently being provided or, if applying for initial services, shall receive the services not in dispute.

SEC. 640. PAYOR OF LAST RESORT.

(a) NONSUBSTITUTION- Funds provided under section 643 may not be used to satisfy a financial commitment for services that would have been paid for from another public or private source, including any medical program administered by the Secretary of Defense, but for the enactment of this part, except that whenever considered necessary to prevent a delay in the receipt of appropriate early intervention services by an infant, toddler, or family in a timely fashion, funds provided under section 643 may be used to pay the provider of services pending reimbursement from the agency that has ultimate responsibility for the payment.

(b) OBLIGATIONS RELATED TO AND METHODS OF ENSURING SERVICES-

(1) ESTABLISHING FINANCIAL RESPONSIBILITY FOR SERVICES-

(A) IN GENERAL- The Chief Executive Officer of a State or designee of the officer shall ensure that an interagency agreement or other mechanism for interagency coordination is in effect between each public agency and the designated lead agency, in order to ensure—

(i) the provision of, and financial responsibility for, services provided under this part; and

(ii) such services are consistent with the requirements of section 635 and the State's application pursuant to section 637, including the provision of such services during the pendency of any such dispute.

(B) CONSISTENCY BETWEEN AGREEMENTS OR MECHANISMS UNDER PART B- The Chief Executive Officer of a State or designee of the officer shall ensure that the terms and conditions of such agreement or mechanism are consistent with the terms and conditions of the State's agreement or mechanism under section 612(a)(12), where appropriate.

(2) REIMBURSEMENT FOR SERVICES BY PUBLIC AGENCY-

(A) IN GENERAL- If a public agency other than an educational agency fails to provide or pay for the services pursuant to an agreement required under paragraph (1), the local educational agency or State agency (as determined by the Chief Executive Officer or designee) shall provide or pay for the provision of such services to the child.

(B) REIMBURSEMENT- Such local educational agency or State agency is authorized to claim reimbursement for the services from the public agency that failed to provide or pay for such services and such public agency shall reimburse the local educational agency or State agency pursuant to the terms of the interagency agreement or other mechanism required under paragraph (1).

(3) SPECIAL RULE- The requirements of paragraph (1) may be met through—

(A) State statute or regulation;

(B) signed agreements between respective agency officials that clearly identify the responsibilities of each agency relating to the provision of services; or

(C) other appropriate written methods as determined by the Chief Executive Officer of the State or designee of the officer and approved by the Secretary through the review and approval of the State's application pursuant to section 637.

(c) REDUCTION OF OTHER BENEFITS- Nothing in this part shall be construed to permit the State to reduce medical or other assistance available or to alter eligibility under title V of the Social Security Act (relating to maternal and child health) or title XIX of the Social Security Act (relating to medicaid for infants or toddlers with disabilities) within the State.

SEC. 641. STATE INTERAGENCY COORDINATING COUNCIL.

(a) ESTABLISHMENT-

(1) IN GENERAL- A State that desires to receive financial assistance under this part shall establish a State interagency coordinating council.

(2) APPOINTMENT- The council shall be appointed by the Governor. In making appointments to the council, the Governor shall ensure that the membership of the council reasonably represents the population of the State.

(3) CHAIRPERSON- The Governor shall designate a member of the council to serve as the chairperson of the council, or shall require the council to so designate such a member. Any member of the council who is a representative of the lead agency designated under section 635(a)(10) may not serve as the chairperson of the council.

(b) COMPOSITION-

(1) IN GENERAL- The council shall be composed as follows:

(A) PARENTS- Not less than 20 percent of the members shall be parents of infants or toddlers with disabilities or children with disabilities aged 12 or younger, with knowledge of, or experience with, programs for infants and toddlers with disabilities. Not less than 1 such member shall be a parent of an infant or toddler with a disability or a child with a disability aged 6 or younger.

(B) SERVICE PROVIDERS- Not less than 20 percent of the members shall be public or private providers of early intervention services.

(C) STATE LEGISLATURE- Not less than 1 member shall be from the State legislature.

(D) PERSONNEL PREPARATION- Not less than 1 member shall be involved in personnel preparation.

(E) AGENCY FOR EARLY INTERVENTION SERVICES- Not less than 1 member shall be from each of the State agencies involved in the provision of, or payment for, early intervention services to infants and toddlers with disabilities and their families and shall have sufficient authority to engage in policy planning and implementation on behalf of such agencies.

(F) AGENCY FOR PRESCHOOL SERVICES- Not less than 1 member shall be from the State educational agency responsible for preschool services to children with disabilities and shall have sufficient authority to engage in policy planning and implementation on behalf of such agency.

(G) STATE MEDICAID AGENCY- Not less than 1 member shall be from the agency responsible for the State medicaid program.

(H) HEAD START AGENCY- Not less than 1 member shall be a representative from a Head Start agency or program in the State.

(I) CHILD CARE AGENCY- Not less than 1 member shall be a representative from a State agency responsible for child care.

(J) AGENCY FOR HEALTH INSURANCE- Not less than 1 member shall be from the agency responsible for the State regulation of health insurance.

(K) OFFICE OF THE COORDINATOR OF EDUCATION OF HOMELESS CHILDREN AND YOUTH- Not less than 1 member shall be a representative designated by the Office of Coordinator for Education of Homeless Children and Youths.

(L) STATE FOSTER CARE REPRESENTATIVE- Not less than 1 member shall be a representative from the State child welfare agency responsible for foster care.

(M) MENTAL HEALTH AGENCY- Not less than 1 member shall be a representative from the State agency responsible for children's mental health.

(2) OTHER MEMBERS- The council may include other members selected by the Governor, including a representative from the Bureau of Indian Affairs (BIA), or where there is no BIA-operated or BIA-funded school, from the Indian Health Service or the tribe or tribal council.

(c) MEETINGS- The council shall meet, at a minimum, on a quarterly basis, and in such places as the council determines necessary. The meetings shall be publicly announced, and, to the extent appropriate, open and accessible to the general public.

(d) MANAGEMENT AUTHORITY- Subject to the approval of the Governor, the council may prepare and approve a budget using funds under this part to conduct hearings and forums, to reimburse members of the council for reasonable and necessary expenses for attending council meetings and performing council duties (including child care for parent representatives), to pay compensation to a member of the council if the member is not employed or must forfeit wages from other employment when performing official council business, to hire staff, and to obtain the services of such professional, technical, and clerical personnel as may be necessary to carry out its functions under this part.

(e) FUNCTIONS OF COUNCIL-

(1) DUTIES- The council shall—

(A) advise and assist the lead agency designated or established under section 635(a)(10) in the performance of the responsibilities set forth in such section, particularly the identification of the sources of fiscal and other support for services for early intervention programs, assignment of financial responsibility to the appropriate agency, and the promotion of the interagency agreements;

(B) advise and assist the lead agency in the preparation of applications and amendments thereto;

(C) advise and assist the State educational agency regarding the transition of toddlers with disabilities to preschool and other appropriate services; and

(D) prepare and submit an annual report to the Governor and to the Secretary on the status of early intervention programs for infants and toddlers with disabilities and their families operated within the State.

(2) AUTHORIZED ACTIVITY- The council may advise and assist the lead agency and the State educational agency regarding the provision of appropriate services for children from birth through age 5. The council may advise appropriate agencies in the State with respect to the integration of services for infants and toddlers with disabilities and at-risk infants and toddlers and their families, regardless of whether at-risk infants and toddlers are eligible for early intervention services in the State.

(f) CONFLICT OF INTEREST- No member of the council shall cast a vote on any matter that is likely to provide a direct financial benefit to that member or otherwise give the appearance of a conflict of interest under State law.

SEC. 642. FEDERAL ADMINISTRATION.

Sections 616, 617, and 618 shall, to the extent not inconsistent with this part, apply to the program authorized by this part, except that—

(1) any reference in such sections to a State educational agency shall be considered to be a reference to a State's lead agency established or designated under section 635(a)(10);

(2) any reference in such sections to a local educational agency, educational service agency, or a State agency shall be considered to be a reference to an early intervention service provider under this part; and

(3) any reference to the education of

children with disabilities or the education of all children with disabilities shall be considered to be a reference to the provision of appropriate early intervention services to infants and toddlers with disabilities.

SEC. 643. ALLOCATION OF FUNDS.

(a) RESERVATION OF FUNDS FOR OUTLYING AREAS-

(1) IN GENERAL- From the sums appropriated to carry out this part for any fiscal year, the Secretary may reserve not more than 1 percent for payments to Guam, American Samoa, the United States Virgin Islands, and the Commonwealth of the Northern Mariana Islands in accordance with their respective needs for assistance under this part.

(2) CONSOLIDATION OF FUNDS- The provisions of Public Law 95-134, permitting the consolidation of grants to the outlying areas, shall not apply to funds those areas receive under this part.

(b) PAYMENTS TO INDIANS-

(1) IN GENERAL- The Secretary shall, subject to this subsection, make payments to the Secretary of the Interior to be distributed to tribes, tribal organizations (as defined under section 4 of the Indian Self-Determination and Education Assistance Act), or consortia of the above entities for the coordination of assistance in the provision of early intervention services by the States to infants and toddlers with disabilities and their families on reservations served by elementary schools and secondary schools for Indian children operated or funded by the Department of the Interior. The amount of such payment for any fiscal year shall be 1.25 percent of the aggregate of the amount available to all States under this part for such fiscal year.

(2) ALLOCATION- For each fiscal year, the Secretary of the Interior shall distribute the entire payment received under paragraph (1) by providing to each tribe, tribal organization, or consortium an amount based on the number of infants and toddlers residing on the reservation, as determined annually, divided by the total of such children served by all tribes, tribal organizations, or consortia.

(3) INFORMATION- To receive a payment under this subsection, the tribe, tribal organization, or consortium shall submit such information to the Secretary of the Interior as is needed to determine the amounts to be distributed under paragraph (2).

(4) USE OF FUNDS- The funds received by a tribe, tribal organization, or consortium shall be used to assist States in child find, screening, and other procedures for the early identification of Indian children under 3 years of age and for parent training. Such funds may also be used to provide early intervention services in accordance with this part. Such activities may be carried out directly or through contracts or cooperative agreements with the Bureau of Indian Affairs, local educational agencies, and other public or private nonprofit organizations. The tribe, tribal organization, or consortium is encouraged to involve Indian parents in the development and implementation of these activities. The above entities shall, as appropriate, make referrals to local, State, or Federal entities for the provision of services or further diagnosis.

(5) REPORTS- To be eligible to receive a payment under paragraph (2), a tribe, tribal organization, or consortium shall make a biennial report to the Secretary of the Interior of activities undertaken under this subsection, including the number of contracts and cooperative agreements entered into, the number of infants and toddlers contacted and receiving services for each year, and the estimated number of infants and toddlers needing services during the 2 years following the year in which the report is made. The Secretary of the Interior shall include a summary of this information on a biennial basis to the Secretary of Education along with such other information as required under section 611(h)(3)(E). The Secretary of Education may require any additional information from the Secretary of the Interior.

(6) PROHIBITED USES OF FUNDS- None of the funds under this subsection may be used by the Secretary of the Interior for administrative purposes, including child count, and the provision of technical assistance.

(c) STATE ALLOTMENTS-

(1) IN GENERAL- Except as provided in paragraphs (2) and (3), from the funds remaining for each fiscal year after the reservation and payments under subsections (a), (b), and (e), the Secretary shall first allot to each State an amount that bears the same ratio to the amount of such remainder as the number of infants and toddlers in the State bears to the number of infants and toddlers in all States.

(2) MINIMUM ALLOTMENTS- Except as provided in paragraph (3), no State shall receive an amount under this section for any fiscal year that is less than the greater of—

(A) 1/2 of 1 percent of the remaining amount described in paragraph (1); or

(B) $500,000.

(3) RATABLE REDUCTION-

(A) IN GENERAL- If the sums made available under this part for any fiscal year are insufficient to pay the full amounts that all States are eligible to receive under this subsection for such year, the Secretary shall ratably reduce the allotments to such States for such year.

(B) ADDITIONAL FUNDS- If additional funds become available for making payments under this subsection for a fiscal year, allotments that were reduced under subparagraph (A) shall be increased on the same basis the allotments were reduced.

(4) DEFINITIONS- In this subsection—

(A) the terms 'infants' and 'toddlers' mean children under 3 years of age; and

(B) the term 'State' means each of the 50 States, the District of Columbia, and the Commonwealth of Puerto Rico.

(d) REALLOTMENT OF FUNDS- If a State elects not to receive its allotment under subsection (c), the Secretary shall reallot, among the remaining States, amounts from such State in accordance with such subsection.

(e) RESERVATION FOR STATE INCENTIVE GRANTS-

(1) IN GENERAL- For any fiscal year for which the amount appropriated pursuant to the authorization of appropriations under section 644 exceeds $460,000,000, the Secretary shall reserve 15 percent of such appropriated amount to provide grants to States that are carrying out the policy described in section 635(c) in order to facilitate the implementation of such policy.

(2) AMOUNT OF GRANT-

(A) IN GENERAL- Notwithstanding paragraphs (2) and (3) of subsection (c), the Secretary shall provide a grant to each State under paragraph (1) in an amount that bears the same ratio to the amount reserved under such paragraph as the number of infants and toddlers in the State bears to the number of infants and toddlers in all States receiving grants under such paragraph.

(B) MAXIMUM AMOUNT- No State shall receive a grant under paragraph (1) for any fiscal year in an amount that is greater than 20 percent of the amount reserved under such paragraph for the fiscal year.

(3) CARRYOVER OF AMOUNTS-

(A) FIRST SUCCEEDING FISCAL YEAR- Pursuant to section 421(b) of the General Education Provisions Act, amounts under a grant provided under paragraph (1) that are not obligated and expended prior to the beginning of the first fiscal year succeeding the fiscal year for which such amounts were appropriated shall remain available for obligation and expenditure during such first succeeding fiscal year.

(B) SECOND SUCCEEDING FISCAL YEAR- Amounts under a grant provided under paragraph (1) that are not obligated and expended prior to the beginning of the second fiscal year succeeding the fiscal year for which such amounts were appropriated shall be returned to the Secretary and used to make grants to States under section 633 (from their allotments under this section) during such second succeeding fiscal year.

SEC. 644. AUTHORIZATION OF APPROPRIATIONS.

For the purpose of carrying out this part, there are authorized to be appropriated such sums as may be necessary for each of the fiscal years 2005 through 2010.

PART D—NATIONAL ACTIVITIES TO IMPROVE EDUCATION OF CHILDREN WITH DISABILITIES

SEC. 650. FINDINGS.

Congress finds the following:

(1) The Federal Government has an ongoing obligation to support activities that contribute to positive results for children with disabilities, enabling those children to lead productive and independent adult lives.

(2) Systemic change benefiting all students, including children with disabilities, requires the involvement of States, local educational agencies, parents, individuals with disabilities and their families, teachers and other service providers, and other interested individuals and organizations to develop and implement comprehensive strategies that improve educational results for children with disabilities.

(3) State educational agencies, in partnership with local educational agencies, parents of children with disabilities, and other individuals and organizations, are in the best position to improve education for children with disabilities and to address their special needs.

(4) An effective educational system serving students with disabilities should—

(A) maintain high academic achievement standards and clear performance goals for children with disabilities, consistent with the standards and expectations for all students in the educational system, and provide for appropriate and effective strategies and methods to ensure that all children with disabilities have the opportunity to achieve those standards and goals;

(B) clearly define, in objective, measurable terms, the school and post-school results that children with disabilities are expected to achieve; and

(C) promote transition services and coordinate State and local education, social, health, mental health, and other services, in addressing the full range of student needs, particularly the needs of children with disabilities who need significant levels of support to participate and learn in school and the community.

(5) The availability of an adequate number of qualified personnel is critical—

(A) to serve effectively children with disabilities;

(B) to assume leadership positions in administration and direct services;

(C) to provide teacher training; and

(D) to conduct high quality research to improve special education.

(6) High quality, comprehensive professional development programs are essential to ensure that the persons responsible for the education or transition of children with disabilities possess the skills and knowledge necessary to address the educational and related needs of those children.

(7) Models of professional development should be scientifically based and reflect successful practices, including strategies for recruiting, preparing, and retaining personnel.

(8) Continued support is essential for the development and maintenance of a coordinated and high quality program of research to inform successful teaching practices and model curricula for educating children with disabilities.

(9) Training, technical assistance, support, and dissemination activities are necessary to ensure that parts B and C are fully implemented and achieve high quality early intervention, educational, and transitional results for children with disabilities and their families.

(10) Parents, teachers, administrators, and related services personnel need technical assistance and information in a timely, coordinated, and accessible manner in order to improve early intervention, educational, and transitional services and results at the State and local levels for children with disabilities and their families.

(11) Parent training and information activities assist parents of a child with a disability in dealing with the multiple pressures of parenting such a child and are of particular importance in—

(A) playing a vital role in creating and preserving constructive relationships between parents of children with disabilities and schools by facilitating open communication between the parents and schools; encouraging dispute resolution at the earliest possible point in time; and discouraging the escalation of an adversarial process between the parents and schools;

(B) ensuring the involvement of parents in planning and decisionmaking with respect to early intervention, educational, and transitional services;

(C) achieving high quality early intervention, educational, and transitional results for children with disabilities;

(D) providing such parents information on their rights, protections, and responsibilities under this title to ensure improved early intervention, educational, and transitional results for children with disabilities;

(E) assisting such parents in the development of skills to participate effectively in the education and development of their children and in the transitions described in section 673(b)(6);

(F) supporting the roles of such parents as participants within partnerships seeking to improve early intervention, educational, and transitional services and results for children with disabilities and their families; and

(G) supporting such parents who may have limited access to services and supports, due to economic, cultural, or linguistic barriers.

(12) Support is needed to improve technological resources and integrate technology, including universally designed technologies, into the lives of children with disabilities, parents of children with disabilities, school personnel, and others through curricula, services, and assistive technologies.

Subpart 1—State Personnel Development Grants

SEC. 651. PURPOSE; DEFINITION OF PERSONNEL; PROGRAM AUTHORITY.

(a) PURPOSE- The purpose of this subpart is to assist State educational agencies in reforming and improving their systems for personnel preparation and professional development in early intervention, educational, and transition services in order to improve results for children with disabilities.

(b) DEFINITION OF PERSONNEL- In this subpart the term 'personnel' means special education teachers, regular education teachers, principals, administrators, related services personnel, paraprofessionals, and early intervention personnel serving infants, toddlers, preschoolers, or children with disabilities, except where a particular category of personnel, such as related services personnel, is identified.

(c) COMPETITIVE GRANTS-

(1) IN GENERAL- Except as provided in subsection (d), for any fiscal year for which the amount appropriated under section 655, that remains after the Secretary reserves funds under subsection (e) for the fiscal year, is less than $100,000,000, the Secretary shall award grants, on a competitive basis, to State educational agencies to carry out the activities described in the State plan submitted under section 653.

(2) PRIORITY- In awarding grants under paragraph (1), the Secretary may give priority to State educational agencies that—

(A) are in States with the greatest personnel shortages; or

(B) demonstrate the greatest difficulty meeting the requirements of section 612(a)(14).

(3) MINIMUM AMOUNT- The Secretary shall make a grant to each State educational agency selected under paragraph (1) in an amount for each fiscal year that is—

(A) not less than $500,000, nor more than $4,000,000, in the case of the 50 States, the District of Columbia, and the Commonwealth of Puerto Rico; and

(B) not less than $80,000 in the case of an outlying area.

(4) INCREASE IN AMOUNT- The Secretary may increase the amounts of grants under paragraph (4) to account for inflation.

(5) FACTORS- The Secretary shall determine the amount of a grant under paragraph (1) after considering—

(A) the amount of funds available for making the grants;

(B) the relative population of the State or outlying area;

(C) the types of activities proposed by the State or outlying area;

(D) the alignment of proposed activities with section 612(a)(14);

(E) the alignment of proposed activities with the State plans and applications submitted under sections 1111 and 2112, respectively, of the Elementary and Secondary Education Act of 1965; and

(F) the use, as appropriate, of scientifically based research activities.

(d) FORMULA GRANTS-

(1) IN GENERAL- Except as provided in paragraphs (2) and (3), for the first fiscal year for which the amount appropriated under section 655, that remains after the Secretary reserves funds under subsection (e) for the fiscal year, is equal to or greater than $100,000,000, and for each fiscal year thereafter, the Secretary shall allot to each State educational agency, whose application meets the requirements of this subpart, an amount that bears the same relation to the amount remaining as the amount the State received under section 611(d) for that fiscal year bears to the amount of funds received by all States (whose applications meet the requirements of this subpart) under section 611(d) for that fiscal year.

(2) MINIMUM ALLOTMENTS FOR STATES THAT RECEIVED COMPETITIVE GRANTS-

(A) IN GENERAL- The amount allotted under this subsection to any State educational agency that received a competitive multi-year grant under subsection (c) for which the grant period has not expired shall be not less than the amount specified for that fiscal year in the State educational agency's grant award document under that subsection.

(B) SPECIAL RULE- Each such State educational agency shall use the minimum amount described in subparagraph (A) for the activities described in the State educational agency's competitive grant award document for that year, unless the Secretary approves a request from the State educational agency to spend the funds on other activities.

(3) MINIMUM ALLOTMENT- The amount of any State educational agency's allotment under this subsection for any fiscal year shall not be less than—

(A) the greater of $500,000 or 1/2 of 1 percent of the total amount available under this subsection for that year, in the case of each of the 50 States, the District of Columbia, and the Commonwealth of Puerto Rico; and

(B) $80,000, in the case of an outlying area.

(4) DIRECT BENEFIT- In using grant funds allotted under paragraph (1), a State educational agency shall, through grants, contracts, or cooperative agreements, undertake activities that significantly and

directly benefit the local educational agencies in the State.

(e) CONTINUATION AWARDS-

(1) IN GENERAL- Notwithstanding any other provision of this subpart, from funds appropriated under section 655 for each fiscal year, the Secretary shall reserve the amount that is necessary to make a continuation award to any State educational agency (at the request of the State educational agency) that received a multi-year award under this part (as this part was in effect on the day before the date of enactment of the Individuals with Disabilities Education Improvement Act of 2004), to enable the State educational agency to carry out activities in accordance with the terms of the multi-year award.

(2) PROHIBITION- A State educational agency that receives a continuation award under paragraph (1) for any fiscal year may not receive any other award under this subpart for that fiscal year.

SEC. 652. ELIGIBILITY AND COLLABORATIVE PROCESS.

(a) ELIGIBLE APPLICANTS- A State educational agency may apply for a grant under this subpart for a grant period of not less than 1 year and not more than 5 years.

(b) PARTNERS-

(1) IN GENERAL- In order to be considered for a grant under this subpart, a State educational agency shall establish a partnership with local educational agencies and other State agencies involved in, or concerned with, the education of children with disabilities, including—

(A) not less than 1 institution of higher education; and

(B) the State agencies responsible for administering part C, early education, child care, and vocational rehabilitation programs.

(2) OTHER PARTNERS- In order to be considered for a grant under this subpart, a State educational agency shall work in partnership with other persons and organizations involved in, and concerned with, the education of children with disabilities, which may include—

(A) the Governor;

(B) parents of children with disabilities ages birth through 26;

(C) parents of nondisabled children ages birth through 26;

(D) individuals with disabilities;

(E) parent training and information centers or community parent resource centers funded under sections 671 and 672, respectively;

(F) community based and other nonprofit organizations involved in the education and employment of individuals with disabilities;

(G) personnel as defined in section 651(b);

(H) the State advisory panel established under part B;

(I) the State interagency coordinating council established under part C;

(J) individuals knowledgeable about vocational education;

(K) the State agency for higher education;

(L) public agencies with jurisdiction in the areas of health, mental health, social services, and juvenile justice;

(M) other providers of professional development that work with infants, toddlers, preschoolers, and children with disabilities; and

(N) other individuals.

(3) REQUIRED PARTNER- If State law assigns responsibility for teacher preparation and certification to an individual, entity, or agency other than the State educational agency, the State educational agency shall—

(A) include that individual, entity, or agency as a partner in the partnership under this subsection; and

(B) ensure that any activities the State educational agency will carry out under this subpart that are within that partner's jurisdiction (which may include activities described in section 654(b)) are carried out by that partner.

SEC. 653. APPLICATIONS.

(a) IN GENERAL-

(1) SUBMISSION- A State educational agency that desires to receive a grant under this subpart shall submit to the Secretary an application at such time, in such manner, and including such information as the Secretary may require.

(2) STATE PLAN- The application shall include a plan that identifies and addresses the State and local needs for the personnel preparation and professional development of personnel, as well as individuals who provide direct supplementary aids and services to children with disabilities, and that—

(A) is designed to enable the State to meet the requirements of section 612(a)(14) and section 635(a) (8) and (9);

(B) is based on an assessment of State and local needs that identifies critical aspects and areas in need of improvement related to the preparation, ongoing training, and professional development of personnel who serve infants, toddlers, preschoolers, and children with disabilities within the State, including—

(i) current and anticipated personnel vacancies and shortages; and

(ii) the number of preservice and inservice programs; and

(C) is integrated and aligned, to the maximum extent possible, with State plans and activities under the Elementary and Secondary Education Act of 1965, the Rehabilitation Act of 1973, and the Higher Education Act of 1965.

(3) REQUIREMENT- The State application shall contain an assurance that the State educational agency will carry out each of the strategies described in subsection (b)(4).

(b) ELEMENTS OF STATE PERSONNEL DEVELOPMENT PLAN- Each State personnel development plan under subsection (a)(2) shall—

(1) describe a partnership agreement that is in effect for the period of the grant, which agreement shall specify—

(A) the nature and extent of the partnership described in section 652(b) and the respective roles of each member of the partnership, including the partner described in section 652(b)(3) if applicable; and

(B) how the State educational agency will work with other persons and organizations involved in, and concerned with, the education of children with disabilities, including the respective roles of each of the persons and organizations;

(2) describe how the strategies and activities described in paragraph (4) will be coordinated with activities supported with other public resources (including part B and part C funds retained for use at the State level for personnel and professional development purposes) and private resources;

(3) describe how the State educational agency will align its personnel development plan under this subpart with the plan and application submitted under sections 1111 and 2112, respectively, of the Elementary and Secondary Education Act of 1965;

(4) describe those strategies the State educational agency will use to address the professional development and personnel needs identified under subsection (a)(2) and how such strategies will be implemented, including—

(A) a description of the programs and activities to be supported under this subpart that will provide personnel with the knowledge and skills to meet the needs of, and improve the performance and achievement of, infants, toddlers, preschoolers, and children with

disabilities; and

(B) how such strategies will be integrated, to the maximum extent possible, with other activities supported by grants funded under section 662;

(5) provide an assurance that the State educational agency will provide technical assistance to local educational agencies to improve the quality of professional development available to meet the needs of personnel who serve children with disabilities;

(6) provide an assurance that the State educational agency will provide technical assistance to entities that provide services to infants and toddlers with disabilities to improve the quality of professional development available to meet the needs of personnel serving such children;

(7) describe how the State educational agency will recruit and retain highly qualified teachers and other qualified personnel in geographic areas of greatest need;

(8) describe the steps the State educational agency will take to ensure that poor and minority children are not taught at higher rates by teachers who are not highly qualified; and

(9) describe how the State educational agency will assess, on a regular basis, the extent to which the strategies implemented under this subpart have been effective in meeting the performance goals described in section 612(a)(15).

(c) PEER REVIEW-

(1) IN GENERAL- The Secretary shall use a panel of experts who are competent, by virtue of their training, expertise, or experience, to evaluate applications for grants under section 651(c)(1).

(2) COMPOSITION OF PANEL- A majority of a panel described in paragraph (1) shall be composed of individuals who are not employees of the Federal Government.

(3) PAYMENT OF FEES AND EXPENSES OF CERTAIN MEMBERS- The Secretary may use available funds appropriated to carry out this subpart to pay the expenses and fees of panel members who are not employees of the Federal Government.

(d) REPORTING PROCEDURES- Each State educational agency that receives a grant under this subpart shall submit annual performance reports to the Secretary. The reports shall—

(1) describe the progress of the State educational agency in implementing its plan;

(2) analyze the effectiveness of the State educational agency's activities under this subpart and of the State educational agency's

strategies for meeting its goals under section 612(a)(15); and

(3) identify changes in the strategies used by the State educational agency and described in subsection (b)(4), if any, to improve the State educational agency's performance.

SEC. 654. USE OF FUNDS.

(a) PROFESSIONAL DEVELOPMENT ACTIVITIES- A State educational agency that receives a grant under this subpart shall use the grant funds to support activities in accordance with the State's plan described in section 653, including 1 or more of the following:

(1) Carrying out programs that provide support to both special education and regular education teachers of children with disabilities and principals, such as programs that—

(A) provide teacher mentoring, team teaching, reduced class schedules and case loads, and intensive professional development;

(B) use standards or assessments for guiding beginning teachers that are consistent with challenging State student academic achievement and functional standards and with the requirements for professional development, as defined in section 9101 of the Elementary and Secondary Education Act of 1965; and

(C) encourage collaborative and consultative models of providing early intervention, special education, and related services.

(2) Encouraging and supporting the training of special education and regular education teachers and administrators to effectively use and integrate technology—

(A) into curricula and instruction, including training to improve the ability to collect, manage, and analyze data to improve teaching, decisionmaking, school improvement efforts, and accountability;

(B) to enhance learning by children with disabilities; and

(C) to effectively communicate with parents.

(3) Providing professional development activities that—

(A) improve the knowledge of special education and regular education teachers concerning—

(i) the academic and developmental or functional needs of students with disabilities; or

(ii) effective instructional strategies, methods, and skills, and the use of State academic content standards and student academic achievement and functional standards, and State assessments, to improve teaching practices and student academic achievement;

(B) improve the knowledge of special education and regular education teachers and principals and, in appropriate cases, paraprofessionals, concerning effective instructional practices, and that—

(i) provide training in how to teach and address the needs of children with different learning styles and children who are limited English proficient;

(ii) involve collaborative groups of teachers, administrators, and, in appropriate cases, related services personnel;

(iii) provide training in methods of—

(I) positive behavioral interventions and supports to improve student behavior in the classroom;

(II) scientifically based reading instruction, including early literacy instruction;

(III) early and appropriate interventions to identify and help children with disabilities;

(IV) effective instruction for children with low incidence disabilities;

(V) successful transitioning to postsecondary opportunities; and

(VI) using classroom-based techniques to assist children prior to referral for special education;

(iv) provide training to enable personnel to work with and involve parents in their child's education, including parents of low income and limited English proficient children with disabilities;

(v) provide training for special education personnel and regular education personnel in planning, developing, and implementing effective and appropriate IEPs; and

(vi) provide training to meet the needs of students with significant health, mobility, or behavioral needs prior to serving such students;

(C) train administrators, principals, and other relevant school personnel in conducting effective IEP meetings; and

(D) train early intervention, preschool, and related services providers, and other relevant school personnel, in conducting effective individualized family service plan (IFSP) meetings.

(4) Developing and implementing initiatives to promote the recruitment and retention of highly qualified special education teachers, particularly initiatives that have been proven effective in recruiting and retaining highly qualified teachers, including programs that provide—

(A) teacher mentoring from exemplary

special education teachers, principals, or superintendents;

(B) induction and support for special education teachers during their first 3 years of employment as teachers; or

(C) incentives, including financial incentives, to retain special education teachers who have a record of success in helping students with disabilities.

(5) Carrying out programs and activities that are designed to improve the quality of personnel who serve children with disabilities, such as—

(A) innovative professional development programs (which may be provided through partnerships that include institutions of higher education), including programs that train teachers and principals to integrate technology into curricula and instruction to improve teaching, learning, and technology literacy, which professional development shall be consistent with the definition of professional development in section 9101 of the Elementary and Secondary Education Act of 1965; and

(B) the development and use of proven, cost effective strategies for the implementation of professional development activities, such as through the use of technology and distance learning.

(6) Carrying out programs and activities that are designed to improve the quality of early intervention personnel, including paraprofessionals and primary referral sources, such as—

(A) professional development programs to improve the delivery of early intervention services;

(B) initiatives to promote the recruitment and retention of early intervention personnel; and

(C) interagency activities to ensure that early intervention personnel are adequately prepared and trained.

(b) OTHER ACTIVITIES- A State educational agency that receives a grant under this subpart shall use the grant funds to support activities in accordance with the State's plan described in section 653, including 1 or more of the following:

(1) Reforming special education and regular education teacher certification (including recertification) or licensing requirements to ensure that—

(A) special education and regular education teachers have—

(i) the training and information necessary to address the full range of needs of children with disabilities across disability categories; and

(ii) the necessary subject matter knowledge and teaching skills in the academic subjects that the teachers teach;

(B) special education and regular education teacher certification (including recertification) or licensing requirements are aligned with challenging State academic content standards; and

(C) special education and regular education teachers have the subject matter knowledge and teaching skills, including technology literacy, necessary to help students with disabilities meet challenging State student academic achievement and functional standards.

(2) Programs that establish, expand, or improve alternative routes for State certification of special education teachers for highly qualified individuals with a baccalaureate or master's degree, including mid-career professionals from other occupations, paraprofessionals, and recent college or university graduates with records of academic distinction who demonstrate the potential to become highly effective special education teachers.

(3) Teacher advancement initiatives for special education teachers that promote professional growth and emphasize multiple career paths (such as paths to becoming a career teacher, mentor teacher, or exemplary teacher) and pay differentiation.

(4) Developing and implementing mechanisms to assist local educational agencies and schools in effectively recruiting and retaining highly qualified special education teachers.

(5) Reforming tenure systems, implementing teacher testing for subject matter knowledge, and implementing teacher testing for State certification or licensing, consistent with title II of the Higher Education Act of 1965.

(6) Funding projects to promote reciprocity of teacher certification or licensing between or among States for special education teachers, except that no reciprocity agreement developed under this paragraph or developed using funds provided under this subpart may lead to the weakening of any State teaching certification or licensing requirement.

(7) Assisting local educational agencies to serve children with disabilities through the development and use of proven, innovative strategies to deliver intensive professional development programs that are both cost effective and easily accessible, such as strategies that involve delivery through the use of technology, peer networks, and distance learning.

(8) Developing, or assisting local

educational agencies in developing, merit based performance systems, and strategies that provide differential and bonus pay for special education teachers.

(9) Supporting activities that ensure that teachers are able to use challenging State academic content standards and student academic achievement and functional standards, and State assessments for all children with disabilities, to improve instructional practices and improve the academic achievement of children with disabilities.

(10) When applicable, coordinating with, and expanding centers established under, section 2113(c)(18) of the Elementary and Secondary Education Act of 1965 to benefit special education teachers.

(c) CONTRACTS AND SUBGRANTS- A State educational agency that receives a grant under this subpart—

(1) shall award contracts or subgrants to local educational agencies, institutions of higher education, parent training and information centers, or community parent resource centers, as appropriate, to carry out its State plan under this subpart; and

(2) may award contracts and subgrants to other public and private entities, including the lead agency under part C, to carry out the State plan.

(d) USE OF FUNDS FOR PROFESSIONAL DEVELOPMENT- A State educational agency that receives a grant under this subpart shall use—

(1) not less than 90 percent of the funds the State educational agency receives under the grant for any fiscal year for activities under subsection (a); and

(2) not more than 10 percent of the funds the State educational agency receives under the grant for any fiscal year for activities under subsection (b).

(e) GRANTS TO OUTLYING AREAS- Public Law 95-134, permitting the consolidation of grants to the outlying areas, shall not apply to funds received under this subpart.

SEC. 655. AUTHORIZATION OF APPROPRIATIONS.

There are authorized to be appropriated to carry out this subpart such sums as may be necessary for each of the fiscal years 2005 through 2010.

Subpart 2—Personnel Preparation, Technical Assistance, Model Demonstration Projects, and Dissemination of Information

SEC. 661. PURPOSE; DEFINITION OF ELIGIBLE ENTITY.

(a) PURPOSE- The purpose of this subpart is—

(1) to provide Federal funding for personnel preparation, technical assistance, model demonstration projects, information dissemination, and studies and evaluations, in order to improve early intervention, educational, and transitional results for children with disabilities; and

(2) to assist State educational agencies and local educational agencies in improving their education systems for children with disabilities.

(b) DEFINITION OF ELIGIBLE ENTITY-

(1) IN GENERAL- In this subpart, the term eligible entity' means—

(A) a State educational agency;

(B) a local educational agency;

(C) a public charter school that is a local educational agency under State law;

(D) an institution of higher education;

(E) a public agency not described in subparagraphs (A) through (D);

(F) a private nonprofit organization;

(G) an outlying area;

(H) an Indian tribe or a tribal organization (as defined under section 4 of the Indian Self-Determination and Education Assistance Act); or

(I) a for-profit organization, if the Secretary finds it appropriate in light of the purposes of a particular competition for a grant, contract, or cooperative agreement under this subpart.

(2) SPECIAL RULE- The Secretary may limit which eligible entities described in paragraph (1) are eligible for a grant, contract, or cooperative agreement under this subpart to 1 or more of the categories of eligible entities described in paragraph (1).

SEC. 662. PERSONNEL DEVELOPMENT TO IMPROVE SERVICES AND RESULTS FOR CHILDREN WITH DISABILITIES.

(a) IN GENERAL- The Secretary, on a competitive basis, shall award grants to, or enter into contracts or cooperative agreements with, eligible entities to carry out 1 or more of the following objectives:

(1) To help address the needs identified in the State plan described in section 653(a)(2) for highly qualified personnel, as defined in section 651(b), to work with infants or toddlers with disabilities, or children with disabilities, consistent with the qualifications described in section 612(a)(14).

(2) To ensure that those personnel have the necessary skills and knowledge, derived from practices that have been determined, through scientifically based research, to be successful in serving those children.

(3) To encourage increased focus on academics and core content areas in special education personnel preparation programs.

(4) To ensure that regular education teachers have the necessary skills and knowledge to provide instruction to students with disabilities in the regular education classroom.

(5) To ensure that all special education teachers are highly qualified.

(6) To ensure that preservice and in-service personnel preparation programs include training in—

(A) the use of new technologies;

(B) the area of early intervention, educational, and transition services;

(C) effectively involving parents; and

(D) positive behavioral supports.

(7) To provide high-quality professional development for principals, superintendents, and other administrators, including training in—

(A) instructional leadership;

(B) behavioral supports in the school and classroom;

(C) paperwork reduction;

(D) promoting improved collaboration between special education and general education teachers;

(E) assessment and accountability;

(F) ensuring effective learning environments; and

(G) fostering positive relationships with parents.

(b) PERSONNEL DEVELOPMENT; ENHANCED SUPPORT FOR BEGINNING SPECIAL EDUCATORS-

(1) IN GENERAL- In carrying out this section, the Secretary shall support activities—

(A) for personnel development, including activities for the preparation of personnel who will serve children with high incidence and low incidence disabilities, to prepare special education and general education teachers, principals, administrators, and related services personnel (and school board members, when appropriate) to meet the diverse and individualized instructional needs of children with disabilities and improve early intervention, educational, and transitional services and results for children with disabilities, consistent with the objectives described in subsection (a); and

(B) for enhanced support for beginning special educators, consistent with the objectives described in subsection (a).

(2) PERSONNEL DEVELOPMENT- In carrying out paragraph (1)(A), the Secretary shall support not less than 1 of the following activities:

(A) Assisting effective existing, improving existing, or developing new, collaborative personnel preparation activities undertaken by institutions of higher education, local educational agencies, and other local entities that incorporate best practices and scientifically based research, where applicable, in providing special education and general education teachers, principals, administrators, and related services personnel with the knowledge and skills to effectively support students with disabilities, including—

(i) working collaboratively in regular classroom settings;

(ii) using appropriate supports, accommodations, and curriculum modifications;

(iii) implementing effective teaching strategies, classroom-based techniques, and interventions to ensure appropriate identification of students who may be eligible for special education services, and to prevent the misidentification, inappropriate overidentification, or underidentification of children as having a disability, especially minority and limited English proficient children;

(iv) effectively working with and involving parents in the education of their children;

(v) utilizing strategies, including positive behavioral interventions, for addressing the conduct of children with disabilities that impedes their learning and that of others in the classroom;

(vi) effectively constructing IEPs, participating in IEP meetings, and implementing IEPs;

(vii) preparing children with disabilities to participate in statewide assessments (with or without accommodations) and alternate assessments, as appropriate, and to ensure that all children with disabilities are a part of all accountability systems under the Elementary and Secondary Education Act of 1965; and

(viii) working in high need elementary schools and secondary schools, including urban schools, rural schools, and schools operated by an entity described in section 7113(d)(1)(A)(ii) of the Elementary and Secondary Education Act of 1965, and schools that serve high numbers or percentages of limited English proficient children.

(B) Developing, evaluating, and disseminating innovative models for the recruitment, induction, retention, and assessment of new, highly qualified teachers to reduce teacher shortages, especially from groups that are underrepresented in the teaching profession, including individuals with disabilities.

(C) Providing continuous personnel preparation, training, and professional development designed to provide support and ensure retention of special education and general education teachers and personnel who teach and provide related services to children with disabilities.

(D) Developing and improving programs for paraprofessionals to become special education teachers, related services personnel, and early intervention personnel, including interdisciplinary training to enable the paraprofessionals to improve early intervention, educational, and transitional results for children with disabilities.

(E) In the case of principals and superintendents, providing activities to promote instructional leadership and improved collaboration between general educators, special education teachers, and related services personnel.

(F) Supporting institutions of higher education with minority enrollments of not less than 25 percent for the purpose of preparing personnel to work with children with disabilities.

(G) Developing and improving programs to train special education teachers to develop an expertise in autism spectrum disorders.

(H) Providing continuous personnel preparation, training, and professional development designed to provide support and improve the qualifications of personnel who provide related services to children with disabilities, including to enable such personnel to obtain advanced degrees.

(3) ENHANCED SUPPORT FOR BEGINNING SPECIAL EDUCATORS- In carrying out paragraph (1)(B), the Secretary shall support not less than 1 of the following activities:

(A) Enhancing and restructuring existing programs or developing preservice teacher education programs to prepare special education teachers, at colleges or departments of education within institutions of higher education, by incorporating an extended (such as an additional 5th year) clinical learning opportunity, field experience, or supervised practicum into such programs.

(B) Creating or supporting teacher-faculty partnerships (such as professional development schools) that—

(i) consist of not less than—

(I) 1 or more institutions of higher education with special education personnel preparation programs;

(II) 1 or more local educational agencies that serve high numbers or percentages of low-income students; or

(III) 1 or more elementary schools or secondary schools, particularly schools that have failed to make adequate yearly progress on the basis, in whole and in part, of the assessment results of the disaggregated subgroup of students with disabilities;

(ii) may include other entities eligible for assistance under this part; and

(iii) provide—

(I) high-quality mentoring and induction opportunities with ongoing support for beginning special education teachers; or

(II) inservice professional development to beginning and veteran special education teachers through the ongoing exchange of information and instructional strategies with faculty.

(c) LOW INCIDENCE DISABILITIES; AUTHORIZED ACTIVITIES-

(1) IN GENERAL- In carrying out this section, the Secretary shall support activities, consistent with the objectives described in subsection (a), that benefit children with low incidence disabilities.

(2) AUTHORIZED ACTIVITIES- Activities that may be carried out under this subsection include activities such as the following:

(A) Preparing persons who—

(i) have prior training in educational and other related service fields; and

(ii) are studying to obtain degrees, certificates, or licensure that will enable the persons to assist children with low incidence disabilities to achieve the objectives set out in their individualized education programs described in section 614(d), or to assist infants and toddlers with low incidence disabilities to achieve the outcomes described in their individualized family service plans described in section 636.

(B) Providing personnel from various disciplines with interdisciplinary training that will contribute to improvement in early intervention, educational, and transitional results for children with low incidence disabilities.

(C) Preparing personnel in the innovative uses and application of technology, including universally designed technologies, assistive technology devices, and assistive technology services—

(i) to enhance learning by children with low incidence disabilities through early intervention, educational, and transitional services; and

(ii) to improve communication with parents.

(D) Preparing personnel who provide services to visually impaired or blind children to teach and use Braille in the provision of services to such children.

(E) Preparing personnel to be qualified educational interpreters, to assist children with low incidence disabilities, particularly deaf and hard of hearing children in school and school related activities, and deaf and hard of hearing infants and toddlers and preschool children in early intervention and preschool programs.

(F) Preparing personnel who provide services to children with significant cognitive disabilities and children with multiple disabilities.

(G) Preparing personnel who provide services to children with low incidence disabilities and limited English proficient children.

(3) DEFINITION- In this section, the term 'low incidence disability' means—

(A) a visual or hearing impairment, or simultaneous visual and hearing impairments;

(B) a significant cognitive impairment; or

(C) any impairment for which a small number of personnel with highly specialized skills and knowledge are needed in order for children with that impairment to receive early intervention services or a free appropriate public education.

(4) SELECTION OF RECIPIENTS- In selecting eligible entities for assistance under this subsection, the Secretary may give preference to eligible entities submitting applications that include 1 or more of the following:

(A) A proposal to prepare personnel in more than 1 low incidence disability, such as deafness and blindness.

(B) A demonstration of an effective collaboration between an eligible entity and a local educational agency that promotes recruitment and subsequent retention of highly qualified personnel to serve children with low incidence disabilities.

(5) PREPARATION IN USE OF BRAILLE- The Secretary shall ensure that all recipients of awards under this subsection who will use that assistance to prepare personnel to provide services to visually impaired or blind children that can appropriately be provided in Braille, will prepare those individuals to provide those services in Braille.

(d) LEADERSHIP PREPARATION; AUTHORIZED ACTIVITIES-

(1) IN GENERAL- In carrying out this section, the Secretary shall support leadership preparation activities that are consistent with the objectives described in subsection (a).

(2) AUTHORIZED ACTIVITIES- Activities that may be carried out under this subsection include activities such as the following:

(A) Preparing personnel at the graduate, doctoral, and postdoctoral levels of training to administer, enhance, or provide services to improve results for children with disabilities.

(B) Providing interdisciplinary training for various types of leadership personnel, including teacher preparation faculty, related services faculty, administrators, researchers, supervisors, principals, and other persons whose work affects early intervention, educational, and transitional services for children with disabilities, including children with disabilities who are limited English proficient children.

(e) APPLICATIONS-

(1) IN GENERAL- An eligible entity that wishes to receive a grant, or enter into a contract or cooperative agreement, under this section shall submit an application to the Secretary at such time, in such manner, and containing such information as the Secretary may require.

(2) IDENTIFIED STATE NEEDS-

(A) REQUIREMENT TO ADDRESS IDENTIFIED NEEDS- An application for assistance under subsection (b), (c), or (d) shall include information demonstrating to the satisfaction of the Secretary that the activities described in the application will address needs identified by the State or States the eligible entity proposes to serve.

(B) COOPERATION WITH STATE EDUCATIONAL AGENCIES- An eligible entity that is not a local educational agency or

a State educational agency shall include in the eligible entity's application information demonstrating to the satisfaction of the Secretary that the eligible entity and 1 or more State educational agencies or local educational agencies will cooperate in carrying out and monitoring the proposed project.

(3) ACCEPTANCE BY STATES OF PERSONNEL PREPARATION REQUIREMENTS- The Secretary may require eligible entities to provide in the eligible entities' applications assurances from 1 or more States that such States intend to accept successful completion of the proposed personnel preparation program as meeting State personnel standards or other requirements in State law or regulation for serving children with disabilities or serving infants and toddlers with disabilities.

(f) SELECTION OF RECIPIENTS-

(1) IMPACT OF PROJECT- In selecting eligible entities for assistance under this section, the Secretary shall consider the impact of the proposed project described in the application in meeting the need for personnel identified by the States.

(2) REQUIREMENT FOR ELIGIBLE ENTITIES TO MEET STATE AND PROFESSIONAL QUALIFICATIONS- The Secretary shall make grants and enter into contracts and cooperative agreements under this section only to eligible entities that meet State and professionally recognized qualifications for the preparation of special education and related services personnel, if the purpose of the project is to assist personnel in obtaining degrees.

(3) PREFERENCES- In selecting eligible entities for assistance under this section, the Secretary may give preference to eligible entities that are institutions of higher education that are—

(A) educating regular education personnel to meet the needs of children with disabilities in integrated settings;

(B) educating special education personnel to work in collaboration with regular educators in integrated settings; and

(C) successfully recruiting and preparing individuals with disabilities and individuals from groups that are underrepresented in the profession for which the institution of higher education is preparing individuals.

(g) SCHOLARSHIPS- The Secretary may include funds for scholarships, with necessary stipends and allowances, in awards under subsections (b), (c), and (d).

(h) SERVICE OBLIGATION-

(1) IN GENERAL- Each application for assistance under subsections (b), (c), and (d) shall include an assurance that the eligible entity will ensure that individuals who receive a scholarship under the proposed project agree to subsequently provide special education and related services to children with disabilities, or in the case of leadership personnel to subsequently work in the appropriate field, for a period of 2 years for every year for which the scholarship was received or repay all or part of the amount of the scholarship, in accordance with regulations issued by the Secretary.

(2) SPECIAL RULE- Notwithstanding paragraph (1), the Secretary may reduce or waive the service obligation requirement under paragraph (1) if the Secretary determines that the service obligation is acting as a deterrent to the recruitment of students into special education or a related field.

(3) SECRETARY'S RESPONSIBILITY- The Secretary—

(A) shall ensure that individuals described in paragraph (1) comply with the requirements of that paragraph; and

(B) may use not more than 0.5 percent of the funds appropriated under subsection (i) for each fiscal year, to carry out subparagraph (A), in addition to any other funds that are available for that purpose.

(i) AUTHORIZATION OF APPROPRIATIONS- There are authorized to be appropriated to carry out this section such sums as may be necessary for each of the fiscal years 2005 through 2010.

SEC. 663. TECHNICAL ASSISTANCE, DEMONSTRATION PROJECTS, DISSEMINATION OF INFORMATION, AND IMPLEMENTATION OF SCIENTIFICALLY BASED RESEARCH.

(a) IN GENERAL- The Secretary shall make competitive grants to, or enter into contracts or cooperative agreements with, eligible entities to provide technical assistance, support model demonstration projects, disseminate useful information, and implement activities that are supported by scientifically based research.

(b) REQUIRED ACTIVITIES- Funds received under this section shall be used to support activities to improve services provided under this title, including the practices of professionals and others involved in providing such services to children with disabilities, that promote academic achievement and improve results for children with disabilities through—

(1) implementing effective strategies for addressing inappropriate behavior of students with disabilities in schools, including strategies to prevent children with emotional and behavioral problems from developing emotional disturbances that require the provision of special education and related services;

(2) improving the alignment, compatibility, and development of valid and reliable assessments and alternate assessments for assessing adequate yearly progress, as described under section 1111(b)(2)(B) of the Elementary and Secondary Education Act of 1965;

(3) providing training for both regular education teachers and special education teachers to address the needs of students with different learning styles;

(4) disseminating information about innovative, effective, and efficient curricula designs, instructional approaches, and strategies, and identifying positive academic and social learning opportunities, that—

(A) provide effective transitions between educational settings or from school to post school settings; and

(B) improve educational and transitional results at all levels of the educational system in which the activities are carried out and, in particular, that improve the progress of children with disabilities, as measured by assessments within the general education curriculum involved; and

(5) applying scientifically based findings to facilitate systemic changes, related to the provision of services to children with disabilities, in policy, procedure, practice, and the training and use of personnel.

(c) AUTHORIZED ACTIVITIES- Activities that may be carried out under this section include activities to improve services provided under this title, including the practices of professionals and others involved in providing such services to children with disabilities, that promote academic achievement and improve results for children with disabilities through—

(1) applying and testing research findings in typical settings where children with disabilities receive services to determine the usefulness, effectiveness, and general applicability of such research findings in such areas as improving instructional methods, curricula, and tools, such as textbooks and media;

(2) supporting and promoting the coordination of early intervention and educational services for children with disabilities with services provided by health,

rehabilitation, and social service agencies;

(3) promoting improved alignment and compatibility of general and special education reforms concerned with curricular and instructional reform, and evaluation of such reforms;

(4) enabling professionals, parents of children with disabilities, and other persons to learn about, and implement, the findings of scientifically based research, and successful practices developed in model demonstration projects, relating to the provision of services to children with disabilities;

(5) conducting outreach, and disseminating information, relating to successful approaches to overcoming systemic barriers to the effective and efficient delivery of early intervention, educational, and transitional services to personnel who provide services to children with disabilities;

(6) assisting States and local educational agencies with the process of planning systemic changes that will promote improved early intervention, educational, and transitional results for children with disabilities;

(7) promoting change through a multistate or regional framework that benefits States, local educational agencies, and other participants in partnerships that are in the process of achieving systemic-change outcomes;

(8) focusing on the needs and issues that are specific to a population of children with disabilities, such as providing single-State and multi-State technical assistance and in-service training—

(A) to schools and agencies serving deaf-blind children and their families;

(B) to programs and agencies serving other groups of children with low incidence disabilities and their families;

(C) addressing the postsecondary education needs of individuals who are deaf or hard-of-hearing; and

(D) to schools and personnel providing special education and related services for children with autism spectrum disorders;

(9) demonstrating models of personnel preparation to ensure appropriate placements and services for all students and to reduce disproportionality in eligibility, placement, and disciplinary actions for minority and limited English proficient children; and

(10) disseminating information on how to reduce inappropriate racial and ethnic disproportionalities identified under section 618.

(d) BALANCE AMONG ACTIVITIES AND AGE RANGES- In carrying out this section, the Secretary shall ensure that there is an appropriate balance across all age ranges of children with disabilities.

(e) LINKING STATES TO INFORMATION SOURCES- In carrying out this section, the Secretary shall support projects that link States to technical assistance resources, including special education and general education resources, and shall make research and related products available through libraries, electronic networks, parent training projects, and other information sources, including through the activities of the National Center for Education Evaluation and Regional Assistance established under part D of the Education Sciences Reform Act of 2002.

(f) APPLICATIONS-

(1) IN GENERAL- An eligible entity that wishes to receive a grant, or enter into a contract or cooperative agreement, under this section shall submit an application to the Secretary at such time, in such manner, and containing such information as the Secretary may require.

(2) STANDARDS- To the maximum extent feasible, each eligible entity shall demonstrate that the project described in the eligible entity's application is supported by scientifically valid research that has been carried out in accordance with the standards for the conduct and evaluation of all relevant research and development established by the National Center for Education Research.

(3) PRIORITY- As appropriate, the Secretary shall give priority to applications that propose to serve teachers and school personnel directly in the school environment.

SEC. 664. STUDIES AND EVALUATIONS.

(a) STUDIES AND EVALUATIONS-

(1) DELEGATION- The Secretary shall delegate to the Director of the Institute of Education Sciences responsibility to carry out this section, other than subsections (d) and (f).

(2) ASSESSMENT- The Secretary shall, directly or through grants, contracts, or cooperative agreements awarded to eligible entities on a competitive basis, assess the progress in the implementation of this title, including the effectiveness of State and local efforts to provide—

(A) a free appropriate public education to children with disabilities; and

(B) early intervention services to infants and toddlers with disabilities, and infants and toddlers who would be at risk of having substantial developmental delays if early intervention services were not provided to the infants and toddlers.

(b) ASSESSMENT OF NATIONAL ACTIVITIES-

(1) IN GENERAL- The Secretary shall carry out a national assessment of activities carried out with Federal funds under this title in order—

(A) to determine the effectiveness of this title in achieving the purposes of this title;

(B) to provide timely information to the President, Congress, the States, local educational agencies, and the public on how to implement this title more effectively; and

(C) to provide the President and Congress with information that will be useful in developing legislation to achieve the purposes of this title more effectively.

(2) SCOPE OF ASSESSMENT- The national assessment shall assess activities supported under this title, including—

(A) the implementation of programs assisted under this title and the impact of such programs on addressing the developmental needs of, and improving the academic achievement of, children with disabilities to enable the children to reach challenging developmental goals and challenging State academic content standards based on State academic assessments;

(B) the types of programs and services that have demonstrated the greatest likelihood of helping students reach the challenging State academic content standards and developmental goals;

(C) the implementation of the professional development activities assisted under this title and the impact on instruction, student academic achievement, and teacher qualifications to enhance the ability of special education teachers and regular education teachers to improve results for children with disabilities; and

(D) the effectiveness of schools, local educational agencies, States, other recipients of assistance under this title, and the Secretary in achieving the purposes of this title by—

(i) improving the academic achievement of children with disabilities and their performance on regular statewide assessments as compared to nondisabled children, and the performance of children with disabilities on alternate assessments;

(ii) improving the participation of children with disabilities in the general education curriculum;

(iii) improving the transitions of children

with disabilities at natural transition points;

(iv) placing and serving children with disabilities, including minority children, in the least restrictive environment appropriate;

(v) preventing children with disabilities, especially children with emotional disturbances and specific learning disabilities, from dropping out of school;

(vi) addressing the reading and literacy needs of children with disabilities;

(vii) reducing the inappropriate overidentification of children, especially minority and limited English proficient children, as having a disability;

(viii) improving the participation of parents of children with disabilities in the education of their children; and

(ix) resolving disagreements between education personnel and parents through alternate dispute resolution activities, including mediation.

(3) INTERIM AND FINAL REPORTS- The Secretary shall submit to the President and Congress—

(A) an interim report that summarizes the preliminary findings of the assessment not later than 3 years after the date of enactment of the Individuals with Disabilities Education Improvement Act of 2004; and

(B) a final report of the findings of the assessment not later than 5 years after the date of enactment of such Act.

(c) STUDY ON ENSURING ACCOUNTABILITY FOR STUDENTS WHO ARE HELD TO ALTERNATIVE ACHIEVEMENT STANDARDS- The Secretary shall carry out a national study or studies to examine—

(1) the criteria that States use to determine—

(A) eligibility for alternate assessments; and

(B) the number and type of children who take those assessments and are held accountable to alternative achievement standards;

(2) the validity and reliability of alternate assessment instruments and procedures;

(3) the alignment of alternate assessments and alternative achievement standards to State academic content standards in reading, mathematics, and science; and

(4) the use and effectiveness of alternate assessments in appropriately measuring student progress and outcomes specific to individualized instructional need.

(d) ANNUAL REPORT- The Secretary shall provide an annual report to Congress that—

(1) summarizes the research conducted under part E of the Education Sciences Reform Act of 2002;

(2) analyzes and summarizes the data reported by the States and the Secretary of the Interior under section 618;

(3) summarizes the studies and evaluations conducted under this section and the timeline for their completion;

(4) describes the extent and progress of the assessment of national activities; and

(5) describes the findings and determinations resulting from reviews of State implementation of this title.

(e) AUTHORIZED ACTIVITIES- In carrying out this section, the Secretary may support objective studies, evaluations, and assessments, including studies that—

(1) analyze measurable impact, outcomes, and results achieved by State educational agencies and local educational agencies through their activities to reform policies, procedures, and practices designed to improve educational and transitional services and results for children with disabilities;

(2) analyze State and local needs for professional development, parent training, and other appropriate activities that can reduce the need for disciplinary actions involving children with disabilities;

(3) assess educational and transitional services and results for children with disabilities from minority backgrounds, including—

(A) data on—

(i) the number of minority children who are referred for special education evaluation;

(ii) the number of minority children who are receiving special education and related services and their educational or other service placement;

(iii) the number of minority children who graduated from secondary programs with a regular diploma in the standard number of years; and

(iv) the number of minority children who drop out of the educational system; and

(B) the performance of children with disabilities from minority backgrounds on State assessments and other performance indicators established for all students;

(4) measure educational and transitional services and results for children with disabilities served under this title, including longitudinal studies that—

(A) examine educational and transitional services and results for children with disabilities who are 3 through 17 years of age and are receiving special education and related services under this title, using a national, representative sample of distinct age cohorts and disability categories; and

(B) examine educational results, transition services, postsecondary placement, and employment status for individuals with disabilities, 18 through 21 years of age, who are receiving or have received special education and related services under this title; and

(5) identify and report on the placement of children with disabilities by disability category.

(f) STUDY- The Secretary shall study, and report to Congress regarding, the extent to which States adopt policies described in section 635(c)(1) and on the effects of those policies.

SEC. 665. INTERIM ALTERNATIVE EDUCATIONAL SETTINGS, BEHAVIORAL SUPPORTS, AND SYSTEMIC SCHOOL INTERVENTIONS.

(a) PROGRAM AUTHORIZED- The Secretary may award grants, and enter into contracts and cooperative agreements, to support safe learning environments that support academic achievement for all students by—

(1) improving the quality of interim alternative educational settings; and

(2) providing increased behavioral supports and research-based, systemic interventions in schools.

(b) AUTHORIZED ACTIVITIES- In carrying out this section, the Secretary may support activities to—

(1) establish, expand, or increase the scope of behavioral supports and systemic interventions by providing for effective, research-based practices, including—

(A) training for school staff on early identification, prereferral, and referral procedures;

(B) training for administrators, teachers, related services personnel, behavioral specialists, and other school staff in positive behavioral interventions and supports, behavioral intervention planning, and classroom and student management techniques;

(C) joint training for administrators, parents, teachers, related services personnel, behavioral specialists, and other school staff on effective strategies for positive behavioral interventions and behavior management strategies that focus on the prevention of behavior problems;

(D) developing or implementing specific curricula, programs, or interventions aimed at

addressing behavioral problems;

(E) stronger linkages between school-based services and community-based resources, such as community mental health and primary care providers; or

(F) using behavioral specialists, related services personnel, and other staff necessary to implement behavioral supports; or

(2) improve interim alternative educational settings by—

(A) improving the training of administrators, teachers, related services personnel, behavioral specialists, and other school staff (including ongoing mentoring of new teachers) in behavioral supports and interventions;

(B) attracting and retaining a high quality, diverse staff;

(C) providing for referral to counseling services;

(D) utilizing research-based interventions, curriculum, and practices;

(E) allowing students to use instructional technology that provides individualized instruction;

(F) ensuring that the services are fully consistent with the goals of the individual student's IEP;

(G) promoting effective case management and collaboration among parents, teachers, physicians, related services personnel, behavioral specialists, principals, administrators, and other school staff;

(H) promoting interagency coordination and coordinated service delivery among schools, juvenile courts, child welfare agencies, community mental health providers, primary care providers, public recreation agencies, and community-based organizations; or

(I) providing for behavioral specialists to help students transitioning from interim alternative educational settings reintegrate into their regular classrooms.

(c) DEFINITION OF ELIGIBLE ENTITY- In this section, the term eligible entity' means—

(1) a local educational agency; or

(2) a consortium consisting of a local educational agency and 1 or more of the following entities:

(A) Another local educational agency.

(B) A community-based organization with a demonstrated record of effectiveness in helping children with disabilities who have behavioral challenges succeed.

(C) An institution of higher education.

(D) A community mental health provider.

(E) An educational service agency.

(d) APPLICATIONS- Any eligible entity that wishes to receive a grant, or enter into a contract or cooperative agreement, under this section shall—

(1) submit an application to the Secretary at such time, in such manner, and containing such information as the Secretary may require; and

(2) involve parents of participating students in the design and implementation of the activities funded under this section.

(e) REPORT AND EVALUATION- Each eligible entity receiving a grant under this section shall prepare and submit annually to the Secretary a report on the outcomes of the activities assisted under the grant.

SEC. 667. AUTHORIZATION OF APPROPRIATIONS.

(a) IN GENERAL- There are authorized to be appropriated to carry out this subpart (other than section 662) such sums as may be necessary for each of the fiscal years 2005 through 2010.

(b) RESERVATION- From amounts appropriated under subsection (a) for fiscal year 2005, the Secretary shall reserve $1,000,000 to carry out the study authorized in section 664(c). From amounts appropriated under subsection (a) for a succeeding fiscal year, the Secretary may reserve an additional amount to carry out such study if the Secretary determines the additional amount is necessary.

Subpart 3—Supports To Improve Results for Children With Disabilities

SEC. 670. PURPOSES.

The purposes of this subpart are to ensure that—

(1) children with disabilities and their parents receive training and information designed to assist the children in meeting developmental and functional goals and challenging academic achievement goals, and in preparing to lead productive independent adult lives;

(2) children with disabilities and their parents receive training and information on their rights, responsibilities, and protections under this title, in order to develop the skills

necessary to cooperatively and effectively participate in planning and decision making relating to early intervention, educational, and transitional services;

(3) parents, teachers, administrators, early intervention personnel, related services personnel, and transition personnel receive coordinated and accessible technical assistance and information to assist such personnel in improving early intervention, educational, and transitional services and results for children with disabilities and their families; and

(4) appropriate technology and media are researched, developed, and demonstrated, to improve and implement early intervention, educational, and transitional services and results for children with disabilities and their families.

SEC. 671. PARENT TRAINING AND INFORMATION CENTERS.

(a) PROGRAM AUTHORIZED-

(1) IN GENERAL- The Secretary may award grants to, and enter into contracts and cooperative agreements with, parent organizations to support parent training and information centers to carry out activities under this section.

(2) DEFINITION OF PARENT ORGANIZATION- In this section, the term parent organization' means a private nonprofit organization (other than an institution of higher education) that—

(A) has a board of directors—

(i) the majority of whom are parents of children with disabilities ages birth through 26;

(ii) that includes—

(I) individuals working in the fields of special education, related services, and early intervention; and

(II) individuals with disabilities; and

(iii) the parent and professional members of which are broadly representative of the population to be served, including low-income parents and parents of limited English proficient children; and

(B) has as its mission serving families of children with disabilities who—

(i) are ages birth through 26; and

(ii) have the full range of disabilities described in section 602(3).

(b) REQUIRED ACTIVITIES- Each parent training and information center that receives assistance under this section shall—

(1) provide training and information that meets the needs of parents of children with disabilities living in the area served by the

center, particularly underserved parents and parents of children who may be inappropriately identified, to enable their children with disabilities to—

(A) meet developmental and functional goals, and challenging academic achievement goals that have been established for all children; and

(B) be prepared to lead productive independent adult lives, to the maximum extent possible;

(2) serve the parents of infants, toddlers, and children with the full range of disabilities described in section 602(3);

(3) ensure that the training and information provided meets the needs of low-income parents and parents of limited English proficient children;

(4) assist parents to—

(A) better understand the nature of their children's disabilities and their educational, developmental, and transitional needs;

(B) communicate effectively and work collaboratively with personnel responsible for providing special education, early intervention services, transition services, and related services;

(C) participate in decisionmaking processes and the development of individualized education programs under part B and individualized family service plans under part C;

(D) obtain appropriate information about the range, type, and quality of—

(i) options, programs, services, technologies, practices and interventions based on scientifically based research, to the extent practicable; and

(ii) resources available to assist children with disabilities and their families in school and at home;

(E) understand the provisions of this title for the education of, and the provision of early intervention services to, children with disabilities;

(F) participate in activities at the school level that benefit their children; and

(G) participate in school reform activities;

(5) in States where the State elects to contract with the parent training and information center, contract with State educational agencies to provide, consistent with subparagraphs (B) and (D) of section 615(e)(2), individuals who meet with parents to explain the mediation process to the parents;

(6) assist parents in resolving disputes in the most expeditious and effective way possible, including encouraging the use, and explaining the benefits, of alternative methods of dispute resolution, such as the mediation process described in section 615(e);

(7) assist parents and students with disabilities to understand their rights and responsibilities under this title, including those under section 615(m) upon the student's reaching the age of majority (as appropriate under State law);

(8) assist parents to understand the availability of, and how to effectively use, procedural safeguards under this title, including the resolution session described in section 615(e);

(9) assist parents in understanding, preparing for, and participating in, the process described in section 615(f)(1)(B);

(10) establish cooperative partnerships with community parent resource centers funded under section 672;

(11) network with appropriate clearinghouses, including organizations conducting national dissemination activities under section 663 and the Institute of Education Sciences, and with other national, State, and local organizations and agencies, such as protection and advocacy agencies, that serve parents and families of children with the full range of disabilities described in section 602(3); and

(12) annually report to the Secretary on—

(A) the number and demographics of parents to whom the center provided information and training in the most recently concluded fiscal year;

(B) the effectiveness of strategies used to reach and serve parents, including underserved parents of children with disabilities; and

(C) the number of parents served who have resolved disputes through alternative methods of dispute resolution.

(c) OPTIONAL ACTIVITIES- A parent training and information center that receives assistance under this section may provide information to teachers and other professionals to assist the teachers and professionals in improving results for children with disabilities.

(d) APPLICATION REQUIREMENTS- Each application for assistance under this section shall identify with specificity the special efforts that the parent organization will undertake—

(1) to ensure that the needs for training and information of underserved parents of children with disabilities in the area to be served are effectively met; and

(2) to work with community based organizations, including community based organizations that work with low-income parents and parents of limited English

proficient children.

(e) DISTRIBUTION OF FUNDS-

(1) IN GENERAL- The Secretary shall—

(A) make not less than 1 award to a parent organization in each State for a parent training and information center that is designated as the statewide parent training and information center; or

(B) in the case of a large State, make awards to multiple parent training and information centers, but only if the centers demonstrate that coordinated services and supports will occur among the multiple centers.

(2) SELECTION REQUIREMENT- The Secretary shall select among applications submitted by parent organizations in a State in a manner that ensures the most effective assistance to parents, including parents in urban and rural areas, in the State.

(f) QUARTERLY REVIEW-

(1) MEETINGS- The board of directors of each parent organization that receives an award under this section shall meet not less than once in each calendar quarter to review the activities for which the award was made.

(2) CONTINUATION AWARD- When a parent organization requests a continuation award under this section, the board of directors shall submit to the Secretary a written review of the parent training and information program conducted by the parent organization during the preceding fiscal year.

SEC. 672. COMMUNITY PARENT RESOURCE CENTERS.

(a) PROGRAM AUTHORIZED-

(1) IN GENERAL- The Secretary may award grants to, and enter into contracts and cooperative agreements with, local parent organizations to support community parent resource centers that will help ensure that underserved parents of children with disabilities, including low income parents, parents of limited English proficient children, and parents with disabilities, have the training and information the parents need to enable the parents to participate effectively in helping their children with disabilities—

(A) to meet developmental and functional goals, and challenging academic achievement goals that have been established for all children; and

(B) to be prepared to lead productive independent adult lives, to the maximum extent possible.

(2) DEFINITION OF LOCAL PARENT ORGANIZATION- In this section, the term local parent organization' means a parent organization, as defined in section 671(a)(2), that—

(A) has a board of directors the majority of whom are parents of children with disabilities ages birth through 26 from the community to be served; and

(B) has as its mission serving parents of children with disabilities who—

(i) are ages birth through 26; and

(ii) have the full range of disabilities described in section 602(3).

(b) REQUIRED ACTIVITIES- Each community parent resource center assisted under this section shall—

(1) provide training and information that meets the training and information needs of parents of children with disabilities proposed to be served by the grant, contract, or cooperative agreement;

(2) carry out the activities required of parent training and information centers under paragraphs (2) through (9) of section 671(b);

(3) establish cooperative partnerships with the parent training and information centers funded under section 671; and

(4) be designed to meet the specific needs of families who experience significant isolation from available sources of information and support.

SEC. 673. TECHNICAL ASSISTANCE FOR PARENT TRAINING AND INFORMATION CENTERS.

(a) PROGRAM AUTHORIZED-

(1) IN GENERAL- The Secretary may, directly or through awards to eligible entities, provide technical assistance for developing, assisting, and coordinating parent training and information programs carried out by parent training and information centers receiving assistance under section 671 and community parent resource centers receiving assistance under section 672.

(2) DEFINITION OF ELIGIBLE ENTITY- In this section, the term eligible entity' has the meaning given the term in section 661(b).

(b) AUTHORIZED ACTIVITIES- The Secretary may provide technical assistance to a parent training and information center or a community parent resource center under this section in areas such as—

(1) effective coordination of parent training efforts;

(2) dissemination of scientifically based research and information;

(3) promotion of the use of technology,

including assistive technology devices and assistive technology services;

(4) reaching underserved populations, including parents of low-income and limited English proficient children with disabilities;

(5) including children with disabilities in general education programs;

(6) facilitation of transitions from—

(A) early intervention services to preschool;

(B) preschool to elementary school;

(C) elementary school to secondary school; and

(D) secondary school to postsecondary environments; and

(7) promotion of alternative methods of dispute resolution, including mediation.

(c) COLLABORATION WITH THE RESOURCE CENTERS- Each eligible entity receiving an award under subsection (a) shall develop collaborative agreements with the geographically appropriate regional resource center and, as appropriate, the regional educational laboratory supported under section 174 of the Education Sciences Reform Act of 2002, to further parent and professional collaboration.

SEC. 674. TECHNOLOGY DEVELOPMENT, DEMONSTRATION, AND UTILIZATION; MEDIA SERVICES; AND INSTRUCTIONAL MATERIALS.

(a) PROGRAM AUTHORIZED-

(1) IN GENERAL- The Secretary, on a competitive basis, shall award grants to, and enter into contracts and cooperative agreements with, eligible entities to support activities described in subsections (b) and (c).

(2) DEFINITION OF ELIGIBLE ENTITY- In this section, the term eligible entity' has the meaning given the term in section 661(b).

(b) TECHNOLOGY DEVELOPMENT, DEMONSTRATION, AND USE-

(1) IN GENERAL- In carrying out this section, the Secretary shall support activities to promote the development, demonstration, and use of technology.

(2) AUTHORIZED ACTIVITIES- The following activities may be carried out under this subsection:

(A) Conducting research on and promoting the demonstration and use of innovative, emerging, and universally designed technologies for children with disabilities, by improving the transfer of technology from research and development to practice.

(B) Supporting research, development, and dissemination of technology with universal design features, so that the technology is accessible to the broadest range of individuals with disabilities without further modification or adaptation.

(C) Demonstrating the use of systems to provide parents and teachers with information and training concerning early diagnosis of, intervention for, and effective teaching strategies for, young children with reading disabilities.

(D) Supporting the use of Internet-based communications for students with cognitive disabilities in order to maximize their academic and functional skills.

(c) EDUCATIONAL MEDIA SERVICES-

(1) IN GENERAL- In carrying out this section, the Secretary shall support—

(A) educational media activities that are designed to be of educational value in the classroom setting to children with disabilities;

(B) providing video description, open captioning, or closed captioning, that is appropriate for use in the classroom setting, of—

(i) television programs;

(ii) videos;

(iii) other materials, including programs and materials associated with new and emerging technologies, such as CDs, DVDs, video streaming, and other forms of multimedia; or

(iv) news (but only until September 30, 2006);

(C) distributing materials described in subparagraphs (A) and (B) through such mechanisms as a loan service; and

(D) providing free educational materials, including textbooks, in accessible media for visually impaired and print disabled students in elementary schools and secondary schools, postsecondary schools, and graduate schools.

(2) LIMITATION- The video description, open captioning, or closed captioning described in paragraph (1)(B) shall be provided only when the description or captioning has not been previously provided by the producer or distributor, or has not been fully funded by other sources.

(d) APPLICATIONS-

(1) IN GENERAL- Any eligible entity that wishes to receive a grant, or enter into a contract or cooperative agreement, under subsection (b) or (c) shall submit an application to the Secretary at such time, in such manner, and containing such information as the Secretary may require.

(2) SPECIAL RULE- For the purpose of an application for an award to carry out activities described in subsection (c)(1)(D), such eligible

entity shall—

(A) be a national, nonprofit entity with a proven track record of meeting the needs of students with print disabilities through services described in subsection (c)(1)(D);

(B) have the capacity to produce, maintain, and distribute in a timely fashion, up-to-date textbooks in digital audio formats to qualified students; and

(C) have a demonstrated ability to significantly leverage Federal funds through other public and private contributions, as well as through the expansive use of volunteers.

(e) NATIONAL INSTRUCTIONAL MATERIALS ACCESS CENTER-

(1) IN GENERAL- The Secretary shall establish and support, through the American Printing House for the Blind, a center to be known as the National Instructional Materials Access Center' not later than 1 year after the date of enactment of the Individuals with Disabilities Education Improvement Act of 2004.

(2) DUTIES- The duties of the National Instructional Materials Access Center are the following:

(A) To receive and maintain a catalog of print instructional materials prepared in the National Instructional Materials Accessibility Standard, as established by the Secretary, made available to such center by the textbook publishing industry, State educational agencies, and local educational agencies.

(B) To provide access to print instructional materials, including textbooks, in accessible media, free of charge, to blind or other persons with print disabilities in elementary schools and secondary schools, in accordance with such terms and procedures as the National Instructional Materials Access Center may prescribe.

(C) To develop, adopt and publish procedures to protect against copyright infringement, with respect to the print instructional materials provided under sections 612(a)(23) and 613(a)(6).

(3) DEFINITIONS- In this subsection:

(A) BLIND OR OTHER PERSONS WITH PRINT DISABILITIES- The term blind or other persons with print disabilities' means children served under this Act and who may qualify in accordance with the Act entitled An Act to provide books for the adult blind', approved March 3, 1931 (2 U.S.C. 135a; 46 Stat. 1487) to receive books and other publications produced in specialized formats.

(B) NATIONAL INSTRUCTIONAL MATERIALS ACCESSIBILITY STANDARD- The term National Instructional Materials Accessibility Standard' means the standard established by the Secretary to be used in the preparation of electronic files suitable and used solely for efficient conversion into specialized formats.

(C) PRINT INSTRUCTIONAL MATERIALS- The term print instructional materials' means printed textbooks and related printed core materials that are written and published primarily for use in elementary school and secondary school instruction and are required by a State educational agency or local educational agency for use by students in the classroom.

(D) SPECIALIZED FORMATS- The term specialized formats' has the meaning given the term in section 121(d)(3) of title 17, United States Code.

(4) APPLICABILITY- This subsection shall apply to print instructional materials published after the date on which the final rule establishing the National Instructional Materials Accessibility Standard was published in the Federal Register.

(5) LIABILITY OF THE SECRETARY- Nothing in this subsection shall be construed to establish a private right of action against the Secretary for failure to provide instructional materials directly, or for failure by the National Instructional Materials Access Center to perform the duties of such center, or to otherwise authorize a private right of action related to the performance by such center, including through the application of the rights of children and parents established under this Act.

(6) INAPPLICABILITY- Subsections (a) through (d) shall not apply to this subsection.

SEC. 675. AUTHORIZATION OF APPROPRIATIONS.

There are authorized to be appropriated to carry out this subpart such sums as may be necessary for each of the fiscal years 2005 through 2010.

Subpart 4—General Provisions

SEC. 681. COMPREHENSIVE PLAN FOR SUBPARTS 2 AND 3.

(a) COMPREHENSIVE PLAN-

(1) IN GENERAL- After receiving input

from interested individuals with relevant expertise, the Secretary shall develop and implement a comprehensive plan for activities carried out under subparts 2 and 3 in order to enhance the provision of early intervention services, educational services, related services, and transitional services to children with disabilities under parts B and C. To the extent practicable, the plan shall be coordinated with the plan developed pursuant to section 178(c) of the Education Sciences Reform Act of 2002 and shall include mechanisms to address early intervention, educational, related service and transitional needs identified by State educational agencies in applications submitted for State personnel development grants under subpart 1 and for grants under subparts 2 and 3.

(2) PUBLIC COMMENT- The Secretary shall provide a public comment period of not less than 45 days on the plan.

(3) DISTRIBUTION OF FUNDS- In implementing the plan, the Secretary shall, to the extent appropriate, ensure that funds awarded under subparts 2 and 3 are used to carry out activities that benefit, directly or indirectly, children with the full range of disabilities and of all ages.

(4) REPORTS TO CONGRESS- The Secretary shall annually report to Congress on the Secretary's activities under subparts 2 and 3, including an initial report not later than 12 months after the date of enactment of the Individuals with Disabilities Education Improvement Act of 2004.

(b) ASSISTANCE AUTHORIZED- The Secretary is authorized to award grants to, or enter into contracts or cooperative agreements with, eligible entities to enable the eligible entities to carry out the purposes of such subparts in accordance with the comprehensive plan described in subsection (a).

(c) SPECIAL POPULATIONS-

(1) APPLICATION REQUIREMENT- In making an award of a grant, contract, or cooperative agreement under subpart 2 or 3, the Secretary shall, as appropriate, require an eligible entity to demonstrate how the eligible entity will address the needs of children with disabilities from minority backgrounds.

(2) REQUIRED OUTREACH AND TECHNICAL ASSISTANCE- Notwithstanding any other provision of this title, the Secretary shall reserve not less than 2 percent of the total amount of funds appropriated to carry out subparts 2 and 3 for either or both of the following activities:

(A) Providing outreach and technical assistance to historically Black colleges and universities, and to institutions of higher education with minority enrollments of not less than 25 percent, to promote the participation of such colleges, universities, and institutions in activities under this subpart.

(B) Enabling historically Black colleges and universities, and the institutions described in subparagraph (A), to assist other colleges, universities, institutions, and agencies in improving educational and transitional results for children with disabilities, if the historically Black colleges and universities and the institutions of higher education described in subparagraph (A) meet the criteria established by the Secretary under this subpart.

(d) PRIORITIES- The Secretary, in making an award of a grant, contract, or cooperative agreement under subpart 2 or 3, may, without regard to the rulemaking procedures under section 553 of title 5, United States Code, limit competitions to, or otherwise give priority to—

(1) projects that address 1 or more—

(A) age ranges;

(B) disabilities;

(C) school grades;

(D) types of educational placements or early intervention environments;

(E) types of services;

(F) content areas, such as reading; or

(G) effective strategies for helping children with disabilities learn appropriate behavior in the school and other community based educational settings;

(2) projects that address the needs of children based on the severity or incidence of their disability;

(3) projects that address the needs of—

(A) low achieving students;

(B) underserved populations;

(C) children from low income families;

(D) limited English proficient children;

(E) unserved and underserved areas;

(F) rural or urban areas;

(G) children whose behavior interferes with their learning and socialization;

(H) children with reading difficulties;

(I) children in public charter schools;

(J) children who are gifted and talented; or

(K) children with disabilities served by local educational agencies that receive payments under title VIII of the Elementary and Secondary Education Act of 1965;

(4) projects to reduce inappropriate identification of children as children with disabilities, particularly among minority children;

(5) projects that are carried out in particular areas of the country, to ensure broad

geographic coverage;

(6) projects that promote the development and use of technologies with universal design, assistive technology devices, and assistive technology services to maximize children with disabilities' access to and participation in the general education curriculum; and

(7) any activity that is authorized in subpart 2 or 3.

(e) ELIGIBILITY FOR FINANCIAL ASSISTANCE- No State or local educational agency, or other public institution or agency, may receive a grant or enter into a contract or cooperative agreement under subpart 2 or 3 that relates exclusively to programs, projects, and activities pertaining to children aged 3 through 5, inclusive, unless the State is eligible to receive a grant under section 619(b).

SEC. 682. ADMINISTRATIVE PROVISIONS.

(a) APPLICANT AND RECIPIENT RESPONSIBILITIES-

(1) DEVELOPMENT AND ASSESSMENT OF PROJECTS- The Secretary shall require that an applicant for, and a recipient of, a grant, contract, or cooperative agreement for a project under subpart 2 or 3—

(A) involve individuals with disabilities or parents of individuals with disabilities ages birth through 26 in planning, implementing, and evaluating the project; and

(B) where appropriate, determine whether the project has any potential for replication and adoption by other entities.

(2) ADDITIONAL RESPONSIBILITIES- The Secretary may require a recipient of a grant, contract, or cooperative agreement under subpart 2 or 3 to—

(A) share in the cost of the project;

(B) prepare any findings and products from the project in formats that are useful for specific audiences, including parents, administrators, teachers, early intervention personnel, related services personnel, and individuals with disabilities;

(C) disseminate such findings and products; and

(D) collaborate with other such recipients in carrying out subparagraphs (B) and (C).

(b) APPLICATION MANAGEMENT-

(1) STANDING PANEL-

(A) IN GENERAL- The Secretary shall establish and use a standing panel of experts who are qualified, by virtue of their training, expertise, or experience, to evaluate each application under subpart 2 or 3 that requests more than $75,000 per year in Federal financial assistance.

(B) MEMBERSHIP- The standing panel shall include, at a minimum—

(i) individuals who are representatives of institutions of higher education that plan, develop, and carry out high quality programs of personnel preparation;

(ii) individuals who design and carry out scientifically based research targeted to the improvement of special education programs and services;

(iii) individuals who have recognized experience and knowledge necessary to integrate and apply scientifically based research findings to improve educational and transitional results for children with disabilities;

(iv) individuals who administer programs at the State or local level in which children with disabilities participate;

(v) individuals who prepare parents of children with disabilities to participate in making decisions about the education of their children;

(vi) individuals who establish policies that affect the delivery of services to children with disabilities;

(vii) individuals who are parents of children with disabilities ages birth through 26 who are benefiting, or have benefited, from coordinated research, personnel preparation, and technical assistance; and

(viii) individuals with disabilities.

(C) TERM- No individual shall serve on the standing panel for more than 3 consecutive years.

(2) PEER-REVIEW PANELS FOR PARTICULAR COMPETITIONS-

(A) COMPOSITION- The Secretary shall ensure that each subpanel selected from the standing panel that reviews an application under subpart 2 or 3 includes—

(i) individuals with knowledge and expertise on the issues addressed by the activities described in the application; and

(ii) to the extent practicable, parents of children with disabilities ages birth through 26, individuals with disabilities, and persons from diverse backgrounds.

(B) FEDERAL EMPLOYMENT LIMITATION- A majority of the individuals on each subpanel that reviews an application under subpart 2 or 3 shall be individuals who are not employees of the Federal Government.

(3) USE OF DISCRETIONARY FUNDS

FOR ADMINISTRATIVE PURPOSES-

(A) EXPENSES AND FEES OF NON-FEDERAL PANEL MEMBERS- The Secretary may use funds available under subpart 2 or 3 to pay the expenses and fees of the panel members who are not officers or employees of the Federal Government.

(B) ADMINISTRATIVE SUPPORT- The Secretary may use not more than 1 percent of the funds appropriated to carry out subpart 2 or 3 to pay non-Federal entities for administrative support related to management of applications submitted under subpart 2 or 3, respectively.

(c) PROGRAM EVALUATION- The Secretary may use funds made available to carry out subpart 2 or 3 to evaluate activities carried out under subpart 2 or 3, respectively.

(d) MINIMUM FUNDING REQUIRED-

(1) IN GENERAL- Subject to paragraph (2), the Secretary shall ensure that, for each fiscal year, not less than the following amounts are provided under subparts 2 and 3 to address the following needs:

(A) $12,832,000 to address the educational, related services, transitional, and early intervention needs of children with deaf-blindness.

(B) $4,000,000 to address the postsecondary, vocational, technical, continuing, and adult education needs of individuals with deafness.

(C) $4,000,000 to address the educational, related services, and transitional needs of children with an emotional disturbance and those who are at risk of developing an emotional disturbance.

(2) RATABLE REDUCTION- If the sum of the amount appropriated to carry out subparts 2 and 3, and part E of the Education Sciences Reform Act of 2002 for any fiscal year is less than $130,000,000, the amounts listed in paragraph (1) shall be ratably reduced for the fiscal year.'.

TITLE II—NATIONAL CENTER FOR SPECIAL EDUCATION RESEARCH

SEC. 201. NATIONAL CENTER FOR SPECIAL EDUCATION RESEARCH.

(a) AMENDMENT- The Education Sciences Reform Act of 2002 (20 U.S.C. 9501 et seq.) is amended—

(1) by redesignating part E as part F; and

(2) by inserting after part D the following:

PART E—NATIONAL CENTER FOR SPECIAL EDUCATION RESEARCH

SEC. 175. ESTABLISHMENT.

(a) ESTABLISHMENT- There is established in the Institute a National Center for Special Education Research (in this part referred to as the Special Education Research Center').

(b) MISSION- The mission of the Special Education Research Center is—

(1) to sponsor research to expand knowledge and understanding of the needs of infants, toddlers, and children with disabilities in order to improve the developmental, educational, and transitional results of such individuals;

(2) to sponsor research to improve services provided under, and support the implementation of, the Individuals with Disabilities Education Act (20 U.S.C. 1400 et seq.); and

(3) to evaluate the implementation and effectiveness of the Individuals with Disabilities Education Act in coordination with the National Center for Education Evaluation and Regional Assistance.

(c) Applicability of Education Sciences Reform Act of 2002- Parts A and F, and the standards for peer review of applications and for the conduct and evaluation of research under sections 133(a) and 134, respectively, shall apply to the Secretary, the Director, and the Commissioner in carrying out this part.

SEC. 176. COMMISSIONER FOR SPECIAL EDUCATION RESEARCH.

The Special Education Research Center shall be headed by a Commissioner for Special Education Research (in this part referred to as the Special Education Research Commissioner') who shall have substantial knowledge of the Special Education Research Center's activities, including a high level of expertise in the fields of research, research management, and the education of children with disabilities.

SEC. 177. DUTIES.

(a) GENERAL DUTIES- The Special Education Research Center shall carry out research activities under this part consistent with the mission described in section 175(b), such as activities that—

(1) improve services provided under the Individuals with Disabilities Education Act in order to improve—

(A) academic achievement, functional outcomes, and educational results for children with disabilities; and

(B) developmental outcomes for infants or toddlers with disabilities;

(2) identify scientifically based educational practices that support learning and improve academic achievement, functional outcomes, and educational results for all students with disabilities;

(3) examine the special needs of preschool aged children, infants, and toddlers with disabilities, including factors that may result in developmental delays;

(4) identify scientifically based related services and interventions that promote participation and progress in the general education curriculum and general education settings;

(5) improve the alignment, compatibility, and development of valid and reliable assessments, including alternate assessments, as required by section 1111(b) of the Elementary and Secondary Education Act of 1965 (20 U.S.C. 6311(b));

(6) examine State content standards and alternate assessments for students with significant cognitive impairment in terms of academic achievement, individualized instructional need, appropriate education settings, and improved post-school results;

(7) examine the educational, developmental, and transitional needs of children with high incidence and low incidence disabilities;

(8) examine the extent to which overidentification and underidentification of children with disabilities occurs, and the causes thereof;

(9) improve reading and literacy skills of children with disabilities;

(10) examine and improve secondary and postsecondary education and transitional outcomes and results for children with disabilities;

(11) examine methods of early intervention for children with disabilities, including children with multiple or complex developmental delays;

(12) examine and incorporate universal design concepts in the development of standards, assessments, curricula, and

instructional methods to improve educational and transitional results for children with disabilities;

(13) improve the preparation of personnel, including early intervention personnel, who provide educational and related services to children with disabilities to increase the academic achievement and functional performance of students with disabilities;

(14) examine the excess costs of educating a child with a disability and expenses associated with high cost special education and related services;

(15) help parents improve educational results for their children, particularly related to transition issues;

(16) address the unique needs of children with significant cognitive disabilities; and

(17) examine the special needs of limited English proficient children with disabilities.

(b) STANDARDS- The Special Education Research Commissioner shall ensure that activities assisted under this section—

(1) conform to high standards of quality, integrity, accuracy, validity, and reliability;

(2) are carried out in accordance with the standards for the conduct and evaluation of all research and development established by the National Center for Education Research; and

(3) are objective, secular, neutral, and nonideological, and are free of partisan political influence, and racial, cultural, gender, regional, or disability bias.

(c) PLAN- The Special Education Research Commissioner shall propose to the Director a research plan, developed in collaboration with the Assistant Secretary for Special Education and Rehabilitative Services, that—

(1) is consistent with the priorities and mission of the Institute and the mission of the Special Education Research Center;

(2) is carried out, updated, and modified, as appropriate;

(3) is consistent with the purposes of the Individuals with Disabilities Education Act;

(4) contains an appropriate balance across all age ranges and types of children with disabilities;

(5) provides for research that is objective and uses measurable indicators to assess its progress and results; and

(6) is coordinated with the comprehensive plan developed under section 681 of the Individuals with Disabilities Education Act.

(d) GRANTS, CONTRACTS, AND COOPERATIVE AGREEMENTS-

(1) IN GENERAL- In carrying out the duties under this section, the Director may

award grants to, or enter into contracts or cooperative agreements with, eligible applicants.

(2) ELIGIBLE APPLICANTS- Activities carried out under this subsection through contracts, grants, or cooperative agreements shall be carried out only by recipients with the ability and capacity to conduct scientifically valid research.

(3) APPLICATIONS- An eligible applicant that wishes to receive a grant, or enter into a contract or cooperative agreement, under this section shall submit an application to the Director at such time, in such manner, and containing such information as the Director may require.

(e) DISSEMINATION- The Special Education Research Center shall—

(1) synthesize and disseminate, through the National Center for Education Evaluation and Regional Assistance, the findings and results of special education research conducted or supported by the Special Education Research Center; and

(2) assist the Director in the preparation of a biennial report, as described in section 119.

(f) AUTHORIZATION OF APPROPRIATIONS- There are authorized to be appropriated to carry out this part such sums as may be necessary for each of fiscal years 2005 through 2010.'.

(b) CONFORMING AMENDMENTS-

(1) AMENDMENTS TO THE TABLE OF CONTENTS- The table of contents in section 1 of the Act entitled An Act to provide for improvement of Federal education research, statistics, evaluation, information, and dissemination, and for other purposes', approved November 5, 2002 (116 Stat. 1940; Public Law 107-279), is amended—

(A) by redesignating the item relating to part E as the item relating to part F; and

(B) by inserting after the item relating to section 174 the following:

Part E—National Center for Special Education Research

SEC. 175. ESTABLISHMENT

SEC. 176. COMMISSIONER FOR SPECIAL EDUCATION RESEARCH.

SEC. 177. DUTIES.

(2) EDUCATION SCIENCES REFORM ACT OF 2002- The Education Sciences Reform Act of 2002 (20 U.S.C. 9501 et seq.) is amended—

(A) in section 111(b)(1)(A) (20 U.S.C. 9511(b)(1)(A)), by inserting and special education' after early childhood education';

(B) in section 111(c)(3) (20 U.S.C. 9511(c)(3))—

(i) in subparagraph (B), by striking and' after the semicolon;

(ii) in subparagraph (C), by striking the period and inserting ; and'; and

(iii) by adding at the end the following:

(D) the National Center for Special Education Research (as described in part E).';

(C) in section 115(a) (20 U.S.C. 9515(a)), by striking including those' and all that follows through such as' and inserting including those associated with the goals and requirements of the Elementary and Secondary Education Act of 1965 (20 U.S.C. 6301 et seq.), the Individuals with Disabilities Education Act (20 U.S.C. 1400 et seq.), and the Higher Education Act of 1965 (20 U.S.C. 1001 et seq.), such as'; and

(D) in section 116(c)(4)(A)(ii) (20 U.S.C. 9516(c)(4)(A)(ii), by inserting special education experts,' after early childhood experts,'.

(3) ELEMENTARY AND SECONDARY EDUCATION ACT OF 1965- Section 1117(a)(3) of the Elementary and Secondary Education Act of 1965 (20 U.S.C. 6317(a)(3)) is amended by striking part E' and inserting part D'.

SEC. 202. NATIONAL BOARD FOR EDUCATION SCIENCES.

Section 116(c)(9) of the Education Sciences Reform Act of 2002 (20 U.S.C. 9516(c)(9)) is amended by striking the third sentence and inserting the following: Meetings of the Board are subject to section 552b of title 5, United States Code (commonly referred to as the Government in the Sunshine Act).'.

SEC. 203. REGIONAL ADVISORY COMMITTEES.

Section 206(d)(3) of the Educational Technical Assistance Act of 2002 (20 U.S.C. 9605(d)(3)) is amended by striking Academy' and inserting Institute'.

TITLE III—
MISCELLANEOUS
PROVISIONS

SEC. 301. AMENDMENT TO CHILDREN'S HEALTH ACT OF 2000.

Section 1004 of the Children's Health Act of 2000 (42 U.S.C. 285g note) is amended—

(1) in subsection (b), by striking Agency' and inserting Agency, and the Department of Education'; and

(2) in subsection (c)—

(A) in paragraph (2), by striking and' after the semicolon;

(B) in paragraph (3), by striking the period at the end and inserting ; and'; and

(C) by adding at the end the following:

(4) be conducted in compliance with section 444 of the General Education Provisions Act (20 U.S.C. 1232g), including the requirement of prior parental consent for the disclosure of any education records, except without the use of authority or exceptions granted to authorized representatives of the Secretary of Education for the evaluation of Federally-supported education programs or in connection with the enforcement of the Federal legal requirements that relate to such programs.

SEC. 302. EFFECTIVE DATES.

(a) Parts A, B, and C, and subpart 1 of part D-

(1) IN GENERAL- Except as provided in paragraph (2), parts A, B, and C, and subpart 1 of part D, of the Individuals with Disabilities Education Act, as amended by title I, shall take effect on July 1, 2005.

(2) HIGHLY QUALIFIED DEFINITION- Subparagraph (A), and subparagraphs (C) through (F), of section 602(10) of the Individuals with Disabilities Education Act, as amended by title I, shall take effect on the date of enactment of this Act for purposes of the Elementary and Secondary Education Act of 1965.

(b) SUBPARTS 2, 3, AND 4 OF PART D- Subparts 2, 3, and 4 of part D of the Individuals with Disabilities Education Act, as amended by title I, shall take effect on the date of enactment of this Act.

(c) Education Sciences Reform Act of 2002-

(1) NATIONAL CENTER FOR SPECIAL EDUCATION RESEARCH- Sections 175, 176, and 177 (other than section 177(c)) of the Education Sciences Reform Act of 2002, as enacted by section 201(a)(2) of this Act, shall take effect on the date of enactment of this Act.

(2) PLAN- Section 177(c) of the Education Sciences Reform Act of 2002, as enacted by section 201(a)(2) of this Act, shall take effect on October 1, 2005.

SEC. 303. TRANSITION.

(a) ORDERLY TRANSITION-

(1) IN GENERAL- The Secretary of Education (in this section referred to as the Secretary') shall take such steps as are necessary to provide for the orderly transition from the Individuals with Disabilities Education Act, as such Act was in effect on the day preceding the date of enactment of this Act, to the Individuals with Disabilities Education Act and part E of the Education Sciences Reform Act of 2002, as amended by this Act.

(2) LIMITATION- The Secretary's authority in paragraph (1) shall terminate 1 year after the date of enactment of this Act.

(b) MULTI-YEAR AWARDS- Notwithstanding any other provision of law, the Secretary may use funds appropriated under part D of the Individuals with Disabilities Education Act to make continuation awards for projects that were funded under section 618, and part D, of the Individuals with Disabilities Education Act (as such section and part were in effect on September 30, 2004), in accordance with the terms of the original awards.

(c) RESEARCH- Notwithstanding section 302(b) or any other provision of law, the Secretary may award funds that are appropriated under the Department of Education Appropriations Act, 2005 for special education research under either of the headings SPECIAL EDUCATION' or INSTITUTE OF EDUCATION SCIENCES' in accordance with sections 672 and 674 of the Individuals with Disabilities Education Act, as such sections were in effect on October 1, 2004.

SEC. 304. REPEALER.

Section 644 of the Individuals with Disabilities Education Act, as such section was in effect on the day before the enactment of this Act, is repealed.

SEC. 305. IDEA TECHNICAL AMENDMENTS TO OTHER LAWS.

(a) Title 10- Section 2164(f) of title 10, United States Code is amended—

(1) in paragraph (1)(B)—

(A) by striking infants and toddlers' each place the term appears and inserting infants or toddlers';

(B) by striking part H' and inserting part C'; and

(C) by striking 1471' and inserting 1431'; and

(2) in paragraph (3)—

(A) in subparagraph (A)—

(i) by striking 602(a)(1)' and inserting 602'; and

(ii) by striking 1401(a)(1)' and inserting 1401';

(B) by striking subparagraph (B);

(C) by redesignating subparagraph (C) as subparagraph (B); and

(D) in subparagraph (B) (as so redesignated)—

(i) by striking and toddlers' and inserting or toddlers';

(ii) by striking 672(1)' and inserting 632'; and

(iii) by striking 1472(1)' and inserting 1432'.

(b) Defense Dependents Education Act of 1978- Section 1409(c)(2) of the Defense Dependents Education Act of 1978 (20 U.S.C. 927(c)(2)) is amended—

(1) by striking 677' and inserting 636'; and

(2) by striking part H' and inserting part C'.

(c) Higher Education Act of 1965- The Higher Education Act of 1965 (20 U.S.C. 1001 et seq.) is amended—

(1) in section 465(a)(2)(C) (20 U.S.C. 1087ee(a)(2)(C), by striking Individuals With' and inserting Individuals with' and;

(2) in section 469(c) (20 U.S.C. 1087ii(c)), by striking 602(a)(1) and 672(1)' and inserting 602 and 632'.

(d) EDUCATION OF THE DEAF ACT- The matter preceding subparagraph (A) of section 104(b)(2) of the Education of the Deaf Act (20 U.S.C. 4304(b)(2)) is amended by striking 618(a)(1)(A)' and inserting 618(a)(1)'.

(e) Goals 2000: Educate America Act- Section 3(a)(9) of the Goals 2000: Educate America Act (20 U.S.C. 5802(a)(9)) is amended by striking 602(a)(17)' and inserting 602'.

(f) School-to-Work Opportunities Act of 1994- Section 4(15) of the School-to-Work Opportunities Act of 1994 (20 U.S.C.

6103(15)) is amended—

(1) by striking 602(a)(17)' and inserting 602'; and

(2) by striking 1401(17)' and inserting 1401'.

(g) Elementary and Secondary Education Act of 1965- The Elementary and Secondary Education Act of 1965 (20 U.S.C. 6301 et seq.) is amended—

(1) in section 1111(b)(2)(I)(ii) (20 U.S.C. 6311(b)(2)(I)(ii)), by striking 612(a)(17)(A)' and inserting 612(a)(16)(A)';

(2) in section 5208 (20 U.S.C. 7221g), by striking 602(11)' and inserting 602'; and

(3) in section 5563(b)(8)(C) (20 U.S.C. 7273b(b)(8)(C)), by striking 682' and inserting 671'.

(h) Rehabilitation Act of 1973- The Rehabilitation Act of 1973 (29 U.S.C. 701 et seq.) is amended—

(1) in section 101(a)(11)(D)(ii) (29 U.S.C. 721(a)(11)(D)(ii)), by striking (as added by section 101 of Public Law 105-17)';

(2) in section 105(b)(1)(A)(ii) (29 U.S.C. 725(b)(1)(A)(ii)), by striking 682(a) of the Individuals with Disabilities Education Act (as added by section 101 of the Individuals with Disabilities Education Act Amendments of 1997; Public Law 105-17)' and inserting 671 of the Individuals with Disabilities Education Act';

(3) in section 105(c)(6) (29 U.S.C. 725(c)(6))—

(A) by striking 612(a)(21)' and inserting 612(a)(20)';

(B) by striking Individual with' and inserting Individuals with'; and

(C) by striking (as amended by section 101 of the Individuals with Disabilities Education Act Amendments of 1997; Public Law 105-17)';

(4) in section 302(f)(1)(D)(ii) (29 U.S.C. 772 (f)(1)(D)(ii)), by striking (as amended by section 101 of the Individuals with Disabilities Education Act Amendments of 1997 (Public Law 105-17))';

(5) in section 303(c)(6) (29 U.S.C. 773(c)(6))—

(A) by striking 682(a)' and inserting 671'; and

(B) by striking (as added by section 101 of the Individuals with Disabilities Education Act Amendments of 1997; Public Law 105-17)'; and

(6) in section 303(c)(4)(A)(ii) (29 U.S.C. 773(c)(4)(A)(ii)), by striking 682(a) of the Individuals with Disabilities Education Act (as added by section 101 of the Individuals with

Disabilities Education Act Amendments of 1997; Public Law 105-17)' and inserting 671 of the Individuals with Disabilities Education Act'.

(i) PUBLIC HEALTH SERVICE ACT- The Public Health Service Act (42 U.S.C. 201 et seq.) is amended—

(1) in section 399A(f) (42 U.S.C. 280d(f), by striking part H' and inserting part C';

(2) in section 399(n)(3) (42 U.S.C. 280c-6(n)(3)), by striking part H' and inserting part C';

(3) in section 399A(b)(8) (42 U.S.C. 280d(b)(8)), by striking part H' and inserting part C';

(4) in section 562(d)(3)(B) (42 U.S.C. 290ff-1(d)(3)(B)), by striking and H' and inserting and C'; and

(5) in section 563(d)(2) (42 U.S.C. 290ff-2(d)(2)), by striking 602(a)(19)' and inserting 602'.

(j) SOCIAL SECURITY ACT- The Social Security Act (42 U.S.C. 301 et seq.) is amended—

(1) in section 1903(c) (42 U.S.C. 1396b(c)), by striking part H' and inserting part C'; and

(2) in section 1915(c)(5)(C)(i) (42 U.S.C. 1396n(c)(5)(C)(i)), by striking (as defined in section 602(16) and (17) of the Education of the Handicapped Act (20 U.S.C. 1401(16), (17))' and inserting (as such terms are defined in section 602 of the Individuals with Disabilities Education Act (20 U.S.C. 1401))'.

(k) Domestic Volunteer Service Act of 1973- Section 211(a) of the Domestic Volunteer Service Act of 1973 (42 U.S.C. 5011(a)) is amended—

(1) by striking part H' and inserting part C'; and

(2) by striking 1471' and inserting 1431'.

(l) HEAD START ACT- The Head Start Act (42 U.S.C. 9831 et seq.) is amended—

(1) in section 640(a)(5)(C)(iv) (42 U.S.C. 9835(a)(5)(C)(iv)), by striking 1445' and inserting 1444';

(2) in section 640(d) (42 U.S.C. 9835(d))—

(A) by striking U.S.C' and inserting U.S.C.'; and

(B) by striking 1445' and inserting 1444';

(3) in section 641(d)(3) (42 U.S.C. 9836(d)(3)), by striking U.S.C 1431-1445' and inserting U.S.C. 1431-1444'; and

(4) in section 642(c) (42 U.S.C. 9837(c)), by striking 1445' and inserting 1444'.

(m) National and Community Service Act of 1990- Section 101(21)(B) of the National and Community Service Act of 1990 (42 U.S.C. 12511(21)(B)) is amended—

(1) by striking 602(a)(1)' and inserting 602'; and

(2) by striking 1401(a)(1)' and inserting 1401'.

(n) Developmental Disabilities Assistance and Bill of Rights Act of 2000- The Developmental Disabilities Assistance and Bill of Rights Act of 2000 (42 U.S.C. 15001 et seq.) is amended—

(1) in section 125(c)(5)(G)(i) (42 U.S.C. 15025(c)(5)(G)(i)), by striking subtitle C' and inserting part C'; and

(2) in section 154(a)(3)(E)(ii)(VI) (42 U.S.C. 15064(a)(3)(E)(ii)(VI))—

(A) by striking 682 or 683' and inserting 671 or 672'; and

(B) by striking (20 U.S.C. 1482, 1483)'.

(o) District of Columbia School Reform Act of 1995- The District of Columbia School Reform Act of 1995 (Public Law 104-134) is amended—

(1) in section 2002(32)—

(A) by striking 602(a)(1)' and inserting 602'; and

(B) by striking 1401(a)(1)' and inserting 1401';

(2) in section 2202(19), by striking Individuals With' and inserting Individuals with'; and

(3) in section 2210—

(A) in the heading for subsection (c), by striking WITH DISABILITIES' and inserting WITH DISABILITIES'; and

(B) in subsection (c), by striking Individuals With' and inserting Individuals with'.

SEC. 306. COPYRIGHT.

Section 121 of title 17, United States Code, is amended—

(1) by redesignating subsection (c) as subsection (d);

(2) by inserting after subsection (b) the following:

(c) Notwithstanding the provisions of section 106, it is not an infringement of copyright for a publisher of print instructional materials for use in elementary or secondary schools to create and distribute to the National Instructional Materials Access Center copies of the electronic files described in sections 612(a)(23)(C), 613(a)(6), and section 674(e) of the Individuals with Disabilities Education Act that contain the contents of print instructional materials using the National Instructional Material Accessibility Standard (as defined in section 674(e)(3) of that Act), if—

(1) the inclusion of the contents of such print instructional materials is required by any State educational agency or local educational agency;

(2) the publisher had the right to publish such print instructional materials in print formats; and

(3) such copies are used solely for reproduction or distribution of the contents of such print instructional materials in specialized formats; and

(3) in subsection (d), as redesignated by this section—

(A) in paragraph (2), by striking 'and' after the semicolon; and

(B) by striking paragraph (3) and inserting the following:

(3) 'print instructional materials' has the meaning given under section 674(e)(3)(C) of the Individuals with Disabilities Education Act; and

(4) 'specialized formats' means—

(A) braille, audio, or digital text which is exclusively for use by blind or other persons with disabilities; and

(B) with respect to print instructional materials, includes large print formats when such materials are distributed exclusively for use by blind or other persons with disabilities.

APPENDIX B

Federal Regulations Implementing
The 2006 IDEA Amendments

[The most important federal regulations affecting the education of children with disabilities, Parts 300 and 104 of Title 34 of the Code of Federal Regulations, as well as sections 76.532 and 76.654, have been reproduced here in their entirety as promulgated by the U.S. Department of Education.]

PART 300—ASSISTANCE TO STATES FOR THE EDUCATION OF CHILDREN WITH DISABILITIES

Subpart A—General Purposes and Applicability

Sec.
300.1 Purposes.
300.2 Applicability of this part to State and local agencies.

Definitions Used in This Part

300.4 Act.
300.5 Assistive technology device.
300.6 Assistive technology service.
300.7 Charter school.
300.8 Child with a disability.
300.9 Consent.
300.10 Core academic subjects.
300.11 Day; business day; school day.
300.12 Educational service agency.
300.13 Elementary school.
300.14 Equipment.
300.15 Evaluation.
300.16 Excess costs.
300.17 Free appropriate public education.
300.18 Highly qualified special education teachers.
300.19 Homeless children.
300.20 Include.
300.21 Indian and Indian tribe.

300.22 Individualized education program.
300.23 Individualized education program team.
300.24 Individualized family service plan.
300.25 Infant or toddler with a disability.
300.26 Institution of higher education.
300.27 Limited English proficient.
300.28 Local educational agency.
300.29 Native language.
300.30 Parent.
300.31 Parent training and information center.
300.32 Personally identifiable.
300.33 Public agency.
300.34 Related services.
300.35 Scientifically based research.
300.36 Secondary school.
300.37 Services plan.
300.38 Secretary.
300.39 Special education.
300.40 State.
300.41 State educational agency.
300.42 Supplementary aids and services.
300.43 Transition services.
300.44 Universal design.
300.45 Ward of the State.

Part B Regulations (34 CFR Part 300)
Authority: 20 U.S.C. 1221e–3, 1406, 1411–1419, unless otherwise noted.

Subpart A—General Purposes and Applicability

§ 300.1 Purposes.
The purposes of this part are—
(a) To ensure that all children with disabilities have available to them a free appropriate public education that emphasizes special education and related services designed to meet their unique needs and prepare them for further education, employment, and independent living;
(b) To ensure that the rights of children with disabilities and their parents are protected;
(c) To assist States, localities, educational service agencies, and Federal agencies to provide for the education of all children with disabilities; and
(d) To assess and ensure the effectiveness of efforts to educate children with disabilities.
(Authority: 20 U.S.C. 1400(d))

§ 300.2 Applicability of this part to State and local agencies.

(a) States. This part applies to each State that receives payments under Part B of the Act, as defined in § 300.4.
(b) Public agencies within the State. The provisions of this part—
(1) Apply to all political subdivisions of the State that are involved in the education of children with disabilities, including:
(i) The State educational agency (SEA).
(ii) Local educational agencies (LEAs), educational service agencies (ESAs), and public

charter schools that are not otherwise included as LEAs or ESAs and are not a school of an LEA or ESA.

(iii) Other State agencies and schools (such as Departments of Mental Health and Welfare and State schools for children with deafness or children with blindness).

(iv) State and local juvenile and adult correctional facilities; and

(2) Are binding on each public agency in the State that provides special education and related services to children with disabilities, regardless of whether that agency is receiving funds under Part B of the Act.

(c) Private schools and facilities. Each public agency in the State is responsible for ensuring that the rights and protections under Part B of the Act are given to children with disabilities—

(1) Referred to or placed in private schools and facilities by that public agency; or

(2) Placed in private schools by their parents under the provisions of § 300.148.

(Authority: 20 U.S.C. 1412)

Definitions Used in This Part

§ 300.4 Act.

Act means the Individuals with Disabilities Education Act, as amended.

(Authority: 20 U.S.C. 1400(a))

§ 300.5 Assistive technology device.

Assistive technology device means any item, piece of equipment, or product system, whether acquired commercially off the shelf, modified, or customized, that is used to increase, maintain, or improve the functional capabilities of a child with a disability. The term does not include a medical device that is surgically implanted, or the replacement of such device.

(Authority: 20 U.S.C. 1401(1))

§ 300.6 Assistive technology service.

Assistive technology service means any service that directly assists a child with a disability in the selection, acquisition, or use of an assistive technology device. The term includes—

(a) The evaluation of the needs of a child with a disability, including a functional evaluation of the child in the child's customary environment;

(b) Purchasing, leasing, or otherwise providing for the acquisition of assistive technology devices by children with disabilities;

(c) Selecting, designing, fitting, customizing, adapting, applying, maintaining, repairing, or replacing assistive technology devices;

(d) Coordinating and using other therapies, interventions, or services with assistive technology devices, such as those associated with

existing education and rehabilitation plans and programs;

(e) Training or technical assistance for a child with a disability or, if appropriate, that child's family; and

(f) Training or technical assistance for professionals (including individuals providing education or rehabilitation services), employers, or other individuals who provide services to, employ, or are otherwise substantially involved in the major life functions of that child.

(Authority: 20 U.S.C. 1401(2))

§ 300.7 Charter school.

Charter school has the meaning given the term in section 5210(1) of the Elementary and Secondary Education Act of 1965, as amended, 20 U.S.C. 6301 et seq. (ESEA).

(Authority: 20 U.S.C. 7221i(1))

§ 300.8 Child with a disability.

(a) General. (1) Child with a disability means a child evaluated in accordance with §§ 300.304 through 300.311 as having mental retardation, a hearing impairment (including deafness), a speech or language impairment, a visual impairment (including blindness), a serious emotional disturbance (referred to in this part as "emotional disturbance"), an orthopedic impairment, autism, traumatic brain injury, an other health impairment, a specific learning disability, deafblindness, or multiple disabilities, and who, by reason thereof, needs special education and related services.

(2)(i) Subject to paragraph (a)(2)(ii) of this section, if it is determined, through an appropriate evaluation under §§ 300.304 through 300.311, that a child has one of the disabilities identified in paragraph (a)(1) of this section, but only needs a related service and not special education, the child is not a child with a disability under this part.

(ii) If, consistent with § 300.39(a)(2), the related service required by the child is considered special education rather than a related service under State standards, the child would be determined to be a child with a disability under paragraph (a)(1) of this section.

(b) Children aged three through nine experiencing developmental delays. Child with a disability for children aged three through nine (or any subset of that age range, including ages three through five), may, subject to the conditions described in § 300.111(b), include a child—

(1) Who is experiencing developmental delays, as defined by the State and as measured by appropriate diagnostic instruments and procedures, in one or more of the following areas: Physical development, cognitive development, communication development, social or emotional development, or adaptive development; and

(2) Who, by reason thereof, needs special

education and related services.

(c) Definitions of disability terms. The terms used in this definition of a child with a disability are defined as follows:

(1)(i) Autism means a developmental disability significantly affecting verbal and nonverbal communication and social interaction, generally evident before age three, that adversely affects a child's educational performance. Other characteristics often associated with autism are engagement in repetitive activities and stereotyped movements, resistance to environmental change or change in daily routines, and unusual responses to sensory experiences.

(ii) Autism does not apply if a child's educational performance is adversely affected primarily because the child has an emotional disturbance, as defined in paragraph (c)(4) of this section.

(iii) A child who manifests the characteristics of autism after age three could be identified as having autism if the criteria in paragraph (c)(1)(i) of this section are satisfied.

(2) Deaf-blindness means concomitant hearing and visual impairments, the combination of which causes such severe communication and other developmental and educational needs that they cannot be accommodated in special education programs solely for children with deafness or children with blindness.

(3) Deafness means a hearing impairment that is so severe that the child is impaired in processing linguistic information through hearing, with or without amplification that adversely affects a child's educational performance.

(4)(i) Emotional disturbance means a condition exhibiting one or more of the following characteristics over a long period of time and to a marked degree that adversely affects a child's educational performance:

(A) An inability to learn that cannot be explained by intellectual, sensory, or health factors.

(B) An inability to build or maintain satisfactory interpersonal relationships with peers and teachers.

(C) Inappropriate types of behavior or feelings under normal circumstances.

(D) A general pervasive mood of unhappiness or depression.

(E) A tendency to develop physical symptoms or fears associated with personal or school problems.

(ii) Emotional disturbance includes schizophrenia. The term does not apply to children who are socially maladjusted, unless it is determined that they have an emotional disturbance under paragraph (c)(4)(i) of this section.

(5) Hearing impairment means an impairment in hearing, whether permanent or fluctuating, that adversely affects a child's educational performance but that is not included under the definition of deafness in this section.

(6) Mental retardation means significantly subaverage general intellectual functioning, existing concurrently with deficits in adaptive behavior and manifested during the developmental period, that adversely affects a child's educational performance.

(7) Multiple disabilities means concomitant impairments (such as mental retardation-blindness or mental retardation-orthopedic impairment), the combination of which causes such severe educational needs that they cannot be accommodated in special education programs solely for one of the impairments. Multiple disabilities does not include deaf-blindness.

(8) Orthopedic impairment means a severe orthopedic impairment that adversely affects a child's educational performance. The term includes impairments caused by a congenital anomaly, impairments caused by disease (e.g., poliomyelitis, bone tuberculosis), and impairments from other causes (e.g., cerebral palsy, amputations, and fractures or burns that cause contractures).

(9) Other health impairment means having limited strength, vitality, or alertness, including a heightened alertness to environmental stimuli, that results in limited alertness with respect to the educational environment, that—

(i) Is due to chronic or acute health problems such as asthma, attention deficit disorder or attention deficit hyperactivity disorder, diabetes, epilepsy, a heart condition, hemophilia, lead poisoning, leukemia, nephritis, rheumatic fever, sickle cell anemia, and Tourette syndrome; and

(ii) Adversely affects a child's educational performance.

(10) Specific learning disability—

(i) General. Specific learning disability means a disorder in one or more of the basic psychological processes involved in understanding or in using language, spoken or written, that may manifest itself in the imperfect ability to listen, think, speak, read, write, spell, or to do mathematical calculations, including conditions such as perceptual disabilities, brain injury, minimal brain dysfunction, dyslexia, and developmental aphasia.

(ii) Disorders not included. Specific learning disability does not include learning problems that are primarily the result of visual, hearing, or motor disabilities, of mental retardation, of emotional disturbance, or of environmental, cultural, or economic disadvantage.

(11) Speech or language impairment means a communication disorder, such as stuttering, impaired articulation, a language impairment, or a voice impairment, that adversely affects a child's educational performance.

(12) Traumatic brain injury means an acquired injury to the brain caused by an external physical force, resulting in total or partial functional disability or psychosocial impairment, or both, that adversely affects a child's educational performance. Traumatic brain injury applies to open or closed head injuries resulting in impairments in one or more areas, such as cognition; language; memory; attention; reasoning; abstract thinking; judgment; problem-solving; sensory, perceptual, and motor abilities; psychosocial behavior; physical functions; information processing; and speech. Traumatic brain injury does not apply to brain injuries that are congenital or degenerative, or to brain injuries induced by birth trauma.

(13) Visual impairment including blindness means an impairment in vision that, even with correction, adversely affects a child's educational performance. The term includes both partial sight and blindness.

(Authority: 20 U.S.C. 1401(3); 1401(30))

§ 300.9 Consent.

Consent means that—

(a) The parent has been fully informed of all information relevant to the activity for which consent is sought, in his or her native language, or other mode of communication;

(b) The parent understands and agrees in writing to the carrying out of the activity for which his or her consent is sought, and the consent describes that activity and lists the records (if any) that will be released and to whom; and

(c)(1) The parent understands that the granting of consent is voluntary on the part of the parent and may be revoked at anytime.

(2) If a parent revokes consent, that revocation is not retroactive (i.e., it does not negate an action that has occurred after the consent was given and before the consent was revoked).

(3)) If the parent revokes consent in writing for their child's receipt of special education services after the child is initially provided special education and related services, the public agency is not required to amend the child's education records to remove any references to the child's receipt of special education and related services because of the revocation of consent.

(Authority: 20 U.S.C. 1414(a)(1)(D))

§ 300.10 Core academic subjects.

Core academic subjects means English, reading or language arts, mathematics, science, foreign languages, civics and government, economics, arts, history, and geography.

(Authority: 20 U.S.C. 1401(4))

§ 300.11 Day; business day; school day.

(a) Day means calendar day unless otherwise indicated as business day or school day.

(b) Business day means Monday through Friday, except for Federal and State holidays (unless holidays are specifically included in the designation of business day, as in § 300.148(d)(1)(ii)).

(c)(1) School day means any day, including a partial day that children are in attendance at school for instructional purposes.

(2) School day has the same meaning for all children in school, including children with and without disabilities.

(Authority: 20 U.S.C. 1221e–3)

§ 300.12 Educational service agency.

Educational service agency means—

(a) A regional public multiservice agency—

(1) Authorized by State law to develop, manage, and provide services or programs to LEAs;

(2) Recognized as an administrative agency for purposes of the provision of special education and related services provided within public elementary schools and secondary schools of the State;

(b) Includes any other public institution or agency having administrative control and direction over a public elementary school or secondary school; and

(c) Includes entities that meet the definition of intermediate educational unit in section 602(23) of the Act as in effect prior to June 4, 1997.

(Authority: 20 U.S.C. 1401(5))

§ 300.13 Elementary school.

Elementary school means a nonprofit institutional day or residential school, including a public elementary charter school, that provides elementary education, as determined under State law.

(Authority: 20 U.S.C. 1401(6))

§ 300.14 Equipment.

Equipment means—

(a) Machinery, utilities, and built-in equipment, and any necessary enclosures or structures to house the machinery, utilities, or equipment; and

(b) All other items necessary for the functioning of a particular facility as a facility for the provision of educational services, including items such as instructional equipment and necessary furniture; printed, published and audiovisual instructional materials; telecommunications, sensory, and other technological aids and devices; and books, periodicals, documents, and other related materials.

(Authority: 20 U.S.C. 1401(7))

§ 300.15 Evaluation.

Evaluation means procedures used in accordance with §§ 300.304 through 300.311 to determine whether a child has a disability and the nature and extent of the special education and related services that the child needs.

(Authority: 20 U.S.C. 1414(a) (c))

§ 300.16 Excess costs.

Excess costs means those costs that are in excess of the average annual perstudent expenditure in an LEA during the preceding school year for an elementary school or secondary school student, as may be appropriate, and that must be computed after deducting—

(a) Amounts received—

(1) Under Part B of the Act;

(2) Under Part A of title I of the ESEA; and

(3) Under Parts A and B of title III of the ESEA and;

(b) Any State or local funds expended for programs that would qualify for assistance under any of the parts described in paragraph (a) of this section, but excluding any amounts for capital outlay or debt service. (See Appendix A to part 300 for an example of how excess costs must be calculated.)

(Authority: 20 U.S.C. 1401(8))

§ 300.17 Free appropriate public education.

Free appropriate public education or FAPE means special education and related services that—

(a) Are provided at public expense, under public supervision and direction, and without charge;

(b) Meet the standards of the SEA, including the requirements of this part;

(c) Include an appropriate preschool, elementary school, or secondary school education in the State involved; and

(d) Are provided in conformity with an individualized education program (IEP) that meets the requirements of §§ 300.320 through 300.324.

(Authority: 20 U.S.C. 1401(9))

§ 300.18 Highly qualified special education teachers.

(a) Requirements for special education teachers teaching core academic subjects. For any public elementary or secondary school special education teacher teaching core academic subjects, the term highly qualified has the meaning given the term in section 9101 of the ESEA and 34 CFR 200.56, except that the requirements for highly qualified also—

(1) Include the requirements described in paragraph (b) of this section; and

(2) Include the option for teachers to meet the requirements of section 9101 of the ESEA by

meeting the requirements of paragraphs (c) and (d) of this section.

(b) Requirements for special education teachers in general. (1) When used with respect to any public elementary school or secondary school special education teacher teaching in a State, highly qualified requires that—

(i) The teacher has obtained full State certification as a special education teacher (including certification obtained through alternative routes to certification), or passed the State special education teacher licensing examination, and holds a license to teach in the State as a special education teacher, except that when used with respect to any teacher teaching in a public charter school, highly qualified means that the teacher meets the certification or licensing requirements, if any, set forth in the State's public charter school law;

(ii) The teacher has not had special education certification or licensure requirements waived on an emergency, temporary, or provisional basis; and (iii) The teacher holds at least a bachelor's degree.

(2) A teacher will be considered to meet the standard in paragraph (b)(1)(i) of this section if that teacher is participating in an alternative route to special education certification program under which—

(i) The teacher—

(A) Receives high-quality professional development that is sustained, intensive, and classroom-focused in order to have a positive and lasting impact on classroom instruction, before and while teaching;

(B) Participates in a program of intensive supervision that consists of structured guidance and regular ongoing support for teachers or a teacher mentoring program;

(C) Assumes functions as a teacher only for a specified period of time not to exceed three years; and

(D) Demonstrates satisfactory progress toward full certification as prescribed by the State; and

(ii) The State ensures, through its certification and licensure process, that the provisions in paragraph (b)(2)(i) of this section are met.

(3) Any public elementary school or secondary school special education teacher teaching in a State, who is not teaching a core academic subject, is highly qualified if the teacher meets the requirements in paragraph (b)(1) or the requirements in (b)(1)(iii) and (b)(2) of this section.

(c) Requirements for special education teachers teaching to alternate achievement standards. When used with respect to a special education teacher who teaches core academic subjects exclusively to children who are assessed against alternate achievement standards established under 34 CFR 200.1(d), highly qualified means the teacher, whether new or not new to the profession, may either—

(1) Meet the applicable requirements of section 9101 of the ESEA and 34 CFR 200.56 for any elementary, middle, or secondary school teacher who is new or not new to the profession; or

(2) Meet the requirements of paragraph (B) or (C) of section 9101(23) of the ESEA as applied to an elementary school teacher, or, in the case of instruction above the elementary level, meet the requirements of paragraph (B) or (C) of section 9101(23) of the ESEA as applied to an elementary school teacher and have subject matter knowledge appropriate to the level of instruction being provided and needed to effectively teach to those standards, as determined by the State.

(d) Requirements for special education teachers teaching multiple subjects. Subject to paragraph (e) of this section, when used with respect to a special education teacher who teaches two or more core academic subjects exclusively to children with disabilities, highly qualified means that the teacher may either—

(1) Meet the applicable requirements of section 9101 of the ESEA and 34 CFR 200.56(b) or (c);

(2) In the case of a teacher who is not new to the profession, demonstrate competence in all the core academic subjects in which the teacher teaches in the same manner as is required for an elementary, middle, or secondary school teacher who is not new to the profession under 34 CFR 200.56(c) which may include a single, high objective uniform State standard of evaluation (HOUSSE) covering multiple subjects; or

(3) In the case of a new special education teacher who teaches multiple subjects and who is highly qualified in mathematics, language arts, or science, demonstrate, not later than two years after the date of employment, competence in the other core academic subjects in which the teacher teaches in the same manner as is required for an elementary, middle, or secondary school teacher under 34 CFR 200.56(c), which may include a single HOUSSE covering multiple subjects.

(e) Separate HOUSSE standards for special education teachers. Provided that any adaptations of the State's HOUSSE would not establish a lower standard for the content knowledge requirements for special education teachers and meets all the requirements for a HOUSSE for regular education teachers—

(1) A State may develop a separate HOUSSE for special education teachers; and

(2) The standards described in paragraph (e)(1) of this section may include single HOUSSE evaluations that cover multiple subjects.

(f) Rule of construction. Notwithstanding any other individual right of action that a parent or student may maintain under this part, nothing in this part shall be construed to create a right of action on behalf of an individual student or class of students for the failure of a particular SEA or LEA employee to be highly qualified, or to prevent a parent from filing a complaint under §§ 300.151 through 300.153 about staff qualifications with the SEA as provided for under this part. (g) Applicability of definition to ESEA; and clarification of new special education teacher. (1) A teacher who is highly qualified under this section is considered highly qualified for purposes of the ESEA.

(2) For purposes of § 300.18(d)(3), a fully certified regular education teacher who subsequently becomes fully certified or licensed as a special education teacher is a new special education teacher when first hired as a special education teacher.

(h) Private school teachers not covered. The requirements in this section do not apply to teachers hired by private elementary schools and secondary schools including private school teachers hired or contracted by LEAs to provide equitable services to parentally-placed private school children with disabilities under § 300.138.

(Authority: 20 U.S.C. 1401(10))

§ 300.19 Homeless children.

Homeless children has the meaning given the term homeless children and youths in section 725 (42 U.S.C. 11434a) of the McKinney-Vento Homeless Assistance Act, as amended, 42 U.S.C. 11431 et seq.

(Authority: 20 U.S.C. 1401(11))

§ 300.20 Include.

Include means that the items named are not all of the possible items that are covered, whether like or unlike the ones named.

(Authority: 20 U.S.C. 1221e–3)

§ 300.21 Indian and Indian tribe.

(a) Indian means an individual who is a member of an Indian tribe.

(b) Indian tribe means any Federal or State Indian tribe, band, rancheria, pueblo, colony, or community, including any Alaska Native village or regional village corporation (as defined in or established under the Alaska Native Claims Settlement Act, 43 U.S.C. 1601 et seq.).

(c) Nothing in this definition is intended to indicate that the Secretary of the Interior is required to provide services or funding to a State Indian tribe that is not listed in the Federal Register list of Indian entities recognized as eligible to receive services from the United States, published pursuant to Section 104 of the Federally Recognized Indian Tribe List Act of 1994, 25 U.S.C. 479a–1.

(Authority: 20 U.S.C. 1401(12) and (13))

§ 300.22 Individualized education program.

Individualized education program or IEP means a written statement for a child with a disability that is developed, reviewed, and revised in accordance with §§ 300.320 through 300.324.

(Authority: 20 U.S.C. 1401(14))

§ 300.23 Individualized education program team.

Individualized education program team or IEP Team means a group of individuals described in § 300.321 that is responsible for developing, reviewing, or revising an IEP for a child with a disability.

(Authority: 20 U.S.C. 1414(d)(1)(B))

§ 300.24 Individualized family service plan.

Individualized family service plan or IFSP has the meaning given the term in section 636 of the Act.

(Authority: 20 U.S.C. 1401(15))

§ 300.25 Infant or toddler with a disability.

Infant or toddler with a disability—

(a) Means an individual under three years of age who needs early intervention services because the individual—

(1) Is experiencing developmental delays, as measured by appropriate diagnostic instruments and procedures in one or more of the areas of cognitive development, physical development, communication development, social or emotional development, and adaptive development; or

(2) Has a diagnosed physical or mental condition that has a high probability of resulting in developmental delay; and

(b) May also include, at a State's discretion—

(1) At-risk infants and toddlers; and

(2) Children with disabilities who are eligible for services under section 619 and who previously received services under Part C of the Act until such children enter, or are eligible under State law to enter, kindergarten or elementary school, as appropriate, provided that any programs under Part C of the Act serving such children shall include—

(i) An educational component that promotes school readiness and incorporates pre-literacy, language, and numeracy skills; and (ii) A written notification to parents of their rights and responsibilities in determining whether their child will continue to receive services under Part C of the Act or participate in preschool programs under section 619.

(Authority: 20 U.S.C. 1401(16) and 1432(5))

§ 300.26 Institution of higher education.

Institution of higher education—

(a) Has the meaning given the term in section 101 of the Higher Education Act of 1965, as amended, 20 U.S.C. 1021 et seq. (HEA); and

(b) Also includes any community college receiving funds from the Secretary of the Interior under the Tribally Controlled Community College or University Assistance Act of 1978, 25 U.S.C. 1801, et seq.

(Authority: 20 U.S.C. 1401(17))

§ 300.27 Limited English proficient.

Limited English proficient has the meaning given the term in section 9101(25) of the ESEA.

(Authority: 20 U.S.C. 1401(18))

§ 300.28 Local educational agency.

(a) General. Local educational agency or LEA means a public board of education or other public authority legally constituted within a State for either administrative control or direction of, or to perform a service function for, public elementary or secondary schools in a city, county, township, school district, or other political subdivision of a State, or for a combination of school districts or counties as are recognized in a State as an administrative agency for its public elementary schools or secondary schools.

(b) Educational service agencies and other public institutions or agencies. The term includes—

(1) An educational service agency, as defined in § 300.12; and

(2) Any other public institution or agency having administrative control and direction of a public elementary school or secondary school, including a public nonprofit charter school that is established as an LEA under State law.

(c) BIA funded schools. The term includes an elementary school or secondary school funded by the Bureau of Indian Affairs, and not subject to the jurisdiction of any SEA other than the Bureau of Indian Affairs, but only to the extent that the inclusion makes the school eligible for programs for which specific eligibility is not provided to the school in another provision of law and the school does not have a student population that is smaller than the student population of the LEA receiving assistance under the Act with the smallest student population.

(Authority: 20 U.S.C. 1401(19))

§ 300.29 Native language.

(a) Native language, when used with respect to an individual who is limited English proficient, means the following:

(1) The language normally used by that individual, or, in the case of a child, the language normally used by the parents of the child, except as provided in paragraph (a)(2) of this section.

(2) In all direct contact with a child (including evaluation of the child), the language normally used by the child in the home or

learning environment.

(b) For an individual with deafness or blindness, or for an individual with no written language, the mode of communication is that normally used by the individual (such as sign language, Braille, or oral communication).

(Authority: 20 U.S.C. 1401(20))

§ 300.30 Parent.

(a) Parent means—

(1) A biological or adoptive parent of a child;

(2) A foster parent, unless State law, regulations, or contractual obligations with a State or local entity prohibit a foster parent from acting as a parent;

(3) A guardian generally authorized to act as the child's parent, or authorized to make educational decisions for the child (but not the State if the child is a ward of the State);

(4) An individual acting in the place of a biological or adoptive parent (including a grandparent, stepparent, or other relative) with whom the child lives, or an individual who is legally responsible for the child's welfare; or

(5) A surrogate parent who has been appointed in accordance with § 300.519 or section 639(a)(5) of the Act.

(b)(1) Except as provided in paragraph (b)(2) of this section, the biological or adoptive parent, when attempting to act as the parent under this part and when more than one party is qualified under paragraph (a) of this section to act as a parent, must be presumed to be the parent for purposes of this section unless the biological or adoptive parent does not have legal authority to make educational decisions for the child.

(2) If a judicial decree or order identifies a specific person or persons under paragraphs (a)(1) through (4) of this section to act as the "parent" of a child or to make educational decisions on behalf of a child, then such person or persons shall be determined to be the "parent" for purposes of this section.

(Authority: 20 U.S.C. 1401(23))

§ 300.31 Parent training and information center.

Parent training and information center means a center assisted under sections 671 or 672 of the Act.

(Authority: 20 U.S.C. 1401(25))

§ 300.32 Personally identifiable.

Personally identifiable means information that contains—

(a) The name of the child, the child's parent, or other family member;

(b) The address of the child;

(c) A personal identifier, such as the child's social security number or student number; or

(d) A list of personal characteristics or other information that would make it possible to identify the child with reasonable certainty.

(Authority: 20 U.S.C. 1415(a))

§ 300.33 Public agency.

Public agency includes the SEA, LEAs, ESAs, nonprofit public charter schools that are not otherwise included as LEAs or ESAs and are not a school of an LEA or ESA, and any other political subdivisions of the State that are responsible for providing education to children with disabilities.

(Authority: 20 U.S.C. 1412(a)(11))

§ 300.34 Related services.

(a) General. Related services means transportation and such developmental, corrective, and other supportive services as are required to assist a child with a disability to benefit from special education, and includes speechlanguage pathology and audiology services, interpreting services, psychological services, physical and occupational therapy, recreation, including therapeutic recreation, early identification and assessment of disabilities in children, counseling services, including rehabilitation counseling, orientation and mobility services, and medical services for diagnostic or evaluation purposes. Related services also include school health services and school nurse services, social work services in schools, and parent counseling and training.

(b) Exception; services that apply to children with surgically implanted devices, including cochlear implants.

(1) Related services do not include a medical device that is surgically implanted, the optimization of that device's functioning (e.g., mapping), maintenance of that device, or the replacement of that device.

(2) Nothing in paragraph (b)(1) of this section— (i) Limits the right of a child with a surgically implanted device (e.g., cochlear implant) to receive related services (as listed in paragraph (a) of this section) that are determined by the IEP Team to be necessary for the child to receive FAPE.

(ii) Limits the responsibility of a public agency to appropriately monitor and maintain medical devices that are needed to maintain the health and safety of the child, including breathing, nutrition, or operation of other bodily functions, while the child is transported to and from school or is at school; or

(iii) Prevents the routine checking of an external component of a surgically implanted device to make sure it is functioning properly, as required in § 300.113(b).

(c) Individual related services terms defined. The terms used in this definition are defined as follows:

(1) Audiology includes—

(i) Identification of children with hearing loss;

(ii) Determination of the range, nature, and degree of hearing loss, including referral for medical or other professional attention for the habilitation of hearing;

(iii) Provision of habilitative activities, such as language habilitation, auditory training, speech reading (lipreading), hearing evaluation, and speech conservation;

(iv) Creation and administration of programs for prevention of hearing loss;

(v) Counseling and guidance of children, parents, and teachers regarding hearing loss; and

(vi) Determination of children's needs for group and individual amplification, selecting and fitting an appropriate aid, and evaluating the effectiveness of amplification.

(2) Counseling services means services provided by qualified social workers, psychologists, guidance counselors, or other qualified personnel.

(3) Early identification and assessment of disabilities in children means the implementation of a formal plan for identifying a disability as early as possible in a child's life.

(4) Interpreting services includes—

(i) The following, when used with respect to children who are deaf or hard of hearing: Oral transliteration services, cued language transliteration services, sign language transliteration and interpreting services, and transcription services, such as communication access real-time translation (CART), C-Print, and TypeWell; and

(ii) Special interpreting services for children who are deaf-blind.

(5) Medical services means services provided by a licensed physician to determine a child's medically related disability that results in the child's need for special education and related services.

(6) Occupational therapy—

(i) Means services provided by a qualified occupational therapist; and

(ii) Includes—

(A) Improving, developing, or restoring functions impaired or lost through illness, injury, or deprivation;

(B) Improving ability to perform tasks for independent functioning if functions are impaired or lost; and

(C) Preventing, through early intervention, initial or further impairment or loss of function.

(7) Orientation and mobility services—

(i) Means services provided to blind or visually impaired children by qualified personnel to enable those students to attain systematic orientation to and safe movement within their environments in school, home, and community; and

(ii) Includes teaching children the following, as appropriate:

(A) Spatial and environmental concepts and use of information received by the senses (such as sound, temperature and vibrations) to establish, maintain, or regain orientation and line of travel (e.g., using sound at a traffic light to cross the street);

(B) To use the long cane or a service animal to supplement visual travel skills or as a tool for safely negotiating the environment for children with no available travel vision;

(C) To understand and use remaining vision and distance low vision aids; and

(D) Other concepts, techniques, and tools.

(8)(i) Parent counseling and training means assisting parents in understanding the special needs of their child;

(ii) Providing parents with information about child development; and

(iii) Helping parents to acquire the necessary skills that will allow them to support the implementation of their child's IEP or IFSP.

(9) Physical therapy means services provided by a qualified physical therapist.

(10) Psychological services includes—

(i) Administering psychological and educational tests, and other assessment procedures;

(ii) Interpreting assessment results;

(iii) Obtaining, integrating, and interpreting information about child behavior and conditions relating to learning;

(iv) Consulting with other staff members in planning school programs to meet the special educational needs of children as indicated by psychological tests, interviews, direct observation, and behavioral evaluations;

(v) Planning and managing a program of psychological services, including psychological counseling for children and parents; and

(vi) Assisting in developing positive behavioral intervention strategies.

(11) Recreation includes—

(i) Assessment of leisure function;

(ii) Therapeutic recreation services;

(iii) Recreation programs in schools and community agencies; and

(iv) Leisure education.

(12) Rehabilitation counseling services means services provided by qualified personnel in individual or group sessions that focus specifically on career development, employment preparation, achieving independence, and integration in the workplace and community of a student with a disability. The term also includes vocational rehabilitation services provided to a student with a disability by vocational rehabilitation programs funded under the Rehabilitation Act of 1973, as amended, 29 U.S.C. 701 et seq.

(13) School health services and school nurse services means health services that are

designed to enable a child with a disability to receive FAPE as described in the child's IEP. School nurse services are services provided by a qualified school nurse. School health services are services that may be provided by either a qualified school nurse or other qualified person.

(14) Social work services in schools includes—

(i) Preparing a social or developmental history on a child with a disability;

(ii) Group and individual counseling with the child and family;

(iii) Working in partnership with parents and others on those problems in a child's living situation (home, school, and community) that affect the child's adjustment in school;

(iv) Mobilizing school and community resources to enable the child to learn as effectively as possible in his or her educational program; and

(v) Assisting in developing positive behavioral intervention strategies.

(15) Speech-language pathology services includes—

(i) Identification of children with speech or language impairments;

(ii) Diagnosis and appraisal of specific speech or language impairments;

(iii) Referral for medical or other professional attention necessary for the habilitation of speech or language impairments;

(iv) Provision of speech and language services for the habilitation or prevention of communicative impairments; and

(v) Counseling and guidance of parents, children, and teachers regarding speech and language impairments.

(16) Transportation includes—

(i) Travel to and from school and between schools;

(ii) Travel in and around school buildings; and

(iii) Specialized equipment (such as special or adapted buses, lifts, and ramps), if required to provide special transportation for a child with a disability.

(Authority: 20 U.S.C. 1401(26))

§ 300.35 Scientifically based research.

Scientifically based research has the meaning given the term in section 9101(37) of the ESEA.

(Authority: 20 U.S.C. 1411(e)(2)(C)(xi))

§ 300.36 Secondary school.

Secondary school means a nonprofit institutional day or residential school, including a public secondary charter school that provides secondary education, as determined under State law, except that it does not include any education beyond grade 12.

(Authority: 20 U.S.C. 1401(27))

§ 300.37 Services plan.

Services plan means a written statement that describes the special education and related services the LEA will provide to a parentally-placed child with a disability enrolled in a private school who has been designated to receive services, including the location of the services and any transportation necessary, consistent with § 300.132, and is developed and implemented in accordance with §§ 300.137 through 300.139.

(Authority: 20 U.S.C. 1412(a)(10)(A))

§ 300.38 Secretary.

Secretary means the Secretary of Education.

(Authority: 20 U.S.C. 1401(28))

§ 300.39 Special education.

(a) General. (1) Special education means specially designed instruction, at no cost to the parents, to meet the unique needs of a child with a disability, including—

(i) Instruction conducted in the classroom, in the home, in hospitals and institutions, and in other settings; and

(ii) Instruction in physical education.

(2) Special education includes each of the following, if the services otherwise meet the requirements of paragraph (a)(1) of this section—

(i) Speech-language pathology services, or any other related service, if the service is considered special education rather than a related service under State standards;

(ii) Travel training; and

(iii) Vocational education.

(b) Individual special education terms defined. The terms in this definition are defined as follows:

(1) At no cost means that all specially-designed instruction is provided without charge, but does not preclude incidental fees that are normally charged to nondisabled students or their parents as a part of the regular education program.

(2) Physical education means—

(i) The development of—

(A) Physical and motor fitness;

(B) Fundamental motor skills and patterns; and

(C) Skills in aquatics, dance, and individual and group games and sports (including intramural and lifetime sports); and

(ii) Includes special physical education, adapted physical education, movement education, and motor development.

(3) Specially designed instruction means adapting, as appropriate to the needs of an eligible child under this part, the content, methodology, or delivery of instruction—

(i) To address the unique needs of the child

that result from the child's disability; and

(ii) To ensure access of the child to the general curriculum, so that the child can meet the educational standards within the jurisdiction of the public agency that apply to all children.

(4) Travel training means providing instruction, as appropriate, to children with significant cognitive disabilities, and any other children with disabilities who require this instruction, to enable them to—

(i) Develop an awareness of the environment in which they live; and

(ii) Learn the skills necessary to move effectively and safely from place to place within that environment (e.g., in school, in the home, at work, and in the community).

(5) Vocational education means organized educational programs that are directly related to the preparation of individuals for paid or unpaid employment, or for additional preparation for a career not requiring a baccalaureate or advanced degree.

(Authority: 20 U.S.C. 1401(29))

§ 300.40 State.

State means each of the 50 States, the District of Columbia, the Commonwealth of Puerto Rico, and each of the outlying areas.

(Authority: 20 U.S.C. 1401(31))

§ 300.41 State educational agency.

State educational agency or SEA means the State board of education or other agency or officer primarily responsible for the State supervision of public elementary schools and secondary schools, or, if there is no such officer or agency, an officer or agency designated by the Governor or by State law.

(Authority: 20 U.S.C. 1401(32))

§ 300.42 Supplementary aids and services.

Supplementary aids and services means aids, services, and other supports that are provided in regular education classes, other education-related settings, and in extracurricular and nonacademic settings, to enable children with disabilities to be educated with nondisabled children to the maximum extent appropriate in accordance with §§ 300.114 through 300.116.

(Authority: 20 U.S.C. 1401(33))

§ 300.43 Transition services.

(a) Transition services means a coordinated set of activities for a child with a disability that—

(1) Is designed to be within a results-oriented process, that is focused on improving the academic and functional achievement of the child with a disability to facilitate the child's movement from school to post-school activities, including postsecondary education, vocational education, integrated employment (including supported employment), continuing and adult education, adult services, independent living, or community participation;

(2) Is based on the individual child's needs, taking into account the child's strengths, preferences, and interests; and includes—

(i) Instruction;

(ii) Related services;

(iii) Community experiences;

(iv) The development of employment and other post-school adult living objectives; and

(v) If appropriate, acquisition of daily living skills and provision of a functional vocational evaluation.

(b) Transition services for children with disabilities may be special education, if provided as specially designed instruction, or a related service, if required to assist a child with a disability to benefit from special education.

(Authority: 20 U.S.C. 1401(34))

§ 300.44 Universal design.

Universal design has the meaning given the term in section 3 of the Assistive Technology Act of 1998, as amended, 29 U.S.C. 3002.

(Authority: 20 U.S.C. 1401(35))

§ 300.45 Ward of the State.

(a) General. Subject to paragraph (b) of this section, ward of the State means a child who, as determined by the State where the child resides, is—

(1) A foster child;

(2) A ward of the State; or

(3) In the custody of a public child welfare agency.

(b) Exception. Ward of the State does not include a foster child who has a foster parent who meets the definition of a parent in § 300.30.

(Authority: 20 U.S.C. 1401(36))

Subpart B—State Eligibility

General

§ 300.100 Eligibility for assistance.

A State is eligible for assistance under Part B of the Act for a fiscal year if the State submits a plan that provides assurances to the Secretary that the State has in effect policies and procedures to ensure that the State meets the conditions in §§ 300.101 through 300.176.

(Approved by the Office of Management and Budget under control number 1820– 0030)

(Authority: 20 U.S.C. 1412(a))

FAPE Requirements

§ 300.101 Free appropriate public education (FAPE).

(a) General. A free appropriate public

education must be available to all children residing in the State between the ages of 3 and 21, inclusive, including children with disabilities who have been suspended or expelled from school, as provided for in § 300.530(d).

(b) FAPE for children beginning at age 3.

(1) Each State must ensure that—

(i) The obligation to make FAPE available to each eligible child residing in the State begins no later than the child's third birthday; and

(ii) An IEP or an IFSP is in effect for the child by that date, in accordance with § 300.323(b).

(2) If a child's third birthday occurs during the summer, the child's IEP Team shall determine the date when services under the IEP or IFSP will begin.

(c) Children advancing from grade to grade. (1) Each State must ensure that FAPE is available to any individual child with a disability who needs special education and related services, even though the child has not failed or been retained in a course or grade, and is advancing from grade to grade.

(2) The determination that a child described in paragraph (a) of this section is eligible under this part, must be made on an individual basis by the group responsible within the child's LEA for making eligibility determinations.

(Approved by the Office of Management and Budget under control number 1820–0030)

(Authority: 20 U.S.C. 1412(a)(1)(A))

§ 300.102 Limitation—exception to FAPE for certain ages.

(a) General. The obligation to make FAPE available to all children with disabilities does not apply with respect to the following:

(1) Children aged 3, 4, 5, 18, 19, 20, or 21 in a State to the extent that its application to those children would be inconsistent with State law or practice, or the order of any court, respecting the provision of public education to children of those ages.

(2)(i) Children aged 18 through 21 to the extent that State law does not require that special education and related services under Part B of the Act be provided to students with disabilities who, in the last educational placement prior to their incarceration in an adult correctional facility—

(A) Were not actually identified as being a child with a disability under § 300.8; and

(B) Did not have an IEP under Part B of the Act.

(ii) The exception in paragraph (a)(2)(i) of this section does not apply to children with disabilities, aged 18 through 21, who—

(A) Had been identified as a child with a disability under § 300.8 and had received services in accordance with an IEP, but who left school prior to their incarceration; or

(B) Did not have an IEP in their last

educational setting, but who had actually been identified as a child with a disability under § 300.8.

(3)(i) Children with disabilities who have graduated from high school with a regular high school diploma.

(ii) The exception in paragraph (a)(3)(i) of this section does not apply to children who have graduated from high school but have not been awarded a regular high school diploma.

(iii) Graduation from high school with a regular high school diploma constitutes a change in placement, requiring written prior notice in accordance with § 300.503.

(iv) As used in paragraphs (a)(3)(i) through (a)(3)(iii) of this section, the term regular high school diploma does not include an alternative degree that is not fully aligned with the State's academic standards, such as a certificate or a general educational development credential (GED).

(4) Children with disabilities who are eligible under subpart H of this part, but who receive early intervention services under Part C of the Act.

(b) Documents relating to exceptions. The State must assure that the information it has provided to the Secretary regarding the exceptions in paragraph (a) of this section, as required by § 300.700 (for purposes of making grants to States under this part), is current and accurate.

(Approved by the Office of Management and Budget under control number 1820–0030)

(Authority: 20 U.S.C. 1412(a)(1)(B)–(C))

Other FAPE Requirements

§ 300.103 FAPE—methods and payments.

(a) Each State may use whatever State, local, Federal, and private sources of support are available in the State to meet the requirements of this part. For example, if it is necessary to place a child with a disability in a residential facility, a State could use joint agreements between the agencies involved for sharing the cost of that placement.

(b) Nothing in this part relieves an insurer or similar third party from an otherwise valid obligation to provide or to pay for services provided to a child with a disability.

(c) Consistent with § 300.323(c), the State must ensure that there is no delay in implementing a child's IEP, including any case in which the payment source for providing or paying for special education and related services to the child is being determined.

(Approved by the Office of Management and Budget under control number 1820–0030)

(Authority: 20 U.S.C. 1401(8), 1412(a)(1)).

§ 300.104 Residential placement

If placement in a public or private residential program is necessary to provide special education and related services to a child with a disability, the program, including non-medical care and room and board, must be at no cost to the parents of the child.

(Approved by the Office of Management and Budget under control number 1820–0030)

(Authority: 20 U.S.C. 1412(a)(1), 1412(a)(10)(B))

§ 300.105 Assistive technology.

(a) Each public agency must ensure that assistive technology devices or assistive technology services, or both, as those terms are defined in §§ 300.5 and 300.6, respectively, are made available to a child with a disability if required as a part of the child's—

(1) Special education under § 300.36;

(2) Related services under § 300.34; or

(3) Supplementary aids and services under §§ 300.38 and 300.114(a)(2)(ii).

(b) On a case-by-case basis, the use of school-purchased assistive technology devices in a child's home or in other settings is required if the child's IEP Team determines that the child needs access to those devices in order to receive FAPE.

(Approved by the Office of Management and Budget under control number 1820–0030)

(Authority: 20 U.S.C. 1412(a)(1), 1412(a)(12)(B)(i))

§ 300.106 Extended school year services.

(a) General. (1) Each public agency must ensure that extended school year services are available as necessary to provide FAPE, consistent with paragraph (a)(2) of this section.

(2) Extended school year services must be provided only if a child's IEP Team determines, on an individual basis, in accordance with §§ 300.320 through 300.324, that the services are necessary for the provision of FAPE to the child.

(3) In implementing the requirements of this section, a public agency may not—

(i) Limit extended school year services to particular categories of disability; or

(ii) Unilaterally limit the type, amount, or duration of those services.

(b) Definition. As used in this section, the term extended school year services means special education and related services that—

(1) Are provided to a child with a disability—

(i) Beyond the normal school year of the public agency;

(ii) In accordance with the child's IEP; and

(iii) At no cost to the parents of the child; and

(2) Meet the standards of the SEA.

(Approved by the Office of Management and Budget under control number 1820–0030)

(Authority: 20 U.S.C. 1412(a)(1))

§ 300.107 Nonacademic services.

The State must ensure the following:

(a) Each public agency must take steps, including the provision of supplementary aids and services determined appropriate and necessary by the child's IEP Team, to provide nonacademic and extracurricular services and activities in the manner necessary to afford children with disabilities an equal opportunity for participation in those services and activities.

(b) Nonacademic and extracurricular services and activities may include counseling services, athletics, transportation, health services, recreational activities, special interest groups or clubs sponsored by the public agency, referrals to agencies that provide assistance to individuals with disabilities, and employment of students, including both employment by the public agency and assistance in making outside employment available.

(Approved by the Office of Management and Budget under control number 1820–0030)

(Authority: 20 U.S.C. 1412(a)(1))

§ 300.108 Physical education.

The State must ensure that public agencies in the State comply with the following:

(a) General. Physical education services, specially designed if necessary, must be made available to every child with a disability receiving FAPE, unless the public agency enrolls children without disabilities and does not provide physical education to children without disabilities in the same grades.

(b) Regular physical education. Each child with a disability must be afforded the opportunity to participate in the regular physical education program available to nondisabled children unless—

(1) The child is enrolled full time in a separate facility; or

(2) The child needs specially designed physical education, as prescribed in the child's IEP.

(c) Special physical education. If specially designed physical education is prescribed in a child's IEP, the public agency responsible for the education of that child must provide the services directly or make arrangements for those services to be provided through other public or private programs.

(d) Education in separate facilities. The public agency responsible for the education of a child with a disability who is enrolled in a separate facility must ensure that the child receives appropriate physical education services in compliance with this section.

(Approved by the Office of Management and Budget under control number 1820–0030)

(Authority: 20 U.S.C. 1412(a)(5)(A))

§ 300.109 Full educational opportunity goal (FEOG).

The State must have in effect policies and procedures to demonstrate that the State has established a goal of providing full educational opportunity to all children with disabilities, aged birth through 21, and a detailed timetable for accomplishing that goal.

(Approved by the Office of Management and Budget under control number 1820–0030)

(Authority: 20 U.S.C. 1412(a)(2))

§ 300.110 Program options.

The State must ensure that each public agency takes steps to ensure that its children with disabilities have available to them the variety of educational programs and services available to nondisabled children in the area served by the agency, including art, music, industrial arts, consumer and homemaking education, and vocational education.

(Approved by the Office of Management and Budget under control number 1820–0030)

(Authority: 20 U.S.C. 1412(a)(2), 1413(a)(1))

§ 300.111 Child find.

(a) General. (1) The State must have in effect policies and procedures to ensure that—

(i) All children with disabilities residing in the State, including children with disabilities who are homeless children or are wards of the State, and children with disabilities attending private schools, regardless of the severity of their disability, and who are in need of special education and related services, are identified, located, and evaluated; and

(ii) A practical method is developed and implemented to determine which children are currently receiving needed special education and related services.

(b) Use of term developmental delay. The following provisions apply with respect to implementing the child find requirements of this section:

(1) A State that adopts a definition of developmental delay under § 300.8(b) determines whether the term applies to children aged three through nine, or to a subset of that age range (e.g., ages three through five).

(2) A State may not require an LEA to adopt and use the term developmental delay for any children within its jurisdiction.

(3) If an LEA uses the term developmental delay for children described in § 300.8(b), the LEA must conform to both the State's definition of that term and to the age range that has been adopted by the State.

(4) If a State does not adopt the term developmental delay, an LEA may not independently use that term as a basis for

establishing a child's eligibility under this part.

(c) Other children in child find. Child find also must include—

(1) Children who are suspected of being a child with a disability under § 300.8 and in need of special education, even though they are advancing from grade to grade; and

(2) Highly mobile children, including migrant children.

(d) Construction. Nothing in the Act requires that children be classified by their disability so long as each child who has a disability that is listed in § 300.8 and who, by reason of that disability, needs special education and related services is regarded as a child with a disability under Part B of the Act.

(Approved by the Office of Management and Budget under control number 1820–0030)

(Authority: 20 U.S.C. 1401(3)); 1412(a)(3))

§ 300.112 Individualized education programs (IEP).

The State must ensure that an IEP, or an IFSP that meets the requirements of section 636(d) of the Act, is developed, reviewed, and revised for each child with a disability in accordance with §§ 300.320 through 300.324, except as provided in § 300.300(b)(3)(ii).

(Approved by the Office of Management and Budget under control number 1820–0030)

(Authority: 20 U.S.C. 1412(a)(4))

§ 300.113 Routine checking of hearing aids and external components of surgically implanted medical devices.

(a) Hearing aids. Each public agency must ensure that hearing aids worn in school by children with hearing impairments, including deafness, are functioning properly.

(b) External components of surgically implanted medical devices. (1) Subject to paragraph (b)(2) of this section, each public agency must ensure that the external components of surgically implanted medical devices are functioning properly.

(2) For a child with a surgically implanted medical device who is receiving special education and related services under this part, a public agency is not responsible for the post-surgical maintenance, programming, or replacement of the medical device that has been surgically implanted (or of an external component of the surgically implanted medical device).

(Approved by the Office of Management and Budget under control number 1820–0030)

(Authority: 20 U.S.C. 1401(1), 1401(26)(B))

Least Restrictive Environment (LRE)

§ 300.114 LRE requirements.

(a) General. (1) Except as provided in § 300.324(d)(2) (regarding children with disabilities in adult prisons), the State must have in effect policies and procedures to ensure that public agencies in the State meet the LRE requirements of this section and §§ 300.115 through 300.120.

(2) Each public agency must ensure that—

(i) To the maximum extent appropriate, children with disabilities, including children in public or private institutions or other care facilities, are educated with children who are nondisabled; and

(ii) Special classes, separate schooling, or other removal of children with disabilities from the regular educational environment occurs only if the nature or severity of the disability is such that education in regular classes with the use of supplementary aids and services cannot be achieved satisfactorily.

(b) Additional requirement—State funding mechanism—(1) General. (i) A State funding mechanism must not result in placements that violate the requirements of paragraph (a) of this section; and

(ii) A State must not use a funding mechanism by which the State distributes funds on the basis of the type of setting in which a child is served that will result in the failure to provide a child with a disability FAPE according to the unique needs of the child, as described in the child's IEP.

(2) Assurance. If the State does not have policies and procedures to ensure compliance with paragraph (b)(1) of this section, the State must provide the Secretary an assurance that the State will revise the funding mechanism as soon as feasible to ensure that the mechanism does not result in placements that violate that paragraph.

(Approved by the Office of Management and Budget under control number 1820–0030)

(Authority: 20 U.S.C. 1412(a)(5))

§ 300.115 Continuum of alternative placements.

(a) Each public agency must ensure that a continuum of alternative placements is available to meet the needs of children with disabilities for special education and related services.

(b) The continuum required in paragraph (a) of this section must—

(1) Include the alternative placements listed in the definition of special education under § 300.38 (instruction in regular classes, special classes, special schools, home instruction, and instruction in hospitals and institutions); and

(2) Make provision for supplementary services (such as resource room or itinerant instruction) to be provided in conjunction with regular class placement.

(Approved by the Office of Management and Budget under control number 1820–0030)

(Authority: 20 U.S.C. 1412(a)(5))

§ 300.116 Placements.

In determining the educational placement of a child with a disability, including a preschool child with a disability, each public agency must ensure that—

(a) The placement decision—

(1) Is made by a group of persons, including the parents, and other persons knowledgeable about the child, the meaning of the evaluation data, and the placement options; and

(2) Is made in conformity with the LRE provisions of this subpart, including §§ 300.114 through 300.118;

(b) The child's placement—

(1) Is determined at least annually;

(2) Is based on the child's IEP; and

(3) Is as close as possible to the child's home;

(c) Unless the IEP of a child with a disability requires some other arrangement, the child is educated in the school that he or she would attend if nondisabled;

(d) In selecting the LRE, consideration is given to any potential harmful effect on the child or on the quality of services that he or she needs; and

(e) A child with a disability is not removed from education in ageappropriate regular classrooms solely because of needed modifications in the general education curriculum.

(Approved by the Office of Management and Budget under control number 1820–0030)

(Authority: 20 U.S.C. 1412(a)(5))

§ 300.117 Nonacademic settings.

In providing or arranging for the provision of nonacademic and extracurricular services and activities, including meals, recess periods, and the services and activities set forth in § 300.107, each public agency must ensure that each child with a disability participates with nondisabled children in the extracurricular services and activities to the maximum extent appropriate to the needs of that child.

The public agency must ensure that each child with a disability has the supplementary aids and services determined by the child's IEP Team to be appropriate and necessary for the child to participate in nonacademic settings.

(Approved by the Office of Management and Budget under control number 1820–0030)

(Authority: 20 U.S.C. 1412(a)(5))

§ 300.118 Children in public or private institutions.

Except as provided in § 300.149(d) (regarding agency responsibility for general supervision for some individuals in adult prisons), an SEA must ensure that § 300.114 is effectively implemented, including, if necessary, making arrangements with public and private institutions (such as a memorandum of agreement or special implementation procedures).

(Approved by the Office of Management and Budget under control number 1820–0030)

(Authority: 20 U.S.C. 1412(a)(5))

§ 300.119 Technical assistance and training activities.

Each SEA must carry out activities to ensure that teachers and administrators in all public agencies—

(a) Are fully informed about their responsibilities for implementing § 300.114; and

(b) Are provided with technical assistance and training necessary to assist them in this effort.

(Approved by the Office of Management and Budget under control number 1820–0030)

(Authority: 20 U.S.C. 1412(a)(5))

§ 300.120 Monitoring activities.

(a) The SEA must carry out activities to ensure that § 300.114 is implemented by each public agency.

(b) If there is evidence that a public agency makes placements that are inconsistent with § 300.114, the SEA must—

(1) Review the public agency's justification for its actions; and

(2) Assist in planning and implementing any necessary corrective action.

(Approved by the Office of Management and Budget under control number 1820–0030)

(Authority: 20 U.S.C. 1412(a)(5))

Additional Eligibility Requirements

§ 300.121 Procedural safeguards.

(a) General. The State must have procedural safeguards in effect to ensure that each public agency in the State meets the requirements of §§ 300.500 through 300.536.

(b) Procedural safeguards identified. Children with disabilities and their parents must be afforded the procedural safeguards identified in paragraph (a) of this section.

(Approved by the Office of Management and Budget under control number 1820–0030)

(Authority: 20 U.S.C. 1412(a)(6)(A))

§ 300.122 Evaluation.

Children with disabilities must be evaluated in accordance with §§ 300.300 through 300.311 of subpart D of this part.

(Approved by the Office of Management and Budget under control number 1820–0030)

(Authority: 20 U.S.C. 1412(a)(7))

§ 300.123 Confidentiality of personally identifiable information.

The State must have policies and procedures in effect to ensure that public agencies in the State comply with §§ 300.610 through 300.626 related to protecting the confidentiality of any personally identifiable information collected, used, or maintained under Part B of the Act.

(Approved by the Office of Management and Budget under control number 1820–0030)

(Authority: 20 U.S.C. 1412(a)(8); 1417(c))

§ 300.124 Transition of children from the Part C program to preschool programs.

The State must have in effect policies and procedures to ensure that—

(a) Children participating in early intervention programs assisted under Part C of the Act, and who will participate in preschool programs assisted under Part B of the Act, experience a smooth and effective transition to those preschool programs in a manner consistent with section 637(a)(9) of the Act;

(b) By the third birthday of a child described in paragraph (a) of this section, an IEP or, if consistent with § 300.323(b) and section 636(d) of the Act, an IFSP, has been developed and is being implemented for the child consistent with § 300.101(b); and

(c) Each affected LEA will participate in transition planning conferences arranged by the designated lead agency under section 635(a)(10) of the Act.

(Approved by the Office of Management and Budget under control number 1820–0030)

(Authority: 20 U.S.C. 1412(a)(9))

§§ 300.125–300.128 [Reserved]

Children in Private Schools

§ 300.129 State responsibility regarding children in private schools.

The State must have in effect policies and procedures that ensure that LEAs, and, if applicable, the SEA, meet the private school requirements in §§ 300.130 through 300.148.

(Approved by the Office of Management and Budget under control number 1820–0030)

(Authority: 20 U.S.C. 1412(a)(10))

Children With Disabilities Enrolled by Their Parents in Private Schools

§ 300.130 Definition of parentally-placed private school children with disabilities.

Parentally-placed private school children with disabilities means children with disabilities enrolled by their parents in private, including religious, schools or facilities that meet the definition of elementary school in § 300.13 or secondary school in § 300.36, other than children with disabilities covered under §§ 300.145

through 300.147.

(Approved by the Office of Management and Budget under control number 1820–0030)

(Authority: 20 U.S.C. 1412(a)(10)(A))

§ 300.131 Child find for parentally-placed private school children with disabilities.

(a) General. Each LEA must locate, identify, and evaluate all children with disabilities who are enrolled by their parents in private, including religious, elementary schools and secondary schools located in the school district served by the LEA, in accordance with paragraphs (b) through (e) of this section, and §§ 300.111 and 300.201.

(b) Child find design. The child find process must be designed to ensure—

(1) The equitable participation of parentally-placed private school children; and

(2) An accurate count of those children.

(c) Activities. In carrying out the requirements of this section, the LEA, or, if applicable, the SEA, must undertake activities similar to the activities undertaken for the agency's public school children.

(d) Cost. The cost of carrying out the child find requirements in this section, including individual evaluations, may not be considered in determining if an LEA has met its obligation under § 300.133.

(e) Completion period. The child find process must be completed in a time period comparable to that for students attending public schools in the LEA consistent with § 300.301.

(f) Out-of-State children. Each LEA in which private, including religious, elementary schools and secondary schools are located must, in carrying out the child find requirements in this section, include parentally-placed private school children who reside in a State other than the State in which the private schools that they attend are located.

(Approved by the Office of Management and Budget under control number 1820–0030)

(Authority: 20 U.S.C. 1412(a)(10)(A)(ii))

§ 300.132 Provision of services for parentally-placed private school children with disabilities—basic requirement.

(a) General. To the extent consistent with the number and location of children with disabilities who are enrolled by their parents in private, including religious, elementary schools and secondary schools located in the school district served by the LEA, provision is made for the participation of those children in the program assisted or carried out under Part B of the Act by providing them with special education and related services, including direct services determined in accordance with § 300.137, unless the Secretary has arranged for services to those children under the by-pass provisions in §§ 300.190 through 300.198.

(b) Services plan for parentally-placed private school children with disabilities. In accordance with paragraph (a) of this section and §§ 300.137 through 300.139, a services plan must be developed and implemented for each private school child with a disability who has been designated by the LEA in which the private school is located to receive special education and related services under this part.

(c) Record keeping. Each LEA must maintain in its records, and provide to the SEA, the following information related to parentally-placed private school children covered under §§ 300.130 through 300.144:

(1) The number of children evaluated;

(2) The number of children determined to be children with disabilities; and

(3) The number of children served.

(Approved by the Office of Management and Budget under control numbers 1820–0030 and 1820–0600)

(Authority: 20 U.S.C. 1412(a)(10)(A)(i))

§ 300.133 Expenditures.

(a) Formula. To meet the requirement of § 300.132(a), each LEA must spend the following on providing special education and related services (including direct services) to parentally-placed private school children with disabilities:

(1) For children aged 3 through 21, an amount that is the same proportion of the LEA's total subgrant under section 611(f) of the Act as the number of private school children with disabilities aged 3 through 21 who are enrolled by their parents in private, including religious, elementary schools and secondary schools located in the school district served by the LEA, is to the total number of children with disabilities in its jurisdiction aged 3 through 21.

(2)(i) For children aged three through five, an amount that is the same proportion of the LEA's total subgrant under section 619(g) of the Act as the number of parentally-placed private school children with disabilities aged three through five who are enrolled by their parents in a private, including religious, elementary school located in the school district served by the LEA, is to the total number of children with disabilities in its jurisdiction aged three through five.

(ii) As described in paragraph (a)(2)(i) of this section, children aged three through five are considered to be parentally-placed private school children with disabilities enrolled by their parents in private, including religious, elementary schools, if they are enrolled in a private school that meets the definition of elementary school in § 300.13.

(3) If an LEA has not expended for equitable services all of the funds described in paragraphs (a)(1) and (a)(2) of this section by the end of the fiscal year for which Congress appropriated the funds, the LEA must obligate the remaining funds for special education and

related services (including direct services) to parentally-placed private school children with disabilities during a carry-over period of one additional year.

(b) Calculating proportionate amount. In calculating the proportionate amount of Federal funds to be provided for parentally-placed private school children with disabilities, the LEA, after timely and meaningful consultation with representatives of private schools under § 300.134, must conduct a thorough and complete child find process to determine the number of parentally-placed children with disabilities attending private schools located in the LEA. (See Appendix B for an example of how proportionate share is calculated).

(c) Annual count of the number of parentally-placed private school children with disabilities. (1) Each LEA must—

(i) After timely and meaningful consultation with representatives of parentally-placed private school children with disabilities (consistent with § 300.134), determine the number of parentally-placed private school children with disabilities attending private schools located in the LEA; and

(ii) Ensure that the count is conducted on any date between October 1 and December 1, inclusive, of each year.

(2) The count must be used to determine the amount that the LEA must spend on providing special education and related services to parentally-placed private school children with disabilities in the next subsequent fiscal year.

(d) Supplement, not supplant. State and local funds may supplement and in no case supplant the proportionate amount of Federal funds required to be expended for parentally-placed private school children with disabilities under this part.

(Approved by the Office of Management and Budget under control number 1820–0030)

(Authority: 20 U.S.C. 1412(a)(10)(A))

§ 300.134 Consultation.

To ensure timely and meaningful consultation, an LEA, or, if appropriate, an SEA, must consult with private school representatives and representatives of parents of parentally-placed private school children with disabilities during the design and development of special education and related services for the children regarding the following:

(a) Child find. The child find process, including—

(1) How parentally-placed private school children suspected of having a disability can participate equitably; and

(2) How parents, teachers, and private school officials will be informed of the process.

(b) Proportionate share of funds. The determination of the proportionate share of Federal funds available to serve parentally-placed private school children with disabilities under § 300.133(b), including the determination of how the proportionate share of those funds was calculated.

(c) Consultation process. The consultation process among the LEA, private school officials, and representatives of parents of parentally-placed private school children with disabilities, including how the process will operate throughout the school year to ensure that parentally-placed children with disabilities identified through the child find process can meaningfully participate in special education and related services.

(d) Provision of special education and related services. How, where, and by whom special education and related services will be provided for parentally-placed private school children with disabilities, including a discussion of—

(1) The types of services, including direct services and alternate service delivery mechanisms; and

(2) How special education and related services will be apportioned if funds are insufficient to serve all parentally-placed private school children; and

(3) How and when those decisions will be made;

(e) Written explanation by LEA regarding services. How, if the LEA disagrees with the views of the private school officials on the provision of services or the types of services (whether provided directly or through a contract), the LEA will provide to the private school officials a written explanation of the reasons why the LEA chose not to provide services directly or through a contract.

(Approved by the Office of Management and Budget under control numbers 1820–0030 and 1820–0600)

(Authority: 20 U.S.C. 1412(a)(10)(A)(iii))

§ 300.135 Written affirmation.

(a) When timely and meaningful consultation, as required by § 300.134, has occurred, the LEA must obtain a written affirmation signed by the representatives of participating private schools.

(b) If the representatives do not provide the affirmation within a reasonable period of time, the LEA must forward the documentation of the consultation process to the SEA.

(Approved by the Office of Management and Budget under control numbers 1820–0030 and 1820–0600)

(Authority: 20 U.S.C. 1412(a)(10)(A)(iv))

§ 300.136 Compliance.

(a) General. A private school official has the right to submit a complaint to the SEA that the LEA—

(1) Did not engage in consultation that was

meaningful and timely; or

(2) Did not give due consideration to the views of the private school official.

(b) Procedure. (1) If the private school official wishes to submit a complaint, the official must provide to the SEA the basis of the noncompliance by the LEA with the applicable private school provisions in this part; and

(2) The LEA must forward the appropriate documentation to the SEA.

(3)(i) If the private school official is dissatisfied with the decision of the SEA, the official may submit a complaint to the Secretary by providing the information on noncompliance described in paragraph (b)(1) of this section; and

(ii) The SEA must forward the appropriate documentation to the Secretary.

(Approved by the Office of Management and Budget under control numbers 1820–0030 and 1820–0600)

(Authority: 20 U.S.C. 1412(a)(10)(A)(v))

§ 300.137 Equitable services determined.

(a) No individual right to special education and related services. No parentally-placed private school child with a disability has an individual right to receive some or all of the special education and related services that the child would receive if enrolled in a public school.

(b) Decisions. (1) Decisions about the services that will be provided to parentally-placed private school children with disabilities under §§ 300.130 through 300.144 must be made in accordance with paragraph (c) of this section and § 300.134(c). (2) The LEA must make the final decisions with respect to the services to be provided to eligible parentally-placed private school children with disabilities.

(c) Services plan for each child served under §§ 300.130 through 300.144. If a child with a disability is enrolled in a religious or other private school by the child's parents and will receive special education or related services from an LEA, the LEA must—

(1) Initiate and conduct meetings to develop, review, and revise a services plan for the child, in accordance with § 300.138(b); and

(2) Ensure that a representative of the religious or other private school attends each meeting. If the representative cannot attend, the LEA shall use other methods to ensure participation by the religious or other private school, including individual or conference telephone calls.

(Approved by the Office of Management and Budget under control number 1820–0030)

(Authority: 20 U.S.C. 1412(a)(10)(A))

§ 300.138 Equitable services provided.

(a) General. (1) The services provided to parentally-placed private school children with disabilities must be provided by personnel meeting the same standards as personnel providing services in the public schools, except that private elementary school and secondary school teachers who are providing equitable services to parentally-placed private school children with disabilities do not have to meet the highly qualified special education teacher requirements of § 300.18.

(2) Parentally-placed private school children with disabilities may receive a different amount of services than children with disabilities in public schools.

(b) Services provided in accordance with a services plan. (1) Each parentally-placed private school child with a disability who has been designated to receive services under § 300.132 must have a services plan that describes the specific special education and related services that the LEA will provide to the child in light of the services that the LEA has determined, through the process described in §§ 300.134 and 300.137, it will make available to parentally-placed private school children with disabilities.

(2) The services plan must, to the extent appropriate—

(i) Meet the requirements of § 300.320, or for a child ages three through five, meet the requirements of § 300.323(b) with respect to the services provided; and

(ii) Be developed, reviewed, and revised consistent with §§ 300.321 through 300.324.

(c) Provision of equitable services. (1) The provision of services pursuant to this section and §§ 300.139 through 300.143 must be provided:

(i) By employees of a public agency; or

(ii) Through contract by the public agency with an individual, association, agency, organization, or other entity.

(2) Special education and related services provided to parentally-placed private school children with disabilities, including materials and equipment, must be secular, neutral, and nonideological.

(Approved by the Office of Management and Budget under control number 1820–0030)

(Authority: 20 U.S.C. 1412(a)(10)(A)(vi))

§ 300.139 Location of services and transportation.

(a) Services on private school premises. Services to parentally-placed private school children with disabilities may be provided on the premises of private, including religious, schools, to the extent consistent with law.

(b) Transportation—(1) General. (i) If necessary for the child to benefit from or participate in the services provided under this part, a parentally-placed private school child with a disability must be provided transportation—

(A) From the child's school or the child's home to a site other than the private school; and

(B) From the service site to the private school, or to the child's home, depending on the timing of the services.

(ii) LEAs are not required to provide transportation from the child's home to the private school.

(2) Cost of transportation. The cost of the transportation described in paragraph (b)(1)(i) of this section may be included in calculating whether the LEA has met the requirement of § 300.133.

(Approved by the Office of Management and Budget under control number 1820–0030)

(Authority: 20 U.S.C. 1412(a)(10)(A))

§ 300.140 Due process complaints and State complaints.

(a) Due process not applicable, except for child find. (1) Except as provided in paragraph (b) of this section, the procedures in §§ 300.504 through 300.519 do not apply to complaints that an LEA has failed to meet the requirements of §§ 300.132 through 300.139, including the provision of services indicated on the child's services plan.

(b) Child find complaints—to be filed with the LEA in which the private school is located. (1) The procedures in §§ 300.504 through 300.519 apply to complaints that an LEA has failed to meet the child find requirements in § 300.131, including the requirements in §§ 300.300 through 300.311.

(2) Any due process complaint regarding the child find requirements (as described in paragraph (b)(1) of this section) must be filed with the LEA in which the private school is located and a copy must be forwarded to the SEA.

(c) State complaints. (1) Any complaint that an SEA or LEA has failed to meet the requirements in §§ 300.132 through 300.135 and 300.137 through 300.144 must be filed in accordance with the procedures described in §§ 300.151 through 300.153.

(2) A complaint filed by a private school official under § 300.136(a) must be filed with the SEA in accordance with the procedures in § 300.136(b).

(Approved by the Office of Management and Budget under control number 1820–0030)

(Authority: 20 U.S.C. 1412(a)(10)(A))

§ 300.141 Requirement that funds not benefit a private school.

(a) An LEA may not use funds provided under section 611 or 619 of the Act to finance the existing level of instruction in a private school or to otherwise benefit the private school.

(b) The LEA must use funds provided under Part B of the Act to meet the special education and related services needs of parentally-placed private school children with disabilities, but not for meeting—

(1) The needs of a private school; or

(2) The general needs of the students enrolled in the private school.

(Approved by the Office of Management

and Budget under control number 1820–0030)

(Authority: 20 U.S.C. 1412(a)(10)(A))

§ 300.142 Use of personnel.

(a) Use of public school personnel. An LEA may use funds available under sections 611 and 619 of the Act to make public school personnel available in other than public facilities—

(1) To the extent necessary to provide services under §§ 300.130 through 300.144 for parentally-placed private school children with disabilities; and

(2) If those services are not normally provided by the private school.

(b) Use of private school personnel. An LEA may use funds available under sections 611 and 619 of the Act to pay for the services of an employee of a private school to provide services under §§ 300.130 through 300.144 if—

(1) The employee performs the services outside of his or her regular hours of duty; and (2) The employee performs the services under public supervision and control.

(Approved by the Office of Management and Budget under control number 1820–0030)

(Authority: 20 U.S.C. 1412(a)(10)(A))

§ 300.143 Separate classes prohibited.

An LEA may not use funds available under section 611 or 619 of the Act for classes that are organized separately on the basis of school enrollment or religion of the children if—'

(a) The classes are at the same site; and

(b) The classes include children enrolled in public schools and children enrolled in private schools.

(Approved by the Office of Management and Budget under control number 1820–0030)

(Authority: 20 U.S.C. 1412(a)(10)(A))

§ 300.144 Property, equipment, and supplies.

(a) A public agency must control and administer the funds used to provide special education and related services under §§ 300.137 through 300.139, and hold title to and administer materials, equipment, and property purchased with those funds for the uses and purposes provided in the Act.

(b) The public agency may place equipment and supplies in a private school for the period of time needed for the Part B program.

(c) The public agency must ensure that the equipment and supplies placed in a private school—

(1) Are used only for Part B purposes; and

(2) Can be removed from the private school without remodeling the private school facility.

(d) The public agency must remove equipment and supplies from a private school if—

(1) The equipment and supplies are no longer needed for Part B purposes; or

(2) Removal is necessary to avoid

unauthorized use of the equipment and supplies for other than Part B purposes.

(e) No funds under Part B of the Act may be used for repairs, minor remodeling, or construction of private school facilities.

(Approved by the Office of Management and Budget under control number 1820–0030)

(Authority: 20 U.S.C. 1412(a)(10)(A)(vii))

Children With Disabilities in Private Schools Placed or Referred by Public Agencies

§ 300.145 Applicability of §§ 300.146 through 300.147.

Sections 300.146 through 300.147 apply only to children with disabilities who are or have been placed in or referred to a private school or facility by a public agency as a means of providing special education and related services.

(Approved by the Office of Management and Budget under control number 1820–0030)

(Authority: 20 U.S.C. 1412(a)(10)(B))

§ 300.146 Responsibility of SEA.

Each SEA must ensure that a child with a disability who is placed in or referred to a private school or facility by a public agency—

(a) Is provided special education and related services—

(1) In conformance with an IEP that meets the requirements of §§ 300.320 through 300.325; and

(2) At no cost to the parents;

(b) Is provided an education that meets the standards that apply to education provided by the SEA and LEAs including the requirements of this part, except for § 300.18 and § 300.156(c); and

(c) Has all of the rights of a child with a disability who is served by a public agency.

(Approved by the Office of Management and Budget under control number 1820–0030)

(Authority: 20 U.S.C. 1412(a)(10)(B))

§ 300.147 Implementation by SEA.

In implementing § 300.146, the SEA must—

(a) Monitor compliance through procedures such as written reports, onsite visits, and parent questionnaires;

(b) Disseminate copies of applicable standards to each private school and facility to which a public agency has referred or placed a child with a disability; and

(c) Provide an opportunity for those private schools and facilities to participate in the development and revision of State standards that apply to them.

(Approved by the Office of Management and Budget under control number 1820–0030)

(Authority: 20 U.S.C. 1412(a)(10)(B))

Children With Disabilities Enrolled by Their Parents in Private Schools When FAPE Is at Issue

§ 300.148 Placement of children by parents when FAPE is at issue.

(a) General.

This part does not require an LEA to pay for the cost of education, including special education and related services, of a child with a disability at a private school or facility if that agency made FAPE available to the child and the parents elected to place the child in a private school or facility. However, the public agency must include that child in the population whose needs are addressed consistent with §§ 300.131 through 300.144.

(b) Disagreements about FAPE. Disagreements between the parents and a public agency regarding the availability of a program appropriate for the child, and the question of financial reimbursement, are subject to the due process procedures in §§ 300.504 through 300.520.

(c) Reimbursement for private school placement. If the parents of a child with a disability, who previously received special education and related services under the authority of a public agency, enroll the child in a private preschool, elementary school, or secondary school without the consent of or referral by the public agency, a court or a hearing officer may require the agency to reimburse the parents for the cost of that enrollment if the court or hearing officer finds that the agency had not made FAPE available to the child in a timely manner prior to that enrollment and that the private placement is appropriate. A parental placement may be found to be appropriate by a hearing officer or a court even if it does not meet the State standards that apply to education provided by the SEA and LEAs.

(d) Limitation on reimbursement. The cost of reimbursement described in paragraph (c) of this section may be reduced or denied—

(1) If—

(i) At the most recent IEP Team meeting that the parents attended prior to removal of the child from the public school, the parents did not inform the IEP Team that they were rejecting the placement proposed by the public agency to provide FAPE to their child, including stating their concerns and their intent to enroll their child in a private school at public expense; or

(ii) At least ten (10) business days (including any holidays that occur on a business day) prior to the removal of the child from the public school, the parents did not give written notice to the public agency of the information described in paragraph (d)(1)(i) of this section;

(2) If, prior to the parents' removal of the child from the public school, the public agency informed the parents, through the notice requirements described in § 300.503(a)(1), of its intent to evaluate the child (including a statement of the purpose of the evaluation that was

appropriate and reasonable), but the parents did not make the child available for the evaluation; or

(3) Upon a judicial finding of unreasonableness with respect to actions taken by the parents.

(e) Exception. Notwithstanding the notice requirement in paragraph (d)(1) of this section, the cost of reimbursement—

(1) Must not be reduced or denied for failure to provide the notice if—

(i) The school prevented the parents from providing the notice;

(ii) The parents had not received notice, pursuant to § 300.504, of the notice requirement in paragraph (d)(1) of this section; or

(iii) Compliance with paragraph (d)(1) of this section would likely result in physical harm to the child; and

(2) May, in the discretion of the court or a hearing officer, not be reduced or denied for failure to provide this notice if—

(i) The parents are not literate or cannot write in English; or

(ii) Compliance with paragraph (d)(1) of this section would likely result in serious emotional harm to the child.

(Approved by the Office of Management and Budget under control number 1820–0030)

(Authority: 20 U.S.C. 1412(a)(10)(C))

SEA Responsibility for General Supervision and Implementation of Procedural Safeguards

§ 300.149 SEA responsibility for general supervision.

(a) The SEA is responsible for ensuring—

(1) That the requirements of this part are carried out; and

(2) That each educational program for children with disabilities administered within the State, including each program administered by any other State or local agency (but not including elementary schools and secondary schools for Indian children operated or funded by the Secretary of the Interior)—

(i) Is under the general supervision of the persons responsible for educational programs for children with disabilities in the SEA; and

(ii) Meets the educational standards of the SEA (including the requirements of this part).

(3) In carrying out this part with respect to homeless children, the requirements of subtitle B of title VII of the McKinney-Vento Homeless Assistance Act (42 U.S.C. 11431 et seq.) are met.

(b) The State must have in effect policies and procedures to ensure that it complies with the monitoring and enforcement requirements in §§ 300.600 through 300.602 and §§ 300.606 through 300.608.

(c) Part B of the Act does not limit the responsibility of agencies other than educational agencies for providing or paying some or all of the costs of FAPE to children with disabilities in the State.

(d) Notwithstanding paragraph (a) of this section, the Governor (or another individual pursuant to State law) may assign to any public agency in the State the responsibility of ensuring that the requirements of Part B of the Act are met with respect to students with disabilities who are convicted as adults under State law and incarcerated in adult prisons.

(Approved by the Office of Management and Budget under control number 1820–0030)

(Authority: 20 U.S.C. 1412(a)(11); 1416)

§ 300.150 SEA implementation of procedural safeguards.

The SEA (and any agency assigned responsibility pursuant to § 300.149(d)) must have in effect procedures to inform each public agency of its responsibility for ensuring effective implementation of procedural safeguards for the children with disabilities served by that public agency.

(Approved by the Office of Management and Budget under control number 1820–0030)

(Authority: 20 U.S.C. 1412(a)(11); 1415(a))

State Complaint Procedures

§ 300.151 Adoption of State complaint procedures.

(a) General. Each SEA must adopt written procedures for—

(1) Resolving any complaint, including a complaint filed by an organization or individual from another State, that meets the requirements of § 300.153 by—

(i) Providing for the filing of a complaint with the SEA; and

(ii) At the SEA's discretion, providing for the filing of a complaint with a public agency and the right to have the SEA review the public agency's decision on the complaint; and

(2) Widely disseminating to parents and other interested individuals, including parent training and information centers, protection and advocacy agencies, independent living centers, and other appropriate entities, the State procedures under §§ 300.151 through 300.153.

(b) Remedies for denial of appropriate services. In resolving a complaint in which the SEA has found a failure to provide appropriate services, an SEA, pursuant to its general supervisory authority under Part B of the Act, must address—

(1) The failure to provide appropriate services, including corrective action appropriate to address the needs of the child (such as compensatory services or monetary reimbursement); and

(2) Appropriate future provision of services for all children with disabilities.

(Approved by the Office of Management

and Budget under control numbers 1820–0030 and 1820–0600)
(Authority: 20 U.S.C. 1221e–3)

§ 300.152 Minimum State complaint procedures.

(a) Time limit; minimum procedures. Each SEA must include in its complaint procedures a time limit of 60 days after a complaint is filed under § 300.153 to—

(1) Carry out an independent on-site investigation, if the SEA determines that an investigation is necessary;

(2) Give the complainant the opportunity to submit additional information, either orally or in writing, about the allegations in the complaint;

(3) Provide the public agency with the opportunity to respond to the complaint, including, at a minimum—

(i) At the discretion of the public agency, a proposal to resolve the complaint; and

(ii) An opportunity for a parent who has filed a complaint and the public agency to voluntarily engage in mediation consistent with § 300.506;

(4) Review all relevant information and make an independent determination as to whether the public agency is violating a requirement of Part B of the Act or of this part; and

(5) Issue a written decision to the complainant that addresses each allegation in the complaint and contains—

(i) Findings of fact and conclusions; and

(ii) The reasons for the SEA's final decision.

(b) Time extension; final decision; implementation. The SEA's procedures described in paragraph (a) of this section also must—(1) Permit an extension of the time limit under paragraph (a) of this section only if—

(i) Exceptional circumstances exist with respect to a particular complaint; or

(ii) The parent (or individual or organization, if mediation or other alternative means of dispute resolution is available to the individual or organization under State procedures) and the public agency involved agree to extend the time to engage in mediation pursuant to paragraph (a)(3)(ii) of this section, or to engage in other alternative means of dispute resolution, if available in the State; and

(2) Include procedures for effective implementation of the SEA's final decision, if needed, including—

(i) Technical assistance activities;

(ii) Negotiations; and

(iii) Corrective actions to achieve compliance.

(c) Complaints filed under this section and due process hearings under § 300.507 and §§ 300.530 through 300.532. (1) If a written complaint is received that is also the subject of a due process hearing under § 300.507 or §§ 300.530 through 300.532, or contains multiple issues of which one or more are part of that hearing, the State must set aside any part of the complaint that is being addressed in the due process hearing until the conclusion of the hearing. However, any issue in the complaint that is not a part of the due process action must be resolved using the time limit and procedures described in paragraphs (a) and (b) of this section.

(2) If an issue raised in a complaint filed under this section has previously been decided in a due process hearing involving the same parties—

(i) The due process hearing decision is binding on that issue; and

(ii) The SEA must inform the complainant to that effect.

(3) A complaint alleging a public agency's failure to implement a due process hearing decision must be resolved by the SEA. Approved by the Office of Management and Budget under control numbers 1820–0030 and 1820–0600)
(Authority: 20 U.S.C. 1221e–3)

§ 300.153 Filing a complaint.

(a) An organization or individual may file a signed written complaint under the procedures described in §§ 300.151 through 300.152.

(b) The complaint must include—

(1) A statement that a public agency has violated a requirement of Part B of the Act or of this part;

(2) The facts on which the statement is based;

(3) The signature and contact information for the complainant; and

(4) If alleging violations with respect to a specific child—

(i) The name and address of the residence of the child;

(ii) The name of the school the child is attending;

(iii) In the case of a homeless child or youth (within the meaning of section 725(2) of the McKinney-Vento Homeless Assistance Act (42 U.S.C. 11434a(2)), available contact information for the child, and the name of the school the child is attending;

(iv) A description of the nature of the problem of the child, including facts relating to the problem; and

(v) A proposed resolution of the problem to the extent known and available to the party at the time the complaint is filed.

(c) The complaint must allege a violation that occurred not more than one year prior to the date that the complaint is received in accordance with § 300.151.

(d) The party filing the complaint must forward a copy of the complaint to the LEA or public agency serving the child at the same time the party files the complaint with the SEA.

(Approved by the Office of Management and Budget under control numbers 1820–0030 and 1820–0600)

(Authority: 20 U.S.C. 1221e–3)

Methods of Ensuring Services

§ 300.154 Methods of ensuring services.

(a) Establishing responsibility for services. The Chief Executive Officer of a State or designee of that officer must ensure that an interagency agreement or other mechanism for interagency coordination is in effect between each noneducational public agency described in paragraph (b) of this section and the SEA, in order to ensure that all services described in paragraph (b)(1) of this section that are needed to ensure FAPE are provided, including the provision of these services during the pendency of any dispute under paragraph (a)(3) of this section. The agreement or mechanism must include the following:

(1) An identification of, or a method for defining, the financial responsibility of each agency for providing services described in paragraph (b)(1) of this section to ensure FAPE to children with disabilities. The financial responsibility of each noneducational public agency described in paragraph (b) of this section, including the State Medicaid agency and other public insurers of children with disabilities, must precede the financial responsibility of the LEA (or the State agency responsible for developing the child's IEP).

(2) The conditions, terms, and procedures under which an LEA must be reimbursed by other agencies.

(3) Procedures for resolving interagency disputes (including procedures under which LEAs may initiate proceedings) under the agreement or other mechanism to secure reimbursement from other agencies or otherwise implement the provisions of the agreement or mechanism.

(4) Policies and procedures for agencies to determine and identify the interagency coordination responsibilities of each agency to promote the coordination and timely and appropriate delivery of services described in paragraph (b)(1) of this section.

(b) Obligation of noneducational public agencies. (1)(i) If any public agency other than an educational agency is otherwise obligated under Federal or State law, or assigned responsibility under State policy or pursuant to paragraph (a) of this section, to provide or pay for any services that are also considered special education or related services (such as, but not limited to, services described in § 300.5 relating to assistive technology devices, § 300.6 relating to assistive technology services, § 300.34 relating to related

services, § 300.41 relating to supplementary aids and services, and § 300.42 relating to transition services) that are necessary for ensuring FAPE to children with disabilities within the State, the public agency must fulfill that obligation or responsibility, either directly or through contract or other arrangement pursuant to paragraph (a) of this section or an agreement pursuant to paragraph (c) of this section.

(ii) A noneducational public agency described in paragraph (b)(1)(i) of this section may not disqualify an eligible service for Medicaid reimbursement because that service is provided in a school context.

(2) If a public agency other than an educational agency fails to provide or pay for the special education and related services described in paragraph

(b)(1) of this section, the LEA (or State agency responsible for developing the child's IEP) must provide or pay for these services to the child in a timely manner. The LEA or State agency is authorized to claim reimbursement for the services from the noneducational public agency that failed to provide or pay for these services and that agency must reimburse the LEA or State agency in accordance with the terms of the interagency agreement or other mechanism described in paragraph (a) of this section.

(c) Special rule. The requirements of paragraph (a) of this section may be met through—

(1) State statute or regulation;

(2) Signed agreements between respective agency officials that clearly identify the responsibilities of each agency relating to the provision of services; or

(3) Other appropriate written methods as determined by the Chief Executive Officer of the State or designee of that officer and approved by the Secretary.

(d) Children with disabilities who are covered by public benefits or insurance.

(1) A public agency may use the Medicaid or other public benefits or insurance programs in which a child participates to provide or pay for services required under this part, as permitted under the public benefits or insurance program, except as provided in paragraph (d)(2) of this section.

(2) With regard to services required to provide FAPE to an eligible child under this part, the public agency—

(i) May not require parents to sign up for or enroll in public benefits or insurance programs in order for their child to receive FAPE under Part B of the Act;

(ii) May not require parents to incur an out-of-pocket expense such as the payment of a deductible or co-pay amount incurred in filing a claim for services provided pursuant to this part, but pursuant to paragraph (g)(2) of this section, may pay the cost that the parents otherwise would be required to pay;

(iii) May not use a child's benefits under a public benefits or insurance program if that use would—

(A) Decrease available lifetime coverage or any other insured benefit;

(B) Result in the family paying for services that would otherwise be covered by the public benefits or insurance program and that are required for the child outside of the time the child is in school;

(C) Increase premiums or lead to the discontinuation of benefits or insurance; or

(D) Risk loss of eligibility for home and community-based waivers, based on aggregate health-related expenditures; and

(iv)(A) Must obtain parental consent, consistent with § 300.9, each time that access to public benefits or insurance is sought; and

(B) Notify parents that the parents' refusal to allow access to their public benefits or insurance does not relieve the public agency of its responsibility to ensure that all required services are provided at no cost to the parents.

(e) Children with disabilities who are covered by private insurance. (1) With regard to services required to provide FAPE to an eligible child under this part, a public agency may access the parents' private insurance proceeds only if the parents provide consent consistent with § 300.9.

(2) Each time the public agency proposes to access the parents' private insurance proceeds, the agency must—

(i) Obtain parental consent in accordance with paragraph (e)(1) of this section; and

(ii) Inform the parents that their refusal to permit the public agency to access their private insurance does not relieve the public agency of its responsibility to ensure that all required services are provided at no cost to the parents.

(f) Use of Part B funds. (1) If a public agency is unable to obtain parental consent to use the parents' private insurance, or public benefits or insurance when the parents would incur a cost for a specified service required under this part, to ensure FAPE the public agency may use its Part B funds to pay for the service.

(2) To avoid financial cost to parents who otherwise would consent to use private insurance, or public benefits or insurance if the parents would incur a cost, the public agency may use its Part B funds to pay the cost that the parents otherwise would have to pay to use the parents' benefits or insurance (e.g., the deductible or co-pay amounts).

(g) Proceeds from public benefits or insurance or private insurance. (1) Proceeds from public benefits or insurance or private insurance will not be treated as program income for purposes of 34 CFR 80.25.

(2) If a public agency spends reimbursements from Federal funds (e.g., Medicaid) for services under this part, those funds will not be considered "State or local" funds for purposes of the maintenance of effort provisions in §§ 300.163 and 300.203.

(h) Construction. Nothing in this part should be construed to alter the requirements imposed on a State Medicaid agency, or any other agency administering a public benefits or insurance program by Federal statute, regulations or policy under title XIX, or title XXI of the Social Security Act, 42 U.S.C. 1396 through 1396v and 42 U.S.C. 1397aa through 1397jj, or any other public benefits or insurance program.

(Approved by the Office of Management and Budget under control number 1820–0030)

(Authority: 20 U.S.C. 1412(a)(12) and (e))

Additional Eligibility Requirements

§ 300.155 Hearings relating to LEA eligibility.

The SEA must not make any final determination that an LEA is not eligible for assistance under Part B of the Act without first giving the LEA reasonable notice and an opportunity for a hearing under 34 CFR 76.401(d).

(Approved by the Office of Management and Budget under control number 1820–0030)

(Authority: 20 U.S.C. 1412(a)(13))

§ 300.156 Personnel qualifications.

(a) General. The SEA must establish and maintain qualifications to ensure that personnel necessary to carry out the purposes of this part are appropriately and adequately prepared and trained, including that those personnel have the content knowledge and skills to serve children with disabilities.

(b) Related services personnel and paraprofessionals. The qualifications under paragraph (a) of this section must include qualifications for related services personnel and paraprofessionals that—

(1) Are consistent with any Stateapproved or State-recognized certification, licensing, registration, or other comparable requirements that apply to the professional discipline in which those personnel are providing special education or related services; and

(2) Ensure that related services personnel who deliver services in their discipline or profession—

(i) Meet the requirements of paragraph (b)(1) of this section; and

(ii) Have not had certification or licensure requirements waived on an emergency, temporary, or provisional basis; and

(iii) Allow paraprofessionals and assistants who are appropriately trained and supervised, in accordance with State law, regulation, or written policy, in meeting the requirements of this part to be used to assist in the provision of special education and related services under this part to children with disabilities.

(c) Qualifications for special education teachers. The qualifications described in paragraph (a) of this section must ensure that each person employed as a public school special education teacher in the State who teaches in an elementary school, middle school, or secondary school is highly qualified as a special education teacher by the deadline established in section 1119(a)(2) of the ESEA.

(d) Policy. In implementing this section, a State must adopt a policy that includes a requirement that LEAs in the State take measurable steps to recruit, hire, train, and retain highly qualified personnel to provide special education and related services under this part to children with disabilities.

(e) Rule of construction. Notwithstanding any other individual right of action that a parent or student may maintain under this part, nothing in this part shall be construed to create a right of action on behalf of an individual student or a class of students for the failure of a particular SEA or LEA employee to be highly qualified, or to prevent a parent from filing a complaint about staff qualifications with the SEA as provided for under this part.

(Approved by the Office of Management and Budget under control number 1820–0030)

(Authority: 20 U.S.C. 1412(a)(14))

§ 300.157 Performance goals and indicators.

The State must—

(a) Have in effect established goals for the performance of children with disabilities in the State that—

(1) Promote the purposes of this part, as stated in § 300.1;

(2) Are the same as the State's objectives for progress by children in its definition of adequate yearly progress, including the State's objectives for progress by children with disabilities, under section 1111(b)(2)(C) of the ESEA, 20 U.S.C. 6311;

(3) Address graduation rates and dropout rates, as well as such other factors as the State may determine; and

(4) Are consistent, to the extent appropriate, with any other goals and academic standards for children established by the State;

(b) Have in effect established performance indicators the State will use to assess progress toward achieving the goals described in paragraph (a) of this section, including measurable annual objectives for progress by children with disabilities under section 1111(b)(2)(C)(v)(II)(cc) of the ESEA, 20 U.S.C. 6311; and

(c) Annually report to the Secretary and the public on the progress of the State, and of children with disabilities in the State, toward meeting the goals established under paragraph (a) of this section, which may include elements of the reports required under section 1111(h) of the ESEA.

(Approved by the Office of Management and Budget under control number 1820–0030)

(Authority: 20 U.S.C. 1412(a)(15))

§§ 300.158–300.161 [Reserved]

§ 300.162 Supplementation of State, local, and other Federal funds.

(a) Expenditures. Funds paid to a State under this part must be expended in accordance with all the provisions of this part.

(b) Prohibition against commingling.

(1) Funds paid to a State under this part must not be commingled with State funds.

(2) The requirement in paragraph (b)(1) of this section is satisfied by the use of a separate accounting system that includes an audit trail of the expenditure of funds paid to a State under this part. Separate bank accounts are not required. (See 34 CFR 76.702 (Fiscal control and fund accounting procedures).)

(c) State-level nonsupplanting. (1) Except as provided in § 300.202, funds paid to a State under Part B of the Act must be used to supplement the level of Federal, State, and local funds (including funds that are not under the direct control of the SEA or LEAs) expended for special education and related services provided to children with disabilities under Part B of the Act, and in no case to supplant those Federal, State, and local funds.

(2) If the State provides clear and convincing evidence that all children with disabilities have available to them FAPE, the Secretary may waive, in whole or in part, the requirements of paragraph (c)(1) of this section if the Secretary concurs with the evidence provided by the State under § 300.164.

(Approved by the Office of Management and Budget under control number 1820–0030)

(Authority: 20 U.S.C. 1412(a)(17))

§ 300.163 Maintenance of State financial support.

(a) General. A State must not reduce the amount of State financial support for special education and related services for children with disabilities, or otherwise made available because of the excess costs of educating those children, below the amount of that support for the preceding fiscal year.

(b) Reduction of funds for failure to maintain support. The Secretary reduces the allocation of funds under section 611 of the Act for any fiscal year following the fiscal year in which the State fails to comply with the requirement of paragraph (a) of this section by the same amount by which the State fails to meet the requirement.

(c) Waivers for exceptional or uncontrollable circumstances. The Secretary may waive the requirement of paragraph (a) of this section for a State, for one fiscal year at a time, if the Secretary determines that—

(1) Granting a waiver would be equitable due to exceptional or uncontrollable circumstances such as a natural disaster or a precipitous and unforeseen decline in the financial resources of the State; or

(2) The State meets the standard in § 300.164 for a waiver of the requirement to supplement, and not to supplant, funds received under Part B of the Act.

(d) Subsequent years. If, for any fiscal year, a State fails to meet the requirement of paragraph (a) of this section, including any year for which the State is granted a waiver under paragraph (c) of this section, the financial support required of the State in future years under paragraph (a) of this section shall be the amount that would have been required in the absence of that failure and not the reduced level of the State's support.

(Approved by the Office of Management and Budget under control number 1820–0030)

(Authority: 20 U.S.C. 1412(a)(18))

§ 300.164 Waiver of requirement regarding supplementing and not supplanting with Part B funds.

(a) Except as provided under §§ 300.202 through 300.205, funds paid to a State under Part B of the Act must be used to supplement and increase the level of Federal, State, and local funds (including funds that are not under the direct control of SEAs or LEAs) expended for special education and related services provided to children with disabilities under Part B of the Act and in no case to supplant those Federal, State, and local funds. A State may use funds it retains under § 300.704(a) and (b) without regard to the prohibition on supplanting other funds.

(b) If a State provides clear and convincing evidence that all eligible children with disabilities throughout the State have FAPE available to them, the Secretary may waive for a period of one year in whole or in part the requirement under § 300.162 (regarding State-level nonsupplanting) if the Secretary concurs with the evidence provided by the State.

(c) If a State wishes to request a waiver under this section, it must submit to the Secretary a written request that includes—

(1) An assurance that FAPE is currently available, and will remain available throughout the period that a waiver would be in effect, to all eligible children with disabilities throughout the State, regardless of the public agency that is responsible for providing FAPE to them. The assurance must be signed by an official who has

the authority to provide that assurance as it applies to all eligible children with disabilities in the State;

(2) All evidence that the State wishes the Secretary to consider in determining whether all eligible children with disabilities have FAPE available to them, setting forth in detail—

(i) The basis on which the State has concluded that FAPE is available to all eligible children in the State; and

(ii) The procedures that the State will implement to ensure that FAPE remains available to all eligible children in the State, which must include—

(A) The State's procedures under § 300.111 for ensuring that all eligible children are identified, located and evaluated;

(B) The State's procedures for monitoring public agencies to ensure that they comply with all requirements of this part;

(C) The State's complaint procedures under §§ 300.151 through 300.153; and

(D) The State's hearing procedures under §§ 300.511 through 300.516 and §§ 300.530 through 300.536;

(3) A summary of all State and Federal monitoring reports, and State complaint decisions (see §§ 300.151 through 300.153) and hearing decisions (see §§ 300.511 through 300.516 and §§ 300.530 through 300.536), issued within three years prior to the date of the State's request for a waiver under this section, that includes any finding that FAPE has not been available to one or more eligible children, and evidence that FAPE is now available to all children addressed in those reports or decisions; and

(4) Evidence that the State, in determining that FAPE is currently available to all eligible children with disabilities in the State, has consulted with the State advisory panel under § 300.167.

(d) If the Secretary determines that the request and supporting evidence submitted by the State makes a prima facie showing that FAPE is, and will remain, available to all eligible children with disabilities in the State, the Secretary, after notice to the public throughout the State, conducts a public hearing at which all interested persons and organizations may present evidence regarding the following issues:

(1) Whether FAPE is currently available to all eligible children with disabilities in the State.

(2) Whether the State will be able to ensure that FAPE remains available to all eligible children with disabilities in the State if the Secretary provides the requested waiver.

(e) Following the hearing, the Secretary, based on all submitted evidence, will provide a waiver, in whole or in part, for a period of one year if the Secretary finds that the State has provided clear and convincing evidence that

FAPE is currently available to all eligible children with disabilities in the State, and the State will be able to ensure that FAPE remains available to all eligible children with disabilities in the State if the Secretary provides the requested waiver.

(f) A State may receive a waiver of the requirement of section 612(a)(18)(A) of the Act and § 300.164 if it satisfies the requirements of paragraphs (b) through (e) of this section.

(g) The Secretary may grant subsequent waivers for a period of one year each, if the Secretary determines that the State has provided clear and convincing evidence that all eligible children with disabilities throughout the State have, and will continue to have throughout the one-year period of the waiver, FAPE available to them.

(Approved by the Office of Management and Budget under control number 1820–0030)

(Authority: 20 U.S.C. 1412(a)(17)(C), (18)(C)(ii))

§ 300.165 Public participation.

(a) Prior to the adoption of any policies and procedures needed to comply with Part B of the Act (including any amendments to those policies and procedures), the State must ensure that there are public hearings, adequate notice of the hearings, and an opportunity for comment available to the general public, including individuals with disabilities and parents of children with disabilities.

(b) Before submitting a State plan under this part, a State must comply with the public participation requirements in paragraph (a) of this section and those in 20 U.S.C. 1232d(b)(7).

(Approved by the Office of Management and Budget under control number 1820–0030)

(Authority: 20 U.S.C. 1412(a)(19); 20 U.S.C. 1232d(b)(7))

§ 300.166 Rule of construction.

In complying with §§ 300.162 and 300.163, a State may not use funds paid to it under this part to satisfy State-law mandated funding obligations to LEAs, including funding based on student attendance or enrollment, or inflation.

(Approved by the Office of Management and Budget under control number 1820–0030)

(Authority: 20 U.S.C. 1412(a)(20))

State Advisory Panel

§ 300.167 State advisory panel.

The State must establish and maintain an advisory panel for the purpose of providing policy guidance with respect to special education and related services for children with disabilities in the State.

(Approved by the Office of Management

and Budget under control number 1820–0030)

(Authority: 20 U.S.C. 1412(a)(21)(A))

§ 300.168 Membership.

(a) General. The advisory panel must consist of members appointed by the Governor, or any other official authorized under State law to make such appointments, be representative of the State population and be composed of individuals involved in, or concerned with the education of children with disabilities, including—

(1) Parents of children with disabilities (ages birth through 26);

(2) Individuals with disabilities;

(3) Teachers;

(4) Representatives of institutions of higher education that prepare special education and related services personnel;

(5) State and local education officials, including officials who carry out activities under subtitle B of title VII of the McKinney-Vento Homeless Assistance Act, (42 U.S.C. 11431 et seq.);

(6) Administrators of programs for children with disabilities;

(7) Representatives of other State agencies involved in the financing or delivery of related services to children with disabilities;

(8) Representatives of private schools and public charter schools;

(9) Not less than one representative of a vocational, community, or business organization concerned with the provision of transition services to children with disabilities;

(10) A representative from the State child welfare agency responsible for foster care; and

(11) Representatives from the State juvenile and adult corrections agencies.

(b) Special rule. A majority of the members of the panel must be individuals with disabilities or parents of children with disabilities (ages birth through 26).

(Approved by the Office of Management and Budget under control number 1820–0030)

(Authority: 20 U.S.C. 1412(a)(21)(B) and (C))

§ 300.169 Duties.

The advisory panel must—

(a) Advise the SEA of unmet needs within the State in the education of children with disabilities;

(b) Comment publicly on any rules or regulations proposed by the State regarding the education of children with disabilities;

(c) Advise the SEA in developing evaluations and reporting on data to the Secretary under section 618 of the Act;

(d) Advise the SEA in developing corrective action plans to address findings identified in Federal monitoring reports under Part B of the Act; and

(e) Advise the SEA in developing and implementing policies relating to the coordination of services for children with disabilities.

(Approved by the Office of Management and Budget under control number 1820–0030)

(Authority: 20 U.S.C. 1412(a)(21)(D))

Other Provisions Required for State Eligibility

§ 300.170 Suspension and expulsion rates.

(a) General. The SEA must examine data, including data disaggregated by race and ethnicity, to determine if significant discrepancies are occurring in the rate of long-term suspensions and expulsions of children with disabilities—

(1) Among LEAs in the State; or

(2) Compared to the rates for nondisabled children within those agencies.

(b) Review and revision of policies. If the discrepancies described in paragraph (a) of this section are occurring, the SEA must review and, if appropriate, revise (or require the affected State agency or LEA to revise) its policies, procedures, and practices relating to the development and implementation of IEPs, the use of positive behavioral interventions and supports, and procedural safeguards, to ensure that these policies, procedures, and practices comply with the Act.

(Approved by the Office of Management and Budget under control number 1820–0030)

(Authority: 20 U.S.C. 1412(a)(22))

§ 300.171 Annual description of use of Part B funds.

(a) In order to receive a grant in any fiscal year a State must annually describe—

(1) How amounts retained for State administration and State-level activities under § 300.704 will be used to meet the requirements of this part; and

(2) How those amounts will be allocated among the activities described in § 300.704 to meet State priorities based on input from LEAs.

(b) If a State's plans for use of its funds under § 300.704 for the forthcoming year do not change from the prior year, the State may submit a letter to that effect to meet the requirement in paragraph (a) of this section.

(c) The provisions of this section do not apply to the Virgin Islands, Guam, American Samoa, the Commonwealth of the Northern Mariana Islands, and the freely associated States.

(Approved by the Office of Management and Budget under control number 1820–0030)

(Authority: 20 U.S.C. 1411(e)(5))

§ 300.172 Access to instructional materials.

(a) General. The State must—

(1) Adopt the National Instructional Materials Accessibility Standard (NIMAS), published as appendix C to part 300, for the purposes of providing instructional materials to blind persons or other persons with print disabilities, in a timely manner after publication of the NIMAS in the Federal Register on July 19, 2006 (71 FR 41084); and

(2) Establish a State definition of "timely manner" for purposes of paragraphs (b)(2) and (b)(3) of this section if the State is not coordinating with the National Instructional Materials Access Center (NIMAC) or (b)(3) and (c)(2) of this section if the State is coordinating with the NIMAC.

(b) Rights and responsibilities of SEA.

(1) Nothing in this section shall be construed to require any SEA to coordinate with the NIMAC.

(2) If an SEA chooses not to coordinate with the NIMAC, the SEA must provide an assurance to the Secretary that it will provide instructional materials to blind persons or other persons with print disabilities in a timely manner.

(3) Nothing in this section relieves an SEA of its responsibility to ensure that children with disabilities who need instructional materials in accessible formats, but are not included under the definition of blind or other persons with print disabilities in § 300.172(e)(1)(i) or who need materials that cannot be produced from NIMAS files, receive those instructional materials in a timely manner.

(4) In order to meet its responsibility under paragraphs (b)(2), (b)(3), and (c) of this section to ensure that children with disabilities who need instructional materials in accessible formats are provided those materials in a timely manner, the SEA must ensure that all public agencies take all reasonable steps to provide instructional materials in accessible formats to children with disabilities who need those instructional materials at the same time as other children receive instructional materials.

(c) Preparation and delivery of files. If an SEA chooses to coordinate with the NIMAC, as of December 3, 2006, the SEA must—

(1) As part of any print instructional materials adoption process, procurement contract, or other practice or instrument used for purchase of print instructional materials, must enter into a written contract with the publisher of the print instructional materials to— (i) Require the publisher to prepare and, on or before delivery of the print instructional materials, provide to NIMAC electronic files containing the contents of the print instructional materials using the NIMAS; or (ii) Purchase instructional materials from the publisher that are produced in, or may be rendered in, specialized formats.

(2) Provide instructional materials to blind persons or other persons with print disabilities in a timely manner.

(d) Assistive technology. In carrying out this section, the SEA, to the maximum extent possible, must work collaboratively with the State agency responsible for assistive technology programs.

(e) Definitions. (1) In this section and § 300.210—

(i) Blind persons or other persons with print disabilities means children served under this part who may qualify to receive books and other publications produced in specialized formats in accordance with the Act entitled "An Act to provide books for adult blind," approved March 3, 1931, 2 U.S.C 135a;

(ii) National Instructional Materials Access Center or NIMAC means the center established pursuant to section 674(e) of the Act;

(iii) National Instructional Materials Accessibility Standard or NIMAS has the meaning given the term in section 674(e)(3)(B) of the Act;

(iv) Specialized formats has the meaning given the term in section 674(e)(3)(D) of the Act.

(2) The definitions in paragraph (e)(1) of this section apply to each State and LEA, whether or not the State or LEA chooses to coordinate with the NIMAC.

(Approved by the Office of Management and Budget under control number 1820–0030)

(Authority: 20 U.S.C. 1412(a)(23), 1474(e))

§ 300.173 Overidentification and disproportionality.

The State must have in effect, consistent with the purposes of this part and with section 618(d) of the Act, policies and procedures designed to prevent the inappropriate overidentification or disproportionate representation by race and ethnicity of children as children with disabilities, including children with disabilities with a particular impairment described in § 300.8.

(Approved by the Office of Management and Budget under control number 1820–0030)

(Authority: 20 U.S.C. 1412(a)(24))

§ 300.174 Prohibition on mandatory medication.

(a) General. The SEA must prohibit State and LEA personnel from requiring parents to obtain a prescription for substances identified under schedules I, II, III, IV, or V in section 202(c) of the Controlled Substances Act (21 U.S.C. 812(c)) for a child as a condition of attending school, receiving an evaluation under §§ 300.300 through 300.311, or receiving services under this part.

(b) Rule of construction. Nothing in paragraph (a) of this section shall be construed to create a Federal prohibition against teachers and other school personnel consulting or sharing classroom-based observations with parents or guardians regarding a student's academic and functional performance, or behavior in the classroom or school, or regarding the need for evaluation for special education or related services under § 300.111 (related to child find).

(Approved by the Office of Management and Budget under control number 1820–0030)

(Authority: 20 U.S.C. 1412(a)(25))

§ 300.175 SEA as provider of FAPE or direct services.

If the SEA provides FAPE to children with disabilities, or provides direct services to these children, the agency—

(a) Must comply with any additional requirements of §§ 300.201 and 300.202 and §§ 300.206 through 300.226 as if the agency were an LEA; and

(b) May use amounts that are otherwise available to the agency under Part B of the Act to serve those children without regard to § 300.202(b) (relating to excess costs).

(Approved by the Office of Management and Budget under control number 1820–0030)

(Authority: 20 U.S.C. 1412(b))

§ 300.176 Exception for prior State plans.

(a) General. If a State has on file with the Secretary policies and procedures approved by the Secretary that demonstrate that the State meets any requirement of § 300.100, including any policies and procedures filed under Part B of the Act as in effect before, December 3, 2004, the Secretary considers the State to have met the requirement for purposes of receiving a grant under Part B of the Act.

(b) Modifications made by a State. (1) Subject to paragraph (b)(2) of this section, policies and procedures submitted by a State in accordance with this subpart remain in effect until the State submits to the Secretary the modifications that the State determines necessary.

(2) The provisions of this subpart apply to a modification to an application to the same extent and in the same manner that they apply to the original plan.

(c) Modifications required by the Secretary. The Secretary may require a State to modify its policies and procedures, but only to the extent necessary to ensure the State's compliance with this part, if—

(1) After December 3, 2004, the provisions of the Act or the regulations in this part are amended;

(2) There is a new interpretation of this Act by a Federal court or a State's highest court; or

(3) There is an official finding of noncompliance with Federal law or regulations.

(Approved by the Office of Management and Budget under control number 1820–0030)

(Authority: 20 U.S.C. 1412(c)(2) and (3))

§ 300.177 States' sovereign immunity and positive efforts to employ and advance qualified individuals with disabilities.

(a) States' sovereign immunity.

(1) A State that accepts funds under this part waives its immunity under the 11th amendment of the Constitution of the United States from suit in Federal court for a violation of this part.

(2) In a suit against a State for a violation of this part, remedies (including remedies both at law and in equity) are available for such a violation in the suit against any public entity other than a State.

(3) Paragraphs (a)(1) and (a)(2) of this section apply with respect to violations that occur in whole or part after the date of enactment of the Education of the Handicapped Act Amendments of 1990.

(b) Positive efforts to employ and advance qualified individuals with disabilities. Each recipient of assistance under Part B of the Act must make positive efforts to employ, and advance in employment, qualified individuals with disabilities in programs assisted under Part B of the Act.

(Authority: 20 U.S.C. 1403, 1405)

Department Procedures

§ 300.178 Determination by the Secretary that a State is eligible to receive a grant.

If the Secretary determines that a State is eligible to receive a grant under Part B of the Act, the Secretary notifies the State of that determination.

(Authority: 20 U.S.C. 1412(d)(1))

§ 300.179 Notice and hearing before determining that a State is not eligible to receive a grant.

(a) General. (1) The Secretary does not make a final determination that a State is not eligible to receive a grant under Part B of the Act until providing the State—

(i) With reasonable notice; and

(ii) With an opportunity for a hearing.

(2) In implementing paragraph (a)(1)(i) of this section, the Secretary sends a written notice to the SEA by certified mail with return receipt requested.

(b) Content of notice. In the written notice described in paragraph (a)(2) of this section, the Secretary—

(1) States the basis on which the Secretary proposes to make a final determination that the State is not eligible;

(2) May describe possible options for resolving the issues;

(3) Advises the SEA that it may request a hearing and that the request for a hearing must be made not later than 30 days after it receives the notice of the proposed final determination that the State is not eligible; and

(4) Provides the SEA with information about the hearing procedures that will be followed.

(Authority: 20 U.S.C. 1412(d)(2))

§ 300.180 Hearing official or panel.

(a) If the SEA requests a hearing, the Secretary designates one or more individuals, either from the Department or elsewhere, not responsible for or connected with the administration of this program, to conduct a hearing.

(b) If more than one individual is designated, the Secretary designates one of those individuals as the Chief Hearing Official of the Hearing Panel. If one individual is designated, that individual is the Hearing Official.

(Authority: 20 U.S.C. 1412(d)(2))

§ 300.181 Hearing procedures.

(a) As used in §§ 300.179 through 300.184 the term party or parties means the following:

(1) An SEA that requests a hearing regarding the proposed disapproval of the State's eligibility under this part.

(2) The Department official who administers the program of financial assistance under this part.

(3) A person, group or agency with an interest in and having relevant information about the case that has applied for and been granted leave to intervene by the Hearing Official or Hearing Panel.

(b) Within 15 days after receiving a request for a hearing, the Secretary designates a Hearing Official or Hearing Panel and notifies the parties.

(c) The Hearing Official or Hearing Panel may regulate the course of proceedings and the conduct of the parties during the proceedings. The Hearing Official or Hearing Panel takes all steps necessary to conduct a fair and impartial proceeding, to avoid delay, and to maintain order, including the following:

(1) The Hearing Official or Hearing Panel may hold conferences or other types of appropriate proceedings to clarify, simplify, or define the issues or to consider other matters that may aid in the disposition of the case.

(2) The Hearing Official or Hearing Panel may schedule a prehearing conference with the Hearing Official or Hearing Panel and the parties.

(3) Any party may request the Hearing Official or Hearing Panel to schedule a prehearing or other conference. The Hearing Official or Hearing Panel decides whether a conference is necessary and notifies all parties.

(4) At a prehearing or other conference, the Hearing Official or Hearing Panel and the parties may consider subjects such as—

(i) Narrowing and clarifying issues;

(ii) Assisting the parties in reaching agreements and stipulations;

(iii) Clarifying the positions of the parties;

(iv) Determining whether an evidentiary hearing or oral argument should be held; and

(v) Setting dates for—

(A) The exchange of written documents;

(B) The receipt of comments from the parties on the need for oral argument or evidentiary hearing;

(C) Further proceedings before the Hearing Official or Hearing Panel (including an evidentiary hearing or oral argument, if either is scheduled);

(D) Requesting the names of witnesses each party wishes to present at an evidentiary hearing and estimation of time for each presentation; or

(E) Completion of the review and the initial decision of the Hearing Official or Hearing Panel.

(5) A prehearing or other conference held under paragraph (b)(4) of this section may be conducted by telephone conference call.

(6) At a prehearing or other conference, the parties must be prepared to discuss the subjects listed in paragraph (b)(4) of this section.

(7) Following a prehearing or other conference the Hearing Official or Hearing Panel may issue a written statement describing the issues raised, the action taken, and the stipulations and agreements reached by the parties.

(d) The Hearing Official or Hearing Panel may require parties to state their positions and to provide all or part of the evidence in writing.

(e) The Hearing Official or Hearing Panel may require parties to present testimony through affidavits and to conduct cross-examination through interrogatories.

(f) The Hearing Official or Hearing Panel may direct the parties to exchange relevant documents or information and lists of witnesses, and to send copies to the Hearing Official or Panel.

(g) The Hearing Official or Hearing Panel may receive, rule on, exclude, or limit evidence at any stage of the proceedings.

(h) The Hearing Official or Hearing Panel may rule on motions and other issues at any stage of the proceedings.

(i) The Hearing Official or Hearing Panel may examine witnesses.

(j) The Hearing Official or Hearing Panel may set reasonable time limits for submission of written documents.

(k) The Hearing Official or Hearing Panel may refuse to consider documents or other submissions if they are not submitted in a timely manner unless good cause is shown.

(l) The Hearing Official or Hearing Panel may interpret applicable statutes and regulations but may not waive them or rule on their validity.

(m)(1) The parties must present their positions through briefs and the submission of other documents and may request an oral argument or evidentiary hearing. The Hearing Official or Hearing Panel shall determine whether an oral argument or an evidentiary hearing is needed to clarify the positions of the parties.

(2) The Hearing Official or Hearing Panel gives each party an opportunity to be represented by counsel.

(n) If the Hearing Official or Hearing Panel determines that an evidentiary hearing would materially assist the resolution of the matter, the Hearing Official or Hearing Panel gives each party, in addition to the opportunity to be represented by counsel—

(1) An opportunity to present witnesses on the party's behalf; and

(2) An opportunity to cross-examine witnesses either orally or with written questions.

(o) The Hearing Official or Hearing Panel accepts any evidence that it finds is relevant and material to the proceedings and is not unduly repetitious.

(p)(1) The Hearing Official or Hearing Panel—

(i) Arranges for the preparation of a transcript of each hearing;

(ii) Retains the original transcript as part of the record of the hearing; and

(iii) Provides one copy of the transcript to each party.

(2) Additional copies of the transcript are available on request and with payment of the reproduction fee.

(q) Each party must file with the Hearing Official or Hearing Panel all written motions, briefs, and other documents and must at the same time provide a copy to the other parties to the proceedings.

(Authority: 20 U.S.C. 1412(d)(2))

§ 300.182 Initial decision; final decision.

(a) The Hearing Official or Hearing Panel prepares an initial written decision that addresses each of the points in the notice sent by the Secretary to the SEA under § 300.179 including any amendments to or further clarifications of the issues, under § 300.181(c)(7).

(b) The initial decision of a Hearing Panel is made by a majority of Panel members.

(c) The Hearing Official or Hearing Panel mails, by certified mail with return receipt requested, a copy of the initial decision to each party (or to the party's counsel) and to the Secretary, with a notice stating that each party has an opportunity to submit written comments regarding the decision to the Secretary.

(d) Each party may file comments and recommendations on the initial decision with the Hearing Official or Hearing Panel within 15 days of the date the party receives the Panel's decision.

(e) The Hearing Official or Hearing Panel sends a copy of a party's initial comments and recommendations to the other parties by certified mail with return receipt requested. Each party may file responsive comments and recommendations with the Hearing Official or Hearing Panel within seven days of the date the party receives the initial comments and recommendations.

(f) The Hearing Official or Hearing Panel forwards the parties' initial and responsive comments on the initial decision to the Secretary who reviews the initial decision and issues a final decision.

(g) The initial decision of the Hearing Official or Hearing Panel becomes the final decision of the Secretary unless, within 25 days after the end of the time for receipt of written comments and recommendations, the Secretary informs the Hearing Official or Hearing Panel and the parties to a hearing in writing that the decision is being further reviewed for possible modification.

(h) The Secretary rejects or modifies the initial decision of the Hearing Official or Hearing Panel if the Secretary finds that it is clearly erroneous.

(i) The Secretary conducts the review based on the initial decision, the written record, the transcript of the Hearing Official's or Hearing Panel's proceedings, and written comments.

(j) The Secretary may remand the matter to the Hearing Official or Hearing Panel for further proceedings.

(k) Unless the Secretary remands the matter as provided in paragraph (j) of this section, the Secretary issues the final decision, with any necessary modifications, within 30 days after notifying the Hearing Official or Hearing Panel that the initial decision is being further reviewed.

(Approved by the Office of Management and Budget under control number 1820–0030)

(Authority: 20 U.S.C. 1412(d)(2))

§ 300.183 Filing requirements.

(a) Any written submission by a party under §§ 300.179 through 300.184 must be filed by hand delivery, by mail, or by facsimile transmission. The Secretary discourages the use of facsimile transmission for documents longer than five pages.

(b) The filing date under paragraph (a) of this section is the date the document is—

(1) Hand-delivered;

(2) Mailed; or

(3) Sent by facsimile transmission.

(c) A party filing by facsimile transmission is responsible for confirming that a complete and legible copy of the document was received by the Department.

(d) If a document is filed by facsimile transmission, the Secretary, the Hearing Official, or the Hearing Panel, as applicable, may require the filing of a follow-up hard copy by hand delivery or by mail within a reasonable period of time.

(e) If agreed upon by the parties, service of a document may be made upon the other party by facsimile transmission.

(Authority: 20 U.S.C. 1412(d))

§ 300.184 Judicial review.

If a State is dissatisfied with the Secretary's final decision with respect to the eligibility of the State under section 612 of the Act, the State may, not later than 60 days after notice of that decision, file with the United States Court of Appeals for the circuit in which that State is located a petition for review of that decision. A copy of the petition must be transmitted by the clerk of the court to the Secretary. The Secretary then files in the court the record of the proceedings upon which the Secretary's decision was based, as provided in 28 U.S.C. 2112.

(Authority: 20 U.S.C. 1416(e)(8))

§ 300.185 [Reserved]

§ 300.186 Assistance under other Federal programs.

Part B of the Act may not be construed to permit a State to reduce medical and other assistance available, or to alter eligibility, under titles V and XIX of the Social Security Act with respect to the provision of FAPE for children with disabilities in the State.

(Authority: 20 U.S.C. 1412(e))

By-pass for Children in Private Schools

§ 300.190 By-pass—general.

(a) If, on December 2, 1983, the date of enactment of the Education of the Handicapped Act Amendments of 1983, an SEA was prohibited by law from providing for the equitable participation in special programs of children with disabilities enrolled in private elementary schools and secondary schools as required by section 612(a)(10)(A) of the Act, or if the Secretary determines that an SEA, LEA, or other public agency has substantially failed or is unwilling to provide for such equitable participation then the Secretary shall, notwithstanding such provision of law, arrange for the provision of services to these children through arrangements which shall be subject to the requirements of section 612(a)(10)(A) of the Act.

(b) The Secretary waives the requirement of section 612(a)(10)(A) of the Act and of §§ 300.131 through 300.144 if the Secretary implements a by-pass.

(Authority: 20 U.S.C. 1412(f)(1))

§ 300.191 Provisions for services under a by-pass.

(a) Before implementing a by-pass, the Secretary consults with appropriate public and private school officials, including SEA officials, in the affected State, and as appropriate, LEA or other public agency officials to consider matters such as—

(1) Any prohibition imposed by State law that results in the need for a bypass; and

(2) The scope and nature of the services required by private school children with disabilities in the State, and the number of children to be served under the by-pass.

(b) After determining that a by-pass is required, the Secretary arranges for the provision of services to private school children with disabilities in the State, LEA or other public agency in a manner consistent with the requirements of section 612(a)(10)(A) of the Act and §§ 300.131 through 300.144 by providing services through one or more agreements with appropriate parties.

(c) For any fiscal year that a by-pass is implemented, the Secretary determines the maximum amount to be paid to the providers of services by multiplying—

(1) A per child amount determined by dividing the total amount received by the State under Part B of the Act for the fiscal year by the number of children with disabilities served in the prior year as reported to the Secretary under section 618 of the Act; by

(2) The number of private school children with disabilities (as defined in §§ 300.8(a) and 300.130) in the State, LEA or other public agency, as determined by the Secretary on the basis of the most recent satisfactory data available, which may include an estimate of the number of those children with disabilities.

(d) The Secretary deducts from the State's allocation under Part B of the Act the amount the Secretary determines is necessary to implement a by-pass and pays that amount to the provider of services. The Secretary may withhold this amount from the State's allocation pending final resolution of any investigation or complaint that could result in a determination that a by-pass must be implemented.

(Authority: 20 U.S.C. 1412(f)(2))

§ 300.192 Notice of intent to implement a by-pass.

(a) Before taking any final action to implement a by-pass, the Secretary provides the SEA and, as appropriate, LEA or other public agency with written notice.

(b) In the written notice, the Secretary—

(1) States the reasons for the proposed by-pass in sufficient detail to allow the SEA and, as appropriate, LEA or other public agency to respond; and

(2) Advises the SEA and, as appropriate, LEA or other public agency that it has a specific period of time (at least 45 days) from receipt of the written notice to submit written objections to the proposed by-pass and that it may request in writing the opportunity for a hearing to show cause why a by-pass should not be implemented.

(c) The Secretary sends the notice to the SEA and, as appropriate, LEA or other public agency by certified mail with return receipt requested.

(Authority: 20 U.S.C. 1412(f)(3)(A))

§ 300.193 Request to show cause.

An SEA, LEA or other public agency in receipt of a notice under § 300.192 that seeks an opportunity to show cause why a by-pass should not be implemented must submit a written request for a show cause hearing to the Secretary, within the specified time period in the written notice in § 300.192(b)(2).

(Authority: 20 U.S.C. 1412(f)(3))

§ 300.194 Show cause hearing.

(a) If a show cause hearing is requested, the Secretary—

(1) Notifies the SEA and affected LEA or other public agency, and other appropriate public and private school officials of the time and place for the hearing;

(2) Designates a person to conduct the show cause hearing. The designee must not have had any responsibility for the matter brought for a hearing; and

(3) Notifies the SEA, LEA or other public agency, and representatives of private schools that they may be represented by legal counsel and submit oral or written evidence and arguments at the hearing.

(b) At the show cause hearing, the designee considers matters such as—

(1) The necessity for implementing a by-pass;

(2) Possible factual errors in the written notice of intent to implement a by-pass; and

(3) The objections raised by public and private school representatives.

(c) The designee may regulate the course of the proceedings and the conduct of parties during the pendency of the proceedings. The designee takes all steps necessary to conduct a fair and impartial proceeding, to avoid delay, and to maintain order.

(d) The designee has no authority to require or conduct discovery. (e) The designee may interpret applicable statutes and regulations, but may not waive them or rule on their validity.

(f) The designee arranges for the preparation, retention, and, if appropriate, dissemination of the record of the hearing.

(g) Within 10 days after the hearing, the designee—

(1) Indicates that a decision will be issued on the basis of the existing record; or

(2) Requests further information from the SEA, LEA, other public agency, representatives of private schools or Department officials.

(Authority: 20 U.S.C. 1412(f)(3))

§ 300.195 Decision.

(a) The designee who conducts the show cause hearing—

(1) Within 120 days after the record of a show cause hearing is closed, issues a written decision that includes a statement of findings; and

(2) Submits a copy of the decision to the Secretary and sends a copy to each party by certified mail with return receipt requested.

(b) Each party may submit comments and recommendations on the designee's decision to the Secretary within 30 days of the date the party receives the designee's decision.

(c) The Secretary adopts, reverses, or modifies the designee's decision and notifies all parties to the show cause hearing of the Secretary's final action. That notice is sent by certified mail with return receipt requested.

(Authority: 20 U.S.C. 1412(f)(3))

§ 300.196 Filing requirements.

(a) Any written submission under § 300.194 must be filed by hand-delivery, by mail, or by facsimile transmission. The Secretary discourages the use of facsimile transmission for documents longer than five pages.

(b) The filing date under paragraph (a) of this section is the date the document is—

(1) Hand-delivered;

(2) Mailed; or

(3) Sent by facsimile transmission.

(c) A party filing by facsimile transmission is responsible for confirming that a complete and legible copy of the document was received by the Department.

(d) If a document is filed by facsimile transmission, the Secretary or the hearing officer, as applicable, may require the filing of a follow-up hard copy by hand-delivery or by mail within a reasonable period of time.

(e) If agreed upon by the parties, service of a document may be made upon the other party by facsimile transmission.

(f) A party must show a proof of mailing to establish the filing date under paragraph (b)(2) of this section as provided in 34 CFR 75.102(d).

(Authority: 20 U.S.C. 1412(f)(3))

§ 300.197 Judicial review.

If dissatisfied with the Secretary's final action, the SEA may, within 60 days after notice of that action, file a petition for review with the United States Court of Appeals for the circuit in which the State is located. The procedures for judicial review are described in section 612(f)(3)(B) through (D) of the Act.

(Authority: 20 U.S.C. 1412(f)(3)(B)–(D))

§ 300.198 Continuation of a by-pass.

The Secretary continues a by-pass until the Secretary determines that the SEA, LEA or other public agency will meet the requirements for providing services to private school children.

(Authority: 20 U.S.C. 1412(f)(2)(C))

State Administration

§ 300.199 State administration.

(a) Rulemaking. Each State that receives funds under Part B of the Act must—

(1) Ensure that any State rules, regulations, and policies relating to this part conform to the purposes of this part;

(2) Identify in writing to LEAs located in the State and the Secretary any such rule, regulation, or policy as a State-imposed requirement that is not required by Part B of the Act and Federal regulations; and

(3) Minimize the number of rules, regulations, and policies to which the LEAs and schools located in the State are subject under Part B of the Act.

(b) Support and facilitation. State rules, regulations, and policies under Part B of the Act must support and facilitate LEA and school-level system improvement designed to enable children with disabilities to meet the challenging State student academic achievement standards.

(Approved by the Office of Management and Budget under control number 1820–0030)

(Authority: 20 U.S.C. 1407)

Subpart C—Local Educational Agency Eligibility

§ 300.200 Condition of assistance.

An LEA is eligible for assistance under Part B of the Act for a fiscal year if the agency submits a plan that provides assurances to the SEA that the LEA meets each of the conditions in §§ 300.201 through 300.213.

(Authority: 20 U.S.C. 1413(a))

§ 300.201 Consistency with State policies.

The LEA, in providing for the education of children with disabilities within its jurisdiction, must have in effect policies, procedures, and programs that are consistent with the State policies and procedures established under §§ 300.101 through 300.163, and §§ 300.165 through 300.174.

(Approved by the Office of Management and Budget under control number 1820–0600)

(Authority: 20 U.S.C. 1413(a)(1))

§ 300.202 Use of amounts.

(a) General. Amounts provided to the LEA under Part B of the Act—

(1) Must be expended in accordance with the applicable provisions of this part;

(2) Must be used only to pay the excess costs of providing special education and related services to children with disabilities, consistent with paragraph (b) of this section; and

(3) Must be used to supplement State, local, and other Federal funds and not to supplant those funds.

(b) Excess cost requirement—(1) General. (i) The excess cost requirement prevents an LEA from using funds provided under Part B of the Act to pay for all of the costs directly attributable to the education of a child with a disability, subject to paragraph (b)(1)(ii) of this section.

(ii) The excess cost requirement does not prevent an LEA from using Part B funds to pay for all of the costs directly attributable to the education of a child with a disability in any of the ages 3, 4, 5, 18, 19, 20, or 21, if no local or State funds are available for nondisabled children of these ages. However, the LEA must comply with the nonsupplanting and other requirements of this part in providing the education and services for these children.

(2)(i) An LEA meets the excess cost requirement if it has spent at least a minimum average amount for the education of its children with disabilities before funds under Part B of the Act are used.

(ii) The amount described in paragraph (b)(2)(i) of this section is determined in accordance with the definition of excess costs in § 300.16. That amount may not include capital outlay or debt service.

(3) If two or more LEAs jointly establish eligibility in accordance with § 300.223, the minimum average amount is the average of the combined minimum average amounts determined in accordance with the definition of excess costs in § 300.16 in those agencies for elementary or secondary school students, as the case may be.

(Approved by the Office of Management and Budget under control number 1820–0600)

(Authority: 20 U.S.C. 1413(a)(2)(A))

§ 300.203 Maintenance of effort.

(a) General. Except as provided in §§ 300.204 and 300.205, funds provided to an LEA under Part B of the Act must not be used to reduce the level of expenditures for the education of children with disabilities made by the LEA from local funds below the level of those expenditures for the preceding fiscal year.

(b) Standard. (1) Except as provided in paragraph (b)(2) of this section, the SEA must determine that an LEA complies with paragraph (a) of this section for purposes of establishing the LEA's eligibility for an award for a fiscal year if the LEA budgets, for the education of children with disabilities, at least the same total or per

capita amount from either of the following sources as the LEA spent for that purpose from the same source for the most recent prior year for which information is available:

(i) Local funds only.

(ii) The combination of State and local funds.

(2) An LEA that relies on paragraph (b)(1)(i) of this section for any fiscal year must ensure that the amount of local funds it budgets for the education of children with disabilities in that year is at least the same, either in total or per capita, as the amount it spent for that purpose in the most recent fiscal year for which information is available and the standard in paragraph (b)(1)(i) of this section was used to establish its compliance with this section.

(3) The SEA may not consider any expenditures made from funds provided by the Federal Government for which the SEA is required to account to the Federal Government or for which the LEA is required to account to the Federal Government directly or through the SEA in determining an LEA's compliance with the requirement in paragraph (a) of this section.

(Approved by the Office of Management and Budget under control number 1820–0600)

(Authority: 20 U.S.C. 1413(a)(2)(A))

§ 300.204 Exception to maintenance of effort.

Notwithstanding the restriction in § 300.203(a), an LEA may reduce the level of expenditures by the LEA under Part B of the Act below the level of those expenditures for the preceding fiscal year if the reduction is attributable to any of the following:

(a) The voluntary departure, by retirement or otherwise, or departure for just cause, of special education or related services personnel.

(b) A decrease in the enrollment of children with disabilities.

(c) The termination of the obligation of the agency, consistent with this part, to provide a program of special education to a particular child with a disability that is an exceptionally costly program, as determined by the SEA, because the child—

(1) Has left the jurisdiction of the agency;

(2) Has reached the age at which obligation of the agency to provide FAPE to the child has terminated; or

(3) No longer needs the program of special education.

(d) The termination of costly expenditures for long-term purchases, such as the acquisition of equipment or the construction of school facilities.

(e) The assumption of cost by the high cost fund operated by the SEA under § 300.704(c).

(Approved by the Office of Management and Budget under control number 1820–0600)

(Authority: 20 U.S.C. 1413(a)(2)(B))

§ 300.205 Adjustment to local fiscal efforts in certain fiscal years.

(a) Amounts in excess. Notwithstanding § 300.202(a)(2) and (b) and § 300.203(a), and except as provided in paragraph (d) of this section and § 300.230(e)(2), for any fiscal year for which the allocation received by an LEA under § 300.705 exceeds the amount the LEA received for the previous fiscal year, the LEA may reduce the level of expenditures otherwise required by § 300.203(a) by not more than 50 percent of the amount of that excess.

(b) Use of amounts to carry out activities under ESEA. If an LEA exercises the authority under paragraph (a) of this section, the LEA must use an amount of local funds equal to the reduction in expenditures under paragraph (a) of this section to carry out activities that could be supported with funds under the ESEA regardless of whether the LEA is using funds under the ESEA for those activities.

(c) State prohibition. Notwithstanding paragraph (a) of this section, if an SEA determines that an LEA is unable to establish and maintain programs of FAPE that meet the requirements of section 613(a) of the Act and this part or the SEA has taken action against the LEA under section 616 of the Act and subpart F of these regulations, the SEA must prohibit the LEA from reducing the level of expenditures under paragraph (a) of this section for that fiscal year.

(d) Special rule. The amount of funds expended by an LEA for early intervening services under § 300.226 shall count toward the maximum amount of expenditures that the LEA may reduce under paragraph (a) of this section.

(Approved by the Office of Management and Budget under control number 1820–0600)

(Authority: 20 U.S.C. 1413(a)(2)(C))

§ 300.206 Schoolwide programs under title I of the ESEA.

(a) General. Notwithstanding the provisions of §§ 300.202 and 300.203 or any other provision of Part B of the Act, an LEA may use funds received under Part B of the Act for any fiscal year to carry out a schoolwide program under section 1114 of the ESEA, except that the amount used in any schoolwide program may not exceed—

(1)(i) The amount received by the LEA under Part B of the Act for that fiscal year; divided by

(ii) The number of children with disabilities in the jurisdiction of the LEA; and multiplied by

(2) The number of children with disabilities participating in the schoolwide program.

(b) Funding conditions. The funds described in paragraph (a) of this section are subject to the following conditions:

(1) The funds must be considered as Federal Part B funds for purposes of the calculations required by § 300.202(a)(2) and

(a)(3).

(2) The funds may be used without regard to the requirements of § 300.202(a)(1).

(c) Meeting other Part B requirements. Except as provided in paragraph (b) of this section, all other requirements of Part B of the Act must be met by an LEA using Part B funds in accordance with paragraph (a) of this section, including ensuring that children with disabilities in schoolwide program schools—

(1) Receive services in accordance with a properly developed IEP; and

(2) Are afforded all of the rights and services guaranteed to children with disabilities under the Act.

(Approved by the Office of Management and Budget under control number 1820–0600)

(Authority: 20 U.S.C. 1413(a)(2)(D))

§ 300.207 Personnel development.

The LEA must ensure that all personnel necessary to carry out Part B of the Act are appropriately and adequately prepared, subject to the requirements of § 300.156 (related to personnel qualifications) and section 2122 of the ESEA.

(Approved by the Office of Management and Budget under control number 1820–0600)

(Authority: 20 U.S.C. 1413(a)(3))

§ 300.208 Permissive use of funds.

(a) Uses. Notwithstanding §§ 300.202, 300.203(a), and 300.162(b), funds provided to an LEA under Part B of the Act may be used for the following activities:

(1) Services and aids that also benefit nondisabled children. For the costs of special education and related services, and supplementary aids and services, provided in a regular class or other education-related setting to a child with a disability in accordance with the IEP of the child, even if one or more nondisabled children benefit from these services.

(2) Early intervening services. To develop and implement coordinated, early intervening educational services in accordance with § 300.226.

(3) High cost special education and related services. To establish and implement cost or risk sharing funds, consortia, or cooperatives for the LEA itself, or for LEAs working in a consortium of which the LEA is a part, to pay for high cost special education and related services.

(b) Administrative case management. An LEA may use funds received under Part B of the Act to purchase appropriate technology for recordkeeping, data collection, and related case management activities of teachers and related services personnel providing services described in the IEP of children with disabilities, that is needed for the implementation of those case management activities.

(Approved by the Office of Management

and Budget under control number 1820–0600)

(Authority: 20 U.S.C. 1413(a)(4))

§ 300.209 Treatment of charter schools and their students.

(a) Rights of children with disabilities. Children with disabilities who attend public charter schools and their parents retain all rights under this part.

(b) Charter schools that are public schools of the LEA. (1) In carrying out Part B of the Act and these regulations with respect to charter schools that are public schools of the LEA, the LEA must—

(i) Serve children with disabilities attending those charter schools in the same manner as the LEA serves children with disabilities in its other schools, including providing supplementary and related services on site at the charter school to the same extent to which the LEA has a policy or practice of providing such services on the site to its other public schools; and

(ii) Provide funds under Part B of the Act to those charter schools—

(A) On the same basis as the LEA provides funds to the LEA's other public schools, including proportional distribution based on relative enrollment of children with disabilities; and

(B) At the same time as the LEA distributes other Federal funds to the LEA's other public schools, consistent with the State's charter school law.

(2) If the public charter school is a school of an LEA that receives funding under § 300.705 and includes other public schools—

(i) The LEA is responsible for ensuring that the requirements of this part are met, unless State law assigns that responsibility to some other entity; and

(ii) The LEA must meet the requirements of paragraph (b)(1) of this section.

(c) Public charter schools that are LEAs. If the public charter school is an LEA, consistent with § 300.28, that receives funding under § 300.705, that charter school is responsible for ensuring that the requirements of this part are met, unless State law assigns that responsibility to some other entity.

(d) Public charter schools that are not an LEA or a school that is part of an LEA. (1) If the public charter school is not an LEA receiving funding under § 300.705, or a school that is part of an LEA receiving funding under § 300.705, the SEA is responsible for ensuring that the requirements of this part are met.

(2) Paragraph (d)(1) of this section does not preclude a State from assigning initial responsibility for ensuring the requirements of this part are met to another entity. However, the SEA must maintain the ultimate responsibility for ensuring compliance with this part, consistent with § 300.149.

(Approved by the Office of Management and Budget under control number 1820–0600)

(Authority: 20 U.S.C. 1413(a)(5))

§ 300.210 Purchase of instructional materials.

(a) General. Not later than December 3, 2006, an LEA that chooses to coordinate with the National Instructional Materials Access Center (NIMAC), when purchasing print instructional materials, must acquire those instructional materials in the same manner, and subject to the same conditions as an SEA under § 300.172.

(b) Rights of LEA. (1) Nothing in this section shall be construed to require an LEA to coordinate with the NIMAC.

(2) If an LEA chooses not to coordinate with the NIMAC, the LEA must provide an assurance to the SEA that the LEA will provide instructional materials to blind persons or other persons with print disabilities in a timely manner.

(3) Nothing in this section relieves an LEA of its responsibility to ensure that children with disabilities who need instructional materials in accessible formats but are not included under the definition of blind or other persons with print disabilities in § 300.172(e)(1)(i) or who need materials that cannot be produced from NIMAS files, receive those instructional materials in a timely manner.

(Approved by the Office of Management and Budget under control number 1820–0600)

(Authority: 20 U.S.C. 1413(a)(6))

§ 300.211 Information for SEA.

The LEA must provide the SEA with information necessary to enable the SEA to carry out its duties under Part B of the Act, including, with respect to §§ 300.157 and 300.160, information relating to the performance of children with disabilities participating in programs carried out under Part B of the Act.

(Approved by the Office of Management and Budget under control number 1820–0600)

(Authority: 20 U.S.C. 1413(a)(7))

§ 300.212 Public information.

The LEA must make available to parents of children with disabilities and to the general public all documents relating to the eligibility of the agency under Part B of the Act.

(Approved by the Office of Management and Budget under control number 1820–0600)

(Authority: 20 U.S.C. 1413(a)(8))

§ 300.213 Records regarding migratory children with disabilities.

The LEA must cooperate in the Secretary's efforts under section 1308 of the ESEA to ensure the linkage of records pertaining to migratory children with disabilities for the purpose of electronically exchanging, among the States, health and educational information regarding those children.

(Approved by the Office of Management and Budget under control number 1820–0600)

(Authority: 20 U.S.C. 1413(a)(9))

§§ 300.214–300.219 [Reserved]

§ 300.220 Exception for prior local plans.

(a) General. If an LEA or a State agency described in § 300.228 has on file with the SEA policies and procedures that demonstrate that the LEA or State agency meets any requirement of § 300.200, including any policies and procedures filed under Part B of the Act as in effect before December 3, 2004, the SEA must consider the LEA or State agency to have met that requirement for purposes of receiving assistance under Part B of the Act.

(b) Modification made by an LEA or State agency. Subject to paragraph (c) of this section, policies and procedures submitted by an LEA or a State agency in accordance with this subpart remain in effect until the LEA or State agency submits to the SEA the modifications that the LEA or State agency determines are necessary.

(c) Modifications required by the SEA. The SEA may require an LEA or a State agency to modify its policies and procedures, but only to the extent necessary to ensure the LEA's or State agency's compliance with Part B of the Act or State law, if—

(1) After December 3, 2004, the effective date of the Individuals with Disabilities Education Improvement Act of 2004, the applicable provisions of the Act (or the regulations developed to carry out the Act) are amended;

(2) There is a new interpretation of an applicable provision of the Act by Federal or State courts; or

(3) There is an official finding of noncompliance with Federal or State law or regulations.

(Authority: 20 U.S.C. 1413(b))

§ 300.221 Notification of LEA or State agency in case of ineligibility.

If the SEA determines that an LEA or State agency is not eligible under Part B of the Act, then the SEA must—

(a) Notify the LEA or State agency of that determination; and

(b) Provide the LEA or State agency with reasonable notice and an opportunity for a hearing.

(Authority: 20 U.S.C. 1413(c))

§ 300.222 LEA and State agency compliance.

(a) General.

If the SEA, after reasonable notice and an opportunity for a hearing, finds that an LEA or State agency that has been determined to be eligible under this subpart is failing to comply with any requirement described in §§ 300.201 through 300.213, the SEA must reduce or must not provide any further payments to the LEA or State agency until the SEA is satisfied that the LEA or State agency is complying with that requirement.

(b) Notice requirement. Any State agency or LEA in receipt of a notice described in paragraph (a) of this section must, by means of public notice, take the measures necessary to bring the pendency of an action pursuant to this section to the attention of the public within the jurisdiction of the agency.

(c) Consideration. In carrying out its responsibilities under this section, each SEA must consider any decision resulting from a hearing held under §§ 300.511 through 300.533 that is adverse to the LEA or State agency involved in the decision.

(Authority: 20 U.S.C. 1413(d))

§ 300.223 Joint establishment of eligibility.

(a) General. An SEA may require an LEA to establish its eligibility jointly with another LEA if the SEA determines that the LEA will be ineligible under this subpart because the agency will not be able to establish and maintain programs of sufficient size and scope to effectively meet the needs of children with disabilities.

(b) Charter school exception. An SEA may not require a charter school that is an LEA to jointly establish its eligibility under paragraph (a) of this section unless the charter school is explicitly permitted to do so under the State's charter school statute.

(c) Amount of payments. If an SEA requires the joint establishment of eligibility under paragraph (a) of this section, the total amount of funds made available to the affected LEAs must be equal to the sum of the payments that each LEA would have received under § 300.705 if the agencies were eligible for those payments.

(Authority: 20 U.S.C. 1413(e)(1) and (2))

§ 300.224 Requirements for establishing eligibility.

(a) Requirements for LEAs in general. LEAs that establish joint eligibility under this section must—

(1) Adopt policies and procedures that are consistent with the State's policies and procedures under §§ 300.101 through 300.163, and §§ 300.165 through 300.174; and

(2) Be jointly responsible for implementing programs that receive assistance under Part B of the Act.

(b) Requirements for educational service agencies in general. If an educational service agency is required by State law to carry out programs under Part B of the Act, the joint responsibilities given to LEAs under Part B of the Act—

(1) Do not apply to the administration and disbursement of any payments received by that educational service agency; and

(2) Must be carried out only by that educational service agency.

(c)   Additional   requirement. Notwithstanding any other provision of §§ 300.223 through 300.224, an educational service agency must provide for the education of children with disabilities in the least restrictive environment, as required by § 300.112.

(Approved by the Office of Management and Budget under control number 1820–0600)

(Authority: 20 U.S.C. 1413(e)(3) and (4))

§ 300.225 [Reserved]

§ 300.226 Early intervening services.

(a) General. An LEA may not use more than 15 percent of the amount the LEA receives under Part B of the Act for any fiscal year, less any amount reduced by the LEA pursuant to § 300.205, if any, in combination with other amounts (which may include amounts other than education funds), to develop and implement coordinated, early intervening services, which may include interagency financing structures, for students in kindergarten through grade 12 (with a particular emphasis on students in kindergarten through grade three) who are not currently identified as needing special education or related services, but who need additional academic and behavioral support to succeed in a general education environment. (See Appendix D for examples of how § 300.205(d), regarding local maintenance of effort, and § 300.226(a) affect one another.)

(b) Activities. In implementing coordinated, early intervening services under this section, an LEA may carry out activities that include—

(1) Professional development (which may be provided by entities other than LEAs) for teachers and other school staff to enable such personnel to deliver scientifically based academic and   behavioral   interventions,   including scientifically based literacy instruction, and, where appropriate, instruction on the use of adaptive and instructional software; and

(2) Providing educational and behavioral evaluations, services, and supports, including scientifically based literacy instruction.

(c) Construction. Nothing in this section shall be construed to either limit or create a right to FAPE under Part B of the Act or to delay appropriate evaluation of a child suspected of having a disability.

(d) Reporting. Each LEA that develops and maintains coordinated, early intervening services under this section must annually report to the SEA on—

(1) The number of children served under this section who received early intervening services; and

(2) The number of children served under this section who received early intervening services and subsequently receive special education and related services under Part B of the Act during the preceding two year period.

(e) Coordination with ESEA. Funds made available to carry out this section may be used to carry out coordinated, early intervening services aligned with activities funded by, and carried out under the ESEA if those funds are used to supplement, and not supplant, funds made available under the ESEA for the activities and services assisted under this section.

(Approved by the Office of Management and Budget under control number 1820–0600)

(Authority: 20 U.S.C. 1413(f))

§ 300.227 Direct services by the SEA.

(a) General. (1) An SEA must use the payments that would otherwise have been available to an LEA or to a State agency to provide special education and related services directly to children with disabilities residing in the area served by that LEA, or for whom that State agency is responsible, if the SEA determines that the LEA or State agency—

(i) Has not provided the information needed to establish the eligibility of the LEA or State agency, or elected not to apply for its Part B allotment, under Part B of the Act;

(ii) Is unable to establish and maintain programs of FAPE that meet the requirements of this part;

(iii) Is unable or unwilling to be consolidated with one or more LEAs in order to establish and maintain the programs; or

(iv) Has one or more children with disabilities who can best be served by a regional or State program or service delivery system designed to meet the needs of these children.

(2) SEA administrative procedures. (i) In meeting the requirements in paragraph (a)(1) of this section, the SEA may provide special education and related services directly, by contract, or through other arrangements.

(ii) The excess cost requirements of § 300.202(b) do not apply to the SEA.

(b) Manner and location of education and services. The SEA may provide special education and related services under paragraph (a) of this section in the manner and at the locations (including regional or State centers) as the SEA considers appropriate. The education and services must be provided in accordance with this part.

(Authority: 20 U.S.C. 1413(g))

§ 300.228 State agency eligibility.

Any State agency that desires to receive a subgrant for any fiscal year under § 300.705 must demonstrate to the satisfaction of the SEA that—

(a) All children with disabilities who are participating in programs and projects funded under Part B of the Act receive FAPE, and that those children and their parents are provided all the rights and procedural safeguards described in this part; and

(b) The agency meets the other conditions of this subpart that apply to LEAs.

(Authority: 20 U.S.C. 1413(h))

§ 300.229 Disciplinary information.

(a) The State may require that a public agency include in the records of a child with a disability a statement of any current or previous disciplinary action that has been taken against the child and transmit the statement to the same extent that the disciplinary information is included in, and transmitted with, the student records of nondisabled children.

(b) The statement may include a description of any behavior engaged in by the child that required disciplinary action, a description of the disciplinary action taken, and any other information that is relevant to the safety of the child and other individuals involved with the child.

(c) If the State adopts such a policy, and the child transfers from one school to another, the transmission of any of the child's records must include both the child's current IEP and any statement of current or previous disciplinary action that has been taken against the child.

(Authority: 20 U.S.C. 1413(i))

§ 300.230 SEA flexibility.

(a) Adjustment to State fiscal effort in certain fiscal years. For any fiscal year for which the allotment received by a State under § 300.703 exceeds the amount the State received for the previous fiscal year and if the State in school year 2003–2004 or any subsequent school year pays or reimburses all LEAs within the State from State revenue 100 percent of the non-Federal share of the costs of special education and related services, the SEA, notwithstanding §§ 300.162 through 300.163 (related to State-level nonsupplanting and maintenance of effort), and § 300.175 (related to direct services by the SEA) may reduce the level of expenditures from State sources for the education of children with disabilities by not more than 50 percent of the amount of such excess.

(b) Prohibition. Notwithstanding paragraph (a) of this section, if the Secretary determines that an SEA is unable to establish, maintain, or oversee programs of FAPE that meet the requirements of this part, or that the State needs assistance, intervention, or substantial intervention under § 300.603, the Secretary

prohibits the SEA from exercising the authority in paragraph (a) of this section.

(c) Education activities. If an SEA exercises the authority under paragraph (a) of this section, the agency must use funds from State sources, in an amount equal to the amount of the reduction under paragraph (a) of this section, to support activities authorized under the ESEA, or to support need-based student or teacher higher education programs.

(d) Report. For each fiscal year for which an SEA exercises the authority under paragraph (a) of this section, the SEA must report to the Secretary—

(1) The amount of expenditures reduced pursuant to that paragraph; and

(2) The activities that were funded pursuant to paragraph (c) of this section.

(e) Limitation. (1) Notwithstanding paragraph (a) of this section, an SEA may not reduce the level of expenditures described in paragraph (a) of this section if any LEA in the State would, as a result of such reduction, receive less than 100 percent of the amount necessary to ensure that all children with disabilities served by the LEA receive FAPE from the combination of Federal funds received under Part B of the Act and State funds received from the SEA.

(2) If an SEA exercises the authority under paragraph (a) of this section, LEAs in the State may not reduce local effort under § 300.205 by more than the reduction in the State funds they receive.

(Authority: 20 U.S.C. 1413(j))

Subpart D—Evaluations, Eligibility Determinations, Individualized Education Programs, and Educational Placements

Parental Consent

§ 300.300 Parental consent.

(a) Parental consent for initial evaluation.

(1)(i) The public agency proposing to conduct an initial evaluation to determine if a child qualifies as a child with a disability under § 300.8 must, after providing notice consistent with §§ 300.503 and 300.504, obtain informed consent, consistent with § 300.9, from the parent of the child before conducting the evaluation.

(ii) Parental consent for initial evaluation must not be construed as consent for initial provision of special education and related services.

(iii) The public agency must make reasonable efforts to obtain the informed consent from the parent for an initial evaluation to determine whether the child is a child with a disability.

(2) For initial evaluations only, if the child is a ward of the State and is not residing with the child's parent, the public agency is not required to obtain informed consent from the parent for an

initial evaluation to determine whether the child is a child with a disability if—

(i) Despite reasonable efforts to do so, the public agency cannot discover the whereabouts of the parent of the child;

(ii) The rights of the parents of the child have been terminated in accordance with State law; or

(iii) The rights of the parent to make educational decisions have been subrogated by a judge in accordance with State law and consent for an initial evaluation has been given by an individual appointed by the judge to represent the child.

(3)(i) If the parent of a child enrolled in public school or seeking to be enrolled in public school does not provide consent for initial evaluation under paragraph (a)(1) of this section, or the parent fails to respond to a request to provide consent, the public agency may, but is not required to, pursue the initial evaluation of the child by utilizing the procedural safeguards in subpart E of this part (including the mediation procedures under § 300.506 or the due process procedures under §§ 300.507 through 300.516), if appropriate, except to the extent inconsistent with State law relating to such parental consent.

(ii) The public agency does not violate its obligation under § 300.111 and §§ 300.301 through 300.311 if it declines to pursue the evaluation.

(b) Parental consent for services. (1) A public agency that is responsible for making FAPE available to a child with a disability must obtain informed consent from the parent of the child before the initial provision of special education and related services to the child.

(2) The public agency must make reasonable efforts to obtain informed consent from the parent for the initial provision of special education and related services to the child.

(3) If the parent of a child fails to respond to a request for, or refuses to consent to, the initial provision of special education and related services, the public agency--

(i) May not use the procedures in subpart E of this part (including the mediation procedures under § 300.506 or the due process procedures under §§ 300.507 through 300.516) in order to obtain agreement or a ruling that the services may be provided to the child;

(ii) Will not be considered to be in violation of the requirement to make FAPE available to the child because of the failure to provide the child with the special education and related services for which the parent refuses to or fails to provide consent; and

(iii) Is not required to convene an IEP Team meeting or develop an IEP under §§ 300.320 and 300.324 for the child.

(4)(4) If, at any time subsequent to the initial provision of special education and related services, the parent of a child revokes consent in writing for the continued provision of special education and related services, the public agency-

(i) May not continue to provide special education and related services to the child, but must provide prior written notice in accordance with § 300.503 before ceasing the provision of special education and related services;

(ii) May not use the procedures in subpart E of this part (including the mediation procedures under § 300.506 or the due process procedures under §§ 300.507 through 300.516) in order to obtain agreement or a ruling that the services may be provided to the child;

(iii) Will not be considered to be in violation of the requirement to make FAPE available to the child because of the failure to provide the child with further special education and related services; and

(iv) Is not required to convene an IEP Team meeting or develop an IEP under §§ 300.320 and 300.324 for the child for further provision of special education and related services.

(c) Parental consent for reevaluations.

(1) Subject to paragraph (c)(2) of this section, each public agency—

(i) Must obtain informed parental consent, in accordance with § 300.300(a)(1), prior to conducting any reevaluation of a child with a disability.

(ii) If the parent refuses to consent to the reevaluation, the public agency may, but is not required to, pursue the reevaluation by using the consent override procedures described in paragraph (a)(3) of this section.

(iii) The public agency does not violate its obligation under § 300.111 and §§ 300.301 through 300.311 if it declines to pursue the evaluation or reevaluation.

(2) The informed parental consent described in paragraph (c)(1) of this section need not be obtained if the public agency can demonstrate that—

(i) It made reasonable efforts to obtain such consent; and

(ii) The child's parent has failed to respond.

(d) Other consent requirements.

(1) Parental consent is not required before—

(i) Reviewing existing data as part of an evaluation or a reevaluation; or

(ii) Administering a test or other evaluation that is administered to all children unless, before administration of that test or evaluation, consent is required of parents of all children.

(2) In addition to the parental consent requirements described in paragraph (a) of this section, a State may require parental consent for other services and activities under this part if it ensures that each public agency in the State establishes and implements effective procedures to ensure that a parent's refusal to consent does

curriculum (or for a preschool child, to participate in appropriate activities);

(2) Not use any single measure or assessment as the sole criterion for determining whether a child is a child with a disability and for determining an appropriate educational program for the child; and

(3) Use technically sound instruments that may assess the relative contribution of cognitive and behavioral factors, in addition to physical or developmental factors.

(c) Other evaluation procedures. Each public agency must ensure that—

(1) Assessments and other evaluation materials used to assess a child under this part—

(i) Are selected and administered so as not to be discriminatory on a racial or cultural basis;

(ii) Are provided and administered in the child's native language or other mode of communication and in the form most likely to yield accurate information on what the child knows and can do academically, developmentally, and functionally, unless it is clearly not feasible to so provide or administer;

(iii) Are used for the purposes for which the assessments or measures are valid and reliable;

(iv) Are administered by trained and knowledgeable personnel; and

(v) Are administered in accordance with any instructions provided by the producer of the assessments.

(2) Assessments and other evaluation materials include those tailored to assess specific areas of educational need and not merely those that are designed to provide a single general intelligence quotient.

(3) Assessments are selected and administered so as best to ensure that if an assessment is administered to a child with impaired sensory, manual, or speaking skills, the assessment results accurately reflect the child's aptitude or achievement level or whatever other factors the test purports to measure, rather than reflecting the child's impaired sensory, manual, or speaking skills (unless those skills are the factors that the test purports to measure).

(4) The child is assessed in all areas related to the suspected disability, including, if appropriate, health, vision, hearing, social and emotional status, general intelligence, academic performance, communicative status, and motor abilities;

(5) Assessments of children with disabilities who transfer from one public agency to another public agency in the same school year are coordinated with those children's prior and subsequent schools, as necessary and as expeditiously as possible, consistent with § 300.301(d)(2) and (e), to ensure prompt completion of full evaluations.

(6) In evaluating each child with a disability under §§ 300.304 through 300.306, the evaluation is sufficiently comprehensive to identify all of the child's special education and related services needs, whether or not commonly linked to the disability category in which the child has been classified.

(7) Assessment tools and strategies that provide relevant information that directly assists persons in determining the educational needs of the child are provided.

(Authority: 20 U.S.C. 1414(b)(1)-(3), 1412(a)(6)(B))

§ 300.305 Additional requirements for evaluations and reevaluations.

(a) Review of existing evaluation data. As part of an initial evaluation (if appropriate) and as part of any reevaluation under this part, the IEP Team and other qualified professionals, as appropriate, must—

(1) Review existing evaluation data on the child, including—

(i) Evaluations and information provided by the parents of the child;

(ii) Current classroom-based, local, or State assessments, and classroom-based observations; and

(iii) Observations by teachers and related services providers; and

(2) On the basis of that review, and input from the child's parents, identify what additional data, if any, are needed to determine—

(i)(A) Whether the child is a child with a disability, as defined in § 300.8, and the educational needs of the child; or

(B) In case of a reevaluation of a child, whether the child continues to have such a disability, and the educational needs of the child;

(ii) The present levels of academic achievement and related developmental needs of the child;

(iii)(A) Whether the child needs special education and related services; or

(B) In the case of a reevaluation of a child, whether the child continues to need special education and related services; and

(iv) Whether any additions or modifications to the special education and related services are needed to enable the child to meet the measurable annual goals set out in the IEP of the child and to participate, as appropriate, in the general education curriculum.

(b) Conduct of review. The group described in paragraph (a) of this section may conduct its review without a meeting.

(c) Source of data. The public agency must administer such assessments and other evaluation measures as may be needed to produce the data identified under paragraph (a) of this section.

(d) Requirements if additional data are not needed.

(1) If the IEP Team and other qualified professionals, as appropriate, determine that no

additional data are needed to determine whether the child continues to be a child with a disability, and to determine the child's educational needs, the public agency must notify the child's parents of'—

(i) That determination and the reasons for the determination; and

(ii) The right of the parents to request an assessment to determine whether the child continues to be a child with a disability, and to determine the child's educational needs.

(2) The public agency is not required to conduct the assessment described in paragraph (d)(1)(ii) of this section unless requested to do so by the child's parents.

(e) Evaluations before change in eligibility. (1) Except as provided in paragraph (e)(2) of this section, a public agency must evaluate a child with a disability in accordance with §§ 300.304 through 300.311 before determining that the child is no longer a child with a disability.

(2) The evaluation described in paragraph (e)(1) of this section is not required before the termination of a child's eligibility under this part due to graduation from secondary school with a regular diploma, or due to exceeding the age eligibility for FAPE under State law.

(3) For a child whose eligibility terminates under circumstances described in paragraph (e)(2) of this section, a public agency must provide the child with a summary of the child's academic achievement and functional performance, which shall include recommendations on how to assist the child in meeting the child's postsecondary goals.

(Authority: 20 U.S.C. 1414(c))

§ 300.306 Determination of eligibility.

(a) General.

Upon completion of the administration of assessments and other evaluation measures—

(1) A group of qualified professionals and the parent of the child determines whether the child is a child with a disability, as defined in § 300.8, in accordance with paragraph (b) of this section and the educational needs of the child; and

(2) The public agency provides a copy of the evaluation report and the documentation of determination of eligibility at no cost to the parent.

(b) Special rule for eligibility determination. A child must not be determined to be a child with a disability under this part—

(1) If the determinant factor for that determination is—

(i) Lack of appropriate instruction in reading, including the essential components of reading instruction (as defined in section 1208(3) of the ESEA);

(ii) Lack of appropriate instruction in math; or

(iii) Limited English proficiency; and

(2) If the child does not otherwise meet the eligibility criteria under § 300.8(a).

(c) Procedures for determining eligibility and educational need. (1) In interpreting evaluation data for the purpose of determining if a child is a child with a disability under § 300.8, and the educational needs of the child, each public agency must—

(i) Draw upon information from a variety of sources, including aptitude and achievement tests, parent input, and teacher recommendations, as well as information about the child's physical condition, social or cultural background, and adaptive behavior; and

(ii) Ensure that information obtained from all of these sources is documented and carefully considered.

(2) If a determination is made that a child has a disability and needs special education and related services, an IEP must be developed for the child in accordance with §§ 300.320 through 300.324.

(Authority: 20 U.S.C. 1414(b)(4) and (5))

Additional Procedures for Identifying Children With Specific Learning Disabilities

§ 300.307 Specific learning disabilities.

(a) General. A State must adopt, consistent with § 300.309, criteria for determining whether a child has a specific learning disability as defined in § 300.8(c)(10). In addition, the criteria adopted by the State—

(1) Must not require the use of a severe discrepancy between intellectual ability and achievement for determining whether a child has a specific learning disability, as defined in § 300.8(c)(10);

(2) Must permit the use of a process based on the child's response to scientific, research-based intervention; and

(3) May permit the use of other alternative research-based procedures for determining whether a child has a specific learning disability, as defined in § 300.8(c)(10).

(b) Consistency with State criteria. A public agency must use the State criteria adopted pursuant to paragraph (a) of this section in determining whether a child has a specific learning disability.

(Authority: 20 U.S.C. 1221e–3; 1401(30); 1414(b)(6))

§ 300.308 Additional group members.

The determination of whether a child suspected of having a specific learning disability is a child with a disability as defined in § 300.8, must be made by the child's parents and a team of qualified professionals, which must include—

(a)(1) The child's regular teacher; or

(2) If the child does not have a regular

teacher, a regular classroom teacher qualified to teach a child of his or her age; or

(3) For a child of less than school age, an individual qualified by the SEA to teach a child of his or her age; and

(b) At least one person qualified to conduct individual diagnostic examinations of children, such as a school psychologist, speech-language pathologist, or remedial reading teacher.

(Authority: 20 U.S.C. 1221e–3; 1401(30); 1414(b)(6))

§ 300.309 Determining the existence of a specific learning disability.

(a) The group described in § 300.306 may determine that a child has a specific learning disability, as defined in § 300.8(c)(10), if—

(1) The child does not achieve adequately for the child's age or to meet State-approved grade-level standards in one or more of the following areas, when provided with learning experiences and instruction appropriate for the child's age or State-approved grade-level standards:

(i) Oral expression.

(ii) Listening comprehension.

(iii) Written expression.

(iv) Basic reading skill.

(v) Reading fluency skills.

(vi) Reading comprehension.

(vii) Mathematics calculation.

(viii) Mathematics problem solving.

(2)(i) The child does not make sufficient progress to meet age or State-approved grade-level standards in one or more of the areas identified in paragraph (a)(1) of this section when using a process based on the child's response to scientific, research-based intervention; or

(ii) The child exhibits a pattern of strengths and weaknesses in performance, achievement, or both, relative to age, State-approved grade-level standards, or intellectual development, that is determined by the group to be relevant to the identification of a specific learning disability, using appropriate assessments, consistent with §§ 300.304 and 300.305; and

(3) The group determines that its findings under paragraphs (a)(1) and (2) of this section are not primarily the result of—

(i) A visual, hearing, or motor disability;

(ii) Mental retardation;

(iii) Emotional disturbance;

(iv) Cultural factors;

(v) Environmental or economic disadvantage; or

(vi) Limited English proficiency.

(b) To ensure that underachievement in a child suspected of having a specific learning disability is not due to lack of appropriate instruction in reading or math, the group must consider, as part of the evaluation described in §§ 300.304 through 300.306—

(1) Data that demonstrate that prior to, or as

a part of, the referral process, the child was provided appropriate instruction in regular education settings, delivered by qualified personnel; and

(2) Data-based documentation of repeated assessments of achievement at reasonable intervals, reflecting formal assessment of student progress during instruction, which was provided to the child's parents.

(c) The public agency must promptly request parental consent to evaluate the child to determine if the child needs special education and related services, and must adhere to the timeframes described in §§ 300.301 and 300.303, unless extended by mutual written agreement of the child's parents and a group of qualified professionals, as described in § 300.306(a)(1)—

(1) If, prior to a referral, a child has not made adequate progress after an appropriate period of time when provided instruction, as described in paragraphs (b)(1) and (b)(2) of this section; and

(2) Whenever a child is referred for an evaluation.

(Authority: 20 U.S.C. 1221e–3; 1401(30); 1414(b)(6))

§ 300.310 Observation.

(a) The public agency must ensure that the child is observed in the child's learning environment (including the regular classroom setting) to document the child's academic performance and behavior in the areas of difficulty.

(b) The group described in § 300.306(a)(1), in determining whether a child has a specific learning disability, must decide to—

(1) Use information from an observation in routine classroom instruction and monitoring of the child's performance that was done before the child was referred for an evaluation; or

(2) Have at least one member of the group described in § 300.306(a)(1) conduct an observation of the child's academic performance in the regular classroom after the child has been referred for an evaluation and parental consent, consistent with § 300.300(a), is obtained.

(c) In the case of a child of less than school age or out of school, a group member must observe the child in an environment appropriate for a child of that age.

(Authority: 20 U.S.C. 1221e–3; 1401(30); 1414(b)(6))

§ 300.311 Specific documentation for the eligibility determination.

(a) For a child suspected of having a specific learning disability, the documentation of the determination of eligibility, as required in § 300.306(a)(2), must contain a statement of—

(1) Whether the child has a specific learning disability;

(2) The basis for making the determination, including an assurance that the determination has been made in accordance with § 300.306(c)(1);

(3) The relevant behavior, if any, noted during the observation of the child and the relationship of that behavior to the child's academic functioning;

(4) The educationally relevant medical findings, if any;

(5) Whether—

(i) The child does not achieve adequately for the child's age or to meet State-approved grade-level standards consistent with § 300.309(a)(1); and

(ii)(A) The child does not make sufficient progress to meet age or State-approved grade-level standards consistent with § 300.309(a)(2)(i); or

(B) The child exhibits a pattern of strengths and weaknesses in performance, achievement, or both, relative to age, State-approved grade-level standards or intellectual development consistent with § 300.309(a)(2)(ii);

(6) The determination of the group concerning the effects of a visual, hearing, or motor disability; mental retardation; emotional disturbance; cultural factors; environmental or economic disadvantage; or limited English proficiency on the child's achievement level; and

(7) If the child has participated in a process that assesses the child's response to scientific, research-based intervention—

(i) The instructional strategies used and the student-centered data collected; and

(ii) The documentation that the child's parents were notified about—

(A) The State's policies regarding the amount and nature of student performance data that would be collected and the general education services that would be provided;

(B) Strategies for increasing the child's rate of learning; and

(C) The parents' right to request an evaluation.

(b) Each group member must certify in writing whether the report reflects the member's conclusion. If it does not reflect the member's conclusion, the group member must submit a separate statement presenting the member's conclusions.

(Authority: 20 U.S.C. 1221e–3; 1401(30); 1414(b)(6))

Individualized Education Programs

§ 300.320 Definition of individualized education program.

(a) General. As used in this part, the term individualized education program or IEP means a written statement for each child with a disability that is developed, reviewed, and revised in a meeting in accordance with §§ 300.320 through 300.324, and that must include—

(1) A statement of the child's present levels of academic achievement and functional performance, including—

(i) How the child's disability affects the child's involvement and progress in the general education curriculum (i.e., the same curriculum as for nondisabled children); or

(ii) For preschool children, as appropriate, how the disability affects the child's participation in appropriate activities;

(2)(i) A statement of measurable annual goals, including academic and functional goals designed to—

(A) Meet the child's needs that result from the child's disability to enable the child to be involved in and make progress in the general education curriculum; and

(B) Meet each of the child's other educational needs that result from the child's disability;

(ii) For children with disabilities who take alternate assessments aligned to alternate achievement standards, a description of benchmarks or short-term objectives;

(3) A description of—

(i) How the child's progress toward meeting the annual goals described in paragraph (2) of this section will be measured; and

(ii) When periodic reports on the progress the child is making toward meeting the annual goals (such as through the use of quarterly or other periodic reports, concurrent with the issuance of report cards) will be provided;

(4) A statement of the special education and related services and supplementary aids and services, based on peer-reviewed research to the extent practicable, to be provided to the child, or on behalf of the child, and a statement of the program modifications or supports for school personnel that will be provided to enable the child—

(i) To advance appropriately toward attaining the annual goals;

(ii) To be involved in and make progress in the general education curriculum in accordance with paragraph (a)(1) of this section, and to participate in extracurricular and other nonacademic activities; and

(iii) To be educated and participate with other children with disabilities and nondisabled children in the activities described in this section;

(5) An explanation of the extent, if any, to which the child will not participate with nondisabled children in the regular class and in the activities described in paragraph (a)(4) of this section;

(6)(i) A statement of any individual appropriate accommodations that are necessary to measure the academic achievement and functional performance of the child on State and districtwide assessments consistent with section

612(a)(16) of the Act; and

(ii) If the IEP Team determines that the child must take an alternate assessment instead of a particular regular State or districtwide assessment of student achievement, a statement of why—

(A) The child cannot participate in the regular assessment; and

(B) The particular alternate assessment selected is appropriate for the child; and

(7) The projected date for the beginning of the services and modifications described in paragraph (a)(4) of this section, and the anticipated frequency, location, and duration of those services and modifications.

(b) Transition services. Beginning not later than the first IEP to be in effect when the child turns 16, or younger if determined appropriate by the IEP Team, and updated annually, thereafter, the IEP must include—

(1) Appropriate measurable postsecondary goals based upon age appropriate transition assessments related to training, education, employment, and, where appropriate, independent living skills; and

(2) The transition services (including courses of study) needed to assist the child in reaching those goals.

(c) Transfer of rights at age of majority. Beginning not later than one year before the child reaches the age of majority under State law, the IEP must include a statement that the child has been informed of the child's rights under Part B of the Act, if any, that will transfer to the child on reaching the age of majority under § 300.520.

(d) Construction. Nothing in this section shall be construed to require—

(1) That additional information be included in a child's IEP beyond what is explicitly required in section 614 of the Act; or

(2) The IEP Team to include information under one component of a child's IEP that is already contained under another component of the child's IEP.

(Authority: 20 U.S.C. 1414(d)(1)(A) and (d)(6))

§ 300.321 IEP Team.

(a) General. The public agency must ensure that the IEP Team for each child with a disability includes—

(1) The parents of the child;

(2) Not less than one regular education teacher of the child (if the child is, or may be, participating in the regular education environment);

(3) Not less than one special education teacher of the child, or where appropriate, not less then one special education provider of the child;

(4) A representative of the public agency who—

(i) Is qualified to provide, or supervise the provision of, specially designed instruction to meet the unique needs of children with disabilities;

(ii) Is knowledgeable about the general education curriculum; and

(iii) Is knowledgeable about the availability of resources of the public agency.

(5) An individual who can interpret the instructional implications of evaluation results, who may be a member of the team described in paragraphs (a)(2) through (a)(6) of this section;

(6) At the discretion of the parent or the agency, other individuals who have knowledge or special expertise regarding the child, including related services personnel as appropriate; and

(7) Whenever appropriate, the child with a disability.

(b) Transition services participants. (1) In accordance with paragraph (a)(7) of this section, the public agency must invite a child with a disability to attend the child's IEP Team meeting if a purpose of the meeting will be the consideration of the postsecondary goals for the child and the transition services needed to assist the child in reaching those goals under § 300.320(b).

(2) If the child does not attend the IEP Team meeting, the public agency must take other steps to ensure that the child's preferences and interests are considered.

(3) To the extent appropriate, with the consent of the parents or a child who has reached the age of majority, in implementing the requirements of paragraph (b)(1) of this section, the public agency must invite a representative of any participating agency that is likely to be responsible for providing or paying for transition services.

(c) Determination of knowledge and special expertise. The determination of the knowledge or special expertise of any individual described in paragraph (a)(6) of this section must be made by the party (parents or public agency) who invited the individual to be a member of the IEP Team.

(d) Designating a public agency representative. A public agency may designate a public agency member of the IEP Team to also serve as the agency representative, if the criteria in paragraph (a)(4) of this section are satisfied.

(e) IEP Team attendance. (1) A member of the IEP Team described in paragraphs (a)(2) through (a)(5) of this section is not required to attend an IEP Team meeting, in whole or in part, if the parent of a child with a disability and the public agency agree, in writing, that the attendance of the member is not necessary because the member's area of the curriculum or related services is not being modified or discussed in the meeting.

(2) A member of the IEP Team described in paragraph (e)(1) of this section may be excused

from attending an IEP Team meeting, in whole or in part, when the meeting involves a modification to or discussion of the member's area of the curriculum or related services, if—

(i) The parent, in writing, and the public agency consent to the excusal; and

(ii) The member submits, in writing to the parent and the IEP Team, input into the development of the IEP prior to the meeting.

(f) Initial IEP Team meeting for child under Part C. In the case of a child who was previously served under Part C of the Act, an invitation to the initial IEP Team meeting must, at the request of the parent, be sent to the Part C service coordinator or other representatives of the Part C system to assist with the smooth transition of services.

(Authority: 20 U.S.C. 1414(d)(1)(B)–(d)(1)(D))

§ 300.322 Parent participation.

(a) Public agency responsibility— general. Each public agency must take steps to ensure that one or both of the parents of a child with a disability are present at each IEP Team meeting or are afforded the opportunity to participate, including—

(1) Notifying parents of the meeting early enough to ensure that they will have an opportunity to attend; and

(2) Scheduling the meeting at a mutually agreed on time and place.

(b) Information provided to parents. (1) The notice required under paragraph (a)(1) of this section must—

(i) Indicate the purpose, time, and location of the meeting and who will be in attendance; and

(ii) Inform the parents of the provisions in § 300.321(a)(6) and (c) (relating to the participation of other individuals on the IEP Team who have knowledge or special expertise about the child), and § 300.321(f) (relating to the participation of the Part C service coordinator or other representatives of the Part C system at the initial IEP Team meeting for a child previously served under Part C of the Act).

(2) For a child with a disability beginning not later than the first IEP to be in effect when the child turns 16, or younger if determined appropriate by the IEP Team, the notice also must—

(i) Indicate—

(A) That a purpose of the meeting will be the consideration of the postsecondary goals and transition services for the child, in accordance with § 300.320(b); and

(B) That the agency will invite the student; and

(ii) Identify any other agency that will be invited to send a representative.

(c) Other methods to ensure parent participation. If neither parent can attend an IEP

Team meeting, the public agency must use other methods to ensure parent participation, including individual or conference telephone calls, consistent with § 300.328 (related to alternative means of meeting participation).

(d) Conducting an IEP Team meeting without a parent in attendance. A meeting may be conducted without a parent in attendance if the public agency is unable to convince the parents that they should attend. In this case, the public agency must keep a record of its attempts to arrange a mutually agreed on time and place, such as—

(1) Detailed records of telephone calls made or attempted and the results of those calls;

(2) Copies of correspondence sent to the parents and any responses received; and

(3) Detailed records of visits made to the parent's home or place of employment and the results of those visits.

(e) Use of interpreters or other action, as appropriate. The public agency must take whatever action is necessary to ensure that the parent understands the proceedings of the IEP Team meeting, including arranging for an interpreter for parents with deafness or whose native language is other than English.

(f) Parent copy of child's IEP. The public agency must give the parent a copy of the child's IEP at no cost to the parent.

(Authority: 20 U.S.C. 1414(d)(1)(B)(i))

§ 300.323 When IEPs must be in effect.

(a) General. At the beginning of each school year, each public agency must have in effect, for each child with a disability within its jurisdiction, an IEP, as defined in § 300.320.

(b) IEP or IFSP for children aged three through five. (1) In the case of a child with a disability aged three through five (or, at the discretion of the SEA, a two-year- old child with a disability who will turn age three during the school year), the IEP Team must consider an IFSP that contains the IFSP content (including the natural environments statement) described in section 636(d) of the Act and its implementing regulations (including an educational component that promotes school readiness and incorporates pre-literacy, language, and numeracy skills for children with IFSPs under this section who are at least three years of age), and that is developed in accordance with the IEP procedures under this part. The IFSP may serve as the IEP of the child, if using the IFSP as the IEP is—

(i) Consistent with State policy; and

(ii) Agreed to by the agency and the child's parents.

(2) In implementing the requirements of paragraph (b)(1) of this section, the public agency must—

(i) Provide to the child's parents a detailed explanation of the differences between an IFSP and an IEP; and

(ii) If the parents choose an IFSP, obtain written informed consent from the parents.

(c) Initial IEPs; provision of services. Each public agency must ensure that—

(1) A meeting to develop an IEP for a child is conducted within 30 days of a determination that the child needs special education and related services; and

(2) As soon as possible following development of the IEP, special education and related services are made available to the child in accordance with the child's IEP.

(d) Accessibility of child's IEP to teachers and others. Each public agency must ensure that—

(1) The child's IEP is accessible to each regular education teacher, special education teacher, related services provider, and any other service provider who is responsible for its implementation; and

(2) Each teacher and provider described in paragraph (d)(1) of this section is informed of—

(i) His or her specific responsibilities related to implementing the child's IEP; and

(ii) The specific accommodations, modifications, and supports that must be provided for the child in accordance with the IEP.

(e) IEPs for children who transfer public agencies in the same State. If a child with a disability (who had an IEP that was in effect in a previous public agency in the same State) transfers to a new public agency in the same State, and enrolls in a new school within the same school year, the new public agency (in consultation with the parents) must provide FAPE to the child (including services comparable to those described in the child's IEP from the previous public agency), until the new public agency either—

(1) Adopts the child's IEP from the previous public agency; or

(2) Develops, adopts, and implements a new IEP that meets the applicable requirements in §§ 300.320 through 300.324.

(f) IEPs for children who transfer from another State. If a child with a disability (who had an IEP that was in effect in a previous public agency in another State) transfers to a public agency in a new State, and enrolls in a new school within the same school year, the new public agency (in consultation with the parents) must provide the child with FAPE (including services comparable to those described in the child's IEP from the previous public agency), until the new public agency—

(1) Conducts an evaluation pursuant to §§ 300.304 through 300.306 (if determined to be necessary by the new public agency); and

(2) Develops, adopts, and implements a new IEP, if appropriate, that meets the applicable requirements in §§ 300.320 through 300.324.

(g) Transmittal of records. To facilitate the transition for a child described in paragraphs (e) and (f) of this section—

(1) The new public agency in which the child enrolls must take reasonable steps to promptly obtain the child's records, including the IEP and supporting documents and any other records relating to the provision of special education or related services to the child, from the previous public agency in which the child was enrolled, pursuant to 34 CFR 99.31(a)(2); and

(2) The previous public agency in which the child was enrolled must take reasonable steps to promptly respond to the request from the new public agency.

(Authority: 20 U.S.C. 1414(d)(2)(A)–(C))

Development of IEP

§ 300.324 Development, review, and revision of IEP.

(a) Development of IEP—(1) General. In developing each child's IEP, the IEP Team must consider—

(i) The strengths of the child;

(ii) The concerns of the parents for enhancing the education of their child;

(iii) The results of the initial or most recent evaluation of the child; and

(iv) The academic, developmental, and functional needs of the child.

(2) Consideration of special factors. The IEP Team must—

(i) In the case of a child whose behavior impedes the child's learning or that of others, consider the use of positive behavioral interventions and supports, and other strategies, to address that behavior;

(ii) In the case of a child with limited English proficiency, consider the language needs of the child as those needs relate to the child's IEP;

(iii) In the case of a child who is blind or visually impaired, provide for instruction in Braille and the use of Braille unless the IEP Team determines, after an evaluation of the child's reading and writing skills, needs, and appropriate reading and writing media (including an evaluation of the child's future needs for instruction in Braille or the use of Braille), that instruction in Braille or the use of Braille is not appropriate for the child;

(iv) Consider the communication needs of the child, and in the case of a child who is deaf or hard of hearing, consider the child's language and communication needs, opportunities for direct communications with peers and professional personnel in the child's language and communication mode, academic level, and full range of needs, including opportunities for direct instruction in the child's language and communication mode; and

(v) Consider whether the child needs assistive technology devices and services.

(3) Requirement with respect to regular education teacher. A regular education teacher of a child with a disability, as a member of the IEP Team, must, to the extent appropriate, participate in the development of the IEP of the child, including the determination of—

(i) Appropriate positive behavioral interventions and supports and other strategies for the child; and

(ii) Supplementary aids and services, program modifications, and support for school personnel consistent with § 300.320(a)(4).

(4) Agreement. (i) In making changes to a child's IEP after the annual IEP Team meeting for a school year, the parent of a child with a disability and the public agency may agree not to convene an IEP Team meeting for the purposes of making those changes, and instead may develop a written document to amend or modify the child's current IEP.

(ii) If changes are made to the child's IEP in accordance with paragraph (a)(4)(i) of this section, the public agency must ensure that the child's IEP Team is informed of those changes.

(5) Consolidation of IEP Team meetings. To the extent possible, the public agency must encourage the consolidation of reevaluation meetings for the child and other IEP Team meetings for the child.

(6) Amendments. Changes to the IEP may be made either by the entire IEP Team at an IEP Team meeting, or as provided in paragraph (a)(4) of this section, by amending the IEP rather than by redrafting the entire IEP. Upon request, a parent must be provided with a revised copy of the IEP with the amendments incorporated.

(b) Review and revision of IEPs—(1) General. Each public agency must ensure that, subject to paragraphs (b)(2) and (b)(3) of this section, the IEP Team—

(i) Reviews the child's IEP periodically, but not less than annually, to determine whether the annual goals for the child are being achieved; and

(ii) Revises the IEP, as appropriate, to address—

(A) Any lack of expected progress toward the annual goals described in § 300.320(a)(2), and in the general education curriculum, if appropriate;

(B) The results of any reevaluation conducted under § 300.303;

(C) Information about the child provided to, or by, the parents, as described under § 300.305(a)(2);

(D) The child's anticipated needs; or

(E) Other matters.

(2) Consideration of special factors. In conducting a review of the child's IEP, the IEP Team must consider the special factors described in paragraph (a)(2) of this section.

(3) Requirement with respect to regular education teacher. A regular education teacher of the child, as a member of the IEP Team, must, consistent with paragraph (a)(3) of this section, participate in the review and revision of the IEP of the child.

(c) Failure to meet transition objectives— (1) Participating agency failure. If a participating agency, other than the public agency, fails to provide the transition services described in the IEP in accordance with § 300.320(b), the public agency must reconvene the IEP Team to identify alternative strategies to meet the transition objectives for the child set out in the IEP.

(2) Construction. Nothing in this part relieves any participating agency, including a State vocational rehabilitation agency, of the responsibility to provide or pay for any transition service that the agency would otherwise provide to children with disabilities who meet the eligibility criteria of that agency.

(d) Children with disabilities in adult prisons—(1) Requirements that do not apply. The following requirements do not apply to children with disabilities who are convicted as adults under State law and incarcerated in adult prisons:

(i) The requirements contained in section 612(a)(16) of the Act and § 300.320(a)(6) (relating to participation of children with disabilities in general assessments).

(ii) The requirements in § 300.320(b) (relating to transition planning and transition services) do not apply with respect to the children whose eligibility under Part B of the Act will end, because of their age, before they will be eligible to be released from prison based on consideration of their sentence and eligibility for early release.

(2) Modifications of IEP or placement.

(i) Subject to paragraph (d)(2)(ii) of this section, the IEP Team of a child with a disability who is convicted as an adult under State law and incarcerated in an adult prison may modify the child's IEP or placement if the State has demonstrated a bona fide security or compelling penological interest that cannot otherwise be accommodated.

(ii) The requirements of §§ 300.320 (relating to IEPs), and 300.112 (relating to LRE), do not apply with respect to the modifications described in paragraph (d)(2)(i) of this section.

(Authority: 20 U.S.C. 1412(a)(1), 1412(a)(12)(A)(i), 1414(d)(3), (4)(B), and (7); and 1414(e))

§ 300.325 Private school placements by public agencies.

(a) Developing IEPs. (1) Before a public agency places a child with a disability in, or refers a child to, a private school or facility, the agency must initiate and conduct a meeting to develop an IEP for the child in accordance with §§ 300.320 and 300.324.

(2) The agency must ensure that a representative of the private school or facility attends the meeting. If the representative cannot attend, the agency must use other methods to ensure participation by the private school or facility, including individual or conference telephone calls.

(b) Reviewing and revising IEPs.

(1) After a child with a disability enters a private school or facility, any meetings to review and revise the child's IEP may be initiated and conducted by the private school or facility at the discretion of the public agency.

(2) If the private school or facility initiates and conducts these meetings, the public agency must ensure that the parents and an agency representative—

(i) Are involved in any decision about the child's IEP; and

(ii) Agree to any proposed changes in the IEP before those changes are implemented.

(c) Responsibility. Even if a private school or facility implements a child's IEP, responsibility for compliance with this part remains with the public agency and the SEA.

(Authority: 20 U.S.C. 1412(a)(10)(B))

§ 300.326 [Reserved]

§ 300.327 Educational placements.

Consistent with § 300.501(c), each public agency must ensure that the parents of each child with a disability are members of any group that makes decisions on the educational placement of their child.

(Authority: 20 U.S.C. 1414(e))

§ 300.328 Alternative means of meeting participation.

When conducting IEP Team meetings and placement meetings pursuant to this subpart, and subpart E of this part, and carrying out administrative matters under section 615 of the Act (such as scheduling, exchange of witness lists, and status conferences), the parent of a child with a disability and a public agency may agree to use alternative means of meeting participation, such as video conferences and conference calls.

(Authority: 20 U.S.C. 1414(f))

Subpart E—Procedural Safeguards Due Process Procedures for Parents and Children

§ 300.500 Responsibility of SEA and other public agencies.

Each SEA must ensure that each public agency establishes, maintains, and implements procedural safeguards that meet the requirements of §§ 300.500 through 300.536.

(Authority: 20 U.S.C. 1415(a))

§ 300.501 Opportunity to examine records; parent participation in meetings.

(a) Opportunity to examine records. The parents of a child with a disability must be afforded, in accordance with the procedures of §§ 300.613 through 300.621, an opportunity to inspect and review all education records with respect to—

(1) The identification, evaluation, and educational placement of the child; and

(2) The provision of FAPE to the child.

(b) Parent participation in meetings.

(1) The parents of a child with a disability must be afforded an opportunity to participate in meetings with respect to—

(i) The identification, evaluation, and educational placement of the child; and

(ii) The provision of FAPE to the child.

(2) Each public agency must provide notice consistent with § 300.322(a)(1) and (b)(1) to ensure that parents of children with disabilities have the opportunity to participate in meetings described in paragraph (b)(1) of this section.

(3) A meeting does not include informal or unscheduled conversations involving public agency personnel and conversations on issues such as teaching methodology, lesson plans, or coordination of service provision. A meeting also does not include preparatory activities that public agency personnel engage in to develop a proposal or response to a parent proposal that will be discussed at a later meeting.

(c) Parent involvement in placement decisions. (1) Each public agency must ensure that a parent of each child with a disability is a member of any group that makes decisions on the educational placement of the parent's child.

(2) In implementing the requirements of paragraph (c)(1) of this section, the public agency must use procedures consistent with the procedures described in § 300.322(a) through (b)(1).

(3) If neither parent can participate in a meeting in which a decision is to be made relating to the educational placement of their child, the public agency must use other methods to ensure their participation, including individual or conference telephone calls, or video conferencing.

(4) A placement decision may be made by a group without the involvement of a parent, if the public agency is unable to obtain the parent's participation in the decision. In this case, the public agency must have a record of its attempt to ensure their involvement.

(Authority: 20 U.S.C. 1414(e), 1415(b)(1))

§ 300.502 Independent educational evaluation.

(a) General. (1) The parents of a child with a disability have the right under this part to obtain an independent educational evaluation of the child, subject to paragraphs (b) through (e) of this section.

(2) Each public agency must provide to parents, upon request for an independent educational evaluation, information about where an independent educational evaluation may be obtained, and the agency criteria applicable for independent educational evaluations as set forth in paragraph (e) of this section.

(3) For the purposes of this subpart—

(i) Independent educational evaluation means an evaluation conducted by a qualified examiner who is not employed by the public agency responsible for the education of the child in question; and

(ii) Public expense means that the public agency either pays for the full cost of the evaluation or ensures that the evaluation is otherwise provided at no cost to the parent, consistent with § 300.103.

(b) Parent right to evaluation at public expense.

(1) A parent has the right to an independent educational evaluation at public expense if the parent disagrees with an evaluation obtained by the public agency, subject to the conditions in paragraphs (b)(2) through (4) of this section.

(2) If a parent requests an independent educational evaluation at public expense, the public agency must, without unnecessary delay, either—

(i) File a due process complaint to request a hearing to show that its evaluation is appropriate; or

(ii) Ensure that an independent educational evaluation is provided at public expense, unless the agency demonstrates in a hearing pursuant to §§ 300.507 through 300.513 that the evaluation obtained by the parent did not meet agency criteria.

(3) If the public agency files a due process complaint notice to request a hearing and the final decision is that the agency's evaluation is appropriate, the parent still has the right to an independent educational evaluation, but not at public expense.

(4) If a parent requests an independent educational evaluation, the public agency may ask for the parent's reason why he or she objects to the public evaluation. However, the public agency may not require the parent to provide an explanation and may not unreasonably delay either providing the independent educational evaluation at public expense or filing a due process complaint to request a due process hearing to defend the public evaluation.

(5) A parent is entitled to only one independent educational evaluation at public expense each time the public agency conducts an evaluation with which the parent disagrees.

(c) Parent-initiated evaluations. If the parent obtains an independent educational evaluation at public expense or shares with the

public agency an evaluation obtained at private expense, the results of the evaluation—

(1) Must be considered by the public agency, if it meets agency criteria, in any decision made with respect to the provision of FAPE to the child; and

(2) May be presented by any party as evidence at a hearing on a due process complaint under subpart E of this part regarding that child.

(d) Requests for evaluations by hearing officers. If a hearing officer requests an independent educational evaluation as part of a hearing on a due process complaint, the cost of the evaluation must be at public expense.

(e) Agency criteria. (1) If an independent educational evaluation is at public expense, the criteria under which the evaluation is obtained, including the location of the evaluation and the qualifications of the examiner, must be the same as the criteria that the public agency uses when it initiates an evaluation, to the extent those criteria are consistent with the parent's right to an independent educational evaluation.

(2) Except for the criteria described in paragraph (e)(1) of this section, a public agency may not impose conditions or timelines related to obtaining an independent educational evaluation at public expense.

(Authority: 20 U.S.C. 1415(b)(1) and (d)(2)(A))

§ 300.503 Prior notice by the public agency; content of notice.

(a) Notice. Written notice that meets the requirements of paragraph (b) of this section must be given to the parents of a child with a disability a reasonable time before the public agency—

(1) Proposes to initiate or change the identification, evaluation, or educational placement of the child or the provision of FAPE to the child; or

(2) Refuses to initiate or change the identification, evaluation, or educational placement of the child or the provision of FAPE to the child.

(b) Content of notice. The notice required under paragraph (a) of this section must include—

(1) A description of the action proposed or refused by the agency;

(2) An explanation of why the agency proposes or refuses to take the action;

(3) A description of each evaluation procedure, assessment, record, or report the agency used as a basis for the proposed or refused action;

(4) A statement that the parents of a child with a disability have protection under the procedural safeguards of this part and, if this notice is not an initial referral for evaluation, the means by which a copy of a description of the

procedural safeguards can be obtained;

(5) Sources for parents to contact to obtain assistance in understanding the provisions of this part;

(6) A description of other options that the IEP Team considered and the reasons why those options were rejected; and

(7) A description of other factors that are relevant to the agency's proposal or refusal.

(c) Notice in understandable language. (1) The notice required under paragraph (a) of this section must be—

(i) Written in language understandable to the general public; and

(ii) Provided in the native language of the parent or other mode of communication used by the parent, unless it is clearly not feasible to do so.

(2) If the native language or other mode of communication of the parent is not a written language, the public agency must take steps to ensure—

(i) That the notice is translated orally or by other means to the parent in his or her native language or other mode of communication;

(ii) That the parent understands the content of the notice; and

(iii) That there is written evidence that the requirements in paragraphs (c)(2)(i) and (ii) of this section have been met.

(Authority: 20 U.S.C. 1415(b)(3) and (4), 1415(c)(1), 1414(b)(1))

§ 300.504 Procedural safeguards notice.

(a) General. A copy of the procedural safeguards available to the parents of a child with a disability must be given to the parents only one time a school year, except that a copy also must be given to the parents—

(1) Upon initial referral or parent request for evaluation;

(2) Upon receipt of the first State complaint under §§ 300.151 through 300.153 and upon receipt of the first due process complaint under § 300.507 in a school year;

(3) In accordance with the discipline procedures in § 300.530(h); and

(4) Upon request by a parent.

(b) Internet Web site. A public agency may place a current copy of the procedural safeguards notice on its Internet Web site if a Web site exists.

(c) Contents. The procedural safeguards notice must include a full explanation of all of the procedural safeguards available under § 300.148, §§ 300.151 through 300.153, § 300.300, §§ 300.502 through 300.503, §§ 300.505 through 300.518, § 300.520, §§ 300.530 through 300.536 and §§ 300.610 through 300.625 relating to—

(1) Independent educational evaluations;

(2) Prior written notice;

(3) Parental consent;

(4) Access to education records;

(5) Opportunity to present and resolve complaints through the due process complaint and State complaint procedures, including—

(i) The time period in which to file a complaint;

(ii) The opportunity for the agency to resolve the complaint; and

(iii) The difference between the due process complaint and the State complaint procedures, including the jurisdiction of each procedure, what issues may be raised, filing and decisional timelines, and relevant procedures;

(6) The availability of mediation;

(7) The child's placement during the pendency of any due process complaint;

(8) Procedures for students who are subject to placement in an interim alternative educational setting;

(9) Requirements for unilateral placement by parents of children in private schools at public expense;

(10) Hearings on due process complaints, including requirements for disclosure of evaluation results and recommendations;

(11) State-level appeals (if applicable in the State);

(12) Civil actions, including the time period in which to file those actions; and

(13) Attorneys' fees.

(d) Notice in understandable language. The notice required under paragraph (a) of this section must meet the requirements of § 300.503(c).

(Approved by the Office of Management and Budget under control number 1820–0600)

(Authority: 20 U.S.C. 1415(d))

§ 300.505 Electronic mail.

A parent of a child with a disability may elect to receive notices required by §§ 300.503, 300.504, and 300.508 by an electronic mail communication, if the public agency makes that option available.

(Authority: 20 U.S.C. 1415(n))

§ 300.506 Mediation.

(a) General. Each public agency must ensure that procedures are established and implemented to allow parties to disputes involving any matter under this part, including matters arising prior to the filing of a due process complaint, to resolve disputes through a mediation process.

(b) Requirements. The procedures must meet the following requirements:

(1) The procedures must ensure that the mediation process—

(i) Is voluntary on the part of the parties;

(ii) Is not used to deny or delay a parent's right to a hearing on the parent's due process complaint, or to deny any other rights afforded under Part B of the Act; and

(iii) Is conducted by a qualified and impartial mediator who is trained in effective mediation techniques.

(2) A public agency may establish procedures to offer to parents and schools that choose not to use the mediation process, an opportunity to meet, at a time and location convenient to the parents, with a disinterested party—

(i) Who is under contract with an appropriate alternative dispute resolution entity, or a parent training and information center or community parent resource center in the State established under section 671 or 672 of the Act; and

(ii) Who would explain the benefits of, and encourage the use of, the mediation process to the parents.

(3)(i) The State must maintain a list of individuals who are qualified mediators and knowledgeable in laws and regulations relating to the provision of special education and related services.

(ii) The SEA must select mediators on a random, rotational, or other impartial basis.

(4) The State must bear the cost of the mediation process, including the costs of meetings described in paragraph (b)(2) of this section.

(5) Each session in the mediation process must be scheduled in a timely manner and must be held in a location that is convenient to the parties to the dispute.

(6) If the parties resolve a dispute through the mediation process, the parties must execute a legally binding agreement that sets forth that resolution and that—

(i) States that all discussions that occurred during the mediation process will remain confidential and may not be used as evidence in any subsequent due process hearing or civil proceeding; and

(ii) Is signed by both the parent and a representative of the agency who has the authority to bind such agency.

(7) A written, signed mediation agreement under this paragraph is enforceable in any State court of competent jurisdiction or in a district court of the United States. Discussions that occur during the mediation process must be confidential and may not be used as evidence in any subsequent due process hearing or civil proceeding of any Federal court or State court of a State receiving assistance under this part.

(c) Impartiality of mediator. (1) An individual who serves as a mediator under this part—

(i) May not be an employee of the SEA or the LEA that is involved in the education or care of the child; and

(ii) Must not have a personal or professional interest that conflicts with the

person's objectivity.

(2) A person who otherwise qualifies as a mediator is not an employee of an LEA or State agency described under § 300.228 solely because he or she is paid by the agency to serve as a mediator.

(Approved by the Office of Management and Budget under control number 1820–0600)

(Authority: 20 U.S.C. 1415(e))

§ 300.507 Filing a due process complaint.

(a) General.

(1) A parent or a public agency may file a due process complaint on any of the matters described in § 300.503(a)(1) and (2) (relating to the identification, evaluation or educational placement of a child with a disability, or the provision of FAPE to the child).

(2) The due process complaint must allege a violation that occurred not more than two years before the date the parent or public agency knew or should have known about the alleged action that forms the basis of the due process complaint, or, if the State has an explicit time limitation for filing a due process complaint under this part, in the time allowed by that State law, except that the exceptions to the timeline described in § 300.511(f) apply to the timeline in this section.

(b) Information for parents. The public agency must inform the parent of any free or low-cost legal and other relevant services available in the area if—

(1) The parent requests the information; or

(2) The parent or the agency files a due process complaint under this section.

(Approved by the Office of Management and Budget under control number 1820–0600)

(Authority: 20 U.S.C. 1415(b)(6))

§ 300.508 Due process complaint.

(a) General. (1) The public agency must have procedures that require either party, or the attorney representing a party, to provide to the other party a due process complaint (which must remain confidential).

(2) The party filing a due process complaint must forward a copy of the due process complaint to the SEA.

(b) Content of complaint. The due process complaint required in paragraph (a)(1) of this section must include—

(1) The name of the child;

(2) The address of the residence of the child;

(3) The name of the school the child is attending;

(4) In the case of a homeless child or youth (within the meaning of section 725(2) of the McKinney-Vento Homeless Assistance Act (42 U.S.C. 11434a(2)), available contact information for the child, and the name of the school the child is attending;

(5) A description of the nature of the problem of the child relating to the proposed or refused initiation or change, including facts relating to the problem; and

(6) A proposed resolution of the problem to the extent known and available to the party at the time.

(c) Notice required before a hearing on a due process complaint. A party may not have a hearing on a due process complaint until the party, or the attorney representing the party, files a due process complaint that meets the requirements of paragraph (b) of this section.

(d) Sufficiency of complaint. (1) The due process complaint required by this section must be deemed sufficient unless the party receiving the due process complaint notifies the hearing officer and the other party in writing, within 15 days of receipt of the due process complaint, that the receiving party believes the due process complaint does not meet the requirements in paragraph (b) of this section.

(2) Within five days of receipt of notification under paragraph (d)(1) of this section, the hearing officer must make a determination on the face of the due process complaint of whether the due process complaint meets the requirements of paragraph (b) of this section, and must immediately notify the parties in writing of that determination.

(3) A party may amend its due process complaint only if—

(i) The other party consents in writing to the amendment and is given the opportunity to resolve the due process complaint through a meeting held pursuant to § 300.510; or

(ii) The hearing officer grants permission, except that the hearing officer may only grant permission to amend at any time not later than five days before the due process hearing begins.

(4) If a party files an amended due process complaint, the timelines for the resolution meeting in § 300.510(a) and the time period to resolve in § 300.510(b) begin again with the filing of the amended due process complaint.

(e) LEA response to a due process complaint. (1) If the LEA has not sent a prior written notice under § 300.503 to the parent regarding the subject matter contained in the parent's due process complaint, the LEA must, within 10 days of receiving the due process complaint, send to the parent a response that includes—

(i) An explanation of why the agency proposed or refused to take the action raised in the due process complaint;

(ii) A description of other options that the IEP Team considered and the reasons why those options were rejected;

(iii) A description of each evaluation procedure, assessment, record, or report the agency used as the basis for the proposed or refused action; and

(iv) A description of the other factors that are relevant to the agency's proposed or refused action.

(2) A response by an LEA under paragraph (e)(1) of this section shall not be construed to preclude the LEA from asserting that the parent's due process complaint was insufficient, where appropriate.

(f) Other party response to a due process complaint. Except as provided in paragraph (e) of this section, the party receiving a due process complaint must, within 10 days of receiving the due process complaint, send to the other party a response that specifically addresses the issues raised in the due process complaint.

(Authority: 20   U.S.C.   1415(b)(7), 1415(c)(2))

§ 300.509 Model forms.

(a) Each SEA must develop model forms to assist parents and public agencies in filing a due process complaint in accordance with §§ 300.507(a) and 300.508(a) through (c) and to assist parents and other parties in filing a State complaint under §§ 300.151 through 300.153. However, the SEA or LEA may not require the use of the model forms.

(b) Parents, public agencies, and other parties may use the appropriate model form described in paragraph (a) of this section, or another form or other document, so long as the form or document that is used meets, as appropriate, the content requirements in § 300.508(b) for filing a due process complaint, or the requirements in § 300.153(b) for filing a State complaint.

(Authority: 20 U.S.C. 1415(b)(8))

§ 300.510 Resolution process.

(a) Resolution meeting. (1) Within 15 days of receiving notice of the parent's due process complaint, and prior to the initiation of a due process hearing under § 300.511, the LEA must convene a meeting with the parent and the relevant member or members of the IEP Team who have specific knowledge of the facts identified in the due process complaint that—

(i) Includes a representative of the public agency who has decision-making authority on behalf of that agency; and

(ii) May not include an attorney of the LEA unless the parent is accompanied by an attorney.

(2) The purpose of the meeting is for the parent of the child to discuss the due process complaint, and the facts that form the basis of the due process complaint, so that the LEA has the opportunity to resolve the dispute that is the basis for the due process complaint.

(3) The meeting described in paragraph (a)(1) and (2) of this section need not be held if—

(i) The parent and the LEA agree in writing

to waive the meeting; or

(ii) The parent and the LEA agree to use the mediation process described in § 300.506.

(4) The parent and the LEA determine the relevant members of the IEP Team to attend the meeting.

(b) Resolution period. (1) If the LEA has not resolved the due process complaint to the satisfaction of the parent within 30 days of the receipt of the due process complaint, the due process hearing may occur.

(2) Except as provided in paragraph (c) of this section, the timeline for issuing a final decision under § 300.515 begins at the expiration of this 30-day period.

(3) Except where the parties have jointly agreed to waive the resolution process or to use mediation, notwithstanding paragraphs (b)(1) and (2) of this section, the failure of the parent filing a due process complaint to participate in the resolution meeting will delay the timelines for the resolution process and due process hearing until the meeting is held.

(4) If the LEA is unable to obtain the participation of the parent in the resolution meeting after reasonable efforts have been made (and documented using the procedures in § 300.322(d)), the LEA may, at the conclusion of the 30-day period, request that a hearing officer dismiss the parent's due process complaint.

(5) If the LEA fails to hold the resolution meeting specified in paragraph (a) of this section within 15 days of receiving notice of a parent's due process complaint or fails to participate in the resolution meeting, the parent may seek the intervention of a hearing officer to begin the due process hearing timeline.

(c) Adjustments to 30-day resolution period. The 45-day timeline for the due process hearing in § 300.515(a) starts the day after one of the following events:

(1) Both parties agree in writing to waive the resolution meeting;

(2) After either the mediation or resolution meeting starts but before the end of the 30-day period, the parties agree in writing that no agreement is possible;

(3) If both parties agree in writing to continue the mediation at the end of the 30-day resolution period, but later, the parent or public agency withdraws from the mediation process.

(d) Written settlement agreement. If a resolution to the dispute is reached at the meeting described in paragraphs (a)(1) and (2) of this section, the parties must execute a legally binding agreement that is—

(1) Signed by both the parent and a representative of the agency who has the authority to bind the agency; and

(2) Enforceable in any State court of competent jurisdiction or in a district court of the United States, or, by the SEA, if the State has

other mechanisms or procedures that permit parties to seek enforcement of resolution agreements, pursuant to § 300.537.

(e) Agreement review period. If the parties execute an agreement pursuant to paragraph (c) of this section, a party may void the agreement within 3 business days of the agreement's execution.

(Authority: 20 U.S.C. 1415(f)(1)(B))

§ 300.511 Impartial due process hearing.

(a) General. Whenever a due process complaint is received under § 300.507 or § 300.532, the parents or the LEA involved in the dispute must have an opportunity for an impartial due process hearing, consistent with the procedures in §§ 300.507, 300.508, and 300.510.

(b) Agency responsible for conducting the due process hearing. The hearing described in paragraph (a) of this section must be conducted by the SEA or the public agency directly responsible for the education of the child, as determined under State statute, State regulation, or a written policy of the SEA.

(c) Impartial hearing officer. (1) At a minimum, a hearing officer—

(i) Must not be—

(A) An employee of the SEA or the LEA that is involved in the education or care of the child; or

(B) A person having a personal or professional interest that conflicts with the person's objectivity in the hearing;

(ii) Must possess knowledge of, and the ability to understand, the provisions of the Act, Federal and State regulations pertaining to the Act, and legal interpretations of the Act by Federal and State courts;

(iii) Must possess the knowledge and ability to conduct hearings in accordance with appropriate, standard legal practice; and

(iv) Must possess the knowledge and ability to render and write decisions in accordance with appropriate, standard legal practice.

(2) A person who otherwise qualifies to conduct a hearing under paragraph (c)(1) of this section is not an employee of the agency solely because he or she is paid by the agency to serve as a hearing officer.

(3) Each public agency must keep a list of the persons who serve as hearing officers. The list must include a statement of the qualifications of each of those persons.

(d) Subject matter of due process hearings. The party requesting the due process hearing may not raise issues at the due process hearing that were not raised in the due process complaint filed under § 300.508(b), unless the other party agrees otherwise.

(e) Timeline for requesting a hearing. A parent or agency must request an impartial hearing on their due process complaint within

not result in a failure to provide the child with FAPE.

(3) A public agency may not use a parent's refusal to consent to one service or activity under paragraphs (a) or (d)(2) of this section to deny the parent or child any other service, benefit, or activity of the public agency, except as required by this part.

(4)(i) If a parent of a child who is home schooled or placed in a private school by the parents at their own expense does not provide consent for the initial evaluation or the reevaluation, or the parent fails to respond to a request to provide consent, the public agency may not use the consent override procedures (described in paragraphs (a)(3) and (c)(1) of this section); and

(ii) The public agency is not required to consider the child as eligible for services under §§ 300.132 through 300.144.

(5) To meet the reasonable efforts requirement in paragraphs (a)(1)(iii), (a)(2)(i), (b)(2), and (c)(2)(i) of this section, the public agency must document its attempts to obtain parental consent using the procedures in § 300.322(d).

(Authority: 20 U.S.C. 1414(a)(1)(D) and 1414(c))

Evaluations and Reevaluations

§ 300.301 Initial evaluations.

(a) General. Each public agency must conduct a full and individual initial evaluation, in accordance with §§ 300.305 and 300.306, before the initial provision of special education and related services to a child with a disability under this part.

(b) Request for initial evaluation. Consistent with the consent requirements in § 300.300, either a parent of a child or a public agency may initiate a request for an initial evaluation to determine if the child is a child with a disability.

(c) Procedures for initial evaluation. The initial evaluation—

(1)(i) Must be conducted within 60 days of receiving parental consent for the evaluation; or

(ii) If the State establishes a timeframe within which the evaluation must be conducted, within that timeframe; and

(2) Must consist of procedures—

(i) To determine if the child is a child with a disability under § 300.8; and

(ii) To determine the educational needs of the child.

(d) Exception. The timeframe described in paragraph (c)(1) of this section does not apply to a public agency if—

(1) The parent of a child repeatedly fails or refuses to produce the child for the evaluation; or

(2) A child enrolls in a school of another public agency after the relevant timeframe in paragraph (c)(1) of this section has begun, and prior to a determination by the child's previous public agency as to whether the child is a child with a disability under § 300.8.

(e) The exception in paragraph (d)(2) of this section applies only if the subsequent public agency is making sufficient progress to ensure a prompt completion of the evaluation, and the parent and subsequent public agency agree to a specific time when the evaluation will be completed.

(Authority: 20 U.S.C. 1414(a))

§ 300.302 Screening for instructional purposes is not evaluation.

The screening of a student by a teacher or specialist to determine appropriate instructional strategies for curriculum implementation shall not be considered to be an evaluation for eligibility for special education and related services.

(Authority: 20 U.S.C. 1414(a)(1)(E))

§ 300.303 Reevaluations.

(a) General. A public agency must ensure that a reevaluation of each child with a disability is conducted in accordance with §§ 300.304 through 300.311—

(1) If the public agency determines that the educational or related services needs, including improved academic achievement and functional performance, of the child warrant a reevaluation; or

(2) If the child's parent or teacher requests a reevaluation.

(b) Limitation. A reevaluation conducted under paragraph (a) of this section—

(1) May occur not more than once a year, unless the parent and the public agency agree otherwise; and

(2) Must occur at least once every 3 years, unless the parent and the public agency agree that a reevaluation is unnecessary.

(Authority: 20 U.S.C. 1414(a)(2))

§ 300.304 Evaluation procedures.

(a) Notice. The public agency must provide notice to the parents of a child with a disability, in accordance with § 300.503, that describes any evaluation procedures the agency proposes to conduct.

(b) Conduct of evaluation. In conducting the evaluation, the public agency must—

(1) Use a variety of assessment tools and strategies to gather relevant functional, developmental, and academic information about the child, including information provided by the parent, that may assist in determining—

(i) Whether the child is a child with a disability under § 300.8; and

(ii) The content of the child's IEP, including information related to enabling the child to be involved in and progress in the general education

two years of the date the parent or agency knew or should have known about the alleged action that forms the basis of the due process complaint, or if the State has an explicit time limitation for requesting such a due process hearing under this part, in the time allowed by that State law.

(f) Exceptions to the timeline. The timeline described in paragraph (e) of this section does not apply to a parent if the parent was prevented from filing a due process complaint due to—

(1) Specific misrepresentations by the LEA that it had resolved the problem forming the basis of the due process complaint; or

(2) The LEA's withholding of information from the parent that was required under this part to be provided to the parent.

(Approved by the Office of Management and Budget under control number 1820–0600)

(Authority: 20 U.S.C. 1415(f)(1)(A), 1415(f)(3)(A)–(D))

§ 300.512 Hearing rights.

(a) General. Any party to a hearing conducted pursuant to §§ 300.507 through 300.513 or §§ 300.530 through 300.534, or an appeal conducted pursuant to § 300.514, has the right to—

(1) Be accompanied and advised by counsel and by individuals with special knowledge or training with respect to the problems of children with disabilities, except that whether parties have the right to be represented by non-attorneys at due process hearings is determined under State law;

(2) Present evidence and confront, cross-examine, and compel the attendance of witnesses;

(3) Prohibit the introduction of any evidence at the hearing that has not been disclosed to that party at least five business days before the hearing;

(4) Obtain a written, or, at the option of the parents, electronic, verbatim record of the hearing; and

(5) Obtain written, or, at the option of the parents, electronic findings of fact and decisions.

(b) Additional disclosure of information. (1) At least five business days prior to a hearing conducted pursuant to § 300.511(a), each party must disclose to all other parties all evaluations completed by that date and recommendations based on the offering party's evaluations that the party intends to use at the hearing.

(2) A hearing officer may bar any party that fails to comply with paragraph (b)(1) of this section from introducing the relevant evaluation or recommendation at the hearing without the consent of the other party.

(c) Parental rights at hearings. Parents involved in hearings must be given the right to—

(1) Have the child who is the subject of the hearing present;

(2) Open the hearing to the public; and

(3) Have the record of the hearing and the findings of fact and decisions described in paragraphs (a)(4) and (a)(5) of this section provided at no cost to parents.

(Authority: 20 U.S.C. 1415(f)(2), 1415(h))

§ 300.513 Hearing decisions.

(a) Decision of hearing officer on the provision of FAPE. (1) Subject to paragraph (a)(2) of this section, a hearing officer's determination of whether a child received FAPE must be based on substantive grounds.

(2) In matters alleging a procedural violation, a hearing officer may find that a child did not receive a FAPE only if the procedural inadequacies—

(i) Impeded the child's right to a FAPE;

(ii) Significantly impeded the parent's opportunity to participate in the decision-making process regarding the provision of a FAPE to the parent's child; or

(iii) Caused a deprivation of educational benefit.

(3) Nothing in paragraph (a) of this section shall be construed to preclude a hearing officer from ordering an LEA to comply with procedural requirements under §§ 300.500 through 300.536.

(b) Construction clause. Nothing in §§ 300.507 through 300.513 shall be construed to affect the right of a parent to file an appeal of the due process hearing decision with the SEA under § 300.514(b), if a State level appeal is available.

(c) Separate request for a due process hearing. Nothing in §§ 300.500 through 300.536 shall be construed to preclude a parent from filing a separate due process complaint on an issue separate from a due process complaint already filed.

(d) Findings and decision to advisory panel and general public. The public agency, after deleting any personally identifiable information, must—

(1) Transmit the findings and decisions referred to in § 300.512(a)(5) to the State advisory panel established under § 300.167; and

(2) Make those findings and decisions available to the public.

(Authority: 20 U.S.C. 1415(f)(3)(E) and (F), 1415(h)(4), 1415(o))

§ 300.514 Finality of decision; appeal; impartial review.

(a) Finality of hearing decision. A decision made in a hearing conducted pursuant to §§ 300.507 through 300.513 or §§ 300.530 through 300.534 is final, except that any party involved in the hearing may appeal the decision under the provisions of paragraph (b) of this section and § 300.516.

(b) Appeal of decisions; impartial review. (1) If the hearing required by § 300.511 is conducted by a public agency other than the

SEA, any party aggrieved by the findings and decision in the hearing may appeal to the SEA.

(2) If there is an appeal, the SEA must conduct an impartial review of the findings and decision appealed. The official conducting the review must—

(i) Examine the entire hearing record;

(ii) Ensure that the procedures at the hearing were consistent with the requirements of due process;

(iii) Seek additional evidence if necessary. If a hearing is held to receive additional evidence, the rights in § 300.512 apply;

(iv) Afford the parties an opportunity for oral or written argument, or both, at the discretion of the reviewing official;

(v) Make an independent decision on completion of the review; and

(vi) Give a copy of the written, or, at the option of the parents, electronic findings of fact and decisions to the parties.

(c) Findings and decision to advisory panel and general public. The SEA, after deleting any personally identifiable information, must—

(1) Transmit the findings and decisions referred to in paragraph (b)(2)(vi) of this section to the State advisory panel established under § 300.167; and

(2) Make those findings and decisions available to the public.

(d) Finality of review decision. The decision made by the reviewing official is final unless a party brings a civil action under § 300.516.

(Authority: 20 U.S.C. 1415(g) and (h)(4), 1415(i)(1)(A), 1415(i)(2))

§ 300.515 Timelines and convenience of hearings and reviews.

(a) The public agency must ensure that not later than 45 days after the expiration of the 30 day period under § 300.510(b), or the adjusted time periods described in § 300.510(c)—

(1) A final decision is reached in the hearing; and

(2) A copy of the decision is mailed to each of the parties.

(b) The SEA must ensure that not later than 30 days after the receipt of a request for a review—

(1) A final decision is reached in the review; and

(2) A copy of the decision is mailed to each of the parties.

(c) A hearing or reviewing officer may grant specific extensions of time beyond the periods set out in paragraphs (a) and (b) of this section at the request of either party.

(d) Each hearing and each review involving oral arguments must be conducted at a time and place that is reasonably convenient to the parents and child involved.

(Authority: 20 U.S.C. 1415(f)(1)(B)(ii), 1415(g), 1415(i)(1))

§ 300.516 Civil action.

(a) General. Any party aggrieved by the findings and decision made under §§ 300.507 through 300.513 or §§ 300.530 through 300.534 who does not have the right to an appeal under § 300.514(b), and any party aggrieved by the findings and decision under § 300.514(b), has the right to bring a civil action with respect to the due process complaint notice requesting a due process hearing under § 300.507 or §§ 300.530 through 300.532. The action may be brought in any State court of competent jurisdiction or in a district court of the United States without regard to the amount in controversy.

(b) Time limitation. The party bringing the action shall have 90 days from the date of the decision of the hearing officer or, if applicable, the decision of the State review official, to file a civil action, or, if the State has an explicit time limitation for bringing civil actions under Part B of the Act, in the time allowed by that State law.

(c) Additional requirements. In any action brought under paragraph (a) of this section, the court—

(1) Receives the records of the administrative proceedings;

(2) Hears additional evidence at the request of a party; and

(3) Basing its decision on the preponderance of the evidence, grants the relief that the court determines to be appropriate.

(d) Jurisdiction of district courts. The district courts of the United States have jurisdiction of actions brought under section 615 of the Act without regard to the amount in controversy.

(e) Rule of construction. Nothing in this part restricts or limits the rights, procedures, and remedies available under the Constitution, the Americans with Disabilities Act of 1990, title V of the Rehabilitation Act of 1973, or other Federal laws protecting the rights of children with disabilities, except that before the filing of a civil action under these laws seeking relief that is also available under section 615 of the Act, the procedures under §§ 300.507 and 300.514 must be exhausted to the same extent as would be required had the action been brought under section 615 of the Act.

(Authority: 20 U.S.C. 1415(i)(2) and (3)(A), 1415(l))

§ 300.517 Attorneys' fees.

(a) In general. (1) In any action or proceeding brought under section 615 of the Act, the court, in its discretion, may award reasonable attorneys' fees as part of the costs to—

(i) The prevailing party who is the parent of a child with a disability;

(ii) To a prevailing party who is an SEA or LEA against the attorney of a parent who files a complaint or subsequent cause of action that is frivolous, unreasonable, or without foundation, or against the attorney of a parent who continued to litigate after the litigation clearly became frivolous, unreasonable, or without foundation; or

(iii) To a prevailing SEA or LEA against the attorney of a parent, or against the parent, if the parent's request for a due process hearing or subsequent cause of action was presented for any improper purpose, such as to harass, to cause unnecessary delay, or to needlessly increase the cost of litigation.

(2) Nothing in this subsection shall be construed to affect section 327 of the District of Columbia Appropriations Act, 2005.

(b) Prohibition on use of funds. (1) Funds under Part B of the Act may not be used to pay attorneys' fees or costs of a party related to any action or proceeding under section 615 of the Act and subpart E of this part.

(2) Paragraph (b)(1) of this section does not preclude a public agency from using funds under Part B of the Act for conducting an action or proceeding under section 615 of the Act.

(c) Award of fees. A court awards reasonable attorneys' fees under section 615(i)(3) of the Act consistent with the following:

(1) Fees awarded under section 615(i)(3) of the Act must be based on rates prevailing in the community in which the action or proceeding arose for the kind and quality of services furnished. No bonus or multiplier may be used in calculating the fees awarded under this paragraph.

(2)(i) Attorneys' fees may not be awarded and related costs may not be reimbursed in any action or proceeding under section 615 of the Act for services performed subsequent to the time of a written offer of settlement to a parent if—

(A) The offer is made within the time prescribed by Rule 68 of the Federal Rules of Civil Procedure or, in the case of an administrative proceeding, at any time more than 10 days before the proceeding begins;

(B) The offer is not accepted within 10 days; and

(C) The court or administrative hearing officer finds that the relief finally obtained by the parents is not more favorable to the parents than the offer of settlement.

(ii) Attorneys' fees may not be awarded relating to any meeting of the IEP Team unless the meeting is convened as a result of an administrative proceeding or judicial action, or at the discretion of the State, for a mediation described in § 300.506.

(iii) A meeting conducted pursuant to § 300.510 shall not be considered—

(A) A meeting convened as a result of an administrative hearing or judicial action; or

(B) An administrative hearing or judicial action for purposes of this section.

(3) Notwithstanding paragraph (c)(2) of this section, an award of attorneys' fees and related costs may be made to a parent who is the prevailing party and who was substantially justified in rejecting the settlement offer.

(4) Except as provided in paragraph (c)(5) of this section, the court reduces, accordingly, the amount of the attorneys' fees awarded under section 615 of the Act, if the court finds that—

(i) The parent, or the parent's attorney, during the course of the action or proceeding, unreasonably protracted the final resolution of the controversy;

(ii) The amount of the attorneys' fees otherwise authorized to be awarded unreasonably exceeds the hourly rate prevailing in the community for similar services by attorneys of reasonably comparable skill, reputation, and experience;

(iii) The time spent and legal services furnished were excessive considering the nature of the action or proceeding; or

(iv) The attorney representing the parent did not provide to the LEA the appropriate information in the due process request notice in accordance with § 300.508.

(5) The provisions of paragraph (c)(4) of this section do not apply in any action or proceeding if the court finds that the State or local agency unreasonably protracted the final resolution of the action or proceeding or there was a violation of section 615 of the Act.

(Authority: 20 U.S.C. 1415(i)(3)(B)–(G))

§ 300.518 Child's status during proceedings.

(a) Except as provided in § 300.533, during the pendency of any administrative or judicial proceeding regarding a due process complaint notice requesting a due process hearing under § 300.507, unless the State or local agency and the parents of the child agree otherwise, the child involved in the complaint must remain in his or her current educational placement.

(b) If the complaint involves an application for initial admission to public school, the child, with the consent of the parents, must be placed in the public school until the completion of all the proceedings.

(c) If the complaint involves an application for initial services under this part from a child who is transitioning from Part C of the Act to Part B and is no longer eligible for Part C services because the child has turned three, the public agency is not required to provide the Part C services that the child had been receiving. If the child is found eligible for special education and related services under Part B and the parent consents to the initial provision of special education and related services under §

300.300(b), then the public agency must provide those special education and related services that are not in dispute between the parent and the public agency.

(d) If the hearing officer in a due process hearing conducted by the SEA or a State review official in an administrative appeal agrees with the child's parents that a change of placement is appropriate, that placement must be treated as an agreement between the State and the parents for purposes of paragraph (a) of this section.

(Authority: 20 U.S.C. 1415(j))

§ 300.519 Surrogate parents.

(a) General. Each public agency must ensure that the rights of a child are protected when—

(1) No parent (as defined in § 300.30) can be identified;

(2) The public agency, after reasonable efforts, cannot locate a parent;

(3) The child is a ward of the State under the laws of that State; or

(4) The child is an unaccompanied homeless youth as defined in section 725(6) of the McKinney-Vento Homeless Assistance Act (42 U.S.C. 11434a(6)).

(b) Duties of public agency. The duties of a public agency under paragraph (a) of this section include the assignment of an individual to act as a surrogate for the parents. This must include a method—

(1) For determining whether a child needs a surrogate parent; and

(2) For assigning a surrogate parent to the child.

(c) Wards of the State. In the case of a child who is a ward of the State, the surrogate parent alternatively may be appointed by the judge overseeing the child's case, provided that the surrogate meets the requirements in paragraphs (d)(2)(i) and (e) of this section.

(d) Criteria for selection of surrogate parents. (1) The public agency may select a surrogate parent in any way permitted under State law.

(2) Public agencies must ensure that a person selected as a surrogate parent—

(i) Is not an employee of the SEA, the LEA, or any other agency that is involved in the education or care of the child;

(ii) Has no personal or professional interest that conflicts with the interest of the child the surrogate parent represents; and

(iii) Has knowledge and skills that ensure adequate representation of the child.

(e) Non-employee requirement; compensation. A person otherwise qualified to be a surrogate parent under paragraph (d) of this section is not an employee of the agency solely because he or she is paid by the agency to serve as a surrogate parent.

(f) Unaccompanied homeless youth. In the case of a child who is an unaccompanied homeless youth, appropriate staff of emergency shelters, transitional shelters, independent living programs, and street outreach programs may be appointed as temporary surrogate parents without regard to paragraph (d)(2)(i) of this section, until a surrogate parent can be appointed that meets all of the requirements of paragraph (d) of this section.

(g) Surrogate parent responsibilities. The surrogate parent may represent the child in all matters relating to—

(1) The identification, evaluation, and educational placement of the child; and

(2) The provision of FAPE to the child.

(h) SEA responsibility. The SEA must make reasonable efforts to ensure the assignment of a surrogate parent not more than 30 days after a public agency determines that the child needs a surrogate parent.

(Authority: 20 U.S.C. 1415(b)(2))

§ 300.520 Transfer of parental rights at age of majority.

(a) General. A State may provide that, when a child with a disability reaches the age of majority under State law that applies to all children (except for a child with a disability who has been determined to be incompetent under State law)—

(1)(i) The public agency must provide any notice required by this part to both the child and the parents; and

(ii) All rights accorded to parents under Part B of the Act transfer to the child;

(2) All rights accorded to parents under Part B of the Act transfer to children who are incarcerated in an adult or juvenile, State or local correctional institution; and

(3) Whenever a State provides for the transfer of rights under this part pursuant to paragraph (a)(1) or (a)(2) of this section, the agency must notify the child and the parents of the transfer of rights.

(b) Special rule. A State must establish procedures for appointing the parent of a child with a disability, or, if the parent is not available, another appropriate individual, to represent the educational interests of the child throughout the period of the child's eligibility under Part B of the Act if, under State law, a child who has reached the age of majority, but has not been determined to be incompetent, can be determined not to have the ability to provide informed consent with respect to the child's educational program.

(Authority: 20 U.S.C. 1415(m))

§§ 300.521–300.529 [Reserved]

Discipline Procedures

§ 300.530 Authority of school personnel.

(a) Case-by-case determination. School personnel may consider any unique circumstances on a case-by-case basis when determining whether a change in placement, consistent with the other requirements of this section, is appropriate for a child with a disability who violates a code of student conduct.

(b) General. (1) School personnel under this section may remove a child with a disability who violates a code of student conduct from his or her current placement to an appropriate interim alternative educational setting, another setting, or suspension, for not more than 10 consecutive school days (to the extent those alternatives are applied to children without disabilities), and for additional removals of not more than 10 consecutive school days in that same school year for separate incidents of misconduct (as long as those removals do not constitute a change of placement under § 300.536).

(2) After a child with a disability has been removed from his or her current placement for 10 school days in the same school year, during any subsequent days of removal the public agency must provide services to the extent required under paragraph (d) of this section.

(c) Additional authority. For disciplinary changes in placement that would exceed 10 consecutive school days, if the behavior that gave rise to the violation of the school code is determined not to be a manifestation of the child's disability pursuant to paragraph (e) of this section, school personnel may apply the relevant disciplinary procedures to children with disabilities in the same manner and for the same duration as the procedures would be applied to children without disabilities, except as provided in paragraph (d) of this section.

(d) Services. (1) A child with a disability who is removed from the child's current placement pursuant to paragraphs (c), or (g) of this section must—

(i) Continue to receive educational services, as provided in § 300.101(a), so as to enable the child to continue to participate in the general education curriculum, although in another setting, and to progress toward meeting the goals set out in the child's IEP; and

(ii) Receive, as appropriate, a functional behavioral assessment, and behavioral intervention services and modifications, that are designed to address the behavior violation so that it does not recur.

(2) The services required by paragraph (d)(1), (d)(3), (d)(4), and (d)(5) of this section may be provided in an interim alternative educational setting.

(3) A public agency is only required to provide services during periods of removal to a child with a disability who has been removed from his or her current placement for 10 school days or less in that school year, if it provides services to a child without disabilities who is similarly removed.

(4) After a child with a disability has been removed from his or her current placement for 10 school days in the same school year, if the current removal is for not more than 10 consecutive school days and is not a change of placement under § 300.536, school personnel, in consultation with at least one of the child's teachers, determine the extent to which services are needed, as provided in § 300.101(a), so as to enable the child to continue to participate in the general education curriculum, although in another setting, and to progress toward meeting the goals set out in the child's IEP.

(5) If the removal is a change of placement under § 300.536, the child's IEP Team determines appropriate services under paragraph (d)(1) of this section.

(e) Manifestation determination. (1) Within 10 school days of any decision to change the placement of a child with a disability because of a violation of a code of student conduct, the LEA, the parent, and relevant members of the child's IEP Team (as determined by the parent and the LEA) must review all relevant information in the student's file, including the child's IEP, any teacher observations, and any relevant information provided by the parents to determine—

(i) If the conduct in question was caused by, or had a direct and substantial relationship to, the child's disability; or

(ii) If the conduct in question was the direct result of the LEA's failure to implement the IEP.

(2) The conduct must be determined to be a manifestation of the child's disability if the LEA, the parent, and relevant members of the child's IEP Team determine that a condition in either paragraph (e)(1)(i) or (1)(ii) of this section was met.

(3) If the LEA, the parent, and relevant members of the child's IEP Team determine the condition described in paragraph (e)(1)(ii) of this section was met, the LEA must take immediate steps to remedy those deficiencies.

(f) Determination that behavior was a manifestation. If the LEA, the parent, and relevant members of the IEP Team make the determination that the conduct was a manifestation of the child's disability, the IEP Team must—

(1) Either—

(i) Conduct a functional behavioral assessment, unless the LEA had conducted a functional behavioral assessment before the behavior that resulted in the change of placement occurred, and implement a behavioral intervention plan for the child; or

(ii) If a behavioral intervention plan already has been developed, review the behavioral intervention plan, and modify it, as necessary, to address the behavior; and

(2) Except as provided in paragraph (g) of this section, return the child to the placement from which the child was removed, unless the parent and the LEA agree to a change of placement as part of the modification of the behavioral intervention plan.

(g) Special circumstances. School personnel may remove a student to an interim alternative educational setting for not more than 45 school days without regard to whether the behavior is determined to be a manifestation of the child's disability, if the child—

(1) Carries a weapon to or possesses a weapon at school, on school premises, or to or at a school function under the jurisdiction of an SEA or an LEA;

(2) Knowingly possesses or uses illegal drugs, or sells or solicits the sale of a controlled substance, while at school, on school premises, or at a school function under the jurisdiction of an SEA or an LEA; or

(3) Has inflicted serious bodily injury upon another person while at school, on school premises, or at a school function under the jurisdiction of an SEA or an LEA.

(h) Notification. On the date on which the decision is made to make a removal that constitutes a change of placement of a child with a disability because of a violation of a code of student conduct, the LEA must notify the parents of that decision, and provide the parents the procedural safeguards notice described in § 300.504.

(i) Definitions. For purposes of this section, the following definitions apply:

(1) Controlled substance means a drug or other substance identified under schedules I, II, III, IV, or V in section 202(c) of the Controlled Substances Act (21 U.S.C. 812(c)).

(2) Illegal drug means a controlled substance; but does not include a controlled substance that is legally possessed or used under the supervision of a licensed health-care professional or that is legally possessed or used under any other authority under that Act or under any other provision of Federal law.

(3) Serious bodily injury has the meaning given the term "serious bodily injury" under paragraph (3) of subsection (h) of section 1365 of title 18, United States Code.

(4) Weapon has the meaning given the term "dangerous weapon" under paragraph (2) of the first subsection (g) of section 930 of title 18, United States Code.

(Authority: 20 U.S.C. 1415(k)(1) and (7))

§ **300.531 Determination of setting.**

The child's IEP Team determines the interim alternative educational setting for services under § 300.530(c), (d)(5), and (g).

(Authority: 20 U.S.C. 1415(k)(2))

§ **300.532 Appeal.**

(a) General. The parent of a child with a disability who disagrees with any decision regarding placement under §§ 300.530 and 300.531, or the manifestation determination under § 300.530(e), or an LEA that believes that maintaining the current placement of the child is substantially likely to result in injury to the child or others, may appeal the decision by requesting a hearing. The hearing is requested by filing a complaint pursuant to §§ 300.507 and 300.508(a) and (b).

(b) Authority of hearing officer. (1) A hearing officer under § 300.511 hears, and makes a determination regarding an appeal under paragraph (a) of this section.

(2) In making the determination under paragraph (b)(1) of this section, the hearing officer may—

(i) Return the child with a disability to the placement from which the child was removed if the hearing officer determines that the removal was a violation of § 300.530 or that the child's behavior was a manifestation of the child's disability; or

(ii) Order a change of placement of the child with a disability to an appropriate interim alternative educational setting for not more than 45 school days if the hearing officer determines that maintaining the current placement of the child is substantially likely to result in injury to the child or to others.

(3) The procedures under paragraphs (a) and (b)(1) and (2) of this section may be repeated, if the LEA believes that returning the child to the original placement is substantially likely to result in injury to the child or to others.

(c) Expedited due process hearing. (1) Whenever a hearing is requested under paragraph (a) of this section, the parents or the LEA involved in the dispute must have an opportunity for an impartial due process hearing consistent with the requirements of §§ 300.507 and 300.508(a) through (c) and §§ 300.510 through 300.514, except as provided in paragraph (c)(2) through (4) of this section.

(2) The SEA or LEA is responsible for arranging the expedited due process hearing, which must occur within 20 school days of the date the complaint requesting the hearing is filed. The hearing officer must make a determination within 10 school days after the hearing.

(3) Unless the parents and LEA agree in writing to waive the resolution meeting described in paragraph (c)(3)(i) of this section, or agree to use the mediation process described in § 300.506—

(i) A resolution meeting must occur within seven days of receiving notice of the due process complaint; and

(ii) The due process hearing may proceed unless the matter has been resolved to the satisfaction of both parties within 15 days of the receipt of the due process complaint.

(4) A State may establish different State-imposed procedural rules for expedited due process hearings conducted under this section than it has established for other due process hearings, but, except for the timelines as modified in paragraph (c)(3) of this section, the State must ensure that the requirements in §§ 300.510 through 300.514 are met.

(5) The decisions on expedited due process hearings are appealable consistent with § 300.514.

(Authority: 20 U.S.C. 1415(k)(3) and (4)(B), 1415(f)(1)(A))

§ 300.533 Placement during appeals.

When an appeal under § 300.532 has been made by either the parent or the LEA, the child must remain in the interim alternative educational setting pending the decision of the hearing officer or until the expiration of the time period specified in §300.530(c) or (g), whichever occurs first, unless the parent and the SEA or LEA agree otherwise.

(Authority: 20 U.S.C. 1415(k)(4)(A))

§ 300.534 Protections for children not determined eligible for special education and related services.

(a) General. A child who has not been determined to be eligible for special education and related services under this part and who has engaged in behavior that violated a code of student conduct, may assert any of the protections provided for in this part if the public agency had knowledge (as determined in accordance with paragraph (b) of this section) that the child was a child with a disability before the behavior that precipitated the disciplinary action occurred.

(b) Basis of knowledge. A public agency must be deemed to have knowledge that a child is a child with a disability if before the behavior that precipitated the disciplinary action occurred—

(1) The parent of the child expressed concern in writing to supervisory or administrative personnel of the appropriate educational agency, or a teacher of the child, that the child is in need of special education and related services;

(2) The parent of the child requested an evaluation of the child pursuant to §§ 300.300 through 300.311; or

(3) The teacher of the child, or other personnel of the LEA, expressed specific concerns about a pattern of behavior demonstrated by the child directly to the director of special education of the agency or to other supervisory personnel of the agency.

(c) Exception. A public agency would not be deemed to have knowledge under paragraph (b) of this section if—

(1) The parent of the child—

(i) Has not allowed an evaluation of the child pursuant to §§ 300.300 through 300.311; or

(ii) Has refused services under this part; or

(2) The child has been evaluated in accordance with §§ 300.300 through 300.311 and determined to not be a child with a disability under this part.

(d) Conditions that apply if no basis of knowledge. (1) If a public agency does not have knowledge that a child is a child with a disability (in accordance with paragraphs (b) and (c) of this section) prior to taking disciplinary measures against the child, the child may be subjected to the disciplinary measures applied to children without disabilities who engage in comparable behaviors consistent with paragraph (d)(2) of this section.

(2)(i) If a request is made for an evaluation of a child during the time period in which the child is subjected to disciplinary measures under § 300.530, the evaluation must be conducted in an expedited manner.

(ii) Until the evaluation is completed, the child remains in the educational placement determined by school authorities, which can include suspension or expulsion without educational services.

(iii) If the child is determined to be a child with a disability, taking into consideration information from the evaluation conducted by the agency and information provided by the parents, the agency must provide special education and related services in accordance with this part, including the requirements of §§ 300.530 through 300.536 and section 612(a)(1)(A) of the Act.

(Authority: 20 U.S.C. 1415(k)(5))

§ 300.535 Referral to and action by law enforcement and judicial authorities.

(a) Rule of construction. Nothing in this part prohibits an agency from reporting a crime committed by a child with a disability to appropriate authorities or prevents State law enforcement and judicial authorities from exercising their responsibilities with regard to the application of Federal and State law to crimes committed by a child with a disability.

(b) Transmittal of records. (1) An agency reporting a crime committed by a child with a disability must ensure that copies of the special education and disciplinary records of the child are transmitted for consideration by the appropriate authorities to whom the agency reports the crime.

(2) An agency reporting a crime under this section may transmit copies of the child's special education and disciplinary records only to the extent that the transmission is permitted by the

Family Educational Rights and Privacy Act.
(Authority: 20 U.S.C. 1415(k)(6))

§ 300.536 Change of placement because of disciplinary removals.

(a) For purposes of removals of a child with a disability from the child's current educational placement under §§ 300.530 through 300.535, a change of placement occurs if—

(1) The removal is for more than 10 consecutive school days; or

(2) The child has been subjected to a series of removals that constitute a pattern—

(i) Because the series of removals total more than 10 school days in a school year;

(ii) Because the child's behavior is substantially similar to the child's behavior in previous incidents that resulted in the series of removals; and

(iii) Because of such additional factors as the length of each removal, the total amount of time the child has been removed, and the proximity of the removals to one another.

(b)(1) The public agency determines on a case-by-case basis whether a pattern of removals constitutes a change of placement.

(2) This determination is subject to review through due process and judicial proceedings.

(Authority: 20 U.S.C. 1415(k))

§ 300.537 State enforcement mechanisms.

Notwithstanding §§ 300.506(b)(7) and 300.510(d)(2), which provide for judicial enforcement of a written agreement reached as a result of mediation or a resolution meeting, there is nothing in this part that would prevent the SEA from using other mechanisms to seek enforcement of that agreement, provided that use of those mechanisms is not mandatory and does not delay or deny a party the right to seek enforcement of the written agreement in a State court of competent jurisdiction or in a district court of the United States.

(Authority: 20 U.S.C. 1415(e)(2)(F), 1415(f)(1)(B))

§§ 300.538–300.599 [Reserved]

Subpart F—Monitoring, Enforcement, Confidentiality, and Program Information

Monitoring, Technical Assistance, and Enforcement

§ 300.600 State monitoring and enforcement.

(a)The State must--

(1) Monitor the implementation of this part;

(2) Make determinations annually about the performance of each LEA using the categories in § 300.603(b)(1);

(3) Enforce this part, consistent with § 300.604, using appropriate enforcement

mechanisms, which must include, if applicable, the enforcement mechanisms identified in § 300.604(a)(1) (technical assistance), (a)(3) (conditions on funding of an LEA), (b)(2)(i) (a corrective action plan or improvement plan), (b)(2)(v) (withholding funds, in whole or in part, by the SEA), and (c)(2) (withholding funds, in whole or in part, by the SEA); and

(4) Report annually on the performance of the State and of each LEA under this part, as provided in § 300.602(b)(1)(i)(A) and (b)(2).

(b) The primary focus of the State's monitoring activities must be on—

(1) Improving educational results and functional outcomes for all children with disabilities; and

(2) Ensuring that public agencies meet the program requirements under Part B of the Act, with a particular emphasis on those requirements that are most closely related to improving educational results for children with disabilities.

(c) As a part of its responsibilities under paragraph (a) of this section, the State must use quantifiable indicators and such qualitative indicators as are needed to adequately measure performance in the priority areas identified in paragraph (d) of this section, and the indicators established by the Secretary for the State performance plans.

(d) The State must monitor the LEAs located in the State, using quantifiable indicators in each of the following priority areas, and using such qualitative indicators as are needed to adequately measure performance in those areas:

(1) Provision of FAPE in the least restrictive environment.

(2) State exercise of general supervision, including child find, effective monitoring, the use of resolution meetings, mediation, and a system of transition services as defined in § 300.43 and in 20 U.S.C. 1437(a)(9).

(3) Disproportionate representation of racial and ethnic groups in special education and related services, to the extent the representation is the result of inappropriate identification.

(e) In exercising its monitoring responsibilities under paragraph (d) of this section, the State must ensure that when it identifies noncompliance with the requirements of this part by LEAs, the noncompliance is corrected as soon as possible, and in no case later than one year after the State's identification of the noncompliance.

(Approved by the Office of Management and Budget under control number 1820–0624)

(Authority: 20 U.S.C. 1416(a))

§ 300.601 State performance plans and data collection.

(a) General. Not later than December 3, 2005, each State must have in place a performance plan that evaluates the State's efforts to implement the requirements and purposes of Part B of the Act, and describes how the State will improve such implementation.

(1) Each State must submit the State's performance plan to the Secretary for approval in accordance with the approval process described in section 616(c) of the Act.

(2) Each State must review its State performance plan at least once every six years, and submit any amendments to the Secretary.

(3) As part of the State performance plan, each State must establish measurable and rigorous targets for the indicators established by the Secretary under the priority areas described in § 300.600(d).

(b) Data collection. (1) Each State must collect valid and reliable information as needed to report annually to the Secretary on the indicators established by the Secretary for the State performance plans.

(2) If the Secretary permits States to collect data on specific indicators through State monitoring or sampling, and the State collects the data through State monitoring or sampling, the State must collect data on those indicators for each LEA at least once during the period of the State performance plan.

(3) Nothing in Part B of the Act shall be construed to authorize the development of a nationwide database of personally identifiable information on individuals involved in studies or other collections of data under Part B of the Act.

(Approved by the Office of Management and Budget under control number 1820–0624)

(Authority: 20 U.S.C. 1416(b))

§ 300.602 State use of targets and reporting.

(a) General. Each State must use the targets established in the State's performance plan under § 300.601 and the priority areas described in § 300.600(d) to analyze the performance of each LEA.

(b) Public reporting and privacy—(1) Public report. (i) Subject to paragraph (b)(1)(ii) of this section, the State must--

(A) Report annually to the public on the performance of each LEA located in the State on the targets in the State's performance plan as soon as practicable but no later than 120 days following the State's submission of its annual performance report to the Secretary under paragraph (b)(2) of this section; and

(B) Make each of the following items available through public means: the State's performance plan, under § 300.601(a); annual performance reports, under paragraph (b)(2) of this section; and the State's annual reports on the performance of each LEA located in the State, under paragraph (b)(1)(i)(A) *73028 of this section. In doing so, the State must, at a minimum, post the plan and reports on the SEA's Web site, and distribute the plan and reports to

the media and through public agencies.

(ii) If the State, in meeting the requirements of paragraph (b)(1)(i) of this section, collects performance data through State monitoring or sampling, the State must include in its report under paragraph (b)(1)(i)(A) of this section the most recently available performance data on each LEA, and the date the data were obtained.

(2) State performance report. The State must report annually to the Secretary on the performance of the State under the State's performance plan.

(3) Privacy. The State must not report to the public or the Secretary any information on performance that would result in the disclosure of personally identifiable information about individual children, or where the available data are insufficient to yield statistically reliable information. (Approved by the Office of Management and Budget under control number 1820–0624)

(Authority: 20 U.S.C. 1416(b)(2)(C))

§ 300.603 Secretary's review and determination regarding State performance.

(a) Review. The Secretary annually reviews the State's performance report submitted pursuant to § 300.602(b)(2).

(b) Determination—(1) General. Based on the information provided by the State in the State's annual performance report, information obtained through monitoring visits, and any other public information made available, the Secretary determines if the State—

(i) Meets the requirements and purposes of Part B of the Act;

(ii) Needs assistance in implementing the requirements of Part B of the Act;

(iii) Needs intervention in implementing the requirements of Part B of the Act; or

(iv) Needs substantial intervention in implementing the requirements of Part B of the Act.

(2) Notice and opportunity for a hearing. (i) For determinations made under paragraphs (b)(1)(iii) and (b)(1)(iv) of this section, the Secretary provides reasonable notice and an opportunity for a hearing on those determinations.

(ii) The hearing described in paragraph (b)(2) of this section consists of an opportunity to meet with the Assistant Secretary for Special Education and Rehabilitative Services to demonstrate why the Department should not make the determination described in paragraph (b)(1) of this section.

(Authority: 20 U.S.C. 1416(d))

§ 300.604 Enforcement.

(a) Needs assistance. If the Secretary determines, for two consecutive years, that a State needs assistance under § 300.603(b)(1)(ii) in implementing the requirements of Part B of the Act, the Secretary takes one or more of the following actions:

(1) Advises the State of available sources of technical assistance that may help the State address the areas in which the State needs assistance, which may include assistance from the Office of Special Education Programs, other offices of the Department of Education, other Federal agencies, technical assistance providers approved by the Secretary, and other federally funded nonprofit agencies, and requires the State to work with appropriate entities. Such technical assistance may include—

(i) The provision of advice by experts to address the areas in which the State needs assistance, including explicit plans for addressing the area for concern within a specified period of time;

(ii) Assistance in identifying and implementing professional development, instructional strategies, and methods of instruction that are based on scientifically based research;

(iii) Designating and using distinguished superintendents, principals, special education administrators, special education teachers, and other teachers to provide advice, technical assistance, and support; and

(iv) Devising additional approaches to providing technical assistance, such as collaborating with institutions of higher education, educational service agencies, national centers of technical assistance supported under Part D of the Act, and private providers of scientifically based technical assistance.

(2) Directs the use of State-level funds under section 611(e) of the Act on the area or areas in which the State needs assistance.

(3) Identifies the State as a high-risk grantee and imposes special conditions on the State's grant under Part B of the Act.

(b) Needs intervention. If the Secretary determines, for three or more consecutive years, that a State needs intervention under § 300.603(b)(1)(iii) in implementing the requirements of Part B of the Act, the following shall apply:

(1) The Secretary may take any of the actions described in paragraph (a) of this section.

(2) The Secretary takes one or more of the following actions:

(i) Requires the State to prepare a corrective action plan or improvement plan if the Secretary determines that the State should be able to correct the problem within one year.

(ii) Requires the State to enter into a compliance agreement under section 457 of the General Education Provisions Act, as amended, 20 U.S.C. 1221 et seq. (GEPA), if the Secretary has reason to believe that the State cannot correct the problem within one year.

(iii) For each year of the determination, withholds not less than 20 percent and not more than 50 percent of the State's funds under section 611(e) of the Act, until the Secretary determines the State has sufficiently addressed the areas in which the State needs intervention.

(iv) Seeks to recover funds under section 452 of GEPA.

(v) Withholds, in whole or in part, any further payments to the State under Part B of the Act.

(vi) Refers the matter for appropriate enforcement action, which may include referral to the Department of Justice.

(c) Needs substantial intervention. Notwithstanding paragraph (a) or (b) of this section, at any time that the Secretary determines that a State needs substantial intervention in implementing the requirements of Part B of the Act or that there is a substantial failure to comply with any condition of an SEA's or LEA's eligibility under Part B of the Act, the Secretary takes one or more of the following actions:

(1) Recovers funds under section 452 of GEPA.

(2) Withholds, in whole or in part, any further payments to the State under Part B of the Act.

(3) Refers the case to the Office of the Inspector General at the Department of Education.

(4) Refers the matter for appropriate enforcement action, which may include referral to the Department of Justice.

(d) Report to Congress. The Secretary reports to the Committee on Education and the Workforce of the House of Representatives and the Committee on Health, Education, Labor, and Pensions of the Senate within 30 days of taking enforcement action pursuant to paragraph (a), (b), or (c) of this section, on the specific action taken and the reasons why enforcement action was taken.

(Authority: 20 U.S.C. 1416(e)(1)–(e)(3), (e)(5))

§ 300.605 Withholding funds.

(a) Opportunity for hearing. Prior to withholding any funds under Part B of the Act, the Secretary provides reasonable notice and an opportunity for a hearing to the SEA involved, pursuant to the procedures in §§ 300.180 through 300.183.

(b) Suspension. Pending the outcome of any hearing to withhold payments under paragraph (a) of this section, the Secretary may suspend payments to a recipient, suspend the authority of the recipient to obligate funds under Part B of the Act, or both, after the recipient has been given reasonable notice and an opportunity to show cause why future payments or authority to obligate funds under Part B of the Act should not be suspended.

(c) *Nature of withholding.* (1) If the Secretary determines that it is appropriate to withhold further payments under § 300.604(b)(2) or (c)(2), the Secretary may determine—

(i) That the withholding will be limited to programs or projects, or portions of programs or projects, that affected the Secretary's determination under § 300.603(b)(1); or

(ii) That the SEA must not make further payments under Part B of the Act to specified State agencies or LEAs that caused or were involved in the Secretary's determination under § 300.603(b)(1).

(2) Until the Secretary is satisfied that the condition that caused the initial withholding has been substantially rectified—

(i) Payments to the State under Part B of the Act must be withheld in whole or in part; and

(ii) Payments by the SEA under Part B of the Act must be limited to State agencies and LEAs whose actions did not cause or were not involved in the Secretary's determination under § 300.603(b)(1), as the case may be.

(Authority: 20 U.S.C. 1416(e)(4), (e)(6))

§ 300.606 Public attention.

Whenever a State receives notice that the Secretary is proposing to take or is taking an enforcement action pursuant to § 300.604, the State must, by means of a public notice, take such actions as may be necessary to notify the public within the State of the pendency of an action pursuant to § 300.604, including, at a minimum, by posting the notice on the SEA's Web site and distributing the notice to the media and through public agencies.

(Authority: 20 U.S.C. 1416(e)(7))

§ 300.607 Divided State agency responsibility.

For purposes of this subpart, if responsibility for ensuring that the requirements of Part B of the Act are met with respect to children with disabilities who are convicted as adults under State law and incarcerated in adult prisons is assigned to a public agency other than the SEA pursuant to § 300.149(d), and if the Secretary finds that the failure to comply substantially with the provisions of Part B of the Act are related to a failure by the public agency, the Secretary takes appropriate corrective action to ensure compliance with Part B of the Act, except that—

(a) Any reduction or withholding of payments to the State under § 300.604 must be proportionate to the total funds allotted under section 611 of the Act to the State as the number of eligible children with disabilities in adult prisons under the supervision of the other public agency is proportionate to the number of eligible individuals with disabilities in the State under the supervision of the SEA; and

(b) Any withholding of funds under § 300.604 must be limited to the specific agency responsible for the failure to comply with Part B of the Act.

(Authority: 20 U.S.C. 1416(h))

§ 300.608 State enforcement.

(a) If an SEA determines that an LEA is not meeting the requirements of Part B of the Act, including the targets in the State's performance plan, the SEA must prohibit the LEA from reducing the LEA's maintenance of effort under § 300.203 for any fiscal year.

(b) Nothing in this subpart shall be construed to restrict a State from utilizing any other authority available to it to monitor and enforce the requirements of Part B of the Act.

(Authority: 20 U.S.C. 1416(f); 20 U.S.C. 1412(a)(11))

§ 300.609 Rule of construction.

Nothing in this subpart shall be construed to restrict the Secretary from utilizing any authority under GEPA, including the provisions in 34 CFR parts 76, 77, 80, and 81 to monitor and enforce the requirements of the Act, including the imposition of special conditions under 34 CFR 80.12.

(Authority: 20 U.S.C. 1416(g))

Confidentiality of Information

§ 300.610 Confidentiality.

The Secretary takes appropriate action, in accordance with section 444 of GEPA, to ensure the protection of the confidentiality of any personally identifiable data, information, and records collected or maintained by the Secretary and by SEAs and LEAs pursuant to Part B of the Act, and consistent with §§ 300.611 through 300.627.

(Authority: 20 U.S.C. 1417(c))

§ 300.611 Definitions.

As used in §§ 300.611 through 300.625—

(a) *Destruction* means physical destruction or removal of personal identifiers from information so that the information is no longer personally identifiable.

(b) *Education records* means the type of records covered under the definition of "education records" in 34 CFR part 99 (the regulations implementing the Family Educational Rights and Privacy Act of 1974, 20 U.S.C. 1232g (FERPA)).

(c) *Participating agency* means any agency or institution that collects, maintains, or uses personally identifiable information, or from which information is obtained, under Part B of the Act.

(Authority: 20 U.S.C. 1221e–3, 1412(a)(8), 1417(c))

§ 300.612 Notice to parents.

(a) The SEA must give notice that is adequate to fully inform parents about the requirements of § 300.123, including—

(1) A description of the extent that the notice is given in the native languages of the various population groups in the State;

(2) A description of the children on whom personally identifiable information is maintained, the types of information sought, the methods the State intends to use in gathering the information (including the sources from whom information is gathered), and the uses to be made of the information;

(3) A summary of the policies and procedures that participating agencies must follow regarding storage, disclosure to third parties, retention, and destruction of personally identifiable information; and

(4) A description of all of the rights of parents and children regarding this information, including the rights under FERPA and implementing regulations in 34 CFR part 99.

(b) Before any major identification, location, or evaluation activity, the notice must be published or announced in newspapers or other media, or both, with circulation adequate to notify parents throughout the State of the activity.

(Authority: 20 U.S.C. 1412(a)(8); 1417(c))

§ 300.613 Access rights.

(a) Each participating agency must permit parents to inspect and review any education records relating to their children that are collected, maintained, or used by the agency under this part. The agency must comply with a request without unnecessary delay and before any meeting regarding an IEP, or any hearing pursuant to § 300.507 or §§ 300.530 through 300.532, or resolution session pursuant to § 300.510, and in no case more than 45 days after the request has been made.

(b) The right to inspect and review education records under this section includes—

(1) The right to a response from the participating agency to reasonable requests for explanations and interpretations of the records;

(2) The right to request that the agency provide copies of the records containing the information if failure to provide those copies would effectively prevent the parent from exercising the right to inspect and review the records; and

(3) The right to have a representative of the parent inspect and review the records.

(c) An agency may presume that the parent has authority to inspect and review records relating to his or her child unless the agency has been advised that the parent does not have the authority under applicable State law governing such matters as guardianship, separation, and divorce.

(Authority: 20 U.S.C. 1412(a)(8); 1417(c))

§ 300.614 Record of access.

Each participating agency must keep a record of parties obtaining access to education records collected, maintained, or used under Part B of the Act (except access by parents and authorized employees of the participating agency), including the name of the party, the date access was given, and the purpose for which the party is authorized to use the records.

(Authority: 20 U.S.C. 1412(a)(8); 1417(c))

§ 300.615 Records on more than one child.

If any education record includes information on more than one child, the parents of those children have the right to inspect and review only the information relating to their child or to be informed of that specific information.

(Authority: 20 U.S.C. 1412(a)(8); 1417(c))

§ 300.616 List of types and locations of information.

Each participating agency must provide parents on request a list of the types and locations of education records collected, maintained, or used by the agency.

(Authority: 20 U.S.C. 1412(a)(8); 1417(c))

§ 300.617 Fees.

(a) Each participating agency may charge a fee for copies of records that are made for parents under this part if the fee does not effectively prevent the parents from exercising their right to inspect and review those records.

(b) A participating agency may not charge a fee to search for or to retrieve information under this part.

(Authority: 20 U.S.C. 1412(a)(8); 1417(c))

§ 300.618 Amendment of records at parent's request.

(a) A parent who believes that information in the education records collected, maintained, or used under this part is inaccurate or misleading or violates the privacy or other rights of the child may request the participating agency that maintains the information to amend the information.

(b) The agency must decide whether to amend the information in accordance with the request within a reasonable period of time of receipt of the request.

(c) If the agency decides to refuse to amend the information in accordance with the request, it must inform the parent of the refusal and advise the parent of the right to a hearing under § 300.619.

(Authority: 20 U.S.C. 1412(a)(8); 1417(c))

§ 300.619 Opportunity for a hearing.

The agency must, on request, provide an

opportunity for a hearing to challenge information in education records to ensure that it is not inaccurate, misleading, or otherwise in violation of the privacy or other rights of the child.

(Authority: 20 U.S.C. 1412(a)(8); 1417(c))

§ 300.620 Result of hearing.

(a) If, as a result of the hearing, the agency decides that the information is inaccurate, misleading or otherwise in violation of the privacy or other rights of the child, it must amend the information accordingly and so inform the parent in writing.

(b) If, as a result of the hearing, the agency decides that the information is not inaccurate, misleading, or otherwise in violation of the privacy or other rights of the child, it must inform the parent of the parent's right to place in the records the agency maintains on the child a statement commenting on the information or setting forth any reasons for disagreeing with the decision of the agency.

(c) Any explanation placed in the records of the child under this section must—

(1) Be maintained by the agency as part of the records of the child as long as the record or contested portion is maintained by the agency; and

(2) If the records of the child or the contested portion is disclosed by the agency to any party, the explanation must also be disclosed to the party.

(Authority: 20 U.S.C. 1412(a)(8); 1417(c))

§ 300.621 Hearing procedures.

A hearing held under § 300.619 must be conducted according to the procedures in 34 CFR 99.22.

(Authority: 20 U.S.C. 1412(a)(8); 1417(c))

§ 300.622 Consent.

(a) Parental consent must be obtained before personally identifiable information is disclosed to parties, other than officials of participating agencies in accordance with paragraph (b)(1) of this section, unless the information is contained in education records, and the disclosure is authorized without parental consent under 34 CFR part 99.

(b)(1) Except as provided in paragraphs (b)(2) and (b)(3) of this section, parental consent is not required before personally identifiable information is released to officials of participating agencies for purposes of meeting a requirement of this part.

(2) Parental consent, or the consent of an eligible child who has reached the age of majority under State law, must be obtained before personally identifiable information is released to officials of participating agencies providing or paying for transition services in accordance with

§ 300.321(b)(3). (3) If a child is enrolled, or is going to enroll in a private school that is not located in the LEA of the parent's residence, parental consent must be obtained before any personally identifiable information about the child is released between officials in the LEA where the private school is located and officials in the LEA of the parent's residence.

(Authority: 20 U.S.C. 1412(a)(8); 1417(c))

§ 300.623 Safeguards.

(a) Each participating agency must protect the confidentiality of personally identifiable information at collection, storage, disclosure, and destruction stages.

(b) One official at each participating agency must assume responsibility for ensuring the confidentiality of any personally identifiable information.

(c) All persons collecting or using personally identifiable information must receive training or instruction regarding the State's policies and procedures under § 300.123 and 34 CFR part 99.

(d) Each participating agency must maintain, for public inspection, a current listing of the names and positions of those employees within the agency who may have access to personally identifiable information.

(Authority: 20 U.S.C. 1412(a)(8); 1417(c))

§ 300.624 Destruction of information.

(a) The public agency must inform parents when personally identifiable information collected, maintained, or used under this part is no longer needed to provide educational services to the child.

(b) The information must be destroyed at the request of the parents. However, a permanent record of a student's name, address, and phone number, his or her grades, attendance record, classes attended, grade level completed, and year completed may be maintained without time limitation.

(Authority: 20 U.S.C. 1412(a)(8); 1417(c))

§ 300.625 Children's rights.

(a) The SEA must have in effect policies and procedures regarding the extent to which children are afforded rights of privacy similar to those afforded to parents, taking into consideration the age of the child and type or severity of disability.

(b) Under the regulations for FERPA in 34 CFR 99.5(a), the rights of parents regarding education records are transferred to the student at age 18.

(c) If the rights accorded to parents under Part B of the Act are transferred to a student who reaches the age of majority, consistent with § 300.520, the rights regarding educational records in §§ 300.613 through 300.624 must also be transferred to the student. However, the public agency must provide any notice required under section 615 of the Act to the student and the parents.

(Authority: 20 U.S.C. 1412(a)(8); 1417(c))

§ 300.626 Enforcement.

The SEA must have in effect the policies and procedures, including sanctions that the State uses, to ensure that its policies and procedures consistent with §§ 300.611 through 300.625 are followed and that the requirements of the Act and the regulations in this part are met.

(Authority: 20 U.S.C. 1412(a)(8); 1417(c))

§ 300.627 Department use of personally identifiable information.

If the Department or its authorized representatives collect any personally identifiable information regarding children with disabilities that is not subject to the Privacy Act of 1974, 5 U.S.C. 552a, the Secretary applies the requirements of 5 U.S.C. 552a(b)(1) and (b)(2), 552a(b)(4) through (b)(11); 552a(c) through 552a(e)(3)(B); 552a(e)(3)(D); 552a(e)(5) through (e)(10); 552a(h); 552a(m); and 552a(n); and the regulations implementing those provisions in 34 CFR part 5b.

(Authority: 20 U.S.C. 1412(a)(8); 1417(c))

Reports—Program Information

§ 300.640 Annual report of children served—report requirement.

(a) The SEA must annually report to the Secretary on the information required by section 618 of the Act at the times specified by the Secretary.

(b) The SEA must submit the report on forms provided by the Secretary.

(Approved by the Office of Management and Budget under control numbers 1820–0030, 1820–0043, 1820–0659, 1820–0621, 1820–0518, 1820–0521, 1820–0517, and 1820– 0677)

(Authority: 20 U.S.C. 1418(a))

§ 300.641 Annual report of children served—information required in the report.

(a) For purposes of the annual report required by section 618 of the Act and § 300.640, the State and the Secretary of the Interior must count and report the number of children with disabilities receiving special education and related services on any date between October 1 and December 1 of each year.

(b) For the purpose of this reporting provision, a child's age is the child's actual age on the date of the child count.

(c) The SEA may not report a child under more than one disability category.

(d) If a child with a disability has more than one disability, the SEA must report that child in accordance with the following procedure:

(1) If a child has only two disabilities and those disabilities are deafness and blindness, and the child is not reported as having a developmental delay, that child must be reported under the category "deaf-blindness."

(2) A child who has more than one disability and is not reported as having deaf-blindness or as having a developmental delay must be reported under the category "multiple disabilities."

(Approved by the Office of Management and Budget under control numbers 1820–0030, 1820–0043, 1820–0621, 1820–0521, and 1820–0517)

(Authority: 20 U.S.C. 1418(a), (b))

§ 300.642 Data reporting.

(a) Protection of personally identifiable data. The data described in section 618(a) of the Act and in § 300.641 must be publicly reported by each State in a manner that does not result in disclosure of data identifiable to individual children.

(b) Sampling. The Secretary may permit States and the Secretary of the Interior to obtain data in section 618(a) of the Act through sampling.

(Approved by the Office of Management and Budget under control numbers 1820–0030, 1820–0043, 1820–0518, 1820–0521, and 1820–0517)

(Authority: 20 U.S.C. 1418(b))

§ 300.643 Annual report of children served—certification.

The SEA must include in its report a certification signed by an authorized official of the agency that the information provided under § 300.640 is an accurate and unduplicated count of children with disabilities receiving special education and related services on the dates in question.

(Approved by the Office of Management and Budget under control numbers 1820–0030 and 1820–0043)

(Authority: 20 U.S.C. 1418(a)(3))

§ 300.644 Annual report of children served—criteria for counting children.

The SEA may include in its report children with disabilities who are enrolled in a school or program that is operated or supported by a public agency, and that—

(a) Provides them with both special education and related services that meet State standards;

(b) Provides them only with special education, if a related service is not required, that meets State standards; or

(c) In the case of children with disabilities enrolled by their parents in private schools, counts those children who are eligible under the Act and receive special education or related services or both that meet State standards under §§ 300.132 through 300.144.

(Approved by the Office of Management and Budget under control numbers 1820–0030, 1820–0043, 1820–0659, 1820–0621, 1820–0521, and 1820–0517)

(Authority: 20 U.S.C. 1418(a))

§ 300.645 Annual report of children served—other responsibilities of the SEA.

In addition to meeting the other requirements of §§ 300.640 through 300.644, the SEA must—

(a) Establish procedures to be used by LEAs and other educational institutions in counting the number of children with disabilities receiving special education and related services;

(b) Set dates by which those agencies and institutions must report to the SEA to ensure that the State complies with § 300.640(a);

(c) Obtain certification from each agency and institution that an unduplicated and accurate count has been made;

(d) Aggregate the data from the count obtained from each agency and institution, and prepare the reports required under §§ 300.640 through 300.644; and

(e) Ensure that documentation is maintained that enables the State and the Secretary to audit the accuracy of the count.

(Approved by the Office of Management and Budget under control numbers 1820–0030, 1820–0043, 1820–0659, 1820–0621, 1820–0518, 1820–0521, and 1820–0517)

(Authority: 20 U.S.C. 1418(a))

§ 300.646 Disproportionality.

(a) General. Each State that receives assistance under Part B of the Act, and the Secretary of the Interior, must provide for the collection and examination of data to determine if significant disproportionality based on race and ethnicity is occurring in the State and the LEAs of the State with respect to—

(1) The identification of children as children with disabilities, including the identification of children as children with disabilities in accordance with a particular impairment described in section 602(3) of the Act;

(2) The placement in particular educational settings of these children; and

(3) The incidence, duration, and type of disciplinary actions, including suspensions and expulsions.

(b) Review and revision of policies, practices, and procedures. In the case of a determination of significant disproportionality with respect to the identification of children as children with disabilities, or the placement in

particular educational settings of these children, in accordance with paragraph (a) of this section, the State or the Secretary of the Interior must—

(1) Provide for the review and, if appropriate revision of the policies, procedures, and practices used in the identification or placement to ensure that the policies, procedures, and practices comply with the requirements of the Act.

(2) Require any LEA identified under paragraph (a) of this section to reserve the maximum amount of funds under section 613(f) of the Act to provide comprehensive coordinated early intervening services to serve children in the LEA, particularly, but not exclusively, children in those groups that were significantly overidentified under paragraph (a) of this section; and

(3) Require the LEA to publicly report on the revision of policies, practices, and procedures described under paragraph (b)(1) of this section.

(Authority: 20 U.S.C. 1418(d))

Subpart G—Authorization, Allotment, Use of Funds, and Authorization of Appropriations

Allotments, Grants, and Use of Funds

§ 300.700 Grants to States.

(a) Purpose of grants. The Secretary makes grants to States, outlying areas, and freely associated States (as defined in § 300.717), and provides funds to the Secretary of the Interior, to assist them to provide special education and related services to children with disabilities in accordance with Part B of the Act.

(b) Maximum amount. The maximum amount of the grant a State may receive under section 611 of the Act is—

(1) For fiscal years 2005 and 2006—

(i) The number of children with disabilities in the State who are receiving special education and related services—

(A) Aged three through five, if the State is eligible for a grant under section 619 of the Act; and

(B) Aged 6 through 21; multiplied by—

(ii) Forty (40) percent of the average per-pupil expenditure in public elementary schools and secondary schools in the United States (as defined in § 300.717); and

(2) For fiscal year 2007 and subsequent fiscal years—

(i) The number of children with disabilities in the 2004–2005 school year in the State who received special education and related services—

(A) Aged three through five if the State is eligible for a grant under section 619 of the Act; and

(B) Aged 6 through 21; multiplied by

(ii) Forty (40) percent of the average per-pupil expenditure in public elementary schools and secondary schools in the United States (as defined in § 300.717);

(iii) Adjusted by the rate of annual change in the sum of—

(A) Eighty-five (85) percent of the State's population of children aged 3 through 21 who are of the same age as children with disabilities for whom the State ensures the availability of FAPE under Part B of the Act; and

(B) Fifteen (15) percent of the State's population of children described in paragraph (b)(2)(iii)(A) of this section who are living in poverty.

(Authority: 20 U.S.C. 1411(a) and (d))

§ 300.701 Outlying areas, freely associated States, and the Secretary of the Interior.

(a) Outlying areas and freely associated States.

(1) Funds reserved. From the amount appropriated for any fiscal year under section 611(i) of the Act, the Secretary reserves not more than one percent, which must be used—

(i) To provide assistance to the outlying areas in accordance with their respective populations of individuals aged 3 through 21; and

(ii) To provide each freely associated State a grant in the amount that the freely associated State received for fiscal year 2003 under Part B of the Act, but only if the freely associated State—

(A) Meets the applicable requirements of Part B of the Act that apply to States.

(B) Meets the requirements in paragraph (a)(2) of this section.

(2) Application. Any freely associated State that wishes to receive funds under Part B of the Act must include, in its application for assistance—

(i) Information demonstrating that it will meet all conditions that apply to States under Part B of the Act.

(ii) An assurance that, notwithstanding any other provision of Part B of the Act, it will use those funds only for the direct provision of special education and related services to children with disabilities and to enhance its capacity to make FAPE available to all children with disabilities;

(iii) The identity of the source and amount of funds, in addition to funds under Part B of the Act, that it will make available to ensure that FAPE is available to all children with disabilities within its jurisdiction; and

(iv) Such other information and assurances as the Secretary may require.

(3) Special rule. The provisions of Public Law 95–134, permitting the consolidation of grants by the outlying areas, do not apply to funds provided to the outlying areas or to the freely associated States under Part B of the Act.

(b) Secretary of the Interior. From the amount appropriated for any fiscal year under section 611(i) of the Act, the Secretary reserves 1.226 percent to provide assistance to the Secretary of the Interior in accordance with §§ 300.707 through 300.716.

(Authority: 20 U.S.C. 1411(b))

§ 300.702 Technical assistance.

(a) In general. The Secretary may reserve not more than one-half of one percent of the amounts appropriated under Part B of the Act for each fiscal year to support technical assistance activities authorized under section 616(i) of the Act.

(b) Maximum amount. The maximum amount the Secretary may reserve under paragraph (a) of this section for any fiscal year is $25,000,000, cumulatively adjusted by the rate of inflation as measured by the percentage increase, if any, from the preceding fiscal year in the Consumer Price Index For All Urban Consumers, published by the Bureau of Labor Statistics of the Department of Labor.

(Authority: 20 U.S.C. 1411(c))

§ 300.703 Allocations to States.

(a) General. After reserving funds for technical assistance under § 300.702, and for payments to the outlying areas, the freely associated States, and the Secretary of the Interior under § 300.701 (a) and (b) for a fiscal year, the Secretary allocates the remaining amount among the States in accordance with paragraphs (b), (c), and (d) of this section.

(b) Special rule for use of fiscal year 1999 amount. If a State received any funds under section 611 of the Act for fiscal year 1999 on the basis of children aged three through five, but does not make FAPE available to all children with disabilities aged three through five in the State in any subsequent fiscal year, the Secretary computes the State's amount for fiscal year 1999, solely for the purpose of calculating the State's allocation in that subsequent year under paragraph (c) or (d) of this section, by subtracting the amount allocated to the State for fiscal year 1999 on the basis of those children. (c) Increase in funds. If the amount available for allocations to States under paragraph (a) of this section for a fiscal year is equal to or greater than the amount allocated to the States under section 611 of the Act for the preceding fiscal year, those allocations are calculated as follows:

(1) Allocation of increase.—(i) General. Except as provided in paragraph (c)(2) of this section, the Secretary allocates for the fiscal year—

(A) To each State the amount the State received under this section for fiscal year 1999;

(B) Eighty-five (85) percent of any remaining funds to States on the basis of the States' relative populations of children aged 3 through 21 who are of the same age as children with disabilities for whom the State ensures the availability of FAPE under Part B of the Act; and

(C) Fifteen (15) percent of those remaining funds to States on the basis of the States' relative populations of children described in paragraph (c)(1)(i)(B) of this section who are living in poverty.

(ii) Data. For the purpose of making grants under this section, the Secretary uses the most recent population data, including data on children living in poverty, that are available and satisfactory to the Secretary.

(2) Limitations. Notwithstanding paragraph (c)(1) of this section, allocations under this section are subject to the following:

(i) Preceding year allocation. No State's allocation may be less than its allocation under section 611 of the Act for the preceding fiscal year.

(ii) Minimum. No State's allocation may be less than the greatest of—

(A) The sum of—

(1) The amount the State received under section 611 of the Act for fiscal year 1999; and

(2) One third of one percent of the amount by which the amount appropriated under section 611(i) of the Act for the fiscal year exceeds the amount appropriated for section 611 of the Act for fiscal year 1999;

(B) The sum of—

(1) The amount the State received under section 611 of the Act for the preceding fiscal year; and

(2) That amount multiplied by the percentage by which the increase in the funds appropriated for section 611 of the Act from the preceding fiscal year exceeds 1.5 percent; or

(C) The sum of—

(1) The amount the State received under section 611 of the Act for the preceding fiscal year; and

(2) That amount multiplied by 90 percent of the percentage increase in the amount appropriated for section 611 of the Act from the preceding fiscal year.

(iii) Maximum. Notwithstanding paragraph (c)(2)(ii) of this section, no State's allocation under paragraph (a) of this section may exceed the sum of—

(A) The amount the State received under section 611 of the Act for the preceding fiscal year; and

(B) That amount multiplied by the sum of 1.5 percent and the percentage increase in the amount appropriated under section 611 of the Act from the preceding fiscal year.

(3) Ratable reduction. If the amount available for allocations to States under paragraph (c) of this section is insufficient to pay those allocations in full, those allocations are ratably reduced, subject to paragraph (c)(2)(i) of this section.

(d) Decrease in funds. If the amount available for allocations to States under paragraph (a) of this section for a fiscal year is less than the amount allocated to the States under section 611 of the Act for the preceding fiscal year, those allocations are calculated as follows:

(1) Amounts greater than fiscal year 1999 allocations. If the amount available for allocations under paragraph (a) of this section is greater than the amount allocated to the States for fiscal year 1999, each State is allocated the sum of—

(i) 1999 amount. The amount the State received under section 611 of the Act for fiscal year 1999; and

(ii) Remaining funds. An amount that bears the same relation to any remaining funds as the increase the State received under section 611 of the Act for the preceding fiscal year over fiscal year 1999 bears to the total of all such increases for all States.

(2) Amounts equal to or less than fiscal year 1999 allocations.—(i) General. If the amount available for allocations under paragraph (a) of this section is equal to or less than the amount allocated to the States for fiscal year 1999, each State is allocated the amount it received for fiscal year 1999.

(ii) Ratable reduction. If the amount available for allocations under paragraph (d) of this section is insufficient to make the allocations described in paragraph (d)(2)(i) of this section, those allocations are ratably reduced.

(Authority: 20 U.S.C. 1411(d))

§ 300.704 State-level activities.

(a) State administration. (1) For the purpose of administering Part B of the Act, including paragraph (c) of this section, section 619 of the Act, and the coordination of activities under Part B of the Act with, and providing technical assistance to, other programs that provide services to children with disabilities—

(i) Each State may reserve for each fiscal year not more than the maximum amount the State was eligible to reserve for State administration under section 611 of the Act for fiscal year 2004 or $800,000 (adjusted in accordance with paragraph (a)(2) of this section), whichever is greater; and

(ii) Each outlying area may reserve for each fiscal year not more than five percent of the amount the outlying area receives under § 300.701(a) for the fiscal year or $35,000, whichever is greater.

(2) For each fiscal year, beginning with fiscal year 2005, the Secretary cumulatively adjusts—

(i) The maximum amount the State was eligible to reserve for State administration under section 611 of the Act for fiscal year 2004; and

(ii) $800,000, by the rate of inflation as measured by the percentage increase, if any, from the preceding fiscal year in the Consumer Price

Index For All Urban Consumers, published by the Bureau of Labor Statistics of the Department of Labor.

(3) Prior to expenditure of funds under paragraph (a) of this section, the State must certify to the Secretary that the arrangements to establish responsibility for services pursuant to section 612(a)(12)(A) of the Act are current.

(4) Funds reserved under paragraph (a)(1) of this section may be used for the administration of Part C of the Act, if the SEA is the lead agency for the State under that Part.

(b) Other State-level activities. (1) States may reserve a portion of their allocations for other State-level activities. The maximum amount that a State may reserve for other State-level activities is as follows:

(i) If the amount that the State sets aside for State administration under paragraph (a) of this section is greater than $850,000 and the State opts to finance a high cost fund under paragraph (c) of this section:

(A) For fiscal years 2005 and 2006, 10 percent of the State's allocation under § 300.703.

(B) For fiscal year 2007 and subsequent fiscal years, an amount equal to 10 percent of the State's allocation for fiscal year 2006 under § 300.703 adjusted cumulatively for inflation.

(ii) If the amount that the State sets aside for State administration under paragraph (a) of this section is greater than $850,000 and the State opts not to finance a high cost fund under paragraph (c) of this section—

(A) For fiscal years 2005 and 2006, nine percent of the State's allocation under § 300.703.

(B) For fiscal year 2007 and subsequent fiscal years, an amount equal to nine percent of the State's allocation for fiscal year 2006 adjusted cumulatively for inflation.

(iii) If the amount that the State sets aside for State administration under paragraph (a) of this section is less than or equal to $850,000 and the State opts to finance a high cost fund under paragraph (c) of this section:

(A) For fiscal years 2005 and 2006, 10.5 percent of the State's allocation under § 300.703.

(B) For fiscal year 2007 and subsequent fiscal years, an amount equal to 10.5 percent of the State's allocation for fiscal year 2006 under § 300.703 adjusted cumulatively for inflation.

(iv) If the amount that the State sets aside for State administration under paragraph (a) of this section is equal to or less than $850,000 and the State opts not to finance a high cost fund under paragraph (c) of this section:

(A) For fiscal years 2005 and 2006, nine and one-half percent of the State's allocation under § 300.703.

(B) For fiscal year 2007 and subsequent fiscal years, an amount equal to nine and one-half percent of the State's allocation for fiscal year 2006 under § 300.703 adjusted cumulatively for inflation.

(2) The adjustment for inflation is the rate of inflation as measured by the percentage of increase, if any, from the preceding fiscal year in the Consumer Price Index for All Urban Consumers, published by the Bureau of Labor Statistics of the Department of Labor.

(3) Some portion of the funds reserved under paragraph (b)(1) of this section must be used to carry out the following activities:

(i) For monitoring, enforcement, and complaint investigation; and

(ii) To establish and implement the mediation process required by section 615(e) of the Act, including providing for the costs of mediators and support personnel;

(4) Funds reserved under paragraph (b)(1) of this section also may be used to carry out the following activities:

(i) For support and direct services, including technical assistance, personnel preparation, and professional development and training;

(ii) To support paperwork reduction activities, including expanding the use of technology in the IEP process;

(iii) To assist LEAs in providing positive behavioral interventions and supports and mental health services for children with disabilities;

(iv) To improve the use of technology in the classroom by children with disabilities to enhance learning;

(v) To support the use of technology, including technology with universal design principles and assistive technology devices, to maximize accessibility to the general education curriculum for children with disabilities;

(vi) Development and implementation of transition programs, including coordination of services with agencies involved in supporting the transition of students with disabilities to postsecondary activities;

(vii) To assist LEAs in meeting personnel shortages;

(viii) To support capacity building activities and improve the delivery of services by LEAs to improve results for children with disabilities;

(ix) Alternative programming for children with disabilities who have been expelled from school, and services for children with disabilities in correctional facilities, children enrolled in State-operated or State-supported schools, and children with disabilities in charter schools;

(x) To support the development and provision of appropriate accommodations for children with disabilities, or the development and provision of alternate assessments that are valid and reliable for assessing the performance of children with disabilities, in accordance with sections 1111(b) and 6111 of the ESEA; and

(xi) To provide technical assistance to schools and LEAs, and direct services, including supplemental educational services as defined in section 1116(e) of the ESEA to children with disabilities, in schools or LEAs identified for improvement under section 1116 of the ESEA on the sole basis of the assessment results of the disaggregated subgroup of children with disabilities, including providing professional development to special and regular education teachers, who teach children with disabilities, based on scientifically based research to improve educational instruction, in order to improve academic achievement to meet or exceed the objectives established by the State under section 1111(b)(2)(G) of the ESEA.

(c) Local educational agency high cost fund. (1) In general—

(i) For the purpose of assisting LEAs (including a charter school that is an LEA or a consortium of LEAs) in addressing the needs of high need children with disabilities, each State has the option to reserve for each fiscal year 10 percent of the amount of funds the State reserves for other State-level activities under paragraph (b)(1) of this section—

(A) To finance and make disbursements from the high cost fund to LEAs in accordance with paragraph (c) of this section during the first and succeeding fiscal years of the high cost fund; and

(B) To support innovative and effective ways of cost sharing by the State, by an LEA, or among a consortium of LEAs, as determined by the State in coordination with representatives from LEAs, subject to paragraph (c)(2)(ii) of this section.

(ii) For purposes of paragraph (c) of this section, local educational agency includes a charter school that is an LEA, or a consortium of LEAs.

(2)(i) A State must not use any of the funds the State reserves pursuant to paragraph (c)(1)(i) of this section, which are solely for disbursement to LEAs, for costs associated with establishing, supporting, and otherwise administering the fund. The State may use funds the State reserves under paragraph (a) of this section for those administrative costs.

(ii) A State must not use more than 5 percent of the funds the State reserves pursuant to paragraph (c)(1)(i) of this section for each fiscal year to support innovative and effective ways of cost sharing among consortia of LEAs.

(3)(i) The SEA must develop, not later than 90 days after the State reserves funds under paragraph (c)(1)(i) of this section, annually review, and amend as necessary, a State plan for the high cost fund. Such State plan must—

(A) Establish, in consultation and coordination with representatives from LEAs, a definition of a high need child with a disability that, at a minimum—

(1) Addresses the financial impact a high need child with a disability has on the budget of the child's LEA; and

(2) Ensures that the cost of the high need child with a disability is greater than 3 times the average per pupil expenditure (as defined in section 9101 of the ESEA) in that State;

(B) Establish eligibility criteria for the participation of an LEA that, at a minimum, take into account the number and percentage of high need children with disabilities served by an LEA;

(C) Establish criteria to ensure that placements supported by the fund are consistent with the requirements of §§ 300.114 through 300.118;

(D) Develop a funding mechanism that provides distributions each fiscal year to LEAs that meet the criteria developed by the State under paragraph(c)(3)(i)(B) of this section;

(E) Establish an annual schedule by which the SEA must make its distributions from the high cost fund each fiscal year; and

(F) If the State elects to reserve funds for supporting innovative and effective ways of cost sharing under paragraph (c)(1)(i)(B) of this section, describe how these funds will be used.

(ii) The State must make its final State plan available to the public not less than 30 days before the beginning of the school year, including dissemination of such information on the State Web site.

(4)(i) Each SEA must make all annual disbursements from the high cost fund established under paragraph (c)(1)(i) of this section in accordance with the State plan published pursuant to paragraph (c)(3) of this section.

(ii) The costs associated with educating a high need child with a disability, as defined under paragraph (c)(3)(i)(A) of this section, are only those costs associated with providing direct special education and related services to the child that are identified in that child's IEP, including the cost of room and board for a residential placement determined necessary, consistent with § 300.114, to implement a child's IEP.

(iii) The funds in the high cost fund remain under the control of the State until disbursed to an LEA to support a specific child who qualifies under the State plan for the high cost funds or distributed to LEAs, consistent with paragraph (c)(9) of this section.

(5) The disbursements under paragraph (c)(4) of this section must not be used to support legal fees, court costs, or other costs associated with a cause of action brought on behalf of a child with a disability to ensure FAPE for such child.

(6) Nothing in paragraph (c) of this section—

(i) Limits or conditions the right of a child with a disability who is assisted under Part B of the Act to receive FAPE pursuant to section

612(a)(1) of the Act in the least restrictive environment pursuant to section 612(a)(5) of the Act; or

(ii) Authorizes an SEA or LEA to establish a limit on what may be spent on the education of a child with a disability.

(7) Notwithstanding the provisions of paragraphs (c)(1) through (6) of this section, a State may use funds reserved pursuant to paragraph (c)(1)(i) of this section for implementing a placement neutral cost sharing and reimbursement program of high need, low incidence, catastrophic, or extraordinary aid to LEAs that provides services to high need children based on eligibility criteria for such programs that were created not later than January 1, 2004, and are currently in operation, if such program serves children that meet the requirement of the definition of a high need child with a disability as described in paragraph (c)(3)(i)(A) of this section.

(8) Disbursements provided under paragraph (c) of this section must not be used to pay costs that otherwise would be reimbursed as medical assistance for a child with a disability under the State Medicaid program under Title XIX of the Social Security Act.

(9) Funds reserved under paragraph (c)(1)(i) of this section from the appropriation for any fiscal year, but not expended pursuant to paragraph (c)(4) of this section before the beginning of their last year of availability for obligation, must be allocated to LEAs in the same manner as other funds from the appropriation for that fiscal year are allocated to LEAs under § 300.705 during their final year of availability.

(d) Inapplicability of certain prohibitions. A State may use funds the State reserves under paragraphs (a) and (b) of this section without regard to—

(1) The prohibition on commingling of funds in § 300.162(b).

(2) The prohibition on supplanting other funds in § 300.162(c).

(e) Special rule for increasing funds. A State may use funds the State reserves under paragraph (a)(1) of this section as a result of inflationary increases under paragraph (a)(2) of this section to carry out activities authorized under paragraph (b)(4)(i), (iii), (vii), or (viii) of this section.

(f) Flexibility in using funds for Part C. Any State eligible to receive a grant under section 619 of the Act may use funds made available under paragraph (a)(1) of this section, § 300.705(c), or § 300.814(e) to develop and implement a State policy jointly with the lead agency under Part C of the Act and the SEA to provide early intervention services (which must include an educational component that promotes school readiness and incorporates preliteracy, language, and numeracy skills) in accordance with Part C of

the Act to children with disabilities who are eligible for services under section 619 of the Act and who previously received services under Part C of the Act until the children enter, or are eligible under State law to enter, kindergarten, or elementary school as appropriate.

(Approved by the Office of Management and Budget under control number 1820–0600)

(Authority: 20 U.S.C. 1411(e))

§ 300.705 Subgrants to LEAs.

(a) Subgrants required. Each State that receives a grant under section 611 of the Act for any fiscal year must distribute any funds the State does not reserve under §300.704 to LEAs (including public charter schools that operate as LEAs) in the State that have established their eligibility under section 613 of the Act for use in accordance with Part B of the Act. Effective with funds that become available on the July 1, 2009, each State must distribute funds to eligible LEAs, including public charter schools that operate as LEAs, even if the LEA is not serving any children with disabilities.

(b) Allocations to LEAs. For each fiscal year for which funds are allocated to States under § 300.703, each State shall allocate funds as follows:

(1) Base payments. The State first must award each LEA described in paragraph (a) of this section the amount the LEA would have received under section 611 of the Act for fiscal year 1999, if the State had distributed 75 percent of its grant for that year under section 611(d) of the Act, as that section was then in effect.

(2) Base payment adjustments. For any fiscal year after 1999—

(i) If a new LEA is created, the State must divide the base allocation determined under paragraph (b)(1) of this section for the LEAs that would have been responsible for serving children with disabilities now being served by the new LEA, among the new LEA and affected LEAs based on the relative numbers of children with disabilities ages 3 through 21, or ages 6 through 21 if a State has had its payment reduced under § 300.703(b), currently provided special education by each of the LEAs;

(ii) If one or more LEAs are combined into a single new LEA, the State must combine the base allocations of the merged LEAs;

(iii) If, for two or more LEAs, geographic boundaries or administrative responsibility for providing services to children with disabilities ages 3 through 21 change, the base allocations of affected LEAs must be redistributed among affected LEAs based on the relative numbers of children with disabilities ages 3 through 21, or ages 6 through 21 if a State has had its payment reduced under § 300.703(b), currently provided special education by each affected LEA; and

(iv) If an LEA received a base payment of

zero in its first year of operation, the SEA must adjust the base payment for the first fiscal year after the first annual child count in which the LEA reports that it is serving any children with disabilities. The State must divide the base allocation determined under paragraph (b)(1) of this section for the LEAs that would have been responsible for serving children with disabilities now being served by the LEA, among the LEA and affected LEAs based on the relative numbers of children with disabilities ages 3 through 21, or ages 6 through 21 currently provided special education by each of the LEAs. This requirement takes effect with funds that become available on July 1, 2009.

(3) Allocation of remaining funds. After making allocations under paragraph (b)(1) of this section, as adjusted by paragraph (b)(2) of this section, the State must—

(i) Allocate 85 percent of any remaining funds to those LEAs on the basis of the relative numbers of children enrolled in public and private elementary schools and secondary schools within the LEA's jurisdiction; and

(ii) Allocate 15 percent of those remaining funds to those LEAs in accordance with their relative numbers of children living in poverty, as determined by the SEA.

(c) Reallocation of LEA funds. (1) If an SEA determines that an LEA is adequately providing FAPE to all children with disabilities residing in the area served by that agency with State and local funds, the SEA may reallocate any portion of the funds under this part that are not needed by that LEA to provide FAPE, to other LEAs in the State that are not adequately providing special education and related services to all children with disabilities residing in the areas served by those other LEAs. The SEA may also retain those funds for use at the State level to the extent the State has not reserved the maximum amount of funds it is permitted to reserve for State-level activities pursuant to § 300.704.

(2) After an SEA distributes funds under this part to an eligible LEA that is not serving any children with disabilities, as provided in paragraph (a) of this section, the SEA must determine, within a reasonable period of time prior to the end of the carryover period in 34 CFR 76.709, whether the LEA has obligated the funds. The SEA may reallocate any of those funds not obligated by the LEA to other LEAs in the State that are not adequately providing special education and related services to all children with disabilities residing in the areas served by those other LEAs. The SEA may also retain those funds for use at the State level to the extent the State has not reserved the maximum amount of funds it is permitted to reserve for State-level activities pursuant to § 300.704.

(Approved by the Office of Management

and Budget under control number 1820–0030)
(Authority: 20 U.S.C. 1411(f))

§ 300.706 [Reserved]

Secretary of the Interior

§ 300.707 Use of amounts by Secretary of the Interior.

(a) Definitions. For purposes of §§ 300.707 through 300.716, the following definitions apply:

(1) Reservation means Indian Country as defined in 18 U.S.C. 1151.

(2) Tribal governing body has the definition given that term in 25 U.S.C. 2021(19).

(b) Provision of amounts for assistance. The Secretary provides amounts to the Secretary of the Interior to meet the need for assistance for the education of children with disabilities on reservations aged 5 to 21, inclusive, enrolled in elementary schools and secondary schools for Indian children operated or funded by the Secretary of the Interior. The amount of the payment for any fiscal year is equal to 80 percent of the amount allotted under section 611(b)(2) of the Act for that fiscal year. Of the amount described in the preceding sentence, after the Secretary of the Interior reserves funds for administration under § 300.710, 80 percent must be allocated to such schools by July 1 of that fiscal year and 20 percent must be allocated to such schools by September 30 of that fiscal year.

(c) Additional requirement. With respect to all other children aged 3 to 21, inclusive, on reservations, the SEA of the State in which the reservation is located must ensure that all of the requirements of Part B of the Act are implemented.

(Authority: 20 U.S.C. 1411(h)(1))

§ 300.708 Submission of information.

The Secretary may provide the Secretary of the Interior amounts under § 300.707 for a fiscal year only if the Secretary of the Interior submits to the Secretary information that—

(a) Meets the requirements of section 612(a)(1), (3) through (9), (10)(B) through (C), (11) through (12), (14) through (16), (19), and (21) through (25) of the Act (including monitoring and evaluation activities);

(b) Meets the requirements of section 612(b) and (e) of the Act;

(c) Meets the requirements of section 613(a)(1), (2)(A)(i), (7) through (9) and section 613(i) of the Act (references to LEAs in these sections must be read as references to elementary schools and secondary schools for Indian children operated or funded by the Secretary of the Interior);

(d) Meets the requirements of section 616 of the Act that apply to States (references to LEAs in section 616 of the Act must be read as references to elementary schools and secondary schools for Indian children operated or funded by the Secretary of the Interior).

(e) Meets the requirements of this part that implement the sections of the Act listed in paragraphs (a) through (d) of this section;

(f) Includes a description of how the Secretary of the Interior will coordinate the provision of services under Part B of the Act with LEAs, tribes and tribal organizations, and other private and Federal service providers;

(g) Includes an assurance that there are public hearings, adequate notice of the hearings, and an opportunity for comment afforded to members of tribes, tribal governing bodies, and affected local school boards before the adoption of the policies, programs, and procedures related to the requirements described in paragraphs (a) through (d) of this section;

(h) Includes an assurance that the Secretary of the Interior provides the information that the Secretary may require to comply with section 618 of the Act;

(i)(1) Includes an assurance that the Secretary of the Interior and the Secretary of Health and Human Services have entered into a memorandum of agreement, to be provided to the Secretary, for the coordination of services, resources, and personnel between their respective Federal, State, and local offices and with the SEAs and LEAs and other entities to facilitate the provision of services to Indian children with disabilities residing on or near reservations.

(2) The agreement must provide for the apportionment of responsibilities and costs, including child find, evaluation, diagnosis, remediation or therapeutic measures, and (where appropriate) equipment and medical or personal supplies, as needed for a child with a disability to remain in a school or program; and

(j) Includes an assurance that the Department of the Interior will cooperate with the Department in its exercise of monitoring and oversight of the requirements in this section and §§ 300.709 through 300.711 and §§ 300.713 through 300.716, and any agreements entered into between the Secretary of the Interior and other entities under Part B of the Act, and will fulfill its duties under Part B of the Act. The Secretary withholds payments under § 300.707 with respect to the requirements described in this section in the same manner as the Secretary withholds payments under section 616(e)(6) of the Act.

(Authority: 20 U.S.C. 1411(h)(2) and (3))

§ 300.709 Public participation.

In fulfilling the requirements of § 300.708 the Secretary of the Interior must provide for public participation consistent with § 300.165.

(Authority: 20 U.S.C. 1411(h))

§ 300.710 Use of funds under Part B of the Act.

(a) The Secretary of the Interior may reserve five percent of its payment under § 300.707(b) in any fiscal year, or $500,000, whichever is greater, for administrative costs in carrying out the provisions of §§ 300.707 through 300.709, 300.711, and 300.713 through 300.716.

(b) Payments to the Secretary of the Interior under § 300.712 must be used in accordance with that section.

(Authority: 20 U.S.C. 1411(h)(1)(A))

§ 300.711 Early intervening services.

(a) The Secretary of the Interior may allow each elementary school and secondary school for Indian children operated or funded by the Secretary of the Interior to use not more than 15 percent of the amount the school receives under § 300.707(b) for any fiscal year, in combination with other amounts (which may include amounts other than education funds), to develop and implement coordinated, early intervening services, which may include interagency financing structures, for children in kindergarten through grade 12 (with a particular emphasis on children in kindergarten through grade three) who have not been identified as needing special education or related services but who need additional academic and behavioral support to succeed in a general education environment, in accordance with section 613(f) of the Act.

(b) Each elementary school and secondary school for Indian children operated or funded by the Secretary of the Interior that develops and maintains coordinated early intervening services in accordance with section 613(f) of the Act and § 300.226 must annually report to the Secretary of the Interior in accordance with section 613(f) of the Act.

(Authority: 20 U.S.C. 1411(h) and 1413(f))

§ 300.712 Payments for education and services for Indian children with disabilities aged three through five.

(a) General. With funds appropriated under section 611(i) of the Act, the Secretary makes payments to the Secretary of the Interior to be distributed to tribes or tribal organizations (as defined under section 4 of the Indian Self-Determination and Education Assistance Act) or consortia of tribes or tribal organizations to provide for the coordination of assistance for special education and related services for children with disabilities aged three through five on reservations served by elementary schools and secondary schools for Indian children operated or funded by the Department of the Interior. The amount of the payments under paragraph (b) of this section for any fiscal year is equal to 20 percent of the amount allotted under § 300.701(b).

(b) Distribution of funds. The Secretary of the Interior must distribute the total amount of the payment under paragraph (a) of this section by allocating to each tribe, tribal organization, or consortium an amount based on the number of children with disabilities aged three through five residing on reservations as reported annually, divided by the total of those children served by all tribes or tribal organizations.

(c) Submission of information. To receive a payment under this section, the tribe or tribal organization must submit the figures to the Secretary of the Interior as required to determine the amounts to be allocated under paragraph (b) of this section. This information must be compiled and submitted to the Secretary.

(d) Use of funds. (1) The funds received by a tribe or tribal organization must be used to assist in child find, screening, and other procedures for the early identification of children aged three through five, parent training, and the provision of direct services. These activities may be carried out directly or through contracts or cooperative agreements with the BIA, LEAs, and other public or private nonprofit organizations. The tribe or tribal organization is encouraged to involve Indian parents in the development and implementation of these activities.

(2) The tribe or tribal organization, as appropriate, must make referrals to local, State, or Federal entities for the provision of services or further diagnosis.

(e) Biennial report. To be eligible to receive a grant pursuant to paragraph (a) of this section, the tribe or tribal organization must provide to the Secretary of the Interior a biennial report of activities undertaken under this section, including the number of contracts and cooperative agreements entered into, the number of children contacted and receiving services for each year, and the estimated number of children needing services during the two years following the year in which the report is made. The Secretary of the Interior must include a summary of this information on a biennial basis in the report to the Secretary required under section 611(h) of the Act. The Secretary may require any additional information from the Secretary of the Interior.

(f) Prohibitions. None of the funds allocated under this section may be used by the Secretary of the Interior for administrative purposes, including child count and the provision of technical assistance.

(Authority: 20 U.S.C. 1411(h)(4))

§ 300.713 Plan for coordination of services.

(a) The Secretary of the Interior must develop and implement a plan for the coordination of services for all Indian children with disabilities residing on reservations served by elementary schools and secondary schools for Indian children operated or funded by the Secretary of the Interior.

(b) The plan must provide for the coordination of services benefiting those children from whatever source, including tribes, the Indian Health Service, other BIA divisions, other Federal agencies, State educational agencies, and State, local, and tribal juvenile and adult correctional facilities.

(c) In developing the plan, the Secretary of the Interior must consult with all interested and involved parties.

(d) The plan must be based on the needs of the children and the system best suited for meeting those needs, and may involve the establishment of cooperative agreements between the BIA, other Federal agencies, and other entities.

(e) The plan also must be distributed upon request to States; to SEAs, LEAs, and other agencies providing services to infants, toddlers, and children with disabilities; to tribes; and to other interested parties.

(Authority: 20 U.S.C. 1411(h)(5))

§ 300.714 Establishment of advisory board.

(a) To meet the requirements of section 612(a)(21) of the Act, the Secretary of the Interior must establish, under the BIA, an advisory board composed of individuals involved in or concerned with the education and provision of services to Indian infants, toddlers, children, and youth with disabilities, including Indians with disabilities, Indian parents or guardians of such children, teachers, service providers, State and local educational officials, representatives of tribes or tribal organizations, representatives from State Interagency Coordinating Councils under section 641 of the Act in States having reservations, and other members representing the various divisions and entities of the BIA. The chairperson must be selected by the Secretary of the Interior.

(b) The advisory board must—

(1) Assist in the coordination of services within the BIA and with other local, State, and Federal agencies in the provision of education for infants, toddlers, and children with disabilities;

(2) Advise and assist the Secretary of the Interior in the performance of the Secretary of the Interior's responsibilities described in section 611(h) of the Act;

(3) Develop and recommend policies concerning effective inter- and intra-agency collaboration, including modifications to regulations, and the elimination of barriers to inter- and intra-agency programs and activities;

(4) Provide assistance and disseminate information on best practices, effective program coordination strategies, and recommendations for improved early intervention services or educational programming for Indian infants, toddlers, and children with disabilities; and

(5) Provide assistance in the preparation of information required under § 300.708(h).

(Authority: 20 U.S.C. 1411(h)(6))

§ 300.715 Annual reports.

(a) In general. The advisory board established under § 300.714 must prepare and submit to the Secretary of the Interior and to Congress an annual report containing a description of the activities of the advisory board for the preceding year.

(b) Availability. The Secretary of the Interior must make available to the Secretary the report described in paragraph (a) of this section.

(Authority: 20 U.S.C. 1411(h)(7))

§ 300.716 Applicable regulations.

The Secretary of the Interior must comply with the requirements of §§ 300.103 through 300.108, 300.110 through 300.124, 300.145 through 300.154, 300.156 through 300.160, 300.165, 300.170 through 300.186, 300.226, 300.300 through 300.606, 300.610 through 300.646, and 300.707 through 300.716.

(Authority: 20 U.S.C. 1411(h)(2)(A))

Definitions that Apply to this Subpart

§ 300.717 Definitions applicable to allotments, grants, and use of funds.

As used in this subpart—

(a) Freely associated States means the Republic of the Marshall Islands, the Federated States of Micronesia, and the Republic of Palau;

(b) Outlying areas means the United States Virgin Islands, Guam, American Samoa, and the Commonwealth of the Northern Mariana Islands;

(c) State means each of the 50 States, the District of Columbia, and the Commonwealth of Puerto Rico; and

(d) Average per-pupil expenditure in public elementary schools and secondary schools in the United States means—

(1) Without regard to the source of funds—

(i) The aggregate current expenditures, during the second fiscal year preceding the fiscal year for which the determination is made (or, if satisfactory data for that year are not available, during the most recent preceding fiscal year for which satisfactory data are available) of all LEAs in the 50 States and the District of Columbia; plus

(ii) Any direct expenditures by the State for the operation of those agencies; divided by (2) The aggregate number of children in average daily attendance to whom those agencies provided free public education during that preceding year.

(Authority: 20 U.S.C. 1401(22), 1411(b)(1) (C) and (g))

Acquisition of Equipment and Construction or Alteration of Facilities

§ 300.718 Acquisition of equipment and construction or alteration of facilities.

(a) General. If the Secretary determines that a program authorized under Part B of the Act will be improved by permitting program funds to be used to acquire appropriate equipment, or to construct new facilities or alter existing facilities, the Secretary may allow the use of those funds for those purposes.

(b) Compliance with certain regulations. Any construction of new facilities or alteration of existing facilities under paragraph (a) of this section must comply with the requirements of—

(1) Appendix A of part 36 of title 28, Code of Federal Regulations (commonly known as the "Americans with Disabilities Accessibility Standards for Buildings and Facilities"); or

(2) Appendix A of subpart 101–19.6 of title 41, Code of Federal Regulations (commonly known as the "Uniform Federal Accessibility Standards").

(Authority: 20 U.S.C. 1404)

Subpart H—Preschool Grants for Children with Disabilities

§ 300.800 In general.

The Secretary provides grants under section 619 of the Act to assist States to provide special education and related services in accordance with Part B of the Act—

(a) To children with disabilities aged three through five years; and

(b) At a State's discretion, to two-year-old children with disabilities who will turn three during the school year.

(Authority: 20 U.S.C. 1419(a))

§§ 300.801–300.802 [Reserved]

§ 300.803 Definition of State.

As used in this subpart, State means each of the 50 States, the District of Columbia, and the Commonwealth of Puerto Rico.

(Authority: 20 U.S.C. 1419(i))

§ 300.804 Eligibility.

A State is eligible for a grant under section 619 of the Act if the State— (a) Is eligible under section 612 of the Act to receive a grant under Part B of the Act; and

(b) Makes FAPE available to all children with disabilities, aged three through five, residing in the State.

(Approved by the Office of Management and Budget under control number 1820–0030)

(Authority: 20 U.S.C. 1419(b))

§ 300.805 [Reserved]

§ 300.806 Eligibility for financial assistance.

No State or LEA, or other public institution or agency, may receive a grant or enter into a contract or cooperative agreement under subpart 2 or 3 of Part D of the Act that relates exclusively to programs, projects, and activities pertaining to children aged three through five years, unless the State is eligible to receive a grant under section 619(b) of the Act.

(Authority: 20 U.S.C. 1481(e))

§ 300.807 Allocations to States.

The Secretary allocates the amount made available to carry out section 619 of the Act for a fiscal year among the States in accordance with §§ 300.808 through 300.810.

(Authority: 20 U.S.C. 1419(c)(1))

§ 300.808 Increase in funds.

If the amount available for allocation to States under § 300.807 for a fiscal year is equal to or greater than the amount allocated to the States under section 619 of the Act for the preceding fiscal year, those allocations are calculated as follows:

(a) Except as provided in § 300.809, the Secretary—

(1) Allocates to each State the amount the State received under section 619 of the Act for fiscal year 1997;

(2) Allocates 85 percent of any remaining funds to States on the basis of the States' relative populations of children aged three through five; and

(3) Allocates 15 percent of those remaining funds to States on the basis of the States' relative populations of all children aged three through five who are living in poverty.

(b) For the purpose of making grants under this section, the Secretary uses the most recent population data, including data on children living in poverty, that are available and satisfactory to the Secretary.

(Authority: 20 U.S.C. 1419(c)(2)(A))

§ 300.809 Limitations.

(a) Notwithstanding § 300.808, allocations under that section are subject to the following:

(1) No State's allocation may be less than its allocation under section 619 of the Act for the preceding fiscal year.

(2) No State's allocation may be less than the greatest of—

(i) The sum of—

(A) The amount the State received under section 619 of the Act for fiscal year 1997; and

(B) One-third of one percent of the amount by which the amount appropriated under section 619(j) of the Act for the fiscal year exceeds the amount appropriated for section 619 of the Act for fiscal year 1997;

(ii) The sum of—

(A) The amount the State received under section 619 of the Act for the preceding fiscal year; and

(B) That amount multiplied by the percentage by which the increase in the funds appropriated under section 619 of the Act from the preceding fiscal year exceeds 1.5 percent; or

(iii) The sum of—

(A) The amount the State received under section 619 of the Act for the preceding fiscal year; and

(B) That amount multiplied by 90 percent of the percentage increase in the amount appropriated under section 619 of the Act from the preceding fiscal year.

(b) Notwithstanding paragraph (a)(2) of this section, no State's allocation under § 300.808 may exceed the sum of—

(1) The amount the State received under section 619 of the Act for the preceding fiscal year; and

(2) That amount multiplied by the sum of 1.5 percent and the percentage increase in the amount appropriated under section 619 of the Act from the preceding fiscal year.

(c) If the amount available for allocation to States under § 300.808 and paragraphs (a) and (b) of this section is insufficient to pay those allocations in full, those allocations are ratably reduced, subject to paragraph (a)(1) of this section.

(Authority: 20 U.S.C. 1419(c)(2)(B) and (c)(2)(C))

§ 300.810 Decrease in funds.

If the amount available for allocations to States under § 300.807 for a fiscal year is less than the amount allocated to the States under section 619 of the Act for the preceding fiscal year, those allocations are calculated as follows:

(a) If the amount available for allocations is greater than the amount allocated to the States for fiscal year 1997, each State is allocated the sum of—

(1) The amount the State received under section 619 of the Act for fiscal year 1997; and

(2) An amount that bears the same relation to any remaining funds as the increase the State received under section 619 of the Act for the preceding fiscal year over fiscal year 1997 bears to the total of all such increases for all States.

(b) If the amount available for allocations is equal to or less than the amount allocated to the States for fiscal year 1997, each State is allocated the amount the State received for fiscal year 1997, ratably reduced, if necessary.

(Authority: 20 U.S.C. 1419(c)(3))

§ 300.811 [Reserved]
§ 300.812 Reservation for State activities.

(a) Each State may reserve not more than

the amount described in paragraph (b) of this section for administration and other State-level activities in accordance with §§ 300.813 and 300.814.

(b) For each fiscal year, the Secretary determines and reports to the SEA an amount that is 25 percent of the amount the State received under section 619 of the Act for fiscal year 1997, cumulatively adjusted by the Secretary for each succeeding fiscal year by the lesser of—

(1) The percentage increase, if any, from the preceding fiscal year in the State's allocation under section 619 of the Act; or

(2) The rate of inflation, as measured by the percentage increase, if any, from the preceding fiscal year in the Consumer Price Index For All Urban Consumers, published by the Bureau of Labor Statistics of the Department of Labor.

(Authority: 20 U.S.C. 1419(d))

§ 300.813 State administration.

(a) For the purpose of administering section 619 of the Act (including the coordination of activities under Part B of the Act with, and providing technical assistance to, other programs that provide services to children with disabilities), a State may use not more than 20 percent of the maximum amount the State may reserve under § 300.812 for any fiscal year.

(b) Funds described in paragraph (a) of this section may also be used for the administration of Part C of the Act.

(Authority: 20 U.S.C. 1419(e))

§ 300.814 Other State-level activities.

Each State must use any funds the State reserves under § 300.812 and does not use for administration under § 300.813—

(a) For support services (including establishing and implementing the mediation process required by section 615(e) of the Act), which may benefit children with disabilities younger than three or older than five as long as those services also benefit children with disabilities aged three through five;

(b) For direct services for children eligible for services under section 619 of the Act;

(c) For activities at the State and local levels to meet the performance goals established by the State under section 612(a)(15) of the Act;

(d) To supplement other funds used to develop and implement a statewide coordinated services system designed to improve results for children and families, including children with disabilities and their families, but not more than one percent of the amount received by the State under section 619 of the Act for a fiscal year;

(e) To provide early intervention services (which must include an educational component that promotes school readiness and incorporates preliteracy, language, and numeracy skills) in accordance with Part C of the Act to children

with disabilities who are eligible for services under section 619 of the Act and who previously received services under Part C of the Act until such children enter, or are eligible under State law to enter, kindergarten; or

(f) At the State's discretion, to continue service coordination or case management for families who receive services under Part C of the Act, consistent with § 300.814(e).

(Authority: 20 U.S.C. 1419(f))

§ 300.815 Subgrants to LEAs.

Each State that receives a grant under section 619 of the Act for any fiscal year must distribute all of the grant funds the State does not reserve under § 300.812 to LEAs (including public charter schools that operate as LEAs) in the State that have established their eligibility under section 613 of the Act. Effective with funds that become available on July 1, 2009, each State must distribute funds to eligible LEAs that are responsible for providing education to children aged three through five years, including public charter schools that operate as LEAs, even if the LEA is not serving any preschool children with disabilities.

(Authority: 20 U.S.C. 1419(g)(1))

§ 300.816 Allocations to LEAs.

(a) Base payments. The State must first award each LEA described in § 300.815 the amount that agency would have received under section 619 of the Act for fiscal year 1997 if the State had distributed 75 percent of its grant for that year under section 619(c)(3), as such section was then in effect.

(b) Base payment adjustments. For fiscal year 1998 and beyond—

(1) If a new LEA is created, the State must divide the base allocation determined under paragraph (a) of this section for the LEAs that would have been responsible for serving children with disabilities now being served by the new LEA, among the new LEA and affected LEAs based on the relative numbers of children with disabilities ages three through five currently provided special education by each of the LEAs;

(2) If one or more LEAs are combined into a single new LEA, the State must combine the base allocations of the merged LEAs;

(3) If for two or more LEAs, geographic boundaries or administrative responsibility for providing services to children with disabilities ages three through five changes, the base allocations of affected LEAs must be redistributed among affected LEAs based on the relative numbers of children with disabilities ages three through five currently provided special education by each affected LEA; and

(4) If an LEA received a base payment of zero in its first year of operation, the SEA must adjust the base payment for the first fiscal year

after the first annual child count in which the LEA reports that it is serving any children with disabilities aged three through five years. The State must divide the base allocation determined under paragraph (a) of this section for the LEAs that would have been responsible for serving children with disabilities aged three through five years now being served by the LEA, among the LEA and affected LEAs based on the relative numbers of children with disabilities aged three through five years currently provided special education by each of the LEAs. This requirement takes effect with funds that become available on July 1, 2009.

(c) Allocation of remaining funds. After making allocations under paragraph (a) of this section, the State must—

(1) Allocate 85 percent of any remaining funds to those LEAs on the basis of the relative numbers of children enrolled in public and private elementary schools and secondary schools within the LEA's jurisdiction; and

(2) Allocate 15 percent of those remaining funds to those LEAs in accordance with their relative numbers of children living in poverty, as determined by the SEA.

(d) Use of best data. For the purpose of making grants under this section, States must apply on a uniform basis across all LEAs the best data that are available to them on the numbers of children enrolled in public and private elementary and secondary schools and the numbers of children living in poverty.

(Authority: 20 U.S.C. 1419(g)(1))

§ 300.817 Reallocation of LEA funds.

(a) If an SEA determines that an LEA is adequately providing FAPE to all children with disabilities aged three through five years residing in the area served by the LEA with State and local funds, the SEA may reallocate any portion of the funds under section 619 of the Act that are not needed by that LEA to provide FAPE, to other LEAs in the State that are not adequately providing special education and related services

to all children with disabilities aged three through five years residing in the areas served by those other LEAs. The SEA may also retain those funds for use at the State level to the extent the State has not reserved the maximum amount of funds it is permitted to reserve for State-level activities pursuant to § 300.812.

(b) After an SEA distributes section 619 funds to an eligible LEA that is not serving any children with disabilities aged three through five years, as provided in § 300.815, the SEA must determine, within a reasonable period of time prior to the end of the carryover period in 34 CFR 76.709, whether the LEA has obligated the funds. The SEA may reallocate any of those funds not *73029 obligated by the LEA to other LEAs in the State that are not adequately providing special education and related services to all children with disabilities aged three through five years residing in the areas served by those other LEAs. The SEA may also retain those funds for use at the State level to the extent the State has not reserved the maximum amount of funds it is permitted to reserve for State-level activities pursuant to § 300.812.

(Authority: 20 U.S.C. 1419(g)(2))

§ 300.818 Part C of the Act inapplicable.

Part C of the Act does not apply to any child with a disability receiving FAPE, in accordance with Part B of the Act, with funds received under section 619 of the Act.

(Authority: 20 U.S.C. 1419(h))

Appendix A to Part 300—Excess Costs Calculation

Except as otherwise provided, amounts provided to an LEA under Part B of the Act may be used only to pay the excess costs of providing special education and related services to children with disabilities. Excess costs are those costs for the education of an elementary school or secondary school student with a disability that are in excess of the average annual per student expenditure in an LEA during the preceding school year for an elementary school or secondary school student, as may be appropriate. An LEA must spend at least the average annual per student expenditure on the education of an elementary school or secondary school child with a disability before funds under Part B of the Act are used to pay the excess costs of providing special education and related services.

Section 602(8) of the Act and § 300.16 require the LEA to compute the minimum average amount separately for children with disabilities in its elementary schools and for children with disabilities in its secondary schools. LEAs may not compute the minimum average amount it must spend on the education of children with disabilities based on a combination of the enrollments in its elementary schools and secondary schools. The following example shows how to compute the minimum average amount an LEA must spend for the education of each of its elementary school children with disabilities under section 602(3) of the Act before it may use funds under Part B of the Act.

a. First the LEA must determine the total amount of its expenditures for elementary school students from all sources—local, State, and Federal (including Part B)—in the preceding school year. Only capital outlay and debt services are excluded. Example: The following is an example of a computation for children with disabilities enrolled in an LEA's elementary schools. In this example, the LEA had an average elementary school enrollment for the preceding school year of 800 (including 100 children with disabilities). The LEA spent the following amounts last year for elementary school students (including its elementary school children with disabilities):

(1) From State and local tax funds.	$6,500,000
(2) From Federal funds	+ 600,000
Total expenditures	7,100,000

Of this total, $60,000 was for capital outlay and debt service relating to the education of elementary school students. This must be subtracted from total expenditures.

(1) Total Expenditures	$7,100,000
(2) Less capital outlay and debt.	-60,000
Total expenditures for elementary school students less capital outlay and debt.	$7,040,000

b. Next, the LEA must subtract from the total expenditures amounts spent for:
(1) IDEA, Part B allocation,
(2) ESEA, Title I, Part A allocation,
(3) ESEA, Title III, Parts A and B allocation,
(4) State and local funds for children with disabilities, and
(5) State or local funds for programs under ESEA, Title I, Part A, and Title III, Parts A and B. These are funds that the LEA actually spent, not funds received last year but carried over for the current school year. Example: The LEA spent the following amounts for elementary school students last year:

(1) From funds under IDEA, Part B allocation.	$ 200,000
(2) From funds under ESEA, Title I, Part A allocation.	250,000
(3) From funds under ESEA, Title III, Parts A and B allocation.	50,000
(4) From State funds and local funds for children with disabilities.	500,000
(5) From State and local funds for programs under ESEA, Title I, Part A, and Title III, Parts A and B.	150,000
Total	1,150,000

(1) Total expenditures less capital outlay and debt.	7,040,000
(2) Other deductions.	-1,150,000
Total	$5,890,000

c. Except as otherwise provided, the LEA next must determine the average annual per student expenditure for its elementary schools dividing the average number of students enrolled in the elementary schools of the agency during the preceding year (including its children with disabilities) into the amount computed under the above paragraph. The amount obtained through this computation is the minimum amount the LEA must spend (on the average) for the education of each of its elementary school children with disabilities. Funds under Part B of the Act may be used only for costs over and above this minimum.

(1) Amount from Step b	$5,890,000
(2) Average number of students enrolled.	800
(3) $5,890,000/800 Average annual per student expenditure	$ 7,362

d. Except as otherwise provided, to determine the total minimum amount of funds the LEA must spend for the education of its elementary school children with disabilities in the LEA (not including capital outlay and debt service), the LEA must multiply the number of elementary school children with disabilities in the LEA times the average annual per student expenditure obtained in paragraph c above. Funds under Part B of the Act can only be used for excess costs over and above this minimum.

(1) Number of children with disabilities in the LEA's elementary schools.	100
(2) Average annual per student expenditure.	$ 7,362
(3) $7,362 x 100. Total minimum amount of funds the LEA must spend for the education of children with disabilities enrolled in the LEA's elementary schools before using Part B funds.	$736,200

Appendix B to Part 300—Proportionate Share Calculation

Each LEA must expend, during the grant period, on the provision of special education and related services for the parentally-placed private school children with disabilities enrolled in private elementary schools and secondary schools located in the LEA an amount that is equal to—

(1) A proportionate share of the LEA's subgrant under section 611(f) of the Act for children with disabilities aged 3 through 21. This is an amount that is the same proportion of the LEA's total subgrant under section 611(f) of the Act as the number of parentally-placed private school children with disabilities aged 3 through 21 enrolled in private elementary schools and secondary schools located in the LEA is to the total number of children with disabilities enrolled in public and private elementary schools and secondary schools located in the LEA aged 3 through 21; and

(2) A proportionate share of the LEA's subgrant under section 619(g) of the Act for children with disabilities aged 3 through 5. This is an amount that is the same proportion of the LEA's total subgrant under section 619(g) of the Act as the total number of parentally-placed private school children with disabilities aged 3 through 5 enrolled in private elementary schools located in the LEA is to the total number of children with disabilities enrolled in public and private elementary schools located in the LEA aged 3 through 5.

Consistent with section 612(a)(10)(A)(i) of the Act and § 300.133 of these regulations, annual expenditures for parentally-placed private school children with disabilities are calculated based on the total number of children with disabilities enrolled in public and private elementary schools and secondary schools located in the LEA eligible to receive special education and related services under Part B, as compared with the total number of eligible parentally-placed private school children with disabilities enrolled in private elementary schools located in the LEA. This ratio is used to determine the proportion of the LEA's total Part B subgrants under section 611(f) of the Act for children aged 3 through 21, and under section 619(g) of the Act for children aged 3 through 5, that is to be expended on services for parentally-placed private school children with disabilities enrolled in private elementary schools and secondary schools located in the LEA.

The following is an example of how the proportionate share is calculated: There are 300 eligible children with disabilities enrolled in the Flintstone School District and 20 eligible parentally-placed private school children with disabilities enrolled in private elementary schools and secondary schools located in the LEA for a total of 320 eligible public and private school children with disabilities (note: proportionate share for parentally-placed private school children is based on total children eligible, not children served). The number of eligible parentally-placed private school children with disabilities (20) divided by the total number of eligible public and private school children with disabilities (320) indicates that 6.25 percent of the LEA's subgrant must be spent for the group of eligible parentally-placed children with disabilities enrolled in private elementary schools and secondary schools located in the LEA. Flintstone School District receives $152,500 in Federal flow through funds.

Therefore, the LEA must spend $9,531.25 on special education or related services to the group of parentally-placed private school children with disabilities enrolled in private elementary schools and secondary schools located in the LEA. (Note: The LEA must calculate the proportionate share of IDEA funds before earmarking funds for any early intervening activities in § 300.226).

The following outlines the calculations for the example of how the proportionate share is calculated.

Proportionate Share Calculation for Parentally-Placed Private School Children with Disabilities For Flintstone School District:

Number of eligible children with disabilities in public schools in the LEA	300
Number of parentally-placed eligible children with disabilities in private elementary schools and secondary schools located in the LEA	+20
Total number of eligible children	320

FEDERAL FLOW-THROUGH FUNDS TO FLINTSTONE SCHOOL DISTRICT

Total allocation to Flintstone	$152,500
Calculating Proportionate Share:	
Total allocation to Flinstone	152,500
Divided by total number of eligible children	320
Average allocation per eligible child	476.5625
Multiplied by the number of parentally placed children with disabilities	20
Amount to be expended for parentally-placed children with disabilities	9,531.25

Appendix C to Part 300—National Instructional Materials Accessibility Standard (NIMAS)

Under sections 612(a)(23)(A) and 674(e)(4) of the Individuals with Disabilities Education Act, as amended by the Individuals with Disabilities Education Improvement Act of 2004, the Secretary of Education establishes the NIMAS. Under section 674(e)(4) of the Act, the NIMAS applies to print instructional materials published after July 19, 2006. The purpose of the NIMAS is to help increase the availability and timely delivery of print instructional materials in accessible formats to blind or other persons with print disabilities in elementary and secondary schools.

Technical Specifications—The Baseline Element Set

The Baseline Element Set details the minimum requirement that must be delivered to fulfill the NIMAS. It is the responsibility of publishers to provide this NIMAS-conformant XML content file, a package file (OPF), a PDF-format copy of the title page (or whichever page(s) contain(s) ISBN and copyright information), and a full set of the content's images. All of the images included within a work must be provided in a folder and placeholders entered in the relevant XML document indicating their location (all images must be included). The preferred image type is SVG, next is either PNG or JPG format. Images should be rendered in the same size/proportion as their originals at 300 dpi. Images should be named with relative path filenames in XML files (example: img id="staricon4" src="./images/U10C02/ staricon4.jpg" alt="star icon").

NIMAS-conformant content must be valid to the NIMAS 1.1 [see ANSI/NISO Z39.86 2005 or subsequent revisions]. In addition, files are required to use the tags from the Baseline Element Set when such tags are appropriate. Publishers are encouraged to augment the required Baseline Element Set with tags from the Optional Element Set (elements not included in the Standard) as applicable. For the purposes of NIMAS, appropriate usage of elements, both baseline and optional, is defined by the DAISY Structure Guidelines. Files that do not follow these guidelines in the selection and application of tags are not conformant to this Standard. Both optional elements and appropriate structure guidelines may be located within Z39.86–2002 and Z39.86– 2005 available from http://www.daisy.org/ z3986/. Use of the most current standard is recommended.

Appendix D to Part 300—Maintenance of Effort and Early Intervening Services

LEAs that seek to reduce their local maintenance of effort in accordance with § 300.205(d) and use some of their Part B funds for early intervening services under § 300.226 must do so with caution because the local maintenance of effort reduction provision and the authority to use Part B funds for early intervening services are interconnected. The decisions that an LEA makes about the amount of funds that it uses for one purpose affect the amount that it may use for the other. Below are examples that illustrate how §§ 300.205(d) and 300.226(a) affect one another.

Example 1: In this example, the amount that is 15 percent of the LEA's total grant (see § 300.226(a)), which is the maximum amount that the LEA may use for early intervening services (EIS), is greater than the amount that may be used for local maintenance of effort (MOE) reduction (50 percent of the increase in the LEA's grant from the prior year's grant) (see § 300.205(a)).

Prior Year's Allocation	$900,000.
Current Year's Allocation	1,000,000.
Increase	100,000.
Maximum Available for MOE Reduction	50,000.
Maximum Available for EIS	150,000.

If the LEA chooses to set aside $150,000 for EIS, it may not reduce its MOE (MOE maximum $50,000 less $150,000 for EIS means $0 can be used for MOE).

If the LEA chooses to set aside $100,000 for EIS, it may not reduce its MOE (MOE maximum $50,000 less $100,000 for EIS means $0 can be used for MOE).

If the LEA chooses to set aside $50,000 for EIS, it may not reduce its MOE (MOE maximum $50,000 less $50,000 for EIS means $0 can be used for MOE).

If the LEA chooses to set aside $30,000 for EIS, it may reduce its MOE by $20,000 (MOE maximum $50,000 less $30,000 for EIS means $20,000 can be used for MOE).

If the LEA chooses to set aside $0 for EIS, it may reduce its MOE by $50,000 (MOE maximum $50,000 less $0 for EIS means $50,000 can be used for MOE).

Example 2: In this example, the amount that is 15 percent of the LEA's total grant (see § 300.226(a)), which is the maximum amount that the LEA may use for EIS, is less than the amount that may be used for MOE reduction (50 percent of the increase in the LEA's grant from the prior year's grant) (see § 300.205(a)).

Prior Year's Allocation	$1,000,000.
Current Year's Allocation	2,000,000.
Increase	1,000,000.
Maximum Available for MOE Reduction	500,000.
Maximum Available for EIS	300,000.

If the LEA chooses to use no funds for MOE, it may set aside $300,000 for EIS (EIS maximum $300,000 less $0 means $300,000 for EIS).

If the LEA chooses to use $100,000 for MOE, it may set aside $200,000 for EIS (EIS maximum $300,000 less $100,000 means $200,000 for EIS).

If the LEA chooses to use $150,000 for MOE, it may set aside $150,000 for EIS (EIS maximum $300,000 less $150,000 means $150,000 for EIS).

If the LEA chooses to use $300,000 for MOE, it may not set aside anything for EIS (EIS maximum $300,000 less $300,000 means $0 for EIS).

If the LEA chooses to use $500,000 for MOE, it may not set aside anything for EIS (EIS maximum $300,000 less $500,000 means $0 for EIS).

Appendix E to Part 300—Index for IDEA—Part B Regulations (34 CFR Part 300)

PART 104—NONDISCRIMINATION ON THE BASIS OF HANDICAP IN PROGRAMS AND ACTIVITIES RECEIVING OR BENEFITING FROM FEDERAL FINANCIAL ASSISTANCE

AUTHORITY: Sec. 504, Rehabilitation Act of 1973, Pub. L. 93–112, 87 Stat. 394 (29 U.S.C. 794); sec. 111(a), Rehabilitation Act Amendments of 1974, Pub. L 93–516, 88 Stat. 1619 (29 U.S.C. 706); sec. 606, Education of the Handicapped Act (20 U.S.C. 1405), as amended by Pub. L 94–142, 89 Stat. 795.

Subpart A—General Provisions

§ 104.1 Purpose.

The purpose of this part is to effectuate section 504 of the Rehabilitation Act of 1973, which is designed to eliminate discrimination on the basis of handicap in any program or activity receiving Federal financial assistance.

§ 104.2 Application.

This part applies to each recipient of Federal financial assistance from the Department of Education and to each program or activity that receives or benefits from such assistance.

§ 104.3 Definitions.

As used in this part, the term:

(a) *The Act* means the Rehabilitation Act of 1973, Pub. L. 93–112, as amended by the Rehabilitation Act Amendments of 1974, Pub. L. 93–516, 29 U.S.C. 794

(b) *Section 504* means section 504 of the Act.

(c) *Education of the Handicapped Act* means that statute as amended by the Education for all Handicapped Children Act of 1975, Pub. L 94–142, 20 U.S.C. 1401 et seq.

(d) *Department* means the Department of Education.

(e) *Assistant Secretary* means the Assistant Secretary for Civil Rights of the Department of Education.

(f) *Recipient* means any state or its political subdivision, any instrumentality of a state or its political subdivision, any public or private agency, institution, organization, or other entity, or any person to which Federal financial assistance is extended directly or through another recipient, including any successor, assignee, or transferee of a recipient, but excluding the ultimate beneficiary of the assistance.

(g) *Applicant for assistance* means one who submits an application, request, or plan required to be approved by a Department official or by a recipient as a condition to becoming a recipient.

(h) *Federal financial assistance* means any grant, loan, contract (other than a procurement contract or a contract of insurance or guaranty), or any other arrangement by which the Department provides or otherwise makes available assistance in the form of:

(1) Funds;

(2) Services of Federal personnel; or

(3) Real and personal property or any interest in or use of such property, including:

(i) Transfers or leases of such property for less than fair market value or for reduced consideration; and

(ii) Proceeds from a subsequent transfer or lease of such property if the Federal share of its fair market value is not returned to the Federal Government.

(i) *Facility* means all or any portion of buildings, structures, equipment, roads, walks, parking lots, or other real or personal property or interest in such property.

(j) *Handicapped person.* (1) "Handicapped persons" means any person who (i) has a physical or mental impairment which substantially limits one or more major life activities, (ii) has a record of such an impairment, or (iii) is regarded as having such an impairment.

(2) As used in paragraph (j)(1) of this section, the phrase:

(i) Physical or mental impairment means (A) any physiological disorder or condition, cosmetic disfigurement, or anatomical loss affecting one or more of the following body systems: neurological; musculoskeletal: special sense organs; respiratory, including speech organs; cardiovascular, reproductive, digestive, genito-urinary; hemic and lymphatic; skin; and endocrine; or (B) any mental or psychological disorder, such as mental retardation, organic brain syndrome, emotional or mental illness, and specific learning disabilities.

(ii) *Major life activities* means functions such as caring for one's self, performing manual tasks, walking, seeing, hearing, speaking, breathing, learning, and working.

(iii) *Has a record of such an impairment* means has a history of, or has been misclassified as having, a mental or physical impairment that substantially limits one or more major life activities.

(iv) *Is regarded as having an impairment* means (A) has a physical or mental impairment that does not substantially limit major life activities but that is treated by a recipient as constituting such a limitation; (B) has a physical or mental impairment that substantially limits major life activities only as a result of the attitudes of others toward such impairment; or (C) has none of the impairments defined in paragraph (j)(2)(i) of this section but is treated by a recipient as having such an impairment.

(k) *Qualified handicapped person* means:

(1) With respect to employment, a handicapped person who, with reasonable accommodation, can perform the essential functions of the job in question;

(2) With respect to public preschool elementary, secondary, or adult educational services, a handicapped person (i) of an age during which nonhandicapped persons are provided such services, (ii) of any age during which it is mandatory under state law to provide such services to handicapped persons, or (iii) to whom a state is required to provide a free appropriate public education under section 612 of the Education of the Handicapped Act; and

(3) With respect to postsecondary and vocational education services, a handicapped person who meets the academic and technical standards requisite to admission or participation in the recipient's education program or activity;

(4) With respect to other services, a handicapped person who meets the essential eligibility requirements for the receipt of such services.

(l) *Handicap* means any condition or characteristic that renders a person a handicapped person as defined in paragraph (j) of this section.

§ 104.4 Discrimination prohibited.

(a) *General.* No qualified handicapped person shall, on the basis of handicap, be excluded from participation in, be denied the benefits of, or otherwise be subjected to discrimination under any program or activity which receives or benefits from Federal financial assistance.

(b) *Discriminatory actions prohibited.* (1) A recipient, in providing any aid, benefit, or service, may not, directly or through contractual, licensing, or other arrangements, on the basis of handicap:

(i) Deny a qualified handicapped person the opportunity to participate in or benefit from the aid, benefit, or service;

(ii) Afford a qualified handicapped person an opportunity to participate in or benefit from the aid, benefit, or service that is not equal to that afforded others;

(iii) Provide a qualified handicapped person with an aid, benefit, or service that is not as effective as that provided to others;

(iv) Provide different or separate aid, benefits, or services to handicapped persons or to any class of handicapped persons unless such action is necessary to provide qualified handicapped persons with aid, benefits, or services that are as effective as those provided to others;

(v) Aid or perpetuate discrimination against a qualified handicapped person by providing significant assistance to an agency, organization, or person that discriminates on the basis of handicap in providing any aid, benefit, or service to beneficiaries of the recipients program;

(vi) Deny a qualified handicapped person the opportunity to participate as a member of planning or advisory boards; or

(vii) Otherwise limit a qualified handicapped person in the enjoyment of any right, privilege, advantage, or opportunity enjoyed by others receiving an aid, benefit, or service.

(2) For purposes of this part, aids, benefits, and services, to be equally effective, are not required to produce the identical result or level of achievement for handicapped and nonhandicapped persons, but must afford handicapped persons equal opportunity to obtain the same result, to gain the same benefit, or to reach the same level of achievement, in the most integrated setting appropriate to the person's needs.

(3) Despite the existence of separate or different programs or activities provided in accordance with this part, a recipient may not deny a qualified handicapped person the opportunity to participate in such programs or activities that are not separate or different.

(4) A recipient may not, directly or through contractual or other arrangements, utilize criteria or methods of administration (i) that have the effect of subjecting qualified handicapped

persons to discrimination on the basis of handicap, (ii) that have the purpose or effect of defeating or substantially impairing accomplishment of the objectives of the recipient's program with respect to handicapped persons, or (iii) that perpetuate the discrimination of another recipient if both recipients are subject to common administrative control or are agencies of the same State.

(5) In determining the site or location of a facility, an applicant for assistance or a recipient may not make selections (i) that have the effect of excluding handicapped persons from, denying them the benefits of, or otherwise subjecting them to discrimination under any program or activity that receives or benefits from Federal financial assistance or (ii) that have the purpose or effect of defeating or substantially impairing the accomplishment of the objectives of the program or activity with respect to handicapped persons.

(6) As used in this section, the aid, benefit, or service provided under a program or activity receiving or benefiting from Federal financial assistance includes any aid, benefit, or service provided in or through a facility that has been constructed, expanded, altered, leased or rented, or otherwise acquired, in whole or in part, with Federal financial assistance.

(c) *Programs limited by Federal law.* The exclusion of nonhandicapped persons from the benefits of a program limited by Federal statute or executive order to handicapped persons or the exclusion of a specific class of handicapped persons from a program limited by Federal statute or executive order to a different class of handicapped persons is not prohibited by this part.

§ 104.5 Assurances required.

(a) *Assurances.* An applicant for Federal financial assistance for a program or activity to which this part applies shall submit an assurance, in a form specified by the Assistant Secretary that the program will be operated in compliance with this part. An applicant may incorporate these assurances by reference in subsequent applications to the Department.

(b) *Duration of Obligation.* (1) In the case of Federal financial assistance extended in the form of real property or to provide real property or structures on the property, the assurances will obligate the recipient or, in the case of a subsequent transfer, the transferee, for the period during which the real property or structures are for the purpose for which Federal financial assistance is extended or for another purpose involving the provision of similar services or benefits.

(2) In the case of Federal financial assistance extended to provide personal property, the assurance will obligate the recipient for the period during which it retains ownership or possession of the property.

(3) In all other cases the assurance will obligate the recipient for the period during which Federal financial assistance is extended.

(c) *Covenants.* (1) Where Federal financial assistance is provided in the form of real property or interest in the property from the Department, the instrument effecting or recording this transfer shall contain a covenant running with the land to assure nondiscrimination for the period during which the real property is used for a purpose for which the Federal financial assistance is extended or for another purpose involving the provision of similar services or benefits.

(2) Where no transfer of property is involved but property is purchased or improved with Federal financial assistance, the recipient shall agree to include the covenant described in paragraph (b)(2) of this section in the instrument effecting or recording any subsequent transfer of the property.

(3) Where Federal financial assistance is provided in the form of real property or interest in the property from the Department, the covenant shall also include a condition coupled with a right to be reserved by the Department to revert title to the property in the event of a breach of the covenant. If a transferee of real property proposes to mortgage or otherwise encumber the real property as security for financing construction of new, or improvement of existing, facilities on the property for the purposes for which the property was transferred, the Assistant Secretary may, upon request of the transferee and if necessary to accomplish such financing and upon such conditions as he or she deems appropriate, agree to forbear the exercise of such right to revert title for so long as the lien of such mortgage or other encumbrance remains effective.

§ 104.6 Remedial action, voluntary action, and self-evaluation.

(a) *Remedial action.* (1) If the Assistant Secretary finds that a recipient has discriminated against persons on the basis of handicap in violation of section 504 or this part, the recipient shall take such remedial action as the Assistant Secretary deems necessary to overcome the effects of the discrimination.

(2) Where a recipient is found to have discriminated against persons on the basis of

handicap in violation of section 504 or this part and where another recipient exercises control over the recipient that has discriminated, the Assistant Secretary, where appropriate, may require either or both recipients to take remedial action.

(3) The Assistant Secretary may, where necessary to overcome the effects of discrimination in violation of section 504 or this part, require a recipient to take remedial action (i) with respect to handicapped persons who are no longer participants in the recipient's program but who were participants in the program when such discrimination occurred or (ii) with respect to handicapped persons who would have been participants in the program had the discrimination not occurred.

(b) *Voluntary action.* A recipient may take steps, in addition to any action that is required by this part, to overcome the effects of conditions that resulted in limited participation in the recipient's program or activity by qualified handicapped persons.

(c) *Self-evaluation.* (1) A recipient shall, within one year of the effective date of this part:

(i) Evaluate, with the assistance of interested persons, including handicapped persons or organizations representing handicapped persons, its current policies and practices and the effects thereof that do not or may not meet the requirements of this part;

(ii) Modify, after consultation with interested persons, including handicapped persons or organizations representing handicapped persons, any policies and practices that do not meet the requirements of this part; and

(iii) Take, after consultation with interested persons, including handicapped persons or organizations representing handicapped persons, appropriate remedial steps to eliminate the effects of any discrimination that resulted from adherence to these policies and practices.

(2) A recipient that employs fifteen or more persons shall, for at least three years following completion of the evaluation required under paragraph (c)(1) of this section, maintain on file, make available for public inspection, and provide to the Assistant Secretary upon request: (i) A list of the interested persons consulted, (ii) a description of areas examined and any problems identified, and (iii) a description of any modifications made and of any remedial steps taken.

§ 104.7 Designation of responsible employee and adoption of grievance procedures.

(a) *Designation of responsible employee.* A recipient that employs fifteen or more persons shall designate at least one person to coordinate its efforts to comply with this part.

(b) *Adoption of grievance procedures.* A recipient that employs fifteen or more persons shall adopt grievance procedures that incorporate appropriate due process standards and that provide for the prompt and equitable resolution of complaints alleging any action prohibited by this part. Such procedures need not be established with respect to complaints from applicants for employment or from applicants for admission to postsecondary educational institutions.

§ 104.8 Notice.

(a) A recipient that employs fifteen or more persons shall take appropriate initial and continuing steps to notify participants, beneficiaries, applicants, and employees, including those with impaired vision or hearing, and unions or professional organizations holding collective bargaining or professional agreements with the recipient that it does not discriminate on the basis of handicap in violation of section 504 and this part. The notification shall state, where appropriate, that the recipient does not discriminate in admission or access to, or treatment or employment in, its programs and activities. The notification shall also include an identification of the responsible employee designated pursuant to § 104.7(a). A recipient shall make the initial notification required by this paragraph within 90 days of the effective date of this part. Methods of initial and continuing notification may include the posting of notices, publication in newspapers and magazines, placement of notices in recipients' publication, and distribution of memoranda or other written communications.

(b) If a recipient publishes or uses recruitment materials or publications containing general information that it makes available to participants, beneficiaries, applicants, or employees, it shall include in those materials or publications a statement of the policy described in paragraph (a) of this section. A recipient may meet the requirement of this paragraph either by including appropriate inserts in existing materials and publications or by revising and reprinting the materials and publications.

§ 104.9 Administrative requirements for small recipients.

The Assistant Secretary may require any recipient with fewer than fifteen employees, or any class of such recipients, to comply with §§ 104.7 and 104.8, in whole or in part, when the Assistant Secretary finds a violation of this part

or finds that such compliance will not significantly impair the ability of the recipient or class of recipients to provide benefits or services.

§ 104.10 Effect of state or local law or other requirements and effect of employment opportunities.

(a) The obligation to comply with this part is not obviated or alleviated by the existence of any state or local law or other requirement that, on the basis of handicap, imposes prohibitions or limits upon the eligibility of qualified handicapped persons to receive services or to practice any occupation or profession.

(b) The obligation to comply with this part is not obviated or alleviated because employment opportunities in any occupation or profession are or may be more limited for handicapped persons than for nonhandicapped persons.

Subpart B—Employment Practices

§ 104.11 Discrimination prohibited.

(a) *General.* (1) No qualified handicapped person shall, on the basis of handicap, be subjected to discrimination in employment under any program or activity to which this part applies.

(2) A recipient that receives assistance under the Education of the Handicapped Act shall take positive steps to employ and advance in employment qualified handicapped persons in programs assisted under that Act.

(3) A recipient shall make all decisions concerning employment under any program or activity to which this part applies in a manner which ensures that discrimination on the basis of handicap does not occur and may not limit, segregate, or classify applicants or employees in any way that adversely affects their opportunities or status because of handicap.

(4) A recipient may not participate in a contractual or other relationship that has the effect of subjecting qualified handicapped applicants or employees to discrimination prohibited by this subpart. The relationships referred to in this subparagraph include relationships with employment and referral agencies, with labor unions, with organizations providing or administering fringe benefits to employees of the recipient, and with organizations providing training and apprenticeship programs

(b) *Specific activities.* The provisions of this subpart apply to:

(1) Recruitment, advertising, and the

processing of applications for employment;

(2) Hiring, upgrading, promotion, award of tenure, demotion, transfer, layoff, termination, right of return from layoff and rehiring;

(3) Rates of pay or any other form of compensation and changes in compensation;

(4) Job assignments, job classifications, organizational structures, position descriptions, lines of progression, and seniority lists;

(5) Leaves of absence, sick leave, or any other leave;

(6) Fringe benefits available by virtue of employment, whether or not administered by the recipient;

(7) Selection and financial support for training, including apprenticeship, professional meetings, conferences, and other related activities, and selection for leaves of absence to pursue training;

(8) Employer sponsored activities, including social or recreational programs; and

(9) Any other term, condition, or privilege of employment.

(c) A recipient's obligation to comply with this subpart is not affected by any inconsistent term of any collective bargaining agreement to which it is a party.

§ 104.12 Reasonable accommodation.

(a) A recipient shall make reasonable accommodation to the known physical or mental limitations of an otherwise qualified handicapped applicant or employee unless the recipient can demonstrate that the accommodation would impose an undue hardship on the operation of its program.

(b) Reasonable accommodation may include:

(1) Making facilities used by employees readily accessible to and usable by handicapped persons, and

(2) job restructuring, part-time or modified work schedules, acquisition or modification of equipment or devices, the provision of readers or interpreters, and other similar actions.

(c) In determining pursuant to paragraph (a) of this section whether an accommodation would impose an undue hardship on the operation of a recipient's program, factors to be considered include:

(1) The overall size of the recipient's program with respect to number of employees, number and type of facilities, and size of budget;

(2) The type of the recipient's operation, including the composition and structure of the recipient's workforce; and

(3) The nature and cost of the accommodation needed.

(d) A recipient may not deny any employment opportunity to a qualified handicapped employee or applicant if the basis for the denial is the need to make reasonable accommodation to the physical or mental limitations of the employee or applicant.

§ 104.13 Employment criteria.

(a) A recipient may not make use of any employment test or other selection criterion that screens out or tends to screen out handicapped persons or any class of handicapped persons unless: (1) The test score or other selection criterion, as used by the recipient, is shown to be job-related for the position in question, and (2) alternative job-related tests or criteria that do not screen out or tend to screen out as many handicapped persons are not shown by the Assistant Secretary to be available.

(b) A recipient shall select and administer tests concerning employment so as best to ensure that, when administered to an applicant or employee who has a handicap that impairs sensory, manual, or speaking skills, the test results accurately reflect the applicant's or employee's job skills, aptitude, or whatever other factor the test purports to measure, rather than reflecting the applicant's or employee's impaired sensory, manual, or speaking skills (except where those skills are the factors that the test purports to measure).

§ 104.14 Preemployment inquiries.

(a) Except as provided in paragraphs (b) and (c) of this section, a recipient may not conduct a preemployment medical examination or may not make preemployment inquiry of an applicant as to whether the applicant is a handicapped person or as to the nature or severity of a handicap. A recipient may, however, make preemployment inquiry into an applicant's ability to perform job-related functions.

(b) When a recipient is taking remedial action to correct the effects of past discrimination pursuant to 104.6(a), when a recipient is taking voluntary action to overcome the effects of conditions that resulted in limited participation in its federally assisted program or activity pursuant to 104.6(b), or when a recipient is taking affirmative action pursuant to section 503 of the Act, the recipient may invite applicants for employment to indicate whether and to what extent they are handicapped, *Provided*, That:

(1) The recipient states clearly on any written questionnaire used for this purpose or makes clear orally if no written questionnaire is used that the information requested is intended

for use solely in connection with its remedial action obligations or its voluntary or affirmative action efforts; and

(2) The recipient states clearly that the information is being requested on a voluntary basis, that it will be kept confidential as provided in paragraph (d) of this section, that refusal to provide it will not subject the applicant or employee to any adverse treatment, and that it will be used only in accordance with this part.

(c) Nothing in this section shall prohibit a recipient from conditioning an offer of employment on the results of a medical examination conducted prior to the employee's entrance on duty, *Provided,* That: (1) All entering employees are subjected to such an examination regardless of handicap, and (2) the results of such an examination are used only in accordance with the requirements of this part.

(d) Information obtained in accordance with this section as to the medical condition or history of the applicant shall be collected and maintained on separate forms that shall be accorded confidentiality as medical records, except that:

(1) Supervisors and managers may be informed regarding restrictions on the work or duties of handicapped persons and regarding necessary accommodations;

(2) First aid and safety personnel may be informed, where appropriate, if the condition might require emergency treatment; and

(3) Government officials investigating compliance with the Act shall be provided relevant information upon request.

Subpart C—Program accessibility

§ 104.21 Discrimination prohibited.

No qualified handicapped person shall, because a recipient's facilities are inaccessible to or unusable by handicapped persons, be denied the benefits of, be excluded from participation in, or otherwise be subjected to discrimination under any program or activity to which this part applies.

§ 104.22 Existing facilities.

(a) *Program accessibility.* A recipient shall operate each program or activity to which this part applies so that the program or activity, when viewed in its entirety, is readily accessible to handicapped persons. This paragraph does not require a recipient to make each of its existing facilities or every part of a facility accessible to and usable by handicapped persons.

(b) *Methods.* A recipient may comply with the requirements of paragraph (a) of this section through such means as redesign of equipment, reassignment of classes or other services to accessible buildings, assignment of aides to beneficiaries, home visits, delivery of health, welfare, or other social services at alternate accessible sites, alteration of existing facilities and construction of new facilities in conformance with the requirements of § 104.23, or any other methods that result in making its program or activity accessible to handicapped persons. A recipient is not required to make structural changes in existing facilities where other methods are effective in achieving compliance with paragraph (a) of this section. In choosing among available methods for meeting the requirement of paragraph (a) of this section, a recipient shall give priority to those methods that offer programs and activities to handicapped persons in the most integrated setting appropriate.

(c) *Small health, welfare, or other social service providers.* If a recipient with fewer than fifteen employees that provides health, welfare, or other social services finds, after consultation with a handicapped person seeking its services, that there is no method of complying with paragraph (a) of this section other than making a significant alteration in its existing facilities, the recipient may, as an alternative, refer the handicapped person to other providers of those services that are accessible.

(d) *Time period.* A recipient shall comply with the requirement of paragraph (a) of this section within sixty days of the effective date of this part except that where structural changes in facilities are necessary, such changes shall be made within three years of the effective date of this part, but in any event as expeditiously as possible.

(e) *Transition plan.* In the event that structural changes to facilities are necessary to meet the requirement of paragraph (a) of this section, a recipient shall develop, within six months of the effective date of this part, a transition plan setting forth the steps necessary to complete such changes. The plan shall be developed with the assistance of interested persons, including handicapped persons or organizations representing handicapped persons. A copy of the transition plan shall be made available for public inspection. The plan shall, at a minimum:

(1) Identify physical obstacles in the recipient's facilities that limit the accessibility of its program or activity to handicapped persons;

(2) Describe in detail the methods that will be used to make the facilities accessible;

(3) Specify the schedule for taking the steps necessary to achieve full program accessibility and, if the time period of the transition plan is longer than one year, identify steps that will be taken during each year of the transition period; and

(4) Indicate the person responsible for implementation of the plan.

(f) *Notice.* The recipient shall adopt and implement procedures to ensure that interested persons, including persons with impaired vision or hearing, can obtain information as to the existence and location of services, activities, and facilities that are accessible to and usable by handicapped persons.

§ 104.23 New construction.

(a) *Design and construction.* Each facility or part of a facility constructed by, on behalf of, or for the use of a recipient shall be designed and constructed in such manner that the facility or part of the facility is readily accessible to and usable by handicapped persons, if the construction was commenced after the effective date of this part.

(b) *Alteration.* Each facility or part of a facility which is altered by, on behalf of, or for the use of a recipient after the effective date of this part in a manner that affects or could affect the usability of the facility or part of the facility shall, to the maximum extent feasible, be altered in such manner that the altered portion of the facility is readily accessible to and usable by handicapped persons.

(c) *Conformance with Uniform Federal Accessibility Standards.* (1) Effective as of January 18, 1991, design, construction, or alteration of buildings in conformance with sections 3-8 of the Uniform Federal Accessibility Standards (UFAS)(Appendix A to 41 CFR subpart 101-19.6) shall be deemed to comply with the requirements of this section with respect to those buildings. Departures from particular technical and scoping requirements of UFAS by the use of other methods are permitted where substantially equivalent or greater access to and usability of the building is provided.

(2) For purposes of this section, section 4.1.6(g) of UFAS shall be interpreted to exempt from the requirements of UFAS only mechanical rooms and other spaces that, because of their intended use, will not require accessibility to the public or beneficiaries or result in the employment or residence therein of persons with physical handicaps.

(3) This section does not require recipients to make building alterations that have little likelihood of being accomplished without removing or altering a load-bearing structural member.

Subpart D—Preschool, Elementary, and Secondary Education

§ 104.31 Application of this subpart.

Subpart D applies to preschool, elementary, secondary, and adult education programs and activities that receive or benefit from Federal financial assistance and to recipients that operate, or that receive or benefit from Federal financial assistance for the operation of, such programs or activities.

§ 104.32 Location and notification.

A recipient that operates a public elementary or secondary education program shall annually:

(a) Undertake to identify and locate every qualified handicapped person residing in the recipient's jurisdiction who is not receiving a public education; and

(b) Take appropriate steps to notify handicapped persons and their parents or guardians of the recipient's duty under this subpart.

§ 104.33 Free appropriate public education.

(a) *General.* A recipient that operates a public elementary or secondary education program shall provide a free appropriate public education to each qualified handicapped person who is in the recipient's jurisdiction, regardless of the nature or severity of the person's handicap.

(b) *Appropriate education.* (1) For the purpose of this subpart, the provision of an appropriate education is the provision of regular or special education and related aids and services that (i) are designed to meet individual educational needs of handicapped persons as adequately as the needs of nonhandicapped persons are met and (ii) are based upon adherence to procedures that satisfy the requirements of §§ 104.34, 104.35, and 104.36.

(2) Implementation of an individualized education program developed in accordance with the Education of the Handicapped Act is one means of meeting the standard established in paragraph (b)(1)(i) of this section.

(3) A recipient may place a handicapped person in or refer such person to a program other than the one that it operates as its means of carrying out the requirements of this subpart. If so, the recipient remains responsible for ensuring that the requirements of this subpart are met with respect to any handicapped person so placed or referred.

(c) *Free education*—(1) *General.* For the purpose of this section, the provision of a free education is the provision of educational and related services without cost to the handicapped person or to his or her parents or guardian, except for those fees that are imposed on nonhandicapped persons or their parents or guardian. It may consist either of the provision of free services or, if a recipient places a handicapped person in or refers such person to a program not operated by the recipient as its means of carrying out the requirements of this subpart, of payment for the costs of the program. Funds available from any public or private agency may be used to meet the requirements of this subpart. Nothing in this section shall be construed to relieve an insurer or similar third party from an otherwise valid obligation to provide or pay for services provided to a handicapped person.

(2) *Transportation.* If a recipient places a handicapped person in or refers such person to a program not operated by the recipient as its means of carrying out the requirements of this subpart, the recipient shall ensure that adequate transportation to and from the program is provided at no greater cost than would be incurred by the person or his or her parents or guardian if the person were placed in the program operated by the recipient.

(3) *Residential placement.* If placement in a public or private residential program is necessary to provide a free appropriate public education to a handicapped person because of his or her handicap, the program, including nonmedical care and room and board, shall be provided at no cost to the person or his or her parents or guardian.

(4) *Placement of handicapped persons by parents.* If a recipient has made available, in conformance with the requirements of this section and § 104.34, a free appropriate public education to a handicapped person and the person's parents or guardian choose to place the person in a private school, the recipient is not required to pay for the person's education in the private school. Disagreements between a parent or guardian and a recipient regarding whether the recipient has made such a program available or otherwise regarding the question of financial responsibility are subject to the due process procedures of § 104.36.

(d) *Compliance.* A recipient may not exclude any qualified handicapped person from a public elementary or secondary education after the effective date of this part. A recipient that is not, on the effective date of this regulation, in full compliance with the other requirements of the preceding paragraphs of this section shall meet such requirements at the earliest practicable time and in no event later than September 1, 1978.

§ 104.34 Educational setting.

(a) *Academic setting.* A recipient to which this subpart applies shall educate, or shall provide for the education of, each qualified handicapped person in its jurisdiction with persons who are not handicapped to the maximum extent appropriate to the needs of the handicapped person. A recipient shall place a handicapped person in the regular educational environment operated by the recipient unless it is demonstrated by the recipient that the education of the person in the regular environment with the use of supplementary aids and services cannot be achieved satisfactorily. Whenever a recipient places a person in a setting other than the regular educational environment pursuant to this paragraph, it shall take into account the proximity of the alternate setting to the person's home.

(b) *Nonacademic settings.* In providing or arranging for the provision of nonacademic and extracurricular services and activities, including meals, recess periods, and the services and activities set forth in § 104.37(a)(2), a recipient shall ensure that handicapped persons participate with nonhandicapped persons in such activities and services to the maximum extent appropriate to the needs of the handicapped person in question.

(c) *Comparable facilities.* If a recipient, in compliance with paragraph (a) of this section, operates a facility that is identifiable as being for handicapped persons, the recipient shall ensure that the facility and the services and activities provided therein are comparable to the other facilities, services, and activities of the recipient.

§ 104.35 Evaluation and placement.

(a) *Preplacement evaluation.* A recipient that operates a public elementary or secondary education program shall conduct an evaluation in accordance with the requirements of paragraph (b) of this section of any person who, because of handicap, needs or is believed to need special education or related services before taking any action with respect to the initial placement of the person in a regular or special education program and any subsequent significant change in placement.

(b) *Evaluation procedures.* A recipient to which this subpart applies shall establish standards and procedures for the evaluation and placement of persons who, because of handicap, need or are believed to need special education or related services which ensure that:

(1) Tests and other evaluation materials have been validated for the specific purpose for which they are used and are administered by trained personnel in conformance with the instructions provided by their producer;

(2) Tests and other evaluation materials include those tailored to assess specific areas of educational need and not merely those which are designed to provide a single general intelligence quotient; and

(3) Tests are selected and administered so as best to ensure that, when a test is administered to a student with impaired sensory, manual, or speaking skills, the test results accurately reflect the student's aptitude or achievement level or whatever other factor the test purports to measure, rather than reflects the student's impaired sensory, manual, or speaking skills (except where those skills are the factors that the test purports to measure).

(c) *Placement procedures.* In interpreting evaluation data and in making placement decisions, a recipient shall (1) draw upon information from a variety of sources, including aptitude and achievement tests, teacher recommendations, physical condition, social or cultural background, and adaptive behavior, (2) establish procedures to ensure that information obtained from all such sources is documented and carefully considered, (3) ensure that the placement decision is made by a group of persons, including persons knowledgeable about the child, the meaning of the evaluation data, and the placement options, and (4) ensure that the placement decision is made in conformity with § 104.34.

(d) *Reevaluation.* A recipient to which this section applies shall establish procedures, in accordance with paragraph (b) of this section, for periodic reevaluation of students who have been provided special education and related services. A reevaluation procedure consistent with the Education of the Handicapped Act is one means of meeting this requirement.

§ 104.36 Procedural safeguards.

A recipient that operates a public elementary or secondary education program shall establish and implement, with respect to actions regarding the identification, evaluation, or educational placement of persons who, because of handicap, need or are believed to need special instruction or related services, a system of procedural safeguards that includes notice, an opportunity for the parents or guardian of the person to examine relevant records, an impartial hearing with opportunity for participation by the person's parents or guardian and representation by counsel, and a review procedure. Compliance with the procedural safeguards of section 615 of the Education of the Handicapped Act is one means of meeting this requirement.

§ 104.37 Nonacademic services.

(a) *General.* (1) A recipient to which this subpart applies shall provide non-academic and extracurricular services and activities in such manner as is necessary to afford handicapped students an equal opportunity for participation in such services and activities.

(2) Nonacademic and extracurricular services and activities may include counseling services, physical recreational athletics, transportation, health services, recreational activities, special interest groups or clubs sponsored by the recipient referrals to agencies which provide assistance to handicapped persons, and employment of students, including both employment by the recipient and assistance in making available outside employment.

(b) *Counseling services.* A recipient to which this subpart applies that provides personal, academic, or vocational counseling, guidance, or placement services to its students shall provide these services without discrimination on the basis of handicap. The recipient shall ensure that qualified handicapped students are not counseled toward more restrictive career objectives than are nonhandicapped students with similar interests and abilities.

(c) *Physical education and athletics.* (1) In providing physical education courses and athletics and similar programs and activities to any of its students, a recipient to which this subpart applies may not discriminate on the basis of handicap. A recipient that offers physical education courses or that operates or sponsors interscholastic, club, or intramural athletics shall provide to qualified handicapped students an equal opportunity for participation in these activities.

(2) A recipient may offer to handicapped students physical education and athletic activities that are separate or different from those offered to nonhandicapped students only if separation or differentiation is consistent with the requirements of § 104.34 and only if no qualified handicapped student is denied the opportunity to compete for teams or to participate in courses that are not separate or different.

§ 104.38 Preschool and adult education programs.

A recipient to which this subpart applies that operates a preschool education or day care program or activity or an adult education program or activity may not, on the basis of handicap, exclude qualified handicapped persons from the program or activity and shall take into account the needs of such persons in determining the aid, benefits, or services to be provided under the program or activity.

§ 104.39 Private education programs.

(a) A recipient that operates a private elementary or secondary education program may not, on the basis of handicap, exclude a qualified handicapped person from such program if the person can, with minor adjustments, be provided an appropriate education, as defined in 104.33(b)(1), within the recipient's program.

(b) A recipient to which this section applies may not charge more for the provision of an appropriate education to handicapped persons than to nonhandicapped persons except to the extent that any additional charge is justified by a substantial increase in cost to the recipient.

(c) A recipient to which this section applies that operates special education programs shall operate such programs in accordance with the provisions of §§ 104.35 and 104.36. Each recipient to which this section applies is subject to the provisions of §§ 104.34, 104.37, and 104.38.

Subpart E—Postsecondary Education

§ 104.41 Application of this subpart.

Subpart E applies to postsecondary education programs and activities, including postsecondary vocational education programs and activities, that receive or benefit from Federal financial assistance and to recipients that operate, or that receive or benefit from Federal financial assistance for the operation of, such programs or activities.

§ 104.42 Admissions and recruitment.

(a) *General.* Qualified handicapped persons may not, on the basis of handicap, be denied admission or be subjected to discrimination in admission or recruitment by a recipient to which this subpart applies.

(b) *Admissions.* In administering its admission policies, a recipient to which this subpart applies:

(1) May not apply limitations upon the number or proportion of handicapped persons who may be admitted;

(2) May not make use of any test or criterion for admission that has a disproportionate, adverse effect on handicapped persons or any class of handicapped persons unless (i) the test or criterion, as used by the recipient, has been validated as a predictor of success in the education program or activity in question and (ii) alternate tests or criteria that have a less disproportionate, adverse effect are not shown by the Assistant Secretary to be available.

(3) Shall assure itself that (i) admissions tests are selected and administered so as best to ensure that, when a test is administered to an applicant who has a handicap that impairs sensory, manual, or speaking skills, the test results accurately reflect the applicant's aptitude or achievement level or whatever other factor the test purports to measure, rather than reflecting the applicant's impaired sensory, manual, or speaking skills (except where those skills are the factors that the test purports to measure); (ii) admissions tests that are designed for persons with impaired sensory, manual, or speaking skills are offered as often and in as timely a manner as are other admissions tests; and (iii) admissions tests are administered in facilities that, on the whole, are accessible to handicapped persons; and

(4) Except as provided in paragraph (c) of this section, may not make preadmission inquiry as to whether an applicant for admission is a handicapped person but, after admission, may make inquiries on a confidential basis as to handicaps that may require accommodation.

(c) *Preadmission inquiry exception.* When a recipient is taking remedial action to correct the effects of past discrimination pursuant to § 104.6(a) or when a recipient is taking voluntary action to overcome the effects of conditions that resulted in limited participation in its federally assisted program or activity pursuant to 104.6(b), the recipient may invite applicants for admission to indicate whether and to what extent they are handicapped, *Provided,* That:

(1) The recipient states clearly on any written questionnaire used for this purpose or makes clear orally if no written questionnaire is used that the information requested is intended for use solely in connection with its remedial action obligations or its voluntary action efforts; and

(2) The recipient states clearly that the information is being requested on a voluntary basis, that it will be kept confidential, that refusal to provide it will not subject the applicant to any adverse treatment, and that it

will be used only in accordance with this part.

(d) *Validity studies.* For the purposes of paragraph (b)(2) of this section, a recipient may base prediction equations on first year grades, but shall conduct periodic validity studies against the criterion of overall success in the education program or activity in question in order to monitor the general validity of the test scores.

§ 104.43 Treatment of students; general.

(a) No qualified handicapped student shall, on the basis of handicap, be excluded from participation in, be denied the benefits of, or otherwise be subjected to discrimination under any academic, research, occupational training, housing, health insurance, counseling, financial aid, physical education, athletics, recreation, transportation, other extracurricular, or other postsecondary education program or activity to which this subpart applies.

(b) A recipient to which this subpart applies that considers participation by students in education programs or activities not operated wholly by the recipient as part of, or equivalent to, an education program or activity operated by the recipient shall assure itself that the other education program or activity, as a whole, provides an equal opportunity for the participation of qualified handicapped persons.

(c) A recipient to which this subpart applies may not, on the basis of handicap, exclude any qualified handicapped student from any course, course of study, or other part of its education program or activity.

(d) A recipient to which this subpart applies shall operate its programs and activities in the most integrated setting appropriate.

§ 104.44 Academic adjustments.

(a) *Academic requirements.* A recipient to which this subpart applies shall make such modifications to its academic requirements as are necessary to ensure that such requirements do not discriminate or have the effect of discriminating, on the basis of handicap, against a qualified handicapped applicant or student. Academic requirements that the recipient can demonstrate are essential to the program of instruction being pursued by such student or to any directly related licensing requirement will not be regarded as discriminatory within the meaning of this section. Modifications may include changes in the length of time permitted for the completion of degree requirements, substitution of specific courses required for completion of degree requirements, and adaptation of the manner in which specific

courses are conducted.

(b) *Other rules.* A recipient to which this subpart applies may not impose upon handicapped students other rules such as the prohibition of tape recorders in classrooms or of dog guides in campus buildings, that have the effect of limiting the participation of handicapped students in the recipient's education program or activity.

(c) *Course examinations.* In its course examinations or other procedures for evaluating students' academic achievement in its program, a recipient to which this subpart applies shall provide such methods for evaluating the achievement of students who have a handicap that impairs sensory, manual, or speaking skills as will best ensure that the results of the evaluation represents the student's achievement in the course, rather than reflecting the student's impaired sensory, manual, or speaking skills (except where such skills are the factors that the test purports to measure).

(d) *Auxiliary aids.* (1) A recipient to which this subpart applies shall take such steps as are necessary to ensure that no handicapped student is denied the benefits of, excluded from participation in, or otherwise subjected to discrimination under the education program or activity operated by the recipient because of the absence of educational auxiliary aids for students with impaired sensory, manual, or speaking skills.

(2) Auxiliary aids may include taped texts, interpreters or other effective methods of making orally delivered materials available to students with hearing impairments, readers in libraries for students with visual impairments, classroom equipment adapted for use by students with manual impairments, and other similar services and actions. Recipients need not provide attendants, individually prescribed devices, readers for personal use or study, or other devices or services of a personal nature.

§ 104.45 Housing.

(a) *Housing provided by the recipient.* A recipient that provides housing to its nonhandicapped students shall provide comparable, convenient, and accessible housing to handicapped students at the same cost as to others. At the end of the transition period provided for in Subpart C, such housing shall be available in sufficient quantity and variety so that the scope of handicapped students' choice of living accommodations is, as a whole, comparable to that of nonhandicapped students.

(b) *Other housing.* A recipient that assists any agency, organization, or person in making housing available to any of its students shall take such action as may be necessary to assure itself that such house is, as a whole, made available in a manner that does not result in discrimination on the basis of handicap.

§ 104.46 Financial and employment assistance to students.

(a) *Provision of financial assistance.* (1) In providing financial assistance to qualified handicapped persons, a recipient to which this subpart applies may not (i), on the basis of handicap, provide less assistance than is provided to nonhandicapped persons, limit eligibility for assistance, or otherwise discriminate or (ii) assist any entity or person that provides assistance to any of the recipient's students in a manner that discriminates against qualified handicapped persons on the basis of handicap.

(2) A recipient may administer or assist in the administration of scholarships, fellowships, or other forms of financial assistance established under wills, trusts, bequests, or similar legal instruments that require awards to be made on the basis of factors that discriminate or have the effect of discriminating on the basis of handicap only if the overall effect of the award of scholarships, fellowships, and other forms of financial assistance is not discriminatory on the basis of handicap.

(b) *Assistance in making available outside employment.* A recipient that assists any agency, organization, or person in providing employment opportunities to any of its students shall assure itself that such employment opportunities, as a whole, are made available in a manner that would not violate Subpart B if they were provided by the recipient.

(c) *Employment of students by recipients.* A recipient that employs any of its students may not do so in a manner that violates Subpart B.

§ 104.47 Nonacademic services.

(a) *Physical education and athletics.* (1) In providing physical education courses and athletics and similar programs and activities to any of its students, a recipient to which this subpart applies may not discriminate on the basis of handicap. A recipient that offers physical education courses or that operates or sponsors intercollegiate, club, or intramural athletics shall provide to qualified handicapped students an equal opportunity for participation in these activities.

(2) A recipient may offer to handicapped students physical education and athletic activities that are separate or different only if separation or differentiation is consistent with

the requirements of § 104.43(d) and only if no qualified handicapped student is denied the opportunity to compete for teams or to participate in courses that are not separate or different.

(b) *Counseling and placement services.* A recipient to which this subpart applies that provides personal, academic, or vocational counseling, guidance, or placement services to its students shall provide these services without discrimination on the basis of handicap. The recipient shall ensure that qualified handicapped students are not counseled toward more restrictive career objectives than are nonhandicapped students with similar interests and abilities. This requirement does not preclude a recipient from providing factual information about licensing and certification requirements that may present obstacles to handicapped persons in their pursuit of particular careers.

(c) *Social organizations.* A recipient that provides significant assistance to fraternities, sororities, or similar organizations shall assure itself that the membership practices of such organizations do not permit discrimination otherwise prohibited by this subpart.

Subpart F—Health, Welfare, and Social Services

§ 104.51 Application of this subpart.

Subpart F applies to health, welfare, and other social service programs and activities that receive or benefit from Federal financial assistance and to recipients that operate, or that receive or benefit from Federal financial assistance for the operation of, such programs or activities.

§ 104.52 Health, welfare, and other social services.

(a) *General.* In providing health, welfare, or other social services or benefits, a recipient may not, on the basis of handicap:

(1) Deny a qualified handicapped person these benefits or services;

(2) Afford a qualified handicapped person an opportunity to receive benefits or services that is not equal to that offered nonhandicapped persons;

(3) Provide a qualified handicapped person with benefits or services that are not as effective (as defined in § 104.4(b)) as the benefits or services provided to others;

(4) Provide benefits or services in a manner that limits or has the effect of limiting the participation of qualified handicapped persons; or

(5) Provide different or separate benefits or services to handicapped persons except where

necessary to provide qualified handicapped persons with benefits and services that are as effective as those provided to others.

(b) *Notice.* A recipient that provides notice concerning benefits or services or written material concerning waivers of rights or consent to treatment shall take such steps as are necessary to ensure that qualified handicapped persons, including those with impaired sensory or speaking skills, are not denied effective notice because of their handicap.

(c) *Emergency treatment for the hearing impaired.* A recipient hospital that provides health services or benefits shall establish a procedure for effective communication with persons with impaired hearing for the purpose of providing emergency health care.

(d) *Auxiliary aids.* (1) A recipient to which this subpart applies that employs fifteen or more persons shall provide appropriate auxiliary aids to persons with impaired sensory, manual, or speaking skills, where necessary to afford such persons an equal opportunity to benefit from the service in question.

(2) The Assistant Secretary may require recipients with fewer than fifteen employees to provide auxiliary aids where the provision of aids would not significantly impair the ability of the recipient to provide its benefits or services.

(3) For the purpose of this paragraph, auxiliary aids may include brailled and taped material, interpreters, and other aids for persons with impaired hearing or vision.

§ 104.53 Drug and alcohol addicts.

A recipient to which this subpart applies that operates a general hospital or outpatient facility may not discriminate in admission or treatment against a drug or alcohol abuser or alcoholic who is suffering from a medical condition, because of the person's drug or alcohol abuse or alcoholism.

§ 104.54 Education of institutionalized persons.

A recipient to which this subpart applies and that operates or supervises a program or activity for persons who are institutionalized because of handicap shall ensure that each qualified handicapped person, as defined in § 104.3(k)(2), in its program or activity is provided an appropriate education, as defined in § 104.33(b). Nothing in this section shall be interpreted as altering in any way the obligations of recipients under Subpart D.

Subpart G—Procedures

§ 104.61 Procedures

The procedural provisions applicable to title VI of the Civil Rights Act of 1964 apply to this part. These procedures are found in §§ 100.6—100.10 and Part 101 of this title.

34 CFR § 76.532 Use of funds for religion prohibited.

(a) No state or subgrantee may use its grant or subgrant to pay for any of the following:

(1) Religious worship, instruction, or proselytization.

(2) Equipment or supplies to be used for any of the activities specified in paragraph (a)(1) of this section.

(3) Construction, remodeling, repair, operation, or maintenance of any facility or part of a facility to be used for any of the activities specified in paragraph (a)(1) of this section.

(4) An activity of a school or department of divinity.

(b) As used in this section, *school or department of divinity* means an institution or a component of an institution whose program is specifically for the education of students to:

(1) Prepare them to enter into a religious vocation; or

(2) Prepare them to teach theological subjects.

34 CFR § 76.654 Benefits for private school students.

(a) *Comparable benefits.* The program benefits that a subgrantee provides for students enrolled in private schools must be comparable in quality, scope, and opportunity for participation to the program benefits that the subgrantee provides for students enrolled in public schools.

(b) *Same Benefits.* If a subgrantee uses funds under a program for public school students in a particular attendance area, or grade or age level, the subgrantee shall insure equitable opportunities for participation by students enrolled in private schools who:

(1) Have the same needs as the public school student to be served; and

(2) Are in that group, attendance area, or age or grade level.

(c) *Different benefits.* If the needs of students enrolled in private schools are different from the needs of students enrolled in public schools, a subgrantee shall provide program benefits for the private school students that are different from the benefits the subgrantee provides for the public school students.

APPENDIX C

Table of Special Education Cases
Decided by the U.S. Supreme Court

Title and Citation (in chronological order)

Southeastern Community College v. Davis, 442 U.S. 397, 99 S.Ct. 2361, 60 L.Ed.2d 980 (1979).

Univ. of Texas v. Camenisch, 451 U.S. 390, 101 S.Ct. 1830, 68 L.Ed.2d 175 (1981).

Pennhurst State School and Hospital v. Halderman, 451 U.S. 1, 101 S.Ct. 1531, 67 L.Ed.2d 694 (1981) (*Pennhurst I*).

Board of Educ. v. Rowley, 458 U.S. 176, 102 S.Ct. 3034, 73 L.Ed.2d 690 (1982).

Pennhurst State School and Hospital v. Halderman, 465 U.S. 89, 104 S.Ct. 900, 79 L.Ed.2d 67 (1984) (*Pennhurst II*).

Irving Independent School Dist. v. Tatro, 468 U.S. 883, 104 S.Ct. 3371, 82 L.Ed.2d 664 (1984).

Smith v. Robinson, 468 U.S. 992, 104 S.Ct. 3457, 82 L.Ed.2d 746 (1984).

Honig v. Students of California School for the Blind, 471 U.S. 148, 105 S.Ct. 1820, 85 L.Ed.2d 114 (1985).

Burlington School Committee v. Dep't of Educ. of Massachusetts, 471 U.S. 359, 105 S.Ct. 1996, 85 L.Ed.2d 385 (1985).

City of Cleburne, Texas v. Cleburne Living Center, 473 U.S. 432, 105 S.Ct. 3249, 87 L.Ed.2d 313 (1985).

Witters v. Washington Dep't of Services for the Blind, 474 U.S. 481, 106 S.Ct. 748, 88 L.Ed.2d 846 (1986).

School Board of Nassau County v. Arline, 480 U.S. 273, 107 S.Ct. 1123, 94 L.Ed.2d 307 (1987).

Honig v. Doe, 484 U.S. 305, 108 S.Ct. 592, 98 L.Ed.2d 686 (1988).

Traynor v. Turnage, 485 U.S. 535, 108 S.Ct. 1372, 99 L.Ed.2d 618 (1988).

Dellmuth v. Muth, 491 U.S. 223, 109 S.Ct. 2397, 105 L.Ed.2d 181 (1989).

Zobrest v. Catalina Foothills School Dist., 509 U.S. 1, 113 S.Ct. 2462, 125 L.Ed.2d 1 (1993).

Florence County School Dist. Four v. Carter, 510 U.S. 7, 114 S.Ct. 361, 126 L.Ed.2d 284 (1993).

Board of Educ. of Kiryas Joel Village School Dist. v. Grumet, 512 U.S. 687, 114 S.Ct. 2481, 129 L.Ed.2d 546 (1994).

Cedar Rapids Community School Dist. v. Garret F., 526 U.S. 66, 119 S.Ct. 992, 143 L.Ed. 2d 154 (1999).

Owasso Independent School Dist. No. I-011 v. Falvo, 534 U.S. 426, 122 S.Ct. 934, 151 L.Ed. 2d 896 (2002).

Locke v. Davey, 540 U.S. 712, 124 S.Ct. 1307, 158 L.Ed.2d 1 (2004).

Schaffer v. Weast, 546 U.S. 49, 126 S.Ct. 528, 163 L.Ed.2d 387 (2005).

Arlington Cent. School Dist. Board of Educ. v. Murphy, 548 U.S. 291, 126 S.Ct. 2455, 165 L.Ed.2d 526 (2006).

Winkelman v. Parma City School Dist., 550 U.S. 516, 127 S.Ct. 1994, 167 L.Ed.2d 904 (2007).

Fitzgerald v. Barnstable School Committee, 555 U.S. 246, 129 S.Ct. 788, 172 L.Ed.2d 582 (2009).

Ysursa v. Pocatello Educ. Ass'n, 555 U.S. 353 129 S.Ct. 1093, 172 L.Ed.2d 770 (2009).

Forest Grove School Dist. v. T.A., 129 S.Ct. 2484 (U.S. 2009).

The Judicial System

In order to allow you to determine the relative importance of a judicial decision, the cases included in *Students with Disabilities and Special Education Law* identify the particular court from which a decision has been issued. For example, a case decided by a state supreme court generally will be of greater significance than a state circuit court case. Hence, a basic knowledge of the structure of our judicial system is important to an understanding of school law.

Almost all the reports in this volume are taken from appellate court decisions. Although most education law decisions occur at trial court and administrative levels, appellate court decisions have the effect of binding lower courts and administrators so that appellate court decisions have the effect of law within their court systems.

State and federal court systems generally function independently of each other. Each court system applies its own law according to statutes and the determinations of its highest court. However, judges at all levels often consider opinions from other court systems to settle issues which are new or arise under unique fact situations. Similarly, lawyers look at the opinions of many courts to locate authority that supports their clients' cases.

Once a lawsuit is filed in a particular court system, that system retains the matter until its conclusion. Unsuccessful parties at the administrative or trial court level generally have the right to appeal unfavorable determinations of law to appellate courts within the system. When federal law issues or constitutional grounds are present, lawsuits may be appropriately filed in the federal court system. In those cases, the lawsuit is filed initially in the federal district court for that area.

On rare occasions, the U.S. Supreme Court considers appeals from the highest courts of the states if a distinct federal question exists and at least four justices agree on the question's importance. The federal courts occasionally send cases to state courts for application of state law. These situations are infrequent and, in general, the state and federal court systems should be considered separate from each other.

The most common system, used by nearly all states and also the federal judiciary, is as follows: a legal action is commenced in district court (sometimes called trial court, county court, common pleas court or superior court) where a decision is initially reached. The case may then be appealed to the court of appeals (or appellate court), and in turn this decision may be appealed to the supreme court.

Several states, however, do not have a court of appeals; lower court decisions are appealed directly to the state's supreme court. Additionally, some states have labeled their courts in a nonstandard fashion.

In Maryland, the highest state court is called the Court of Appeals. In the state of New York, the trial court is called the Supreme Court. Decisions of this court may be appealed to the Supreme Court, Appellate Division. The highest court in New York is the Court of Appeals. Pennsylvania has perhaps the most complex court system. The lowest state court is the Court of Common Pleas. Depending on the circumstances of the case, appeals may be taken to either the Commonwealth Court or the Superior Court. In certain instances the Commonwealth Court functions as a trial court as well as an appellate court. The Superior Court, however, is strictly an intermediate appellate court. The highest court in Pennsylvania is the Supreme Court.

While supreme court decisions are generally regarded as the last word in legal matters, it is important to remember that trial and appeals court decisions also create important legal precedents. For the hierarchy of typical state and federal court systems, please see the diagram below.

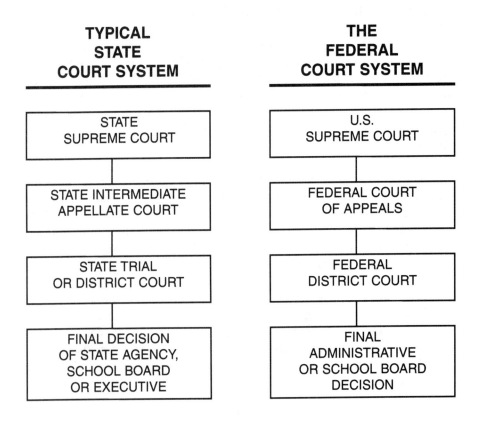

Federal courts of appeals hear appeals from the district courts which are located in their circuits. Below is a list of states matched to the federal circuits in which they are located.

First Circuit — Puerto Rico, Maine, New Hampshire, Massachusetts, Rhode Island

Second Circuit — New York, Vermont, Connecticut

Third Circuit — Pennsylvania, New Jersey, Delaware, Virgin Islands

Fourth Circuit — West Virginia, Maryland, Virginia, North Carolina, South Carolina

Fifth Circuit — Texas, Louisiana, Mississippi

Sixth Circuit — Ohio, Kentucky, Tennessee, Michigan

Seventh Circuit — Wisconsin, Indiana, Illinois

Eighth Circuit — North Dakota, South Dakota, Nebraska, Arkansas, Missouri, Iowa, Minnesota

Ninth Circuit — Alaska, Washington, Oregon, California, Hawaii, Arizona, Nevada, Idaho, Montana, Northern Mariana Islands, Guam

Tenth Circuit — Wyoming, Utah, Colorado, Kansas, Oklahoma, New Mexico

Eleventh Circuit — Alabama, Georgia, Florida

District of Columbia Circuit — Hears cases from the U.S. District Court for the District of Columbia.

Federal Circuit — Sitting in Washington, D.C., the U.S. Court of Appeals, Federal Circuit hears patent and trade appeals and certain appeals on claims brought against the federal government and its agencies.

How to Read a Case Citation

Generally, court decisions can be located in case reporters at law school or governmental law libraries. Some cases can also be located on the Internet through legal Web sites or official court Web sites.

Each case summary contains the citation, or legal reference, to the full text of the case. The diagram below illustrates how to read a case citation.

case name (parties)   case reporter name and series   court location

A.P v. Woodstock Board of Educ.,   572 F.Supp.2d   221   (D. Conn. 2008).

volume number   first page   year of decision

Some cases may have two or three reporter names such as U.S. Supreme Court cases and cases reported in regional case reporters as well as state case reporters. For example, a U.S. Supreme Court case usually contains three case reporter citations.

first reporter

Schaffer v. Weast,   546 U.S. 49,   126 S.Ct. 528,   163 L.Ed.2d 1387 (2005).

second reporter   third reporter

The citations are still read in the same manner as if only one citation has been listed.

Occasionally, a case may contain a citation which does not reference a case reporter. For example, a citation may contain a reference such as:

case name   year of decision   first page

Amy S. v. Danbury Local School Dist.,   2006   WL   891178,
No. 04-1279JTM,   (6th Cir. 3/31/06).

court file number   court location   date of decision   Westlaw®[1]

---

[1] Westlaw® is a computerized database of court cases available for a fee.

The court file number indicates the specific number assigned to a case by the particular court system deciding the case. In our example, the Sixth Circuit Court has assigned the case of *Amy S. v. Danbury Local School District* the case number of "No. 04-1279JTM" which will serve as the reference number for the case and any matter relating to the case. Locating a case on the Internet generally requires either the case name and date of the decision, and/or the court file number.

Below, we have listed the full names of the regional reporters. As mentioned previously, many states have individual state reporters. The names of those reporters may be obtained from a reference law librarian.

P.	**Pacific Reporter**
	Alaska, Arizona, California, Colorado, Hawaii, Idaho, Kansas, Montana, Nevada, New Mexico, Oklahoma, Oregon, Utah, Washington, Wyoming
A.	**Atlantic Reporter**
	Connecticut, Delaware, District of Columbia, Maine, Maryland, New Hampshire, New Jersey, Pennsylvania, Rhode Island, Vermont
N.E.	**Northeastern Reporter**
	Illinois, Indiana, Massachusetts, New York, Ohio
N.W.	**Northwestern Reporter**
	Iowa, Michigan, Minnesota, Nebraska, North Dakota, South Dakota, Wisconsin
So.	**Southern Reporter**
	Alabama, Florida, Louisiana, Mississippi
S.E.	**Southeastern Reporter**
	Georgia, North Carolina, South Carolina, Virginia, West Virginia
S.W.	**Southwestern Reporter**
	Arkansas, Kentucky, Missouri, Tennessee, Texas
F.	**Federal Reporter**
	The thirteen federal judicial circuits courts of appeals decisions. See *The Judicial System*, p. 641, for specific state circuits.
F.Supp.	**Federal Supplement**
	The thirteen federal judicial circuits district court decisions.
Fed.Appx.	**Federal Appendix**
	Contains unpublished opinions of the U.S. Circuit Courts of Appeal. See *The Judicial System*, p. 641, for specific state circuits.
U.S.	**United States Reports**
S.Ct.	**Supreme Court Reporter** ⎫ U.S. Supreme Court Decisions
L.Ed.	**Lawyers' Edition** ⎭

GLOSSARY

Age Discrimination in Employment Act (ADEA) - The ADEA, 29 U.S.C. § 621 *et seq.*, is part of the Fair Labor Standards Act. It prohibits discrimination against persons who are at least 40 years old, and applies to employers that have 20 or more employees and that affect interstate commerce.

Americans with Disabilities Act (ADA) - Key provisions of the ADA, 42 U.S.C. § 12101 *et seq.*, went into effect on July 26, 1992. Among other things, it prohibits discrimination against a qualified individual with a disability because of that person's disability with respect to job application procedures, the hiring, advancement or discharge of employees, employee compensation, job training, and other terms, conditions and privileges of employment.

Bona Fide - Latin term meaning "good faith." Generally used to note a party's lack of bad intent or fraudulent purpose.

Class Action Suit - Federal Rule of Civil Procedure 23 allows members of a class to sue as representatives on behalf of the whole class provided that the class is so large that joinder of all parties is impractical, there are questions of law or fact common to the class, the claims or defenses of the representatives are typical of the claims or defenses of the class, and the representative parties will adequately protect the interests of the class. In addition, there must be some danger of inconsistent verdicts or adjudications if the class action were prosecuted as separate actions. Most states also allow class actions under the same or similar circumstances.

Collateral Estoppel - Also known as issue preclusion. The idea that once an issue has been litigated, it may not be re-tried. Similar to the doctrine of *Res Judicata* (see below).

Due Process Clause - The clauses of the Fifth and Fourteenth Amendments to the Constitution that guarantee the citizens of the United States "due process of law" (see below). The Fifth Amendment's Due Process Clause applies to the federal government, and the Fourteenth Amendment's Due Process Clause applies to the states.

Due Process of Law - The idea of "fair play" in the government's application of law to its citizens, guaranteed by the Fifth and Fourteenth Amendments. Substantive due process is just plain *fairness*, and procedural due process is accorded when the government utilizes adequate procedural safeguards for the protection of an individual's liberty or property interests.

Education for All Handicapped Children Act (EAHCA) - See Individuals with Disabilities Education Act (IDEA).

Education of the Handicapped Act (EHA) - See Individuals with Disabilities Education Act (IDEA).

Enjoin - See Injunction.

Equal Pay Act - Federal legislation which is part of the Fair Labor Standards Act. It applies to discrimination in wages which is based on gender. For race discrimination, employees paid unequally must utilize Title VII or 42 U.S.C. § 1981. Unlike many labor statutes, there is no minimum number of employees necessary to invoke the act's protection.

Equal Protection Clause - The clause of the Fourteenth Amendment that prohibits a state from denying any person within its jurisdiction equal protection of its laws. Also, the Due Process Clause of the Fifth Amendment that pertains to the federal government. This has been interpreted by the Supreme Court to grant equal protection even though there is no explicit grant in the Constitution.

Establishment Clause - The clause of the First Amendment that prohibits Congress from making "any law respecting an establishment of religion." This clause has been interpreted as creating a "wall of separation" between church and state. The test now used to determine whether government action violates the Establishment Clause, referred to as the *Lemon* test, asks whether the action has a secular purpose, whether its primary effect promotes or inhibits religion, and whether it requires excessive entanglement between church and state.

Fair Labor Standards Act (FLSA) - Federal legislation that mandates the payment of minimum wages and overtime compensation to covered employees. The overtime provisions require employers to pay at least time-and-one-half to employees who work more than 40 hours per week.

Federal Tort Claims Act - Federal legislation that determines the circumstances under which the United States waives its sovereign immunity (see below) and agrees to be sued in court for money damages. The government retains its immunity in cases of intentional torts committed by its employees or agents, and where the tort is the result of a "discretionary function" of a federal employee or agency. Many states have similar acts.

42 U.S.C. §§ 1981, 1983 - Section 1983 of the federal Civil Rights Act prohibits any person acting under color of state law from depriving any other person of rights protected by the Constitution or by federal laws. A vast majority of lawsuits claiming constitutional violations are brought under § 1983. Section 1981 provides that all persons enjoy the same right to make and enforce contracts as "white citizens." Section 1981 applies to employment contracts. Further, unlike § 1983, § 1981 applies even to private actors. It is not limited to those acting under color of state law. These sections do not apply to the federal government, though the government may be sued directly under the Constitution for any violations.

Free Appropriate Public Education (FAPE) - The IDEA requires local educational agencies to provide students with disabilities with a free appropriate public education. Under the federal FAPE standard, a student receives a FAPE through an individually developed education program that allows the student to receive educational benefit. States can enact higher standards under the IDEA, but at a minimum must comply with the federal standard governing the provision of a FAPE.

Free Exercise Clause - The clause of the First Amendment that prohibits Congress from interfering with citizens' rights to the free exercise of their religion. Through the Fourteenth Amendment, it has also been made applicable to the states and their sub-entities. The Supreme Court has held that laws of general applicability that have an incidental effect on persons' free exercise rights are not violative of the Free Exercise Clause.

Handicapped Children's Protection Act (HCPA) - (See also Individuals with Disabilities Education Act (IDEA).) The HCPA, enacted as an amendment to the EHA, provides for the payment of attorneys' fees to a prevailing parent or guardian in a lawsuit brought under the EHA (IDEA).

Hearing Officer - Also known as an administrative law judge. The hearing officer decides disputes that arise *at the administrative level*, and has the power to administer oaths, take testimony, rule on evidentiary questions, and make determinations of fact.

Immunity (Sovereign Immunity) - Federal, state and local governments are free from liability for torts committed except in cases in which they have consented to be sued (by statute or by court decisions).

Incorporation Doctrine - By its own terms, the Bill of Rights applies only to the federal government. The Incorporation Doctrine states that the Fourteenth Amendment makes the Bill of Rights applicable to the states.

Individuals with Disabilities Education Act (IDEA) - Also known as the Education of the Handicapped Act (EHA), the Education for All Handicapped Children Act (EAHCA), and the Handicapped Children's Protection Act (HCPA). Originally enacted as the EHA, the IDEA is the federal legislation that provides for the free, appropriate public education of all children with disabilities.

Individualized Education Program (IEP) - The IEP is designed to give children with disabilities a free, appropriate education. It is updated annually, with the participation of the child's parents or guardian.

Injunction - An equitable remedy (see Remedies) wherein a court orders a party to do or refrain from doing some particular action.

Issue Preclusion - Also known as collateral estoppel, the legal rule that prohibits a court from reconsideration of a particular issue in litigation arising from the same set of facts, involving the same parties and requesting similar relief to a matter previously heard by the court.

Jurisdiction - The power of a court to determine cases and controversies. The Supreme Court's jurisdiction extends to cases arising under the Constitution and under federal law. Federal courts have the power to hear cases where there is diversity of citizenship or where a federal question is involved.

Least Restrictive Environment/Mainstreaming - Part of what is required for a free, appropriate education is that each child with a disability be educated in the "least restrictive environment." To the extent that disabled children are educated with non-disabled children in regular education classes, those children are being mainstreamed.

Negligence per se - Negligence on its face. Usually, the violation of an ordinance or statute will be treated as negligence per se because no careful person would have been guilty of it.

Per Curiam - Latin phrase meaning "by the court." Used in court reports to note an opinion written by the court rather than by a single judge or justice.

Placement - A special education student's placement must be appropriate (as well as responsive to the particular child's needs). Under the IDEA's "stay-put" provision, school officials may not remove a special education child from his or her "then current placement" over the parents' objections until the completion of administrative or judicial review proceedings.

Preemption Doctrine - Doctrine which states that when federal and state law attempt to regulate the same subject matter, federal law prevents the state law from operating. Based on the Supremacy Clause of Article VI, Clause 2, of the Constitution.

Pro Se - A party appearing in court, without the benefit of an attorney, is said to be appearing pro se.

Rehabilitation Act - Section 504 of the Rehabilitation Act prohibits employers who receive federal financial assistance from discriminating against otherwise qualified individuals with handicaps solely because of their handicaps. An otherwise qualified individual is one who can perform the "essential functions" of the job with "reasonable accommodation."

Related Services - As part of the free, appropriate education due to children with disabilities, school districts may have to provide related services such as transportation, physical and occupational therapy, and medical services that are for diagnostic or evaluative purposes relating to education.

Remand - The act of an appellate court in returning a case to the court from which it came for further action.

Remedies - There are two general categories of remedies, or relief: legal remedies, which consist of money damages, and equitable remedies, which consist of a court mandate that a specific action be prohibited or required. For example, a claim for compensatory and punitive damages seeks a legal remedy; a claim for an injunction seeks an equitable remedy. Equitable remedies are generally unavailable unless legal remedies are inadequate to address the harm.

Res Judicata - The judicial notion that a claim or action may not be tried twice or re-litigated, or that all causes of action arising out of the same set of operative facts should be tried at one time. Also known as claim preclusion.

Section 1981 & Section 1983 - (see 42 U.S.C. §§ 1981, 1983).

Sovereign Immunity - The idea that the government cannot be sued without its consent. It stems from the English notion that "the King can do no wrong." This immunity from suit has been abrogated in most states and by the federal government through legislative acts known as "tort claims acts."

Standing - The judicial doctrine which states that in order to maintain a lawsuit a party must have some real interest at stake in the outcome of the trial.

Statute of Limitations - A statute of limitation provides the time period in which a specific cause of action may be brought.

Summary Judgment - Federal Rule of Civil Procedure 56 provides for the summary adjudication of a case before trial if either party can show that there is no genuine issue as to any material fact and that, given the facts agreed upon, the party is entitled to judgment as a matter of law. In general, summary judgment is used to dispose of claims which do not support a legally recognized claim.

Supremacy Clause - Clause in Article VI of the Constitution, which states that federal legislation is the supreme law of the land. This clause is used to support the Preemption Doctrine (see above).

Title VII, Civil Rights Act of 1964 (Title VII) - Title VII prohibits discrimination in employment based upon race, color, sex, national origin, or religion. It applies to any employer having fifteen or more employees. Under Title VII, where an employer intentionally discriminates, employees may obtain money damages unless the claim is for race discrimination. For those claims, monetary relief is available under 42 U.S.C. § 1981.

Tort - A tort is a civil wrong, other than breach of contract. Torts include negligence, assault, battery, trespass, defamation, infliction of emotional distress and wrongful death.

U.S. Equal Employment Opportunity Commission (EEOC) - The EEOC is the government entity that is empowered to enforce Title VII (see above) and other federal laws against discrimination through investigation and/or lawsuits. Private individuals alleging discrimination must pursue administrative remedies within the EEOC before they are allowed to file suit under Title VII.

Vacate - The act of annulling the judgment of a court either by an appellate court or by the court itself. The Supreme Court will generally vacate a lower court's judgment without deciding the case itself, and remand the case to the lower court for further consideration in light of some recent controlling decision.

Writ of Certiorari - The device used by the Supreme Court to transfer cases from the appellate court's docket to its own. Since the Supreme Court's appellate jurisdiction is largely discretionary, it need only issue such a writ when it desires to rule in the case.

INDEX